The
OLD BOOK
Value Guide

25,000 Listings of Old Books with Current Values

By the Editors of Collector Books

COLLECTOR BOOKS
A Division of Schroeder Publishing Co., Inc.

The current values in this book should be used only as a guide. They are not intended to set prices, which vary from one section of the country to another. Auction prices as well as dealer prices vary greatly and are affected by condition as well as demand. Neither the Author nor the Publisher assumes responsibility for any losses that might be incurred as a result of consulting this guide.

Introduction

This book was compiled to help the owner of old books evaluate his holdings and find a buyer for them. Most of us have a box, trunk, stack, or bookcase of old books. Chances are they are not rare books, but they may have value. Two questions that we are asked most frequently are 'Can you tell me the value of my old books?' and 'Where can I sell them?' *The Old Book Value Guide* will help answer both of these questions. Not only does this book place retail values on over 25,000 old books, it also lists scores of buyers along with the type of material each is interested in purchasing. Note that we list retail values (values that an interested party would be willing to pay to obtain possession of the book.) These prices are taken from recent dealer's selling lists.

If you were to sell your books to a dealer, you would expect to receive no more than 50% of the values listed in this book unless the dealer had a specific buyer in mind for some of your material. In many cases, a dealer will pay less than 50% of retail for a book to stock.

Do not ask a dealer to evaluate your old books unless you intend to sell your books to him. Most Antiquarian book dealers in the larger cities will appraise your books and ephemera for a fee that ranges from a low of $10.00 per hour to $50.00 per hour. If you were to have an extensive library of rare books, the $50.00-an-hour figure would be money well spent (assuming, of course, the appraiser to be qualified and honest).

The Old Book Value Guide places values on the more common holdings that many seem to accumulate. You will notice that the majority of the books listed are in the $5.00 to $20.00 range. Many such guides list only the rare, almost non-existent books that the average person will never see. The format is very simple: the listings are alphabetized first by the name of the author or illustrator; if more than one book is listed for a particular author, each title is listed alphabetically under his or her name.

In the back of the book, we have listed buyers of books and book-related material. When you correspond with these dealers, be sure to enclose a self-addressed, stamped envelope if you want a reply. Please do not send lists of books for an appraisal. If you wish to sell your books, quote the price that you want or negotiate price only on the items the buyer is interested in purchasing. When you list your books, do so by author, full title, publisher and place, date, and edition. Indicate condition, noting any defects on cover or contents.

When shipping your books, first wrap each book in paper such as brown kraft or a similar type of material. Never use newspaper for the inner wrap, since newsprint tends to rub off. (It may, however be used as a cushioning material within the outer carton.) Place your books in a sturdy corrugated box, and use a good shipping tape to seal it. Tape impregnated with nylon string is preferable, as it will not tear.

Books shipped by parcel post may be sent at a special fourth class book rate, which is much lower than regular parcel post zone rates.

The Editors of Collector Books

Listing of Standard Abbreviations

Am	American	inscr	inscription
decor	decoration	Ltd	limited
dj	dust jacket	pb	paperback
ed	edition	pl	plate
Eng	English	pp	page
EX	excellent	Pr	press
ex-lib	ex-library	SftCvr	soft cover
fld	folded	T.B.	textbook
G	good	trans	translated
Ills	illustrated	VG	very good

ABAJIAN. *Blacks & Their Contributions to American West.* 1974. 1st ed. 487 pp. EX $50.00

ABBEY, Edward. *Black Sun.* 1971. Simon & Schuster. 1st ed. dj. $35.00

ABBEY, Edward. *Slickrock.* 1973. San Francisco. 1st ed. dj. EX $60.00

ABBEY. *Desert Images.* 1974. 1st ed. sgn. dj. EX $60.00

ABBOT, A.E. *A Guide to Occult Books.* 1963. London. 66 pp. wrappers. EX $10.00

ABBOT, J. *In the Belly of the Beast.* 1981. New York. 1st revised ed. dj. EX $15.00

ABBOT, John. *Home Book of Wonders.* 1869. Hartford. Ills. 800 pp. $15.00

ABBOT, Willis J. *American Merchant Ships & Sailors.* 1902. Ills. Brown. G $30.00

ABBOT, Willis J. *Battlefields & Victory.* 1891. New York. 329 pp. $15.00

ABBOT, Willis J. *Bluejackets of 1812.* 1887. Dodd Mead. Ills. Abbot. $8.00

ABBOT, Willis J. *Panama & the Canal: In Picture & Prose.* 1913. New York. photos. 444 pp. $12.50

ABBOT, Willis J. *The Naval History of the United States.* 1890. Ills. 2 vol set. G $20.00

ABBOT & COBERT. *Creative Figure Photography.* 1961. Philadelphia. wrappers. VG $7.50

ABBOT. *Grimm's Fairy Tales.* 1935. Scribner. Ills. $10.00

ABBOTT, Bernice. *Changing New York.* 1939. 1st ed. dj. EX $45.00

ABBOTT, Charles C., M.D. *Wasteland Wanderings.* 1887. New York. DE Naturalist Observ. VG $25.00

ABBOTT, Charles. *Smithsonian Scientific Series.* 1929-1932. Patrons Ed. Ills. 12 vol set. $87.50

ABBOTT, Jacob *Rollo's Tour in Europe.* 1864. New York. Sheldon. Ills. 10 vol set. VG $75.00

ABBOTT, Jacob. *Makers of History, Charles I.* 1902. New York. Harper. G $5.00

ABBOTT, Jacob. *Makers of History, Cleopatra.* 1902. New York. Harper. G $5.00

ABBOTT, Jacob. *Makers of History, Louis XIV.* 1902. New York. Harper. Ills. G $5.00

ABBOTT, Jacob. *Queen Elizabeth.* (ca.1910-20) VG $5.00

ABBOTT, Jacob. *Rollo at School.* 1839. Boston. Ills. $35.00

ABBOTT, Jacob. *Rollo's Vacation.* 1839. Boston. $35.00

ABBOTT, Jacob. *The Schoolboy.* 1839. Boston. 1st ed. $25.00

ABBOTT, John S.C. *Lives of the Presidents.* 1882. Boston. Ills. 1st printing. 640 pp. VG $20.00

ABBOTT, John S.C. *The History of Maine.* 1875. Boston. 1st ed. 556 pp. VG $30.00

ABBOTT, John S.C. *The History of the State of Ohio.* 1875. Detroit. Ills. 1st ed. 876 pp. $65.00

ABBOTT, John S.C. *The Life of Christopher Columbus.* 1875. Dodd Mead. Ills. G $11.00

ABBOTT, R. Tucker. *American Seashells.* 1955. Van Norstrand. 3rd printing. VG $25.00

ABDILL, G.B. *Locomotive Engineers' Album. Steam Engine Saga.* 1965. 1st ed. dj. EX $25.00

ABDILL, G.B. *This Was Railroading.* 1958. Seattle. Ills. dj. VG $25.00

ABDY, H. Bennett. *Old California.* 1924. San Francisco. Ltd. ed. 1/400. EX $85.00

ABE, Kobo. *Secret Rendezvous.* 1979. Knopf. 1st Am. ed. dj. VG $15.00

ABE, Kobo. *The Face of Another.* 1966. Knopf. 1st Am. ed. dj. VG $25.00

ABEL, Annie H. & Klingberg, F. *Sidelight on American-Anglo Relations, 1839-1858.* 1927. 407 pp. VG $40.00

ABEL. *Correspondence of J.C. Calhoun, Indian Affairs.* 1915. Washington. fld maps. $100.00

ABELE. *The Violin & Its Story.* 1905. London. 121 pp. $20.00

ABERNATHY, John R. *Catch 'Em Alive Jack.* 1936. New York. Ills. VG $20.00

ABOTT, N.C. *Montana in the Making.* 1954. Billings. 562 pp. EX $15.00

ABRAHAMS, William. *Children of Capricorn.* 1963. Random House. 1st ed. dj. VG $20.00

ABRAMS, B.Z. *Gluckel of Hamlen, by Herself.* 1963. New York. Ills. dj. EX $20.00

ABRAMS, Henry. *Treasures of the Library of Congress.* 1980. New York. Ills. 318 pp. folio. dj. EX $25.00

ABRAMS. *Transactions of the Antiseptic Club.* 1895. New York. Ltd. 1st ed. 1/1000. $27.50

ABRAMSON, David. *Vascular Disorders of the Extremities.* 1974. Harper. 2nd ed. $30.00

ABZUG, R.H. *Inside the Vicious Heart.* 1984. New York. Oxford U.P. Ills. EX $20.00

ACACREON. *The Works of Acacreon* 1735. London. Greek/English text. 1st ed. $85.00

ACHAD, Frater. *The Chalice of Ecstasy.* 1923. Chicago. Yogi Pub. 1st ed. 82 pp. EX $35.00

ACHAD, Frater. *The Egyptian Revival.* 1969. New York. Weisers. Ltd. ed. 1/750. dj. $40.00

ACHESON, Dean. *Present at the Creation.* 1969. NY. Norton. 798 pp. dj. VG $5.50

ACHESON, Dean. *Sketches from Lives of Men I Have Known.* 1960. New York. Harper. 206 pp. dj. VG $4.50

ACHILLEOS, Chris. *Beauty & the Beast: Collection of Heroic Fantasy.* 1978. Fireside Book. Ills. wrappers. VG $25.00

ACKER, E.D. *A Brief History of the Acker-Halbert Family.* 1928. Lincoln, AL. 179 pp. VG $15.00

ACKER, Kathy. *Don Quixote Which Was a Dream.* 1986. Grove Press. proof copy. wrappers. EX $40.00

ACKER, W. *The Hermit, Sixty Poems by T'ao Ch'ien.* 1952. London. 1st ed. 157 pp. dj. VG $25.00

ACKERLY, Mary D. & Parker, L. *Our Kin, Bedford County Virginia Families.* 1981. Harrisonburg. Ills. 840 pp. $42.50

ACKERMAN, James S. *The Architecture of Michelangelo.* 1961. New York. Ills. 1st ed. dj. VG $20.00

ACKERMAN. *Germany. The Next Republic.* New York. Ills. 1st ed. G $7.50

ACOSTA, Joseph. *The Naturall & Morall Historie of E. & W. Indies.* 1604. London. 1st Eng. ed. 590 pp. VG $1,500.00

ADACHI, Barbara. *Backstage at Bunraku.* 1985. Weatherhill. Ills. 1st ed. 143 pp. dj. EX $65.00

ADAIR, Ian. *Conjuring as a Craft.* 1970. Barnes. dj. EX $6.00

ADAIR, John. *The Navajo & Pueblo Silversmiths.* 1946. U. of OK Press. Ills. 220 pp. index. dj. VG $15.00

ADAM, W. *First Lessons in Geology.* 1857. London. 173 pp. $10.00

ADAMI. *Letters of G. Puccini.* 1931. Philadelphia. Ills. 1st ed. dj. VG $15.00

ADAMIC, Louis. *Two-Way Passage.* 1941. New York. Harper. 328 pp. $6.50

ADAMS, A.L. *Notes of a Naturalist in the Nile Valley.* 1870. Edinburgh. 25 Ills. 295 pp. VG $95.00

ADAMS, Alexander. *Eternal Quest, Story of The Great Naturalists.* 1969. Putnams. photos. 509 pp. $17.00

ADAMS, Alice. *Families & Survivors.* 1974. Knopf. 1st ed. dj. VG $30.00

ADAMS, Alice. *Superior Women.* 1984. New York. 1st ed. dj. $15.00

ADAMS, Alice. *To See You Again.* 1982. Knopf. 1st ed. dj. EX $15.00

ADAMS, Andy. *Cattle Brands: Collection of Campfire Stories.* 1906. Boston. 315 pp. VG $20.00

ADAMS, Andy. *The Outlet.* 1905. Houghton Mifflin. Ills. Smith. $20.00

ADAMS, Ansel & Newhall, Nancy. *This is the American Earth.* 1960. San Francisco. Sierra Club. folio. dj. VG $75.00

ADAMS, Ansel. *The Portfolios of Ansel Adams.* 1977. Garden City. 3rd printing. EX $35.00

ADAMS, Ansel. *The Print: Contact Printing & Enlarging.* 1967. New York. Morgan. new ed. dj. $15.00

ADAMS, Ansel. *These We Inherit, Parklands of America.* 1962. Sierra Club. dj. EX $60.00

ADAMS, B. *Rust in Peace.* 1976. Austin. dj. mint. $37.50

ADAMS, Bess Porter. *About Books & Children.* 1953. New York. Holt. Ills. inscr. dj. $15.00

ADAMS, C. *Complete Book of Bow Hunting.* 1978. dj. EX $12.50

ADAMS, Carsbie C. *Space Flight.* 1958. New York. McGraw Hill. photos. 373 pp. $6.50

ADAMS, Clinton. *Fritz Scholder Lithographs.* 1975. Boston. Ills. 1st ed. dj. EX $15.00

ADAMS, D. *Life, the Universe & Everything.* 1982. Harmony. 1st ed. dj. EX $17.50

ADAMS, D. *Restaurant at the End of the Universe.* 1980. Harmony. 1st ed. dj. EX $25.00

ADAMS, Daniel. *The Scholars Arithmetic or Federal Accountant.* 1808. Keene, NH. 216 pp. $10.00

ADAMS, Dorothy Dort. *My Mother Told Me.* 1939. New York. 1st ed. VG $10.00

ADAMS, Dorothy. *We Stood Alone.* 1944. New York. 1st ed. 284 pp. dj. 6.50

ADAMS, Douglas. *So Long & Thanks for All the Fish.* 1985. Harmony. 1st ed. sgn. dj. EX $20.00

ADAMS, Douglas. *So Long & Thanks for All the Fish.* London. sgn. $22.00

ADAMS, Edgar. *Private Gold Coinage of California, 1849-55.* Stackpole. $15.00

ADAMS, F.P. *The Melancholy Lute.* 1936. Ltd. ed. 1/400. sgn. boxed. $26.50

ADAMS, Frank. *Arizona Feud.* 1st ed. $6.00

ADAMS, Frank. *Book of Nursery Rhymes, Stories, & Pictures.* London. Blackie. Ills. $30.00

ADAMS, George. *Doctors in Blue.* 1952. New York. Ills. 1st ed. sgn. dj. EX $15.00

ADAMS, Hannah. *Hist. of New Eng. from First Settlement Plymouth.* 1799. Dedham, MA. 516 pp. $50.00

ADAMS, James Truslow. *Album of American History.* 1944. New York. 411 pp. dj. $10.00

ADAMS, James Truslow. *History of the United States.* 1933. Scribner. Ills. 1st ed. 4 vol set. $15.00

ADAMS, James Truslow. *The Epic of America.* 1931. Boston. Ills. 433 pp. $7.50

ADAMS, James Truslow. *The March of Democracy.* 1933. New York. Scribner. 6 vol set. VG $25.00

ADAMS, James Truslow. *The March of Democracy.* 1932. New York. 1st ed. 428 pp. $10.00

ADAMS, Joey. *On the Road for Uncle Sam.* 1963. 1st ed. dj. VG $5.50

ADAMS, John F. *Backyard Poultry Raising.* 1977. Garden City. 139 pp. dj. EX $4.00

ADAMS, John Quincy. *Letters of John Quincy Adams to His Son.* 1848. Auburn, NY. 128 pp. $10.00

ADAMS, John Quincy. *Life in a New England Town: 1787-1788.* 1903. Boston. Ills. 204 pp. $25.00

ADAMS, John Quincy. *Oration on Life & Character of Lafayette.* 1935. Washington. $12.50

ADAMS, L.A. & Eddy, S. *Comparative Anatomy, Introduction to Vertebrates.* 1949. Wiley. Ills. 520 pp. VG $10.00

ADAMS, R.H. *White Churches of Plains, Examples from Colorado.* 1970. Boulder. 57 photos. dj. VG $17.50

ADAMS, Ramon. *The Cowman & His Code of Ethics.* 1969. Austin. Encino Pr. Ills. Ltd. ed. dj. $35.00

ADAMS, Ramon F. *From the Pecos to the Powder.* 1965. U. of OK Press. 1st ed. dj. VG $20.00

ADAMS, Ramon F. *The Best of the American Cowboy.* 1957. Norman. Ills. 1st ed. dj. EX $22.50

ADAMS, Richard & Lockley, R. *Voyage Through the Antarctic.* 1982. Knopf. 1st Am. ed. dj. VG $15.00

ADAMS, Richard. *The Girl in the Swing.* 1980. Knopf. 1st ed. dj. VG $15.00

ADAMS, Richard. *The Iron Wolf A.O.S.* 1980. London. Allen. 1st ed. dj. EX $35.00

ADAMS, Richard. *The Plague Dogs.* 1978. Knopf. 1st Am. ed. dj. VG $15.00

ADAMS, Richard. *The Ship's Cat.* 1977. 1st Am. ed. dj. $18.00

ADAMS, Richard. *The Tyger Voyage.* 1976. New York. Ills. Bayley. 1st Am. ed. dj. $15.00

ADAMS, Richard. *The Unbroken Web.* 1980. New York. Ills. Bilbert & Campbell. EX $10.00

ADAMS, Richard. *Watership Down.* 1972. New York. 1st Am. ed. 429 pp. dj. EX $27.50

ADAMS, S. & Mathias, Roland. *Shining Pyramid & Other Stories by Welsh Authors.* 1970. 1st ed. $20.00

ADAMS, Samuel Hopkins. *A. Woollcott, His Life & His World.* 1945. New York. photos. 386 pp. $4.50

ADAMS, Samuel Hopkins. *Banner by the Wayside.* 1947. New York. Random House. 376 pp. dj. $4.50

ADAMS, Samuel Hopkins. *Canal Town.* 1945. New York. World. 469 pp. dj. $4.50

ADAMS, Samuel Hopkins. *Sunrise to Sunset.* 1950. New York. Random House. 314 pp. dj. $4.50

ADAMS, Sherman. *Firsthand Report.* 1961. New York. Harper. 1st ed. 481 pp. dj. $7.50

ADAMS, Thomas B. *Letters of Thomas Boylston Adams.* 1917. Cincinnati. 47 pp. wrappers. $8.50

ADAMS, Will & Drake, John. *Dan Beard Talks to Scouts.* 1940. Garden City. 14 pp+78rpm record. dj. VG $15.00

ADAMS, William Davenport. *By-Ways in Book-Land.* 1889. New York. 1st Am.. ed. 224 pp. $12.50

ADAMS, William Davenport. *With Poet & Player.* New York. no date. 228 pp. $10.00

ADAMS & CUNNINGHAM. *The Swiss Confederation.* 1889. London. map. G $20.00

ADAMS. *Death Valley.* New York. 1st ed. wrappers. $45.00

ADAMS. *Empire on Seven Seas.* 1940. 1st ed. VG $15.00

ADAMS. *Life of George C. Lodge.* 1911. Boston. 1st ed. VG $7.50

ADAMS. *Polaroid Land Photography.* 1978. dj. VG $30.00

ADAMS. *Tenderloin.* 1959. New York. 1st ed. dj. VG $7.50

ADAMS. *Yosemite Album.* New York. 1st ed. wrappers. $15.00

ADAMSON, Hans Christian. *Eddie Rickenbacker.* 1946. New York. 1st ed. dj. VG $10.00

ADAMSON, Hans. *Keepers of the Lights.* 1955. Greenburg. 1st ed. dj. $10.00

ADAMSON, Joy. *Born Free, Lioness of Two Worlds.* 1960. Pantheon. photos. 220 pp. dj. $5.00

ADAMSON, Joy. *Spotted Sphinx.* 1969. Harcourt Brace. 1st Am. ed. photos. 313 pp. $9.00

ADAMSON, Joy. *The Story of Elsa.* 1966. Pantheon. photos. 318 pp. VG $5.00

ADDAMS, Charles. *Homebodies.* 1954. New York. 1st ed. dj. VG $20.00

ADDAMS, Jane. *Forty Years at Hull House.* 1935. Macmillan. Ills. 1st ed. 459 pp. VG $37.50

ADDAMS, Jane. *Jane Addams Centennial Reader.* 1960. New York. 330 pp. dj. VG $7.50

ADDAMS, Jane. *The Spirit of Youth & the City Streets.* 1916. New York. Macmillan Co. 162 pp. $5.00

ADDAMS, Jane. *Twenty Years at Hull House.* 1911. New York. 1st ed. EX $10.00

ADDISON, J.D.W. *Arts & Crafts in the Middle Ages.* 1908. London. Bell. $40.00

ADE, George. *Forty Modern Fables.* 1901. New York. Ills. 1st ed. VG $10.00

ADE, George. *Knocking the Neighbors.* 1912. Doubleday $12.50

ADE, George. *More Fables.* 1900. NY/Chicago. Ills. Newman. 1st ed. 222 pp. $10.00

ADE, George. *Nettie, a Play in One Act.* 1923. France. 1st ed. inscr. wrappers. $5.50

ADE, John. *Newton County Indiana, 1853-1911.* 1911. Indianapolis. Bobbs Merrill. sgn. $60.00

ADELMAN. *Confessions of a Master Criminal.* 1973. New York. 1st ed. VG $10.00

ADKINS, J. *Upland Game Habitat Development Evaluation.* 1980. Washington. Wash. Game Div. photos. map. $4.00

ADLER, Bill. *The Churchill Wit.* 1965. New York. Ills. dj. VG $8.50

ADLER, Mortimer. *How to Think About God.* 1980. dj. EX $10.00

ADLER, Renata. *Pitch Dark.* Doubleday. 2nd printing. sgn. dj. EX $12.50

ADLER, Renata. *Speedboat.* 1976. Random House. 1st ed. dj. VG $15.00

ADNEY, E.T. & Chapelle, H.I. *Bark Canoes & Skin Boats of North America.* 1964. Smithsonian. 224 photos & drawings. 242 pp. $32.50

ADSHEAD, Gladys. *Casco.* 1943. New York. Ills. E. Bostleman. 1st ed. EX $10.00

AESOP. *Aesop's Fables.* 1939. New York. Ills. Arthur Rackham. G $30.00

AESOP. *The Aesop for Children.* 1941. Chicago. Ills. Milo Winter. VG $35.00

AESOP. *The Fables of Aesop.* 1931. New York. Ills. C.H. Bennett. Deluxe ed. $20.00

AFARQUAR, Carley. *The Sports Almanac.* 1965. Ills. Kalmenoff. 1st ed. $5.50

AFLALO, F.G. *British Salt-Water Fish.* 1904. London. Ills. 1st ed. VG $35.00

AGAR, H. *A Time for Greatness.* 1942. 1st ed. $6.50

AGASSIZ, Louis. *Geological Sketches.* 1866. Boston. Ills. 1st ed. $55.00

AGATE, James. *Around Cinemas.* 1946. 1st ed. 280 pp. $17.50

AGATE, James. *Ego 7.* 1945. London. Ills. 1st ed. 323 pp. $17.50

AGATE, James. *Kingdoms for Horses.* 1936. London. Ills. Rex Whistler. 1st ed. VG $35.00

AGATHA, Sister. *Texas Prose Writings.* 1936. Dallas. 1st ed. $30.00

AGEE, J. *Collected Poems.* 1968. dj. $16.50

AGEE, James & Evans, Walker. *Let Us Now Praise Famous Men.* 1960. Boston. Ills. 2nd ed. 471 pp. $22.50

AGEE, James. *A Death in the Family.* 1957. McDowell. 1st ed. dj. $40.00

AGEE, James. *A Death in the Family.* 1957. McDowell. 2nd ed. dj. VG $20.00

AGEE, James. *Letters of James Agee.* 1962. Braziller. 1st ed. dj. $12.50

AGEE, James. *The Collected Short Prose of James Agee.* 1968. Boston. 1st ed. 243 pp. dj. $15.00

AGILION, R. *Fighting French. French Resistance Fighters WW II.* 1943. Ills. G $13.75

AGNEW, Brad. *Fort Gibson, Terminal On The Trail Of Tears.* 1978. 274 pp. $12.50

AGNEW, Georgette. *Let's Pretend.* 1927. London. Ills. Shepard. 1st ed. VG $15.00

AGNON, S.Y. *A Guest for the Night.* 1968. Schocken. 1st Am. ed. dj. VG $20.00

AGRESTI, Olivia Rossetti. *David Lubin.* 1941. Berkley, CA. 2nd ed. 372 pp. dj. VG $5.00

AGRICOLA, G. *De Re Metallica.* 1950. 289 Ills. 638 pp. EX $30.00

AHRENFELDT, R.H. *Psychiatry in British Army in Second World War.* 1958. G $17.50

AI. *Cruelty.* 1973. dj. $10.00

AI. *Killing Floor.* 1979. Boston. 1st ed. dj. VG $12.50

AICKMAN, Duncan. *The Taming of the Frontier.* 1925. New York. Ills. 1st ed. 319 pp. $15.00

AIKEN, Conrad. *A Seizure of Limericks.* 1968. 1st ed. dj. VG $15.00

AIKEN, Conrad. *Blue Voyage.* 1927. New York. Scribner. 1st trade ed. $17.50

AIKEN, Conrad. *Mr. Arcularis. A Play.* 1957. Cambridge. Harvard U. Pr. 1st ed. 83 pp. $15.00

AIKEN, Conrad. *Preludes for Memnon.* 1931. 1st ed. dj. VG $35.00

AIKEN, Conrad. *Sheepfold Hill.* 1958. New York. Sagamore Press. 1st ed. dj. VG $20.00

AIKEN, Conrad. *Thee.* 1967. Braziller. 1st ed. dj. $12.50

AIKEN, Conrad. *Time in the Rock.* 1936. 1st ed. VG $22.50

AIKEN, Conrad. *Ushant.* 1963. Allen. 1st English ed. dj. VG $25.00

AIKEN, Conrad. *Who's Zoo.* 1977. Atheneum. Ills. J.V. Lord. 1st ed. dj $10.00

AIKEN, Dr. & Barbauld, Mrs. *Evenings at Home; or, The Juvenile Budget Opened.* 1865. $8.00

AIKEN, J. *The Wolves of Willoughby Chase.* 1962. 1st Am. ed. dj. EX $17.50

AIKEN, Joan. *Castle Barebane.* 1976. advance copy. wrappers. VG $12.50

AIKEN, Joan. *The Far Forests.* 1977. New York. Viking. 1st ed. dj. EX $17.50

AIKIN, John, M.D. *The Arts of Life.* 1803. Boston. 1st Am. ed. $150.00

AIKMAN, Duncan. *Calamity Jane & the Lady Wildcats.* 1927. New York. Ills. 346 pp. dj. VG $17.50

AIKMAN, J.M. *Distribution & Structure of East Nebraska Forests.* Nebraska U. photos. maps. 73 pp. $8.00

AIKMAN, Lonnelle. *Nature's Healing Arts.* 1977. Nat. Geo. Soc. photos. dj. EX $4.50

AIKMAN. *The History of Scotland.* 1862. London. Ills. 2 vol set. VG $60.00

AINSWORTH, Edward Maddin. *Beckoning Desert.* 1962. Prentice Hall. Ills. 264 pp. $15.00

AINSWORTH, W. Harrison. *Mervyn Clitheroe.* 1858. London. Ills. Brown. 1st ed. VG $17.50

AINSWORTH, William. *The Tower of London.* 1840. London. Ills. Geo. Cruikshank. 1st ed. $40.00

AINSWORTH. *Golden Checkerboard.* 1965. Palm Desert. Ills. dj. EX $125.00

AINSWORTH. *The Cowboy in Art.* 1968. 1st printing. dj. EX $27.50

AIRD, Catherine. *A Most Contagious Game.* 1967. London. 1st ed. VG $30.00

AIRD, Catherine. *Some Die Eloquent.* 1979. London. Collins. 1st ed. dj. EX $20.00

AIRD, Catherine. *The Complete Steel.* 1969. London. 1st ed. dj. VG $22.50

AKEHURST, Richard. *The World of Guns by Richard Akehurst.* 1972. London. Ills. $10.00

AKELEY, Carl. *In Brightest Africa.* Garden City. reprint. photos. 267 pp. $10.00

AKELEY, M.L.J. *Carl Akeley's Africa.* 1930. G $35.00

AKELEY, M.L.J. *Congo Eden.* 1950. Dodd Mead. photos. map. 356 pp. VG $13.00

AKELEY, M.L.J. *Restless Jungle.* 1936. Nat. Travel Club. 1st ed. $15.00

AKERLUND, Harold. *Fartygsfynden I Den Forna Hamne I Kalmar.* 1951. Stockholm. 1st ed. stiff wrappers. $20.00

AKERS, Dwight. *Drivers Up. Story of American Harness Racing.* 1938. New York. 1st ed. dj. EX $45.00

AKINARI, Uyeda. *Tales of Moonlight & Rain, Japanese Gothic Tales.* 1972. Columbia U. Ills. 150 pp. dj. EX $48.00

AKINARI, Uyeda. *Ugetsu Monogatari, Tales of Moonlight & Rain.* 1974. Ills. 279 pp. dj. rare. EX $58.00

AKIYAMA, Aisaburo. *Sights of Old Capital.* 1930. Kyoto. 3rd ed. 149 pp. dj. rare. VG $75.00

AKIYAMA, Terukazu. *Treasures of Asia, Japanese Printings.* 1977. Geneva/Paris. Ills. 216 pp. dj. scarce. EX $85.00

AKSYONOV, Vassily. *The Island of Crimea.* 1983. Random House. 1st ed. dj. $20.00

ALAMARAZ, S. *Petroleo en Bolivia.* 1958. La Paz. 292 pp. EX $22.50

ALBAUGH, William. *Confederate Arms.* 1957. Ills. 1st ed. $27.50

ALBAUGH, William. *Confederate Edged Weapons.* 1960. New York. Ills. 1st ed. $27.50

ALBAUGH, William. *Confederate Handguns.* Bonanza. Ills. 250 pp. dj. VG $12.50

ALBEE, E. *A Delicate Balance.* 1966. 1st ed. dj. EX $27.50

ALBEE, E. *A Walk on the Wild Side.* 1956. 1st ed. dj. G $20.00

ALBEE, Edward. *Everything in the Garden.* 1968. Atheneum. 1st ed. dj. VG $20.00

ALBEE, Edward. *The Wounding: Essay on Education.* 1981. Mountain State. 1st ed. sgn. wrappers. VG $30.00

ALBERT, Allen D., ed. *History of the Forty-Fifth Regiment.* 1912. Williamsport. Ills. 530 pp. $85.00

ALBERT, Harvey. *In Out.* 1978. Salt Works. Ltd. ed. 1/400. sgn. VG $25.00

ALBERT, Herman. *Odyssey of a Desert Prospector.* 1967. Norman. 1st ed. inscr. dj. EX $15.00

ALBERT, J.S. *Button Collector's Second Journal.* 1941. Hightstown. $20.00

ALBERTI, Guiseppe Antonio. *Istruzioni Pratcher per I'Ingegnero Civile.* 1782. Venezia. 25 fld pls. VG $425.00

ALBERTS, R.C. *Adventures of Major Robert Stobo.* 1965. $12.50

ALBERTS, Robert C. *The Good Provider: H.J. Heinz & His 57 Varieties.* 1973. Boston. 1st printing. 297 pp. dj. VG $7.00

ALBERTSON. *Bessie.* 1973. New York. Ills. dj. VG $6.50

ALBION, Baker & Labaree. *New England & the Sea.* 1972. $10.00

ALBION, R. *The Rise of New York Port.* 1970. New York. 1st ed. dj. VG $17.50

ALBISETTI & VENTURELLI. *Encyclopedia Bororo. Vol. I.* 1962. Brazil. Portugese text. 1047 pp. $45.00

ALBRIGHT, H. & Taylor, O.H. *Ohio Range.* 1935. Dodd Mead. Ills. Ruth Taylor. 4th print. $35.00

ALBRIGHT, H.M. & Taylor, F.J. *Oh, Ranger, a Book of National Parks.* 1941. Dodd Mead. photos. 272 pp. $10.00

ALCOTT, Louisa May. *A Garland for Girls.* New York. Grosset & Smith. 286 pp. dj. $10.00

ALCOTT, Louisa May. *An Old-Fashioned Girl.* 1928. Philadelphia. Winston. 342 pp. $10.00

ALCOTT, Louisa May. *Aunt Jo's Scrap Bag.* 1929. New York. Grosset & Dunlap. 354 pp. $10.00

ALCOTT, Louisa May. *Eight Cousins.* 1928. Ills. H.L. Price. VG $10.00

ALCOTT, Louisa May. *Eight Cousins.* 1940. Racine. Whitman. 237 pp. $10.00

ALCOTT, Louisa May. *Hospital Sketches.* 1863. Boston. 1st ed. VG $200.00

ALCOTT, Louisa May. *Jo's Boys.* 1899. Boston. Little, Brown & Co. Ills. $16.50

ALCOTT, Louisa May. *Jo's Boys.* 1933. Little, Brown. Ills. Clara M. Burd. $25.00

ALCOTT, Louisa May. *Kitty's Class Day.* Grosset & Dunlap. dj. VG $10.00

ALCOTT, Louisa May. *Little Men.* 1949. New York. Grosset & Dunlap. 338 pp. dj. $10.00

ALCOTT, Louisa May. *Little Men.* 1955. Racine. Whitman. 283 pp. pb. $2.50

ALCOTT, Louisa May. *Little Women.* 1922. Boston. Ills. Jessie W. Smith. G $12.50

ALCOTT, Louisa May. *Rose in Bloom.* 1945. Boston. 344 pp. dj. EX $7.50

ALCOTT, Louisa May. *Silver Pitchers & Independence.* 1876. Boston. 1st ed. 315 pp. VG $20.00

ALCOTT, Louisa May. *The Frost King.* Racine. (ca.1929) Ills. Frobisher. G $20.00

ALCOTT, Louisa May. *Under the Lilacs.* 1928. Boston. Ills. M. Davis. 1st ed. $25.00

ALDANOV, Mark. *The Fifth Seal.* 1943. Scribner. trans. Wreden. 1st ed. VG $10.00

ALDEN, Raymond MacDonald. *The Christmas Tree Forest.* 1958. Bobbs Merrill. Ills. Busoni. 1st ed. dj. VG $20.00

ALDERMAN, Dr. E.A. *In Memoriam.* 1924. $5.00

ALDERSON, E. *With Mounted Infantry & Mashonaland Field Force.* 1898. London. VG $42.50

ALDERSON. *Andrew Carnegie. The Man & His Work.* 1902. Garden City. Ills. G $7.50

ALDIN, Cecil. *Just Among Friends.* 1934. Scribner. Ills. 1st ed. VG $35.00

ALDINGTON, R. *Images, Old & New.* 1916. Boston. 1st Am. ed. wrappers. VG $40.00

ALDINGTON, Richard. *At All Costs.* 1930. London. Heinemann. 1st ed. sgn. 45 pp. $40.00

ALDINGTON, Richard. *D.H. Lawrence.* 1930. Chatto. 1st ed. wrappers. VG $20.00

ALDINGTON, Richard. *Lawrence of Arabia.* 1955. London. dj. VG $10.00

ALDINGTON, Richard. *Pinorman.* 1954. London. 1st ed. dj. EX $15.00

ALDIS, Mary. *The Princess Jack.* 1915. EX $8.00

ALDISS, Brian. *Barefoot in the Head.* 1970. New York. 1st Am. ed. dj. EX $10.00

ALDISS, Brian. *Frankenstein Unbound.* 1973. New York. 1st Am. ed. dj. VG $20.00

ALDISS, Brian. *Space Opera.* 1974. London. 1st ed. dj. EX $17.50

ALDISS, Brian. *Space, Time & Nathaniel.* 1957. London. 1st ed. dj. EX $40.00

ALDISS, Brian. *The Saliva Tree & Other Strange Growths.* 1966. London. 1st ed. dj. EX $20.00

ALDISS, Brian. *This World & Nearer Ones.* London. sgn. $15.00

ALDISS & HARRISON, eds. *Decade, the 1940's.* 1978. St.Martins. 1st Am. ed. dj. VG $10.00

ALDRICH, Bess Streeter. *Miss Bishop.* 1933. New York. Appleton. 336 pp. VG $4.00

ALDRICH, Bess Streeter. *Spring Came on Forever.* 1935. New York. Appleton. 332 pp. G $3.50

ALDRICH, Chilsan. *The Real Log Cabin.* 1945. Ills. 278 pp. dj. $6.00

ALDRICH, R.S. *Gertrude Lawrence as Mrs. A.* 1954. Ills. $7.50

ALDRICH, T. *A Book of Famous Explorers.* 1902. Hall & Locke. Ills. VG $5.00

ALDRICH, Thomas Bailey. *At Sea Turn & Other Matters.* 1902. Boston. Ltd. 1st ed. 1/200. VG $35.00

ALDRICH, Thomas Bailey. *Ponkapog Paper.* 1903. Boston. Ltd. 1st ed. VG $35.00

ALDRICH, Thomas Bailey. *Stillwater Tragedy.* 1880. Boston. Houghton Mifflin. 1st ed. $25.00

ALDRICH, Thomas Bailey. *The Poems of Thomas Bailey Aldrich.* 1893. New York. Ills. ex-lib. 290 pp. VG $3.50

ALDRICH, Thomas Bailey. *The Story of a Bad Boy.* 1932. NY/Boston. 1st ed. 179 pp. $15.00

ALDRICH, Thomas Bailey. *The Story of a Bad Boy.* 1870. Boston. Ills. 1st ed. $100.00

ALDRIDGE, Allan. *The Beatles Illustrated Lyrics.* 1969. New York. 1st Am. ed. dj. VG $16.00

ALDRIDGE, James. *Goodbye Un-America.* 1979. 1st Am. ed. 157 pp. dj. $27.50

ALDRIDGE, James. *Signed with Their Honor.* 1942. New York. Black League of America. EX $4.50

ALDRIDGE, Janet. *Meadowbrook Girls.* 1913. Altemus. Ills. $3.00

ALDRIDGE, Janet. *The Meadowbrook Girls Across the Country.* 1913. Saalfield. Ills. G $3.50

ALDRIDGE, Janet. *The Meadowbrook Girls by the Sea.* 1914. Saalfield. Ills. G $3.50

ALDRIN, Col. Edwin E. Jr. *Return to Earth.* 1973. New York. Random House. photos. 338 pp. $4.00

ALEGRIA, C. *Broad & Alien is the World.* 1941. NY. Farrar & Rinehart. dj. VG $15.00

ALEXANDER, A. *25 Years in a Wagon: Sport & Travel in So. Africa.* 1888. London. 2nd ed. VG $120.00

ALEXANDER, B. *From the Niger to the Nile.* 1907. London. 2 vol set. VG $95.00

ALEXANDER, Constance. *Francesca Alexander.* 1927. Harvard. Ltd. ed. 233 pp. VG $27.50

ALEXANDER, De Alva S. *A Political History of the State of New York.* 1909. New York. 3 vol set. $25.00

ALEXANDER, E.P. *Iron Horses.* 1941. New York. Ills. VG $30.00

ALEXANDER, Francesca. *The Story of Ida.* 1894. Portland. Ltd. ed. 1/925. VG $10.00

ALEXANDER, Harold H. *Design, Criteria for Decisions.* 1976. Macmillan. 555 pp. dj. $4.50

ALEXANDER, Hartley. *World's Rim/Great Mysteries of North Am. Indians.* 1953. U. of NB. 1st ed. dj. $10.00

ALEXANDER, Holmes. *The Spirit of '76. Political Novel of Near Future.* 1966. New York. 386 pp. dj. $8.00

ALEXANDER, James W. *History of the University Club of New York.* 1915. New York. dj. $15.00

ALEXANDER, Karl. *Time After Time.* 1979. New York. 1st ed. dj. VG $15.00

ALEXANDER, M. *Discovering the New World.* 1976. New York. Ills. 1st Am. ed. maps. dj. EX $26.00

ALEXANDER, Michael. *Mrs. Fraser on the Fatal Shore.* 1971. $5.50

ALEXANDER, Michael. *True Blue, Life & Adventures of Col. F. Barnaby.* 1958. New York. Ills. 215 pp. dj. G $10.00

ALEXANDER, of Yugoslavia. *Prince Philip, A Family Portrait.* 1960. New York. Bobbs Merrill. 256 pp. dj. $5.00

ALEXANDER, Rev. Dr. A. *Advice to A Young Christian.* 1843. New York. 168 pp. $12.50

ALEXANDER, Roy. *The Cruise of the Raider 'Wolf.'* 1941. Garden City. 270 pp. dj. EX $5.00

ALEXANDER, W.B. *Birds of the Ocean.* 1954. Putnam. Ills. 2nd ed. $12.00

ALEXANDER. *Model Balloons & Flying Machines.* 1910. London. Ills. 1st ed. VG $70.00

ALFVEN, H. *Cosmical Electrodynamics.* 1950. Oxford U. Press. G $15.00

ALGEO, Sara. *The Story of the Sub-Pioneer.* 1925. Providence. sgn. dj. VG $12.50

ALGER, Horatio, Jr. *Brave & Bold.* New York. no date. 161 pp. $3.00

ALGER, Horatio, Jr. *Chester Rand; or, The New Path to Fortune.* 1905. New York. 284 pp. $4.00

ALGER, Horatio, Jr. *Driven from Home.* Chicago. Donahue. $3.00

ALGER, Horatio, Jr. *Facing the World.* 1908. New York. New York Book Co. 168 pp. $3.50

ALGER, Horatio, Jr. *Frank Hunter's Peril.* 1896. Philadelphia. 335 pp. $4.50

ALGER, Horatio, Jr. *In a New World.* New York. 289 pp. VG $3.50

ALGER, Horatio, Jr. *Jacob Marlowe's Secret.* New York. A.L. Burt. 262 pp. $3.00

ALGER, Horatio, Jr. *Making His Way.* 1909. New York. New York Book Co. $3.50

ALGER, Horatio, Jr. *Mark, the Match Boy.* 1869. Boston. Loring. Ills. 1st ed. $35.00

ALGER, Horatio, Jr. *Mark Mason, His Trails, & Triumphs.* New York. Hurst. 320 pp. $3.50

ALGER, Horatio, Jr. *Only an Irish Boy.* 1909. New York. New York Book Co. 168 pp. $3.50

ALGER, Horatio, Jr. *The Young Adventurer.* Chicago. Donahue. 255 pp. $3.00

ALGER, Horatio, Jr. *The Young Salesman.* Chicago. Donahue. 252 pp. $3.00

ALGER, Horatio, Jr. *Tom, The Bootblack; or, The Road to Success.* 1889. New York. A.L. Burt. 280 pp. $5.00

ALGER, Horatio, Jr. *Young Adventurers.* 1910. New York. $6.00

ALGER. *Abraham Lincoln.* 1883. 1st ed. $8.00

ALGER. *Cast Upon the Breakers.* 1974. Doubleday. 1st ed. dj. VG $12.00

ALGER. *Do & Dare.* Goldsmith. no date. G $5.50

ALGER. *Frank's Companion.* 1892. Winston. VG $6.50

ALGER. *Hector's Inheritance.* Donohue. no date. $3.50

ALGER. *Sink or Swim.* A.L. Burt. no date. G $4.50

ALGER. *Struggling Upward.* 1910. New York New York Book Co. VG $6.50

ALGER. *Struggling Upward.* Hurst. no date. G $5.50

ALGREN, Nelson. *A Walk on the Wild Side.* 1956. Farrar. 1st ed. dj. VG $25.00

ALGREN, Nelson. *The Last Carousel.* 1973. Putnam. 1st ed. dj. EX $15.00

ALGREN, Nelson. *The Man with the Golden Arm.* 1959. London. 1st English ed. dj. VG $30.00

ALGREN, Nelson. *The Neon Wilderness.* 1965. London. Deutsch. 1st Eng. ed. dj. VG $30.00

ALGREN, Nelson. *Who Lost an American?* 1963. New York. Macmillan. dj. EX $20.00

ALI, Muhammad & Durham, R. *The Greatest, My Own Story.* 1975. New York. Random House. 416 pp. VG $3.50

ALI, Salim. *Book of Indian Birds.* 1946. Bombay Nat. Hist. Soc. dj. EX $35.00

ALI, Salim. *Field Guide to the Birds of Eastern Himalayas.* 1979. Oxford U. Press. 265 pp. dj. $25.00

ALIGHIERI, Dante. *Divine Comedy.* 1932. boxed. VG $50.00

ALIGHIERI, Dante. *La Divina Commedia in English & Italian.* 1928. Nonesuch. Ltd. ed. gilt decor. $150.00

ALIMEN, H. *Prehistory of Africa.* 1957. London. Ills. 438 pp. 25 pls. index. $17.50

ALINGTON, C.A. *Midnight Wireless.* 1947. London. Macdonald. 1st ed. dj. VG $30.00

ALLA, Ogal. *Blue Eye. A Story of the People of the Plains.* 1905. Portland. 245 pp. $20.00

ALLAN, Doug. *Facing Danger in the Last Wilderness.* 1962. Rolton House. 214 pp. dj. EX $20.00

ALLAN, P.B.M. *The Book-Hunter at Home.* 1922. New York. 2nd ed. 1/500. VG $20.00

ALLAN, William. *History of the Campaign of Gen. T.J. Jackson.* 1974. Dayton. Morningside Pr. dj. VG $20.00

ALLARD. *Faces of Bronze.* 1960. New York. Ills. 1st Am. ed. dj. VG $12.50

ALLBEURY, Ted. *Moscow Quadrille.* 1976. London. 1st ed. dj. VG $20.00

ALLBUT, Robert. *The Tourist's Handbook to Switzerland.* 1892. London. Ills. 7th ed. maps. G $20.00

ALLEGRO, J. *Treasure of Copper Scroll.* 1960. New York. 1st ed. dj. EX $22.50

ALLEN, A. *Stalking Birds with Color Camera.* 1951. Nat. Geog. Soc. 1st ed. 331 photos. 328 pp. $15.00

ALLEN, C. & B. *The Man Wonderful in the House Beautiful.* 1887. New York. VG $7.50

ALLEN, Capt Quincy. *The Outdoor Chums on the Lake.* 1911. Goldsmith. 229 pp. G $2.50

ALLEN, Caroline S. *The Well-Bred Dolls.* 1913. Boston. Ills. EX $20.00

ALLEN, Charlotte Vale. *Intimate Friends.* 1983. Dutton. proof copy. wrappers. VG $15.00

ALLEN, D.L. *Michigan Fox Squirrel Management.* 1943. Mich. Dept. Conserv. 404 pp. $7.00

ALLEN, D.L. *Pheasants in North America.* 1956. Stackpole. photos. 409 pp. EX $45.00

ALLEN, Douglas. *Frederic Remington & the Spanish-American War.* 1971. New York. Ltd. ed. 1/150. sgn. boxed. $100.00

ALLEN, Edward & Kelley, B.F. *Fun by the Ton.* 1941. New York. Ills. 116 pp. $9.00

ALLEN, Edward L. *Pilot Lore from Sail to Steam.* 1922. New York. Deluxe ed. $30.00

ALLEN, Edward. *Merchants of Menace. The Mafia.* 1962. Springfield. Ills. 1st ed. 326 pp. dj. VG $25.00

ALLEN, Everett S. *The Black Ships.* 1979. dj. $12.50

ALLEN, Everett. *Arctic Odyssey. Life of Admiral Donald Macmillan.* 1963. Dodd Mead. dj. sgn. $35.00

ALLEN, F.M. *Brayhard.* 1890. Ward & Downey. 1st ed. ex-lib. $65.00

ALLEN, Fred. *Letters.* 1965. Garden City. Doubleday. 359 pp. $5.00

ALLEN, Fred. *Much Ado About Me.* 1956. Boston. Little, Brown. 380 pp. $6.50

ALLEN, Frederick Lewis. *Since Yesterday. The 1930's in America.* 1940. New York. Harper. photos. $6.50

ALLEN, G. *Birds & Their Attributes.* 1948. Jones. Ills. 338 pp. $13.00

ALLEN, G.R. *Fishes of Western Australia.* 1985. 526 color photos. 329 pp. $30.00

ALLEN, George F. *Francis' Metallic Life Boat Company.* 1852. New York. Ills. 1st ed. map. VG $75.00

ALLEN, George H. *The Great War.* 1915. Philadelphia. Ills. 5 vol set. EX $45.00

ALLEN, Grant. *The Story of Plants.* 1904. Appleton. Ills. 218 pp. $3.50

ALLEN, Grant. *The Woman Who Did.* 1895. 1st Am. ed. G $20.00

ALLEN, Hervey. *Action at Aquila.* 1938. New York. 1st ed. dj. VG $7.50

ALLEN, Hervey. *Anthony Adverse.* 1933. New York. 1st ed. 1224 pp. EX $30.00

ALLEN, Hervey. *Christmas Epithalamium.* 1925. New York. Ltd. ed. 1/295. dj. $15.00

ALLEN, Hervey. *Israfel. Life & Times of Edgar Allan Poe.* 1934. New York. Farrar. Ills. 748 pp. $4.50

ALLEN, Hervey. *The City in the Dawn.* 1950. New York. 696 pp. $4.00

ALLEN, Hervey. *Toward the Morning.* 1948. New York. 458 pp. $4.50

ALLEN, Hugh. *Rubber's Home Town.* 1949. New York. Ills. 1st ed. 265 pp. dj. VG $37.50

ALLEN, Hugh. *The House of Goodyear.* 1949. photos. $6.00

ALLEN, Ivan. *Atlanta from the Ashes.* 1928. Atlanta. Ills. Ltd ed. sgn. 114 pp. $17.50

ALLEN, James Lane. *Bride of Mistletoe.* 1909. 1st ed. $10.00

ALLEN, James Lane. *The Choir Invisible.* 1897. EX $7.50

ALLEN, James Lane. *The Doctor's Christmas Eve.* 1910. New York. 1st ed. 304 pp. $12.50

ALLEN, James Lane. *The Reign of Law: A Tale of KY Hemp Fields.* 1900. New York. 1st ed. VG $15.00

ALLEN, James. *As a Man Thinketh.* Mount Vernon. Pauper Press. 60 pp. dj. $17.50

ALLEN, John Houghton. *Southwest.* 1952. Philadelphia. Lippencott. 1st ed. $12.50

ALLEN, Joseph Chase. *The Wheelhouse Loafer.* 1966. Little, Brown. 1st ed. $8.50

ALLEN, Jules Verne. *Cowboy Lore.* 1933. San Antonio. 1st ed. 165 pp. dg. VG $30.00

ALLEN, L.A. *Time Before Morning.* 1975. Crowell. Ills. 1st ed. VG $20.00

ALLEN, Leonard L. *History of New York State Grange.* 1934. Watertown, NY. 215 pp. VG $10.00

ALLEN, Lt. H.T. *Expedition to Copper, Tanana & Koyukuk Rivers.* 1985. photos. maps. 96 pp. $7.00

ALLEN, Mark. *Falconry in Arabia.* 1980. London. Ills. 1st ed. dj. EX $32.00

ALLEN, Mrs. J. *Samantha Among the Brethren.* 1891. H.J. Smith. Ills. $9.50

ALLEN, Mrs. J. *Samantha at Coney Island.* 1911. Christian Herald. 349 pp. $12.50

ALLEN, Mrs. J. *Samantha at Saratoga.* 1887. Hurst. Ills. 374 pp. $8.50

ALLEN, Mrs. J. *Samantha at the World's Fair.* 1893. Funk & Wagnalls. Ills. $9.50

ALLEN, P.S. *Correspondence of Early Printing House.* 1932. Glasgow. 36 pp. $27.50

ALLEN, Paul. *A History of the American Revolution.* 1819. Baltimore. Hopkins. 1st ed. 2 vol set. $175.00

ALLEN, Ralph B. *Poems.* 1963. inscr. dj. $10.00

ALLEN, Robert. *Birds of the Caribbean.* 1961. Viking. Ills. 1st ed. map. dj. $25.00

ALLEN, Stookie. *Men of Daring.* 1933. New York. Ills. 86 pp. $7.50

ALLEN, T. *Vanishing Wildlife of North America.* 1974. Nat. Geog. Soc.Ills. photos. 207 pp. dj. $15.00

ALLEN, T.G. & Sachtleben, W.L.*Across Asia on a Bicycle.* 1894. New York. Century. Ills. EX $35.00

ALLEN, T.L. *Blue Green Grass Region of Kentucky.* 1900. New York. 1st ed. VG $12.50

ALLEN, Van Nes. *I Found Africa.* 1939. Indianapolis. Ills. 1st ed. 306 pp. $12.50

ALLEN, Willis Boyd. *The Head of Pasht.* 1900. New York. Dutton. 1st ed. VG $40.00

ALLEN, Woody. *Side Effects.* 1980. Random House. 1st ed. dj. G $17.00

ALLEN, Woody. *Without Feathers.* 1975. Random House. 1st ed. dj. VG $20.00

ALLEN. *Battles of the British Navy.* 1842. London. 2 vol set. VG $90.00

ALLEN. *N.C. Wyeth: Collected Paintings, Ills. & Murals.* 1972. Crown. 1st ed. dj. EX $50.00

ALLEN. *The Sea Years of Joseph Conrad.* 1965. Doubleday. 368 pp. dj. EX $7.50

ALLENDE, Isabel. *The House of the Spirits.* 1985. Knopf. 1st Am. ed. dj. VG $17.50

ALLERS, C. *Capri.* 1892. Munich. 53 pls. folio. $40.00

ALLHANDS, J.L. *Railroads to the Rio.* 1960. Salado, TX. Ills. Ltd. 1st ed. 213 pp. $45.00

ALLILUYEVA, Svetlana. *Only One Year.* 1969. New York. 439 pp. dj. VG $5.00

ALLILUYEVA, Svetlana. *Twenty Letters to a Friend.* 1967. Harper. 1st ed. 246 pp. G $37.50

ALLINGHAM, Margery. *Crime & Mr. Campion.* 1937. New York. Doubleday. 575 pp. $3.50

ALLINGHAM, Margery. *Take Two at Bedtime.* 1950. Surrey. 1st ed. presentation copy. $65.00

ALLINGHAM, Margery. *The Beckoning Lady.* 1955. London. Chatto & Windus. 1st ed. dj. $35.00

ALLINGHAM, Margery. *Three Cases for Mr. Campion.* 1941. New York. Book Club Ed. 604 pp. dj. EX $12.50

ALLISON, J. Murray. *The Five Black Cousins.* 1924. London. Ills. Austen. 1st ed. sgn. dj. $35.00

ALLISON, W.L. *Adventures of Famous Sailors.* New York. (ca.1860-1900) 300 pp. $22.50

ALLWARD, Maurice & Taylor, J. *Spitfire.* 1946. Leicester. Harborough Pub. EX $19.00

ALLWARD, Maurice. *Hurricane Special.* 1975. London. Allan Ltd. 1st ed. $14.50

ALLYN, John. *The Forty-Seven Ronin Story.* 1972. Tuttle. 240 pp. dj. scarce. VG $18.00

ALMANSI, Guido, ed. *Photos/Letters of Lewis Carroll to Child Friends.* 1975. $85.00

ALMY, Frank. *Life, Trial & Confession of Frank Almy.* Laconia, NH. (ca.1892) 1st ed. EX $50.00

ALPINI, Prosperi. *De Medicine Aegyptorium, Libri Quotuor.* 1591. $625.00

ALSBERG, Henry G. *The American Guide.* 1949. New York. Hastings House. 1348 pp. dj. $4.50

ALSOP, George. *Character of the Province of Maryland.* 1880. Baltimore. Ills. Ltd. ed. ex-lib. 125 pp. $50.00

ALSOP, George. *Character of the Province of Maryland.* 1902. Cleveland. Burrows. Ltd. ed. EX $50.00

ALSOP, Stewart. *Stay of Execution.* 1973. New York. Lippincott. 305 pp. dj. $5.00

ALTER, Stephen. *Neglected Lives.* 1978. Farrar. 1st ed. dj. VG $12.50

ALTER. *James Bridger.* 1951. Ltd. ed. 1/1000. sgn. $50.00

ALTHER, Lisa. *Other Women.* 1984. Knopf. 1st ed. dj. VG $15.00

ALTMAN, Seymour & Violet. *Book of Buffalo Pottery.* 1969. New York. Crown. Ills. 1st ed. dj. VG $17.50

ALTSHELER, Joseph. *The Hosts of the Air.* 1942. Appleton Century. G $10.00

ALVAREZ. *Savage God.* 1972. 4th ed. dj. VG $8.50

ALVAREZ. *Travel on Southern Antebellum Railroads 1826-1860.* 1974. U. of AL. 1st ed. dj. VG $20.00

ALVORD, C. & Carter, C. *Trade & Politics 1767-1769.* 1921. Springfield. 760 pp. $18.50

AMADO, Jorge. *Gabriela.* London. 1st ed. dj. VG $25.00

AMADO, Jorge. *Home is the Sailor.* 1964. New York. 1st ed. dj. EX $20.00

AMADO, Jorge. *Pen, Sword, Camisole.* 1986. Godine. 1st Am. ed. dj. VG $15.00

AMADO, Jorge. *The Swallow & the Tom Cat.* 1982. Delacorte. Ills. Carybe. 1st Am. ed. dj. $10.00

AMADO, Jorge. *The Swallow & the Tom Cat.* 1982. Delacorte. proof copy. wrappers. EX $35.00

AMADO, Jorge. *The Two Deaths of Quincas Wateryell.* 1965. Knopf. Ills. 1st Am. ed. dj. VG $30.00

AMADON, Dean. *A Child's Book of Wild Birds.* 1955. New York. Maxton Pub. Ills. 1st ed. EX $10.00

AMBASZ, E. *Italy: New Domestic Landscape.* 1972. EX $25.00

AMBER, J, ed. *Gun Digest Treasury.* 1961. wrappers. VG $10.00

AMBER, J. *Guns Illustrated.* 2nd ed. dj. VG $7.50

AMBLER, E. *Passage of Arms.* 1960. New York. 1st Am. ed. dj. EX $12.00

AMBLER, Eric, ed. *To Catch a Spy.* 1965. Atheneum. 1st Am. ed. dj. VG $20.00

AMBLER, Eric. *A Kind of Anger.* 1964. Atheneum. 1st ed. dj. EX $15.00

AMBLER, Eric. *Doctor Frigo.* 1974. New York. Atheneum. dj. EX $15.00

AMBLER, Eric. *The Care of Time.* 1981. NY. Farrar. proof copy. wrappers. EX $35.00

AMBLER, Eric. *The Intercom Conspiracy.* 1969. Atheneum. 1st ed. dj. EX $25.00

AMBLER, Eric. *The Levanter.* 1972. New York. Atheneum. dj. VG $20.00

AMBLER, Eric. *The Schirmer.* 1953. Knopf. 1st Am. ed. dj. EX $20.00

AMBLER, Eric. *The Seige of the Villa Lipp.* 1977. New York. Random House. dj. EX $20.00

AMBLER, R.P. *The Spiritual Teacher.* 1860. New York. A.J. Davis. 149 pp. $35.00

AMBROSE, D. *Under Gas-Light: or, Lights & Shadows IL Capital.* 1879. Springfield. T.W. Kidd, Pub. 144 pp. $30.00

AMBROSINI, M.L. & Willis, M. *The Secret Archives of the Vatican.* 1969. Boston. Ills. 1st ed. 366 pp. dj. $10.00

AMERICAN HERITAGE. *Historic Houses of America.* 1971. New York. American Heritage Pub. 320 pp. $5.00

AMERICAN HOME. *American Home Garden Book & Plant Encyclopedia.* 1972. 512 pp. EX $5.50

AMERICAN KENNEL CLUB. *Pure-Bred Dogs.* 1935. New York. Ills. G $50.00

AMERICAN KENNEL CLUB. *American Kennel Club Blue Book of Dogs.* 1938. New York. G $35.00

AMERICAN ROSE SOCIETY. *What Every Rose-Grower Should Know.* 1940. Am. Rose Soc. Ills. 80 pp. $2.50

AMERINGER, Oscar. *Communism, Socialism, & the Church.* 1913. Milwaukee. 1st ed. wrappers. VG $15.00

AMERINGER, Oscar. *If You Don't Weaken.* 1940. New York. Holt. 1st ed. dj. EX $35.00

AMES, Joseph. *Loudon from Laramie.* 1925. New York. 1st ed. dj. VG $12.50

AMES, Mary C. *Eirene, or a Woman's Right.* 1871. New York. $21.50

AMES, Mary C. *Ten Years in Washington.* 1874. Ills. VG $12.50

AMES, P.L. & Stickney, E.H. *Avian Anatomical Specimens in Peabody Museum.* 1968. Yale U. Press. 40 pp. $2.00

AMES, Seth. *Works of Fisher Ames Vol. II.* 1854. Little, Brown. 442 pp. $3.00

AMHERST, A. *History of Gardening in England.* 1895. 1st ed. G $18.00

AMIS, Kingsley. *Colonel Sun.* 1968. New York. Harper. dj. VG $20.00

AMIS, Kingsley. *Girl 20.* London. 1st Eng. ed. dj. EX $10.00

AMIS, Kingsley. *I Like It Here.* 1958. Harcourt. 1st ed. dj. $12.50

AMIS, Kingsley. *On Drink.* 1972. London. Ills. Nicolas Bentley. 1st ed. $25.00

AMIS, Kingsley. *Take a Girl Like You.* 1960. 1st Am. ed. dj. VG $12.50

AMIS, Kingsley. *The Green Man.* 1970. Harcourt. 1st Am. ed. dj. VG $20.00

AMIS, Kingsley. *The Riverside Villas Murder.* 1973. New York. Harcourt. dj. EX $15.00

AMIS, Martin. *Dead Babies.* 1975. London. Cape. 1st ed. VG $35.00

AMIS. *That Uncertain Feeling.* 1956. New York. 1st Am. ed. dj. VG $10.00

AMMEN. *The Navy in the Civil War: The Atlantic Coast.* 1898. Ills. 272 pp. $12.50

AMMONS, A.R. *Corsons Inlet.* 1965. Ithaca. Cornell. advance copy. dj. EX $65.00

AMORY, Cleveland & Bradlee, F. *Vanity Fair.* 1960. New York. Viking. 327 pp. $6.00

AMORY, Cleveland. *Who Killed Society?* 1960. New York. Harper. Ills. 599 pp. $5.00

AMOS, Andrew. *Great Oyer of Poisoning Trial in Tower of London.* 1846. London. 1st ed. G $30.00

AMSDEN, Charles Avery. *Navaho Weaving, Its Technique & History.* 1974. Rio Grande. Ills. 261 pp. $30.00

AMSDEN, Charles Avery. *Navaho Weaving.* 1934. Southwest Museum. 1st ed. sgn. $180.00

AMSDEN, Dora & Happer, J.S. *Heritage of Heroshige: Glimpse Japanese Landscape.* 1912. Elder. Ills. $40.00

AMSDEN, Dora. *Impressions of Ukiyo-e, School Japanese Artists.* 1905. Ills. 84 pp. G $52.00

AMSDEN, Dora. *The Macaroni Tree.* 1927. Santa Barbara. Ills. Paget-Fredericks. VG $25.00

AMUNDSEN, R. & Ellsworth, L. *First Crossing of the Polar Sea.* 1928. Doubleday Doran. VG $45.00

ANATOLI, A. *Babi Yar.* 1970. New York. 1st ed. dj. VG $10.00

ANCHORS, Don. *Common Folks. A Group of Original Poems.* 1926. Kansas City. radio gift ed. sgn. 94 pp. $12.50

ANDERS, Gen. W. *Hitler's Defeat in Russia.* 1953. 1st ed. $35.00

ANDERS, Nedda Casson. *Cookbook for Infra-Red Broiler & Rotisserie.* 1955. New York. Barrows. 5th printing. 219 pp. $5.50

ANDERSEN, Hans Christian. *Fairy Tales.* 1957. Flensted. World Edition. 3 vol set. EX $15.00

ANDERSEN, Hans Christian. *Fairy Tales.* New York. Brentano. Ills. Clarke. VG $95.00

ANDERSEN, Hans Christian. *Story of a Mother.* 1929. Cincinnati. 18 pls. VG $30.00

ANDERSEN, Hans Christian. *The Sand Hills of Jutland.* 1860. Boston. VG $40.00

ANDERSEN, Hans Christian. *The Tumble-Bug & Other Tales.* 1940. New York. Ills. Hertha List. 1st ed. VG $30.00

ANDERSEN, Hans Christian. *The Wild Swans & Other Stories.* 1922. Jacobs & Co. Ills. Abbott & Shenton. EX $4.50

ANDERSON, Alex. *Father of Wood Engraving in America.* Am. Tract Soc. (ca.1820) Ills. $125.00

ANDERSON, Anne. *The Patsy Book.* Ills. Thomas Nelson. G $40.00

ANDERSON, Anne. *The Wonder Storybook.* London. 6 color pls. VG $45.00

ANDERSON, Bernice G. *Topsy Turvy & the Tin Clown.* 1934. Chicago. Rand McNally. Ills. Friend. $15.00

ANDERSON, Betty Baxter. *Julia Brent of the WAAC.* 1943. New York. 248 pp. $3.50

ANDERSON, Bruce. *The Solar Home Book.* 1977. Brick House Pub. Ills. photos. $4.50

ANDERSON, C. *Megellan.* 1970. New York. 1st ed. dj. EX $10.00

ANDERSON, C.W. *A Touch of Greatness.* 1945. Macmillan. Ills. 1st ed. VG $20.00

ANDERSON, Charles. *Bookselling in America & the World.* 1975. New York. Times Book Co. dj. VG $10.00

ANDERSON, Clinton & Viorst, M. *Outsider in the Senate.* 1970. New York. World. 328 pp. dj. $4.50

ANDERSON, D. *American Flower Painting.* 1980. New York. Watson-Guptill. $15.00

ANDERSON, D. *Claudie's Kinfolks.* 1954. Boston. inscr. $20.00

ANDERSON, Duncan. *History of the Abbey & Palace of Holyrood.* 1857. Edinburgh. Ills. wrappers. VG $45.00

ANDERSON, F.B. *A Grandfather for Benjamin Franklin.* 1940. VG $12.50

ANDERSON, I. *Spell of the Hawaiian Islands & Philippines.* 1916. Ills. 1st ed. dj. VG $12.50

ANDERSON, Isabel. *Presidents & Pies.* 1920. Boston. 290 pp. $5.00

ANDERSON, Isabel. *Yacht in Mediterranean Waters.* 1930. Boston. 1st ed. dj. EX $17.50

ANDERSON, J.M. *The Changing World of Birds.* 1973. Holt. Ills. 1st ed. 122 pp. dj. $5.00

ANDERSON, James H. *Life & Letters of Judge Thomas J. Anderson & Wife.* 1904. Columbus. 535 pp. $20.00

ANDERSON, Jean & Hanna, E. *The Doubleday Cookbook Vol. I.* 1975. New York. Doubleday. 780 pp. $3.50

ANDERSON, John. *Box Office.* 1929. 121 pp. dj. VG $12.50

ANDERSON, Ken. *Winky Lost in the Rockies.* 1944. Grand Rapids. 66 pp. dj. $2.50

ANDERSON, Kenneth. *Man Eaters & Jungle Killers.* 1957. New York. Nelson. Ills. $17.50

ANDERSON, M. *Candle in the Wind.* 1941. 1st ed. $10.00

ANDERSON, M. *Wingless Victory.* 1937. 2nd ed. dj. $10.00

ANDERSON, P. *Orion Shall Rise.* 1983. Phantasia Press. Ltd. ed. $50.00

ANDERSON, P. *Vault of the Ages.* 1952. Philadelphia. author's 1st book. dj. $40.00

ANDERSON, Paul. *The Merman's Children.* 1979. New York. Putnam. proof copy. wrappers. $30.00

ANDERSON, Rudolph E. *The Story of the American Automobile.* 1950. Washington. Ills. 301 pp. dj. VG $12.50

ANDERSON, Rufus. *Memoir of Catherine Brown, a Christian Indian.* 1827. Cincinnati. 3rd ed. 143 pp. $100.00

ANDERSON, S. *Horses & Men.* 1923. 1st ed. VG $25.00

ANDERSON, Sherwood. *A Story Teller's Story.* 1924. Heubsch. dj. VG $55.00

ANDERSON, Sherwood. *Dark Laughter.* 1925. New York. 6th printing. VG $25.00

ANDERSON, Sherwood. *Hello Towns.* 1929. 1st ed. $26.50

ANDERSON, Sherwood. *Puzzled America.* 1935. Scribner. 1st ed. VG $15.00

ANDERSON, Sherwood. *Return to Winesburg.* 1967. Chapel Hill. Ills. 1st ed. 223 pp. dj. $75.00

ANDERSON, Sherwood. *Sherwood Anderson's Memoirs.* 1942. 1st ed. $10.00

ANDERSON, Sherwood. *Sherwood Anderson's Notebook.* 1926. 1st ed. EX $15.00

ANDERSON, Sherwood. *Winesburg, Ohio.* 1919. New York. 1st ed. VG $25.00

ANDERSON, Sparky. *The Main Spark.* 1978. Doubleday. 1st ed. sgn. dj. VG $17.50

ANDERSON, William. *Japanese Wood Engravings, Their History.* 1895. London. Ills. 80 pp. $125.00

ANDERSON. *Gem Testing.* 1971. New York. $15.00

ANDERSON. *Southwestern American Literature.* 1980. 1st ed. 445 pp. dj. EX $30.00

ANDERSON. *Sparks of Laughter, 5th Annual Compilation.* 1924. Spruce Printing. 299 pp. G $4.50

ANDERSON. *The Craftsman in America.* 1975. Nat. Geo. Soc. Ills. 200 pp. $6.50

ANDERSON. *They are Human Too.* 1957. Chicago. Ills. 1st ed. dj. VG $7.50

ANDOM, R. *The Strange Adventure of Roger Wilkins.* 1895. Ills. Tylston. 1st ed. VG $50.00

ANDRE, Eugene. *A Naturalist in the Guianas.* 1904. London. Smith Elder. fld map. 310 pp. $145.00

ANDREE, S.A. *Andree's Story: Complete Record of Polar Flight.* 1930. Blue Ribbon Books. VG $30.00

ANDRETTI, Mario & Collins, B. *What's It Like Out There?* 1970. Chicago. photos. 282 pp. dj. VG $4.50

ANDREWS, Allen. *The Pig Plantagent.* 1980. New York. Viking. Ills. Foreman. dj. $25.00

ANDREWS, Charles. *The Colonial Period of American History.* 1937-1938. Yale. 4 vol set. $60.00

ANDREWS, Clarence L. *The Eskimo & His Reindeer in Alaska.* 1939. Caldwell, ID. 253 pp. photos. $15.00

ANDREWS, Edward. *The People Called Shakers.* 1953. Oxford. 1st ed. dj. $10.00

ANDREWS, Henry. *Decendants of John Porter of Windsor, CT, 1635-39.* 1893. Saratoga Springs. Vol. II. G $25.00

ANDREWS, Israel Ward. *Washington County & Early Settlement of Ohio.* 1877. Cincinnati. Ills. 251 pp. $60.00

ANDREWS, Marietta Minnigerode. *George Washington's Country.* 1930. New York. Dutton. Ills. 318 pp. dj. $3.50

ANDREWS, Mary R.S. *The Eternal Masculine.* 1913. New York. Ills. 1st ed. VG $10.00

ANDREWS, Mary Raymond Shipman. *Joy in the Morning.* 1919. New York. Scribner. $10.00

ANDREWS, R.H. *A Corner of Chicago.* 1963. 1st ed. $5.50

ANDREWS, Ralph W. *Indians as the Westerners Saw Them.* 1973. New York. Ills. dj. 176 pp. $7.00

ANDREWS, Raymond. *Appalachee Red.* 1978. New York. Dial. proof copy. wrappers. EX $20.00

ANDREWS, Raymond. *Rosiebelle Lee Wildcat of Tennessee.* 1980. Dial Press. advance copy. wrappers. EX $20.00

ANDREWS, Roger. *Old Fort Mackinac on the Hill of History.* 1938. Menominee, MI. Ills. 190 pp. $25.00

ANDREWS, Roy & Andrews, Y. *Camps & Trails in China.* 1918. presentation copy. sgn. $95.00

ANDREWS, Roy & Andrews, Y. *Camps & Trails in China.* 1919. New York. Ills. map. 334 pp. $75.00

ANDREWS, Roy. *Across Mongolian Plains.* 1921. Blue Ribbon Books. 276 pp. $15.00

ANDREWS, Roy. *An Explorer Comes Home.* 1947. Doubleday. 1st ed. 276 pp. $13.00

ANDREWS, Roy. *Meet Your Ancestors, Biography of Primitive Man.* 1945. New York. Viking. Ills. 259 pp. $5.00

ANDREWS, Roy. *My Favorite Stories of the Great Outdoors.* 1950. Greystone. 404 pp. dj. G $10.00

ANDREWS, Roy. *On the Trail of Ancient Man.* 1926. Putnam. photos. fld map. 375 pp. VG $20.00

ANDREYEV, Vladimir. *Gamailis & Other Tales from Stalin's Russia.* 1963. Chicago. 240 pp. dj. VG $7.50

ANDRONOW & CHAIKIN. *Theory of Oscillations.* 1949. $15.00

ANDRY, R. *African Genesis, Personal Investigation.* 1963. Atheneum. Ills. 1st ed. 390 pp. VG $10.00

ANELL, Bengt. *Hunting & Trapping Methods in Australia.* 1960. 1st ed. stiff wrappers. $25.00

ANGELO, Valenti. *Hill of Little Miracles.* 1942. New York. Ills. dj. G $15.00

ANGELO, Valenti. *Nino.* 1938. Lit. Guild. 1st ed. $20.00

ANGELOU, Maya. *Gather Together in My Name.* 1974. Random House. 1st ed. sgn. dj. VG $30.00

ANGELOU, Maya. *I Know Why the Caged Bird Sings.* 1969. New York. Random House. 1st ed. dj. EX $25.00

ANGELOU, Maya. *Shaker, Why Don't You Sing.* 1983. Random House. 1st ed. dj. VG $7.50

ANGELOU, Maya. *Shaker, Why Don't You Sing.* 1983. Random House. proof copy. wrappers. VG $35.00

ANGELUCCI, Enzo. *Airplanes, from the Dawn of Flight to Present Day.* 1973. New York. McGraw Hill. dj. EX $15.00

ANGER, K. *Hollywood Babylon.* 1984. New York. Dutton. 1st ed. dj. EX $15.00

ANGIER, Bradford. *Living off the Country.* 1971. Stackpole. Ills. 241 pp. dj. $10.00

ANGIER, Bradford. *Survival with Style.* 1970. Ills. 320 pp. $4.00

ANGLE, Paul. *A Shelf of Lincoln Books.* 1946. Ltd. ed. 1/1000. VG $15.00

ANGLE, Paul. *Here I Have Lived: Hist. of Lincoln's Springfield.* 1935. Springfield. 1st ed. inscr. sgn. EX $25.00

ANGLE, Paul. *The Great Chicago Fire.* 1946. Chicago. Ills. 85 pp. VG $8.50

ANGLE, Paul. *The Lincoln Reader.* 1947. New York. photos. 564 pp. $6.00

ANGLO, Michael. *Penny Dreadfuls & Other Victorian Horrors.* 1977. London. Jupiter. Ills. 1st ed. dj. VG $25.00

ANGLUND, Jean. *In a Pumpkin Shell. A Mother Goose ABC.* 1961. Collins. Ills. 1st Eng. ed. 30 pp. dj. $20.00

ANGLUND, Joan. *Morning is a Little Child.* 1969. New York. Ills. 1st ed. EX $8.50

ANGOFF. *World of George Jean Nathan.* 1952. $15.00

ANGUS, W. Mack. *Rivalry on the Atlantic.* 1939. Furman. 1st ed. dj. $15.00

ANNABELL, R. *Tales of a Big Game Guide.* 1938. New York. Derrydale Pr. Ltd. ed. EX $375.00

ANNENBERG, M. *Typographic Journey Through Inland Printer.* 1977. Baltimore. Moane Press. EX $45.00

ANNES, Milford E. *Song of Metamoris.* 1964. Caldwell, ID. 509 pp. dj. VG $20.00

ANNIXGER, Paul. *Wilderness Ways.* 1930. Philadelphia. Ills. C.L. Bull. 1st ed. EX $25.00

ANNO, Mutsumasa. *Anno's Alphabet.* 1975. 1st Am. ed. dj. EX $17.50

ANNO, Mutsumasa. *Anno's Counting House.* 1982. Philomel. Ills. 1st ed. dj. VG $10.00

ANOBILE, Rich, ed. *Why a Duck?* 1971. New York. intro Groucho. photos. 288 pp. $20.00

ANON. *When a Man's a Man.* 1916. Book Supply. 1st ed. $4.00

ANON. *A Centennial View of Our Country & Its Resources.* 1876. foxing, covered scarred. G $20.00

ANON. *A Century of Progress: General Electric Story.* 1981. 4 vols in 1. Photohistory. $17.50

ANON. *A Complete History of the World War.* 1919. 5 vol. set. $14.50

ANON. *A Little Cookbook for a Little Girl.* 1905. Boston. soiled, disbound. $8.00

ANON. *A New Alice in an Old Wonderland.* 1874. Philadelphia. 1st ed. VG $30.00

ANON. *Achievement. By Leaders of World Affairs.* 1928. New York. Am. Educational Pr. 225 pp. VG $15.00

ANON. *American Almanac.* 1832. Boston. 312 pp. VG $75.00

ANON. *American Almanac.* 1837. Boston. 336 pp. VG $75.00

ANON. *American Wildlife Illustrated.* 1940. New York. VG $15.00

ANON. *American Woman's Cookbook.* 1938. Thumb, Indiana. $18.00

ANON. *Animal Stories for Little People.* Philadelphia. Altemus. Ills. 192 pp. G $4.50

ANON. *Animaux Domestiques.* Paris. (ca.1950) Ills. French text. $10.00

ANON. *Annual Encyclopedia For 1872* 1873. New York Ills. 700 pp. $11.50

ANON. *Anton, the Peasant Boy, a Tyrolese Story.* 1861. Carlton & Porter. 118 pp. $3.50

ANON. *As We Knew Adlai.* 1966. Harper. by 22 friends. 288 pp. $4.00

ANON. *Big Budget Book for Boys.* London. no date. Ills. VG $15.00

ANON. *Bradford's History of Plymouth Plantation.* 1898. Boston 1st ed. 555 pp. $21.00

ANON. *Chicken Little.* Chicago. Peter Rabbit Series. Ills. EX $7.50

ANON. *Children. Playtime.* 1896. London. Raphael Tuck & Sons. G $10.00

ANON. *Civil War Medical.* (ca. 1860). 104 pp. $175.00

ANON. *Coal Miners Pocketbook.* 1916. McGraw Hill. 1172 pp. EX $12.50

ANON. *Color Treasury of Model Soldiers.* 1972. Crescent Books. Ills. 64 pp. $3.50

ANON. *Contemporary American Sculpture.* 1929. G $20.00

ANON. *Contemporary Chinese Woodcuts.* 1950. London. scarce. $30.00

ANON. *Covered Bridges on the Byways of Ohio.* 1969. Cincinnati. Ills. 1st ed. 224 pp. $95.00

ANON. *Damon Runyan, Gentleman of Broadway.* 1964. Boston. Ills. 1st ed. ex-lib. 369 pp. $4.00

ANON. *Decorum.* 1880. 352 pp. $9.50

ANON. *Dewdrops.* Boston. American Tract Society. $40.00

ANON. *Farmers & Breeders Directory of Knox Co. IL.* 1917. Chicago. 197 pp. G $30.00

ANON. *Faulty Diction.* 1915. New York. Funk & Wagnalls. 80 pp. $3.50

ANON. *Fifty Years in Chains; or, Life of American Slave.* 1859. New York. Dayton. fair. $50.00

ANON. *Good Housekeeping's Book of Menus.* 1922. New York. G $10.00

ANON. *Grand Army War Songs.* 1885. Chicago. 162 pp. $10.00

ANON. *Great Pirate Stories.* 1937. New York. Tudor Pub. $7.50

ANON. *Great Restaurants of America.* 1960. $8.00

ANON. *Hawaiian Phrase Book.* 1900. 1st ed. $10.00

ANON. *He, a Companion to She.* 1887. N.L. Munro. rare $65.00

ANON. *Hist. of Dearborn & Ohio Counties of Indiana.* 1885. Chicago. reprint. 987 pp. $50.00

ANON. *Historical Places Unearthed in New China.* 1972. Peking. Foreign Language Press. Ills. $25.00

ANON. *History of Hillsdale, Michigan.* 1879. Philadelphia. 333 pp. $80.00

ANON. *History of Ireland, Vol I.* 1833. 285 pp. $10.00

ANON. *History of Palestine or Holy Land.* 1839. 330 pp. $12.50

ANON. *History of Pike County Illinois.* 1880. Chicago. Chas. Chapman Co. 966 pp. G $85.00

ANON. *History of the Town of Millbury, Massachusetts.* 1915. Worcester, MA. index. G $50.00

ANON. *History of the United States of America.* 1823. Keene, NH. $35.00

ANON. *How to Ride A Bicycle.* 1884. New York. Tousey. Ills. VG $22.50

ANON. *Iowa & History & Foremost Citizens, Vol. II.* 1915. Chicago. Clarke. G $30.00

ANON. *Life, Explorations & Public Services of Fremont.* 1856. Ticknor & Fields. 356 pp. $17.50

ANON. *Life of Peter the Great.* 1834. 318 pp. $15.00

ANON. *Linen Nursery ABC & Simple Speller.* 1905. McLoughlin. Ills. cloth. VG $12.00

ANON. *Lion Annual 1969.* London. Fleetway Pub. Ills. 159 pp. G $4.00

ANON. *Lives of Distinguished Shoemakers.* 1849. Portland. 340 pp. $15.00

ANON. *Manners & Customs of the French.* 1893. London. Ills. Ltd. ed. 1/250. $280.00

ANON. *Memorial Book of Princeton Sesquicentennial.* 1898. New York. Ltd ed. 500 copies. Ills. VG $65.00

ANON. *Men of Wyoming: Bios & Photos of 300 Residents.* 1915. Denver. VG $30.00

ANON. *Pearls.* Boston. American Tract Society. $40.00

ANON. *Peeps-At-Many-Lands Series.* 1915. London. 1st ed. 12 colorplates. VG $20.00

ANON. *Picturesque Bloomington, Illinois.* 1907. Bloomington. Pantograph Printing. photos. $20.00

ANON. *Rainy Day Stories.* 1915. Akron. Saalfield. Ills. $10.00

ANON. *Remarks on Tour from Hartford & Quebec in Autumn.* 1820. New Haven. G $70.00

ANON. *Rural Directory of Ottawa County, Michigan.* 1918. Philadelphia. Wilmer Atkinson Co. 223 pp. VG $20.00

ANON. *Salem & Marion County Directory, 1921.* 1921. Portland, OR. Polk & Co. G $15.00

ANON. *Secret Societies of the Middle Ages.* 1848. London. 408 pp. G $90.00

ANON. *Somehow It Works.* 1965. Doubleday. 1st ed. 223 pp. dj. EX $20.00

ANON. *Stories of King Arthur.* Donohue. no date. G $3.50

ANON. *Stories of Robin Hood & the Little Lame Prince.* Barse & Hopkins. no date. G $4.50

ANON. *Story of Robin Hood.* 1889. New York. McLoughlin. VG $5.00

ANON. *Tales from American History. Vol I.* 1839. 238 pp. G $12.50

ANON. *Tell It All: Story Life's Experience in Mormonism.* 1875. Hartford. Ills. VG $75.00

ANON. *The Adventures of John Wetherell.* 1953. Doubleday. $6.50

ANON. *The All Together Book.* 1975. G $5.00

ANON. *The American Home Cookbook by Ladies of Detroit.* 1878. Detroit. $45.00

ANON. *The Arabian Nights Entertainments.* Rand McNally. no date. 632 pp. G $4.50

ANON. *The Babes in the Woods.* 1886. McLoughlin. G $5.00

ANON. *The Boatman's Manual.* 1951. Lane, Norton & Co. 596 pp. $7.50

ANON. *The Book of a Thousand Tongues.* 1938. Am. Bible Soc. 386 pp. $12.00

ANON. *The Boy's Own Conjuring Book.* New York. (ca.1859) 416 pp. VG $50.00

ANON. *The Complete Angler's Guide, 1966.* Fin Pub. FL & Bahamas ed. $3.50

ANON. *The Eighth Wonder.* 1928. Boston. Ills. 2nd ed. 68 pp. $10.00

ANON. *The Experts Book of Shooting Sports.* 1972. Simon & Schuster. 320 pp. $4.00

ANON. *The Groans of the Plantations.* 1689. London. 1st ed. 35 pp. VG $775.00

ANON. *The Little Aesop.* London. Tilts & Bogue. Ills. $160.00

ANON. *The Man Who Killed Hitler.* 1939. Hollywood. Putnam. 1st ed. dj. EX $15.00

ANON. *The Mother's Journal.* 1848. New York. Ills. 376 pp. $8.50

ANON. *The Recreation of Brian Kent.* Book Supply. Ills. St.John. 1st ed. $3.00

ANON. *The Story of Bing Crosby.* 1945. foreword Bob Hope. 239 pp. $6.00

ANON. *The Weekend Book.* 1929. VG $6.00

ANON. *Their Yesterday.* 1912. Book Supply. Ills. Cootes, 1st ed. $3.00

ANON. *Thirteen Months in the Rebel Army.* 1862. New York. Ills. 1st ed. 232 pp. $27.50

ANON. *Towns of New & Old England, Ireland & Scotland.* 1920. Boston. Ills. 2 vols in 1. $25.00

ANON. *Trial of Josef Kramer & Forty-Four Others.* 1949. London. Hodge. Ills. 2 vol set. G $45.00

ANON. *War Lyrics & Songs of the South.* 1866. London. Ills. 261 pp. $27.50

ANON. *Weird Tid-Bits.* New York. White & Allen. 1st Am. ed. EX $15.00

ANON. *Welch & Allied Families.* 1969. Charleston. 312 pp. $15.00

ANON. *Western Star.* 1941. 1st ed. $6.00

ANON. *Women of Achievement.* 1940. New York City. Ltd ed. Ills. Kesslere. $47.00

ANSON, George. *A Voyage Round the World in the Years 1740-44.* 1748. London. Walter. 1st ed. plates. maps. $850.00

ANSON, George. *A Voyage Round the World in the Years 1740-44.* 1756. London. 8th ed. VG $100.00

ANSON, George. *Authentic Account of Commodore Anson's Expedition.* 1744. London. $875.00

ANSON, P.F. *Fishermen & Fishing Ways.* 1975. 150 Ills. 285 pp. dj. $8.00

ANSTED, David. *The Goldseeker's Manual.* 1849. London. 172 pp. $100.00

ANSTEY, F. *Salted Almonds.* 1906. London. 1st ed. VG $25.00

ANTEVS, E. *Quaternary Climates, Big Tree as Climatic Measure.* 1925. Carnegie Inst. Ills. $4.00

ANTHAM, E.A. *The Principle of War.* 1914. Macmillan. 1st ed. ex-lib. 2 vol set. VG $12.50

ANTHEIL, George. *Bad Boy of Music.* 1945. 1st ed. $8.50

ANTHOLOGY. *Mary, Mary, Quite Contrary, & Other Rhymes.* 1897. New York. McLoughlin. Ills. wrappers. VG $15.00

ANTHOLOGY. *Santa Claus Parade: Charming Holiday Stories.* 1903. Chicago. Conkey Co. Ills. 1st ed. VG $12.50

ANTHONY, Edward. *O Rare Don Marquis.* 1962. Garden City. Ills. 1st ed. 670 pp. $10.00

ANTHONY, Irvin. *Decatur.* 1931. New York. $12.50

ANTHONY, Irvin. *Paddle Wheels & Pistols.* 1929. New York. Grosset & Dunlap reprint. dj. $10.00

ANTHONY, Katharine. *Margaret Fuller. A Psychological Biography.* 1920. New York. 1st ed. 223 pp. index. VG $5.00

ANTHONY, Katherine. *Catherine the Great.* 1925. New York. Garden City. 331 pp. $4.00

ANTHONY, Katherine. *Louisa May Alcott.* 1938. New York. Knopf. 304 pp. VG $5.50

ANTHONY, Piers. *Ghost.* proof copy. $25.00

ANTHONY, Piers. *Shade of the Tree.* 1986. 1st ed. dj. $15.00

ANTHONY, Piers. *Wielding a Red Sword.* proof copy. wrappers. $30.00

ANTIN, Mary. *The Promised Land.* 1912. NY/Boston. Houghton Mifflin. 1st ed. sgn. $15.00

APENSZLAK, Jacob. *The Black Book of Polish Jewry.* 1943. New York. Ills. 343 pp. index. dj. EX $55.00

APOLLINAIRE, G. *The Poet Assassinated.* 1923. New York. Broom Pub. Ills. VG $25.00

APOLLINAIRE, G. *The Poet Assassinated.* 1968. New York. Ills. Jim Dine. dj. VG $30.00

APOLLINAIRE, Guillaume. *Le Bestiaire, ou Cortege D'Orphee.* 1977. New York. Ills. Raoul Duffy. boxed. VG $25.00

APPEL, Benjamin. *Brain Guy.* 1934. 1st ed. $10.00

APPELL. *Gunman's Grudge.* Lion. pb. $3.00

APPERLEY, Charles J. *Nimrod's Hunting Tours.* 1903. London. Ltd. ed. 1/50. VG $225.00

APPLE, Max. *Free Agents.* 1984. New York. Harper. dj. EX $15.00

APPLE, Max. *The Oranging of America.* 1976. New York. 1st ed. dj. EX $35.00

APPLEFELD, Aaron. *The Age of Wonders.* 1981. Godine. 1st Am. ed. dj. VG $15.00

APPLETON, Le Roy H. *Indian Art of the Americas.* 1950. New York. Ills. 1st ed. dj. VG $40.00

APPLETON, Victor. *Don Sturdy Among the Gorillas.* New York. Grosset & Dunlap. Ills. $3.00

APPLETON, Victor. *The Moving Picture Boys in Earthquake Land.* 1913. New York. Grosset & Dunlap. 214 pp. dj. $3.50

APPLETON, Victor. *Tom Swift-Wireless-Arabian Nights.* 1924. Winston. Ills. Adeline B. Winston. $15.00

APPLETON. *God & the Groceryman.* 1927. 1st ed. $12.00

APPLETON. *Nile Journal.* 1876. Boston. $40.00

APRIL, Jack. *Feud at Five Rivers.* 1st ed. dj. $6.00

APTHEKER, Herbert. *The Colonial Era.* 1970. New York. International. 158 pp. $4.00

APULEIUS, Lucius. *The Golden Ass.* 1930. private print. Ills. Gockinga. 295 pp. $12.50

ARADI, Zsolt. *Pius XI, the Pope & the Man.* 1958. New York. Hanover House. 262 pp. dj. $6.00

ARBON & CHRISTENSEN. *The Bismarck Sea Ran Red.* 1979. dj. VG $15.00

ARBUTHNOT, May Hill. *Children & Books.* Scott Foresman.(ca.1957) VG $10.00

ARBUTHNOT, May Hill. *Children & Books.* 1947. New York. Ills. 626 pp. index. $12.50

ARBUTHNOT. *African Hunt.* 1954. New York. Ills. 1st ed. VG $10.00

ARCH, E.L. *Double-Minded Man.* 1966. 1st ed. dj. EX $7.50

ARCH, E.L. *Man with Three Eyes.* 1967. 1st ed. dj. EX $7.50

ARCHER, Fred. *Fred Archer on Portraiture.* 1954. San Francisco. Camera Craft. 2nd ed. dj. VG $15.00

ARCHER, G.W. *The Dismemberment of Maryland: Historical Essay.* 1880. Baltimore. 1st ed. 135 pp. $35.00

ARCHER, Jeffrey. *A Matter of Honor.* 1986. 1st ed. sgn. dj. EX $22.00

ARCHER, Jeffrey. *First Among Equals.* 1984. 1st ed. dj. EX $15.00

ARCHER, Jeffrey. *Shall We Tell the President.* 1977. advance ready copy. EX $25.00

ARCHER, Lou Ella. *Canyon Shadows.* 1931. Phoenix. Ills. VG $35.00

ARCHER, William. *Ibsen's Prose Dramas.* 1903. London. 6 vol set. VG $30.00

ARCHIBALD, William. *The Innocents. Play from Turn of the Screw.* 1950. New York. 1st ed. dj. VG $15.00

ARCHINIEGAS, G. *Caribbean, Sea of the New World.* 1946. 1st ed. $7.50

ARD. *Hell is a City.* 1955. 1st Am. ed. dj. EX $15.00

ARDIZZONE, Edward. *Daddy Long Legs.* 1966. Merideth Press.1st ed. dj. VG $8.50

ARDIZZONE, Edward. *Great Expectations.* Heritage Press.Ills. boxed. EX $12.50

ARDIZZONE, Edward. *Hey Nonny Yes.* 1947. London. Ills. 1st ed. dj. EX $65.00

ARDIZZONE, Edward. *Little Bookroom.* 1956. New York. 1st ed. dj. $7.50

ARDIZZONE, Edward. *Peter Pan.* 1962. Scribner. Ills. 1st ed. VG $20.00

ARDIZZONE, Edward. *The Old Ballad of the Babes in the Wood.* 1972. New York. Ills. $20.00

ARDIZZONE, Edward. *Tunnel of Hugsy Goode.* 1972. New York. 1st ed. dj. $7.50

ARDIZZONE, Edward. *Young Ardizzone.* 1970. London. 1st ed. dj. EX $15.00

ARDREY, R. *The Hunting Hypothesis.* 1976. Atheneum. 242 pp. dj. $8.00

ARDREY. *The Social Contract.* 1970. New York. Ills. dj. VG $7.50

ARENSBERG, Ann. *Sister Wolf.* 1981. London. Sidgwick & Jackson. 1st ed. $15.00

ARETINO, Peter. *Raccolta Di Poesie Satiriche.* 1808. Milano. Italian text. $37.50

ARFWEDSPM. *The U.S. & Canada.* 1834. London. 2 vol set. $130.00

ARGENZIO. *Fascination of Diamonds.* 1966. New York. 184 pp. dj. $15.00

ARIS, Stephen. *But There Are No Jews in England.* 1971. New York. 1st Am. ed. 255 pp. index. VG $12.50

ARISTOPHANES. *The Eleven Comedies.* 1928. New York. Ills. Bosschere. Ltd ed. VG $50.00

ARKHAM HOUSE. *30 Years of Arkham House 1939-1969.* 1970. Sauk City. 1st ed. dj. EX $32.50

ARLEN, M. *Man's Mortality.* 1933. Heinemann. 1st ed. dj. VG $50.00

ARLEN, Michael. *Young Men in Love.* 1927. New York. Doran. 1st ed. VG $10.00

ARMER, Laura Adams. *Waterless Mountain.* 1931. NY/Toronto. Ills. 3rd ed. 212 pp. $18.50

ARMISTEAD, Wilson. *Trout Waters.* 1908. London. 1st ed. VG $20.00

ARMITAGE, M. *Homage to the Santa Fe.* 1973. Yucca Valley. Ills. dj. EX $20.00

ARMITAGE, Merle. *The Lithographs of Richard Day.* 1932. Ltd. ed. 1/500. $35.00

ARMONAS, Barbara. *Leave Your Tears in Moscow.* 1961. 6th ed. dj. $27.50

ARMSTRONG, B.L. & Murphy, J.B.*The Natural History of Mexican Rattlesnakes.* 1979. Kansas U. 43 photos. maps. 88 pp. $6.00

ARMSTRONG, Charlotte. *A Dram of Poison.* 1956. New York. dj. VG $7.00

ARMSTRONG, Hamilton F. *Those Days.* 1963. New York. Harper & Row. 151 pp. dj. $5.00

ARMSTRONG, Margaret. *Fanny Kemble a Passionate Victorian.* 1938. New York. Macmillan. 387 pp. VG $5.00

ARMSTRONG, Margaret. *Trelawny, a Man's Life.* 1940. New York. Macmillan. 379 pp. VG $6.00

ARMSTRONG, Martin. *Adrian Glynde.* 1930. London. Ltd. 1st ed. 1/100. sgn. VG $17.50

ARMSTRONG, W. *Red Duster at War. The Merchant Marine in WW II.* 1942. London. G $15.00

ARMSTRONG, William H. *Organs for America.* 1967. ex-lib. EX $10.00

ARMSTRONG. *Mother Church.* 1937. Boston. Ills. dj. VG $17.50

ARMSTRONG. *200 Years American Sculpture.* 1976. Whitney/Godine. $15.00

ARNAC, Marcel. *Thirty-Six Inches of Adventure.* 1930. New York. Planet Press. Ills. 245 pp. $10.00

ARNDT, John Stover. *The Story of the Arndts.* 1922. Philadelphia. Ills. 427 pp. index. VG $27.50

ARNHEIM, Rudolf. *Entropy & Art: Essay on Disorder & Order.* 1971. U. of California. dj. $7.00

ARNO PRESS, eds. *Battlefields of the Civil War.* 1979. Ills. 524 ppl $12.50

ARNOLD, Arthur Z. *Banks, Credit, & Money in Soviet Russia.* 1937. New York. Columbia U. Pr. 1st ed. VG $22.50

ARNOLD, Edward. *The Voyage of the Ithobal.* 1901. NY/London. VG $15.00

ARNOLD, Edwin Lester. *Lieutenant Gullivar Jones, His Vacation.* 1905. London. 1st ed. VG $185.00

ARNOLD, Edwin. *The Light of Asia.* 1880. New York. 121 pp. $35.00

ARNOLD, Edwin. *The Light of Asia.* 1932. Ills. Willy Pogany. $35.00

ARNOLD, Edwin. *The Song Celestial.* 1934. Ills. Willy Pogany. $30.00

ARNOLD, Isaac. *Life of Abraham Lincoln.* 1887. Chicago. VG $12.50

ARNOLD, Matthew. *Essays in Criticism.* 1888. London. 2nd series. 1st ed. 132 pp. $120.00

ARNOLD, Matthew. *Essays in Criticism.* 1865. London. Macmillan. 1st ed. $125.00

ARNOLD, Matthew. *Irish Essays & Others.* 1882. London. Smith, Elder. 1st ed. VG $45.00

ARNOLD, Matthew. *Literature & Dogma.* 1897. London. VG $18.00

ARNOLD, Matthew. *Literature & Dogma.* 1873. London. 1st ed. EX $125.00

ARNOLD, Oren. *Arizona Brags.* 1947. SftCvr. $7.50

ARNOLD, Oren. *Wildlife in the Southwest.* 1936. Upshaw. photos. color pls. 274 pp. $12.00

ARNOLD. *Bill Bruce in the Trans-Continental Race.* 1928. A.L. Burt. EX $5.50

ARNOLD. *Matthew Arnold's Letters.* 1968. U. of Virginia.1st ed. EX $30.00

ARNOLD. *Potiphar's Wife & Other Poems.* 1892. New York. 1st ed. G $15.00

ARNOLD. *Ventures in Book Collecting.* 1923. New York. posthumous work. inscr. widow. $30.00

ARNOLD. E.C. *British Waders: Water-Colour & Description.* 1924. Cambridge. 51 color pls. $95.00

ARNOLD-FORSTER, M. *The World at War.* 1973. Ills. Book Club ed. map. dj. $10.00

ARNOW, Harriet. *Hunter's Horn.* 1949. New York. dj. EX $10.00

ARTHUR, T.S. *Ten Nights in a Barroom.* Altemus. no date (ca.1895) $6.50

ARTHUR. *Life of Lord Kitchener.* 1920. New York. 1st ed. 3 vol set. dj. VG $25.00

ARTIZIBASHEV, Michael. *Sinine, a Russian Love Novel.* 1932. New York. Ills. Wright. Ltd. ed. 328 pp. $20.00

ARTMAN, Samuel R. *The Legalized Outlaw.* 1908. Indianapolis. 295 pp. $10.00

ARTZYBASHEFF, Boris. *As I See.* 1954. Dodd Mead. 1st ed. dj. VG $50.00

ARTZYBASHEFF, Boris. *Poor Shaydullah.* 1931. New York. 1st ed. VG $20.00

ARTZYBASHEFF, Boris. *Seven Simeons.* 1937. London. Cassell. Ltd. ed. 1st ed. VG $35.00

ARUNDALE, George S. *Mount Everest. It's Spiritual Attainment.* 1933. 1st ed. 197 pp. VG $30.00

ARVIK, Charles L. *Fluorescent Lighting.* 1942. New York. 312 pp. VG $10.00

ASBURY, Herbert. *Great Illusion. Informal History of Prohibition.* 1950. New York. 1st ed. 344 pp. dj. VG $17.50

ASBURY, Herbert. *Up From Methodism.* 1926. New York. 1st ed. dj. VG $30.00

ASBURY. *Gem of the Prairie.* 1960. Chicago. Knopf. Ills. 1st ed. VG $10.00

ASCH. *War Goes On.* 1936. New York. 1st ed. G $10.00

ASCHER, Amalie Adler. *The Complete Flower Arranger.* 1974. New York. 228 pp. dj. VG $5.00

ASH, Christopher. *Whaler's Eye.* 1962. Macmillan. 1st ed. dj. $10.00

ASHBEE, C.R. *Kingfisher Out of Egypt.* 1934. London. Ills. Ltd. ed. dj. $25.00

ASHBERY, John. *Some Trees.* 1956. New Haven. Yale U. Press. Ltd. ed. sgn. $150.00

ASHBROOK, William. *Donizetti.* 1965. London. Ills. 1st. ed. dj. VG $20.00

ASHBY, R.C. *He Arrived by Dusk.* 1933. New York. Macmillan. 1st ed. VG $20.00

ASHDOWN, Dulcie M. *Princess of Wales.* 1979. New York. Ills. 240 pp. index. dj. VG $5.00

ASHE, Capt. S.A. *Southern View of Invasion Southern States & War.* 1938. Raleigh. wrappers. VG $15.00

ASHE, R.P. *Chronicles of Uganda.* 1894. London. VG $35.00

ASHE, Thomas. *Travels in America in 1806.* 1808. London. 1st ed. 3 vol set VG $465.00

ASHE, Thomas. *Travels in America in 1806.* 1809. London. 3rd Eng. ed. 316 pp. wrappers. $150.00

ASHFORD, Daisy. *The Young Visitors.* 1919. New York. Doran. G $7.50

ASHFORD. *A Soldier in Science.* 1934. Ills. 2nd printing. VG $10.00

ASHLEY, Ossian D. *Railways & Their Employees.* 1895. Chicago. 213 pp. $15.00

ASHLEY. *Christmas Shadows. The Poor Needle Women.* 1850. New York. 1st ed. rebound. VG $10.00

ASHTON, Francis. *That Great City.* 1940. London. 1st ed. dj. EX $20.00

ASHTON, Francis. *The Breaking Seals.* 1946. London. Andrew Dakers. $50.00

ASHTON, John. *Chap-Books of the 18th Century.* 1882. London. 1st ed. $115.00

ASHTON. *Hyde Park from Domesday Book to Date.* 1896. London. Ills. map. 282 pp. VG $25.00

ASHTON-WARNER, Sylvia. *I Passed This Way.* 1979. New York. Knopf. 1st ed. $7.50

ASHTON-WARNER, Sylvia. *Spinster.* 1959. New York. Simon & Schuster. 1st ed. dj. $30.00

ASIMOV, Carr & Greenberg, eds. *100 Great Fantasy Short Short Stories.* 1984. 1st ed. dj. EX $15.00

ASIMOV, Isaac. *Earth is Room Enough.* 1957. Garden City. dj. EX $50.00

ASIMOV, Isaac. *Fantastic Voyage.* 1966. Boston. Houghton Mifflin. 1st ed. dj. $25.00

ASIMOV, Isaac. *Foundation & Earth.* proof copy. $65.00

ASIMOV, Isaac. *Foundation & Empire.* 1952. Gnome Press. 1st ed. 1st issue. rebound. $125.00

ASIMOV, Isaac. *Foundation.* 1951. Gnome Press. 1st ed. 1st issue. rebound. $150.00

ASIMOV, Isaac. *Foundation's Edge.* 1982. Garden City. 1st ed. dj. VG $15.00

ASIMOV, Isaac. *Foundations's Edge.* 1982. Whispers Press.Ltd. ed. 1/1000. sgn. $100.00

ASIMOV, Isaac. *I, Robot.* 1950. New York. Gnome Press. sgn. $250.00

ASIMOV, Isaac. *Lucky Starr & the Big Sun of Mercury.* 1956. Garden City. 1st ed. dj. G $30.00

ASIMOV, Isaac. *Opus 100.* 1969. Boston. 1st ed. dj. VG $20.00

ASIMOV, Isaac. *Pebble in the Sky.* 1950. 1st Am. ed. dj. $65.00

ASIMOV, Isaac. *Robots & Empire.* 1985. Phantasia Press. Ltd. ed. $50.00

ASIMOV, Isaac. *Second Foundation.* 1953. Gnome Press. 1st ed. 1st printing. rebound. $125.00

ASIMOV, Isaac. *The Best Science Fiction of I. Asimov.* proof copy. $25.00

ASIMOV, Isaac. *The Ends of the Earth.* 1975. New York. 2nd printing. dj. VG $7.50

ASIMOV, Isaac. *The Naked Sun.* 1957. 1st ed. dj. VG $95.00

ASIMOV, Isaac. *The Robots of Dawn.* 1983. Phantasia Press. Ltd. ed. sgn. $100.00

ASIMOV, Isaac. *The Robots of Dawn.* 1983. Garden City. 1st ed. dj. VG $10.00

ASIMOV, Isaac. *Winds of Change.* 1983. Garden City. 1st ed. dj. EX $10.00

ASIMOV, Isaac. *X Stands for Unknown.* 1984. Garden City. 1st ed. dj. VG $10.00

ASIMOV. *Of Matters Great & Small.* 1975. 1st ed. dj. VG $10.00

ASKINS, C. *The African Hunt.* 1958. Harrisburg. 1st ed. dj. EX $20.00

ASKINS, Col. Charles. *Texans, Guns & History.* 1970. New York. Bonanza Books. 246 pp. dj. EX $15.00

ASKINSON. *Perfumes & Their Properties.* 1900. New York. 2nd ed. EX $15.00

ASPETO, M. *The Misbound Volumes.* 1924. London. Dane. 1st ed. VG $40.00

ASPIAZU, Agustin. *Paginas Escogidas.* 1956. La Paz. EX $15.00

ASQUITH, Mary. *We Actor Folks: Story of an Ugly Actress.* 1931. Pittsburgh. White Squaw Pr. 1st ed. inscr. $10.00

ASQUITH. *The Flying Carpet.* 1925. New York. color pls. VG $15.00

ASSOC. for CHILDHOOD ED. *Told Under the Blue Umbrella.* 1934. New York. Macmillan. 161 pp. $3.00

ASTOR, John Jacob. *A Journey in Other Worlds.* 1894. Appleton. 1st ed. dj. $40.00

ATCHERLY, R. *A Trip to Boerland.* 1879. London. VG $47.50

ATGET. *Vision of Paris.* 1963. New York. 1st ed. $250.00

ATHERAN, Robert. *Rebel of the Rockies.* 1962. Yale U. Press. Ills. 1st ed. 395 pp. dj. VG $35.00

ATHERTON, Gertrude. *American Wives & English Husbands.* 1898. New York. Dodd Mead. 1st ed. sgn. G $12.00

ATHERTON, Gertrude. *Black Oxen.* 1923. Boni. Ltd. 1st ed. 1/250. sgn. G $20.00

ATHERTON, Gertrude. *Rezanov.* 1906. New York. 320 pp. $3.00

ATHERTON, Gertrude. *White Morning.* 1918. New York. Ills. inscr. 195 pp. $15.00

ATHERTON, J.S. *The Books at the Wake.* 1960. 1st Am. ed. dj. EX $15.00

ATHERTON. *Conqueror.* 1902. New York. 1st ed. VG $18.00

ATHERTON. *Immortal Marriage.* 1927. New York. 1st ed. 2nd printing. VG $7.50

ATKINS, Elizabeth Howard. *Toby's Goblin.* 1930. Chicago. Ills. U. Trippe. 1st ed. VG $25.00

ATKINS, Robert C. *Dr. Atkins' Diet Revolution.* 1973. New York. McKay. 310 pp. $5.00

ATKINS, William Giles. *History of the Town of Hawley.* 1887. W. Cummington. ex-lib. 132 pp. VG $45.00

ATKINSON, B. *This Bright Land.* 1972. Ills. 1st ed. 201 pp. $5.00

ATKINSON, Edward. *The Margin of Profit.* 1887. New York. Putnam. 1st ed. wrappers. VG $25.00

ATKINSON, Eleanor. *Greyfriars Bobby.* 1912. A.L. Burt. 292 pp. dj. EX $4.50

ATKINSON, J. Brooks. *Henry Thoreau the Cosmic Yankee.* 1927. Knopf. Ills. 1st ed. EX $25.00

ATKINSON, T. *Oriental & Western Siberia.* 1970. Ills. map. 611 pp. VG $45.00

ATTENBOROUGH, David. *Life on Earth, A Natural History.* 1979. Little, Brown. 1st ed. EX $12.50

ATTENBOROUGH, David. *Life on Earth. A Natural History.* 1970. 1st Am. ed. dj. EX $12.50

ATTENBOROUGH, David. *The Living Planet.* 1984. Ills. dj. EX $5.00

ATTENBOROUGH, David. *The Tribal Eye.* 1976. New York. Ills. dj. EX $17.50

ATTERIDGE. *First Phase of the Great War.* 1914. Ills. 244 pp. $14.50

ATTLA, G. *Everything I Know-Training & Racing Sled Dogs.* 1972. dj. VG $10.00

ATTWELL. *Water Babies.* Kingsley, Tuck. 12 pls. VG $35.00

ATWOOD, J. *Daggers & Edged Weapons of Hitler's Germany.* 1965. Berlin. 1st ed. color pls. EX $65.00

ATWOOD, Margaret. *Bluebeard's Egg & Other Stories.* 1986. Boston. Houghton Mifflin. 1st Am. ed. $35.00

ATWOOD, Margaret. *Bodily Harm.* 1982. Simon & Schuster. 1st ed. dj. $15.00

ATWOOD, Margaret. *Dancing Girls.* 1977. Toronto. McClelland & Stewart. dj. EX $30.00

ATWOOD, Margaret. *Dancing Girls.* 1982. New York. Simon & Schuster. dj. VG $15.00

ATWOOD, Margaret. *Lady Oracle.* 1976. Simon & Schuster. 1st ed. dj. $20.00

ATWOOD, Margaret. *Life Before Man.* 1979. New York. 1st ed. sgn. dj. EX $25.00

ATWOOD, Margaret. *Surfacing.* 1972. Toronto. McClelland & Stuart. dj. VG $30.00

ATWOOD, Margaret. *The Handmaid's Tale.* Toronto. 1st ed. inscr. $35.00

ATWOOD, Margaret. *The Handmaid's Tale.* 1986. Houghton Mifflin. 1st ed. sgn. $40.00

ATWOOD. *Encounters with Element Man.* 1982. Ills. Ltd. ed. 1/100. wrappers. $40.00

AUBERTIN, J.J. *A Flight to Mexico.* 1882. London. 325 pp. fld map. $15.00

AUBREY, Frank. *The Devil-Tree of El Dorado.* 1897. New Amsterdam. 1st Am. ed. VG $65.00

AUBRY. *Joseph Conrad, Life & Letters.* 1927. Doubleday Page. 2 vol set. VG $25.00

AUCHINCLOSS, L. *Diary of a Yuppie.* 1986. proof copy. VG $20.00

AUCHINCLOSS, L. *Quotations from Henry James.* 1984. Ltd. 1st ed. 1/500. slipcase. $35.00

AUCHINCLOSS, L. *Reading Henry James.* 1975. Minneapolis. 1st ed. dj. EX $10.00

AUCHINCLOSS, L. *The House of the Prophet.* 1st ed. dj. VG $6.00

AUCHINCLOSS, L. *The Romantic Egoists.* 1954. 1st ed. dj. EX $7.00

AUCHINCLOSS, Louis A. *Writer's Capital.* 1974. U. MN Press. Ills. 160 pp. dj. $7.50

AUCHINCLOSS, Louis. *Second Chance.* 1970. Boston. Houghton Mifflin. 1st ed. dj. $20.00

AUCHINCLOSS, Louis. *The Country Cousin.* 1978. Boston. Houghton Mifflin. 1st ed. dj. $15.00

AUCHINCLOSS, Louis. *The Dark Lady.* 1977. Boston. Houghton Mifflin. 1st ed. dj. $20.00

AUCHINCLOSS, Louis. *The Partners.* 1974. Boston. Houghton Mifflin. 1st ed. dj. $15.00

AUCHINCLOSS, Louis. *The Rector of Justin.* 1964. Boston. Houghton Mifflin. 1st ed. dj. $20.00

AUCHINCLOSS. *Portrait in Brownstone.* 1962. Boston. 1st ed. dj. VG $15.00

AUCHTER, E.C. & Knapp, H.B. *Orchard & Small Fruit Culture.* 1937. New York. Ills. VG $20.00

AUDEN, W.H. *About the House.* 1965. New York. dj. VG $20.00

AUDEN, W.H. *Good-Bye to the Mezzogiorno.* 1958. Milano. 1st ed. wrappers. $50.00

AUDEN, W.H. *Poems.* 1930. London. 1st ed. VG $300.00

AUDEN, W.H. *Poems.* 1934. 1st ed. dj. $150.00

AUDEN, W.H. *Secondary Worlds.* 1968. New York. 1st ed. dj. VG $22.50

AUDEN, W.H. *Thank You Fog. Last Poems by W.H. Auden.* 1974. New York. 1st ed. dj. VG $15.00

AUDEN, W.H. *The Orators.* 1932. London. 1st ed. sgn. $350.00

AUDEN, W.H. *The Shield of Achilles.* 1955. New York. 1st ed. dj. VG $25.00

AUDEN, W.H., Shapiro & Arheim. *Poets at Work.* 1948. Harcourt. 1st ed. dj. $12.50

AUDEN, W.H. & MacNeice, L. *Letters from Iceland.* 1937. 1st ed. G $17.50

AUDEN, W.H. & Taylor, P.B. *The Elder Edda.* 1970. 1st printing. dj. VG $20.00

AUDEN & ISHERWOOD. *On the Frontier.* 1938. London. 1st ed. dj. VG $65.00

AUDEN. *Collected Shorter Poems 1930-44.* 1950. London. dj. EX $50.00

AUDEN. *Journey to a War.* 1939. New York. VG $25.00

AUDREY, R. *Territorial Imperative.* 1966. Atheneum. Ills. 1st ed. $8.00

AUDUBON, John J. *Birds of America.* 1941. Macmillan. Ills. 2nd ed. $25.00

AUDUBON, John J. *Birds of America.* 1937. New York. Ltd. ed. 1/2500. 500 pls. VG $245.00

AUDUBON, John J. *Delineations of American Scenery & Character.* 1926. New York. 1st ed. 349 pp. $20.00

AUEL, Jean M. *The Valley of Horses.* 1982. Crown. proof copy. wrappers. VG $20.00

AUEL, Jean. *Clan of the Cave Bear.* 1980. New York. 1st ed. dj. EX $37.50

AUER, Leopold. *Violin Master Works & Their Interpretation.* 1925. New York. Ills. 166 pp. VG $20.00

AUERBACH, Jessica. *Winter Wife.* 1983. Ticknor. proof copy. dj. VG $15.00

AUFFENBERG, W. *Herpetofauna of Komoda & Notes of Adjacent Areas.* 1980. photos. maps. $15.00

AUGUSTA, J. & Burian, Z. *Prehistoric Animals.* London. no date. Ills. 47 pp. dj. $17.00

AULD, Joseph. *Picturesque Burlington.* 1893. Burlington, VT. Ills. 180 pp. G $17.50

AULD, William Muir. *Christmas Traditions.* 1941. New York. dj. VG $7.50

AULTMAN, Richard. *Learning to Play Golf.* 1969. New York. Rand McNally. Ills. 72 pp. VG $4.00

AURAND, A. Monroe, Jr. *Slants on the Origin of Bundling in Old World.* 1938. Harrisburg. 32 pp. wrappers. $3.00

AURTHUR, Robert. *The Third Marine Division in World War II.* 1948. Infantry Journal Press. $27.50

AUSLANDER, Joseph. *Letters to Women.* 1929. Harper. Ills. Leighton. 1st ed. 85 pp. $10.00

AUSONIUS, Decimus Magnus. *Patchwork Quilt.* London. Ills. Bawden. Ltd. ed. 1/400. $35.00

AUSPURGER, Marie M. *Yellowstone National Park.* 1948. Middletown, OH. inscr. 247 pp. dj. $17.50

AUSTEN, Jane. *Love & Friendship.* 1922. New York. 1st printing. VG $17.50

AUSTEN, Jane. *Pride & Prejudice.* 1940. New York. Heritage Press. Ills. Sewell. $12.50

AUSTEN, Jane. *Three Evening Prayers.* 1940. San Francisco. Cold Press. Ltd. ed. sgn. $50.00

AUSTEN, John. *As You Like It.* 1930. Ills. VG $22.50

AUSTEN, John. *Everyman & Other Plays.* 1925. Ills. VG $30.00

AUSTEN, John. *Five Black Cousins.* 1932. Cape. Ills. VG $20.00

AUSTEN, John. *Madame Bovary.* 1928. NY/London. Ills. 1st Am. ed. dj. VG $25.00

AUSTEN, John. *Perfection.* 1923. Ills. VG $20.00

AUSTEN, John. *Rogues in Porclean.* 1924. Ills. VG $30.00

AUSTEN, John. *Tales of Lost Times.* 1922. VG $25.00

AUSTEN, Mary. *One-Smoke Stories.* 1934. Boston. Houghton Mifflin. 295 pp. $12.50

AUSTEN, Michael. *Love Act.* 1982. Crown. proof copy. wrappers. VG $15.00

AUSTIN, H.H. *With MacDonald in Uganda.* 1903. London. EX $85.00

AUSTIN, James C. *Fields of Atlantic Monthly, Letters to an Editor.* 1953. San Marino, CA. 445 pp. $10.00

AUSTIN, Mary. *Land of Little Rain.* 1903. 1st ed. EX $35.00

AUSTIN, Mary. *The Arrow-Maker. A Drama in Three Acts.* 1915. Houghton Mifflin. SftCvr. $15.00

AUSTIN, O.L. *Birds of the World.* 1961. Golden Press. 300 Ills. Singer. 319 pp. EX $23.00

AUSTIN, Stephen F. *The Austin Papers.* 1924-28. Washington. 1st ed. 3 vol set. $200.00

AUSTIN, William. *Letters from London. Written During 1802-1803.* 1804. Boston. 312 pp. $25.00

AUTHURS, Stanley. *The American Historical Scene.* 1936. New York. Ills. dj. VG $40.00

AVADON. *Portraits.* 1977. New York. inscr. $100.00

AVAKIAN, L. *Cross & Crescent.* 1965. 1st ed. sgn. EX $17.50

AVARY, M.L. *A Virginia Girl in the Civil War.* 1903. New York. $40.00

AVARY, M.L. *Dixie After the War.* 1906. New York. EX $35.00

AVEDON, R. *Photographs 1947-1977.* 1978. New York. 1st ed. dj. EX $37.50

AVEDON & CAPOTE. *Observations.* 1959. 1st ed. VG $175.00

AVEDON. *Nothing Personal.* 1965. Dell Books. wrappers. VG $25.00

AVERELL, William Woods. *Ten Years In The Saddle.* 1978. Ills. 443 pp. $12.50

AVERILL, C.V. *Placer Mining for Gold in California.* 1946. San Francisco. Ills. 1st ed. 377 pp. EX $25.00

AVERILL, Charles. *A Short Treatise on Operative Surgery.* 1823. Philadelphia. 1st Am. ed. VG $65.00

AVERY, C. Louise. *Early American Silver.* 1930. New York. Ills. 1st ed. 387 pp. $37.50

AVERY. *A Yankee Flier in Italy.* 1944. Grosset & Dunlap. Ills. G $3.50

AVERY. *A Yankee Flier in Normandy.* 1945. Grosset & Dunlap. Ills. G $3.50

AVERY. *A Yankee Flyer Over Berlin.* 1944. Grosset & Dunlap. Ills. $3.50

AVERY. *History of the United States & Its People.* 1904-1910. Cleveland. Ills. 7 vol set. $175.00

AVI-YONAH, M. *A History of the Holy Land.* 1969. Jerusalem. Ills. 323 pp. $15.00

AWOONEOR, Kofi. *This Earth, My Brother.* 1971. New York. Doubleday. 232 pp. $5.00

AXELROD, H.R. *African ,Chichlids of Lakes Malawi & Tanganyika.* 1974. photos. 256 pp. $15.00

AXELROD, Tod. *Collecting Historical Documents.* 1984. 1st ed. color pls. VG $30.00

AXELSON, Eric. *Congo to Cape, Early Portuguese Explorers.* 1973. Harper. 10 Ills. 3 maps. 224 pp. dj. $20.00

AYER, A.J. *The Problem of Knowledge.* 1956. London. dj. VG $20.00

AYER, E.B. *Motor Flight Through Algeria & Tunisia.* 1911. Chicago. VG $20.00

AYER, F., Jr. *Before the Colors Fade.* 1971. Ills. VG $15.00

AYER, Mary F. *Boston Common in Colonial & Provincial Days.* 1903. Merrymount Pr. Ills. Updike. Ltd. ed. 1/175. $25.00

AYMAR, Brandt & Sagarin, Ed. *A Pictorial History of the World's Great Trials.* 1967. Ills. 373 pp. dj. $12.50

AYMAR, G.C. *A Treasury of Sea Stories.* 1948. New York. Ils. Kent. 1st ed. VG $10.00

AYMAR, G.C. *Bird Flight.* 1938. Deluxe ed. dj. EX $37.50

AYMAR, G.C. *Bird Flight.* 1936. Dodd Mead. 200 action photos. 234 pp. $15.00

AYRES, H. *Carroll's Alice.* 1936. Columbia U. Pr. 1st ed. VG $12.50

AYRTON, M. & Denvir, B. *Hogarth's Drawings.* 1948. London. 1st ed. 78 plates. $36.00

AYRTON, Michael. *Here are Ghosts & Witches.* 1954. London. Ills. 1st ed. dj. VG $40.00

AYTRON, M. *Summer's Last Will & Testament.* 1946. Ltd. ed. 1/100. sgn. $200.00

AZARIAN, Mary. *A Farmer's Alphabet.* 1981. Boston. Godine. 61 pp. wrappers. EX $15.00

AZECHENYI, Zsigmond. *Land of Elephants.* 1935. London. VG $70.00

AZIZ, P. *Doctors of Death.* 1976. Geneva. Ferni. Ills. EX $35.00

BAARSLAG, Karl. *Coast Guard to the Rescue.* 1937. Chicago. photos. 328 pp. EX $4.50

BABB, T.A. *In the Bosom of the Comanche Texas Border Lands.* 1923. Amarillo. Ills. 2nd ed. 146 pp. scarce. $45.00

BABCOCK, Bernie. *The Soul of Abe Lincoln.* 1923. Lippincott. 238 pp. dj. $52.50

BABCOCK, George. *Yezad: Romance of the Unknown.* Conn. Co-Operative Pub. sgn. G $40.00

BABCOCK, Havilah. *Education of Pretty Boy.* 1961. New York. 1st ed. dj. EX $35.00

BABCOCK, Havilah. *My Health is Better in November.* 1966. New York. Ills. 7th printing. VG $35.00

BABCOCK, Havilah. *My Health is Better in November.* 1948. Columbia. 2nd ed. dj. VG $30.00

BABCOCK, Havilah. *Tales of Quails & Such.* 1951. Greenberg. 1st ed. dj. VG $55.00

BABCOCK, William H. *Clan of the Chariots.* 1898. Boston. Lathrop. 1st ed. VG $17.50

BABCOCK, William H. *The Tower of Wye.* 1901. Philadelphia. Coates. 1st Am. ed. EX $15.00

BABER, Daisy F. *Injun Summer. An Old Cowhand Rides Ghost Trails.* 1952. Caldwell, ID. Ills. 1st ed. 223 pp. dj. $17.50

BABITZ, Eve. *L.A. Woman.* 1982. Linden. proof copy. dj. EX $15.00

BABITZ, Eve. *Slow Days, Fast Company.* 1977. New York. 1st ed. dj. EX $10.00

BABSON, Roger W. *Actions & Reactions.* 1935. 1st ed. sgn. dj. VG $15.00

BACH, J. *America's Germany.* 1946. Random House. G $10.00

BACH, Marcus. *Will to Believe.* 1956. New York. sgn. dj. VG $8.00

BACH & HALL. *4th Div.: Services & Achievements in Great War.* 1920. photos. G $12.00

BACHE, Alexander. *Report of Showing Progress of Coast Survey 1850.* 1850. Washington. 22 fld charts. VG $75.00

BACHELLOR, Irving. *A Man for All Ages.* 1919. Ills. 1st ed. $6.50

BACHELLOR, Irving. *D'ri and I, 1812.* 1901. Ills. F.C. Yohn. $4.00

BACHELLOR, Irving. *Keeping Up with Lizzie.* 1911. 1st ed. $6.50

BACHELLOR. *In the Days of Poor Richard.* 1922. Bobbs Merrill. Ills. J.W. Adams. EX $4.50

BACHMAN, Richard. *Rage.* 1977. New York. Signet. 1st ed. VG $25.00

BACHMAN, Richard. *Running Man.* New York. Signet. 1st ed. pb. EX $25.00

BACHMAN, Richard. *Talisman.* 1984. Grant. Ltd. ed. slipcase. EX $75.00

BACON, Admiral. *Warfare Today.* 1940. London. $13.50

BACON, E.M. *Rambles Around Old Boston.* 1914. Boston. Ltd. ed. 1/150. VG $30.00

BACON, Edgar M. *Narragansett Bay.* 1904. New York. Ills. 377 pp. $25.00

BACON, F. *Essays.* 1900. London. Humphreys. $12.50

BACON, H. *Sacred Flora: Flowers from Grave of a Child.* 1847. Boston. Tompkins & Mussey. 160 pp. VG $20.00

BACON, Matthew. *A New Abridgment of the Law. Vol. I.* 1736. folio. $25.00

BACON, Mrs. J. Daskam. *On Our Hill.* 1918. New York. Ills. T.M. & M.T. Bevans. $12.00

BACON, Mrs. J. Daskam. *The Memoirs of a Baby.* 1904. NY/London. Ills. F.Y. Cory. 1st ed. $10.00

BACON, Oliver. *History of Nantick, Massachusetts.* 1856. Boston. Damrell & Moore Pub. 261 pp. $35.00

BACON, Sir Francis. *Novum Organum.* 1844. London. 335 pp. rebound. $60.00

BACON, Sir Francis. *The Works of Francis Bacon.* 1824. London. Barnes. 10 vol set. rebound. $490.00

BACON, William J. *History of the 55th Field Artillery Brigade.* (ca.1920) VG $25.00

BACON. *The Yankee Magazine Book of Forgotten Arts.* 1978. Simon & Schuster. 219 pp. EX $4.50

BADEAU, A. *Military History of Ulysses S. Grant.* 1881. New York. 3 vol set. VG $65.00

BADEN-POWELL. *Handbook for Girl Scouts.* 1917. $15.00

BADEN-POWELL. *The Matabele Campaign.* 1897. London. VG $35.00

BADER, Barbara. *Am. Picture-Books from Noah's Ark to Beast Within.* 1976. Macmillan. $35.00

BADER, Capt. Douglas. *Fight for the Sky, Story of Spitfire & Hurricane.* 1973. Sidgwick & Jackson. 1st ed. $15.00

BAEDEKER, Karl. *Baedeker Guide. The Rhine.* 1926. Liepzig/London. maps. dj. EX $22.50

BAEDEKER, Karl. *Baedeker Guides. Belgium & Holland.* 1897. Leipzig. $20.00

BAEDEKER, Karl. *Baedeker Guides. Belgium & Holland.* 1910. $10.00

BAEDEKER, Karl. *Baedeker Guides. Eastern Alps.* 1899. Leipzig. 9th ed. 586 pp. $25.00

BAEDEKER, Karl. *Baedeker Guides. Egypt & the Sudan.* 1908. Leipzig. 6th ed. 439 pp. VG $45.00

BAEDEKER, Karl. *Baedeker Guides. Greece.* 1894. $10.00

BAEDEKER, Karl. *Baedeker Guides. London & Environs.* 1905. $10.00

BAEDEKER, Karl. *Baedeker Guides. Northern Germany.* 1910. New York. G $12.50

BAEDEKER, Karl. *Baedeker Guides. Southern Germany.* 1914. New York. G $12.50

BAEDEKER, Karl. *Baedeker Guides. Spain & Portugal.* 1913. Leipzig. 4th ed. 594 pp. map. $20.00

BAEDEKER, Karl. *Norway, Sweden & Denmark. Handbook for Travelers.* 1903. Leipzig. 8th ed. 486 pp. fld map. $16.50

BAEDEKER, Karl. *Palestine & Syria. Handbook for Travelers.* 1906. Leipzig. Ills. 4th ed. 436 pp. VG $15.00

BAGG, Edward P., M.D. *Another Canterbury Tale.* 1938. 1st ed. inscr. $15.00

BAGGULEY, Wm. H., ed. *Andrew Marvell 1621-1678.* 1922. London. Ills. 1st ed. dj. VG $35.00

BAGLEY, C.B. *Early Catholic Missions in Old Oregon.* 1932. Seattle. 2 vol set. EX $200.00

BAGLEY, Clarence B. *The Acquisition & Pioneering of Old Oregon.* 1924. Seattle. Argus. Ills. 1st ed. $125.00

BAGLEY, D. *Bahama Crisis.* 1980. Summit. 1st Am. ed. dj. EX $8.50

BAGNASCO, E. *Submarines of World War II.* 1978. Ills. 256 pp. index. dj. EX $30.00

BAGNIS, Ramond. *Fishes of Polynesia.* 1974. Lansdowne. 1st Australiian ed. dj. $40.00

BAGNOLD, Enid. *National Velvet.* 1935. New York. Morrow. Ills. L. Jones. dj. EX $30.00

BAGNOLD, Enid. *The Loved & Envied.* 1951. New York. 1st ed. dj. VG $10.00

BAGROW, Leo. *History of Russian Cartography Up to 1800.* 1975. Ontario. 1st eds. 2 vol set. $75.00

BAHR, Fritz. *Commercial Floriculture. A Practical Manual.* 1922. New York. Ills. G $20.00

BAIGELL, Matthew. *Thomas Cole.* 1981. New York. 1st ed. dj. EX $22.50

BAIKIE, James. *The Charm of the Scott Country.* 1927. London. Ills. G. Home. VG $35.00

BAILEY, A.M. & Niedrach, R.J. *Birds of Colorado.* 1965. Denver Museum. photos. map. 895 pp. 2 vol set. $150.00

BAILEY, Alice Cooper. *Kimo, the Whistling Boy.* 1928. Wise-Parslow. Ills. Lucille Holling. 96 pp. $4.50

BAILEY, Alice Cooper. *The Skating Gander.* 1927. Joliet. Voland. Ills. M.H. Myers. VG $20.00

BAILEY, Arthur Scott. *The Tale of Frisky Squirrel.* 1916. Ills. Eleanore Fagan. G $6.50

BAILEY, Arthur Scott. *The Tale of Jolly Robin.* 1917. New York. Ills. H.L. Smith. VG $7.50

BAILEY, B. *A Town Under Fire.* 1980. dj. G $12.50

BAILEY, B. *Meal Planning, Table Service.* 1924. Manuel Arts Press. Ills. G $8.00

BAILEY, Bernadine. *Abraham Lincoln's Other Mother.* 1946. 5th ed. sgn. dj. VG $15.00

BAILEY, Carolyn Sherwin. *Finnegan II, His Nine Lives.* 1953. New York. Ills. Kate Seredy. dj. G $25.00

BAILEY, Carolyn Sherwin. *Miss Hickory.* 1946. New York. Ills. R. Gannett. 1st ed. dj. $25.00

BAILEY, David C. *Viva Cristo Rey!* 1974. Austin. 346 pp. $10.00

BAILEY, Emma. *Sold to the Lady in the Green Hat.* 1962. $5.00

BAILEY, H.C. *Mr. Fortune Finds a Pig.* 1943. Garden City. 1st ed. dj. VG $10.00

BAILEY, Henry T. *Photography & Fine Art.* 1918. Davis Press. VG $40.00

BAILEY, Horace W. *Historical Booklet of Discovery of Lake Champlain.* 1909. 30 pp. map. wrappers. VG $17.50

BAILEY, J. & Culley, G. *General View of County of Northumberland.* 1794. London. $17.50

BAILEY, J.O. *Pilgrims Through Times & Space.* 1947. New York. 1st ed. dj. EX $35.00

BAILEY, John. *Our Wild Animals.* 1965. Nelson. photos. 216 pp. dj. EX $7.00

BAILEY, L.H. *Cultivated Evergreens.* 1923. Macmillan. 1st ed. $20.00

BAILEY, L.H. *Principles of Fruit Growing with Applications.* 1916. New York. 432 pp. VG $6.00

BAILEY, L.H. & Bailey, E. *Hortus Second. Dictionary of Gardening.* 1941. New York. $20.00

BAILEY, L.H. & Bailey, E. *Plant Breeding.* 1910. New York. Rural Science Series. Ills. VG $12.00

BAILEY, L.H. & Bailey, E. *The Principles of Vegetable Gardening.* 1913. New York. Rural Science Series. Ills. $10.00

BAILEY, P., Buchanan & Bucy. *Intracranial Tumors of Infancy & Childhood.* 1939. Chicago Press. 1st ed. 598 pp. $220.00

BAILEY, Pearl. *Hurry Up, America, & Spit.* 1976. New York. Harcourt. 1st ed. dj. EX $20.00

BAILEY, Pearl. *Talking to Myself.* 1971. New York. 233 pp. dj. $3.50

BAILEY, Percival & Cushing, H. *A Classification of Tumores of Glioma Group.* 1926. Philadelphia. 1st ed. 171 pp. $300.00

BAILEY, Philip James. *Festus, a Poem.* 1847. Boston. 7th Am. ed. 412 pp. $18.50

BAILEY & HOLLOWAY. *Book of Color Photography.* 1979. New York. 1st Am. ed. dj. EX $12.50

BAILEY. *Letters on Occult Meditation.* 1926. New York. Ills. G $10.00

BAILLIE, G.H. *Watchmakers & Clockmakers of the World.* 1969. London. 388 pp. 14 maps. dj. VG $12.50

BAIMBRIDGE, John. *The Super Americans.* 1961. 1st ed. dj. VG $6.50

BAIN, Robert. *The Clans & Tartans of Scotland.* London. Collins. (ca.1930's) VG $10.00

BAIN. *Tobacco in Song & Story.* 1896. 1st ed. $20.00

BAIN. *Tobacco Leaves.* 1903. Caldwell. EX $20.00

BAINBRIDGE, Beryl. *English Journey.* 1984. Braziller. proof copy. wrappers. EX $15.00

BAINBRIDGE, Beryl. *The Secret Glass.* 2nd ed. sgn. dj. EX $12.50

BAINBRIDGE, Peter Carl. *Faberge: Goldsmith & Jeweler to Jeweler at Court.* 1966. London. dj. EX $25.00

BAINBRIDGE, Peter Carl. *Faberge.* 1949. London. Batsford. 1st ed. $150.00

BAIRD, Robert. *Impressions & Experiences of West Indies/North Am.* 1850. Philadelphia. 1st Am. ed. VG $40.00

BAIRD, Robert. *Religion in America.* 1856. New York. 1st Am. ed. VG $75.00

BAIRD, Spencer F. *Biographical Memoirs of Spencer Fullerton Baird.* 1888. Washington. Smithsonian Report. 42 pp. $10.00

BAITSELL, G.A. *The Evolution of Earth & Man.* 1929. Yale U. Press. Ills. 476 pp. $9.00

BAKELESS, John. *Turncoats, Traitors, & Heroes.* 1959. New York. Lippincott. ex-lib. 406 pp. $4.00

BAKER, C.H. Collins. *Lely & the Stuart Portrait Painters.* 1912. London. Ltd. ed. 1/405. 2 vol set. VG $225.00

BAKER, Carlos. *A Friend in Power.* 1958. New York. Scribner. 1st ed. dj. VG $30.00

BAKER, Carlos. *A Year & a Day.* 1963. Vandguard. 1st ed. inscr. dj. VG $25.00

BAKER, Carlos. *Selected Letters of Ernest Hemingway 1917-1961.* 1981. New York. 1st ed. 948 pp. dj. VG $12.50

BAKER, Denys Val. *The Face in the Mirror.* 1971. Sauk City. 1st ed. 113 pp. dj. EX $10.00

BAKER, Dorothy. *Our Gifted Son.* 1948. Boston. 1st ed. dj. VG $10.00

BAKER, Dorothy. *Young Man with a Horn.* 1946. Tower. reprint. dj. VG $8.50

BAKER, E. *Introduction to Steel Shipbuilding.* 1953. Ills. 2nd ed. VG $15.00

BAKER, Elliot. *Klynt's Law.* 1976. New York. Harcourt. 1st ed. dj. EX $20.00

BAKER, F.C. *The Mollusca of the Chicago Area.* 1898 & 1902. Chicago. Ills. 2 vol set. VG $25.00

BAKER, Frank. *Miss Hargreaves.* 1941. New York. Coward McCann. 1st Am. ed. dj. $12.50

BAKER, G.P. *Dramatic Technique.* 1919. 531 pp. $10.00

BAKER, Geoffrey & Funaro, B. *Shopping Centers, Design & Operation.* 1954. New York. Ills. dj. VG $35.00

BAKER, Karle Wilson. *The Garden of the Plynck.* 1920. Yale U. Press. 1st ed. EX $125.00

BAKER, L.C. *History of U.S. Secret Service.* 1867. Philadelphia. 1st ed. 704 pp. G $22.50

BAKER, Michael. *The Doyle Diary, Charles Altamont Doyle.* 1978. Ballantine Books. Ills. 90 pp. $3.50

BAKER, Michael. *The Doyle Diary.* 1978. NY/London. Ills. dj. VG $10.00

BAKER, Michael. *The Doyle Diary: Last Great Conan Doyle Mystery.* 1978. Paddington Pr. 1st ed. dj. VG $15.00

BAKER, Pearl. *The Wild Bunch at Robbers Roost.* 1971. New York. Ills. maps. 224 pp. dj. $8.50

BAKER, R.S.B. *Green Glory, Forests of the World.* 1949. Wyn. 253 pp. $9.00

BAKER, Russell. *Growing Up.* 1982. New York. Cogdon & Weed. 278 pp. dj. $4.00

BAKER, Russell. *No Cause for Panic.* 1964. New York. Lippincott. 248 pp. dj. EX $4.00

BAKER, S.W. *Ismailia, Narrative of Expedition to Africa.* 1874. Macmillan. Ills. sgn & dated. 2 vol set. $165.00

BAKER, S.W. *Nile Tributaries of Abyssinia & Sword Hunters.* 1869. Ills. fld map. 413 pp. $45.00

BAKER, S.W. *The Rifle & Hound in Ceylon.* 1873. Philadelphia. VG $40.00

BAKER, Scott. *Night Child.* 1979. New York. 1st ed. dj. EX $10.00

BAKER & KUNZ. *The Collector's Book of Railroadiana.* 1976. Ills. EX $20.00

BAKER. *Cassandra at the Wedding.* 1962. Boston. 1st ed. dj. EX $10.00

BAKER. *Colonial Vessels.* 1962. 1st ed. 3 pls. dj. VG $10.00

BAKER. *Hemingway-Writer as Artist.* 1956. Princeton. dj. VG $7.50

BAKUNIN, Michael. *God & the State.* New York. Mother Earth. 1st Am. ed. VG $35.00

BALAKAIN. *Critical Encounters.* 1st ed. dj. VG $7.50

BALANO, James W. *The Log of the Skipper's Wife.* 1979. $4.50

BALCH, Thomas W. *The Alabama Arbitration.* 1900. Philadelphia. 1st ed. 150 pp. $35.00

BALCON, Michael & others. *Twenty Years of British Film 1925-1945.* 1947. London. Ills. 1st ed. $22.50

BALD, F.C. *Michigan in Four Centuries.* 1961. New York. G $5.00

BALDENSPERGER, P.J. *The Immovable East, Studies of People & Customs.* 1906. London. Ills. 309 pp. $17.50

BALDERSON, L.R. *Housewifery. A Manual & Textbook.* 1919. Philadelphia. Ills. VG $30.00

BALDERSTON, M. *Here Is England.* 1927. New York. fld maps. $10.00

BALDET, M. *Lead Soldiers & Figurines.* New York. (ca.1965) dj. EX $35.00

BALDINUCCI, Filippo. *The Life of Berniini.* 1966. PA State U. Pr.1st ed. dj. $12.50

BALDT, *Dressmaking Made Easy.* 1928. McCall Co. Ills. 181 pp. $4.50

BALDWIN, Billy. *Billy Baldwin Decorates.* 1972. Chartwell Books. photos. dj. $20.00

BALDWIN, C.S. *Essays Out of Hours.* 1907. Longman Green. University Pr. G $7.50

BALDWIN, Capt. J.H. *Large & Small Game of Bengal & India.* 1876. London. King. Ills. 380 pp. $300.00

BALDWIN, Christopher C. *Diary of Christopher C. Baldwin, 1829-1835.* 1901. Worcester. Ills. 1st ed. 380 pp. $35.00

BALDWIN, Faith. *Harvest of Hope.* 1962. New York. Holt. 148 pp. $10.00

BALDWIN, Faith. *Testament of Trust.* 1960. New York. Holt. 223 pp. $10.00

BALDWIN, Hanson W. *Sea Fights & Ship Wrecks.* 1955. $12.50

BALDWIN, Hanson W. *Sea Fights & Shipwrecks.* 1956. Garden City. dj. VG $7.50

BALDWIN, J. *Reading from Another Country.* 1963. Calliope. 1st ed. $12.50

BALDWIN, J. *The Story of Siegfried.* 1931. Scribner. Ills. Hurd. $10.00

BALDWIN, J. *The Story of Siegfried.* 1911. Scribner. Ills. Pyle. EX $17.50

BALDWIN, J. & Mead, Margaret. *A Rap on Race.* 1971. Lippincott. 1st ed. inscr. dj. VG $12.50

BALDWIN, James. *Blues for Mr. Charlie.* 1965. London. 1st Eng. ed. dj. EX $20.00

BALDWIN, James. *Blues for Mr. Charlie.* 1964. New York. 1st ed. dj. VG $17.50

BALDWIN, James. *Giovanni's Room.* 1956. New York. dj. VG $20.00

BALDWIN, James. *Go Tell It on the Mountain.* 1953. New York. 1st ed. dj. VG $90.00

BALDWIN, James. *Going to Meet the Man.* 1965. New York. 1st ed. dj. VG $15.00

BALDWIN, James. *Just Above My Head.* 1979. Dial Press. 1st trade ed. dj. VG $15.00

BALDWIN, James. *Just Above My Head.* 1979. proof copy. VG $45.00

BALDWIN, James. *Little Man, Little Man: Story of Childhood.* 1976. London. Joseph. Ills. Cazac. 1st ed. $27.50

BALDWIN, James. *No Name on the Street.* 1972. Dial Press. 1st ed. dj. VG $17.50

BALDWIN, James. *Nobody Knows My Name.* 1961. Dial. dj. VG $35.00

BALDWIN, James. *Reading from Giovanni's Room.* 1963. Calliope. 1st ed. $12.50

BALDWIN, James. *The Fire Next Time.* 1963. Dial Press. 1st ed. dj. VG $25.00

BALDWIN, John D. *Ancient America, Notes on American Archaeology.* 1872. New York. 1st ed. 299 pp. EX $45.00

BALDWIN, Joseph G. *Flush Times of Alabama & Mississippi.* 1876. San Francisco. VG $40.00

BALDWIN, Leland. *Pittsburgh. Story of a City.* 1938. Ills. Ward Hunter. G $10.00

BALDWIN, Leland. *Whiskey Rebels.* 1939. U. PA Press. 1st ed. 326 pp. dj. $32.50

BALDWIN, W.C. *African Hunting & Adventure: Natal to Zambezi.* 1893. London. Ills. 2nd ed. VG $145.00

BALDWIN, W.C. *African Hunting & Adventure: Natal to Zambezi.* 1981. Bulawayo. Ills. 451 pp. dj. EX $25.00

BALDWIN. *Baldwin's Readers, Fourth & Fifth Years Combined.* 1897. Am. Book Co. Ills. 208 pp. $3.50

BALESTIER, Joseph. *The Annals of Chicago.* 1876. 2nd ed. wrappers. VG $45.00

BALFOUR, A.B. *Twelve Hundred Miles in a Wagon.* 1895. London. Arnold. Ills. map. 265 pp. VG $90.00

BALFOUR, W. *An Inquiry, Devil & Satan.* 1827. Charlestown. 2nd ed. $30.00

BALFOUR. *How to Tell Nationality of Old Violins.* 1901. London. 28 pp. $20.00

BALFOUR. *Life of Robert Louis Stevenson.* 1901. New York. Scribner. 2 vol set. VG $9.00

BALFOUR. *Life of Robert Louis Stevenson.* 1901. London. 2 vol set. VG $30.00

BALIETT, Whitney. *Super Drummer: Profile of Buddy Rich.* 1968. Indianapolis. photos Fred Seligo. dj. VG $18.00

BALL, George J. Inc. *The Ball Red Book.* 1965. 11th ed. photos. EX $5.00

BALL, I.J. *Ecology & Management of Western Canada Goose.* 1891. Washington. Ills. maps. 68 pp. $5.00

BALL, Ian M. *Pitcairn: Children of Mutiny.* 1973. $10.00

BALL, John. *Singapore.* 1986. 1st ed. dj. EX $25.00

BALL, Max W. *This Fascinating Oil Business.* 1940. Bobbs Merrill. dj. VG $10.00

BALL, W. *Valentine Reminiscences & Letters Sir Robert Ball.*1915. 1st ed. ex-lib. 408 pp. VG $20.00

BALL. *Pioneers of '49.* 1891. Boston. 1st ed. $75.00

BALLANTINE, Bill. *Wild Tigers & Tame Fleas.* 1958. Rinehart. 344 pp. $10.00

BALLANTINE, D.S. *U.S. Naval Logistics in Second World War.* 1949. ex-lib. VG $15.00

BALLANTINE, W. *Ballantine's Problems in Law.* 1937. St.Paul. 1275 pp. $5.00

BALLANTYNE, R.M. *Wild Man of the West. A Tale of Rocky Mountains.* Philadelphia. Porter & Coates. Alta ed. $10.00

BALLANTYNE, Sheila. *Imaginary Crimes.* 1982. Viking Press. 1st ed. sgn. dj. VG $30.00

BALLARD, J.G. *Atrocity Exhibition.* 1970. London. Cape. 1st ed. dj. EX $47.50

BALLARD, J.G. *Best of J.G. Ballard.* 1977. London. Futura. 1st ed. pb. EX $25.00

BALLARD, J.G. *Billenium.* 1962. New York. Berkley. 1st ed. pb. VG $15.00

BALLARD, J.G. *Burning World.* 1964. New York. Berkley. 1st ed. pb. EX $22.50

BALLARD, J.G. *Concrete Island.* 1974. New York. 1st U.S. ed. dj. EX $25.00

BALLARD, J.G. *Crash.* 1973. New York. 1st Am. ed. dj. EX $27.50

BALLARD, J.G. *Crystal World.* 1966. New York. 1st Am. ed. dj. EX $32.50

BALLARD, J.G. *Disaster Area.* 1973. London. Panther. pb. EX $7.50

BALLARD, J.G. *Disaster Area.* 1967. 1st Eng. ed. inscr. dj. VG $125.00

BALLARD, J.G. *Empire of the Sun.* 1984. Gollancz. 1st ed. sgn. dj. EX $45.00

BALLARD, J.G. *Hello America.* 1981. London. Cape. 1st ed. dj. EX $35.00

BALLARD, J.G. *High-Rise.* 1977. New York. 1st Am. ed. dj. EX $27.50

BALLARD, J.G. *Love & Napalm.* 1972. New York. Grove. 1st Am. ed. dj. EX $35.00

BALLARD, J.G. *Low-Flying Aircraft.* 1976. London. 1st ed. dj. EX $27.50

BALLARD, J.G. *Passport to Eternity.* 1976. London. Cape. 1st ed. dj. EX $27.50

BALLARD, J.G. *The Unlimited Dream Company.* 1979. New York. Holt. proof copy. wrappers. EX $50.00

BALLINGER, Bill. *49 Days of Death.* 1969. Los Angeles. 1st ed. dj. VG $6.00

BALLOU, Arthur W. *Bound for Mars.* 1970. Boston. Little, Brown. dj. EX $15.00

BALLOU, M.M. *Aztec Land.* 1890. Boston/NY. 355 pp. $12.50

BALLOU, M.M. *New Eldorado.* 1890. 2nd ed. VG $22.50

BALLOU, M.M. *Under the Southern Cross.* 1887. Boston. G $35.00

BALLOWE. *The Lawd Sayin the Same: Negro Folk Tales.* 1947. L.S.U. 1st ed. VG $10.00

BALMER, Edwin. *Resurrection Rock.* 1920. Boston. Little, Brown. VG $15.00

BALSDON, Dacre. *Oxford Life.* 1959. London. Ills. 3rd ed. 279 pp. EX $7.50

BALSTON, Thomas. *English Wood Engraving 1900-1950.* 1950. London. Ills. wrappers. VG $15.00

BALZAC, Honore de. *Droll Stories.* 1874. London. Ills. Dore. 1st ed. $26.50

BALZAC, Honore de. *Droll Tales: the Second Decade.* 1929. Ills. de Bosschere. Ltd. ed. $35.00

BALZAC, Honore de. *Pere Goriot & Eugenie Grandet.* 1946. Modern Library. dj. $3.00

BALZAC, Honore de. *Pere Goriot.* 1939. Appleby. ex-lib. $3.00

BALZAC, Honore de. *Pere Goriot.* 1951. New York. VG $7.00

BALZAC, Honore de. *Ten Droll Tales.* Abby Library. no date. Ills. de Bosschere. $15.00

BANASIAK, C.F. *Deer in Maine.* 1964. Maine Game Comm. Ills. 163 pp. $8.00

BANCROFT, Aaron. *Life of George Washington.* 1826. Boston. 2 vol set. G $30.00

BANCROFT, Caroline. *Unique Ghost Towns & Mountain Spots.* 1961. Boulder, CO. Johnson. 96 pp. wrappers. $27.50

BANCROFT, G. *History of Formation of Constitution of U.S.A.* 1896. Appleton. 495 pp. $15.00

BANCROFT, Hubert H. *History of Alaska, 1730-1885.* 1959. New York. Ltd. ed. 1/750. 775 pp. $60.00

BANCROFT, Hubert H. *History of Northern Mexican States & Texas.* San Francisco. 1st ed. 2 vol set. $50.00

BANCROFT. *History of the Life of Leland Stanford.* 1952. Oakland. Ltd ed. 1/750. EX $60.00

BANCROFT. *The Life & Death of Jefferson Davis.* 1890. Ills. 256 pp. $13.50

BANGS, John Kendrick. *A Houseboat on the Styx.* 1895. New York. Ills. Peter Newell. VG $10.00

BANGS, John Kendrick. *A Houseboat on the Styx.* 1900. Harper. Ills. VG $5.00

BANGS, John Kendrick. *From Pillar to Post.* 1916. Century. Ills. Neill. VG $15.00

BANGS, John Kendrick. *Line of Cheer for Each Day of the Year.* 1913. Little, Brown. VG $5.00

BANGS, John Kendrick. *Mr. Munchausen.* 1901. Boston. Ills. Peter Newell. 1st ed. VG $35.00

BANGS, John Kendrick. *New Waggins of Old Tales by Two Wags.* 1888. Boston. Ills. 165 pp. $12.50

BANGS, John Kendrick. *The Bicycler & Three Other Farces.* 1896. New York. 1st ed. EX $35.00

BANIGAN, Sharon. *Puppies.* 1966. Lowe Co. Ills. pop-up. SftCvr. VG $3.50

BANISTER, M. *Pictorial Manual of Bookbinding.* 1958. New York. Ronald Press. 40 pp. VG $12.50

BANJAMIN, Israel. *Drei Jahre in Amerika, 1859-1862.* 1862. Hanover. 3 vols. in 2. wrappers. $500.00

BANK, Ted *Birthplace of the Winds.* 1956. New York. 274 pp. dj. $7.50

BANKHEAD, Tallulah. *Tallulah, My Autobiography.* 1952. Chicago. Sears. 335 pp. dj. $4.50

BANKO, Winston. *The Trumpeter Swan.* 1980. Neb. U. Press. photos. maps. 214 pp. EX $8.00

BANKS, Charles E. *Able Men of Suffolk in 1638.* 1931. Boston. 536 pp. $25.00

BANKS, Louis Albert. *Immortal Songs of Camp & Field.* 1899. Cleveland. Ills. inscr. VG $35.00

BANKS, R.C. *Birds of the Belvedere Expedition to Gulf of CA.* 1963. San Diego Nat. Hist. Soc. $2.00

BANNERMAN, D.A. *Birds of West & Equatorial Africa.* 1953. Edinburgh. Ills. 1st ed. 2 vol set. $195.00

BANNERMAN. *Black Sambo.* 1922. 16th ed. $35.00

BANNERMAN. *Story of White Squibba.* 1967. 1st ed. $15.00

BANNING. *Six Horses.* 1930. New York. 1st ed. VG $20.00

BANNISTER, Don. *Burning Leaves.* 1982. London. Rutledge & Paul. 1st Eng. ed. $25.00

BANNISTER, Don. *Sam Chard.* 1979. New York. Knopf. 1st ed. dj. VG $20.00

BANNISTER, M. *Pictorial Manual of Bookbinding.* 1958. New York. Ronald Press. 40 pp. VG $12.50

BANTA, R.E., ed. *Indiana Authors & Their Books, 1816-1916.* 1949. Crawfordsville. Ltd. ed. 1/2000. 352 pp. VG $45.00

BANVARD, John. *Description of Banvard's Panorama of Miss. River.* 1847. Boston. original printed wrappers. $185.00

BANVARD. *Private Life of a King.* 1875. New York. Ills. 1st ed. VG $40.00

BARAKA, Imamu Amira. *It's National Time.* 1970. Chicago. Third World. wrappers. $20.00

BARAKA, Imamu Amira. *Jello.* 1970. Chicago. Third World. wrappers. EX $20.00

BARASH, David. *Sociobiology & Behavior.* 1977. photos. 378 pp. dj. $18.00

BARBAROUX, C.O. *L'Histoire des Etats-Unis d'Amerique.* 1836. Philadelphia. 304 pp. $60.00

BARBAULT, Armand. *Gold of a Thousand Mornings.* 1975. London. 130 pp. dj. $30.00

BARBE, Waitman. *Famous Poems Explained. Helps in Reading.* 1909. New York. 237 pp. G $5.00

BARBE, Waitman. *Going to College, with Opinions of 50 Educators.* 1899. New York. 104 pp. $8.00

BARBE, Waitman. *Great Poems Interpreted with Biographical Notes.* 1914. New York. sgn. 368 pp. $7.50

BARBE, Waitman. *In the Virginias. Stories & Sketches.* 1896. Akron. Ills. 184 pp. $10.00

BARBEAU, C.M. *Huron & Wyandot Mythology.* 1915. Ottawa. Ills. 437 pp. scarce. $60.00

BARBEAU, Marius. *Alaska Beckons.* 1947. Cladwell, ID. Ills. 343 pp. $40.00

BARBEAU, Marius. *Indian Days in the Canadian Rockies.* 1923. Toronto. Ills. W.L. Kihn. 1st ed. dj. $100.00

BARBEAU, Marius. *The Golden Phoenix.* 1965. 9 French-Canadian fairy tales. $5.00

BARBER, E.A. *American Glassware Old & New.* 1900. Philadelphia. $30.00

BARBER, E.A. *Anglo-American Pottery.* 1901. Philadelphia. $30.00

BARBER, E.A. *Pottery & Porcelain of the U.S.* 1901. New York. $100.00

BARBER, E.A. *Tin Enamelled Pottery.* 1907. New York. $35.00

BARBER, H. *Aerobatics*. 1918. New York. Ills. 1st ed. 61 pp. $65.00

BARBER, Joel. *Wildfowl Decoys*. 1970. wrappers. EX $12.50

BARBER, John W. *History & Antiquities of New England*. 1841. New York. Dorr, Howland & Co. VG $35.00

BARBER, John W. *The Handbook of Illustrated Proverbs*. 1857. Cincinnati. Howe Pub. 2 vols in 1. 164 pp. $20.00

BARBER, John. *Incidents in American History*. 1856. Boston. VG $11.00

BARBER, Lynn. *Heyday of Natural History 1820-1870*. 1980. Doubleday. Ills. 1st Am. ed. 320 pp. $15.00

BARBER, N. *A Sinister Twilight. Account of Fall of Singapore*. 1968. ex-lib. dj. $8.00

BARBER & HOWE. *Historical Collection of State of New Jersey*. 1860. Newark. Ills. map. $45.00

BARBER & HOWE. *Historical Collection of State of New York*. 1841. New York. Ills. ex-lib. $25.00

BARBER. *The Aeroplane Speaks*. 1917. New York. Ills. 144 pp. $25.00

BARBICAN, James. *Confessions of a Rum-Runner*. 1928. New York. VG $7.50

BARBOUR, George M. *Florida for Tourist, Invalids & Settlers*. 1881 & 1882. New York. Ills. 2 vols. VG $75.00

BARBOUR, Thomas. *Cuban Ornithology*. 1943. Nuttall Ornith. Club. 144 pp. $35.00

BARBOUR, Thomas. *Naturalist at Large*. 1943. Little, Brown. Ills. 1st ed. 314 pp. $15.00

BARBOUR. *Little Jack Rabbit & Chippy Chipmunk*. 1921. Grosset & Dunlap. 4 pls. $11.00

BARBOUR. *Little Jack Rabbit & the Squirrel Brothers*. 1921. Grosset & Dunlap. 4 pls. dj. $17.00

BARBOUR. *Little Jack Rabbit & Uncle John Hare*. 1922. Grosset & Dunlap. 4 pls. VG $10.00

BARCLAY, A. *Medical Diagnosis*. 1864. $10.00

BARCLAY, Anthony. *Wilde's Summer Rose*. 1871. Savannah. G $35.00

BARCLAY, R. *True Christian Divinity, Vindication of Quakers*. 1805. Philadelphia. G $9.00

BARCSAY. *Anatomy for Artist*. 1958. $38.00

BARCUS, F. *Freshwater Fury*. 1961. Detroit. 2nd printing. dj. EX $8.50

BARD, Emil. *Chinese Life in Town & Country*. 1905. New York. Ills. EX $30.00

BARDACH, John. *Downstream: Natural History of the River*. 1964. Harper & Row. 1st ed. ex-lib. dj. $2.50

BARDECHE, Maurice. *History of Motion Pictures*. 1938. 1st ed. $10.00

BARDIN, John Franklin. *Purloining Tiny*. 1978. Harper. dj. $5.00

BAREA, Arturo. *The Forging of a Rebel*. 1946. New York. 1st ed. 736 pp. dj. $7.00

BARGER, Edgar H. & Card, L. *Diseases & Parasites of Poultry*. 1943. Philadelphia. 399 pp. VG $4.00

BARIES, George F., ed. & pub. *History of Madison Township, Franklin Co. Ohio*. 1902. Winchester, OH.515 pp. Fair $15.00

BARING-GOULD, C. *Cliff Castles & Cave Dwellings of Europe*. 1911. Lippincott. $17.50

BARING-GOULD, William S. *Sherlock Holmes of Baker Street*. 1962. Bramhall. dj. VG $20.00

BARING-GOULD, William S. *The Annotated Mother Goose*. 1962. Bramhall House.Ills. Rackham/Parrish/others. $20.00

BARING-GOULD, William S. *The Annotated Sherlock Holmes*. 1973. New York. 2nd ed. 9th printing. 2 vols. $45.00

BARINGER, W. *Lincoln's Rise to Power*. 1937. Boston. Ills. 1st ed. VG $7.50

BARJANSKY, Catherine. *Portraits with Backgrounds*. 1948. London. 1st ed. VG $10.00

BARKELEY, Richard. *Road to Mayerling*. 1958. New York. Ills. 1st ed. 292 pp. dj. VG $12.50

BARKER, A.J. *Dunkirk, the Great Escape*. 1977. Ills. maps. dj. EX $14.00

BARKER, Benjamin. *Ellen Grafton, Lily of Lexington: Romance*. 1845. Boston. 1st ed. EX $75.00

BARKER, Clive. *Books of Blood*. 1985. Scream Press. 3 vol in 1. dj. EX $45.00

BARKER, Clive. *Books of Blood*. 1985. London. Ltd. ed. 1/200. sgn. slipcase. $275.00

BARKER, Clive. *Damnation Game*. 1985. 1st ed. EX $30.00

BARKER, Clive. *The Inhuman Condition*. 1985. New York. proof copy. wrappers. EX $40.00

BARKER, Dudley. *Writer by Trade*. 1966. New York. Atheneum. 1st Am. ed. 260 pp. $5.00

BARKER, George. *Janus*. 1935. London. 1st ed. sgn. wrappers. $80.00

BARKER, Joseph. *Recollections of the First Settlement of Ohio*. 1958. Marietta. Ills. 96 pp. $15.00

BARKER, Mrs. Sale. *Lily at Her Grandmama's*. 1879. London. Routledge. Ills. VG $20.00

BARKER, Mrs. Sale. *Little Silverlocks Story Book*. 1880. London. Routledge. 200 Ills. VG $38.50

BARKER, R. *Rufiji*. 1956. London. Hale. Ills. 157 pp. $25.00

BARKER, Virgil. *American Painting History & Interpretation*. 1950. New York. dj. $12.50

BARKER, Will. *Familiar Reptiles & Amphibians of America*. 1964. Harper & Row. Ills. 1st ed. 220 pp. VG $12.00

BARKLEY, Alben W. *That Reminds Me*. 1954. Doubleday. Ills. 288 pp. VG $5.00

BARLETT & CORMACK. *The Racket*. 1928. London/NY. G $10.00

BARLEY, Carolyn Sherwin. *Miss Hickory*. 1946. Viking. Ills. Ruth Gannett. 1st ed. $25.00

BARLEY, Carolyn Sherwin. *Pioneer Art in America*. 1944. Viking. Ills. Grace Paul. 1st ed. VG $5.00

BARLEY, Carolyn Sherwin. *Tops & Whistles*. 1937. Viking. Ills. Grace Paul. 1st ed. VG $15.00

BARLOSKY. *Infinite Jest-Wit & Humour in Italian Renaissance*.1978. U. of MO Press. $15.00

BARLOW, R. *Lisbeth Holly*. 1947. New York. Ills. LaRiviere. sgn. dj. VG $7.50

BARLOW, T.D. *Woodcuts of Albrecht Durer*. 1948. London. King Penguin Bk. 1st ed. VG $20.00

BARLOW. *In Memorium*. 1923. Albany. Ills. VG $30.00

BARNABY, R. *Gliders & Gliding*. 1930. New York. Ronald Press. VG $25.00

BARNARD, Evan G. *Rider of the Cherokee Strip*. 1936. 1st ed. $22.50

BARNARD, H. *Chats on Wedgwood Ware*. New York. (ca.1924) dj. $30.00

BARNARD, Julian. *Victorian Ceramic Tiles*. 1972. London. Studio Vista. Ills. 1st ed. VG $20.00

BARNES, Albert. *An Inquiry Into the Scriptural Views of Slavery*. 1846. Philadelphia. ex-lib. 384+12 pp. ads. $20.00

BARNES, Alfred Smith. *Memorial. Family & Publishing History*. 1889. New York. private print. EX $45.00

BARNES, D. *Nightwood*. 1963. Deluxe ed. dj. VG $45.00

BARNES, Djuna. *Ladies Almanac*. 1972. New York. dj. EX $15.00

BARNES, Djuna. *Ryder*. 1928. New York. Liveright. Ltd. 1st ed. dj. $35.00

BARNES, E.W. *The Lady of Fashion. Anna Cora Mowatt*. 1954. Ills. $7.50

BARNES, J. *Picture Analysis of Golf Strokes*. 1919. Philadelphia. $35.00

BARNES, M. *The Mountain World*. Harper. photos. maps. 200 pp. dj. EX $20.00

BARNES, Melvyn. *Murder in Print*. 1986. London. 1st ed. dj. EX $35.00

BARNES, Ruth A. *I Hear America Singing*. 1937. Philadelphia. Ills. Lawson. 1st ed. sgn. $10.00

BARNETT, Annie A. *The Penlee Recipe Book*. 1932. London. $10.00

BARNETT, F. *Dictionary of Prehistoric Indian Artifacts*. 1974. 2nd ed. wrappers. VG $12.50

BARNETT. *Antiquities of India*. 1914. New York. 1st ed. dj. VG $12.50

BARNEY. *Tales of Apache Warfare*. 1933. Pheonix. 45 pp. wrappers. $48.00

BARNEY. *Yuma. History of Yuma, Arizona*. 1953. Pheonix. 43 pp. wrappers. $18.00

BARNHAM, Richard H. *The Ingoldsby Legends*. 1898. London. Ills. Rackham. 1st ed. EX $150.00

BARNOW, Erik. *The Magician & the Cinema*. 1981. VG $4.00

BARNUM, P.T. *Funny Stories*. 1890. Ills binding. VG $35.00

BARNUM, P.T. *Life of P.T. Barnum Written by Himself*. 1888. Buffalo. inscr. VG $35.00

BARNUM, P.T. *Struggles & Triumphs*. 1872. Buffalo. G $10.00

BARNUM. *An Exposition of the Roman Catholic System*. 1876. Conn Pub. Ills. 848 pp. G $6.50

BARNWELL. *Death Rider*. Signet. pb. $3.00

BARO, Gene. *Beat Poets*. 1961. London. Vista Books. wrappers. EX $25.00

BARR, A. *Remember the Alamo*. 1979. Gregg. reprint. dj. EX $10.00

BARR, Louise F. *Presses of North California & Their Books 1900-33*. 1939. Berkeley. Ltd. ed. 1/400. $75.00

BARR, Robert. *From Whose Bourne*. 1896. New York. Stokes. 1st Am. ed. dj. VG $35.00

BARR, Robert. *The Face & the Mask*. 1895. Stokes. 1st Am. ed. dj. VG $65.00

BARR, Robert. *The Triumphs of Eugene Valmont*. 1906. New York. 1st Am. ed. VG $100.00

BARR, Stringfellow. *Copydog in India*. 1955. New York. Ills. Kurt Wiese. dj. G $10.00

BARR. *Picasso: 50 Years of His Art*. 1946. Simon & Schuster. $15.00

BARRES, Wm. A. *Selections from the Poetry of Robert Browning*. 1930. Chicago. Laurel Books. 172 pp. G $3.00

BARRETT, C. *Australian Bird Life*. 1947. Oxford U. Press. Ills. 239 pp. $10.00

BARRETT, Francis. *The Magus, or Celestial Intelligencer*. 1967. New Hyde Park. University Books. 2 vols in 1. $32.50

BARRETT, J.O. *The Spiritual Pilgrim*. 1871. Boston. 303 pp. $45.00

BARRETT, Joseph. *Life of Abraham Lincoln*. 1865. New York. Ills. VG $22.50

BARRETT, P. *Treasury of African Hunting*. 1960. dj. EX $20.00

BARRETT, Roger & Jackson, W. *Nazi Conspiracy & Aggression*. 1946. Washington. 8 vol set. $125.00

BARRETT, S.M. *Geronimo, His Own Story*. 1970. New York. reprint. 190 pp. 11 pls. dj. $12.50

BARRETT, S.M. *Geronimo's Story*. 1906. New York. Ills. 1st ed. 216 pp. $60.00

BARRETT, Walter. *Old Merchants of New York City*. 1863. New York. VG $15.00

BARRIE, J.M. *A Window in Thrums*. 1892. London. Ills. Hole. 1st ed. 1/50. sgn. $57.50

BARRIE, J.M. *Auld Licht Idylls*. 1888. London. 1st ed. G $50.00

BARRIE, J.M. *Peter & Wendy*. 1920. photoplay ed. $40.00

BARRIE, J.M. *Peter & Wendy*. 1911. New York. Ills. F.D. Bedford. 1st ed. VG $22.00

BARRIE, J.M. *Peter Pan & Wendy*. 1921. New York. Scribner. 1st ed. G $35.00

BARRIE, J.M. *Peter Pan in Kensington Gardens*. 1916. London. Ills. Rackham. $85.00

BARRIE, J.M. *Picture Story Book of Peter Pan*. 1931. Ills. Roy Best.1st ed. VG $25.00

BARRIE, J.M. *Sentimental Tommy*. 1896. New York. Ills. Hatherell. 1st Am. ed. $20.00

BARRIE, J.M. *Sentimental Tommy*. 1896. London. 1st ed. dj. VG $15.00

BARRIE, J.M. *The Novels, Tales, & Sketches of J.M. Barrie*. 1898. Scribner. 10 vol set. $125.00

BARRIERE & LELAND. *A Dictionary of Slang, Jargon, & Cant*. 1889. Ltd. 1st ed. 1/675. $85.00

BARRINGER, Marie. *The Four & Lena*. 1938. New York. Ills. Petersham. 1st ed. dj. $25.00

BARRON, Leonard. *The Complete Book of Gardening*. 1936. New York. Ills. VG $6.00

BARRON, Milton L. *The Juvenile in Delinquent Society*. 1954. New York. Knopf. 347 pp. dj. VG $4.00

BARROS, James. *The Corfu Incident of 1923*. 1965. Princeton, NJ. ex-lib. 339 pp. dj. EX $4.50

BARROWS, Edward M. *Great Commodore: Exploits of Matthew C. Perry*. 1935. Indianapolis. Ills. 1st ed. 397 pp. dj. $10.00

BARROWS, J.S. *Fryeburg, Maine: An Historical Sketch*. 1938. 1st ed. 309 pp. $30.00

BARROWS, Marjorie. *Little Duck*. 1935. Grosset & Dunlap. Ills. Myers. $3.50

BARROWS, William. *Twelve Nights in a Hunter's Camp*. Boston. Ills. 268 pp. VG $17.50

BARRY, Joe. *The Pay-Off*. 1943. New York. Mystery House. 1st ed. dj. VG $15.00

BARRY, John J. *How to Make Etchings*. 1929. 1st American ed. $25.00

BARRY, T.A. & Patton, B.A. *San Francisco, California, 1850*. 1947. San Francisco. Biobooks. Ills. Ltd. ed. sgn. $50.00

BARRY, Tom. *Courage*. 1929. New York. S. French. 119 pp. dj. $3.00

BARRY. *Rutledge of South Carolina*. 2nd ed. sgn. $10.00

BARRYMORE, Diana & Frank, G. *Too Much, Too Soon*. 1957. New York. Holt. photos. 380 pp. $4.50

BARSIS, Max. *Common Man Through Centuries: Book of Drawings*. 1973. New York. Ungar. Ills. dj. VG $17.50

BARSNESS, L. *Gold Camp*. 1962. 1st ed. dj. VG $10.00

BART, Sheldon. *Ruby Sweetwater & the Ringo Kid*. 1981. McGraw Hill. 1st ed. dj. EX $20.00

BART, Sir Humphry Davy. *Consolations in Travel*. 1830. Philadelphia. $30.00

BARTH, Heinrich. *Travels & Discoveries in North & Central Africa*. 1859. Bradley. Ills. 1st Am. ed. 538 pp. VG $85.00

BARTH, Heinrich. *Travels & Discoveries in North & Central Africa*. 1857-1859. New York. 3 vol set. VG $130.00

BARTH, John. *Chimera*. 1974. London. 1st Eng. ed. dj. EX $17.50

BARTH, John. *Chimera*. 1972. New York. Random House. 1st ed. dj. VG $20.00

BARTH, John. *Giles Goatboy*. 1966. New York. 1st ed. dj. VG $22.50

BARTH, John. *Letters*. 1979. New York. proof copy. $40.00

BARTH, John. *Lost in the Funhouse*. 1968. Doubleday. 1st ed. dj. $25.00

BARTH, John. *Sabbatical*. 1982. Putnam. 1st ed. dj. VG $20.00

BARTH, John. *Sot Weed Factor*. 1960. Garden City. 1st ed. dj. VG $50.00

BARTH, John. *Sot Weed Factor*. London. 1st English ed. dj. VG $45.00

BARTH, John. *The Friday Book*. 1984. New York. Putnam. 1st ed. dj. EX $20.00

BARTH, John. *Todd Andrews to the Author*. 1979. Lord John. Ltd. ed. 1/300. sgn. VG $50.00

BARTHELME, Abbe. *From the Log of the Velsa*. 1920. Ltd. ed. 1/110. G $50.00

BARTHELME, Abbe. *Travels of Anacharsis the Younger in Greece*. 1830. Ills. fld map. VG $50.00

BARTHELME, D. & Milik, J.T. *Discoveries in the Judean Desert.* 1956. Oxford. Ills. ex-lib. 165 pp. index. $27.50

BARTHELME, Donald. *City Life.* 1970. Farrar. 1st ed. dj. VG $35.00

BARTHELME, Donald. *Come Back, Dr. Caligari.* 1964. Little, Brown. 1st ed. dj. VG $90.00

BARTHELME, Donald. *Guilty Pleasures.* 1974. Farrar. 1st ed. dj. VG $25.00

BARTHELME, Donald. *Overnight to Many Distant Cities.* 1983. New York. Putnam. 1st ed. EX $15.00

BARTHELME, Donald. *Sixty Stories.* 1981. Putnam. Ltd. ed. 1/500. sgn. slipcase. $75.00

BARTHELME, Donald. *Sixty Stories.* 1981. Putnam. 1st ed. dj. EX $15.00

BARTHELME, Donald. *Snow White.* 1967. Atheneum. 1st ed. dj. VG $55.00

BARTHELME, Donald. *Unspeakable Practices, Unnatural Acts.* 1968. Farrar. dj. EX $40.00

BARTHELME, Frederick. *Moon Deluxe.* 1983. New York. Simon & Schuster. 1st ed. dj. $25.00

BARTHOLOMEW. *Mechanical Toys.* 1979. dj. VG $12.50

BARTLETT, D.W. *Life & Public Services of Hon. Abraham Lincoln.* 1860. Cincinnati. 354 pp. VG $40.00

BARTLETT, Dana. *The Better City.* 1907. Aeuner Co., CA.Ills. ex-lib. 248 pp. G $6.00

BARTLETT, Des & Jen. *The Flight of the Snow Geese.* 1975. Stein & Day. 1st Am. ed. photos. 189 pp. $8.00

BARTLETT, Fred. *The Prodigal Pro Tem.* 1910. Boston. Small, Maynard. 1st ed. VG $8.50

BARTLETT, Jen. *Nature's Paradise.* 1967. Boston. 1st printing. photos. dj. EX $25.00

BARTLETT, John H. *History of the Wanton Family of Newport.* 1878. Providence. 1st ed. $40.00

BARTLETT, John Russell. *Dictionary of Americanisms.* 1860. Boston. 3rd ed. G $75.00

BARTLETT, John; Morley, C. *Familiar Quotations.* 1938. Boston. Little, Brown. 11th ed. $6.00

BARTLETT, Kim. *The Finest Kind.* 1977. $7.50

BARTLETT, N. *Military Record of Louisiana.* 1964. Baton Rouge. 259 pp. VG $20.00

BARTLETT, V. *The Past of Pastimes.* 1969. London. Ills. 1st ed. dj. VG $18.00

BARTLETT, William H. *Pilgrim Fathers in the Reign of James the First.* 1853. London. 256 pp. 28 pls. $75.00

BARTLETT, William H. *Walks about City & Environs of Jerusalem, 1842.* 1974. Jerusalem. Ills. 1st ed. dj. VG $25.00

BARTLETT. *A Son of the Wild Pack.* 1934. Wilde Co. $3.50

BARTON, Bruce. *The Book Nobody Knows.* 1926. New York. Grosset & Dunlap. 305 pp. dj. $3.50

BARTON, C. Josephine. *Evangel Ahvalliah.* 1895. dj. VG $30.00

BARTON, Clara. *Story of My Childhood.* 1907. $15.00

BARTON, Clara. *The Red Cross of the Geneva Convention.* 1878. Washington. 8 pp. wrappers. $15.00

BARTON, Ralph. *God's Country.* 1929. New York. Knopf. 330 pp. $3.00

BARTON, Roger. *How to Watch Birds.* 1961. Bonanza. Ills. 170 pp. VG $5.00

BARTON, William. *Abraham Lincoln & His Books.* 1920. VG $15.00

BARTON, William. *The Paternity of Abraham Lincoln.* 1920. New York. G $10.00

BARTON. *The Hollow Crown.* Dial Press. Ills. 271 pp. dj. $8.50

BARTON. *The Vengeance Riders.* Popular. pb. $3.00

BARTONLINI, L. *Bicycle Thieves.* 1950. 1st ed. dj. VG $15.00

BARUCH, Bernard M. *Baruch, My Own Story.* 1957. New York. Holt. 337 pp. dj. $4.50

BARUCH, Bernard M. *Baruch, the Public Years.* 1960. New York. 1st ed. 431 pp. dj. VG $8.00

BARZUN, J. & Taylor, W.H. *A Catalogue of Crime.* 1974. New York. Harper. 2nd impression. dj. EX $50.00

BARZUN, Jacques. *Berlioz & the Romantic Century.* 1950. Century. 1st ed. ex-lib. 2 vol set. EX $25.00

BASCH, P. *Put a Girl in Your Pocket.* 1969. Greenwich. pb. EX $7.50

BASHEFF, Artzy. *As I See.* 1954. Dodd Mead. 1st ed. dj. VG $47.50

BASHFORD, Dean. *A Miscellany of Arms & Armor.* 1928. New York. Rudge. Ltd. ed. 1/100. $45.00

BASHLINE, L.J. & Saults, eds. *America's Great Outdoors.* 1976. Ferguson. Ills. 367 pp. dj. EX $21.00

BASIGER, David. *The Lincoln Conspiracy.* 1977. Ills. $3.50

BASILE, Giambattista. *The Pentameron.* 1952. London. Ills. M. Ayrton. 1st ed. dj. $20.00

BASKETT, John. *Constable Oil Sketches.* 1966. New York. Watson-Cuptill Pub. 82 pp. dj. $15.00

BASKETT, John. *The Horse in Art.* 1980. 1st Am. ed. 160 pp. boxed. EX $55.00

BASKIN, L. *Caprices & Grotesques.* 1965. Ltd. 1st ed. 1/500. slipcase. $295.00

BASKIN, Leonard. *Baskin's Miniature Natural History, 1st Series.* 1983. Pantheon Books.1st ed. 4 vols set. slipcase. $20.00

BASLER, Roy P. *The Collected Works of Abraham Lincoln.* 1953. New Brunswick. 8 vol set. $7.00

BASON, Fred. *Fred Bason's Diary.* 1950. London. 1st ed. 4 vol set. $95.00

BASSANI. *Garden Finzi-Continis.* 1st Am. ed. dj. VG $35.00

BASSETT, John. *The Lost Fruits of Waterloo.* 1919. New York. Macmillan. 280 pp. $3.50

BASSETT, John. *William Faulkner/Annotated Checklist of Criticism.*1972. New York. Lewis. 551 pp. dj. $10.00

BATCHELDER, Ann. *New Delineator Recipes.* 1930. Butterick Pub. Ills. 222 pp. $3.50

BATCHELOR. *British Boxing.* 1948. London. Ills. 1st ed. VG $15.00

BATE, P. *English Table Glass.* London. no date. $35.00

BATE, William. *George Cruikshank.* 1879. London. Ills. 94 pp. $125.00

BATEMAN, C. *First Ascent of the Kasai.* 1869. London. EX $47.50

BATEMAN, Robert. *The Art of Robert Bateman.* 1983. Viking Press. 82 color pls. 178 pp. dj. EX $45.00

BATES, Charles Auston. *Short Talks on Advertising.* 1898. C.A. Bates Press. 211 pp. $3.50

BATES, Ernest. *Story of the Supreme Court.* 1936. Bobbs-Merrill. 1st ed. VG $12.50

BATES, F.L. *Escape & Suicide of John Wilkes Booth.* (ca.1905) $35.00

BATES, Gordon. *The Khaki Boys at the Front.* 1918. New York. 202 pp. G $2.50

BATES, H.E. *Day of the Tortoise.* 1961. London. 1st ed. sgn. dj. EX $35.00

BATES, H.E. *Fair Stood the Wind for France.* 1944. Little, Brown. 1st ed. dj. $10.00

BATES, H.E. *Oh! To Be in England.* 1964. New York. Farrar. 1st ed. dj. VG $15.00

BATES, H.E. *The Darling Buds of May.* 1958. Boston. Little, Brown. 1st ed. dj. VG $15.00

BATES, H.E. *The Purple Plain.* 1947. Boston. 1st ed. EX $8.50

BATES, H.E. *Through the Woods.* 1936. New York. Ills. 141 pp. dj. $22.50

BATES, Jerome P. *The Imperial Highway.* 1885. Chicago. Ills. 811 pp. VG $12.50

BATES, Joseph. *Spinning for American Game Fish.* 1950. VG $15.00

BATES, K. *Basic Design, Principles, & Practice.* 1970. New York. dj. EX $12.50

BATES, K. *Once Upon a Time, Book of Old Time Fairy Tales.* 1939. Rand McNally. Junior ed. 127 pp. VG $4.50

BATES, Marston. *Where Winter Never Comes.* 1952. Scribner. Ills. 1st ed. maps. 310 pp. VG $14.00

BATES. *The Face of England.* 1952. London. Ills. 1st ed. dj. EX $12.50

BATHAN, Cyril N. *Grand Lodge of England According to Constitutions.* 1981. London. 71 pp. EX $3.00

BATHELME, D. *Sadness.* 1972. 1st ed. dj. $10.00

BATSFORD & FRY. *Cathedrals of England.* 1941. London. Ills. 5th revised ed. dj. VG $12.50

BATTEN, Jack. *The Leaves in Autumn.* 1975. Toronto. Macmillan. Ills. 143 pp. dj. $10.00

BATTERBERRY, Michael & Ariane. *Fashion, Mirror of History.* 1982. New York. Greenwich. dj. VG $20.00

BATTERSON, James G. *Gold & Silver as Currency.* 1896. Case, Lockwood & Brainard Co. $10.00

BATTY, J.H. *Practical Taxidermy.* 1894. New York. Ills. VG $17.50

BAUDER, Emma Pow. *Ruth & Marie.* 1895. 363 pp. $12.50

BAUER, Erwin. *Treasury of Big Game Animals.* 1975. Outdoor Life. color photos. 398 pp. dj. $10.00

BAUER, Erwin. *Treasury of Big Game Animals.* 1972. New York. Ills. 1st ed. dj. VG $17.50

BAUER, Joseph M. *As Far as My Feet Will Carry Me.* 1957. New York. 1st printing. dj. VG $10.00

BAUER, Max. *Precious Stones Vol. II.* 1968. G $5.00

BAUER, S. *Saturday.* 1980. Putnam. 1st ed. dj. EX $17.50

BAUGH, Albert C. *Chaucer's Major Poetry.* 1963. Appleton Century. 1st ed. VG $10.00

BAUGHMAN, James. *The Mallorys of Mystic.* 1972. Wesleyan U. Pr. Ills. Ltd. ed. sgn. boxed. EX $45.00

BAUGHMAN, Theodore. *The Oklahoma Scout.* Chicago. Ills. 216 pp. $20.00

BAUGHMAN. *Aviation Dictionary & Reference Guide.* 1942. Glendale. 2nd ed. 1st issue. VG $12.50

BAUM, James E. *Unknown Ethiopia. New Lights on Abyssinia.* 1935. New York. G $18.00

BAUM, L. Frank. *Dorothy & the Wizard in Oz.* 1908. Chicago. reprint. Ills. Neill. $30.00

BAUM, L. Frank. *Dorothy & the Wizard in Oz.* 1908. Chicago. 1st ed. 1st issue. EX $500.00

BAUM, L. Frank. *Dot & Tot of Merryland.* 1901. Indianapolis. Ills. W.W. Denslow. $375.00

BAUM, L. Frank. *Father Goose's Year Book.* 1907. Chicago. 1st ed. $100.00

BAUM, L. Frank. *Glinda of Oz.* 1920. Chicago. Reilly & Lee. Ills. Neill. $100.00

BAUM, L. Frank. *Glinda of Oz.* 1920. Chicago. Ills. Neill. 2nd printing. $75.00

BAUM, L. Frank. *Glinda of Oz.* Chicago. (ca.1920) EX $35.00

BAUM, L. Frank. *Glinda of Oz.* 1920. 1st issue. G $50.00

BAUM, L. Frank. *John Dough & the Cherub.* 1906. Reilly/Britton. Ills. Denslow. 1st ed. $150.00

BAUM, L. Frank. *Kabumpo in Oz.* 1922. Chicago. Ills. Thompson & Plumly. VG $40.00

BAUM, L. Frank. *Ozma of Oz.* 1907. Chicago. Reilly & Lee. Ills. 270 pp. $55.00

BAUM, L. Frank. *Purple Dragon & Other Fantasies.* 1976. Kirk & Greene. 1st ed. dj. EX $35.00

BAUM, L. Frank. *Rinkitink in Oz.* 1916. Chicago. Reilly & Lee. Ills. Neill. VG $55.00

BAUM, L. Frank. *Road to Oz.* Reilly & Lee. no date. reprint. Ills. Neill. $20.00

BAUM, L. Frank. *Road to Oz.* 1909. Reilly/Britton. 1st ed. 1st issue. $100.00

BAUM, L. Frank. *Sky Island.* 1912. Reilly & Lee. Ills. Neill. 1st ed. VG $100.00

BAUM, L. Frank. *The Emerald City of Oz.* 1910. Chicago. Reilly & Lee. Ills. Neill. $75.00

BAUM, L. Frank. *The Emerald City of Oz.* 1918. Ills. Neill. 1st ed. 3rd impression. VG $45.00

BAUM, L. Frank. *The Emerald City of Oz.* 1910. Reilly & Britton. 1st ed. VG $137.50

BAUM, L. Frank. *The Gnome King of Oz.* 1927. Chicago. Ills. Thompson & Plumly. VG $60.00

BAUM, L. Frank. *The Land of Oz.* 1939. oversized. $18.00

BAUM, L. Frank. *The Lost Princess of Oz.* 1917. Chicago. Ills. J.R. Neill. 1st ed. VG $80.00

BAUM, L. Frank. *The Magic of Oz.* 1919. Reilly & Lee. Ills. Neil. $55.00

BAUM, L. Frank. *The Magical Monarch of Mo.* 1903. Chicago. Ills. Frank Verbeck. G $75.00

BAUM, L. Frank. *The New Wizard of Oz.* 1944. Bobbs Merrill. Ills. E. Copelman. 209 pp. VG $12.50

BAUM, L. Frank. *The New Wizard of Oz.* 1903. Indianapolis. Bobbs Merrill. Ills. Denslow. $50.00

BAUM, L. Frank. *The Patchwork Girl of Oz.* 1922. Chicago. Reilly & Lee. Ills. Neill. $35.00

BAUM, L. Frank. *The Scalawagons of Oz.* 1941. Chicago. Ills. J.R. Neill. EX $65.00

BAUM, L. Frank. *The Sea Fairies.* 1911. Chicago. Ills. Neill. 1st ed. $100.00

BAUM, L. Frank. *The Silver Princess of Oz.* 1938. Chicago. Ills. Thompson & Plumly. VG $40.00

BAUM, L. Frank. *The Tin Woodman of Oz.* 1918. Chicago. Ills. J.R. Neill. VG $30.00

BAUM, L. Frank. *The Tin Woodman of Oz.* Chicago. Reilly & Lee. Ills. Ulrey. $20.00

BAUM, L. Frank. *The Wishing Horse of Oz.* 1935. Chicago. Ills. Thompson/Plumly & Neill. $125.00

BAUM, L. Frank. *The Wizard of Oz.* 1950. New York. Random House. 64 pp. VG $3.50

BAUM, L. Frank. *The Wizard of Oz.* 1985. New Jersey. Ills. Hildebrandt. 191 pp. $17.50

BAUM, L. Frank. *The Wizard of Oz.* 1950. Random House. Ills. Anton Loeb. 1st ed. EX $10.00

BAUM, L. Frank. *The Wizard of Oz.* 1956. Chicago. Reilly & Lee. Ills. Denslow. $17.50

BAUM, L. Frank. *The Yellow Knight of Oz.* 1930. Chicago. Ills. J.R. Neill. G $40.00

BAUM, L. Frank. *Tik-Tok of Oz.* 1914. Chicago. Ills. J.R. Neill. VG $30.00

BAUM, L. Frank. *Wizard of Oz Pop Up Classic.* Random House. (ca.1960) Ills. VG $12.50

BAUM, Vicki. *Falling Star.* 1934. New York. Doubleday Doran. 307 pp. G $2.50

BAUM, Vicki. *Grand Hotel.* 1930. London. 1st ed. dj. VG $12.00

BAUMANN, P. *Collecting Antique Marbles.* 1970. Des Moines. $10.00

BAUMANN. *Leica Book in Color.* 1938. Munich. 72 color pls. VG $22.50

BAUR, John. *Dogs on the Frontier.* 1964. Naylor. Ills. 238 pp. $18.00

BAUSCH, Edward. *Manipulation of the Microscope.* 1901. Rochester. 202 pp. index. VG $12.50

BAUSCH, Robert. *The Lives of Riley Chance.* 1984. St. Martins. dj. VG $15.00

BAX, Clifford, ed. *B. Shaw & W.B. Yeats. Letters to Florence Farr.* 1946. London. 67 pp. dj. EX $30.00

BAX, Emily. *Miss Bax of the Embassy.* 1939. Boston. photos. 331 pp. G $5.00

BAXT. *Queer Kind of Death.* 1966. 1st ed. dj. EX $20.00

BAXTER, Austin. *History of the New York Society Library.* 1908. New York. Ltd. ed. 1/500. inscr. 607 pp. $100.00

BAXTER, George Owen. *Shadow of Silver Tip.* 1925. New York. 1st ed. dj. VG $35.00

BAXTER, James Phinney. *New France in New England.* 1894. Munsell. 450 pp. $22.50

BAXTER, W.E. *Winter in India.* 1883. New York. 1st Am. ed. wrappers. EX $30.00

BAXTER, William. *Life of Knowles Shaw, the Singing Evangelist.* 1879. Cincinnati. 237 pp. $17.50

BAXTER. *Gallant Fourteenth.* 1980. Traverse City. Ills. dj. EX $25.00

BAY, J.C. *Second Handful of Western Books.* 1936. Torch Press. Ltd. ed. 1/400. VG $20.00

BAY, J.C. *Third Handful of Western Books.* 1937. Torch Press. Ltd. ed. 1/400. VG $20.00

BAY, K. *American Fly Tyer's Handbook.* 1974. dj. EX $12.50

BAYER, Herbert. *World Geo-Graphic Atlas.* 1953. Chicago. private print. Ills. 368 pp. $44.00

BAYER, William. *Peregrine.* 1981. Congdon. dj. EX $8.00

BAYER, William. *Switch.* 1984. Simon & Schuster. dj. EX $10.00

BAYER, William. *Tangier.* 1978. Congdon. dj. VG $9.00

BAYLER, Walter. *Last Man Off Wake Island.* 1943. Bobbs Merrill. Ills. Ltd. ed. 367 pp. index. $27.50

BAYLES, Richard M. *History of Windham County, Connecticut.* 1889. New York. Preston Co. 1204 pp. VG $80.00

BAYLOCK, J.P. *Paper Dragons.* Ltd. ed. 1/100. Intro Tim Powers. sgns. $45.00

BAYNARD, Samuel H., Jr. *History of the Supreme Council, 33rd Degree.* 1938. Boston. 1st ed. 2 vol set. djs. boxed. VG $30.00

BAYNE, Marie. *Toy Soldiers.* New York. Sully & Kleinteich. Ills. $30.00

BAYNE, Samuel Gamble. *Derricks of Destiny, an Autobiography.* 1924. New York. $10.00

BAYS, Davis H. *Doctrines/Dogmas of Mormonism, Examined & Refuted.* 1897. St. Louis. Ills. 1st ed. 459 pp. $75.00

BAYS. *The Orphic Vision.* 1964. dj. VG $7.50

BAZE, W. *Just Elephants.* 1955. London. Elek Books. photos. 244 pp. $13.00

BAZIN, Andre. *Jean Renoir.* 1971. New York. Ills. 1st ed. 320 pp. dj. VG $8.50

BAZIN, Germain. *History of World Sculpture.* 1968. Holland. Ills. 1st ed. folio. dj. $30.00

BAZIN, Germain. *Italian Painting in the XIV & XV Centuries.* 1938. Paris. Hyperion Press. dj. VG $45.00

BAZIN. *Fra Angelico.* 1949. 130 plates. VG $29.00

BEACH, Charles Amory. *Air Service Boys Flying for Victory.* 1920. New York. 218 pp. dj. $3.50

BEACH, Charles Amory. *Air Service Boys Over the Enemy's Lines.* 1919. New York. World Syndicated Pub. 216 pp. $3.50

BEACH, E.L. *Dust on the Sea.* 1972. dj. EX $10.00

BEACH, Edward L. *Submarine!* 1952. New York. 301 pp. VG $3.50

BEACH, Joseph Warren. *The Making of the Auden Canon.* 1957. U. of MN. 1st ed. dj. $8.50

BEACH, Marjorie. *The Mayor's Wife: Crusade in Kansas City.* 1953. New York. inscr. dj. VG $12.50

BEACH, Rex. *Son of the Gods.* 1929. New York. Harper. 392 pp. G $3.50

BEACH, Rex. *The Auction Block.* 1914. New York. Harper. 441 pp. $3.50

BEACH, Rex. *The Iron Trail, an Alaskan Romance.* 1913. New York. 1st ed. 390 pp. $17.50

BEACH, Rex. *The Miracle of Coral Gables.* 1926. Hartford. Ills. Edw. Wilson. Ltd. ed. VG $30.00

BEACH, Rex. *The Silver Horde.* 1909. Ills. 1st ed. VG $6.00

BEACH, Rex. *The Spoilers.* 1906. A.L. Burt. Ills. $6.50

BEACH, Sylvia. *Shakespeare & Company.* 1959. New York. Harcourt. Ills. 1st ed. dj. $15.00

BEACH, W.A. *Treatise on Anatomy, Physiology & Health.* 1847. $295.00

BEACH & MOORE. *The Big Game 1913-1947.* 1948. New York. 1st ed. photos. VG $15.00

BEACH. *Obsessive Images/Symbolism in Poetry of 1930-40's.* 1960. U. of MN. VG $12.50

BEACH. *The Winds of Chance.* 1918. 1st ed. dj. EX $35.00

BEADLE, George & Muriel. *The Language of Life, Introduction to Genetics.* 1966. Doubleday. Ills. 242 pp. dj. $9.00

BEADLE, J.H. *Life in Utah; or, Mysteries & Crimes of Mormonism.* 1870. Philadelphia. Ills. 1st ed. fld map. VG $60.00

BEADLE, J.H. *Western Wilds & the Men Who Redeem Them.* 1878. Cincinnati. fld map. 624 pp. $25.00

BEADLEY, Mercer. *How to Play Tennis.* 1936. New York. Garden City. Ills. 172 pp. $5.00

BEAGLE, Peter S. *A Fine & Private Place.* 1960. Viking. 1st ed. dj. VG $45.00

BEAGLE, Peter S. *I See My Outfit.* 1965. Viking Press. 1st ed. dj. VG $25.00

BEAL, M. *Story of Man in Yellowstone.* 1949. Caxton Press. presentation copy. $95.00

BEAL, Samuel. *Travels of Fah-Hian & Sung-Yun, China to India.* 1964. London. 2nd ed. 208 pp. dj. $28.00

BEAL. *The Gladiolus & Its Culture.* 1931. Orange Judd Pub. Ills. 124 pp. $6.50

BEALE, H.P. *Bibliography of Plant Viruses & Index to Research.* 1976. Columbia Press. 1495 pp. VG $15.00

BEALER, Alex. *The Successful Craftsman.* 1975. Barre. $2.50

BEALLE, M.A. *Gangway for Navy, Football at USNA, 1879-1950.* 1951. 1st ed. dj. EX $8.50

BEALS, Carleton. *Our Yankee Heritage.* 1955. New York. 1st ed. 311 pp. dj. EX $10.00

BEAMAN, S.G. Hulme, retold by. *Aladdin.* 1925. New York. McBride. Ills. 1st Am. ed. dj. $25.00

BEAMISH, North Ludlow. *Discovery of America by Northmen in 10th Century.* 1841. London. 1st ed. Ills. maps. EX $100.00

BEAMISH, Richard J. *The Boy's Story of Lindbergh, the Lone Eagle.* 1928. Chicago. Winston. Ills. 320 pp. VG $6.50

BEAMISH, Richard J. *The Boy's Story of Lindbergh, the Lone Eagle.* 1928. Philadelphia. Ills. 320 pp. VG $7.50

BEAMISH, Richard J. *The Story of Lindbergh, the Lone Eagle.* 1927. Dayton. Ills. 320 pp. VG $12.50

BEAMISH, Richard. *The Psychomony of the Hand.* 1865. London. 2nd ed. 94 pp. 31 pls. $45.00

BEAMISH, Tody, *Aldabra Alone.* 1970. Sierra Club. 24 color photos. 222 pp. dj. $15.00

BEAN, P. *Winslow Homer's Magazine Engravings.* 1979. Harper & Row. 1st ed. $25.00

BEAN, W. *Boss Ruef's San Francisco.* 1952. CA U. Press. dj. VG $12.50

BEAR, Gilly. *When I Grow Up.* 1915. New York. Ills. Brundage & Kaucher. $10.00

BEAR, Greg. *Eon.* 1985. New York. Blue Jay. proof copy. EX $40.00

BEAR, Robert. *Delivered Unto Satan.* 1974. Carlisle, PA. 1st ed. 331 pp. dj. VG $20.00

BEARD, Charles. *Lucks & Talismans.* 1972. Detroit. reprint ed. 258 pp. $25.00

BEARD, Charles. *Wither Mankind.* 1928. 1st ed. dj. $6.50

BEARD, Dan. *American Boys' Book of Birds & Brownies of Woods.* 1931. Ills. 2nd ed. dj. VG $18.50

BEARD, Dan. *Moonblight & Six Feet of Romance.* 1904. New York. Ills. $7.50

BEARD, Dan. *The American Boy's Handy Book.* 1983. Godine. Ills. reprint of 1890 ed. $15.00

BEARD, James. *Fowl & Game Cookery.* 1944. 1st ed. dj. VG $15.00

BEARD, James. *Menus for Entertaining.* 1965. Delacorte. 398 pp. dj. EX $4.50

BEARD, James. *Treasury of Outdoor Cooking.* 1960. 1st ed. VG $20.00

BEARDSLEY, A. *His Best Fifty Drawings.* 1955. London. Ltd. 1st ed. dj. VG $25.00

BEARDSLEY, A. *Selected Drawings.* 1967. New York. Grove Press. 1st ed. $47.50

BEARDSLEY, Aubrey. *A Second Book of Fifty Drawings.* 1899. London. Ltd. ed. 1/1050. pls. VG $85.00

BEARDSLEY, Aubrey. *Bon-Mots of Sydney Smith & R. Brinsley Sheridan.* 1893. London. Ills. 1st ed. $60.00

BEARDSLEY, Aubrey. *Brian Reade.* 1967. New York. dj. VG $25.00

BEARDSLEY, D.B. *History of Hancock County, Ohio.* 1881. Springfield. 472 pp. G $40.00

BEARDWOOD, W. *The Still Hunt.* 1965. McKay. Ills. 148 pp. $3.00

BEASSE, Pierre. *A New & Rational Treatise of Dowsing.* 1941. Ills. 1st Eng. ed. wrappers. $35.00

BEATIE, R.H., Jr. *Road to Manassas.* 1961. New York. 1st ed. dj. VG $10.00

BEATON, Cecil. *Cecil Beaton's New York.* 1938. 1st ed. EX $32.50

BEATON, Cecil. *I Take Great Pleasure.* 1956. Day. 1st Am. ed. dj. VG $7.50

BEATON, Cecil. *Memoirs of the '40s.* 1972. New York. McGraw Hill. Ills. 310 pp. $10.00

BEATON, Cecil. *Quail in Aspic.* 1963. Indianapolis. Ills. 1st ed. dj. VG $35.00

BEATON & BOLTON. *A German Source Book in Physics.* 1969. Oxford U. Press. dj. $20.00

BEATON & TYNAN, Kenneth. *Personal Grata.* 1954. Putnam. 1st Am. ed. dj. EX $15.00

BEATON. *An Indian Album.* 1945. dj. $25.00

BEATTIE, Ann. *Distortions.* 1976. Garden City. Doubleday. 1st ed. dj. VG $75.00

BEATTIE, Ann. *Falling in Place.* 1980. Random House. 1st ed. sgn. dj. EX $35.00

BEATTIE, Ann. *Secrets & Surprises.* 1978. New York. Random House. 1st ed. dj. EX $25.00

BEATTIE, Ann. *The Burning House.* 1982. Random House. review copy. dj. VG $17.50

BEATTIE, James. *Essays on Truth.* 1777. Edinburgh. Scotland. $150.00

BEATTY, Clyde. *Jungle Performers.* New York. McBride. 1st ed. sgn. VG $22.50

BEATTY, Jerome, Jr. *Double Take.* 1971. Brattleboro. Stephen Green Press. 117 pp. $6.50

BEAUCHAMP, Wilbur & Compton. *Science Stories.* 1933. Chicago. Scott, Foreman. 144 pp. $3.50

BEAULIEU, Victor-Levy. *Jack Kerouac. A Chicken-Essay.* 1975. Toronto. Ltd. ed. 1/1000. wrappers. EX $25.00

BEAUMONT, Cyril. *Five Centuries of Ballet Design.* London. Ills. 127 pp. VG $20.00

BEAUMONT, Cyril. *Puppets & Puppetry.* 1958. Studio Pub. 1st ed. dj. $15.00

BEAUMONT, Edouard De. *The Sword & Womankind.* 1929. New York. Ltd. ed. 1/760. 237 pp. VG $12.50

BEAUMONT, William. *Physiology of Digestion with Experiments.* 1847. Burlington. Ills. 2nd ed. 304 pp. VG $375.00

BEAUVOIR, Simone de, *The Prime of Life.* 1962. New York. 1st ed. dj. VG $10.00

BEAUVOIR, Simone de. *The Blood of Others.* 1948. New York. Knopf. dj. EX $35.00

BEBEL, August. *Woman in Past, Present, & Future.* 1897. VG $30.00

BEBERMAN, Herbert. *Salt of the Earth.* 1965. Boston. Beacon Pr. 1st ed. inscr. dj. $40.00

BEBEY, Francis. *African Music: People's Art.* 1975. New York. Ills. 184 pp. $8.00

BECATTI. *Art of Ancient Greece & Rome.* 1967. VG $49.00

BECHDOLT, Jack. *Roscoe.* 1939. New York. Ills. Decie Merwin. 1st ed. $10.00

BECHDOLT, Jack. *The Modern Handy Book for Boys.* 1933. New York. 421 pp. $4.00

BECHDOLT, Jack. *The Torch.* 1948. Philadelphia. Prime Press. 1st ed. dj. EX $20.00

BECK, B.F. *Honey & Health.* 1938. New York. Ills. 1st ed. index. dj. VG $17.50

BECK, E.M. *Sailor Historian. Best of Samuel Eliot Morison.* 1977. VG $15.00

BECK, Fred & Barnes, O.K. *73 Years in a Sand Trap.* 1949. New York. Ills. 5th printing. 159 pp. $10.00

BECK, Henry H. *Cuba's Fight for Freedom & the War with Spain.* 1898. Philadelpia. Globe Pub. 2 vols in 1. G $12.50

BECK, Horace. *Folklore & the Sea.* 1973. $7.50

BECK, James M. *The War & Humanity.* 1917. New York. Putnam. 360 pp. $3.50

BECK, Lois & Keddie, N. *Women in the Muslim World.* 1978. Cambridge. Harvard U. Press. 698 pp. $12.50

BECK, Louis. *Ebbing of the Tide.* 1896. New York. 292 pp. G $20.00

BECKE, Louis. *By Reef & Palm.* 1895. Philadelphia. 1st Am. ed. $45.00

BECKER, A.C. *Waterfowl in the Marshes.* 1969. Barnes. Ills. 155 pp. dj. $13.00

BECKER, Anthony J. *Biography of a Country Town U.S.A.* 1954. no place. Ills. 217 pp. $10.00

BECKER, Carl. *Freedom & Responsibility.* 1945. Knopf. 1st ed. $27.50

BECKER, Ethel Anderson. *Klondike '98. Hegg's Album 1898 Alaska Gold Rush.* 1958. Portland. Ills. 2nd printing. 126 pp. $18.50

BECKER, Peter. *Dingane, King of the Zulu 1828-1840.* 1965. Crowell. Ills. 1st Am. ed. 283 pp. dj. $20.00

BECKER, Stephen. *Comic Art in America.* 1959. New York. 1st ed. VG $12.50

BECKER, Stephen. *Season of the Stranger.* 1951. New York. 1st ed. dj. EX $15.00

BECKER. *Dog Tags.* 1973. 1st Am. ed. dj. EX $15.00

BECKER. *The Last Mandarin.* 1979. 1st ed. dj. EX $12.50

BECKER. *The Outcasts.* 1967. 1st Am. ed. dj. EX $22.50

BECKER. *When the War is Over.* 1969. 1st Am. ed. dj. EX $20.00

BECKETT, S. *Catastrophe.* 1983. Ltd. ed. 1/100. sgn. $90.00

BECKETT, S. *Poems in English.* 1963. New York. 1st ed. dj. $12.50

BECKETT, Samuel. *Footfalls.* 1976. London. Faber. proof copy. EX $75.00

BECKETT, Samuel. *Molloy/Malone Dies/The Unnamable.* 1959. Paris. Olympia Press. wrappers. EX $65.00

BECKETT, Samuel. *The Unnamable.* 1958. New York. Grove. 1st Am. ed. dj. EX $25.00

BECKETT. *Endgame.* 1958. 1st Eng. ed. dj. VG $50.00

BECKETT. *Play.* 1964. 1st Eng. ed. dj. VG $25.00

BECKETT. *Proust.* 1931. 1st Eng. ed. VG $110.00

BECKETT. *Waiting for Godot.* 1956. 1st Eng. ed. dj. VG $50.00

BECKFORD, William. *Vathek.* 1929. Nonesuch Press. Ills. Dorn. Ltd. ed. 1/1050. $50.00

BECKWITH, M. Helen. *Story Telling with the Scissors.* 1923. Springfield. G $7.50

BECKWITH, Thomas. *The Indian; or, Mound Builder.* 1911. Cape Girardeau. Ills. 135 pp. $45.00

BEDDALL, Barbara. *Wallace & Bates in the Tropics.* 1969. Macmillan. Ills. 1st printing. 241 pp. EX $18.00

BEDELL, C.T. *The Valley of Bones.* 1847. Boston. 140 pp. $12.50

BEDFORD, G. *Timescape.* 1980. New York. Simon & Schuster. 1st ed. dj. $40.00

BEDFORD. *Peter & Wendy.* 1911. Scribner. Ills. 1st Am. ed. $38.00

BEDFORD, Sybille. *A Compass Error.* 1969. New York. 1st ed. dj. EX $8.50

BEDFORD, Sybille. *A Legacy.* 1957. New York. 1st ed. dj. EX $15.00

BEDFORD-JONES. *D'Artagnan's Letter.* 1931. New York. Covici. 1st ed. dj. EX $20.00

BEDFORD-JONES. *Saint Michael's Gold.* 1926. New York. Putnam. 1st ed. dj. EX $30.00

BEDFORD-JONES. *The Mesa Trail.* 1920. New York. Doubleday. 1st ed. dj. $10.00

BEDICHEK, Roy. *Adventures with a Texas Naturalist.* 1966. Texas U. Press.Ills. Lockwood. revised ed. $15.00

BEE, J.W. & others. *Mammals in Kansas.* 1981. Kansas U. Press. Ills. 300 pp. $18.00

BEEBE, B.F. *American Lions & Cats.* 1963. McKay. Ills. 177 pp. dj. $15.00

BEEBE, C. William. *Two Bird-Lovers in Mexico.* 1905. Boston/NY. Riverside Pr. Ills. 1st ed. EX $75.00

BEEBE, F.L. & Webster, H.M. *North American Falconry & Hunting Hawks.* 1976. Denver. Ills. 331 pp. dj. EX $25.00

BEEBE, Lucius & Clegg, C. *Hear the Train Blow.* 1952. New York. 1st ed. dj. VG $20.00

BEEBE, Lucius & Clegg, C. *San Francisco's Golden Era.* 1960. Berkley. Ills. 2nd printing. 255 pp. VG $18.00

BEEBE, Lucius & Clegg, C. *Steamcars to the Comstock.* 1957. Berkeley, CA. Ills. sgns. dj. VG $25.00

BEEBE, Lucius. *Big Spenders.* 1958. London. Ills. 1st ed. dj. VG $10.00

BEEBE, Lucius. *Highball.* 1945. Bonanza. Ills. 223 pp. dj. EX $3.00

BEEBE, Lucius. *Stork Club Bar Book.* 1946. 1st ed. dj. VG $10.00

BEEBE, William. *Beneath Tropic Seas, Diving Among Coral Reefs.* 1928. Putnam. Ills. $10.00

BEEBE, William. *Edge of the Jungle.* 1921. Garden City. 303 pp. $7.00

BEEBE, William. *Galapagos: World's End.* 1924. New York. 1st ed. $30.00

BEEBE, William. *Half Mile Down.* 1957. Ills. map. 344 pp. VG $15.00

BEEBE, William. *Jungle Days.* 1925. Garden City. 201 pp. $5.00

BEEBE, William. *Pheasant Jungles.* 1927. Putnam. 60 Ills. 1st ed. VG $17.50

BEEBE, William. *Pheasants, Their Lives & Homes.* 1936. New York. 309 pp. dj. $30.00

BEEBE, William. *The Arcturus Adventure.* 1926. Putnam. photos. maps. 439 pp. $10.00

BEEBE, William. *The Log of the Sun.* 1927. Garden City. 321 pp. $10.00

BEEBE, William. *The Log of the Sun.* 1906. Holt. Ills. W.K. Strong. 1st ed. VG $50.00

BEEBE & BULKLEY. *Bibliography of the Writings of E.A. Robinson.* 1931. Dunster House. Ltd. ed. 1/300. VG $30.00

BEECHER, C. & Stowe, H.B. *The American Woman's Home.* 1869. New York. 1st ed. VG $17.50

BEECHER, E. *Walt Disney's Tonka.* Golden Press. Ills. G $3.50

BEECHER, Elizabeth. *Roy Rogers King of the Cowboys.* 1953. New York. Simon & Schuster. 112 pp. $2.50

BEECROFT, John. *Kipling, a Selection of His Stories & Poems.* 1956. New York. Doubleday. 531 pp. $5.00

BEECROFT, John. *Mr. Maugham Himself by W. Somerset Maugham.* 1954. New York. Doubleday. 688 pp. VG $5.00

BEECROFT, John. *The Gentlemen from Indianapolis.* 1957. New York. Doubleday. 732 pp. dj. $5.00

BEEM, Frances. *Three Little Pigs & the Foolish Pig.* 1918. Chicago. Rand McNally. Ills. $10.00

BEER, Thomas. *Hanna.* 1929. New York. 325 pp. index. $7.50

BEERBOHM, Max. *A Survey.* 1921. London. 1st ed. VG $80.00

BEERBOHM, Max. *Caricatures from Collection In Asmolean Museum.* 1958. Oxford. Ills. 1st ed. dj. VG $30.00

BEERBOHM, Max. *Lytton Strachy.* 1943. 1st Am. ed. dj. EX $20.00

BEERBOHM, Max. *More.* 1899. London. 1st ed. slipcase. VG $95.00

BEERBOHM, Max. *Observations.* 1926. London. Ltd. ed. 1/280. sgn. dj. VG $200.00

BEERBOHM, Max. *Seven Men.* 1919. London. Heinemann. 1st ed. $35.00

BEERBOHM, Max. *The Dreadful Dragon of Hay Hill.* 1928. London. 1st ed. dj. VG $22.50

BEERBOHM, Max. *The Guerdon.* 1925. private print. Ltd. 1st ed. 1/110. VG $17.50

BEERBOHM, Max. *The Works of Max Beerbohm.* 1896. New York. 1st ed. VG $125.00

BEERBOHM, Max. *Things New & Old.* 1923. London. Heinemann. 1st ed. sgn. $275.00

BEERBOHM, Max. *Zuleika Dobson.* 1911. London. 1st ed. wrappers. VG $37.50

BEERBOHM. *Fin De Siecle.* 1957. London. Ills. author, Wilde, Alfie. VG $25.00

BEERS, Frank. *The Green Signal or Life on the Rail.* 1904. Kansas City. Ills. 239 pp. scarce $20.00

BEETON, Isabella. *Mrs. Beeton's Cookery & Household Management.* 1967. London. Ills. 8th impression. 1344 pp. $20.00

BEETON. *Beeton's All About Cookery. Collection of Recipes.*1892. London. Ills. $17.50

BEETON. *Mrs. Beeton's Household Management.* 1926. London. $27.50

BEETS, Henry. *Het Leven van William McKinley.* 1901. Holland. scarce. $15.00

BEGG, A. *History of British Columbia.* 1894. Toronto. 1st ed. $50.00

BEHAN, Brendan. *Behan's New York.* 1964. $15.00

BEHAN, Brendan. *Brendan Behan's Island.* 1962. Ills. Hogarth. 1st Am. ed. dj. VG $35.00

BEHAN, Brendan. *Confessions of an Irish Rebel.* 1965. New York. 1st ed. dj. EX $15.00

BEHAN, Brendan. *Richard's Cork Leg.* 1974. Grove Press. 1st Am. ed. dj. VG $15.00

BEHAN, Brendan. *The Scarperer.* 1964. Doubleday. 1st ed. dj. VG $25.00

BEHME, R.L. *Shasta & Rogue.* 1974. Simon & Schuster. 1st ed. sgn. $7.00

BEHN, Jack. *'.45-70' Rifles.* 1956. Harrisburg, PA.Ills. 1st ed. 137 pp. dj. $25.00

BEHN, Noel. *Seven Silent Men.* 1984. Arbor House. advance copy. wrappers. $25.00

BEHRMAN, S.N. *Duveen.* 1972. Boston. Ills. 1st ed. dj. VG $7.50

BEHRMAN, S.N. *Fanny.* 1955. New York. Ills. dj. VG $7.50

BEHRMAN, S.N. *The Pirate.* 1943. New York. Ills. 1st ed. dj. VG $7.50

BEHRMAN, S.N. *Wine of Choice.* 1938. New York. Random House. 213 pp. $5.00

BEIGEL, H.M. *Battleship Country.* 1984. Ills. 72 pp. wrappers. EX $7.50

BEILEUSON, Edna. *Holiday Party Desserts.* 1956. Peter Pauper Press. 61 pp. $4.50

BEIRNE, Francis F. *Baltimore, a Picture History 1858-1958.* 1957. New York. 1st printing. 153 pp. sgn. VG $18.00

BEIRNE, Francis F. *The Amiable Baltimoreans.* 1951. New York. sgn. VG $4.50

BEITZELL, Edwin. *Life on the Potomac River.* 1968. 1st ed. sgn. dj. $20.00

BEKEN, A.K. *Beauty of Sail.* 1954. 2nd impression. $7.00

BEKEN, A.K. *Yacts.* 1960. Ills. $7.50

BELANGER, Jerry. *Raising Milk Goats the Modern Way.* 1975. Charlotte, VT. 152 pp. SftCvr. VG $4.50

BELANGER. *Memoires d'un Cultivateur.* 1936. Quebec. Ills. 1st ed. wrappers. $20.00

BELASCO, David. *The Return of Peter Grimm.* 1912. New York. Ills. J. Rae. 1st ed. VG $15.00

BELCHER, Lady. *Mutineers of the Bounty & Their Descendants.* 1871. New York. map. VG $45.00

BELDEN, Charles J. *Spurs Were a-Jinglin'.* dj. VG $8.00

BELDEN, David. *Life of David Belden.* 1891. New York. Ills. 1st ed. 472 pp. $150.00

BELDEN, H. *Illustrated Historical Atlas of Wayne Co. MI.* 1876. Chicago. 79 pp. $295.00

BELITSKII, Iakov. *Slovo O Moskve.* 1984. Moscow. 159 pp. $5.00

BELKNAP, E. *Milk Glass.* 1959. New York. $15.00

BELKNAP. *Fred Kabotie: Hopi Indian Artist.* 1977. Northland. 1st ed. $20.00

BELL, A.H. *Practical Dowsing. A Symposium.* 1965. London. Bell. 1st ed. 198 pp. $20.00

BELL, Alexander Graham. *Establishment for the Study of Vocal Physiology.* 1872. Boston. 1st ed. 16 pp. wrappers. $125.00

BELL, Charles. *The Hand: Its Mechanism & Vital Endowments.* 1833. scarce. $295.00

BELL, Dorothy Briggs. *Musical Jingles for the Very Young.* 1932. Ditson Co. Ills. Parker. wrappers. $12.00

BELL, Douglas. *Seamen of Britain.* 1943. $8.00

BELL, Ernest. *Fighting Traffic in Young Girls.* 1910. Ills. 481 pp. $17.50

BELL, Gertrude. *The Letters of Gertrude Bell.* 1927. London. Ills. 2 vol set. djs. VG $30.00

BELL, Isaac. *Foxiana.* 1929. London. 1st ed. 16 pls. EX $40.00

BELL, Jessica LaForge. *Ward's Land.* 1967. San Antonio. Ltd. ed. 272 pp. EX $12.50

BELL, John. *Bulletin of Medical Science: Pilcher on the Ear.* 1843. 1st ed. 299 pp. $35.00

BELL, Madison Smartt. *Straight Cut.* 1986. New York. Ticknor & Fields. wrappers. $12.50

BELL, Margaret. *Margaret Fuller.* 1930. Boni. 1st ed. $15.00

BELL, Quentin. *Virginia Woolf.* 1972. New York. Harcourt. 2 vols in 1. $7.50

BELL, Robert W. & Lockerbie. *In Peril on the Sea, a Personal Remembrance.* 1984. Garden City. Doubleday. 284 pp. dj. $3.50

BELL, Thomas. *From This Day Forward.* 1946. New York. Grosset & Dunlap. 1st ed. dj. $15.00

BELL, W. *Wanderings of an Elephant Hunter.* 1958. 2nd ed. $75.00

BELL, W.D.M. *Karamojo Safari.* 1949. 1st Eng. ed. dj. VG $155.00

BELL. *Abraham Lincoln, a Poetical Interpretation.* 1913. Ltd. ed. 1/125. VG $75.00

BELL. *Reminiscences of a Ranger.* 1881. Los Angeles. 1st ed. $125.00

BELLAIRS, A. & Attridge, J. *Reptiles.* 1975. London. Ills. revised ed. 240 pp. $20.00

BELLAIRS, George. *Death in the Night Watches.* 1946. Macmillan. 1st printing. 223 pp. dj. $75.00

BELLAMY, Edward. *Equality.* 1897. New York. 1st ed. VG $22.50

BELLAMY, Edward. *Looking Backward.* 1888. Boston. 1st ed. 1st issue. VG $100.00

BELLAMY, Edward. *Looking Backward.* 1945. World. Ltd. 1st ed. 1/950. slipcase. $40.00

BELLAMY, Edward. *The Blindman's World & Other Stories.* 1898. Boston. Houghton Mifflin. $75.00

BELLEGARRIQUE, A. *Les Femmes d'Amerique.* 1853. Paris. 1st ed. 96 pp. wrappers. $75.00

BELLEMIN, George. *Physical Anthropology.* 1956. TB. 70 pp. G $5.00

BELLEU, Frank. *The Art of Amusing.* 1866. New York. Charleton. 302 pp. VG $20.00

BELLMANN, Henry & Katherine. *Parris Mitchell of King's Row.* 1948. New York. Simon & Schuster. 333 pp. dj. $75.00

BELLOC, H. & Chesterton, C. *The Party System.* 1911. London. presentation copy. 1st ed. VG $40.00

BELLOC, Hilaire. *The Bad Child's Book of Beasts.* 1930. New York. Knopf. Ills. 1st Am. ed. $15.00

BELLOW, Saul. *Henderson, the Rain King.* 1959. Viking. 1st ed. 1st issue. dj. VG $80.00

BELLOW, Saul. *Henderson, the Rain King.* 1959. Weidenfield. 1st English ed. dj. VG $65.00

BELLOW, Saul. *Humbold's Gift.* 1975. New York. Viking. 1st ed. dj. VG $25.00

BELLOW, Saul. *Mr. Sammler's Planet.* 1970. New York. Viking. 1st ed. dj. VG $22.50

BELLOW, Saul. *Nobel Lecture.* 1979. Targ. Ltd. ed. 1/350. sgn. VG $50.00

BELLOW, Saul. *The Dean's December.* 1982. New York. Harper. 1st ed. dj. VG $15.00

BELLOW, Saul. *The Dean's December.* 1952. Ltd. 1st ed. 1/500. sgn. VG $65.00

BELLOW, Saul. *The Victim.* 1947. New York. 1st ed. $125.00

BELLOW, Saul. *To Jerusalem & Back.* 1976. 1st ed. dj. $10.00

BELLOW. *American Fiction.* New York. 1st ed. wrappers. VG $20.00

BELLOWS, George. *George W. Bellows: Lithographs & Paintings.* 1927 & 1929. Knopf. 1st eds. 2 vol set. VG $250.00

BELLOWS, I.H. *Old Mechanical Banks.* 1940. Chicago. $35.00

BELLROSE, F.C. *Ducks, Geese, & Swans of North America.* 1976. Stackpole. Ills. 540 pp. $15.00

BELOTE & BELOTE. *Typhoons of Steel. The Battle for Okinawa.* 1970. Ills. ex-lib. dj. G $9.00

BELSHAM, W. *Memoirs of the Reign of George III to Parliament.* 1795. London. 4 vol set. $65.00

BELSHAW, Cyril. *In Search of Wealth.* 1955. 1st ed. wrappers. $8.50

BEMELMANS, Ludwig. *Hotel Splendide.* 1941. Ltd. 1st ed. sgn. boxed. VG $75.00

BEMELMANS, Ludwig. *Madeline in London.* 1961. Viking. Ills. 1st ed. folio. dj. EX $40.00

BEMELMANS, Ludwig. *Madeline.* 1939. New York. Ills. 1st ed. folio. EX $50.00

BEMELMANS, Ludwig. *Madeline's Rescue.* 1953. Viking. 1st ed. dj. $45.00

BEMELMANS, Ludwig. *My Life in Art.* 1958. New York. Harper. Ills. 69 pp. dj. VG $22.50

BEMELMANS, Ludwig. *My War with the United States.* 1937. New York. Ills. author. 1st ed. VG $25.00

BEMELMANS, Ludwig. *Now I Lay Me Down to Sleep.* 1943. Viking. 1st ed. VG $10.00

BEMELMANS, Ludwig. *Now I Lay Me Down to Sleep.* 1945. Ltd. ed. 1/400. sgn. slipcase. $120.00

BEMELMANS, Ludwig. *Quito Express.* 1938. New York. Ills. author. 1st ed. VG $30.00

BEMELMANS, Ludwig. *The Blue Danube.* 1945. New York. Ills. author. 1st ed. dj. EX $20.00

BEMELMANS, Ludwig. *The Eye of God.* 1949. New York. 1st ed. $30.00

BEMELMANS, Ludwig. *The High World.* 1954. Harper. Ills. 1st ed. dj. VG $25.00

BEMENT, C.N. *American Poulterer's Companion.* 1847. Ills. 5th ed. $18.00

BEMIS, Samuel Flagg. *John Q. Adams & Foundations of American Policy.* 1949. New York. Ills. 1st ed. 588 pp. dj. $15.00

BENABO, Brian. *Moonlight Kingdom.* 1972. London. 1st Eng. ed. inscr. dj. EX $40.00

BENADAC, C. *Naked Puppet: Auschwitz.* 1978. Ferni. Ills. EX $35.00

BENARD, Robert. *A Catholic Education.* 1982. Holt. dj. VG $15.00

BENCH, Johnny. *Catch You Later.* 1979. Harper. 1st ed. sgn. dj. VG $17.50

BENCHLEY, Belle. *My Animal Babies.* 1946. Little, Brown. 264 pp. $10.00

BENCHLEY, Nathaniel. *The Visitors.* 1965. 1st ed. dj. $37.50

BENCHLEY, Robert. *Chips Off the Old Benchley.* 1949. Ills. Gluyas Williams. VG $7.50

BENCHLEY, Robert. *Inside Benchley.* 1942. Harper. 1st ed. dj. VG $20.00

BENCHLEY, Robert. *My Ten Years in a Quandary.* 1940. 1st ed. $10.00

BENCHLEY, Robert. *No Poems.* 1932. 1st ed. VG $65.00

BENCHLEY, Robert. *Pluck & Luck.* 2nd ed. VG $6.50

BENCHLEY, Robert. *The Early Worm.* 1927. 1st ed. VG $15.00

BENCHLEY, Robert. *The Reel Benchley.* 1950. 1st ed. photos. $26.50

BENET, Stephen V. *John Brown's Body.* 1928. Garden City. Doubleday Doran. 1st ed. dj. $40.00

BENEDICTINE. *Oeuvres Completes de Saint Augustin.* 1872. Paris. French & Latin texts. 34 vols. $300.00

BENES, E. *Democracy Today & Tomorrow.* 1939. New York. 244 pp. $6.00

BENET, Stephen V. *John Brown's Body.* 1928. Doubleday. Ltd. 1st ed. sgn. EX $80.00

BENET, Stephen V. *John Brown's Body: A Poem.* 1948. Heritage Press.Ills. Curry. boxed. EX $7.50

BENET, Stephen V. *Tales Before Midnight.* 1939. New York. Rinehart. 1st ed. dj. EX $15.00

BENET, Stephen V. *The Devil & Daniel Webster.* 1945. Kingsport, TN. Ills. Eichenberg. 1st ed. EX $15.00

BENET, Stephen V. *Western Star.* 1943. Farrar & Rinehart. dj. G $15.00

BENET, W.R. *The Reader's Encyclopedia.* 1948. New York. 4 vols. 1242 pp. EX $7.50

BENET, W.R. & Aiken, C., eds. *An Anthology of Famous English & American Poetry.* 1945. New York. Modern Library. 956 pp. EX $17.50

BENET. *Blacks.* 1st Eng. ed. dj. VG $50.00

BENEVOLUS, Hilaris. *The Pleasures of Human Life.* 1807. London. Ills. rare. $2.50

BENFORD, G. *Jupiter Project.* 1975. Nelson. 1st ed. dj. EX $17.50

BENFORD, G. & Eklund, G. *If the Stars are Gods.* 1977. 1st ed. dj. EX $25.00

BENFORD, Gregory & Brin, D. *Heart of the Comet.* 1986. New York. Bantam. 1st ed. dj. EX $12.50

BENFORD, Gregory. *Timescape.* 1980. New York. Simon & Schuster. 1st ed. sgn. $35.00

BENHAM, W. Gurney. *Playing Cards.* London. (ca.1940) 196 pp. dj. $45.00

BENHAM, W.H. *Trade & Trade Centers of History.* 1907. New York. De Vinne Press. Ills. 63 pp. $12.50

BENJAMIN, L.N. *The St. Alban's Raid.* 1865. wrappers. $40.00

BENJAMIN, Philip. *Quick Before It Melts.* 1964. New York. 1st ed. dj. $10.00

BENJAMIN. *Our American Artist.* 1879. $33.00

BENNETT, Arnold. *From the Log of the Velsa.* 1920. Ltd. 1st ed. 1/110. sgn. G $50.00

BENNETT, Arnold. *Imperial Palace; Riceyman Steps.* 1923. 1st ed. $6.50

BENNETT, Arnold. *Journal of Arnold Bennett.* 1932. 1st ed. $6.50

BENNETT, Arnold. *Journalism for Women: Practical Guide.* 1898. London. Lane. 1st ed. rare. VG $140.00

BENNETT, Arnold. *Old Wives' Tale.* 1911. EX $5.00

BENNETT, Arnold. *The Night Visitor & Other Stories.* 1913. Edinburgh. 1st ed. VG $15.00

BENNETT, Charles. H. *Bennett's Fables.* 1978. New York. Ills. reprint of 1857 ed. EX $10.00

BENNETT, Edward. *Amenities of Social Life.* 1887. London. 1st ed. 220 pp. $12.50

BENNETT, Gary L. *The Star Sailors.* 1980. New York. review copy. dj. EX $15.00

BENNETT, Geoffrey. *Nelson the Commander.* 1972. New York. Scribner. Ills. 322 pp. dj. $4.50

BENNETT, Ira E. *History of the Panama Canal.* 1915. Washington. 1st ed. folio. VG $50.00

BENNETT, John. *The Treasure of Pyre Gaillard.* 1906. New York. Ills. 1st ed. G $45.00

BENNETT, Joseph D. *Baudelaire. A Criticism.* 1944. Princeton. 165 pp. $5.00

BENNETT, Margot. *The Long Way Back.* 1955. New York. 1st Am. ed. dj. EX $8.00

BENNETT, Richard. *Mich & Mack & Mary Jane.* 1948. Garden City. Ills. author. 1st ed. VG $10.00

BENNETT, Robert Ames. *The Bowl of Baal.* 1975. Grant. 1st ed. dj. VG $15.00

BENNETT, Robert Ames. *Thyra: Romance of the Polar Pit.* 1901. New York. Holt. 1st ed. dj. VG $95.00

BENNETT, Russell. *Complete Rancher.* 1946. Rinehart. dj. EX $15.00

BENNETT, Sanford. *Old Age, Its Cause & Prevention.* 1921. New York. 390 pp. dj. $10.00

BENNETT, W.C. *Excavations at LaMata, Marcay, Venezuela.* 1937. photos & drawings. 137 pp. $9.00

BENNETT, W.C. *The North Highlands of Peru.* 1944. 1st ed. stiff wrappers. $12.50

BENNETT. *Illustrated Child.* 1979. VG $22.00

BENNETT. *Sweet By & By.* 1887. Dutton. Ills. $6.50

BENOIST, Elizabeth. *Swift as a Shadow.* 1980. St.Louis. Sunrise Pub. 249 pp. VG $3.00

BENSEN, E.F. *Visible & Invisible.* 1924. Doran. 2nd printing. G $45.00

BENSON, Adolph B. & Hedin, N. *Americans From Sweden.* 1950. New York. Lippincott. ex-lib. 448 pp. VG $8.00

BENSON, Adolph B. & Hedin, N. *Swedes in America 1638-1938.* 1938. New Haven, CT. Yale U. Press. ex-lib. 614 pp. $10.00

BENSON, B.K. *Bayard's Courier.* 1902. New York. 2nd printing. 402 pp. $12.50

BENSON, E. *Vindication Captors of Major Andre.* 1865. Ltd. ed. VG $30.00

BENSON, E.F. *Daisy's Aunt.* 1910. London. 1st ed. VG $20.00

BENSON, Ezra Taft. *Freedom to Farm.* 1960. 1st ed. 239 pp. dj. $27.50

BENSON, Henry C. *Life Among the Choctaw & Sketches of Southwest.* 1860. Cincinnati. 1st ed. 314 pp. $250.00

BENSON, Herbert. *The Mind/Body Effect.* 1979. Simon & Schuster. 1st ed. $2.00

BENSON, Lyman. *The Cacti of Arizona.* 1981. AZ U. Press. photos. maps. 218 pp. $12.00

BENSON, S.V. *Birds of Lebanon & the Jordon Area.* 1970. Ills. 218 pp. dj. EX $25.00

BENSON, Sally. *Meet Me in St. Louis.* 1944. Cleveland. World Pub. 2nd ed. 290 pp. $3.50

BENSON, Stella. *Tobit Transplanted.* 1931. London. 1st ed. VG $10.00

BENSON. *Campfire Girls Rural Retreat.* 1918. Donahue. Ills. G $4.50

BENSON. *Life of Alcibiades.* 1929. 1st ed. dj. VG $10.00

BENTHAM, T. *Asiatic Horns & Antlers in the Indian Museum.* 1908. Calcutta. Ills. 95 pp. heavy wrappers. $28.00

BENTLEY, E.C. *Elephant's Work.* 1950. Knopf. 1st Am. ed. dj. VG $15.00

BENTLEY, E.C. & Allen, H. W. *Trent's Own Case.* 1936. London. 1st ed. VG $35.00

BENTLEY, John. *It Was Murder They Said.* 1948. London. 1st ed. dj. VG $18.00

BENTLEY, Phyllis. *Freedom, Farewell.* 1936. presentation copy. $35.00

BENTLEY, Phyllis. *The Rise of Henry Morcar.* 1946. London. Gollancz. 1st ed. dj. $25.00

BENTON, Frank. *Cowboy Life on the Sidetrack.* 1903. Denver. Ills. G $60.00

BENTON, Joel. *Greeley on Lincoln & Mr. Greeley's Letters.* 1893. VG $15.00

BENTON, Joel. *Life of Hon. Phineas T. Barnum.* 1891. Edgewood Pub. Ills. 621pp. $15.00

BENTON, Josiah H. *John Baskerville. Type Founder & Printer 1706-75.* 1945. Ltd. ed. 1/625. 101 pp. VG $22.00

BENTON, William & Elizabeth. *How Does My Garden Grow?* 1969. Racine. Ills. Goldsborough. VG $7.50

BENTON. *A Little Cookbook for a Little Girl.* 1921. Page Pub. 179 pp. $9.50

BENVENUTI. *Russian Fairy Tales.* 1960. Golden Press. trans. Ponsot. Ills. folio. VG $17.50

BENZAQUIN, P. *Holocaust! Boston's Coconut Grove Fire.* 1959. Ills. 1st ed. dj. VG $10.00

BERCKMAN, Evelyn. *Stalemate.* 1966. Doubleday. $5.00

BERCKMAN, Evelyn. *The Victorial Album.* 1973. Doubleday. $5.00

BERCKMAN, Evelyn. *The Voice of Air.* 1970. Doubleday. $5.00

BERE, Rennie. *Antelopes.* 1970. London. Barker. Ills. 1st ed. dj. $10.00

BERENSON, B. *Essays in the Study of Sienese Painting.* 1928. $20.00

BERENSON, B. *Italian Painters of Renaissance.* 1953. New York. VG $25.00

BERENSTAIN. *The Sorcerer's Scrapbook.* 1981. Rand McNally. Ills. 1st ed. dj. EX $9.00

BERESFORD, J.D. *The Hampdenshire Wonder.* 1911. London. 1st ed. Sidgwick. VG $50.00

BERESFORD, J.D. *The Meeting Place.* 1929. Faber. 1st ed. $10.00

BERESFORD-HOWE, Constance. *The Book of Eve.* 1970. Boston. 1st ed. dj. EX $10.00

BERG, A. Scott. *Max Perkins, Editor of Genius.* 1979. New York. Dutton. Ills. 498 pp. dj. $10.00

BERG, Bengt. *Der Lammergeier im Himalaga.* 1931. Berlin. 101 photos. 208 pp. $30.00

BERGAMINI, D. *The Land & Wildlife of Australia.* 1976. photos. 198 pp. VG $14.00

BERGANST, Erik. *Rocket to the Planets.* 1961. Putman. VG $3.00

BERGER, Howard & Bennett, B. *On Sticks & Pucks.* 1985. Coombe Books. Ills. dj. EX $12.50

BERGER, Thomas. *Killing Time.* 1967. Dial Press. 1st ed. dj. VG $17.50

BERGER, Thomas. *Little Big Man.* 1964. New York. Dial Press. 1st ed. dj. EX $85.00

BERGER, Thomas. *Nowhere.* 1985. Delacorte. proof copy. wrappers. VG $65.00

BERGER, Thomas. *Regiment of Women.* 1973. New York. 1st ed. dj. EX $10.00

BERGER, Thomas. *Reinhart's Women.* 1981. New York. Delacorte. 1st ed. dj. EX $20.00

BERGER, Thomas. *The Feud.* 1983. Delacorte. proof copy. wrappers. EX $42.50

BERGER. *Sneaky People.* 1975. 1st Am. ed. dj. EX $15.00

BERGHOLD, Alexander. *The Indians' Revenge.* 1891. San Francisco. 1st ed. wrappers. G $95.00

BERGLAND, B. *Wilderness Living.* 1976. Scribner. Ills. 192 pp. $7.00

BERGMAN, I. *Scenes from a Marriage.* 1974. 1st Am. ed. dj. EX $7.00

BERGMAN, R. *Just Fishing.* 1941. sgn. dj. VG $10.00

BERGMAN, R. *Trout.* 1952. New York. Knopf. 2nd ed. 21 col pls. VG $15.00

BERGMAN, Sten. *Sport & Exploration in the Far East.* 1933. London. Methuen. Ills. 1st ed. 246 pp. $80.00

BERGREEN, Lawrence. *James Agee, a Life.* 1984. New York. 1st ed. 467 pp. dj. VG $12.50

BERGSON, Henri. *Creative Evolution.* 1911. New York. EX $25.00

BERGSTROM, Evangeline. *Old Glass Paperweights.* 1948. Crown. 2nd printing. dj. $12.50

BERKELEY, E. & D. *Dr. John Mitchell, Man Who Mapped North America.* 1975. NC U. Press. Ills. 283 pp. dj. VG $16.00

BERKELEY, Grantley F. *The English Sportsman in the Western Prairies.* 1861. London. Hurst & Blackett. 1st ed. $145.00

BERKEY, William. *The Money Question.* 1876. Grand Rapids. 384 pp. $25.00

BERKOWITZ, H. Chonon. *Perez Galdos Spanish Liberal Crusader.* 1948. U. of Wis. 1st ed. dj. $15.00

BERLING, E.M. *Art in Confectionery & Pastry.* 1930. EX $25.00

BERLIOZ, Hector. *Evenings with the Orchestra.* 1969. New York. trans. J. Barzun. VG $8.50

BERLITZ, Charles. *The Bermuda Triangle.* 1974. $7.50

BERMANN, Eric. *Scapegoat/Impact of Death-Fear on American Family.* 1973. Ann Arbor. 357 pp. $10.00

BERNADAC, C. *Camp for Women: Ravensbruck.* 1978. Geneva. Ferni. Ills. EX $35.00

BERNADAC, C. *Death Train.* 1978. Geneva. Ferni. Ills. EX $35.00

BERNADAC, C. *Doctors of Mercy.* 1977. Geneva. Ferni. Ills. EX $35.00

BERNARD, David. *Light on Masonry: Collection of Documents.* 1829. Utica. Williams. 1st ed. 568 pp. G $100.00

BERNARD, Kenneth. *Lincoln & the Music of the Civil War.* 1966. Caxton Press. 333 pp. dj. VG $17.50

BERNARD, Raymond. *The Hollow Earth.* 1964. Fieldcrest. New ed. pb. $15.00

BERNARD, W. *Jailbait! Story of Juvenile Delinquency.* 1951. Garden City. dj. VG $10.00

BERNARD, W. *Rider of the Cherokee Strip.* 1936. $12.00

BERNAYS, Anne. *The School Book.* 1980. Harper. dj. VG $10.00

BERNER, Jeff. *The Innerspace Project.* 1972. New York. World Pub. dj. EX $25.00

BERNHARD. *The Big Heart.* 1957. sgn. dj. $35.00

BERNSEN. *The North American Waterfowler.* 1972. Salisbury Press. Ills. 206 pp. $10.50

BERNSTEIN, Aline. *Three Blue Suits.* 1933. New York City. Ltd. ed. 1/600. sgn. 74 pp. $115.00

BERNSTEIN, Burton. *Thurber. A Biography.* 1975. New York. Ills. 532 pp. $7.50

BERNSTEIN, M.H. *The Job of the Federal Executive.* 1958. Washington. Brookings Inst. 241 pp. dj. VG $6.00

BERNSTEIN, Theodore M. *Do's, Don'ts, & Maybe's of the English Usage.* 1977. Time Books. 250 pp. $4.00

BEROLZHEIMER, Ruth. *The American Woman's Cookbook.* 1939. Chicago. 815 pp. $5.00

BERRA, TIM. *Atlas of Distribution of Freshwater Fish Families.* 1981. NB U. Press. maps. 197 pp. $15.00

BERRALL, Julia. *A History of Flower Arrangement.* 1953. Crowell. Ills. dj. $8.00

BERRIGAN, Daniel. *Night Flight to Hanoi. War Diary with G.I. Poems.* 1968. New York. Macmillan. 1st printing. dj. $10.00

BERRIGAN, Daniel. *The World for Wedding Ring.* 1962. Macmillan. dj. VG $20.00

BISCOE, C.E.T. *Kashmir in Sunlight & Shade.* 1922. Philadelphia. Ills. 315 pp. fld map. index. $15.00

BISH. *Home Gunsmithing Digest.* 1970. DBI Books. 319 pp. $4.50

BISHCHOF, Werner. *Japan.* 1954. New York. Simon & Schuster. dj. VG $42.50

BISHOP, Claire Huchet. *Pancakes-Paris.* 1947. New York. Viking. Ills. Schreiber. $20.00

BISHOP, Claire Huchet. *The Ferryman.* 1941. New York. Ills. K. Wiese. 1st ed. dj. $10.00

BISHOP, Elizabeth. *Collected Prose.* 1984. New York. Farrar. proof copy. EX $40.00

BISHOP, George. *Encyclopedia of Motorcycling.* 1980. New York. Putnam. 192 pp. SftCvr. EX $6.00

BISHOP, Glenn A. *Chicago's Accomplishments & Leaders.* 1932. Chicago. 550 pp. $12.50

BISHOP, J.B. *Chronicle of 150 Years: Chamber of Commerce of NY.* 1918. New York. dj. VG $25.00

BISHOP, J.B. *Teddy Roosevelt's Letters to His Children.* 1919. Scribner. VG $10.00

BISHOP, Jim. *A Day in the Life of President Johnson.* 1967. 1st printing. 274 pp. dj. $65.00

BISHOP, Jim. *The Day Christ Died.* 1957. New York. Harper. 336 pp. dj. $4.00

BISHOP, Jim. *The Day Christ Was Born.* 1960. New York. Harper. 107 pp. $4.00

BISHOP, Jim. *The Murder Trial of Judge Peel.* 1962. New York. Simon & Schuster. 210 pp. dj. $3.00

BISHOP, M. *Transfigurations.* 1979. Putnam. 1st ed. dj. EX $25.00

BISHOP, M.C. *Prison Life of Marie Antoinette.* 1894. London. EX $10.00

BISHOP, Michael. *A Little Knowledge.* 1977. New York. Berkley. 1st ed. dj. EX $20.00

BISHOP, Michael. *Catacomb Years.* 1979. New York. Berkley. 1st ed. dj. VG $17.50

BISHOP, Michael. *Stolen Faces.* 1977. New York. 1st ed. dj. EX $10.00

BISHOP, N.H. *Voyage of the Paper Canoe.* 1878. Boston. Ills. G $50.00

BISHOP, R. & Coblentz, P. *Gallery of American Weathervanes & Whirligigs.* 1984. New York. Bonanza. Ills. dj. VG $10.50

BISHOP, Richard. *Bishop's Wildfowl.* 1948. Brown & Bigelow. Ills. 282 pp. $200.00

BISHOP, Richard. *The Ways of Wildfowl.* 1971. Ferguson. Ills. author & Hines. 260 pp. $95.00

BISHOP, Richard. *The Ways of Wildfowl.* 1971. Chicago. Ills. dj. $80.00

BISHOP, Robert & Coblentz, P. *American Decorative Arts.* 1982. New York. Abrams. Ills. dj. VG $27.50

BISHOP, Robert. *The American Chair: Three Centuries of Style.* 1983. New York. Bonanza. Ills. dj. VG $17.50

BISHOP, W.W. *The Backs of Books.* 1926. Baltimore. EX $25.00

BISHOP, William Henry. *Old Mexico & Her Lost Provinces-Journey in Mexico.* 1883. New York. Ills. 1st ed. G $25.00

BISHOP, Zealia. *The Curse of Yig.* 1953. Sauk City. Arkham House. Ltd. ed. 1/1200. $125.00

BISHOP. *Project Sherwood: U.S. Program Controlled Fusion.* 1958. 1st ed. dj. EX $10.00

BISS, Gerald. *Door of the Unreal.* 1920. New York. Putnam. 1st Am. ed. VG $50.00

BISSELL, Emily P. *Happiness & Other Verses.* Philadelphia. (ca.1908) 224 pp. sgn. $12.50

BISSELL, Richard. *A Stretch on the River.* 1951. 1st ed. dj. VG $25.00

BISSETT, Clark P. *Abraham Lincoln. Universal Man.* 1923. Ltd. ed. 1/125. sgn. VG $75.00

BJERKOE, Ethel. *How to Decorate for & with Antiques.* 1959. Garden City. Doubleday. Ills. 256 pp. dj. $6.50

BJERRE, J. *Kalahari.* 1960. Hill Wang. photos. 227 pp. $10.00

BJORKLUND, Gustaf. *Death & Resurrection.* 1910. Chicago. Open Court Pub. G $7.50

BLACH, William R. *Perfect Jewels: Collection of Choicest Literature.* 1884. Adrian, MI. Ills. 608 pp. $12.50

BLACK, Arthur D. *Index of Periodical Dental Literature.* 1923. NY/London. ex-lib. 577 pp. index. VG $15.00

BLACK, Lionel. *Outbreak.* 1968. London. 1st ed. dj. VG $22.00

BLACK, Mary. *New Key to Weaving: Text book of Hand Weaving.* 1971. Bruce. 573 pp. dj. VG $20.00

BLACK. *Black's Picturesque Tourist, Road, Railway Guide.* 1851. Edinburgh. 538 pp. fld maps & views. $62.00

BLACKBURN, J. *The Cyclops Goblet.* 1977. London. 1st ed. dj. EX $25.00

BLACKBURN, John. *A Book of the Dead.* 1984. London. Hale. 1st ed. dj. EX $25.00

BLACKER, I.R. *Hakluyt's Voyages.* 1965. Viking. Ills. 522 pp. dj. $20.00

BLACKER, I.R. *Old West in Fiction.* 1961. Obolensky Pub. 1st ed. dj. EX $15.00

BLACKFORD, Katherine M.H. *Character Analysis by the Observational Method.* 1922. New York. 6th ed. 5 vol set. $60.00

BLACKFORD, S. *Letter's From Lee's Army.* 1947. New York. 1st ed. dj. VG $10.00

BLACKFORD & NEWCOMB. *Analyzing Character.* 1916. New York. Ills. G $10.00

BLACKFORD. *War Years with Jeb Stuart.* 1945. Ills. 322 pp. $21.00

BLACKIE. *Blackie's Little One's Annual.* Blackie & Son. no date. Ills. Ltd ed. 136 pp. $3.50

BLACKINGTON, Alton Hall. *More Yankee Yarns.* 1956. New York. Ills. 245 pp. $5.00

BLACKMAN, Wm. F. *The Making of Hawaii: Study in Social Evolution.* 1899. New York. 1st ed. 267 pp. $35.00

BLACKMAN. *History of Susquehanna County.* 1873. Caxton. Ills. maps. VG $50.00

BLACKMAR, Frank W. *Higher Education in Kansas.* 1900. Washington. 1st ed. 166 pp. wrappers. $40.00

BLACKMORE, Howard L. *Guns & Rifles of the World.* 1965. Viking. Ills. 1st printing. 124 pp. $35.00

BLACKMORE, R.D. *Erema.* 1878. London. Ills. 1st ed. inscr. $50.00

BLACKMORE, R.D. *Lorna Doone.* 1921. Ills. Harold Brett. EX $30.00

BLACKMORE, R.D. *Lorna Doone.* 1924. New York. Ills. Wheelright & Swell. $20.00

BLACKMORE, R.D. *Lorna Doone.* 1873. Philadelphia. Ills. Helen Mason Grose. G $7.50

BLACKWALL. *Inquiry into the Life & Writings of Homer.* 1736. London. 2nd ed. fld map. VG $200.00

BLACKWOOD, Algernon. *John Silence.* 1914. Ltd. 2nd Am. ed. 1/500. $45.00

BLACKWOOD, Algernon. *Tales of the Uncanny & Supernatural.* 1966. London. Spring Books. 426 pp. dj. $10.50

BLACKWOOD, Algernon. *The Doll & One Other.* 1946. Sauk City. 1st ed. 138 pp. dj. EX $30.00

BLACKWOOD, Easley. *Bridge Humanics.* 1949. Indianapolis. 255 pp. dj. $5.00

BLACKWOOD, Harry. *Artistic Travel.* 1895. London. Ills. Caldecott/Dore, etc. EX $25.00

BLAINE, G. *Falconry.* 1970. London. Spearman. Ills. 253 pp. dj. $19.00

BLAINE, James G. *Twenty Years of Congress.* 1884. Norwich. 2 vol set. VG $25.00

BLAINE, James G. *Twenty Years of Congress: Lincoln to Garfield.* 1886. Norwich, CT. ex-lib. Vol. II. 723 pp. G $3.50

BLAIR, Claude. *Pistols of the World.* 1968. Viking Press. Ills. 206 pp. dj. VG $32.50

BLAIR, Frank & Smith, Jack. *Let's Be Frank About It.* 1979. Garden City. proof copy. wrappers. EX $35.00

BLAIR & MEINE. *Half Horse/Half Alligator. Mike Fink Legend.* 1956. 1st ed. dj. EX $30.00

BLAKE, A. Hope. *60 Years in New Zealand.* New Zealand. (ca.1909) VG $35.00

BLAKE, J.L. *Conversations on Natural Philosophy.* 1833. Boston. Ills. 23 pls. $27.50

BLAKE, John F. *Astronomical Myths.* 1877. London. 1st ed. 431 pp. G $60.00

BLAKE, N. *William Mahone of Virginia.* 1935. 1st ed. VG $15.00

BLAKE, Nicholas. *The Sad Variety.* 1964. London. 1st ed. dj. VG $25.00

BLAKE, Patricia & Howard, Max. *Dissonant Voices in Soviet Literature.* 1962. New York. Pantheon. 308 pp. $5.00

BLAKE, W.H. *Brown Waters & Other Sketches.* 1915. Ills. VG $25.00

BLAKE, W.O. *Hist. of Slavery & Slave Trade, Ancient & Modern.* 1857. Columbus. Ills. 1st ed. 832 pp. $30.00

BLAKE, William. *Russian America. 1868.* 1868. Washington. 1st ed. maps. $90.00

BLAKE, William. *Songs of Experience.* 1927. London. Ills. facsimile ed. dj. VG $100.00

BLAKE, William. *Songs of Innocence.* 1927. London/Boston. Ills. Parsons. VG $22.50

BLAKE, William. *Songs of Innocence.* 1926. London. Ills. facsimile ed. VG $65.00

BLAKE, William. *The Land of Dreams.* 1928. New York. Ills. Bianco. 1st Am. ed. dj. $15.00

BLAKE, William. *The Poetical Works.* 1913. London. Ills. 1st ed. $30.00

BLAKEY, Robert. *Historical Sketches of the Angling Literature.* 1856. London. 1st ed. EX $80.00

BLANCHAN, Neltje. *Birds Worth Knowing.* 1923. Garden City. Ills. 257 pp. EX $27.50

BLANCHAN, Neltje. *Birds.* 1922. Garden City. Ills. Fuertes/Horsfall. VG $12.50

BLANCHAN, Neltje. *The American Flower Garden.* 1909. New York. Ills. Ltd. ed. EX $95.00

BLANCHAN, Neltje. *Wild Flowers Worth Knowing.* 1923. Garden City. Ills. 270 pp. 48 pls. EX $22.50

BLANCHAN, Neltje. *Wildflowers.* 1922. Garden City. Ills. 48 plates. EX $12.50

BLANCHE. *Masterpieces of French Painting to 16th Cent.* 1934. $30.00

BLANCK, Jacob. *Harry Castleman, Boy's Own Author.* 1969. Waltham, Mass. Ills. 2nd ed. 142 pp. $20.00

BLANCO, Antonio de Fierro. *The Journey of the Flame.* 1933. Literary Guild.Ills. Alfedo de Fierro. G $10.00

BLAND. *Currier & Ives, a Manual for Collectors.* 1931. Doubleday Doran. 349 pp. $65.00

BLAND-SUTTON. *Man & Beast in Eastern Ethiopia.* 1911. London. VG $85.00

BLANDING, Don. *Hula Moons.* 1949. Ills. dj. VG $25.00

BLANDING, Don. *Pilot Bails Out.* 1943. inscr. VG $10.00

BLANDING, Don. *Stowaways in Paradise.* 1934. New York. Dodd Mead. Ills. dj. EX $15.00

BLANDING, Don. *Vagabond's House.* 1940. sgn. VG $12.50

BLANDING, Don. *Vagabond's House.* 1936. New York. Ills. sgn. VG $10.00

BLANKENBURG, Lucretia L. *The Blankenburgs of Philadelphia.* 1928. Philadelphia. sgn. 220 pp. VG $15.00

BLANSHARD, Paul. *God & Man in Washington.* 1960. Boston. Beacon Press. 241 pp. dj. VG $5.00

BLATTY, William P. *The Exorcist.* 1971. 1st ed. dj. EX $25.00

BLAVATSKY, H.P. *A Modern Panarion.* 1895. London. 1st ed. 504 pp. $60.00

BLAW. *Jews of the U.S. 1790-1840.* 3 vol set. boxed. $12.00

BLECH, Rudi & Janis, Harriet. *They All Played Ragtime.* 1950. New York. Knopf. 1st ed. dj. EX $45.00

BLEDSOE, Albert Taylor. *A Theodicy; or, Vindication of the Divine Glory.* 1856. New York. 368 pp. $17.50

BLEGEN, C.W. *Troy & Trojans.* 1964. New York. Prager. $12.50

BLENNERHASSETT, R. & Sleeman. *Adventures in Mashonaland.* 1975. Books of Rodesia. 340 pp. $15.00

BLEUNARD, Albert. *Babylon Electrified.* 1890. London. Chapman & Hall. 1st ed. G $40.00

BLEUNARD, Albert. *Babylon Electrified.* 1889. Philadelphia. Gebbie & Co. 1st ed. VG $135.00

BLIGH, William. *A Voyage to the South Sea.* 1979. Australian Facsimile Editions. $25.00

BLIGH, William. *Narrative of Mutiny on Board Ship Bounty.* 1790. London. 1st ed. maps & charts. 88 pp. $2,150.00

BLINDMAN. *The Complete Graphic Works of William Blake.* 1978. Putnam. 1st ed. VG $55.00

BLISH, James & Lowndes, R. *The Duplicated Man.* 1959. New York. Avalon. 1st ed. dj. VG $30.00

BLISH, James. *Black Easter.* 1968. Garden City. dj. VG $20.00

BLISH, James. *Earthman, Come Home.* 1955. New York. 1st ed. dj. VG $35.00

BLISH, James. *Jack of Eagles.* 1952. New York. Greenberg. 1st ed. dj. VG $35.00

BLISH, James. *Star Trek Reader III.* 1977. New York. 1st ed. dj. EX $27.50

BLISH, James. *Star Trek.* 1967. New York. Bantam. 1st ed. pb. VG $5.00

BLISH, James. *The Seedling Stars.* 1957. New York. Gnome. 1st ed. dj. VG $17.50

BLISH, James. *The Vanished Jet.* 1968. 1st ed. dj. EX $35.00

BLISH, James. *They Shall Have Stars.* 1974. Faber. reprint. dj. VG $7.50

BLISHCHENKO, I. & Zhdanov. *Terrorism & International Law.* 1984. Moscow. 286 pp. $6.00

BLISS, Edwin. *Turkey & the Armenian Atrocities.* 1896. photos. 574 pp. $6.00

BLITS, H. *Blits' Method of Canning Fruits & Vegetables.* 1890. Brooklyn, NY. $50.00

BLOCH, I. *Odoratus Sexualis.* 1935. New York. Ltd. ed. 1/2000. VG $20.00

BLOCH, Robert. *Cold Chills.* 1977. Garden City. 1st ed. dj. EX $15.00

BLOCH, Robert. *Cold Chills.* 1977. New York. 1st ed. dj. EX $15.00

BLOCH, Robert. *Dragons & Nightmares.* 1968. Baltimore, MD. Ltd. ed. 1/1000. $85.00

BLOCH, Robert. *Is There a Serpent in Eden?* Zebra pb. VG $70.00

BLOCH, Robert. *Out of My Head.* 1968. Ltd 1st ed. 1/800. dj. EX $35.00

BLOCH, Robert. *Pleasant Dreams, Nightmares.* 1969. Arkham. 1st ed. dj. EX $50.00

BLOCH, Robert. *Pleasant Dreams.* 1960. Sauk City. Arkham House. $75.00

BLOCH, Robert. *The King of Terrors.* 1977. New York. Mysterious Press. 2nd ed. $8.00

BLOCH, Robert. *The Opener of the Way.* 1945. Sauk City. Arkham House. scarce. EX $150.00

BLOCK, Lawrence. *Burglars Can't Be Choosers.* 1977. Random House. Ltd. ed. sgn. dj. EX $25.00

BLOCK. *Pop Wiener: Naive Painter.* 1974. U. of Mass. $7.00

BLOCK. *Straight Herblock.* 1964. 1st ed. sgn. dj. VG $10.00

BLOM, Ed. *Grove's Dictionary of Music.* 1955. St.Martins. 5th ed. 10 vol set. VG $210.00

BLOMBERG, Rolf. *Buried Gold & Anacondas.* 1959. New York. Nelson. Ills. maps. 144 pp. EX $12.50

BLOND, G. *The Great Migrations.* 1961. Macmillan. 192 pp. dj. $5.00

BLONDIN, Frances. *The New Encyclopedia of Modern Sewing.* 1949. New York. Wise & Co. 366 pp. VG $6.00

BLONDIN, Francis. *The New Encyclopedia of Modern Sewing.* 1946. Wise. Ills. 430 pp. G $4.50

BLOOM, John Porter. *Territorial Papers of United States Vol. XXVIII.* 1975. Washington. 1319 pp. $20.00

BLOOM, M.T. *The Trouble with Lawyers.* 1968. Simon & Schuster. 1st ed. dj. $15.00

BLOOM, Sol. *The Story of the Constitution.* 1937. Washington. 192 pp. $15.00

BLOOMFIELD, Robert. *Wild Flowers; or, Pastoral & Local Poetry.* 1809. London. 132 pp. pls. $40.00

BLOOMSTER, Edgar L. *Sailing & Small Craft Down the Ages.* 1940. Annapolis. reprint Nov. 1957. EX $22.50

BLOSS, G.M. *Historic & Literary Miscellany.* 1875. Cincinnati. 468 pp. $12.50

BLOSSOM, F.A. *Told at the Explorers Club.* 1932. 425 pp. VG $13.00

BLOWER, James M. & Korach, R. *The N. O. T. & L. Story.* 1966. Chicago. Ills. 1st ed. 268 pp. $50.00

BLUESTONE, George. *Novels into Film.* 1957. Hopkins. dj. EX $7.50

BLUM, Daniel. *American Theatre 1900-1951.* 1951. New York. Greenburg. 304 pp. $5.00

BLUM, Daniel. *Pictorial History of the Talkies.* 1958. New York. Grosset & Dunlap. 318 pp. $6.00

BLUM, Daniel. *Screen World.* 1949. New York. $9.00

BLUM, Daniel. *Theatre World: 1947-1948.* New York. dj. VG $30.00

BLUM, E. *Poems.* 1937. Golden Eagle Press. 1st ed. VG $16.50

BLUME, Judy. *Tiger Eyes.* 1981. Bradbury Press.dj. VG $10.00

BLUMENAU, L. *Art & Craft of Hand Weaving.* 1955. New York. dj. $20.00

BLUMENSON, Martin. *Breakout & Pursuit.* 1961. Washington. Ills. 1st ed. maps. VG $27.50

BLUMENTHAL, J. *Typographic Years.* 1982. New York. inscr. dj. EX $35.00

BLUMENTHAL, Walter Hart. *A Charm of Books.* 1861. Philadelphia. 110 pp. EX $6.50

BLUMENTHAL, Walter Hart. *Brides from Bridewell Female Falons Sent to Amer.* 1962. Tuttle. 1st ed. dj. $10.00

BLUMENTHAL, Walter Hart. *Women Camp Followers of American Revolution.* 1952. Philadelphia. Ltd. ed. 1/300. dj. VG $35.00

BLUMENTHAL. *Art of the Printed Book.* 1978. Boston. 3rd ed. EX $30.00

BLUMENTHAL. *The Printed Book in America.* 1977. Boston. 1st ed. EX $30.00

BLUNDEN, Edmund. *Japanese Garland.* 1928. Beaumont Pr. Ills. Ltd. ed. sgn. VG $47.50

BLUNDEN, Edmund. *Masks of Time.* 1925. London. Beaumont Press. Ltd. ed. VG $65.00

BLUNDEN, Edmund. *Near & Far.* 1929. Ltd. ed. sgn. VG $32.50

BLUNDEN, Edmund. *To Nature.* 1923. London. Beaumont Press. Ltd. ed. VG $25.00

BLUNDEN, Edmund. *Undertones of War.* 1928. London. Cobden-Sanderson. 1st ed. dj. $150.00

BLUNDEN, Edmund. *Winter Nights. Ariel Poem #17.* Ills. Ltd. ed. sgn. VG $15.00

BLUNT, Lady Anne. *Pilgrimage to Nejd.* 1881. London. Ills. ex-lib. 2 vol set. $115.00

BLUNT, Wilfred J. *Japanese Colour Prints from Harunobu to Utamaro.* 1952. London. Ills. wrappers. scarce. $40.00

BLUNT, Wilfred S. *Cockerell.* New York. 1st ed. dj. $15.00

BLUNT, Wilfred S. *Love Lyrics & Natalia's Resurrection.* 1892. London. 1st ed. $45.00

BLUNT, Wilfred S. *My Diaries.* 1921. Knopf. 1st ed. 2 vol set. EX $50.00

BLUNT, Wilfred S. *Poems.* 1923. New York. Knopf. 1st ed. VG $7.00

BLUNT, Wilfrid. *Art of William Blake.* 1959. Columbia U. Press. $12.00

BLUNT, Wilfrid. *The Art of Botanical Illustration.* 1951. NY/London. Ills. 1st ed. 304 pp. dj. EX $50.00

BLY, Robert. *The Light Around the Body.* 1968. Rapp & Whiting.1st English ed. dj. VG $35.00

BLYTH, Henry. *Card the Fatal Passion.* 1972. New York. 278 pp. dj. EX $5.00

BLYTHE. *Hornet's Nest: Charlotte & Mecklenburg County.* 1961. 1st ed. 511 pp. $25.00

BLYTON. *Five Go Down to the Sea.* 1961. Reilly & Lee. Ills. Aloise. 1st ed. dj. VG $10.00

BOAG, D. *The Kingfisher.* 1982. Blandforn. Ills. 120 pp. dj. EX $16.00

BOARDMAN. *Archaic Greek Gems.* 1968. Evanston. 236 pp. dj. $35.00

BOAS, Franz. *Decorative Art of Indians of North Pacific Coast.* 1897. Am. Mus. Nat. Hist. SftCvr. $10.00

BOAS, Frederick. *Songs & Lyrics of English Masques & Light Operas.* 1949. Harrap. 1st ed. dj. $8.50

BOATNER, Mark M. *Civil War Dictionary.* 1961. New York. 974 pp. maps. dj. EX $20.00

BOATRIGHT, Mody C. *Family Saga & Other Phases of American Folklore.* 1958. Urbana. U. of IL Pr. review copy. dj. $15.00

BOCCACCIO, Giovanni. *The Decameron.* 1940. Heritage Press.boxed. EX $7.50

BOCCACCIO, Giovanni. *The Decameron.* 1930. Ills. Bosschere. dj. $10.00

BOCKRIS, Victor. *With William Burroughs.* 1981. Seaver. dj. VG $15.00

BODART, Anne. *The Blue Dog.* 1956. trans. Toklas. 1st ed. dj. VG $17.50

BODENHEIM, Maxwell. *Ninth Avenue.* 1926. 1st ed. $12.50

BODENHEIM, Maxwell. *Replenishing Jessica.* 1925. New York. Boni & Liveright. VG $15.00

BODINE, Aubrey. *Chesapeake Bay.* 1954. $20.00

BODINE, Aubrey. *My Maryland.* 1952. $20.00

BOECKL, Wilhelm Richard. *Willy Boeckl on Figure Skating.* 1937. no place. Ills. 212 pp. $20.00

BOEHME, Jacob. *Personal Christianity, a Science.* 1919. New York. 1st ed. 336 pp. G $65.00

BOEHME, Jacob. *Six Theosophic Points & Other Writings.* 1920. New York. ex-lib. 220 pp. VG $45.00

BOEHN, E. *We Survived.* 1949. 1st ed. dj. EX $20.00

BOERKER, Richard. *Behold Our Green Mansions.* 1945. Chapel Hill. photos. dj. $12.50

BOESCH, Mark. *The Lawless Land, Story of Vigilantes.* 1953. Philadelphia. Ills. Bjorklund. 181 pp. dj. $12.50

BOESE. *John C. Greenaway & Opening of Western Mesabi.* 1975. 1st ed. dj. EX $15.00

BOESEN, G. & Boje, C. *Old Danish Silver.* 1948. Ills. $38.00

BOESEN, G. & Boje, C. *Old Danish Silver.* 1949. Copenhagen. Ills. 1st translation. VG $45.00

BOETHEL, P.C. *The Big Guns of Fayette.* 1965. Austin. sgn. 98 pp. dj. EX $25.00

BOETLE, Ed. *Singa Hipsy Doodle & Folk Songs of West Virginia.* 1971. Parkersburg. 177 pp. dj. EX $15.00

BOGAN, Louise. *A Poet's Alphabet.* 1970. 1st ed. dj. EX $15.00

BOGARDE, Dirk. *A Gentle Occupation.* 1981. New York. 1st ed. sgn. dj. $10.00

BOGARDUS, A.H. *Field, Cover & Trap Shooting.* 1891. 3rd ed. VG $50.00

BOGART, W.H. *Daniel Boone & Hunters of Kentucky.* 1854. Auburn. 24 Ills. VG $40.00

BOHN, H.G. *Guide to Pottery.* 1887. London. $25.00

BOHROD, Aaron. *A Pottery Sketchbook.* 1967. U. of WI Press.2nd ed. dj. VG $20.00

BOILEAU, T. & Narcejac, P. *Choice Cuts.* 1966. NY. Dutton. 1st ed. dj. VG $15.00

BOJE, C. *Danish Gold & Silver Marks Before 1870.* 1946. Dane text. 587 pp. $39.00

BOK, Edward W. *A Man From Maine.* 1923. New York. Scribner. ex-lib. 278 pp. G $4.50

BOLAND, John. *No Refuge.* 1956. London. 1st ed. dj. EX $10.00

BOLINDER, G. *We Dared the Andes.* London. Adventurers Club. 192 pp. dj. $12.00

BOLITHO, Hector. *A Batsford Century.* 1943. London. Ills. 1st ed. VG $20.00

BOLITHO, Hector. *Empty Clothes.* 1934. London. Centaur Press. sgn. $20.00

BOLITHO, Hector. *Judith Silver.* 1929. New York. 1st ed. sgn. VG $20.00

BOLITHO, Hector. *The British Empire.* 1947. London. ex-lib. 246 pp. VG $4.50

BOLL, Heinrich. *A Soldier's Legacy.* 1985. proof copy. $20.00

BOLL, Heinrich. *A Soldier's Legacy.* 1985. Knopf. 1st Am. ed. dj. VG $12.50

BOLL, Heinrich. *Acquainted With the Night.* 1954. Holt. 1st Am. ed. dj. VG $40.00

BOLL, Heinrich. *Adam & the Death: Two Novels.* 1970. McGraw Hill. 1st Am. ed. dj. VG $20.00

BOLL, Heinrich. *Adam & the Train: Two Novels.* 1970. McGraw Hill. review copy. dj. VG $20.00

BOLL, Heinrich. *And Never Said a Word.* 1978. McGraw Hill. 1st Am. ed. dj. VG $15.00

BOLL, Heinrich. *Bred of Those Early Years.* 1976. New York. 1st ed. dj. VG $7.50

BOLL, Heinrich. *Children Are Civilians Too.* 1970. McGraw Hill. review copy. dj. VG $20.00

BOLL, Heinrich. *Group Portrait with Lady.* 1973. McGraw Hill. 1st Am. ed. dj. VG $20.00

BOLL, Heinrich. *Irish Journal.* 1967. McGraw Hill. 1st Am. ed. dj. VG $25.00

BOLL, Heinrich. *The Lost Honor of Katharina Blum.* 1975. McGraw Hill. 1st Am. ed. dj. VG $12.50

BOLL, Heinrich. *The Safety Net.* 1982. Knopf. 1st Am. ed. dj. VG $15.00

BOLL, Heinrich. *Tomorrow & Yesterday.* 1957. Criterion. 1st Am. ed. dj. VG $30.00

BOLL, Heinrich. *What's to Become of the Boy?* 1984. Knopf. 1st Am. ed. dj. VG $12.50

BOLLAERT, William. *Bollaert's Texas.* 1956. U. of OK. 1st ed. dj. $10.00

BOLLER, Willy. *Masterpieces of the Japanese Color Woodcut.* 1957. London. Ills. 1st ed. folio. VG $155.00

BOLLES, A. *Industrial History of the U.S.* (ca.1878) Ills. G $22.50

BOLOGNA, G. *The World of Birds.* 1975. Abbeville. Ills. 256 pp. EX $10.00

BOLTON, Herbert E. *Coronado, Knight of Pueblo & Plains.* 1949. Albuquerque. 491 pp. $20.00

BOLTON, Herbert. *Coronado, Knight of Pueblo & Plains.* 1949. New York. McGraw Hill. dj. VG $12.50

BOLTON, Isabel. *Many Mansions.* 1952. New York. 1st ed. dj. EX $25.00

BOLTON, Robert. *History County Westchester.* 1848. New York. 1st ed. 2 vol set. $175.00

BOLTON. *History of 2nd Illinois Infantry.* 1899. Chicago. photos. roster. VG $35.00

BOMBAL, Maria Luisa. *New Islands.* 1982. Farrar. 1st Am. ed. dj. VG $15.00

BOMBECK, E. & Keane, B. *Just Wait Till Kids Own D-Day.* 1971. 1st ed. dj. VG $10.00

BONATTI. *I Giorni Grandi.* 1972. dj. EX $20.00

BONC, J. Harvey. *The Other World.* 1963. 1st ed. dj. EX $7.50

BOND, Beverly W. *Intimate Letters of John Cleves Symmes & Family.* 1956. Cincinnati. 174 pp. dj. $15.00

BOND, Frederick Bligh. *The Gate of Remembrance.* 1918. Oxford. Blackwell. 2nd ed. VG $15.00

BOND, J. Harvey. *The Other World.* 1963. 1st ed. dj. EX $7.50

BOND, James. *Birds of the West Indies.* 1960. London. Collins. Ills. Eckelberry. EX $12.00

BOND, Nelson. *Nightmares & Daydreams.* 1968. Arkham House. 1st ed. dj. VG $17.50

BOND, Nelson. *No Time Like the Future.* Avon. pb. EX $12.50

BOND, Nelson. *Thirty-First of February: 13 Flights of Fantasy.* 1949. New York. Gnome Press. $110.00

BONE, James. *The London Perambulator.* 1925. New York. Ills. Muirhead Bone. VG $20.00

BONEHILL, Ralph. *With Custer in the Black Hills.* 1902. New York. Grosset & Dunlap. 244 pp. $3.00

BONETT, Richard C. *Iowa School Laws & Decisions.* 1902. 150 pp. $3.00

BONFIGLIOLI, Kyril. *All the Tea in China.* 1978. London. Secker & Warburg. 1st ed. dj. $20.00

BONI, Margaret B. *Fireside Book of Folk Songs.* 1947. New York. Simon & Schuster. 323 pp. dj. $5.00

BONINGTON, C. *Annapurna, South Face.* 1971. 1st ed. dj. EX $20.00

BONKER, F. & Thornber, J.J. *The Sage of the Desert.* 1930. Stratford. Ills. 106 pp. EX $9.00

BONNER, T.D. *Life & Adventures J.P. Beckworth.* 1856. 1st ed. $115.00

BONNER, Thomas. *The Kansas Doctor. A Century of Pioneering.* 1959. U. of Kansas. 1st ed. dj. $7.50

BONNER. *Superstition Range.* Popular. pb. $3.00

BONNEY, Catharine V.R. *A Legacy of Historical Gleanings.* 1875. Albany. 2nd ed. 2 vol set. index. VG $15.00

BONOSKY, P. *Dragon Pink on Old White.* 1963. New York. Marzani & Munsell. sgn. dj. $10.00

BONSELS, Waldemar. *The Adventures of Maya the Bee.* 1929. New York. Ills. Vera Bock. VG $22.50

BONTEMPS, Arna & Conroy, J. *Anyplace but Here.* 1966. New York. Hill & Wang. 1st ed. dj. EX $30.00

BONYON, Bill & Gene. *Full Hold & Splendid Passage.* 1969. $5.50

BOOKS, W.K. *The Oyster, a Scientific Study.* 1905. Baltimore. Johns Hopkins Press. 225 pp. $30.00

BOONE & CROCKETT. *Trefethan. Crusade for Wildlife.* 1961. Stackpole. 1st ed. VG $37.50

BOORAEM, V.V. *Internal Energy.* 1960. Brooklyn, NY. 1st ed. VG $10.00

BOOTHBY, Guy. *Farewell Nikola.* 1901. Philadelphia. Lippincott. 1st Am. ed. VG $17.50

BOOTHROYD, Geoffrey. *The Handgun.* Bonanza. Ills. 564 pp. dj. VG $20.00

BOR, N.L. & Raizada, M.B. *Some Beautiful Indian Climbers & Shrubs.* 1954. Bombay. Ills. 286 pp. $18.00

BORD, J. & C. *Alien Animals.* 1981. Stackpole. photos. 258 pp. dj. $15.00

BORDEAUX, Henry. *Guynemer Knight of the Air.* 1918. London. dj. $40.00

BORDEN, Mrs. John. *Cruise of the Northern Light.* 1928. G $35.00

BORDEN, Spencer. *The Arab Horse.* 1906. New York. Ills. 1st ed. 104 pp. VG $60.00

BORDON, Elizabeth. *Bird Children.* 1912. Volland. Ills. M.T. Moss. 96 pp. G $17.50

BOREHAM. *A Temple of Topaz.* 1951. Judson. ex-lib. 272 pp. $37.50

BORGENSON, G. & Jaqderquist. *Sport & Classic Cars.* 1955. New York. Bonanza. 466 pp. $6.00

BORGES, J. & Bioy-Casares, A. *Six Problems for Don Isidro Parodi.* 1981. London. trans. Giovanni. 1st Eng. ed. $30.00

BORGES, Jorge Luis. *Evaristo Carriego.* 1983. Dutton. advance copy. wrappers. EX $30.00

BORGES, Jorge Luis. *Evaristo Carriego.* 1984. New York. Dutton. 1st ed. dj. EX $40.00

BORLAND, Hal. *Beyond Your Doorstep.* 1962. 1st ed. 377 pp. dj. EX $12.50

BORLAND, Hal. *Country Editor's Boy.* 1970. Lippincott. 313 pp. dj. $8.00

BORLAND, Hal. *Homeland, a Report from the Country.* 1969. Lippincott. 187 pp. dj. $5.00

BORLAND, Hal. *Sundial of the Seasons.* 1964. Lippincott. 350 pp. $5.00

BORLAND, Hal. *The Enduring Pattern.* 1959. Simon & Schuster. 247 pp. $6.00

BORMANN, Maj. Gen. *Shrapnel Shell in England & Belgium.* 1859. Brussels. Librairie Europeenne. 166 pp. $20.00

BORN, Max. *My Life & My Views.* 1968. New York. 1st ed. 216 pp. index. VG $15.00

BORROR, D.J. & White, R.E. *Insects of North America North of Mexico.* 1984. Easton. Ills. 404 pp. EX $30.00

BORROW. *Lavengro & the Romany Rye.* Wisconsin. 374 pp. VG $5.50

BORTHWICK, Rev. J. Douglas. *Poems & Songs on the South African War.* 1901. Montreal. $12.50

BORTHWICK. *Three Years in California.* 1857. London. ex-lib. $175.00

BORTHWICK. *Three Years in California.* 1948. Oakland. Ills. Ltd. ed. 318 pp. EX $60.00

BORTON. *The Walton Boys & Gold in the Snow.* 1948. Whitman. VG $4.50

BORTONE, S.A. *Revision of Sea Basses of the Genus Diplectrum.* 1977. Ills. 49 pp. $4.00

BORUP, George. *A Tenderfoot with Peary.* 1911. Stokes. Ills. souvenir ed. 317 pp. VG $27.50

BOSANKO, W. *Collecting Old Lustre Ware.* 1926. New York. $25.00

BOSCH, R. & others. *An Introduction to Biological Control.* 1982. Plenum. photos. 247 pp. $15.00

BOSHER, Kate L. *Mary Cary Frequently Martha.* 1910. Harper. Ills. 168 pp. VG $15.00

BOSHER, Kate L. *The Man in Lonely Land.* 1912. Harper. Ills. 1st ed. $7.50

BOSSARD, Chandler. *The Spanish Scene.* 1968. Viking. 1st ed. dj. VG $22.50

BOSTON, Bernard. *History of the 398th Infantry Regiment in W.W.II.* 1947. Washington. Ills. 208 pp. VG $17.50

BOSWELL, James. *Journal of Tour to Hebrides.* 1974. New York. Ltd. Eds. Club. Ills. boxed. $40.00

BOSWELL, James. *Journal of Tour to Hebrides.* 1928. London. Ills. photos. 361 pp. VG $5.00

BOSWELL, James. *The Life of Samuel Johnson.* 1946. 631 pp. EX $4.00

BOSWELL, James. *The Life of Samuel Johnson.* London. (ca.1851) 4 vol set. $20.00

BOSWELL, Peyton Jr. *Modern American Painting.* 1940. New York. Dodd Mead. Ills. 166 pp. G $10.00

BOTKIN, B. *A Civil War Treasury.* 1960. Random House. 1st ed. dj. VG $12.50

BOTKIN, B. *A Treasury of American Folklore.* 1944. New York. Crown Pub. 932 pp. $3.50

BOTKIN & HARLOW. *A Treasury of Railroad Folklore.* 1953. New York. Crown. 1st ed. VG $17.50

BOTT. *The Londoner's England.* 1947. EX $20.00

BOTTA, Charles. *History of War of Independence of U.S of America.* New Haven. 4th ed. 2 vol set. G $75.00

BOTTOME, Phyllis. *Survival.* 1943. Little, Brown. $4.50

BOTTOME, Phyllis. *The Heart of a Child.* 1940. New York. inscr. sgn. dj. EX $12.50

BOTTOMLEY, Gordon. *The Gate of Smargadus.* 1904. London. Ills. Balmer. 1st ed. VG $25.00

BOTUME, Elizabeth. *First Days Amongst the Contrabands.* 1893. Boston. 1st ed. $40.00

BOUCHER, Anthony. *The Compleat Werewolf.* 1969. Simon & Schuster. 4th print. $40.00

BOUCHER, F. *20,000 Years of Fashion.* 1966. $55.00

BOUCHER, Jonathan. *Reminiscences of an American Loyalist, 1738-1789.* 1925. Boston. Ills. Ltd. 1st ed. 201 pp. $50.00

BOUCHER, M. *Birds of Prey of Britain & Europe.* 1977. London. Hamlyn. Ills. 235 pp. dj. $12.50

BOUGAINVILLE, Louis Antoine. *A Voyage Round the World in Years 1766-1769.* 1772. London. 1st Eng. ed. maps. $1,675.00

BOULDING, K. *The Image.* 1956. Ann Arbor. 1st ed. dj. VG $15.00

BOULENGER, E.G. *Wildlife the World Over.* 1954. Wise. Ills. 624 pp. VG $6.00

BOULESTIN, Marcel *What Shall We Have To-Day?* 1932. Heinemann. 1st ed. dj. $20.00

BOULESTIN, Marcel. *Having Crossed the Channel.* 1934. Heinemann. 1st ed. $12.50

BOULESTIN, Marcel. *Herbs, Salads, & Seasonings.* 1930. Heinemann. 1st ed. $12.50

BOULESTIN, Marcel. *Myself, My Two Countries.* 1936. Cassell. 1st ed. dj. $15.00

BOULESTIN, Marcel. *Potatoes.* 1932. Heinemann. 1st ed. $12.50

BOULLE, Pierre. *Ears of the Jungle.* 1972. New York. ex-lib. 224 pp. dj. EX $4.50

BOULLE, Pierre. *Garden on the Moon.* 1965. Vanguard. 1st Am. ed. dj. VG $20.00

BOULLE, Pierre. *The Bridge over the River Kwai.* 1954. Vanguard. 1st Am. ed. dj. VG $40.00

BOULLE, Pierre. *The Good Leviathan.* 1978. Vanguard. 1st ed. dj. VG $15.00

BOULLE, Pierre. *The Marvelous Palace.* 1977. Vanguard. 1st Am. ed. dj. VG $15.00

BOULLE, Pierre. *The Photographer.* 1967. Vanguard. 1st Am. ed. dj. VG $15.00

BOULLERAY, Yvonne. *California Wine Country Cooking.* 1975. sgn. 97 pp. $7.00

BOULTON, Agnes. *Part of a Long Story.* 1958. Garden City. Doubleday. 1st ed. 331 pp. $10.00

BOURDELLE, Pierre. *War.* 1945. New York. color plts of WWII & Europe. $165.00

BOURJAILY, Vance. *The Hound of Earth.* 1955. New York. Scribner. 1st ed. $45.00

BOURKE, John G. *An Apache Compaign in Sierra Madre.* 1958. New York. reprint 1886 ed. dj. EX $15.00

BOURKE, John G. *On the Border with Crook.* 1891. $125.00

BOURKE-WHITE, Margaret. *Dear Fatherland. Rest Quietly.* 1946. New York. Simon & Schuster. Ills. dj. G $35.00

BOURKE-WHITE, Margaret. *One Thing Leads to Another.* 1936. $22.50

BOURKE-WHITE, Margaret. *Portrait of Myself.* 1963. New York. Ills. 1st ed. 383 pp. dj. G $12.50

BOURKE-WHITE, Margaret. *Purple Heart Valley.* 1944. $17.50

BOURKE-WHITE, Margaret. *Say Is This the U.S.A.?* 1941. Duell. 1st ed. dj. $35.00

BOURKE-WHITE, Margaret. *Shooting the Russian War.* 1942. $25.00

BOURNE, Benjamin Franklin. *The Captive in Patagonia; Life Among the Giants.* 1853. Boston. Ills. Brown. 233 pp. G $150.00

BOURNE, Peter. *Drums of Destiny.* 1947. New York. Putnam. 414 pp. VG $3.50

BOURRIT, M.T. *Nouvelle Description Des Glacieres.* 1785. Geneva. 2 vol set. $70.00

BOUSCAREN, Anthony. *Imperial Communism.* 1953. Washington. ex-lib. 256 pp. $4.50

BOUTELL, Charles. *British Archaeology.* 1858. London. 1st ed. 20 color pls. EX $25.00

BOUTELL, H.S. *First Editions.* 1929. Philadelphia. VG $16.00

BOUTON, Jim. *Ball Four.* 1970. New York. World Pub. 407 pp. VG $4.50

BOUTON. *Bibliographie Bernardine.* 1958. Paris. 164 pp. wrappers. VG $7.50

BOUZEK, J. *Anatolian Collection of Charles University.* 1974. Prague. 1st ed. 217 pp. 52 pls. $20.00

BOVERY, M. *The Saga of the Waterfowl.* 1949. Ills. F.L. Jaques. 140 pp. $8.00

BOVILL, E.W. *The Niger Explored.* 1968. Oxford U. Press. Ills. 263 pp. $30.00

BOWAN, H. & Dickinson, S. *Westward from Rio.* 1936. Willett Clark. Ills. map. 351 pp. VG $9.00

BOWAN, Isaiah. *Desert Trails of Atacama.* 1924. New York. Am. Geographical Soc. 362 pp. $10.00

BOWDEN, Edwin. *James Thurber, a Bibliography.* 1968. OH State U. Pr.dj. EX $12.50

BOWDITCH, N.I. *Suffolk Surnames.* 1857. Boston. 108 pp. sgn. $21.00

BOWEN, Catherine D. *Beloved Friend.* 1937. New York. Random House. 484 pp. EX $6.00

BOWEN, Catherine D. *Family Portrait.* 1970. Boston. 1st ed. dj. VG $10.00

BOWEN, Catherine D. *The Writing of Biography.* 1951. $7.50

BOWEN, Catherine D. *Yankee From Olympus.* 1945. Boston. 465 pp. dj. $4.50

BOWEN, Catherine D. *Yankee From Olympus; Justice Holmes & His Family.* 1944. Little, Brown. dj. $7.50

BOWEN, Croswell. *The Curse of the Misbegotten.* 1959. New York. 1st ed. 3rd printing. 386 pp. $10.00

BOWEN, Dana Thomas. *Lore of the Lakes Told in Story & Picture.* 1948. Daytona Beach. Ills. 5th printing. sgn. dj. $10.00

BOWEN, Elizabeth. *A Time in Rome.* 1960. New York. 3rd printing. dj. EX $7.50

BOWEN, Elizabeth. *Anthony Trollope.* 1946. New York. Ills. 1st Am. ed. $10.00

BOWEN, Elizabeth. *Bowen's Court.* 1942. New York. 1st ed. dj. VG $10.00

BOWEN, Elizabeth. *Collected Impressions.* 1950. New York. 1st ed. dj. $25.00

BOWEN, Elizabeth. *Early Stories.* 1951. New York. 1st ed. dj. VG $15.00

BOWEN, Elizabeth. *Eva Trout.* 1968. New York. Knopf. 1st ed. dj. EX $25.00

BOWEN, Elizabeth. *The Death of the Heart.* 1939. Knopf. 1st Am. ed. dj. VG $45.00

BOWEN, Elizabeth. *The Heat of the Day.* 1949. Knopf. 1st Am. ed. dj. VG $25.00

BOWEN, Elizabeth. *The Hotel.* 1928. Dial Press. 1st Am. ed. dj. VG $50.00

BOWEN, Elizabeth. *The House in Paris.* 1936. New York. 1st ed. dj. VG $20.00

BOWEN, Elizabeth. *The Little Girls.* 1964. Knopf. 1st Am. ed. dj. VG $20.00

BOWEN, Elizabeth. *World of Love.* 1955. Knopf. 1st Am. ed. dj. VG $15.00

BOWEN, F.C. *From Carrack to Clipper. Book of Sailing Models.* 1927. London. Ills. G $47.50

BOWEN, Louise De Koven. *Safeguards for City Youth at Work & Play.* 1914. New York. 1st ed. inscr. 241 pp. index. $15.00

BOWEN, R. Sidney. *Red Randall in Burma.* 1945. Grosset & Dunlap. 212 pp. G $3.50

BOWEN. *Beloved Friend Story of Tchaikowsky.* 1937. 1st ed. VG $20.00

BOWEN. *Dave Dawson at Dunkirk.* 1941. Saalfield. dj. VG $5.50

BOWEN. *Red Randall on New Guinea.* 1944. Grosset & Dunlap. $4.50

BOWERS, R.L. *The U.S. Air Force in South-East Asia.* 1983. EX $12.50

BOWIE, Theodore Robert. *The Drawings of Hokusai.* 1964. IN U. Press. 130 drawings. 190 pp. VG $35.00

BOWKER, John. *Jesus & the Pharisees.* 1973. Cambridge. dj. EX $22.50

BOWLES, Jane. *In the Summer House.* 1954. New York. Ills. 1st ed. dj. EX $75.00

BOWLES, P. *In Red Room.* 1981. Los Angeles. Ltd. ed. 1/330. sgn. $50.00

BOWLES, P. *Let It Come Down.* 1952. 1st ed. dj. VG $30.00

BOWLES, P. *Next to Nothing.* Ltd. ed. 1/300. sgn. $25.00

BOWLES, P. *Spider House.* Ltd. ed. 1/350. sgn. $30.00

BOWLES, P. *The Lemon. By Mohammed Mrabet.* 1972. McGraw Hill. 1st Am. ed. dj. VG $15.00

BOWLES, P. *Up Above the World.* 1966. Simon & Schuster. 1st ed. dj. $30.00

BOWLES, P. *Without Stopping.* 1972. 1st ed. dj. EX $15.00

BOWLES, Samuel. *Across the Continent to the Rocky Mountains.* 1865. New York. 452 pp. fld map. VG $40.00

BOWLES, Samuel. *Across the Continent to the Rocky Mountains.* 1866. Massachusetts. fld map. G $25.00

BOWLES, Samuel. *Across the Continent/Summer's Journey to Rockies.* 1866. Springfield. fld map. VG $27.50

BOWLES, Samuel. *Across the Continent/Summer's Journey to Rockies.* 1865. Springfield. 1st ed. fld map. G $50.00

BOWMAN, Albert H. *The Struggle for Neutrality.* 1974. Knoxville, TN. Tenn. Press. 460 pp. $4.50

BOWMAN & DICKINSON. *Westward from Rio.* 1936. Chicago. Clark. 1st ed. ex-lib. sgns. $10.00

BOWNE, E. *House in Paris.* 1936. 1st ed. dj. VG $7.00

BOWRA, C.M. *Primitive Song.* 1962. Cleveland. Ills. 1st ed. VG $20.00

BOWYER, Charles. *Bomber Group at War.* 1981. London. 1st ed. EX $15.00

BOWYER, Charles. *Hampden Special.* 1976. London. 1st ed. EX $12.50

BOWYER, Charles. *Hurricane at War.* 1974. London. 1st ed. EX $15.00

BOWYER, Charles. *Images of Air War 1939-45.* 1983. London. $12.00

BOWYER, Charles. *The Encyclopedia of British Military Aircraft.* 1982. New York. Crescent. 1st ed. EX $15.00

BOWYER, Michael J.F. *Bombing Colours.* 1973. Cambridge. Patrick Stephens. 1st ed. $15.00

BOYCE, William D. *Australia & New Zealand Illustrated.* 1922. Chicago. 381 pp. $18.00

BOYCE, William D. *Illustrated Africa.* 1925. Chicago. presentation copy. dj. VG $20.00

BOYCE, William D. *United States Colonies & Dependencies.* 1914. Chicago/NY. Ills. 638 pp. index. $17.50

BOYCE. *A Strike.* 1894. Ltd. ed. $35.00

BOYD, Denny. *The Vancouver Canuck's Story.* 1973. McGraw Hill. Ills. 139 pp. dj. EX $7.50

BOYD, Ernest. *Collected Novels & Stories of Guy de Maupassant.* 1922. New York. Knopf. 262 pp. $3.00

BOYD, J. *Girl with Jade Green Eyes.* 1978. Viking. 1st ed. dj. EX $15.00

BOYD, J. *Marching On.* 1927. $10.00

BOYD, J. *Roman Antiquities.* 1837. New York. Ills. G $60.00

BOYD, J.P. *Stanley in Africa.* 1899. Stanley Pub. Ills. 800 pp. $6.00

BOYD, J.P. *The Life of General William T. Sherman.* 1891. 608 pp. $12.50

BOYD, John. *Barnard's Planet.* 1975. New York. Berkley. 1st ed. dj. EX $15.00

BOYD, Louise. *The Fiord Region of East Greenland.* 1935. Am. Geo. Soc. 1st ed. 2 vol set. $22.50

BOYD, T. *Shadow of the Long Knives.* 1928. New York. $10.00

BOYER, Dwight. *True Tales of the Great Lakes.* 1971. New York. Ills. 2nd printing. 340 pp. $12.50

BOYER, Josephine & Cowdin, K. *Hay Dieting Menus & Receipts for All Occasions.* 1934. New York. Scribner. 383 pp. $3.00

BOYER, Mary G. *Arizona in Literature.* 1935. Clark. EX $25.00

BOYER, Rick. *The Daisy Ducks.* 1986. Boston. Houghton Mifflin. 1st ed. dj. $15.00

BOYES, Kate & Virgil. *Langford of the Three Bars.* 1907. Chicago. Ills. N.C. Wyeth. 1st ed. $45.00

BOYESEN, Hjalmar H. *Works of Goethe.* 1885. Barrie. Ills. 1st ed. 3 vol set. VG $65.00

BOYINGTON, Gregory. *Baa Baa Black Sheep by Pappy Boyington.* 1958. New York. 1st ed. 384 pp. dj. $8.50

BOYKIN, Edward. *Congress & the Civil War.* 1955. McBride. 1st ed. dj. $10.00

BOYLE, Elizabeth. *Scrap Basket Sam.* 1923. Chicago. Ills. D.L. Gregory. VG $15.00

BOYLE, John Richards. *Soldiers True.* 1903. New York. Ills. 1st ed. maps. 386 pp. $125.00

BOYLE, K. *American Citizen: A Poem.* 1944. 1st ed. wrappers. VG $15.00

BOYLE, K. *Generation Without Farewell.* 1960. 1st ed. sgn. $16.50

BOYLE, Kay. *The Long Walk at San Francisco State.* 1970. Grove. dj. VG $20.00

BOYLE, Kay. *The Seagull on the Step.* 1955. 1st ed. VG $25.00

BOYLE, Kay. *The Underground Woman.* 1975. Doubleday. dj. EX $15.00

BOYLE, Kay. *His Human Majesty.* 1949. New York. VG $10.00

BOYLE, T. Coraghessan. *Budding Prospects.* 1984. New York. Viking. 1st ed. dj. EX $25.00

BOYLE, T. Coraghessan. *Greasy Lake A.O.S.* 1985. New York. Viking. 1st ed. dj. EX $20.00

BOYLE, T.C. *Descent of Man.* London. 1st ed. dj. VG $30.00

BOYN. *Glacier Bay.* 1967. dj. EX $40.00

BOYSTON, E.D. *Sketch of a Busy Life at 'Busyfield' & Elsewhere.* 1892. Amherst, NH. 184 pp. pls. $12.50

BOZMAN, John L. *A Sketch of the History of Maryland.* 1811. Baltimore. 1st ed. VG $50.00

BRACK & KELLEY. *Early Biographies.* 1974. U. Of Iowa. 1st ed. $20.00

BRACKEN, Peg. *I Hate to Cook Book Appendix.* 1966. New York. Ills. Hilary Knight. 1st ed. $10.00

BRACKEN, Peg. *I Hate to Cook Book.* 1960. New York. Harcourt. $5.00

BRACKENRIDGE, H.H. *History of the Western Insurrection.* 1859. 1st ed. VG $40.00

BRACKENRIDGE, H.H. *Modern Chivalry; or, Adventures of Capt. Farrago.* 1856. Philadelphia. Ills. 2 vol., 4 parts. $30.00

BRACKETT, Albert G. *History of the United States Cavalry.* 1863. Ills. 337 pp. $24.50

BRACKETT, Leigh. *The Starmen.* 1952. New York. Gnome. 1st ed. dj. VG $25.00

BRADBURY, John M. *The Fugitives: A Critical Account.* 1958. U. NC Press. 1st ed. dj. VG $20.00

BRADBURY, Malcolm. *Rates of Exchange.* 1983. New York. Knopf. 1st ed. dj. EX $20.00

BRADBURY, Ray. *A Medicine for Melancholy.* 1959. New York. Doubleday. 1st ed. sgn. dj. VG $65.00

BRADBURY, Ray. *Autumn People.* 1965. Ballantine. Ills. Frazetta. pb. EX $25.00

BRADBURY, Ray. *Beyond 1984: Remembrance of Things Future.* 1983. New York. Ltd. 1st ed. 1/350. sgn. EX $50.00

BRADBURY, Ray. *Dandelion Wine.* 1957. Garden City. 1st ed. dj. VG $55.00

BRADBURY, Ray. *Dark Carnival.* 1947. Arkham House. 1st ed. dj. EX $400.00

BRADBURY, Ray. *Dark Carnival.* 1948. Hamilton. 1st English ed. dj. VG $225.00

BRADBURY, Ray. *Death is a Lonely Business.* 1985. Franklin Lib. Ltd. 1st ed. sgn. dj. VG $40.00

BRADBURY, Ray. *Death is a Lonely Business.* 1985. Knopf. 1st ed. dj. EX $15.00

BRADBURY, Ray. *Dinosaur Tales.* 1983. 1st ed. dj. EX $10.00

BRADBURY, Ray. *Forever & the Earth.* 1984. Croissant. 1st ed. dj. VG $55.00

BRADBURY, Ray. *Ghosts of Forever.* 1980. New York. Rizzoli. Ills. Sessa. 1st ed. $30.00

BRADBURY, Ray. *Halloween Tree.* 1972. 1st ed. dj. VG $20.00

BRADBURY, Ray. *I Sing the Body Electric.* 1969. Knopf. 1st ed. dj. VG $35.00

BRADBURY, Ray. *Long After Midnight.* 1976. New York. 1st ed. dj. EX $12.50

BRADBURY, Ray. *S is for Space.* 1966. London. Hart Davis. review copy. dj. $75.00

BRADBURY, Ray. *S is for Space.* 1966. New York. 1st ed. inscr. sgn. dj. VG $75.00

BRADBURY, Ray. *Stories of Ray Bradbury.* 1980. Knopf. 1st ed. dj. EX $20.00

BRADBURY, Ray. *The Golden Apples of the Sun.* 1953. 1st ed. dj. EX $65.00

BRADBURY, Ray. *The Halloween Tree.* 1972. 1st ed. dj. EX $25.00

BRADBURY, Ray. *The Last Circus & Electrocution.* 1980. Northridge. Ltd. 1st ed. sgn. slipcase. EX $65.00

BRADBURY, Ray. *The Last Circus & Electrocution.* 1980. New York. 1st ed. sgn. dj. VG $40.00

BRADBURY, Ray. *The Martian Chronicles.* 1974. Ltd. Ed. Club. Ills. Mugnaini. sgns. EX $150.00

BRADBURY, Ray. *The Martian Chronicles.* 1963. Time Books. 1st ed. wrappers. EX $25.00

BRADBURY, Ray. *This Attic Where the Meadow Greens.* 1979. Ltd. ed. 1/300. sgn. VG $70.00

BRADBURY, Ray. *Where Robot Mice.* 1977. New York. Knopf. 1st ed. dj. EX $15.00

BRADDON, Mary Elizabeth. *Lady Audley's Secret.* 1862. Tauchnitz. 1st ed. VG $60.00

BRADDY, H. *Paradox of Pancho Villa.* 1978. Texas U. Press. Ills. 1st ed. dj. EX $15.00

BRADEN. *The Lone Indian.* 1936. Saalfield. G $3.50

BRADFORD, Ernie. *Southward the Caravels.* 1961. $6.50

BRADFORD, Gamaliel. *Bare Souls.* 1924. 1st ed. $6.50

BRADFORD, Gershom. *The Secret of Mary Celeste.* 1966. $8.50

BRADFORD, N. *Battles & Leaders of Civil War.* 1956. 1st ed. VG $20.00

BRADFORD, Roark. *A Legend of the River People.* 1937. Washington. sgn. EX $22.50

BRADFORD, Roark. *How Come Christmas.* 1948. Harper. dj. VG $20.00

BRADFORD, Roark. *John Henry.* 1931. Harper. 1st ed. G $10.00

BRADFORD, Roark. *The Green Roller.* 1949. New York. Harper. 1st ed. 118 pp. $6.00

BRADISH, Sarah P. *Stories of Country Life.* 1901. New York. Eclectic series. $8.50

BRADLEE, Benjamin. *Conversations with Kennedy.* 1975. New York. Norton. 1st ed. 251 pp. dj. $50.00

BRADLEE, Francis. *Blockade Running During the Civil War.* 1925. Salem, MA. Ills. 340 pp. $23.50

BRADLEY, A.G. *Sketches from Old Virginia.* 1897. London. Macmillan. 284 pp. $25.00

BRADLEY, A.G. *Wolfe.* 1895. London. 214 pp. $15.00

BRADLEY, David. *The Chaneyville Incident.* 1981. New York. Harper. 1st ed. dj. EX $30.00

BRADLEY, Joshua. *Some of the Beauties of Free-Masonry.* 1816. Rutland. Fay & Davison. 1st ed. 318 pp. $150.00

BRADLEY, M.H. *On the Gorilla Trail.* 1922. Appleton. 1st ed. photos. maps. VG $35.00

BRADLEY, M.H. *Trailing the Tiger.* 1929. Appleton. photos. map. 246 pp. $25.00

BRADLEY, M.Z. *Castle Terror.* Lancer. pb. VG $10.00

BRADLEY, M.Z. *Catch Trap.* 1979. Ballentine. 1st ed. sgn. dj. EX $25.00

BRADLEY, M.Z. *Planet Savers & Sword of Aldones.* 1962. New York. wrappers. $15.00

BRADLEY, M.Z. *The Colors of Space.* Monarch. pb. EX $10.00

BRADLEY, Omar N. *A Soldier's Story.* 1951. New York. Holt. 1st ed. 618 pp. boxed. $35.00

BRADLEY, Omar N. & Blair, C. *A General's Life.* 1983. New York. Simon & Schuster. 752 pp. dj. $6.00

BRADLEY, Van A. *More Gold in Your Attic.* 1962. New York. 2nd printing. 415 pp. dj. VG $8.50

BRADSHAW, Terry w/Diles, D. *Terry Bradshaw: Man of Steel.* 1979. Grand Rapids. 195 pp. dj. $5.00

BRADSHAW, William. *The Goddess of Atvatabar.* 1892. New York. 1st Am. ed. VG $65.00

BRADY, Cyrus Townsend. *A Little Traitor to the South.* 1904. New York. Grosset & Dunlap. 1st ed. VG $12.50

BRADY, Cyrus Townsend. *The West Wind.* 1912. McClurg. Ills. Dixon. $5.50

BRADY, James. *Strange Encounters.* London. (ca.1950's) Ills. VG $35.00

BRADY, Ryder. *Instar.* 1976. 1st ed. dj. EX $15.00

BRADY. *Historian with a Camera.* 1955. $25.00

BRAGDON, Claude. *A Primer of Higher Space.* 1938. New York. 2nd ed. 81 pp. G $31.00

BRAGG, Paul C. *Health Cookbook.* 1947. New York. Knopf. 402 pp. index. $5.00

BRAINE. *Room at the Top.* 1st ed. dj. VG $30.00

BRAININ. *The Early Potters & Potteries of Maine.* 1978. Wesleyan. $10.00

BRAITHWAITE, David. *Fairground Architecture.* 1968. Ills. 1st ed. $25.00

BRAITHWAITE, Wm. Stanley. *Anthology of Magazine Verse for 1921.* 1921. Boston. Small, Maynard. 294 pp. $10.00

BRAITHWAITE, Wm. Stanley. *Anthology of Magazine Verse for 1923.* 1923. Boston. Brimmer. 188 pp. $12.50

BRAITHWAITE, Wm. Stanley. *The Golden Treasury of Magazine Verse.* 1918. $4.50

BRAKEFIELD. *Hunting Big Game Trophies.* 1976. Ills. 446 pp. $8.50

BRAMAH, Ernest. *Kai Lung Beneath the Mulberry Tree.* 1978. New York. Arno Press. EX $15.00

BRAMAH, Ernest. *Kai Lung Unrolls His Mat.* 1928. New York. Doubleday. 1st Am. ed. dj. VG $30.00

BRAMAH, Ernest. *The Mirror of Kong Ho.* 1930. New York. Doubleday. 1st Am. ed. dj. EX $35.00

BRAMAH, Ernest. *The Return of Kai Lung.* 1937. Sheridan House.1st Am. ed. VG $35.00

BRAMAH, Ernest. *The Wallet of Kai Lung.* New York. Doran. G $50.00

BRAMAH, Ernest. *The Wallet of Kai Lung.* 1923. London. Ltd. ed. 1/200. sgn. dj. VG $145.00

BRAMANTI, Bruno. *Life of Christ.* 1951. New York. Pellegrini & Cudahy. 130 pp. $22.50

BRAMELD, Theodore. *Design for America.* 1945. 1st ed. dj. $8.50

BRANCH, E.D. *Cowboy & His Intrepreters.* 1926. 1st ed. $35.00

BRANCH, E.D. *Hunting of the Buffalo.* 1929. Appleton. 1st ed. $50.00

BRANCH, E.D. *The Sentimental Years 1836-1860.* 1934. Appleton Century. 432 pp. $15.00

BRAND, Christina. *Tour de Force.* 1955. London. Joseph. 1st ed. dj. VG $20.00

BRAND, John. *Observations on Popular Antiquities.* 1900. London. Chatto & Windus. 807 pp. $15.00

BRAND, Max. *The Thunderer.* 1933. VG $60.00

BRAND, Millen. *Local Lives. Poems About Pennsylvania Dutch.* 1975. New York. 1st ed. $10.00

BRANDAU, R. *History of Homes & Gardens of Tennessee.* 1936. Nashville. Ltd. ed. 1/1500. 502 pp. VG $125.00

BRANDE, W.T. *A Dictionary of Science, Literature & Art.* 1843. New York. Harper. VG $30.00

BRANDER, A.A.D. *Wild Animals in Central India.* 1982. Natraj, India. 1st Indian ed. photos. 296 pp. $42.00

BRANDER, Michael. *Hunting & Shooting from Earliest Times to Present.*1971. New York. Putnam. Ills. 255 pp. VG $15.00

BRANDES, George. *Poland: Land, People, Literature.* 1904. New York. VG $10.00

BRANDES, Joseph. *Herbert Hoover & Economic Diplomacy.* 1962. Pittsburgh. 237 pp. dj. VG $6.00

BRANDON, Helen P. *Gay Bar.* 1957. San Francisco. Ltd. ed. sgn. dj. EX $20.00

BRANDT, Francis B. *The Wissahickon Valley.* 1927. Philadelphia. 142 pp. $13.50

BRANDT, Herbert. *Alaska Bird Trails.* 1943. Cleveland. Ills. 1st ed. 464 pp. index. $95.00

BRANGWYN, Frank. *Windmills.* 1923. 1st ed. $20.00

BRANHAM & KUTASH. *Encyclopedia of Criminology.* 1949. New York. Philosophical Soc. 527 pp. VG $25.00

BRANNON. *Yellow Kid Weil.* 1948. Chicago. Davis. 1st ed. inscr. dj. $30.00

BRASCH & ROTHENSTEINS. *Dictionary of Berlin.* 1883. Ills. 150 pp. VG $15.00

BRASHER, Rex. *Birds & Trees of North America.* 1969. New York. Rowman & Littlefield. Ills. VG $20.00

BRASHLER, William. *The Bingo Long Traveling All Stars & Motor Kings.* 1973. Harper. 1st ed. dj. VG $15.00

BRASSAI. *Picasso & Co.* 1966. dj. $45.00

BRASSEY, Mrs. *Around the World in the Yacht Sunbeam.* 1879. New York. Ills. map. VG $12.50

BRASSEY, Mrs. *The Last Voyage.* 1889. London. Ills. ex-lib. VG $12.50

BRASSEY, Mrs. *Voyage on Sunbeam, Our Home on Ocean 11 Months.* 1879. Toronto. Ills. 6th ed. 511 pp. $22.50

BRATCHER, J.T. & Kendall, L.H.*Some Victorian Forged Rarities.* 1970. Austin. Ltd. ed. 1/500. dj. EX $55.00

BRATHWAIT, Richard. *The Law of Drinking.* 1903. New Haven. reprint. VG $45.00

BRATLEY, George H. *The Power of Gems & Charms.* 1907. London. 197 pp. $45.00

BRATT. *Trails of Yesterday.* 1921. Chicago. Ills. 1st ed. EX $75.00

BRAUDEL, Fernand. *Civilization & Capitalism 15-18th Cent.; Vol 3.* 1984. New York. Harper. 699 pp. dj. EX $12.50

BRAUN, Adolphe Armand. *Figures, Faces, & Folds.* 1928. London. Ills. photos. 152 pp. $17.50

BRAUTIGAN, Richard. *Abortion: Historical Romance.* 1966. 1st ed. dj. VG $10.00

BRAUTIGAN, Richard. *Dreaming of Babylon.* 1977. Delacorte. 1st ed. dj. VG $20.00

BRAUTIGAN, Richard. *Hawkline Monster.* 1974. New York. Simon & Schuster. dj. EX $15.00

BRAUTIGAN, Richard. *Sombrero Fallout.* 1976. New York. Simon & Schuster. 1st ed. dj. $25.00

BRAUTIGAN, Richard. *The Tokyo-Montana Express.* 1980. Delacorte. 1st trade ed. dj. VG $15.00

BRAWNE, Fanny. *Letters of Fanny Brawne to Fanny Keats 1820-1824.* 1937. New York. Ills. dj. EX $20.00

BRAYNARD, F.O. *Famous American Ships.* 1978. Ills. new revised ed. dj. VG $15.00

BRAYNARD, F.O. *Famous American Ships.* 1957. New York. $20.00

BRAYNARD, F.O. *Lives of the Liners.* 1947. Ills. author. VG $20.00

BRAYTON, George A. *A Defense of Samuel Gorton & Settlers of Shawomet.* 1883. Providence. 1st ed. 120 pp. wrappers. $25.00

BRAZER, E.S. *Early American Decoration.* 1947. Springfield. Ills. dj. EX $75.00

BRAZIER, Marion. *Stage & Screen.* 1920. Boston. Brazier. Ills. 130 pp. $37.50

BRAZILLER, George. *Japanese Ghosts & Demons.* 1985. U. of Kansas. Ills. 192 pp. wrappers. $45.00

BREAKENRIDGE, William M. *Helldorado.* 1982. EX $12.50

BREBNER, Percy. *Princess Maritza.* 1906. New York. Ills. Fisher. EX $8.50

BRECHT, Bertolt. *Tales from the Calendar.* 1961. London. Methuen. 1st ed. dj. EX $25.00

BRECK, J. *New Book of Flowers.* 1896. Ills. 1st ed. 480 pp. $12.00

BRECKENRIDGE, Gerald. *The Radio Boys on the Mexican Border.* 1922. New York. A.L. Burt. 231 pp. G $2.00

BRECKINRIDGE, Mary. *Wide Neighbors.* 1952. 1st ed. 366 pp. $6.00

BREDES, Don. *Muldoon.* 1982. Holt. dj. EX $15.00

BREESKIN. *Mary Cassatt: Cataloque Raisonne of Graphic Work.* 1979. Smithsonian Institute Press. $20.00

BREFFNY, B.D. *The Synagogue.* 1978. New York. Macmillan. Ills. G $25.00

BREIHAN, Carl W. *Quantrill & His Civil War Guerillas.* 1959. New York. Promontory Pr. Ills. 174 pp. $7.50

BREIHAN, Carl W. *The Bandit Belle.* 1970. Seattle. Ills. 143 pp. $15.00

BREIHAN, Carl W. *The Killer Legions of Quantrill.* 1971. Vancouver. Ills. 144 pp. $17.00

BREISACH, Ernest. *Caterina Sforza.* 1967. U. Chicago. proof copy. wrappers. VG $30.00

BREMER, Fredrika. *The Homes of the New World Impressions of America.* 1853. New York. 2 vol set. G $25.00

BREMSER, R. *Angel.* 1967. 1st ed. $12.50

BRENNAN, J.P. & Grant, D.M. *Act of Providence.* 1979. Ltd. ed. 1/250. sgn. boxed. EX $25.00

BRENNAN, Louis. *American Dawn. New Model of American Prehistory.* 1971. New York. Ills. 1st ed. sgn. dj. EX $15.00

BRENNAN, Niall. *The Making of a Moron.* 1953. New York. 1st ed. dj. VG $20.00

BRENNER, S. *Pennsylvania Dutch: Plain & Fancy.* 1957. Stackpole. 1st ed. dj. VG $12.50

BRENNER. *Idols Behind Altars.* 1929. photo ed. $25.00

BRENT. *The Hell Hole. The Yuma Prison Story.* 1962. Ills. 61 pp. SftCvr. $7.50

BRENTANO. *Light of Christmas.* 1964. 1st ed. dj. VG $12.50

BRENTANO. *Tale of Cockel, Hinkel & Gackeliah.* 1961. Ills. Sendak. dj. VG $15.00

BRENTON, Myron. *The Privacy Invaders.* 1964. New York. Coward McCann. 240 pp. dj. VG $5.00

BRENTON, Nicholas. *The Bower of Delights.* 1893. London. 1st ed. VG $25.00

BRENTON, Nicholas. *Twelve Months.* 1927. Ltd. ed. 1/500. dj. VG $75.00

BRERETON, F.S. *Under the Spangled Banner.* 1903. VG $10.00

BRESSON, Henri Cartier. *From One China to the Other.* 1955. 1st ed. VG $95.00

BRETON, P.N. *Popular Ills. Guide to Canadian Coins & Metals.* 1912. Montreal. 1st ed. $15.00

BRETT, Simon. *A Shock to the System.* 1984. London. Macmillan. 1st ed. sgn. dj. VG $22.50

BRETT, Simon. *Situation Tragedy.* 1981. London. 1st ed. dj. sgn. EX $30.00

BRETT-SMITH. *Peacock's Memoirs of Shelley w/Shelley's Letters.* 1909. London. Frowde. EX $25.00

BRETZ, J.H. *Caves of Missouri.* 1956. dj. VG $25.00

BREUIL, H. & Lantier, R. *The Men of the Stone Age.* 1965. St.Martins. Ills. 272 pp. dj. $10.00

BREWER, David H. *Adventures in Fairyland.* 1894. Collins Press. Ills. VG $27.50

BREWER, David J. *The Twentieth Century from Another Viewpoint.* 1899. 1st ed. $8.50

BREWER, E. *Character Sketches of Romance, Fiction & Drama.* 1896. New York. Ills. 4 vol set. $65.00

BREWER, J. *Wings in the Meadow.* 1967. Houghton Mifflin. Ills. dj. $10.00

BREWER, Leighton. *Riders of the Sky.* 1934. Boston. $10.00

BREWER, S. *The Chimps of Mount Asserik.* 1978. Knopf. 1st U.S. ed. photos. 302 pp. $12.00

BREWER. *Joys & Sorrows of a Book Collector.* 1928. Ltd. ed. 1/300. VG $20.00

BREWITT, Ross. *A Spin of the Wheel.* 1975. Vantage Press. 197 pp. dj. EX $7.50

BREWSTER, David. *Memoirs of Life, Writings & Discoveries of Newton.* 1855. Edinburgh. 2nd ed. ex-lib. G $75.00

BREWSTER, George. *The Western Literary Magazine & Journal of Ed.* 1854. Cleveland. Ills. 400 pp. $35.00

BREWSTER, Jerry. *Zuniga.* Alpine Fine Arts. $35.00

BREWSTER, William. *Birds of Cambridge Region of Mass.* 1906. Ills. 1st ed. 3 maps. $45.00

BREWSTER, William. *Concord River.* 1937. Cambridge. Ills. Benson. 1st ed. dj. EX $47.50

BREYTENBACH, Breyten. *The True Confessions of an Alfino Terrorist.* 1985. Farrar. 1st Am. ed. dj. VG $20.00

BRICE, Marshall Moore. *Daughter of the Stars.* 1973. McClure Press. Ills. 309 pp. dj. $12.50

BRICKDALE, Eleanor Fortescue. *Fleur & Blanchefleur.* 1922. London. O'Connor Pub. Ills. 1st ed. VG $25.00

BRICKELL, Herschel. *O'Henry Memorial Award Prize Stories of 1943.* 1943. Doubleday Doran. Book Club ed. $4.50

BRICKELL, Herschel. *Prize Stories of 1951.* 1951. Doubleday. 1st ed. 325 pp. $7.50

BRIDDLE, G. *Artist at War.* 1944. dj. VG $20.00

BRIDGE, Ann. *Facts & Fictions. Some Literary Recollections.* 1968. New York. 1st ed. 207 pp. dj. VG $5.00

BRIDGE, B.A. *Treatise on the Elements of Algebra.* 1841. Philadelphia. $10.00

BRIDGEMAN, Thomas. *Florist's Guide.* 1840. 3rd ed. G $45.00

BRIDGEMAN, Thomas. *The Young Gardener's Assistant.* 1837. 7th ed. $39.00

BRIDGEMAN, Thomas. *The Young Gardener's Assistant.* 1857. New York. new ed. 189 pp. VG $35.00

BRIDGES, E.L. *Uttermost Part of the Earth.* 1949. Dutton. 97 Ills. 5 maps. 558 pp. $25.00

BRIDGES, R. *The Shorter Poems.* 1894. 4th ed. G $15.00

BRIDGES, Robert. *The Roosevelt Book.* 1908. New York. Scribner. 189 pp. G $4.00

BRIDGES, T.C. *Men of the Mist.* 1923. Philadelphia. McKay. 1st Am. ed. VG $35.00

BRIDGES, T.C. *Young Folks Book of Invention.* 1926. Boston. 1st ed. VG $7.50

BRIDGES. *Testament of Beauty.* 1930. New York. 1st revised ed. VG $20.00

BRIDGMAN, Betty. *Lullaby for Eggs.* 1955. New York. Ills. E. Orton Jones. dj. EX $20.00

BRIDGMAN-METCHIM. *Atlantis.* 1900. $50.00

BRIFFAULT, Robert. *The Troubadours.* 1965. Bloomington. Ills. dj. EX $10.00

BRIGGS, Clare. *Selected Drawings.* 1930. New York City. 7 vol set. $87.00

BRIGGS, Ellis. *Shots Heard Round the World.* 1957. Viking. Ills. 149 pp. $3.50

BRIGGS, L. Cabot. *The Living Races of the Sahara Desert.* 1958. 1st ed. stiff wrappers. $20.00

BRIGGS, Martin. *Wren the Incomparable.* 1953. Geo. Allen. 1st ed. dj. $12.50

BRIGGS, Peter. *Buccaneer Harbor.* 1970. $10.00

BRIGGS, Sam. *The Essays, Humor & Poems of Nathaniel Ames.* 1891. Cleveland. Ills. 490 pp. $35.00

BRIGGS. *Bull Terriers.* 1940. Derrydale Pr. Ltd. ed. 1/500. EX $500.00

BRIGGS. *Without Noise of Arms.* 1976. Ills. dj. VG $45.00

BRIGHAM, B. *Heaved from the Earth.* 1971. Knopf. 1st ed. inscr. dj. VG $15.00

BRIGHAM, Clarence S. *Fifty Years of Collecting Americana.* 1958. Worcester. Ltd. ed. 1/1000. wrappers. EX $45.00

BRILLAT-SAVARIN, Jean A. *Handbook of Gastronomy.* 1915. Boston. Riverside Pr. Ltd. ed. VG $125.00

BRILLAT-SAVARIN, Jean A. *Physiology of Taste.* 1948. $10.00

BRIMBLE, L.J.F. *Flowers in Britain.* 1945. Macmillan. 2nd printing. dj. $8.50

BRIMM, Daniel & Boggess, E. *Aircraft Engine Maintenance.* 1939. Pitman Pub. Ills. 470 pp. $7.50

BRIMMER, F.E. *Motor Campcraft.* 1923. New York. Ills. $10.00

BRIN, D. *River of Time.* Ltd. ed. 1/400. sgn. $35.00

BRINDLE, John & White, J. *Talking in Flowers: Japanese Botanical Art.* 1982. Pittsburgh. Ills. wrappers. scarce. $26.00

BRINE, Lindesay. *Travels Amongst American Indians.* 1894. London. Ills. 1st ed. fld map. 429 pp. $45.00

BRINK, Andre. *Ambassador.* Cape Town. 1st ed. dj. VG $35.00

BRINK, Andre. *Looking on Darkness.* 1975. Morrow. 1st Am. ed. dj. VG $35.00

BRINK, Andre. *Rumours of Rain.* 1978. Morrow. 1st Am. ed. ex-lib. dj. VG $20.00

BRINK, Carol. *Harps in the Wind.* 1947. New York. dj. VG $8.50

BRINK, Carol. *Mademoiselle Misfortune.* 1936. New York. Ills. Kate Seredy. 1st ed. $25.00

BRINKLEY, William. *Don't Go Near the Water.* 1956. New York. Random House. 1st ed. dj. EX $40.00

BRINNIN, John M. *Sextet. T.S. Eliot & Truman Capote & Others.* 1981. Delacorte. proof copy. wrappers. EX $15.00

BRINNIN, John M. *The Third Rose.* 1959. Boston. 1st ed. dj. VG $10.00

BRINSMADE, E.M. *Children's Books on Alaska, Annotated List.* 1956. Fairbanks. ex-lib. 31 pp. wrappers. $5.00

BRINTON, Henry. *Drug on the Market.* 1st ed. dj. $7.00

BRION, Marcel. *The Medici.* 1969. New York. dj. EX $17.50

BRION. *Romantic Art.* 1960. New York. VG $38.00

BRISBANE, Albert. *Social Destiny of Man.* 1840. Philadelphia. 1st ed. 2 pls. $175.00

BRISTER, Bob. *The Golden Crescent.* 1969. Houston. Ills. Cowan. sgns. EX $140.00

BRISTER. *Moss, Mallards, & Mules.* 1969. Winchester Press. 216 pp. dj. $14.00

BRISTOWE, W.S. *A Book of Spiders.* 1947. London. 24 color pls. 58 pp. EX $10.00

BRITTEN, Emma Hardinge. *Nineteenth Century Miracles.* 1884. New York. 1st ed. 556 pp. $45.00

BRITTEN, F.J. *Old Clocks & Watches & Their Makers.* 1899. London. $45.00

BRITTON, D. & Hayashida, T. *The Japanese Crane, Bird of Happiness.* 1981. Tokoyo. Kodansha. Ills. 1st ed. dj. EX $25.00

BRITTON, Nan. *The President's Daughter.* 1927. New York. 1st ed. EX $50.00

BRITTON, Nathaniel L & Brown. *An Illustrated Flora of Northern U.S. Canada.* 1913. New York. Scribner. 2nd ed. $120.00

BROADHOUSE. *The Violin: How to Make It.* London. (ca.1890) 112 pp. $20.00

BROADSTONE, M.A. *History of Greene County Ohio.* 1918. Bohen & Co. G $22.00

BROBECK, Florence. *Chafing Dish Cookery.* 1950. New York. Barrows. 256 pp. $6.50

BROCK, Theodore. *The Mountains Wait.* 1942. 1st ed. $37.00

BROCKMAN, C.F. *Trees of North America.* 1968. Golden Press. Ills. maps. 380 pp. $12.00

BROCKWAY, W. & Winer, B. *Homespun America. A Collection of Writings.* 1958. New York. 1st printing. 831 pp. $10.00

BROCKWAY, Wallace & Weinstock.*The World of Opera: Origins & Lore of Performance.*1962. New York. Ills. VG $25.00

BROCKWELL, Maurice W. *Erasmus: Humanist & Painter.* 1918. no place. Ltd. ed. 1/100. 98 pp. $85.00

BRODEUR, Paul. *The Stunt Man.* 1970. New York. 1st ed. dj. EX $20.00

BRODHAY, Chester O. *Veiled Victory.* 1941. Philadelphia. Dorrace. 1st ed. inscr. sgn. $30.00

BRODIE, B. *A Layman's Guide to Naval Strategy.* 1943. maps. diagrams. G $9.00

BRODIE, F.M. *No Man Knows My History. Life of Joseph Smith.* 1945. New York. Knopf. $12.50

BRODSKY, L. & Hamblin. *The Degaulle Story.* 1985. U. Press Miss. 1st ed. dj. VG $35.00

BRODTKORB, R. *Flying Free.* 1965. Rand McNally. photos. dj. $10.00

BRODY, Alter. *A Family Album & Other Poems.* 1918. New York. ex-lib. 132 pp. $3.50

BRODY, Iles. *Gone with the Windsors.* 1953. Philadelphia. Winston. 327 pp. dj. $5.00

BRODY, Iles. *The Colony Portrait & Recipes.* 1945. New York. trade ed. 296 pp. $6.00

BRODY, Iles. *The Colony.* 1945. New York. Ltd. ed. 1/750. sgn. boxed. VG $32.50

BRODY. *Indian Painting & White Patrons.* 1971. U. of New Mexico. $20.00

BRODY. *Mimbres Painted Pottery.* 1977. U. of New Mexico. $12.00

BROGAN, D.W. *Politics in America.* 1954. New York. Harper. ex-lib. dj. VG $3.00

BROGAN, D.W. *The Price of Revolution.* 1952. London. 280 pp. dj. VG $6.00

BROKAW, Irving. *The Art of Skating. Its History & Development.* 1926. New York. Ills. 1st Am. ed. $25.00

BROM, J.L. *African Odyssey.* 1966. Living Books. photos. map. dj. VG $15.00

BROM, J.L. *The Pitiless Jungle.* 1955. McKay. photos. dj. $10.00

BROMAGE, Mary C. *Churchill & Ireland.* 1964. Notre Dame, IN.ex-lib. 222 pp. dj. $3.50

BROMFIELD, L. *Animals & Other People.* 1955. Harper. Ills. 272 pp. $5.00

BROMFIELD, Louis. *A Bromfield Galaxy.* 1957. New York. Harper. 639 pp. $8.00

BROMFIELD, Louis. *A Few Brass Tacks.* 1946. New York. Harper. ex-lib. 303 pp. G $3.00

BROMFIELD, Louis. *A Good Woman.* 1927. New York. Stokes. 1st ed. 432 pp. $4.50

BROMFIELD, Louis. *Colorado.* 1947. New York. Harper. 263 pp. dj. VG $5.00

BROMFIELD, Louis. *From My Experience.* 1955. New York. Harper. 355 pp. dj. VG $8.00

BROMFIELD, Louis. *Modern Hero.* 1932. New York. Ltd. 1st ed. 1/250. sgn. $40.00

BROMFIELD, Louis. *Mrs. Parkington.* 1943. Collier. $5.00

BROMFIELD, Louis. *Mrs. Parkington.* 1943. New York. Harper. 330 pp. dj. $3.50

BROMFIELD, Louis. *Out of the Earth.* 1950. New York. Ills. 1st ed. 305 pp. dj. VG $20.00

BROMFIELD, Louis. *The Louis Bromfield Trilogy.* 1926. New York. inscr. 307 pp. $10.00

BROMFIELD, Louis. *The Rains Came.* 1937. New York. Harper. 597 pp. VG $3.50

BROMFIELD, Louis. *The Rains Came.* 1937. New York. Grosset & Dunlap. sgn. G $5.00

BROMFIELD, Louis. *The Strange Case of Miss Annie Spragg.* 1928. New York. 1st ed. 314 pp. G $10.00

BROMFIELD, Louis. *The World We Live In.* 1944. Philadelphia. 339 pp. VG $3.50

BROMWELL, J.H. *Masonic Code of the Grand Lodge of Ohio.* 1908. no place. 473 pp. $5.00

BRONGERSMA, L.D. & Venema, G. *The Mountains of the Stars.* 1963. Doubleday. Ills. 1st Am. ed. map. EX $15.00

BRONIEWSKI, W. *Le Combat La Mort Le Souvenir 1939-1945.* Ills. French text. G $40.00

BRONSON, B.H. *The Traditional Tunes of the Child Ballads.* 1966. Princeton. dj. VG $45.00

BRONSON, Charles Cook. *The Bronson Book.* no place. (ca.1976). 145 pp. EX $10.00

BRONSON, Wilfrid Swancourt. *Water People.* 1935. New York. Wise-Parslow. Ills. 1st ed. $25.00

BRONTE, Charlotte. *Jane Eyre.* 1944. 343 pp. pictorial board cover. $3.50

BRONTE, Charlotte. *Twelve Adventurers & Other Stories.* 1925. London. EX $20.00

BRONTE, P. *Detroit Murders.* 1948. New York. 1st ed. 218 pp. dj. VG $16.00

BROOK, Mary B. *Reasons for the Necessity of Silent Waiting.* 1780. Philadelphia. 1st Am. ed. wrappers. $50.00

BROOKE, Rupert. *Democracy & the Arts.* 1946. London. 1st ed. dj. VG $28.00

BROOKER, Anita. *A Start in Life.* 1981. London. Cape. 1st Am. ed. VG $55.00

BROOKES, L. *The Automobile Handbook.* 1908. Ills. VG $20.00

BROOKES, Richard. *The Art of Angling, Rock & Sea-Fishing.* 1740. London. Ills. 249 pp. $225.00

BROOKHOUSER, Frank. *She Made the Big Town.* 1952. U. of Kansas. Twayne Press. dj. $7.50

BROOKINGS INSTITUTION. *Major Problems of U.S. Foreign Policy 1954.* 1954. Menasha, WI. Banta Pub. ex-lib. 429 pp. VG $3.50

BROOKNER, Anita. *Family & Friends.* 1985. Cape. Ltd. 1st ed. 1/250. sgn. VG $75.00

BROOKNER, Anita. *Providence.* 1982. London. Cape. 1st ed. VG $35.00

BROOKNER, Anita. *The Debut.* 1981. New York. Linden. 1st ed. dj. EX $30.00

BROOKNER, Anita. *The Debut.* 1982. New York. Simon & Schuster. 1st Am. ed. $25.00

BROOKS, Charles. *Sensory Awareness.* 1974. New York. Viking. Esalen Book. $2.50

BROOKS, Charles. *Texas Missions.* 1936. Dallas. Ltd. ed. 1/200. sgn. VG $25.00

BROOKS, Elbridge. *The Story of the American Indian.* 1887. Boston. Ills. index. G $10.00

BROOKS, Fred Emerson. *Patriotic Toasts.* 1919. $4.00

BROOKS, G.S. *James Durand, an Able Seaman of 1812.* 1926. G $17.50

BROOKS, Helen M. *The Days of the Spinning Wheel in New England.* 1886. Boston. Ills. 99 pp. $10.00

BROOKS, Joe. *Bass Bug Fishing.* 1947. 1st ed. dj. VG $20.00

BROOKS, Joe. *Complete Book of Fly Fishing.* 1958. 1st ed. dj. EX $12.50

BROOKS, Joe. *Fly Fishing.* 1966. 1st ed. dj. EX $15.00

BROOKS, Joe. *Greatest Fishing.* 1957. 1st ed. dj. EX $10.00

BROOKS, Joe. *Salt Water Game Fishing.* 1968. 1st ed. dj. VG $15.00

BROOKS, John. *American Syndicalism.* 1913. New York. Macmillan. 1st ed. VG $50.00

BROOKS, John. *The Fate of Edsel & Other Business Adventures.* 1963. Harper & Row. 182 pp. dj. G $8.00

BROOKS, Noah. *First Across the Continent/Story of Lewis & Clark.* 1901. New York. Ills. 1st ed. map. VG $25.00

BROOKS, Noah. *The Boy Emigrants.* 1912. New York. Ills. Moran & Shephard. VG $12.00

BROOKS, Noah. *The Boy Emigrants.* 1925. New York. Ills. Dunn. 381 pp. $12.00

BROOKS, Philip Coolidge. *Diplomacy & Borderlands: Adams-Onis Treaty 1819.* 1939. Berkeley. Ills. 262 pp. wrappers. $75.00

BROOKS, T.R. *Toil & Trouble.* 1964. New York. dj. VG $10.00

BROOKS, Terry. *Magic Kingdom for Sale/Sold.* 1986. New York. 1st ed. inscr. sgn. dj. VG $20.00

BROOKS, Terry. *The Elfstones of Shannara.* 1982. New York. Del Ray. 1st ed. sgn. dj. EX $35.00

BROOKS, Terry. *The Sword of Shannara.* 1976. New York. Special Preview ed. wrappers. $25.00

BROOKS, Terry. *The Sword of Shannara.* 1977. Random House. 1st ed. dj. EX $25.00

BROOKS, Terry. *The Wishsong of Shannara.* 1985. New York. 1st ed. dj. VG $8.00

BROOKS, Van Wyck & Bettmann. *Our Literary Heritage.* 1956. New York. Dutton. Ills. 246 pp. dj. $15.00

BROOKS, Van Wyck. *New England: Indian Summer, 1865-1915.* 1940. New York. Dutton. 557 pp. $5.00

BROOKS, Van Wyck. *The Flowering of New England 1815-1865.* 1937. Dutton. new revised ed. 550 pp. $5.00

BROOKS, Van Wyck. *The Flowering of New England.* 1936. Dutton. 1st ed. dj. $25.00

BROOKS, Van Wyck. *The World of Washington Irving.* 1944. New York. Dutton. 387 pp. dj. $4.00

BROPHY, A. *The Air Force.* 1956. New York. 362 pp. dj. $5.00

BROPHY, B. *Flesh.* 1962. World. 1st ed. dj. $10.00

BRORUP, R.P. *Truth & Poetry.* 1897. Chicago. International Book Co. 114 pp. $12.50

BROSSARD, Chandler. *Dirty Books for Little Folks.* 1978. 1st ed. wrappers. EX $35.00

BROSSARD, Chandler. *The Spanish Scene.* 1968. Viking. 1st ed. dj. VG $27.50

BROTHER JONATHAN. *The Butchers of Ghent.* 1842. New York. $40.00

BROUGH, Robert B. *The Life of Sir John Falstaff.* 1858. London. Ills. Cruikshank. rebound. VG $225.00

BROUGHTON, Alan. *Winter Journey.* 1980. New York. Dutton. 1st ed. dj. EX $25.00

BROUGHTON, J. *Thud Ridge.* 1960. 1st ed. dj. EX $17.50

BROUGHTON, James. *A Long Undressing. Collected Poems 1949-1969.* 1971. New York. 1st ed. dj. EX $15.00

BROUGHTON, James. *Musical Chairs.* 1950. Centaur. inscr. dj. EX $20.00

BROUGHTON, James. *The Playground.* 1949. Centaur. Ills. dj. VG $7.50

BROUGHTON, James. *The Right Playmate.* 1952. Hart Davis. Ills. Hoffnug. dj. VG $7.50

BROUGHTON, Rhoda. *Twilight Stories.* 1947. London. 99 pp. dj. VG $12.50

BROUGHTON. *The Magistrates of the Roman Republic.* 2 vol set. VG $25.00

BROUMAS, O. *Beginning with O.* 1977. 1st ed. wrappers. $10.00

BROUMAS, O. *Caritas.* 1976. Jackrabbit Press. 1st ed. $26.50

BROUN, Haywood & Leech, M. *Anthony Comstock, Roundsman of the Lord.* 1927. New York. Boni. Ills. 285 pp. dj. VG $15.00

BROUN, Haywood. *A Shepherd.* 1926. New York. Ltd. ed. 1/245. dj. $15.00

BROUN, Haywood. *Our Army at the Front.* 1918. New York. Scribner. Ills. 265 pp. $3.50

BROWER, C.D. *Fifty Years Below Zero.* 1948. Dodd Mead. photos. 310 pp. VG $10.00

BROWER, David. *The Meaning of Wilderness to Science.* 1960. Sierra Club. photos. AL map. 129 pp. dj. $8.00

BROWER, J.H. *The Mills of Mammon.* 1909. Joliet. 2nd ed. dj. $100.00

BROWN, A.J. *New Forces in Old China.* 1904. New York. Revell. 2nd ed. fld map. G $20.00

BROWN, Aaron V. *Speeches, Congressional & Political, & Writings.* 1854. Nashville. Ills. 1st ed. 706 pp. $45.00

BROWN, Alec, trans. *The Voyage of the Chelyuskin.* 1935. New York. Ills. 325 pp. maps. pls. dj. $27.50

BROWN, Alexander. *The Cabells & Their Kin.* 1978. Harrisonburg. reprint. Ills. 708 pp. $42.50

BROWN, B. *Gems, a Censored Anthology.* 1931. Paris. Roving Eye Press. wrappers. $125.00

BROWN, B. *Globe-Gliding.* 1930. Diessen. Roving Eye Press. wrappers. $46.50

BROWN, B. *Texas.* 1938. Naylor. 1st ed. sgn. VG $40.00

BROWN, Barrington. *Canoe & Camp Life in British Columbia.* 1876. London. color pls. $90.00

BROWN, Beth. *Universal Station.* 1944. Regent House. 1st ed. dj. $15.00

BROWN, Bob, Rose, & Cora. *Most for Your Money Cookbook.* 1938. New York. Modern Age. 1st ed. dj. VG $35.00

BROWN, Bolton. *Lithography.* 1923. Ltd. ed. 1/500. VG $18.00

BROWN, C. *Manchild in the Promised Land.* 1965. New York. advance copy. wrappers. VG $65.00

BROWN, C. *My Ditty Bag.* 1925. Boston. dj. EX $10.00

BROWN, C.W. *Salt Dishes.* 1968. Des Moines. dj. $35.00

BROWN, Cecil. *Days Without Weather.* 1982. New York. Farrar. advance copy. EX $30.00

BROWN, Cecil. *The Life & Loves of Mr. Jiveass Nigger.* 1969. 1st ed. dj. EX $10.00

BROWN, Christy. *A Shadow on Summer.* 1975. Stein & Day. 1st Am. ed. dj. VG $15.00

BROWN, Christy. *Down All the Days.* 1970. Stein & Day. 1st Am. ed. dj. VG $25.00

BROWN, D.C. *Yukon Trophy Trails.* 1971. map. 213 pp. dj. $30.00

BROWN, D.E. *Grizzly in Southwest, Documentary of Extinction.* 1985. OK U. Press. Ills. 1st ed. 274 pp. $20.00

BROWN, Dale & Time Life Eds. *American Cooking.* 1968. New York. Ills. 208 pp. $10.00

BROWN, Dee & Schmitt, M.F. *Fighting Indians of the West.* 1948. 1st ed. VG $50.00

BROWN, Dee. *Bury My Heart at Wounded Knee.* 1970. New York. 487 pp. dj. $6.00

BROWN, Dee. *Creek Mary's Blood.* 1980. New York. 1st ed. 433 pp. dj. EX $20.00

BROWN, Dee. *Creek Mary's Blood.* 1980. Winston. 433 pp. dj. VG $20.00

BROWN, Dee. *Killdeer Mountain.* 1983. New York. Holt. 1st ed. dj. EX $25.00

BROWN, Dee. *The Westerners.* 1974. New York. Ills. photos. 288 pp. $6.00

BROWN, Dee. *Trail Driving Days.* 1952. 1st ed. dj. EX $35.00

BROWN, Dorothy F. *Button Parade.* 1942. Chicago. Ills. 2nd ed. 143 pp. VG $20.00

BROWN, E.K. *Willa Cather.* 1953. Knopf. 1st ed. dj. $12.50

BROWN, E.R. *27th Indiana Volunteer Infantry.* 1899. Monticello. 1st ed. inscr. rare $200.00

BROWN, Eleanor & Bob. *Culinary Americana.* 1961. 1st ed. index. $30.00

BROWN, Elijah P. *Blasts from a Ram's Horn.* 1893. Cincinnati. 388 pp. $12.50

BROWN, F. *Honeymoon in Hell.* 1958. Bantam pb. 1st ed. VG $12.50

BROWN, F. *The Screaming Mimi.* 1949. 1st ed. dj. $10.00

BROWN, F. *What a Mad Universe.* 1949. New York. 1st ed. dj. $17.50

BROWN, F.C. *Letters & Lettering.* 1906. Boston. G $12.50

BROWN, Francis H. *Harvard University in the War of 1861-1865.* 1886. Boston. G $20.00

BROWN, Fredric. *Madman's Holiday.* 1985. Ltd. ed. 1/350. sgn. dj. EX $30.00

BROWN, Fredric. *The Case of the Dancing Sandwiches.* 1985. Ltd. ed. 1/400. dj. EX $30.00

BROWN, Fredric. *The Late Lamented.* 1959. New York. Dutton. 1st ed. dj. VG $25.00

BROWN, George. *Harold the Klansman.* 1923. Kansas City. Western Baptist Pub. G $25.00

BROWN, H.B. *Cotton.* 1938. New York. Ills. VG $6.00

BROWN, Henry Collins. *From Alley Pond to Rockefeller Center.* 1936. New York. Ills. 1st ed. dj. VG $15.00

BROWN, Henry Collins. *Valentine's City of New York Guide Book.* 1920. wrappers. VG $7.50

BROWN, Henry Collins. *Valentine's Manual of Old New York.* 1927. New York. Ills. 4 color pls. $40.00

BROWN, Irving. *Gypsy Fires in America.* 1924. Harper. Ills. 1st ed. VG $30.00

BROWN, J.F. *Abnormal Psychodynamics.* 1940. $6.00

BROWN, J.P.S. *Jim Kane.* 1970. New York. 1st ed. dj. EX $27.50

BROWN, Jesse & Willard, A.M. *Black Hills Trails/Hist. of Struggles of Pioneers.* 1924. Rapid City. VG $100.00

BROWN, Jimmy & Cope, Myron. *Off My Chest.* 1964. New York. Doubleday. dj. VG $5.00

BROWN, John J. *American Angler's Guide.* 1850. 4th ed. 332 pp. $95.00

BROWN, John M. *Daniel Boone.* 1951. New York. Random House. 177 pp. $4.00

BROWN, John M. *To All Hands.* 1943. New York. photos. 236 pp. VG $3.50

BROWN, John. *A Short Catechism.* 1822. Pittsburg. Andrews. 80 pp. wrappers. $35.00

BROWN, John. *Jeems the Doorkeeper & Other Essays.* 1912. Edinburgh. Ills. Macgoun. 1st ed. VG $20.00

BROWN, Joseph E. *The Mormon Trek West.* 1980. Garden City. Ills. 184 pp. index. dj. EX $20.00

BROWN, Julia. *The Enchanted Peacock.* 1911. Rand McNally. Ills. Lucy Fitch Perkins. VG $25.00

BROWN, K.F. *California Missions.* 1939. Garden City. Ills. VG $7.50

BROWN, Leslie. *Birds of Prey, Their Biology & Ecology.* 1976. London. Ills. 1st ed. 256 pp. dj. $25.00

BROWN, Leslie. *Eagles of the World.* 1976. David & Charles. Ills. 224 pp. $20.00

BROWN, Leslie. *Eagles.* 1955. London. Sci. Book Club. map. 274 pp. $15.00

BROWN, Leslie. *The African Fish Eagle.* 1980. England. Bailey Swinfen. Ills. 168 pp. $15.00

BROWN, Lloyd L. *Lift Every Voice for Paul Robeson.* 1951. New York. Freedom Associates. wrappers. $20.00

BROWN, Lloyd L. *Stand Up for Freedom!* 1952. New York. Century. 1st ed. wrappers. VG $20.00

BROWN, Lucinda W. *Aunty Brown in the New Shoe.* Akron. Ills. 79 pp. wrappers. $22.50

BROWN, Lucinda W. *Aunty Brown's Story, Token of Love & Friendship.* 1908. Akron. Ills. 60 pp. $22.50

BROWN, M. *Before Barbed Wire.* 1956. New York. Holt. 1st ed. 256 pp. dj. $40.00

BROWN, M. *Jacob Lawrence.* 1974. Whitney Museum. 1st ed. dj. EX $10.00

BROWN, M. *Madagascar Rediscovered.* 1979. Archon. Ills. 1st ed. 9 maps. 310 pp. $22.00

BROWN, M.W. *When the Wind Blew.* 1977. Ills. Hayes. 1st ed. dj. VG $12.50

BROWN, Marcia. *Cinderella.* 1954. Scribner. Ills. VG $15.00

BROWN, Marcia. *Dick Whittington & His Cat.* 1950. New York. dj. VG $17.50

BROWN, Marcia. *Henry-Fisherman.* 1949. New York. Ills. author. 1st ed. VG $40.00

BROWN, Marcia. *The Blue Jackal.* 1977. New York. Ills. author. 1st printing. VG $15.00

BROWN, Marcia. *The Flying Carpet.* 1956. Scribner. 1st ed. dj. VG $20.00

BROWN, Margaret Wise. *Little Pigs Picnic.* 1939. Boston. Ills. Disney Studio. $30.00

BROWN, Margaret Wise. *The Important Book.* 1949. Harper. Ills. Weisgard. VG $12.00

BROWN, R.M. *A Plain Brown Rapper.* 1976. Diana Press. 1st ed. wrappers. $10.00

BROWN, R.M. *In Her Day.* 1976. Daughters, Inc.1st ed. wrappers. $10.00

BROWN, R.M. *Sudden Death.* 1983. Bantam. review copy. dj. EX $15.00

BROWN, Robert H. *Farm Electrification.* 1956. New York. McGraw Hill. 367 pp. VG $3.50

BROWN, Rosellen. *Cora Fry.* 1977. Norton. sgn. dj. EX $25.00

BROWN, Rosellen. *Some Deaths in the Delta.* 1970. U. of MA. Pr. 1st ed. wrappers. VG $35.00

BROWN, Rosellen. *Street Games.* 1974. Doubleday. sgn. dj. VG $35.00

BROWN, Rosellen. *Tender Mercies.* 1978. Knopf. 1st ed. sgn. dj. VG $37.50

BROWN, Rosellen. *The Autobiography of My Mother.* 1976. Garden City. Doubleday. 1st ed. dj. EX $30.00

BROWN, Rosemary. *Unfinished Symphonies.* 1971. New York. Morrow. 192 pp. dj. $4.00

BROWN, S.A. *The Guide to South & East Africa.* 1913. London. 19th ed. $40.00

BROWN, Samuel R. *The Western Gazetteer; or, Emigrant's Directory.* 1817. Auburn, NY. 360 pp. EX $200.00

BROWN, T. *Taxidermist's Manual.* 1883. VG $17.50

BROWN, William Griffee. *History of Nicholas County, West Virginia.* 1981. Richwood. reprint. Ills. 425 pp. $25.00

BROWN, William H. *Glory Seekers; Early Days of Great Southwest.* 1906. Chicago. Ills. 1st ed. 347 pp. $25.00

BROWN, William H. *Hear That Lonesome Whistle Blow.* 1977. 1st ed. dj. VG $20.00

BROWN, William H. *The History of the First Locomotive in America.* 1871. New York. Ills. EX $125.00

BROWN & ARBUTHNOT. *Story of England.* Random House. (ca.1943) Ills. Tenggren. G $7.50

BROWNE, B. *Conquest of Mt. McKinley.* 1956. Ills. new ed. VG $10.00

BROWNE, Charles. *Gun Club Cookbook.* 1934. G $10.00

BROWNE, D.G. *The American Bird Fancier.* 1881. New York. Ills. 116 pp. wrappers. VG $20.00

BROWNE, D.J. *The Trees of America Native & Foreign.* 1851. Harper. Ills. 520 pp. $65.00

BROWNE, D.J. *Trees of America.* 1857. 520 pp. $38.00

BROWNE, Francis. *Bugle-Echoes.* 1886. New York. 1st ed. 336 pp. VG $20.00

BROWNE, Francis. *Granny's Wonderful Chair.* 1924. New York. Ills. Emma Brock. 1st ed. VG $20.00

BROWNE, Howard. *Warrior of the Dawn.* 1943. 1st ed. dj. G $40.00

BROWNE, J.R. *Washoe Revisited: Notes on Silver Regions of NV.* 1957. Oakland. Ltd. 1st CA ed. EX $60.00

BROWNE, M. *Artistic & Scientific Taxidermy.* 1896. London. VG $45.00

BROWNE, Thomas. *Religio Medici.* 1939. Eugene, OR. Ltd. ed. 1/1500. 113 pp. VG $65.00

BROWNELL, Charles DeWolf. *The Indian Races of North & South America.* 1853. New York. Ills. 640 pp. $47.50

BROWNELL, Henry Howard. *Pioneer Heroes of the New World.* 1859. Ills. rebound. VG $25.00

BROWNELL, Henry Howard. *Pioneer Heroes of the New World.* 1856. Cincinnati. Ills. 736 pp. G $35.00

BROWNELL, Henry Howard. *The New World Embracing American History.* 1855. New York. Ills. 46 color pls. $40.00

BROWNELL, Sam. *Rodeos & Tipperary.* 1961. Denver. 126 pp. wrappers. $20.00

BROWNING, Elizabeth Barrett. *Last Poems.* 1862. London. 1st ed. $35.00

BROWNING, Elizabeth Barrett. *Sonnets from Portuguese.* London. (ca.1900's) Ills. EX $125.00

BROWNING, Elizabeth Barrett. *The Poet's Enchiridion.* 1914. Boston. Bibliophile Soc. VG $15.00

BROWNING, Meshach. *Forty-Four Years of the Life of a Hunter.* 1859. Ills. Stabler. VG $55.00

BROWNING, Robert. *Complete Poems.* 1895. Boston. 1033 pp. $150.00

BROWNING, Robert. *Pied Piper of Hamelin.* 1934. Whitman. Ills. 39 pp. SftCvr. G $3.50

BROWNING, Robert. *Pied Piper of Hamelin.* Warne. Ills. Greenaway. 48 pp. VG $17.50

BROWNING, Robert. *Poems.* 1896. G $75.00

BROWNING, Robert. *Prince Hohenstiel-Schwangau, Savior of Society.* 1871. London. 1st ed. $45.00

BROWNING, Robert. *Rabbi Ben Ezra.* London. Hodder Stoughton. Ills. VG $30.00

BROWNING, Robert. *Red Cotton Night-Cap Country.* 1873. London. 1st ed. VG $45.00

BROWNING, Robert. *Ring & the Book.* 1868. Smith Elder. 1st eds. 4 vol set. $150.00

BROWNING, Robert. *The Inn Album.* 1875. London. 1st ed. VG $35.00

BROWNING, S. *Enju.* 1982. Northland Pr. 1st ed. dj. VG $15.00

BROWNING, Tod. *The Mocking Bird.* 1925. Jacobsen-Hodgkinson Co. Ills. $5.50

BROWNLEE, Richard. *Gray Ghosts of the Confederacy.* 1958. L.S.U. Press. 1st ed. sgn. dj. VG $12.50

BROWNLOW, Kevin. *The War, the West, & the Wilderness.* 1979. New York. Ills. 1st ed. 602 pp. dj. VG $15.00

BROWNLOW, W.G. *Sketches/Rise, Progress, & Decline of Successsion.* 1862. 1st ed. $16.50

BROWNSTONE PRESS, INC. *The Republican Cookbook.* 1969. Brownstone Press. 200 pp. dj. $4.50

BROZEK, Joseph. *The Biology of Human Variation.* 1966. NY. stiff wrappers. $10.00

BRUBAKER. *The Last Capital: Danville, VA.* 1979. dj. VG $15.00

BRUCATO, J. *The Farmer Goes to Town.* 1949. San Francisco. Burke. VG $10.00

BRUCCOLI, Matthew. *Selected Letters of John O'Hara.* 1978. New York. Random House. 1st ed. 538 pp. $7.50

BRUCCOLI, SMITH & KERR. *The Romantic Egoists.* 1974. Scribner. dj. EX $20.00

BRUCE, James. *Little Things to Please Little Minds.* 1979. Cambridge. Ltd 1st ed. 1/400. 22 pp. $20.00

BRUCE, P.A. *History of University of Virginia 1819-1919.* 1920. New York. 1st ed. 5 vol set. VG $60.00

BRUCE, Robert. *Pawnee Naming Ceremonial.* 1932. Private Pub. Ills. 1st ed. 36 pp. map. VG $10.00

BRUMBAUGH, Gaius Marcus. *Genealogy of Descendants of Theobald Fauss.* 1914. Baltimore. Ills. 1st ed. 289 pp. VG $27.50

BRUNER, Jane W. *Free Prisoners. A Story of California Life.* 1877. Philadelphia. 258 pp. G $10.00

BRUNFORD, Sheila. *Bel Ria.* 1978. Boston. 1st ed. dj. EX $10.00

BRUNHOFF, Jean de. *Les Vacances de Zephir Librairie Hachett.* 1936. G $80.00

BRUNHOUSE, Robert L. *The Counter-Revolution in Pennsylvania 1776-1790.* 1942. Harrisburg. 368 pp. $10.00

BRUNK, Max E. & Darrah, L.B. *Marketing of Agricultural Products.* 1955. New York. Ronald Press Co. 419 pp. VG $4.50

BRUNNER, J. *Sanctuary in the Sky.* 1960. Ace Double Novel. 1st ed. $12.50

BRUNNER, John. *Dreaming Earth.* 1963. New York. Pyramid. 1st ed. EX $7.50

BRUNNER, John. *From This Day Forward.* 1972. 1st ed. dj. $10.00

BRUNNER, John. *The Crucible of Time.* 1983. New York. 1st ed. dj. VG $10.00

BRUNNER, John. *The Sheep Look Up.* 1972. New York. Harper. 1st ed. dj. EX $35.00

BRUNNER, John. *The Shockwave Rider.* 1975. 1st ed. dj. $10.00

BRUNNER, Joseph. *Tracks & Tracking.* 1909. New York. Ills. $10.00

BRUNNER, Lousene. *Casserole Treasury.* 1964. New York. Harper. 310 pp. $5.00

BRUNO, Harry. *Wings Over America.* 1942. New York. Ills. 1st ed. VG $10.00

BRUNO, Harry. *Wings: Story of American Aviation, Illustrated.* 1944. Garden City. photos. 333 pp. dj. $7.50

BRUNS, Vincent G. *The Red Harvest. A Cry for Peace.* 1930. New York. presentation copy. 433 pp. $7.50

BRUNTON, Paul. *A Search in Secret India.* 1945. photos. $2.00

BRUNVAND, Jan Harold. *The Study of American Folklore.* 1968. New York. Norton. Ills. 383 pp. $12.50

BRUSH, Daniel Harmon. *Growing Up with Southern Illinois, 1820-1861.* 1944. Chicago. Ills. $8.50

BRUSTEIN, Robert. *The Culture Watch. Essays on Theatre & Society.* 1975. New York. Knopf. 1st ed. 197 pp. dj. $7.50

BRUUN, B. *Birds of Europe.* 1971. Golden Press. Ills. Singer. maps. 321 pp. $25.00

BRUUN, L. *Promised Isle.* 1922. 1st ed. $6.50

BRYAN, C.D.B. *Wilkinson.* 1965. Harper. dj. EX $25.00

BRYAN, John. *Fables & Essays, Vol. I.* 1895. New York. 244 pp. $17.50

BRYAN, William Jennings. *The Royal Art.* 1914. Revell. VG $40.00

BRYANT, Arthur. *Nelson.* 1970. 1st ed. dj. $8.50

BRYANT, Arthur. *The Turn of the Tide.* 1957. New York. Doubleday. 624 pp. EX $8.00

BRYANT, B. *Children of Ol' Man River.* 1936. Ills. VG $10.00

BRYANT, E. *What I Saw in California.* 1967. Haines. reprint. Ltd. ed. EX $12.50

BRYANT, E. *What I Saw in California.* 1848. New York. 1st ed. 455 pp. VG $125.00

BRYANT, H. Stafford, Jr. *The Georgian Locomotive.* 1962. dj. $5.00

BRYANT, Jacob. *A New System or Analysis of Ancient Mythology.* 1807. London. 3rd ed. 41 pls. 6 vol set. VG $85.00

BRYANT, Louise. *Six Months in Red Russia.* 1918. Doran. VG $32.50

BRYANT, Sara Cone. *Best Stories to Tell to Children.* 1912. New York. Ills. P. Wilson. $25.00

BRYANT, William Cullen. *Picturesque America.* 1872. New York. folio. 6 vol set. EX $250.00

BRYANT, William Cullen. *Picturesque America; or, The Land We Live In.* 1872. New York. Ills. 2 vol set. $150.00

BRYANT, Edwin. *Voyage en Californie.* Paris. (ca.1850) fld map. $80.00

BRYANT. *Poems.* Heritage Press. boxed. VG $7.50

BRYANT. *Railways, a Reader's Guide.* 1968. 1st ed. dj. VG $25.00

BRYANT. *The New Standard Commercial Bookkeeping.* 1885. 160 pp. $3.50

BRYCE, George. *The Old Settlers of Red River.* 1885. Winnipeg. 1st ed. wrappers. $75.00

BRYCE, James. *International Relations.* 1922. New York. Macmillan. 275 pp. $3.50

BRYCE, James. *Social Institutions of the United States.* 1891. New York. Chautauqua Press. 298 pp. $12.50

BRYCE, James. *The American Commonwealth. Vol. II* 1920. New York. Macmillan. new ed. VG $4.00

BRYER, Jackson R. *Conversations with Lillian Hellman.* 1986. U. Press MS. 1st ed. dj. VG $20.00

BRYHER, W. *Ruan.* 1960. New York. 1st ed. dj. EX $12.50

BRYNNER, Yul. *The Yul Brynner Cookbook.* 1983. New York. VG $15.00

BRYSON, Lyman. *Smoky Roses.* 1916. New York. Putnam. 1st ed. 104 pp. $5.00

BRZEZINSKI, Zbigniew. *Africa & the Communist World.* 1963. Stanford, CA. exlib. 272 pp. dj. VG $4.50

BUBER, Martin. *Tales of the Hasidim: the Late Masters.* 1948. 1st ed. dj. VG $17.50

BUCHAN, John. *A History of the Great War.* 1922. Boston. Ills. Ltd. ed. sgn. dj. VG $135.00

BUCHAN, John. *Augustus.* 1937. Boston. 1st ed. VG $12.50

BUCHAN, John. *Castle Gay.* 1930. London. 1st ed. dj. VG $120.00

BUCHAN, John. *Greenmantle.* London. 1923 reprint. VG $25.00

BUCHAN, John. *Island of Sheep.* 1936. London. 1st ed. VG $15.00

BUCHAN, John. *Lake of Gold.* 1944. Toronto. Musson. 1st Canadian ed. dj. $20.00

BUCHAN, John. *Lord Minto.* 1925. London. Ills. 4th ed. VG $22.50

BUCHAN, John. *Montrose.* London. 1st ed. sgn. scarce $40.00

BUCHAN, John. *Principles of Social Service.* 1933. Glasgow. wrappers. rare. EX $95.00

BUCHAN, John. *Salute to Adventurers.* 1915. New York. Doran. 1st Am. ed. VG $20.00

BUCHAN, John. *The Battle of Jutland.* London. Nelson. Ills. wrappers. EX $20.00

BUCHAN, John. *The Blanket of the Dark.* 1931. London. 1st printing. dj. VG $110.00

BUCHAN, John. *The Power House.* 1916. Blackwood. 1st ed. $35.00

BUCHAN, John. *The Thirty-Nine Steps.* 1915. Edinburgh. 1st ed. G $80.00

BUCHAN, John. *The Thirty-Nine Steps.* 1964. London. Ills. Adrizzone. 1st ed. EX $15.00

BUCHAN, William. *Buchan's Domestic Medicine.* 1824. Edinburgh. rebound. G $190.00

BUCHAN, William. *Domestic Medicine.* 1799. Philadelphia. 512 pp. $100.00

BUCHAN, William. *Domestic Medicine. With Advice to Mothers.* 1807. Charleston, SC. $75.00

BUCHANAN, Andrew. *The Art of Film Production.* 1936. London. Pitman. Ills. 1st ed. 99 pp. $27.50

BUCHANAN, H. *Treasury of Natural History Books.* 1979. Mayflower. Ills. 1st Am. ed. 220 pp. dj. $50.00

BUCHANAN, James. *Utah Territory. Message from Buchanan.* 1860. Washington. 1st ed. 51 pp. $65.00

BUCHANAN, Lamont. *A Pictorial History of the Confederacy.* 1951. Ills. 288 pp. $13.50

BUCHANAN. *Canadian Painters.* 1945. $38.00

BUCHENHOLZ, B. *Doctor in the Zoo.* 1975. David & Charles. Ills. 191 pp. $12.00

BUCHER, Francois. *The Pamplona Bibles.* 1970. New Haven. 2 vol set. boxed. EX $150.00

BUCHER, L. *Man in the Past, Present, & Future.* 1872. Lippincott. 1st Am. ed. $15.00

BUCHER, Lloyd M. *Bucher: My Story.* 1970. New York. Ills. 447 pp. dj. VG $10.00

BUCHWALD, Art. *'I Am Not a Crook.'* 1974. New York. Putnam. 250 pp. dj. $3.50

BUCHWALD, Art. *Laid Back in Washington.* 1981. New York. 1st ed. 311 pp. dj. EX $7.50

BUCHWALD, Art. *The Buchwald Stops Here.* 1978. New York. Putnam. 295 pp. VG $3.50

BUCK, Bob. *Burning Up the Sky.* 1931. New York. sgn. dj. VG $12.50

BUCK, Carl Darling. *Comparative Grammar of Greek & Latin.* 1969. Chicago. 11th impression. $17.50

BUCK, Charles. *Memoirs of Chas. Buck Interspersed with Anecdotes.* 1941. Walnut House. $12.50

BUCK, Edward. *Massachusetts Ecclesiastical Law.* 1866. 310 pp. $5.00

BUCK, Margaret W. *Animals Through the Year.* 1941. Rand McNally. Ills. dj. VG $10.00

BUCK, Pearl & Romulo, Carlos. *Friend to Friend.* 1958. New York. ex-lib. 126 pp. dj. $3.50

BUCK, Pearl S. *All Under Heaven.* 1973. New York. John Day. 1st ed. dj. EX $25.00

BUCK, Pearl S. *Command the Morning.* 1959. John Day. 1st ed. dj. VG $20.00

BUCK, Pearl S. *Dragon Seed.* 1943. $4.00

BUCK, Pearl S. *Dragon Seed.* 1946. Philadelphia. 378 pp. VG $3.50

BUCK, Pearl S. *Fighting Angel, Portrait of a Soul.* 1936. New York. 302 pp. $4.50

BUCK, Pearl S. *Fighting Angel.* 1972. John Day. sgn. dj. $15.00

BUCK, Pearl S. *House Divided.* 1935. EX $12.50

BUCK, Pearl S. *Imperial Woman.* 1956. New York. 346 pp. dj. VG $3.50

BUCK, Pearl S. *My Several Worlds, A Personal Record.* 1954. New York. 407 pp. dj. VG $5.00

BUCK, Pearl S. *Of Men & Women.* 1971. John Day. dj. $15.00

BUCK, Pearl S. *Pearl Buck's America.* 1971. Bartholomew House. Ills. dj. $5.00

BUCK, Pearl S. *Peony.* 1948. John Day. 312 pp. VG $7.50

BUCK, Pearl S. *The Exile.* 1936. New York. 315 pp. VG $4.50

BUCK, Pearl S. *The Living Reed.* 1963. New York. 478 pp. $3.50

BUCK, Pearl S. *The Patriot.* 1939. New York. 372 pp. G $2.50

BUCK, Pearl S. *The Promise.* 1942. John Day. 248 pp. dj. VG $4.50

BUCK, Pearl S. *The Time Is Noon.* 1966. New York. John Day. 1st ed. dj. VG $30.00

BUCK, Pearl S. *The Woman Who Was Changed & Other Stories.* 1979. New York. John Day. 1st ed. dj. EX $25.00

BUCK, Pearl S. *To My Daughters, with Love.* 1972. John Day. Ltd. ed. sgn. $20.00

BUCK, Solon. *Planting of Civilization in Western Pennsylvania.* 1939. U. of Pittsburgh. 1st ed. dj. $12.50

BUCK, William J. *History of Montgomery County.* 1859. Norristown. $25.00

BUCKBEE, Edna. *Pioneer Days of Angel Camp.* 1932. wrappers. $20.00

BUCKINGHAM, J. *Travels in Palestine.* 1822. London. 2nd ed. 2 vol set. VG $95.00

BUCKINGHAM, James. *Ancestors of Ebenezer Buckingham & Descendants.* 1892. Chicago. G $25.00

BUCKINGHAM, Nash. *Blood Lines, Tales of Shooting & Fishing.* 1947. New York. 1st trade ed. dj. EX $45.00

BUCKINGHAM, Nash. *Blood Lines.* Derrydale Pr. Ltd. ed. 1/1250. VG $250.00

BUCKINGHAM, Nash. *Game Bag.* 1945. Putnam. dj. VG $45.00

BUCKINGHAM, Nash. *Ole Miss'.* Derrydale Pr. Ltd. ed. 1/1250. VG $300.00

BUCKINGHAM, Nash. *Shootin'est Gent'man & Other Hunting Tales.* 1961. Nelson. Ills. Greene. 1st ed. dj. $45.00

BUCKINGHAM, Nash. *Tattered Coat.* 1944. Putnam. 2nd ed. dj. VG $30.00

BUCKINGHAM. *America, Historical, Statistic, & Descriptive.* 1841. New York. 2 vol set. $40.00

BUCKLES, M.P. *Animals of the World.* 1978. Ridge Press. Ills. 240 pp. dj. $18.00

BUCKLEY, Arthur. *Principles & Deceptions.* 1948. Springfield. Ills. 1st ed. 224 pp. $45.00

BUCKLEY, L.J. *Antiques & Their History.* 1927. Binghampton. $25.00

BUCKLEY, W. *Art of Glass.* 1939. London. Ills. 1st ed. EX $55.00

BUCKLEY, William F. *Airborne.* 1976. Macmillan. 1st ed. dj. VG $45.00

BUCKLEY, William. F. *A Hymnal.* 1978. New York. Putnam. 1st ed. inscr. dj. EX $30.00

BUCKMAN, George R. *Colorado Springs.* 1893. CO Springs, CO. 2nd ed. photos Jackson. EX $85.00

BUCOVICH, Marie V. *Berlin in Photograph.* 1928. Berlin. 256 pp. $20.00

BUDAY, G. *History of the Christmas Card.* 1964. London. dj. $45.00

BUDD, Anne Lockwood. *Richland County Ohio Abstracts of Willis, 1813-73.* 1974. Mansfield, OH. 241 pp. EX $22.50

BUDD, J.L. & Hanses, N.E. *American Horticultural Manual Part I.* 1911. New York. Wiley. 417 pp. VG $4.50

BUDD, Lillian. *Tekla's Easter.* 1962. Ills. 1st ed. EX $20.00

BUDGE, E.A. Wallis. *Book of the Dead.* 1895. 1st Eng. trans. ex-lib. $185.00

BUDGE, E.A. Wallis. *Book of the Dead: Papyrus of Ani.* 1913. New York. Ills. 1st Am. ed. 3 vol set. $225.00

BUDGE, E.A. Wallis. *Cook's Handbook for Egypt & Egyptian Sudan.* 1921. London. Ills. 4th ed. 956 pp. 9 maps. $85.00

BUDGE, E.A. Wallis. *Egyptian Language.* 1958. London. 7th ed. 246 pp. $28.00

BUDGEN, Frank. *James Joyce & the Making of Ulysses.* 1934. Grayson & Grayson. 1st ed. VG $7.50

BUECHNER, Frederick. *A Long Day's Dying.* 1949. Knopf. 1st ed. dj. VG $50.00

BUECHNER, Frederick. *Norman Rockwell, a Sixty Year Retrospective.* 1972. Abrams. 159 Ills. dj. EX $17.50

BUECHNER, Frederick. *The Entrance to Porlock.* 1970. Atheneum. 1st ed. dj. VG $22.50

BUECHNER, Frederick. *The Hungered Dark.* 1969. Seabury. 1st ed. dj. VG $25.00

BUECHNER, Frederick. *The Return of Ansel Gibbs.* 1958. Knopf. 1st ed. dj. VG $40.00

BUEL, J.W. *Glimpses of America.* New York. Langan & Bro. Ills. dj. VG $27.50

BUEL, J.W. *Heroes of the Dark Continent.* 1889. North Am. Pub. 500 engravings. $100.00

BUEL, R. *The Native Problem in Africa.* 1928. New York. 2 vol set. VG $35.00

BUEL. *America's Wonderlands. Country's Scenic Marvels.* 1893. Boston. Ills. 1st ed. folio. $110.00

BUEL. *America's Wonderlands. Country's Scenic Marvels.* 1893. Cincinnati. Ills. 503 pp. VG $85.00

BUFFET-CHALLIE. *Flower Decoration in European Homes.* 1969. Morrow. dj. EX $30.00

BUFFEY, Vern. *Black & White & Never Right.* 1980. Toronto. Wiley. 151 pp. dj. EX $8.50

BUFFUM, George T. *Smith of Bear City & Other Frontier Sketches.* 1906. New York. Grafton Press. VG $45.00

BUFKIN, J. Earl. *Handling Your Hunting Dogs.* 1947. St.Louis, MO. 9th ed. Ills. 64 pp. EX $4.00

BUGATTI, L'Ebe. *Bugatti Story.* 1967. Pittsburgh. 1st ed. photos. dj. EX $12.50

BUHL, H. *Nanga Parbat Pilgrimage.* 1956. London. Ills. 1st ed. VG $15.00

BUIST, R. *Family Kitchen Garden.* 1852. 216 pp. $23.00

BUITENHUIS, Peter. *Grasping Imagination. Am. Writings of Henry James.* 1973. Toronto. dj. VG $10.00

BUKOWSKI, C. *Burning in Water/Drowning in Flame.* 1974. Ltd. ed. 1/300. sgn. $26.50

BUKOWSKI, C. *Crucifix in a Deathhand.* 1965. Loujon Press. EX $45.00

BUKOWSKI, C. *Dangling in Turnefortia.* 1981. Ltd. ed. 1/100. sgn. $10.00

BUKOWSKI, C. *It Catches My Heart in Its Hands.* 1963. Loujon Press. Ltd. ed. 1/777. sgn. $95.00

BUKOWSKI, C. *Love Poem.* 1979. Ltd. ed. 1/176. sgn. $30.00

BUKOWSKI, C. *Poems Written Before Jumping Out 8 Story Window.* 1968. 1st ed. wrappers. $10.00

BUKOWSKI, C. *What They Want.* Ltd. ed. 1/75. sgn. $45.00

BUKOWSKI-WAKOSKI. *Tough Company.* 1976. Ltd. ed. 1/176. sgns. $55.00

BULEY, E.C. *The Old Northwest.* 1962. Indianapolis. 3rd printing. 2 vols boxed. EX $35.00

BULEY, E.C. *The Old Northwest: Pioneer Period 1815-1840.* 1950. Ills. 1st ed. maps. VG $50.00

BULFINCH, Thomas. *Age of Chivalry.* 1859. Boston. Crosby/Nichols. dj. VG $200.00

BULL. *The Teddy Bear Book.* 1970. Random House. Ills. 1st ed. 207 pp. dj. EX $30.00

BULLA, Clyde Robert. *Song of St.Francis.* 1952. Crowell. Ills. Angelo. 1st printing. $20.00

BULLA, Clyde Robert. *The Secret Valley.* 1949. New York. Ills. G. Paull. 1st printing. $20.00

BULLARD, F. Lauriston. *Abraham Lincoln & the Widow Bixby.* 1946. New Brunswick. 154 pp. dj. $7.50

BULLATY, S. *Sudek.* 1978. New York. 1st ed. dj. EX $32.50

BULLEN, F. *The Cruise of the Cachalot After Sperm Whales.* 1906. Appleton. Ills. 379 pp. G $20.00

BULLEN, Frank T. *The Cruise of the Cachalot After Sperm Whales.* 1898. London. 1st ed. blue cloth binding. $265.00

BULLEN, Frank T. *The Cruise of the Cachalot After Sperm Whales.* 1928. New York. Ills. Mead Schaeffer. dj. $37.50

BULLETT, Gerald. *Dreaming.* 1928. London. Ltd. ed. VG $20.00

BULLINS. *The Hungered One.* 1971. Morrow. dj. VG $10.00

BULLITT, William C. *The Great Globe Itself.* 1946. Scribner. 310 pp. dj. VG $8.00

BULLOCK, T.I. *Exercises in the Chinese Written Language.* 1902. London. 263 pp. $37.50

BULMER, H.K. *Empire of Chaos.* 1953. London. Hamilton Prather. 1st ed. dj. $20.00

BULMER, H.K. *The Stars are Ours.* 1953. London. Hamilton Prather. 1st ed. dj. $20.00

BULPETT, C. *A Picnic Party in Wildest Africa.* 1907. London. VG $47.50

BULPIN, T.V. *Lost Trails of Transvaal.* 1983. Cape Town. Books of Africa. 474 pp. EX $18.00

BULPIN, T.V. *The Ivory Trail.* 1973. Cape Town. Books of Africa. Ills. EX $15.00

BULWER-LYTTON, Edward. *A Strange Story.* 1862. Boston. Fuller. 1st Am. ed. VG $60.00

BULWER-LYTTON, Edward. *Night & Morning.* 1841. New York. 1st ed. VG $20.00

BULWER-LYTTON, Edward. *The Ring of Amasis.* 1863. New York. Harper. 1st Am. ed. VG $65.00

BUMP, G. *Ruffled Grouse: History, Propagation, Management.* 1947. New York. State Conservation Dept. EX $65.00

BUNCE, W.H. *Chula Son of the Mound Builders.* 1942. Ills. 1st ed. G $7.50

BUNKER, Alonzo. *Soo Than. Tale of Making of Karen Nation.* 1902. New York. Ills. VG $26.00

BUNKER, Robert. *Other Men's Skies.* 1956. 1st ed. dj. VG $10.00

BUNKLEY, J.M. *Testimony of an Escaped Novice from Sisterhood.* 1855. New York. Harper. 338 pp. 4 pls. $15.00

BUNNELL, L.H. *The Yosemite.* 1892. $45.00

BUNNER, H.C. *Zadoc Pine & Other Stories.* New York. Scribner. 256 pp. $10.00

BUNTING, B. *What the Chairman Told Tom.* 1967. Ltd. 1st ed. 1/226. sgn. EX $36.50

BUNYAN, John. *Pilgrim's Progress.* 1842. Honolulu. Hawaiian text. $250.00

BUNYAN, John. *Pilgrim's Progress.* 1879. EX $75.00

BURACK, A.S. *Television Plays for Writers.* 1957. Boston. 1st ed. EX $15.00

BURBRIDGE, B. *Gorilla Tracking & Capturing Ape-Man of Africa.* 1928. Century. 1st printing. photos. 320 pp. $27.00

BURCH, John P. *Charles W. Quantrell.* 1923. Texas. Ills. 1st ed. dj. G $25.00

BURCH, M. *Shotgunner's Guide.* 1980. dj. EX $12.50

BURCHAN, John. *Greenmantle.* 1924. London. reprint. inscr. $25.00

BURCHENAL, Elizabeth. *Dances of the People.* 1934. New York. Ills. revised ed. $20.00

BURCHETT, W.G. *Pacific Treasure Island, New Caledonia.* 1941. Melbourne. Cheshire. Ills. 230 pp. $12.00

BURCKHARDT, Carl J. *Kleinasiatsche Reise.* 1926. Munchen. Bremmer Presse. Ltd. ed. EX $250.00

BURD, Clara M. *Dickens' Stories About Children.* 1929. Chicago. Winston. Ills. 1st ed. VG $15.00

BURDETT. *Gems of Wit & Humor.* 1903. Stahl. Ills. VG $25.00

BURDETTE, R.J. *The Drums of the 47th.* 1914. VG $20.00

BURDICK, E. & Lederer, W.J. *Sarkhan.* 1st ed. dj. EX $12.00

BURDO, A. *A Voyage Up the Niger Benueh.* 1880. London. VG $57.50

BUREAU OF NATIONAL LITERATURE. *Messages & Papers of the Presidents.* New York. 20 vols cover 1897-1916. EX $45.00

BURGER, J. *Horned Death.* 1947. Cape Buffalo. VG $175.00

BURGESS, Anthony. *A Vision of the Battlements.* 1965. $10.00

BURGESS, Anthony. *Clockwork Orange.* 1962. 1st Eng. ed. dj. VG $45.00

BURGESS, Anthony. *Enderby Outside.* 1968. London. Heinemann. 1st ed. dj. VG $50.00

BURGESS, Anthony. *Enderby.* 1963. Norton. 1st Am. ed. dj. VG $25.00

BURGESS, Anthony. *Honey for the Bears.* 1963. London. 1st ed. dj. VG $75.00

BURGESS, Anthony. *Little Wilson & Big God.* 1986. New York. advance proof. wrappers. EX $25.00

BURGESS, Anthony. *MF.* 1971. Knopf. 1st ed. $52.50

BURGESS, Anthony. *Moses.* 1976. New York. Stonehill Press. 1st ed. dj. $20.00

BURGESS, Anthony. *On Going to Bed.* 1982. Abbeville. 1st Am. ed. dj. VG $12.50

BURGESS, Anthony. *The Clockwork Testament, or Enderby's End.* 1975. New York. Knopf. 1st ed. dj. VG $30.00

BURGESS, Anthony. *The Earthly Powers.* 1980. New York. Simon & Schuster. 1st ed. dj. $25.00

BURGESS, Anthony. *The End of the World News.* 1983. New York. McGraw Hill. 1st ed. dj. EX $20.00

BURGESS, Anthony. *The Kingdom of the Wicked.* 1985. New York. Arbor House. advance copy. EX $25.00

BURGESS, Anthony. *The Novel Today.* 1963. London. Ills. 1st ed. dj. EX $30.00

BURGESS, Anthony. *The Right to an Answer.* 1960. London. 1st ed. dj. VG $90.00

BURGESS, Dorothy. *Dream & Deed. Story of Katharine Lee Bates.* 1952. Norman, OK. Ills. 1st ed. 241 pp. index. $4.00

BURGESS, Fred W. *Antique Jewelry & Trinkets.* 1937. Ills. 1st ed. $20.00

BURGESS, Fred W. *Silver, Pewter, & Sheffield Plate.* 1921. London. Ills. 299 pp. index. $25.00

BURGESS, Gelett. *The Maxims of Methuselah.* 1907. New York. Ills. Francher. 1st ed. VG $35.00

BURGESS, Gelett. *The Purple Cow.* 1895. San Francisco. 1st ed. slipcase. EX $150.00

BURGESS, Gelett. *Vivette; or, Memoirs of the Romance Association.* 1897. Boston. 1st ed. G $45.00

BURGESS, John W. *The Middle Period, 1817-1858.* 1897. New York. Scribner. maps. G $3.00

BURGESS, Joyce. *Here Comes Everybody.* 1965. London. 1st ed. dj. $35.00

BURGESS, Lorraine M. *Garden Art.* 1981. New York. Walker. Ills. dj. VG $10.00

BURGESS, R. *The Sharks.* 1970. Doubleday. 1st ed. photos. 159 pp. $13.00

BURGESS, Thomas. *Foreign Born Americans & Their Children.* 1923. New York. Dept of Missions. VG $3.50

BURGESS, Thornton W. *Adventures of Chatterer, the Red Squirrel.* 1923. Boston. Ills. Harrison Cady. sgn. dj. $35.00

BURGESS, Thornton W. *Adventures of Johnny Chuck.* 1930. Little, Brown. Ills. Johnny Chuck. dj. VG $15.00

BURGESS, Thornton W. *Bedtime Stories.* 1959. New York. Ills. Carl & Mary Hauge. $8.50

BURGESS, Thornton W. *Flower Book for Children.* 1923. Little, Brown. Ills. $20.00

BURGESS, Thornton W. *Happy Jack.* 1920. Boston. Ills. Harrison Cady. VG $25.00

BURGESS, Thornton W. *Lightfoot the Deer.* 1921. Boston. Ills. H. Cady. VG $6.00

BURGESS, Thornton W. *Mother West Wind 'Where' Stories.* 1919. New York. Grosset & Dunlap. 244 pp. G $2.50

BURGESS, Thornton W. *Mother West Wind's Children.* 1911. New York. Grosset & Dunlap. 240 pp. $5.00

BURGESS, Thornton W. *Now I Remember.* 1960. Little, Brown. ex-lib. $4.00

BURGESS, Thornton W. *Old Granny Fox.* 1920. New York. Grosset & Dunlap. 202 pp. $3.50

BURGESS, Thornton W. *The Adventures of Grandfather Frog.* 1923. Boston. Ills. Harrison Cady. VG $20.00

BURGESS, Thornton W. *The Adventures of Poor Mrs. Quack.* 1919. Boston. Ills. Harrison Cady. VG $10.00

BURGESS, Thornton W. *The Adventures of Reddy Fox.* 1919. Boston. Ills. Harrison Dady. VG $10.00

BURGESS, Thornton W. *The Adventures of Unc'Billy Possum.* 1922. Boston. Ills. Harrison Cady. EX $20.00

BURGESS, Thornton W. *The Burgess Bird Book for Children.* 1937. Boston. Ills. Louis Agassiz Furetes. $17.50

BURGESS, Thornton W. *The Burgess Bird Book for Children.* 1919. Little, Brown. Ills. Fuertes. dj. EX $25.00

BURGESS, Thornton W. *The Little Burgess Animal Book for Children.* 1941. Rand McNally. Ills. L.A. Fuertes. 64 pp. G $3.50

BURGESS, Thornton W. *50 Favorite Burgess Stories.* 1944. New York. Grosset & Dunlap. 184 pp. $5.00

BURGESS, Thorton W. *Book of Nature Lore.* Little, Brown. 1st ed. VG $4.00

BURGESS, Tristam. *Battle of Lake Erie.* 1839. Providence. 132 pp. $75.00

BURGHEIM, Fanny Louise. *The First Circus.* 1930. New York. Platt & Munk. Ills. EX $10.00

BURGOYNE, J. *Dramatic & Poetical Works.* 1807. London. 2 vol set. $95.00

BURHAM, Clara Louis. *Clever Betsy.* 1910. Ills. Rose O'Neill. VG $12.00

BURK, B. *Game Bird Carving.* 1972. dj. $10.00

BURK, B. *Waterfowl Studies.* 1976. Winchester. 700 photos. dj. $18.00

BURK, John N. *Great Concert Music.* 1939. Garden City. 400 pp. $3.50

BURKE, Ashworth P. *Family Records.* 1965. New York. Ills. 709 pp. index. VG $25.00

BURKE, Billie. *With Powder on My Nose.* 1959. Coward McCann. 1st ed. 215 pp. dj. EX $35.00

BURKE, John. *Dreams & Derisions.* 1927. New York. Ills. Kent. Ltd. ed. slipcase. $100.00

BURKE, K. *Collected Poems.* 1968. 1st ed. dj. $12.50

BURKE, Kenneth A. *Grammar of Motives.* 1955. New York. 503 pp. dj. $5.00

BURKE, Padraic. *A History of the Port of Seattle.* 1976. Seattle, WA. 134 pp. dj. VG $5.00

BURKE, Thomas. *Song Book of Quong Lee of Limehouse.* 1920. London. 1st ed. VG $30.00

BURKE, Thomas. *Victorian Grotesque.* 1941. London. 1st ed. $25.00

BURKE, Thomas. *Whispering Windows.* 1921. London. Richards. 1st ed. dj. VG $50.00

BURKERT, Nancy Ekholm. *Acts of Light.* 1980. Garden City. 1st ed. dj. VG $35.00

BURKERT, Nancy Ekholm. *The Fir Tree.* 1970. Harper & Row. Ills. VG $20.00

BURKETT, Charles Wm. *Our Domestic Animals.* 1907. Boston. Ills. $20.00

BURKS, Arthur J. *Black Medicine.* 1966. Sauk City. 1st ed. 308 pp. dj. EX $25.00

BURKS, Arthur J. *Look Behind You.* 1954. Buffalo. Ills. dj. $15.00

BURLAND, Cottie. *North American Indian Mythology.* 1965. London. Ills. 1st ed. dj. EX $20.00

BURLAND, Harris. *The Princess Thora.* 1904. Boston. Little, Brown. 1st ed. VG $125.00

BURLEIGH, T. *Georgia Birds.* 1958. OK U. Press. Ills. G.M. Sutton. 1st ed. dj. $75.00

BURLEND, Rebecca. *A True Picture of Emigration.* 1936. Chicago. Ills. ex-lib. $8.50

BURLESON, Clyde W. *The Jennifer Project.* 1977. photos. 179 pp. dj. EX $4.50

BURLINGAME, R. *Life & Times of Elmer Davis.* 1961. New York. 1st ed. ex-lib. 352 pp. $3.00

BURLINGAME, Roger. *Endless Frontiers.* 1959. New York. McGraw Hill. Ills. 1st ed. $7.50

BURLINGAME, Roger. *I Have Known Many Worlds.* 1959. Doubleday. 283 pp. $5.50

BURLINGAME, Roger. *Of Making Many Books.* 1946. New York. Scribner. 1st ed. 347 pp. EX $20.00

BURLS. *Science & Technology Industrial Diamonds.* 1967. 2 vol set. djs. $25.00

BURMAN, Ben L. *Children of Noah.* 1951. New York. Ills. sgn. dj. EX $10.00

BURNAND. *Die Gleichniss Jesu.* 1900. Baden. 42 plates. 204 pp. $44.00

BURNE, A.H. *The Art of War on Land.* 1958. Ills. 23 maps. 11 diagrams. VG $12.00

BURNE-JONES, Dan. *The Prints of Rockwell Kent.* 1975. Chicago. Ills. 1st ed. dj. VG $27.50

BURNELL, George R. *Rudimentary Treatise of Limes, Cements, etc.* 1850. London. $20.00

BURNELL, Whit & Foley, Martha. *A Story Anthology 1931-1933.* 1933. New York. Vanguard Press. 346 pp. $5.00

BURNETT, Frances Hodgson. *A Fair Barbarian.* 1881. Boston. 1st ed. 1st issue. G $25.00

BURNETT, Frances Hodgson. *A Little Princess.* 1905. New York. Ills. Betts. 1st ed. VG $50.00

BURNETT, Frances Hodgson. *Children's Book.* 1909. New York. Ills. 1st ed. VG $25.00

BURNETT, Frances Hodgson. *Editha's Burglar.* 1888. Boston. Ills. Sandham. 1st ed. $20.00

BURNETT, Frances Hodgson. *In the Closed Room.* 1904. New York. Ills. Jessie Willcox Smith. VG $60.00

BURNETT, Frances Hodgson. *Little Lord Fauntleroy.* 1932. New York. Scribner. Ills. Birch. $12.50

BURNETT, Frances Hodgson. *Little Lord Fauntleroy.* 1887. New York. Scribner. VG $37.50

BURNETT, Frances Hodgson. *Little Lord Fauntleroy.* 1886. New York. Ills. Birch. 1st ed. G $55.00

BURNETT, Frances Hodgson. *Little Princess.* 1963. Lippincott. Ills. Tasha Tudor. $15.00

BURNETT, Frances Hodgson. *Racketty-Packetty House.* 1922. Century. Ills. Harrison Cady. VG $20.00

BURNETT, Frances Hodgson. *The Dawn of Tomorrow.* 1906. Scribner. 1st ed. VG $25.00

BURNETT, Frances Hodgson. *The Head of the House of Coombe.* 1922. New York. 374 pp. VG $3.50

BURNETT, Frances Hodgson. *The Secret Garden.* 1911. Stokes. 1st ed. 375 pp. $95.00

BURNETT, Frances Hodgson. *The Secret Garden.* 1962. Lippincott. Ills. Tasha Tudor. 1st ed. dj. $25.00

BURNETT, Frances Hodgson. *World of Fun & Story.* 1915. New York. Cupples & Leon. VG $15.00

BURNETT, Hallie. *The Daughter-in-Law Cookbook.* 1969. Old Tappan, NJ. Hewitt House. 318 pp. $10.00

BURNETT, Peter H. *An Old California Pioneer.* 1946. Oakland. Ltd. ed. 1/675. maps. index. $40.00

BURNETT, W. *The Maker of Signs.* 1934. 1st ed. sgn. dj. $10.00

BURNETT, W.R. *Dark Hazard.* 1933. New York. Harper. 295 pp. G $2.50

BURNETT, W.R. *The Goodhues of Sinking Creek.* 1934. New York. Harper. Ills. Lankes. dj. EX $45.00

BURNETT, Whit. *The World's Best.* 1950. New York. Dial Press. 1186 pp. dj. $4.00

BURNEY, F. *Evelina.* 1903. London. Ills. Hugh Thompson. 1st ed. $15.00

BURNEY, James. *Chronological Hist. of N.E. Voyages of Discovery.* 1819. London. 1st ed. 310 pp. 2 fld maps. VG $300.00

BURNS, Eugene. *Advanced Fly Fishing.* 1953. Stackpole. 1st ed. $40.00

BURNS, George. *I Love Her That's Why.* 1955. Simon & Schuster. 1st ed. dj. $17.50

BURNS, J.M. *Roosevelt: Soldier of Freedom 1940-1945.* 1956. New York. 1st ed. 533 pp. dj. EX $7.50

BURNS, John Horne. *Lucifer with a Book.* 1949. London. Secker & Warburg. 1st ed. dj. $20.00

BURNS, Rex. *The Farnsworth Score.* 1977. New York. Harper. 1st ed. dj. VG $25.00

BURNS, Robert. *An Address to the Devil.* London. Ills. Thomas Landseer. VG $35.00

BURNS, Robert. *Complete Poetical Works.* 1880. Nimmo. VG $15.00

BURNS, Robert. *I Am a Fugitive from Georgia Chain Gang.* 1932. New York. Grosset & Dunlap. 257 pp. $2.50

BURNS, Vincent G. *Out of These Chains.* 1942. Los Angeles. 464 pp. dj. $15.00

BURNS, W.N. *Tombstone: Gun-Toting Days in Old Arizona.* New York. Ills. dj. VG $12.50

BURNS. *Fresh & Salt-Water Spinning.* 1952. Barnes. Ills. 96 pp. $3.00

BURNSIDE. *Maynard Dixon: Artist of West.* 1974. Bringham Young U. Pr. Ltd. ed. $30.00

BURR, A.R. *Portrait of a Banker, Jason Stillman.* 1928. New York. 370 pp. $15.00

BURR, Grace H. *Hispanic Furniture.* 1964. New York. Ills. 2nd ed. dj. EX $40.00

BURR, Samuel Engle Jr. *Small Town Merchant.* 1957. NY/Washington. 1st ed. sgn. 354 pp. dj. $10.00

BURR & HYDE. *Great Industries of the United States.* 1872. Hartford. Ills. 1st ed. VG $35.00

BURR. *The Life of Gen. Philip H. Sheridan.* 1888. Ills. 1st ed. 445 pp. $13.50

BURRAGE, E. Harcourt. *The Twin Castaways.* 1900. London. 1st ed. VG $40.00

BURRELL, Angus & Bennett, ed. *The Bedside Book of Famous American Stories.* 1936. New York. Random House. 1273 pp. $4.00

BURRELL, H. *The Platypus.* 1927. Sydney. Ills. 1st ed. 227 pp. $60.00

BURRITT, Elijah H. *Geography of the Heavens.* 1941. New York. 305 pp. G $10.00

BURROUGHS, Edgar Rice. *Escape on Venus.* 1946. Tarzana. Ills. 1st ed. 347 pp. dj. $47.50

BURROUGHS, Edgar Rice. *Fighting Men of Mars.* New York. 1st ed. VG $60.00

BURROUGHS, Edgar Rice. *Gods of Mars.* 1940. Tarzana. tan-gray binding. dj. EX $37.50

BURROUGHS, Edgar Rice. *Jungle Girl.* 1933. 1st Eng. ed. dj. VG $45.00

BURROUGHS, Edgar Rice. *Jungle Tales of Tarzan.* 1919. London. 1st Eng. ed. VG $80.00

BURROUGHS, Edgar Rice. *Jungle Tales of Tarzan.* 1919. McClurg. 1st ed. G $60.00

BURROUGHS, Edgar Rice. *Lost Empire.* 1929. Metro Books. 1st ed. $100.00

BURROUGHS, Edgar Rice. *Lost on Venus.* 1935. Tarzana. tan-gray binding. dj. EX $35.00

BURROUGHS, Edgar Rice. *Odhams.* 1933. 1st Eng. ed. dj. $90.00

BURROUGHS, Edgar Rice. *Pellucidar.* McClurg. 1st ed. VG $70.00

BURROUGHS, Edgar Rice. *Sword of Mars.* 1936. Tarzana. dj. EX $85.00

BURROUGHS, Edgar Rice. *Synthetic Men of Mars.* 1940. Tarzana, CA. 2nd ed. 315 pp. dj. VG $57.50

BURROUGHS, Edgar Rice. *Tanar of Pellucidar.* 1930. New York. Metropolitan. 1st ed. dj. VG $65.00

BURROUGHS, Edgar Rice. *Tarzan & the City of Gold.* 1954. Racine. Whitman. 282 pp. pb. $3.00

BURROUGHS, Edgar Rice. *Tarzan & the Foreign Legion.* 1947. Tarzana. Ills. 1st ed. 314 pp. $50.00

BURROUGHS, Edgar Rice. *Tarzan & the Lost Empire.* 1929. Metropolitan. 1st ed. dj. $400.00

BURROUGHS, Edgar Rice. *Tarzan & the Lost Empire.* 1929. New York. 1st ed. VG $65.00

BURROUGHS, Edgar Rice. *Tarzan & the Lost Safari.* 1957. Racine. Whitman. 282 pp. pb. $3.00

BURROUGHS, Edgar Rice. *Tarzan of the Apes.* 1964. Racine. Whitman. 285 pp. pb. $2.50

BURROUGHS, Edgar Rice. *Tarzan of the Apes.* 1914. McClurg. 1st ed. VG $650.00

BURROUGHS, Edgar Rice. *Tarzan of the Apes.* 1914. McClurg. 1st ed. G $500.00

BURROUGHS, Edgar Rice. *The Girl from Hollywood.* 1923. New York. 1st ed. 320 pp. EX $65.00

BURROUGHS, Edgar Rice. *The Mucher.* 1921. New York. Grosset & Dunlap. Ills. G $12.50

BURROUGHS, Edgar Rice. *The Outlaw of Torn.* 1927. A.C. McClurg. 1st ed. inscr. $750.00

BURROUGHS, Edgar Rice. *The Son of Tarzan.* 1917. Grosset & Dunlap. 312 pp. $12.50

BURROUGHS, Edgar Rice. *The Son of Tarzan.* 1918. New York. A.L. Burt. dj. EX $50.00

BURROUGHS, Edgar Rice. *Thuvia, Maid of Mars.* New York. Grosset & Dunlap. 256 pp. $15.00

BURROUGHS, Edgar Rice. *Thuvia, Maid of Mars.* McClurg. 1st ed. $70.00

BURROUGHS, J. *Under the Maples.* 1921. 1st ed. $6.50

BURROUGHS, John Rolfe. *Headfirst in the Pickle Barrel.* 1963. New York. Morrow. 423 pp. dj. $52.50

BURROUGHS, John. *Bird & Bough.* 1906. Boston. Ltd. 1st ed. 1/150. $22.50

BURROUGHS, John. *Camping & Tramping with Roosevelt.* 1907. Boston. Houghton Mifflin. 111 pp. VG $10.00

BURROUGHS, John. *In the Catskills.* 1910. Boston/NY. Ills. Johnson. 1st ed. G $12.50

BURROUGHS, Joseph B. *Titan, Son of Saturn.* 1907. Ohio. Emeth. G $17.50

BURROUGHS, Polly. *A Celebrated Schooner Life.* 1972. $7.50

BURROUGHS, Stephen. *Memoirs of the Notorious Stephen Burroughs.* New York. (ca.1825) 299 pp. $9.00

BURROUGHS, William. *Cities of the Red Night.* 1981. New York. Holt. Ltd. ed. 1/500. sgn. EX $75.00

BURROUGHS, William. *Cities of the Red Night.* 1981. New York. Holt. sgn. dj. EX $35.00

BURROUGHS, William. *Cities of the Red Night.* 1981. Holt. 1st trade ed. dj. VG $15.00

BURROUGHS, William. *Cobble Stone Gardens.* 1976. Cherry Valley. 1st ed. wrappers. EX $20.00

BURROUGHS, William. *Naked Lunch.* 1959. New York. 1st Am. ed. dj. EX $40.00

BURROUGHS, William. *Nova Express.* 1964. Grove Press. 1st ed. dj. $10.00

BURROUGHS, William. *Queer.* 1985. New York. Viking. 1st ed. dj. EX $20.00

BURROUGHS, William. *So Who Owns Death TV?* 1967. Beach Books. Ltd. ed. 1/200. EX $45.00

BURROUGHS, William. *The Book of Breathing.* 1976. Berkeley. Blue Wind. 1st Am. ed. EX $20.00

BURROWS, Abe. *Song Book.* 1955. Doubleday. Ills. Macdonald. sgn. EX $17.50

BURROWS, G. *Land of the Pygmies.* New York. (ca.1898) $35.00

BURT, Struthers. *Powder River Let'er Buck.* 1938. New York. Ills. $12.00

BURT, W.H. *Field Guide to the Mammals.* 1961. Houghton Mifflin. Ills. maps. $6.00

BURT. *Burt's Guide to the Connecticut Valley.* 1867. Northampton. map. $37.50

BURTON, Alfred. *The Adventures of Johnny Newcome in the Navy.* 1904. London. Ills. Rowlandson. $15.00

BURTON, Hal. *The Walton Boys.* 1958. Racine. Whitman. 282 pp. pb. G $2.00

BURTON, Isabel. *The Life of Captain Sir Richard F. Burton.* 1893. London. Ills. 1st ed. 664 pp. 2 vol set. $225.00

BURTON, J. *Birds of the Tropics.* 1973. Ills. 128 pp. dj. $6.00

BURTON, J. *Small Mammals.* 1977. Ills. 1st ed. 64 pp. dj. $7.00

BURTON, Katherine. *The Great Mantle.* 1950. New York. Longman. 238 pp. EX $4.00

BURTON, M. *A Smell of Smoke.* 1959. London. 1st ed. dj. VG $30.00

BURTON, M. *Animal Legends.* 1957. Coward McCann. Ills. 1st Am. ed. 318 pp. dj. $7.00

BURTON, M. *Death Takes a Detour.* 1958. London. 1st ed. dj. EX $35.00

BURTON, M. *Infancy In Animals.* 1956. London. Ills. 1st ed. 228 pp. dj. $10.00

BURTON, M. *Just Like an Animal.* 1978. Scribner. Ills. 215 pp. dj. $8.00

BURTON, M. *Margins of the Sea.* 1954. Harper. Ills. 212 pp. dj. VG $5.00

BURTON, M. *Systematic Dictionary of Mammals of the World.* 1962. Crowell. Ills. 307 pp. dj. $12.00

BURTON, M. & R. *Encyclopedia of Insects & Arachnids.* 1984. Finsbury. Ills. 252 pp. dj. $24.00

BURTON, R. *Lake Regions of Central Africa.* 1860. New York. VG $85.00

BURTON, R. *Mission to Glele.* 1893. London. 2 vol set. VG $65.00

BURTON, R. *The Life & Death of Whales.* 1980. London. 185 pp. dj. $10.00

BURTON, Richard. *A Christmas Story.* 1964. New York. Morrow. 31 pp. $3.00

BURTON, Richard. *Secret Places of the Human Body.* 1935. Golden Hind. Ills. VG $60.00

BURTON, Richard. *The Kasidah of Haji Abdu El-Yezdi.* 1931. Philadelphia. McKay. Ills. 1st ed. boxed. EX $60.00

BURTON, Richard. *The Perfumed Garden.* 1933. Golden Hind. Ltd. ed. 10 pls. VG $60.00

BURTON, Richard. *Vikram the Vampire.* Dover. pb. VG $30.00

BURTON, Richard. *Wanderings in Three Continents.* 1901. London. 1st ed. dj. VG $40.00

BURTON, Robert. *The English Hero; or, Sir Francis Drake Revived.* 1710. London. Ills. 8th ed. VG $350.00

BURTON, William. *A General History of Porcelain.* 1921. Cassell. 1st ed. 2 vol set. VG $50.00

BUSBY, F.M. *The Long View.* 1976. Putnam. 1st ed. dj. VG $12.50

BUSCH, Capt. F. *Holocaust at Sea. Drama of the Scharnhorst.* 1957. Ills. dj. G $17.50

BUSCH, Frederick. *Breathing Trouble.* 1973. London. Calder & Boyars. 1st Eng. ed. $30.00

BUSCH, Frederick. *Hardwater Country.* 1979. Knopf. 1st ed. dj. VG $22.50

BUSCH, Frederick. *Invisible Mending.* 1984. Godine. dj. VG $15.00

BUSCH, Frederick. *Rounds.* 1979. Farrar. 1st ed. dj. VG $15.00

BUSCH, Frederick. *Take This Man.* 1981. Farrar. 1st ed. dj. VG $12.50

BUSCH, Frederick. *Take This Man.* 1981. New York. Farrar. proof copy. EX $40.00

BUSCH, Frederick. *The Mutual Friend.* 1978. Harper. 1st ed. dj. EX $20.00

BUSCH, Noel F. *Adlai Stevenson of Illinois.* 1952. New York. 236 pp. dj. EX $10.00

BUSCH, Wilhelm. *Santlighe Werke Munchen.* 1949. Ills. 7 vol set. djs. EX $90.00

BUSCHOR. *On the Meaning of Greek Statues.* 1980. U. of MA. $6.00

BUSH, Fritz. *Pages from a Musician's Life.* 1953. London. 1st ed. VG $22.50

BUSH, Vannerar. *Pieces of the Action.* 1970. New York. Morrow. 366 pp. EX $5.00

BUSH. *Doris Caesar.* 1970. Syracuse U. Press. $12.00

BUSHNEL, Nelson. *A Walk After John Keats.* 1936. New York. Ills. 1st ed. 318 pp. dj. EX $20.00

BUSHONG, M.K. *History of Jefferson County West Virginia.* 1941. Charles Town. 1st ed. EX $35.00

BUSSBY, Frederick. *Jane Austen in Winchester.* 1969. Winchester. 1st ed. wrappers. VG $15.00

BUSTARD, R. *Sea Turtles, Natural History & Conservation.* 1972. London. Ills. 1st ed. 220 ppl. dj. $25.00

BUTLER, A. *British Birds with Their Nests & Eggs.* London. (ca.1908) 6 vol set. VG $150.00

BUTLER, A.C. *Persimmons. A Story for Boys & Girls.* 1895. Taylorville. Ills. 112 pp. $10.00

BUTLER, A.G. *Bird Eggs of the British Isles.* 1904. London. Gill. Ills. 105 pp. $20.00

BUTLER, Benjamin F. *Butler's Book.* 1892. 1st ed. $37.50

BUTLER, E.I. & Dale, G.A. *Alaska, Land & People.* 1959. Viking Press. Ills. photos. maps. 159 pp. $10.00

BUTLER, Ellis Parker. *Philo Gubb: Correspondence School Detective.* 1918. Boston. Houghton Mifflin. 1st ed. EX $65.00

BUTLER, F. *Sketches of Universal History.* 1832. Hartford. $30.00

BUTLER, F.H. *Wine & Winelands of the World.* 1926. London. Ills. 1st ed. EX $20.00

BUTLER, Francis. *Breeding, Training, Management, Disease of Dogs.* 1860. New York. Ills. G $25.00

BUTLER, Joseph T. *American Antiques 1800-1900.* 1965. New York. Odyssey. Ills. dj. VG $15.50

BUTLER, Joseph T. *Candleholders in America 1650-1900.* 1967. New York. dj. $15.00

BUTLER, June Rainsford. *Floralia: Garden Paths & By-Paths of 18th Cent.* 1938. U. NC Press. Ltd ed. 1/500. 4 color pls. $100.00

BUTLER, Mann. *A History of the Commonwealth of Kentucky.* 1834. Louisville. 1st ed. 396 pp. $200.00

BUTLER, Margaret Manor. *Pictorial History of Western Reserve, 1796-1860.* 1963. Cleveland. Ills. 155 pp. dj. VG $25.00

BUTLER, S. *The Way of All Flesh.* 1903. London. slipcase. VG $250.00

BUTLER, Samuel. *An Atlas of Ancient Geography.* 1839. Philadelphia. Lea & Blanchard. VG $35.00

BUTLER, Samuel. *Dr. Butler's Atlas of Ancient Geography.* 1854. Philadelphia. 21 pls. 44 pp. index. $45.00

BUTLER, Samuel. *Hudibras, with a Life & Annotations.* 1829. New York. VG $37.50

BUTLER, Samuel. *Hudibras.* 1819. London. 2nd ed. 3 vol set. $35.00

BUTLER, T. Harrison. *An Illustrated Guide to the Slit-Lamp.* 1927. Oxford. G $20.00

BUTLER, W.F. *The Great Lone Land.* 1873. London. Ills. fld map. 386 pp. $30.00

BUTLER, W.F. *The Great Lone Land.* 1889. London. $20.00

BUTLER. *Patternmaster.* 1976. 1st ed. dj. EX $15.00

BUTLER. *The Analogy of Religion.* 1843. Newman. G $6.50

BUTLER. *Wild Seed.* 1980. 1st Am. ed. dj. EX $20.00

BUTTERFIELD. *Saturday Evening Post Treasury.* 1954. Simon & Schuster. 544 pp. dj. $12.50

BUTTERWORTH, H. *Pinocchio's Adventure in Wonderland.* 1898. New York. Ills. Quentin. 212 pp. $8.50

BUTTERWORTH, H. *Story of Magellan & Discovery of Philippines.* 1899. New York. Ills. Merrill. 235 pp. VG $7.00

BUTTERWORTH, H. *The Knight of Liberty.* 1896. New York. Ills. Pierce. 225 pp. $7.00

BUTTERWORTH, H. *The Log School-House on the Columbia.* 1890. New York. Ills. 1st ed. ex-lib. $15.00

BUTTERWORTH, H. *True to His Home.* 1907. New York. Ills. H. Winthrop Pierce. VG $10.00

BUTTERWORTH, H. *Zig-Zag Stories.* 1896. Boston. Ills. 357 pp. $8.00

BUTTERWORTH, H. *Zigzag Journeys Around the World.* 1895. Boston. Dana Estes. Ills. $15.00

BUTTERWORTH, H. *Zigzag Journeys in the British Isles.* 1889. Boston. Dana Estes. Ills. $15.00

BUTTEWORTH, Charles. *The English Primers 1529-1545.* 1953. U. of Pittsburgh. 1st ed. dj. $12.50

BUTTITTA, Tony. *After the Good Gay Times.* New York. Viking Press. 1st ed. $5.00

BUTTREE, Julia M. *Rhythm of the Red Man in Song, Dance & Decoration.* 1937. New York. Ills. Thompson. 280 pp. dj. $45.00

BUTTS, Mary. *Ashe of Rings.* 1926. New York. 1st ed. VG $60.00

BUXTON, A. *Traveling Naturalist.* 1948. London. Collins. Ills. maps. 224 pp. $20.00

BYAM-SHAW, J. *Drawings of Domenico Tiepolo.* 1962. London. Ills. dj. VG $15.00

BYERS, S.H.M. *Switzerland & the Swiss.* 1885. Boston. Ills. G $25.00

BYINGTON, Margaret F. *Homestead. The Households of a Mill Town.* 1910. New York. 292 pp. VG $5.00

BYNNER, Witter. *Take Away the Darkness.* 1947. Knopf. 1st ed. dj. VG $20.00

BYRD, Max. *Fly Away, Jill.* 1984. London. Allison & Busby. 1st Eng. ed. $15.00

BYRD, R.E. *Discovery.* 1935. New York. 1st ed. dj. EX $65.00

BYRD, Richard. *Alone.* 1938. New York. 1st ed. 296 pp. $17.50

BYRD, Richard. *Autobiography of Byrd's Polar Journey.* 1928. 1st ed. ex-lib. 359 pp. VG $22.00

BYRD, Richard. *Skyward.* 1928. New York. Putnam. 1st ed. sgn. 359 pp. $20.00

BYRD, Richard. *Skyward.* 1981. Chicago. Lakeside Classic. EX $10.00

BYRD, William. *Another Secret Diary of William Byrd of Westover.* 1942. Richmond, VA. Ills. 490 pp. dj. $150.00

BYRD, William. *The Writings of William Byrd.* 1901. New York. Ills. Ltd. ed. 1/500. 461 pp. $175.00

BYRD. *The Big Aviation Book for Boys.* 1929. McLoughlin Bros. Ills. dj. EX $8.50

BYRNE, Beverly. *Woman's Rites.* 1985. Villard Press. advance copy. VG $50.00

BYRNES, Gene. *Regular Fellers in the Navy.* New York. (ca.1930) Ills. dj. VG $20.00

BYRNES, James F. *Speaking Frankly.* 1947. New York. Harper. 324 pp. $3.00

BYRNES, Lt. L.G. *History of the 94th Infantry Division in WWII.* (ca.1981) Ills. maps. EX $25.00

BYRON, Lord. *England Bards & Scotch Reviewers.* 1811. London. 4th ed. VG $65.00

BYRON, Lord. *The Poetical Works of Lord Byron.* 1854. Philadelphia. 715 pp. G $37.50

BYTWERK, R.L. *Julius Streicher.* 1983. New York. Stein & Day. Ills. dj. EX $15.00

BYWATER, H.C. *A Searchlight on the Navy.* 1935. London. new ed. G $20.00

C

CABANNE. *Outlaws of Art.* London. no date. dj. EX $10.00

CABELL, James Branch. *Domnei, Comedy of Woman-Worship.* 1930. New York. Ills. 1st ed. dj. $20.00

CABELL, James Branch. *Figures of Earth.* 1925. London. Ills. Pape. 1st ed. VG $12.50

CABELL, James Branch. *Jurgen, a Comedy of Justice.* 1921. Bodley Head. Ills. Frank Pape. Ltd. ed. G $35.00

CABELL, James Branch. *Lineage of Litchfield.* 1922. New York. Ltd. 1st ed. 1/365. sgn. dj. $65.00

CABELL, James Branch. *Preface to the Past.* 1936. New York. McBride. 2nd ed. dj. VG $10.00

CABELL, James Branch. *Some of Us.* 1930. New York. Ltd. ed. sgn. boxed. VG $25.00

CABELL, James Branch. *Something About Eve.* 1929. New York. Ills. Pape. 1st impression. EX $20.00

CABELL, James Branch. *Something About Eve.* 1927. Ltd. 1st Am. ed. sgn. VG $30.00

CABELL, James Branch. *Straws & Prayer Books.* 1924. New York. Ltd. 1st ed. sgn. VG $25.00

CABELL, James Branch. *Taboo.* 1921. Ltd. 1st Am. ed. 1/920. VG $17.50

CABELL, James Branch. *The High Place.* 1923. McBride. Ills. Ltd. ed. VG $75.00

CABELL, James Branch. *The Jewell Merchants.* 1921. New York. Ltd. 1st ed. 1/1040. dj. $20.00

CABELL, James Branch. *The Music from Behind the Moon.* 1926. John Day. 1st ed. EX $45.00

CABELL, James Branch. *The Silver Stallion.* 1926. New York. Ltd. ed. 1/850. sgn. G $50.00

CABELL, James Branch. *The Way of Ecben.* 1929. Ills. Frank Pape. 1st ed. G $12.50

CABELL, James Branch. *The White Robe.* 1928. McBride. Ills. Ltd. ed. 1/3250. VG $40.00

CABELL, James Branch. *The White Robe. A Saint's Summary.* 1923. New York. Ills. Ltd. ed. slipcase. $50.00

CABELL, James Branch. *These Restless Heads.* 1932. New York. Literary Guild. 2nd printing. $7.50

CABLE, George W. *The Grandissmes.* 1899. New York. 448 pp. $15.00

CABLE, George W. *The Grandissmes.* 1898. Scribner. VG $16.50

CABLE, M. & French, F. *The Gobi Desert.* 1946. London. Hodder Stoughton. 303 pp. $14.00

CABOT, P.S. *Juvenile Delinquency. A Critical Annotated Biblio.* 1946. New York. 166 pp. G $10.00

CADE, Stanford. *Radium Treatment of Cancer.* 1929. William Wood. 1st ed. $20.00

CADE, Tom. *Falcons of the World.* 1982. London. Collins. Ills. 192 pp. dj. EX $40.00

CADIEUX, C. *Coyotes, Predators & Survivors.* 1983. Stone Wall. 1st ed. photos. 233 pp. dj. EX $16.00

CADY, Daniel L. *Adventures of Bob White.* 1923. Little, Brown. 6 Ills. $17.00

CADY, Daniel L. *Rhymes of Vermont Rural Life.* 1923. Tuttle. 279 pp. $5.00

CAEMMERER, H.P. *Washington, D.C. the National Capital.* 1932. Ills. G $35.00

CAEN, H. *Baghdad by the Bay.* 1949. Doubleday. 1st ed. sgn. dj. VG $20.00

CAEN, H. *Only in San Francisco.* 1960. Doubleday. 1st ed. G $10.00

CAEN, H. *San Francisco. City on Golden Hills.* 1967. Ills. Kingman. 1st ed. dj. VG $25.00

CAEN, H. *The San Francisco Book.* 1948. Houghton. Ills. Yavano. G $10.00

CAESAR, G. *The Wild Hunters, the Wolves, Bears, & Big Cats.* 1957. Putnam. Ills. 252 pp. dj. VG $11.00

CAFFIN, Charles H. *American Masters of Painting.* 1902. New York. $18.00

CAHILL. *Pop Art: 24 Selections from His Work.* 1928. New York. Downtown Gallery. $18.00

CAHN. *Our Brother's Keeper. Indian in White America.* 1970. Ills. SftCvr. $7.50

CAHPIN, Howard. *The Artistic Motives in the U.S. Flag.* 1930. Providence. 1st ed. $7.50

CAIN, James M. *Galatea.* 1953. Knopf. 1st ed. dj. $12.50

CAIN, James M. *Madonna Red.* 1976. Little, Brown. 1st ed. dj. VG $25.00

CAIN, James M. *Past All Dishonor.* 1946. Knopf. 1st ed. dj. $15.00

CAIN, James M. *Serenade.* 1937. New York. 1st ed. VG $20.00

CAIN, James M. *The Baby in the Icebox.* 1981. New York. 1st ed. dj. VG $10.00

CAIN, James M. *The Butterfly.* 1947. New York. Knopf. 1st ed. dj. EX $25.00

CAIN, James M. *The Magician's Wife.* 1965. New York. 1st ed. dj. VG $20.00

CAIN, James M. *The Moth.* 1948. New York. 1st ed. dj. VG $25.00

CAIN, James M. *The Postman Always Rings Twice.* 1934. New York. Knopf. 1st ed. dj. $400.00

CAIN, James M. *Three of a Kind.* 1943. New York. Knopf. 1st ed. dj. VG $100.00

CAINE, Hall. *Life of Christ.* 1938. New York. Doubleday Doran. 1310 pp. EX $7.00

CAINE, Hall. *Life of Samuel Taylor Coleridge.* 1887. London. Scott. Great Writers Series. $25.00

CAINE, Hall. *The Bondman.* 4th ed. EX $6.00

CAINE, Hall. *The Christian.* 1897. EX $10.00

CAINE, Hall. *The Eternal City.* 1929. Ills. EX $8.00

CAINE, Hall. *The Master of Man.* 1922. 6th ed. EX $6.00

CAINE, Hall. *The Prodigal Son.* 1904. New York. 408 pp. $15.00

CAINE, Hall. *The Woman Thou Gavest Me.* 1915. EX $8.00

CAINE, W.S. *Picturesque India.* 1898. London. Ills. EX $30.00

CAIRNS. *Grand Lake in the Olden Days.* 1971. private print. sgn. VG $20.00

CAIRNS. *Great Paintings from the National Gallery of Art.* 1952. Macmillan. dj. $12.00

CALAHAN. *Learning to Sail.* 1946. Ills. 345 pp. VG $6.50

CALAMANDREI, Piero. *Eulogy of Judges.* 1942. Princeton. trans. Adams & Phillips. dj. $10.00

CALDECOTT, Andrew. *Fire Burn Blue.* 1948. London. Arnold. 1st ed. dj. EX $25.00

CALDECOTT, Andrew. *Yours Pictorially.* 1976. London. Ills. dj. $25.00

CALDECOTT, Randolph. *A Sketch Book of R. Caldecott's.* 1883. London/NY. Ills. 48 pp. VG $70.00

CALDECOTT, Randolph. *Bracebridge Hall.* 1892. London. 117 Ills. VG $20.00

CALDECOTT, Randolph. *Old Christmas.* 1882. London. Macmillan. Ills. 1st ed. $25.00

CALDECOTT, Randolph. *Randolph Caldecott's Sketches.* 1890. London. Ills. 1st ed. VG $30.00

CALDER. *Einstein's Universe.* 1979. New York. Viking. 154 pp. dj. EX $3.50

CALDIN, Martin. *Golden Wings.* 1974. reprint. dj. VG $12.50

CALDWELL, Erskine. *A Place Called Estherville.* 1949. Duell. 1st ed. dj. VG $25.00

CALDWELL, Erskine. *All Night Long.* 1942. New York. Book League. G $17.50

CALDWELL, Erskine. *Around About America.* 1964. Farrar. Ills. 1st ed. dj. VG $20.00

CALDWELL, Erskine. *Claudelle Inglish.* 1958. Little, Brown. 1st ed. dj. VG $20.00

CALDWELL, Erskine. *Close to Home.* 1962. Farrar. 1st ed. dj. VG $25.00

CALDWELL, Erskine. *God's Little Acre.* 1962. Ills. Glaser. 1st ed. sgn. dj. VG $26.50

CALDWELL, Erskine. *Journeyman.* 1935. New York. Ltd. ed. 1/1475. 195 pp. G $15.00

CALDWELL, Erskine. *Journeyman.* 1935. 1st ed. dj. VG $22.50

CALDWELL, Erskine. *Kneel to the Rising Sun & Other Stories.* 1935. New York. Viking. 1st ed. dj. VG $35.00

CALDWELL, Erskine. *Men & Women. Twenty-Two Stories.* 1961. Boston. 1st ed. 313 pp. dj. $10.00

CALDWELL, Erskine. *The Earnshaw Neighborhood.* 1971. New York. World. proof copy. wrappers. $60.00

CALDWELL, Erskine. *The Sure Hand of God.* 1947. New York. Grosset & Dunlap. 243 pp. dj. $3.50

CALDWELL, Erskine. *The Weather Shelter.* 1969. New York. World. 1st ed. dj. EX $15.00

CALDWELL, Erskine. *The Weather Shelter.* 1969. Cleveland. 1st ed. dj. $5.00

CALDWELL, Erskine. *Tobacco Road.* 1948. New York. Grosset & Dunlap. 241 pp. $4.50

CALDWELL, Erskine. *Tobacco Road.* 1973. New York. 1st ed. 241 pp. G $6.00

CALDWELL, Howard W. *Education in Nebraska.* 1902. Washington. 1st ed. 268 pp. wrappers. $45.00

CALDWELL, Taylor. *Bright Flows the River.* New York. 1st ed. dj. EX $7.00

CALDWELL, Taylor. *Captains & Kings.* 1972. $10.00

CALDWELL, Taylor. *Dear & Glorious Physician.* 1959. New York. Am. Book Club ed. dj. $7.50

CALDWELL, Taylor. *Great Lion of God.* 1970. New York. Doubleday. dj. EX $3.50

CALDWELL, Taylor. *Let Love Come Last.* New York. 1st ed. $6.50

CALDWELL, Taylor. *On Growing Up Tough.* 1971. New York. inscr. $50.00

CALDWELL, Taylor. *Prologue to Love.* New York. 1st ed. $6.50

CALDWELL, Taylor. *There Was a Time.* New York. 1st ed. $6.50

CALDWELL, Taylor. *This Side of Innocence.* 1946. New York. Scribner. 1st ed. VG $7.00

CALISHER, Hortense. *Extreme Magic.* 1964. Little, Brown. 1st ed. dj. VG $20.00

CALISHER, Hortense. *False Entry.* 1961. Boston. 1st ed. dj. VG $20.00

CALISHER, Hortense. *On Keeping Women.* 1977. Arbor House. 1st ed. dj. VG $10.00

CALISHER, Hortense. *Standard Dreaming.* 1972. Arbor House. 1st ed. dj. VG $15.00

CALKINS, F. *Rocky Mountain Warden.* 1971. Knopf. 1st ed. 265 pp. dj. $18.00

CALKINS, Franklin W. *My Host the Enemy & Other Tales.* 1901. Chicago/NY. Ills. 1st ed. 302 pp. $15.00

CALLAGHAN, M. *No Man's Meat.* 1931. Paris. Titus. Ltd. ed. sgn. slipcase. $100.00

CALLAGHAN, Morley. *More Joy in Heaven.* 1937. Random House. 1st ed. dj. $20.00

CALLAGHAN, Morley. *That Summer in Paris.* 1963. $5.00

CALLAGHAN, Morley. *The Many Colored Coat.* 1960. Coward. 1st ed. dj. $10.00

CALLAHAN, H. *Color 1941-1980.* 1980. Providence. 1st ed. slipcase. $60.00

CALLAHAN, Jack. *Man's Grim Justice. My Life Outside the Law.* 1928. New York. 1st ed. dj. VG $30.00

CALLAHAN, Jason M. *History of West Virginia.* 1923. Chicago. Ltd. ed. 3 vol set. VG $75.00

CALLCOTT. *Santa Anna.* 1936. U. of OK Press. 1st ed. VG $30.00

CALMAN, G. *Ehret, Flower Painter Extraordinary.* 1977. New York. Ills. 1st ed. 160 pp. dj. EX $27.00

CALTHROP, Dion C. *English Costume, Painted & Described.* 1923. London. Black. Ills. 61 color pls. $35.00

CALVERT. *Spain.* 1924. Ills. 2 vol set. $68.00

CALVIN. *Square-Rigged.* 1929. Little, Brown. $8.00

CALVINO, Italo. *Difficult Loves.* 1984. Harcourt. trans. 1st Am. ed. dj. VG $15.00

CALVINO, Italo. *If on a Winter's Night a Traveler.* 1979. New York. 1st ed. $7.50

CALVINO, Italo. *Invisible Cities.* 1974. London. Secker & Warburg. dj. EX $25.00

CALVINO, Italo. *Mr. Palomar.* proof copy. $40.00

CALVINO, Italo. *The Baron in the Trees.* 1959. Random House. 1st Am. ed. dj. VG $35.00

CALVINO, Italo. *The Castle of Crossed Destinies.* 1977. Harcourt. 1st Am. ed. dj. VG $20.00

CALVINO, Italo. *The Path to the Nest of Spiders.* 1957. Beacon. 1st Am. ed. VG $50.00

CALVINO, Italo. *The Silent Mr. Palomar.* 1981. Targ. Ltd. ed. 1/250. sgn. dj. VG $85.00

CALVINO, Italo. *The Watcher.* 1971. Harcourt. 1st Am. ed. dj. VG $25.00

CAMBELL, Archibald. *Capt. Macdonald's Daughter. A Novel.* 1887. New York. 331 pp. $5.00

CAMBELL, Frank S. *The Story of Hamilton County Indiana.* 1962. 223 pp. pb. $14.00

CAMBELL, George F. *Soldier of the Sky.* 1918. Chicago. Ills. 232 pp. $45.00

CAMBELL-PRAED, Mrs. Rosa. *The Head Station.* 1890. London. Ward & Downey. new ed. $45.00

CAMDEN, William. *Hist. of Renowned & Victorious Princess Elizabeth.* 1630. London. 1st ed. G $150.00

CAMEHL, A.W. *Blue China Book.* New York. (ca.1950) dj. $20.00

CAMERON, A. & Parnall, P. *The Nightwatchers.* 1978. Four Winds. Ills. 111 pp. dj. EX $22.00

CAMERON, Agnes. *The New North.* 1910. Appleton. photos. maps. 398 pp. $30.00

CAMERON, Kenneth. *Shelley & His Circle 1773-1822.* 1961-1973. 1st ed. 6 vol set. $150.00

CAMERON, Lucy. *The Little Dog Flora, with Her Silver Bell.* 1835. New York. John Day. Ills. wrappers. $35.00

CAMERON, V.L. *Across Africa.* 1969. Negro U. Press. Ills. fld map. 508 pp. EX $23.00

CAMERON, V.L. *Across Africa.* 1877. New York. VG $47.50

CAMERON. *Water Babies.* 1911. Stokes. 8 color pls. VG $38.00

CAMERSON, Robert. *Above San Francisco.* 1969. San Francisco. Ills. 1st ed. dj. EX $40.00

CAMP, Raymond. *Fireside Book of Fishing.* 1959. Ills. 1st ed. VG $20.00

CAMP, Raymond. *The Hunter's Encyclopedia.* 1948. Harrisburg. 1st ed. dj. EX $40.00

CAMP, Wendell H. *The World in Your Garden.* 1957. Washington. 1st ed. dj. $10.00

CAMP, William. *San Francisco. Port of Gold.* 1948. Doubleday. Ills. maps. photos. dj. VG $15.00

CAMPBELL, A. *The Heart of Africa.* 1954. 1st ed. $7.50

CAMPBELL, Bruce. *Dictionary of Birds in Color.* 1983. Exeter. 1,008 color bird photos. EX $28.00

CAMPBELL, Bruce. *Dictionary of Birds.* 1974. New York. Ills. 1st ed. dj. VG $17.50

CAMPBELL, D. *On Trail of Veiled Tuareg.* Philadelphia. (ca.1938) VG $45.00

CAMPBELL, D. *The Lairds of Glenlyon.* 1984. Strathtay. reprint. 351 pp. dj. $30.00

CAMPBELL, D. *Wanderings in Central Africa.* 1929. London. VG $42.50

CAMPBELL, D. *Wanderings in Wildest Africa.* 1931. London. Tract Soc. photos. fld map. VG $13.00

CAMPBELL, H.J. *Beyond the Visible.* 1952. London. Hamilton. 1st ed. sgn. dj. VG $15.00

CAMPBELL, Helen. *Darkness & Daylight/Lights & Shadows of NY Life.* 1892. Connecticut. 740 pp. VG $22.50

CAMPBELL, Helen. *Darkness & Daylight/Lights & Shadows of NY Life.* 1899. Ills. VG $27.50

CAMPBELL, Hope. *Legend of Lost Earth.* 1977. New York. Four Winds. 1st ed. $10.00

CAMPBELL, Hugh. *State of Rise & Progress of Disputes with Spain.* 1739. London. 1st ed. marbled wrappers. $250.00

CAMPBELL, J. *Voyages to & from the Cape of Good Hope.* 1840. Philadelphia. 1st Am. ed. 271 pp. $20.00

CAMPBELL, James. *The Bombing of Nuremburg.* 1974. New York. Ills. Book Club ed. VG $10.00

CAMPBELL, Jason B. *Illus. History of Paris International Exposition.* 1900. Chicago. 12 vol set. wrappers. $35.00

CAMPBELL, John W., Jr. *Cloak of Aesir.* 1952. Chicago. 1st ed. dj. EX $20.00

CAMPBELL, John W., Jr. *Islands of Space.* 1956. Reading. Fantasy. 1st trade ed. dj. VG $20.00

CAMPBELL, John W., Jr. *The Mightiest Machine.* 1947. Hadley Pub. Ills. 1st ed. dj. $40.00

CAMPBELL, John W., Jr. *The Moon is Hell.* 1951. Reading. Fantasy. 1st trade ed. dj. VG $20.00

CAMPBELL, John W., Jr. *Invaders from the Infinite.* 1961. Hicksville. Gnome. Ltd. 1st ed. dj. EX $35.00

CAMPBELL, Libby Marsh. *Make Me a Falcon.* 1974. 100 pp. dj. $9.00

CAMPBELL, R. *Cold Print.* 1985. Scream Press. Ltd. ed. 1/250. sgn. EX $60.00

CAMPBELL, R. *Face That Must Die.* 1983. Scream Press. Ltd. ed. sgn. boxed. EX $300.00

CAMPBELL, R. *Obsession.* London. sgn. $28.00

CAMPBELL, R.T. *Bodies in the Bookshop.* 1946. London. 1st ed. VG $35.00

CAMPBELL, R.T. *Take Thee a Sharp Knife.* 1946. London. 1st ed. dj. VG $20.00

CAMPBELL, Roy. *Pomegranates.* 1932. London. Ills. Boswell. Ltd. 1st ed. EX $100.00

CAMPBELL, Roy. *The Wayzgoose. A South African Satire.* 1928. London. 1st ed. dj. VG $30.00

CAMPBELL, Ruth. *Small Fry & the Winged Horse.* 1927. Volland. Ills. Gustaf Tenggren. 1st ed. $50.00

CAMPBELL, Ruth. *The Cat Whose Whiskers Slipped & Other Stories.* 1938. New York. Ills. V.E. Cadie. EX $20.00

CAMPBELL, Tom W. *Two Fighters & Two Fines.* 1941. Little Rock. 557 pp. dj. VG $15.00

CAMPBELL SOUP CO. *Easy Ways to Delicious Meals.* 1967. 203 pp. $6.00

CAMPBELL. *Demons by Daylight.* 1973. Arkham House. dj. VG $30.00

CAMPBELL. *The Mythis Image.* 1974. Princeton U. Press. $30.00

CAMPION, Thomas. *Selected Songs.* 1973. Boston/London. 1st ed. dj. EX $50.00

CAMUS, Albert. *A Happy Death.* 1972. New York. Knopf. 1st Am. ed. $7.50

CAMUS, Albert. *Le Minotaure ou Le Halte D'Oran.* 1950. Ltd. 1st ed. wrappers. VG $17.50

CAMUS, Albert. *Notebooks 1935-1942.* 1963. New York. 1st ed. dj. VG $10.00

CAMUS, Albert. *Resistance, Rebellion, & Death.* 1961. Knopf. trans. 1st Am. ed. dj. VG $30.00

CAMUS, Albert. *Two Plays: Caligula & Cross Purpose.* 1947. London. 1st ed. dj. $10.00

CANAVOR, Frederick. *Rape One.* 1982. Madonna. dj. VG $10.00

CANBY, Henry Seidel. *Thoreau.* 1939. Boston. Houghton Mifflin. 508 pp. $7.50

CANBY, Henry Seidel. *Turn West Turn East-Mark Twain & Henry James.* 1951. 1st ed. dj. $10.00

CANDEE, H.C. *The Tapestry Book.* 1935. New York. Ills. dj. boxed. EX $25.00

CANE, Melville. *So That It Flower.* 1966. New York. 1st ed. $5.00

CANFIELD, C.L. *The City of Six.* 1910. McClurg. Ills. VG $15.00

CANFIELD, C.L. *The Diary of a '49er.* 1920. Boston. 250 pp. $12.50

CANFIELD, Dorothy. *Decorations by Robert Ball. Basque People.* 1931. Harcourt Brace.dj. VG $15.00

CANFIELD, Dorothy. *Hillsboro People.* 1915. New York. 1st ed. VG $15.00

CANFIELD, Dorothy. *Raw Material.* 1923. New York. VG $8.50

CANFIELD, Dorothy. *Rough-Hewn.* 1922. New York. VG $10.00

CANNELL, J.C. *The Secrets of Houdini.* 1973. G $2.00

CANNON, Le Grand B. *Personal Reminiscences of the Rebellion.* 1895. 1st ed. 228 pp. $32.50

CANNON, Poppy & Brooks, P. *The President's Cookbook.* 1968. New York. Funk & Wagnalls. 545 pp. $15.00

CANNON, R. *The Sea of Cortez.* 1966. Menlo Park. Ills. 1st ed. dj. EX $25.00

CANNON, R. *The Sea of Cortez.* 1966. San Francisco. dj. EX $20.00

CANTOR, Bert. *The Bernie Cornfield Story.* 1970. Lyle Stuart. 320 pp. dj. G $5.00

CANTOR, Eddie. *Take My Life.* 1957. Ills. 1st ed. sgn. dj. $45.00

CANTWELL, R. *Alexander Wilson, Naturalist & Pioneer.* 1961. Lippincott. Ills. 1st ed. 319 pp. dj. $45.00

CANZIANI. *Through the Appenines & Abruzzi.* 1928. Houghton Mifflin. Ills. VG $35.00

CAPEK, Karel. *Meteor.* 1935. New York. Putnam. 1st Am. ed. dj. VG $12.50

CAPEK, Karel. *Tales from Two Pockets.* 1943. New York. 1st Am. ed. dj. VG $60.00

CAPEK, Karel. *The Makropoulos Secret.* 1925. Boston. 1st ed. G $25.00

CAPEK, Thomas. *The Slovaks of Hungary. Slavs & Panslavism.* 1906. New York. 1st ed. 215 pp. index. $15.00

CAPELLO & IREAUS. *From Benquella to the Territory of Yacca.* 1882. London. 2 vol set. VG $95.00

CAPES, Bernard. *The Lake of Wine.* 1898. New York. 364 pp. $10.00

CAPES, Bernard. *The Skeleton Key.* 1918. New York. Doran. VG $12.50

CAPON, Robert Farrar. *Capon On Cooking.* 1983. Boston. Houghton Mifflin. 1st ed. dj. $7.50

CAPOTE, Truman. *A Christmas Memory.* 1966. Random House. 1st trade ed. slipcase. EX $30.00

CAPOTE, Truman. *A Tree of Night.* 1949. Random House. 1st ed. dj. VG $95.00

CAPOTE, Truman. *Breakfast at Tiffany's.* 1958. Random House. 1st ed. dj. VG $90.00

CAPOTE, Truman. *Christmas Memory.* 1956. New York. Ltd. ed. sgn. slipcase. EX $75.00

CAPOTE, Truman. *In Cold Blood.* Ltd. 1st ed. 1/500. sgn. $140.00

CAPOTE, Truman. *In Cold Blood.* 1965. New York. Random House. 343 pp. $10.00

CAPOTE, Truman. *Local Color.* 1950. New York. 1st ed. dj. VG $75.00

CAPOTE, Truman. *Music for Chameleons.* 1980. Random House. 1st trade ed. dj. VG $15.00

CAPOTE, Truman. *Observations.* 1959. New York. Simon & Schuster. VG $60.00

CAPOTE, Truman. *Other Voices/Other Rooms.* 1948. London. Heinemann. 1st Eng. ed. dj. VG $65.00

CAPOTE, Truman. *Other Voices/Other Rooms.* 1948. Random House. dj. EX $60.00

CAPOTE, Truman. *Selected Writings.* 1963. Random House. 1st ed. dj. VG $40.00

CAPOTE, Truman. *The Dogs Bark.* 1973. Random House. dj. EX $30.00

CAPOTE, Truman. *The Muses are Heard.* 1957. Heineman. 1st English ed. dj. VG $35.00

CAPOTE, Truman. *The Muses are Heard.* 1956. New York. Random House. 1st ed. dj. EX $75.00

CAPPON, Daniel. *Toward an Understanding of Homosexuality.* 1965. New York. dj. VG $12.50

CAPPS, C.M. *Indian Legends & Poems.* Dalton, GA. Tennessee Pub. VG $15.00

CAPUTO, P. *Horn of Africa.* 1980. Ltd. ed. 1/250. sgn. slipcase $35.00

CAPUTO, Philip. *Rumor of War.* 1977. New York. 1st ed. ed. EX $27.50

CARAS, R. *Dangerous to Man.* 1964. Chilton. Ills. 1st ed. 433 pp. $15.00

CARAS, R. *Monarch of Deadman Bay, Life & Death of a Kodiak.* 1969. Little, Brown & Co. 1st ed. $10.00

CARAS, R. *North American Mammals.* 1967. Galahad. photos. maps. 578 pp. dj. EX $20.00

CARAS, R. *Panther!* 1969. Little, Brown. 1st ed. $7.00

CARAS, R. *Venomous Animals of the World.* 1974. Prentice Hall. Ills. 1st ed. 362 pp. dj. $20.00

CARAS, Roger. *North American Mammals/Fur-Bearing Animals of U.S.* 1967. New York. 1st ed. 4 color pls. dj. VG $22.50

CARDWELL, P. *America's Camping Book.* 1969. Scribner. photos. 591 pp. dj. VG $9.00

CARELL, P. *They're Coming. German Account Battle for France.* 1984. Ills. pb. EX $4.00

CAREY, C. *A General History of Oregon.* 1936. Portland. 2 vol set. $37.50

CAREY, Gary. *All the Stars in Heaven.* 1981. New York. 1st ed. 320 pp. dj. VG $7.50

CAREY. *Little Miss Muffet.* 1893. Lippincott. Ills. VG $14.00

CARGILL, M. *Gallery of Nazis.* 1978. Lyle Stuart. Ills. dj. VG $28.00

CARHART, A. *Hunting North American Deer.* 1946. 1st ed. VG $12.50

CARHART, Arthur. *Hi, Stranger: Complete Guide to Dude Ranches.* 1949. New York. photos. 222 pp. dj. $3.50

CARL, G.C. *The Amphibians of British Columbia.* 1950. England. Ills. Frank Beebe. 62 pp. $10.00

CARLBORG, U. *Vascular Studies in Pseudoxanthoma Elasticum.* 1959. Stockholm. 1st ed. stiff wrappers. $12.50

CARLELL, Lodowick. *Fool Would Be a Favorite.* Golden Cockerel Pr. Ltd. ed. $35.00

CARLETON, Will. *City Ballads & Farm Legends.* 1885. New York. $5.00

CARLETON, Will. *Farm Ballads.* 1882. Harper. Ills. $15.00

CARLETON, Will. *Farm Festivals.* 1881. Harper. Ills. $15.00

CARLETON. *Farm Legends.* 1876. Harper. Ills. VG $14.00

CARLETON. *The Seat of Empire.* 1870. 1st ed. 232 pp. $45.00

CARLOVA, John. *Mistress of the Seas.* 1964. 1st ed. dj. VG $7.50

CARLSON, J.R. *Under Cover.* 1943. New York. 544 pp. EX $4.00

CARLSON, L.H. *An Alaska Gold Mine.* 1951. N. Western U. G $16.00

CARLSON, R.E. *Liverpool & Manchester Railway Project 1821-31.* 1969. Ills. EX $27.50

CARLSON, William K. *Elysium.* 1982. Garden City. review copy. dj. VG $10.00

CARLSON & BATES. *Hearst, Lord of San Simoeon.* 1936. New York. 332 pp. $10.00

CARLTON, W.N.C. *Pauline, Favorite Sister of Napoleon.* 1930. New York. Harper. 372 pp. $4.00

CARLYLE, Thomas. *Latter Day Pamphlets.* 1850. Boston. wrappers. VG $25.00

CARLYLE, Thomas. *Oliver Cromwell's Letters & Speeches.* 1846. New York. Colyer. 336 pp. G $57.50

CARLYLE, Thomas. *The Early Kings of Norway.* 1875. New York. Harper. 257 pp. VG $6.00

CARMAN, B. & Hovey, R. *More Songs from Vagabondia.* 1896. Ltd. 2nd ed. 1/750. VG $20.00

CARMAN, Harry J. & Syrett, H. *A History of the American People to 1865. Vol I.* 1952. New York. Knopf. G $3.00

CARMER, Carl. *Dark Trees to the Wind.* 1st ed. dj. EX $12.00

CARMER, Carl. *Listen for a Lonesome Drum.* 1950. New York. Ills. Cosgrave. 430 pp. dj. VG $4.00

CARMER, Carl. *Songs of R.O.A.* 1942. 1st ed. dj. EX $25.00

CARMER, Carl. *Songs of the Rivers of America.* 1942. New York. dj. VG $65.00

CARMER, Carl. *Stars Fell on Alabama.* 1934. New York. Literary Guild. 294 pp. $3.00

CARMICHAEL, Jim. *The Modern Rifle.* 1975. New York. Wincester Pr. Ills. 342 pp. $12.50

CARNEGIE, Andrew. *An American Four-in-Hand in Britain.* 1884. Scribner. 339 pp. VG $65.00

CARNEGIE, Andrew. *Around the World.* 1895. New York. presentation copy. sgn. $50.00

CARNEGIE, Dale. *Biographical Roundup.* 1944. 1st ed. dj. $8.50

CARNEGIE, Dale. *How to Win Friends.* 1937. VG $7.50

CARNER, M. *The Waltz.* 1948. London. dj. EX $8.50

CARNEVALI, Emanuel. *A Hurried Man.* Paris. VG $125.00

CARNOCHAN, F.L. & Adamson, H. *Out of Africa.* 1936. 1st ed. dj. $7.50

CARO. *The Power Broker.* 1974. New York. 1st ed. dj. $7.00

CAROE, Olaf. *Soviet Empire: Turks of Central Asia & Stalinism.* 1967. London. 2nd ed. ex-lib. 308 pp. $10.00

CARPENTER, Edward. *Love's Coming of Age.* 1911. New York. 1st ed. dj. EX $45.00

CARPENTER, Ernest C. *The Boyhood Days of President Calvin Coolidge.* 1926. Rutland, VT. Tuttle. photos. 192 pp. EX $5.50

CARPENTER, F.B. *Six Months at White House with Abraham Lincoln.* 1867. New York. VG $17.50

CARPENTER, F.D. *Adventures in Geyser Land.* 1935. Caldwell. Caxton. 1st ed. VG $65.00

CARPENTER, Frances. *Tales of a Chinese Grandmother.* 1937. Jr. Literary Guild. dj. VG $10.00

CARPENTER, John A. *Sword & Olive Branch.* 1964. Pittsburgh. Ills. 1st ed. 379 pp. $15.00

CARPENTER, Liz. *Ruffles & Flourishes.* 1970. 1st ed. dj. $8.50

CARPENTER, R.G. & Stiegler, H. *Fishes of New Hampshire.* 1947. NH Fish & Game. Ills. 87 pp. $10.00

CARPENTER, Scott. *We Seven.* 1962. New York. Simon & Schuster. photos. dj. $4.00

CARPENTER, Will Tomas. *Lucky 7. A Cowman's Autobiography.* 1957. TX U. Press. Ills. Lee Hart. 1st ed. dj. VG $25.00

CARPENTER. *A Naturalist on Lake Victoria.* 1920. Dutton. VG $20.00

CARR, Archie. *So Excellent a Fish, Natural Hist. of Sea Turtles.* 1967. Nat. Hist. Press. 1st ed. $20.00

CARR, Archie. *The Reptiles.* 1963. Life Nature Lib. Ills. 192 pp. $13.00

CARRYL, G.W. *Fables for the Frivolous.* 1898. New York. Ills. Newell. 1st ed. VG $35.00

CARSON, Gerald. *History of Bourbon. Unhurried Account of Drink.* 1963. New York. Ills. 280 pp. index. $12.50

CARSON, James. *The Saddle Boys on Mexican Trails.* 1915. New York. 208 pp. G $2.00

CARSON, Kit. *Life & Adventures of Kit Carson.* 1874. Hartford. $50.00

CARSON, Rachel L. *The Sea Around Us.* 1951. New York. Oxford Press. 230 pp. dj. VG $4.00

CARSON, Robert. *The Magic Lantern.* 1952. Holt. 1st ed. 504 pp. $52.50

CARSON, W.E. *Mexico.* 1909. New York. Macmillan. Ills. 1st ed. VG $16.00

CARTER, A.C. *The Kingdom of Siam.* 1904. Putnam. 1st ed. photos. 280 pp. VG $13.00

CARTER, A.E. *Battle of South America.* 1941. VG $10.00

CARTER, Angela. *Fireworks.* 1981. New York. Harper. 1st ed. dj. EX $15.00

CARTER, Angela. *Heroes & Villains.* 1970. New York. Simon & Schuster. 1st ed. dj. $25.00

CARTER, Angela. *Nights at the Circus.* London. sgn. $30.00

CARTER, Angela. *Nights at the Circus.* 1985. 1st Am. review copy. dj. EX $20.00

CARTER, Angela. *The Bloody Chamber.* 1979. New York. Harper. 1st ed. dj. VG $20.00

CARTER, Clarence Edwin. *Territorial Papers of the United States.* 1934. Washington. 694 pp. $16.50

CARTER, David. *Butterflies & Moths in Britain & Europe.* 1982. British Museum.1st ed. 300 photos. dj. EX $35.00

CARTER, H. *The Histories of Herodotus.* 1958. Heritage. Ills. map. 2 vol set. $10.00

CARTER, Isabel Hopestill. *Shipmates.* 1934. 1st ed. $12.50

CARTER, Jimmy. *Keeping the Faith.* 1982. New York. Bantam. 622 pp. dj. $10.00

CARTER, Jimmy. *Keeping the Faith.* Ltd. ed. sgn. slipcase. EX $45.00

CARTER, John & Muir, P. *Printing & the Mind of Man.* 1967. London. 1st ed. dj. EX $240.00

CARTER, John & Pollard, G. *Firm of Charles Ottley, Landon & Co.* 1948. London/NY. Ills. 1st ed. wrappers. VG $45.00

CARTER, John & Pollard, G. *Gorfin's Stock.* 1970. Oxford. Blackwell. Ltd. 1st ed. EX $50.00

CARTER, John & Pollard, G. *The Mystery of 'The Death of Balder.'* 1969. Oxford. Blackwell. Ltd. 1st ed. EX $60.00

CARTER, John & Sadleir, M. *Victorian Fiction.* 1947. London. 50 pp. wrappers. VG $25.00

CARTER, John. *ABC for Book Collectors.* 1952. London. Hart Davis. 1st ed. dj. VG $45.00

CARTER, John. *Books & Book Collectors.* 1956. London. Hart Davis. 2nd impression. EX $30.00

CARTER, John. *Handlist of Writings of Stanley Morison.* 1950. Cambridge. Ltd. ed. VG $65.00

CARTER, John. *Taste & Technique in Book Collecting.* 1949. Cambridge. 2nd impression. dj. VG $30.00

CARTER, Lin. *Invisible Death.* 1975. Doubleday. dj. VG $15.00

CARTER, Lin. *Lovecraft.* 1972. New York. Ballantine. 1st ed. pb. EX $8.50

CARTER, Lin. *The Earth-Shaker.* 1982. Garden City. 1st ed. dj. VG $10.00

CARTER, Lin. *The Spawn of Cthulhu.* Ballantine. pb. VG $6.50

CARTER, Lin. *The Volcano Ogre.* 1976. Doubleday. dj. VG $15.00

CARTER, R. *Those Devils in Baggy Pants.* 1951. New York. 1st ed. VG $15.00

CARTER, Robert A. *American Revolution Bicentennial 1776-1976.* 1976. Mansfield, OH. 60 pp. wrappers. $7.50

CARTER, Rosalynn. *First Lady from Plains.* Ltd. 1st ed. 1/750. sgn. $20.00

CARTER, Thomas. *The Invention of Printing in China.* 1931. revised ed. dj. VG $80.00

CARTER, William Harding. *The Horses of the World.* 1923. Washington. 95 Ills. 118 pp. $20.00

CARTER & MUIR. *Printing & the Mind of Man.* 1967. 1st ed. dj. $100.00

CARTER. *The Boy Scouts First Camp Fire.* 1913. A.L. Burt. dj. EX $7.50

CARTER. *101st Field Artillery, AEF, 1917-1919.* 1940. dj. VG $15.00

CARTIER-BRESSON, Henri. *People of Moscow.* 1955. Simon Schuster. dj. EX $35.00

CARTIER-BRESSON, Henri. *The Europeans.* 1955. New York. EX $57.50

CARTWRIGHT, A.P. *The Corner House: Early History of Johannesburg.* 1965. Capetown. Purnell. Ills. dj. EX $20.00

CARTWRIGHT, Edward. *Life, Writings, Inventions of Dr. Ed. Cartwright.* 1843. 1st ed. ex-lib. 372 pp. G $42.00

CARUS, Paul. *Chinese Thought.* 1907. Open Court Pub.EX $25.00

CARUS, Paul. *Point of View.* 1927. Open Court Pub.VG $12.50

CARUS, Paul. *Story of Samson.* 1907. Open Court Pub.VG $30.00

CARUS, Paul. *Truth on Trial.* 1911. Open Court Pub.dj. EX $30.00

CARUSO, John Anthony. *Appalachian Frontier/America's First Surge West.* 1956. Indianapolis. Ills. 408 pp. VG $7.50

CARVER, C. *Bookplates of Princeton & Princetonians.* 1912. Princeton. Ltd. ed. EX $45.00

CARVER, C. *Brann & the Iconoclast.* 1957. 1st ed. dj. VG $20.00

CARVER, Raymond. *Cathedral.* 1983. Knopf. 1st ed. sgn. dj. VG $30.00

CARVER, Raymond. *Cathedral.* 1983. New York. Knopf. proof copy. VG $50.00

CARVER, Raymond. *Cathedral.* 1983. Knopf. advance copy. VG $50.00

CARVER, Raymond. *Early for the Dance.* 1986. Ewert. Ltd. ed. 1/100. sgn. wrappers. $45.00

CARVER, Raymond. *Fires: Essay-Poems-Stories.* 1983. Capra. Ltd. 1st ed. dj. EX $30.00

CARVER, Raymond. *If It Please You.* 1984. Lord John. Ltd. ed. 1/200. $50.00

CARVER, Raymond. *If It Please You.* 1984. Lord John. Ltd. ed. 1/26. sgn. EX $150.00

CARVER, Raymond. *Ultramarine.* 1986. proof copy. $60.00

CARVER, Raymond. *Where Water Comes Together with Other Water.* 1985. Random House. 1st ed. dj. VG $15.00

CARVER, Raymond. *Where Water Comes Together with Other Water.* 1985. review copy. dj. VG $25.00

CARVER. *Three Years Travel Interior North America.* 1798. Edinburgh. $125.00

CARY, Alice. *From Year to Year.* 1884. Chicago/NY. 312 pp. $12.50

CARY, Alice. *From Year to Year.* 1890. Henneberry. 312 pp. $4.50

CARY, Diana S. *The Hollywood Posse.* 1975. Boston. Ills. 268 pp. $9.00

CARY, Joyce. *Cock Jarvis.* 1974. London. 1st ed. dj. $15.00

CARY, Joyce. *Not Honour More.* 1955. London. Joseph. 1st ed. dj. EX $25.00

CARY, Joyce. *The Captive & the Free.* 1959. New York. Harper. 1st Am. ed. dj. VG $15.00

CARY, Joyce. *The Horse's Mouth.* 1944. London. Joseph. 1st ed. dj. VG $65.00

CARY, Joyce. *The Horse's Mouth.* 1957. London. Ills. VG $15.00

CARY, Joyce. *The Horse's Mouth.* 1944. New York. Harper. 1st Am. ed. 311 pp. VG $15.00

CASANOVA, Carlamaria. *Renata Tebaldi: La Voce d'Angelo.* 1981. Milano. Ills. sgns. dj. VG $35.00

CARR, E.H. *A History of Soviet Russia; Interregnum 1923-1924.*1954. New York. Macmillan. 392 pp. $8.00

CARR, H.G. *Flags of the World.* 1953. London. 209 pp. 300 flags in color. EX $14.50

CARR, Harry, ed. *The Collected Prestonian Lectures, 1925-1960.* 1984. London. Lewis Masonic. 491 pp. dj. EX $12.50

CARR, J. Scott. *The Devil in Robes; or, The Sin of Priests.* Aurora, MO. no date. $4.00

CARR, Jayge. *Navigator's Syndrome.* 1983. Garden City. review copy. dj. VG $10.00

CARR, John Dickson. *Captain Cut-Throat.* 1955. New York. Harper. 1st ed. dj. EX $30.00

CARR, John Dickson. *Deadly Hall.* 1971. New York. Harper. 1st ed. dj. EX $20.00

CARR, John Dickson. *He Who Whispers.* 1946. New York. Harper. 1st ed. dj. EX $60.00

CARR, John Dickson. *Life of Sir Arthur Conan Doyle.* 1949. London. 1st ed. dj. VG $30.00

CARR, John Dickson. *Panic in Box C.* 1966. New York. Harper. 1st ed. dj. EX $30.00

CARR, John Dickson. *The Bride of Newgate.* 1950. Harper. 1st ed. dj. $15.00

CARR, John Dickson. *The Dead Sleep Lightly.* 1983. Doubleday. dj. VG $7.50

CARR, John Dickson. *The Life of Sir Arthur Conan Doyle.* 1949. New York. 1st ed. 304 pp. index. EX $55.00

CARR, John Dickson. *The Men Who Explained Miracles.* 1964. London. Hamilton. 1st Eng. ed. dj. VG $22.50

CARR, M.F. *Life Among the Shakers.* New York. (ca.1885-90) 36 pp. wrappers. $45.00

CARR, Norman. *The White Impala.* 1969. London. Collins. Ills. 1st ed. 190 pp. $20.00

CARR, Terry, ed. *Universe 11.* 1981. Garden City. 1st ed. dj. $10.00

CARR, Terry, ed. *Universe 14.* 1984. Garden City. 1st ed. dj. VG $8.00

CARR, Terry, ed. *Universe 3.* 1973. New York. 1st ed. dj. EX $12.50

CARRASCO, Pedro. *Land & Polity in Tibet.* 1959. WA U. 1st ed. $15.00

CARRICK, A. Van L. *History of American Silhouettes.* 1968. Rutland. dj. $17.50

CARRIGHAR, S. *Icebound Summer.* 1953. Knopf. Ills. 262 pp. dj. VG $9.00

CARRIGHAR, S. *Moonlight at Midday.* 1959. Knopf. photos. map. dj. EX $9.00

CARRIGHAR, Sally. *One Day at Teton Marsh.* 1955. London. Ills. G. & P. Mattson. 1st ed. $15.00

CARRINGTON, Fitztrey, ed. *Essays on England & Etchers.* 1912. New York. 1st ed. $20.00

CARRINGTON, Gen. Henry B. *Washington the Soldier.* 1899. Boston. 2nd ed. inscr. G $25.00

CARRINGTON, Grant. *Time's Fool.* 1981. Garden City. review copy. dj. VG $15.00

CARRINGTON, Hereward. *True Ghost Stories.* 1915. 1st ed. dj. VG $35.00

CARRINGTON, Mrs. Margaret I. *Absaraka, Home of the Crows.* 1950. EX $30.00

CARRINGTON, R. *Elephants.* 1958. London. Chatto & Windus. Ills. 272 pp. $18.00

CARRIQUE, Jean. *In Monument Rose.* 1953. Noonday. 1st ed. dj. VG $12.50

CARRIQUE, Jean. *The Monument Rose.* 1953. Harper. 1st ed. dj. VG $75.00

CARROL, Ruth. *Chessie by Ruth Carrol.* 1936. VG $12.50

CARROLL, Alice. *Complete Guide to Modern Knitting & Crocheting.* 1942. New York. Wise & Co. Ills. 310 pp. G $5.00

CARROLL, George. *Art Stationery & Usages of Polite Society.* 1880. New York. embossed pls. VG $35.00

CARROLL, Gladys H. *Few Foolish Ones.* 1935. 1st ed. dj. VG $15.00

CARROLL, J.A. *Reflections of Western Historians.* 1969. dj. VG $10.00

CARROLL, James. *Family Trade.* 1982. Little, Brown. proof copy. sgn. wrappers. VG $25.00

CARROLL, James. *Mortal Friends.* 1978. Little, Brown. dj. VG $15.00

CARROLL, John. *Eggenhofer: Pulp Years.* Ltd. ed. 1/250. sgn. boxed. $75.00

CARROLL, Lewis. *Adventures in Wonderland & Through Looking-Glass.* 1923. Philadelphia. Ills. Prittie & Tenniel. VG $20.00

CARROLL, Lewis. *Alice au Pays de Merveilles.* 1949. Paris. Ills. Jourcin. VG $25.00

CARROLL, Lewis. *Alice in Wonderland.* Boston. (ca.1930) Ills. 252 pp. $6.00

CARROLL, Lewis. *Alice in Wonderland.* 1941. Ills. G $25.00

CARROLL, Lewis. *Alice in Wonderland.* London. Ills. Gwenedd Hudson. dj. VG $40.00

CARROLL, Lewis. *Alice in Wonderland.* 1899. New York. Mansfield & Wessels. VG $70.00

CARROLL, Lewis. *Alice's Adventures & Through the Looking Glass.* Philadelphia. Macrae-Smith. Ills. Tenniel. $15.00

CARROLL, Lewis. *Alice's Adventures in Wonderland.* 1923. Philadelphia. Ills. Tenniel & Prittie. $9.00

CARROLL, Lewis. *Alice's Adventures in Wonderland.* 1923. Philadelphia. Ills. Kay & Tenniel. VG $55.00

CARROLL, Lewis. *Alice's Adventures in Wonderland.* 1982. Berkeley. reprint Pennyroyal trade ed. $30.00

CARROLL, Lewis. *Alice's Adventures in Wonderland.* 1941. New York. Heritage. Ills. Tenniel. dj. $15.00

CARROLL, Lewis. *Alice's Adventures in Wonderland.* 1941. New York. Book League of Am. Ills. EX $15.00

CARROLL, Lewis. *Alice's Adventures Underground.* 1964. Ann Arbor. Ills. slipcase. EX $20.00

CARROLL, Lewis. *Alices's Adventures Underground.* 1965. New York. Dover. exlib. 95 pp. G $3.50

CARROLL, Lewis. *Handbook of Literature of Rev. C.L. Dodgson.* 1931. Oxford. Ltd. ed. 1/750. VG $20.00

CARROLL, Lewis. *Lewis Carroll's the Hunting of the Snark.* 1982. Los Altos. Centennial Ed. dj. VG $15.00

CARROLL, Lewis. *Rhyme? Reason?* 1883. London. 1st ed. Ills. A.B. Frost. G $35.00

CARROLL, Lewis. *Rhyme? Reason?* 1884. New York. 1st Am. ed. VG $20.00

CARROLL, Lewis. *The Hunting of the Snark & Other Poems.* 1903. NY/London. Harper. Ills. Newell. 1st ed. $35.00

CARROLL, Lewis. *The Hunting of the Snark & Other Poems.* 1937. Macmillan. Ills. Holiday. $25.00

CARROLL, Lewis. *The Road to Nowhere.* 1900. New York. Ills. Morse & Livingston. VG $30.00

CARROLL, Lewis. *Through Looking Glass & What Alice Found There.* 1983. Berkeley. U. of CA Press. Ills. Moser. $30.00

CARROLL, Lewis. *Through Looking Glass & What Alice Found There.* 1946. New York. Random House special ed. Ills. $18.00

CARROLL, Lewis. *Through Looking Glass & What Alice Found There.* 1902. NY/London. Ills. Peter Newell. 1st ed. $75.00

CARROLL, P. *Odes.* 1969. 1st ed. dj. $10.00

CARROLL. *Photography with the Graflex 22.* 1954. 1st ed. VG $10.00

CARROLL. *The Night Before Christmas.* (ca.1920) Ills. Tasha Tudor. $22.50

CARRUTH, Hayden. *For You. Poems.* 1970. New Directions.1st ed. dj. VG $20.00

CARRUTHERS, Douglas. *Beyond the Caspian, A Naturalist in Central Asia.* 1949. Edinburgh. Oliver & Boyd. 1st ed. 290 pp. $135.00

CARRUTHERS, George. *The Story of Paper-Making.* 1901. Chicago. Butler Paper Co. VG $15.00

CARRYL, Charles E. *Davy & the Goblin.* 1886. Boston. 1st ed. $85.00

CASANOVA. *Memoirs of Casanova.* 1894. trans. Machen. 6 vol set. VG $175.00

CASATI, G. *Ten Years in Equatoria.* 1891. NY/London. VG $127.50

CASE, Frank. *Keeping the Lions, an Algonquin Cookbook.* 1942. Graystone. 1st ed. dj. VG $25.00

CASE, Frank. *Tales of the Wayward Inn.* 1938. Philadelphia. Ills. index. VG $25.00

CASE, Josephine Young. *At Midnight on the 31st of March.* 1938. Boston. 1st ed. inscr. 132 pp. dj. $10.00

CASEY, Bernie. *Look at the People.* 1969. Garden City. 1st ed. dj. EX $20.00

CASEY, Brig. Gen. Silas. *Infantry Tactics.* 1865. Ills. 3 vol set. $57.50

CASLER, J.O. *Four Years in the Stonewall Brigade.* 1951. Marietta, GA. Continental Books. 365 pp. VG $25.00

CASLER. *Cape Vincent & Its History.* 1906. New York. 1st ed. $15.00

CASS, William. *In the Heart of the Heart of the Country.* 1968. Harper. 1st ed. dj. VG $75.00

CASSERES, Benjamin de. *Mencken & Shaw.* 1930. New York. $10.00

CASSON, Herbert N. *History of the Telephone.* 1911. Chicago. Ills. 315 pp. $8.50

CASSON, P. *Decoys Simplified.* 1972. dj. EX $12.50

CASSON, Stanley. *Murder by Burial.* 1938. New York. 1st ed. dj. VG $12.50

CASTANEDA, Carlos. *A Separate Reality.* 1971. New York. 2nd printing. dj. VG $10.00

CASTANEDA, Carlos. *Tales of Power.* 1974. New York. Simon & Schuster. 1st ed. dj. $20.00

CASTANEDA, Carlos. *The Eagle's Gift.* 1981. New York. Simon & Schuster. 1st ed. dj. $20.00

CASTANEDA, Carlos. *The Eagle's Gift.* 1981. 2nd ed. dj. VG $7.50

CASTANEDA, Carlos. *The Second Ring of Power.* 1977. New York. Simon & Schuster. 1st ed. dj. $25.00

CASTANEDA. *Teachings of Don Juan.* 1973. New York. Simon & Schuster. dj. VG $12.50

CASTEL, Albert *William Clarke Quantrill: His Life.* 1962. Ills. 250 pp. $12.50

CASTELLO. *The Theory & Practice of Fencing.* 1933. Scribner. Ills. 272 pp. $12.50

CASTELLS, F. *Antiquity of the Holy Royal Arch.* 1960. London. Lewis. 299 pp. EX $17.50

CASTELLS, F. *Our Ancient Brethren, Originators of Freemasonry.* 1932. London. 1st ed. 308 pp. VG $37.50

CASTELLS, F. *The Genuine Secrets in Freemasonry Prior to 1717.* 1971. London. Lewis. EX $22.50

CASTILLO, B.D.D. *Discovery & the Conquest of Mexico 1517-1521.* 1936. London. Routledge. Ills. 3rd ed. dj. $12.50

CASTIN, M. & Phipps, D. *Racing & Sports Car Chassis Design.* 1963. Bentley, MA. 3rd impression. 147 pp. dj. $10.00

CASTLE, Pat. *Descriptive Angling.* 1935. 1st ed. $8.50

CASTLEMOLE. *On Winged Arrow Medicine.* 1909. VG $7.00

CASTLEMON, Harry. *Elam Storm the Wolfer.* 1895. Winston Co. VG $6.50

CASTLEMON, Harry. *Frank Among the Rancheros.* 1896. Winston. Rocky Mountain Series. VG $6.50

CASTLEMON, Harry. *Frank at Don Carlos Rancho.* Hurst. Rocky Mountain Series. G $5.50

CASTLEMON, Harry. *Frank Before Vicksburg. The Gun Boat Series.* 1856. Philadelphia. Ills. 256 pp. $7.50

CASTLEMON, Harry. *Frank Before Vicksburg. The Rocky Mountain Series.* 1892. Winston. G $5.50

CASTLEMON, Harry. *Frank in the Woods. The Gun Boat Series.* 1865. Philadelphia. Ills. 256 pp. $7.50

CASWELL. *Arctic Frontiers.* 1956. dj. VG $12.50

CATER, Harold Dean. *Henry Adams & His Friends.* 1947. Boston. dj. $15.00

CATHAM, D. & M. *Cape Coddities.* 1920. Boston. Ills. 166 pp. $5.00

CATHER, Willa S. *Alexander's Bridge.* 1912. Boston/NY. Houghton Mifflin. 1st ed. EX $75.00

CATHER, Willa. *A Lost Lady.* 1923. New York. Knopf. 1st ed. 174 pp. $17.50

CATHER, Willa. *A Lost Lady.* 1923. New York. 1st ed. 5th printing. dj. VG $18.00

CATHER, Willa. *Alexander's Bridge.* 1912. Boston/NY. 1st ed. 3rd printing. VG $40.00

CATHER, Willa. *Death Comes for the Archbishop.* 1927. NY. 303 pp. dj. VG $10.00

CATHER, Willa. *Death Comes for the Archbishop.* 1959. New York. dj. VG $6.00

CATHER, Willa. *Lucy Gayheart.* 1935. New York. 1st ed. dj. VG $16.50

CATHER, Willa. *My Antonia.* 1949. New York. 266 pp. VG $5.00

CATHER, Willa. *My Mortal Enemy.* 1926. 1st ed. 5th printing. dj. slipcase. EX $25.00

CATHER, Willa. *O Pioneers!* 1913. 1st ed. VG $75.00

CATHER, Willa. *On Writing.* 1949. Knopf. 1st ed. dj. VG $32.50

CATHER, Willa. *Sapphira & the Slave Girl.* 1940. New York. 1st ed. 295 pp. dj. VG $20.00

CATHER, Willa. *Shadows on the Rock.* 1931. New York. 1st ed. dj. VG $30.00

CATHER, Willa. *The Old Beauty & Others.* 1948. Knopf. 1st ed. dj. VG $30.00

CATHER, Willa. *The Troll Garden.* 1905. New York. McClure. 1st ed. VG $50.00

CATHER, Willa. *Uncle Valentine & Other Stories.* 1973. U. NB Press. dj. VG $12.50

CATHER, Willa. *Willa Cather in Europe.* 1956. Knopf. 1st ed. dj. $12.50

CATHROP, Dion C. *English Costume in the Middle Ages.* 1906. London. Ills. VG $15.00

CATLIN, George. *Letters & Notes on Customs of N. American Indians.* 1841. London. 1st ed. 1st issue. 2 vol set. $350.00

CATLIN, George. *The Breath of Life.* 1861. New York. wrappers. G $75.00

CATLIN, George. *The Catlin Book of American Indians.* 1977. New York. dj. EX $30.00

CATTON, Bruce. *American Heritage Pictorial History of Civil War.* 1960. 2 vol set. boxed. G $45.00

CATTON, Bruce. *Grant Moves South.* 1960. Boston. 1st ed. dj. G $8.00

CATTON, Bruce. *Hallowed Ground. Story of Union Side of Civil War.* 1956. Garden City. Ills. 1st ed. 437 pp. $10.00

CATTON, Bruce. *Terrible Swift Sword.* 1963. New York. Doubleday. 559 pp. $5.50

CATTON, Bruce. *The Army of the Potomac: Glory Road.* 1952. New York. Doubleday. 389 pp. VG $6.50

CAVE, R.C. *The Men in Gray.* 1911. Nashville. 143 pp. $25.00

CAVE-BROWN, A. *Last Hero Wild Bill Donovan.* 1982. New York. VG $10.00

CAVENDISH, William. *A General System of Horsemanship.* 1970. New York. Winchester Pr. Ills. dj. VG $65.00

CAVETT, Dick & Chris. *Cavett.* 1974. Porterfield. Ills. 1st ed. photos. VG $12.00

CEASARIS, J. *J. Ceasaris Quae Extant Omnia.* 1713. Leyden. w/notes by J. Celsus. 16 Ills. $65.00

CECIL, Henry. *Daughters in Law.* 1961. London. 1st ed. dj. VG $15.00

CECIL, Henry. *Just Within the Law.* 1975. London. 1st ed. dj. VG $20.00

CECIL, Henry. *The Wanted Man.* 1972. London. 1st ed. dj. EX $25.00

CECIL, Lord David. *Two Quiet Lives.* 1948. Indianapolis. Ills. 256 pp. VG $5.00

CELINE, Louis-Ferdinand. *Death on the Installment Plan.* 1938. Boston. Little, Brown. 1st ed. dj. EX $75.00

CELIZ, Francisco. *Diary of Alarcon Expedition into Texas, 1718-1719.*1935. Quivira Soc. Ills. Ltd. 1st ed. 124 pp. $250.00

CELLI, Lisa. *The Pasta Diet.* 1984. New York. 256 pp. dj. EX $5.00

CELLINI. *The Autobiography of Benvenuto Cellini.* 1948. Ills. Dali. $6.50

CENNINI, C.D. *The Craftsman's Handbook.* 1933. Yale U. Press. trans. Thompson. Ills. 169 pp. $15.00

CERAM, C.W. *Gods, Graves, & Scholars.* 1954. Knopf. Ills. photos. $3.00

CERAM, C.W. *Hands on the Past.* 1966. Knopf. Ills. 434 pp. dj. EX $6.50

CERAM, C.W. *The Secret of the Hittites.* 1956. New York. VG $8.00

CERF, Bennett. *An Encyclopedia of Modern American Humor.* 1954. Garden City. Doubleday & Co. 688 pp. VG $4.00

CERF, Bennett. *At Random. The Reminiscences of Bennett Cerf.* 1977. New York. Random House. $5.00

CERF, Bennett. *Bennett Cerf's Bumper Crop.* 1956. Garden City. 733 pp. $3.50

CERF, Bennett. *Laugh Day.* 1965. New York. Doubleday. 496 pp. $3.50

CERF, Bennett. *The Arabian Nights; or, Book of 1001 Nights.* 1932. New York. Blue Ribbon Books. 823 pp. $4.00

CERF, Bennett. *The Bedside Book of Famous British Stories.* 1940. New York. Am. Literary Guild. 1233 pp. $5.00

CERF, Bennett. *The Sound of Laughter.* 1970. Doubleday. 1st ed. sgn. dj. $12.50

CERF, Bennett. *Try & Stop Me.* 1945. New York. Simon & Schuster. 378 pp. $6.00

CERF, Jay & Pozen, Walter. *Strategy for the 60's.* 1961. New York. 155 pp. $3.50

CERF & CARTMELL. *Thirty Famous One Act Plays.* 1943. New York. 617 pp. VG $10.00

CERVANTES, Saavedra. *Don Quixote De La Mancha.* 1941. New York. Ills. Mueller. $20.00

CESCINSKY, H. *English Furniture from Gothic to Sheraton.* 1929. Grand Rapids. Dean-Hicks. folio. VG $60.00

CESCINSKY, H. *English Furniture of the 18th Century.* London. 3 vol set. $150.00

CESCINSKY, H. & Hunter, G.L. *English & American Furniture.* 1929. Garden City. $30.00

CHADWICH. *Little Churches in France.* 1930. 125 pls. $66.00

CHADWICK, D.H. *A Beast of Winter, the Mountain Goat Observed.* 1983. Sierra Club. Ills. maps. 1st ed. dj. EX $20.00

CHADWICK, Nora K. *Celtic Britain.* 1963. New York. Praeger. Ills. maps. 238 pp. $30.00

CHADWICK, Winifred E. *The Borzoi Handbook.* 1952. Ills. $10.00

CHAFFEE, Allen. *The Adventures of Twinkly Eyes, Little Black Bear.*1919. Springfield. Ills. Peter Da Ru. EX $10.00

CHAFFERS, William. *Hall Marks on Gold & Silver Plate.* 1905. London. $90.00

CHAFLIN, Mary B. *Brampton Sketches. Old-Time New England Life.* 1890. New York. Ills. 158 pp. $4.00

CHAGALL, Bella. *Burning Lights.* 1946. New York. Ills. Marc Chagall. 1st ed. EX $75.00

CHAGALL, Marc. *The Jerusalem Windows.* 1967. Braziler. 1st revised ed. $25.00

CHAGALL, Marc. *The Jerusalem Windows.* 1962. New York. 2 lithos. EX $85.00

CHAGALL, Marc. *The Lithographs of Chagall. Vol. 3. 1962-1968.* 1969. Boston. 1st Am. ed. dj. slipcase. EX $200.00

CHAGALL. *Diary of a Horse.* 1956. New York. 1st ed. dj. EX $20.00

CHAGALL. *Jean Sans Terre.* 1955. New York. 1st ed. dj. EX $20.00

CHALFANT, W.A. *Death Valley: the Facts.* 1930. Stanford. Ills. VG $20.00

CHALFANT, W.A. *Gold Guns & Ghost Towns.* 1947. 1st ed. dj. VG $12.00

CHALFANT, W.A. *Outposts of Civilization.* 1928. Boston. G $35.00

CHALLONER, Bishop. *Memoirs of Missionary Priests & Other Catholics.* 1803. Manchester. 2 vols in 1. 2 engraved pls. $22.50

CHALMERS, Harvey. *Drums Against Frontenac.* 1949. New York. 440 pp. $3.50

CHALMERS, Harvey. *Last Stand of Nez Perce.* 1962. New York. Twayne. Ills. 1st ed. dj. VG $27.50

CHALMERS, P. *Sport & Travel in East Africa.* 1930. $50.00

CHALMERS, W.S. *Max Horton & the Western Approaches.* 1954. London. Ills. dj. $20.00

CHALMERS. *On Political Economy.* 1883. 2nd Am. ed. VG $30.00

CHAMALES, Tom T. *Never So Few.* 1957. New York. 1st ed. 499 pp. $22.50

CHAMBERLAIN, Allen. *Beacon Hill/Its Ancient Pastures & Early Mansions.*1925. Boston/NY. G $15.00

CHAMBERLAIN, Anne. *The Darkest Bough.* 1958. Indianapolis. 1st ed. 186 pp. $6.00

CHAMBERLAIN, Anne. *The Soldier Room.* 1956. Indianapolis. 1st ed. 227 pp. dj. $8.50

CHAMBERLAIN, Ethel Clere. *Shoes & Ships & Sealing Wax.* 1928. Akron. Saalfield. Ills. Scott. EX $15.00

CHAMBERLAIN, Ethel Clere. *Shoes & Ships & Sealing Wax.* 1928. New York. Ills. Scott. 1st ed. EX $25.00

CHAMBERLAIN, G.A. *African Hunting Among the Thongas.* 1923. Harper. 1st ed. 286 pp. $35.00

CHAMBERLAIN, H.D. *Riding & Schooling Horses.* 1934. New York. Derrydale Pr. Ltd. ed. dj. VG $40.00

CHAMBERLAIN, Joshua L. *Yale University; Its History, Influence.* 1900. Boston. 259 pp. photos. $42.50

CHAMBERLAIN, Mellen. *Documentary History of Chelsea.* 1902. Boston. 2 vol set. 1st ed. $85.00

CHAMBERLAIN, Narcissa. *French Menus for Parties.* 1968. New York. Hastings. 241 pp. $10.00

CHAMBERLAIN, S. & Flynt, H.N. *Frontier of Freedom.* 1952. Deerfield. Ills. Chamberlain. dj. VG $10.00

CHAMBERLAIN, S. & N. *Southern Interiors of Charleston, South Carolina.* 1956. New York. Ills. 171 pp. index. dj. $20.00

CHAMBERLAIN, Samuel. *Beyond New England Thresholds.* 1937. New York. Hastings House. Ills. 96 pp. $12.50

CHAMBERLAIN, Samuel. *Fair Is Our Land.* 1942. Chicago. Ills. 252 pp. dj. $4.50

CHAMBERLAIN, Samuel. *Open House in New England.* 1937. Battleboro, VT.217 photos. map. dj. VG $12.50

CHAMBERLAIN, Samuel. *Open House in New England.* 1948. Ills. author. dj. VG $10.00

CHAMBERLAIN, Samuel. *Springtime in Virginia.* 1947. New York. VG $10.00

CHAMBERLAIN, Samuel. *The Coast of Maine.* 1941. $12.50

CHAMBERLAIN & Harrington, K.P. *Songs of All the Colleges.* 1903. New York. 330 pp. VG $4.00

CHAMBERLIN, William H. *Japan over Asia.* 1939. Boston. ex-lib. 463 pp. $5.50

CHAMBERS, A.J. *Recollections by Andrew Jackson Chambers.* 1947. 1st ed. 40 pp. wrappers. $75.00

CHAMBERS, D. & Sanford, C. *Cock-a-Hoop: Bibliography Golden Cockerel Press.* London. dj. EX $15.00

CHAMBERS, E.K. *English Literature at the Close of Middle Ages.* 1947. New York. Oxford U. Pr. 2nd impression. $6.50

CHAMBERS, I.M. *The Modern Devil.* 1903. Ills. 520 pp. $3.50

CHAMBERS, K. *A Country-Lovers Guide to Wildlife.* 1979. Johns Hopkins U. Ills. 228 pp. $15.00

CHAMBERS, L. *Stonewall Jackson.* 1959. New York. 1st ed. 2 vol set. boxed. EX $40.00

CHAMBERS, Robert W. *The Book of Days.* 1863. Edinburgh. Ills. 2 vol set. $30.00

CHAMBERS, Robert W. *The Cambric Mask.* 1899. New York. Stokes. 1st ed. VG $25.00

CHAMBERS, Robert W. *The Girl in Golden Rags.* 1936. New York. Grosset & Dunlap. 314 pp. VG $7.50

CHAMBERS, Robert W. *The Happy Parrot.* 1931. Appleton. Ills. Price. 37 pls. dj. EX $35.00

CHAMBERS, Robert W. *The King in Yellow.* 1902. New York. Harper. Ills. 1st ed. inscr. $25.00

CHAMBERS, Robert W. *The King in Yellow.* 1895. 2nd ed. VG $50.00

CHAMBERS, Robert W. *The Maid-at-Arms.* 1902. Ills. H.C. Christy. $6.00

CHAMBERS, Robert W. *The Maker of Moons.* 1954. Buffalo. Shroud. dj. $50.00

CHAMBERS, Robert W. *The Maker of Moons.* 1896. 1st ed. VG $75.00

CHAMBERS, Robert W. *The Maker of Moons.* 1954. reprint. wrappers. VG $10.00

CHAMBERS, Robert W. *The Rogue's Moon.* 1929. Appleton. Ills. Price. 35 pls. EX $35.00

CHAMBERS, Whittaker. *Witness.* 1952. New York. Random House. 808 pp. EX $6.50

CHAMBLISS, J.E. *Lives & Travels of Livingstone & Stanley.* 1881. VG $15.00

CHAMPION, F.W. *With Camera in Tiger Land.* 1927. Chatto & Windus. Ills. 228 pp. $15.00

CHAMPION, Frank. *Campaign Handbook & Citizens Manual.* 1872. Ills. 232 pp. $10.00

CHAMPLIN, John D. *Encyclopedia of Painters & Paintings.* 1887. New York. Ills. 4 vol set. G $125.00

CHAMPLIN, John D. *Orations, Addresses, & Speeches of Chauncy Depew.* 1910. New York. Vol. III. ex-lib. 378 pp. $3.00

CHAMPNEY, Elizabeth W. *Three Vassar Girls in Switzerland.* 1890. Ills. author & others. $18.00

CHANCELLOR, J. *Audubon, a Biography.* 1978. New York. Viking. Ills. 224 pp. $12.00

CHANCELLOR, J. *The Dark God.* 1928. New York. Century. 1st Am. ed. VG $10.00

CHANCY, Louise & Davis, F. *The Believer. Story of Mrs. H. Ford.* 1960. Coward McCann. dj. VG $8.00

CHANDLER, A. Bertram. *The Rim of Space.* 1961. New York. 1st ed. dj. VG $20.00

CHANDLER, Raymond. *Playback.* 1958. London. 1st ed. dj. EX $85.00

CHANDLER, Raymond. *The Little Sister.* 1949. Boston. Houghton Mifflin. dj. VG $35.00

CHANDLER, Raymond. *The Long Good-Bye.* 1959. London. Penguin. 1st ed. wrappers. $22.00

CHANDLER, Raymond. *The Long Good-Bye.* 1953. 1st Eng. ed. inscr. dj. VG $45.00

CHANDLER, Raymond. *The Raymond Chandler Omnibus.* 1953. London. Hamilton. 1st ed. dj. VG $45.00

CHANDLER, Raymond. *Unknown Thriller.* Ltd. 1st ed. 1/250. sgn. $45.00

CHANDLER, Zachariah. *An Outline Sketch of His Life & Public Services.* 1880. Detroit. VG $30.00

CHANDLER. *Farewell My Lovely.* Tower. 1st Am. ed. dj. VG $18.00

CHANDLER. *Gateway to the Peninsula.* Daly City. slipcase. $15.00

CHANDRASEKHAR, S. *Ellipsoidal Figures of Equilibrium.* 1969. Yale U. Press. EX $14.00

CHANG, K.C. *Food in Chinese Culture.* 1977. Yale. dj. EX $20.00

CHANIN, Paul. *The Natural History of Otters.* 1985. 1st ed. photos. dj. $25.00

CHANLER, W. *Through Jungle & Desert.* 1896. NY/London. VG $50.00

CHANNING, Ed. *The Barrington-Bernard Correspondence 1760-1770.* 1912. Cambridge. 1st ed. 306 pp. $12.50

CHANNING, Mark. *India Mosaic.* 1936. London. Lippincott. 316 pp. dj. EX $3.50

CHANNING, Mark. *Nine Lives.* 1937. Philadelphia. 1st Am. ed. dj. EX $45.00

CHANNING, Mark. *The Poisoned Mountain.* 1936. Philadelphia. Lippincott. 1st Am. ed. dj. EX $45.00

CHANNING, Mark. *White Python.* 1934. Philadelphia. Lippincott. 1st ed. dj. EX $40.00

CHANNING, William E. *Slavery.* 1835. Boston. 1st ed. G $45.00

CHANT, Joy. *Grey Mane of Morning.* London. 1st ed. VG $25.00

CHAO, L.N. *Basis for Classifying Western Atlantic Sciaenidae.* 1978. Ills. 64 pp. $3.00

CHAPEL, C.E. *Complete Guide to Gunsmithing.* 1962. 2nd revised ed. dj. $15.00

CHAPEL, C.E. *Guns of the Old West.* 1961. New York. Coward-McCann. Ills. dj. VG $22.50

CHAPEL, C.E. *Simplified Pistol & Revolver Shooting.* 1950. New York. dj. VG $15.00

CHAPEL, C.E. *The Gun Collector's Handbook of Values.* 1970. New York. 9th revised ed. Ills. 398 pp. $10.00

CHAPEL, C.E. *The Gun Collector's Handbook of Values.* 1958. New York. Ills. 4th ed. dj. VG $7.50

CHAPEL, C.E. *The Gun Collector's Handbook of Values.* 1947. VG $12.50

CHAPEL, C.E. *The Gun Collector's Handbook of Values.* 1960. New York. $5.00

CHAPELLE, Howard I. *History of American Sailing Ships.* Bonanza. dj. EX $17.50

CHAPELLE, Howard I. *The History of the American Sailing Navy.* 1949. New York. Ills. 1st ed. $35.00

CHAPELLE, Howard I. *Yacht Designing & Planning.* 1936. New York. Norton. 319 pp. dj. $7.50

CHAPIN, Carl M. *Manchester in Vermont History.* 1932. 1st ed. EX $10.00

CHAPIN, Hyman & Carroll. *The Suburbs of San Francisco.* San Francisco. Chronicle Books. dj. VG $15.00

CHAPIN, William. *Complete Reference Gazetteer of the United States.* 1839. New York. 1st ed. VG $55.00

CHAPLIN, Ralph. *Bars & Shadows.* 1923. Ridgewood. 2nd ed. sgn. wrappers. VG $30.00

CHAPLIN, Ralph. *Bars & Shadows: Prison Poems of Ralph Chaplin.* 1922. Leonard Press. dj. VG $10.00

CHAPLIN, Ralph. *Somewhat Barbaric.* 1944. Seattle. 1st ed. dj. EX $40.00

CHAPLIN, Ralph. *Wobbly.* 1948. Chicago Pr. 1st ed. dj. EX $35.00

CHAPMAN, Arthur. *The Pony Express.* 1932. New York. 1st ed. $65.00

CHAPMAN, C.F. *Piloting Seamanship & Small Boat Handling.* 1958. $5.50

CHAPMAN, Ervin S. *Particeps Criminis.* 1910. New York. Ills. 107 pp. $5.00

CHAPMAN, F.M. *Autobiography of a Bird Lover.* 1933. Appleton. 1st ed. photos. 420 pp. $15.00

CHAPMAN, F.M. *Camps & Curses of an Ornithologist.* 1908. Appleton. 1st ed. photos. 432 pp. $18.00

CHAPMAN, F.M. *Color Key to North American Birds.* 1912. Appleton. Ills. revised 2nd ed. 356 pp. $19.00

CHAPMAN, Isaac. *A Sketch of the History of Wyoming.* 1830. 1st ed. VG. $95.00

CHAPMAN, J.A. & Morgan, R.P. *Systematic Status of the Cottontail.* 1973. Wildlife Society. 54 pp. $2.00

CHAPMAN, John. *The Burns Mantle Best Plays of 1949-1950.* 1950. New York. Dodd Mead. Ills. sgn. 437 pp. $12.50

CHAPMAN, Maria Weston. *Harriet Matineau's Autobiography.* 1877. Boston. 1st ed. 2 vol set. G $100.00

Date 11/6/55 19___

M_____

Address_____

Reg. No.	Clerk	Account Forward		
1	1 PAPER BACK			75¢
2	BOOK			
3				
4				
5				
6				
7				
8				
9				
10				
11				
12				
13				
14				
15	197-1			

Your Account Stated to Date—If Error Is Found Return at Once
1200 B

THANK YOU
Call Again

We appreciate your patronage
and hope we may continue to
merit it. If we please you, tell
your friends. If we don't, tell us.
We strive to satisfy.

CHAPMAN, Paul & Sheffer, L.M. *Livestock Farming.* 1936. Turner E. Smith. 720 pp. G $4.50

CHAPMAN, Ronald. *The Laurel & the Thorn. A Study of G.F. Watts.* 1955. 2nd printing. dj. $10.00

CHAPMAN, W. *The Loneliest Continent.* 1964. New York. Ills. 1st ed. dj. VG $15.00

CHAPMAN. *Life & Work of D.L. Moody.* 1900. New York. Ills. $8.50

CHAPMAN. *Memoirs of a Mountaineer.* London. Travel Book Club. G $10.00

CHAPPELL, George S. *A Basket of Poses.* 1942. New York. Boni. Ills. Hogarth. 1st ed. $25.00

CHAPPELL, George S. *Through the Alimentary Canal with Gun & Camera.* 1930. New York. Stokes. Ills. 4th printing. $4.00

CHAPPLE, Mitchell. *Warren G. Harding, the Man.* 1920. Boston. Ills. sgn. 128 pp. rare. $15.00

CHAPSTICK, P.H. *Death in Silent Places.* 1981. St.Martins. dj. EX $14.00

CHAPSTICK, P.H. *Death in the Long Grass.* 1977. St.Martins. photos M. Phillip Kahl. VG $15.00

CHAPSTICK, P.H. *Maneaters.* 1981. Peterson. Ills. 178 pp. dj. EX $15.00

CHAR, Rene. *Picasso, His Recent Drawings. 1966-1968.* 1969. New York. Abrams. folio. VG $50.00

CHARBONNEAU, Louis. *No Place on Earth.* 1958. 1st ed. dj. VG $20.00

CHARDIN, Pierre Teilhard de. *The Making of a Mind.* 1st Eng. ed. dj. EX $15.00

CHARELL, Ralph. *How I Turn Complaints into Thousands of Dollars.* Stein & Day. 192 pp. dj. VG $3.50

CHARLES, Robert. *A Roundabout Turn.* 1930. London. 1st ed. 4 color pls. VG $45.00

CHARLOT, Jean. *The Mexican Mural Renaissance 1820-1915.* 1963. Yale. 1st ed. $25.00

CHARLTON, Warwick. *The Second Mayflower Adventure.* 1957. Boston. Ills. 1st ed. 245 pp. dj. $12.50

CHARMAIN. *The Book of Jack London.* London. 2 vol set. G $90.00

CHARPENTIER, H. & Sparkes, B. *Life a la Henri.* 1934. New York. Simon & Schuster. sgn. $10.00

CHARTERIS, L. *Saint at the Thieves Picnic.* 1951. Avon. #347. pb. EX $8.50

CHARTERIS, L. *Saint in Europe.* 1954. London. 1st Eng. ed. dj. VG $18.00

CHARTERIS, L. & Sanderson, H. *Saint Magazine Reader.* 1966. New York. 1st ed. VG $10.00

CHARYN, Jerome. *Pinocchio's Nose.* 1983. Arbor House. 1st ed. dj. VG $15.00

CHARYN, Jerome. *The Tar Baby.* 1973. Holt. 1st ed. dj. EX $15.00

CHASE, A.W. *Bishop Chase's Reminiscences.* 1848. Boston. 2nd ed. 2 vol set. $22.50

CHASE, A.W. *Dr. Chase's New Receipt Book & Medical Advisor.* 1927. Chicago. 348 pp. $7.50

CHASE, A.W. *Dr. Chase's Recipes or Information for Everybody.* 1880. Beal. 400 pp. $6.50

CHASE, Agnes. *First Book of Grasses.* 1922. Macmillan. 121 pp. EX $5.00

CHASE, J.S. *Yosemite Trails.* 1911. Boston. 1st ed. EX $35.00

CHASE, Mary Ellen. *Abby Aldrich Rockefeller.* 1950. New York. Macmillan. 159 pp. dj. $4.50

CHASE, Mary Ellen. *Dawn in Lyonesse.* 1938. Macmillan. 1st ed. dj. VG $12.50

CHASE, Mary Ellen. *The Fishing Fleets of New England.* 1961. $10.00

CHASE, Rhoda. *The Second Bubble Book.* 1918. Harper. Ills. complete w/3 records. $20.00

CHASE, Salmon P. *Diary & Correspondence.* 1903. Washington. 1st ed. 527 pp. $25.00

CHASE, Stuart. *Government in Business.* 1940. New York. Macmillan. ex-lib. 296 pp. $3.50

CHASE, Stuart. *Idle Money Idle Men.* 1940. New York. ex-lib. 249 pp. $3.50

CHASE, Stuart. *Men & Machines.* 1929. New York. Ills. W.T. Murch. 1st ed. dj. $10.00

CHASE, Stuart. *The Ecomony of Abundance.* 1934. New York. Macmillan. 327 pp. $3.50

CHATALBASH, Ron. *Dr. Blackfoot's Carnival Extraordinaire.* 1982. Boston. Ills. author. 1st ed. VG $12.50

CHATEUBRIAND. *Atala.* 1889. Excelsior, NY. Ills. Dore. VG $50.00

CHATFIELD, TAYLOR & OBER. *The Aircraft & Its Engine.* 1936. McGraw Hill. Ills. 401 pp. G $6.50

CHATFIELD, TAYLOR & OBER. *The Airplane & Its Engine.* 1940. New York. Ills. 4th ed. 412 pp. index. $15.00

CHATTERTON, E. K. *Fore & Aft.* 1912. London. Ills. VG $65.00

CHATTERTON, E. K. *Sailing Ships & Their Story.* 1914. London. Ills. $40.00

CHATTERTON, E. K. *Seamen All.* Stokes. $9.00

CHATTERTON, E.K. *In Great Waters. Novel of the Sea.* 1929. $6.00

CHATTERTON, E.K. *Romance of a Ship. Story of Origin & Evolution.* 1913. London. Ills. G $15.00

CHATTERTON, E.K. *Ship Models.* London. Ltd. 1/1000. Ills. VG $100.00

CHATTERTON. *Whalers & Whaling.* 1926. 251 pp. VG $25.00

CHAUCER, G. *Canterbury Tales, in Modern English.* 1934. Garden City. Ills. R. Kent. Deluxe ed. VG $50.00

CHAUCER, G. *Canterbury Tales.* 1934. Garden City. Ills. R. Kent. not Deluxe ed. $20.00

CHAUCER, G. *Canterbury Tales.* Medici Society.Ills. Flint. Ltd. ed. 3 vol set. $450.00

CHAUCER, G. *Canterbury Tales.* 1946. Ltd. Eds. Club.1/1500. boxed. EX $125.00

CHAUCER, G. *The Canterbury Tales.* 1904. New York. Fox, Duffield. Ills. W.Clark. $40.00

CHAUCER, G. *Troilus & Cressida.* 1932. Literary Guild.Ills. Eric Gill. $10.00

CHAUVIN, R. *Animal Societies from the Bee to the Gorilla.* 1968. Hill Wang. 1st Am. ed. photos. 281 pp. $10.00

CHAUVIN, R. *The World of an Insect.* 1967. McGraw Hill. ex-lib. photos. 254 pp. $3.00

CHEEVER, H.T. *The Whale & His Captors.* 1849. New York. 1st ed. G $100.00

CHEEVER, John. *Bullet Park.* 1969. New York. 1st ed. sgn. dj. VG $32.50

CHEEVER, John. *Collected Stories.* Pulitzer Prize Winner ed. $60.00

CHEEVER, John. *Falconer.* 1977. Knopf. 1st ed. dj. VG $20.00

CHEEVER, John. *Oh What A Paradise It Seems.* 1982. Knopf. 1st ed. dj. VG $12.50

CHEEVER, John. *Stories.* 1978. 1st ed. sgn. dj. $35.00

CHEEVER, John. *The Brigadier & the Gold Widow.* 1964. Harper. 1st ed. dj. VG $35.00

CHEEVER, John. *The Enormous Radio & Other Stories.* 1953. New York. 1st ed. 237 pp. $17.50

CHEEVER, John. *The Wapshot Chronicle.* 1957. New York. Harper. 1st ed. VG $30.00

CHEEVER, John. *The Wapshot Chronicle/The Wapshot Scandal.* 1979. Harper. proof copy. wrappers. VG $40.00

CHEEVER, John. *The Way Some People Live.* 1943. New York. 1st ed. $40.00

CHEEVER, John. *The World of Apples.* 1973. New York. Knopf. 1st ed. VG $17.50

CHEEVER, Rev. George B. *Guilt of Slavery & Crime of Slaveholding.* 1860. New York. Ills. 472 pp. $18.50

CHEEVER, Susan. *Looking for Work.* 1979. New York. Simon & Schuster. 1st ed. dj. $25.00

CHEEVER, Susan. *Looking for Work.* 1979. Simon & Schuster. proof copy. $45.00

CHEIRO. *Fate in the Making.* 1931. New York. Ills. 1st ed. 335 pp. VG $38.00

CHEIRO. *How I Foretold the Lives of Great Men.* 1935. Bombay. 1st ed. 111 pp. G $35.00

CHEKHOV, Anton. *The Works of Anton Chekhov.* 1929. New York. 1 vol ed. 632 pp. $3.50

CHELTHAM, J. *The Life of Thomas Paine.* 1809. New York. $15.00

CHEN MONG HOCK. *Early Chinese Newspapers of Singapore, 1881-1912.* 1967. Singapore. Ills. 171 pp. index. $17.50

CHENEY, Edna Dow. *Louisa May Alcott. Her Life, Letters & Journals.* 1890. Boston. Ills. 404 pp. VG $5.00

CHENEY, Sheldon. *Theatre. 3,000 Years of Drama, Acting, Stagecraft.* 1935. Ills. 558 pp. $9.00

CHENEY, Sheldon. *Theatre. 3,000 Years of Drama, Acting, Stagecraft.* 1929. London. Longmans. 204 Ills. 1st ed. $37.50

CHENNAULT, Anna. *A Thousand Springs.* 1963. sgn. dj. VG $17.50

CHENNAULT, C. *Way of a Fighter.* 1949. New York. 1st ed. dj. EX $37.50

CHERKAS, Selma. *Dining with Celebrities.* 1966. Rutland. 160 pp. $6.50

CHERKASOV, N. *Notes of a Soviet Actor.* 1935. $15.00

CHERNEV & HARKNESS. *An Invitation to Chess.* 1945. Simon & Schuster. 221 pp. EX $4.50

CHERNEV & REINFELD. *The Fireside Book of Chess.* 1949. 6th ed. 401 pp. $37.50

CHERNEV. *Winning Chess Traps.* 1946. Philadelphia. dj. VG $8.00

CHERRY-GARRARD. *The Worst Journey in the World.* 1965. London. Ills. 584 pp. maps. index. $37.50

CHERRYH, C.J. *Chanur's Venture.* 1984. Phantasia. Ltd. ed. 1/300. sgn. boxed. EX $45.00

CHERRYH, C.J. *Cuckoo's Egg.* 1985. Phantasia. Ltd. ed. 1/350. sgn. boxed. VG $40.00

CHERRYH, C.J. *Forty Thousand in Ghenna.* 1983. Phantasia. Ltd. ed. 1/350. sgn. boxed. EX $45.00

CHERRYH, C.J. *Kif Strike Back.* 1985. Phantasia. Ltd. ed. 1/350. sgn. boxed. EX $40.00

CHERRYH, C.J. *Visible Light.* 1968. Phantasia. Ltd. ed. 1/300. sgn. boxed. EX $40.00

CHESELDEN, Wm. *The Anatomy of the Human Body.* 1795. Boston. Ills. 1st Am. ed. 350 pp. $225.00

CHESNUT, M. *A Diary from Dixie.* 1949. Houghton Mifflin. dj. VG $12.50

CHESSON, W.H. *George Cruikshank.* 1905. London. 1st ed. VG $18.00

CHESTER. *French Cooking for English Homes.* 1929. London. 3rd ed. $20.00

CHESTERFIELD, Lord & Waller. *Case of Hanover Forces in Pay of Great Britain.* 1743. London. Cooper. 1st ed. 83 pp. $60.00

CHESTERFIELD, Lord. *Letters, Sentences, & Maxims.* Chesterfield Soc. Deluxe ed. $8.50

CHESTERTON, G.K. *A Miscellany of Men.* 1912. New York. 1st Am. ed. EX $25.00

CHESTERTON, G.K. *Essays of Today & Yesterday.* 1928. London. Harrap. 1st ed. dj. VG $20.00

CHESTERTON, G.K. *Manalive.* 1912. London. Nelson. 1st ed. VG $30.00

CHESTERTON, G.K. *Queen of Seven Swords.* 1926. London. 1st Eng. ed. 50 pp. VG $12.50

CHESTERTON, G.K. *The Coloured Lands.* 1938. London. Ills. author. dj. VG $175.00

CHESTERTON, G.K. *The Common Man.* 1950. London. Sheed & Ward. 1st ed. dj. VG $25.00

CHESTERTON, G.K. *The Napoleon of Notting Hill.* 1904. London. Ills. Robertson. 1st ed. VG $195.00

CHESTERTON, G.K. *The Poet & the Lunatic.* 1929. London. Cassell. 1st ed. VG $40.00

CHESTERTON, G.K. *The Possessors.* 1964. New York. Simon & Schuster. dj. VG $17.50

CHESTERTON, G.K. *The Sword of Wood.* 1938. Woburn Books. Ltd. ed. sgn. $50.00

CHESTNUTT, Charles W. *The Wife of His Youth.* 1899. Houghton Mifflin. 1st ed. VG $100.00

CHETLAM, Augustus L. *Recollections of Seventy Years.* 1899. Galena, IL. $20.00

CHEUSE, Alan. *The Grandmother's Club.* 1986. Layton. Gibbs M. Smith. advance copy. $25.00

CHEVALIER, Haakon. *Oppenheimer: Story of a Friendship.* 1965. New York. Braziller. 1st ed. dj. EX $20.00

CHEVALIER, Maurice. *I Remember It Well.* 1970. New York. 1st ed. dj. VG $15.00

CHEYNEY, Peter. *Dark Hero.* 1946. New York. Dodd Mead. 1st ed. dj. VG $10.00

CHIANG, Cecilia Sun Yun. *The Mandarin Way.* 1974. Boston. Little, Brown. 1st ed. sgn. G $7.00

CHIBA, Reiko. *The Making of a Japanese Print.* 1984. Tokyo. 11th printing. VG $15.00

CHIBBETT, David. *History of Japanese Printing & Book Illustration.* 1977. Kodansha. 1st ed. 264 pp. dj. EX $135.00

CHICAGO, Judy. *The Birth Project.* 1985. NY. Doubleday. Ills. 231 pp. VG $22.00

CHICHESTER, Francis. *Alone Across the Pacific.* 1961. 1st Am. ed. dj. $9.00

CHICHESTER, Francis. *Along the Clipper Way.* 1967. New York. 1st Am. ed. $12.50

CHIDECKEL, M. *Female Perversion.* 1935. $15.00

CHIDIMIAN, C. *Book of Cacti & Other Succulents.* 1958. Am. Garden Guild. 1st ed. VG $10.00

CHIDSEY, Donald Barr. *Five Stories.* 1956. New York. Vintage Books. 214 pp. $2.50

CHIDSEY, Donald Barr. *Goodbye to Gunpowder.* 1964. Ills. 224 pp. VG $6.50

CHIDSEY, Donald Barr. *Panama Passage.* 1946. New York. Doubleday. 442 pp. VG $3.50

CHIEF STANDING BEAR. *My People, the Sioux.* 1928. intro Wm. S. Hart. $35.00

CHILD, Julia. *Mastering the Art of French Cooking.* 1961. Knopf. 726 pp. dj. EX $8.50

CHILD, Julia. *The French Chef Cookbook.* 1968. New York. Knopf. Book Club Ed. 440 pp. $7.50

CHILD, L. Maria. *Letters from New York.* 1845. New York. 1st ed. VG $35.00

CHILD, Mrs. *Family Nurse; or, Companion of Frugal Housewife.* 1837. Boston. Hendee. 156 pp. $20.00

CHILDE, Wilfred Rowland. *Dream English: Fantastical Romance.* London. (ca.1920) $15.00

CHILDERS, J.S. *War Eagles.* 1943. New York. Ills. 1st ed. VG $22.00

CHILDRESS, Mark. *A World Made of Fire.* 1984. Knopf. 1st ed. sgn. dj. VG $30.00

CHILDS. *Hanover, a Bicentennial Book. 1761-1961.* Hanover, NH. Ills. VG $10.00

CHILDS, H. *Gazetteer of Grafton County.* 1886. $50.00

CHILDS, Marquis F. *The Cabin.* 1944. New York. Harper. 1st ed. dj. VG $30.00

CHILDS, Marquis F. *The Peacemakers.* 1961. New York. Harcourt. 1st ed. dj. VG $25.00

CHILDS, Marquis. *Eisenhower: Captive Hero.* 1950. New York. 310 pp. dj. $6.50

CHILVERS, Hedley A. *Seven Wonders of South Africa.* 1929. Johannesburg. $15.00

CHINERY, M. *Killers of the Wild.* 1979. Ills. 224 pp. dj. EX $17.50

CHINIQUY, Father. *The Priest, the Woman, & the Confessional.* 1880. Revell Co. $6.50

CHIPMAN, N.P. *The Tragedy of Andersonville.* 1911. San Francisco. G $25.00

CHIPPENDALE, Thomas. *Gentleman & Cabinet Maker's Director.* 1938. New York. Towse Pub. reprint. folio. VG $55.00

CHIPPERFIELD, J. *My Wild Life.* 1976. Putnam. Ills. 219 pp. dj. EX $7.50

CHIROL, Valentine. *Indian Unrest.* 1910. London. Macmillan. 371 pp. $3.50

CHISHOLM, A.H. *Bird Wonders of Australia.* 1935. Angus & Robertson. 2nd ed. VG $20.00

CHISHOLM, Lovey. *In Fairyland.* 1904. New York. Ills. Camerson. 30 color pls. $75.00

CHITTENDEN, Hiram. *Yellowstone National Park.* U. of OK Press.dj. VG $7.00

CHITTENDEN, Larry. *Ranch Verses.* 1893. New York. Ills. gilt decor. VG $45.00

CHITTENDEN, Wm. L. *Ranch Verses.* 1895. New York. Ills. 3rd ed. 195 pp. $35.00

CHOPPING, Richard. *The Fly.* 1965. New York. 1st ed. dj. VG $15.00

CHORLEY, Henry & Newman, E. *Thirty Years' Musical Recollections.* 1926. New York. Knopf. G $20.00

CHRISTENSEN, E.O. *Early American Wood Carvings.* 1952. Cleveland. 1st ed. dj. VG $20.00

CHRISTENSEN, E.O. *Index of American Design.* 1950. New York. $37.50

CHRISTIE, Agatha. *A Caribbean Mystery.* 1964. London. 1st ed. no dj. VG $10.00

CHRISTIE, Agatha. *A Murder is Announced.* 1950. London. Collins. 1st ed. dj. VG $35.00

CHRISTIE, Agatha. *Adventure of the Christmas Pudding.* 1960. London. 1st ed. dj. EX $15.00

CHRISTIE, Agatha. *After the Funeral.* 1953. London. 1st ed. no dj. VG $12.50

CHRISTIE, Agatha. *At Bertram's Hotel.* 1965. London. 1st ed. no dj. EX $10.00

CHRISTIE, Agatha. *By Pricking of My Thumbs.* 1968. London. 1st ed. dj. VG $12.50

CHRISTIE, Agatha. *Cat Among the Pigeons.* 1959. London. 1st ed. no dj. VG $12.50

CHRISTIE, Agatha. *Clocks.* 1963. London. 1st ed. no dj. VG $10.00

CHRISTIE, Agatha. *Crooked House.* 1949. London. 1st ed. no dj. VG $17.50

CHRISTIE, Agatha. *Dead Man's Folly.* 1956. London. 1st ed. dj. EX $15.00

CHRISTIE, Agatha. *Death Comes as the End.* 1945. London. 1st ed. dj. VG $20.00

CHRISTIE, Agatha. *Death on the Nile.* 1937. London. 1st ed. VG $25.00

CHRISTIE, Agatha. *Elephants Can Remember.* 1972. London. 1st ed. dj. EX $15.00

CHRISTIE, Agatha. *Elephants Can Remember.* Taiwan. piracy copy. dj. EX $20.00

CHRISTIE, Agatha. *Endless Night.* 1967. London. 1st ed. dj. VG $10.00

CHRISTIE, Agatha. *First Lady of Crime.* 1977. Ills. Keating. 1st ed. dj. EX $15.00

CHRISTIE, Agatha. *Hercule Poirot's Christmas.* 1939. London. Collins. 1st ed. $45.00

CHRISTIE, Agatha. *Hickory Dickory Dock.* 1955. London. 1st ed. no dj. EX $12.50

CHRISTIE, Agatha. *Hound of Death.* 1936. London. G $15.00

CHRISTIE, Agatha. *Hound of Death.* 1933. London. VG $40.00

CHRISTIE, Agatha. *Mrs. McGinty's Dead.* 1952. London. 1st ed. no dj. VG $15.00

CHRISTIE, Agatha. *Murder in the Mews.* 1937. London. 1st ed. dj. G $25.00

CHRISTIE, Agatha. *Mysterious Affair at Styles.* 1975. New York. Commemorative ed. dj. VG $10.00

CHRISTIE, Agatha. *N or M?* 1941. London. 1st ed. no dj. VG $20.00

CHRISTIE, Agatha. *Nemeses.* 1971. Boston. Dodd Mead. 3rd printing. EX $10.00

CHRISTIE, Agatha. *Ordeal by Innocence.* 1958. London. 1st ed. no dj. EX $12.50

CHRISTIE, Agatha. *Partners in Crime.* 1929. New York. 1st Am. ed. VG $20.00

CHRISTIE, Agatha. *Passenger to Frankfort.* 1970. London. 1st ed. dj. EX $17.50

CHRISTIE, Agatha. *Poems.* 1973. London. Collins. proof copy. wrappers. $65.00

CHRISTIE, Agatha. *Poirot's Last Case.* 1975. London. Collins. 1st ed. proof copy. $45.00

CHRISTIE, Agatha. *Postern of Fate.* 1973. London. 1st ed. no dj. VG $10.00

CHRISTIE, Agatha. *Seven Dials Mystery.* 1929. 1st Am. ed. dj. VG $30.00

CHRISTIE, Agatha. *Sleeping Murder.* 1976. New York. 1st Am. ed. dj. EX $10.00

CHRISTIE, Agatha. *Sparkling Cyanide.* 1945. London. 1st ed. VG $20.00

CHRISTIE, Agatha. *Taken at the Flood.* 1948. London. 1st ed. VG $17.50

CHRISTIE, Agatha. *The Adventure of the Christmas Pudding.* 1960. London. Collins. 1st ed. dj. VG $35.00

CHRISTIE, Agatha. *The Big Four.* 1927. London. 1st ed. $30.00

CHRISTIE, Agatha. *The Clocks.* 1963. 1st Am. ed. dj. EX $15.00

CHRISTIE, Agatha. *The Hollow.* 1946. London. 1st ed. VG $17.50

CHRISTIE, Agatha. *The Labours of Hercules.* 1947. London. 1st ed. dj. VG $17.50

CHRISTIE, Agatha. *The Mirror Cracked from Side to Side.* 1962. London. 1st ed. dj. EX $15.00

CHRISTIE, Agatha. *The Third Girl.* 1966. London. 1st ed. dj. EX $20.00

CHRISTIE, Agatha. *They Came to Baghdad.* 1951. 1st ed. dj. VG $20.00

CHRISTIE, Agatha. *They Do It with Mirrors.* 1952. London. 1st ed. dj. VG $15.00

CHRISTIE, Agatha. *Towards Zero.* 1944. London. 1st ed. dj. VG $20.00

CHRISTIE, Agatha. *4.50 from Paddington.* 1957. London. 1st ed. dj. EX $15.00

CHRISTOPHER, Milbourne. *Houdini: Untold Story.* 1969. New York. 1st ed. dj. EX $8.00

CHRISTOPHER, Milbourne. *Medium, Mystics & the Occult.* 1975. EX $6.00

CHRISTOPHER. *Petunia Be Keerful.* 1934. G $14.00

CHRISTOPHERSON, Ed. *The Story of Montana-Yellowstone Earthquake.* 1960. Ills. 88 pp. $3.50

CHRISTY, Howard Chandler. *Drawings in Black & White.* 1905. New York. 1st ed. folio. VG $60.00

CHRISTY, Howard Chandler. *Evangeline.* 1905. Indianapolis. VG $35.00

CHRISTY, Howard Chandler. *Our Girls: An Anthology.* 1907. G $15.00

CHRISTY, Howard Chandler. *The Christy Girl.* 1906. Bobbs Merrill. 16 color pls. G $80.00

CHRITTENDEN, L.E. *Recollections of Lincoln & His Administration.* 1891. VG $20.00

CHU, A. & G. *Oriental Cloisonne & Other Enamels.* 1975. New York. Ills. $15.00

CHUIKOV. *Battle for Stalingrad.* 1964. New York. $18.50

CHUMBLEY, G.L. *Colonial Justice in Virginia.* 1938. Richmond. 1st ed. dj. VG $20.00

CHUNN, Maj. C.E. *Of Rice & Men.* 1946. 1st ed. $28.50

CHURCH, Alonzo. *Discourse Delivered Before GA Historical Society.* 1845. Savannah. 1st ed. 40 pp. wrappers. $45.00

CHURCH, Charles A. *History of Republican Party in Illinois 1854-1912.* 1912. Rockford. Ills. VG $22.50

CHURCH, Peggy. *The House at Otowi Bridge.* 1960. U. NM Press. 1st ed. dj. EX $15.00

CHURCH, Ruth Ellen. *Mary Meade's Country Cookbook.* 1964. Chicago. Rand McNally. Ills. 376 pp. $10.00

CHURCH, Thomas. *History of Great Indian War of 1675-1676.* Hartford. (ca.1850) Ills. $35.00

CHURCHILL, Caroline Nichols. *Active Footsteps.* 1909. Colorado Springs. 258 pp. $75.00

CHURCHILL, John Wesley. *History of First Church in Dunstable-Nashua, NH.* 1918. Boston. Ills. 99 pp. $35.00

CHURCHILL, R. *Men, Mines & Animals in South Africa.* 1892. New York. VG $67.50

CHURCHILL, Winston S. *A Far Country.* 1915. New York. Ills. Herman Pfeifer. G $5.00

CHURCHILL, Winston S. *Blood, Sweat, & Tears.* 1941. New York. Putnam. 462 pp. $5.50

CHURCHILL, Winston S. *Ian Hamilton's March.* VG $55.00

CHURCHILL, Winston S. *India: Speeches.* 1931. 1st Eng. ed. wrappers. VG $375.00

CHURCHILL, Winston S. *Inside the Cup.* 1912. G $10.00

CHURCHILL, Winston S. *London to Ladysmith.* 1900. 1st Eng. ed. VG $350.00

CHURCHILL, Winston S. *My African Journey.* 1908. 1st Eng. ed. VG $300.00

CHURCHILL, Winston S. *Richard Carvel.* 1899. New York. Macmillan. 538 pp. G $3.00

CHURCHILL, Winston S. *The Age of Revolution.* 1957. New York. Dodd Mead. VG $5.00

CHURCHILL, Winston S. *The Crisis.* 1901. New York. 516 pp. $5.50

CHURCHILL, Winston S. *The Inside of the Cup.* 1913. New York. Grosset & Dunlap. 513 pp. VG $3.50

CHURCHILL, Winston S. *The River War.* 1899. 1st Eng. ed. 2 vol set. VG $1,650.00

CHURCHILL, Winston S. *The Second World War.* 1961. New York. 6 vol set. G $10.00

CHURCHILL, Winston S. *The Second World War.* 1948-1954. London. 1st eds. 6 vol set. EX $75.00

CHURTON, E. *The Railroad Book of England. 1851.* 1973. London. Ills. dj. EX $27.50

CHUSE, Anne. *Costume Design.* 1930. New York. Bridgman. Ills. dj. VG $10.50

CHUTE, B.J. *One Touch of Nature.* 1965. New York. 1st ed. $7.50

CHUTE, Carolyn. *The Beans of Egypt Maine.* 1985. New York. Ticknor & Fields. 1st ed. sgn. $65.00

CHUTE, Carolyn. *The Beans of Egypt Maine.* 1985. New York. Ticknor & Fields. proof copy. $85.00

CHUTE, Carolyn. *The Beans of Egypt Maine.* 1985. London. Chatto & Windus. 1st Eng. ed. $35.00

CIANO, G. *Ciano Diaries, 1939-43.* 1946. Garden City. G $10.00

CIARDI, J. *The Monster Den.* 1966. 1st ed. dj. VG $10.00

CIARDI, John. *Look What Happened at My House.* Ills. Gorey. sgns. dj. EX $30.00

CIARDI, John. *This Strangest Everything.* 1966. Rutgers. 1st ed. dj. VG $30.00

CIARDI. *Other Skies.* 1st ed. dj. $45.00

CICERO. *De Finibus Bonorum et Malorum.* 1741. Cambridge. (ed. J. Davisius) 2nd ed. $25.00

CICERO. *Letters of a Roman Gentleman.* 1926. Houghton Mifflin. trans. VG $20.00

CIECHANOWSKI, Jan. *Defeat in Victory.* 1947. New York. 397 pp. $5.50

CILL. *Gay Bandit of the Border.* Popular. pb. $3.00

CIRTOS. G.W. *Prue & I.* Harper. (ca.1856) $20.00

CIST, Charles. *Sketches & Statistics of Cincinnati in 1851.* Ills. William H. Moore. $25.00

CLADWELL, Erskine. *Before I Change My Mind.* 1982. Minneapolis. sgn. wrappers. EX $25.00

CLAFLIN, Bert. *Muskie Fishing.* 1948. Knopf. Ills. 1st ed. 219 pp. index. $22.50

CLAIN-STEFFANELLI, E. & V. *Beauty & Lore of Coins, Currency & Medals.* 1974. dj. $15.00

CLAIRBORNE, Craig. *A Feast Made for Laughter.* 1982. Garden City. Doubleday. dj. VG $7.50

CLAIRBORNE, Craig. *An Herb & Spice Cook Book.* 1963. New York. Harper. 334 pp. $6.50

CLAIRBORNE, Craig. *Favorites from the NY Times, Series IV.* 1984. New York. Bonanza Books. dj. VG $6.50

CLAIRBORNE, J.F.H. *Life & Times of Gen. Sam Dale, MS Partisan.* 1860. New York. 1st ed. $45.00

CLAIRMONTE, Glenn. *Calamity Was the Name for Jane.* 1959. Denver. dj. VG $22.50

CLANCY, T. *Red Storm Rising.* 1986. 1st ed. sgn. dj. EX $30.00

CLAPHAM, Richard. *Foxes, Foxhounds, Foxhunting.* 1922. New York. 40 photos. VG $30.00

CLAPHAM, Richard. *The Book of the Fox.* 1931. Derrydale Pr. Ltd. ed. 1/750. EX $125.00

CLARK, A. *Barbarossa.* 1965. New York. 1st ed. dj. EX $35.00

CLARK, A. *Brave Against the Enemy.* 1944. Lawrence, KS. Ills. 215 pp. wrappers. VG $15.00

CLARK, A.C. *Abraham Lincoln in the National Capital.* 1925. Washington. Ills. 179 pp. $17.50

CLARK, A.C. *Fountains of Paradise.* 1978. 1st ed. dj. EX $17.50

CLARK, Adm. Jocko & Reynolds. *Carrier Admiral.* 1967. New York. presentation ed. sgn. dj. $25.00

CLARK, Ann. *Singing Sioux Cowboy Reader.* U.S. Indian Bureau. SftCvr. EX $3.50

CLARK, Ann. *Who Wants to Be a Prairie Dog?* 1940. Phoenix. Ills. Van Tsinahjinnie. $20.00

CLARK, Badger. *Sun & Saddle Leather.* 1922. Goram Press. Ills. Huffman. 11th ed. VG $9.00

CLARK, C. *How to Become a Successful Hostess.* 1930. Boston. $8.50

CLARK, Champ. *My Quarter Century of American Politics.* 1920. New York. Ills. 1st ed. 2 vol set. $25.00

CLARK, Charles & Eubank, E. *Lockstep & Corridor. 35 Years of Prison Life.* 1927. Cincinnati. Ills. sgns. 177 pp. $15.00

CLARK, Cottonseed. *Brushwood Poetry & Philosophy.* 1945. SftCvr. $6.00

CLARK, D.K. *The Steam Engine.* 1891. London. 4 vol set. $37.50

CLARK, Dan. *Samuel Jordan Kirwood.* 1917. Iowa city. 464 pp. VG $17.50

CLARK, Dick. *Rock, Roll & Remember.* 1976. Crowell. New York. 2nd ed. photos. dj. $9.00

CLARK, Douglas. *Roast Eggs.* 1981. London. 1st ed. dj. EX $20.00

CLARK, E.L. *Daleth, Egypt Illustrated.* 1864. Boston. Ills. 8 color pls. dj. VG $35.00

CLARK, Eleanor. *Doctor Heart. A Novella & Other Stories.* 1974. New York. 1st ed. sgn. dj. EX $20.00

CLARK, Eleanor. *The Oysters of Locmariaquer.* 1964. New York. 1st ed. dj. EX $17.50

CLARK, Elmer T. *The Chiangs of China.* 1943. G $2.50

CLARK, Henry W. *History of Alaska.* 1930. New York. Ills. 1st ed. VG $22.50

CLARK, J. *Desiderii Erasmi.* 1810. Philadelphia. $25.00

CLARK, James (1788-1870). *A Treatise on Pulmonary Consumption.* 1935. Philadelphia. ex-lib. 296 pp. rebound. $17.50

CLARK, Kenneth, ed. *The Negro Protest.* 1963. Boston. Beacon Press. 1st ed. dj. EX $25.00

CLARK, Kenneth. *Civilization.* 1969. Harper. 359 pp. dj. EX $10.00

CLARK, Kenneth. *The Best of Audrey Beardsley.* 1979. London. Ills. 1st Eng. ed. 173 pp. EX $17.50

CLARK, Leonard. *The River Ran East.* 1953. 366 pp. dj. VG $15.00

CLARK, M. *Track of the Kodiak.* 1984. Ills. 1st ed. 224 pp. dj. EX $20.00

CLARK, Margery. *The Poppy Seed Cakes.* 1924. Garden City. Doubleday. Ills. Petersham. $20.00

CLARK, R.S. & Sowerby, A. *Through Shen-Kan.* 1912. London/Leipzig.Ills. maps. VG $395.00

CLARK, Rene. *Goeth's Faust.* 1932. Ltd. Ed. Club. 1/1500. sgn. boxed. $25.00

CLARK, S. *All the Best in Cuba.* 1946. 1st ed. $7.50

CLARK, S. *The Pumas Claw.* 1959. London. Ills. 1st ed. G $12.50

CLARK, Steven. *Fight Against Time.* 1979. Atheneum. dj. EX $3.50

CLARK, Thomas D. *Rampaging Frontier Manners/Humors of Pioneer Days.*1939. Indianapolis. 1st ed. dj. $22.50

CLARK, W.M. *Manual of Mechanical Movements.* 1948. VG $8.00

CLARK, William J. *Great American Sculptures.* 1878. Philadelphia. Ills. G $25.00

CLARK, William. *Ben Franklin's Privateers.* 1956. LA State U. 1st ed. dj. $8.50

CLARK, William. *Memorial of the State of Missouri.* 1826. Washington. 1st ed. 90 pp. $250.00

CLARK. *Civilization.* 1969. Harper. Ills. dj. EX $6.50

CLARK. *Lynchburg.* 1971. photos. dj. VG $7.50

CLARK. *Yensie Walton's Womanhood.* 1882. Lathrop. $4.50

CLARKE, A. *Flavouring Materials.* 1922. London. 166 pp. VG $17.50

CLARKE, A. *The Reefs of Taprobane.* 1957. Harper. Ills. 1st ed. 205 pp. map. $12.50

CLARKE, A.C. *2010: Odyssey Two.* 1982. Phantasia Pr. Ltd. 1st ed. sgn. boxed. EX $160.00

CLARKE, Adam. *Dissertation on Use & Abuse of Tobacco.* 1798. London. 2nd ed. wrappers. $75.00

CLARKE, Arthur C. *Dolphin Island.* 1963. Winston. 1st ed. dj. VG $15.00

CLARKE, Arthur C. *Imperial Earth.* 1976. Harcourt. 1st Am. ed. dj. VG $15.00

CLARKE, Arthur C. *Islands in the Sky.* 1952. Philadelphia. 1st ed. dj. EX $65.00

CLARKE, Arthur C. *Rendezvous with Rama.* 1973. dj. VG $8.00

CLARKE, Arthur C. *The Exploration of Space.* 1951. New York. 1st ed. dj. VG $30.00

CLARKE, Arthur C. & Wilson, M.*The Treasure of the Great Reef.* Harper. photos. 233 pp. $3.50

CLARKE, Arthur. *Ascent to Orbit.* 1984. Wiley. proof copy. VG $50.00

CLARKE, Asia Booth. *The Unlocked Book. Memoir of John Wilkes Booth.* 1938. New York. Ills. 1st ed. 205 pp. dj. VG $10.00

CLARKE, C. *Eichmann: Man & His Crimes.* 1960. Ballentine. Ills. G $10.00

CLARKE, Covington. *The Lost Canyon.* 1925. Chicago. Reilly & Lee. 269 pp. VG $3.50

CLARKE, Herman F. *John Hull, Builder of Bay Colony.* 1940. Portland. Ills. 1st ed. 221 pp. boxed. $225.00

CLARKE, Ida Clyde. *Men that Wouldn't Stay Dead.* 1936. London. Ills. Braby. 1st ed. dj. VG $40.00

CLARKE, Kit. *Practical Angler.* 1892. 2nd ed. wrappers. VG $20.00

CLARKE, L. & M. *Narratives of the Sufferings.* 1846. Boston. 144 pp. $27.00

CLARKE, Mary Cowden. *Best Loved Plays of William Shakespeare.* no date. Spencer Press. 630 pp. G $3.00

CLARKE, Mary Cowden. *The Girlhood of Shakespeare's Heroines.* 1873. New York. Putnam. ex-lib. 473 pp. G $3.00

CLARKE, S.A. *Pioneer Days of Oregon History.* 1905. Cleveland. Clark. 1st ed. 2 vol set. $150.00

CLARKE, S.J. *History of McDonough Co. Illinois.* 1878. Springfield. 692 pp. G $80.00

CLARKE, Wood T. *Emigres in the Wilderness.* 1941. Macmillan. 1st printing. inscr. VG $18.50

CLARKE. *A Biographical Dictionary of Fiddlers.* 1895. London. 360 pp. $25.00

CLARKE. *Prelude to Space.* 1st Am. ed. dj. EX $25.00

CLARKE. *Travels in Greece & Egypt.* 1818. 2 vol set. 7 fld map. $250.00

CLARKSON, Jesse D. *History of Russia.* 1961. 857 pp. maps. photos. dj. EX $12.50

CLARKSON, L. *Buttercup's Visit to Little Stay at Home.* 1881. Dutton. Ills. G $55.00

CLARKSON, Rosetta E. *Green Enchantment.* 1940. Macmillan. Ills. 1st ed. dj. $4.50

CLARY, James. *M.T. Halbouty. Last Boom.* 1972. Random House. Ills. 305 pp. index. $17.50

CLARY, Martin. *The Facts about Muscle Shoals.* 1924. New York. Ocean Pub. ex-lib. 254 pp. $3.00

CLAUDY, Carl. *The Mystery Men of Mars.* 1933. Ills. Valentine. 1st ed. dj. $32.50

CLAVELL, James. *Noble House.* 1981. Delacorte. Ltd. ed. 1/2000. EX $25.00

CLAVELL, James. *Shogun.* 1975. 1st ed. dj. VG $25.00

CLAY, John. *My Life on the Range.* 1924. Chicago. private print. Ills. 1st ed. $350.00

CLAYTON, Frances. *Revelation of St. John the Divine.* Curwen Press. Ills. Ltd. ed. 1/1000. sgn. VG $20.00

CLEAR, Charles. *John Palmer Mail Coach Pioneer.* 1955. London. 1st ed. dj. $8.50

CLEARWATER, Alphonso. *History of Ulster County New York.* 1907. Kingston, NY. Van Dusen Pub. $60.00

CLEARY, Beverly. *The Mouse the Mototcycle.* 1965. Weekly Reader. Ills. Louis Darling. 156 pp. $3.50

CLEAVES, Francis W. *Manual of Mongolian Astrology & Divination.* 1969. Harvard, Mass. 127 pp. wrappers. EX $40.00

CLELAND, John. *Memoirs of a Coxcomb.* 1926. Fortune Press. reprint. Ltd. ed. 1/575. G $40.00

CLELAND, R.G. *California in Our Time.* 1947. Knopf. dj. EX $20.00

CLEM, Deloris Kitchel. *The Cookie Cookbook.* 1966. New York. Barnes. 2nd ed. dj. VG $7.50

CLEMEAU, Carol. *The Ariadne Clue.* 1982. Scribner. 1st ed. dj. VG $12.50

CLEMENS, Clara. *My Father Mark Twain.* 1931. New York. 1st ed. inscr. dj. VG $45.00

CLEMENS, Clara. *My Husband Gabrilowitsch.* 1938. New York. Ills. 1st ed. sgn. VG $35.00

CLEMENS, Samuel L. *A Connecticut Yankee in King Arthur's Court.* 1890. 2nd ed. $26.50

CLEMENS, Samuel L. *A Connecticut Yankee in King Arthur's Court.* 1949. Ltd. Ed. Club. Ills. H. Guibeau. 275 pp. VG $65.00

CLEMENS, Samuel L. *A Dog's Tale.* 1904. G $16.50

CLEMENS, Samuel L. *Adventures of Huckleberry Finn.* 1933. New York. Ltd. Ed. Club. Ills. 494 pp. $125.00

CLEMENS, Samuel L. *Captain Stromfield's Visit to Heaven.* 1909. $26.50

CLEMENS, Samuel L. *English as She is Taught.* 1900. Boston. 1st ed. $60.00

CLEMENS, Samuel L. *Following the Equator.* 1897. Hartford. 1st ed. 1st issue. G $60.00

CLEMENS, Samuel L. *Life on the Mississippi.* 1883. Boston. 1st Am. ed. 2nd state. VG $100.00

CLEMENS, Samuel L. *Mark Twain, Notes on His Life.* 1928. wrappers. VG $40.00

CLEMENS, Samuel L. *Mark Twain's Autobiography & First Romance.* 1871. G $27.50

CLEMENS, Samuel L. *Mark Twain's Autobiography.* 1924. NY/London. 1st ed. 1st state. 2 vol set. $80.00

CLEMENS, Samuel L. *Million Pound Bank Note.* 1893. 1st ed. $57.50

CLEMENS, Samuel L. *The American Claimant.* 1892. New York. 1st ed. VG $75.00

CLEMENS, Samuel L. *The Innocents Abroad; or, New Pilgrim's Progress.* 1869. Hartford. Am. Pub. Co. Ills. VG $450.00

CLEMENS, Samuel L. *Tragedy of Pudd'nhead Wilson & Comedy of Twins.* 1894. Hartford. 1st Am. ed. 432 pp. VG $150.00

CLEMENT, Clara Erskine. *Charlotte Cushman.* 1882. Boston. Ills. 1st ed. 193 pp. index. $4.00

CLEMENT, Clara Erskine. *Constantinople.* 1895. Boston. Ills. 309 pp. 17 pls. $10.00

CLEMENT, Clara Erskine. *Handbook of Legendary & Mythological Art.* 1881. Boston. Ills. 498 pp. VG $17.50

CLEMENT, E. *Hildreth's Japan as It Was & Is.* 1906. McClurg. 100 Ills. 1st ed. maps. $15.00

CLEMENT, H. *Zoo Man.* 1969. Macmillan. Ills. 179 pp. dj. VG $10.00

CLEMENT, Hal. *Iceworld.* 1953. New York. Gnome. 1st ed. dj. VG $12.50

CLEMENT, Mrs. *Painters, Sculptors, Architects.* 1875. New York. Ills. G $12.50

CLEMENTS, Edith. *Flowers of Mountain & Plain.* 1926. New York. 43 color plates. $25.00

CLEMENTS, Robert J. *Michelangelo's Theory of Art.* 1961. New York. 1st ed. VG $22.50

CLERGUE, L. *Naisances D'Aphrodite.* 1966. New York. 1st ed. dj. EX $47.50

CLERGUE, L. *Toros Muertos.* 1966. New York. 1st ed. dj. EX $47.50

CLEVELAND, Grover. *Message Relating to the Hawaiian Islands.* 1893. Washington. Ills. 1st ed. 684 pp. $75.00

CLEVELAND, H.A. *Golden Sheaves Gathered from Fields of Literature.* 1870. Philadelphia. 583 pp. $12.50

CLEVELAND, H.W.S. *Hints to Riflemen.* 1864. Appleton. $40.00

CLEVELAND, Henry. *Alexander H. Stephens, in Public & Private.* 1866. Philadelphia. 833 pp. $20.00

CLEVELAND & GRAHAM. *Aviation Annual of 1945.* VG $10.00

CLEWES, Dorothy. *The Wildwood.* 1948. New York. Ills. Hawkins. 1st Am. ed. $20.00

CLIFFORD, Sir Hugh. *Bushwacking & Other Asiatic Tales & Memories.* 1929. NY/London. Ills. Blaine. 1st ed. $50.00

CLIFTON, Mark. *When They Come from Space.* 1962. New York. Doubleday. dj. EX $30.00

CLINCH, Bryan J. *California & Its Old Missions.* 1904. San Francisco. Ills. 2 vol set. rare. VG $150.00

CLINE, I.M. *Tropical Cyclones: an Exhaustive Study.* 1926. New York. Ills. 301 pp. VG $20.00

CLINTON-BRADDELEY, V.C. *All Right on the Night.* 1954. London. Putnam. 1st ed. dj. VG $15.00

CLINTON-BRADDELEY, V.C. *The Burlesque Tradition.* 1952. Ills. 152 pp. dj. $12.50

CLOETE, Stuart. *Watch for the Dawn.* 1939. Boston. 489 pp. dj. VG $3.50

CLOOS, H. *Conversation with the Earth.* 1952. Knopf. Ills. 1st ed. 413 pp. dj. EX $12.50

CLOUD, Virgil. *Pioneer Blood.* 1948. Raleigh. presentation copy. sgn. EX $20.00

CLOUD, Virginia Woodward. *Down Durley Land & Other Ballads.* 1898. New York. Ills. Birch. 1st ed. 99 pp. $20.00

CLOUDSLEY-THOMPSON, J. *Animal Twilight, Man & Game in Eastern Africa.* 1967. London. Ills. 1st ed. 204 pp. EX $12.50

CLOUDSLEY-THOMPSON, J. *Wildlife of the Deserts.* 1979. Hamlyn. Ills. 96 pp. dj. $12.50

CLOUGH, Arthur Hugh. *The Bothie & Other Poems.* 1896. London/NY. Scott. 1st ed. 222 pp. VG $35.00

CLOUGH, Arthur Hugh. *The Poetical Works.* 1906. London. Routledge. VG $30.00

CLOUGH, B. & P. *World Guide to Covered Bridges.* 1959. Ills. 1st ed. 141 pp. $20.00

CLOUSTON, J. Storer. *The Chemical Baby.* 1934. London. Jenkins. 1st ed. VG $30.00

CLOUTH & CUMING. *World Encyclopedia of Recorded Music.* 1952, 53, 57. London. 3 vol set. $75.00

CLOUZOT, H. *Painted & Printed Fabrics. 1760-1815.* 1927. New York. Ltd. ed. 1/2000. $50.00

CLOWES, W.L. *The Captain of the Mary Rose.* 1893. Ills. 2nd ed. $40.00

CLYNE, Gerldine. *Jolly Jump-Ups Vacation Trip.* 1942. McLoughlin. pop up book. VG $7.50

CLYNE, N. *Ballads & Lays Scottish History.* 1844. Edinburgh. G $8.00

COATES, George. *Herd Book. Pedigrees of Improved Short-Horn Bulls.* 1843. Doncaster. Ills. $25.00

COATES, Robert. *Outlaw Years/Hist. of Land Pirates Natchez Trace.* 1930. Literary Guild. Ills. 308 pp. VG $15.00

COATES, Robert. *The Hour After Westerly & Other Stories.* 1957. New York. Harcourt. 1st ed. $10.00

COATES, Robert. *The Man Just Ahead of You.* 1964. New York. Sloan. dj. $7.50

COATS, A. *The Amateur Keeper.* 1962. London. Ills. 1st ed. 125 pp. EX $10.00

COATS, Alice-Leone. *Lupescu, Story of a Royal Love Affair.* 1955. New York. Holt. 220 pp. dj. EX $6.00

COATS, Peter. *Great Gardens of the Western Worlds.* 1963. London. Spring Books. Ills. 288 pp. $15.00

COATSWORTH, Elizabeth. *Desert Dan.* 1960. New York. Ills. Harper Johnson. 1st ed. $15.00

COATSWORTH, Elizabeth. *Good Night.* 1972. New York. Macmillan. Ills. Aruego. dj. $10.00

COATSWORTH, Elizabeth. *Mouse Chorus.* 1955. New York. Ills. G. Vaughan-Jackson. EX $15.00

COATSWORTH, Elizabeth. *The Creaking Stair.* New York. Ills. W.A. Dwiggins. dj. VG $45.00

COATSWORTH, Elizabeth. *The Enchanted.* 1951. Pantheon. 1st ed. VG $12.50

COATSWORTH. *The Big Green Umbrella.* 1944. Ills. Sewell. dj. VG $18.00

COBB, B. *A Field Guide to the Ferns.* 1960. Houghton Mifflin. Ills. VG $7.00

COBB, Elijah. *A Cape Cod Skipper.* 1925. New Haven. Ills. 111 pp. $10.00

COBB, I.S. *Local Color.* 1916. New York. 460 pp. $5.00

COBB, Irvin & Rinehart, Mary. *Oh! Well! You Know How Women Are!* 1920. Doran. 1st ed. dj. VG $40.00

COBB, Irvin S. *Irvin Cobb at His Best.* 1942. EX $10.00

COBB, Irvin S. *Many Laughs for Many Days.* 1925. New York. Garden City. 243 pp. VG $2.50

COBB, Irvin S. *Speaking of Operations.* 1915. Grosset & Dunlap. VG $5.00

COBB, Irvin S. *The Glory of the Coming.* 1918. New York. 463 pp. VG $3.50

COBB, Mrs. Wilton P. *History of Dodge County.* 1932. Atlanta. Ills. 1st ed. 258 pp. $45.00

COBB, Sylvanus. *The Gunmaker of Moscow.* 1888. New York. 1st ed. scarce. G $150.00

COBBAN, J. MacLaren. *An African Treasure.* 1900. New York. New Amsterdam. 1st Am. ed. VG $25.00

COBBETT, William. *Cottage Economy.* 1824. New York. 1st Am. ed. EX $100.00

COBBETT, William. *Life & Adventures of Peter Porcupine.* 1927. Nonesuch Press. Ltd. 1st ed. 1/1800. $12.50

COBBOLD, Richard. *Valentine Verses/Lines of Truth, Love & Virtue.* 1827. Ipswich. 100 litho pls. $125.00

COBLENTZ, Stanton A. *Under the Triple Suns.* 1955. Reading, PA. Fantasy Press. dj. $85.00

COBLENTZ, Stanton. *After 12,000 Years.* 1950. Los Angeles. 1st ed. dj. EX $25.00

COBLENTZ, Stanton. *The Blue Barbarians.* 1958. New York. Avalon. 1st ed. dj. EX $20.00

COBLENTZ, Stanton. *The Crimson Capsule.* 1967. New York. 1st ed. dj. VG $10.00

COBLENTZ, Stanton. *The Runaway World.* 1961. New York. 1st ed. dj. EX $20.00

COBLENTZ, Stanton. *Under the Triple Suns.* 1955. Reading. Fantasy. 1st trade ed. dj. VG $25.00

COBURN, Alvin L. *More Men of Mark.* 1922. New York. photos. VG $125.00

COBURN, Alvin Langdon. *Men of Mark.* 1913. NY/London. Ills. folio. $275.00

COBURN, Wallace D. *Rhymes From a Round-Up Camp.* 1899. Ills. Russell. 1st ed/issue. $675.00

COCHRAN, Alan. *Two Plus Two.* 1980. Doubleday. 1st ed. dj. VG $6.00

COCHRAN, Emory. *Philatelic Therapy.* 1964. Federalsburg. Ills. 1st ed. inscr. 102 pp. $35.00

COCHRAN, Hamilton. *Buccaneer Islands.* 1941. New York. Nelson. Ills. Zhenya Gay. EX $15.00

COCHRAN, Louis. *The Fool of God.* 1985. Joplin, MO. 407 pp. EX $8.00

COCHRAN, Robert. *Vance Randolph, an Ozark Life.* 1985. U. IL Press. 1st ed. EX $15.00

COCHRAN. *Blockade Runners of The Confederacy.* 1958. Ills. 1st ed. 350 pp. $12.50

COCKBURN, Claud. *In Time of Trouble: Autobiography.* 1956. London. Hart-Davis. ex-lib. $6.00

COCKE, Mr. *Intercourse with the Indians.* 1826. Washington. 1st ed. $35.00

COCKE, Sarah. *Bypaths in Dixie: Folk Tales of the South.* 1911. New York. Dutton. Ills. 2nd printing. VG $25.00

COCKERELL, Douglas. *A Note on Bookbinding.* 1904. London. W.H. Smith. 34 pp. wrappers. $25.00

COCKERELL, T.D.A. *Zoology of Colorado.* 1927. CO U. Press. Ills. 262 pp. VG $20.00

COCKERELL. *Old Testament Miniatures.* 1975. New York City. color plates. 207 pp. $46.00

COCKRELL, Cathy. *Undershirts.* 1982. Hanging Loose. 1st ed. dj. EX $4.00

COCKRUM, E.L. *Mammals of the Southwest.* 1982. AZ U. Press. Ills. 176 pp. pb. EX $6.00

COCKTON, Henry. *Life & Adventures of Valentine Vox, Ventriloquist.* London/NY. Routledge. Ills. 691 pp. $30.00

COCTEAU, Jean. *My Contemporaries.* 1968. 1st ed. dj. $10.00

COCTEAU, Jean. *The Difficulty of Being.* 1967. New York. Coward McCann. 1st Am. ed. dj. $7.50

CODDINGTON, Edwin B. *The Gettysburg Campaign.* Ills. 1st ed. dj. EX $20.00

CODMAN, John. *Sailor's Life & Sailor's Yarns.* 1847. New York. 1st ed. presentation copy. $65.00

CODMAN & SHURTLEFF. *Catalogue of Dental Furniture, Instruments, etc.* 1870. Boston. Ills. 95 pp. $15.00

CODY, C.S. *The Witching Night.* 1952. NY/Cleveland. 1st ed. dj. EX $10.00

CODY, Morill. *This Must Be the Place.* 1937. New York. Lee Furman. dj. VG $20.00

CODY, William F. *Buffalo Bill's Own Story of Life & Deeds.* 1917. Stanton. Ills. $22.50

CODY. *Bitter Creek.* Pocketbook. pb. $3.00

CODY. *Homestead Range.* Mac Fadden. $30.00

CODY. *The Big Corral.* Popular. pb. $3.00

CODY. *West of the Law.* Pocketbooks. pb. $3.00

COE, G.W. *Frontier Fighter.* 1984. Lakeside Press. Ills. VG $10.00

COE, Joseph. *True America.* 1840. $35.00

COFFIN, C.C. *Old Times in the Colonies.* 1899. New York. Ills. 460 pp. $7.50

COFFIN, Charles C. *My Days & Nights on the Battlefield.* (ca.1890) VG $6.50

COFFIN, Charleton. *Redeeming the Republic.* 1890. Harper. Ills. $27.50

COFFIN, George. *Pioneer Voyage-California & Round World 1849-52.* 1908. Chicago. private print. 235 pp. VG $35.00

COFFIN, Margaret. *History & Folklore of American Country Tinware.* 1968. Galahad, NY. Ills. dj. VG $15.50

COFFIN, Robert P. Tristram. *Golden Falcon.* 1929. New York. $50.00

COFFIN, Robert P. Tristram. *Red Sky in the Morning.* 1935. New York. 1st ed. dj. EX $30.00

COFFIN, Robert P. Tristram. *Tristram. Book of Crowns & Cottages.* 1925. New Haven. Ills. VG $30.00

COFFIN, Robert. *Portrait of an American.* 1931. New York. 1st ed. 182 pp. $5.00

COFFIN, Tristam. *Senator Fulbright.* 1967. London. 378 pp. dj. VG $5.00

COFFIN. *Our New Way Round the World.* 1880. Ills. 508 pp. VG $7.50

COFFMAN, I. Wade. *Laws of Masonry in West Virginia.* 1944. Charleston, WV. 10th ed. 211 pp. index. $7.50

COGGINS, Jack & Pratt, F. *By Space Ship to the Moon.* 1958. Random House. 58 pp. $3.00

COGGINS, Jack & Pratt, F. *Satellites & Space Travel.* 1958. New York. Random House. ex-lib. 64 pp. $37.50

COGGINS, Jack. *The Campaign for Guadalcanal.* 1972. New York. Doubleday. Ills. 208 pp. VG $7.50

COGGINS, James C. *Eugenics of Abraham Lincoln.* 1940. dj. VG $25.00

COGHLAN, H.H. *Notes on Prehistoric & Early Iron in Old World.* 1956. Pitt Rivers Museum. 1st ed. $15.00

COGSWELL, H.L. *Water Birds of California.* 1977. CA U. Press. Ills. 399 pp. dj. EX $12.50

COHANE. *Yale Football Story.* 1951. 1st ed. VG $15.00

COHEN, Albert K. *Delinquent Boys/The Culture of the Gang.* 1955. Free Press. 198 pp. dj. VG $4.50

COHEN, Arthur A. *In the Days of Simon Stern.* 1973. Random House. 1st ed. dj. EX $15.00

COHEN, Felix S. *Handbook of Federal Indian Law.* 1945. Washington. VG $35.00

COHEN, Isidor. *Historical Sketches & Sidelights of Miami, FL.* 1925. Miami. private print. 1st ed. 209 pp. $50.00

COHEN, Joseph E. *Socialism for Students.* 1915. Chicago. Kerr. EX $15.00

COHEN-PORTHEIM. *Spirit of London.* 1937. $15.00

COHN, Art. *Michael Todd's Around World in 80 Days Almanac.* 1956. Ills. 71 pp. $4.50

COHN, David L. *The Fabulous Democrats.* 1956. New York. Putnam. photos. 191 pp. dj. $5.00

COHN. *Chinese Painting.* 1948. Phaidon. 220 pls. dj. EX $45.00

COIL, Henry Wilson. *Freemasonry Through Six Centuries.* 1967. Richmond. Macoy. 2 vol set. djs. EX $25.00

COIT, M. *J.C. Calhoun.* 1950. Boston. G $10.00

COIT, Thomas W. *Puritanism; or, A Churchman's Defense.* 1845. New York. 527 pp. $20.00

COKE. *Nordfeldt the Painter.* 1972. U. of NM. 1st ed. $10.00

COLANGE, Leo de. *Voyages & Travels. Scenes in Many Lands.* 1887. $130.00

COLBERT, E.H. *Men & Dinosaurs.* 1968. Dutton. Ills. 283 pp. $10.00

COLBERT, E.H. *The Age of Reptiles.* 1965. Norton. Ills. 228 pp. dj. EX $12.50

COLBERT, E.H. *The Great Dinosaur Hunters & Their Discoveries.* 1984. Dover. Ills. map. EX $10.00

COLBY, Constance Taber. *The View from Morningside.* 1987. Philadelphia. Lippincott. 1st ed. dj. EX $15.00

COLBY, Henry W. *Rhymes of the Local Philosopher.* 1899. Taunton, MA. 208 pp. $10.00

COLE, Cyrenus. *A History of the People of Iowa*. 1921. Cedar Rapids. 1st ed. inscr. VG $55.00

COLE, Cyrenus. *Iowa Through the Years*. 1940. Iowa City. 547 pp. $12.50

COLE, Harry Ellsworth. *Barboo Bear Tales*. 1915. Wisconsin. Ills. 110 pp. G $22.50

COLE, S.W. *American Fruit Book*. 1849. Ills. 1st ed. G $12.00

COLE, William. *Folk Songs of England, Ireland, Scotland & Wales*. 1961. Doubleday. 1st ed. dj. $12.50

COLE. *The Death Riders*. Pyramid. pb. $3.00

COLEMAN, L. Vail. *Historic House Museums*. 1933. Washington. Ills. 155 pp. EX $25.00

COLEMAN, Lyman. *Historical Text Book & Atlas: Biblical Geography*. 1868. Lippincott. 330 pp. $5.00

COLEMAN, Satis N. *The Drum Book*. 1931. New York. 189 pp. dj. $3.50

COLERIDGE, Samuel Taylor. *Rime of the Ancient Mariner*. 1883. New York. Ills. Dore. 52 pp. $17.50

COLERIDGE, Samuel Taylor. *The Literary Remains of Samuel Taylor Coleridge*. 1839. London. Pickering. 1st ed. 4 vol set. $180.00

COLERIDGE, Samuel Taylor. *The Poetical Works*. 1840. London. Pickering. 4 vol set. VG $115.00

COLERIDGE, Samuel Taylor. *The Poetical Works*. 1901. London. Bell. Aldine ed. $30.00

COLERIDGE. *Christabel*. 1905. New York. Dutton. VG $12.00

COLES, G. & M. *Double Blackmail*. 1939. New York. Macmillan. 1st ed. $15.00

COLETTE, J. *The Difficulty of Being a Christian*. 1968. Notre Dame. 1st ed. dj. VG $10.00

COLETTE. *The Collected Stories of Colette*. New York. Farrar. proof copy. wrappers. $35.00

COLLETTE. *Break of Day*. 1961. Farrar Strauss. 1st ed. dj. VG $22.50

COLLETTE. *Cheri & the Last of Cheri*. 1951. Farrar. dj. VG $10.00

COLLIDGE, Dane & Mary. *The Last of the Seris*. 1939. New York. 1st ed. 264 pp. 38 pls. dj. VG $22.50

COLLIE, George. *The Aurignacians & Their Culture*. 1928. Beloit College. 1st ed. stiff wrappers. $12.50

COLLIER, E. *Three Against the Wilderness*. 1960. Dutton. Ills. 349 pp. dj. VG $10.00

COLLIER, John. *Defy the Foul Fiend*. 1934. New York. Knopf. 1st ed. dj. $50.00

COLLIER, John. *Fancies & Goodnights*. 1951. New York. 1st ed. dj. VG $45.00

COLLIER, John. *His Monkey Wife*. 1930. London. Davies. 1st ed. dj. EX $150.00

COLLIER, John. *Presenting Moonshine*. 1941. New York. Viking. 1st Am. ed. VG $20.00

COLLIER, Peter. *Downriver*. 1978. Holt. proof copy. wrappers. EX $10.00

COLLIER, R. *City That Would Not Die. The Bombing of London*. 1960. Ills. ex-lib. dj. G $7.00

COLLIN, Hedvig. *Wind Island*. 1945. New York. Ills. 1st ed. $15.00

COLLIN, Rodney. *The Theory of Celestial Influence*. 1968. London. 392 pp. dj. $30.00

COLLINGWOOD, Herbert W. *Hope Farm Notes*. 1921. 1st ed. $8.50

COLLINS, A. Frederick. *A Birds Eye View of Invention*. 1926. New York. Ills. index. VG $10.00

COLLINS, A. Frederick. *Book of Stars*. 1915. New York. Ills. 1st ed. 230 pp. dj. $15.00

COLLINS, A. Frederick. *Going Somewhere*. 1929. $15.00

COLLINS, Alan C. *The Story of America in Pictures*. 1953. Garden City. Doubleday. 480 pp. dj. EX $5.00

COLLINS, Charles F. *Notes on Chase of Wild Red Deer*. 1902. London. Ills. E. Caldwell. VG $63.00

COLLINS, Dennis. *The Indians' Last Fight or the Dull Knife Raid*. 1915. Girard, KS. 1st ed. EX $100.00

COLLINS, Francis. *The Boys Book of Model Aeroplanes*. 1910. Ills. 1st ed. photos. EX $75.00

COLLINS, H.H. & Boyajian, N.R. *Familiar Garden Birds of America*. 1965. Harper. Ills. 309 pp. EX $7.50

COLLINS, Henry Hill, Jr. *Complete Field Guide to American Wildlife*. 1959. Harper. Ills. Peterson/others. 683 pp. $4.50

COLLINS, Hubert E. *Warpath & Cattle Trail*. 1928. New York. Ills. 1st ed. ex-lib. 296 pp. $30.00

COLLINS, J. Lawton. *War in Peacetime*. 1969. Boston. Ills. 1st ed. 416 pp. dj. $15.00

COLLINS, J.S. *My Experiences in the West*. 1980. Lakeside Press. VG $10.00

COLLINS, Jimmy. *Test Pilot*. 1935. 178 pp. dj. $50.00

COLLINS, Max Allan. *Midnight Haul*. 1986. Woodstock. Foul Play. 1st ed. dj. EX $15.00

COLLINS, Randall. *The Case of the Philosopher's Ring*. 1978. New York. Crown. 1st ed. dj. VG $25.00

COLLINS, Wilkie. *The Legacy of Cain*. 1888. Tauchnitz. 1st ed. 2 vol set. VG $85.00

COLLINS, Wilkie. *The Moonstone*. 1868. Tauchnitz. 1st ed. VG $70.00

COLLINS & LA PIERRE. *O Jerusalem!* 1972. Ills. Book Club ed. dj. VG $8.50

COLLINS. *Across the Plains in '64*. 1904. 1st ed. ex-lib. $75.00

COLLISON, Robert L. *Indexes & Indexing*. 1953. London. Benn. 1st ed. dj. VG $15.00

COLLISON, T. *This Winged World*. 1943. New York. $10.00

COLLODI, Carlo. *Pinocchio, Story of a Puppet*. 1920. Philadelphia. Ills. Maria L. Birk. 1st ed. $20.00

COLLODI, Carlo. *Pinocchio*. 1932. Garden City. Ills. Maud & Petersham. VG $25.00

COLLODI, Carlo. *Pinocchio*. 1916. Philadelphia. Lippincott. Ills. M. Kirk. G $15.00

COLLODI, Carlo. *Pinocchio*. Philadelphia. McKay. no date. Ills. Folkard. $35.00

COLLODI, Carlo. *Pinocchio*. 1986. New Jersey. Ills. Hildebrandt. 178 pp. $17.00

COLLODI, Carlo. *Pinocchio*. Winston. no date. Ills. Richardson. G $6.50

COLLODI, Carlo. *Pinocchio*. 1924. Saalfield. Ills. Brundage. 247 pp. EX $50.00

COLLODI, Carlo. *The Adventures of Pinochio*. 1927. Macmillan. Ills. Mussino. 1st ed. VG $25.00

COLLODI, Carlo. *The Adventures of Pinocchio*. Philadelphia. Ills. Richardson & Folkard. EX $25.00

COLMAN, Julia. *Boys & Girls*. 1857. New York. Ills. 1st ed. $45.00

COLMAN, Julia. *New Stories for Little Boys & Little Girls*. 1850 & 1855. NY. Raynor. Ills. 2 vol set. $50.00

COLMERY, R.C. *Memoir of Life & Character of Josiah Scott*. 1881. Columbus. 190 pp. G $17.50

COLOMBO, John R. *Colombo's Hollywood*. 1979. Toronto. 192 pp. dj. $3.50

COLQUHOUN, A.R. *The Mystery of the Pacific*. 1904. New York. Macmillan. Ills. 2nd ed. G $15.00

COLT, C.E. *The Early Piano*. 1981. London. Stainer & Bell. Ills. dj. VG $16.50

COLT, Daniel Wadsworth. *Drawings & Letters*. 1937. San Francsico. Grabhorn Press. Ills. Ltd. ed. $60.00

COLT, Terry Strickland. *Knights, Goats & Battleships*. 1930. Garden City. Ills. M. Flack. dj. EX $25.00

COLT. *Quick-Trigger Country*. Signet. pb. $3.00

COLTON, Harold S. *Black Sand. Prehistory in Northern Arizona*. 1960. Albuquerque. Ills. 1st ed. dj. EX $30.00

COLTON, Matthew M. *Frank Armstrong at College*. 1914. New York. Hurst & Co. 302 pp. G $2.00

COLTON, S. *Hopi Kachina Dolls.* 1949. U. of NM. 1st ed. dj. VG $25.00

COLTON, Walter. *Three Years in California.* 1850. New York. Barnes. Ills. 1st ed. map. VG $225.00

COLTON. *The California Diary.* 1948. Oakland. Ills. Ltd. CA ed. 1/100. EX $60.00

COLUM, Padraic. *Creatures.* 1927. Macmillan. Ills. Artzybasheff. VG $15.00

COLUM, Padraic. *Poems of the Irish Revolutionary Brotherhood.* 1916. Maynard. 1st ed. $35.00

COLUM, Padraic. *The Stone of Victory & Other Tales.* 1966. New York. Ills. Judith Gwyn Brown. EX $15.00

COLUM, Padriac. *Adventures of Odysseus & Tale of Troy.* 1918. New York. Ills. Pogany. 1st ed. 254 pp. $35.00

COLVER, Anne. *Mr. Lincoln's Wife.* 1943. New York. Farrar & Rinehart. 406 pp. $5.50

COLVIN, Sidney. *John Keats.* 1917. New York. Ills. 1st ed. 598 pp. EX $50.00

COLVIN, Sidney. *John Keats.* 1887. London. 1st ed. VG $45.00

COLVIN, Sidney. *Letters of Robert Louis Stevenson.* 1902. New York. 2 vol set. VG $12.50

COLWIN, Laurie. *Family Happiness.* 1982. 1st ed. sgn. VG $25.00

COLWIN, Laurie. *Happy All the Time.* 1978. Knopf. 1st ed. dj. VG $17.50

COLWIN, Laurie. *Passion & Affect.* 1974. Viking. 1st ed. dj. VG $35.00

COLWIN, Laurie. *The Lone Pilgrim.* 1981. Knopf. 1st ed. dj. VG $15.00

COLYTON, Henry John. *Sir Pagan.* 1947. New York. 376 pp. VG $3.50

COMBE, G. *Lectures on Phrenology.* 1840. New York. Fowler & Wells. 3rd ed. Ills. $12.50

COMBS, G.H. *Himmler, Nazi Spider Man.* 1942. 1st ed. VG $20.00

COMBS. *Kill Devil Hill. Secret of the Wright Brothers.* 1979. Boston. inscr. $7.00

COMMAGER & NEVINS. *Heritage of America.* 1947. reprint. Ills. VG $6.50

COMMAGER. *Illustrated History of the Civil War.* 1976. Ills. 284 pp. $14.50

COMMONER, Barry. *The Closing Circle.* 1972. Rodale Book Club. $2.50

COMOLLI, G.B. *Project D'Une Fontaine Publique.* 1808. Parma. 14 pls. folio. VG $75.00

COMPTON, D.G. *Windows.* 1979. Putnam. 1st ed. dj. EX $15.00

COMPTON, Margaret. *American Indian Fairy Tales.* 1907. New York. Ills. 201 pp. VG $15.00

COMPTON-BURNETT, Ivy. *Mother & Son.* 1955. London. 1st ed. dj. EX $22.50

COMPTON-BURNETT. *Two Worlds & Their Ways.* 1949. 1st Am. ed. VG $10.00

COMPTON-HALL, R. *Submarine Warfare. Monsters & Midgets.* 1985. Poole. Ills. dj. EX $20.00

COMSTOCK, F.A. *A Gothic Vision: F.L. Griggs & His Work.* 1966. Boston. Ltd. ed. 1/600. sgn. $50.00

COMSTOCK, Helen. *100 Most Beautiful Rooms in America.* 1968. New York. Viking. revised ed. dj. $15.00

COMSTOCK, J.H. & COMSTOCK, A. *Manual for the Study of Insects.* 1895. Comstock Pub. Ills. 1st ed. $125.00

COMSTOCK, Jim. *Pa & Ma & Fiddlin' Clyde.* 1965. Richwood. sgn. 121 pp. $7.50

COMSTOCK, Joseph. *The Tongue of Time & Star of the States.* 1840. Hartford. Ills. 487 pp. $95.00

CONACHER, Brian. *Hockey in Canada. The Way It Is!* 1970. Gateway Press. Ills. 151 pp. VG $10.00

CONANT, E. *Geography, History, Constitution & VT Government.* 1895. Rutland, VT. Ills. $20.00

CONARD, J. *Within the Tides.* 1st Eng. ed. VG $60.00

CONATSER. *Sterling Legend. Facts Behind Lost Dutchman Mine.* 1972. Ills. 1st ed. 98 pp. map. SftCvr. $12.50

CONDE. *Narrow Gauge in a Kingdom. Hawaiian Railroad Co.* 1971. Ills. 96 pp. SftCvr. $10.00

CONDON, George. *Stars in the Water.* 1974. Garden City. 338 pp. $10.00

CONDON, Richard. *A Talent for Loving.* 1961. McGraw Hill. 1st ed. dj. EX $20.00

CONDON, Richard. *An Infinity of Mirrors.* 1964. 1st ed. dj. EX $20.00

CONDON, Richard. *Any God Will Do.* 1966. Random House. 1st ed. dj. VG $15.00

CONDON, Richard. *Mile High.* 1969. 1st ed. dj. EX $15.00

CONDON, Richard. *Money is Love.* 1975. 1st ed. dj. VG $12.00

CONDON, Richard. *Prizzi's Honor.* 1982. advance copy. $35.00

CONDON, Richard. *Some Angry Angel.* 1960. McGraw Hill. 1st ed. dj. EX $25.00

CONDON, Richard. *The Ecstasy Business.* 1967. Dial Press. 1st Am. ed. dj. VG $15.00

CONDON, Richard. *The Vertical Smile.* 1971. Dial Press. 1st ed. dj. VG $15.00

CONDON, Richard. *Winter Kills.* 1974. Dial Press. 1st ed. dj. EX $15.00

CONE, Arthur L., Jr. *Fishing Made Easy.* 1968. Macmillan. Ills. 1st printing. EX $7.50

CONEY, Michael. *Gods of the Greataway.* 1984. Boston. 1st ed. dj. VG $10.00

CONEY, Michael. *The Celestial Steam Locomotive. Vol. I.* 1983. Boston. 1st ed. dj. VG $10.00

CONGDON. *The Covered Bridge.* 1946. $17.50

CONGER, Sarah Pike. *Letters from China.* 1909. Chicago. Ills. 2nd ed. map. VG $30.00

CONGRESS. *Land Claims in the Territory of New Mexico.* 1858. Washington. 1st ed. 326 pp. EX $250.00

CONGREVE, William. *The Way of the World.* 1929. New York. Dodd Mead. Ills. Kettelwell. $23.00

CONKLING, Hilda. *Silverhorn.* 1924. New York. Ills. Dorothy P. Lathrop. EX $50.00

CONKLING, Roscoe. *The Butterfield Overland Mail.* 1947. Glendale Clark. 1st ed. 2 vol set. VG $200.00

CONKLING. *Memoirs of the Mother & the Wife of Washington.* 1850. Derby, Miller & Co. 248 pp. VG $8.50

CONLAN, Jocko. *Jocko.* 1967. 1st ed. dj. VG $7.50

CONLEY, Philip. *History of West Virginia Coal Industry.* 1960. Charleston. presentation copy. 311 pp. $12.50

CONN, Charles P. *The Winner's Circle.* 1979. Revell Co. $5.50

CONN, G.H. *The Arabian Horse in Fact, Fantasy, & Fiction.* 1959. Barnes. 384 pp. EX $10.00

CONN, H.W. *Practical Dairy Bacteriology.* 1907. New York. Judd Pub. 314 pp. G $3.50

CONNELL, Brian. *The Plains of Abraham.* 1959. London. Ills. maps. 288 pp. $20.00

CONNELL, Evan S. *A Long Desire.* 1979. Holt. 1st ed. dj. VG $20.00

CONNELL, Evan S. *Mr. Bridge.* 1969. Knopf. 1st ed. dj. VG $30.00

CONNELL, Evan S. *Son of the Morning Star/Custer & Little Bighorn.* 1984. N. Point Press. 441 pp. dj. EX $6.00

CONNELL, Evan S. *The Connoisseur.* 1974. Knopf. 1st ed. dj. VG $25.00

CONNELL, Evan S. *The White Lantern.* 1980. Holt. 1st ed. dj. VG $15.00

CONNELL. *Diary of a Rapist.* New York. 1st ed. dj. VG $10.00

CONNELL. *Note in a Bottle.* New York. 1st ed. dj. VG $10.00

CONNELLEY. *Doniphan's Expedition.* 1907. 1st ed. $60.00

CONNELLEY. *Wild Bill & His Ear.* 1933. New York. $50.00

CONNELLY, Marc. *The Green Pastures.* 1930. New York. Ills. Jones. Ltd. ed. sgns. VG $45.00

CONNELLY, Marc. *The Green Pastures.* 1929. 1st ed. 173 pp. dj. EX $20.00

CONNER, A.Z. *Red Army Order of Battle in Great Patriotic War.* 1985. Navato, CA. 408 pp. $10.00

CONNETT, Eugene. *American Big Game Fishing.* 1935. Derrydale. Ltd. 1st ed. 1/850. $350.00

CONNETT, Eugene. *Duck Shooting Along Atlantic Tidewater.* 1947. Morrow. Ills. 1st ed. 308 pp. $57.50

CONNETT, Eugene. *Duck Shooting Along the Atlantic Tidewater.* 2nd ed. $35.00

CONNETT, Eugene. *Duck Shooting Along the Atlantic Tidewater.* Bonanza. pb. VG $16.00

CONNETT, Eugene. *Wildfowling in Mississippi Flyway.* 1949. Van Nostrand. Ills. 1st ed. 387 pp. index. $125.00

CONNINGHAM. *Currier & Ives Prints, an Illustrated Checklist.* 1983. revised ed. dj. EX $15.00

CONNINGTON, J.J. *Jack-in-the-Box.* 1944. Boston. Little, Brown. dj. EX $10.00

CONNOLLY, B. *Gullible's Travels with Campbell.* 1982. 1st ed. dj. EX $14.00

CONNOLLY, Cornelius. *External Morphology of the Primate Brain.* 1950. Charles Thomas.1st ed. $25.00

CONNOLLY, Cyril. *The Rock Pool.* 1936. Scribner. 1st ed. G $20.00

CONNOLLY, James B. *Gloucestermen.* 1930. New York. $7.50

CONNOLLY, James B. *Out of Gloucester.* 1905. New York. inscr. VG $20.00

CONNOLLY, Margaret. *Friendship Year Book.* 1910. Crowell. 120 pp. SftCvr. VG $10.00

CONNOR, Ralph. *Rock, a Tale of the Selkirks.* Illinois. D. Cook. VG $3.50

CONNOR. *The Sky Pilot.* 1899. Grosset & Dunlap. Ills. $5.50

CONQUEST, Robert. *Soviet Nationalities Policy in Practice.* 1967. New York. Praeger. ex-lib. 160 pp. $6.00

CONQUEST, Robert. *The Soviet Deportation of Nationalities.* 1960. London. Macmillan. ex-lib. 203 pp. $9.00

CONRAD, B. *Encyclopedia of Bullfighting.* 1962. London. Ills. 1st ed. 271 pp. EX $10.00

CONRAD, Earl. *Jim Crow America.* 1947. Duell. dj. VG $10.00

CONRAD, Joseph & Hueffer, F.M.*The Nature of a Crime.* 1924. London. 1st ed. dj. VG $25.00

CONRAD, Joseph. *A Conrad Argosy.* 1942. New York. Ills. Mueller. 713 pp. VG $5.00

CONRAD, Joseph. *An Outcast of the Islands.* 1896. London. 1st ed. G $25.00

CONRAD, Joseph. *Arrow of Gold.* 1919. London. 1st ed. dj. $45.00

CONRAD, Joseph. *Laughing Anne & One Day More.* 1924. London. dj. EX $50.00

CONRAD, Joseph. *Mirror of the Sea.* 1906. London. 1st ed. VG $50.00

CONRAD, Joseph. *Suspense.* 1925. Garden City. 1st trade ed. dj. VG $40.00

CONRAD, Joseph. *Tales of Hearsay.* 1925. London. Unwin. Ltd. 1st ed. dj. $150.00

CONRAD, Joseph. *Tales of Unrest.* 1898. New York. 1st ed. G $40.00

CONRAD, Joseph. *The Arrow of Gold.* 1919. New York. Doubleday. 1st ed. G $25.00

CONRAD, Joseph. *The Complete Works of Joseph Conrad.* 1920. New York. Dial Press. 24 vol set. sgn. $550.00

CONRAD, Joseph. *The Rescue.* 1920. London. 1st Eng. ed. dj. $40.00

CONRAD, Joseph. *The Rover.* 1913. New York. 1st ed. G $12.50

CONRAD, Joseph. *The Rover.* 1932. London. dj. $40.00

CONRAD, Joseph. *The Secret Agent. A Drama in Three Acts.* 1923. Ltd ed. 1/1000. sgn. $145.00

CONRAD, Joseph. *Twixt Land & Sea.* 1912. 1st ed. VG $72.50

CONRAD, Joseph. *Victory.* London. 1st Eng. ed. EX $45.00

CONRAD, Joseph. *Within the Tides.* 1915. London. 1st ed. EX $45.00

CONRAD, Joseph. *Youth & Other Stories.* 1903. New York. Doubleday. 339 pp. $3.50

CONRAD, Joseph. *Youth & Two Other Stories.* 1929. Leipzig. 1st ed. VG $70.00

CONRAD, Will C. & Wilson. *The Milwaukee Journal, the First 80 Years.* 1964. Madison, Wis. 372 pp. dj. VG $5.00

CONROTTO, Eugene L. *Lost Desert Bonanzas.* 1963. Best West. 1st ed. 91 maps. dj. EX $22.50

CONROY, Frank. *Midair.* 1985. New York. Dutton. 1st ed. dj. EX $20.00

CONROY, Jack. *Midland Humor. A Harvest of Fun & Folklore.* 1947. New York. 446 pp. $5.00

CONROY, Pat. *The Great Santini.* 1976. Houghton. proof copy. wrappers. VG $20.00

CONROY, Pat. *The Great Santini.* 1976. Houghton Mifflin. 1st ed. dj. $25.00

CONROY, Pat. *The Water is Wide.* 1972. Houghton. 1st ed. dj. VG $50.00

CONSTAINTINE, M. *Tina Modotti.* 1975. New York. dj. EX $37.50

CONSTANTINE, K.C. *A Fix Like This.* 1975. New York. Dutton. 1st ed. dj. EX $15.00

CONSTANTINE, K.C. *The Man Who Liked Slow Tomatoes.* 1982. Boston. Library of Congress duplicate. $10.00

CONSUMER GUIDE. *Guns 1977 & Hunting Equipment.* 1976. Skokie, IL. 130 pp. SftCvr. VG $3.50

CONTINI, M. *Fashion from Ancient Egypt to the Present Day.* 1965. New York. dj. EX $20.00

CONTOSTA, David R. *Henry Adams & the American Experiment.* 1980. Boston. 1st ed. dj. $10.00

CONWAY, J. Gregory. *Flowers East & West.* 1938. Knopf. $20.00

CONWAY, J. Gregory. *Treasury of Flower Arrangements.* 1953. Knopf. $30.00

CONWAY, Moncure. *Solomon & Solomonic Literature.* 1899. Open Court Pub.VG $25.00

CONWELL, Col. R. *History of the Great Fire in Boston.* 1873. Boston. Ills. VG $15.00

COOK, Chris. *A History of the Great Trains.* 1977. New York. photos. 144 pp. dj. EX $12.50

COOK, David J. *Hands Up; or, 35 Years of Detective Life.* 1897. Denver. enlarged ed. $120.00

COOK, E.T. *Gardens of England.* 1908. London. Ills. Parsons. 20 color pls. $67.50

COOK, Frances Kerr. *Red & Gold Stories.* 1973. New York. Viking. Ills. 127 pp. dj. EX $4.50

COOK, Frederick A. *My Attainment of the Pole.* 1912. Kennerley. G $90.00

COOK, Frederick. *Through the First Antarctic Night.* 1909. New York. sgn. inscr. VG $125.00

COOK, James H. *50 Years on Old Frontier as Cowboy, Hunter, Guide.*1923. New Haven. Ills. 1st ed. VG $35.00

COOK, James. *A Voyage to the Pacific Ocean.* 1784. Dublin. Ills. 1st Irish ed. 4 vol set. $975.00

COOK, James. *Fifty Years On The Old Frontier.* 1954. Ills. 253 pp. $12.50

COOK, James. *Journal of Capt. Cook's Last Voyage to Pacific.* 1781. London. Ills. 1st ed. maps. chart. VG $2,450.00

COOK, James. *Three Voyages of Capt. Cook Round the World.* 1821. London. 7 vol set. rebound. $250.00

COOK, James. *Three Voyages of Capt. Cook Round the World.* 1821. London. Longman, Hurst. Ills. 7 vol. set. $575.00

COOK, James. *Voyages Round World Towards North & South Poles.* 1799. Manchester. 5 pls. appendix. $400.00

COOK, Joel. *America. Picturesque & Description.* 1900. New York. Ills. EX $33.00

COOK, John R. *Border & Buffalo.* 1907. Topeka. 1st ed. 352 pp. $55.00

COOK, R.B. *Washington's Western Lands.* 1930. Strasburg. 1st ed. 176 pp. $15.00

COOK, Robin. *Mindbend.* 1985. proof copy. $22.00

COOK, Robin. *Mindbend.* 1985. Putnam. 1st ed. dj. VG $15.00

COOK, Roy T. *101 Famous Poems.* 1958. 181 pp. $4.50

COOK, S.F. & Heizer, R.F. *Physical Analysis of Nine Indian Mounds.* 1951. Berkeley. 32 pp. wrappers. $8.50

COOK, Samuel Newton. *Norma Lane. Daughter of an Absent Brother.* 1909. Columbus, OH. 245 pp. $7.50

COOK, William Wallace. *Around the World in Eighty Hours.* 1925. New York. Chelsea House. 1st ed. VG $30.00

COOK Sherwin. *Torchlight Parade. Our Presidential Pageant.* 1929. New York. Ills. 1st ed. VG $15.00

COOK. *Return from the Pole.* 1951. 1st ed. VG $12.50

COOK. *Secret Mission.* 1943. Grosset & Dunlap. Ills. G. $4.50

COOK. *Spitfire Pilot.* 1942. Grosset & Dunlap. Ills. VG $5.50

COOK. *Wit & Wisdom of Reverend Charles H. Spurgeon.* 1892. Treat Co. Ills. 527 pp. $6.50

COOKE, A.H. *Molluscs, Brachipods, & Brachiopods.* 1895. Macmillan. Ills. 535 pp. $20.00

COOKE, Alistair. *Alistair Cooke's America.* 1973. Knopf. Ills. 399 pp. EX $4.50

COOKE, Alistair. *One Man's America.* 1952. Knopf. 1st Am. ed. VG $10.00

COOKE, David. *My Best Murder Story.* 1955. New York. 1st ed. dj. VG $17.50

COOKE, David. *Deca: A Village in India.* 1967. Ills. 1st ed. 155 pp. $3.00

COOKE, Edmund Vance. *Told to the Little Tot.* 1906. New York. Dodge. Ills. Pease. $15.00

COOKE, Edward. *Voyage to South Sea & Round World in 1708-1711.* 1712. London. Ills. 1st complete ed. 2 vol set. $1,750.00

COOKE, Grace MacGowan. *Their First Formal Call.* 1906. NY/London. Harper. 1st ed. $40.00

COOKE, J. *America Picturesque & Descriptive.* 1900. Winston. Ills. 3 vol set. $45.00

COOKE, J.H. *Virginia: History of the People.* 1883. Boston. 1st ed. VG $15.00

COOKE, John Esten. *Hammer & Rapier.* 1871. London. 307 pp. G $10.00

COOKE, John Esten. *Outlines from the Outpost.* 1961. Lakeside Classic. VG $20.00

COOKE, John Esten. *Surry of Eagle's Nest.* 1866. New York. Ills. Winslow. 3rd ed. $45.00

COOKE, Matthew. *Injurious Insects of the Orchard, Vineyard, (etc.).* 1883. Sacramento. Ills. 472 pp. $20.00

COOKE, Rose Terry. *A Lay Preacher.* 1884. Boston. 1st ed. EX $25.00

COOKRIDGE, E.H. *Orient Express.* 1978. New York. Random House. 1st ed. 288 pp. $5.00

COOLEY. *Domestic Art in Women's Education.* 1911. Scribner. 274 pp. $3.50

COOLIDGE, Calvin. *The Autobiography of Coolidge.* 1929. New York. Ltd. 1st ed. 1/1000. sgn. $175.00

COOLIDGE, Dane. *Fighting Men of the West.* 1932. New York. Ills. 1st ed. VG $30.00

COOLIDGE, Dane. *Gringo Gold.* 1939. New York. 249 pp. dj. $6.50

COOLIDGE, Dane. *Not Afraid.* 1926. New York. Dutton. 299 pp. dj. $6.00

COOLIDGE, Dane. *Rawhide Johnny.* 1936. New York. Dutton. 1st ed. dj. $8.50

COOLIDGE, Dane. *Sheriff Killer.* 1932. New York. Dutton. 286 pp. dj. $6.50

COOLIDGE. *Klondike & the Yukon Country.* 1897. map. 18 pls. VG $125.00

COOMARASWAMY, A.L. *Elements of Buddhist Inconography.* 1935. Harvard. 1st ed. 95 pp. 15 pls. VG $28.00

COOMBS, David. *Sport & Countryside in English Paintings.* 1973. Oxford. Ills. VG $25.00

COON, C. *The Hunting People.* 1971. Little, Brown. Ills. 1st ed. 413 pp. dj. EX $22.50

COONEY, Barbara. *Little Juggler.* 1961. Hastings House. Ills. dj. VG $8.00

COOPER, . *The Prairie; The Pioneers; The Pathfinder.* J.B. Alden. no date. 3 vol set. $12.50

COOPER, A.E. *Sea Fishing.* London. 120 Ills. VG $25.00

COOPER, Bryan & Batchelor, J. *Fighter, History of Fighter Aircraft.* 1973. New York. Scribner. 1st ed. EX $15.00

COOPER, C. *Lions 'N' Tigers 'N' Everything.* 1924. Little, Brown. Ills. 260 pp. $10.00

COOPER, F. *Lionel Lincoln or the Leaguer of Boston.* London. (ca.1845) 378 pp. G $15.00

COOPER, Frederic Taber. *The Book of Fables.* 1921. New York. Hampton. Ills. Bransom. VG $25.00

COOPER, James Fenimore. *Correspondence of James Fenimore Cooper.* 1922. Yale U. Press. 1st ed. 776 pp. 2 vol set. $45.00

COOPER, James Fenimore. *The Deerslayer.* 1929. Scribner. Ills. N.C. Wyeth. G $18.50

COOPER, James Fenimore. *The Deerslayer.* 1841. London. 2nd ed. 3 vol set. EX $250.00

COOPER, James Fenimore. *The Last of the Mohicans.* 1946. New York. Scribner. Ills. Wyeth. dj. $30.00

COOPER, James Fenimore. *The Last of the Mohicans.* New York. Book League. EX $40.00

COOPER, James Fenimore. *The Leather Stocking Tales.* New York. (ca.1890's) 5 vol set. VG $35.00

COOPER, James Fenimore. *The Leather Stocking Tales.* 1954. Pantheon. Ills. Marsh. 833 pp. $7.50

COOPER, James Fenimore. *The Redskins; or Indian & Injin.* Chicago. no date. 442 pp. G $3.50

COOPER, John G. *The Life of Socrates.* 1771. London. Ills. 179 pp. $38.00

COOPER, M. *Cruising to Florida.* 1946. New York. VG $10.00

COOPER, Margaret. *The Inventions of Leonardo Da Vinci.* 1965. Macmillan. 1st ed. dj. $15.00

COOPER, Marion D. *Descendants of John Dean (1650-1727) of Dedham.* 1957. (private printing) 217 pp. $15.00

COOPER, Paul Fenimore. *Island of the Lost.* 1961. New York. 1st ed review copy. $15.00

COOPER, S. *First Lines of Practice of Surgery.* 1828. Boston. 9 pls. VG $75.00

COOPER, T. *The Emporium of Arts & Sciences.* 1813. Philadelphia. fld pls. 3 vol set. VG $120.00

COOPER, W.T. *Portfolio of Australian Birds.* 1968. Rutland. Ills. folio. 25 pls. dj. VG $60.00

COOPER, Wendy. *Hair.* 1971. 1st ed. dj. EX $20.00

COOPER, William. *An Account of Triumphant Death of Mr. Moses Abbot.* 1807. Boston. $15.00

COOPER. *Hope Glynne's Awakening.* Pickering & Inglis. Ills. VG $4.50

COOPER. *Toulouse-Lautrec.* 1956. $29.00

COOPER-OAKLEY, Isabel. *The Count of Saint Germain.* 1970. New York. Rudolf Steiner. 248 pp. dj. EX $17.50

COOTES. *The Eyes of the World.* 1914. Chicago. Book Supply. Ills. Cootes. $52.50

COOVER, Robert. *Pricksongs & Descants.* 1969. Dutton. 1st ed. dj. VG $60.00

COOVER, Robert. *The Public Burning.* 1977. New York. Viking. 1st ed. dj. VG $15.00

COOVER. *The Origin of the Brunists.* 1966. New York. 1st ed. dj. EX $60.00

COPE, E.D. *The Batrachis of North America.* 1963. Lundberg. Ills. 86 pls. 525 pp. index. $30.00

CORLEY, Edwin. *Farewell, My Slightly Tarnished Hero.* 1971. Dodd Mead. dj. EX $10.00

CORLEY, Edwin. *Shadows.* 1975. Stein. 1st ed. dj. VG $12.50

CORLISS. *Propulsion Systems for Space Flight.* 1960. $8.50

CORMACK, Malcolm. *Constable.* 1986. 1st ed. dj. EX $30.00

CORMACK, Mrs. J.G. *Everyday Customs in China.* 1935. London. Moray Press. dj. VG $10.00

CORMAN, Avery. *Kramer vs. Kramer.* 1977. Random House. 1st ed. dj. VG $15.00

CORMAN, Avery. *Oh, God!* 1971. Simon & Schuster. 1st ed. dj. $20.00

CORMAN, Avery. *The Old Neighborhood.* 1980. Linden. 1st ed. ex-lib. dj. VG $10.00

CORMAN, Cid. *Living/Dying.* 1970. New Directions.1st ed. dj. VG $10.00

CORN. *The Art of Andrew Wyeth.* 1973. San Francisco. Ills. dj. EX $45.00

CORNELISEN, Ann. *Strangers & Pilgrims.* 1980. New York. 304 pp. dj. EX $6.00

CORNELIUS, Brian Keith. *Old Master of California.* 1942 & 1957. 1st ed. 2 vol set. inscr. dj. $250.00

CORNELIUS, C.O. *Early American Furniture.* 1926. New York. $15.00

CORNELIUS, Elias. *The Little Osage Captive.* 1822. Boston. 1st ed. 108 pp. VG $250.00

CORNELIUS & SHORT. *Ding Hao, America's Air War in China 1937-1945.* 1980. dj. $10.00

CORNELL, Fred C. *A Rip Van Winkle of the Kalahari.* 1915. London. Unwin. 1st ed. VG $65.00

CORNER. *San Antonio de Bexar.* 1890. $85.00

CORNEWALL-JONES, R.J. *Ships, Sailors, & the Sea.* 1887. $9.50

CORNFIELD, J. *Photo Illustration: Bert Stern.* 1974. New York. wrappers. EX $10.00

CORNING, Howard. *Letters of John James Audubon 1826-1840.* 1969. New York. 278 pp. $30.00

CORNING GLASS WORKS. *Pyrex Prize Recipes.* 1953. Corning. 128 pp. EX $3.50

CORNYN. *Glooskap Stories.* 1930. Little, Brown. Ills. $3.50

CORRINGTON, John. *Lines to the South & Other Poems.* 1965. LA U. Press. 3rd book verse. dj. VG $20.00

CORSARO, Frank. *The Love for Three Oranges.* 1984. New York. Ills. Sendak. 1st Am. ed. dj. $20.00

CORTAZAR, Julio. *A Certain Lucas.* 1984. New York. Knopf. 1st ed. dj. VG $20.00

CORTAZAR, Julio. *End of the Game.* 1967. Pantheon. 1st ed. dj. EX $35.00

CORTAZAR, Julio. *Hopscotch.* 1966. New York. Pantheon. 1st ed. dj. VG $45.00

CORTAZAR, Julio. *Hopscotch.* 1967. London. Collins. 1st Eng. ed. VG $40.00

CORTAZAR, Julio. *The Winners.* 1965. New York. Pantheon. 1st ed. EX $40.00

CORTAZAR, Julio. *We Love Glenda So Much.* 1983. Knopf. proof copy. wrappers. VG $35.00

CORTAZAR, Julio. *A Manual for Manuel.* 1978. Pantheon. 1st Am. ed. dj. VG $12.50

CORTI, Egon. *Maximilian & Charlotte of Mexico.* 1928. New York. 2 vol set. slipcase. EX $75.00

CORY, David. *Billy Bunny & the Friendly Elephant.* 1920. New York. Cupples & Leon. Ills. Spencer. $7.50

CORY, David. *Billy Bunny & Uncle Lucky Lefthindfoot.* 1920. New York. Cupples & Leon. Ills. Spencer. $7.50

COSGROVE, George. *Early California Justice. 1849-1944.* 1948. San Francisco. Grabhorn Press. folio. EX $62.50

COSHELL, Harold. *F.D.R. Champion Campaigner.* 1952. 223 pp. EX $4.00

COSSELL, Howard. *Like It Is.* 1974. inscr. dj. VG $10.00

COSTAIN, Thomas. *A History of the Plantagenets.* 1962. Garden City. 4 vol set. slipcase. $40.00

COSTAIN, Thomas. *Below the Salt.* 1958. London. 1st ed. dj. VG $40.00

COSTAIN, Thomas. *Last Love.* 1963. Garden City. 1st ed. dj. VG $25.00

COSTAIN, Thomas. *The Darkness & the Dawn.* 1959. Garden City. Doubleday. 1st ed. dj. VG $35.00

COSTAIN, Thomas. *The Silver Chalice.* 1952. Garden City. Doubleday. 1st ed. dj. VG $30.00

COSTANZO, Gerald. *Wage the Improbable Happiness.* 1982. Bits. 1st ed. wrappers. EX $5.00

COTLOW, L. *In Search of the Primitive.* 1966. Little, Brown. Ills. 454 pp. VG $10.00

COTLOW, L. *The Twilight of the Primitive.* 1971. Macmillan. Ills. 257 pp. dj. EX $12.50

COTLOW, L. *Zanzabuku (Dangerous Safari).* 1956. Rinehart. Ills. 1st ed. 370 pp. VG $12.50

COTTAM. *Whitewings.* 1968. 1st ed. dj. EX $20.00

COTTEN, Sallie. *The White Doe; or, The Fate of Virginia Dare.* 1901. Philadelphia. VG $15.00

COTTER, Arundel. *United States Steel.* 1921. Doubleday Page.1st ed. VG $10.00

COTTERELL, Howard H. *National Types of Old Pewter.* Weathervane. New York. Ills. dj. VG $10.00

COTTINGHAM, Clive. *The Game of Billiards.* 1964. Lippincott. Ills. 165 pp. $7.50

COTTLE, Delmer L. & Cottle, E. *Index to Atlas of Washington County Ohio.* 1971. Knightstown. 116 pp. wrappers. VG $12.50

COTTON, Henry. *List of Eds. of Bible & Parts Thereof in English.* 1821. Oxford. 1st ed. $100.00

COTTON, Leo. *Mr. Boston Deluxe Official Bartender's Guide.* 1967. Boston. 149 pp. VG $2.50

COUFFER, J. *Song of Wild Laughter.* 1963. Simon & Schuster. Ills. VG $6.00

COUGHLAN, Robert. *The Private World of William Faulkner.* 1954. Ills. 1st ed. dj. EX $40.00

COULSON, Thomas. *Joseph Henry; His Life & Work.* 1950. Princeton. 1st ed. dj. $8.50

COULTER, Douglas. *Columbia Workshop Plays.* 1939. New York. Whittlesey House. 378 pp. $4.00

COULTER, E. *The Civil War & Readjustment in Kentucky.* 1926. 1st ed. EX $50.00

COULTER, John. *Galveston Horror.* 1900. United Pub. photos. 362 pp. VG $5.00

COULTER, John. *Our Martyr Presidents.* 1901. Ills. VG $12.50

COULTON, G. *Medieval Panorama. The English Scene.* 1939. Cambridge. $10.00

COUPERUS, Louis. *Arrogance.* 1930. New York. Ills. Nadejen. 1st ed. EX $35.00

COURLANDER, H. *The Fourth World of the Hopis.* 1971. New York. Ills. 239 pp. dj. $12.00

COURTAULD, Augustine. *From Ends of Earth: Anthology of Polar Writings.* 1958. Oxford. 1st ed. VG $30.00

COUSE, L.E. & Maple, M. *Button Classics.* 1948. Chicago. 4th printing. Ills. 225 pp. $12.50

COUSINS, Norman. *Dr. Schweitzer of Lambarene.* 1960. New York. Harper. photos. 254 pp. $5.50

COUSINS, Norman. *Human Options.* 1981. Norton. 1st ed. dj. VG $10.00

COUSINS, Norman. *Who Speaks for Man?* 1953. New York. 2nd printing. dj. VG $17.50

COUSTEAU, Jacques-Yves. *Octopus & Squid.* 1973. Doubleday. Ills. 1st Am. ed. dj. $12.50

COUSTEAU, Jacques-Yves. *The Shark, Splendid Savage of the Sea.* 1970. Doubleday. Ills. 1st Am. ed. 277 pp. EX $12.50

COUSTEAU, Jacques-Yves. *The Shark.* 1970. New York. Doubleday Doran. 124 photos. $9.50

COUSTEAU, Jacques-Yves. *The Living Sea.* 1963. Harper & Row. Ills. 325 pp. VG $5.00

COUSTILLAS, Pierre. *George Gissing at Alderley Edge.* 1969. London. Ltd. 1st ed. 1/250. dj. EX $25.00

COUTANT. *History of Wyoming.* 1890. Laramie. G $115.00

COVARRUBIAS, M. *Mexico South, Isthmus of Tehuantepec.* 1946. New York. 1st ed. pls. $30.00

COVARRUBIAS, Miguel. *Eagle, Jaguar, Serpent; Indian Art of Americas.* 1954. New York. Ills. 1st ed. 314 pp. dj. EX $65.00

COVARRUBIAS, Miguel. *Indian Art of Mexico & Central America.* 1957. New York. Ills. author. dj. EX $50.00

COVARRUBIAS, Miguel. *Negro Drawings.* 1927. New York. Knopf. 1st ed. dj. scarce. VG $165.00

COVARRUBIAS, Miguel. *The Prince of Wales & Other Famous Americans.* 1925. New York. Ills. 1st ed. VG $40.00

COWAN, Frank. *Revi-Lona: Romance of Love in a Marvelous Land.* Greensburg, PA.(ca.1879) VG $200.00

COWAN, Robert Ernest. *A Bibliography of History of California.* 1914. San Francisco. 1st ed. VG $250.00

COWAN, Sam K. *Sergeant York & His People.* 1922. New York. Grosset & Dunlap. 292 pp. $4.50

COWARD, Noel. *Spangles Unicorn.* 1932. London. Hutchinson. 1st ed. dj. $75.00

COWDEN, J. *Chameleons, Little Lions of the Reptile World.* 1977. McKay. Ills. 1st ed. dj. EX $12.50

COWELL, A. *The Heart of the Forest.* 1971. Knopf. Ills. maps. 238 pp. VG $10.00

COWELL, A. *The Tribe That Hides from Man.* 1974. Stein Day. Ills. 1st ed. map. 251 pp. EX $10.00

COWIE, Donald. *England, the Land, & the People.* 1972. Barnes. Ills. 236 pp. dj. VG $4.50

COWIE, M. *I Walk with Lions.* 1961. 1st ed. dj. EX $8.50

COWLES, Fleur. *Flair Annual.* 1953. EX $50.00

COWLES, Fleur. *The Case of Salvador Dali.* 1959. Little Brown. Ills. 1st ed. 334 pp. dj. VG $15.00

COWLES, Julia. *Our Little Saxon Cousin of Long Ago.* 1930. Boston. Ills. H.W. Packard. $7.50

COWLEY, Abraham. *Mistress & Other Poems.* Nonsuch Press. Ltd. ed. 1/1050. VG $35.00

COWLEY, Abraham. *The Works of Cowley.* 1860. London. 6th ed. $110.00

COWLEY, Malcolm. *Writers at Work.* 1958. London. 2nd impression. dj. VG $15.00

COWLEY, Malcolm. *A Second Flowering.* 1973. Viking Press. 1st ed. dj. VG $15.00

COWLEY, Malcolm. *Adventures of an African Slaver.* 1928. New York. Boni. 1st ed. VG $65.00

COWLEY, Malcolm. *And I Worked at the Writer's Trade.* 1978. Viking Press. 1st ed. dj. VG $15.00

COWLEY, Malcolm. *The Dream of the Golden Mountains.* 1980. New York. Viking Press. 1st ed. dj. EX $20.00

COWLEY, Malcolm. *The View from 80.* 1980. Viking Press. 1st ed. dj. VG $15.00

COWLEY, Malcolm. *The View from 80.* 1980. New York. 1st ed. dj. EX $25.00

COWLEY, Malcolm. *Think Back on Us/Contemporary Chronicle on 1930's.* 1967. S.I.U. Press. 1st ed. dj. VG $20.00

COWLEY, Malcolm. *Unshaken Friend.* 1985. Ltd. ed. 1/250. sgn. $35.00

COWPER, William. *Diverting History of John Gilpin.* 1953. King Penguin. Ills. Ronald Searle. dj. EX $15.00

COWPER, William. *The Task, a Poem.* 1819. Boston. $25.00

COX, A.B. *Professor on Paws.* 1927. New York. Dial Press. 1st Am. ed. VG $35.00

COX, B. *Prehistoric Animals.* 1970. Ills. 159 pp. dj. EX $6.00

COX, Charles E., Jr. *John Tobias, Sportsman.* 1937. Derrydale Pr. Ills. A.L. Ripley. Ltd. ed. $50.00

COX, E.G. *Reference Guide to the Literature of Travel.* 1969. New York. Greenwood Pr. 2nd ed. 3 vol set. $45.00

COX, Erle. *Out of the Silence.* 1947. Melbourne. reprint. $40.00

COX, Harding. *Chasing & Racing.* 1922. New York. 282 pp. $10.00

COX, J.H. *Folk-Songs Mainly from West Virginia.* 1939. 23 pp. wrappers. VG $25.00

COX, John Jr. *Quakerism in the City of New York, 1657-1930.* 1930. New York. 1st ed. sgn. 244 pp. $15.00

COX, Marian Buckley. *Glimpse of Glory/George Mason of Gunston Hall.* 1954. Richmond. Ills. 254 pp. dj. VG $10.00

COX, Palmer. *Another Brownie Book.* 1890. Century. Ills. 1st ed. scarce. $75.00

COX, Palmer. *Queer People.* 1888. Hubbard Bros. 1st ed. VG $50.00

COX, Palmer. *The Brownies Around the World.* 1894. New York. 1st ed. 144 pp. $35.00

COX, Palmer. *The Brownies: Their Book.* 1887. New York. Ills. 144 pp. $45.00

COX, Ross. *Adventures on the Columbia River.* 1832. New York. $125.00

COX, Warren E. *Book of Pottery & Porcelain.* 1970. Crown. 2 vol set. slipcase. VG $50.00

COX, Warren F. *Book of Pottery & Porcelain.* 1944. New York. Crown. Ills. 2 vol set. $35.00

COX. *Dare Boys in Virginia.* Petell & Peck. Ills. Mencl. G $4.50

COXE, George Harmon. *The Man Who Died Too Soon.* 1962. Knopf. 1st ed. dj. VG $15.00

COXE, Louis. *The Middle Passage.* 1960. U. Chicago Pr. Ills. 155 pp. $7.50

COYNER, David H. *The Lost Trappers.* 1847. Cincinnati. rebound. $40.00

COYNER, David H. *The Lost Trappers.* 1859. Cincinnati. Ills. 240 pp. G $27.50

COZZENS, J.G. *Morning, Noon, & Night.* 1968. $10.00

COZZENS, J.G. *S.S. San Pedro. A Sea Story.* no date. pb. G $2.50

COZZENS, Samuel Woodworth. *The Ancient Cibola. The Marvellous Country.* 1876. Boston. Ills. G $40.00

CRABB, A.L. *Dinner at Belmont.* 1942. Belmont. VG $15.00

CRADDOCK, Charles Egbert. *In the Tennessee Mountains.* 1884. Boston/NY. 322 pp. $8.00

CRADDOCK, Charles Egbert. *In the Tennessee Mountains.* 1896. Boston. $10.00

CRADDOCK, Charles Egbert. *In the Tennessee Mountains.* 1895. Boston. EX $16.00

CRADDOCK, Charles Egbert. *The Prophet of the Great Smoky Mountains.* 1885. Boston/NY. 308 pp. $8.50

CRADDOCK, Charles. *The Frontierman.* 1904. VG $12.50

CRADO, Thomas. *Strange, True-Life & Adventures of Capt. Crado.* 1893. New Bedford. $40.00

CRAFT, Mabel. *Hawaii.* 1899. San Francisco. Ills. G $20.00

CRAFT, Robert. *Prejudices in Disguise.* 1974. New York. 1st ed. dj. EX $15.00

CRAFTS, W.A. *The Southern Rebellion.* 1867. Boston. Ills. 2 vol set. VG $35.00

CRAIG, Alec. *The Banned Books of England.* 1937. London. foreword by Forster. 1st ed. $45.00

CRAIG, E.G. *The Theatre, Advancing.* 1928. 1st Am. ed. 298 pp. $20.00

CRAIG, John. *The Locks of the Oxford Canal.* 1984. Whittington Pr. Ills. Ltd. ed. 1/350. VG $60.00

CRAIGE, John Houston. *The Practical Book of American Guns.* 1950. New York. Bramhall House. Ills. 352 pp. $10.00

CRAIGHEAD, F.C. *Track of the Grizzly.* 1979. Sierra Club. Ills. maps. 261 pp. dj. EX $10.00

CRAIK, D. Mullock. *Adventures of a Brownie & Some Children's Poems.* 1908. McLoughlin. 128 pp. VG $10.00

CRAINE, E.J. *Airplane Boys with the Revolutionists in Bolivia.* 1931. New York. 201 pp. dj. $3.00

CRAINE, E.R. & Reindorp, R.C. *The Chronicles of Michoacan.* 1970. OK U. Press. Ills. 1st ed. map. 253 pp. dj. $15.00

CRAINE, Edith J. & Burton, A. *Happy Days Out West for Littlebits.* 1927. Chicago. Ills. Gregory. 1st ed. $15.00

CRAM, Mildred. *Old Seaport Towns of the South.* 1917. New York. Ills. 1st ed. 364 pp. VG $25.00

CRAM, Ralph. *Walled Town.* 1919. 1st ed. dj. VG $25.00

CRAMER, Carl. *Eagle in the Wind.* 1948. New York. Aladdin. Ills. E. Cramer. dj. $25.00

CRAMER, Carl. *Songs of Rivers of America.* 1942. Farrar Rinehart. 1st ed. dj. $65.00

CRAMER, Zadock. *The Navigator.* 1818. Pittsburgh. 10th ed. 304 pp. maps. VG $250.00

CRANCH, Christopher Pearse. *The Last of the Huggermuggers.* 1856. Boston. 1st ed. G $45.00

CRANDALL, Elizabeth Brownell. *Shellac.* 1924. Chicago. Ills. Robert Hyman. 1st ed. VG $10.00

CRANE, Aimee. *Marines at War.* 1943. New York. Ills. 128 pp. $15.00

CRANE, C.E. *Let Me Show You Vermont.* 1937. 1st ed. $7.50

CRANE, Hart. *The Collected Poems of Hart Crane.* 1933. Liveright. VG $10.00

CRANE, Leo. *Indians of the Enchanted Desert.* 1925. Boston. Ills. 1st ed. fld map. 364 pp. $35.00

CRANE, Nathalia. *The Janitor's Boy.* 1924. New York. Ltd. 1st ed. 1/500. sgn. $20.00

CRANE, R.S. & Kaye, F.B. *A Census of British Newspapers & Periodicals.* London. 205 pp. $25.00

CRANE, Stephen. *Active Service.* 1899. New York. 1st ed. dj. $70.00

CRANE, Stephen. *George's Mother.* London. 1st Eng. ed. $22.50

CRANE, Stephen. *George's Mother.* 1896. New York. 1st ed. dj. $80.00

CRANE, Stephen. *Great Battles of the World.* 2nd ed. VG $25.00

CRANE, Stephen. *Maggie.* 1896. 1st Eng. ed. rare. VG $350.00

CRANE, Stephen. *The Monster.* 1899. New York. 1st ed. VG $50.00

CRANE, Stephen. *The Red Badge of Courage.* 1951. New York. EX $10.00

CRANE, Stephen. *The Red Badge of Courage.* 1896. New York. Appleton. 2nd ed. $30.00

CRANE, Stephen. *The Third Violet.* 1897. New York. 1st ed. dj. $80.00

CRANE, Stephen. *The Works of Stephen Crane.* 1926. New York. 12 vol set. $325.00

CRANE, Stephen. *War is Kind.* 1899. New York. $360.00

CRANE, Stephen. *Whilomville Stories.* 1900. New York. 1st ed. dj. $80.00

CRANE, Walter. *Don Quixote.* 1940. Dodd Mead. Ills. VG $45.00

CRANE, Walter. *Flora's Feast. A Masque of Flowers.* 1889. London. Ills. 1st ed. $60.00

CRANE, Walter. *Ideals in Art.* 1905. London. 1st ed. VG $85.00

CRANE. *The Automobile Girls at Palm Beach.* 1913. Altemus Co. Ills. VG $5.50

CRANKSHAW, Edward. *Bismark.* 1981. Ills. 451 pp. dj. EX $4.00

CRANKSHAW, Edward. *The Fall of the House of Hapsburg.* 1966. New York. Viking. 459 pp. VG $5.00

CRAPSEY, Algernon Sidney. *The Last of the Heretics.* 1924. New York. 1st ed. inscr. dj. VG $22.50

CRARKE, R. *Old & New Lights on Columbus.* 1893. New York. 600 pp. $25.00

CRAVEN, Avery. *Edmund Ruffin, Southerner.* 1932. 1st ed. $13.50

CRAVEN, Thomas. *A Treasury of American Prints.* 1939. New York. $20.00

CRAVEN, Wayne. *Sculpture in America.* 1968. New York. dj. VG $20.00

CRAVEN & CATE. *Army Air Force in WWII.* 1950-1958. Chicago. 7 vol set. VG $225.00

CRAWFORD, A.C. *Customs & Culture of Vietnam.* 1966. Ills. ex-lib. G $7.00

CRAWFORD, D. *Thinking Black.* 1912. New York. Ills. VG $25.00

CRAWFORD, F. Marion. *Khaled: Tale of Arabia.* 1891. Macmillan. 1st ed. G $50.00

CRAWFORD, F.M. *Man Overboard.* 1903. Macmillan. 1st ed. VG $30.00

CRAWFORD, Isabel. *Joyful Journey.* 1951. Philadelphia. Judson Press. Ills. 1st ed. $75.00

CRAWFORD, James M. *Studies in Southeastern Indian Languages.* 1975. U. of GA. 453 pp. EX $12.50

CRAWFORD, Lucy. *The History of the White Mountains.* 1886. Portland. G $45.00

CRAWFORD, Marion. *The Little Princesses.* 1950. New York. Harcourt Brace. 1st ed. dj. $5.00

CRAWFORD, Mary & Welton, T. *Before the Doctor Comes.* 1909. New York. Christian Herald. Ills. $8.00

CRAWFORD, Theron Clark. *A Man & His Soul.* New York. Reed. VG $50.00

CRAWFORD. *An American Politician.* 1884. Collier. $4.50

CRAWFORD. *Rekindling Camp Fires.* 1926. Bismark. dj. $35.00

CRAWFORD. *The Children of the King.* 1885. Collier. $4.50

CRAWLEY, E. & Besterman. *The Mystic Rose. Study of Primitive Marriage.* 1927. New York. 2nd revised ed. 2 vol set. VG $27.50

CRAWNINSHIELD, Frank, ed. *Unofficial Palace of New York, Tribute to Waldorf.* 1939. New York. Ills. VG $30.00

CREASEY, J. *Death in the Rising Sun.* 1976. $10.00

CREASEY, J. *Make-Up for the Toff.* 1967. $10.00

CREASY, E.D. *The Fifteen Decisive Battles of the World.* New York. no date. 386 pp. $5.00

CREEKMORE, Hubert. *The Fingers of Night.* 1946. New York. Appleton. 1st ed. dj. VG $25.00

CREEKMORE, Hubert. *The Long Reprieve & Other Poems.* 1946. New Directions.Ltd. ed. 1/1000. dj. EX $30.00

CREEL, George. *Rebel at Large. Recollections of 50 Crowded Years.* 1947. New York. 384 pp. $8.00

CREEL, George. *Sam Houston, Colossus in Buckskin.* 1928. New York. 340 pp. $12.50

CREEL, George. *War Criminals & Punishment.* 1944. New York. McBride. G $15.00

CREELEY, Robert. *A Calendar.* 1984. Morning Coffee.Ltd. ed. 1/600. sgn. wrappers. $12.50

CREELEY, Robert. *Mary's Fancy.* 1970. New York. Ltd. ed. sgn. dj. EX $50.00

CREELEY, Robert. *Pieces.* 1969. New York. Scribner. 81 pp. wrappers. $5.00

CREELEY, Robert. *The Island.* 1963. New York. Scribner. 1st ed. 190 pp. dj. $7.50

CREELEY. *The Charm.* 1969. San Francisco. Ltd. 1st ed. sgn. EX $100.00

CREELY, R. *Poems 1950-1965.* 1st ed. VG $10.00

CREENE, Gael. *Doctor Love.* 1882. St. Martins. 1st ed. dj. VG $15.00

CREMER, Jan. *Jan Cremer Writes Again.* 1969. New York. Grove Press. 1st ed. dj. VG $35.00

CREMERS VAN DER DOES, Eline C.*The Agony of Fashion.* 1980. Blanford. Dorset. Ills. dj. VG $7.50

CRESSEY, G. *Indiana Sand Dunes & Shore Line of Lake Michigan.* 1928. Chicago. 80 pp. dj. EX $10.00

CRESSWELL. *The Journal of Nicholas Cresswell, 1774-1777.* 1925. VG $25.00

CREWDSON, Charles N. *Tales of the Road.* 1905. Chicago. 16 Ills. J.J. Gould. 2nd ed. $10.00

CREWS, Harry. *A Childhood.* 1978. Harper. 1st ed. dj. VG $15.00

CREWS, Harry. *Karate is a Thing of the Spirit.* 1971. Morrow. 1st ed. dj. VG $50.00

CREWS, Harry. *The Hawk is Dying.* 1973. Knopf. 1st ed. dj. VG $17.50

CREWS, Harry. *Two by Crews.* 1984. Lord John. Ltd. ed. 1/200. sgn. EX $50.00

CREWS, Harry. *Two by Crews.* 1984. Lord John. Ltd. ed. 1/26. sgn. EX $125.00

CREWSON, E.A. *Old Times. A Collection of Poems.* 1893. Kansas City. G $7.50

CRICHTON, A. *The History of Arabia.* 1845. New York. 2 vol set. $20.00

CRICHTON, A. *The History of Arabia.* 1835. New York. 2 vol set. $37.50

CRICHTON, M. *Andromeda Strain.* 1969. New York. 1st ed. dj. VG $12.50

CRICHTON, Michael. *Eaters of the Dead.* 1976. Knopf. 1st ed. dj. VG $15.00

CRICHTON, Michael. *Electronic Life.* 1983. Knopf. 1st ed. dj. VG $12.50

CRICHTON, Michael. *The Terminal Man.* 1972. New York. Knopf. proof copy. wrappers. $35.00

CRICHTON, Michael. *The Terminal Man.* 1972. Knopf. 1st ed. dj. EX $15.00

CRICHTON. *Law & Order.* 1926. Santa Fe. Ltd. 1st ed. ex-lib. dj. $40.00

CRIDDLE, Russell. *Love is Not Blind.* 1953. New York. Norton. 272 pp. dj. $4.00

CRILE, Grace. *George Crile, an Autobiography.* 1947. Philadelphia. Ills. 1st ed. 2 vol. boxed. $18.00

CRILE. *Skyways to a Jungle Laboratory.* 1936. Norton. Ills. 1st ed. $4.50

CRIPPS, W. *Old English Plate. Its Makers & Marks.* 1899. London. Ills. 6th ed. 477 pp. $50.00

CRIPPS, W.J. *Old English Plate. Its Makers & Marks.* 1899. New York. $40.00

CRIPPS-DAY, Francis H. *The Manor Farm.* 1931. London. $45.00

CRISLER, Lois. *Artic Wild.* 1958. New York. Harper. photos. 301 pp. $4.00

CRISP, N.J. *The Brink.* 1982. Viking Press. review copy. wrappers. VG $10.00

CRISPIN, Edmund. *Fen Country.* 1979. London. Gollancz. 1st ed. dj. EX $25.00

CRISPIN, Edmund. *Frequent Hearses.* 1950. London. Gollancz. 1st ed. dj. VG $65.00

CRISPIN, Edmund. *Holy Disorders.* 1946. Philadelphia. Lippincott. 1st ed. dj. EX $30.00

CRISPIN, Edmund. *Swan Song.* 1947. London. Gollancz. 1st ed. dj. VG $75.00

CRISPIN, Edmund. *The Moving Toyshop.* London. 1st Eng. ed. dj. VG $125.00

CRISS, Mildred. *Isabella, Young Queen of Spain.* 1941. New York. Ills. Marc Simont. VG $10.00

CRISSEY, Forrest. *Alexander Legge 1866-1933.* 1936. private printing. VG $18.50

CRISTENSEN, E.O. *The Index of American Design.* 1950. New York. 1st printing. EX $30.00

CRITES, A. *Hunter's Tales of the Great Outdoors.* 1952. Los Angeles. sgn. photos. scarce. VG $90.00

CROCKER, Betty. *Picture Cook Book.* 1950. 1st ed. VG $20.00

CROCKER. *Hawaiian Numerals of the Kingdom.* 1909. San Francisco. Ills. 22 pls. G $45.00

CROCKETT, David. *The Autobiography of David Crockett.* 1923. NY/Chicago. 328 pp. $7.50

CROCKETT, Davy. *Davy Crockett's Own Story.* 1955. Citadel. 1st ed. dj. $7.50

CROCKETT, L.P. *Life & Times of Abraham Lincoln.* 1865. Philadelphia. rebound. VG $17.50

CROCKETT, S.R. *The Surprising Adventures of Sir Toady Lion.* 1897. New York. Stokes. Ills. Browne. 314 pp. $6.50

CROCKETT, Walter Hill. *A History of Lake Champlain.* 1909. Ills. 1st ed. VG $25.00

CROFTS, Freeman Wills. *Antidote to Venom.* 1938. London. Hodder & Stoughton. 1st ed. $35.00

CROFTS, Freeman Wills. *Inspector French & the Cheyne Mystery.* 1926. London. Collins. 1st ed. VG $30.00

CROFTS, Freeman Wills. *Mystery in the Channel.* 1931. London. 1st ed. VG $50.00

CROFTS, Freeman Wills. *Sir John Magill's Last Journey.* 1930. London. Collins. 1st ed. VG $70.00

CROFTS, Freeman Wills. *The Loss of the Jane Vosper.* 1936. London. Collins. 1st ed. EX $55.00

CROFUT, W.A. *50 Years in Camp & Field. Diary of Ethan Allen.* 1909. New York. 1st ed. $48.00

CROLY, Mrs. J.C. *Jennie June's American Cookery Book.* 1868. New York. $50.00

CROMER, The Earl of. *Ancient & Modern Imperialism.* 1910. New York. Longmans. 143 pp. $3.00

CROMWELL, Rev. T. *The Orphan Boy's Trials.* 1849. Worcester. $20.00

CRONE, G.R., ed. *The Explorers.* 1962. Ills. 1st ed. maps. 361 pp. EX $12.50

CRONE, G.R. & Kendall, A. *The Voyages of Discovery.* 1970. $10.00

CRONIN, A.J. *A Pocketful of Rye.* 1969. Boston. Little, Brown. 1st ed. dj. EX $25.00

CRONIN, A.J. *A Song of Sixpence.* 1964. Little, Brown. 1st Am. ed. 224 pp. dj. VG $15.00

CRONIN, A.J. *Beyond This Place.* 1953. Boston. 279 pp. EX $5.00

CRONIN, A.J. *Shannon's Way.* 1948. New York. Grosset & Dunlap. 313 pp. dj. $3.50

CRONIN, A.J. *The Citadel.* 1938. Boston. 401 pp. dj. VG $3.50

CRONIN, A.J. *The Green Years.* 1944. Little, Brown. 1st Am. ed. VG $10.00

CRONIN, A.J. *The Judas Tree.* 1961. Boston. 224 pp. $3.50

CRONIN, A.J. *The Keys of the Kingdom.* 1941. Boston. 1st ed. 344 pp. dj. VG $10.00

CRONIN, A.J. *The Northern Lights.* 1958. Little, Brown. 1st Am ed. dj. VG $12.50

CRONYN, George. *The Sandbar Queen.* 1918. New York. wrappers. VG $40.00

CROOK, A.R. *Guide to Mineral Collections in IL State Museum.* 1920. Springfield. G $22.50

CROSBY, Fanny. *Fanny Crosby's Life Story.* 1903. New York. VG $6.00

CROSBY, Frank. *Life of Abraham Lincoln.* 1865. Philadelphia. Potter. 476 pp. $30.00

CROSBY, Gary & Firestone, R. *Going My Own Way.* 1983. New York. Doubleday. 304 pp. dj. VG $4.50

CROSBY, John. *Out of the Blue.* 1952. New York. 1st printing. 301 pp. index. $10.00

CROSBY, Kathryn. *Bing & Other Things.* 1967. New York. Ills. 1st ed. sgn. dj. $12.00

CROSBY, Percy. *Dear Sooky.* 1929. New York. Ills. mounted color pls. $27.50

CROSBY, Percy. *Sport Drawings.* 1933. McLean, VA. Ltd. ed. 1/1000. sgn. VG $50.00

CROSCUP, George E. *United States History with Syncronic Charts.* 1915. New York. Cambridge Book Co. 127 pp. $3.00

CROSLAND, M. *Collette, a Provincial in Paris.* 1954. 1st ed. dj. VG $15.00

CROSS, Amanda. *A Death in the Faculty.* 1981. London. 1st Eng. ed. dj. EX $15.00

CROSS, Amanda. *Poetic Justice.* 1970. New York. Knopf. 1st ed. dj. EX $75.00

CROSS, Amanda. *The James Joyce Murder Case.* 1967. New York. Macmillan. 1st ed. dj. $75.00

CROSS, Clarence. *Descendants of William & Adam Casselman.* 1984. Ltd. ed. 56 pp. wrappers. $20.00

CROSS, F.W. *George Eliot's Life.* Blackwood. 646 pp. VG $15.00

CROSS, J.W. *George Eliot's Life.* 1884. Cabinet ed. 3 vol set. VG $35.00

CROSS, Jeremy L. *The True Masonic Chart; or, Hieroglyphic Monitor.* 1866. New York. Masonic Pub. Ills. 288 pp. VG $30.00

CROSS, John Keir. *The Other Passenger.* 1946. Philadelphia. Lippincott. dj. $40.00

CROSS, Osborn. *A Report of March of Regiment of Mounted Riflemen.* 1850. Washington. 36 pls. VG $325.00

CROSS, R. *Complete Fly Tier.* 1950. dj. VG $20.00

CROSS, Wilbur L. *Connecticut Yankee.* 1943. New Haven. ex-lib. 428 pp. $50.00

CROSS, Wilbur L. *The History of Henry Fielding.* 1918. New Haven. Yale U. Pr. 3 vol set. EX $200.00

CROSS, Wilbur L. *The Life & Times of Lawrence Sterne.* 1925. New Haven. Yale U. Pr. 2 vol set. EX $65.00

CROSSMAN, Carl. *The China Trade.* 1972. Princeton. Ills. 2nd ed. 275 pp. dj. VG $32.50

CROSSMAN, Edward C. *Military & Sporting Rifle Shooting.* 1932. Onslow City. Ills. 499 pp. dj. VG $45.00

CROSSMAN, Edward C. *The Book of the Springfield Rifle.* 1951. Georgetown, SC.Ills. 567 pp. $30.00

CROTHERS, Samuel McChord. *By the Christmas Fire.* 1911. New York. Houghton Mifflin. 226 pp. $4.00

CROTHERS, Samuel McChord. *Miss Muffet's Christmas Party.* 1902. Boston. Ills. Oive M. Long. 1st ed. VG $10.00

CROTHERS, Samuel McChord. *The Children of Dickens.* 1929. New York. Scribner. Ills. J.W. Smith. G $18.50

CROTHERS, Samuel McChord. *The Children of Dickens.* 1931. Scribner. Ills. Jessie W. Smith. ex-lib. $10.00

CROTHERS, Samuel McChord. *The Children of Dickens.* 1925. New York. Ills. J. Wilcox Smith. 1st ed. $35.00

CROTTY. *Glimpses of Don Quixote & La Mancha.* 1963. Los Angeles. Ltd. ed. 1/250. EX $27.50

CROTTY. *Zamorano 80, Selection of Distinguished CA Books.* 1969. reprint. EX $15.00

CROUCH. *Nuclear Ship Propulsion.* 1967. New York. Ills. 1st ed. 347 pp. dj. VG $15.00

CROUSE, M. Elizabeth. *Algiers.* 1906. New York. James Pott & Co. Ills. Hyde. $15.00

CROUSE, William H. *Everyday Automobile Repairs.* 1946. New York. McGraw Hill. 296 pp. $4.00

CROUSE & MAPLE. *Button Classics.* 1944. Chicago. Ills. 3rd ed. 249 pp. VG $25.00

CROW, Carl. *He Opened the Door of Japan.* 1939. New York. Harper. Ills. G $10.00

CROW, Carl. *Japan's Dream of World Empire: Tanaka Memorial.* 1942. New York. Harper. 118 pp. $3.00

CROW, Carl. *The City of Flint Grows Up.* 1945. New York. 1st ed. dj. $6.00

CROWE, John. *Book of Trout Lore.* 1947. New York. Barnes. 50 Ills. VG $6.50

CROWE, P. *Sport is Where You Find It.* 1953. Ltd. ed. sgn. dj. EX $20.00

CROWE, Z. *With Thackeray in America.* 1893. Cassell. 1st ed. VG $17.50

CROWER, J.G. & Whiddington, R. *Science at War.* 1948. New York. 185 pp. VG $4.00

CROWINSHEILD, Francis W. *Manners for the Metropolis.* 1909. Appleton. G $15.00

CROWLEY, Aleister. *Little Essays Toward Truth.* Ontario. Dove Press. 84 pp. dj. EX $10.00

CROWLEY, Aleister. *Magic in Theory & Practice.* 1929. Paris. Lecram Press. 1st ed. 436 pp. $50.00

CROWLEY, Aleister. *Magic Without Tears.* 1973. St.Paul. Llewellyn Pub. 1st printing. $25.00

CROWLEY, Aleister. *Moonchild.* 1929. London. Mandrake Pr. 1st ed. 335 pp. $45.00

CROWLEY, Aleister. *Olla: Anthology of Sixty Years of Song.* London. 1st ed. 128 pp. VG $57.50

CROWLEY, Aleister. *The Confessions of Aleister Crowley.* 1969. New York. Hill & Wang. 960 pp. dj. VG $25.00

CROWLEY, Aleister. *The Diary of a Drug Fiend.* 1923. New York. Dutton. 1st ed. 368 pp. VG $35.00

CROWLEY, Aleister. *The Eye in the Triangle.* 1970. St.Paul. Llewellyn Pub. 1st ed. 517 pp. $25.00

CROWLEY, Aleister. *The Holy Books.* 1972. Dallas. Sangreal Foundation. 116 pp. $10.00

CROWLEY, Aleister. *The Magical Record of the Beast 666.* 1972. Montreal. 1st Am. ed. 326 pp. dj. $30.00

CROWLEY, Aleister. *The Stratagem.* 1929. London. Mandrake Press. 1st ed. dj. EX $125.00

CROWLEY, Aleister. *The Vision & the Voice.* 1972. Dallas. Sangreal Foundation. 261 pp. $12.50

CROWLEY, John. *Little Big.* London. 1st ed. sgn. wrappers. VG $25.00

CROWN PUBLISHERS. *Men at War.* 1942. New York. intro. Hemingway. 1072 pp. $5.00

CROWNOVER, Sims. *The Battle of Franklin.* 1955. reprint. 31 pp. wrappers. $3.50

CROWTHER, Bosley. *Hollywood Rajah. Life & Times of Louis B. Mayer.* 1960. New York. dj. $10.00

CROY, H. *Trigger Marshall.* 1958. Ills. 1st ed. dj. VG $12.50

CROY. *Putnam's Household Handbook.* 1916. Putnam. 327 pp. EX $4.50

CROY. *Retina Way.* 1957. 8th ed. EX $8.50

CROZIER, A.A. *The Cauliflower.* 1891. Ann Arbor. Inland Press. VG $12.00

CROZIER, William. *How the Farm Pays.* 1884. New York. Henderson. 400 pp. VG $15.00

CRUBER. *Gunsight.* Lion. pb. $3.00

CRUICKSHANK, Thomas. *The Practical Planter.* 1830. Edinburgh. Ills. 1st ed. 448 pp. $100.00

CRUIKSHANK, George. *History of Tom Jones.* 1876. London. 1st ed. 2 vol set. dj. VG $30.00

CRUIKSHANK, George. *Omnibus.* 1842. London. 1st ed. $40.00

CRUIKSHANK, George. *Punch & Judy.* 1881. London. Ills. 6th ed. VG $45.00

CRUIKSHANK. *Ingoldsby Legends.* 1884. New York. Ills. VG $25.00

CRUIKSHANKS, Evel. *Hogarth's England, a Selection of Engravings.* 1957. London. Ills. VG $18.00

CRUMLEY, James. *The Last Good Kiss.* 1978. Random House. 1st ed. sgn. dj. VG $30.00

CRUMLEY, James. *The Wrong Case.* 1975. New York. Random House. VG $90.00

CRUMP, Irving. *Teen-Age Boy Scout Stories.* 1948. New York. 254 pp. $3.00

CRUMP, Irving. *The Pilot of the Cloud Patrol.* 1929. New York. Grosset & Dunlap. 220 pp. $3.50

CRUMPACKER, Emily. *Seasonal Gifts from the Kitchen.* 1983. Morrow. 1st ed. dj. VG $6.50

CULBERTSON. *Contract Bridge Complete.* 1937. Winston. 610 pp. $6.50

CULLEN, C. *Copper Sun.* 1927. New York. VG $15.00

CULLEN, Countee. *The Beginning of Black Christ.* 1929. New York. 1st ed. VG $20.00

CULLEN, Countee. *Color.* 1925. Harper. 1st ed. G $25.00

CULLEN, Countee. *Color.* 1925. NY. Harper. presentation copy. sgn. $35.00

CULLEN, Countee. *The Black Christ.* New York. 4th printing. inscr. VG $20.00

CULLUM, Albert. *The Geranium on the Window Sill Just Died.* 1972. Harlin Quist. 2nd printing. $15.00

CULLUM, Ridgwell. *Flaming Wilderness.* 1934. Philadelphia. 1st ed. dj. VG $20.00

CULPEPPER, Nicholas. *Culpepper's Family Physician.* 1824. revised ed. $55.00

CULPEPPER, Nicholas. *Culpepper's Herbal.* 1861. London. 20 colored pls of 180 herbs. $300.00

CULSHAW, John. *Ring Resounding.* 1968. New York. Ills. dj. VG $15.00

CULVER, Dwight. *Negro Segregation in the Methodist Church.* 1953. Yale. 1st ed. dj. $10.00

CULVER, Henry B. *Contemporary Scale Models of Vessels of 17th Cent.* 1926. New York. Ills. Ltd. ed. folio. VG $100.00

CUMING, E.D. *With Rod & Gun.* London/Toronto. Ills. 1st ed. VG $55.00

CUMING E.D. *The Bodley Head Natural History.* 1913. London. J. Land. Ills. Shepherd. $9.00

CUMINGS, E.D. *Idlings in Arcadia.* 1935. Dutton. Ills. J.A. Shepherd. 1st ed. $20.00

CUMMING, C.F. Gordon. *Two Happy Years in Ceylon.* 1892. New York. 2 vol set. EX $60.00

CUMMING, G. *Wild Men & Wild Beasts.* 1872. Scribner. Ills. 372 pp. VG $35.00

CUMMING, R. *Five Years in South Africa.* 1873. $75.00

CUMMINGS, A.P. *The Missionary's Daughter. Memoir of Lucy Goodale.* 1842. New York. 219 pp. $25.00

CUMMINGS, E.E. *Fifty Poems.* 1940. VG $4.00

CUMMINGS, E.E. *Puella Mea.* Golden Eagle Pr. Ills. dj. VG $17.50

CUMMINGS, E.E. *Selected Letters.* 1972. London. dj. $8.00

CUMMINGS, E.E. *Selected Poems 1923-1958.* 1960. London. Faber. 1st Eng. ed. dj. $30.00

CUMMINGS, E.E. *The Enormous Room.* 1922. New York. Boni & Liveright. 1st ed. $250.00

CUMMINGS, E.E. *The Enormous Room.* 1922. New York. Cape & Smith. VG $15.00

CUMMINGS, E.E. *Tulips & Chimneys.* 1924. 2nd printing. G $45.00

CUMMINGS, Ray. *Insect Invasion.* 1967. 1st ed. dj. EX $8.00

CUMMINGS, Rev. Asa. *A Memoir of the Rev. Edward Payson.* 1830. New York. VG $25.00

CUMMINS, Harle O. *Welsh Rarebit Tales.* 1902. Boston. Mutual Bk Co. Ills. 1st ed. G $25.00

CUMONT, Franz. *Astrology & Religion Among the Greeks & Romans.* 1912. New York. 1st ed. 208 pp. VG $55.00

CUNARD, Nancy. *Brave Poet.* 1968. Philadelphia. Ills. 1st ed. dj. $25.00

CUNARD, Nancy. *These Were the Hours.* 1969. 1st ed. dj. $10.00

CUNDALL, Joseph. *A Brief History of Wood Engraving.* 1895. London. 1st ed. VG $25.00

CUNEO, John R. *Robert Rogers of the Rangers.* 1959. New York. Ills. 308 pp. dj. $35.00

CUNEO, John R. *Winged Mars, Vol. I. German Air Weapon 1870-1914.* 1942. Harrisburg. 2nd printing. dj. VG $75.00

CUNLIFFE, Marcus. *George Washington, Man, & Monument.* 1958. Boston. Little, Brown. 234 pp. VG $4.00

CUNNINGHAM, Ann Rowe. *Letters & Diary of John Rowe, Boston Merchant.* 1903. Boston. Ills. 1st ed. 453 pp. EX $150.00

CUNNINGHAM, Charles Henry. *Audencia in the Spanish Colonies.* 1919. Berkeley. Ills. 1st ed. 479 pp. VG $35.00

CUNNINGHAM, Edith Perkins. *Owls Nest: Tribute to Sarah Elliott Perkins.* 1907. Cincinnati. Ills. 1st ed. 323 pp. $150.00

CUNNINGHAM, Eugene. *Buckaroo.* London. 1st Eng. ed. $7.50

CUNNINGHAM, Eugene. *Texas Sheriff.* 1934. Boston. dj. $10.00

CUNNINGHAM, Eugene. *Triggernometry.* 4th ed. $25.00

CUNNINGHAM, Eugene. *Triggernometry. A Gallery of Gunfighters.* 1945. Caldwell, ID. Ills. 441 pp. $30.00

CUNNINGHAM, J.C. & Lancelot. *Soils & Plant Life as Related to Agriculture.* 1915. New York. Macmillan. ex-lib. 348 pp. VG $4.50

CUNNINGHAM, Peter. *The Story of Nell Gwyn & Sayings of Charles II.* 1892. London. Ills. Ltd. ed. index. $55.00

CUNNINGTON. *Chess Traps & Stratagems.* London. 14th ed. $4.00

CUPPER, J. & L. *Hawks in Focus, Study of Australia's Birds of Prey.* 1981. Jaclin. Ills. 1st ed. 208 pp. dj. EX $27.50

CURIE, Eve. *Journey Among Warriors.* 1943. Doubleday. 1st ed. 501 pp. $95.00

CURIE, Eve. *Madame Curie.* 1938. New York. Doubleday Doran. 412 pp. EX $10.00

CURJEL, Hans. *Experiment Krolloper.* Berlin. Ills. German text. boxed. EX $40.00

CURL, Peter. *Designing a Book Jacket.* 1956. London. Ills. 1st ed. 96 pp. $22.50

CURLE, Richard. *Robert Browning & Julia Wedgwood.* 1937. New York. 1st ed. VG $12.50

CURRY. *The American West Painters from Catlin to Russell.* 1972. 1st ed. dj. EX $20.00

CURTIS, Bardella. *Sacred Scriptures & Religious Philosophy.* 1942. Caxton. 1st ed. dj. $8.50

CURTIS, Benjamin R. *Dottings Round the Circle.* 1876. Boston. 1st ed. G $20.00

CURTIS, C. & R. *Hunting in Africa East & West.* 1925. Boston/NY. VG $45.00

CURTIS, Edward S. *The North American Indian: the Southwest.* 1980. Amaranth Press.Ltd. ed. 1/250. folio. EX $95.00

CURTIS, George Ticknor. *Life of Daniel Webster.* 1870. New York. 1318 pp. 2 vol set. $25.00

CURTIS, George William. *Correspondence of John Lothrop Motley.* 1889. New York. 2 vol set. VG $20.00

CURTIS, Lettice. *Forgotten Pilots/Story of Air Transport Auxiliary.* 1985. London. Ills. 337 pp. dj. VG $25.00

CURTIS, M.M. *Book of Snuff & Snuff Boxes.* 1935. New York. dj. $30.00

CURTIS, Natalie. *The Indians Book.* 1923. New York. Ills. 583 pp. $150.00

CURTIS, Newton M. *The Doom of the Tory's Guard. A Tale.* 1843. New York. 1st ed. wrappers. $50.00

CURTIS, William E. *Today in Syria & Palestine.* 1903. New York. Ills. 1st ed. VG $40.00

CURTIS. *Guns & Gunning.* 1943. Knopf. Ills. 384 pp. $5.50

CURTIS. *Sportsmen All.* Derrydale Pr. Ltd. ed. 1/950. $85.00

CURTISS, H.A. & F.H. *The Key of Destiny.* 1923. 6th ed. 328 pp. G $35.00

CURTIUS, Rufus Q. *De Rebus Alex.* 1733. Berlin. 865 pp. 3 indexes. rebound. $120.00

CURWEN, Henry. *History of Booksellers.* 1873. London. Ills. 1st ed. VG $50.00

CURWOOD, James O. *God's Country & the Woman.* Triangle. dj. $5.50

CURWOOD, James O. *God's Country/The Trail to Happiness.* 1921. New York. ex-lib. EX $35.00

CURWOOD, James O. *The Country Beyond.* 1922. New York. Ills. Louderback. 1st ed. dj. $45.00

CURWOOD, James O. *The Gentleman of Courage.* 1924. Ills. Stewart. 1st ed. $6.50

CURWOOD, James O. *The Great Lakes.* 1909. New York. Ills. 1st ed. 72 pls. map. $175.00

CURZON, R. *Ancient Monasteries of the East.* 1854. New York. Ills. 390 pp. $17.50

CUSHING, Caleb. *Treaty of Washington: Its Negotiation & Execution.* 1873. New York. 1st ed. VG $45.00

CUSHING, E. *History of Entomology in World War II.* 1957. Smithsonian. Ills. 117 pp. EX $15.00

CUSHING, Frank H. *The Nation of the Willows.* 1965. Flagstaff. Northland. 75 pp. $7.50

CUSHING, Harvey. *Intracranial Tumors: Notes of 2,000 Cases.* 1932. Springfield. 150 pp. $220.00

CUSHING, Harvey. *Life of Sir William Osler.* 1940. Oxford. 2 vol set. EX $27.50

CUSHING, Harvey. *Life of Sir William Osler.* 1925. Oxford. 1st ed. 2 vol set. VG $50.00

CUSHING, Harvey. *Meningiomas.* 1938. 1st ed. 785 pp. $310.00

CUSHMAN, Dan. *The Great North Trail.* 1966. McGraw Hill. 1st ed. dj. VG $15.00

CUSHMAN, J. *Foraminifera, Their Classification & Economic Use.* 1940. Harvard U. Pr. 3rd ed. 79 pls. 535 pp. VG $17.50

CUSHMAN, Samuel. *The Mines of Clear Creek County, Colorado.* 1876. Denver. 1st ed. 116 pp. wrappers. $300.00

CUSHMAN. *Great North Trail.* 1966. McGraw Hill. dj. VG $15.00

CUSHMAN. *North Fork to Hell.* Gold Medal. pb. $3.00

CUST, Lionel. *Abrecht Durer; Study of His Life & Works.* 1897. London. Ills. 1st ed. VG $36.00

CUSTER, Elizabeth B. *Boots & Saddles.* 1885. Harper. 1st ed. map. 312 pp. VG $30.00

CUSTER, Elizabeth B. *Following the Guidon.* 1890. New York. Harper. G $15.00

CUSTER, Elizabeth B. *Life in Dakota with General Custer.* 1885. New York. 1st ed. VG $30.00

CUSTER, Elizabeth B. *Tenting on the Plains.* 1889. New York. 1st ed. 702 pp. $32.50

CUSTER, George A. *My Life on the Plains.* 1952. EX $27.50

CUTBUSH, James. *The American Artist's Manual, Vol 2.* 1814. Philadelphia. $40.00

CUTCHINS, John A. *History of Twenty-Ninth Division Blue & Grey.* 1921. Philadelphia. Ills. 1st ed. 493 pp. VG $12.50

CUTLER, C. *Greyhounds of the Sea.* 1930. New York. Halcyon House. Ills. 592 pp. $25.00

CUTLER, Harriet Louise Ford. *Harriet Louise Ford Cutler, Teacher, Wife, Mother.* E. Northfield. MA. (ca.1920) Ills. 154 pp. $15.00

CUTTEN, G.B. *Silversmiths of Central New York.* 1937. 8 pp. pamphlet. $5.00

CUTTER, Calvin. *A Treatise on Anatomy, Physiology & Hygiene.* 1850. Boston. Mussey & Co. Ills. 458 pp. G $7.50

CUTTER, William. *New England Families.* 1914. New York. Lewis Hist. Pub. Ills. 4 vol set. $36.00

CUTTING, S. *Fire Ox & Other Years.* 1940. New York. Scribner. Ills. G $20.00

CUTTS, Edward L. *Parish Priests & People in Middle Ages in England.* 1898. London. Ills. 579 pp. $25.00

CUTTS, Richard. *Index to the Youth's Companion 1871-1929.* 1972. Metcuhen, NJ. 1292 pp. 2 vol set. $50.00

CYNK, Jerzy B. *History of the Polish Air Force, 1918-1968.* 1972. Reading. Ills. 307 pp. index. dj. VG $42.50

CZOBOR, Agnes. *Dutch Landscapes.* 1967. New York. 48 color pls. dj. EX $10.00

D'ALVIELLA, Goblet. *The Migration of Symbols.* 1894. Westminster. Constable Co. 1st ed. 277 pp. $60.00

D'AULAIRE, Ingri & Edgar. *Children of the Northern Lights.* 1935. Viking. 1st ed. $75.00

D'AULAIRE, Ingri & Edgar. *East of the Sun & West of the Moon.* 1938. Viking Press. VG $10.00

D'AULAIRE, Ingri & Edgar. *George Washington.* 1936. Garden City. Doubleday. Ills. VG $18.50

D'AULAIRE, Ingri & Edgar. *Norse Gods & Giants.* 1967. Doubleday. Ills. 1st ed. dj. VG $30.00

D'AULAIRE, Ingri & Parin, E. *Pocahontas.* 1946. Garden City. Ills. 1st ed. $40.00

D'AULAIRE. *Lord's Prayer.* 1944. New York. Protestant 1st ed. dj. VG $45.00

D'AULNOY. *D'Aulnoy's Fairy Tales.* 1923. Philadelphia. McKay. Ills. Tenggren. dj. EX $50.00

D'AULNOY. *The White Cat & Other Old French Fairy Tales.* 1928. New York. Ills. MacKinstry. 1st ed. EX $100.00

D'AZEGLIO, Massimo. *I Miei Ricordi.* 1876. Firenze. 7th ed. 2 vol set. G $25.00

D'INDY, Vincent. *Beethoven.* 1913. Boston. trans. Dr. T. Baker. VG $18.00

D'URFE, Honore. *D'Astrea.* 1675. Amsterdam. Dutch text. 12 pls. $35.00

DABNEY. *Virginia, the New Dominion.* 1971. Doubleday. dj. VG $15.00

DACUS & BUEL. *Tour of St. Louis.* 1878. G $15.00

DADD. *American Cattle Doctor.* 1903. New York. 367 pp. $15.00

DAHL, Roald. *Dahl's Book of Ghost Stories.* 1983. New York. 1st ed. dj. EX $10.00

DAHL, Roald. *Going Solo.* 1986. proof copy. wrappers. EX $12.50

DAHL, Roald. *Going Solo.* 1986. New York. Farrar. advance copy. VG $20.00

DAHL, Roald. *My Uncle Oswald.* 1980. Knopf. 1st ed. ex-lib. dj. VG $15.00

DAHL, Roald. *Someone Like You.* 1953. New York. 1st ed. dj. VG $25.00

DAHL, Roald. *Switch Bitch.* 1974. New York. Knopf. 1st ed. dj. EX $15.00

DAHL. *Danny Champion of the World.* 1975. Knopf. Ills. Bennett. 1st ed. dj. EX $15.00

DAHLBERG, Edward. *From Flushing to Calvary.* 1932. New York. dj. EX $30.00

DAHLBERG. *The Confessions of Dahlberg.* 1971. New York. Ltd. 1st ed. 1/200. sgn. EX $85.00

DAHLINGER, Charles W. *Pittsburgh. Sketch of Its Early Social Life.* 1916. NY/London. 216 pp. index. dj. VG $12.50

DAICHES, D. *Two Worlds. An Edinburgh Jewish Childhood.* 1974. Sussex. 2nd ed. EX $10.00

DAICHES, David. *Robert Louis Stevenson.* 1947. 1st ed. $8.50

DAIN, Martin J. *Faulkner's County: Yoknapatawpha.* 1963. Random House. 1st ed. dj. EX $12.50

DAIN, Martin J. *William Faulkner's Country.* 1964. New York. Ills. 1st ed. EX $60.00

DALAFIELD, Francis. *Studies in Pathological Anatomy.* 1882. New York. 1st ed. Vol I (of II). Ills. $145.00

DALBY, Milton A. *Dynamite Johnny O'Brien.* 1933. $7.50

DALE. *Tales of the Tepee.* 1920. Heath. VG $37.50

DALE-GREEN, P. *Cult of the Cat.* 1963. New York. 189 pp. 30 pls. index. $7.50

DALEY, Robert. *Prince of the City.* 1978. Boston. 311 pp. EX $3.50

DALGLEISH. *Christmas.* 1935. New York. Ills. Woodward. sgn. VG $22.50

DALGLIESH, Alice, ed. *Saint George & the Dragon.* 1941. New York. Ills. Lois Maloy. dj. $12.50

DALGLIESH, Alice. *Along Janet's Road.* 1946. New York. sgn. $5.00

DALGLIESH, Alice. *The Courage of Sarah Noble.* 1966. Scribner. Ills. Weisgard. dj. VG $8.50

DALGLIESH, Alice. *The Enchanted Book.* 1947. New York. Ills. Concetta Cacciola. $15.00

DALGLIESH, Alice. *The Little Angel: Story of Old Rio.* 1943. Scribner. Ills. Katherine Milhous. dj. $20.00

DALGLIESH, Alice. *The Silver Pencil.* 1969. Scribner. Ills. K. Milhous. dj. VG $10.00

DALGLIESH, Alice. *They Live in South America.* 1942. New York. Ills. K. Milhous & F. Lichten. $15.00

DALI, S. *Secret Life Salvador Dali.* 1942. Dial Press. 1st ed. VG $50.00

DALI, S. *Study of His Art in Jewels.* 1959. Garden City. slipcase. EX $75.00

DALI. *Conquest of the Irrational.* 1935. New York. Ltd. ed. 1/1000. $65.00

DALI. *Jerusalem Bible.* 1970. red leather binding. boxed. EX $100.00

DALLAWAY, James. *Constantinople: Ancient & Modern.* 1797. London. 1st ed. map. 10 pls. G $100.00

DALLIN, David J. *Soviet Russia's Foreign Policy 1939-1942.* 1942. New Haven, CT. ex-lib. 452 pp. $3.00

DALLIN, David. *Forced Labor in Soviet Russia.* 1947. Yale. 1st ed. dj. $8.50

DALRYMPLE, B.W *Doves & Dove Shooting.* 1949. 1st ed. dj. EX $12.50

DALRYMPLE, B.W. *Complete Guide to Hunting Across North America.* 1970. Harper. Ills. maps. 848 pp. dj. EX $6.50

DALRYMPLE, B.W. *Modern Book of Black Bass.* 1972. Winchester. 206 pp. $7.50

DALRYMPLE, B.W. *North American Game Animals.* 1978. Crown. Ills. 480 pp. G $10.00

DALRYMPLE, B.W. *The Complete Book of Deer Hunting.* 1973. New York. Winchester. 247 pp. dj. $5.00

DALY, Elizabeth. *The House Without the Door.* 1945. London. Hammond. 1st ed. dj. VG $22.00

DALY, J. Carroll. *Snarl of the Beast.* 1927. New York. Clode. 1st ed. VG $20.00

DALY, Kathleen N. *Jingle Bells/New Story Based on Traditional Carol.* 1964. New York. Golden Press. Ills. 1st ed. VG $6.00

DALY, Lloyd. *The Curse of Envy; Aesopic Fable by Avianus Trans.* 1969. Menomonie, WI. Vagabond Press. Ltd. ed. sgn. $20.00

DALY, Margaret. *Diary of a Union Lady.* 1962. Funk & Wagnall. 1st ed. dj. $8.50

DALY, R.W. *How the Merrimac Won. Definitive Account of Ship.* 1957. Ills. maps dj. G $15.00

DALZIEL, Hugh. *The St. Bernard.* London. (ca.1888) 1st ed. VG $40.00

DAME, L.L. & Brooks, H. *Handbook of the Trees of New England.* 1901. Ginn. Ills. 196 pp. EX $10.00

DAMESHEK. *Morphologic Hermatology.* 1947. Ills. G $15.00

DAMON, Bertha. *A Sense of Humus.* 1943. New York. EX $15.00

DAMPIER, William. *A New Voyage Round the World.* London. 6th ed. ex-lib. rebound. $125.00

DANA, Julian. *Sacramento.* 1939. 1st ed. dj. EX $20.00

DANA, Mrs. *How to Know the Wild Flowers.* 1895. 1st ed. 156 pls. G $20.00

DANA, Mrs. *How to Know the Wild Flowers.* 1902. Scribner. Ills. G $5.00

DANA, Richard. *Two Years Before the Mast.* 1907. New York. Ills. 415 pp. EX $20.00

DANDLIKER, Karl. *A Short History of Switzerland.* 1899. London. 2 fld maps. VG $20.00

DANDRIDGE, Raymond Garfield. *Zalka Peetruza & Other Poems.* 1928. Cincinnati. EX $27.50

DANE. *Your Home Cook Book.* 1929. 1st ed. VG $10.00

DANEHOWER. *Lt. Danehower's Narrative of the Jeanette.* 1882. Boston. Osgood. 102 pp. wrappers. $32.50

DANFORD, H.E. *The West Virginian.* 1926. New York. 300 pp. $10.00

DANFORTH, G. *What You Should Know About Snakes.* 1956. Citadel. Ills. 1st ed. 96 pp. dj. VG $12.50

DANFORTH, William. *As a Man Doeth. President Monday Morning Messages.*1924. VG $8.50

DANFORTH, William. *Russia Under the Hammer & Sickle.* 1927. Ralston. private print. scarce $18.50

DANGERFIELD, Clinton. *Blair of Bar XL.* 1930. New York. presentation copy. dj. VG $30.00

DANGERFIELD, Clinton. *Lost Canyon.* 1932. New York. presentation copy. dj. VG $30.00

DANGERFIELD, Elna. *Mad Shelley. A Play by Elna Dangerfield.* 1936. London. VG $15.00

DANIEL, D. *Cut & Engraved Glass. 1771-1905.* 1950. Ills. 1st ed. 441 pp. EX $35.00

DANIEL, H. & Minot, F. *The Inexhaustible Sea.* 1954. Dodd Mead. 261 pp. G $5.00

DANIEL, J.W. *Life & Reminiscences of Jefferson Davis.* 1980. Ills. 1st ed. 490 pp. $16.50

DANIEL, Mr. M. *My Sister Minnie. A Novel.* 1854. Halifax. Milner & Sowerby. $25.00

DANIELS, J. *The Devil's Backbone.* 1962. $10.00

DANIELS, Les. *The Black Castle.* 1978. Scribner. 1st ed. dj. VG $9.00

DANIELS, W.J. & Tucker, H.B. *Model Sailing Yachts.* London. $15.00

DANIELSON, Richard. *Martha Doyle.* 1938. Derrydale Pr. Ltd. ed. 1/1250. VG $45.00

DANILOFF, Nicholas. *The Kremlin & the Cosmos.* 1972. Knopf. 1st ed. dj. EX $15.00

DANN, Jack. *More Wandering Stars.* 1981. Garden City. review copy. dj. VG $10.00

DANNECKER, Haxel. *Fisherman Simms.* 1947. New York. Ills. Bradfield. 1st ed. dj. $20.00

DANNETT, Sylvia. *A Treasury of Civil War Humor.* 1962. Yoseloff. 1st ed. dj. $8.50

DANSON, L. *Max Beerbohm & the Mirror of the Past.* 1982. Princeton. Ills. Ltd. ed. 1/800. dj. VG $35.00

DANTE. *The Divine Comedy.* 1948. Ills. Dore. 186 pp. dj. EX $5.00

DARBY, Ken. *The Brownstone House of Nero Wolfe.* 1983. Boston. Little, Brown. 1st ed. dj. EX $30.00

DARBY, William. *A Tour from New York-Detroit-Michigan Territory.* 1819. New York. 1st ed. 228 pp. 3 fld maps. EX $300.00

DARE, M.P. *Unholy Relics.* 1947. London. Arnold Pub. 1st ed. dj. G $35.00

DARGON. *The Nameless Order.* 1927. London. Lane. reprint. VG $10.00

DARLEY, Felix O.C. *Sketches Abroad with Pen & Pencil.* 1878. Boston. Ills. 192 pp. $45.00

DARLING, F.F. *Wildlife of Britain.* 1943. London. Collins. Ills. 48 pp. G $2.00

DARLING, Graser F. *A Herd of Red Deer.* 1956. London. Oxford U. Press. VG $15.00

DARLING. *Bankrupt Bookseller.* 1947. VG $10.00

DARLINGTON. *My Antarctic Honeymoon.* 1956. 1st ed. dj. EX $17.50

DARRELL, Margery. *The Fairy World of Rackham. Once Upon a Time.* 1972. New York. 1st ed. 56 color pls. dj. $30.00

DARROW, Clarence. *Story of My Life.* 1932. New York. Ills. 1st trade ed. inscr. $47.50

DARROW, Whitney. *Princeton University Press.* 1951. Princeton. Ills. 1st ed. wrappers. EX $10.00

DARTON, F.J. Harvey. *Dickens.* 1933. London. Argonaut Press. Ills. 1st ed. $50.00

DARTON, F.J. Harvey. *The Story of the Canterbury Pilgrims.* 1914. New York. Stokes. Ills. Kirk. 1st ed. $50.00

DARTON. *Story of Grand Canyon.* 1922. Ills. 80 pp. map. SftCvr. $12.50

DARWIN, Bernard. *Every Idle Dream.* 1948. London. 1st ed. dj. VG $22.00

DARWIN, Bernard. *Golf Between Two Wars.* 1944. London. Chatto & Windus. Ills. 1st ed. $45.00

DARWIN, Charles. *Animals Under Domestication.* 1898. New York. 2 vol set. VG $25.00

DARWIN, Charles. *Charles Darwin & the Voyage of the Beagle.* 1946. New York. reprint. dj. VG $27.50

DARWIN, Charles. *Complete Works in Ten Volumes.* 1896. Appleton. (8 of 10 vols) $15.00

DARWIN, Charles. *Darwin's Works in German.* Germany. (ca.1900) 18 vol set. EX $135.00

DARWIN, Charles. *Descent of Man.* 1871. 1st Eng. ed. 2 vol set. VG $600.00

DARWIN, Charles. *Different Forms of Flowers.* 1877. New York. 1st Am. ed. VG $20.00

DARWIN, Charles. *Expression of Emotions.* 1955. New York. reprint. dj. VG $15.00

DARWIN, Charles. *Fertilization of Orchids.* 1895. New York. 2nd ed. $20.00

DARWIN, Charles. *Formation Vegetable Mould Through Action of Worms.*1881. London. 1st ed. VG $85.00

DARWIN, Charles. *Insectivorous Plants.* 1897. New York. 1st ed. dj. EX $17.50

DARWIN, Charles. *On Various Contrivances for Fertilizing Orchids.* 1862. London. Murry. G $165.00

DARWIN, Charles. *The Descent of Man.* 1871. Appleton. 1st Am. ed. 2 vol set. $125.00

DARWIN, Charles. *The Illustrated Origin of Species.* 1979. Hill Wang. Ills. 1st Am. ed. 240 pp. dj. $15.00

DARWIN, Charles. *The Origin of Species.* 1979. Avenel. reprint. Ills. 460 pp. EX $15.00

DARWIN, Charles. *The Structure & Distribution of Coral Reefs.* 1984. AZ U. Press. reprint. Ills. 214 pp. EX $7.50

DARWIN, Charles. *The Voyage of the Beagle.* 1969. Harvard. reprint. Ills. 524 pp. EX $10.00

DARWIN, Francis. *Autobiography & Letters of Charles Darwin.* 1893. New York. 365 pp. VG $25.00

DARY, D. *The Buffalo Book.* 1974. Sage Books. Ills. 1st printing. 374 pp. EX $20.00

DAS, Bhagavan. *The Science of Peace.* 1904. London. 1st ed. 347 pp. G $35.00

DASENT, George. *Story of Burnt Njal.* 1861. Edinburgh. Ills. 2 vol set. G $80.00

DASHKEVICH-PURTO, Victoria. *Japanese Woodcut Book Illustration.* 1982. New York. Ills. stiff wrappers. $15.00

DASKAM, Joseph Dodge. *The Madness of Phillip.* 1902. New York. Ills. F.Y. Cory. 2nd ed. dj. $15.00

DAUBENY, Charles. *Journey of Tour Through U.S. & Canada.* 1843. Oxford. Ltd. ed. 1/100. inscr. rare $1,000.00

DAUGHERTY, James. *Daniel Boone.* 1939. Viking. 1st ed. dj. G $50.00

DAUGHERTY, James. *Of Courage Undaunted.* 1964. Viking. Ills. dj. VG $10.00

DAUGHERTY, James. *Walt Whitman's America.* 1964. New York. World. Ills. dj. VG $10.00

DAUGHERTY, James. *West of Boston.* 1956. New York. 1st ed. dj. VG $10.00

DAUGHTERS AMER. REVOLUTION. *Soldiers of American Revolution Who Lived in Ohio.*1959. $15.00

DAUMAS, Joseph. *Reminiscences of an Officer of the Zouaves.* 1860. New York. 317 pp. G $40.00

DAUMIER, Honore. *Doctors & Medicine in Works of Daumier.* 1960. Boston. 1st Am. ed. $35.00

DAUVILLIER, A. *The Photochemical Origin of Life.* 1965. Academic Press. Ills. 193 pp. dj. EX $15.00

DAVENEY, John. *The Bobby Orr Story.* 1973. Random House. Ills. 148 pp. EX $5.00

DAVENPORT, Basil. *Tales to be Told in the Dark.* 1953. New York. Dodd. 1st ed. dj. EX $12.50

DAVENPORT, Carles B. *Inheritance in Canaries.* 1908. New York. VG $25.00

DAVENPORT, Guy. *The Iliad. A Study Guide.* 1967. Philadelphia. sgn. wrappers. EX $45.00

DAVENPORT, Guy. *The Odyssey. A Study Guide.* 1967. Philadelphia. wrappers. EX $35.00

DAVENPORT, M. *East Side West Side.* 1947. $10.00

DAVENPORT, Marcia. *The Valley of Decision.* 1942. New York. Scribner. 640 pp. G $3.00

DAVENPORT, W. & Derieux, J. *Ladies, Gentlemen & Editor.* 1960. Garden City. Ills. 1st ed. 386 pp. $5.00

DAVEY, John. *Davey's Primer on Trees & Birds.* 1905. no place. Ills. 1st ed. inscr. 165 pp. $37.50

DAVID, Hans & Mendel, A. *The Bach Reader.* 1945. New York. 1st ed. dj. EX $22.50

DAVID, T.W.E. *The Geology of the Commonwealth of Australia.* 1950. London. Ills. 2 vol set. slipcase. EX $115.00

DAVID-NEEL, A. *My Journey to Lhasa.* 1927. New York. Harper. 1st ed. $25.00

DAVIDOFF. *The Connoisseur's Book of the Cigar.* 1967. McGraw Hill. Ills. 1st ed. EX $25.00

DAVIDS, R.C. *Lords of the Arctic.* 1982. Macmillan. Ills. 1st ed. dj. EX $17.50

DAVIDSON, Avram. *Strange Seas & Shores.* 1971. Garden City. 1st ed. dj. EX $8.00

DAVIDSON, Avram. *The Redward Edward Papers.* 1978. Garden City. 1st ed. dj. EX $8.00

DAVIDSON, B. *Subsistence U.S.A.* 1973. New York. 1st ed. dj. EX $37.50

DAVIDSON, H.M. *Fourteen Months in Southern Prisons of Richmond.* 1865. Milwaukee. map. G $50.00

DAVIDSON, John. *The Last Ballad & Other Poems.* 1899. London/NY. gilt decor. VG $35.00

DAVIDSON, L. & Boswick, P. *Literature of Rocky Mountain West 1803-1903.* 1939. Caxton. 1st ed. 449 pp. dj. VG $25.00

DAVIDSON, Marshall B. *American Heritage History of the Writer's America.* 1973. New York. American Heritage. Ills. dj. $20.00

DAVIDSON, Marshall B. *Notable American Houses.* 1971. New York. American Heritage. 383 pp. dj. $17.50

DAVIDSON, Marshall B. *The Horizon Book of Lost Worlds.* 1962. Ills. 431 pp. EX $12.00

DAVIDSON, Marshall. *The Horizon Concise History of France.* 1971. Ills. 219 pp. dj. $4.00

DAVIDSON, N.J. *Modern Exploration & Travel.* 1932. Lippincott. Ills. 318 pp. VG $17.50

DAVIDSON, W. *Where California Began.* 1929. San Diego. 2nd ed. 174 pp. $7.50

DAVIE, O. *Methods in the Art of Taxidermy.* 1900. McKay. Ills. 359 pp. VG $32.50

DAVIES, Charles. *Elements of Surveying & Navigation, etc.* 1849. New York. Barnes. Ills. revised ed. $25.00

DAVIES, Charles. *Primary Arithmetic.* 1869. New York. Ills. $12.00

DAVIES, Dorothy. *A Gentle Murderer.* 1961. Scribner. 187 pp. dj. $37.50

DAVIES, Howell. *South American Handbook.* 1938. London. 698 pp. fld map. index. EX $12.50

DAVIES, Hunter. *The Beatles.* 1978. New York. McGraw Hill. 381 pp. VG $6.50

DAVIES, J.J. *History & Business Directory of Madison County.* 1869. Des Moines. 1st ed. fld map. 254 pp. $150.00

DAVIES, John. *The Legend of Hobey Baker.* 1966. Boston. 1st ed. dj. VG $15.00

DAVIES, Marion. *The Times We Had, Life of William Randolph Hearst.* 1975. Indianapolis. Ills. 1st ed. 276 pp. dj. VG $8.50

DAVIES, Mary Carolyn. *The Slave with Two Faces.* 1918. New York. wrappers. $50.00

DAVIES, N. *Voyagers to the New World.* 1979. Morrow. Ills. 1st Am. ed. 287 pp. dj. $17.50

DAVIES, Rhys. *Rings on Her Fingers.* 1930. Harcourt. 1st Am. ed. dj. VG $15.00

DAVIES, Robertson. *A Voice from the Attic.* 1976. 1st ed. dj. EX $20.00

DAVIES, Robertson. *Fifth Business.* 1970. Macmillan. 1st ed. dj. EX $75.00

DAVIES, Robertson. *The Manticore.* 1972. Toronto. Macmillan. 1st ed. dj. VG $45.00

DAVIES, Robertson. *The Rebel Angels.* 1982. New York. Viking. 1st Am. ed. dj. $25.00

DAVIES, Robertson. *World of Wonders.* 1976. New York. Viking. 1st ed. dj. EX $25.00

DAVIES, Robertson. *World of Wonders.* 1975. New York. Viking. wrappers. EX $25.00

DAVIS, Adelle. *Let's Eat Right to Keep Fit.* 1970. New York. Harcourt. revised ed. 334 pp. $5.00

DAVIS, Andrew Jackson. *Arabula. Or, the Divine Guest.* 1867. Boston. 1st ed. 403 pp. VG $45.00

DAVIS, B. *A Williamsburg Galaxy.* 1968. New York. 1st ed. $10.00

DAVIS, B. *Savage Luxury, Slaughter of Baby Seals.* 1970. London. Souvenir Pr. Ills. 1st ed. dj. $5.00

DAVIS, Benjamin. *The Path of Negro Liberation.* 1947. New York. New Century. wrappers. VG $15.00

DAVIS, Britton. *The Truth About Geronimo.* 1951. Chicago. 380 pp. EX $35.00

DAVIS, Burke *The Gray Fox. Robert E. Lee & the Civil War.* 1956. New York. Ills. 466 pp. $9.50

DAVIS, Charles G. *Build-up Ship Model.* 1933. Salem. $45.00

DAVIS, Charles G. *Ship Models: How to Build Them.* 1925. Salem. Ills. 1st ed. $50.00

DAVIS, Charles G. *Shipping & Craft in Silhouette.* 1929. Salem, MA. Marine Research Soc. 1st ed. $65.00

DAVIS, Charles G. *The Ship Model Builder's Assistant.* 1926. Salem. Ills. 1st ed. dj. VG $25.00

DAVIS, Christopher. *Waiting for It.* 1980. Harper. 1st ed. dj. VG $12.50

DAVIS, Elmer. *Giant Killer.* 1928. John Day. VG $4.50

DAVIS, Elmer. *History of New York Times, 1851-1921.* 1921. 1st ed. G $11.00

DAVIS, Elmer. *Two Minutes Till Midnight.* 1955. New York. ex-lib. 207 pp. VG $3.00

DAVIS, F. Hadland. *Myths & Legends of Japan.* 1928. London. 32 color pls. 432 pp. dj. $25.00

DAVIS, Grania. *Moonbird.* 1986. Garden City. 1st ed. dj. VG $8.00

DAVIS, Hassoldt. *Sorcerer's Village.* 1955. Ills. 1st ed. 334 pp. dj. EX $15.00

DAVIS, Herbert. *The Complete Plays of William Congreve.* 1967. Chicago. U. of Chicago Press. 503 pp. $3.50

DAVIS, J. *Character Assassination.* 1950. 1st ed. dj. $6.50

DAVIS, J.E. *Round About Jamestown Historical Sketches.* 1907. Ills. 1st ed. wrappers. $15.00

DAVIS, James J. *The Iron Puddler.* 1922. Indianapolis. 275 pp. $12.50

DAVIS, Julia. *The Shenandoah.* 1945. NY/Toronto. Ills. Taubes. 1st ed. dj. EX $25.00

DAVIS, Kenneth S. *The Eisenhower College Collection Paintings.* 1972. L.A. 1st ed. $25.00

DAVIS, Kenneth S. *The Hero.* 1959. Garden City. 1st ed. 527 pp. VG $10.00

DAVIS, M.L. *Alaska the Great Bear's Cub.* 1930. Boston. G $25.00

DAVIS, N. *The Toltecs, Until the Fall of Tula.* 1977. OK U. Press. Ills. 1st ed. maps. 320 pp. EX $17.50

DAVIS, Norbert. *Sally's in the Alley.* 1943. $3.00

DAVIS, O. *I's Like to Do It Again.* 1931. Ills. $7.50

DAVIS, Professor A. *History of New Amsterdam.* 1854. New York. Ills. 1st ed. 240 pp. $35.00

DAVIS, R. *Sundari.* 1974. Barre. Ills. 1st ed. dj. EX $5.00

DAVIS, Ralph. *The Rise of the English Industry.* 1962. $12.50

DAVIS, Rebecca H. *Waiting for the Verdict. A Novel.* 1868. New York. 1st ed. $35.00

DAVIS, Richard Harding. *Captain Macklin.* 1902. Scribner. Ills. W.A. Claek. 329 pp. $3.50

DAVIS, Richard Harding. *Her First Appearance.* 1901. NY/London. Ills. Gibson & Ashe. 53 pp. $5.00

DAVIS, Richard Harding. *In the Fog.* 1902. New York. Ills. Pierce & Steele. 155 pp. $3.00

DAVIS, Richard Harding. *In the Fog.* 1901. New York. Ills. 1st ed. VG $10.00

DAVIS, Richard Harding. *Soldiers of Fortune.* 1921. $7.00

DAVIS, Richard Harding. *Soldiers of Fortune.* 1897. New York. Ills. Gibson. 348 pp. $3.50

DAVIS, Richard Harding. *The Bar Sinister.* 1903. New York. Ills. E.M. Ashe. 1st ed. VG $25.00

DAVIS, Richard Harding. *The Exiles & Other Stories.* 1919. New York. Ills. H.C. Christy. VG $7.00

DAVIS, Richard Harding. *The King's Jackal.* 1898. New York. Ills. Charles D. Gibson. $7.00

DAVIS, Richard Harding. *The King's Jackal.* 1903. Scribner. Ills. C. D. Gibson. 218 pp. $3.00

DAVIS, Richard Harding. *The Lost Road.* 1916. Scribner. ex-lib. 330 pp. VG $3.00

DAVIS, Richard Harding. *The Rulers of the Mediterranean.* 1894. New York. Ills. 228 pp. $10.00

DAVIS, Richard Harding. *The West from a Car Window.* 1892. New York. Harper. Ills. Remington. $30.00

DAVIS, Robertson. *Fifth Business.* 1970. Toronto. Macmillan. 1st ed. $75.00

DAVIS, Robertson. *One Half of Robertson Davis.* 1978. 1st ed. dj. EX $30.00

DAVIS, Sammy, Jr. & Boyar. *Yes I Can; Story of Sammy Davis, Jr.* 1965. New York. Straus & Giroux. 630 pp. dj. $6.00

DAVIS, W. Jefferson. *Japan, the Air Menace of the Pacific.* 1927. Boston. 1st ed. dj. $25.00

DAVIS, W.B. *Mammals of Texas.* 1978. TX Parks Dept. Ills. 294 pp. EX $7.50

DAVIS, W.T. *Plymouth Memories of an Octogenarian.* 1906. Plymouth, Mass. 1st ed. 541 pp. $30.00

DAVIS, Webster. *John Bull's Crime.* 1901. New York. 225 pp. $47.50

DAVIS, Wesley Ford. *The Time of the Panther.* 1958. New York. Harper. 1st ed. VG $25.00

DAVIS, William C. *The Orphan Brigade.* 1980. 318 pp. EX $15.00

DAVIS, William Heath. *Seventy-Five Years in California.* 1929. San Francisco. Ills. Howell. VG $75.00

DAVIS, William Heath. *Sixty Years in California.* 1889. San Francisco. fair $12.00

DAVIS, William Stearns. *The Saint of the Dragon Dale.* 1903. New York. Macmillan. 1st ed. VG $22.50

DAVISON, Charles. *A Study of Recent Earthquakes.* 1905. New York. Scribner. Ills. ex-lib. VG $8.00

DAVISON, Peter. *Half Remembered. A Personal History.* 1973. New York. Harper. 1st ed. 245 pp. $6.50

DAVISON, V.E. *Attracting Birds from Prairies to Atlantic.* 1967. Crowell. Ills. 252 pp. dj. EX $5.00

DAWES, Leonard G. *Japanese Illustrated Books.* 1972. Ills. wrappers. $18.00

DAWIDOWICZ, L.S. *War Against the Jews 1933-45.* 1974. New York. Holt Rinehart. dj. G $20.00

DAWSON, E. *Texas Wildlife.* 1955. Upshaw. Ills. 1st ed. 174 pp. EX $22.50

DAWSON, Samuel E. *The Saint Lawrence Basin & Its Border-Lands.* 1905. London. Ills. maps. 451 pp. $15.00

DAWSON, Sarah Morgan. *A Confederate Girl's Diary.* 1960. Bloomington. IN U. Press. Ills. 473 pp. dj. $12.50

DAY, A. Grove. *The Sky Clears, Poetry of the American Indians.* 1951. New York. review copy. dj. VG $17.50

DAY, Albert M. *North American Waterfowl.* 1949. Stackpole. Ills. Hines. 1st ed. dj. VG $27.50

DAY, Clarence. *Life with Father.* 1935. New York. Knopf. 258 pp. G $5.00

DAY, Clarence. *Life with Mother.* New York. Ltd. ed. 1/750. VG $45.00

DAY, Donald. *A Biography of Will Rogers.* 1962. McKay. dj. VG $7.00

DAY, Donald. *Big Country Texas.* 1947. New York. 1st ed. dj. VG $32.50

DAY, Dorothy. *Therese.* 1960. Notre Dame. dj. VG $10.00

DAY, Douglas. *Malcolm Lowry.* 1973. Oxford. Ills. 1st ed. dj. EX $12.50

DAY, E. *Book Typography. 1815-1965 in Europe & U.S.* 1966. London. EX $27.50

DAY, George E. *Productive Swine Husbandry.* 1915. Philadelphia. Lippincott. ex-lib. 315 pp. VG $4.50

DAY, J. Wentworth. *Broadland Adventure.* 1951. London. Country Life. 189 pp. photos. $10.00

DAY, J. Wentworth. *Sporting Adventure.* 1937. London. Ltd. ed. 1/105. sgn. boxed. VG $225.00

DAY. *A History of Commerce.* 1907. New York. maps. 575 pp. $6.50

DAYTON, Edson C. *Dakota Days, May 1886-August, 1898.* 1937. Hartford. Ills. Ltd. 1st ed. 128 pp. $250.00

DAYTON, Fred. *Steamboat Days.* 1925. 436 pp. VG $17.50

DE ANDREA, William L. *Killed in the Ratings.* 1978. New York. Harcourt. 1st ed. dj. VG $35.00

DE ANDREA, William. *Five O'Clock Lightning.* 1982. New York. proof copy. wrappers. EX $25.00

DE ANDREA, William. *The Lunatic Fringe.* 1980. New York. Evans. advance copy. inscr. EX $35.00

DE ANDREA, William. *The Lunatic Fringe.* 1980. Evans. proof copy. yellow wrappers. $30.00

DE ANGELI, Marguerite. *Book of Nursery & Mother Goose Rhymes.* 1953. Garden City. Ills. folio. $17.50

DE ANGELI, Marguerite. *Book of Nursery & Mother Goose Rhymes.* 1954. Doubleday. Ills. dj. VG $10.00

DE ANGELI, Marguerite. *Bright April.* 1946. Doubleday. Ills. dj. VG $20.00

DE ANGELI, Marguerite. *Jared's Island.* 1947. New York. Ills. 1st ed. dj. $20.00

DE ANGELI, Marguerite. *The Door in the Wall.* 1949. New York. Ills. $8.50

DE ANGELI, Marguerite. *Thee, Hannah!* 1940. New York. dj. EX $8.00

DE BALZAC, H. *Eugenia Grandet.* 1843. New York. Winchester. 32 pp. $20.00

DE BALZAC, H. *Ten Troll Tales.* Abbey Library. Ills. DeBosschere. 1st ed. VG $10.00

DE BEAUVOIR, Simone. *A Very Easy Death.* 1st Am. ed. dj. EX $15.00

DE BEAUVOIR, Simone. *The Blood of Others.* 1948. New York. 1st ed. dj. EX $15.00

DE BEAUVOIR, Simone. *When Things of the Spirit Come First.* 1982. Deutsch. 1st English ed. dj. VG $20.00

DE BECKER, J.E. *The Nightless City.* 1905. Bremen. Ills. 4th ed. $50.00

DE BLAISIS, Celeste. *Suffer a Sea Change.* 1976. New York. 1st ed. dj. VG $20.00

DE BODE, C.A. *Travels in Luristan & Arabistan.* 1845. London. 2 vol set. $250.00

DE BONO, Edward. *Eureka! An Illustrated History of Inventions.* 1974. Ills. 248 pp. index. dj. $25.00

DE BOSSCHERE, Jean. *Gulliver's Travels.* 1920. London. Ills. 1st ed. 4 color pls. VG $85.00

DE BOSSCHERE, Jean. *Marthe & the Madman.* 1928. New York. Covici. Ills. 1st ed. VG $20.00

DE BOTH, Jessie Marie. *Modernistic Recipe-Menue.* 1929. Chicago. 1st ed. $12.00

DE BRUNHOFF, Jean. *Babar the King.* 1935. Random House. trans. Haas. 1st ed. folio. VG $50.00

DE BRUNHOFF, Jean. *Les Vacances De Zephir.* 1936. Hachette. 1st ed. $17.50

DE BRUNHOFF, Jean. *The Story of Babar.* 1933. New York. Random House. Ills. ex-lib. G $5.00

DE BRUNHOFF, Laurent. *Babar Comes to America.* 1965. Random House. Ills. 1st ed. dj. EX $20.00

DE BRUNHOFF, Laurent. *Babar the Gardener.* 1969. Random House. Ills. VG $8.50

DE BRUNHOFF, Laurent. *Babar's Birthday Surprise.* 1970. Random House. folio. dj. EX $22.50

DE BRUNHOFF, Laurent. *Babar's Cousin: That Rascal Arthur.* 1948. New York. Random House. 1st Am. ed. VG $35.00

DE BRUNHOFF, Laurent. *Bonhomme & the Huge Beast.* 1974. Random House. Ills. 1st ed. dj. $12.50

DE CAMP, L. Sprague & C. *Science Fiction Handbook. Revised.* 1975. Owlswick. 1st ed. dj. EX $22.50

DE CAMP, L. Sprague & C.C. *The Bones of Zora.* 1983. Phantasia Pr. Ltd. ed. 1/300. sgn. boxed. EX $35.00

DE CAMP, L. Sprague & Pratt. *Wall of Serpents.* 1978. Phantasia Pr. Ltd. ed. 1/200. sgn. boxed. EX $225.00

DE CAMP, L. Sprague. *Demons & Dinosaurs.* 1979. Sauk City. Arkham House. dj. EX $50.00

DE CAMP, L. Sprague. *Divide & Rule.* 1948. Reading. Fantasy. 1st trade ed. dj. VG $35.00

DE CAMP, L. Sprague. *Dragon of the Ishtar Gate.* 1961. New York. Doubleday. dj. EX $65.00

DE CAMP, L. Sprague. *Let Darkness Fall.* 1949. Philadelphia. Prime Press. 1st ed. dj. EX $35.00

DE CAMP, L. Sprague. *Lost Continents.* 1954. New York. Gnome. 1st ed. dj. EX $25.00

DE CAMP, L. Sprague. *Lovecraft.* 1975. Doubleday. 1st ed. dj. EX $22.50

DE CAMP, L. Sprague. *Phantoms & Fancies.* 1972. Baltimore. Mirage Press. Ills. Kirk. sgn. $125.00

DE CAMP, L. Sprague. *The Continent Makers & Other Tales of Viagens.* 1953. New York. 1st ed. dj. VG $30.00

DE CAMP, L. Sprague. *The Continent Makers & Other Tales of Viagens.* 1953. New York. Twayne. dj. $60.00

DE CAMP, L. Sprague. *The Search for Zei.* 1962. New York. Covici. 1st ed. dj. EX $55.00

DE CAMP, L. Sprague. *The Unbeheaded King.* 1983. New York. 1st ed. dj. VG $10.00

DE CAMP, L. Sprague. *Wheels of If.* 1948. Chicago. Shasta. dj. EX $80.00

DE CAMP, L.S. & Miller, P.S. *Genus Homo.* 1950. Reading. Fantasy. 1st ed. $8.00

DE CAMP, L.S. & Pratt, F. *Tales from Gavagan's Bar.* 1953. New York. Twayne. 1st ed. dj. VG $20.00

DE CAMP, L.S. & Pratt, F. *The Castle of Iron.* 1950. New York. 1st ed. dj. VG $40.00

DE CAMP, L.S. & Pratt, F. *The Land of Unreason.* 1922. New York. Holt. 1st ed. dj. EX $150.00

DE CARLE, D. *Practical Watch Repairing.* 1946. Ills. 1st Am. ed. $60.00

DE CASSERES, Benjamin. *Anathema, Litanies of Negation.* 1928. New York. forward O'Neill. dj. boxed. VG $50.00

DE CERVANTES, Miguel. *Don Quixote de la Mancha.* 1951. Paris. Ills. De Dubout. Ltd. 1st ed. $30.00

DE COMEAU, Alexander. *Monk's Magic.* 1931. New York. Dutton. 1st ed. dj. VG $30.00

DE FELICE, Aurelio. *33 Disegni.* Rome. Ltd. ed. 1/535. wrappers. $25.00

DE FOE, D. *The History of the Devil.* 1845. Boston. Dow & Jackson. 6th ed. 296 pp. $25.00

DE FOE, Daniel. *Freebooters & Buccaneers.* 1935. New York. Dial Press. $12.50

DE FOE, Daniel. *Moll Flanders.* 1929. New York. Ills. John Austen. VG $30.00

DE FOE, Daniel. *Robinson Crusoe.* 1914. Chicago. Ills. Milo Winter. EX $25.00

DE FOE, Daniel. *Robinson Crusoe.* 1946. Ills. Jr. Library & Ward. VG $6.50

DE FOE, Daniel. *Robinson Crusoe.* New York. Allison. EX $8.50

DE FOE, Daniel. *Robinson Crusoe.* 1930. Heritage. boxed. EX $20.00

DE FOE, Daniel. *The Life & Adventures of Robin Crusoe.* London. (ca.1830) VG $60.00

DE FOE, Daniel. *The Life & Adventures of Robin Crusoe.* 1924. Saalfield. Ills. F. Brundage. 250 pp. VG $7.50

DE FOREST, B.S. *Random Sketches & Wandering Thoughts.* 1866. New York. 324 pp. G $20.00

DE FOREST, Eleanor. *Armageddon: Tale of the Antichrist.* 1938. Grand Rapids. Eerdmans. 1st ed. VG $15.00

DE FRANCE, Henry. *The Elements of Dowsing.* 1959. London. Bell. 1st Eng. 83 pp. dj. $17.50

DE FRANCIS, Folsom. *Our Police.* 1888. Baltimore. Ills. 546 pp. $125.00

DE GOLYER, E. *Journey of Three Englishmen Across Texas in 1568.* 1947. El Paso. Ltd ed. 1/465. sgn. $275.00

DE GRAFF. *Head Hunters of the Amazon.* 1923. Garden City. Ills. 337 pp. $4.50

DE GROOT, Henry. *Recollections of California Mining Life.* 1884. San Francisco. 1st ed. original wrappers. $120.00

DE GROOT, J.J.M. *Religion in China.* 1912. New York. 1st ed. dj. EX $30.00

DE GROOT, Roy A. *Feasts for All Seasons.* 1966. Knopf. Ills. Tom Funk. 70 pp. $15.00

DE JONGE, G.H. *Dutch Tiles.* 1971. Praeger. 1st ed. dj. VG $20.00

DE KNIGHT. *Date with a Dish.* 1948. 1st ed. dj. VG $20.00

DE KROYFT, Helen A. *The Soul of Eve.* 1904. New York. DeKroyft. VG $8.00

DE KROYFT, S.H. *A Place in Thy Memory.* 1868. New York. VG $15.00

DE L'ISLE-ADMAN, Villiers. *Claire Lenoir.* 1925. New York. Boni. 1st ed. dj. VG $40.00

DE LA MARE, A.T. *Garden Guide.* 1925. $9.00

DE LA MARE, W. *Animal Stories.* 1940. New York. Ills. Topsell. 1st ed. G $8.50

DE LA MARE, W. *Come Hither.* 1923. New York. 1st ed. inscr. sgn. VG $150.00

DE LA MARE, W. *Eight Tales.* 1971. Sauk City. 1st ed. 108 pp. dj. EX $12.50

DE LA MARE, W. *Peacock Pie.* New York. Holt. Ills. C. Lovat Fraser. $25.00

DE LA MARE, W. *Peacock Pie.* 1929. Holt. Ills. W. Heath Robinson. G $40.00

DE LA MARE, W. *Rhymes & Verses.* 1947. Ills. Blaisdell. 1st printing. $7.50

DE LA MARE, W. *Selected Poems.* 1954. London. Faber & Faber. 208 pp. dj. VG $20.00

DE LA MARE, W. *Stories from the Bible.* 1929. NY. Ills. Nadejeh. 1st U.S. ed. $20.00

DE LA MARE, W. *Stuff & Nonsense.* 1927. Ills. Bold. 1st ed. dj. EX $20.00

DE LA MARE, W. *The Return.* 1910. London. 1st ed. boxed. VG $125.00

DE LA MARE, W. *The Three Mulla-Mulgars.* 1910. London. 1st ed. 2nd issue. sgn. inscr. $85.00

DE LA MARE, W. *The Three Mulla-Mulgars.* London. Ills. Shepard. Ltd. ed. sgn. $120.00

DE LA MARTINE. *A History of the French Revolution of 1848 Vol. I.* 1860. Boston. 270 pp. $3.50

DE LA REY. *The Best of C.L. Moore.* 1975. New York. Taplinger. 1st ed. dj. EX $12.50

DE LA ROCHE, Mazo. *Return to Jalna.* 1946. Boston. 1st ed. 402 pp. $50.00

DE LA ROCHE, Mazo. *Ringing the Changes.* 1957. 1st ed. dj. VG $10.00

DE LA TORRE, Lillian. *Dr. Sam Johnson, Detector.* 1946. New York. dj. VG $20.00

DE LILLO, Don. *Great Jones Street.* 1973. Houghton Mifflin. 1st ed. sgn. $30.00

DE LILLO, Don. *Ratner's Star.* 1976. Knopf. 1st ed. dj. VG $20.00

DE LOLME, J.L. *The Constitution of England.* 1781. London. $85.00

DE LUBAC, Henri. *The Un-Marxian Socialist. Study of Proudhon.* 1948. London. trans. Scantlebury. 304 pp. G $8.00

DE MADARIAGA, Salvador. *Sir Bob.* 1930. New York. Harcourt Brace. Ills. $25.00

DE MAISTRE, Xavier. *The Leper of Aoste.* 1842. London. 216 pp. wrappers. $37.50

DE MARINIS, Rick. *A Lovely Monster.* 1975. Simon & Schuster. 1st ed. dj. $15.00

DE MARINIS, Rick. *Jack & Jill.* 1979. Dutton. 1st ed. dj. VG $50.00

DE MAUPASSANT, Guy. *Bel Ami.* 1968. New York. Ills. Ltd ed. 1/1500. EX $65.00

DE MEUN. *Le Plaisant Jeu de Dodecheron.* 1574. Lyon. ex-lib. rebound. rare. $395.00

DE MILLE, James. *A Strange Manuscript Found in a Copper Cylinder.* 1888. Harper. Ills. 1st ed. VG $45.00

DE MONFRIED, H. & Treat, Ida. *Pearls, Arms & Hashish.* 1930. New York. Ills. photos. VG $10.00

DE MONTOLIEU, Baronne. *Le Robinson Suisse Ou Journal.* 1824. Paris. French text. VG $15.00

DE MONVEL, M. Boutet. *Joan of Arc.* 1918. McKay. Ills. VG $30.00

DE MONVEL, M. Boutet. *Joan of Arc.* 1931. New York. Century. 47 pp. VG $60.00

DE MORGAN, John. *In Lighter Vein.* 1907. San Francisco. wrappers. G $22.50

DE NERVAL, Gerard. *Sylvie.* 1887. Routledge. Devinne Press. Ills. Rudaux. $60.00

DE NOGALES, R. *Memoirs of a Soldier of Fortune.* 1932. Garden City. 380 pp. VG $10.00

DE PAOLA, Tomie. *The Comic Adventures of Old Mother Hubbard & Dog.* 1981. New York. Harcourt Brace Jovanovich. $10.00

DE PAOLA, Tomie. *The Mysterious Giant of Barletta.* 1984. Ills. dj. EX $17.50

DE PAOLA, Tomie. *When Everyone Was Fast Asleep.* 1976. New York. Ills. author. 1st ed. dj. VG $10.00

DE POL, John. *The Seasons, or Life in the Country.* 1953. Flushing. Ltd. ed. 1/350. wrappers. EX $20.00

DE PORTE, A.W. *De Gaulle's Foreign Policy 1944-1946.* 1968. Cambridge, MA. ex-lib. 327 pp. dj. $4.00

DE PROROK, B.K. *Digging for Lost African Gods.* 1926. 1st ed. EX $20.00

DE PUY, Henry. *The Mountain Hero.* 1855. 1st ed. $12.50

DE QUEIROZ, Eca. *Cousin Bazilio.* 1953. Noonday. 1st Am. ed. dj. EX $7.50

DE QUESANDO, G. & Northrup, H. *War in Cuba, Full Account of Struggle for Freedom.* 1896. Liberty Pub. VG $4.50

DE QUILLE, William Wright. *The Big Bonanza.* 1947. Knopf. 1st Borzi ed. dj. VG $18.50

DE QUINCY, Thomas. *Letters of De Quincy: English Opium-Eater.* 1843. Philadelphia. $45.00

DE QUINCY, Thomas. *Toilette of the Hebrew Lady.* 1926. Hartford. wrappers. VG $15.00

DE ROSIER, Arthur. *The Removal of the Choctaw Indians.* 1970. Knoxville. sgn. VG $15.00

DE SAINT-EXUPERY, A. *The Little Prince.* 1943. New York. Ltd. ed. 1/500. sgn. $125.00

DE SAINT-EXUPERY, Antoine. *Le Petit Prince.* 1946. Paris. Ills. wrappers. $10.00

DE SAINT-EXUPERY, Antoine. *The Little Prince.* 1943. Harcourt Brace. trans. K. Woods. Ills. dj. EX $15.00

DE SAINT-FUX, Georges. *The Symphonies of Mozart.* 1949. New York. dj. VG $6.00

DE SERVIEZ, Jacques B. *The Roman Empresses.* 1932. New York. Ills. Ltd. ed. 2 vol set. $15.00

DE SEVERSKY, Alexander P. *Victory Through Air Power.* 1942. New York. Simon & Schuster. Ills. sgn. $10.00

DE SEVIGNE, Madame. *Lettres De Sevigne.* 1856. Paris. 6 vol set. VG $45.00

DE SHIELDS. *Border Wars of Texas.* 1912. Tioga, TX. $90.00

DE STAEL, Madame. *Bolte, Amelt/An Historical Novel.* 1869. New York. Putnam. G $15.00

DE TOCQUEVILLE, Alexis. *Democracy in America.* 1863. Cambridge. 3rd ed. 2 vol set. $20.00

DE TOCQUEVILLE, Alexis. *The Old Regime & the Revolution.* 1856. New York. trans. Bonner. VG $57.50

DE TROBRIANT, Philippe R. *Vie Militaire Dan le Dakota: Notes et Souvenirs.* 1926. Paris. 1st ed. 407 pp. wrappers. $75.00

DE TURENNE, Comte Louis. *Quatorze Mois Dans l'Amerique du Nord.* 1879. Paris. 1st ed. 2 vol set. wrappers. $175.00

DE VINNE, Theodore Low. *The First Editor, Aldus Pius Manutius.* 1983. New York. Ills. Frasconi. Ltd. ed. sgn. $95.00

DE VINNE, Theodore Low. *The Invention of Printing.* 1878. New York. Hart. 556 pp. G $95.00

DE VITO, John. *Pawns of Destiny.* 1931. Boston. Humphries. 1st ed. dj. EX $25.00

DE VORE, I. *Primate Behavior.* 1965. Holt/Winston. Ills. 645 pp. photos. maps. $17.50

DE VOTO, Bernard. *Across the Wide Missouri.* 1947. Boston. Houghton Mifflin. 1st ed. dj. $37.50

DE VOTO, Bernard. *Minority Report.* 1940. Little Brown. 1st ed. sgn. dj. VG $40.00

DE VOTO, Bernard. *Mountain Time.* 1947. Boston. 313 pp. dj. $3.50

DE VOTO, Bernard. *The Course of Empire.* 1952. Boston. Houghton Mifflin. 647 pp. dj. $6.00

DE VOTO, Bernard. *The Hour.* Boston. Houghton Mifflin. 84 pp. VG $6.00

DE VOTO, Bernard. *The Year of Decision 1846.* 1943. Boston. Little, Brown. dj. VG $10.00

DE VRIES, Leonard. *Little Wide-Awake.* 1967. London. Barker. Ills. 1st ed. dj. VG $30.00

DE VRIES, Lini. *Up From the Cellar.* 1979. Minneapolis. Vanilla Pr. 1st ed. dj. VG $15.00

DE VRIES, Peter. *But Who Wakes the Bugler.* 1940. Boston. Ills. Addams. 1st ed. VG $175.00

DE VRIES, Peter. *Comfort Me with Apples.* 1956. Little, Brown. 1st ed. dj. VG $50.00

DE VRIES, Peter. *Consenting Adults or the Duchess Will be Furious.* 1980. Little, Brown. 1st ed. dj. VG $15.00

DE VRIES, Peter. *I Hear America Singing.* 1976. Little, Brown. 1st ed. dj. VG $15.00

DE VRIES, Peter. *Into Your Tent I'll Creep.* 1971. Boston. 1st ed. 244 pp. dj. $10.00

DE VRIES, Peter. *Let Me Count the Ways.* 1965. Little, Brown. 1st ed. dj. VG $25.00

DE VRIES, Peter. *Madder Music.* 1977. Little, Brown. 1st ed. dj. VG $15.00

DE VRIES, Peter. *Mrs. Wallop.* 1970. Little, Brown. 1st ed. 310 pp. dj. EX $20.00

DE VRIES, Peter. *Reuben, Reuben.* 1964. Little, Brown. 1st ed. dj. VG $25.00

DE VRIES, Peter. *Sauce for the Goose.* 1981. Little, Brown. 1st ed. dj. VG $12.50

DE VRIES, Peter. *The Cat's Pajamas & Witch's Milk.* 1968. Little, Brown. 1st ed. dj. VG $20.00

DE VRIES, Peter. *The Glory of the Hummingbird.* 1974. $10.00

DE VRIES, Peter. *The Mackerel Plaza.* 1958. Boston. Little, Brown. 1st ed. dj. VG $30.00

DE VRIES, Peter. *The Tents of Wickedness.* 1959. Little, Brown. 1st ed. dj. VG $25.00

DE VRIES, Peter. *Through the Fields of Clover.* 1961. Little, Brown. 1st ed. dj. VG $25.00

DE WAAL. *World Biblio. of Sherlock Holmes & Dr. Watson.* 1974. New York. boxed. EX $35.00

DE WET, Christian. *Three Years War.* 1902. New York. 1st Am. ed. fld map. VG $25.00

DE WOLFE, Elsie. *The House in Good Taste.* 1914. New York. Century. photos. 322 pp. VG $3.50

DE WOLFE, Fiske & Co. *A Run Around the World.* 1891. Boston. Ills. 311 pp. some foxing. G $3.00

DEAN, Capt. *Pedro Gorino: True Adventures of a Negro Sea Capt.* 1929. New York. 1st ed. VG $10.00

DEAN, Graham M. *Herb Kent, West Point Cadet.* 1936. Chicago. Goldsmith Pub. 250 pp. dj. $2.50

DEAN, John. *Blind Ambition & the White House Years.* 1976. New York. Simon & Schuster. 415 pp. dj. $6.50

DEAN, Leon W. *Stark of the North Country.* 1941. New York. Farrar & Rinehart. 277 pp. $3.50

DEAN, Maureen & Gorey, Hays. *'MO,' a Woman's View of Watergate.* 1975. New York. Simon & Schuster. 221 pp. dj. $4.00

DEAN, S.F. *Such Pretty Toys.* 1982. Walker. dj. EX $10.00

DEAN, Spencer. *Murder After a Fashion.* 1960. 1st ed. dj. EX $15.00

DEAN, Vera Micheles. *Foreign Policy Without Fear.* 1953. New York. McGraw Hill. 220 pp. VG $3.00

DEANE, Philip. *I was a Captive in Korea.* 1954. Tokyo. Tuttle. 1st ed. 253 pp. VG $15.00

DEANS, Marjorie. *Meeting at the Sphinx.* London. 1st ed. color pls. dj. EX $45.00

DEARBORN, N. *American Text Book for Letters.* 1846. Boston. 3rd ed. $95.00

DEARING, J.S. *A Drummer's Experience.* 1913. CO Springs, CO. Ills. 1st ed. 567 pp. $75.00

DEAS, W. *Australian Fishes.* 1971. Rigby. Ills. dj. EX $12.50

DEBANS, Camille. *John Bull's Misfortunes.* 1884. New York. Ills. wrappers. $5.00

DEBENHAM, F. *Kalahari Sand.* 1953. London. Bell. Ills. 189 pp. dj. $10.00

DEBO, Angie. *Oklahoma, Foot-Loose & Fancy-Free.* 1949. U. of OK Press. Ills. ex-lib. 258 pp. EX $4.00

DEBO, Angie. *Prairie City. Story of an American Community.* 1944. New York. Knopf. 16 pls. dj. $12.50

DEBO, Angie. *The Rise & Fall of the Choctaw Republic.* 1967. Norman. dj. VG $15.00

DEBS, Eugene V. *Debs: His Life, Writings & Speeches.* Chicago. Kerr. 1st ed. EX $25.00

DEBUS, A. *The English Paracelsians.* 1965. New York. 222 pp. dj. $17.00

DECLE, L. *Three Years in Savage Africa.* 1900. London. VG $70.00

DEDIJER, Vladimir. *The Road to Sarajevo.* 1966. 1st ed. 550 pp. dj. $50.00

DEEGAN, Paul J. *Stickhandling & Passing.* 1976. Ills. Henriksen. 30 pp. EX $3.00

DEEPING, Warwick. *Bluewater.* 1939. Knopf. 1st Am. ed. 424 pp. $75.00

DEEPING, Warwick. *Exile.* 1930. Knopf. 1st ed. $6.50

DEEPING, Warwick. *Old Pybus.* 1928. New York. Knopf. 376 pp. G. $3.00

DEEPING, Warwick. *Seven Men Came Back.* 1934. Knopf. 1st Am. ed. $52.50

DEFENCE, A. *Of Southern Slavery.* 1851. Hamburg, SC. 1st ed. wrappers. EX $75.00

DEFOURI, J.H. *Hist. Sketch of Catholic Church in New Mexico.* 1887. San Francisco. 1st ed. wrappers. VG $285.00

DEIGHTON, Len. *An Expensive Place to Die.* 1967. New York. Putnam. 1st ed. dj. VG $30.00

DEIGHTON, Len. *Bomber.* 1970. Harper. 1st Am. ed. dj. VG $20.00

DEIGHTON, Len. *Catch a Falling Spy.* 1976. New York. Harcourt. 1st ed. dj. VG $25.00

DEIGHTON, Len. *Catch a Falling Spy.* 1976. NY. Harcourt. proof copy. wrappers. $50.00

DEIGHTON, Len. *Close-Up.* 1972. Atheneum. 1st Am. ed. dj. VG $12.50

DEIGHTON, Len. *Eleven Declarations of War.* 1971. Harcourt. 1st Am. ed. dj. VG $15.00

DEIGHTON, Len. *Funeral in Berlin.* 1965. Putnam. 1st Am. ed. dj. VG $40.00

DEIGHTON, Len. *Funeral in Berlin.* 1964. London. Cape. 1st ed. dj. EX $40.00

DEIGHTON, Len. *Goodbye Mickey Mouse.* 1982. Knopf. 1st Am. ed. dj. VG $15.00

DEIGHTON, Len. *Horse Under Water.* 1968. Putnam. 1st Am. ed. dj. VG $35.00

DEIGHTON, Len. *Mexico Set.* 1985. Knopf. 1st Am. ed. dj. VG $17.50

DEIGHTON, Len. *Ou Est Le Garlic.* 1977. New York. Harper. 1st ed. dj. EX $45.00

DEIGHTON, Len. *Spy Story.* 1974. New York. Harcourt. advance copy. dj. VG $30.00

DEIGHTON, Len. *The Billion Dollar Brain.* 1966. New York. Putnam. 1st ed. dj. VG $30.00

DEIGHTON, Len. *Yesterday's Spy.* 1975. Harcourt. 1st ed. dj. VG $20.00

DEIGHTON. *Ipcress File.* 1963. New York. 1st ed. dj. EX $25.00

DEKRUIF. *Hunger Fighters.* 1928. $5.00

DEL MAR. *Around the World Through Japan.* 1904. London. Ills. 435 pp. VG $8.00

DEL RAY, Lester. *Space Flight, Coming Exploration of the Universe.* 1959. Golden Press. Ills. Polgreen. 56 pp. G $4.50

DELAFIELD, E.M. *Jill.* 1927. 1st ed. $6.50

DELAND, Margaret. *An Old Chester Secret.* 1920. New York. 1st ed. inscr. sgn. VG $25.00

DELAND, Margaret. *Florida Days.* 1889. Boston. Ills. 1st ed. VG $25.00

DELAND, Margaret. *The Old Garden & Other Verses.* 1894. Boston. Ills. Crane. 114 pp. $20.00

DELAND, Margaret. *The Old Garden.* 1893. Houghton Mifflin. Ills. Crane. $12.50

DELANY, Samuel R. *Neveryona.* 1983. New York. Bantam. review copy. pb. VG $10.00

DELAUNEY, Charles. *Hot Discography.* 1943. New York. Commodore Record Co. VG $25.00

DELDERFIELD, R.F. *God is an Englishman.* 1970. London. 1st ed. dj. EX $20.00

DELDERFIELD, R.F. *The Spring Madness of Mr. Sermon.* 1963. London. Hodder & Stoughton. 1st ed. VG $35.00

DELESSERT, Etienne. *The Story of Number One.* 1968. Harlin Quist. Ills. 1st Am. ed. VG $15.00

DELESSERT, Etienne. *The Tree.* 1966. Harlin Quist. Ills. 1st ed. dj. VG $15.00

DELINEATOR HOME INSTITUTE. *New Delineator Recipes.* 1930. 222 pp. $4.00

DELITZSCH, Franz. *Jewish Artisan Life.* 1883. New York. 1st Am. ed. wrappers. EX $45.00

DELL, Floyd. *King Arthur's Socks & Village Plays.* 1922. New York. Knopf. 1st ed. dj. EX $65.00

DELLENBAUGH, Frederick S. *Fremont & '49. Story of a Remarkable Career.* 1914. New York. Putnam. Ills. maps. 547 pp. $15.00

DELONEY, Thomas. *The Works of Thomas Deloney.* 1912. Oxford. 1st ed. $65.00

DELVING, Michael. *A Shadow of Himself.* 1972. London. 1st Eng. ed. dj. VG $15.00

DELVING, Michael. *Bored to Death.* 1975. New York. Scribner. 1st ed. dj. VG $25.00

DELVING, Michael. *No Sign of Life.* 1978. London. 1st Eng. ed. dj. VG $15.00

DEMAREST, David P., Jr. *From These Hills. From These Valleys.* 1976. U. Pittsburgh. Ills. 240 pp. dj. $10.00

DEMBECK, H. *Animals & Men.* 1965. Nat. Hist. Pr. Ills. 1st Am. ed. 390 pp. EX $7.50

DEMING. *Cosel with Geronimo on His Last Raid.* 1938. Philadelphia. 6 color pls. dj. VG $15.00

DEMPSEY, Michael. *The Year's Art 1969-'70 Europe & USA.* 1971. New York. $15.00

DEMUTH, Norman. *An Anthology of Musical Criticism.* 1947. London. VG $8.00

DENDY, Dr. W.C. *The Philosophy of Systery.* 1845. New York. 1st Am. ed. $45.00

DENHARDT, R.M. *The Horse of the Americas.* 1949. OK U. Press. Ills. 286 pp. EX $15.00

DENIS, A. *Cats of the World.* 1964. London. Constable. Ills. 119 pp. dj. $10.00

DENIS, M. *Leopard in My Lap.* 1955. Messner. Ills. 254 pp. VG $7.50

DENIS. *On Safari.* 1963. London. 1st ed. dj. VG $10.00

DENISON, E.S. *Pacific Coast Souvenir.* 1888. Oakland. 12 pp. 46 photos. VG $18.50

DENKINGER, Emma Marshall. *Immortal Sidney.* 1931. New York. Ills. 317 pp. index. VG $12.50

DENKSTEIN, V. *Gothic Art of South Bohemia.* 1955. Prague. 1st ed. dj. VG $25.00

DENMAN, Frank. *Shaping of Alphabet: Study of Changing Type Style.* 1955. New York. Ills. 228 pp. dj. $24.00

DENNETT, Raymond & Johnson, J. *Negotiating with the Russians.* 1951. World Peace Foundation. $4.00

DENNETT. *At the Back of the Black Man's Mind.* 1906. London. 1st ed. 157 pp. $60.00

DENNIS, Patrick. *Genius.* 1962. Harcourt. 1st ed. dj. VG $20.00

DENNIS, Patrick. *Little Me.* 1961. New York. 1st ed. dj. VG $20.00

DENNIS, Patrick. *Tony.* 1966. New York. 1st ed. $7.50

DENNIS. *Black People of America.* 1970. New York. dj. VG $10.00

DENNISON, W. & Morey, C.R. *Studies in East Christian & Roman Art.* 1918. New York. Macmillan. EX $75.00

DENNISTON, J.D. *Greek Prose Style.* 1979. Greenwood. reprint 1952 Oxford ed. $20.00

DENNY. *Fabrics, Eighth Edition.* 1962. Lippincott. Ills. 163 pp. EX $3.50

DENNYS, Joyce. *Our Hospital. ABC.* (WWI alphabet) Brodley Head. Ills. 4th ed. $30.00

DENOVAN. *Phenomena of Nature.* 1897. Ills. 648 pp. $5.50

DENSLOW, W.W. *Denslow's Night Before Christmas.* 1902. Dillingham Co. Ills. G $150.00

DENSLOW, W.W. *My Favorite Circus Book.* 1903. Chicago. Ills. G $50.00

DENSLOW, W.W. *Wizard of Oz.* Bobbs Merrill. 8 color pls. VG $15.00

DENSMORE, Frances. *American Indians & Their Music.* 1926. Womans Press. 1st ed. dj. VG $50.00

DENSMORE. *Chippewa Music.* 1910. VG $45.00

DENSON, A. *Printed Writings by George W. Russell.* 1961. Evanston. 255 pp. dj. VG $8.50

DENTER. *Tom Harmon & the Great Gridiron Plot.* 1946. Whitman. Ills. VG $4.50

DENTON, J. *When Hell Was in Session.* 1976. New York. 1st ed. dj. EX $20.00

DENTON, Sherman F. *Incidents of a Collector's Rambles in Australia.* 1889. Boston. Ills. 272 pp. EX $50.00

DENYS, F. Ward. *Our Summer in the Vale of Kashmir.* 1915. 1st ed. dj. EX $12.50

DEPEW, Chauncey M. *Marching on Miscellaneous Speeches.* 1925. New York. ex-lib. 441 pp. $3.00

DER LING, Princess. *Kowtow.* 1930. New York. Dodd Mead. dj. EX $22.50

DERBY, Elias Hasket. *The Overland Route to the Pacific.* 1869. Boston. 1st ed. 97 pp. wrappers. VG $265.00

DERBY, George H. *Phoenixana; or, Sketches & Burlesques.* 1856. New York. 274+14pp ads. G $25.00

DERBY, J.C. *Fifty Years Among Authors, Books, & Publishers.* 1884. New York. Ills. Ltd. ed. 1/500. 739 pp. $25.00

DERBY, J.C. *Fifty Years Among Authors, Books, & Publishers.* 1886. Carlton. Ills. VG $35.00

DERLETH, August. *A Wisconsin Harvest.* 1966. Sauk City. sgn. 338 pp. VG $15.00

DERLETH, August. *Far Boundaries.* 1951. New York. Pellegrini. 1st ed. dj. EX $20.00

DERLETH, August. *New Poetry Out of Wisconsin.* 1969. Sauk City. dj. VG $12.50

DERLETH, August. *The Nightside.* 1947. New York. Rinehart. 1st ed. dj. EX $30.00

DERLETH, August & Schorer, M. *Colonel Markesan & Less Pleasant People.* 1966. Sauk City. Arkham House. dj. $60.00

DERLETH, August. *A Praed Street Dossier.* 1968. Sauk City. 1st ed. 108 pp. dj. EX $25.00

DERLETH, August. *Caitlin.* 1969. Iowa City. Prairie Press. advance copy. $30.00

DERLETH, August. *Dark Things.* 1971. Sauk City. Arkham House. dj. $60.00

DERLETH, August. *Fell Purpose.* 1953. New York. Arcadia House. 1st ed. VG $20.00

DERLETH, August. *Harrigan's File.* 1975. 1st ed. dj. VG $10.00

DERLETH, August. *Mr. Fairlie's Final Journey.* 1968. Sauk City. Arkham House. dj. $65.00

DERLETH, August. *Not Long for This World.* 1948. Sauk City. Arkham House. dj. $80.00

DERLETH, August. *Sleep No More.* 1944. New York. Rinehart. 1st ed. dj. EX $35.00

DERLETH, August. *Something Near.* 1945. Sauk City. Arkham House. dj. $130.00

DERLETH, August. *The Arkham Collector-Nos. 1-10.* Sauk City. Arkham House. $200.00

DERLETH, August. *The House by the River.* 1965. New York. 1st ed. dj. VG $10.00

DERLETH, August. *The Trail of Cthulhu.* 1962. Arkham House. dj. EX $40.00

DERLETH, August. *The Wisconsin, River of a Thousand Isles.* 1942. New York. 1st ed. VG $7.50

DERLETH, August. *Travelers by Night.* 1967. Sauk City. Arkham House. dj. $70.00

DERLETH, August. *Walden Pond.* 1968. Iowa City. 1st ed. dj. VG $12.50

DERLETH, August. *Walden West.* 1961. New York. 1st ed. dj. VG $10.00

DERLETH, August. *Wisconsin Murders.* 1968. Sauk City. dj. $65.00

DERLETH, August. *Writing Fiction.* 1946. Boston. 1st ed. dj. EX $12.50

DERLETH. *Someone in the Dark.* 1941. Arkham House. 1st ed. dj. EX $300.00

DERRICK, Thomas. *Decarmeron of Boccaccio.* 1924. London. Ills. VG $15.00

DERRY, J.T. *Story of the Confederate States.* 1865. Richmond. 448 pp. $60.00

DERWOOD, Gene. *The Poems of Gene Derwood.* 1955. New York. Clarke & Way. Ltd. 1st ed. $15.00

DES MARAIS, Walter. *Making Manuscripts Salable.* 1937. St.Louis. 159 pp. $37.50

DES PRES, T. *The Survivor.* 1976. Oxford. 6th printing. VG $12.50

DESAI, Anita. *In Custody.* 1984. Harper. 1st Am. ed. dj. VG $17.50

DESCHARNES, R. *The World of Salvador Dali.* 1962. New York. 1st ed. dj. EX $50.00

DESCHIN, Jacob. *Photo Tricks & Effects.* 1940. Davis Pub. Ills. 126 pp. VG $4.50

DESMONDE, Kay. *All Color Book of Dolls.* 1974. Octopus Books. 1st ed. dj. VG $20.00

DESTLER, Chester McArthur. *Roger Sherman & the Independent Oil Men.* 1967. New York. 304 pp. index. dj. $8.00

DETMOLD, E.J. *The Book of Baby Pets.* 1913. London. Ills. author. VG $150.00

DEUCHER, Sybil & Wheeler, O. *Giotto Tended the Sheep.* 1938. New York. Dutton. Ills. Bayley. 1st ed. $12.50

DEUTSCH, Babette. *Honey Out of the Rock.* 1925. New York. 1st ed. VG $10.00

DEUTSCH, K. *Science & the Creative Spirit.* 1958. Toronto. 165 pp. $7.50

DEVA, Jaya. *Japan's Kampf.* 1944. India. Allahabad Law Journal Press. $15.00

DEVINE, Dominic. *This is Your Death.* 1982. St.Martins. 1st ed. dj. VG $10.00

DEVINE, E.J. *Historic Caughnawaga Montreal.* 1922. wrappers. VG $60.00

DEVOE, A. *Lives Around Us.* 1942. Creative Age. Ills. 221 pp. dj. G $7.50

DEVOL, George H. *Forty Years as a Gambler on the Mississippi.* 1887. Cincinnati. 1st ed. 300 pp. VG $385.00

DEVOL, William Stowe. *Arizona Agricultural Experiment Station.* 1895. Tucson. $10.00

DEVON, Gary. *Lost.* 1986. New York. Knopf. proof copy. wrappers. $25.00

DEW, Robb Forman. *Dale Loves Sophie to Death.* 1981. Farrar. 1st ed. dj. VG $20.00

DEWEY, Thomas E. *Journey to the Far Pacific.* 1952. New York. 1st ed. 335 pp. dj. VG $15.00

DEWIS, David D. *Fight for the Sea.* 1961. Cleveland. Ills. 1st ed. 350 pp. $17.50

DEXTER, Will. *Everybody's Book of Magic.* 1956. London/NY. dj. VG $7.50

DEXTER, Will. *Famous Magic Secrets.* London. dj. VG $7.50

DEXTER, Will. *Secrets of the Conjurer's Craft.* London. dj. VG $7.50

DEXTER, Will. *This is Magic.* 1958. London. dj. VG $7.50

DHOTRE, D. *Wild Animal Man.* 1973. Taplinger. Ills. 154 pp. dj. EX $7.50

DI CESNOLA, L.P. *Cyprus: Its Ancient Cities, Tombs & Temples.* 1878. New York. Harper. Ills. 456 pp. $45.00

DI PESO, Charles. *Casas Grandes.* 1974. Amerind Found. 1st ed. 3 vol set. djs. EX $75.00

DI PRIMA, Diane. *Dinners & Nightmares.* 1961. New York. Corinth. inscr. wrappers. EX $35.00

DI PRIMA, Diane. *Earthsong.* 1968. New York. Poets Press. wrappers. EX $20.00

DICHTER, Harry. *Early American Sheet Music, 1768-1889.* 1941. 1st ed. VG $85.00

DICK, Philip K. *A Scanner Darkly.* 1977. 1st ed. dj. EX $50.00

DICK, Philip K. *Confessions of a Crap Artist.* Ltd. ed. 1/90. sgn. $175.00

DICK, Philip K. *Confessions of a Crap Artist.* 1974. 1st ed. EX $50.00

DICK, Philip K. *Flow My Tears, the Policeman Said.* 1974. Garden City. 1st ed. dj. EX $30.00

DICK, Philip K. *Martian Time-Slip.* 1964. New York. Ballantine. 1st ed. wrappers. $35.00

DICK, Philip K. *Radio Free Albemuth.* 1985. New York. Arbor House. proof copy. $50.00

DICK, Philip K. *The Collected Stories.* 1986. Underwood-Miller. $50.00

DICK, Philip K. *The Divine Invasion.* 1981. New York. 1st ed. dj. EX $10.00

DICK, Philip K. *The Preserving Machine.* 1969. Gollancz. dj. EX $45.00

DICK, Philip K. *The Transmigration of Timothy Archer.* 1982. New York. Timescape. uncorrected proof. $75.00

DICK, Philip K. *The Unteleported Man.* 1964. New York. Ace. 1st ed. wrappers. EX $25.00

DICK, Philip K. & Zelazny, R. *Deus Irae.* 1976. Garden City. Doubleday. dj. EX $20.00

DICK, R.A. *The Ghost & Mrs. Muir.* 1945. Chicago. 1st ed. VG $22.50

DICK, S. *Master Painters. Stories of Their Romantic Lives.* 1912. London. Ills. G $6.50

DICK. *Celestial Scenery.* 1838. Philadelphia. VG $35.00

DICKENS, Charles. *A Christmas Carol.* Philadelphia. Lippincott & Heinemann. Ills. $100.00

DICKENS, Charles. *A Christmas Carol.* 1924. New York. Ills. Everett. 1st ed. dj. $35.00

DICKENS, Charles. *A Christmas Carol.* 1922. London. Ills. Leech. reprint orig. ed. $55.00

DICKENS, Charles. *A Christmas Carol.* 1938. Philadelphia. Ills. Shinn. 131 pp. EX $20.00

DICKENS, Charles. *A Christmas Carol.* 1843. London. 3rd ed. G $75.00

DICKENS, Charles. *A Christmas Carol: Retold for Children.* 1940. McLoughlin. Ills. Robert Graef. VG $8.50

DICKENS, Charles. *A Christmas Story & The Holly Tree.* McLoughlin. Ills. (2 Christmas Stories) $4.50

DICKENS, Charles. *A Tale of Two Cities.* 1946. New York. World Pub. 348 pp. VG $3.50

DICKENS, Charles. *American Notes for General Circulation.* 1842. London. 1st ed. 2 vol set. rebound. G $200.00

DICKENS, Charles. *American Notes for General Circulation.* 1975. Ltd. Eds. Club.Ills. Houlihan. sgn. boxed. $35.00

DICKENS, Charles. *Battle of Life.* 1846. London. 1st ed. rebound. VG $75.00

DICKENS, Charles. *Beautiful Stories About Children.* 1898. Ills. $15.00

DICKENS, Charles. *Charles Dickens, 1812-1870-A Biography.* 1962. Fife, Scotland.Ills. Russell. Ltd. ed. $28.50

DICKENS, Charles. *Christmas Books.* 1852. London. 1st collected ed. VG $85.00

DICKENS, Charles. *Christmas Stories from Household Words.* 1894. London. Chapman & Hall. Ills. VG $10.00

DICKENS, Charles. *Cricket on the Hearth.* 1846. London. 1st ed. dj. G $175.00

DICKENS, Charles. *David Copperfield.* Ills. Reynolds. Ltd. 1st ed. 1/350. sgn. $300.00

DICKENS, Charles. *Dembey & Son.* 1848. London. 1st ed. gilt decor. VG $250.00

DICKENS, Charles. *Dembey & Son.* Boston. Magnifique ed. 3 vol set. EX $75.00

DICKENS, Charles. *Drawing-Room & Platform Acting.* London. no date. 48 pls. VG $12.00

DICKENS, Charles. *Hunted Down.* 1871. London. Hotten. 1st Eng. ed. VG $125.00

DICKENS, Charles. *Nicholas Nickleby.* Rand McNally. G $65.00

DICKENS, Charles. *Our Mutual Friend.* New York. Hurst. no date. Ills. G $5.50

DICKENS, Charles. *Our Mutual Friend.* 1868. Appleton. wrappers. G $15.00

DICKENS, Charles. *A Tale of Two Cities.* 1859. Leipzig. Tauchnitz. 1st ed. VG $65.00

DICKENS, Charles. *The Annotated Christmas Carol.* 1976. New York. Potter. Ills. Leech. 1st ed. $20.00

DICKENS, Charles. *The Battle of Life.* 1846. London. Ills. Dalziel. 1st ed. $90.00

DICKENS, Charles. *The Centennial Edition of Charles Dickens.* 1970. Heron Books. 1st ed. 36 vol set. VG $75.00

DICKENS, Charles. *The Life of Our Lord.* 1934. New York. Simon & Schuster. 1st ed. dj. $5.00

DICKENS, Charles. *The Life of Our Lord.* 1934. New York. Ltd. ed. 1/123. boxed. EX $25.00

DICKENS, Charles. *The Personal History of David Copperfield.* 1924. New York. Ills. Gertrude Demain Hammond. $25.00

DICKENS, Charles. *The Posthumous Papers of Pickwick Club.* Lombard Street ed. EX $175.00

DICKENS, Charles. *The Posthumous Papers of Pickwick Club.* 1887. London. Chapman & Hall. Ltd. ed. EX $75.00

DICKENS, Charles. *The Works of Charles Dickens.* 1894. Boston. Riverside Pr. Ills. 32 vol set. $265.00

DICKENS, Charles. *Works of Charles Dickens.* 1858-59. Chapman & Hall. 20 vol set. G $110.00

DICKENS, Monica. *An Open Book.* 1978. New York. Mayflower Books. Ills. 210 pp. $7.50

DICKENS; retold by Weedon, L. *Child Characters from Dickens.* London/NY. no date. Ills. Dixon. EX $125.00

DICKERSON, L. *Wilderness Man, Strange Story of Grey Owl.* 1973. Macmillan. Ills. 1st ed. 281 pp. dj. $20.00

DICKERSON, M. *Light House System.* 1837. Washington. 1st ed. 97 pp. $30.00

DICKEY, James. *Deliverance.* 1970. Boston. 1st ed. sgn. dj. VG $37.50

DICKEY, James. *Head-Deep in Strange Sounds.* 1979. Palaemon. Ltd. ed. 1/475. sgn. EX $20.00

DICKEY, James. *Spinning the Crystal Ball.* 1967. Lib. Congress. 1st ed. wrappers. EX $20.00

DICKEY, James. *The Enemy from Eden.* 1978. Lord John. Ills. Sauter. Ltd. ed. sgn. EX $40.00

DICKEY, James. *Tucky the Hunter.* 1978. New York. Crown. Ills. Angel. 1st ed. $20.00

DICKEY, James. *Veteran's Birth.* 1978. Palaemon. Ills. Dance. Ltd. ed. sgn. EX $20.00

DICKEY. *New Mexico Village Arts.* 1949. 1st ed. dj. EX $35.00

DICKINSON, Emily. *Love Poems & Others.* Mount Vernon. Peter Pauper Press. boxed. VG $12.50

DICKINSON, Emily. *Poems, Second Series.* 1891. Boston. VG $150.00

DICKINSON, Emily. *Poems, Second Series.* 1892. Boston. $45.00

DICKINSON, Emily. *Poems.* 1891. 3rd ed. $45.00

DICKINSON, Emily. *The Complete Poems.* 1924. 1st ed. VG $30.00

DICKINSON, Emily. *The Single Hound.* 1915. 2nd ed. VG $35.00

DICKINSON, Gordon. *Time Storm.* 1977. St.Martins. review copy. dj. VG $15.00

DICKINSON, Maude. *When Meals Were Meals.* 1967. New York. Crowell. 185 pp. $7.50

DICKINSON, Peter. *A Pride of Heroes.* 1969. London. 1st ed. dj. VG $25.00

DICKINSON, Peter. *A Summer in the Twenties.* 1981. Pantheon. 1st ed. dj. VG $20.00

DICKINSON, Peter. *City of Gold & Other Stories from Old Testament.* 1980. Pantheon. 1st ed. dj. VG $40.00

DICKINSON, Robert Latou. *Human Sex Anatomy.* 1949. Baltimore. Ills. 2nd ed. 133 pp. VG $30.00

DICKINSON. *The Book of Diamonds.* 1965. New York. 226 pp. dj. $12.50

DICKINSON. *The Book of Pearls.* 1968. New York. 248 pp. dj. $15.00

DICKMAN, J.T. *The Great Crusade. Narrative of the World War.* 1927. Appleton. Ills. Maps. 313 pp. $10.00

DICKSON, Carter. *And So to Murder.* 1940. New York. Morrow. 1st ed. 280 pp. VG $17.50

DICKSON, Carter. *Seeing is Believing.* 1945. Tower Books. 1st ed. dj. VG $10.00

DICKSON, Carter. *Skeleton in the Clock.* 1948. New York. 1st ed. G $12.50

DICKSON, G.R. & Bova, Ben. *Gremlins Go Home.* 1974. New York. Ills. Kelly Freas. sgns. $65.00

DICKSON, Gordon R. *Ancient My Enemy.* 1974. New York. 1st ed. dj. EX $20.00

DICKSON, Gordon R. *Sleepwalker's World.* 1971. Philadelphia. 1st ed. dj. VG $12.50

DICKSON, Gordon R. *Spacepaw.* 1969. New York. 1st ed. dj. EX $17.50

DICKSON, Gordon R. *The Far Call.* 1978. London. 1st ed. dj. EX $20.00

DICKSON, Gordon R. *The Star Road.* 1973. New York. 1st ed. dj. EX $20.00

DICKSON, Gordon R. *Time Storm.* 1977. New York. 1st ed. dj. EX $20.00

DICKSON & Anderson, Paul. *Earthman's Burden.* 1957. New York. Gnome. 1st ed. sgn. inscr. dj. $20.00

DICULAFAOY, Jane. *At Susa. Ancient Capitol of Kings of Persia.* 1890. Philadelphia. Gebbie & Co. wrappers. VG $30.00

DIDION, Joan. *A Book of Common Prayer.* 1977. Simon & Schuster. 1st ed. dj. $20.00

DIDION, Joan. *Play It as It Lays.* 1970. Farrar. 1st ed. dj. VG $30.00

DIDION, Joan. *Salvador.* 1983. Simon & Schuster. 1st ed. dj. $15.00

DIDION, Joan. *The White Album.* 1979. Simon & Schuster. 1st ed. dj. $15.00

DIECK. *The Johnstown Flood.* (ca.1890) Ills. 224 pp. G $4.50

DIEFFENBACH, G. *Fur Unsere Kleinen.* Gotha. Perthes. no date. Ills. $25.00

DIEHL, William. *Sharkey's Machine.* 1978. Delacorte. 1st ed. dj. VG $12.50

DIETZ, Lew. *Full Fathom Five.* 1958. $7.50

DIETZ, Nettie Fowler. *A White Woman in a Black Man's Country.* 1926. Omaha. Ills. 2nd printing. 327 pp. $10.00

DILLARD, Annie. *Holy the Firm.* 1977. Harper. 1st ed. dj. VG $20.00

DILLING, Elizabeth. *Red Network: Who's Who & Handbook of Radicalism.* 1936. Chicago. 352 pp. G $8.00

DILLION, John B. *History of Indiana.* 1843. Indianapolis. 1st ed. 456 pp. $35.00

DILLON, John B. *Oddities of Colonial Legislation in America.* 1879. Indianapolis. Ills. 784 pp. $37.50

DILLON & MILLAY. *Flowers of Evil.* 1936. 1st ed. VG $10.00

DIMOCK, A.W. & Julian. *Florida Enchantments.* 1908. New York. Ills. EX $50.00

DIMSDALE, Thomas J. *The Vigilantes of Montana.* 1882. Virginia City. 2nd ed. 241 pp. wrappers. $165.00

DINE, Jim & Padgett, Ron. *The Adventures of Mr. & Mrs., Jim & Ron.* 1970. New York. 1st ed. dj. VG $20.00

DINE, Jim. *Appollinaire's the Poet Assassinated.* 1968. New York. Crown. dj. VG $45.00

DINES & PRICE. *Dog Soldiers. Cheyenne Warrior Society.* 1961. New York. Ills. Peter Burchard. $8.00

DINESEN, Isak. *Last Tales.* 1957. New York. Random House. 1st ed. EX $20.00

DINESEN, Isak. *Out of Africa.* 1938. Random House. 1st ed. dj. VG $42.50

DINESEN, Isak. *Seven Gothic Tales.* 1934. New York. 1st ed. dj. $40.00

DINESEN, Isak. *Shadows on the Grass.* 1961. New York. 1st ed. dj. EX $15.00

DINESEN, Isak. *Shadows on the Grass.* 1961. Random House. Book Month Club ed. dj. EX $5.00

DINESEN, Isak. *Shadows on the Grass.* 1960. London. Joseph. 1st ed. dj. EX $35.00

DINESEN, Isak. *The Angela Avengers.* 1946. Random House. Book Month Club ed. dj. VG $5.00

DINESEN, Isak. *Winter's Tales.* 1942. New York. 1st ed. dj. EX $20.00

DINESEN, Isak. *Winter's Tales.* Tower Books. 1st ed. dj. VG $7.50

DINESEN, Thomas. *Twilight on the Betzy.* 1952. London. Putnam. 1st ed. dj. EX $17.50

DINGLE. *International Chef.* 1955. EX $8.00

DINGMAN, Larry. *Booksellers' Marks.* 1986. Ltd. 1st ed. 1/438. VG $32.50

DINGWALL, Eric J. *The Haunting of Borley Rectory.* 1956. London. Duckworth. 1st ed. dj. VG $25.00

DINH, Tran Van. *Blue Dragon White Tiger.* 1983. Philadelphia. Triam Press. 1st ed. inscr. VG $30.00

DINNERSTEIN, Leonard. *The Leo Frank Case.* New York. Columbia U. Pr. 248 pp. dj. VG $8.00

DINTENFASS, Mark. *Montgomery Street.* 1978. Harper. 1st ed. dj. VG $20.00

DINTENFASS, Mark. *Old World, New World.* 1982. Morrow. proof copy. wrappers. VG $30.00

DINTENFASS, Mark. *The Case Against Org.* 1970. Little, Brown. 1st ed. dj. VG $25.00

DIONNE & others. *The Dionne Quintuplets. We're Two Years Old.* 1936. Whitman Pub. EX $25.00

DIPPIE. *Custer In Turf, Field & Farm.* 1980. Ills. 174 pp. $12.50

DIRAC, P.A.M. *Principles of QM.* 1947. Oxford U. Pr. 3rd ed. sgn. dj. VG $40.00

DISCH, R. *The Ecological Conscience.* 1970. Prentice Hall. 206 pp. EX $5.00

DISCH, Thomas. *Getting into Death.* 1976. 1st ed. dj. EX $25.00

DISCH, Thomas. *On Wings of Song.* 1979. St.Martin. 1st ed. dj. VG $12.50

DISCH, Thomas. *Ringtime.* 1983. Ills. Ltd. ed. 1/100. sgns. $45.00

DISCH, Thomas. *The Businessman.* 1984. Harper. 1st ed. dj. VG $15.00

DISNEY, Dorothy Cameron. *Crimson Friday.* 1943. Random House. 1st ed. dj. VG $20.00

DISNEY, Walt. *Mickey Detective.* 1933. Paris. French text. Ills. 1st ed. $60.00

DISNEY, Walt. *Mickey Mouse & Pluto.* 1936. Racine. $55.00

DISNEY, Walt. *Mickey Mouse Club Annual.* 1956. New York. Simon & Schuster. 120 pp. $4.00

DISNEY, Walt. *The Black Hole.* 1979. pop up book. $3.50

DISNEY, Walt. *The Golden Touch. Mickey Mouse Presents.* 1937. Whitman. 1st ed. Ills. dj. $55.00

DISNEY, Walt. *White Wilderness: Animals of the Arctic.* 1958. New York. color photos. VG $8.00

DISNEY, Walt. *Mickey Mouse Club Annual.* 1948. London. Ills. 1st Eng. ed. $30.00

DISNEY STUDIOS. *Cinderella.* 1950. New York. Simon & Schuster. $10.00

DISNEY STUDIOS. *Peter & the Wolf.* 1947. New York. Simon & Schuster. $5.00

DISNEY STUDIOS. *Pinocchio.* 1939. New York. Random House. Ills. from film. $20.00

DISNEY STUDIOS. *The Pop-Up Silly Symphonies.* 1932. New York. gift inscr. VG $175.00

DISNEY STUDIOS. *Three Little Pigs.* 1933. New York. VG $35.00

DISNEY STUDIOS. *Walt Disney's Appleseed.* 1949. New York. Simon & Schuster. Ills. VG $4.50

DISSELHOFF-LINNE. *America Precolombina.* 1962. Barcelona. Ills. 295 pp. maps. boxed. VG $20.00

DISTURNELL, J. *Great Lakes or Inland Seas of America.* 1863. 1st ed. $65.00

DITCHFIELD, P.H. *Books Fatal to Their Authors.* 1895. New York. 1st Am. ed. 244 pp. $20.00

DITMARS, R. *A Field Book of North American Snakes.* 1939. Doubleday. Ills. 305 pp. dj. VG $10.00

DITMARS, R. *Snakes of the World.* 1951. Macmillan. Ills. 205 pp. VG $15.00

DITMARS, R. *The Book of Living Reptiles.* 1936. Lippincott. Ills. 64 pp. VG $10.00

DIVINE, David. *The Golden Fool.* 1954. 1st ed. dj. $8.50

DIX, Beulah Marie. *Merrylips.* 1908. Ills. F.T. Merrill. VG $4.00

DIX, John. *A Winter in Maderia & Summer in Spain & Florence.* 1850. New York. EX $30.00

DIXON, C. *Bird Life in a Southern County.* 1899. London. Ills. 303 pp. G $6.00

DIXON, C. *Rural Bird Life in England.* 1895. Werner. Ills. 374 pp. rebound. $10.00

DIXON, Edward H. *Scenes in the Practice of a New York Surgeon.* 1856. New York. $15.00

DIXON, Franklin W. *Across the Pacific.* 1928. Grosset & Dunlap. Ills. dj. EX $4.50

DIXON, Franklin W. *Brushing the Mountain Top.* 1934. New York. 216 pp. $3.50

DIXON, Franklin W. *Following the Sun Shadow.* 1932. Grosset & Dunlap. 215 pp. $4.50

DIXON, Franklin W. *Over the Ocean to Paris.* Grosset & Dunlap. Ills. G $3.50

DIXON, Franklin W. *The Disappearing Floor.* 1940. New York. Grosset & Dunlap. 218 pp. $4.50

DIXON, Franklin W. *The Great Airport Mystery.* 1930. New York. Grosset & Dunlap. 210 pp. dj. $3.50

DIXON, Franklin W. *The Hardy Boys; Hunting for Hidden Gold.* 1928. New York. Grosset & Dunlap. 214 pp. $2.50

DIXON, Franklin W. *The Hardy Boys; The Clue of the Broken Blade.* 1942. New York. Grosset & Dunlap. 218 pp. $3.50

DIXON, Franklin W. *The Hardy Boys; The Secret Panel.* 1946. New York. Grosset & Dunlap. 212 pp. dj. $3.50

DIXON, Franklin W. *The Lone Eagle of the Border.* 1929. New York. Grosset & Dunlap. 214 pp. $2.50

DIXON, George. *Voyage Autour Du Monde.* 1789. Paris. Ills. 1st French ed. VG $450.00

DIXON, George. *Voyage Round World; Particularly NW Coast of Amer.* 1789. London. Ills. 1st ed. 5 fld maps. VG $775.00

DIXON, Martha. *Copper Kettle Cook Book.* 1963. Eerdmans Pub. 480 pp. G $5.50

DIXON, R. & Eddy, B. *Personality of Insects.* 1924. Clark. Ills. 247 pp. VG $5.00

DIXON, Roland B. *Racial History of Man.* 1923. New York. 1st ed. VG $15.00

DIXON, Stephen. *No Relief.* 1976. Ann Arbor. 1st ed. sgn. wrappers. EX $45.00

DIXON, Stephen. *14 Stores.* 1980. Baltimore. Johns Hopkins. 1st ed. dj. EX $20.00

DIXON, Thomas. *The Black Hood.* 1924. Appleton. 1st ed. dj. VG $12.50

DIXON, Thomas. *The Sins of the Father. A Romance of the South.* 1912. New York. Ills. John Cassell. VG $6.00

DIXON, Thomas. *The Victim.* 1914. New York. Ills. J.N. Marchand. VG $10.00

DIXON, William Hepworth. *New America.* 1867. London. Ills. 3rd ed. 2 vol set. $30.00

DIXON, William. *Fox Hunting in the Twentieth Century.* 1925. New York. Ills. VG $25.00

DIXON. *A Figure in Hiding.* 1937. Ills. Laune. dj. VG $7.50

DIXON. *The Clue in the Embers.* 1955. G $3.50

DIXON. *The Flickering Torch Mystery.* 1943. Ills. Laune. dj. VG $7.50

DIXON. *The Hidden Harbor Mystery.* 1935. dj. VG $7.50

DIXON. *The Hooded Hawk Mystery.* 1951. G $3.50

DIXON. *The House on the Cliff.* 1927. dj. VG $7.50

DIXON. *The Mark on the Door.* 1934. dj. VG $7.50

DIXON. *The Melted Coins.* 1944. Ills. Laune. dj. VG $7.50

DIXON. *The Mystery of the Flying Express.* 1941. Ills. Laune. dj. VG $7.50

DIXON. *The Phantom Freighter.* 1947. G $3.50

DIXON. *The Secret of the Old Mill.* 1927. dj. EX $8.50

DIXON. *The Secret Warning.* 1938. Ills. Laune. dj. EX $8.50

DIXON. *The Sign of the Crooked Arrow.* 1949. G $3.50

DIXON. *The Tower Treasure.* 1927. dj. VG $7.50

DIXON. *The Tower Treasure.* 1959. dj. VG $4.50

DIXON. *The Wailing Siren Mystery.* 1951. VG $3.50

DIXON. *What Happened at Midnight.* 1931. G $3.50

DIXON. *While the Clock Ticked.* 1932. G $3.50

DJANG CHU. *The China Problem.* 1947. Washington. $65.00

DMITRI, Ivan. *Flight to Everywhere.* 1944. NY/London. Ills. 1st ed. VG $15.00

DOAK, W. *Fishes of the New Zealand Region.* 1972. New Zealand. Ills. 132 pp. dj. EX $25.00

DOANE, F.H. *Radio Devices & Communications.* 1928. Scranton, PA. 240 pp. $4.00

DOANE, Pelagie. *Tell Me About God.* 1946. Rand McNally. Ills. 70 pp. G $4.00

DOBBIN, E. Virginia. *The Low Fat, Low Cholesterol Diet.* 1951. Garden City. Doubleday. 371 pp. $5.50

DOBBINS, W.W. *History of the Battle of Lake Erie.* 1876. Erie, PA. 96 pp. wrappers. $47.50

DOBEREINER. *Down the 19th Fairway.* 1982. London. Ills. 1st ed. dj. $22.00

DOBIE, C.C. *San Francisco. A Pageant.* 1933. Appleton. Ills. Suydam. 1st ed. VG $12.50

DOBIE, J. Frank. *Coffee in the Gourd.* 1935. Austin. reprint ed. Ills. 110 pp. VG $30.00

DOBIE, J. Frank. *Coronado's Children.* 1931. New York. Literary Guild. Ills. 367 pp. $12.50

DOBIE, J. Frank. *Coronado's Children.* 1930. Dallas. 1st ed. 2nd issue. VG $40.00

DOBIE, J. Frank. *Cow People.* 1964. 306 pp. $4.00

DOBIE, J. Frank. *I'll Tell You a Tale.* 1969. Little, Brown. dj. EX $25.00

DOBIE, J. Frank. *John C. Duval.* Ills. T. Lea. 2nd ed. dj. EX $7.50

DOBIE, J. Frank. *Lost Mines of the Old West.* 1960. London. Hammond. 1st Eng. ed. dj. EX $20.00

DOBIE, J. Frank. *Mustangs & Cow Horses.* 1940. Austin, TX. Ills. 1st ed. 429 pp. dj. $50.00

DOBIE, J. Frank. *Prefaces.* 1975. Little, Brown. 1st ed. EX $15.00

DOBIE, J. Frank. *Rattlesnakes.* 1965. Little, Brown. Ills. 1st ed. 201 pp. dj. $17.50

DOBIE, J. Frank. *The Longhorns.* 1941. Boston. Ills. Lea. ex-lib. 388 pp. $20.00

DOBIE, J. Frank. *The Longhorns.* 1941. New York. Ills. Tom Lea. 387 pp. dj. EX $12.50

DOBIE, J. Frank. *The Mustangs.* 1952. New York. Ills. C.B. Wilson. dj. $15.00

DOBIE, J. Frank. *The Mustangs.* 1952. Boston. Ills. 1st ed. 376 pp. dj. $35.00

DOBIE, J. Frank. *The Voice of the Coyote.* 1949. Little, Brown. Ills. Murie. 1st ed. sgn. VG $65.00

DOBIE. *Guide to Life & Literature of the Southwest.* 1965. revised ed. wrappers. VG $8.00

DOBIE. *Vaquero of Brush Country.* 1929. Dallas. 3rd ed. VG $30.00

DOBREE, Bonamy, ed. *Works of Sir John Vanbrugh.* Nonesuch. Ltd. ed. 1/1300. VG $90.00

DOBSON, Austin. *Old English Songs from Various Sources.* 1894. Ills. Thomson. 1st ed. $15.00

DOBSON. *Ballad of Beau Brocade.* 1892. London. 1st ed. $35.00

DOBYNS, Stephen. *Saratoga Longshot.* 1976. New York. Atheneum. 1st ed. VG $25.00

DOBZHANSKY, Theodosius. *Genetics & Origin of the Species.* 1937. New York. Columbia U. Press. 1st ed. $75.00

DOCK, Lavinia L. & Stewart, I. *A Short History of Nursing.* 1938. New York. Putnam. 435 pp. $5.00

DOCTOROW, E.L. *Drinks Before Dinner.* 1979. New York. Random House. 1st ed. dj. EX $20.00

DOCTOROW, E.L. *Lives of the Poets.* 1984. Random House. Ltd. 1st ed. slipcase. EX $75.00

DOCTOROW, E.L. *Lives of the Poets.* 1984. Random House. 1st ed. sgn. dj. EX $40.00

DOCTOROW, E.L. *Loon Lake.* 1980. New York. Random House. 1st trade ed. $10.00

DOCTOROW, E.L. *Ragtime.* 1975. Random House. 1st ed. dj. VG $25.00

DOCTOROW, E.L. *Welcome to Hard Times.* 1960. New York. 1st ed. dj. VG $100.00

DOCTOROW, E.L. *World's Fair.* Ltd. ed. 1/300. sgn. $65.00

DODD, Martha. *The Searching Light.* 1955. New York. 2nd ed. dj. VG $8.50

DODDS, John. *Age of Paradox a Biography of England 1841-1851.* 1953. Gollancz. 1st ed. dj. $10.00

DODDs, John. *Spirit Manifestations Examined & Explained.* 1854. New York. $20.00

DODDS, Norman. *Gypsies, Didikois & Other Travellers.* 1966. Johnson Pub. Ills. 1st ed. VG $20.00

DODGE, G.M. *The Telegraph Instructor.* 1911. Valparaiso, IN. Ills. 302 pp. $3.50

DODGE, J.R. *WV: Its Farm & Forests, Mines & Oil-Wells.* 1865. Philadelphia. 1st ed. ex-lib. VG $45.00

DODGE, Mary Mapes. *Along the Way.* 1879. New York. 1st ed. G $15.00

DODGE, Mary Mapes. *Hans Brinker; or, The Silver Skates.* 1936. Rand McNally. Windermere Series. G $7.50

DODGE, Mary Mapes. *Hans Brinker; or, The Silver Skates.* 1926. New York. Scribner. Ills. G.W. Edwards. $40.00

DODGE, Mary Mapes. *Hans Brinker; or, The Silver Skates.* 1925. Winston. Ills. Clara M. Budd. dj. EX $7.50

DODGE, Mary Mapes. *Hans Brinker; or, The Silver Skates.* 1932. New York. Garden City. Ills. 305 pp. dj. $35.00

DODGE, Mary Mapes. *Hans Brinker; or, The Silver Skates.* 1925. Philadelphia. Ills. Clara M. Budd. VG $15.00

DODGE, Mary Mapes. *Hans Brinker; or, The Silver Skates.* 1913. New York. Ills. Rudolph Menci. 261 pp. $5.00

DODGE, Mary Mapes. *Hans Brinker; or, The Silver Skates.* 1918. Philadelphia. McKay. Ills. Enright. dj. $20.00

DODGE, Mary Mapes. *Hans Brinker; or, The Silver Skates.* 1915. New York. Ills. Edwards. 1st ed. EX $15.00

DODGE, Mary Mapes. *The Companion Library.* 1963. Grosset & Dunlap. Ills. EX $3.50

DODGE, Richard Irving. *Our Wild Indians.* 1882. Hartford. Ills. 1st ed. $100.00

DODGE, Richard Irving. *Our Wild Indians.* 1883. Hartford, CT. Worthington. Ills. 653 pp. $50.00

DODGE, Robert J. *Isolated Splendor: Put-in-Bay & South Bass Island.*1975. New York. 166 pp. $12.50

DODGE, Theodore A. *Patrocus & Penelope.* 1885. Houghton Mifflin. Ills. VG $30.00

DODWELL, C.R. *Essays on Durer.* 1973. Manchester U. 1st ed. dj. $15.00

DOHERTY. *George Stubbs: Anatomical Works.* 1975. Godine. $40.00

DOLIN, Anton. *Alicia Markova.* 1953. New York. 1st ed. sgn. dj. VG $20.00

DOLINER, Roy. *For Love or Money.* 1974. Simon & Schuster. 1st ed. sgn. $20.00

DOLLAR, Robert. *Memoirs of Robert Dollar.* 1918-1928. 4 vols in 3. Ills. EX $100.00

DOLLFUS, Chas. & Geoffroy, E. *Histoire de la Locomotion Terrestre.* 1925. Paris. Ills. folio. 360 pp. index. VG $200.00

DOLMETSCH, N. *The Viola da Gamba.* 1962. London. Hinrischsen. 27 pls. dj. EX $25.00

DOMENECH, Abbe E.M. *Seven Years Residence in Great Deserts of N. Amer.*1860. London. Ills. 1st ed. 2 vol set. VG $225.00

DOMENECH, Emmanuel H.D. *Missionary Adventures in Texas & Mexico.* 1858. London. Ills. 1st ed. map. 366 pp. $375.00

DOMENECH. *Great Deserts of North America.* 1860. 1st ed. VG $45.00

DOMINIC, R.B. *Epitaph for a Lobbyist.* 1974. London. Macmillan. 1st Eng. ed. dj. VG $35.00

DOMVILLE-FIFE. *Savage Life in the Black Sudan.* 1927. Philadelphia. VG $45.00

DON, Etherl C. *Proud Roxana.* 1909. Philadelphia. Ills. Wireman. 12 color pls. $30.00

DONAHEY, Mary D. *The Calorie Cook Book.* 1923. Chicago. 250 pp. $3.50

DONAHEY, William. *The Children's Mother Goose.* 1921. Rielly & Lee. Ills. 120 pp. G $7.50

DONAHEY. *Teenie Weenie Neighbors.* 1945. London. 2nd ed. dj. VG $2.00

DONAHEY. *The Teenie Weenies Under the Rosebush.* 1922. Reilly Lee. Ills. 1st ed. $22.50

DONAHUE, H.E.F. *Conversations with Nelson Algren.* 1964. New York. Hill & Wang. 1st ed. 333 pp. $6.50

DONAHUE & Co., Phil. *Donahue, My Own Story.* 1979. New York. Simon & Schuster. 247 pp. dj. $5.50

DONALD. *Outlaws of Border/History of Frank & Jessie James.*1st ed. $40.00

DONALDSON, S. *Daughter of Regals.* 1984. Grant. Ills. Ltd. ed. 1/1075. sgn. $75.00

DONALDSON, S. *Gilden-Fire.* 1981. Ills. Fabian. Ltd. ed. 1/270. sgn. boxed. EX $100.00

DONALDSON, S. *Gilden-Fire.* 1981. Underwood & Miller. 1st ed. EX $35.00

DONAN, Peter. *The Dells of the Wisconsin.* 1879. Chicago. Ills. 1st ed. wrappers. $125.00

DONLEAVY, J.P. *A Fairy Tale of New York.* 1973. Delacorte. 1st ed. dj. VG $17.50

DONLEAVY, J.P. *A Singular Man.* 1963. Little, Brown. 1st ed. dj. VG $30.00

DONLEAVY, J.P. *Leila.* 1983. Delacorte. proof copy. wrappers. VG $25.00

DONLEAVY, J.P. *Leila.* 1983. Delacorte. review copy. dj. VG $22.50

DONLEAVY, J.P. *Schultz.* 1979. Delacorte. 1st ed. dj. VG $12.50

DONLEAVY, J.P. *The Beastly Beatitudes of Balthazar.* 1968. New York. Delacourt. 1st ed. dj. VG $25.00

DONLEAVY, J.P. *The Ginger Man.* 1958. New York. 1st Am. ed. dj. VG $45.00

DONLEAVY, J.P. *The Ginger Man.* 1958. Paris. 1st hardcover ed. dj. VG $75.00

DONLEAVY, J.P. *What They Did in Dublin with the Ginger Man.* 1961. London. Macgibbon & Kee. 1st ed. $25.00

DONNE, John. *Complete Poetry & Selected Prose.* 1929. Nonesuch. Ltd. ed. VG $125.00

DONNE, John. *Love Poems.* Mount Vernon. Peter Pauper Press. boxed. VG $12.50

DONNELLY, Ignatius. *Atlantis: Antidiluvian World.* 1882. New York. 1st ed. 490 pp. EX $45.00

DONNELLY, Ignatius. *The Golden Bottle.* 1892. New York. Merrill. 1st ed. dj. $25.00

DONOGHUE, Denis. *An Honored Guest-New Essays on W.B. Yeats.* 1966. St. Martins. 1st ed. dj. $10.00

DONOGHUE, S. *Donoghue Up: Autobiography of Steve Donoghue.* 1938. New York. VG $15.00

DONOHO, M.H. *Circle Dot, Cowboy Life Forty Years Ago.* 1907. Topeka. 1st ed. $55.00

DONOHUE, Ernest J. *Dramatic Character in the English Romantic Age.* 1970. 1st ed. dj. $8.50

DONOSO, Jose. *A House in the Country.* 1984. New York. Knopf. 1st ed. dj. VG $20.00

DONOSO, Jose. *Coronation.* 1965. Knopf. trans. 1st Am. ed. dj. VG $40.00

DONOSO, Jose. *Sacred Families.* 1977. New York. Knopf. 1st ed. dj. EX $25.00

DONOVAN, Edward. *Natural History of British Birds.* 1799. London. 98 colored pls. $300.00

DONOVAN, Robert J. *Conflict & Crisis.* 1977. New York. 473 pp. dj. $10.00

DONOVAN, Robert J. *PT 109: John F. Kennedy in World War II.* 1961. New York. McGraw Hill. 221 pp. dj. EX $4.50

DOOLEY, J.H. *Dem Good Ole Times.* 1906. New York. Ills. 1st ed. dj. VG $25.00

DOOLITTLE, J. *Social Life of the Chinese.* 1865. New York. Harper. Ills. 2 vol set. G $37.50

DOONER, P.W. *Last Days of the Republic.* 1880. San Francisco. Alta CA Pub. 1st ed. ex-lib. $75.00

DORAN, George H. *Chronicles of Barabbas.* 1952. New York. 1st ed. 446 pp. dj. $7.50

DORBIN, S. *A Bibliography of Charles Bukowski.* 1969. Ltd. ed. 1/350. sgns. $66.50

DORE, Gustave & Blanchard, J. *London. A Pilgrimage.* 1872. London. VG $130.00

DOREY, Jacques. *Three & the Moon.* 1929. Knopf. Ills. Artzybasheff. 1st ed. G $40.00

DORIAN, Max. *The Du Ponts from Gunpowder to Nylon.* 1961. Boston/Toronto.Ills. 1st ed. index. VG $10.00

DORING, Clare. *Economical Cook Book, All-Round Cookery & Hints.* 1929. London. $15.00

DORMAN, Caroline. *Wild Flowers of Louisiana.* Doubleday. 1st ed. sgn. $20.00

DORMANN, Genevieve. *Colette: a Passion for Life.* 1985. New York. 1st ed. dj. EX $25.00

DORNBUSCH, C.E. *Military Bibliography of the Civil War. Vol I.* 1961. New York Public Library. $35.00

DORO, Edward. *The Boar & Shibboleth.* 1933. New York. Ills. Landacre. Ltd. ed. VG $15.00

DORSEY, George. *Christopher of San Francisco.* 1962. Macmillan. 1st ed. sgns. dj. VG $40.00

DORSEY, J.M. *Jefferson-Duglison Letters.* 1960. U. of VA. inscr. $15.00

DORSEY. *Indians of the Southwest.* 1903. Ills. 223 pp. SftCvr. $20.00

DORTZBACH, Karl & Debbie. *Kidnapped.* 1975. New York. Harper & Row. 177 pp. dj. $4.00

DOS PASSOS, John. *Brazil on the Move.* 1963. New York. 1st ed. dj. EX $17.50

DOS PASSOS, John. *Chosen Country.* 1951. New York. 485 pp. $10.00

DOS PASSOS, John. *Chosen Country.* 1951. Cambridge. 1st revised copy. slipcase. EX $20.00

DOS PASSOS, John. *Doctor Hudson's Secret Journal.* 1939. Ltd. ed. 1/500. sgn. dj. EX $25.00

DOS PASSOS, John. *Head & Heart of Thomas Jefferson.* 1954. Garden City. Doubleday. dj. VG $20.00

DOS PASSOS, John. *Midcentury.* 1961. Houghton. 1st ed. dj. VG $35.00

DOS PASSOS, John. *Mr. Wilson's War.* 1962. Doubleday. 1st ed. dj. VG $15.00

DOS PASSOS, John. *Nineteen Nineteen.* 1932. Harcourt. 1st ed. dj. EX $30.00

DOS PASSOS, John. *Number One.* 1943. Houghton. 1st ed. dj. VG $40.00

DOS PASSOS, John. *Occasions & Protests.* 1964. Regnery. 1st ed. dj. VG $30.00

DOS PASSOS, John. *The Big Money.* 1936. New York. 1st Am. ed. dj. VG $30.00

DOS PASSOS, John. *The Prospect Before Us.* 1950. Boston. $15.00

DOS PASSOS, John. *The 42nd Parallel.* 1930. New York. 1st ed. dj. VG $65.00

DOS PASSOS, John. *U.S.A.: The 42nd Parellel, 1919, Big Money.* 1946. Boston. Ills. Marsh. 3 vol set. $20.00

DOSSENBACH, H.D. *The Family Life of Birds.* 1971. McGraw Hill. Ills. 185 pp. VG $5.00

DOSTOEVSKY, Fyodor. *A Gentle Spirit.* 1931. New York. Paris. Ills. Berard. Ltd. ed. $40.00

DOSTOEVSKY. *Brothers Karamazov.* Heritage Press.boxed. VG $7.50

DOSTOEVSKY. *Stavrogin's Confession.* 1947. New York. 1st ed. dj. VG $20.00

DOTTORE, Signor. *The Autobiography of F. Michele Daniele.* 1959. New York. Exposition Press. 237 pp. G $5.00

DOTY, B. *Legion of the Damned.* 1928. New York. G $15.00

DOTY, Carolyn. *What She Told Him.* 1985. New York. Viking. 1st ed. dj. VG $45.00

DOTY, Sile. *The Life of Sile Doty 1800-1876.* 1948. Detroit. 1st ed. 288 pp. dj. EX $22.50

DOUBLEDAY, Russ. *Cattle Ranch to College.* 1899. Ills. 1st ed. VG $10.00

DOUGHTY, Charles M. *Travels in Arabia Deserta.* 1949. London. 2 vol set. djs. $50.00

DOUGLAS, Ellen. *A Lifetime Burning.* 1982. Random House. 1st ed. sgn. dj. VG $22.50

DOUGLAS, Ellen. *A Long Night.* 1986. Nouveau. Ltd. ed. 1/300. sgn. EX $25.00

DOUGLAS, Ellen. *The Rock Cried Out.* 1979. Harcourt. 1st ed. sgn. dj. VG $25.00

DOUGLAS, George. *Scottish Fairy Tales.* Burt. (ca.1900). Ills. VG $12.50

DOUGLAS, Lloyd C. *Magnificent Obsession.* 1929. New York. Willett, Clark & Co. 330 pp. $3.50

DOUGLAS, Lloyd C. *The Big Fisherman.* 1948. 581 pp. $4.00

DOUGLAS, Lloyd C. *The Robe.* 1942. Boston. 1st ed. 695 pp. dj. VG $3.50

DOUGLAS, M.S. *The Everglades, River of Grass.* 1947. New York. 406 pp. dj. VG $12.50

DOUGLAS, N. *Summer Islands.* Ltd. ed. 1/500. sgn. boxed. VG $65.00

DOUGLAS, Norman. *Fountains in Sand/Rambles Among Oases of Tunisia.* 1912. New York. Ills. $60.00

DOUGLAS, Norman. *London Street Games.* 1931. London. 2nd revised ed. dj. VG $15.00

DOUGLAS, Norman. *Nerinda.* 1929. Ltd. ed. 1/475. VG $65.00

DOUGLAS, Norman. *Nerinda.* 1929. Day. 1st ed. $10.00

DOUGLAS, Norman. *Siren Land.* 1911. Dent. 1st ed. $100.00

DOUGLAS, Norman. *South Wind.* 1928. Ills. Angelo. 1st ed. dj. EX $55.00

DOUGLAS, Norman. *South Wind.* 1929. Chicago. Argus Books. 15 color pls. VG $45.00

DOUGLAS, Robert. *China.* 1887. London. Ills. 2nd ed. 433 pp. VG $25.00

DOUGLAS, William O. *Democracy's Manifesto.* 1962. Garden City. 1st ed. 48 pp. dj. $12.50

DOUGLAS, William O. *Go East, Young Man-The Early Years.* New York. Random House. 493 pp. dj. $6.00

DOUGLAS, William O. *My Wilderness: East to Katahdin.* 1961. New York. Doubleday. photos. 290 pp. dj. $4.00

DOUGLAS, William. *My Wilderness. The Pacific West.* 1960. Doubleday. Ills. Jaques. 1st ed. 206 pp. $7.50

DOUGLAS & D'HARNONCOURT. *Indian Art of the United States.* 1948. 2nd ed. pls. dj. VG $22.50

DOUGLAS & D'HARNONCOURT. *Indian Art of the United States.* 1969. New York. Ills. 203 pp. dj. $15.00

DOUGLAS & D'HARNONCOURT. *Indian Art of the United States.* 1941. New York. Ills. 1st ed. 219 pp. VG $32.50

DOUGLAS. *Beyond High Himalayas.* 1952. 1st ed. dj. VG $10.00

DOUGLAS. *Endurance Test; or, How Clear Grit Won the West.* 1913. Donahue. Victory Boy Scout Series. dj. $6.50

DOUGLAS-HAMILTON, I. & O. *Among the Elephants.* 1975. Viking Press. Ills. 285 pp. maps. VG $7.50

DOUGLASS, Benjamin Wallace. *The New Deal Comes to Brown County.* 1936. Garden City. 86 pp. dj. $7.50

DOVER, Cedric. *American Negro Art.* 1969. London. Crown. Ills. dj. EX $15.00

DOW, Geo. & Robinson, John. *The Sailing Ships of New England 1607-1907.* 1953. Westminster. 1st ed. dj. $12.50

DOW, George F. *Diary & Letters of Benjamin Pickman of Salem.* 1928. Newport. Wayside Press. Ltd. ed. 1/125. $100.00

DOWDEN, Edward. *A Woman's Relquary.* 1913. Cuala Press. Ltd. 1st ed. 1/300. 59 pp. $52.50

DOWDEY, Clifford. *Bugles Blow No More.* 1967. Dunwoody. 3rd ed. ex-lib. 497 pp. dj. $75.00

DOWDING, Geoffrey. *An Introduction to the History of Printing Types.* 1961. Clerkenwell. Wace & Co. ex-lib. 277 pp. dj. $10.00

DOWLING, Lela. *The Fantasy Art of Lela Dowling.* 1979. 1st ed. dj. wrappers. EX $15.00

DOWLING, Tom. *Coach, a Season with Lombardi.* 1970. New York. Norton. 333 pp. dj. $4.00

DOWNES, William. *John S. Sagent, His Life & Work.* 1925. 1st ed. ex-lib. G $12.50

DOWNEY, Fairfax. *Richard Harding Davis.* 1933. New York. Scribner. Ills. 322 pp. $10.00

DOWNEY, Fairfax. *The Grande Turke.* 1929. New York. 333 pp. 9 pls. index. $12.50

DOWNEY, Fairfax. *The Guns at Gettysburg.* 1958. New York. Ills. 1st ed. 290 pp. dj. VG $25.00

DOWNING, A.F. & Scully, V.J. *Architectural Heritage of Newport, R.I. 1640-1915.* 1952. Cambridge. 1st ed. photos. dj. $75.00

DOWNING, A.J. *Cottage Residences, North America.* 1860. New York. Wiley. 4th ed. G $80.00

DOWNING, A.J. *The Fruit & Fruit Trees of America.* 1892. Wiley & Sons. $45.00

DOWNING, A.J. *Treatise on Theory & Practice of Landscape Garden.* 1859. New York. Ills. 6th ed. 570 pp. $75.00

DOWNING, E.R. *A Naturalist in the Great Lakes Region.* 1922. Chicago. Ills. maps. 328 pp. EX $17.50

DOWNING, Elliot R. *Elementary Euenics.* 1928. Chicago. U. of Chicago Press. 137 pp. $2.50

DOWNS, E.C. *Four Years a Scout & Spy.* 1866. Zanesville, OH.rebound. VG $60.00

DOWNS, J. *American Furniture-Queen Anne & Chippendale.* 1952. New York. Ills. dj. EX $65.00

DOWSON, Ernest, trans. *The Story of Beauty & the Beast.* 1908. London. Ills. Charles Condor. folio. $75.00

DOYLE, Adrian Conan. *Heaven Has Claws.* 1953. New York. 1st ed. dj. VG $20.00

DOYLE, Arthur Conan. *A Desert Drama.* 1898. Lippincott. Ills. Paget. 1st Am. ed. VG $45.00

DOYLE, Arthur Conan. *A Treasury of Sherlock Holmes.* 1955. New York. Hanover House. 686 pp. $3.50

DOYLE, Arthur Conan. *Cases of Sherlock Holmes.* 1947. St Louis. 118 pp. 4 stories. $3.00

DOYLE, Arthur Conan. *Danger & Other Stories.* 1919. New York. 1st ed. G $25.00

DOYLE, Arthur Conan. *Jack the Giant Killer.* 1888. London. 1st ed. VG $200.00

DOYLE, Arthur Conan. *Memorial Edition Complete Sherlock Holmes.* 1930. Doubleday. 2 vol set. $25.00

DOYLE, Arthur Conan. *Micah Clarke. His Statement.* 1889. London. Longman Green. 1st ed. 421 pp. $75.00

DOYLE, Arthur Conan. *Micah Clarke. His Statement.* 1929. New York. Ills. Henry Pitz. EX $20.00

DOYLE, Arthur Conan. *Songs of Action.* 1898. New York. 1st Am. ed. 144 pp. VG $22.50

DOYLE, Arthur Conan. *Strange Secrets.* 1895. New York. Fenno. 1st ed. dj. VG $20.00

DOYLE, Arthur Conan. *The Adventures of Gerard.* 1903. New York. Ills. 1st ed. VG $45.00

DOYLE, Arthur Conan. *The Case for Spirit Photography.* 1923. New York. Doran. Ills. 1st ed. 134 pp. $95.00

DOYLE, Arthur Conan. *The Casebook of Sherlock Holmes.* 1927. London. rebound. VG $250.00

DOYLE, Arthur Conan. *The Hound of the Baskervilles.* 1902. New York. 1st Am. ed. G $60.00

DOYLE, Arthur Conan. *The Parasite.* 1895. New York. Harper. Ills. Pyle. 1st ed. EX $65.00

DOYLE, Arthur Conan. *The Return of Sherlock Holmes.* 1905. New York. 1st Am. ed. G $120.00

DOYLE, Arthur Conan. *The Sign of the Four.* New York. Eureka Detective Series. #19. $15.00

DOYLE, Arthur Conan. *The Sign of the Four.* 1890. Lippincott. VG $700.00

DOYLE, Arthur Conan. *The Stark Munro Letters.* 1895. London. 1st ed. VG $55.00

DOYLE, Arthur Conan. *The Valley of Fear.* 1914. New York. 1st Am. ed. G $22.50

DOYLE, Arthur Conan. *The White Company.* 1922. New York. Ills. Wyeth. 1st ed. $100.00

DOYLE, Arthur Conan. *Three of Them.* 1923. London. Murray. 1st ed. dj. EX $135.00

DOYLE, Arthur Conan. *Vital Message.* 1919. New York. 1st Am. ed. 164 pp. $22.50

DOYLE, J.A. *English Colonies in America.* 1889. New York. 5 vol set. $100.00

DRABBLE, Margaret. *Arnold Bennett.* 1974. New York. Knopf. 397 pp. $5.00

DRABBLE, Margaret. *The Ice Age.* 1977. Weidenfeld. 1st ed. dj. VG $25.00

DRABBLE, Margaret. *The Middle Ground.* 1980. New York. 1st ed. dj. EX $8.50

DRACOPOLI, I. *Through Jubaland to the Lorian Swamp.* 1914. London. 2nd ed. VG $67.50

DRADE, Samuel Adams. *Pine Tree Coast.* 1891. Boston. VG $25.00

DRAGO, Harry. *Buckskin Meadows.* Pocketbooks. pb. $3.00

DRAGO, Harry. *Wild, Wooly & Wicked.* 1960. Bramhall. dj. VG $10.00

DRAGOO, Don W. *Mounds for the Dead: Analysis of Adena Culture.* Pittsburgh. Ills. 315 pp. VG $17.50

DRAKE, Benjamin. *Life & Adventures of Black Hawk.* 1847. Cincinnati. $25.00

DRAKE, Benjamin. *Life of Tecumseh & His Brother the Prophet.* 1856. Cincinnati. Rulison. Ills. G $30.00

DRAKE, Francis. *Indian History for the Young Folks.* 1884. Harper. Ills. 1st ed. VG $15.00

DRAKE, S.A. *Nooks & Corners of the New England Coast.* 1875. New York. Ills. 1st ed. $25.00

DRAKE, S.A. *The Myths & Fables of Today.* 1900. Boston. 1st ed. G $20.00

DRAKE, St. Clair & Cayton, H. *Black Metropolis.* 1945. New York. ex-lib. 807 pp. $5.00

DRAKE. *The Boy Allies with the Flying Squadron.* 1915. A.L. Burt. VG $5.50

DRAKE. *Vertical Warfare.* 1943. New York. dj. $15.00

DRALICE. *Pioneer Life in Kentucky.* 1948. New York. Ills. dj. $12.00

DRANNAN, W.F. *Chief of Scouts Piloting Emigrants Across Plains.* 1910. Chicago. 1st ed. 407 pp. $25.00

DRANNAN, W.F. *Thirty-One Years on the Plains & Mountains.* 1914. Chicago. Ills. 586 pp. $16.50

DRAPER, Muriel. *Music at Midnight.* 1929. New York. Harper. Ills. 237 pp. $10.00

DRAPER, Thomas. *The 84th Division in Battle of Germany.* 1946. New York. 1st ed. dj. slipcase. VG $30.00

DRAPER, W.F. *Recollections of a Varied Career.* 1908. Ills. 412 pp. $13.50

DREER, Henry A. *Dreer's Garden Book 1929.* 1929. Philadelphia. 224 pp. $15.00

DREIFUSS, J. *Furlough from Heaven.* 1946. 1st ed. dj. EX $10.00

DREISER, Theodore. *A Gallery of Women.* 1929. Liveright. 1st ed. 2 vol set. dj. boxed. $30.00

DREISER, Theodore. *A Traveler at Forty.* 1914. New York. 526 pp. $15.00

DREISER, Theodore. *An American Tragedy.* 1925. New York. 1st ed. 2 vol set. VG $25.00

DREISER, Theodore. *Bulwark.* 1946. Doubleday. 1st ed. dj. VG $12.50

DREISER, Theodore. *Chains.* 1927. New York. 1st trade ed. dj. VG $45.00

DREISER, Theodore. *Dawn. A History of Myself.* 1931. London. 1st Eng. ed. 623 pp. $15.00

DREISER, Theodore. *Dreiser Looks at Russia.* 1928. New York. Liveright. 1st ed. 264 pp. $12.50

DREISER, Theodore. *Jennie Gerhardt.* 1911. Harper. 1st ed. $15.00

DREISER, Theodore. *Moods.* 1935. Simon & Schuster. 1st ed. dj. $20.00

DREISER, Theodore. *The Financier.* 1912. Harper. 1st ed. $20.00

DREISER, Theodore. *The Genius.* 1915. John Lane. 1st ed. $20.00

DREISER, Theodore. *The Titan.* 1914. NY/London. Lane. 1st ed. 552 pp. $15.00

DREISER, Theodore. *The Titan.* 1935. Simon & Schuster. 1st ed. $15.00

DREPPERD, C.W. *ABC's of Old Glass.* 1949. Garden City. Ills. 1st ed. $15.00

DREPPERD, C.W. *First Reader for Antique Collectors.* 1946. Garden City. $7.50

DREPPERD, C.W. *Handbook of Antique Chairs.* 1948. Garden City. $10.00

DRIER & DUTEMPLE. *Prehistoric Copper Mining in Lake Superior Region.* private printed. EX $8.00

DRIGGS, Howard. *Rise of Lone Star.* Ills. Deming. 1st ed. VG $25.00

DRIGGS, Howard. *The Old West Speaks.* 1956. New Jersey. Ills. $9.00

DRIMMER, Frederick. *Very Special People.* 1973. New York. Amjon. 411 pp. dj. $37.50

DRINKER, Cecil K. *The Clinical Physiology of Lungs.* 1954. Springfield. 1st ed. 84 pp. $95.00

DRINKWATER, J. *A Book for Bookmen.* 1927. New York. 284 pp. dj. EX $15.00

DRINKWATER, John. *Abraham Lincoln. A Play.* 1919. Boston. 112 pp. $85.00

DRINKWATER, John. *Discovery Being the Second Book of Autobiography.* 1933. Boston. Houghton Mifflin. ex-lib. G $4.50

DRISCOLL, Charles. *The Life of O.O. McIntyre.* 1938. New York. inscr. 344 pp. $125.00

DRISCOLL, J. *War Discovers Alaska.* 1943. Philadelphia. 1st ed. VG $10.00

DRISCOLL, James R. *The Brighton Boys with the Flying Corps.* 1918. Philadelphia. 233 pp. $2.50

DRISKELL. *Two Centuries of Black American Art.* 1976. Los Angeles Museum. 1st ed. EX $15.00

DRIVER. *Cape-Scapes.* 1930. Boston. $6.50

DROWN, Merle. *Plowing Up a Snake.* 1982. New York. Dial Press. 1st ed. dj. EX $10.00

DROZ. *Monsieur, Madame, & Bebe.* 1910. Current Lit. Pub. VG $7.50

DRUAN-REYNALS, M.L. *The Fever Bark Tree: Pageant of Quinine.* 1946. Doubleday. 1st ed. VG $10.00

DRUMMOND, Henry. *Tropical Africa.* 1889. New York. 1st Am. ed. fld maps. VG $25.00

DRUMMOND, Henry. *Tropical Africa.* 1890. Alden. Ills. VG $17.50

DRURY, Allen. *A Shade of Difference.* 1962. New York. Doubleday. 677 pp. dj. EX $3.50

DRURY, John. *The Heritage of Early American Houses.* 1969. New York. Coward. Ills. 298 pp. dj. $17.50

DRURY, S. *Native Birds of Australia.* 1981. Macmillan. Ills. 120 pp. dj. EX $10.00

DRYDEN, Cecil Pear. *Mr. Hunt & the Fabulous Plan.* 1958. Caldwell. Ills. Driessen. 1st ed. dj. VG $12.50

DRYDEN, John. *The Poetical Works of Dryden.* 1855. Edinburgh. VG $25.00

DRYDEN, Ken. *Face-Off at the Summit.* 1973. Boston. Ills. 209 pp. dj. EX $10.00

DRYDEN, Ken. *Let's Play Better Hockey.* 1973. Prosport Productions. 56 pp. $5.00

DRYDEN, Ken. *The Game.* 1983. Toronto. Macmillan. 248 pp. dj. EX $10.00

DRYFHOUT, John & Fox, Beverly. *Agustus Saint-Gaudens: The Portrait Reliefs.* 1969. VG $10.00

DRYFUS, John. *A History of the Nonesuch Press.* 1981. London. Nonesuch Press. Ltd. ed. VG $150.00

DU BIN, Alexander. *Old Philadelphia & Old New York Families.* 1948. Philadelphia. VG $25.00

DU BOIS, F. *Timbuctoo the Mysterious.* 1879. London. VG $45.00

DU BOIS, Theodora. *Solution T-25.* 1951. New York. Doubleday. 1st ed. dj. VG $10.00

DU BOIS, W.E.B. *Darkwater.* 1920. New York. Harcourt. 1st ed. dj. EX $45.00

DU BOIS. *Color & Democracy.* 1945. 1st ed. dj. VG $15.00

DU BOIS. *Gift of Black Folk.* 1924. Boston. 1st ed. $15.00

DU CANE, Florence. *The Flowers & Gardens of Japan.* 1908. A. & C. Black. 249 pp. 50 color pls. $40.00

DU CHAILLU, P. *A Journey to Ashango-Land.* 1867. New York. VG $65.00

DU CHAILLU, P. *Explorations & Adventures in Equatorial Africa.* 1871. Harper. Ills. revised ed. 535 pp. VG $85.00

DU CHAILLU, P. *My Apingi Kingdom.* 1912. Harper. Ills. 254 pp. VG $20.00

DU CHAILLU, P. *Stories of the Gorilla Country.* 1867. Ills. 292 pp. VG $22.50

DU CHAILLU, P. *The Land of the Long Night.* 1901. New York. VG $15.00

DU CHAILLU, P. *The Viking Age.* 1889. Scribner. 2 vol set. w/all gilt intact. $75.00

DU MAURIER, Daphne. *Frenchman's Creek.* 1942. Garden City. $10.00

DU MAURIER, Daphne. *Frenchman's Creek.* 1942. New York. Doubleday Doran. 1st ed. $52.50

DU MAURIER, Daphne. *Hungry Hill.* 1947. Philadelphia. 344 pp. dj. VG $3.00

DU MAURIER, Daphne. *Mary Anne.* London. 1st Eng. ed. dj. VG $20.00

DU MAURIER, Daphne. *My Cousin Rachel.* 1942. New York. Doubleday. 288 pp. EX $3.50

DU MAURIER, Daphne. *Rebecca.* 1938. London. Gollancz. 1st ed. VG $45.00

DU MAURIER, Daphne. *The Apple Tree.* 1952. London. 1st ed. dj. VG $30.00

DU MAURIER, Daphne. *The Flight of the Falcon.* 1965. New York. Doubleday. 253 pp. $3.50

DU MAURIER, Daphne. *The Holly-Tree Inn.* London. Hodder & Stoughton. 40 pp. EX $5.00

DU MAURIER, Daphne. *The Parasites.* 1950. dj. $8.50

DU MAURIER, Daphne. *The Scapegoat.* 1957. New York. 1st ed. dj. VG $7.00

DU MAURIER, Daphne. *Three Romantic Novels of Cornwall.* 1942. New York. Doubleday. dj. $4.00

DU MAURIER, George. *Peter Ibbetson.* 1892. London. Ills. slipcase. VG $27.50

DU MAURIER, George. *Society Pictures by George du Maurier.* London. folio. $25.00

DU PONT. *The Autobiography of an American Enterprise.* 1952. Scribner. dj. VG $11.00

DUANE, William. *Two Americas, Great Britain & the Holy Alliance.* 1824. Washington. 1st ed. 37 pp. $45.00

DUBELLE, G. *Soda Fountain Beverages.* 1911. New York. 4th ed. 161 pp. G $12.50

DUBUS, Andre. *The Lieutenant.* 1967. New York. Dial Press. 1st ed. VG $65.00

DUDLEY, Carrie. *My Peek-A-Boo Show Book.* 1928. Volland Press. Ills. 1st ed. VG $75.00

DUDLEY, Darle W. *The Evolution of Gear Art.* 1969. Am. Gear Mfgs. Assoc. EX $15.00

DUDLEY, E. *Rufus.* 1972. Hart. Ills. 1st Am. ed. 124 pp. dj. $6.00

DUERRENMATT, Friedrich. *The Quarry.* 1962. New York. Greenwich. 1st ed. dj. EX $12.50

DUFF, H. *Nyasaland Under the Foreign Office.* 1903. London. VG $42.50

DUFF, Wilson. *Indians History of British Columbia.* 1969. Victoria. 2nd ed. stiff wrappers. $8.50

DUFFEY, E.B. *What Women Should Know.* 1873. Chicago. VG $20.00

DUFFIELD, K.G. *Four Little Pigs that Didn't Have any Mother.* 1919. Philadelphia. Altemus. Ills. 1st ed. VG $10.00

DUFFUS, R.L. *The Santa Fe Trail.* 1930. New York. 1st ed. ex-lib. G $12.50

DUFFUS, R.L. *The Santa Fe Trail.* 1930. New York. Ills. 1st ed. EX $35.00

DUFFUS, R.L. *The Santa Fe Trail.* 1934. Tudor Pub. Ills. VG $25.00

DUFFUS, R.L. *Waterbury Record.* 1959. 1st ed. dj. VG $10.00

DUFFY, James. *Shipwreck & Empire.* 1955. Harvard. 1st ed. dj. $8.50

DUFFY, Mrs. E.B. *Blue Book Etiquette for Ladies & Gentlemen.* 1911. Winston. VG $12.50

DUFRESNE, F. *No Room for Bears.* 1965. Holt/Winston. Ills. 252 pp. EX $10.00

DUGAN, J. *The Great Iron Ship. Story of the Great Eastern.* 1953. Harper. Ills. 272 pp. G $7.00

DUGAN, J. *World Beneath the Sea.* 1967. Nat. Geog. Soc.Ills. fld map. 204 pp. dj. EX $7.50

DUGAN & STEWART. *Ploesti.* 1962. 1st ed. dj. EX $45.00

DUGGER, S. *Balsam Broves of the Grandfather Mountain.* 1907. Banner Elk. Dugger. 300 pp. 21 pls. $25.00

DUGMORE, A.R. *Camera Adventures in the African Wilds.* 1910. New York. VG $45.00

DUGMORE, A.R. *Wildlife & the Camera.* 1912. Heinemann. Ills. 1st ed. 332 pp. VG $20.00

DUJCEV, Ivan. *The Miniatures of the Chronicle of Manasse.* 1963. Ltd ed. 1/1000. 70 pls. VG $32.00

DUKE, Donald. *Southern Pacific Steam Locomotives.* 1978. dj. EX $6.00

DUKE, Madeline. *Death of a Holy Murderer.* 1975. London. Joseph. 1st ed. dj. EX $15.00

DUKORE, Margaret Mitchell. *A Novel Called Heritage.* 1982. Scribner. 1st ed. dj. VG $12.50

DULAC, Edmond. *Daughters of the Stars.* 1939. London. Ills. Ltd. 1st ed. sgn. $135.00

DULAC, Edmond. *Green Lacquer Pavillion.* 1926. Doran. 10 Ills. 1st ed. dj. $20.00

DULAC, Edmond. *Marriage of Cupid & Psyche.* 1951. Heritage House. 6 pls. boxed. $18.00

DULAC, Edmond. *Princess Badoura.* Hodder & Stoughton. 10 pls. $175.00

DULAC, Edmond. *Sinbad the Sailor.* Hodder & Stoughton. 23 pls. VG $325.00

DULAC, Edmond. *The Bells.* no date. 28 pls. VG $95.00

DULAC, Edmund. *A Fairy Garland.* 1928. London. Ltd. ed. sgn. 12 color pls. VG $150.00

DULAC, Edmund. *Golden Cockerel from Pushkin's Tale.* Heritage Press. Ills. folio. $25.00

DULAC, Edmund. *Rubaiyat of Omar Khayyam.* Doran. (ca.1920) Ills. G $15.00

DULAC, Edmund. *Rubaiyat of Omar Khayyam.* London. Hodder & Stoughton. EX $60.00

DULAC, Edmund. *The Sleeping Beauty & Other Fairy Tales.* New York. Hodder & Stoughton. VG $45.00

DULAC, Edmund. *Treasure Island.* New York. Garden City. 8 pp. Ills. VG $12.50

DULLES, Eleanor. *Chances of a Lifetime.* 1st ed. $12.50

DULLES, Foster R. *Labor in America: a History.* 1950. 3rd ed. dj. VG $10.00

DUMAS, Alexandre. *Camille.* Hurst. 151 pp. $3.00

DUMAS, Alexandre. *The Count of Monte Cristo.* New York. no date. Ills. Schaeffer. VG $25.00

DUMAS, Alexandre. *The Count of Monte Cristo.* 1946. New York. McGraw Hill. 1365 pp. EX $7.50

DUMAS, Alexandre. *The Crusaders. A Sequel to the Duke of Burgundy.* 1846. New York. Graham. 35 pp. wrappers. $35.00

DUMAS, Alexandre. *The Man in the Iron Mask.* 1965. New York. Ills. Legrand. Ltd. ed. $35.00

DUMAS, Alexandre. *The Three Musketeers.* Lupton. no date. $2.00

DUMAS, Alexandre. *The Three Musketeers.* 1923. Rand McNally. Ills. Milo Winter. 547 pp. EX $10.50

DUMAS, Alexandre. *The Three Musketeers.* 1952. Doubleday. Ills. Rasmussen. VG $8.00

DUMAS, Alexandre. *Twenty Years After.* 1958. NY. Ills. Legrand. Ltd. ed. $35.00

DUMONT, Frank. *Burnt Cork; or, the Amateur Minstrel.* 1881. New York. Ills. 114 pp. wrappers. EX $15.00

DUNATHAN, Clint. *As Years Pass By . . . The Century Book 1863-1963.* 1963. Escanaba. ex-lib. 240 pp. dj. $10.00

DUNBAR, Charles S. *Buses, Trolley & Trams.* 1967. London. Ills. 1st ed. dj. VG $10.00

DUNBAR, Paul Lawrence. *In Old Plantation Days.* 1903. New York. 1st ed. VG $65.00

DUNBAR, Paul Lawrence. *Poems of Cabin & Field.* 1896. $37.50

DUNBAR, Seymour. *History of Travel in America.* 1937. New York. Ills. maps. 1530 pp. dj. $15.00

DUNBAR. *Candle Lightin' Time.* 1901. New York. 1st ed. $37.50

DUNCAN, D.D. *I Protest.* 1968. New York. 1st ed. wrappers. EX $35.00

DUNCAN, D.D. *Occam's Razor.* 1957. Ballantine. pb. VG $8.50

DUNCAN, D.D. *Picasso's Picassos.* 1961. New York. Ills. dj. VG $60.00

DUNCAN, D.D. *Self-Portrait: U.S.A.* 1969. New York. 1st ed. dj. EX $32.50

DUNCAN, D.D. *Silent Studio.* 1976. New York. 1st Am. ed. dj. EX $22.50

DUNCAN, D.D. *The Madrone Tree.* 1949. New York. Macmillan. 1st ed. dj. $20.00

DUNCAN, D.D. *This is War!* 1967. New York. Bantam. 1st ed. pb. EX $9.50

DUNCAN, D.D. *This is War!* 1951. New York. 1st ed. dj. EX $25.00

DUNCAN, D.D. *War Without Heroes.* 1970. New York. 1st ed. VG $110.00

DUNCAN, D.D. *Yankee Nomad.* 1966. New York. 1st ed. dj. EX $27.50

DUNCAN, Frances. *Mary's Garden & How It Grew.* 1917. New York. Century. Ills. Zeigler. VG $25.00

DUNCAN, John M. *A Sabbath Among the Tuscarora Indians.* 1819. Glasgow. Ills. 1st ed. VG $125.00

DUNCAN, John M. *Travels Through Part of U.S. & Canada in 1818-19.* 1823. Glasgow. 1st ed. 14 sm. maps. 2 vol set. $275.00

DUNCAN, Norman. *The Suitable Child.* 1909. New York. Ills. E. S. Creen & J. Turner. $40.00

DUNCAN, T.W. *Big River, Big Man.* 1959. Philadelphia. dj. $10.00

DUNCAN, William J. *R.M.S. Queen Mary.* 1969. Anderson. 1st ed. inscr. photos. dj. EX $15.00

DUNDAS, L. *Big Game Pocket-Book for Kenya Colony.* 1927. VG $45.00

DUNHAM, Curtis. *Dancing with Helen Moller.* 1928. NY/London. 115 pp. 43 photos. G $20.00

DUNHAM, Curtis. *The Golden Goblin.* 1906. Indianapolis. Ills. George F. Kerr. $14.00

DUNHAM, Jacob. *Journal of Voyages.* 1856. New York. Ills. 1st ed. 243 pp. $185.00

DUNHILL, Alfred. *The Pipe Book.* 1924. NY/London. Ills. VG $32.50

DUNIWAY, Clyde A. *Development of Freedom of Press in Massachusetts.* 1969. New York. reprint. 202 pp. $20.00

DUNLAP, Roy F. *Gunsmithing.* 1950. 1st ed. 714 pp. $25.00

DUNLOP, R. *Behind Japanese Lines. With O.S.S. in Burma, WWII.* 1979. Book Club ed. dj. VG $12.00

DUNN, J.P. *Massacres of the Mountains.* 1886. New York. Ills. 1st ed. 784 pp. maps. VG $67.50

DUNN, James. *The St. Croix.* 1965. New York. 1st ed. inscr. dj. $25.00

DUNN, Robert L. *William H. Taft, American.* 1908. Boston. $10.00

DUNNE, John Gregory. *Dutch Shea, Jr.* 1982. Linden. 1st ed. sgn. dj. VG $30.00

DUNNE, John Gregory. *True Confessions.* 1977. Dutton. 1st ed. dj. VG $15.00

DUNNETT, D. *Queen's Play.* 1964. Putnam. 1st ed. dj. VG $25.00

DUNNING, A.E. *Congregationalists in America.* 1894. Hill. Ills. VG $20.00

DUNNINGER, Joseph. *Dunninger's Monument to Magic.* 1974. Secaucus. dj. VG $7.50

DUNSANY, Lord. *Alexander & 3 Small Plays.* 1925. Putnam. Ltd. ed. 1/250. VG $25.00

DUNSANY, Lord. *Don Rodriguez.* 1922. New York. Putnam. 1st Am. ed. VG $12.50

DUNSANY, Lord. *Fifty Poems.* 1929. London. 1st ed. VG $20.00

DUNSANY, Lord. *Five Plays.* 1914. Grant Richards. 1st ed. VG $20.00

DUNSANY, Lord. *His Fellow Men.* 1952. London. 1st ed. sgn. EX $50.00

DUNSANY, Lord. *If I Were Dictator.* 1934. London. 1st ed. $15.00

DUNSANY, Lord. *If.* 1921. Putnam. VG $17.00

DUNSANY, Lord. *Jorkens Borrows Another Whiskey.* 1954. London. 1st ed. dj. VG $15.00

DUNSANY, Lord. *Jorkens Remembers Africa.* 1934. 1st ed. dj. $45.00

DUNSANY, Lord. *Little Tales of Smethers & Other Stories.* 1952. London. 1st ed. dj. VG $15.00

DUNSANY, Lord. *Plays of Gods & Men.* 1917. Fisher. 1st ed. VG $25.00

DUNSANY, Lord. *Rory & Bran.* 1937. New York. 1st ed. dj. scarce $30.00

DUNSANY, Lord. *Sword of Welleran & Other Tales of Enchantment.* 1954. New York. Devin Adair. 1st ed. sgn. dj. $30.00

DUNSANY, Lord. *Tales of War.* 1918. 1st Am. ed. G $12.50

DUNSANY, Lord. *The Blessing of Pan.* 1927. London. 1st ed. inscr. VG $50.00

DUNSANY, Lord. *The Book of Wonder.* 1912. London. Ills. Dunsany. $25.00

DUNSANY, Lord. *The Book of Wonder.* 1930. Boston. Luce. Ills. 1st ed. VG $32.50

DUNSANY, Lord. *The Fourth Book of Jorkens.* 1948. Sauk City. Arkham House. dj. $75.00

DUNSANY, Lord. *The Last Book of Wonder.* 1916. Boston. Luce. 1st Am. ed. dj. EX $35.00

DUNSANY, Lord. *The Last Revolution.* 1951. London. 1st ed. sgn. dj. EX $45.00

DUNSANY, Lord. *The Sirens Wake.* 1946. London. 2nd ed. dj. EX $15.00

DUNSANY, Lord. *The Strange Journey of Colonel Polders.* 1950. London. 1st ed. dj. VG $15.00

DUNSANY, Lord. *Time & the Gods.* Heineman. Ills. Dunsany. $25.00

DUNSANY, Lord. *While the Sirens Slept.* 1944. London. Jarrolds. 1st ed. VG $12.50

DUNSHEE, K.H. *As You Pass By.* 1952. New York. Ills. 278 pp. $20.00

DUNTHORNE, Gordon. *Flower-Fruit Prints of 18th & Early 19th Cent.* 1938. Washington. Ills. Deluxe ed. boxed. EX $750.00

DUNTON, S. *Hold That Tiger!* 1957. Greenburg. Ills. 188 pp. dj. EX $6.00

DUPANLOUP, Monseigneur. *A Study of Freemasonry.* 1866. New York. Sadlier. 1st ed. 155 pp. VG $17.50

DUPEE, F.W. *Question of Henry James.* 1945. New York. 1st ed. dj. EX $25.00

DUPLAIX, George. *Popo the Hippopotamus.* 1935. Winston. 28 pp. G $3.50

DUPLAIX, N. & Simon, N. *World Guide to Mammals.* 1983. Greenwich. Ills. 1st ed. 283 pp. dj. EX $15.00

DUPREE, Louis. *Shamshir Ghar: Historic Cave Sites in Kandahar.* 1958. Am. Mus. Nat. Hist. 1st ed. $15.00

DURANG, Mary. *Rich & Poor: History of Virginia & Susan.* 1847. Philadelphia. $45.00

DURANT, John & Alice. *Pictorial History of American Presidents.* 1955. New York. 327 pp. $4.50

DURANT, John & Alice. *Pictorial History of American Ships.* 1953. 312 pp. dj. VG $4.00

DURANT, John & Alice. *The Presidents of the United States.* 1966. Gache, NY. Commemorative ed. 2 vol set. $125.00

DURANT, John & Bettmann, Otto. *Pictorial History of American Sports.* 1952. Barnes. 279 pp. $75.00

DURANT, W.C. *Law Observance.* 1929. New York. 563 pp. $7.50

DURANT, Will & Ariel. *The Lessons of History.* New York. (ca.1968) 1st ed. inscr. dj. $25.00

DURAS, Marguerite. *The Ravishing of Lol Stein.* 1966. New York. Grove Press. dj. EX $25.00

DURAS, Marguerite. *10:30 on a Summer Night.* 1962. New York. Grove Press. 1st ed. dj. EX $30.00

DURDEN, Kent. *A Fine & Peaceful Kingdom.* 1975. Simon & Schuster. 1st ed. dj. $7.50

DURHAM, David. *The Pearl-Headed Pin.* 1925. London. Hodder & Stoughton. 1st ed. $55.00

DURHAM, Marilyn. *Dutch Uncle.* 1973. Harcourt. 1st ed. dj. VG $15.00

DURHAM, Marilyn. *The Man Who Loved Cat Dancing.* 1972. Harcourt. 1st ed. dj. $20.00

DURHAM, Victor G. *The Submarine Boys & the Middies.* 1909. Saalfield. dj. EX $7.50

DURHAM, Victor G. *The Submarine Boys & the Trail Trip.* 1909. Saalfield. Ills. $4.00

DURHAM, Victor G. *The Submarine Boys on Duty.* 1909. Altemus Co. Ills. 253 pp. G $4.50

DURICK, Agnes York. *Father Bear.* 1932. Harter Pub. Ills. 12 pp. $7.00

DURKIN, Barbara Wernecke. *Oh, You Dundalk Girls, Can't You Dance the Polka?* 1984. Morrow. 1st ed. dj. VG $15.00

DUROCHER, Leo w/Linn, Ed. *Nice Guys Finish Last.* 1975. New York. Simon & Schuster. 375 pp. $5.00

DURR, Eleanor. *Lakeside Ohio: First 100 Years.* 1973. New York. 230 pp. dj. VG $10.00

DURRELL, G. *Golden Bats & Pink Pigeons.* 1977. Ills. 1st ed. 190 pp. dj. EX $10.00

DURRELL, G. *The Donkey Rustlers.* 1968. London. 1st ed. dj. EX $15.00

DURRELL, G. *The Mockery Bird.* 1981. London. 1st ed. dj. $15.00

DURRELL, G. *The Overloaded Ark.* 1963. Viking. Ills. 180 pp. dj. $6.00

DURRELL, G. *The Whispering Land.* 1962. Viking. Ills. 1st ed. 235 pp. dj. EX $10.00

DURRELL, Lawrence. *The Henry Miller Reader.* 1959. New Directions. 397 pp. $5.00

DURRELL, Lawrence & Perles, A. *Art & Outrage, Correspondence About Henry Miller.* 1959. London. dj. EX $25.00

DURRELL, Lawrence. *A Smile in the Mind's Eye.* 1982. New York. Universe. 1st ed. dj. EX $20.00

DURRELL, Lawrence. *Collected Poems.* 1960. New York. Dutton. 1st ed. 288 pp. dj. $12.50

DURRELL, Lawrence. *Constance.* 1982. New York. Viking. 1st ed. dj. VG $20.00

DURRELL, Lawrence. *Monsieur.* 1975. New York. Viking. 1st ed. dj. VG $25.00

DURRELL, Lawrence. *Mount-Olive.* 1958. London. 1st ed. dj. VG $50.00

DURRELL, Lawrence. *Mount-Olive.* 1959. New York. Dutton. 1st ed. dj. VG $35.00

DURRELL, Lawrence. *Nun Quam.* 1970. New York. Dutton. 1st ed. dj. VG $45.00

DURRELL, Lawrence. *On Seeming to Presume.* 1948. Faber. 1st ed. dj. VG $40.00

DURRELL, Lawrence. *Pope Joan.* 1960. New York. Overlook. 1st ed. dj. VG $25.00

DURRELL, Lawrence. *Quinx.* London. 1st ed. sgn. $35.00

DURRELL, Lawrence. *Sauve Qui Peut.* 1967. New York. Dutton. $4.00

DURRELL, Lawrence. *Sauve Qui Peut.* 1966. London. Ills. Nicolas Bentley. 1st ed. $9.00

DURRELL, Lawrence. *Sebastian.* 1983. Viking. 1st Am. ed. dj. VG $15.00

DURRELL, Lawrence. *Sicilian Carousel.* 1977. Viking. 1st Am. ed. dj. VG $15.00

DURRELL, Lawrence. *The Alexandria Quartet.* 1960. London. Faber. 1st 1 vol ed. dj. VG $85.00

DURRELL, Lawrence. *Tunc.* 1968. New York. Dutton. 1st ed. dj. VG $45.00

DURRELL, Lawrence. *White Eagles over Serbia.* 1957. London. Faber. 1st ed. sgn. dj. VG $95.00

DURSTON, George. *The Boy Scout's Victory.* 1921. Akron, OH. VG $2.50

DURSTON, George. *The Boy Scouts on the Trail.* 1921. Saalfield. dj. EX $6.50

DURSTON, George. *The Boy Scouts' Champion Recruit.* 1912. New York. 172 pp. $2.50

DURUY, Victor. *History of Rome & of the Roman People.* 1884-85. Estes & Lauriat. 8 vol set. $200.00

DUTORD, Jean. *The Taxis of the Marne.* 1957. London. 1st ed. dj. $10.00

DUTOURD, Jean. *A Dog's Head.* 1953. New York. Simon & Schuster. 1st Am. ed. $15.00

DUVAL, G.R. *R.A.F. Fighters of 1918-1937; Pictorial History.* 1975. London. D. Bradford Barton. $12.50

DUVERGIER DE HAURANNE, Ernest. *A Frenchman in Lincoln's America, 1864-1865.* 1975. Chicago. Ills. 2 vol set. $8.50

DUVOISIN, Roger. *Donkey-Donkey.* 1940. New York. dj. EX $10.00

DUVOISIN, Roger. *They Put Out to Sea.* 1943. New York. Knopf. Ills. 1st ed. $20.00

DUYCKINCK, Evert. *National Portrait Gallery of Americans.* New York. (ca. 1870). 151 engravings. EX $175.00

DUYCKINCK & CORNELL. *The Duyckinck & Allied Families.* 1908. New York. Ltd. ed. VG $11.00

DUYCKINCK. *National Portrait Gallery of Eminent Americans.* 1862. 1st ed. 2 vol set. VG $75.00

DWIGGINS, W.A. *Millenium I.* 1945. New York. 1st ed. dj. VG $15.00

DWIGHT, Benjamin. *Modern Philology-Discoveries, History, Influence.* 1860. New York. Ills. index. VG $20.00

DWIGHT, Theodore. *History of the Hartford Convention.* 1933. New York. G $35.00

DWIGHT, Wilder. *Life & Letters of Wilder Dwight.* 1891. Boston. 2nd ed. $22.50

DWINELLE, William H. *The Casket & the Ribbon; or, The Honors of Ether.* 1849. Baltimore. 28 pp. wrappers. $100.00

DWYER, Pat. *Tales from the Gangway.* 1923. Cleveland. Ills. 1st ed. 450 pp. $12.50

DYAN, Y. *Israel Journal, June 1967.* 1967. Ills. VG $10.00

DYBEK, Stuart. *Childhood & Other Neighborhoods.* 1980. Viking Press. 1st ed. dj. VG $15.00

DYE, Charity. *The James Whitcomb Riley Reader.* 1915. Indianapolis. Ills. ex-lib. 116 pp. G $2.50

DYE, Eva Emery. *McDonald of Oregon.* 1906. Chicago. 1st ed. $12.50

DYE, W. *Moslem Egypt & Christian Abyssinia.* 1880. New York. VG $65.00

DYER. *Textile Fabrics.* 1923. Houghton Mifflin. 352 pp. $4.50

DYKE, A.L. *Dyke's Automobile & Gasoline Engine Encyclopedia.* 1924. Chicago. 13th ed. 1226 pp. EX $30.00

DYKE, Henry van. *Joy & Power.* 1903. Merrymount Press. 1st ed. dj. $10.00

DYKE, Walter. *Son of Old Man Hat, a Navajo Autobiography.* 1938. New York. review copy. dj. VG $60.00

DYKE, Walter. *Son of Old Man Hat, a Navajo Autobiography.* 1938. 1st ed. dj. VG $50.00

DYKES, Jeff. *Fifty Great Western Illustrators.* 1975. 1st ed. dj. EX $35.00

DYKES. *My Dobie Collection.* 1971. 1st ed. sgn. wrappers. EX $25.00

DYKSTRA, Robert R. *The Cattle Towns.* 1968. New York. Ills. 386 pp. index. dj. $20.00

EAKIN, R. *The Third Eye.* 1973. CA U. Press. Ills. dj. EX $12.50

EAKIN, Sue & Logsdon, J. *Twelve Years a Slave by Solomon Northup.* 1968. Baton Rouge. 273 pp. dj. $6.00

EARDLEY-WILMOT, S. *Leaves from an Indian Forest.* 1930. London. Arnold. Ills. 1st ed. 200 pp. $32.50

EARDLEY-WILMOT, S. *The Life of a Tiger.* 1911. London. Ills. 183 pp. VG $20.00

EARDLEY-WILMOT, S. *The Life of an Elephant.* 1912. London. Arnold. Ills. VG $17.50

EARHART, Amelia. *Last Flight.* 1937. New York. Ills. 229 pp. $20.00

EARHART, Amelia. *Last Flight.* 1957. 1st ed. dj. G $15.00

EARL, L. *Crocodile Fever.* 1954. London. Collins. Ills. 255 pp. VG $17.50

EARLE, Alice Morse. *Stage Coach & Tavern Days.* 1900. New York. 1st ed. VG $75.00

EARLE, Alice Morse. *Sun Dials & Roses of Yesterday.* 1902. New York. 1st ed. VG $20.00

EARLE, Charles, M.D. *Scarlatina in Chicago: Epidemic of 1876-7.* 1877. Chicago. 22 pp. wrappers. $35.00

EARLE, Joe. *An Introduction to Japanese Prints.* 1980. Compton Press. Ills. Mint. $18.00

EARLE, P. *Robert E. Lee.* 1973. 1st ed. $12.50

EARLE, Ralph. *Life at the U.S. Naval Academy.* 1917. New York. Putnam. ex-lib. 359 pp. $3.50

EARLY, Eleanor. *An Island Patchwork.* 1941. Boston. Houghton Mifflin. $10.00

EARLY, Eleanor. *Cape Cod Summer.* 1949. Boston. Houghton Mifflin. 306 pp. $10.00

EARLY, Eleanor. *Evangeline & Hill, Grace L.* 1919. Lippincott. dj. VG $6.50

EARLY, Eleanor. *New England Cookbook.* 1954. New York. Random House. 236 pp. $10.00

EASTLAKE, W. *The Long Naked Descent into Boston.* 1977. 1st ed. VG $25.00

EASTLAKE, William. *Castle Keep.* 1965. New York. Simon & Schuster. 1st ed. VG $20.00

EASTMAN, Charles A. *Indian Boyhood.* 1905. New York. Ills. Blumenschein. 1st ed. $22.50

EASTMAN, Charles. *Indian Heroes & Great Chieftans.* 1918. Boston. Little, Brown. Ills. VG $35.00

EASTMAN, Dave. *Carmichael.* 1959. New York. Rinehart. wrappers. VG $10.00

EASTMAN, E. *Pratt, the Red Man's Moses.* 1935. Norman. 1st ed. dj. VG $35.00

EASTMAN, E.R. *Journey to Day Before Yesterday.* 1963. Englewood Cliffs, NJ. 254 pp. $3.50

EASTMAN, G. *Chronicles of an African Trip.* 1927. private print. presentation copy. sgn. VG $42.50

EASTMAN, M.E. *East of the White Hills.* 1900. North Conway. Ills. 139 pp. $25.00

EASTMAN, Mary H. *American Annual: Ills. of Early Hist. No. America.* Philadelphia. Lippincott. (ca.1854) 1st ed. $750.00

EASTMAN, Max. *Journalism Verses Art.* 1916. New York. Knopf. Ills. Art Young. VG $45.00

EASTMAN, Max. *Leon Trotsky: Portrait of a Youth.* 1925. New York. Greenberg. 1st ed. EX $35.00

EASTMAN, Max. *Reflections on the Failure of Socialism.* 1955. New York. Devin-Adair. inscr. dj. $35.00

EASTMAN, Max. *The End of Socialism in Russia.* 1937. Boston. Little, Brown. 1st ed. dj. $45.00

EASTMAN, R.M. *Pilots & Pilot Boats of Boston Harbor.* 1956. Boston. Ills. 91 pp. wrappers. $10.00

EASTMAN KODAK CO. *F.W. Lovejoy, the Story of a Practical Idealist.* 1947. 52 pp. G $3.50

EASTON, M. *Aubrey & the Dying Lady.* 1972. London. Ills. Beardsley. 1st ed. dj. $15.00

EASTON, Robert. *Lord of Beasts. Saga of Buffalo Jones.* 1961. U. of AZ. 2nd printing. dj. $7.50

EASTON. *Art of Augustus John.* 1975. Godine. $20.00

EATON, Allan H. *Beauty Behind Barbed Wire.* 1952. New York. Ills. 208 pp. dj. EX $35.00

EATON, C. *A History of the Southern Confederacy.* 1954. New York. 351pp. $13.50

EATON, C. *Jefferson Davis.* 1977. New York. 1st ed. $12.50

EATON, Walter Prichard. *Skyline Camps.* 1922. no place. Ills. 245 pp. VG $12.50

EBAN. *Promised Land.* 1978. 1st ed. folio. dj. VG $45.00

EBBESEN. *AIDS: Basic Guide.* 1984. 1st ed. dj. VG $10.00

EBBUTT. *Myths & Legends the British Race.* 1910. Ltd. ed. 375 pp. 58 pls. $48.50

EBERHART, Mignon. *Alpine Condo Crossing.* 1984. New York. Random House. 1st ed. dj. VG $20.00

EBERHART, Mignon. *Call After Midnight.* 1964. New York. 1st ed. dj. VG $7.50

EBERHART, Mignon. *Enemy in the House.* 1962. New York. 1st ed. dj. VG $7.50

EBERHART, Mignon. *The Patient in Cabin C.* 1983. New York. Random House. 1st ed. dj. EX $30.00

EBERHART, Mignon. *Two Little Rich Girls.* 1971. New York. 1st ed. dj. EX $12.50

EBERLEIN, H.D. & McClure, A. *Practical Book of American Antiques.* 1928. Philadelphia. $25.00

EBERLEIN, H.D. & McClure, A. *The Practical Book of Period Furniture.* 1914. Philadelphia. Lippincott. Ills. 371 pp. $20.00

EBERLEIN. *American Antiques.* 1927. Garden City. Ills. dj. EX $25.00

EBERSTADT, Fernanda. *Low Tide.* 1985. Knopf. 1st ed. dj. VG $15.00

EBERT, John & Katherine. *Old American Prints for Collectors.* 1974. New York. Scribner. VG $17.00

ECCLI, Eugene. *Low-Cost, Energy-Efficient Shelter.* 1975. VG $5.00

ECHOLS, Lee. *Dead Aim.* 1951. San Diego. Ills. sgn. $8.50

ECKELS, J.H. *Modern Mortuary Science.* 1946. Philadelphia. Ills. 508 pp. G $25.00

ECKERT, A.W. *The Conquerors.* 1970. Boston. 1st ed. dj. VG $10.00

ECKERT, A.W. *The Frontiersmen.* 1967. Boston. Little, Brown. 626 pp. VG $6.50

ECKERT, A.W. *The Owls of North America.* 1974. New York. 1st ed. slipcase. EX $55.00

ECKERT, A.W. *The Owls of North America.* 1974. Doubleday. Ills. 1st trade ed. 278 pp. EX $45.00

ECKERT, A.W. *Wild Season.* 1967. Little, Brown. Ills. 1st ed. dj. EX $10.00

ECKERT, A.W. *Wilderness Empire.* 1969. Boston. 1st ed. dj. VG $10.00

ECKFELDT, J.R. & DuBois, Wm. *New Varieties of Gold & Silver, with Mint Values.* Philadelphia. 60 pp. 3 pls. very rare $1,200.00

ECKHARDT, C.F. *Lost San Saba Mines.* 1982. dj. EX $6.00

ECKHARDT, G. *Pennsylvania Clocks & Clockmakers.* 1955. New York. 229 pp. dj. VG $8.00

ECKLES, C.H., Combs & Macy. *Milk & Milk Products.* 1943. New York. McGraw Hill. TB. 414 pp. VG $4.00

ECKSTROM, J.D. *Time of the Hedrons.* 1968. 1st ed. dj. EX $7.50

ECO, Umberto. *The Name of the Rose.* 1983. New York. trans. Wm. Weaver. 502 pp. dj. $12.50

ECO, Umberto. *Travels in Hyper Reality.* proof copy. $20.00

EDBERG, Rolf. *The Dream of Kilimanjaro.* 1976. New York. 1st Am. ed. dj. VG $10.00

EDDINGS, D. *Pawn of Prophecy.* London. 1st ed. $15.00

EDDINGTON, Arthur. *Relativity Theory of Protons & Electrons.* 1936. Cambridge. VG $30.00

EDDY, A.D. *The Life of Jacob Hodges, an African Negro.* 1842. Philadelphia. 1st ed. EX $45.00

EDDY, Daniel C. *Walter's Tour in the East, Walter in Jerusalem.* 1870. Sheldon Co. Ills. 220 pp. VG $5.00

EDDY, Mary Baker. *Christ & Christmas.* Boston. 1st ed. VG $90.00

EDDY, Mary Baker. *Retrospection & Introspection.* 1920. Boston. 95 pp. G $6.00

EDDY, Mary Baker. *Science & Health.* 1914. Boston. lg print. VG $6.00

EDDY, Mary O. *Ballads & Songs from Ohio.* 1939. New York. Augustin. 1st ed. VG $35.00

EDDY, S. *How to Know the Freshwater Fish.* 1957. Brown. Ills. 253 pp. VG $10.00

EDEL, L. *The Complete Plays of Henry James.* 1949. Philadelphia. Lippincott. 1st ed. dj. EX $50.00

EDEL, L. *Bibliography of Henry James.* 1982. Oxford. 3rd ed. dj. EX $37.50

EDEL, L. *Diary of Alice James.* 1964. New York. Dodd Mead. 1st ed. dj. EX $25.00

EDEL, L. *Henry James.* 1963. Minneapolis. 4th printing. wrappers. VG $10.00

EDEL, L. *Henry James.* Philadelphia. 1st ed. 5 vol set. djs. EX $87.50

EDEL, L. *Selected Fiction.* 1953. New York. Dutton. 1st ed. dj. VG $15.00

EDEL, L. *Selected Letters of Henry James.* 1955. New York. 1st ed. dj. EX $25.00

EDEL, L. *Stories of the Supernatural.* 1970. New York. Taplinger. 1st ed. dj. EX $30.00

EDEL, L. *The American Essays of Henry James.* 1956. New York. Vintage Pr. wrappers. VG $15.00

EDEL, L. *The Complete Tales.* Lippincott. 1st Am. ed. 12 vol set. dj. EX $290.00

EDEL, L. *The Thirties.* 1980. New York. 1st printing. 753 pp. dj. $20.00

EDEL, L. & Laurence, Dan H. *A Bibliography of Henry James.* 1957. London. Hart Davis. 1st ed. dj. VG $125.00

EDEL, L. & Lind, I. *Parisian Sketches.* 1957. NY. NY U. Press. dj. VG $32.50

EDEL, L. & Lind, I. *Parisian Sketches.* 1958. London. Hart Davis. 1st Eng. ed. dj. $25.00

EDEN, Dorothy. *The Storrington Papers.* 1978. Coward. 1st Am. ed. dj. VG $6.00

EDEN, Emily. *The Semi-Attached Couple.* 1947. Boston. 1st ed. dj. EX $15.00

EDERER, B.F. *Through Alaska's Back Door.* 1954. Vantage. Ills. 162 pp. dj. EX $15.00

EDFELDT, Ake. *Silent Speech & Silent Reading.* 1960. Chicago. dj. EX $15.00

EDGAR, John F. *Pioneer Life in Dayton & Vicinity, 1796-1840.* 1896. Dayton. Ills. 1st ed. 289 pp. $75.00

EDGERTON, Gladys. *Walled Garden.* 1934. Berkeley Heights. inscr. VG $75.00

EDGEWORTH, Maria. *Little Dog Trusty, Cherry Orchard & Orange Man.* 1851. Worcester. $20.00

EDGEWORTH, Maria. *Moral Tales.* 1867. Philadelphia. new ed. $7.50

EDGEWORTH, Maria. *Novels & Tales.* 1850. New York. 10 vol set. VG $50.00

EDGEWORTH, Maria. *Popular Tales.* 1823. Boston. Ills. $65.00

EDGEWORTH, Maria. *The Bracelets.* 1850. Philadelphia. Appleton. Ills. wrappers. $25.00

EDIB, Halide. *Memoirs of Halide Ebib.* New York. reprint. Ills. 472 pp. $24.00

EDISON, Thomas. *Diary & Sundry Observations of Thomas A. Edison.* 1948. Philosophical Lib. 1st ed. dj. $8.50

EDITH, Sister St. Mary. *The Secrets of Good Cooking.* 1928. Montreal. Canadian Printing. 309 pp. $5.00

EDMAN, Irwin. *Poems.* 1925. New York. Simon & Schuster. Ltd. ed. VG $12.50

EDMINISTER, Frank. *The Ruffed Grouse.* 1947. Macmillan. Ills. 1st ed. 384 pp. index. $37.50

EDMONDS, Harry. *The Secret Voyage.* 1946. London. MacDonald. 1st ed. dj. VG $10.00

EDMONDS, S. Emma. *Nurse & Spy in the Union Army.* 1865. G $12.50

EDMONDS, Walter. *Chad Hanna.* 1940. Boston. Little, Brown. 1st ed. $10.00

EDMONDS, Walter. *The Big Barn.* 1930. Boston. 1st ed. 333 pp. $10.00

EDMONDS, Walter. *The Boyds of Black River.* 1953. New York. 248 pp. dj. VG $4.00

EDMONDS, Walter. *They Fought with What They Had.* 1951. Boston. 1st ed. G $22.50

EDSON, Russell. *The Boundary.* 1964. Stamford. Ltd. ed. 1/200. EX $10.00

EDSON, Russell. *The Brain Kitchen.* 1965. Stamford. Ltd. ed. 1/250. wrappers. EX $10.00

EDWARD, Ernest. *Finding Birds in Mexico.* 1968. 2nd ed. 282 pp. VG $14.00

EDWARD, George W. *Brittany & the Bretons.* 1910. New York. Ills. 1st ed. inscr. $17.50

EDWARDS, Albert. *A Man's World.* 1912. New York. Macmillan. 1st ed. dj. VG $45.00

EDWARDS, Amelia B. *Egypt & Its Monuments.* 1891. Harper. VG $45.00

EDWARDS, Amelia. *Untrodden Peaks & Unfrequented Valleys.* 1893. Routledge. 2nd ed. $15.00

EDWARDS, Anne & Citron, S. *The Inn & Us.* 1976. New York. Random House. 1st ed. inscr. $30.00

EDWARDS, Anne. *Judy Garland.* 1975. dj. $5.00

EDWARDS, Anne. *The Survivors.* 1968. New York. 1st ed. dj. VG $25.00

EDWARDS, Billy. *Gladiators of the Prize Ring.* 1895. Chicago. G $60.00

EDWARDS, Clayton. *A Treasury of Heroes & Heroines.* 1920. New York. Ills. Choate & Curtis. VG $20.00

EDWARDS, G.W. *Tanglewood Tales.* 1888. Houghton Mifflin. Ills. EX $30.00

EDWARDS, Gawain. *The Earth Tube.* 1927. New York. Appleton. 1st ed. dj. EX $85.00

EDWARDS, George W. *Alsace-Lorraine.* 1918. Philadelphia. Ills. VG $35.00

EDWARDS, George W. *Constantinople.* 1930. Philadelphia. VG $50.00

EDWARDS, George W. *The Book of Christmas.* 1909. New York. Macmillan. Ills. 1st ed. $20.00

EDWARDS, George W. *Vanished Halls & Cathedrals of France.* 1917. Philadelphia. Ills. 1st ed. 324 pp. VG $27.50

EDWARDS, George W. *Vanished Towers & Chimes of Flanders.* 1916. Philadelphia. Ills. 1st ed. 212 pp. EX $35.00

EDWARDS, H. *All Night at Mr. Stanyhurst's.* 1963. London. Cape. 1st ed. dj. EX $35.00

EDWARDS, H. *Sharks & Shipwreck.* 1976. Demeter. Ills. 126 pp. EX $12.50

EDWARDS, H. Sutherland. *Prima Donna: Hist. & Surroundings 17th-19th Cent.* 1888. London. 2 vol set. VG $75.00

EDWARDS, J.H., ed. *Orthodoxy in the Civil Courts.* 1884. Cincinnati. 247 pp. $12.50

EDWARDS, J.O. *Life of David Brainerd.* 1749. Boston. rebound. VG $250.00

EDWARDS, Jonathan. *Memoirs of Rev. David Brainerd.* 1822. New Haven. VG $45.00

EDWARDS, Julie Andrews. *Last of the Really Good Whangdoodles.* 1974. Harper. 1st ed. dj. VG $10.00

EDWARDS, Lewis. *The Law & Custom of Freemasonry.* 1928. London. Lewis. 1st ed. 260 pp. VG $15.00

EDWARDS, Lionel. *Golden Moorland Mousie.* 1930. Scribner. 2nd ed. 106 pp. $30.00

EDWARDS, Lionel. *The Fox.* NY/London. (ca.1940's) Ills. 94 pp. dj. $12.50

EDWARDS, Lionel. *The Wiles of the Fox.* London. Ills. 50 pp. color pls. G $10.00

EDWARDS, Peter. *Terminus.* 1976. New York. 1st Am. ed. dj. VG $8.00

EDWARDS, Robert Dudley. *Church & State in Tudor Ireland.* 1935. Dublin. 1st ed. maps. 352 pp. $15.00

EDWARDS, Samuel. *George Sand.* 1972. New York. 1st ed. 271 pp. index. dj. VG $5.00

EDWARDS, Samuel. *The Ohio Hunter; or, Frontier Life of S. Edwards.* 1866. Battle Creek. 1st ed. $450.00

EDWARDS, William B. *The Story of Colt's Revolver. Biography of Colt.* 1953. New York. Castle. Ills. 470 pp. dj. VG $35.00

EDWARDS, William S. *Into the Yukon.* 1905. Cincinnati. Clarke. Ills. 324 pp. dj. $17.50

EDWARDS. *Eneas Africanus.* 1929. Macon, GA. Burke Co. wrappers. EX $15.00

EDWARDS. *Painter Wall of Mexico from Pre-Historic Times.* 1966. Texas U. Press. $15.00

EDWARDS. *Pharoahs/Fellahs/Explorers.* 1891. New York. Ills. 1st ed. VG $25.00

EDWARDS. *The Art of Wen Cheng Ming (1470-1559).* 1976. U. of MI & Museum of Art. $18.00

EDWARDS. *Valley Whose Name is Death.* 1940. Ltd. 1st ed. 1/1000. $60.00

EDYE, Huish. *Angler & the Trout.* 1945. London. Ills. dj. VG $17.50

EFFINGER, George Alec. *The Nick of Time.* 1985. Garden City. 1st ed. dj. VG $10.00

EFFINGER, George Alec. *The Wolves of Memory.* 1981. New York. 1st ed. dj. VG $12.50

EGAN, M.F. *Confessions of a Book Lover.* 1923. Garden City. Doubleday. G $12.00

EGAN, Michael. *The Flying, Gray-Haired Yank.* 1888. Philadelphia. Ills. 414 pp. $75.00

EGAN & ALCOCK. *Beaudelaire: Flowers of Evil.* 1947. Sylvan Pr. private print. 142 pp. G $20.00

EGE, Robert. *Strike Them Hard.* 1970. Old Army Press.Ltd. ed. 1/50. slipcase. EX $95.00

EGELER. *Challenge of the Andes.* 1955. New York. 1st ed. dj. VG $15.00

EGGLESTON, G.T. *Tahiti, Voyage Through Paradise.* 1953. New York. 252 pp. $15.00

EGGLESTON, George Cary. *Red Eagle & the Wars with Creek Indians of AL.* 1878. New York. Ills. 346 pp. $20.00

EGGLESTON, George Cary. *The Master of Warlock.* 1903. Boston. Lothrop. Ills. Williams. G $6.50

EGGLESTON, J.B. *The Circuit Rider, a Tale of the Heroic Age.* 1874. Ford & Co. Ills. G $22.50

EHERNBERGER, J. & Gschwind, F. *Sherman Hill Union Pacific.* 1973. dj. EX $6.00

EHLE, John. *The Changing Guard.* 1974. New York. Random House. 1st ed. VG $20.00

EHRENFELD, D.W. *Conserving Life on Earth.* 1972. Oxford U. Pr. Ills. 360 pp. dj. EX $10.00

EHRIG, F. *The Williams Family Chronicle.* 1969. EX $20.00

EHRLICHMAN, John. *The Whole Truth.* Simon & Schuster. 1st ed. dj. $10.00

EHWA, Carl. *The Book of Pipes & Tobacco.* 1974. 1st ed. dj. EX $25.00

EICHENBERG, Fritz. *The Wood & the Graver.* 1977. Potter. Ills. 1st ed. 199 pp. dj. EX $25.00

EICHLER, Lillian. *The New Book of Etiquette.* 1924. New York. Garden City. 277 pp. VG $4.00

EICHLER, Lillian. *Today's Etiquette.* 1941. New York. Doubleday Doran. Ills. VG $4.00

EINARSEN, A.S. *Black Brant, Sea Goose of the Pacific Coast.* 1965. WA U. Press. Ills. 142 pp. dj. EX $20.00

EINSTEIN, Alfred. *Essays on Music.* 1956. New York. 1st ed. EX $20.00

EIPPER, Paul. *Circus Men, Beasts, & Joys of the Road.* 1931. New York. Ills. 213 pp. $10.00

EISEN, Edna. *Our Country from the Air.* 1937. Chicago. Ills. 1st ed. maps. 212 pp. VG $25.00

EISENBERG, Philip. *We Were with Charles Darwin on the Beagle.* 1960. $2.00

EISENBERG. *Transactions in Foreign Currency.* 1986. proof copy. $25.00

EISENHART, Luther P. *Transformations of Surfaces.* 1923. Princeton. $30.00

EISENHOWER, D.D. *Crusade in Europe.* 1948. Doubleday. 559 pp. EX $5.50

EISENHOWER, D.D. *Eisenhower College Collection of Paintings.* 1972. VG $27.00

EISENHOWER, D.D. *Mandate for Change.* 1963. Ills. $7.50

EISENHOWER, D.D. *Waging Peace.* 1965. Ills. $7.50

EISENHOWER, John. *The Bitter Woods.* 1969. 3rd printing. dj. EX $10.00

EISENSCHIML, Otto. *Why Was Lincoln Murdered?* 1937. Boston. Ills. 1st ed. sgn. dj. VG $17.50

EISENSTAEDT, Alfred. *Witness to Our Time.* 1966. Viking Studio Book. 1st ed. VG $30.00

EISENSTAEDT. *People.* dj. EX $85.00

EKENRODE & CONRAD. *James Longstreet. Lee's Warhorse.* 1936. 1st ed. dj. VG $55.00

EKERT, Allan. *Wilderness Empire.* 1969. Boston. 653 pp. dj. $6.50

ELBE, Louis. *Future Science.* 1906. Chicago. 382 pp. VG $35.00

ELDER, Donald. *Ring Lardner: a Biography.* 1956. Garden City. 1st ed. 409 pp. $8.50

ELDER, William. *Biography of E. Kent Kane.* 1858. Philadelphia. 1st ed. dj. VG $50.00

ELDRIDGE, Charles J. *Oriental Art of Charming Horses & Colts.* 1857. Cincinnati. 48 pp. wrappers. $150.00

ELDRIDGE, Ed. *Hypnotism.* 1902. Philadelphia. 197 pp. $7.50

ELGIN, Suzette Haden. *And Then There'll be Fireworks.* 1981. Garden City. 1st ed. dj. VG $10.00

ELGIN, Suzette Haden. *The Grand Jubilee.* 1981. Garden City. review copy. dj. VG $12.50

ELGIN. *Gentle Art of Verbal Self-Defense.* 1980. Dorset. dj. VG $15.50

ELIADE, Mircea & Kitagawa, J. *The History of Religions. Essays in Methodology.* 1959. Chicago. 5th impression. 164 pp. dj. EX $12.50

ELIADE, Mircea. *Occultism, Witchcraft & Cultural Fashions.* 1976. Chicago. 1st ed. dj. EX $10.00

ELIADE, Mircea. *Shamanism: Archaic Techniques of Ecstacy.* 1970. Princeton. 2nd printing. 610 pp. VG $15.00

ELIADE, Mircea. *Tow Tales of the Occult.* 1970. New York. Harper. 1st ed. 130 pp. dj. VG $10.00

ELIASON, Joyce. *Fresh Meat/Warm Weather.* 1974. New York. Harper. 1st ed. dj. VG $20.00

ELIOT, Alexander. *Three Hundred Years of American Painting.* 1957. New York. dj. $15.00

ELIOT, George. *Complete Works.* 1900. Boston. 10 vol set. EX $50.00

ELIOT, George. *Silas Marner.* 1861. New York. 1st Am. ed. green cloth. EX $75.00

ELIOT, George. *Silas Marner.* 1950. Lardlaw Bros. TB. EX $2.00

ELIOT, George. *The Works of George Eliot.* Boston. (ca. 1880) Ills. 12 vol set. $125.00

ELIOT, T.S. *Collected Poems, 1909-1935.* 1936. New York. 1st Am. ed. VG $20.00

ELIOT, T.S. *Complete Poems & Plays 1909-1950.* 1958. New York. 392 pp. dj. VG $5.00

ELIOT, T.S. *Essays Ancient & Modern.* 1936. New York. 1st Am. ed. dj. VG $50.00

ELIOT, T.S. *Family Reunion.* 1939. London. 1st ed. dj. $50.00

ELIOT, T.S. *Four Quartets.* 1975. Folio Society. 1st ed. EX $20.00

ELIOT, T.S. *Four Quartets.* 1943. New York. 1st ed. 2nd impression. VG $50.00

ELIOT, T.S. *Four Quartets.* Ltd. 1st Am. ed. 1/788. $690.00

ELIOT, T.S. *Four Quartets.* 1943. New York. 1st Am. ed. dj. VG $250.00

ELIOT, T.S. *John Dryden: Poet, Dramatist, Critic.* 1932. New York. Ltd. 1st ed. 1/1000. dj. EX $75.00

ELIOT, T.S. *Little Gidding.* 1942. London. 1st ed. wrappers. $25.00

ELIOT, T.S. *Murder in the Cathedral.* 1935. New York. Harcourt Brace. 2nd ed. 96 pp. $37.50

ELIOT, T.S. *Murder in the Cathedral.* 1952. Film ed. VG $10.00

ELIOT, T.S. *Notes Toward the Definition of Culture.* 1949. New York. Harcourt. 1st ed. dj. VG $30.00

ELIOT, T.S. *Selected Poems.* 1948. Faber & Faber. 1st ed. wrappers. VG $18.00

ELIOT, T.S. *The Classics & the Man of Letters.* 1942. London. 1st ed. wrappers. VG $25.00

ELIOT, T.S. *The Confidential Clerk.* London. 1st English ed. dj. VG $30.00

ELIOT, T.S. *The Confidential Clerk.* 1954. Harcourt. 1st Am. ed. dj. VG $20.00

ELIOT, T.S. *The Cultivation of Christmas Trees.* 1954. Faber. Ills. Jones. 1st ed. wrappers. $15.00

ELIOT, T.S. *The Cultivation of Christmas Trees.* 1956. Farrar. Ills. Enrico Arno. 1st Am. ed. $15.00

ELIOT, T.S. *The Rock.* 1934. New York. 1st Am. ed. dj. VG $15.00

ELIOT, T.S. *The Rock. A Pageant Play.* 1934. London. 1st ed. dj. $65.00

ELIOT, T.S. *Three Voices of Poetry.* 1953. London. 1st ed. wrappers. $15.00

ELIOT, T.S. *To Criticize the Critic.* 1st Am. ed. VG $10.00

ELIOT, T.S. *What is a Classic?* 1945. Faber. 1st ed. dj. VG $20.00

ELIOT, T.S. *What is a Classic?* 1945. Faber. 2nd ed. dj. VG $10.00

ELIOT. *Ash Wednesday.* 1930. New York. Ltd. ed. 1/600. sgn. $70.00

ELIOT. *The Cocktail Party.* 1950. London. 4th impression. sgn. dj. $200.00

ELIOT, E.C. *Kemlo & the Crazy Planet.* 1954. London. 1st ed. dj. $15.00

ELISOFON. *Color Photography.* 1st ed. dj. EX $27.50

ELKIN, S. & Ravenel, W. *The Best American Short Stories 1980.* 1980. Boston. Houghton Mifflin. 1st ed. dj. $7.50

ELKIN, Stanley. *Boswell.* 1964. New York. Random House. 1st ed. dj. EX $50.00

ELKIN, Stanley. *George Mills.* 1982. New York. 1st ed. dj. EX $10.00

ELKIN, Stanley. *The Bad Man.* 1967. New York. Random House. 1st printing. $7.50

ELKON, Juliette & Ross, E. *Menus for Entertaining.* 1960. New York. Hastings House. 288 pp. $6.50

ELLACOTT, S.E. *Collecting Arms & Armour.* 1964. Arco. Ills. 128 pp. dj. VG $8.50

ELLER, John. *Charlie & the Ice Man.* 1981. St.Martins. review copy. dj. VG $10.00

ELLER, John. *Rage of Heaven.* 1982. St.Martins. 1st ed. dj. VG $10.00

ELLET, Elizabeth. *Pioneer Women of the West.* Philadelphia. (ca. 1860-1880) 434 pp. VG $20.00

ELLIN, Stanley. *Blessington Method.* 1964. New York. 1st ed. dj. EX $40.00

ELLIN, Stanley. *The Dark Fantastic.* 1983. Mysterious Pr. Ltd. ed. 1/250. sgn. slipcase. $75.00

ELLIN, Stanley. *The Speciality of the House A.O.S.* 1979. Mysterious Pr. Ltd. ed. 1/250. sgn. slipcase. $60.00

ELLIOT, Bob & Goulding, Ray. *Write If You Get Work.* 1st Am. ed. dj. EX $10.00

ELLIOT, Robert G. *Agent of Death. Memoirs of an Executioner.* 1940. New York. 3rd printing. 315 pp. dj. $9.00

ELLIOT, S.H. *Attractions of New Haven, Conn. A Guide to City.* 1869. New York. Ills. 141+34 pp. ads. map. G $47.50

ELLIOTT, C. *Fading Trails.* 1947. Macmillan. Ills. 279 pp. VG $12.00

ELLIOTT, Charles. *Life of Rev. Robert R. Roberts.* 1844. Cincinnati. Ills. 1st ed. 407 pp. $100.00

ELLIOTT, D.G. *The Gallinaceous Game Birds of North America.* 1897. London. Ills. $175.00

ELLIOTT, Eleanor. *The Glamour Magazine Party Book.* 1965. Garden City. Doubleday. Book Club Ed. $5.00

ELLIOTT, Henry W. *Our Alaska Province.* 1886. New York. Ills. 1st ed. maps. $75.00

ELLIOTT, Henry W. *Our Arctic Province: Alaska & the Seal Islands.* 1897. New York. Ills. 473 pp. fld map. pls. $27.50

ELLIOTT, J.H. *Imperial Spain 1496-1716.* 1964. 1st Am. ed. dj. EX $10.00

ELLIOTT, James W. *Transport to Disaster.* 1962. Holt Rinehart. Ills. 1st ed. 247 pp. dj. VG $17.50

ELLIOTT, Lawrence. *The Long Hunter.* 1976. New York. 1st ed. 242 pp. dj. $12.50

ELLIOTT, Sarah Barnwell. *An Incident.* 1899. NY/London. Harper. Ills. Smedley. $8.00

ELLIOTT, Stephen. *A High Civilization the Moral Duty of Georgians.* 1844. Savannah. 1st ed. 21 pp. $45.00

ELLIS, A.R. *Under Scott's Command. Lashly's Antarctic Diaries.* 1969. New York. 1st ed. dj. VG $7.50

ELLIS, B.F. *The Dialogue Grammar; or, Book Instructor.* 1834. South Hanover. 252 pp. $20.00

ELLIS, C. *Printing Inks.* 1940. New York. Ills. G $12.50

ELLIS, Chris. *Fighting Vehicles.* 1972. London. 95 pp. $4.50

ELLIS, Chris. *Tanks of WWII.* 1981. London. Ills. 207 pp. $10.50

ELLIS, Chris. *The World of Aviation.* 1977. London. Hamlyn. 1st ed. EX $12.50

ELLIS, Edward. *Great Leaders & National Issues of 1896.* 1896. Philadelphia. World Bible House. 511 pp. $3.50

ELLIS, Edward. *The Life & Times of Col. Daniel Boone.* 1884. Philadelphia. 269 pp. VG $22.50

ELLIS, Elmer. *Henry Moore Teller.* 1941. Caxton. dj. $15.00

ELLIS, Elmer. *Mr. Dooley's America.* 1941. Knopf. 1st ed. dj. VG $17.50

ELLIS, George. *Letters Upon the Annexation of Texas to J. Adams.* 1845. Boston. 1st ed. original wrappers. $200.00

ELLIS, H.F. *The Vexations of A.J. Wentworth, B.A.* 1950. Boston. ex-lib. 152 pp. dj. VG $3.00

ELLIS, Ida. *A Catechism of Palmistry.* 1900. London. Ills. 2nd ed. 155 pp. G $40.00

ELLIS, Joseph. *New England Mind in Transition. Samuel Johnson.* 1973. Yale Press. $10.00

ELLIS, M. *The World of Birds.* 1971. Doubleday. Ills. 140 pp. dj. EX $10.00

ELLIS, M. *Wild Goose, Brother Goose.* 1970. Holt/Winston. 159 pp. dj. EX $7.50

ELLIS, Mrs. *Guide to Social Happiness.* New York. no date. 184 pp. $15.00

ELLIS, William Donohue. *The Cuyahoga.* 1966. New York. Ills. K.T. Shogren. 1st ed. $17.50

ELLIS, William T. *Billy Sunday, the Man & His Message*. 1914. Philadelphia. Winston. photos. 432 pp. VG $4.50

ELLIS, William. *Narrative of a Tour Through Hawaii*. 1826. London. 1st Eng. ed. $300.00

ELLIS, William. *Three Visits to Madagascar During Years 1853-56*. 1859. Philadelphia. 426 pp. $27.50

ELLISON, Beckles. *The Life & Letters of James Wolfe*. 1909. London. Ills. 522 pp. $35.00

ELLISON, H. *Stalking the Nightmare*. 1982. Phantasia. Ltd. ed. 1/700. sgn. boxed. EX $75.00

ELLISON, Harlan. *Medea: Harlan's World*. 1985. New York. Bantam. review copy. wrappers. $15.00

ELLISON, Harlan. *Medea: Harlan's World*. 1985. Huntington Woods. dj. EX $75.00

ELLISON, Harlan. *Alone Against Tomorrow*. 1971. New York. dj. EX $20.00

ELLISON, Harlan. *An Edge in My Voice*. 1985. Ltd. 1st ed. sgn. slipcase. EX $45.00

ELLISON, Harlan. *Approaching Oblivion*. 1st Eng. ed. dj. VG $30.00

ELLISON, Harlan. *Deathbird Stories*. 1975. New York. 1st ed. sgn. dj. EX $45.00

ELLISON, Harlan. *Memos from Purgatory*. 1977. sgn. $6.00

ELLISON, Harlan. *No Doors, No Windows*. 1973. New York. Pyramid. 1st ed. pb. VG $15.00

ELLISON, Harlan. *Repent Harlequin*. 1967. New York. Doubleday. 1st ed. dj. EX $12.50

ELLISON, Harlan. *Shatterday*. 1983. 1st ed. sgn. VG $25.00

ELLISON, Harlan. *Stalking the Nightmare*. 1982. Phantasea. 1st trade ed. dj. VG $20.00

ELLISON, Harlan. *Strange Wine*. 1978. New York. 1st ed. sgn. dj. VG $35.00

ELLISON, Harlan. *The Beast that Shouted Love*. 1969. New York. 1st ed. dj. EX $20.00

ELLISON, Harlan. *The Illustrated Harlan Ellison*. 1978. New York. Ltd. ed. sgn. VG $30.00

ELLISON, Ralph. *Invisible Man*. 1953. Signet. 1st ed. wrappers. VG $5.00

ELLISON, William. *A Self-Governing Dominion California*. 1950. U. of CA. 1st ed. dj. $8.50

ELLISWORTH, Henry L. *Washington Irving on the Prairie*. 1938. Am. Book Co. dj. G $20.00

ELLROY, James. *Brown's Requiem*. 1984. London. Allison & Busby. 1st ed. dj. $15.00

ELLS, B.F. *History of the Romish Inquisition*. 1835. Hanover, IN. 120 pp. G $45.00

ELLSBERG, Edward. *Captain Paul*. 1941. New York. Literary Guild/Am. 607 pp. VG $6.00

ELLSBERG, Edward. *Hell on Ice, Saga of the Jeannette*. 1938. Ills. 1st ed. $7.50

ELLSBERG, Edward. *On the Bottom*. 1929. New York. 320 pp. $5.50

ELLSWORTH, Helen. *The Blue Jays of the Sierras*. 1918. 1st ed. photos. dj. $12.50

ELLSWORTH. *Queen of Household*. 1898. $15.00

ELLWANGER, George H. *The Pleasures of the Table*. 1902. New York. Doubleday Page. Ills. 477 pp. $25.00

ELLWOOD, G.M. *English Furniture & Decoration, 1680-1800*. Stuttgart. Ills. dj. VG $20.00

ELM, Ienar. *Aviation by Dead Reckoning*. 1929. Philadelphia. Ills. map. 120 pp. $17.50

ELMAN, R. *America's Pioneering Naturalists*. 1982. Winchester. Ills. 231 pp. dj. EX $12.50

ELMAN, R. *Great American Shooting Prints*. 1972. Knopf. 1st ed. folio. scarce. $60.00

ELMAN, R. *The Living World of Audubon Mammals*. 1976. Ridge Press. Ills. 271 pp. dj. EX $12.50

ELMENDORF, W.W. *Two Wives*. 1935. Caxton. 1st ed. dj. $35.00

ELMER, R.P. *Target Archery*. 1946. New York. dj. VG $30.00

ELON, Amos. *The Israelis; Founders & Sons*. 1971. London. Weidenfeld. 359 pp. $6.00

ELSAM, Richard. *Practical Builder's Perpetual Price Book*. 1825. London. 180 pp. 8 pls. $185.00

ELSEN, Albert. *Rodin*. 1963. Museum Modern Art. dj. EX $20.00

ELSON, Henry. *Side Lights on American History, Vol. 2*. 1923. New York. ex-lib. 401 pp. $3.50

ELSON, Louis C. *Reminiscences of a Musician's Vacation Abroad*. 1896. Philadelphia. G $8.50

ELSTON. *Laramie*. Pocketbook. pb. $3.00

ELSTON. *Wyoming Manhunt*. Pocketbook. pb. $3.00

ELTING, Mary. *Ships at Work*. 1953. $5.00

ELTON, Charles & Mary. *The Great Book Collectors*. 1893. London. 1st ed. 228 pp. VG $85.00

ELTRINGHAM, S.K. *Elephants*. 1982. Blanford. Ills. 1st Eng. ed. dj. EX $20.00

ELUARD, Paul. *Picasso*. 1947. 1st ed. dj. $40.00

ELVILLE, E.M. *Paperweights & Other Glass Curiosities*. 1967. London. $25.00

ELVIN, C.N. *Orders of Chivalry*. 1893. 32 pls. G $32.00

ELWOOD, Maren. *Characters Make Your Story*. 1942. Boston. $4.00

ELY, David. *Seconds*. 1962. 1st ed. dj. VG $15.00

ELY, Sims. *Lost Dutchman Mine*. 1953. Morrow. 1st ed. dj. VG $17.50

EMANUEL, Walter. *A Dog Day*. 1902. Ills. Cecil Aldin. EX $55.00

EMBREE, Edwin R. *Brown America-The Story of a New Race*. 1931. New York. Viking. ex-lib. 311 pp. $6.00

EMBREE, Edwin R. *Brown Americans-The Story of a 10th of a Nation*. 1944. New York. Viking. 248 pp. $6.00

EMERSON, Alice B. *Ruth Fielding at College*. 1917. New York. 206 pp. G $2.00

EMERSON, Alice B. *Ruth Fielding at Lighthouse Point*. 1913. New York. Cupples & Leon. Ills. 202 pp. $3.50

EMERSON, Alice B. *Ruth Fielding at Snow Camp*. 1913. New York. Cupples & Leon. Ills. $3.50

EMERSON, Alice B. *Ruth Fielding Down in Dixie*. 1916. New York. Cupples & Leon. Ills. VG $5.50

EMERSON, Alice B. *Ruth Fielding Homeward Bound*. 1919. New York. 210 pp. G $2.50

EMERSON, Alice B. *Ruth Fielding in Moving Pictures*. 1916. New York. 208 pp. G $2.50

EMERSON, Alice B. *Ruth Fielding in the Saddle*. 1917. New York. Cupples & Leon. Ills. G $4.50

EMERSON, Earl W. *Fat Tuesday*. 1986. New York. Morrow. proof copy. wrappers. $15.00

EMERSON, Edwin Jr. & Miller. *The Nineteenth Century & After*. 1906. New York. Ills. 3 vol set. EX $10.00

EMERSON, Edwin. *Hoover & His Times*. 1932. Garden City. Ills. 632 pp. $6.00

EMERSON, G.B. *Manual of Agriculture*. 1862. Boston. Ills. faded, stained. $25.00

EMERSON, G.B. *The Trees & Shrubs of Massachusetts*. 1894. Boston. 2 vol set. $75.00

EMERSON, Nathaniel. *Unwritten Literature of HA. Sacred Songs of Hula*. 1909. 288 pp. EX $50.00

EMERSON, R.W. *English Traits*. 1856. Boston. 1st ed. G $45.00

EMERSON, R.W. *Letters & Social Aims*. 1876. Boston. 1st ed. VG $25.00

EMERSON, R.W. *Poems*. 1847. London. 1st ed. $150.00

EMERSON, W. *Seven Types of Ambiguity*. 1930. 1st ed. G $35.00

EMERSON, William A. *History of the Town of Douglass.* 1879. Boston. Ills. 359 pp. fld map. $25.00

EMERSON. *Essays.* Peter Pauper. Ills. Mueller. boxed. $15.00

EMERSON. *Representative Men.* New York. (ca.1890) 265 pp. $5.50

EMERY, Clark. *The World of Dylan Thomas.* 1962. U. of Miami Pr.319 pp. $4.00

EMERY, K.O. *Coastal Pond Studied by Oceanographic Methods.* 1969. Elsevier. Ills. 80 pp. EX $4.00

EMERY, Walter. *Bach's Ornaments.* 1953. London. dj. EX $10.00

EMMITT, Robert. *The Last War Trail. Utes & Settlement of Colorado.*1954. Norman. Ills. 1st ed. 333 pp. index. $22.50

EMORY, Kenneth. *The Island of Lanai.* 1924. Bernice Bishop Mus. 1st ed. $15.00

ENARI. *Ornamental Shrubs of California.* 1962. Ills. dj. VG $25.00

ENDE, Michael. *The Neverending Story.* 1983. New York. Doubleday. 1st ed. dj. EX $25.00

ENDELL, Fritz. *Old Tavern Signs.* 1916. Boston. Ills. Ltd. 1st ed. VG $70.00

ENDEMANN, Dr. F. *Lehrbach Des Burger Lichen Rechts.* 1905. Berlin. VG $45.00

ENDICOTT, W. *Adventures in Alaska & Along the Trail.* 1928. New York. 1st ed. EX $35.00

ENGEL, Lehman. *The American Musical Theatre.* 1967. Ills. 236 pp. $15.00

ENGEL. *Researches into Early History of Violin Family.* 1883. 168 pp. $30.00

ENGEN, Rodney. *Kate Greenaway.* 1981. London. Macdonald Futura. 1st ed. dj. $40.00

ENGEN, Rodney. *Kate Greenaway.* 1976. London. Ills. 1st ed. dj. $28.00

ENGEN, Rodney. *Randolph Caldecott.* 1976. London. Ills. 1st ed. wrappers. VG $20.00

ENGLAND, George. *Keep Off the Grass.* 1919. Boston. Small Maynard. 1st ed. $65.00

ENGLAND, George. *Out of the Abyss.* 1967. 1st ed. dj. EX $8.50

ENGLE, Alice B. *A Story of Four Acorns.* 1881. Boston. Ills. sgn. G $6.50

ENGLE, P. & Langland, J. *Poet's Choice.* 1962. New York. Dial Press. 303 pp. dj. VG $7.50

ENGLEBERT, Omer. *The Last of the Conquistadors Junipero Serra.* 1956. New York. photos. 368 pp. EX $8.50

ENGLEBRECHT. *Merchants of Death.* 1934. 1st ed. G $12.50

ENGLEHARDT, Wolfgang. *Survival of the Free.* 1962. New York. Putnam. 258 pp. $6.50

ENGLEHARDT, Z. *San Francisco or Mission Delores.* 1924. Chicago. Ills. 430 pp. $45.00

ENGLEHARDT, Zaphyrin. *The Franciscans in Arizona.* 1899. Harbor Springs.Ills. 1st ed. maps. $125.00

ENGLEMANN, R. *Pompeii.* 1904. London/NY. VG $15.00

ENNION, E.A.R. *The Lapwing.* 1949. Methuen. Ills. 47 pp. VG $6.00

ENRIGHT, Elizabeth. *Then There Were Five.* 1944. New York. Ills. 1st ed. dj. $20.00

ENSLIN, Theodore. *Fragments. Epigrammata.* 1982. Salt Works. Ltd. 1st ed. 1/100. sgn. VG $25.00

ENSLIN, Theodore. *Songs Without Notes.* 1984. Salt Works. Ltd. ed. 1/350. sgn. VG $25.00

ENTICK, John. *The General History of the Late War.* 1764. London. 1st ed. 5 vol set. VG $585.00

ENTICK. *The Present State of the British Empire.* 1774. London. Ills. 4 vol set. VG $200.00

EPHRON, Nora. *Crazy Salad.* 1975. Knopf. 1st ed. dj. VG $20.00

EPHRON, Nora. *Heartburn.* 1983. Knopf. 1st ed. dj. VG $25.00

EPHRON, Nora. *Scribble, Scribble.* 1978. Knopf. 1st ed. dj. VG $16.00

EPOSITO, Phil & Dew, Dick. *Phil Esposito's Winning Hockey for Beginners.* 1976. Chicago. Ills. 160 pp. EX $8.50

EPP, Margaret. *Prairie Princess.* 1967. dj. $3.00

EPSTEIN, E.J. *Legend.* 1978. McGraw Hill. 1st ed. $10.00

ERASMUS. *Colloquia.* 1664. Leyden & Rott. $50.00

ERASMUS. *Colloquia.* 1693. Amsterdam. $45.00

ERDRICH, Louise. *Love Medicine.* 1984. 1st ed. VG $30.00

ERDRICH, Louise. *The Beet Queen.* 1986. New York. 1st ed. sgn. dj. EX $35.00

ERICHSON-BROWN, C. *Use of Plants for the Past 500 Years.* 1980. Breezy Creek. Ills. 512 pp. EX $20.00

ERICKSON, J. *Road to Stalingrad.* 1975. New York. 1st ed. dj. EX $47.50

ERICKSON, Pamela. *The Duchess.* 1958. $6.50

ERICKSON, Phoebe. *Nature Almanac.* 1949. New York. Ills. 1st ed. inscr. EX $15.00

ERICSON, Maxine & Rock. *Good Neighbor Recipes.* 1952. New York. 403 pp. dj. EX $5.00

ERMINE. *Laramie Rides Alone.* Signet. pb. $3.00

ERMINE. *Longhorn Empire.* Pennant. pb. $3.00

ERMINE. *Singing Lariat.* Pocketbook. pb. $3.00

ERNST, Morris & Lindey, A. *Censor Marches On.* 1940. New York. 1st ed. inscr. Lindey. dj. EX $15.00

ERNST, Morris & Lorentz, P. *Censored: Private Life of the Movie.* 1930. New York. 1st ed. photos. EX $15.00

ERSKINE, Jim & Moran, George. *Throw a Tomato, & 151 Other Ways to Be Mean.* 1979. Crown. Ills. dj. $3.50

ERSKINE, John. *Philharmonic-Symphony Soc. of NY: 1st 100 Yrs.* 1943. New York. Ills. dj. VG $12.00

ERSKINE, John. *Private Life of Helen of Troy.* 1925. Indianapolis. 1st ed. sgn. 304 pp. dj. $17.50

ERSKINE, John. *Uncle Sam in the Eyes of His Family.* Indianapolis. Ltd. 1st ed. sgn. slipcase. VG $30.00

ERVING & TROTT. *The Book of the Beastie.* 1912. Forest Press. Ills. 1st ed. 249 pp. VG $10.00

ESCARRA & SELLA. *Image de L'Himalaya.* Ills. folio. wrappers. VG $25.00

ESCHOLIER. *Daumier.* 1930. Paris. Library Floury. $25.00

ESCRITT, L.B. *Rifle & Gun for Competition & Sport.* 1953. London. 1st ed. VG $20.00

ESDAILE, James. *Mesmerism in India.* 1902. Chicago. $20.00

ESKENAZI, Gerald. *A Thinking Man's Guide to Pro Hockey.* 1972. Dutton. 223 pp. dj. EX $8.00

ESKENAZI, Gerald. *The Derek Sanderson Nobody Knows.* 1973. Chicago. Follett. 219 pp. dj. EX $10.00

ESPINOSA. *Saints in the Valleys.* 1960. New Mexico. 1st ed. dj. EX $35.00

ESPOSITO, Phil & Eskenazi, G. *Hockey Is My Life.* 1972. Dodd Mead. Ills. 207 pp. dj. VG $8.00

ESQUIRE. *Esquire Cook Book.* 1956. London. Muller. Ills. 322 pp. $7.50

ESTLEMAN, Loren. *Motor City Blue.* 1980. Boston. Houghton Mifflin. 1st ed. sgn. $35.00

ESTLEMAN, Loren. *Roses Are Dead.* 1985. Mysterious Press. proof copy. $25.00

ESTLEMAN, Loren. *The Glass Highway.* 1983. Boston. Houghton Mifflin. 1st ed. sgn. $25.00

ESTLEMAN. *Sugartown.* Boston. 1st Am. ed. sgn. dj. EX $25.00

ESTRIN, M. *A Treasury of Hobbies & Crafts.* 1947. New York. Ills. 160 pp. $4.00

ETCHISON, D. *Dark Country.* 1982. Scream Press. Ltd. 1st ed. 1/100. sgn. EX $400.00

ETCHISON, D. *Red Dreams.* Scream Press. Ltd. 1st ed. 1/250. sgn. $65.00

ETS, Marie Hall. *Mr. T.W. Anthony Woo.* 1951. Viking Press. Ills. 1st ed. dj. G $20.00

EUBANK, Thomas. *Key to Harvey's Practical Grammar.* 1886. Cleveland, OH. 5th ed. 204 pp. wrappers. $5.00

EULALIE. *A Child's Garden of Verses.* Platt & Munk. 11 color pls. VG $18.00

EUSTIS, P.S. *Homeward Through America.* 1887. 4 pls. 32 pp. SftCvr. $18.00

EVAN, Paul. *West of the Pecos.* 1st ed. ex-lib. dj. $5.00

EVANOFF. *Hunting Secrets of the Experts.* 1964. Doubleday. Ills. 251 pp. dj. $3.50

EVANOFF. *The Fresh-Water Fisherman's Bible.* 1964. New York. Ills. 1st ed. 180 pp. $7.50

EVANS, A. *Palace of Minos Knossos.* 1964. New York. Biblio & Tannen. 4 vol set. Ills. $300.00

EVANS, C. *Kangchenjunga, Untrodden Peak.* 1957. New York. Ills. maps. VG $12.50

EVANS, C. *On Climbing.* 1955. New York. 6 maps. 32 pls. VG $10.00

EVANS, Donald P. *Super Bird: Story of the Albatross.* 1975. Cranberry, NJ. Ills. 246 pp. dj. $3.50

EVANS, E. Everett. *Man of Many Minds.* 1953. Reading, PA. Fantasy Press. 1st ed. inscr. $40.00

EVANS, Ellwood. *Washington Territory: Past, Present & Future.* 1877. Olympia. 1st ed. original wrappers. $125.00

EVANS, George Bird. *The Upland Shooting Life.* 1971. New York. 1st ed. dj. VG $25.00

EVANS, H. *Falconry for You.* 1973. London. Ills. dj. EX $15.00

EVANS, H. & M. *The Life & Art of George Cruikshank.* 1978. Phillips. $15.00

EVANS, John. *Sketch of Denominations of Christian World.* 1802. London. 7th ed. G $18.00

EVANS, Lawton B. *The Student's History of Georgia.* 1884. Ills. 352 pp. maps. $15.00

EVANS, Pauline Rush. *The Family Treasury of Children's Stories.* 1956. Doubleday. Ills. D. Sibley. 2 vol set. $8.50

EVANS. *The Upland Shooting Life.* 1971. Knopf. Ills. 1st ed. 301 pp. $12.50

EVARTS, H.G. *Ambush Rider.* Popular. pb. $3.00

EVARTS, H.G. *The Passing of the Old West.* 1921. Little, Brown. VG $17.50

EVERETT, M. *Birds of Paradise & Bower Birds.* 1978. Putnam. 60 pls. maps. photos. dj. EX $80.00

EVERETT, M. *Birds of Prey.* 1975. London. Orbis. Ills. maps. 128 pp. dj. $25.00

EVERETT, T.H. *Guide to Wild Flowers: Field Flowers.* 1945. Racine. Ills. Freund. 1st ed. VG $25.00

EVERETT. *Complete Life of William McKinley.* 1901. Ills. Memorial ed. G $6.50

EVERETT. *Fun with Trout.* 1952. Stackpole. 1st ed. inscr. dj. EX $35.00

EVERETT. *The Great Chicago Theater Disaster.* 1904. McCurdy. Ills. fair $3.50

EVERETT. *The Water Babies.* 1930. 8 color pls. dj. VG $12.50

EVERITT, Charles P. *Adventures of a Treasure Hunter.* 1952. London. 1st Eng. ed. dj. VG $15.00

EVERITT, Charles P. *Adventures of a Treasure Hunter.* 1951. Boston. Little, Brown. 1st ed. dj. VG $20.00

EVERITT, Charles. *Birds of the Edward Marshall Boehm Aviaries.* 1973. Lakeside Press.1st ed. $20.00

EVERS, Medgar. *For Us, The Living.* 1967. New York. Doubleday. 378 pp. dj. $5.50

EVERSON, William. *Robinson Jeffers.* 1968. Oyez. 1st ed. $30.00

EVERSON, William. *The Art of W.C. Fields.* 1967. New York. Bonanza Books. 232 pp. dj. $37.50

EWART, Gavin. *The Gavin Ewart Show. Selected Poems 1939-1985.* 1986. Bits Press. 1st ed. dj. VG $15.00

EWELL, J.B. *Bridge Axioms & Laws.* 1907. Dutton. 89 pp. $27.50

EWEN, C. L'Estrange. *Witch Hunting & Witch Trials.* 1929. London. 1st ed. dj. VG $25.00

EWEN. *Encyclopedia of Concert Music.* 1959. 1st ed. dj. VG $10.00

EWEN. *Encyclopedia of Opera.* 1955. Hill & Wang. 594 pp. dj. EX $6.50

EWERS, Hanns Heinz. *Blood.* 1930. New York. Heron Press. Ills. Ltd. ed. VG $45.00

EWERS, John C. *Artists of the Old West.* 1973. Doubleday. Ills. dj. VG $32.50

EWING, Elmore. *Bugles & Bells.* 1899. Cincinnati. VG $15.00

EWING, Julian. *Jackanapes.* Little, Brown. Ills. Caldecott. $12.50

EWING, Julian. *Jackanapes.* 1893. Crowell. Ills. Caldecott. EX $20.00

EWING, Juliana Horatia. *Six to Sixteen.* 1908. London. Ills. M.V. Wheelhouse. 1st ed. $15.00

EWING. James. *Lectures on Tumor Pathology.* 1934. New York. 1st ed. 166 pp. $80.00

EXLEY, Frederick. *A Fan's Notes.* 1968. Harper. 1st ed. dj. VG $75.00

EXLINE. *Valhalla in the Smokies.* 1938. Ltd. sgn. EX $65.00

EXMAN, Eugene. *The House of Harper.* 1967. New York. 1st ed. dj. EX $15.00

EXQUEMELING, John. *History of Buccaneers of America.* 1704. London. Ills. maps. charts. EX $350.00

EYRING. *Quantum Chemistry.* 1947. $15.00

FABENS, Joseph Warren. *Prince of Kashna, a West Indian Story.* 1866. New York. 1st ed. 450 pp. $25.00

FABENS, Joseph Warren. *Story of Life on the Isthmus.* 1853. New York. 1st ed. 215 pp. $50.00

FABRE, Jean Henri. *Fabre's Book of Insects.* 1935. New York. Ills. E.J. Detmold. $60.00

FABRERE, Claude. *Useless Hands.* 1926. New York. Dutton. dj. EX $65.00

FABRI, R. *Painting Cityscapes.* 1973. New York. dj. EX $17.50

FABRI, R. *Painting Outdoors.* 1969. New York. dj. EX $15.00

FADDIS, Margene O. *History of Frances Payne Bolton School of Nursing.* 1948. Cleveland. Ills. 179 pp. index. $7.50

FADIMAN, Clifton. *The Lifetime Reading Plan.* 1960. Cleveland. $5.00

FAGAN, David D. *History of Benton County, Oregon.* 1885. Portland. Ills. 1st ed. 35 pls. $175.00

FAHEY. *Ships & Aircraft of the U.S. Fleet.* 1941. New York. wrappers. $5.00

FAIR, Ronald L. *Hog Butcher.* 1966. New York. Harcourt. 1st ed. inscr. dj. $30.00

FAIR, Ronald. *World of Nothing.* 1970. New York. Harper. proof copy. EX $45.00

FAIRBAIRN, W. *Some Game Birds of West Africa.* 1952. Edinburgh. 1st ed. 9 pls. 92 pp. EX $17.50

FAIRBANK, Alfred. *A Book of Scripts.* 1952. Penguin. 95 pp. $50.00

FAIRBANKS, Douglas. *Laugh & Live.* 1917. New York. 190 pp. VG $15.00

FAIRBANKS, Douglas. *Making Life Worthwhile.* 1918. New York. Ills. 157 pp. EX $25.00

FAIRBROTHER, Nan. *The Cheerful Day.* 1960. New York. 1st ed. dj. VG $15.00

FAIRCHILD, David. *Exploring for Plants.* 1930. Macmillan. 1st ed. 591 pp. dj. VG $40.00

FAIRCHILD, H.N. *Religious Trends in English Poetry. Vol. I.* 1939. $10.00

FAIRLESS, Michael. *The Roadmender.* 1922. Dutton. Ills. Taylor. 1st ed. VG $20.00

FAIRLIE, G. *Flight Without Wings.* 1957. London. 1st ed. dj. EX $15.00

FAIRMONT, Ethel. *Rhymes for Kindly Children.* 1937. New York. Ills. Gruelle. $20.00

FAITHFULL, E. *Three Visits to America.* 1888. New York. EX $20.00

FALCONER, William. *The Shipwreck.* 1802. London. 167 pp. $24.00

FALDWIN, James. *The Devil Finds Work.* 1976. Dial Press. 1st ed. dj. EX $12.50

FALL, Bernard. *Hell in a Small Place.* 1966. Lippincott. Ills. 1st ed. 515 pp. dj. VG $22.50

FALL, Bernard. *Hell in a Very Small Place.* 1967. Philadelphia. dj. VG $15.00

FALLACI, Oriana. *A Man.* 1980. 1st Am. ed. sgn. VG $30.00

FALLACI, Oriana. *Limelighters.* London. 1st ed. dj. VG $25.00

FALLOWS. *Liberty & Union.* 1889. Midland Pub. Ills. 512 pp. VG $12.50

FALORP. *Cape May to Montauk.* 1973. sgn. VG $12.50

FALSTAFF, Jake. *Book Of Rabelais.* 1928. 1st ed. $8.00

FANNING, Edmund. *Voyages & Discoveries in South Seas 1792-1832.* 1924. Salem. Ills. 335 pp. dj. $125.00

FARINA, Richard. *Long Time Coming & a Long Time Gone.* 1969. Random House. 1st ed. dj. VG $30.00

FARIS, J.T. *Old Roads Out of Philadelphia.* 1917. Philadelphia. Lippincott. 1st ed. 327 pp. $17.50

FARIS, J.T. *Seeing Pennsylvania.* 1919. VG $6.00

FARJEON, B.L. *The House of the White Shadows.* 1903. New Amsterdam. 1st ed. VG $25.00

FARJEON, Eleanor & Herbert. *Kings & Queens.* London. Ills. R. Thornycroft. dj. VG $17.50

FARJEON, Eleanor. *Nursery Rhymes of London Town.* 1916. London. Ills. Macdonald Gill. VG $25.00

FARJEON, Eleanor. *Tales from Chaucer.* 1930. rendered in prose. Ills. VG $45.00

FARJEON, Eleanor. *The Unlocked Book.* 1938. Putnam. Ills. 1st ed. 205 pp. dj. VG $25.00

FARLEY, Walter. *How to Stay Out of Trouble with Your Horse.* 1981. 1st ed. photos. dj. EX $9.00

FARLEY, Walter. *Son of the Black Stallion.* 1947. $3.00

FARLEY, Walter. *The Black Stallion & Flame.* 1960. dj. VG $3.00

FARLEY, Walter. *The Black Stallion & Satan.* 1949. New York. Ills. Menasco. 1st printing. $10.00

FARLEY, Walter. *The Black Stallion Mystery.* 1957. $3.00

FARLEY, Walter. *The Island Stallion Races.* 1955. 1st ed. dj. VG $8.50

FARMER, Bernard J. *Death of a Bookseller.* 1956. London. Heinemann. 1st ed. dj. VG $55.00

FARMER, Fannie Merritt. *Boston Cooking School Cookbook.* 1914. Boston. $15.00

FARMER, Fannie Merritt. *Rumford Cook Book.* 1906. Providence. 47 pp. wrappers. VG $12.00

FARMER, Fannie Merritt. *The Boston Cooking School Cookbook.* 1942. Boston. 7th ed. 830 pp. $10.00

FARMER, Fannie Merritt. *The Original Boston Cooking School Cookbook 1896.* 1980. Boston. 1st ed. dj. VG $9.50

FARMER, Florence. *Nature Myths of Many Lands.* 1910. Ills. VG $5.00

FARMER, P.J. *Barnstormer in Oz.* 1982. Phantasia Pr. Ltd. ed. 1/600. sgn. boxed. EX $50.00

FARMER, P.J. *Dayworld.* 1985. Putnam. 1st ed. dj. VG $17.50

FARMER, P.J. *Doc Savage: His Apocalyptic Life.* 1973. 1st ed. dj. VG $10.00

FARMER, P.J. *Gods of Riverworld.* 1983. New York. 1st ed. dj. VG $12.50

FARMER, P.J. *Lord Tyger.* 1970. New York. Doubleday. 1st ed. sgn. dj. VG $75.00

FARMER, P.J. *Private Cosmos.* 1981. Phantasia. Ltd. ed. 1/250. sgn. boxed. EX $50.00

FARMER, P.J. *River of Eternity.* 1983. Phantasia Pr. Ltd. 1st ed. sgn. dj. EX $75.00

FARMER, P.J. *Tarzan Alive.* 1972. 1st ed. dj. EX $30.00

FARMER, P.J. *The Adventure of the Peerless Peer.* 1974. Boulder. dj. EX $45.00

FARMER, P.J. *The Grand Adventure.* New York. Ltd. 1st ed. 1/325. sgn. $65.00

FARMER, P.J. *The Magic Labyrinth.* 1980. New York. 1st ed. dj. VG $10.00

FARMER, P.J. *The Maker of Universes.* 1980. Phantasia Pr. Ltd. ed. 1/200. sgn. dj. EX $125.00

FARMER, P.J. *The Unreasoning Mask.* 1981. New York. review copy. dj. VG $20.00

FARMER. *Ensor.* 1976. Art Institute of Chicago. $6.00

FARNHAM, A. *Taxidermy for Pleasure & Profit.* 1916. VG $27.50

FARNHAM, A.B. *Home Manufacture of Fur & Skins.* 1916. Columbus. VG $15.00

FARNHAM, Benjamin. *Dissertations on the Prophecies.* 1800. E. Windsor, CT. Pratt. 155 pp. $35.00

FARNHAM, Thomas J. *Travels in California.* 1947. Oakland. Ltd. ed. 1/750. map. VG $37.50

FARNOL, Jeffery. *Famous Prize Fights; or, Epics of 'The Fancy.'* 1928. Boston. Little, Brown. 260 pp. G $3.50

FARNOL, Jeffery. *The Amateur Gentleman.* 1913. New York. A.L. Burt. Ills. 625 pp. VG $3.50

FARNOL, Jeffrey *The Shadow & Other Stories.* London. (ca.1929) 1st ed. dj. VG $15.00

FARNOL. *The Broad Highway.* 1910. London. Ills. Brock. $25.00

FARQUHAR, Francis P. *Books of the Colorado River & Grand Canyon.* 1953. Los Angeles. Ills. 1st ed. 75 pp. $35.00

FARQUHAR. *The Sportsman Almanac.* 1965. Harper. 1st ed. 493 pp. dj. $9.50

FARR, F. *Frank Lloyd Wright.* 1961. Scribner. 1st ed. dj. VG $17.50

FARRALL, A.W. *Dairy Engineering.* 1952. New York. Wiley & Sons. 477 pp. VG $4.00

FARRAND, Max. *The Development of the United States.* 1918. Houghton Mifflin. G $3.00

FARRAR, Emmie F. & Hines, E. *Old Virginia Houses.* 1974. Yale. Ills. dj. VG $10.50

FARRAR, Emmie. *Old Virginia Houses. The Mobjack Bay Country.* 1955. Hastings House.1st ed. dj. $12.50

FARRAR, John. *Elementary Treatment on Mechanics.* 1825. Cambridge. Ills. VG $45.00

FARRAR, Mrs. John. *The Young Lady's Friend.* 1843. New York. 432 pp. $12.50

FARRELL, Henry. *What Ever Happened to Baby Jane?* 1960. New York. Rinehart. 1st ed. dj. EX $25.00

FARRELL, James T. *Bernard Clare.* 1946. New York. 1st Am. ed. dj. VG $10.00

FARRELL, James T. *Gas-House McGinty.* 1944. New York. World. 250 pp. dj. $3.50

FARRELL, James T. *It Has Come to Pass.* 1958. Herzl Press. 1st ed. dj. VG $15.00

FARRELL, James T. *Literature & Morality.* 1947. New York. Vanguard. 1st ed. dj. EX $35.00

FARRELL, James T. *My Days of Anger.* 1943. Vanguard. 1st ed. dj. VG $15.00

FARRELL, James T. *Olive & Mary Anne.* 1977. Stonehill. 1st ed. dj. VG $15.00

FARRELL, James T. *The Road Between.* 1949. Vanguard. 1st ed. dj. VG $20.00

FARRELL, James T. *The Young Manhood of Studs Lonigan.* 1944. New York. World. 350 pp. G $3.50

FARRELL, James T. *This Man & This Woman.* 1951. New York. 1st ed. $7.50

FARRER, J. Anson. *Books Condemned to be Burnt.* 1892. London. 1st ed. 206 pp. $22.50

FARRINGTON, Inez M. *My Maine Folks.* 1956. Portland, ME. sgn. 96 pp. dj. $7.50

FARRINGTON, S. Kip. *Atlantic Game Fishing.* 1937. New York. Ills. Lynn B. Hunt. 1st ed. VG $95.00

FARRINGTON, S. Kip. *Fishing the Atlantic.* 1949. dj. EX $20.00

FARRINGTON, S. Kip. *Fishing the Pacific.* 1953. dj. VG $15.00

FARRINGTON, S. Kip. *Gems & Gem Materials.* 1903. Chicago. 229 pp. $125.00

FARRINGTON, S. Kip. *Railroading the Modern Way.* 1951. inscr. dj. VG $10.00

FARRINGTON, S. Kip. *Railroads at War.* 1944. VG $18.00

FARRINGTON, S. Kip. *Railroads of Today.* 1949. inscr. dj. VG $10.00

FARRIS, J. *King Windom.* 1967. New York. Trident. 1st ed. dj. VG $25.00

FARRIS, J. *The Uninvited.* 1982. Delacorte. 1st ed. dj. VG $12.50

FARRIS, J. *Wildwood.* proof copy. $22.00

FARRIS, J.T. *Seeing the Far West.* 1920. Lippincott. Ills. 1st ed. maps. VG $15.00

FARRISH, Edwin Thomas. *History of Arizona.* 1915. San Francisco. Filmer Bros. 1st ed. VG $75.00

FARROW. *Adventures in Wallypugland.* no date. (ca.1900) $20.00

FARSHLER, Earl R. *Riding & Training.* 1945. Louisville. Standard Printing. VG $20.00

FASGIOLI, Marco. *Hitherto Unpublished Erotic Prints by Utamaro.* 1977. Florence. Eng/Italian text. Ltd. ed. VG $55.00

FAST, Howard. *Place in the City.* 1937. Harcourt. 1st ed. dj. VG $15.00

FAST, Howard. *Spartacus.* 1951. private print. 1st ed. VG $25.00

FAST, Howard. *The American; or, A Middle Western Legend.* 1946. New York. 337 pp. dj. VG $3.50

FAST, Howard. *The Case of the Kidnapped Angel.* 1982. Delacorte. 1st ed. dj. VG $10.00

FAST, Howard. *The Last Supper & Other Stories.* 1955. New York. Harcourt. 1st ed. dj. EX $25.00

FAST, Howard. *The Naked God.* 1957. Praeger. 1st ed. dj. VG $20.00

FAST, Howard. *The Unvanquished.* 1942. New York. Black League. 316 pp. G $3.50

FAST, Howard. *Thirty Pieces of Silver.* 1954. Blue Heron Pr. Ltd. ed. sgn. VG $15.00

FAST, Howard. *Torquemada.* 1966. Garden City. Doubleday. 1st ed. dj. VG $25.00

FATOUT, Paul. *Ambrose Bierce & the Black Hills.* 1956. U. of OK Press.1st ed. dj. VG $12.50

FAULK, Odie B. *Geronimo Campaign.* 1969. Oxford. dj. $10.00

FAULK, Odie B. *Tombstone Myth & Reality.* 1972. New York. Oxford U. Press. Ills. 242 pp. $12.50

FAULKNER, Edward H. *Plowman's Folly.* Grosset & Dunlap. dj. $5.50

FAULKNER, Georgene, retold by. *Little Peachling.* 1928. Wise-Parslow. Ills. Fred Richardson. 91 pp. $4.00

FAULKNER, Herbert Waldron. *The Mysteries of the Flowers.* 1917. New York. Stokes. Ills. 238 pp. $75.00

FAULKNER, John. *My Brother Bill.* 1963. Trident Press. dj. EX $20.00

FAULKNER, Raymond O., trans. *The Book of the Dead.* 1972. Lt. Ed. Club. 1/1500. 2 vol set. slipcase. $135.00

FAULKNER, William. *A Fable.* 1954. New York. 1st ed. dj. VG $50.00

FAULKNER, William. *Absalom, Absalom!* 1936. Random House. 2nd ed. VG $15.00

FAULKNER, William. *Big Woods.* 1955. Random House. 1st ed. dj. VG $90.00

FAULKNER, William. *Collected Stories.* 1950. New York. 1st ed. dj. VG $55.00

FAULKNER, William. *Complete Stories.* 1974. 1st Russian ed. dj. VG $22.00

FAULKNER, William. *Fairchild's Story.* 1976. London. Warren. Ltd. ed. 1/175. $30.00

FAULKNER, William. *Father Abraham.* 1983. Random House. 1st trade ed. dj. EX $7.50

FAULKNER, William. *Faulkner at West Point.* 1964. New York. 1st ed. dj. EX $12.00

FAULKNER, William. *Flags in the Dust.* 1973. Random House. 1st ed. dj. EX $10.00

FAULKNER, William. *Go Down, Moses.* 1942. 1st trade ed. VG $35.00

FAULKNER, William. *Go Down, Moses.* 1955. Modern Library.1st ed. dj. EX $10.00

FAULKNER, William. *Intruder in the Dust.* 1948. Random House. 1st ed. dj. VG $45.00

FAULKNER, William. *Intruder in the Dust.* 1949. London. Chatto & Windus. 1st Eng. ed. $75.00

FAULKNER, William. *Knight's Gambit.* 1949. Random House. dj. EX $45.00

FAULKNER, William. *Light in August.* 1932. New York. Smith & Haas. 1st ed. VG $50.00

FAULKNER, William. *Light in August.* 1932. New York. 1st ed. 1st printing. VG $110.00

FAULKNER, William. *Mayday.* 1978. U. Notre Dame. 1st trade ed. dj. VG $10.00

FAULKNER, William. *Mirrors of Chartres Street.* 1953. Faulkner Studies. Ltd. ed. dj. $60.00

FAULKNER, William. *Mosquitoes.* 1927. Boni & Liveright. G $35.00

FAULKNER, William. *New Orleans Sketches.* 1959. Sidgwick. 1st English ed. dj. VG $60.00

FAULKNER, William. *Nobel Speech.* 1951. Ltd. ed. 1/2500. wrappers. VG $50.00

FAULKNER, William. *Notes on a Horse Thief.* 1950. Levee Press. Ltd. ed. inscr. sgn. EX $300.00

FAULKNER, William. *Pylon.* 1935. New York. 1st trade ed. dj. VG $110.00

FAULKNER, William. *Requiem for a Nun.* London. 1st Eng. ed. dj. VG $65.00

FAULKNER, William. *Requiem for a Nun.* 1951. Random House. 1st ed. dj. VG $85.00

FAULKNER, William. *Requiem for a Nun: a Play.* 1959. Random House. 1st ed. dj. VG $20.00

FAULKNER, William. *Sanctuary.* 1931. Cape. 3rd ed. VG $7.50

FAULKNER, William. *Sartoris.* Grosset & Dunlap. reprint. VG $7.50

FAULKNER, William. *Selected Letters of William Faulkner.* 1977. Random House. 1st trade ed. sgn. dj. VG $22.50

FAULKNER, William. *Sherwood Anderson & Other Creoles.* 1926. New Orleans. Ills. Spratling. Ltd. 1st ed. $500.00

FAULKNER, William. *The Faulkner Reader.* 1954. New York. Random House. 682 pp. $5.00

FAULKNER, William. *The Hamlet.* 1940. Random House. dj. VG $55.00

FAULKNER, William. *The Mansion.* 1959. Random House. 1st ed. dj. VG $50.00

FAULKNER, William. *The Marionettes.* 1975. Ltd. ed. folio. slipcase. VG $200.00

FAULKNER, William. *The Portable Faulkner.* 1946. Viking Press. 1st ed. VG $12.50

FAULKNER, William. *The Reivers.* 1962. New York. 1st ed. dj. EX $45.00

FAULKNER, William. *The Reivers.* 1962. 1st trade ed. dj. VG $12.50

FAULKNER, William. *The Town.* 1957. New York. Ltd. ed. 1/450. sgn. $525.00

FAULKNER, William. *The Town.* 1957. Random House. 1st ed. 2nd issue. dj. VG $55.00

FAULKNER, William. *The Town.* 1957. Random House. 1st ed. 1st issue. dj. VG $65.00

FAULKNER, William. *The Unvanquished.* 1938. New York. 1st ed. dj. VG $125.00

FAULKNER, William. *The White Rose of Memphis.* 1953. Coley Taylor. 1st ed. dj. VG $15.00

FAULKNER, William. *The Wild Palms.* 1939. Random House. 1st ed. G $20.00

FAULKNER, William. *The Wishing Tree.* New York. Ills. Bolognese. 1st ed. EX $125.00

FAULKNER, William. *These Thirteen.* 1931. New York. Ltd. 1st ed. 1/299. sgn. $750.00

FAULKNER. *A Comprehensive Guide to the Brodsky Collection.* 1985. U. Press MS 1st ed. dj. VG $35.00

FAULKNER. *What We Hear in Music.* 1924. Victor Talking Machine Co. EX $6.50

FAURE. *Gardens of Rome.* 1924. $35.00

FAUST, Joan Lee. *The New York Times Garden Book.* 1962. New York. Knopf. Ills. 369 pp. $8.50

FAVRETTI & DE WOLF. *Colonial Gardens.* Ills. 1st ed. dj. EX $15.00

FAWCETT, Anthony. *California Rock, California Sound.* 1978. Los Angeles. Ills. 1st ed. dj. EX $20.00

FAWCETT, B. *Railways of the Andes.* 1963. London. 1st ed. 328 pp. pls. maps. dj. $18.00

FAWN, M. Brodie. *Devil Drives. A Life of Sir Richard Burton.* 1967. New York. Norton. Ills. dj. EX $17.50

FAY. *Mary Celeste.* 1942. Salem. G $15.00

FAY. Bernard. *Franklin; Apostle of Modern Times.* 1929. Boston. Little, Brown. 547 pp. $6.50

FAY. Frank. *How to Be Poor.* 1945. New York. Ills. Flagg. 172 pp. $7.50

FAY, Mrs. E. *Original Letters from India.* 1st ed. VG $12.50

FAY, Paul B., Jr. *The Pleasure of His Company.* 1966. New York. Harper & Row. 243 pp. $4.00

FAYETTE, J.B. *Voices from Many Hill Tops.* 1886. Springfield Pr.1st ed. VG $60.00

FEARING, Kenneth. *New & Selected Poems.* 1948. New York. Harcourt. 1st ed. dj. EX $25.00

FEATHER, L. & Gitler, Ira. *Encyclopedia of Jazz in the Seventies.* 1976. New York. 393 pp. EX $5.00

FEATHER, Leonard. *Encyclopedia of Jazz in the 60's.* 1966. New York. Horizon Press. dj. VG $15.00

FEATHER, Leonard. *The Encyclopedia of Jazz.* 1955. New York. Ills. ex-lib. 360 pp. $5.00

FECHTER, Paul. *Des Expressionismus.* 1920. Munchen. VG $30.00

FEDDEN & THOMPSON. *Crusader Castles.* 1957. Beirut. Ills. dj. VG $15.00

FEDDERSON. *Japanese Decorative Art.* 1962. Ills. 1st Am. ed. 296 pp. dj. $25.00

FEDER, Norman. *American Indian Art.* 1965. New York. Ills. 2 vol set. 445 pp. $35.00

FEDER, Norman. *American Indian Art.* 1969. Abrams. Ills. 60 color pls. dj. EX $50.00

FEHRENBACH. *The Battle of Anzio. Account of Operation Shingle.* 1962. pb. G $3.00

FEHRENBACH. *This Kind of War.* 1963. Macmillan. 1st ed. 689 pp. dj. EX $35.00

FEHRENBACHER. *The Dred Scott Case.* 1978. New York. dj. VG $10.00

FEIBLEMAN, Peter. *Charlie Boy.* 1980. Boston. Little, Brown. 1st ed. dj. VG $20.00

FEIBLEMAN, Peter. *The Columbus Tree.* 1973. New York. Atheneum. 1st ed. dj. VG $25.00

FEIDMAN, A. *Crocheting & Creative Design.* 1975. New York. EX $10.00

FEIFFER, Jules. *Passionella & Other Stories.* 1959. New York. 1st ed. SftCvr. VG $15.00

FEIFFER, Jules. *Tantrum.* 1979. Knopf. proof copy. wrappers. EX $40.00

FEIFFER, Jules. *Tantrum.* 1979. Knopf. 1st ed. dj. VG $15.00

FEIFFER, Jules. *The Great Comic Book Heroes.* 1965. VG $8.00

FEILD, Robert. *The Art of Walt Disney.* 1942. Macmillan. 1st ed. dj. $45.00

FEININGER, Andreas. *Feininger on Photography.* 1949. 1st ed. dj. VG $45.00

FEIS, Herbert. *Europe the World's Banker 1870-1914.* 1931. New Haven. Yale U. Pr. 2nd printing. G $15.00

FELCH. *Poultry Culture.* 1903. $9.00

FELIX, Edgar. *Television, Its Methods & Uses.* 1931. McGraw Hill. 1st ed. 272 pp. EX $30.00

FELIX, J. *Animals of Asia.* 1983. London. Ills. photos. 299 pp. dj. EX $15.00

FELLINI, Federico. *La Dolce Vita.* 1961. Ballantine. 1st Am. pb. wrappers. VG $6.00

FELLOWES. *A Visit to the Monastery of La Trappe.* 1818. London. 1st ed. 15 aquatint pls. VG $150.00

FELLOWES. *Boating Trips on North East Rivers.* 1884. Ills. 1st ed. maps. $26.00

FELLOWES. *First Over Everest.* 1934. New York. dj. VG $15.00

FELS. *Vincent Van Gogh.* 1928. Paris. $25.00

FELTON, Harold W. *Legends of Paul Bunyan.* 1950. New York. Knopf. Ills. Bennett. $15.00

FENN, Amor. *Design & Tradition.* New York. Scribner. no date. VG $10.00

FENN, George M. *Off to the Wilds. Two Brothers in South Africa.* 1882. New York. Crowell. Ills. EX $125.00

FENN, George M. *Seven Frozen Sailors.* 1896. New Amsterdam. 1st ed. dj. EX $45.00

FENNELLY. *Steelhead Paradise.* 1970. dj. EX $12.50

FENNER, Phyllis R. *Time to Laugh.* 1942. New York. Ills. Henry C. Pitz. 1st ed. $15.00

FENNY, J. *Time & Again.* 1980. London. 1st ed. dj. EX $25.00

FENOLLOSA, Ernest. *Epochs of Chinese & Japanese Art.* 1921. Heinemann. revised ed. 2 vol set. $50.00

FENTON, C. *Our Amazing Earth.* 1943. Garden City. maps. 346 pp. G $6.00

FENTON, C. *The World of Fossils.* 1933. Appleton. Ills. 183 pp. G $7.50

FENTON, Elijah. *The Poetical Works of Elijah Fenton.* 1798. London. Ills. 140 pp. $30.00

FERBER, Edna. *A Peculiar Treasure.* 1939. New York. $10.00

FERBER, Edna. *Cheerful by Request.* 1918. Doubleday. G $15.00

FERBER, Edna. *Cimarron.* 1930. New York. 1st ed. VG $6.00

FERBER, Edna. *Come & Get It.* 1935. 1st ed. G $6.00

FERBER, Edna. *Giant.* 1952. Doubleday. 1st ed. dj. VG $20.00

FERBER, Edna. *Gigolo.* 1922. Doubleday. 1st ed. G $10.00

FERBER, Edna. *Show Boat.* 1926. Doubleday. Ltd. ed. 1/1000. VG $22.50

FERBER, Edna. *So Big.* 1924. New York. Doubleday. 360 pp. $3.50

FERDINAND, Prince Louis. *Rebel Prince. Memoirs of Prince Louis Ferdinand.* 1952. Chicago. Ills. sgn. 356 pp. index. dj. $15.00

FERGUSEN. *English Springer Spaniel.* Derrydale Pr. Ltd. ed. 1/850. $80.00

FERGUSON, Charles. *The University Militant.* 1911. NY/London. 1st ed. G $15.00

FERGUSON, Donald N. *Masterworks of the Orchestral Repertoire.* 1954. U. of MN. dj. EX $15.00

FERGUSON, Donald N. *Piano Music of Six Great Composers.* 1947. New York. SftCvr. EX $10.00

FERGUSON, John. *Chinese Painting.* 1927. Chicago. G $50.00

FERGUSON, John. *Death Comes to Perigord.* 1931. London. 1st ed. VG $20.00

FERGUSON, Walter. *Birds of All Kinds.* 1959. New York. Golden Press. Ills. 1st ed. VG $4.00

FERGUSON. *Experiences of a Forty-Niner.* 1888. 1st ed. $140.00

FERGUSSON, Edna. *Our Southwest.* 1941. Knopf. 2nd printing. VG $15.00

FERGUSSON, Edna. *Our Southwest.* 1946. Knopf. Ills. 3rd printing. VG $8.50

FERGUSSON, H. *Blood of Conquerors.* 1921. New York. 1st ed. dj. VG $250.00

FERGUSSON, H. *Home in the West.* 1944. New York. Ills. 1st ed. VG $45.00

FERGUSSON, W.N. *Adventures & Sport on the Tibetan Steppes.* 1911. London. Ills. $50.00

FERGUSSON. *Diamonds & Other Gems.* 1927. Los Angeles. 160 pp. $12.50

FERLINGHETTI, Lawrence. *Northwest Ecology.* 1978. San Francisco. 1st ed. wrappers. EX $10.00

FERLINGHETTI, Lawrence. *The Mexican Night.* 1970. New York. New Direction. wrappers. EX $12.50

FERMI, Laura. *Atoms in the Family. My Life with Enrico Fermi.* 1954. Chicago Press. Ills. 2nd printing. 267 pp. $12.50

FERN, S. & L. *Wings Over the Pacific, 7th Air Force in Pictures.* 1947. Gray Printing Co. 118 pp. dj. $7.50

FERRARI. *La Terra Cotta E Pavimenti in Laterizo.* 1928. Milan. $20.00

FERRARS, Elizabeth. *Murder Among Friends.* 1946. London. 1st ed. dj. VG $15.00

FERRAZ. *Pioneer Photographs of Brazil.* 1976. $7.00

FERRIER, Neil. *Churchill. The Man of the Century.* 1965. New York. Doubleday. 62 pp. dj. $4.50

FERRIL, Helen. *The Indoor Bird Watcher's Manual.* 1950. New York. 2nd ed. 64 pp. $37.50

FERRIS, Paul. *Dylan Thomas, a Biography.* 1977. New York. Dial Press. 399 pp. dj. $8.00

FERRIS, Warren A. *Life in the Rocky Mountains.* 1983. Old West Pub. new revised ed. maps. EX $40.00

FESSIER, Michael. *Fully Dressed & in His Right Mind.* 1934. New York. 1st ed. dj. VG $40.00

FETIS. *Notice of Anthony Stradivari.* 1864. London. 132 pp. $25.00

FEUCHTWANGER, Lion. *Jefta und Seine Tochter.* 1957. Berlin. 1st ed. inscr. dj. VG $45.00

FEUER, L.S. *Spinoza & the Rise of Liberalism.* 1958. Boston. 323 pp. index. $12.50

FIALA, Anthony. *Fighting the Polar Ice.* 1906. 1st ed. $100.00

FIELD, D.D. *Genealogy of the Brainerd Family in United States.* 1857. New York. 303 pp. $40.00

FIELD, D.M. *Oriental Rugs.* 1983. New York. Crescent. Ills. dj. VG $10.50

FIELD, Edward. *Diary of Israel Angel 1778-1781.* 1899. Providence. Ills. 158 pp. fld. map. $24.00

FIELD, Edward. *Stand Up, Friend, with Me.* 1963. New York. Grove. 1st ed. dj. EX $20.00

FIELD, Eugene. *A Little Book of Western Verse.* 1896. New York. Scribner. 202 pp. VG $6.00

FIELD, Eugene. *Christmas Tales & Christmas Verse.* 1912. New York. Ills. Storer. 1st ed. 8 pls. $30.00

FIELD, Eugene. *Poems of Childhood.* 1904. Scribner. Ills. Parrish. VG $60.00

FIELD, Eugene. *Sharps & Flats.* 1900. Scribner. 2 vol set. VG $110.00

FIELD, Eugene. *The Gingham Dog & Calico Cat.* 1926. New York. Ills. G $30.00

FIELD, Eugene. *The Poems of Field, Eugene. Complete Edition.* 1911. New York. Scribner. 553 pp. $4.50

FIELD, Eugene. *Wynken, Blynken & Nod/Gingham Dog & Calico Cat.* 1945. Chicago. Wilcox & Follett. Ills. Page. $10.00

FIELD, Henry. *An Anthropological Reconnaissance in Near East.* 1956. Peabody Museum. 1st ed. wrappers. $10.00

FIELD, Henry. *Gibraltar.* 1889. New York. Ills. sgn. 139 pp. $15.00

FIELD, Henry. *The Life of David Dudley Field.* 1898. New York. presentation copy. sgn. VG $15.00

FIELD, Louise A. *Peter Rabbit & His Ma.* 1917. Saalfield. Ills. Virginia Albert. VG $10.00

FIELD, Louise A. *Peter Rabbit & His Pa.* 1916. Akron. Ills. Virginia Albert. $15.00

FIELD, Matthew C. *Prairie & Mountain Sketches.* 1957. Norman. 1st ed. dj. $20.00

FIELD, Michael. *Culinary Classics & Improvisations.* 1967. New York. Knopf. 223 pp. $6.00

FIELD, Peter. *End of the Trail.* Pocketbooks. pb. $3.00

FIELD, Peter. *Powder Valley Ambush.* Pocketbooks. pb. $3.00

FIELD, Peter. *Road to Laramie.* Pocketbooks. pb. $3.00

FIELD, Peter. *The Smoking Iron.* Pocketbooks. pb. $3.00

FIELD, Rachel. *All This & Heaven Too.* 1938. New York. 1st ed. G $25.00

FIELD, Rachel. *Calico Bush.* 1931. Jr. Lit. Guild. Ills. Allen Lewis. G $12.50

FIELD, Rachel. *Calico Bush.* 1966. Macmillan. reprint. 201 pp. $15.00

FIELD, Rachel. *Calico Bush.* 1931. New York. Macmillan. Ills. Allen Lewis. $35.00

FIELD, Rachel. *Calico Bush.* 1931. New York. presentation copy. dj. VG $45.00

FIELD, Rachel. *God's Pocket.* 1934. New York. 1st ed. VG $10.00

FIELD, Rachel. *Hepatica Hawks.* 1932. Macmillan. Ills. Allen Lewis. 1st ed. VG $15.00

FIELD, Rachel. *Hitty: Her First Hundred Years.* 1930. Macmillan. Ills. Lathrop. dj. VG $30.00

FIELD, Roswell. *The Bondage of Ballinger.* 1903. Chicago. 2nd ed. VG $10.00

FIELD, Sara Bard. *Barabbas.* 1932. New York. Boni. 1st ed. dj. EX $40.00

FIELD, Sara Bard. *The Speech of Sara Bard Field.* 1921. San Francisco. Nash. wrappers. VG $25.00

FIELD. *California Alcalde.* 1950. Oakland. Ltd. 1st ed. EX $60.00

FIELDER, Mildred. *Wild Bill & Deadwood.* 1965. Seattle. Ills. 1st ed. 160 pp. dj. $20.00

FIELDER. *Life of Joseph E. Brown.* 1883. VG $25.00

FIELDER. *Sioux Indian Leaders.* 1981. reprint. dj. EX $8.00

FIELDING, Daphne. *Emerald & Nancy.* 1969. London. revised ed. dj. EX $12.50

FIELDING, Henry. *Jonathan Wild.* 1926. New York. Knopf. Ltd ed. 1/3000. VG $13.00

FIELDING, Henry. *Joseph Andrews.* 1929. London. Scolartis Press. Ltd. ed. VG $15.00

FIELDING, Henry. *The History of Tom Jones, a Foundling.* 1948. New York. Literary Guild. 374 pp. VG $5.00

FIELDING, Henry. *The History of Tom Jones.* 1930. New York. Ills. Pryse. 1st ed. $25.00

FIELDING, William J. *Strange Customs of Courtship & Marriage.* 1942. New York. 1st ed. 322 pp. dj. EX $20.00

FIGUIER, Louis. *Earth & Sea.* 1870. London. Nelson. 715 pp. $30.00

FILSON, John. *Histoire de Kentucke.* 1785. Paris. 1st French ed. Ills. 234 pp. $850.00

FINCH, Christopher. *Norman Rockwell's America.* 1975. New York. 313 pp. dj. EX $10.00

FINCH, Christopher. *The Art of Walt Disney.* 1973. New York. Abrams. 1st ed. $75.00

FINCH, Christopher. *The Art of Walt Disney.* 1975. Abrams. dj. wrappers. VG $24.00

FINCH, Christopher. *Walt Disney's America.* 1978. Abbevill Press. Ills. 302 pp. folio. EX $40.00

FINDLAY, J.T. *Wolfe in Scotland.* 1928. New York. Ills. 328 pp. $30.00

FINDLEY, Row. *Great American Deserts.* 1972. Washington. Ills. 207 pp. index. dj. $7.50

FINE, Robert. *The World's Great Chess Games.* 1951. Bonanza. VG $3.50

FINEBERG, S. Andhil. *Punishment Without Crime.* 1949. New York. Doubleday. ex-lib. 337 pp. VG $5.00

FINECKE, Bror Von Blixen. *African Hunter.* 1938. Knopf. Ills. 1st ed. 284 pp. index. $150.00

FINERTY, John F. *War-Path & Bivouac.* 1955. EX $25.00

FINERTY, John F. *World's Best Histories Ireland, Vol. II.* 1904. New York. Co-Operative Pub. G $2.50

FINESHRIBER, W. *Stendhal the Romantic Rationalist.* 1932. Princeton. dj. scarce $10.00

FINESTONE, Harry. *Bacon's Rebellion.* 1956. Charlottesville. 40 pp. $8.50

FINEY, James E. *Pioneer Life in the West.* 1853. Cincinnati/NY. 1st ed. VG $20.00

FINGER, Charles. *Frontier Ballads Heard & Gathered.* 1927. Garden City. Ills. 1st ed. VG $20.00

FINGER, Charles. *High Water in Arkansas.* Grosset & Dunlap. Ills. Pitz. $15.00

FINGER, Charles. *Ozark Fantasia.* 1927. Fayette, Ark. Ills. Paul Honore. sgn. VG $20.00

FINKELSTEIN, L. *The Jews, Their History, Culture, & Religion.* 1949. Philadelphia. 1st ed. 4 vol set. $45.00

FINLEY, J.B. *History of Wyandott Mission, Upper Sandusky, OH.* 1840. Cincinnati. 1st ed. 432 pp. $350.00

FINLEY, James B. *Sketches of Western Methodism.* 1854. Cincinnati. 1st ed. 551 pp. $40.00

FINLEY, Jason. *Life Among the Indians.* Ohio. Cranston-Curts. Ills. 548 pp. $15.00

FINLEY, Martha. *Elsie Dinsmore.* Chicago. Saalfield. 402 pp. fair $4.00

FINLEY, Martha. *Elsie's Girlhood.* 1872. Dodd. Mead. red cloth w/gold lettering. $3.50

FINLEY, Martha. *Elsie's Holiday.* 1868. Grosset & Dunlap. 354 pp. G $3.50

FINLEY, Martha. *Holidays at Roselands.* 1898. New York. Dodd Mead. 354 pp. $4.50

FINLEY, R.E. *Old Patchwork Quilts.* 1929. Philadelphia. $12.50

FINLEY, William & Irene. *Little Bird Blue.* 1915. Boston. Ills. R. Bruce Horsfall. $10.00

FINLEY. *Pioneering Life in West.* 1853. G $12.50

FINN, F. *Indian Sporting Birds.* 1915. London. 1st ed. 100 pls. 280 pp. EX $200.00

FINN, F. *Mammalia of India.* 1929. Calcutta. Ills. revised ed. 347 pp. VG $45.00

FINNEY, C. *Memoirs.* 1876. New York. 1st ed. 477 pp. G $25.00

FINNEY, C. *The Circus of Dr. Lao.* 1948. London. Ills. G.N. Fish. 1st ed. EX $45.00

FINNEY, C. *The Unholy City.* 1937. New York. Vanguard. 1st ed. VG $12.50

FINNEY, Jack. *Forgotten News.* 1982. 1st ed. dj. EX $15.00

FINNEY, Jack. *Good Neighbor Sam.* 1963. New York. advance copy. wrappers. EX $75.00

FINNEY, Jack. *I Love Galesburg in the Springtime.* 1963. Simon & Schuster. 1st ed. dj. $50.00

FINNEY, Jack. *The Body Snatchers.* 1955. Eyre & Spottiswoode. 1st ed. $50.00

FINNEY, Jack. *The House of Numbers.* 1957. Dell. 1st ed. pb. VG $10.00

FINNEY, Jack. *The Night People.* 1977. 1st ed. dj. $35.00

FINNEY, Jack. *The Third Level.* 1957. New York. Rinehart. 1st ed. dj. VG $30.00

FINNEY, Jack. *The Woodrow Wilson Dime.* 1968. New York. 1st ed. dj. VG $30.00

FINNEY, Jack. *Time & Again.* 1970. 1st ed. dj. EX $65.00

FIRBANK, Ronald. *Artificial Princess.* 1934. 1st Eng. ed. VG $70.00

FIRBANK, Ronald. *Concerning the Eccentricities of Cardinal Pirelli.* 1926. London. $85.00

FIRBANK, Ronald. *Five Novels.* New Directions. 1st Am. ed. dj. VG $7.50

FIRBANK, Ronald. *Flower Beneath the Foot.* 1923. London. $65.00

FIRBANK, Ronald. *Flower Beneath the Foot.* 1924. 1st Am. ed. VG $40.00

FIRBANK, Ronald. *Inclinations.* 1916. London. $55.00

FIRBANK, Ronald. *La Princesse aux Soleils & Harmonie.* 1974. Ltd. ed. 1/200. EX $25.00

FIRBANK, Ronald. *Odette: Fairy Tale for Weary People.* 1916. London. Ills. 1st ed. wrappers. VG $50.00

FIRBANK, Ronald. *Prancing Niger.* 1924. New York. Brentano. dj. EX $32.50

FIRBANK, Ronald. *Princess Zoubaroff.* 1920. London. $75.00

FIRBANK, Ronald. *Sorrow Sunlight.* 1925. 1st Eng. ed. 1/1000. VG $45.00

FIRBANK, Ronald. *Three Novels.* New York. New Directions. 1st ed. dj. EX $30.00

FIRBANK, Ronald. *Vainglory.* 1915. London. $75.00

FIRBANK, Ronald. *Valmouth.* 1919. London. Ills. A. John. 1st ed. $75.00

FIRESTONE, Clark B. *Sycamore Shores.* 1936. New York. Ills. 1st ed. 247 pp. dj. $12.50

FIRESTONE, Harvey. *Man on the Move. Ills. Story of Transportation.* 1967. Putnam. dj. VG $11.00

FIRESTONE, Harvey. *Men & Rubber. The Story of Business.* 1926. Garden City. 1st ed. inscr. 279 pp. VG $35.00

FIRSOFF. *On Foot in the Cairngorms.* 1965. Edinburgh. 1st ed. dj. EX $10.00

FISCHEL, O. & Boehn, Max von. *Modes & Manners of the 19th Century.* 1909. London/NY. Ills. 3 vol set. VG $100.00

FISCHER, Helene. *Skiing East & West.* 1946. 1st ed. EX $15.00

FISCHER, Ottokar. *Illustrated Magic.* 1949. New York. dj. EX $10.00

FISCHER. *Bierzig Fahre Glasmalkunst.* 1910. Munich. VG $27.50

FISCHLER, Stan & Baliotti. *This is Hockey.* 1975. Prentice Hall. Ills. 224 pp. dj. EX $17.50

FISCHLER, Stan & Shirley. *Fischlers' Hockey Encyclopedia.* 1975. New York. 628 pp. dj. EX $15.00

FISCHLER, Stan. *Heroes of Pro Hockey.* 1971. Random House. Ills. 140 pp. EX $5.00

FISCHLER, Stan. *Hockey's Great Rivalries.* 1974. Random House. Ills. 151 pp. EX $5.00

FISCHLER, Stan. *Kings of the Rink.* 1978. Dodd Mead. Ills. 104 pp. dj. EX $7.50

FISCHLER, Stan. *Slapshot!* 1973. Grosset & Dunlap. 231 pp. dj. $8.00

FISCHLER, Stan. *Slashing.* 1974. Cromwell. Ills. 266 pp. VG $7.50

FISCHLER, Stan. *Those Were the Days.* 1976. Dodd Mead. 337 pp. dj. EX $10.00

FISH, Donald. *Airline Detective.* 1962. London. Ills. 1st ed. dj. VG $65.00

FISHBERG. *The Jews: Study of Race & Environment.* 1911. New York. Ills. $35.00

FISHER, A. Hugh. *Frolics with Uncle Yule.* 1928. Boston. Ills. $25.00

FISHER, Anne B. *The Salinas, Upside Down River.* 1945. 1st ed. dj. VG $15.00

FISHER, Fred V. *The Translation of Job, Tale of High Sierras.* 1900. Cook Pub. $6.50

FISHER, H.D. *Gun & the Gospel. Brown, Quantrell & Mormons.* 1896. Chicago. Kenwood Press. $20.00

FISHER, Harrison. *A Dream of Fair Women.* 1907. Indianapolis. Ills. 1st ed. VG $75.00

FISHER, Harrison. *American Belles, Decorated by Bertha Stuart.* 1911. New York. mounted color plates. VG $125.00

FISHER, Harrison. *American Girls in Miniature.* 1912. New York. 1st ed. 32 color pls. EX $50.00

FISHER, Harrison. *Bachelor Belles.* 1908. Dunlap. 19 color pls. dj. VG $85.00

FISHER, Harrison. *Bachelor Belles.* 1908. Dodd Mead. 1st ed. boxed. $125.00

FISHER, J. & Peterson, R.T. *World of Birds.* 1964. revised ed. 192 pls. 191 pp. $12.50

FISHER, L. *Life & Death of Stalin.* 1952. Harper. 272 pp. dj. $17.00

FISHER, M.F.K. *A Considerable Town.* 1978. New York. dj. EX $10.00

FISHER, M.F.K. *An Alphabet for Gourmets.* 1949. Viking. 1st printing. dj. $8.50

FISHER, M.F.K. *As They Were.* 1982. New York. dj. EX $10.00

FISHER, M.F.K. *Map of Another Town.* 1964. Boston. 1st ed. dj. VG $17.50

FISHER, M.F.K. *Sister Age.* 1983. 1st ed. dj. EX $15.00

FISHER, M.F.K. *The Art of Eating.* 1954. Cleveland/NY. World. dj. VG $25.00

FISHER, M.F.K. *The Gastronomical Me.* 1948. Cleveland/NY. World. $20.00

FISHER, M.F.K. *With Bold Knife & Fork.* 1969. New York. dj. VG $17.50

FISHER, Miles Mark. *Negro Slave Songs.* 1953. Ithaca. Cornell U. Pr. dj. EX $30.00

FISHER, Ronald M. *The Appalachian Trail.* 1972. Washington. Ills. 199 pp. index. dj. VG $7.50

FISHER, Sydney. *Men, Women & Manners on Colonial Times.* 1898. Philadelphia. 1st ed. 2 vol set. EX $50.00

FISHER, Vardis. *Challenge to Evasion.* 1938. Chicago. Ltd. ed. 1/400. $22.50

FISHER, Vardis. *City of Illusion.* 1941. New York. 3rd ed. EX $20.00

FISHER, Vardis. *City of Illusion.* 1941. Caldwell. Caxton Printers. Ltd. 1st ed. $195.00

FISHER, Vardis. *Forgive Us Our Virtues.* 1938. Caxton. 1st ed. VG $15.00

FISHER, Vardis. *Love & Death.* 1959. Garden City. New York. 1st ed. dj. VG $12.50

FISHER, Vardis. *Orphans in Gethesmane.* 1960. Denver. Ltd. ed. sgn. dj. EX $65.00

FISHER, Vardis. *Tale of Valor.* 1958. 1st ed. VG $15.00

FISHER & ABELL. *Still Waters, White Waters.* 1977. Nat. Geo. Soc. photos. dj. EX $4.50

FISHER. *Children of God.* 1939. New York. Harper. 1st ed. VG $18.00

FISHETTI. *Pompeii, Past & Present.* 1895. Ills. EX $100.00

FISHMAN, J. *Seven Men of Spandu.* 1954. New York. Ills. $7.00

FISHMAN, J.F. *Sex in Prisons.* 1934. New York. Ills. 256 pp. G $15.00

FISHWICK, Marshall W. *The Virginia Tradition.* 1956. Washington. Ills. 111 pp. dj. $7.50

FISKE, D.T. *Faith Working by Love: Exemplified by F. Fiske.* 1868. Boston. 1st ed. 416 pp. $40.00

FISKE, James. *Fighting in the Alps.* 1916. New York. 226 pp. dj. $3.50

FISKE, John. *Essays Historical & Literary.* 1902. New York. 1st ed. sgn. 2 vol set. $20.00

FISKE, John. *How the U.S. Became a Nation.* 1904. Boston. Ginn & Co. 254 pp. VG $2.75

FISKE, John. *Mississippi Valley in the Civil War.* 1900. Boston. Ills. 1st ed. 368 pp. $20.00

FISKE, John. *Myths & Myth Makers.* 1873. Boston. 1st Am. ed. VG $15.00

FISKE, John. *Myths & Myth Makers.* 1900. New York. EX $6.00

FISKE. *Old Virginia & Her Neighbors.* 1899. 2 vol set. 700 pp. $9.50

FISKE. *The Critical Period of American History.* 1897. Ills. 395 pp. $13.50

FITCH, Asa. *1st & 2nd Report on Noxious & Beneficial Insects.* 1856. Albany. Ills. 336 pp. $18.00

FITCH, H.S. *Autecology of the Copperhead.* 1960. KS U. Press. Ills. EX $12.00

FITCH, John. *Annals of the Army of the Cumberland.* 1863. Philadelphia. 1st ed. 671 pp. $37.50

FITCH, Thomas. *Reasons Why Colonies Should Not Be Charged Taxes.* 1764. New Haven. 1st ed. 39 pp. orig. wrappers. $550.00

FITE, Emerson David. *The Presidential Campaign of 1860.* 1911. New York. 1st ed. 356 pp. $25.00

FITINGHOFF, Laura. *Children of the Moor.* 1927. Boston. Ills. Tenggren. 1st ed. $25.00

FITZ, Grancel. *North American Head Hunting.* 1957. Ills. 1st ed. 188 pp. $10.00

FITZ-GIBBON, Bernice. *Macy's, Gimbels, and Me.* 1967. New York. Ills. 1st printing. VG $15.00

FITZ-GIBBON, Bernice. *Macy's, Gimbels, and Me.* 1967. New York. Simon & Schuster. 3rd print. G $4.00

FITZ-SIMMONS, Foster. *Bright Leaf.* 1948. Rinehart. $2.00

FITZGERALD, F. Scott. *Afternoon of an Author.* 1958. New York. 1st trade ed. dj. VG $25.00

FITZGERALD, F. Scott. *Afternoon of an Author.* 1957. New York. Scribner. 226 pp. $12.50

FITZGERALD, F. Scott. *All the Sad Young Men.* 1926. New York. 1st ed. $200.00

FITZGERALD, F. Scott. *Flappers & Philosophers.* 1920. New York. 1st ed. VG $50.00

FITZGERALD, F. Scott. *Tales of the Jazz Age.* 1922. New York. 1st ed. 2nd issue. EX $50.00

FITZGERALD, F. Scott. *Tales of the Jazz Age.* 1922. New York. Scribner. 1st ed. 1st issue. $125.00

FITZGERALD, F. Scott. *Taps at Reveille.* 1935. New York. Scribner. dj. VG $80.00

FITZGERALD, F. Scott. *Tender is the Night.* 1934. New York. 1st ed. 1st issue. $125.00

FITZGERALD, F. Scott. *The Beautiful & the Damned.* 1922. New York. Scribner. 1st ed. dj. VG $57.50

FITZGERALD, F. Scott. *The Great Gatsby.* 1925. Scribner. 1st ed. $65.00

FITZGERALD, F. Scott. *The Portable F. Scott Fitzgerald.* 1945. New York. Viking. 1st ed. 835 pp. $7.50

FITZGERALD, F. Scott. *The Stories of F. Scott Fitzgerald.* 1951. Scribner. dj. VG $20.00

FITZGERALD, F. Scott. *The Vegetable.* 1923. New York. 1st ed. EX $60.00

FITZGERALD, F. Scott. *This Side of Paradise.* 1948. New York. Scribner. 255 pp. VG $4.00

FITZGERALD, John Honey. *The Advance of Boston 1910-1913.* 1913. Boston. Ills. 1st ed. 113 pp. sgn. VG $100.00

FITZGERALD, Nigel. *Black Welcome.* 1961. London. 1st ed. dj. VG $15.00

FITZGERALD, Oscar P. *Three Centuries of American Furniture.* 1985. Grammercy, NY. Ills. dj. VG $12.50

FITZGERALD, Pegeen. *Meatless Cooking. Pegeen's Vegetarian Recipes.* New York. Gramercy. 207 pp. $5.00

FITZGIBBON, Constantine. *The Life of Dylan Thomas.* 1965. Boston. Little, Brown. 1st Am. ed. $5.00

FITZGIBBON, Constantine. *When the Kissing Had to Stop.* 1960. New York. 1st ed. dj. VG $25.00

FITZHUGH, Percy Keese. *Tom Slade on Overlook Mountain.* 1923. New York. Grosset & Dunlap. 229 pp. $3.50

FITZHUGH. *Roy Blakely, Lost, Strayed or Stolen.* 1921. Grosset & Dunlap. Ills. $3.50

FITZPATRICK, John C. *The Autobiography of Martin Van Buren.* 1920. Washington. 808 pp. $30.00

FITZPATRICK, P. *Jock of the Bushveld.* 1979. London. Ills. Caldwell. 474 pp. VG $17.50

FITZSIMMONS, Ben. *Tanks & Weapons of WWI.* 1973. New York. VG $6.00

FITZSIMMONS, F. *The Monkey Folk of South Africa.* 1911. London. VG $45.00

FITZSIMMONS, M. & Fitzsimmons. *You Can Cook If You Can Read.* 1946. New York. Viking. 364 pp. $3.50

FITZSIMONS, Bernard. *Tanks & Weapons of World War I.* 1973. London. photos. Ills. 160 pp. dj. EX $10.00

FITZSIMONS, J. *Pheasants & Their Enemies.* 1979. Spur, England. Ills. 101 pp. dj. EX $10.00

FITZSIMONS, V.F.M. *Field Guide to the Snakes of Southern Africa.* 1980. Collins. Ills. 221 pp. EX $25.00

FIXX, Jim. *Jim Fixx's Second Book of Running.* 1980. Random House. 239 pp. dj. EX $4.50

FIZELL, W.G. & Greenfield, G. *Around the World on the Cleveland.* 1910. sgn. VG $15.00

FLADER, Susan. *Thinking Like a Mountain.* 1974. U. of MO Press.1st ed. dj. $4.00

FLAGG, James Montgomery. *'If', A Guide to Bad Manners.* 1905. New York. Ills. 107 pp. G $27.50

FLAGG, James Montgomery. *Roses & Buckshot.* 1946. New York. Ills. 1st ed. 224 pp. dj. $10.00

FLAHERTY, F.H. *Elephant Dance.* 1937. Scribner. Ills. 136 pp. G $7.50

FLAHERTY, Frances. *The Odyssey of a Film Maker.* 1960. 1st ed. VG $25.00

FLAMMARION, Camille. *Urania.* 1890. Boston. 1st ed. $60.00

FLAMMONDE, Paris. *The Kennedy Conspiracy.* 1969. New York. Ills. 1st ed. 348 pp. index. $17.50

FLANAGAN, Hallie. *Shifting Scenes of European Theatre.* 1928. New York. Coward. 1st ed. dj. EX $20.00

FLANAGAN, Thomas. *The Year of the French.* 1st ed. sgn. dj. EX $30.00

FLANDERS, Bertram Holland. *Early GA Magazines: Literary Periodicals to 1865.* 1944. Athens, GA. 1st ed. 289 pp. dj. $40.00

FLANNAGAN, Roy C. *The Story of Lucky Strike.* 1938. Richmond, VA. VG $4.00

FLANNER, Janet. *Paris Was Yesterday 1925-1939.* 1972. New York. Viking. 5th printing. $4.50

FLAUBERT, G. *Three Tales.* 1923. Ills. Diaz de Soria. $75.00

FLAUBERT, Gustave. *Madame Bovary.* 1957. New York. Random House. 396 pp. Vg. $3.50

FLAUBERT, Gustave. *November.* 1932. Roman Press. Ills. 1st Am. ed. dj. VG $40.00

FLEAY, David. *Nightwatchmen of Bush & Plain. Australian Owls.* 1968. Brisbane. Ills. dj. $15.00

FLECHTNER, Myron. *Springfield & Clark County Ohio.* 1941. Springfield. Ills. 1st ed. 136 pp. maps. VG $35.00

FLECKER, James Elroy. *The Last Generation.* 1908. London. New Age Pr. 1st ed. wrappers. $65.00

FLECKER, James. *Hassan.* 1924. London. Ills. 1st ed. dj. VG $90.00

FLEET, S. *Clocks.* 1972. London. dj. EX $10.00

FLEETWOOD, J. *Life of Jesus Christ.* 1891. Philadelphia. 541 pp. $35.00

FLEISCHER, Nat. *Black Dynamite, Story of Negro in Boxing.* 1938. New York. Ills. 182 pp. EX $15.00

FLEMING, A. *Falconry & Falcons.* 1974. England. Ills. 114 pp. dj. EX $17.50

FLEMING, Ian. *Chitty Chitty Bang Bang.* 1964. London. Ills. 1st ed. dj. VG $40.00

FLEMING, Ian. *Diamonds Are Forever.* 1956. London. Cape. 1st ed. dj. EX $225.00

FLEMING, Ian. *Gilt Edges Bonds.* 1961. Macmillan. 1st printing. VG $28.00

FLEMING, Ian. *Goldfinger.* 1959. London. Cape. 1st ed. VG $150.00

FLEMING, Ian. *Moonraker.* 1955. London. 1st ed. dj. VG $260.00

FLEMING, Ian. *Moonraker.* 1955. New York. Macmillan. 1st Am. ed. dj. VG $60.00

FLEMING, Ian. *Octopussy & Living Daylights.* 1966. London. Cape. 1st ed. dj. EX $45.00

FLEMING, Ian. *On Her Majesty's Secret Service.* 1963. 1st Eng. ed. dj. VG $35.00

FLEMING, Ian. *The Diamond Smugglers.* 1957. London. Cape. 1st ed. dj. EX $75.00

FLEMING, Ian. *The Man with the Golden Gun.* 1965. 1st Eng. ed. dj. VG $40.00

FLEMING, Ian. *The Spy Who Loved Me.* 1962. London. Cape. 1st ed. VG $35.00

FLEMING, Ian. *Thunderball.* 1961. London. Cape. 1st ed. VG $35.00

FLEMING, Ian. *You Only Live Twice.* 1964. Cape. 1st Eng. ed. dj. VG $40.00

FLEMING, N.C. *The Undersea.* 1977. Macmillan. Ills. 1st Am. ed. dj. EX $5.00

FLEMING, P. *Brazilian Adventure.* 1934. Scribner. Ills. 1st ed. 412 pp. EX $15.00

FLEMING, P. *The Flying Visit.* 1940. New York. Scribner. $12.00

FLEMING, S. *God's Gold: Story of Baptist Beginnings in CA.* 1949. Judson Press. VG $12.00

FLEMING, Thomas J. *Now We Are Enemies.* 1960. New York. dj. EX $10.00

FLEMING. *News from Tartary.* 1936. New York. 1st ed. dj. EX $15.00

FLEMING. *Old Violins & Their Makers.* 1883. London. 331 pp. $45.00

FLEMING. *The Fiddle Fancier's Guide.* 1892. London. 309 pp. $40.00

FLETCHER, Archibald Lee. *Boy Scouts in the Everglades.* 1913. $2.00

FLETCHER, Arnold. *Afghanistan, Highway of Conquest.* 1965. Ithaca, NY. Ills. 1st ed. 325 pp. $15.00

FLETCHER, Ernest. *Africa, Trip of a Lifetime.* 1954. 1st ed. inscr. dj. EX $12.50

FLETCHER, George U. *The Well of the Unicorn.* 1948. New York. Sloane. 1st ed. dj. VG $50.00

FLETCHER, Grace N. *The Fabulous Flemings of Kathmandu.* 1964. New York. Dutton. 219 pp. dj. EX $4.50

FLETCHER, Helen Jill. *Adventures in Archaeology.* 1978. dj. EX $4.00

FLETCHER, Inglis. *Bennett's Welcome.* 1950. New York. Garden City. 451 pp. $3.50

FLETCHER, Inglis. *Bennett's Welcome.* 1950. Bobbs Merrill. 1st ed. dj. VG $35.00

FLETCHER, Inglis. *Cormorant's Brood.* 1959. New York. Lippincott. 345 pp. dj. VG $3.50

FLETCHER, Inglis. *Lusty Wind for Carolina.* 1944. Philadelphia. Blakiston. 470 pp. $3.00

FLETCHER, Inglis. *Queen's Gift.* 1952. Bobbs Merrill. Ltd. ed. sgn. dj. VG $50.00

FLETCHER, Inglis. *Roanoke Hundred.* 1948. New York. 492 pp. VG $3.50

FLETCHER, Inglis. *The Scotswoman.* 1954. New York. 414 pp. $3.50

FLETCHER, Inglis. *The Scotswoman.* 1954. Bobbs Merrill. 1st ed. dj. VG $30.00

FLETCHER, Inglis. *The Wind in the Forest.* 1957. Bobbs Merrill. 1st ed. dj. VG $25.00

FLETCHER, Inglis. *Toil of the Brave.* 1946. New York. $4.00

FLETCHER, J. *Studies on Slavery.* 1852. Natchez. $90.00

FLETCHER, J.S. *Beyond the Monocle & Other Stories.* 1930. New York. Doubleday Doran. 1st ed. EX $32.50

FLETCHER, John Gould. *The Burning Mountain.* 1946. Dutton. 1st ed. $10.00

FLETCHER, Phinehas. *Piscatory Eclogues.* Edinburgh. (ca.1771) VG $75.00

FLETCHER, W.Y. *English Bookbinding in the British Museum.* 1895. London. Kagan & Paul. Ltd. ed. Ills. $420.00

FLEURY, Claude. *Manners of the Ancient Israelites.* 1834. New York. G $20.00

FLEXNER. *I Hear America Talking.* 1976. Van Nostrand. Ills. 505 pp. EX $6.50

FLEXNER. *The Wilder Image.* 1962. 1st ed. dj. VG $25.00

FLINN, J. *History of the Chicago Police.* 1887. Chicago. Ills. 1st ed. $45.00

FLINN, J. *Official Guide to the World's Columbian Exposition.* 1893. wrappers. $15.00

FLINN, J. *The Standard Guide to Chicago Illustrated.* 1893. Chicago. World's Fair ed. Ills. 552 pp. $12.50

FLINT, T. *History & Geography of Mississippi Valley.* 1832. Cincinnati. 2nd ed. 2 vols in 1. $65.00

FLINT, T. *Indian Wars of the West.* 1833. Cincinnati. 1st ed. VG $185.00

FLINT, T. *Recollections Last 10 Years.* 1826. $175.00

FLOETHE, Louise. *Fountain of the Friendly Lion.* 1966. New York. Ills. Richard Floethe. G $15.00

FLOETHE, Louise. *Jungle People.* 1971. New York. Ills. Richard Floethe. VG $15.00

FLORESCU, Radu. *In Search of Frankenstein.* 1975. Boston. Ills. 1st ed. dj. VG $15.00

FLORIAN, Chev. de. *William Tell.* 1841. Concord, NH. $25.00

FLOWER, D. *Henry James in Northampton.* 1971. Northampton. 1st ed. wrappers. EX $25.00

FLOWER, Desmond. *The Paper-Back.* 1959. London. Ltd. 1st ed. $40.00

FLOWER, J. Howard. *Florentine Sonnets & Florentine Lyrics.* 1923. Hartland, VT. Solitarian Press. Ltd. ed. $10.00

FLOWER. *Grace Harlows Overland Riders on American Desert.* 1921. Saalfield. Ills. VG $4.50

FLOWER. *Grace Harlows Overland Riders on Old Apache Trail.* 1921. Saalfield. Ills. VG $4.50

FLOWER. *Harlows Overland Riders Among Border Guerillas.* 1924. Saalfield. Ills. G $3.50

FLYNN, E. *Showdown.* 1946. 1st Am. ed. dj. EX $75.00

FLYNN, Elizabeth Gurley. *Women in the War.* 1942. New York. Workers Library. 1st ed. EX $15.00

FLYNT, Josiah. *Tramping with Tramps, Studies & Sketches.* 1901. New York. 398 pp. $8.00

FOCH, General. *The Principles of War.* 1918. H.K. Fly Co. 9 fld maps. EX $30.00

FOEANDER, E.C. *Big Game of Malaya, Types, Distribution & Habits.* 1952. Batchworth. photos. maps. 208 pp. dj. EX $75.00

FOERSTER, Wolfgang. *Wir Kampfer in Weltkreig.* 1929. Munchen. Ills. 519 pp. photos. $32.50

FOGDEN, M. & P. *Animals & Their Colors.* 1974. Crown. Ills. dj. EX $17.50

FOLEY, D., ed. *The Flowering World of 'Chinese' Wilson.* 1969. Macmillan. Ills. 1st printing. dj. EX $17.50

FOLEY, Daniel J. *Gardening by the Sea.* 1965. Philadelphia. Chilton. 1st ed. 285 pp. dj. $7.50

FOLEY, Daniel J. *Vegetable Gardening in Color.* 1943. New York. Macmillan. Ills. 252 pp. VG $5.50

FOLEY, M. & Burnett, D. *The Best American Short Stories.* 1963. Boston. Houghton Mifflin. 1st ed. dj. $7.50

FOLEY, Mason. *Gingham Old & New.* 1935. VG $15.00

FOLEY. *American Authors.* 1897. Boston. G $16.00

FOLLETT, Ken. *The Gentlemen of 16 July.* 1978. Arbor House. 1st Am. ed. dj. VG $15.00

FOLLETT, W. *Works of Stephen Crane.* New York. 12 vol set. djs. boxed. $150.00

FOLSOM. *Great American Mansions.* 1963. Hastings. dj. EX $20.00

FONDA, Jane. *Jane Fonda's Workout Book.* 1981. Ills. Schapiro. 254 pp. dj. EX $4.50

FONER, Philip & Schultz, R. *Das Andere Amerika.* 1983. Berlin. Elefanten Pr. 1st ed. 550 pp. $35.00

FONER, Philip & Schultz, R. *The Other America.* 1985. Journeyman Pr. 176 pp. wrappers. EX $15.00

FONTAINE, Francis. *Etowah.* 1887. Atlanta. Fontaine Pub. $25.00

FONTANA. *Magic Butterfly.* 1963. $18.00

FONTENELLE, Jose F.B. *State of Ceara. Notes for Exposition of Chicago.* 1893. Chicago. presentation copy. photos. VG $30.00

FONTEYN. *Autobiography.* New York. 1st ed. dj. EX $8.00

FONTEYN. *Magic of Dance.* 1979. 1st Am. ed. dj. VG $20.00

FOOTE, Edward B. *Medical Common Sense.* 1863. New York. VG $10.00

FOOTE, J. *Anglers All.* 1947. 1st ed. dj. VG $12.50

FOOTE, J.T. *Blister Jones.* 1913. Indianapolis. Ills. Hambidge. 1st ed. $12.50

FOOTE, J.T. *Jing.* 1936. New York. Derrydale Pr. Ltd. ed. EX $65.00

FOOTE, Shelby. *Follow Me Down.* 1950. Dial Press. 1st ed. dj. VG $30.00

FOOTE, Shelby. *Jordan County.* 1954. Dial Press. 1st ed. dj. VG $35.00

FOOTE, Shelby. *Love in a Dry Season.* 1951. Dial Press. 1st ed. dj. VG $40.00

FOOTE, Shelby. *The Civil War, a Narrative. Vol. 1.* 1958. 1st ed. 840 pp. VG $12.50

FOOTE, Shelby. *Tournament.* 1949. Dial Press. 1st ed. dj. EX $35.00

FORBATH, P. *The River Congo.* 1977. Harper. Ills. maps. 417 pp. dj. $15.00

FORBENIUS, Leo. *The Childhood of Man.* 1909. Philadelphia. 415 Ills. 504 pp. $35.00

FORBES, A. *Towns of New England & Old England.* 1921. Putnam. 2 vol set. EX $50.00

FORBES, Alexander. *Northmost Labrador Mapped from Air.* 1938. Am. Geog. Soc. 1st ed. VG $20.00

FORBES, Alexander. *The Radio Gunner.* 1924. Boston. 1st ed. EX $40.00

FORBES, Esther. *America's Paul Revere.* 1946. Boston. Ills. Lynd Ward. 1st ed. dj. $20.00

FORBES, Esther. *Johnny Tremain.* 1943. Boston. Ills. Lynd Ward. dj. EX $12.00

FORBES, Harold M. *West Virginia History, Bibliography & Guide.* 1981. Morgantown. 359 pp. wrappers. $9.00

FORBES, John. *A Physicians Holiday, or a Month in Switzerland.* 1849. London. fld map. 4 pls. $27.50

FORBES, Rosita. *These Are Real People.* 1939. 1st ed. VG $6.50

FORBUSH, E.H. *Birds of Massachusetts.* 1929. Boston. 3 vol set. VG $115.00

FORCE, Roland. *Leadership & Cultural Change in Palau.* 1960. 1st ed. wrappers. $10.00

FORD, A.E. *History of Clinton, Mass. 1653-1865.* 1896. Clinton. 696 pp. $35.00

FORD, Alice. *John James Audubon.* 1965. OK U. Press. Ills. 488 pp. dj. EX $12.50

FORD, Alice. *The 1826 Journal of John James Audubon.* 1967. OK U. Press. Ills. 1st ed. dj. EX $10.00

FORD, Alla T. & Martin, D. *The Musical Fantasies of Frank L. Baum.* 1958. Chicago. Ills. 80 pp. wrappers. $15.00

FORD, C. *Donovan of O.S.S.* 1970. Boston. G $18.00

FORD, Corey. *Every Dog Should Have a Man.* 1952. New York. 1st ed. EX $20.00

FORD, Corey. *Minutes of the Lower Forty.* 1962. New York. 1st ed. dj. EX $50.00

FORD, Corey. *You Can Always Tell a Fisherman.* 1958. Holt. 1st ed. dj. VG $25.00

FORD, Dan. *Pappy: The Life of John Ford.* 1979. 324 pp. dj. $27.50

FORD, Daniel. *Born Again: or, The Romance of a Dual Life.* 1893. Falmouth, MA. Succansset Press. 356 pp. $35.00

FORD, F.M. *A Man Could Stand Up.* 1926. 1st ed. VG $15.00

FORD, Frank R. *Diseases of the Nervous System.* 1937. Springfield. 1st ed. $55.00

FORD, George D. *These were Actors: Chapmans & Drakes.* 1955. dj. $12.50

FORD, George H. *Study of Novels & Stories of D.H. Lawrence.* 1965. New York. 1st ed. dj. $10.00

FORD, H.J. *Blue Fairy Book.* 1889. Ills. 2nd ed. G $20.00

FORD, H.J. *Blue Poetry Book.* 1981. 1st ed. VG $40.00

FORD, H.J. *Book of Romance.* 1902. 1st ed. 8 color pls. $45.00

FORD, H.J. *Crimson Fairy Book.* 1906. Ills. 8 color pls. $20.00

FORD, H.J. *Green Fairy Book.* 1906. Ills. VG $20.00

FORD, H.J. *Grey Fairy Book.* 1900. Ills. 1st ed. VG $20.00

FORD, H.J. *Olive Fairy Book.* 1915. 8 color pls. G $20.00

FORD, H.J. *Orange Fairy Book.* 1911. Ills. 8 color pls. G $30.00

FORD, H.J. *Pink Fairy Book.* 1897. Ills. 1st ed. $60.00

FORD, H.J. *Red Book of Romance.* 1905. 1st ed. 8 color pls. EX $40.00

FORD, H.J. *Red Fairy Book.* 1890. Ills. Ford & Speed. 1st ed. VG $30.00

FORD, H.J. *Violet Fairy Book.* 1901. Longmans. 1st ed. 8 color pls. VG $50.00

FORD, Henry. *Today & Tomorrow.* 1926. Doubleday Page. 1st ed. VG $30.00

FORD, James L. *Forty-Odd Years in the Literary Shop.* 1921. New York. Dutton. photos. 362 pp. $6.00

FORD, Lauren. *The Little Book About God.* 1934. Ills. tissue dj. VG $45.00

FORD, Leslie. *The Bahamas Murder Case.* 1952. New York. Scribner. 188 pp. $7.50

FORD, Madox. *Your Mirror to My Times.* 1971. New York. Holt. 1st ed. $5.00

FORD, Paul L. *Story of Untold Love.* 1902. New York. 1st ed. sgn. VG $85.00

FORD, Paul L. *The Great K. & A. Train Robbery.* 1897. New York. 1st issue. EX $60.00

FORD, Paul L. *The Many Sided Franklin.* 1899. New York. 1st ed. G $25.00

FORD, Paul L. *The New England Primer.* 1899. New York. 1st ed. VG $30.00

FORD, Paul L. *Wanted: Chaperone.* 1902. New York. Ills. Christy. VG $10.00

FORD, Richard. *A Piece of My Heart.* 1976. New York. Random House. 1st ed. VG $35.00

FORD, Richard. *A Piece of My Heart.* 1976. New York. Harper. 1st ed. dj. VG $50.00

FORD, Richard. *The Sportswriter.* 1986. New York. Vintage. 1st ed. sgn. $25.00

FORD, Thomas. *A History of Illinois I.* 1945. EX $35.00

FORD, Thomas. *A History of Illinois II.* 1946. EX $35.00

FORD, W.C. *The Boston Book Market 1679-1700.* 1917. Boston. Merrymount Pr. Ltd. ed. EX $100.00

FORD, William E. *Dana's Manual of Mineralogy.* 1912. London. 460 pp. $4.00

FORD, Worthington C. *Cycle of Charles Francis Adams Letters, 1861-1865.* 1920. Boston. Ills. 2 vol set. $45.00

FORD, Worthington C. *Letters of Henry Adams, 1858-1891.* 1930. Boston. dj. $15.00

FORD, Worthington C. *List of B. Franklin Papers in Library of Congress.* 1905. Washington. ex-lib. 322 pp. VG $22.50

FORD. *Nothing So Strange.* 1958. 1st ed. dj. VG $20.00

FORDHAM, Elias Pym. *Narrative of Travels in VA, MA, OH, IN, KY, & IL.* 1906. Cleveland. Ills. maps. 248 pp. $65.00

FOREL, Oscar. *Hidden Art in Nature.* 1972. New York. 1st ed. dj. $25.00

FOREMAN, Grant. *Indian Removal. Emigration of 5 Civilized Tribes.* 1956. U. of OK Press. Ills. 2nd printing new ed. dj. $18.50

FOREMAN, Grant. *Indians & Pioneers, Story of American Southwest.* 1930. $70.00

FOREMAN, H.B. *Medwin's Revised Life of Shelley.* 1913. Oxford. VG $35.00

FOREMAN, Grant. *Indians & Pioneers, Story of American Southwest.* 1967. U. of OK Press. VG $25.00

FORESEE, A. *Famous Photographers-Adams, Steichen, Beaton, etc.* 1968. Philadelphia. dj. EX $10.00

FORESTER, C.S. *Commodore Hornblower.* 1945. Boston. Wyeth Ills dj. VG $10.00

FORESTER, C.S. *Commodore Hornblower.* 1945. Little, Brown. 384 pp. $4.50

FORESTER, C.S. *Gold From Crete.* 1970. 1st Am. ed. dj. EX $20.00

FORESTER, C.S. *Good Shepherd.* 1955. 1st Am. ed. dj. VG $25.00

FORESTER, C.S. *Hornblower & the Atropos.* 1953. Boston. 1st ed. dj. EX $15.00

FORESTER, C.S. *Hunting the Bismarck.* 1959. London. 1st ed. dj. $40.00

FORESTER, C.S. *Lieutenant Hornblower.* 1952. Ills. Wyeth. 1st ed. dj. EX $25.00

FORESTER, C.S. *Lord Hornblower.* 1946. Boston. 1st ed. 332 pp. $100.00

FORESTER, C.S. *Marionettes at Home.* 1936. London. Joseph. Ills. 1st ed. $65.00

FORESTER, C.S. *One Wonderful Week.* 1927. Indianapolis. 1st Am. ed. dj. $90.00

FORESTER, C.S. *Sky & Forest.* 1948. Little, Brown. 1st ed. VG $10.00

FORESTER, C.S. *The Commodore.* 1945. London. 1st ed. VG $35.00

FORESTER, C.S. *The Hornblower Companion.* 1964. London. Joseph. 1st ed. dj. $75.00

FORESTER, C.S. *The Sky & the Forest.* 1948. London. 1st Am. ed. dj. EX $30.00

FORESTER, C.S. *Young Hornblower/Three Complete Novels.* 1953. New York. 672 pp. VG $4.00

FORESTER, Frank. *The Complete Manual for Young Sportsmen.* 1856. New York. Stringer/Townsend. 1st ed. G $35.00

FORESTER, Frank. *The Horse of America.* 1857. New York. Ills. 2 vol set. VG $175.00

FORESTER. *The Good Shepherd.* 1945. Boston. VG $6.00

FORLAG, Alb. *Cammermeyers. A Smile Among Friends.* Oslo, Norway. Ills. 139 pp. VG $15.00

FORMAGGIO, Dino. *A Book of Miniatures.* 1962. Tudor. 1st Am. ed. dj. $12.50

FORMAN, H. *Changing China.* 1948. New York. Crown. Ills. dj. G $20.00

FORMAN, H. *Report from Red China.* 1947. New York. Book Find Club. Ills. dj. G $15.00

FORMAN. *Face of Ancient China.* 1960. Spring Books. VG $35.00

FORREST, Leon. *The Bloodworth Orphans.* 1977. New York. Random House. 1st ed. dj. EX $35.00

FORREST, Leon. *There is a Tree More Ancient than Eden.* 1973. New York. Random House. 1st ed. dj. EX $35.00

FORRESTER, I. *This One Mad Act.* 1937. Boston. 500 pp. dj. $25.00

FORSBERG, Franklin. *The Best from Yank.* 1945. New York. photos. Ills. 304 pp. VG $5.00

FORSEY, Maude S. *Jack & Me.* Philadelphia. London. Ills. Jacobs. 1st ed. $25.00

FORSHAW, J. & Cooper, W. *Australian Parrots.* 1981. Lansdowne. Ills. Cooper. 312 pp. dj. EX $75.00

FORSTER, E.M. *A Passage to India.* 1952. New York. 322 pp. $3.50

FORSTER, E.M. *A Passage to India.* 1924. 1st Eng. ed. VG $200.00

FORSTER, E.M. *Battersea Rise.* 1955. New York. 1st ed. dj. VG $35.00

FORSTER, Harold. *Supplements to Dodsley's Collection of Poems.* 1980. Oxford. 1st ed. 106 pp. wrappers. $15.00

FORSTER, Walter. *Zion on the Mississippi.* 1953. St.Louis. Ills. EX $17.50

FORSYTE, Charles. *Decoding of Edwin Drood.* 1980. London. 1st ed. sgn. $22.00

FORSYTH, Frederick. *Day of the Jackal.* 1971. Viking. 1st Am. ed. dj. VG $25.00

FORSYTH, Frederick. *No Comebacks.* 1982. Viking. 1st Am. ed. dj. VG $15.00

FORSYTH, Frederick. *The Devil's Alternative.* 1979. London. Hutchinson. 1st ed. dj. VG $30.00

FORSYTH, Frederick. *The Dogs of War.* 1974. Viking. 1st Am ed. dj. VG $20.00

FORSYTH, Frederick. *The Dogs of War.* 1974. London. Hutchinson. 1st ed. dj. VG $35.00

FORSYTH, Frederick. *The Shepherd.* 1976. Viking. Ills. Fleck. 1st Am. ed. dj. $15.00

FORSYTH, J. *Highlands of Central India.* 1920. New York. G $20.00

FORSYTH, J.S. *Demonologia, or Natural Knowledge Revealed.* 1827. London. 1st ed. 438 pp. $150.00

FORSYTH. *The Odessa File.* 1st Eng. ed. dj. VG $25.00

FORSYTH. *4th Protocol.* Ltd. ed. 1/600. sgn. $55.00

FORSYTHE, Elizabeth Hailey. *Joanna's Husband & David's Wife.* 1986. Delacorte. 1st ed. sgn. dj. VG $40.00

FORSYTHE, George. *Thrilling Days in Army Life.* 1900. New York. Ills. 1st ed. inscr. sgn. VG $45.00

FORTNUM, C.D.E. *Bronzes.* 1877. New York. $5.00

FORTNUM, C.D.E. *Majolica.* 1876. New York. $5.00

FORTTE, Burmester & Stempell. *Das Menicheninftem Offene Volks-Sprache.* 1874. Berlin. 844 pp. G $12.50

FORTUNE, Dion. *Cosmic Doctrine.* 1966. London. 157 pp. dj. VG $15.00

FORTUNE, Dion. *Sane Occultism.* 1967. London. 190 pp. dj. VG $15.00

FORTUNE, Jan. *Elisabet Ney.* 1943. Knopf. 1st ed. $10.00

FOSS, Chris. *World War II Tanks & Vehicles.* 1981. New York. Ills. 160 pp. $6.00

FOSS, Philip. *Yana.* 1978. Tideline Press.Ills. Ltd. ed. sgn. EX $70.00

FOSS, Sam Walter. *Dreams in Homespun.* 1897. Boston. ex-lib. 221 pp. G $2.50

FOSS, Sam Walter. *Whiffs from Wild Meadows.* 1895. Boston. ex-lib. 272 pp. VG $2.50

FOSTER, A.D. *Moment of Magician.* 1984. Phantasia Pr. Ltd. ed. 1/375. sgn. boxed. EX $45.00

FOSTER, A.D. *The Hour of the Gate.* 1984. New York. Warner. proof copy. wrappers. $20.00

FOSTER, E. *Gigi, Story of a Merry-go-Round Horse.* 1943. Ills. Bischoff.1st ed. VG $15.00

FOSTER, E. *Gigi in America.* 1946. Ills. P. Cote. 1st ed. dj. VG $15.00

FOSTER, George. *A Summary of Yuki Culture.* 1944. U. of CA Press.1st ed. wrappers. $10.00

FOSTER, George. *Culture & Conquest: America's Spanish Heritage.* 1960. Viking. 1st ed. wrappers. $12.50

FOSTER, J. *Essay on the Evils of Popular Ignorance.* 1821. Boston. 1st Am. ed. VG $22.50

FOSTER, J. & J. *Wild Country.* 1975. Toronto. Van Nostrand. Ills. 155 pp. VG $7.00

FOSTER, J.J. *Miniature Painters, British & Foreign.* 1903. Dutton. ex-lib. 2 vol set. rebound. G $85.00

FOSTER, J.R. *Great Folktales of Wit & Humor.* 1955. Harper. 1st ed. VG $15.00

FOSTER, Jeanne Cooper. *Ulster Folklore.* 1951. Belfast. Ills. R. Friers. 1st ed. dj. $15.00

FOSTER, R.F. *Foster's Complete Hoyle. Encyclopedia of Games.* 1916. New York. Stokes. 701 pp. $10.00

FOSTER, William Harnden. *New England Grouse Shooting.* 1942. New York. 1st ed. VG $65.00

FOSTER, William Trufant. *Gyps & Swindles.* 1945. New York. 32 pp. wrappers. EX $15.00

FOSTER Alan Dean. *The Time of the Transference.* 1987. New York. Warner. proof copy. wrappers. $15.00

FOSTER. *Rear Admiral Byrd & the Polar Expedition.* 1930. A.L. Burt. Ills. $5.50

FOSTER. *The Married State, Its Obligations & Duties.* Andrus & Sons. (ca.1875) 137 pp. VG $4.50

FOSTER-HARRIS. *The Look of the Old West.* New York. no date. Ills. 316 pp. $10.00

FOTHERGILL, Augusta B. *Peter Jones & Richard Jones Genealogies.* 1924. Richmond, VA. sgn. 363 pp. VG $25.00

FOTHERGILL. *The First Violin.* 1904. Grosset & Dunlap. Ills. $4.50

FOURE, Gabriel. *The Italian Lakes.* Boston. Ills. 143 pp. VG $8.50

FOWKE, Gerald. *The Evolution on the Ohio River.* 1933. Indianapolis. 1st ed. dj. VG $25.00

FOWKE, Gerard. *Archaelogical History of Ohio.* 1902. Columbus. Ills. 760. maps. index. G $35.00

FOWKES, Henry L. *Hist. Encyclopedia of IL & Hist. of Christian Co.* 1918. Munsell Pub. 2 vol set. gilted on top. $65.00

FOWLER, Alfred. *The Romance of Fine Prints.* 1938. Kansas City. Print Society. Ills. VG $45.00

FOWLER, Frank. *The Bronco Rider Boys Down in Arizona.* 1914. New York. A.L. Burt. 249 pp. $2.50

FOWLER, Frank. *The Bronco Rider Boys with the Texas Rangers.* New York. A.L. Burt. 249 pp. G $2.00

FOWLER, Gene. *A Solo in Tom-Toms.* 1946. New York. Viking. 390 pp. dj. $4.50

FOWLER, Gene. *Good Night, Sweet Prince.* 1944. Philadelphia. 474 pp. $5.00

FOWLER, Gene. *Minutes of the Last Meeting.* 1945. New York. Viking Press. $5.00

FOWLER, Gene. *Schnozzola, the Story of Jimmy Durante.* 1951. Viking Press. Ills. 261 pp. $4.50

FOWLER, O.S. *Self Instructor Phrenology.* New York. G $17.50

FOWLER, Will. *The Young Man from Denver.* 1962. Garden City. Doubleday. Ills. 1st ed. $5.00

FOWLER, Wm. M., Jr. *Rebels Under Sail.* 1976. New York. Scribner. 320 pp. dj. $6.50

FOWLER. *The Art of Letter Writing.* 1913. Sully & Kleinteich. 203 pp. $3.50

FOWLES, John. *A Maggot.* 1985. London. Ltd. 1st ed. 1/500. sgn. EX $50.00

FOWLES, John. *A Maggot.* 1985. Ltd. ed. 1/350. sgn. slipcase. $80.00

FOWLES, John. *Aristos.* 1965. 1st Eng. ed. $350.00

FOWLES, John. *Aristos.* Boston. 1st ed. EX $100.00

FOWLES, John. *Cinderella.* 1974. Little, Brown. Ills. 1st Am. ed. dj. VG $30.00

FOWLES, John. *Daniel Martin.* 1977. Little, Brown. 1st ed. $40.00

FOWLES, John. *Mantissa.* 1982. Little, Brown. Ltd. 1st Am. ed. 1/510. sgn. $85.00

FOWLES, John. *Stonehenge.* London. 1st ed. dj. VG $25.00

FOWLES, John. *The Collector.* Boston/Toronto.1st ed. dj. EX $55.00

FOWLES, John. *The Collector.* 1st Eng. ed. dj. VG $65.00

FOWLES, John. *The Ebony Tower.* 1974. Boston. Little, Brown. 1st ed. dj. VG $45.00

FOWLES, John. *The French Lieutenant's Woman.* 1969. Taiwan pirated ed. dj. VG $45.00

FOWLES, John. *The French Lieutenant's Woman.* 1969. Boston. 1st ed. dj. VG $10.00

FOWLES, John. *The French Lieutenant's Woman.* 1969. Ltd. ed. 1/360. sgn. $75.00

FOX, C. *Adventures of Ebenezer Fox in Revolutionary War.* 1847. Boston. VG $40.00

FOX, C. *Book of Lures.* 1975. dj. EX $17.50

FOX, C. *Pictorial History of Performing Horses.* 1960. New York. dj. VG $12.50

FOX, Charles. *Rising Trout.* 1967. Carlisle, PA. Ltd. ed. sgn. VG $45.00

FOX, Charles. *The Wonderful World of Trout.* 1963. Carlisle, PA. Foxcrest. Ltd. ed. sgn. VG $45.00

FOX, Charles. *Who's Who on the Screen.* 1920. New York. Ills. VG $35.00

FOX, H.L. *What the Boys Did Over There.* 1919. New York. 186 pp. $4.00

FOX, John, Jr. *A Knight of Cumberland & Hell-Fer-Sartain.* 1906. New York. Ills. F.C. Yohn. $6.00

FOX, John, Jr. *Christmas Eve on Lonesome & Other Stories.* 1904. New York. Ills. 1st ed. 234 pp. $20.00

FOX, John, Jr. *Erskine Dale, Pioneer.* 1920. New York. 1st ed. $20.00

FOX, John, Jr. *In Happy Valley* 1917. Scribner. Ills. F.C. Yohn. 1st ed. $10.00

FOX, John, Jr. *Little Shepherd of Kingdom Come.* 1909. Scribner. Ills. F.C. Yohn. G $4.00

FOX, John, Jr. *Little Shepherd of Kingdom Come.* 1903. Ills. F.C. Yohn. VG $8.00

FOX, John, Jr. *Little Shepherd of Kingdom Come.* 1904. New York. Scribner. Ills. 404 pp. G $4.50

FOX, John, Jr. *The Trail of the Lonesome Pine.* 1908. New York. Scribner. Ills. 422 pp. VG $7.00

FOX, Stephen R. *The Guardian of Boston, William Monroe Trotter.* 1970. New York. 1st ed. dj. VG $10.00

FOX, W.P. *Doctor Gold.* 1963. Phil/NY. 1st ed. dj. VG $12.50

FOX, W.P. *Doctor Gold.* 1963. Lippincott. 1st ed. dj. EX $30.00

FOX, W.P. *Ruby Red.* 1971. Phil/NY. Book Club ed. dj. VG $10.00

FOX. *Red Lamp of Incest.* 1980. 1st ed. dj. VG $9.00

FOXCROFT, Thomas. *The Day of a Godly Man's Death.* 1722. Boston. B. Green. G $75.00

FOXX, Redd. *Encyclopedia of Black Humor.* 1977. W. Ritchie Pr. 1st ed. dj. VG $15.00

FRAAS, Arthur P. *Aircraft Power Plants.* 1943. McGraw Hill. 1st ed. VG $12.50

FRAENKEL, Michael. *Death Is Not Enough.* London. Carrefour Pub. wrappers. EX $45.00

FRANCE, Anatole. *Bee, Princess of the Dwarfs.* 1922. London/NY. Ills. Robinson. 127 pp. $42.50

FRANCE, Anatole. *Nos Enfants.* Paris. Ills. Boutet de Monvel. $55.00

FRANCE, Anatole. *Thais.* Bodley Head. Ills. Frank Pape. 1st ed. VG $50.00

FRANCE, Anatole. *The Revolt of the Angels.* 1927. New York. Ills. Pape. dj. EX $15.00

FRANCE, Anatole. *The Revolt of the Angels.* Bodley Head. Ills. Frank Pape. 1st ed. VG $45.00

FRANCE, Royal W. *My Native Grounds.* 1957. New York. Cameron Assoc. 255 pp. dj. $4.50

FRANCE, Yvonne. *Mrs. Gaskell.* 1949. London. 1st ed. 112 pp. index. dj. $4.00

FRANCIS, Dick & Welcome, John. *Best Racing & Chasing Stories.* 1966. London. Faber. 1st ed. dj. VG $65.00

FRANCIS, Dick & Welcome, John. *The Racing Man's Bedside Book.* 1969. London. Faber. 1st ed. dj. VG $45.00

FRANCIS, Dick. *Banker.* 1983. Putnam. 1st Am. ed. dj. VG $15.00

FRANCIS, Dick. *Banker.* 1982. 1st English ed. dj. EX $35.00

FRANCIS, Dick. *Blood Sport.* 1967. London. 1st ed. dj. VG $95.00

FRANCIS, Dick. *Blood Sport.* New York. 1st Am. ed. sgn. dj. EX $60.00

FRANCIS, Dick. *Bolt.* 1987. New York. Putnam. proof copy. wrappers. $40.00

FRANCIS, Dick. *Bonecrack.* 1971. London. Joseph. 1st ed. dj. VG $55.00

FRANCIS, Dick. *Break In.* 1986. New York. 1st ed. dj. EX $15.00

FRANCIS, Dick. *Break In.* London. 1st ed. sgn. $32.00

FRANCIS, Dick. *Flying Finish.* 1967. New York. Harper. 1st Am. ed. dj. EX $65.00

FRANCIS, Dick. *Forfeit.* 1968. London. Joseph. 1st ed. dj. VG $95.00

FRANCIS, Dick. *Forfeit.* 1968. London. Joseph. proof copy. wrappers. $185.00

FRANCIS, Dick. *High Stakes.* 1975. 1st Am. ed. sgn. dj. EX $40.00

FRANCIS, Dick. *Knockdown.* 1974. New York. 1st Am. ed. dj. EX $30.00

FRANCIS, Dick. *Knockdown.* 1974. London. dj. VG $30.00

FRANCIS, Dick. *Rat Race.* 1970. London. Joseph. 1st ed. dj. VG $65.00

FRANCIS, Dick. *Reflex.* 1981. Putnam. 1st ed. sgn. dj. VG $40.00

FRANCIS, Dick. *Risk.* 1977. Harper. 1st ed. sgn. dj. VG $45.00

FRANCIS, Dick. *Slay-Ride.* 1973. 1st English ed. dj. EX $50.00

FRANCIS, Dick. *Smoke Screen.* 1972. New York. 1st ed. dj. EX $15.00

FRANCIS, Dick. *Smoke Screen.* 1972. London. Joseph. 1st ed. sgn. dj. EX $75.00

FRANCIS, Dick. *The Danger.* 1984. New York. 1st ed. dj. EX $12.00

FRANCIS, Dick. *The Welcome Collection.* 1972. London. 1st ed. dj. $18.00

FRANCIS, Dick. *Three to Follow.* 1st English ed. dj. VG $65.00

FRANCIS, Dick. *Trial Run.* 1978. New York. 1st ed. dj. VG $25.00

FRANCIS, Dick. *Trial Run.* 1978. London. Joseph. 1st ed. dj. VG $45.00

FRANCIS, Dick. *Twice Shy.* 1981. 1st Eng. ed. dj. EX $45.00

FRANCIS, Dick. *Whiphand.* 1979. New York. Harper. 1st ed. sgn. dj. VG $40.00

FRANCIS, F. *A Book on Angling.* 1867. London. 5 color pls. $75.00

FRANCIS, H.E. *A Disturbance of Gulls A.O.S.* 1983. New York. Braziller. 1st ed. dj. VG $20.00

FRANCIS. *Bowie's Lost Mine.* 1954. 1st ed. VG $10.00

FRANCIS-LEWIS, C. *Art & Craft of Leatherwork.* 1928. England. Ills. EX $25.00

FRANCK, Harry A. *Four Months Afoot in Spain.* 1911. Garden City. Ills. 292 pp. $5.50

FRANCK, Harry A. *Roaming Through the West Indies.* 1920. Ills.. 486 pp. dj. G $10.00

FRANCO, Victor. *The Morning After.* 1963. Praegen, NY. trans. 1st Am. ed. dj. $10.00

FRANCOISE. *Jeanne-Marie Counts Her Sheep.* 1951. Ills. dj. VG $15.00

FRANCOISE. *Noel for Jeanne-Marie.* 1953. dj. VG $10.00

FRANEY, Pierre. *The New York Times 60-Minute Gourmet.* 1979. New York. Times Books. 339 pp. dj. EX $5.00

FRANK, Edgar B. *Old French Ironwork. The Craftsman & His Art.* 1950. Cambridge. Ills. 1st ed. dj. EX $25.00

FRANK, Gerold. *An American Death.* 1972. uncorrected proof. $17.50

FRANK, H., Jr. *Single.* 1978. London. Macmillan. 1st ed. dj. EX $30.00

FRANK, Joseph. *Hobbled Pegasus.* 1968. Albuquerque. 1st ed. dj. EX $40.00

FRANK, Leslie. *Famous Leaders & Battlescenes.* 1896. New York. Ills. large folio. G $150.00

FRANK, Leslie. *The American Soldier in the Civil War.* (ca.1895) Ills. VG $135.00

FRANK, P. *Forbidden Area.* 1956. Lippincott. 1st ed. dj. EX $15.00

FRANK, S. *Pictorial Encyclopedia of Fishes.* 1971. Hamlyn. 902 photos. 552 pp. dj. VG $15.00

FRANK. *America & Alfred Steiglitz.* 1934. Literary Guild.1st ed. EX $35.00

FRANKFURTER, Felix & Green, N.*The Labor Injunction.* 1930. New York. 1st ed. sgn. VG $85.00

FRANKL, Oscar. *Theodor Herzl. The Jew & the Man.* 1949. New York. 1st ed. inscr. 190 pp. $25.00

FRANKL, Paul. *Spacing for Living.* 1938. 1st ed. photos. VG $37.50

FRANKLIN, B. & Bigelow, J.*The Life of Benjamin Franklin.* 1879. Boston. Lippincott. 2nd ed. 3 vol set. $22.50

FRANKLIN, Benjamin. *Experiments & Observations on Electricity.* 1774. London. Ills. 5th ed. VG $450.00

FRANKLIN, Benjamin. *The Complete Poor Richard's Almanacks 1733-1758.* 1970. Barre, MA. Imprint Soc. Ltd. ed. 2 vol set. G $40.00

FRANKLIN, Benjamin. *The Life of the Late Dr. Franklin.* 1813. New York. VG $45.00

FRANKLIN, Benjamin. *The Works, Essays of Benjamin Franklin.* 1835. Baltimore. $30.00

FRANKLIN, Benjamin. *The Works of Franklin.* 1812. Edinburgh. Ills. G $45.00

FRANKLIN, Benjamin. *Works of the Late Dr. Benjamin Franklin.* 1794. New York. 2nd Am. ed. 2 vols in 1. G $95.00

FRANKLIN, John. *Narrative of a Journey to Shores of Polar Sea.* 1823. London. Ills. 1st ed. maps. $575.00

FRANKLIN, Linda C. *From Hearth to Cookstove: Collectibles of Kitchen.*1976. Florence, AL. Ills. dj. VG $15.50

FRANKLIN, Roy. *Franklin Pierce, Young Hickory of Granite Hills.* 1931. Philadelphia. Ills. ex-lib. 615 pp. $10.00

FRANKLIN, Vincent P. *The Education of Black Philadelphia.* 1979. Penn. U. Pub. 298 pp. $10.00

FRANKLIN. *Mr. Franklin: Selection from His Personal Papers.* 1956. New Haven. 2nd printing. dj. EX $15.00

FRANKLYN. *The Cockney.* 1953. revised ed. dj. $15.00

FRARY, I.T. *Early Homes of Ohio.* 1936. Richmond. Ills. 1st ed. 336 pp. dj. $42.50

FRARY, I.T. *Ohio in Homespun & Calico.* 1942. 1st ed. calico cloth cover. VG $20.00

FRARY, I.T. *They Built the Capitol.* 1940. dj. VG $22.50

FRASCONI, Antonio. *A Sunday in Monterey.* 1964. New York. Harcourt Brace. boxed. EX $20.00

FRASER, Antonia. *History of Toys.* 1966. sgn. dj. VG $40.00

FRASER, C. *Heroes of the Air.* 1928. Crowell Co. Ills. 550 pp. VG $6.50

FRASER, Douglas. *Primitive Art.* 1962. Doubleday. Ills. 1st ed. dj. $20.00

FRASER, George MacDonald. *Flashman & the Dragon.* 1985. London. 1st ed. dj. $25.00

FRASER, George MacDonald. *Flashman at the Charge.* 1973. London. Book Club Assoc. dj. VG $22.50

FRASER, George MacDonald. *Flashman.* 1969. Jenkins. 1st Eng. ed. dj. VG $60.00

FRASER, George MacDonald. *Flashman's Lady.* 1977. London. Macmillan. 1st ed. dj. $45.00

FRASER, George MacDonald. *Royal Flash.* 1970. London. 1st ed. dj. EX $40.00

FRASER, George MacDonald. *The Pyrates.* 1984. Knopf. 1st Am. ed. dj. VG $17.50

FRASER, Hugh. *Seven Years on the Pacific Slope.* 1914. New York. 1st ed. $20.00

FRASER, James. *Journey into Khorasan.* 1825. London. $700.00

FRASER, R. *Business of Travel: 50 Years Record of Progress.* 1891. London. 318 pp. VG $22.50

FRASER, R. *Flower Phantoms.* 1926. New York. Boni. 1st Am. ed. dj. VG $35.00

FRASER, R. *Marriage in Heaven.* 1932. 1st ed. dj. VG $20.00

FRASER, Samuel. *The Potato.* 1915. New York. Ills. VG $10.00

FRASER, W.A. *The Eye of a God.* 1899. New York. Doubleday. 1st ed. VG $40.00

FRASER & JONES. *Motor Vehicles & Their Engines.* 1921. New York. 278 Ills. 352 pp. G $10.00

FRASSANITO. *America's Bloodiest Day.* 1978. Ills. 304 pp. $12.50

FRAUCA, H. *Australian Bird Wonders.* 1974. Rigby. Adelaide. Ills. 1st ed. dj. EX $12.50

FRAUCA, H. *Australian Bush Birds.* 1978. Lansdowne. photos. maps. 135 pp. dj. EX $20.00

FRAYNE, Trent. *The Mad Men of Hockey.* 1978. McClelland & Steward. 191 pp. $7.00

FRAZEE, Steve. *The Sky Block.* 1953. New York. 1st ed. dj. $10.00

FRAZER, James. *Folklore in the Old Testament.* 1918. London. 1st ed. 3 vol set. VG $125.00

FRAZER, W.D. *American Pistol Shooting.* 1929. New York. Ills. VG $40.00

FRAZIER, E. Franklin. *Negro Youth at the Crossways.* 1940. Washington. 301 pp. $5.00

FRAZIER, Griffiin. *James Frazier, Kent County Delaware & Descendants.*1965. Arlington, VA. 1st ed. dj. EX $35.00

FRAZIER, Ian. *Dating Your Mom.* 1986. Farrar. 1st Am. ed. sgn. dj. $25.00

FRAZIER, Ida H. *Fort Recovery.* 1941. Columbus. 31 pp. wrappers. $8.50

FRAZIER, S.M. *Secrets of the Rocks.* 1905. Denver. Hall & Williams. Ills. 432 pp. $20.00

FRAZIER, Walt. *Rockin' Steady.* 1974. New York. Prentice Hall. 158 pp. dj. $37.50

FREDDI, Cris. *Pork & Others.* 1981. New York. Knopf. 1st ed. dj. VG $30.00

FREDDI, Cris. *Pork.* 1982. London. Routledge & Paul. 1st ed. $25.00

FREDERICK. *One Hundred Views of Juji.* 1958. 2 vols in 1. Ills. VG rare. $95.00

FREDERICKSON, O. *The Silence of the North.* 1972. Crown. 209 pp. dj. EX $10.00

FREE, Montague. *All About House Plants.* 1947. New York. Doubleday. 329 pp. VG $4.50

FREE, Spencer Michael. *Shawnee Cabin & Other Poems.* 1931. New York. 87 pp. wrappers. $5.00

FREEDMAN, J. *Old News: Resurrection City.* 1970. New York. 1st ed. dj. EX $10.00

FREEHAN, Bill. *Behind the Mask.* 1970. World. Ills. dj. $4.50

FREELING, Nicolas. *The Dresden Green.* 1966. London. Gollancz. 1st ed. dj. EX $15.00

FREEMAN, Andrew. *Abraham Lincoln Goes to New York.* 1960. dj. VG $12.50

FREEMAN, Andrew. *The Case for Doctor Cook.* 1961. New York. review copy. $15.00

FREEMAN, D.S. *George Washington.* 1949-1952. 5 vol set. boxed. EX $50.00

FREEMAN, D.S. *Lee's Dispatches: Unpublished Letters of Gen. Lee.* Putnam. (ca.1957) new ed. EX $20.00

FREEMAN, D.S. *Lee's Lieutenants.* 1942-44. Scribner. sgn. 3 vol set. VG $100.00

FREEMAN, D.S. *Robert E. Lee.* 1947. 4 vol set. VG $60.00

FREEMAN, Dan. *Elephants, the Vanishing Giants.* 1981. Putnam. Ills. 1st ed. dj. EX $17.50

FREEMAN, E.A. *The Story of Cape Cod.* (ca.1920) Ills. 100 pp. $3.50

FREEMAN, Harry C. *History of Butte, World's Greatest Mining Camp.* 1900. Chicago. Ills. Russell/others. 123 pp. $100.00

FREEMAN, Joseph. *The Long Pursuit.* 1947. Rinehart. advance copy. wrappers. EX $40.00

FREEMAN, L. *Iridescent Glass.* 1956. New York. 1st ed. EX $20.00

FREEMAN, L.R. *Down the Columbia.* 1921. New York. 1st ed. EX $40.00

FREEMAN, L.R. *Waterways of Westward Wanderings.* 1927. Dodd Mead. Ills. 368 pp. VG $20.00

FREEMAN, Margaret. *Herbs for the Medieval Household for Cooking.* 1943. New York. Ills. Ltd. 1st ed. inscr. VG $25.00

FREEMAN, O.W. *The Pacific Northwest.* 1942. Willey & Sons. Ills. 1st ed. EX $10.00

FREEMAN, R. *Travels & Life in Ashanti & Japan.* 1898. Westminster. VG $95.00

FREEMAN, R. Austin. *Dr. Thorndyke Intervenes.* 1933. New York. Dodd. 1st Am. ed. G $12.50

FREEMAN, R. Austin. *Dr. Thorndyke's Cases.* 1931. New York. 1st ed. G $25.00

FREEMAN, R. Austin. *Felo De Se?* 1937. London. Hodder. 1st ed. dj. VG $175.00

FREEMAN, R. Austin. *For the Defense: Dr. Thorndyke.* 1934. London. Hodder & Stoughton. 1st ed. $40.00

FREEMAN, R. Austin. *Mr. Pottermack's Oversight.* Burt reprint. VG $8.50

FREEMAN, R. Austin. *Surprising Adventures of Mr. Shuttlebury Cobb.* 1927. London. 1st ed. VG $55.00

FREEMAN, R. Austin. *The Eye of Osiris.* Scribner reprint. VG $8.50

FREEMAN, R. Austin. *The Puzzle Lock.* A.L. Burt. reprint. VG $8.50

FREEMAN, R. Austin. *The Singing Bone.* 1923. New York. 1st ed. G $30.00

FREEMAN, Roger A. *Mustang at War.* 1974. New York. Doubleday Bookclub ed. EX $9.00

FREEMAN, Samuel. *The Massachusetts Justice. Laws of Commonwealth.* 1802. Boston. 2nd ed. 334 pp. rebound. $12.50

FREEMAN. *How to Hunt Deer.* 1960. Stackpole. Ills. 243 pp. dj. $4.50

FREEMAN. *Louis Prang: Color Lithographer.* 1971. Ills. 192 pp. dj. VG $25.00

FREGUALT, Guy. *Canada: War of the Conquest.* 1969. Toronto. maps. 427 pp. $25.00

FREIBERG, E.B. *Bayou St. John in Colonial Louisiana 1699-1803.* 1980. Ills. 1st ed. dj. VG $10.00

FREIDEL, Frank. *The Splendid Little War.* 1958. Boston/Toronto. Ills. 1st ed. 314 pp. VG $15.00

FREMANTLE, Anne & Holme, B. *Europe: A Journey with Pictures.* 1954. Ills. dj. EX $4.00

FREMANTLE, Sir. A.J.L. *Three Months in the Southern States.* 1863. Edinburgh. 1st ed. VG $170.00

FREMONT, James. *Report, Exploring Expedition Rocky Mountains.* 1845. Washington. fld map. pls. 693 pp. $225.00

FREMONT, James. *The Exploring Expedition to the Rocky Mountains.* 1852. Buffalo. 456 pp. fld map. G $210.00

FREMONT, James. *The Exploring Expedition to the Rocky Mountains.* 1846. London. Wiley & Putnam. 1st Eng. ed. $225.00

FREMONT, Jessie B. *Story of the Guard: Chronicle of the War.* 1863. Boston. 1st ed. 227 pp. $40.00

FRENCH, B.F. *Historical Collections of Louisiana & Florida.* 1869. 1st ed. $55.00

FRENCH, George Russell. *Shakespeareana Genealogica.* 1869. London. $25.00

FRENCH, Giles. *Cattle Country of Peter French.* 1965. Portland. Ills. 2nd printing. dj. EX $15.00

FRENCH, H.W. *Castle Foam; or, The Heir of Meerschaum.* 1880. Boston. 371 pp. $17.50

FRENCH, Joseph L. *The Big Aviation Book for Boys.* 1929. Springfield. photos. 285 pp. $2.50

FRENCH, Joseph Lewis. *A Gallery of Old Rogues.* 1931. New York. 1st ed. dj. $12.50

FRENCH; Granger, Ernest, ed. *Contes De La Brume Et Du Soleil.* 1922. Paris. Ills. K. Simunek. VG $30.00

FRENCH-SHELDON. *Sultan to Sultan.* 1892. Boston. VG $65.00

FRESSENDEN. *New American Gardener.* 1833. 7th ed. disbound. $36.00

FRETS, G.P. *Heredity of Headform in Man.* 1921. 1st ed. dj. $15.00

FREUD, Anna. *Introduction to Technique of Child Analysis.* 1928. 1st ed. 61 pp. $30.00

FREUD, Sigmund. *Totem & Taboo.* 1918. New York. VG $60.00

FREUDENTHAL, Elizabeth E. *The Aviation Business.* 1940. New York. Vanguard. 342 pp. $3.50

FREUDENTHAL, Elizabeth. *Flight into History: Wright Brothers & Air Age.* 1949. U. of OK. 1st ed. dj. $12.50

FREY, Col. *Cote Occidentale d'Afrique.* 1890. Paris. VG $85.00

FREY, Laura C. *The Land in the Fork: Pittsburgh 1953-1914.* 1955. Philadelphia. 1st ed. dj. VG $20.00

FREY. *The Campfire Girls at School.* 1916. A.L. Burt. G $4.50

FREY. *The Campfire Girls on the Open Road.* 1918. A.L. Burt. $3.50

FRICKE, Donna & Douglas, eds. *Aeolian Harps, Essays in Literature.* 1976. 1st ed. dj. $8.50

FRIDAY, Nancy. *Men in Love.* 1980. G $4.00

FRIEDBERG, Gertrude. *The Revolving Boy.* 1967. Gollancz. 1st ed. sgn. dj. EX $25.00

FRIEDLANDER, C.P. *The Biology of Insects.* 1977. Pica Press. Ills. 189 pp. dj. EX $10.00

FRIEDLANDER. *Pius XII & the Third Reich.* 1966. Knopf. 1st Am. ed. dj. EX $15.00

FRIEDMAN, Bruce Jay. *About Harry Towns.* 1974. Knopf. 1st ed. dj. VG $15.00

FRIEDMAN, Bruce Jay. *Black Angels.* 1966. Simon & Schuster. 1st ed. dj. $30.00

FRIEDMAN, Bruce Jay. *Stern.* 1962. Simon & Schuster. 1st ed. dj. $50.00

FRIEDMAN, Bruce Jay. *Tokyo Woes.* 1985. New York. proof copy. wrappers. EX $25.00

FRIEDMAN, I.K. *The Autobiography of a Beggar.* 1903. Boston. 1st ed. sgn. EX $100.00

FRIEDMAN, T. *The Hunter.* 1964. New York. Doubleday. G $15.00

FRIEDMAN, Wm. & Elizabeth. *The Shakespeare Cyphers Examined.* 1958. Cambridge. Ills. 302 pp. $5.00

FRIEDMAN. *Bestiary of St. Jerome: Animal Symbolism in Art.* 1980. Smithsonian Institute Press. $20.00

FRIEDMANN, H. *The Parasitic Weaverbirds.* 1960. Smithsonian. Ills. 196 pp. EX $25.00

FRIEDMANN, H. *The Symbolic Goldfinch, History in European Art.* 1946. 1st ed. dj. EX $17.50

FRIEL, Arthur. *Renegade.* 1926. Philadelphia. PA 1st ed. dj. $65.00

FRIPP, Edgar I. *Shakespeare, Man & Artist.* 1938. London. 2 vol set. VG $20.00

FRISBIE, Florence. *Miss Ulysses from Puka Puka.* 1948. Macmillan. 1st ed. $15.00

FRISON-ROCHE. *Mont Blanc & the Seven Valleys.* 1961. Arthaud. 1st ed. dj. EX $15.00

FRITH, H.J. *Birds in the Australian High Country.* 1969. Reed. Ills. Betty Watts. 1st ed. dj. $40.00

FRITH, Henry & Allen, Ed. *The Language of the Hand.* London. Routledge. Ills. Noyes. $17.50

FROBENIUS, L. *The Childhood of Man.* 1909. London. VG $32.50

FROBENIUS, L. *Und Africa Sprache.* Berlin. (ca.1912) VG $67.50

FROEBEL, Julius. *Seven Years Travel in Central America.* 1859. London. Ills. 1st Eng. ed. EX $325.00

FROHMAN, Charles E. *Milan & the Milan Canal.* 1976. Sandusky, OH. Ills. 99 pp. VG $15.00

FROMONDO, Liberto. *Philosophiae Christianae de Anima.* 1649. Louvain. $85.00

FROST, A.B. *A Book of Drawings.* 1904. New York. $32.50

FROST, E.H. *Hovering Shadow.* 1929. 1st ed. sgn. R. Kent. $37.50

FROST, E.H. *The Lost Lyricist.* 1928. New York. Ills. Tuttle. 1st ed. dj. VG $5.00

FROST, J. *Book of Navy/Gen. Hist. Am. Marine & Most Battles.* 1843. Ills. Wm. Croome. G $80.00

FROST, J. *Mexican War & Its Warriors.* 1848. New Haven. Ills. 1st ed. 332 pp. VG $42.50

FROST, Jack. *Cape Cod Sketchbook.* 1939. New York. 3rd ed. dj. VG $15.00

FROST, John. *Indian Battles, Captivities & Adventures.* 1859. New York. Ills. G $60.00

FROST, John. *Pictorial History of the United States.* 1847. Hartford, CT. 4 vols in 1. 960 pp. $25.00

FROST, John. *Thrilling Adventures Among the Indians.* 1854. Boston. Ills. VG $40.00

FROST, Lawrence. *The Phil Sheridan Album.* 1968. Superior. 1st ed. dj. $8.50

FROST, R. *A Witness Tree.* 1942. New York. 1st trade ed. dj. VG $20.00

FROST, R. *A Witness Tree.* 1943. London. 1st English ed. dj. VG $20.00

FROST, Robert A. *A Boy's Will.* 1915. New York. 1st Am. ed. 2nd printing. sgn. $150.00

FROST, Robert. *A Further Range.* 1936. New York. 1st ed. 102 pp. EX $25.00

FROST, Robert. *A Masque of Mercy.* 1947. New York. Ltd. ed. 1/751. sgn. boxed. VG $80.00

FROST, Robert. *A Masque of Mercy.* 1947. New York. 1st ed. dj. VG $30.00

FROST, Robert. *A Masque of Reason.* 1945. Holt. 1st ed. dj. EX $30.00

FROST, Robert. *A Wishing Well.* 1953. New York. $9.00

FROST, Robert. *Accidentally on Purpose.* 1960. New York. $9.00

FROST, Robert. *Cabin in the Clearing.* 1951. New York. wrappers. VG $10.00

FROST, Robert. *Collected Poems.* 1930. Holt. 1st ed. $25.00

FROST, Robert. *Collected Poems.* 1930. Ltd. ed. 1/1000. sgn. VG $85.00

FROST, Robert. *Come In & Other Poems.* 1943. New York. Holt. Ills. John Cosgrove. 1st ed. $20.00

FROST, Robert. *Complete Poems of Robert Frost.* 1949. New York. 1st ed. sgn. dj. EX $65.00

FROST, Robert. *In the Clearing.* 1962. New York. 1st ed. dj. EX $20.00

FROST, Robert. *Kitty Hawk.* 1956. Xmas. 1st ed. wrappers. $25.00

FROST, Robert. *New Hampshire.* 1923. New York. 6th ed. sgn. $10.00

FROST, Robert. *North of Boston.* 1916. New York. 2nd ed. VG $18.00

FROST, Robert. *One Favored Acorn.* 1969. Middleburg. Ltd. ed. 1/400. wrappers. EX $50.00

FROST, Robert. *One More Brevity.* 1953. Xmas. 1st ed. $25.00

FROST, Robert. *Selected Poems.* 1928. Holt. 1st ed. $12.50

FROST, Robert. *Selected Poems.* 1932. New York. sgn. dated. VG $55.00

FROST, Robert. *Several Short Poems.* 1924. New York. 1st ed. VG $65.00

FROST, Robert. *Steeple Bush.* 1947. New York. 1st ed. dj. EX $20.00

FROST, Robert. *Steeple Bush.* 1947. New York. Ltd. ed. 1/751. sgn. boxed. EX $95.00

FROST, Robert. *West Running Brook.* 1928. Holt. 1st ed. G $12.50

FROST. *History of California.* 1853. Auburn. $15.00

FROTHINGHAM, R. *History of the Siege of Boston.* 1872. Boston. Ills. 3rd ed. maps. G $25.00

FROUDE, Chas C. *The Right Food, the Right Remedy.* 1923. 310 pp. $4.00

FROUDE, J.A. *Oceana; or, England & Her Colonies.* 1886. London. 3rd ed. VG $35.00

FROUDE, James. *Caesar.* 1879. leather bound. VG $35.00

FRY, Christopher. *The Dark is Light Enough.* 1954. London. 1st ed. dj. VG $18.00

FRY, Christopher. *Venus Observed.* 1950. London. 1st ed. dj. VG $35.00

FRY, Roger. *Vision & Design.* 1947. Peter Smith reprint. $10.00

FRY, Roger. *Vision & Design.* New York. Ills. 302 pp. $35.00

FRY, Rosalie K. *Deep in the Forest.* 1958. New York. Ills. 1st ed. dj. $20.00

FRY. *The Listener.* 1836. London. VG $45.00

FRYAR, Peter. *Private Case/Public Scandal.* 1966. London. 1st ed. dj. EX $45.00

FRYE, R.M. *Shakespeare's Life & Times. A Pictorial Record.* 1965. VG $12.50

FRYE, R.N. *Heritage of Persia.* 1963. Cleveland. World Publishing. Ills. Maps. $15.00

FRYE. *Fairy Tales Every Child Should Know.* 1915. New York. 8 color pls. VG $20.00

FRYER, Donald S. *Songs & Sonnets Atlantean.* 1971. Sauk City. 1st ed. 134 pp. dj. EX $15.00

FRYER, Jane & Frances, M. *Easy Steps in Cooking.* 1913. Ills. M.G. Hays. VG $35.00

FRYER, Jane & Frances, M. *Easy Steps in Sewing.* 1912. Ills. J.A. Boyer. VG $35.00

FRYER, Jane E. *Mary Frances' First Aid Book.* 1916. Winston. Ills. J.A. Boyer. G $15.00

FRYXELL, Ritiof. *Tetons.* 1938. 1st ed. dj. EX $25.00

FUCHIDA, Mitsuo. *Midway.* 1959. dj. EX $15.00

FUCHS, Daniel. *West of the Rockies.* 1971. New York. Knopf. 1st ed. dj. VG $20.00

FUCHS, E. *Life, Love & Sex: Women's Middle Years.* 1st ed. dj. VG $10.00

FUCHS, Emil. *With Pencil, Brush & Chisel: Life of an Artist.* 1925. New York. Ills. VG $40.00

FUENTES, Carlos. *Distant Relations.* 1982. Farrar. 1st Am. ed. dj. VG $12.50

FUENTES, Carlos. *The Hydra Head.* 1978. New York. 1st ed. dj. VG $25.00

FUERMANN, George. *Reluctant Empire.* 1957. 1st ed. dj. VG $12.50

FUERTES, L.A. & Osgood, W.H. *Artist & Naturalist in Ethiopia.* 1936. Garden City. Ills. dj. $80.00

FUERTES, Louis & Brooks, A. *Portraits of New England Birds.* 1932. MA Commonwealth. 1st ed. G $25.00

FUGE, Fred T. *God & the World in Outer Space.* Fostoria, OH. 19 pp. wrappers. $4.00

FUJIKAWA, Gyo. *Mother Goose.* 1968. New York. Grosset & Dunlap. Ills. VG $10.00

FUKUSAWA, Hanshii. *Kaei Tsugo (Chinese-English Conversation Book).* 1860. Tokyo. $125.00

FULD, George & Melvin. *A Guide to Civil War Store Card Tokens.* 1962. pb. VG $4.00

FULLER, A. *The Gospel Worthy of All Acceptation.* 1809. Otsego, NY. 180 pp. $15.00

FULLER, Anna. *Later Pratt Portraits.* 1911. New York. Putnam. Ills. Maud Faugel. $7.50

FULLER, Burns. *Fenton-My Home Town.* 1966. 1st printing. sgn. SftCvr. G $5.00

FULLER, J.F.C. *Grant & Lee.* 1959. London. dj. VG $10.00

FULLER, Jane Jay. *Uncle John's Flower Gatherers/Companion for Woods.* 1869. New York. Ills. 316 pp. $10.00

FULLER, Jane. *The Grahams.* 1864. New York. 1st ed. VG $125.00

FULLER, Margaret. *One World at a Time.* 1922. New York. 1st ed. dj. VG $15.00

FULLER, Margaret. *Recollections of Richard F. Fuller.* 1926. Boston. private print. 102 pp. $20.00

FULLER, R. *Jubilee Jim, Life of Col. James Fisk, Jr.* 1928. Macmillan. Ills. 566 pp. $6.50

FULLER, R. Buckminster. *Nine Chains to the Moon.* 1938. Philadelphia. 1st trade ed. dj. VG $40.00

FULLER, R. Buckminster. *Nine Chains to the Moon.* 1938. advance copy. dj. VG $50.00

FULLER, R. Buckminster. *Untitled Poem on History of Industrialization.* 1962. EX $20.00

FULLER, Timothy. *Reunion with Murder.* 1941. Boston. 1st ed. 258 pp. EX $15.50

FULLERTON, Alexander. *The Publisher.* 1971. New York. 254 pp. $5.00

FULLERTON, B.M. *Selective Bibliography of American Literature.* 1932. New York. 1st ed. VG $25.00

FULLMER, J.Z. *Sir Humphrey Davy's Published Works.* 1969. Harvard U. Pr. Ills. 112 pp. dj. EX $10.00

FULOP-MILLER, Rene. *Leaders, Dreamers, & Rebels.* 1935. New York. 1st ed. $10.00

FULOP-MILLER, Rene. *Rasputin, Holy Devil.* 1928. New York. Garden City. 386 pp. VG $10.00

FULOP-MILLER, Rene. *The Silver Bacchinal.* 1960. New York. 1st ed. $7.50

FULTON, C.C. *Europe Viewed Through American Spectacles.* 1874. Philadelphia. 312 pp. VG $25.00

FULTON, J.A. *Peach Culture.* 1870. New York. 1st ed. EX $25.00

FULTON, John F. *Harvey Cushing.* 1946. Springfield. VG $27.50

FULTON, John F. *Physiology of the Nervous System.* 1949. Oxford. Ills. 3rd revised ed. 667 pp. $50.00

FULTON, John F. *Physiology.* 1931. New York. 1st ed. Ills. 141 pp. $80.00

FULTON, Justin D. *Why Priests Should Wed.* 1913. Toledo. new ed. 393 pp. $10.00

FUNK, C.E. *A Hog on Ice & Other Curious Expressions.* 1948. Harper. Ills. Tom Funk. VG $15.00

FUNNELL, William. *A Voyage Around the World.* 1707. London. Botham, Knapton. Ills. 1st ed. $1,175.00

FURBANK, P.N. *E.M. Forster, a Life.* 1978. New York. 1st ed. dj. $15.00

FURER-HAIMENDORF, C. *Himalayan Barbary.* 1955. London. Ills. John Murray. G $17.00

FURLONG, Charles Willington. *Let 'Er Buck.* 1921. New York. Ills. 242 pp. $25.00

FURLONG, William Barry. *Season with Solti.* 1974. New York. 1st printing. VG $12.00

FURMAN, Bess. *White House Profile.* 1951. 1st ed. $8.50

FURMAN, Laura. *The Shadow Line.* 1982. Viking. 1st ed. dj. VG $15.00

FURMAN, Laura. *Watch Time Fly.* 1985. Viking. 1st ed. dj. VG $15.00

FURNAS, C.C. *The Next Hundred Years.* 1936. New York. 434 pp. $4.50

FURNAS, J.C. *Voyage to Windward/Life of Robert Louis Stevenson.* 1951. New York. Sloane. Ills. 566 pp. $5.00

FURNEAUX, R. *The Great Treasure Hunts.* 1969. New York. dj. EX $10.00

FURNISS, Harry. *Parliamentary Views.* 1885. London. Ills. Ltd. 1st ed. 1/1000. $70.00

FURNIVALE, E.J. & Munro, John. *Shakespeare, His Life & Work.* 1908. London. Cassell. 279 pp. $5.00

FUSCO & HORWITZ. *La Causa: California Grape Strike.* 1970. New York. wrappers. EX $7.50

FUSCO. *Training Your Filly with Love.* 1977. 1st ed. 144 pp. photos. dj. EX $15.00

FUX, Johann Joseph. *Steps to Parnassus.* 1943. New York. trans. A. Mann. 1st ed. dj. VG $18.00

FYLEMAN, Rose. *Gay Go Up.* 1930. Doubleday. Ills. Decie Merwin. 1st ed. VG $20.00

FYNN, A.J. *The American Indian as a Product of Environment.* 1907. Little, Brown. 1st ed. $15.00

G

GAARDEN, John. *Gold Nuggets of the World.* 1940. Hollywood. Ills. 149 pp. wrappers. VG $20.00

GABRIEL, Ralph H. *Elias Boudinot Cherokee & His America.* 1941. U. of OK Press. 1st ed. dj. $15.00

GABRIEL, Ralph H. *The Pageant of America: Pictorial History of U.S.* 1925. New Haven. 15 vol set. VG $115.00

GABRIELSON. *The Fisherman's Encyclopedia.* 1950. Ills. 968 pp. $14.50

GADD, W.L. *Great Expectations Country.* 1929. London. Ills. 1st ed. $15.00

GADDIS, Thomas. *Birdman of Alcatraz.* 1955. Random House. 1st ed. dj. $15.00

GADDIS, Vincent. *Invisible Horizons.* 1965. $10.00

GAEDDERT, Lou Ann. *The Split-Level Cookbook.* 1967. New York. Crowell. 228 pp. $7.50

GAGE, Nicholas. *Mafia, U.S.A.* 1972. Chicago. Playboy Press. photos. dj. VG $17.00

GAGE, W.L. *Home God's People.* 1873. Dustin-Gilman. 150 maps. VG $100.00

GAGE. *Woman, Church & State.* 1893. VG $10.00

GAGEY, Edmond. *Revolution in American Drama.* 1947. 315 pp. $12.50

GAGGIN, E.R. *An Ear for Uncle Emil.* 1939. New York. Ills. Kate Seredy. VG $10.00

GAIGE, Crosby. *Andre Simon's French Cook Book.* New York. revised ed. 342 pp. $6.50

GAIGE. *Cocktail Guide & Ladies Companion.* 1941. 1st ed. VG $10.00

GAINES, Charles. *Stay Hungry.* 1972. 1st ed. dj. $8.50

GAINES, W.M. *Mad Forever.* 1959. New York. 1st ed. dj. EX $30.00

GAINHAM, Sarah. *Takeover Bid.* 1970. Holt. 1st ed. dj. VG $25.00

GAINHAM, Sarah. *The Right Deadly.* 1960. New York. Walker. 1st ed. dj. VG $40.00

GALATOPOULOS, Stelios. *Maria Callas.* 1970. Ills. ex-lib. 218 pp. dj. $27.50

GALBRAITH, J.K. *A Life in Our Times.* 1981. Ltd. ed. 1/300. sgn. slipcase. $65.00

GALBRAITH, J.K. *Affluent Society.* 1958. Boston. $30.00

GALE, David C. *The Story of a Marble Town.* 1922. Vermont. Ills. 260 pp. VG $15.00

GALE, E.J. *Pewter & the Amateur Collector.* 1909. New York. $30.00

GALE, T.A. *Wonder of 19th Century Oil.* reprint. Ltd. ed. slipcase. EX $35.00

GALE, Zona. *Neighborhood Stories.* 1914. New York. 2nd printing. EX $35.00

GALE, Zona. *The Loves of Pelleas & Etarre.* 1907. Macmillan. 1st ed. $7.50

GALE, Zona. *What Women Won in Wisconsin.* 1921. wrappers. VG $20.00

GALE. *The Court of the Gentiles. Part II: Of Philosophies.* 1671. Oxford. $50.00

GALILEO. *Dialogues Two New Sciences.* 1946. Northwestern. VG $12.50

GALLAGER, Tess. *Instructions to the Double.* Graywolf Press. Ltd. ed. 1/150. G $15.00

GALLAHER, Art, Jr. *Plainville Fifteen Years Later.* 1961. New York. Columbia U. Press. 301 pp. dj. $10.00

GALLATIN, A.E. *Art & the Great War.* 1919. New York. Ills. 1st trade ed. VG $25.00

GALLATIN, Albert. *The Oregon Question.* 1846. New York. 75 pp. wrappers. $100.00

GALLICO, P. *Let Me Not Hunger.* 1st Am. ed. dj. VG $10.00

GALLICO, Paul. *Matilda.* 1970. London. Heinemann. 1st ed. dj. VG $40.00

GALLICO, Paul. *Mrs. 'A-Parl.* 1965. 1st ed. dj. EX $10.00

GALLICO, Paul. *Mrs. 'Arris Goes to Paris.* 1958. New York. Ills. Fiammenghi. 1st ed. VG $8.50

GALLICO, Paul. *Mrs. 'Arris Goes to Parliament.* 1965. Garden City. Ills. Fiammenghi. 1st Am. ed. $12.50

GALLICO, Paul. *Mrs. 'Arris Goes to New York.* 1960. New York. 2nd ed. dj. VG $7.50

GALLICO, Paul. *The Abandoned.* 1950. New York. 1st ed. sgn. dj. VG $16.00

GALLICO, Paul. *The Day Jean-Pierre Joined the Circus.* 1970. New York. Ills. Fiammenghi. 1st ed. dj. $10.00

GALLICO, Paul. *The Foolish Immortals.* 1953. New York. Doubleday. 224 pp. Vg $3.50

GALLICO, Paul. *The Hand of Mary Constable.* 1964. Garden City. 1st ed. dj. VG $35.00

GALLICO, Paul. *The Hurricane Story.* 1959. London. 1st ed. EX $15.00

GALLICO, Paul. *The Man Who Was Magic.* 1966. New York. Doubleday. 203 pp. $4.00

GALLICO, Paul. *The Revealing Eye.* 1967. photos by Nickolas Muray. VG $20.00

GALLICO, Paul. *The Silent Miaow.* 1964. New York. Crown Pub. Ills. $4.00

GALLICO, Paul. *The Small Miracle.* 1952. Garden City. Ills. Lonette. 1st ed. $15.00

GALLICO, Paul. *The Snow Goose.* 1946. Ills. Peter Scott. 1st ed. EX $17.50

GALLICO, Paul. *Thomasina.* 1957. Doubleday. 1st ed. dj. VG $30.00

GALLICO, Paul. *Trial by Terror.* 1951. New York. Knopf. 247 pp. VG $4.00

GALLIENE, Richard. *The Romance of Perfume.* 1928. Hudnut Pub. Ills. 1st ed. VG $25.00

GALLISHAW, John. *Trenching at Gallipoli.* 1916. New York. Ills. sgn. 241 pp. VG $15.00

GALLISHAW, John. *Trenching at Gallipoli.* 1917. New York. Century. $7.00

GALLOWAY, Alexander. *Skeletal Remains of Bambandyanalo.* 1959. Johannesburg. 1st ed. dj. $15.00

GALLUP, Joseph A., M.D. *Sketches of Epidemic Diseases in State of VT.* 1815. Boston. 1st ed. ex-lib. G $65.00

GALLWITZ. *Picasso at 90: Late Works.* 1971. Putnam. dj. VG $90.00

GALSWORTHY, John. *Die Forsyte Saga.* 1926. Berlin. German text. 3 vol set. $15.00

GALSWORTHY, John. *On Forsyte Change.* 1930. New York. 1st Am. ed. VG $15.00

GALSWORTHY, John. *Plays of John Galsworthy.* 1929. Duckworth Pr. Ltd. ed. 1/250. sgn. VG $60.00

GALSWORTHY, John. *Swan Song.* 1928. London. Ltd. 1st ed. sgn. $30.00

GALSWORTHY, John. *Swan Song.* 1928. presentation copy. sgn. EX $35.00

GALSWORTHY, John. *The Forsyte Saga.* 1933. New York. Scribner. 921 pp. EX $4.00

GALSWORTHY, John. *Two Forsyte Interludes.* 1928. New York. 1st Am. ed. VG $10.00

GALSWORTHY. *Awakening.* 1920. London. 1st ed. $30.00

GALT, John. *Annals of the Parish.* 1919. T.N. Foulis. Ills. H. Kerr. $25.00

GALTON, F. *Narrative of Explorer in Tropical South Africa.* 1853. London. VG $125.00

GALTON, Francis. *The Art of Travel.* 1856. London. 2nd ed. VG $30.00

GALVIN, J. *Through the Country of Comanche Indians in 1845.* 1970. San Francisco. Ills. maps. folio. dj. EX $35.00

GANDHI, M.K. *Songs from Prison.* 1934. Macmillan. dj. $20.00

GANDHI, Mahatma. *Young India.* 1923. New York. 1st Am. ed. 1200 pp. scarce. $45.00

GANGULY, Anil Baran. *Fine Arts in Ancient India.* 1979. New Delhi. Ills. 1st ed. inscr. $20.00

GANN, Ernest K. *Blaze of Noon.* 1946. New York. 310 pp. dj. VG $3.50

GANN, Ernest K. *Ernest K. Gann's Flying Circus.* 1974. New York. Macmillan. 1st ed. dj. VG $45.00

GANN, Ernest K. *Fiddler's Green.* 1950. New York. Sloane. 286 pp. dj. $3.50

GANN, Ernest K. *Soldier of Fortune.* 1954. New York. Sloane. 217 pp. dj. $3.50

GANN, Ernest K. *The Antagonists.* 1959. New York. Simon & Schuster. 277 pp. dj. $3.50

GANNETT, Lewis & Holbrook.*The Age of the Moguls.* 1953. 1st ed. dj. $6.50

GANS-RUEDIN, E. *Antique Oriental Carpets.* 1975. Ills. 1st ed. EX $75.00

GANSON, Lewis. *Routined Manipulation Finale.* London. VG $10.00

GANTZ. *Man in Space-U.S.A.F. Program for Developing Crew.*1959. dj. VG $15.00

GARBARINO. *Health Plans & Collective Bargaining.* 1960. dj. $15.00

GARBER, C.M. *Stories & Legends of Bering Strait Eskimos.* 1940. Boston. 1st ed. sgn. 260 pp. EX $50.00

GARBETT, Mike & Goulding, B. *Lancaster at War, Vol. 3.* 1984. London. EX $15.00

GARCES, Francisco. *Record of Travels in Arizona & California 1775-6.* 1965. Howell. EX $37.50

GARCIA, L. *Prehistoric Art of Western Mediterranean & Sahara.*1964. Viking. 1st ed. stiff wrappers. $12.50

GARCIA MARQUEZ, Gabriel. *One Hundred Years of Solitude.* 1970. New York. Harper & Row. 1st Am. ed. dj. $50.00

GARD, Wayne. *Frontier Justice.* 1949. OK U. Press. dj. VG $15.00

GARD, Wayne. *Great Buffalo Hunt.* 1959. Ills. dj. VG $15.00

GARD, Wayne. *Sam Bass.* 1936. 1st ed. $75.00

GARDINER, D. & Walker, K.S. *Raymond Chandler Speaking.* 1962. Boston. Houghton Mifflin. 1st ed. dj. $40.00

GARDINER, John. *Great Dream from Heaven.* 1974. Dutton. 1st ed. dj. VG $20.00

GARDNER, Albert & Field, S. *American Paintings. Vol. I.* 1965. New York. NY Graphic Soc. 1st printing. $12.50

GARDNER, Alexander. *Gardner's Photographic Sketch Book of Civil War.* 1959. Ills. 220 pp. VG $7.50

GARDNER, Brian. *Up to the Line to Death. War Poets: 1914-1918.* 1969. New York. Potter. 1st Am. ed. 184 pp. $5.00

GARDNER, Charles. *The Grange: Friend of the Farmer, 1867-1947.* 1949. National Grange. dj. VG $20.00

GARDNER, Erle Stanley. *Case of the Fabulous Fake.* 1969. New York. 1st ed. $10.00

GARDNER, Erle Stanley. *Case of the Velvet Claws.* 1933. New York. Morrow. 2nd printing. dj. $50.00

GARDNER, Erle Stanley. *Smoking Chimney.* 1943. New York. 1st ed. dj. $150.00

GARDNER, Erle Stanley. *The Case of the Backward Mule.* 1946. Morrow. 1st ed. dj. VG $30.00

GARDNER, Erle Stanley. *The Case of the Buried Clock.* 1945. London. Cassell. 1st Eng. ed. dj. VG $15.00

GARDNER, Erle Stanley. *The Case of the Careless Cupid.* 1968. Morrow. 1st ed. EX $20.00

GARDNER, Erle Stanley. *The Case of the Counterfeit Eye.* 1935. Morrow. 1st ed. VG $30.00

GARDNER, Erle Stanley. *The Case of the Daring Decoy.* 1957. Roslyn. 1st ed. 171 pp. dj. EX $15.00

GARDNER, Erle Stanley. *The Case of the Howling Dog.* 1934. Morrow. 1st ed. VG $30.00

GARDNER, Erle Stanley. *The Case of the Rolling Bones.* 1939. New York. Morrow. 1st ed. 279 pp. $42.50

GARDNER, Erle Stanley. *The Desert is Yours.* 1963. New York. Morrow. Ills. 1st ed. dj. EX $15.00

GARDNER, Herb. *A Thousand Clowns.* 1962. Random House. 1st ed. dj. $15.00

GARDNER, Horace J. *Let's Celebrate Christmas.* 1940. Barnes, NY. VG $8.50

GARDNER, J. *October Light.* 1976. 1st ed. dj. EX $20.00

GARDNER, John & Dunlap, L. *The Forms of Fiction.* 1962. New York. 1st ed. EX $85.00

GARDNER, John & Maier, John. *Gilgamesh.* 1984. New York. Knopf. 1st ed. dj. VG $20.00

GARDNER, John. *For Special Services.* 1982. Coward McCann. 1st Am. ed. dj. VG $12.50

GARDNER, John. *For Special Services.* 1982. Coward McCann. review copy. dj. EX $35.00

GARDNER, John. *Freddy's Book.* 1980. Knopf. Ills. 1st ed. dj. EX $22.50

GARDNER, John. *Grendel.* 1971. New York. Knopf. 1st ed. sgn. EX $200.00

GARDNER, John. *Gudgekin, the Thistle Girl.* Ills. M. Sporn.1st ed. sgn. dj. EX $30.00

GARDNER, John. *Icebreaker.* 1983. Putnam. 1st Am. ed. dj. VG $12.50

GARDNER, John. *Icebreaker.* London. proof copy. $55.00

GARDNER, John. *Icebreaker.* 1983. New York. Putnam. review copy. EX $30.00

GARDNER, John. *In the Suicide Mountains.* 1977. New York. Knopf. 1st ed. dj. VG $45.00

GARDNER, John. *Mickelsson's Ghosts.* 1982. New York. Knopf. proof copy. wrappers. $45.00

GARDNER, John. *Mickelsson's Ghosts.* 1982. New York. Knopf. 1st ed. 590 pp. dj. EX $20.00

GARDNER, John. *Nickel Mountain.* 1973. Knopf. Ills. O'Donohue. 1st ed. dj. $35.00

GARDNER, John. *On Moral Fiction.* 1978. Basic. proof copy. wrappers. EX $100.00

GARDNER, John. *On Moral Fiction.* 1977. 1st ed. dj. EX $12.50

GARDNER, John. *Role of Honor.* 1984. Putnam. 1st Am. ed. dj. VG $12.50

GARDNER, John. *Role of Honor.* 1984. New York. Putnam. review copy. EX $25.00

GARDNER, John. *Sunlight Dialogues.* 1977. Knopf. VG $9.00

GARDNER, John. *The Art of Living.* 1981. New York. Knopf. dj. EX $17.50

GARDNER, John. *The Art of Living.* London. 1st ed. VG $15.00

GARDNER, John. *The King's Indian.* 1975. Cape. 1st English ed. dj. VG $25.00

GARDNER, John. *The King's Indian.* 1974. New York. Ills. Fink. 1st ed. 323 pp. VG $25.00

GARDNER, John. *The King's Indian.* 1974. New York. Knopf. 1st ed. inscr. dj. EX $40.00

GARDNER, John. *Sunlight Dialogues.* 1972. Knopf. 1st ed. dj. VG $70.00

GARDNER, John. *The Wreckage of Agathon.* 1970. Harper. 1st ed. dj. VG $90.00

GARDNER, John. *Understrike.* London. Lib. Congress dup copy. $30.00

GARDNER, L. *Fat City.* 1969. New York. uncorrected proof. wrappers. $40.00

GARDNER, Martin. *The Annotated Snark.* 1962. New York. Ills. 1st ed. dj. $22.50

GARDNER, R.E. *American Arms & Arms Makers.* 1938. Columbus, OH. Ills. ex-lib. 167 pp. $10.00

GARDNER, Robert G. *On the Hill, Story of Shorter College.* 1972. Rome, GA. 476 pp. dj. VG $4.50

GARDNER, S.M. *Some Descendants of Justus Harris of NY State.* 1974. Chicago. 160 pp. $10.00

GARDNER, Will. *The Clock that Talks & What It Tells.* 1954. Nantucket. inscr. dj. $20.00

GARFIELD, Leon, & Blishen, E. *The Golden Shadow.* 1973. Harmondwsorth. Ills. Charles Keeping. 1st ed. $25.00

GARFIELD, Leon. *The House of Cards.* 1982. St.Martins. 1st Am. ed. dj. VG $12.50

GARFIELD, Leon. *The Sound of Coaches.* 1974. Middlesex. Kestrell. 1st ed. dj. VG $30.00

GARFIELD, Leon. *The Strange Affair of Adelaide Harris.* 1971. New York. 1st ed. dj. VG $35.00

GARFIELD & BLISHEN. *The Golden Shadow.* 1973. London. Ills. 1st ed. dj. VG $15.00

GARGAN, J. & Coke, J. *Political Behavior & Public Issues in Ohio.* 1972. Kent State U. 1st ed. 388 pp. index. VG $7.50

GARIN, Eugenio. *Astrology in Renaissance; Zodiac of Life.* 1983. London. Routledge & Paul. 1st ed. dj. $15.00

GARIN, Eugenio. *Giovanni Pico Della Mirandola.* 1963. Parma. Paolo Toschi. 57 pp. EX $12.50

GARIN, Eugenio. *Medioevo e Rinascimento: Studi e Richerche.* 1984. Bari. Laterza ed. 336 pp. EX $15.00

GARIS, Cleo. *Missing at Marshlands, Arden Blake.* 1934. A.L. Burt. Ills. dj. VG $10.00

GARIS, Howard R. *Buddy & His Chums.* 1930. Cupples & Leon. G $3.50

GARIS, Howard R. *Buddy & His Cowboy Pal.* 1935. Cupples & Leon. G $3.50

GARIS, Howard R. *Buddy & the Arrow Club.* 1937. New York. 208 pp. $3.50

GARIS, Howard R. *Buddy & the Flying Balloon.* 1931. Cupples & Leon. VG $4.50

GARIS, Howard R. *Buddy & the G-Man Mystery.* 1944. Cupples & Leon. G $3.50

GARIS, Howard R. *Buddy & the Indian Chief.* 1936. Cupples & Leon. VG $4.50

GARIS, Howard R. *Buddy & the Secret Cave.* 1934. Cupples & Leon. G $3.50

GARIS, Howard R. *Buddy & the Victory Club.* 1943. Cupples & Leon. G $3.50

GARIS, Howard R. *Buddy at Pine Beach.* 1931. Cupples & Leon. VG $4.50

GARIS, Howard R. *Buddy at Rainbow Lake.* 1930. Cupples & Leon. VG $4.50

GARIS, Howard R. *Buddy at Red Gate.* 1941. Cupples & Leon. EX $5.50

GARIS, Howard R. *Buddy in Deep Valley.* 1940. Cupples & Leon. VG $4.50

GARIS, Howard R. *Buddy in School.* 1929. Cupples & Leon. G $3.50

GARIS, Howard R. *Buddy on Floating Island.* 1933. Cupples & Leon. dj. G $5.50

GARIS, Howard R. *Buddy on Mystery Mountain.* 1932. Cupples & Leon. G $3.50

GARIS, Howard R. *Buddy on the Farm.* 1929. Cupples & Leon. VG $4.50

GARIS, Howard R. *Curly Tops at Sunset Beach.* 1924. Cupples & Leon. dj. VG $15.00

GARIS, Howard R. *The Curley Tops on Star Island.* 1918. Cupples & Leon. Ills. VG $4.50

GARIS, Howard R. *The Curly Tops & Their Pets.* 1921. Cupples & Leon. Ills. G $3.50

GARIS, Howard R. *The Curly Tops at Cherry Farm.* 1918. Cupples & Leon. Ills. G $3.50

GARIS, Howard R. *The Curly Tops at Summer Camp.* 1927. Cupples & Leon. Ills. G $3.50

GARIS, Howard R. *The Curly Tops at Uncle Frank's Ranch.* 1918. Cupples & Leon. Ills. G $3.50

GARIS, Howard R. *The Curly Tops in the Woods.* 1923. Cupples & Leon. Ills. G $3.50

GARIS, Howard R. *The Curly Tops Snowed In.* 1918. Cupples & Leon. Ills. G $3.50

GARIS, Howard R. *The Dragon Swamp.* 1942. Cupples & Leon. G $3.50

GARIS, Howard R. *Uncle Wiggily and His Funny Auto.* 1940. Whitman. Ills. Campbell. 34 pp. VG $4.50

GARIS, Howard R. *Uncle Wiggily & His Flying Rug.* 1940. Whitman. Ills. Campbell. VG $4.50

GARIS, Howard R. *Uncle Wiggily on the Farm.* 1939. New York. Platt & Monk. 185 pp. $3.00

GARIS, Howard R. *Uncle Wiggily's Automobile.* 1929. New York. Platt & Monk. 184 pp. dj. $4.00

GARIS, Howard R. *Uncle Wiggily's Story Book.* 1939. Ills. Lansing Campbell. VG $20.00

GARIS, Howard R. *Uncle Wiggily Goes Camping.* 1949. Whitman. Ills. Campbell. 34 pp. VG $4.50

GARIS, Lilian. *Sally Found Out.* 1930. New York. Grosset & Dunlap. 248 pp. $3.50

GARIS. *The Curly Tops & Their Playmates.* Cupples & Leon. Ills. G $3.50

GARLAND, Hamlin. *A Member of the Third House.* 1897. Appleton. presentation copy. sgn. VG $65.00

GARLAND, Hamlin. *A Son of the Middle Border.* 1917. New York. 1st ed. 467 pp. $10.00

GARLAND, Hamlin. *Afternoon Neighbors.* 1934. New York. 1st ed. dj. VG $10.00

GARLAND, Hamlin. *Back Trailers from the Middle Border.* 1928. New York. 1st ed. sgn. VG $25.00

GARLAND, Hamlin. *Cavanagh Forest Ranger.* 1910. New York. 1st ed. $15.00

GARLAND, Hamlin. *My Friendly Contemporaries.* 1932. New York. 1st ed. $15.00

GARLAND, Hamlin. *Roadside Meetings.* 1930. New York. Macmillan. 1st ed. 474 pp. $10.00

GARLAND, Hamlin. *Rose of Dutcher's Cooly.* 1896. New York. 2nd ed. $10.00

GARLAND, Hamlin. *The Book of the American Indian.* 1923. New York. Harper. Ills. Remington. $150.00

GARLAND, Hamlin. *The Book of the American Indian.* 1927. New York. Ills. Remington. dj. boxed. $85.00

GARLAND, Hamlin. *The Moccasin Ranch.* 1909. New York. 1st ed. $15.00

GARLAND, Hamlin. *Trail Makers of the Middle Border.* 1926. New York. $10.00

GARLAND, Hamlin. *Westward March of American Settlement.* 1927. Chicago. $5.00

GARLAND, Hamlin. *Witch's Gold.* 1906. New York. 1st ed. $15.00

GARLAND, Joseph, M.D. *The Doctor's Saddlebag.* 1930. Linotyping Corp. VG $10.00

GARLINSKI. *Hitler's Last Weapons.* 1978. Time Books. Ills. ex-lib. 239 pp. dj. $3.50

GARNER, Alan. *Elidor.* 1965. Collins. 1st ed. dj. EX $85.00

GARNETT, D. *Beany-Eye.* 1935. London. Ltd. ed. 1/110. sgn. VG $60.00

GARNETT, D. *Plough over the Bones.* 1973. London. Macmillan. 1st ed. dj. VG $20.00

GARNETT, D. *Pocahontas.* 1933. New York. 1st ed. $15.00

GARNETT, D. *The Grasshoppers Come.* 1931. New York. 1st ed. VG $12.50

GARNETT, D. *The Sailor's Return.* 1925. Ltd. ed. 1/160. sgn. EX $35.00

GARNETT, Louise Ayres. *The Muffin Shop.* 1910. Rand McNally. Ills. Hope Dunlap. VG $25.00

GARNETT, Lucy M.J. *Mysticism & Magic in Turkey.* 1912. London. Ills. 202 pp. index. VG $40.00

GARNETT, R. *Idylls & Epigrams.* 1869. London. 1st ed. $12.00

GARNETT, R. *Shelley's Letters.* 1882. London. Keagan, Paul, Trench & Co. VG $35.00

GARRARD, Lewis H. *Memoir of Charlotte Chambers.* 1856. Philadelphia. 1st ed. 135 pp. EX $1,250.00

GARRARD, Lewis H. *Wah-To-Yah, & the Taos Trail.* 1850. Cincinnati. Derby. 1st ed. 349 pp. VG $1,250.00

GARRARD, Phillis. *Running Away with Nebby.* 1944. Philadelphia. McKay. Ills. Pogany. 1st ed. $15.00

GARREAU, Emile & Cohen, L. *Billy Mitchell.* 1942. New York. 1st ed. dj. VG $10.00

GARRETSON, Martin S. *The American Bison.* 1938. New York. Ills. 1st ed. dj. VG $47.50

GARRETT, Edmund H. *Elizabethan Songs in Honour of Love & Beautie.* 1891. Boston. VG $15.00

GARRETT, George. *King of the Mountains.* 1957. New York. Scribner. 1st ed. sgn. VG $40.00

GARRETT, George. *Poets of Today IV.* 1957. New York. Scribner. 166 pp. $7.50

GARRETT, George. *The Succession.* 1983. New York. Doubleday. 538 pp. EX $3.50

GARRETT, H. *Rufous Redtail.* 1947. Viking Press. Ills. F.L. Jaques. 1st ed. dj. $10.00

GARRETT, Pat. *Authentic Life of Billy the Kid.* 1954. 1st ed. EX $35.00

GARRETT, Pat. *Authentic Life of Billy the Kid.* 1927. Ills. ex-lib. VG $25.00

GARRETT, Randall. *Unwise Child.* 1962. Garden City. 1st issue. dj. VG $10.00

GARRETT, Richard. *General Wolfe.* 1975. London. Ills. maps. 230 pp. dj. $12.00

GARRETT, Wm. *The Grand Buffalo.* 1926. Ills. Edwards. 1st ed. 147 pp. VG $9.50

GARRICK, David. *Three Plays.* 1926. Ltd. ed. 1/490. VG $15.00

GARRIQUE, Jean. *The Ego & the Centaur.* 1947. New Directions.1st ed. dj. VG $12.50

GARRISON, George P. *Diplomatic Correspondence of Republic of Texas.* 1908-1911. Washington. 1st ed. 3 vol set. $150.00

GARRY, Mrs. A. *Book of Sun-Dials.* 1900. London. Ills. 529 pp. folio. $45.00

GARST, Shannon. *Kit Carson, Trail Blazer & Scout.* 1942. New York. Ills. Daugherty. 1st ed. $15.00

GARSTANG, John. *The Hittite Empire.* 1929. London. 364 pp. 53 pls. index. $32.50

GARTH, D. *Appointment with Danger.* 1940. Popular Library. #136. pb. VG $7.00

GARTH, Will. *Dr. Cyclops.* 1940. New York. Phoenix Press. dj. scarce $75.00

GARVE, Andrew. *Counterstroke.* 1978. New York. 1st Am. ed. dj. VG $5.00

GARVEY & WICK. *The Arts of the French Book 1900-1965.* 1967. Dallas. S. Methodist U. Pr. dj. EX $20.00

GARWOOD, Darrell. *Artist in Iowa: Life of Grant Wood.* 1944. New York. 1st ed. dj. VG $35.00

GARWOOD, Darrell. *Crossroads of America, Story of Kansas City.* Norton. no title pp. VG $8.00

GARY, Elbert H. *Works of Art: Furniture, Fabrics, Rugs.* 1928. Am. Art Assoc. Ills. folio. VG $50.00

GASCOIGNE, B. *The Great Moguls.* 1971. Harper & Row. Ills. 1st Am. ed. dj. EX $7.50

GASH, Jonathan. *Moonspender.* 1986. London. Collins. 1st ed. sgn. dj. VG $30.00

GASH, Jonathan. *Pearlhanger.* London. 1st ed. sgn. $28.00

GASH, Jonathan. *Spend Game.* proof copy. wrappers. VG $25.00

GASH, Jonathan. *The Gondola Scam.* 1984. London. Collins. 1st ed. sgn. dj. VG $30.00

GASH, Jonathan. *The Tartan Ringers.* 1986. London. Collins. 1st ed. dj. sgn. EX $30.00

GASH, Jonathan. *Vatican Rip.* proof copy. wrappers. VG $20.00

GASK, Lilian. *Betty & Bobtail at Pine-Tree Farm.* NY/London. no date. Ills. Helen Jacobs. $25.00

GASKELL, Jane. *The City.* 1966. London. Hodder. 1st ed. EX $25.00

GASKELL, Mrs. *Cranford.* 1899. London/NY. Macmillan. 295 pp. $35.00

GASKELL, T.F. *The Gulf Stream.* 1973. Ills. dj. EX $10.00

GASKILL, J.W. *Footprints Through Dixie.* 1919. Alliance, OH. 1st ed. 186 pp. $95.00

GASPER, Howland. *The Complete Sportsman.* 1893. New York. Ills. gold decor on cover. $25.00

GASQUE, J. *Bass Fishing.* 1945. VG $15.00

GASQUET, Francies A. *Henry VIII & English Monasteries.* 1889. London. 4th ed. 2 vol set. $22.50

GASS, Patrick. *Voyages & Travels Under Capts. Lewis & Clarke.* 1808. London. 1st Eng. ed. 381 pp. $875.00

GASS, William. *Omensetter's Luck.* 1966. New York. 1st ed. dj. EX $100.00

GASS, William. *Willie Masters' Lonesome Wife.* New York. 1st Am. ed. dj. EX $15.00

GASTAFSON, A. *Foundation of Death: Study of the Drink Question.* 1885. Boston. G $15.00

GASTER, M. *The Sword of Moses.* 1975. New York. Weisers. 3rd impression. VG $35.00

GATE, Ethel May. *Tales from the Enchanted Isles.* 1926. New York. Ills. Lathrop. 118 pp. dj. $25.00

GATES, F. *Wildflowers in Kansas.* 1934. Ills. 293 pp. VG $10.00

GATES, Gilman. *Saybrook at the Mouth of the Connecticut.* 1935. Ills. 246 pp. index. EX $20.00

GATES, Josephine S. *Story of Live Dolls.* 1901. Indianapolis. VG $50.00

GATES, Josephine S. *Story of Lost Doll.* 1905. Indianapolis. VG $50.00

GATES, Josephine S. *Sunshine Annie.* 1910. Ills. Fanny Cory. 1st ed. VG $30.00

GATES, Susa Young. *The Life Story of Brigham Young.* 1930. New York. 388 pp. dj. VG $40.00

GATES. *Capt. Billy Leads Way to Land 'I Don't Want To.'* 1914. Dodd Mead. Ills. $3.50

GATTHAAR. *The March to the Sea & Beyond.* 1885. Ills. 310 pp. $9.50

GATTI, A. *Killers All!* 1943. McBride. Ills. 245 pp. dj. EX $25.00

GAUBA, Kanhayalal. *Pathology of Princes.* 1930. Lahore. VG $15.00

GAUDIER-BRZESKA. *Drawings.* 1946. London. Ills. 1st printing. EX $25.00

GAUGUIN, Paul. *Noa Noa.* 1919. 1st ed. dj. VG $40.00

GAULT, John. *The Fans Go Wild.* 1973. Toronto. New Press. Ills. 141 pp. dj. $8.00

GAULT, W.P. *Ohio at Vicksburg.* 1906. Columbus. 1st ed. EX $30.00

GAUNT, W. *Restless Century. Paintings in Britain 1800-1900.* 1972. Phaidon. folio. dj. VG $30.00

GAUNT, W. *Surrealists.* 1972. 92 full pp. color pls. dj. VG $45.00

GAUTIER, Leon. *La Chanson De Rolland. Dune Intro Historique.* 1872. Tours. Ills. 3 vol set. $80.00

GAUVREAU, Emile & Cohen, L. *Billy Mitchell, Founder of Air Force & Prophet.* 1942. New York. 1st ed. 303 pp. $12.50

GAVARNI. *Oeuvres Choisies.* 1944. Paris. wrappers. VG $15.00

GAVIN, J.R. *Air Assault. Development of Airmobile Warfare.* 1979. Ills. maps. G $20.00

GAVIN. *Great Red Dragon or Master Key to Popery.* 1854. New York. G $9.00

GAY, Carlo T.E. *Chalcacingo.* 1972. Portland. Ills. Frances Pratt. no dj. EX $40.00

GAY, John. *The Beggars Opera.* 1922. London. Ills. Ltd. ed. 1/1000. $67.50

GAY, John. *The Letters of Gay.* 1966. London. 1st ed. dj. EX $20.00

GAY, John. *Trivia, Art of Walking the Streets of London.* 1922. London. Ills. folio. EX $40.00

GAY, Zheya. *Ballad of Reading Gaol.* 1937. New York. lithos. slipcase. VG $60.00

GAYARRE, C. *Louisiana: History as a French Colony.* 1852. New York. 1st ed. 380 pp. fld map. $40.00

GAYTON, Bertram. *The Gland Stealers.* 1922. Philadelphia. Lippincott. 1st ed. dj. VG $20.00

GEBLER, Ernest. *The Plymouth Adventure.* 1950. New York. 1st ed. 377 pp. dj. $12.50

GEDDES, H. *Gorilla.* 1955. Melrose. Ills. 1st ed. map. 206 pp. dj. $15.00

GEDDES. *The Evergreen. Part 2.* 1895. VG $16.00

GEDDIE, John. *Beyond the Himalayas.* 1889. London. Ills. Hildibrand. VG $15.00

GEE, E.P. *The Wildlife of India.* 1964. Dutton. Ills. 1st Am. ed. 192 pp. EX $17.50

GEHLEN, Gen. Reinhard. *The Service.* 1972. New York. EX $12.50

GEHMAN, Christian. *Beloved Gravely.* 1984. New York. Scribner. proof copy. VG $45.00

GEIGER, Maynard. *The Life & Times of Fray Junipero Serra.* 1959. 1st ed. 2 vol set. $22.50

GEIKE, A. *Scenery of Scotland.* London/NY. 2nd ed. 481 pp. $40.00

GEIKIE, John C. *Adventures in Canada or Life in the Woods.* Philadelphia. (ca.1875) Ills. 408 pp. $10.00

GEIRER, Christina. *An Adopted Daughter: or, The White Slave.* 1882. Evansville, IN. I. Esslinger, Printer. 134 pp. $35.00

GEISMAR, M. *Henry James & the Jacobites.* 1963. Boston. 1st ed. dj. EX $32.50

GEISSMAR, Berta. *Two Worlds of Music.* 1946. New York. Ills. dj. VG $20.00

GEIST, V. *Mountain Sheep, a Study in Behavior & Evolution.* 1971. Chicago. Ills. 383 pp. EX $15.00

GEISTER. *Ice Breakers, Games & Stunts.* 1918. Woman's Press. 93 pp. EX $4.50

GELHIUS, Aulus. *Noctes Atticae.* 1651. Amsterdam. Elzevir Press. VG $75.00

GELL, William. *Pompeiana.* 1832. London. Ills. 2 vol set. rebound. VG $130.00

GELL, William. *Pompeiana.* 1852. London. Ills. 3rd ed. G $80.00

GELLER, Stephen. *Gad.* 1979. Harper. 1st ed. dj. VG $12.50

GELLER, Stephen. *Gad.* 1979. Harper. 1st ed. sgn. inscr. dj. VG $20.00

GELLHORN, Martha. *Liana.* 1944. New York. dj. VG $7.50

GELLIS, Roberta. *Roselynde.* 1978. Playboy Press. proof copy. wrappers. EX $50.00

GENET, Jean. *The Thief's Journal.* 1964. Grove Press. dj. EX $7.50

GENET. *Balcony.* 1st English ed. dj. VG $50.00

GENT, W.H. *Road to Oregon. Chronicle of Great Emigrant Trail.* 1934. New York. Ills. 274 pp. map. $9.00

GENTHE, Arnold. *Impressions of Old New Orleans.* 1926. New York. 1st ed. 101 pls. $40.00

GENTHE, Arnold. *Pictures of Old Chinatown.* 1908. New York. 57 pp. 56 photos. G $40.00

GENTHE. *As I Remember.* 1936. New York. 1st ed. VG $60.00

GENTHE. *Sanctuary: Bird Masque.* 1914. VG $45.00

GENTILES, Margaret. *Masters of Japanese Print: Moronobu to Utamaro.* 1964. New York. Ills. 171 pp. $60.00

GENTRY, Curt. *Last Days of the Late, Great State of California.* 1968. New York. Putnam. VG $4.00

GEOFFREY, Dennis. *Coronation Commentary.* 1937. New York. 1st ed. 2nd printing. VG $7.50

GEORGE, David Lloyd. *Where Are We Going.* 1923. New York. Doran. 371 pp. dj. $52.50

GEORGE, Henry. *Social Problems.* 1883. Chicago/NY. 1st ed. 367 pp. $35.00

GEORGE, Henry. *The Condition of Labor.* 1891. New York. 1st ed. $40.00

GEORGE, Noah J.T. *The Gentlemen & Ladies' Pocket Dictionary.* 1831. Concord. $15.00

GEORGE, U. *In the Deserts of This Earth.* 1977. Harcourt. Ills. 307 pp. EX $12.50

GEORGE, W. *Animals & Maps.* 1969. CA U. Press. Ills. maps. 235 pp. dj. EX $17.50

GERARD, James W. *My Four Years in Germany.* 1917. Grosset & Dunlap. 328 pp. $4.50

GERARD, James W. *My Four Years in Germany.* 1917. New York. Doran. 448 pp. G $4.00

GERARD, Jules. *La Chasse Au Lion.* 1881. Paris. Ills. Dore. 251 pp. VG $27.50

GERHART, E.C. *America's Advocate.* 1958. Indianapolis. $20.00

GERHART, Genevra. *The Russian's World; Life & Language.* 1974. New York. 257 pp. $8.00

GERMOND, Jack W. & Whitcover. *Blue Smoke & Mirrors.* 1981. New York. Viking. 337 pp. dj. $4.50

GERNSBACK, Hugo. *Ralph 124C 41 +.* 1925. Boston. 1st ed. VG $50.00

GERNSBACK, Hugo. *Ultimate World.* 1971. New York. Walker. dj. VG $15.00

GERNSHEIM, Helmut. *Lewis Carroll-Photographer.* 1949. New York. Chanticleer Press. 121 pp. VG $50.00

GERNSHEIM. *Beautiful London.* 1956. $32.50

GERNSHEIM. *Churchill.* 1955. $30.00

GERNSHEIM. *History of Photography.* 1969. dj. $260.00

GERSHON, Freddie. *Sweetie, Baby, Cookie, Honey.* 1986. New York. Arbor House. advance copy. EX $20.00

GERSTAECKER, F. *Gerstaeckers Travels: Rio, Chili, California.* 1854. G $35.00

GERSTAECKER, F. *Wild Sports in the Far West.* 1876. Lippincott. G $5.00

GERTZ, Ulrich. *Comtemporary Plastic Art.* 1953. Berlin. Ills. 2nd ed. VG $25.00

GESELL, Arnold. *The Child from Five to Ten.* 1946. Harper. 1st ed. 475 pp. $20.00

GESSLER, C. *Tropic Landfall, the Port of Honolulu.* 1942. Doubleday. Ills. 1st ed. 331 pp. VG $15.00

GESSNER, John. *Best American Plays. 1918-1958.* 1963. New York. Crown. 2nd printing. 687 pp. $10.00

GESTON, M.S. *The Siege of Wonder.* 1976. New York. Doubleday. 1st ed. dj. EX $17.50

GHEERBRANT, A. *Journey to the Far Amazon.* 1954. Simon & Schuster. Ills. dj. VG $15.00

GHIRSHAMAN, D.J. Roman. *The Art of Ancient Iran.* 1964. Golden Press. 1st ed. photos. VG $35.00

GHOSE, Sudhin N. *And Gazelles Leaping.* 1949. Macmillan. 1st printing. $47.50

GIBBINGS, R. *Coming Down the Seine.* 1953. London. 1st ed. dj. VG $15.00

GIBBINGS, Robert. *Blue Angels & Whales.* 1946. Dutton. Ills. 1st ed. VG $15.00

GIBBINGS, Robert. *Over the Reefs & Far Away.* 1948. New York. 1st ed. dj. EX $12.50

GIBBON, Edward. *Roman Empire.* 1845. G $35.00

GIBBON, Perceval. *Vrouw Grobelaar.* 1906. New York. McClure. 1st ed. dj. VG $20.00

GIBBONS, Cromwell. *The Bat Woman.* 1938. New York. World. 1st ed. VG $25.00

GIBBONS, Euell & Gibbons, Joe. *Feast on a Diabetic Diet.* 1969. New York. ex-lib. 314 pp. dj. VG $5.00

GIBBONS, Euell. *Stalking the Wild Asparagus.* 1962. New York. 303 pp. dj. EX $5.00

GIBBONS, Phoebe Earl. *Pennsylvania Dutch & Other Essays.* 1882. Philadelphia. Lippincott. VG $12.50

GIBBONS, Reginald. *The Ruined Motel.* 1981. Houghton. 1st ed. dj. VG $12.50

GIBBONS, Stella. *Conference at Cold Comfort Farm.* 1949. London. 1st ed. dj. VG $35.00

GIBBONS, Stella. *The Weather at Tregulla.* 1962. London. Hodder & Stoughton. 1st ed. $40.00

GIBBONS, William F. *Those Black Diamond Men.* 1902. New York. Revell. 1st ed. EX $35.00

GIBBS, George. *Alphabetical Vocabulary of the Chinook Language.* 1863. New York. Cramoisy Pr. 1st ed. 23 pp. $125.00

GIBBS, George. *Dictionary of Chinook Jargon; Trade of Oregon.* 1863. New York. 1st ed. 44 pp. wrappers. $150.00

GIBBS, J.A. *Shipwrecks of the Pacific Coast.* 1981. Ills. wrappers. EX $8.00

GIBBS, Philip. *England Speaks.* 1935. Garden City. 1st ed. dj. G $6.00

GIBBS, Philip. *The Soul of the War.* 1915. New York. A.L. Burt. 371 pp. $3.50

GIBBS-SMITH, Charles. *Rebirth of European Aviation 1902-1908.* 1974. London. 387 pp. dj. EX $22.50

GIBLEY, Walter. *George Morland. His Life & Work.* 1907. London. 1st trade ed. VG $30.00

GIBRAN, K. *Spirits Rebellious.* 1947. New York. Philosophical Library. 121 pp. $50.00

GIBRAN, K. *Tears & Laughter.* 1949. New York. gift ed. 94 pp. EX $12.50

GIBSON, A. *The Chickasaws.* 1971. Norman. dj. VG $10.00

GIBSON, A.M. *Political Crime, History of the Great Fraud.* 1885. New York. 1st ed. 402 pp. $15.00

GIBSON, C. *Enchanted Trails.* 1948. London. Museum Press. Ills. 272 pp. VG $15.00

GIBSON, Charles Dana. *Sketches in Egypt.* 1899. New York. Ltd. ed. 1/250. sgn. VG $30.00

GIBSON, Katharine. *Pictures to Grow Up With.* 1948. London/NY. Ills. 151 pp. dj. VG. $8.50

GIBSON, Thomas. *The Anatomy of Human Bodies Epitomized.* 1688. London. Ills. 3rd ed. index. $150.00

GIBSON, W. *Our Native Orchids.* 1905. Doubleday Page. Ills. 1st ed. EX $25.00

GIBSON, Walter & Young, M. *Houdini's Fabulous Magic.* 1961. Philadelphia. dj. VG $7.50

GIBSON, Walter B. *Houdini's Escapes & Magic.* 1930. New York. Blue Ribbon Books. 317 pp. EX $12.50

GIBSON, Walter. *The Shadow.* 1979. New York. Doubleday. 1st ed. dj. $10.00

GIBSON, William Hamilton. *Camp Life in the Woods & Tricks of Trapping.* 1899. New York. VG $25.00

GIBSON, William Hamilton. *Eye Spy: Afield with Nature & Animate Things.* 1897. Harper. Ills. 264 pp. $125.00

GIBSON, William. *Count Zero.* London. 1st ed. sgn. $35.00

GIBSON, William. *Neuromancer.* Ltd. 1st ed. 1/375. sgn. $80.00

GIBSON, William. *The Institutes & Practice of Surgery;* 1835. Philadelphia. 4th ed. 30 pls. $90.00

GIBSON & HARPER. *The Riddle of Jutland.* 1934. Ills. Ernest Clegg. G $27.50

GIBSON. *The Book of Secrets. Miracles of Ancient & Modern.* 1927. Ills. VG $25.00

GIDART, R. *Albion College 1835-1960; A History.* 1961. dj. EX $5.00

GIDDINGS, Joshua. *The Exiles of Florida.* 1858. Columbus, OH. G $40.00

GIDE, Andre. *Pretexts, Reflections on Literature & Mortality.* 1959. New York. Meridian. 1st printing. $5.00

GIELOW, Martha. *Mammy's Reminiscences & Other Sketches.* 1898. New York. Ills. Clara W. Parrish. $50.00

GIES, Joseph. *Wonders of the Modern World.* 1966. New York. 241 pp. dj. $4.50

GIESY, J.D. *Mouthpiece of Zitu.* 1965. 1st ed. dj. EX $7.50

GIFFORD, Thomas. *Hollywood Gothic.* 1979. New York. Putnam. proof copy. wrappers. $20.00

GIFILLAN, Archer B. *Sheep.* 1929. Boston. Ills. Wiese. 1st ed. $25.00

GIGON, Fernand. *Formula for Death E6MC2. Atom Bombs & After.* 1958. Wingate. 1st ed. dj. $15.00

GIHON, John H. *Geary & Kansas.* 1857. Philadelphia. G $35.00

GILBERT, A.W. *The Potato.* 1920. New York. Rural Science Series. Ills. VG $10.00

GILBERT, Henry. *Robin Hood.* 1943. New York. 348 pp. $4.50

GILBERT, James. *The Flier's World.* 1976. New York. Ridge Press. EX $10.00

GILBERT, John R. *Cats.* 1969. London. P. Hamlyn. Ills. 151 pp. $6.50

GILBERT, Lydia Northrop. *Our Most Popular Trees.* 1929. New York. Ills. 110 pp. $3.50

GILBERT, M. *Mr. Calder & Mr. Behrens.* 1982. Harper. dj. EX $7.50

GILBERT, Michael. *Death Has Deep Roots.* 1951. London. 1st ed. dj. VG $30.00

GILBERT, Michael. *Flash Point.* 1974. London. 1st ed. dj. VG $35.00

GILBERT, Michael. *The Body of a Girl.* 1972. London. Hodder. 1st ed. dj. VG $30.00

GILBERT, Michael. *The Dust & the Heat.* 1967. London. Hodder & Stoughton. 1st ed. VG $40.00

GILBERT, Michael. *The Etuscan Net.* 1969. London. 1st ed. dj. VG $35.00

GILBERT, Michael. *The Long Journey Home.* London. 1st ed. sgn. $25.00

GILBERT, Michael. *The Night of the Twelfth.* 1976. London. Hodder & Stoughton. 1st ed. VG $15.00

GILBERT, Michael. *The Wycherly Woman.* 1962. London. Collins. 1st Eng. ed. dj. VG $20.00

GILBERT, R.A. *A.E. Waite: a Bibliography.* 1983. Aquarian Press. 1st ed. 192 pp. dj. EX $25.00

GILBERT, Rod & Park, Brad. *Playing Hockey the Professional Way.* 1972. Harper & Row. Ills. 1st ed. 270 pp. G $6.00

GILBERT, Stuart. *James Joyce's Ulysses.* 1952. Knopf. 2nd ed. dj. VG $5.00

GILBERT, Stuart. *Letters of James Joyce.* 1957. Viking. 1st Am. ed. dj. VG $10.00

GILBERT, W.S. *Fifty Bab Ballads.* 1877. London. Ills. 1st ed. VG $30.00

GILBERT, W.S. *The Bab Ballads.* 1898. London/NY. 350 Ills. 3rd ed. VG $60.00

GILBERT, W.S. *The Bab Ballads.* 1869. John Camden. Ills. 1st ed. 2 vol set. VG $150.00

GILBERT, W.S. *The Mikado & Other Plays.* New York. Readers League/Am. 581 pp. E $4.50

GILBERT, W.S. *The Mikado; or, The Town of Titipu.* 1979. London. Ills. Flint. & Brock. 1st ed. $12.50

GILBERT, W.S. *Yeoman of the Guard; or, Merryman & His Maid.* 1979. London. Ills. Flint & Brock. EX $15.00

GILBERT. *Historical Survey of County of Cornwall.* 1817. London. Ills. 2 vol set. VG $35.00

GILCHRIST, Ellen. *The Annunciation.* 1983. Little, Brown. proof copy. sgn. wrappers. VG $85.00

GILCHRIST, Ellen. *The Annunciation.* 1983. Boston. Little, Brown. 1st ed. EX $40.00

GILCHRIST, Ellen. *The Land Surveyor's Daughter.* 1979. Lost Roads. 1st ed. sgn. wrappers. VG $85.00

GILCHRIST, Ellen. *Victory Over Japan.* 1984. Little, Brown. 1st ed. sgn. dj. VG $35.00

GILCHRIST, Ellen. *Victory Over Japan.* 1985. London. Faber. 1st Eng ed. VG $45.00

GILDER, Rodman. *The Battery.* 1936. Boston. Ills. Ltd. ed. 1/228. sgn. $10.00

GILES, Barbara. *The Gentle Bush.* 1947. New York. Harcourt. 1st ed. dj. EX $35.00

GILES, Dorothy. *Singing Valleys. The Story of Corn.* 1940. New York. 1st printing. 361 pp. G $10.00

GILES, Edward. *History of the Art of Cutting in England.* 1887. London. inscr. G $25.00

GILES, Janice Holt. *The Damned Engineers.* 1970. Boston. dj. EX $15.00

GILES, Janice Holt. *The G.I. Journal of Sergeant Giles.* 1965. Houghton Mifflin. 1st ed. VG $20.00

GILES, Janice Holt. *The Kinta Years, an Oklahoma Childhood.* 1973. Boston. 337 pp. dj. $5.00

GILES. *Letters & Essays on Irish & Other Subjects.* 1869. New York. 1st ed. $20.00

GILES. *Shata County California: History of Oakland.* 1949. Ills. Ltd. 1st ed. 1/1000. EX $65.00

GILHAM, William. *Manual of Instruction, U.S. Volunteers & Militia.* 1861. Philadelphia Ills. 743 pp. $37.50

GILL, Brendan. *Cole.* 1971. New York. Ills. VG $25.00

GILL, Brendan. *Lindbergh Alone.* 1977. 1st ed. dj. VG $16.00

GILL, Brendan. *The Trouble of One House.* 1950. Garden City. Doubleday. 1st ed. 314 pp. dj. $15.00

GILL, Eric. *Autobiography.* 1941. Devin-Adair. dj. VG $17.50

GILL, Eric. *It All Goes Together. Selected Essays.* 1944. Devin-Adair. dj. VG $15.00

GILL, Eric. *Letters of Eric Gill.* 1947. London. Cape. 1st ed. dj. EX $15.00

GILL, Eric. *The Devil's Devices.* 1915. 1st Eng. ed. VG $225.00

GILL, F. *The Little Days.* 1917. Boston. Ills. Milo Winter. 1st ed. VG $25.00

GILL, F. *Windy Leaf.* 1924. New York. Ills. N.B. Zane. VG $10.00

GILLETT, J.B. *Six Years with the Texas Rangers 1875-1881.* 1925. New Haven. Yale U. Press. Ills. 259 pp. $45.00

GILLETT, J.B. *Six Years with the Texas Rangers.* 1921. Austen. 1st ed. VG $130.00

GILLETTE, F.L. *White House Cookbook.* 1889. G $50.00

GILLIAM, D.T. *The Essentials of Pathology.* 1883. Philadelphia. Ills. 296 pp. $15.00

GILLIAM, Franklin. *Some Unusual California Magazines.* 1975. San Francisco. Ills. wrappers. VG $30.00

GILLIARD, E.T. *Living Birds of the World.* 1967. Doubleday. Ills. 400 pp. dj. EX $15.00

GILLILAN, Strickland. *Including Finnigin.* 1919. Chicago. ex-lib. 124 pp. VG $2.50

GILLISS, J.M. *U.S. Naval Astronomical Expedition So. Hemisphere.* 1855. Washington. Ills. Vol. I. 565 pp. G $45.00

GILLMORE, Parker. *Adventures Afloat & Ashore.* 1873. London. Ills. 1st ed. 2 vol set. $150.00

GILLMORE. *Engineer & Artillery Operations Charleston.* 1865. New York. Ills. $50.00

GILLMORE. *The Rear Guard of the Revolution.* 1899. 322 pp. $12.50

GILLULY, J. *Origin of Granite.* 1959. Ills. 139 pp. $15.00

GILMAN, Alexander W. *Gillmans of Highgate w/Letters of S.T. Coleridge.* 1895. London. Ills. 1st ed. dj. VG $175.00

GILMAN, Caroline. *Recollections of a Southern Matron.* 1838. New York. Harper. ex-lib. G $80.00

GILMAN, Charlotte P. *Charlotte P. Gilman Reader.* 1980. New York. 1st ed. dj. EX $12.50

GILMAN, Charlotte P. *Perkins Herland.* 1979. Pantheon. 1st ed. SftCvr. $7.00

GILMAN, Charlotte P. *Perkins Herland.* 1979. New York. 1st ed. dj. EX $12.50

GILMAN, Lawrence. *Edward MacDowell.* 1921. New York. G $8.00

GILMAN, Lawrence. *Toscanini & Great Music.* 1938. New York. dj. VG $8.50

GILMORE, Anthony. *Space Hawk.* 1952. New York. Greenberg. 1st ed. dj. EX $17.50

GILMORE, J.C. *Art for Conservation, Federal Duck Stamps.* 1971. Barre. Ills. 94 pp. dj. EX $37.50

GILOT, Francoise & Lake, C. *Life with Picasso.* 1969. New York. 1st ed. dj. VG $16.00

GILPATRICK, Guy. *The Canny Mr. Glencannon.* 1948. New York. Dutton. 3rd printing. 213 pp. $15.00

GILPATRICK, Guy. *The First Glencannon Omnibus.* 1956. New York. Dodd Mead. 437 pp. dj. $20.00

GILPATRICK, Guy. *The Last Glencannon Omnibus.* 1957. Dodd Mead. dj. VG $25.00

GILPATRICK, Guy. *The Second Glencannon Omnibus.* 1944. New York. Dodd Mead. dj. $20.00

GILPIN, Laura. *The Hocus-Pocus of the Universe.* 1977. New York. Doubleday. 1st ed. VG $15.00

GILSON, J.H. *History of 126th Regt. Ohio Volunteer Infantry.* 1883. Salem, Ohio. 272 pp. $125.00

GINN, P. & McIlleron, G. *Water Birds of Southern Africa.* 1982. Rensburg. Ills. 1st ed. 143 pp. EX $20.00

GINRICH, Arnold. *The Bedside Esquire.* 1940. New York. 703 pp. VG $4.00

GINSBERG, A. & Cassady, N. *As Ever, the Collected Correspondence.* 1977. 1st ed. EX $10.00

GINSBERG, Allen. *Bixby Canyon Ocean Path World Breeze.* 1972. New York. Gotham Book Mart. wrappers. EX $20.00

GINSBERG, Allen. *Iron Horse.* 1974. City Lights. 1st Am. ed. wrappers. VG $10.00

GINSBERG, Allen. *Planet News.* 1969. City Lights. 1st ed. $15.00

GINSBERG, Allen. *Plutonian Ode.* 1982. City Lights. 1st ed. $5.00

GINSBERG, Allen. *Sad Dust Glories.* 1975. Berkeley. Workingmans Press. wrappers. $15.00

GINSBERG, Allen. *The Fall of America Wins a Prize.* 1974. Gotham Books. 1st ed. wrappers. EX $10.00

GINSBERG, Allen. *The Moments Return.* 1970. Grabhorn-Hoyem.Ltd. 1st ed. 1/200. VG $65.00

GINSBERG. *Baby Poems.* Ltd. ed. 1/100. sgn. $75.00

GINZBERG, Eliza. *The Negro Potential.* 1956. New York. 1st ed. dj. EX $10.00

GINZBURG, Natalia. *Family Sayings.* 1967. Hogarth. 1st ed. dj. VG $30.00

GINZBURG, Ralph. *An Unhurried View of Erotica.* 1958. Helman Press. Collector's ed. 128 pp. $7.50

GIOVANNI, Nikki. *Black Judgement.* 1968. Detroit. 1st ed. wrappers. EX $45.00

GIOVANNI, Nikki. *The Women & the Men.* 1975. New York. Morrow. 1st ed. dj. EX $20.00

GIPSON, Fred. *Hound Dog Man.* 1949. Harper. 247 pp. VG $6.50

GIRAUDOUX, Jean. *Amica America.* 1928. Paris. Ltd. ed. 1/225. folio. VG $22.50

GISSING, George. *Charles Dickens.* 1898. London. Blackie. 1st ed. VG $75.00

GISSING, George. *Letters of Gissing to His Family.* 1927. London. Portrait. ed. by family. VG $65.00

GISSING, George. *Six Sonnets on Shakespearean Heroines.* 1982. London. Ltd. 1st ed. wrappers. VG $20.00

GISSING, George. *The Private Papers of Henry Ryecroft.* 1903. Westminister. 1st ed. VG $175.00

GISSING, George. *Town Traveller.* 1898. Stokes. 1st ed. 293 pp. VG $20.00

GISSING, George. *Vernailda.* 1904. London. 1st ed. VG $95.00

GISSING, Geroge. *Will Warburton.* 1905. London. 1st ed. $85.00

GITLER, Ira. *Make the Team in Ice Hockey.* 1972. New York. Ills. revised ed. 68 pp. EX $5.00

GITTINGS, R. *John Keats: Living Year 1818-1819.* 1954. Harvard. 1st ed. dj. $12.50

GIUDICI. *Tragedy of the Italia.* 1929. $9.00

GIVEN, Meta. *The Modern Family Cook Book.* 1961. Chicago. Ferguson Pub. 632 pp. $5.00

GJERSET, Knut. *History of Iceland.* 1924. New York. 1st ed. fld map. 482 pp. VG $25.00

GLACKENS, Ira. *William Glackens & the Ashcan Group.* 1958. Crown. 1st ed. dj. $20.00

GLADDEN, W. *From the Hub to the Hudson.* 1869. Boston. Ills. 1st ed. VG $20.00

GLADDEN, Washington. *From Hub to Hudson w/Sketches of Nature & History.* 1870. Greenfield. Housac Tunnel. Ills. G $10.00

GLADDEN, Washington. *Live & Learn.* 1914. New York. 159 pp. $10.00

GLADDEN, Washington. *Recollections.* 1909. 1st ed. VG $12.00

GLADKOV. *Meetings with Pasternak.* 1st ed. dj. $6.00

GLASCOW, Ellen. *They Stooped to Folly.* 1929. Garden City. 1st ed. VG $10.00

GLASER. *Graphik der Neuzeit.* 1922. Berlin. $32.00

GLASGOW, Ellen. *In This Our Life.* 1941. New York. Grosset & Dunlap. 467 pp. dj. $3.50

GLASGOW, Ellen. *The Deliverance.* New York. 1st ed. rare dj. $20.00

GLASGOW, Ellen. *The Shadowy Third.* 1923. New York. Doubleday. 1st ed. VG $30.00

GLASGOW, Ellen. *Vein of Iron.* 1935. New York. 1st ed. 462 pp. $10.00

GLASGOW, Ellen. *Voice of the People.* 1900. New York. 1st ed. VG $10.00

GLASGOW, Ellen. *Woman Within.* 1954. New York. 1st ed. dj. $6.00

GLASGOW. *Phases of an Interior Planet.* 1898. 1st impression. VG $75.00

GLASPELL, Susan. *Norma Ashe.* 1942. Philadelphia. Lippincott. 1st ed. dj. VG $45.00

GLASPELL, Susan. *Plays.* 1920. Boston. 1st ed. dj. EX $25.00

GLASS, Mary Lou. *Recipes for Two.* 1947. New York. 387 pp. EX $5.00

GLASSCOCK. *A Golden Highway.* 1934. Bobbs Merrill. Ills. 1st ed. dj. VG $15.00

GLASSE. *The Art of Cookery Made Plain & Easy.* 1799. Dublin. full leather, foxed. worn. $150.00

GLASSER, Ronald. *365 Days.* 1971. New York. 1st ed. inscr. sgn. dj. $50.00

GLASSMAN, Judith. *The Year in Music 1978.* 1978. New York. Columbia House. Ills. 320 pp. $4.50

GLASSMAN, Sidney. *The Flora of Ponape.* 1952. Bishop Museum. 1st ed. stiff wrappers. $12.50

GLAZIER, William. *Down the Great River.* 1889. Philadelphia. Ills. fld map. VG $20.00

GLAZIER, William. *Heroes of Three American Wars.* 1880. Philadelphia. EX $12.50

GLAZIER, William. *Peculiarities & American Cities.* 1886. Philadelphia. Ills. pls. $20.00

GLAZIER, William. *Prison Pen & Escape: Prison Life in the South.* 1868. Hartford. G $15.00

GLAZIER, William. *Sword & Pen.* 1900. 500 pp. $11.50

GLEASON, Oscar. *Gleason's Horse Book.* 1892. Springfield. Ills. 416 pp. wrappers. VG $25.00

GLENDON. *Rowing.* 1923. Ills. 1st ed. VG $7.50

GLENN, Thomas. *Some Colonial Mansions & Those Who Lived in Them.* 1899. Philadelphia. Ills. 1st ed. VG $35.00

GLOSSOP, Reginald. *The Egyptian Venus.* 1946. London. Regency. 1st ed. inscr. dtd. $35.00

GLOVER, T.R. & Calvin, D.D. *A Corner of Empire the Old Ontario Strand.* 1937. Cambridge. 1st ed. dj. $10.00

GLUCKMAN, Arcadi. *United States Muskets, Rifles & Carbines.* 1948. 1st ed. dj. EX $50.00

GLUSKER, Irwin. *A Southern Album.* 1975. Birmingham. Ltd. 1st ed. sgn. VG $30.00

GOBLE, Paul & Dorothy. *Red Hawk's Account of Custer's Last Battle.* 1969. New York. Ills. 63 pp. dj. $6.00

GOBLE, Warwick. *Green Willow.* 1923. Macmillan. 16 color pls. $55.00

GOBLE, Warwick. *Water Babies.* 1910. Macmillan. 16 color pls. $75.00

GOBLE. *Indian Myth & Legend.* London. 8 color pls. $28.00

GOBLE. *The Modern Reader's Chaucer.* 1921. Macmillan. 607 pp. 32 color pls. $185.00

GODDARD, Abba. *The Trojan Sketch Book.* 1846. New York. 1st ed. $45.00

GODDARD, J. *Kayaks Down the Nile.* 1979. Brigham Young U. Ills. dj. VG $10.00

GODDARD, Pliny Earle. *Indians of the Northwest.* 1924. New York. $20.00

GODDARD, Pliny Earle. *Indians of the Southwest.* 1931. New York. Ills. 205 pp. 68 pls. G $12.50

GODDARD, Pliny Earle. *White Mountain Apache Texts.* 1920. 159 pp. SftCvr. $10.00

GODDARD, Robert H. *Papers of Robert H. Goddard.* 1970. New York. Ills. 1707 pp. 3 vol set. $95.00

GODDARD, Robert H. *The Papers of Volume III 1938-1945.* 1970. New York. VG $20.00

GODDARD, Robert. *Rocket Genius-Robert Goddard.* 1963. Ills. 75 pp. $3.00

GODDEN, G. *Coalport & Coalbrookdale Porcelains.* 1970. New York. Praeger. VG $27.00

GODDEN, G. *Encyclopedia British Pottery & Porcelain Marks.* 1964. New York. $25.00

GODDEN, Rumer. *A Fugue in Time.* 1945. London. 1st ed. dj. $25.00

GODDEN, Rumer. *An Episode of Sparrows.* 1955. Viking. 1st Am. ed. dj. VG $25.00

GODDEN, Rumer. *China Court.* 1961. Viking. 1st ed. dj. VG $30.00

GODDEN, Rumer. *In Noah's Ark.* 1949. New York. $10.00

GODDEN, Rumer. *In This House of Brede.* 1969. Viking. 1st Am. ed. dj. EX $20.00

GODDEN, Rumer. *St. Jerome & the Lion.* 1961. London. Ills. Primrose. 1st ed. dj. VG $15.00

GODDEN, Rumer. *The Battle of the Villa Fiorita.* 1963. New York. Viking. 1st ed. dj. VG $30.00

GODDEN, Rumer. *The River.* 1946. London. 1st ed. dj. VG $20.00

GODDEN, Rumer. *The River.* 1946. Boston. 1st ed. dj. VG $8.50

GODEY, Louis A. & Hale, Sarah. *Godey's Lady's Book. Vol. LX & Vol. LXI.* 1860. Philadelphia. Ills. 1145 pp. VG $75.00

GODFREY, Elizabeth. *Home Life Under the Stuarts 1603-1649.* 1903. London. photos. 312 pp. VG $5.50

GODFREY, J. *The Great Outdoors.* 1947. St. Paul. Ills. Chidley. 1st ed. EX $45.00

GODMAN, Dr. John D. *Rambles of a Naturalist. With a Memoir.* 1859. Philadelphia. $25.00

GODMAN, John. *American National History.* 1831. Ills. 2nd ed. 3 vol set. disbound. $35.00

GODOLPHIN, Mary. *Robinson Crusoe. Told in One Syllable Words.* 1882. 1st ed. VG $20.00

GODWIN, Gail. *A Mother & Two Daughters.* 1982. Viking. 1st ed. dj. VG $15.00

GODWIN, Gail. *Dream Children.* New York. 1st ed. VG $15.00

GODWIN, Gail. *Finishing School.* 1985. Viking. proof copy. wrappers. EX $40.00

GODWIN, Gail. *Finishing School.* New York. 1st ed. sgn. $30.00

GODWIN, Gail. *Mr. Bedrord & the Muses.* 1983. Viking. 1st ed. dj. VG $15.00

GODWIN, Gail. *The Odd Woman.* 1974. New York. Knopf. 1st ed. dj. VG $30.00

GODWIN, Gail. *Violet Clay.* 1978. New York. Knopf. 1st ed. dj. VG $25.00

GODWIN, J. *This Baffling World.* 1968. Hart. photos. dj. VG $10.00

GODWIN, Parke. *The Fire When It Comes.* 1984. Garden City. review copy. dj. VG $12.50

GODWIN, William. *Lives of the Necromancers.* 1834. London. 1st ed. sgn. VG $90.00

GODWIN. *Robin Hood.* 1932. Garden City. 4 color pls. VG $10.00

GOEING. *Vom Tropischen Tiefande Zum Ewigen Schnee.* Venezuela. Leipzig. 12 color pls. folio. $100.00

GOERNER, Fred. *The Search for Amelia Earhart.* 1966. New York. Doubleday. 1st ed. $6.00

GOETHE, Johann von. *Faust.* 1823. London. $25.00

GOETHE, Johann von. *Faust.* 1908. London. Hutchinson. Ills. Pogany. VG $35.00

GOETHE, Johann von. *Letters from Goethe.* 1957. Nelson. 1st ed. dj. $15.00

GOETHE, Johann von. *The Story of Reynard the Fox.* 1954. Heritage. Ills. Eichenberg. slipcase. $15.00

GOETZ. *Prophet with Honor, Fred Tuttle Story.* 1965. Phoenix. 91 pp. $20.00

GOETZMAN, W. & Sloan, K. *Looking Far North, Harriman Expedition to Alaska.* 1899. Viking Press. Ills. 1st ed. 244 pp. dj. EX $15.00

GOFF, Clarissa. *Florence.* 1905. Black. Ills. 262 pp. VG $20.00

GOFF, Frederick R. *Incunabula in American Libraries.* 1964. New York. EX $65.00

GOFF, John S. *Robert Todd Lincoln.* 1968. 1st ed. 286 pp. EX $10.00

GOFFIN, Robert. *Louis Armstrong: Le Roi Du Jazz.* 1947. Paris. 1st ed. wrappers. EX $25.00

GOGARTY, O. *Going Native.* 1940. New York. 1st ed. VG $15.00

GOGARTY, Oliver St.John. *An Offering of Swans.* London. presentation copy. sgn. 57 pp. $22.50

GOIN, C. & O. *Introduction to Herpetology.* 1970. Freeman. Ills. 353 pp. VG $15.00

GOLD, H.L. *What Will They Think of Last.* 1976. Ltd. 1st ed. sgn. dj. EX $40.00

GOLD, Herbert. *A Girl of Forty.* 1986. New York. proof copy. wrappers. EX $25.00

GOLD, Herbert. *Family.* 1981. Arbor House. 1st ed. dj. VG $12.50

GOLD, Herbert. *My Last Two Thousand Years.* 1972. Random House. 1st ed. dj. EX $15.00

GOLD, Herbert. *Salt.* 1963. 1st ed. dj. EX $20.00

GOLD, Herbert. *Swiftie the Magician.* 1974. McGraw Hill. VG $12.50

GOLD, Herbert. *True Love.* 1982. Arbor House. 1st ed. dj. VG $15.00

GOLDBARTH, Albert. *Curve.* 1977. New Rivers. 1st ed. wrappers. VG $5.00

GOLDBERG, G.J. *The Lynching of Orin Newfield.* 1970. Dial Press. 1st ed. VG $7.50

GOLDBERG, M. *Name Sake.* 1982. New Haven. Ills. G $10.00

GOLDBERG. *The Man Mencken.* 1925. New York. 2nd printing. $10.00

GOLDEN, G.F. *My Lady Vaudeville & Her White Rats.* 1909. New York. Broadway Press. 199 pp. G $35.00

GOLDEN, I.J. *Precedent.* 1931. New York. Farrar. 1st ed. dj. EX $35.00

GOLDHURST, F.S. *Fizgerald & Contempories.* 1st Am. ed. dj. VG $10.00

GOLDIE, B. *The Piper of Arristoun.* 1935. Ward, Lock. 1st ed. dj. $20.00

GOLDIN, Stephen. *A World Called Solitude.* 1981. Garden City. review copy. dj. VG $10.00

GOLDIN, William. *Darkness Visible.* 1979. Faber. EX $15.00

GOLDING, Harry. *The Wonder Book of Engineering Wonders.* London. Ward, Lock. no date. Ills. $15.00

GOLDING, Harry. *The Wonder Book of the Navy.* London. Ills. G $22.50

GOLDING, Louis. *Honey for the Ghost.* 1949. 1st ed. dj. G $15.00

GOLDING, Louis. *The Doomington Wanderer.* 1934. London. Gollancz. dj. VG $17.50

GOLDING, Louis. *The Glory of Elsie Silver.* Hutchinson. 1st ed. inscr. dj. VG $25.00

GOLDING, William. *A Moving Target.* 1982. New York. Farrar. 1st ed. dj. EX $25.00

GOLDING, William. *Darkness Visible.* 1979. New York. Farrar. 1st ed. dj. VG $35.00

GOLDING, William. *Free Fall.* 1959. London. Faber. 1st ed. dj. VG $85.00

GOLDING, William. *Pyramid.* London. 1st English ed. dj. VG $50.00

GOLDING, William. *Rites of Passage.* 1980. New York. Farrar. 1st ed. dj. EX $25.00

GOLDING, William. *The Pyramid.* 1967. Harcourt. 1st Am. ed. dj. VG $20.00

GOLDING, William. *The Spire.* 1964. New York. Harcourt. 1st ed. dj. VG $45.00

GOLDMAN, Emma. *Living My Life.* 1934. Garden City. VG $25.00

GOLDMAN, Eric. *Rendezvous with Destiny.* 1952. 1st ed. $8.50

GOLDMAN, Eric. *The Tragedy of Lyndon Johnson.* 1969. Knopf. 3rd printing. 535 pp. dj. $50.00

GOLDMAN, Irving. *The Cubeo Indians of the North West Amazon.* 1963. 1st ed. stiff wrappers. $10.00

GOLDMAN, Laurel. *Sounding the Territory.* 1982. Knopf. 1st ed. ex-lib. dj. VG $15.00

GOLDMAN, William. *Control.* 1982. Delacorte. proof copy. wrappers. EX $20.00

GOLDMAN, William. *Marathon Man.* 1974. Delacorte. 1st ed. dj. VG $25.00

GOLDMAN, William. *Soldier in the Rain.* advance copy. wrappers. VG $20.00

GOLDMAN, William. *The Color of Light.* 1984. Warner. advance copy. wrappers. VG $15.00

GOLDMAN, William. *The Temple of Gold.* 1957. New York. 1st ed. dj. VG $40.00

GOLDRING, Douglas. *The Last Pre-Raphaelite.* 1948. London. 1st ed. dj. VG $20.00

GOLDSMITH, J. *On a Popular Plan.* 1818. London. Ills. 744 pp. fld maps. EX $45.00

GOLDSMITH, M.M. *Hobbes' Science of Politics.* 1966. New York. Columbia U. Pr. 274 pp. dj. VG $10.00

GOLDSMITH, Margaret. *Christina of Sweden.* 1935. New York. Doubleday Doran. 308 pp. dj. $4.00

GOLDSMITH, Oliver. *An History of the Earth & Animated Nature.* 1774. London. Nourse. 1st ed. 8 vol set. VG $225.00

GOLDSMITH, Oliver. *Animated Nature: History of Earth & Nature.* 1872. London. Blackie & Son. Ills. 2 vol set. $175.00

GOLDSMITH, Oliver. *Goody Two Shoes.* 1930. Winston. Ills. Harriet Price. 1st ed. $25.00

GOLDSMITH, Oliver. *The Works of Oliver Goldsmith.* 1928. Putnam. Turkshead Ltd. ed. EX $115.00

GOLDSMITH, Oliver. *Vicar of Wakefield.* 1929. Philadelphia. Ills. Arthur Rackham. 1st ed. $100.00

GOLDSMITH, Oliver. *Vicar of Wakefield.* 1929. London. Harrap. Ills. Rackham. 1st ed. $60.00

GOLDSMITH, Oliver. *Vicar of Wakefield.* 1914. London. Ills. Sullivan. Ltd. ed. sgn. $35.00

GOLDSMITH, Richard. *Physiological Genetics.* 1938. New York. McGraw Hill. 1st ed. 374 pp. $100.00

GOLDSMITH. *Goldsmith Official Baseball Score Book, No. 2.* 1939. P. Goldsmith Sons, Inc. $6.50

GOLDSMITH. *Goldsmith's Roman History.* 1808. New York. 4th Am. ed. 275 pp. G $22.50

GOLDSMITH. *Poetical Works of Goldsmith.* 1872. Boston. $17.50

GOLDSTEIN, Rebecca. *The Mind-Body Problem.* 1983. Random House. advance copy. dj. VG $15.00

GOLDSTONE, Adrian H. *Collection of Mystery & Detective Fiction.* 1981. San Francisco. 2 vol set. wrappers. EX $125.00

GOLDTHORPE, John. *The Same Scourge.* 1956. New York. Putnam. 1st Am. ed. ex-lib. $52.50

GOLOWNIN, R.N. *Narrative of My Captivity in Japan.* 1818. London. 1st ed. 2 vol set. VG $475.00

GOLTRA, John N. *Preventative Medicine in the Home.* 1912. Chicago. 5 vol set. VG $135.00

GOMBRICHT, E.H. *The Story of Art.* 1951. Ills. 462 pp. dj. EX $5.00

GONEIM, M.Z. *The Buried Pyramid.* 1956. London. Ills. 1st ed. dj. $15.00

GONZALEZ & SALAZAR. *The Great Rebel, Che Guevara in Boliva.* 1969. Grove Press. 1st ed. dj. VG $10.00

GOOD HOUSEKEEPING. *Good Housekeeping Book of Meals.* 1930. New York. 2nd ed. 256 pp. $5.00

GOOD HOUSEKEEPING. *New Ways to Handle Housework.* 1924. $8.50

GOODE, G. Brown. *Virginia Cousins.* 1981. Harrisonburg. reprint. Ills. 526 pp. $32.50

GOODE, George B. *Fisheries & Fishery Industries of U.S.* 1884. 277 pls. 2 vol set. $75.00

GOODELL, Jane. *They Sent Me to Iceland.* 1943. New York. Washburn. 248 pp. VG $4.50

GOODEN, A.H. *Smoke Tree Range.* 1936. New York. 1st ed. ex-lib. $7.50

GOODMAN, Benny. *Benny; King of Swing.* 1979. Morrow. 1st ed. folio. dj. EX $20.00

GOODMAN, Daniel Carson. *Fan Dance at Cockcrow.* 1970. 1st ed. dj. $8.50

GOODMAN, J. *The Fireside Book of Dog Stories.* 1943. Simon & Schuster. 591 pp. dj. $7.50

GOODMAN, Paul. *A Ceremonial.* 1980. Black Sparrow. Ltd. ed. 1/750. wrappers. EX $25.00

GOODMAN, Paul. *Break-Up of Our Camp.* 1978. Black Sparrow. Ltd. ed. 1/750. wrappers. EX $25.00

GOODRICH, A.L. *Birds in Kansas.* 1946. Topeka. 1st ed. 340 pp. wrappers. VG $15.00

GOODRICH, C.A. *The Universal Traveller: Arts, Customs & Manners.* 1836. Hartford. Ills. foxed. worn. $20.00

GOODRICH, C.A. *Travels & Sketches in North & South America.* 1852. Boston. Ills. $25.00

GOODRICH, John. *The Civil & Executive Officers' Assistant.* 1793. New Haven. 1st ed. $125.00

GOODRICH, Lloyd. *Edward Hopper.* New York. Abrams. Ills. 306 pp. folio. $75.00

GOODRICH, Lloyd. *The Artist in America.* 1967. New York. 1st ed. dj. VG $12.50

GOODRICH, S.G. *A Pictorial Geography of the World.* 1852. Boston. Ills. 400+ pp. $40.00

GOODRICH, S.G. *Ills. Natural History of the Animal Kingdom.* 1861. New York. Derby & Jackson. Ills. 2 vol set. $195.00

GOODRICH, S.G. *Johnson's Natural History of the Animal Kingdom.* 1874. New York. 1550 Ills. G $25.00

GOODRICH, S.G. *Malte Brun School Geography.* 1836. Hartford. Ills. 11th ed. VG $25.00

GOODRICH, S.G. *Pictorial History of the United States.* 1876. Philadelphia. 521 pp. $75.00

GOODRICH, S.G. *Pictorial History of the Western World.* 1849. 830 pp. $30.00

GOODRICH, S.G. *The Animal Kingdom.* 1880. Ann Arbor. Ills. 2 vol set. $50.00

GOODRICH. *A New Universal Pocket Gazetteer.* 1832. Boston. 1st ed. 297 pp. $25.00

GOODSPEED, Charles. *Yankee Bookseller.* 1937. Boston. 1st ed. dj. VG $20.00

GOODSPEED, E. *Things Seen & Heard.* 1925. Chicago. 1st ed. inscr. 226 pp. VG $15.00

GOODSPEED, T.H. *Plant Hunters in the Andes.* 1914. Farrar. sgn. photos. dj. $30.00

GOODWIN, C.C. *As I Remember Them.* 1913. Salt Lake City. 360 pp. $20.00

GOODWIN, C.C. *That Brief.* 1886. Washington. 1st ed. 22 pp. wrappers. $50.00

GOODWIN, C.C. *The Comstock Club.* 1891. Salt Lake City. 1st ed. VG $35.00

GOODWIN, D. *Birds of Man's World.* 1978. Cornell U. Ills. 1st ed. 183 pp. dj. EX $10.00

GOODWIN, D. *Pigeons & Doves of the World.* 1970. British Museum. Ills. 446 pp. dj. EX $40.00

GOODWIN, N. *Foote Family; or, Descendants of Nathaniel Foote.* 1849. Hartford. VG $30.00

GOODWIN, N. *Nat Goodwin's Book.* 1914. Boston. Ills. 1st ed. G $35.00

GOODWIN, W. *Truth About Leif Erickson & the Greenland Voyages.* 1941. Boston. Ills. maps. 445 pp. $40.00

GOODWIN, Wm. B. *Spanish & English Ruins in Jamaica.* 1946. Boston. 239 pp. photos. maps. VG $35.00

GOODYEAR, W.A. *Coal Mines of the Western Coast.* 1877. San Francisco. VG $45.00

GOODYEAR, W.H. *Renaissance & Modern Art.* 1894. Ills. 1st ed. VG $10.00

GOODYKOONTZ, C. *Home Missions on American Frontier.* 1939. Caxton Pub. 460 pp. dj. VG $20.00

GOOKIN, Frederick William. *Japanese Colour Prints & Their Designers.* 1913. New York. Ills. Ltd. ed. 1/100. folio. $145.00

GOOLD, Wm. *Portland in the Past with Historical Notes.* 1886. Portland. Ills. 543 pp. $30.00

GOOLRICK, J.T. *Frederickburg & Cavalier Country.* 1935. dj. VG $10.00

GOOSSEN. *Navajo Made Easier. Course Conversational Navajo.* 1979. revised ed. EX $10.00

GORAN & LINIGOOD. *Different Valor. Story of Gen. Joseph E. Johnson.* 1956. Indianapolis. dj. VG $15.00

GORDI, Tooni. *Contemporary American Women Poets.* 1936. New York. VG $25.00

GORDIMER, Nadine. *Burger's Daughter.* 1979. Cape. 1st English ed. dj. VG $25.00

GORDIMER, Nadine. *Livingstone's Companions.* 1971. Viking. 1st Am. ed. dj. VG $35.00

GORDIMER, Nadine. *Livingstone's Companions.* 1972. London. Cape. 1st ed. VG $40.00

GORDIMER, Nadine. *Not for Publication.* 1965. Viking. 1st Am. ed. dj. VG $30.00

GORDIMER, Nadine. *Not For Publication.* 1965. London. Gollancz. 1st ed. VG $50.00

GORDIMER, Nadine. *Occasion for Loving.* 1963. Viking. 1st Am. ed. dj. VG $25.00

GORDIMER, Nadine. *Soldier's Embrace.* 1980. New York. 1st ed. dj. EX $7.50

GORDIMER, Nadine. *Something Out There.* 1984. Viking. 1st Am. ed. dj. VG $15.00

GORDIMER, Nadine. *Something Out There.* 1984. Cape. 1st ed. dj. VG $25.00

GORDIMER, Nadine. *The Conservationist.* 1974. Viking. 1st Am. ed. dj. VG $25.00

GORDIMER, Nadine. *The Lying Days.* 1953. Simon & Schuster. 1st Am. ed. $60.00

GORDIMER, Nadine. *The Soft Voice of the Serpent.* 1952. New York. 1st Am. ed. dj. VG $65.00

GORDING, Louis. *The Bare-Knuckle Breed.* 1952. London. Ills. VG $35.00

GORDON, Alvin. *Inherit the Earth.* 1963. U. Arizona Pr. 1st ed. dj. EX $20.00

GORDON, Arthur. *American Heritage; History of Flight.* 1962. no place. Ills. dj. VG $22.50

GORDON, Caroline. *How to Read a Novel.* 1957. Viking. 1st ed. dj. VG $40.00

GORDON, Caroline. *Old Red & Other Stories.* 1963. Scribner. 1st ed. dj. EX $35.00

GORDON, Caroline. *The Collected Stories of Caroline Gordon.* 1981. Farrar. 1st ed. dj. VG $20.00

GORDON, Caroline. *The Malefactors.* 1956. New York. 1st ed. VG $65.00

GORDON, Charles. *General Gordon's Khartoum Journal.* 1963. Vanguard. 1st ed. dj. $8.50

GORDON, Elizabeth. *Buddy Jim.* 1922. $10.00

GORDON, Elizabeth. *Mother Earth's Children.* 1914. New York. Ills. M.T. Ross. VG $25.00

GORDON, Elizabeth. *The Turned-Into's.* 1935. New York. Ills. Janet Laura Scott. $20.00

GORDON, Grant. *The Story of the Ship.* 1919. McLoughlin. 1st ed. VG $20.00

GORDON, H.W. & E. *Oriental Lowestoft.* 1963. 3rd ed. $10.00

GORDON, Harry. *On the Columbia.* 1913. New York. A.L. Burt. 256 pp. dj. $3.50

GORDON, Harry. *On the Mississippi.* 1913. New York. A.L. Burt. 256 pp. dj. $3.50

GORDON, Harry. *The River Motor Boat Boys on the Colorado.* 1913. New York. A.L. Burt. 256 pp. $3.50

GORDON, Jan & Cora. *Two Vagabonds in Albania.* 1927. London. John Lane. Ills. VG $15.00

GORDON, Jean. *Pageant of the Rose.* 1961. Woodstock, VT. Red Rose Pub. 2nd ed. dj. $20.00

GORDON, Mary. *Final Payments.* 1978. New York. Random House. 1st ed. dj. EX $25.00

GORDON, Mary. *Men & Angels.* 1985. Random House. 1st ed. dj. VG $17.50

GORDON, Mary. *The Company of Women.* 1980. Knopf. 1st ed. dj. VG $20.00

GORDON, Maurice. *Aesulapius Comes to Colonies. Story of Medicine.* 1949. Ventnor. 1st ed. dj. $15.00

GORDON, Ruth. *My Side: Autobiography of Ruth Gordon.* 1976. New York. 1st ed. dj. EX $12.50

GORDON, Ruth. *Myself Among Others.* 1971. New York. 1st ed. dj. VG $15.00

GORDON, S. *The Golden Eagle.* 1955. Citadel. Ills. 1st Am. ed. dj. EX $10.00

GORDON, S. *Thirty Years of Nature Photography.* 1952. London. Ills. dj. $12.50

GORDON, William R. *A Three-Fold Test of Modern Spiritualism.* 1856. New York. 1st ed. 408 pp. G $60.00

GORE, J.R. *Boyhood of Abraham Lincoln.* 1921. Indianapolis. Ills. G $7.50

GOREN, Charles H. *Better Bridge for Better Players.* 1942. New York. Doubleday. 537 pp. G $3.50

GOREN, Charles H. *Goren Presents the Italian Bridge System.* 1958. New York. Doubleday. ex-lib. 216 pp. dj. $3.50

GORES, Joe. *Final Notice.* 1973. New York. Random House. 1st ed. dj. VG $35.00

GORES, Joe. *Final Notice.* 1974. London. Gollancz. 1st Eng. ed. dj. VG $20.00

GORES, Joe. *Gone, No Forwarding.* 1978. New York. Random House. 1st ed. dj. VG $25.00

GORES, Joe. *Hammett.* 1975. New York. Putnam. 1st ed. dj. EX $20.00

GOREY, E. *Scrap Irony.* 1961. Ills. 1st ed. dj. VG $20.00

GOREY, Edward. *A Mercurial Bear.* 1983. Gotham. Ills. 1st ed. sgn. wrappers. $12.50

GOREY, Edward. *Glorious Nosebleed.* 1974. 1st ed. sgn. dj. VG $20.00

GOREY, Edward. *The Broken Spoke.* 1976. Dodd Mead. 1st ed. sgn. dj. VG $20.00

GOREY, Edward. *The Doubtful Guest.* 1978. New York. Dodd Mead. 1st ed. sgn. dj. $30.00

GOREY, Edward. *The Doubtful Guest.* 1958. London. Ills. 1st Eng. ed. dj. VG $30.00

GOREY, Edward. *The Epileptic Bicycle.* 1969. New York. Ills. author. 1st ed. dj. EX $35.00

GOREY, Edward. *The Listing Attic.* 1954. Boston/NY. Ills. 1st ed. dj. $125.00

GOREY, Edward. *The Unstrung Harp.* 1953. New York. Duell. 1st ed. dj. VG $65.00

GOREY, Edward. *The Vinegar Works.* 1963. New York. 1st ed. 3 vol set. slipcase. $125.00

GOREY, Edward. *Why We Have Day & Night.* 1970. Capra Press. 1st ed. wrappers. $7.50

GOREY. *Amphigorey.* New York. 1st ed. dj. EX $30.00

GOREY. *Clinical Sonnets.* 1953. New York. 1st Ills. ed. $5.00

GOREY. *Fatal Lozenge.* 1960. New York. 1st ed. VG $25.00

GOREY. *Instant Lives.* New York. 1st ed. dj. EX $15.00

GOREY. *Utter Zoo Alphabet.* 1967. New York. 1st ed. $15.00

GOREY. *Very Fine Clock.* New York. 1st ed. dj. EX $15.00

GOREY. *War of the Worlds.* New York. 1st ed. VG $25.00

GORHAM, Maurice. *Television Medium of the Future.* 1949. London. Marshall. 142 pp. dj. $52.50

GORHAM. *Famous Small Bronzes.* 1928. $34.00

GORKY, Maxim. *Foma Gordyeeff.* 1917. New York. Scribner. 448 pp. G $3.50

GORKY, Maxim. *Reminiscences of L.N. Tolstoy.* 1920. New York. 1st Am. ed. dj. VG $30.00

GORMAN, Herbert. *James Joyce.* 1948. Rinehart. 1st ed. dj. VG $7.50

GORMAN, J. *Honour the King.* 1935. London. Ills. VG $12.50

GORMAN, Michael. *The Real Book About Cowboys.* 1952. New York. Ills. 189 pp. $6.00

GORSLINE, Douglas. *What People Wore.* 1952. New York. Bonanza. Ills. dj. VG $10.50

GOSNELL, H. Allen. *Guns on the Western Waters.* 1949. Ills. 273 pp. $18.50

GOSS, Charles F. *The Redemption of David Corson.* 1900. Indianapolis. 418 pp. $15.00

GOSS, Elbridge H. *The Life of Colonel Paul Revere.* 1904. Boston. Ills. 2 vol set. EX $37.50

GOSS, Warren. *The Boy's Life of General Sheridan.* 1913. New York. 318 pp. VG $5.00

GOSSE, Edmund. *Critical Kit-Kats.* 1896. London. Heinemann. 1st ed. VG $40.00

GOSSON, Louis C. *Post-Bellum Campaigns of Blue & Gray. 1881-1882.* 1882. Trenton. Ills. 1st ed. 192 pp. $50.00

GOUGH, John B. *Sunlight & Shadow; or, Gleanings from Life/Work.* 1881. London. 401 pp. $12.50

GOUDGE, Elizabeth. *Pilgrim's Inn.* 1948. $10.00

GOUDGE, Elizabeth. *The Lost Angel.* 1971. New York. Ills. S. Hughs. 1st Am. ed. $15.00

GOUDSMIT, Samuel A. *Alsos: Story of a Nazi A-Bomb.* 1947. New York. Ills. 259 pp. $15.00

GOUGE. *Fiscal History of Texas.* 1852. Philadelphia. 1st ed. $80.00

GOUGH, John B. *Platform Echoes/Leaves from Notebooks of 40 Years.* 1886. Hartford. Ills. VG $15.00

GOUGH, John B. *Sunlight & Shadow.* 1882. Hartford. EX $15.00

GOULART, Ron. *The Hardboiled Dicks.* 1965. Los Angeles. Sherbourne Pr. 1st ed. dj. EX $25.00

GOULART, Ron. *Brinkman.* 1981. Garden City. review copy. dj. EX $12.50

GOULART, Ron. *Hawksaw.* 1972. New York. Doubleday. 1st ed. dj. EX $8.50

GOULD, E.W. *Fifty Years on the Mississippi*. 1889. St. Louis. scarce. VG $135.00

GOULD, John. *Birds of Asia*. 1969. London. Methuen. Ills. 321 pp. dj. EX $85.00

GOULD, John. *Birds of Europe*. 1966. Metheun. 160 color pls. EX $45.00

GOULD, John. *The Parables of Peter Partout*. 1964. Boston/Toronto.Ills. 1st ed. sgn. 171 pp. dj. $9.00

GOULD, Lois. *La Presidenta*. 1981. New York. Simon & Schuster. 349 pp. dj. $4.00

GOULD, Lois. *Necessary Objects*. 1972. New York. Random House. 1st ed. inscr. $45.00

GOULD, Lois. *Such Good Friends*. 1970. New York. Random House. 1st ed. dj. VG $35.00

GOULD, Mary Earle. *Early American Wooden Ware*. 1948. sgn. dj. VG $50.00

GOULD, R.E. *Yankee Storekeeper*. 1946. New York. McGraw Hill. 195 pp. VG $3.50

GOULD, Robert Freke. *Gould's History of Freemasonry Throughout World*. 1936. New York. Scribner. Ills. 6 vol set. VG $60.00

GOULD, Robert Freke. *History of Freemasonry, Antiquities, Symbols, etc.*1890. Cincinnati/NY. Yorston & Co. 4 vol set. VG $100.00

GOULD & PYLE. *Anomalies & Curiosities of Medicine*. 1927. New York. 295 Ills. 986 pp. index. VG $45.00

GOULD. *Dick Tracy Meets the Night Crawler*. 1945. Whitman. Ills. VG $4.50

GOULD. *Report on Invertebrata of Mass.* 1841. Cambridge. Ills. inscr. $35.00

GOULDER, Grace. *John D. Rockefeller, the Cleveland Years*. 1972. Cleveland. 271 pp. $12.50

GOULLART. *Land of the Lamas, Adventure Secret Tibet*. 1959. New York. 1st ed. dj. EX $10.00

GOUZENKO, Igor. *The Fall of a Titan*. 1954. New York. Norton. 1st ed. dj. VG $20.00

GOVIER, Katherine. *Going Through the Motions*. 1982. St. Martins. 1st ed. dj. VG $15.00

GOW, G.F. & Swanson, S. *Snakes & Lizards of Australia*. Australia. photos. 80 pp. EX $17.50

GOWER, Ronald. *My Reminiscences*. 1884. New York. VG $25.00

GOWING, Clara. *The Alcotts as I Knew Them*. 1909. Boston. Ills. 1st ed. 134 pp. VG $7.50

GOYEN, William. *Come, the Restorer*. 1974. Doubleday. 1st ed. dj. VG $25.00

GOYEN, William. *Ghost & Flesh*. 1952. New York. Random House. 1st ed. VG $35.00

GOYEN, William. *The House of Breath*. 1975. New York. Ltd. 1st ed. 1/500. dj. EX $20.00

GOYEN, William. *Nine Poems*. 1976. Albondocani. Ltd. ed. 1/200. sgn. wrappers. $30.00

GOYEN, William. *The Faces of Blood Kindred*. 1960. Random House. 1st ed. dj. VG $35.00

GOYEN, William. *The House of Breath*. 1950. Random House. 1st ed. dj. VG $30.00

GOYTISOLO, Juan. *Makbara*. 1981. Seaver. trans. Lane. 1st Am. ed. dj. $15.00

GRABER, J.W. *Illinois Birds, Wood Warblers*. 1983. Ills. map. 144 pp. EX $10.00

GRABHORN, Robert. *19th Century Type Display*. 1959. 1st ed. sgn. VG $100.00

GRACQ, Julien. *A Dark Stranger*. New York. New Directions. 1st ed. dj. $30.00

GRACQ, Julien. *Balcony in the Forest*. 1959. New York. Braziller. 1st ed. dj. VG $20.00

GRADY, James. *Runner in the Street*. 1984. New York. advance copy. wrappers. EX $25.00

GRAEME, Bruce. *Epilogue*. 1934. Philadelphia. Lippincott. 1st Am. ed. dj. VG $40.00

GRAEME, David. *Monsieur Blackshirt*. 1933. Philadelphia. Lippincott. 1st Am. ed. dj. VG $10.00

GRAETZ, H. *History of the Jews*. 1891. Philadelphia. 6 vol set. VG $75.00

GRAF, Max. *From Beethoven to Shostakovich*. 1947. New York. Ills. dj. VG $12.50

GRAFF. *LIFE History of U.S.A.* 1903. New York. Ills. folio. 12 vol set. $48.00

GRAFTON, Charles. *Home; or, A Short Account of Charles Grafton*. 1820. Andover. $12.50

GRAFTON, Sue. *'A' is for Alibi*. 1982. New York. Holt. 1st ed. dj. EX $20.00

GRAFTON, Sue. *'C' is for Corpse*. 1986. New York. Holt. advance copy. wrappers. $17.50

GRAHAM, A. & F. *Alligators*. 1979. Delacorte. Ills. 130 pp. dj. EX $7.50

GRAHAM, Billy. *The Secret of Happiness*. 1955. New York. Doubleday. 117 pp. dj. $3.50

GRAHAM, D. *Chinese Gardens*. 1938. New York. 1st ed. dj. $30.00

GRAHAM, F. *Gulls, a Social History*. 1975. Random House. Ills. 1st ed. 179 pp. dj. EX $10.00

GRAHAM, F. *Since Silent Spring*. 1970. Houghton Mifflin. 332 pp. dj. $6.00

GRAHAM, Harvey. *Eternal Eve*. 1950. London. 1st ed. dj. $35.00

GRAHAM, J.B. *Handset Reminiscences*. 1915. Salt Lake City.1st ed. 307 pp. VG $75.00

GRAHAM, Jory. *Chicago, an Extraordinary Guide*. 1968. Rand McNally. 499 pp. dj. $3.50

GRAHAM, Martha. *Sixteen Dances in Photographs*. 1945. New York. 1st ed. EX $65.00

GRAHAM, R.B. Cunningham. *Life of B. Diaz del Castillo*. 1915. London. VG $40.00

GRAHAM, W.A. *Story of the Little Big Horn/Custer's Last Fight*. 1952. New York. Ills. 178 pp. $8.00

GRAHAM, W.A. *The Custer Myth*. 1903. New York. Ills. 413 pp. dj. $28.00

GRAHAM, W.A. *The Custer Myth*. 1953. New York. Bonanza. 413 pp. dj. VG $15.00

GRAHAM, W.A. *The Story of the Little Big Horn*. 1959. New York. Ills. maps. 221 pp. $16.00

GRAHAM, W.S. *The White Threshold*. 1949. London. 1st ed. inscr. $15.00

GRAHAM, Winston. *Night Journey*. 1968. Garden City. Doubleday. 1st ed. dj. VG $30.00

GRAHAM, Winston. *Take My Life*. 1967. Garden City. Doubleday. 1st ed. dj. VG $30.00

GRAHAM, Winston. *The Black Moon*. 1973. Garden City. Doubleday. 1st ed. dj. VG $25.00

GRAHAM & BEARD. *Eyelids of Morning*. 1973. SftCvr. VG $20.00

GRAHAM. *Escape from the Nazis*. 1975. Castle Books. Ills. 120 pp. $4.50

GRAHAME, Ken. *On Smoking*. 1946. New York. Ltd. ed. 1/200. slipcase. EX $25.00

GRAHAME, Kenneth. *Dream Days*. 1976. New York. Ills. $25.00

GRAHAME, Kenneth. *Dream Days*. 1899. London. 1st ed. dj. VG $30.00

GRAHAME, Kenneth. *Dream Days*. Ills. Shepard. Ltd. 1st ed. 1/275. sgns. $350.00

GRAHAME, Kenneth. *The Golden Age*. 1915. London. Ills. Enraght-Moony. 1st ed. $40.00

GRAHAME, Kenneth. *The Golden Age*. 1895. London. 1st ed. dj. VG $50.00

GRAHAME, Kenneth. *The Golden Age*. 1900. New York. Lane. Ills. M. Parrish. VG $35.00

GRAHAME, Kenneth. *The Golden Age*. 1899. Ills. Parrish. VG $50.00

GRAHAME, Kenneth. *The Wind in the Willows*. 1959. New York. Ills. Rackham. VG $16.00

GRAHAME, Kenneth. *The Wind in the Willows*. 1940. Heritage House. Ills. Rackham. 1st ed. VG $40.00

GRAHN, Judy. *The Work of a Common Woman.* 1984. proof copy. wrappers. VG $20.00

GRAIL, Shirley Ann. *The Condor Passes.* 1971. Knopf. 1st ed. dj. EX $20.00

GRAINGE, William. *Daemonologia. A Discourse on Witchcraft.* 1882. Harrogate. Ackrill. 1st ed. 189 pp. $90.00

GRAMBERG, Oliver. *AP: Story of News.* 1940. New York. 1st ed. 506 pp. dj. VG $20.00

GRAND, Gordon. *Col. Weatherford.* 1933. Derrydale Press. Ltd. ed. VG $75.00

GRAND, Gordon. *Old Man.* 1934. Derrydale Press. Ltd. ed. VG $75.00

GRAND, Gordon. *The Southborough Fox.* 1939. Derrydale Pr. Ltd. ed. 1/1450. sgn. VG $75.00

GRAND, Gordon. *Young Entry.* 1935. Derrydale Press. Ltd. ed. $75.00

GRANDMA MOSES. *The Grandma Moses Storybook.* 1961. Random House. 1st ed. dj. VG $35.00

GRANDY, W. *Romance of Glass Making.* 1898. London. 160 pp. $20.00

GRANGE, W.B. *The Way to Game Abundance.* 1949. New York. 1st ed. EX $17.50

GRANGE, W.B. *Those of the Forest.* 1953. Ills. Murie. 1st ed. dj. VG $15.00

GRANGER, Bill. *Schism.* 1981. New York. Crown. proof. wrappers. EX $50.00

GRANGER, Bill. *Schism.* 1981. New York. Crown. review copy. dj. EX $40.00

GRANGER, Boyd H. *Arizona Place Names.* Ills. A. Peck. revised ed. VG $25.00

GRANGER. *Hemingway's Notebook.* uncorrected proof copy. $15.00

GRANT, Blanche. *Taos Indians.* 1924. Taos. Ills. 1st ed. 127 pp. $40.00

GRANT, Blanche. *Taos Indians.* 1925. Ills. 127 pp. $35.00

GRANT, Chapman. *The Herpetology of the Cayman Islands.* 1940. 1st ed. stiff wrappers. $15.00

GRANT, Charles L. *Shadows 3.* 1980. Garden City. review copy. dj. VG $12.50

GRANT, Charles L. *Shadows 6.* 1983. Garden City. review copy. dj. VG $12.50

GRANT, D.M. & Hadley, T., eds. *Rhodes Island on Lovecraft.* 1945. Providence. 1st ed. wrappers. $35.00

GRANT, E.M. *Guide to Fishes.* 1965. Queensland. Ills. 280 pp. VG $30.00

GRANT, George Monro. *Picturesque Canada.* 1882. Toronto. Belden Bros. 2 vol set. $50.00

GRANT, Gordon. *Gordon Grant Sketchbook.* 1960. Watson-Guptill. Ills. 1st ed. sgn. dj. EX $35.00

GRANT, Gordon. *The Life & Adventures of John Nicol Mariner.* 1936. Farrar. 1st ed. $15.00

GRANT, Kenneth. *Aleister Cowley & the Hidden God.* 1974. New York. 1st Am. ed. 245 pp. dj. EX $12.50

GRANT, Kenneth. *The Magical Revival.* 1973. New York. Weiser. 244 pp. dj. EX $12.50

GRANT, Michael. *Myths of the Greeks & Romans.* 1963. Weidenfield. EX $25.00

GRANT, Robert A. *Repair Your Plymouth Yourself.* 1962. Pocket Books. 96 pp. SftCvr. $3.50

GRANT, U.S. *Personal Memoirs of U.S. Grant.* 1885 & 1886. Webster, NY. 2 vol set. G $35.00

GRANT, Vernon. *Tinker Tim the Toy Maker.* 1934. Racine. Ills. 1st ed. 10 color pls. VG $40.00

GRANT. *Captain of Old Ironsides.* 1947. 1st ed. dj. G $15.00

GRANTZ, G.J. *Home Book of Taxidermy & Tanning.* 1977. Stackpole. Ills. 160 pp. dj. EX $10.00

GRANVILLE, Austin. *Fallen Race.* 1892. Neely. VG $55.00

GRASS, Gunter. *Headbirths; or, The Germans Are Dying Out.* 1982. New York. Harcourt. 1st ed. dj. EX $20.00

GRASS, Gunter. *The Flounder.* 1978. New York. Harcourt. 1st ed. dj. VG $25.00

GRASS, Gunter. *The Plebians Rehearse the Uprising.* 1966. 1st Am. ed. sgn. wrappers. $7.50

GRASS, Gunter. *The Tin Drum.* 1962. Pantheon. 1st Am. ed. dj. VG $45.00

GRATTON, John. *Journal of Life of John Gratton.* 1805. Stanford. $25.00

GRATZ, D.L. *Bernese Antibaptists & Their American Descendants.* 1953. Ills. dj. VG $12.50

GRAU, Shirley Ann. *Evidence of Love.* 1977. Knopf. 1st ed. dj. VG $15.00

GRAU, Shirley Ann. *Keepers of the House.* 1964. New York. 1st ed. dj. VG $10.00

GRAU, Shirley Ann. *The Black Prince.* 1955. Knopf. 1st ed. dj. VG $20.00

GRAU, Shirley Ann. *The Condor Passes.* 1971. New York. Knopf. 421 pp. dj. VG $10.00

GRAU, Shirley Ann. *The Hard Blue Sky.* 1958. Knopf. 1st ed. dj. VG $30.00

GRAU, Shirley Ann. *The House on Coliseum Street.* 1961. Knopf. 1st ed. dj. VG $20.00

GRAU, Shirley Ann. *The Wind Shifting West.* 1973. Knopf. 1st ed. dj. VG $15.00

GRAUSTEIN, J. *Thomas Nutall-Naturalist, Explorations in America.* 1967. Harvard. Ills. maps. 481 pp. dj. EX $30.00

GRAVE, Andrew. *A Hero for Leanda.* 1959. London. 1st ed. dj. VG $15.00

GRAVE, Andrew. *Counterstroke.* 1978. New York. 1st ed. dj. VG $5.00

GRAVE, J. *My 70 Years in California.* 1927. Los Angeles. 1st ed. VG $25.00

GRAVES, Charles. *Cigars & the Piccadilly.* 1938. London. St. Martins. Ltd. ed. $15.00

GRAVES, E. *Bibliography of English History to 1485.* 1975. Oxford. EX $17.50

GRAVES, John. *Goodbye to a River.* 1960. Knopf. 1st ed. sgn. VG $85.00

GRAVES, Merle Dixon. *Bubblins an' Bilins at the Center.* 1934. Rutland. Tuttle Co. Ills. $12.00

GRAVES, R. & Hodge, A. *The Long Weekend.* 1st English ed. dj. EX $20.00

GRAVES, Robert. *But It Still Goes On.* 1930. London. 1st issue. VG $25.00

GRAVES, Robert. *Collected Poems.* 1961. New York. 1st Am. ed. dj. EX $75.00

GRAVES, Robert. *Collected Short Stories.* 1964. 1st ed. VG $35.00

GRAVES, Robert. *Colophon to Love Respelt.* Ltd. 1st ed. 1/350. wrappers. $55.00

GRAVES, Robert. *Count Belisarius.* 1938. London. 1st ed. maps. dj. VG $45.00

GRAVES, Robert. *Country Sentiment.* 1920. Knopf. 1st Am. ed. VG $15.00

GRAVES, Robert. *Good-Bye to All That.* 1930. New York. Ills. 1st Am. ed. 430 pp. $25.00

GRAVES, Robert. *Hercules, My Shipmate.* 1945. New York. 1st ed. VG $20.00

GRAVES, Robert. *Homer's Daughter.* 1955. London. 1st ed. dj. VG $50.00

GRAVES, Robert. *Love Respelt Again.* 1969. Ltd. ed. 1/1000. sgn. dj. EX $45.00

GRAVES, Robert. *No More Ghosts.* 1940. London. 1st ed. dj. VG $45.00

GRAVES, Robert. *Proceed Sgt. Lamb.* 1941. New York. 1st Am. ed. dj. VG $10.00

GRAVES, Robert. *Seventeen Poems Missing from Love Respelt.* Ltd. 1st ed. 1/330. sgn. VG $50.00

GRAVES, Robert. *They Hanged My Saintly Billy.* 1957. Doubleday. 1st Am. ed. dj. VG $40.00

GRAVES, Robert. *They Hanged My Saintly Billy.* 1957. London. 1st ed. dj. VG $25.00

GRAVES & PAYNE. *American Snapshots.* 1977. New York. 1st ed. dj. EX $12.50

GRAVES. *Beyond Giving.* Ltd. 1st ed. 1/536. sgn. EX $55.00

GRAVES. *Great Dinners from Life.* 1974. wrappers. VG $12.50

GRAY, Alan. *Sailmaking Simplified.* 1940. New York. Ills. 1st ed. VG $5.00

GRAY, Asa. *How Plants Grow.* 1858. New York. American Books. Ills. 233 pp. $25.00

GRAY, Asa. *Scientific Papers of Asa Gray.* 1969. Kraus. 2 vols in 1. index. EX $20.00

GRAY, Basil. *Japanese Woodcuts.* 1957. New York. Citadel Press. Ills. VG scarce $18.00

GRAY, Cecil. *Sibelius.* 1931. London. G $7.00

GRAY, Curme. *Murder in Millennium VI.* 1951. Chicago. 1st ed. dj. VG $15.00

GRAY, E. *Diving Stations.* 1980. dj. EX $10.00

GRAY, E. *The Killing Time.* 1972. New York. Scribner. photos, dj. VG $6.00

GRAY, Grace Viall. *Every Day.* 1932. Illinois. wrappers. VG $8.50

GRAY, Hamilton. *Mrs. Scepulchres of* 1841. 2nd ed. 540 pp. VG $40.00

GRAY, Henry. *Anatomy, Descriptive & Surgical.* 1959. Philadephia. 754 pp. scarce. $385.00

GRAY, Thomas. *William Blake's Water Colours.* 1972. Ills. Keynes. 1st ed. dj. EX $40.00

GRAY, W.G. *The Roll Right Ritual.* 1975. London. 166 pp. dj. EX $25.00

GRAY & ARBUTHNOT. *Our New Friends.* 1947. Scott Foresman. Ills. Ward. $3.50

GRAY. *Cross Trails & Shaparral.* 1925. Carmel. 88 pp. SftCvr. $15.00

GRAYAZNOV, M.P. *The Ancient Civilization of Southern Siberia.* 1969. New York. 170 Ills. 251 pp. index. $17.50

GRAYDON, William Murray. *In Friendship's Guise.* 1899. New York. Street & Smith. 1st ed. VG $10.00

GRAYSON, David. *Adventures in Contentment.* 1907. Garden City. 249 pp. dj. G $5.00

GREAVES, R.H. *Sixty Common Birds of the Nile Delta.* Ills. M. Greaves. 53 pp. VG $20.00

GREELEY, Horace. *The Great Industries of the United States.* 1873. Hartford. 500 Ills. 1304 pp. $30.00

GREELEY, William B. *Forests & Men.* 1951. Garden City. 1st ed. inscr. 255 pp. index. $10.00

GREELY, A.W. *Handbook of Alaska.* 1909. New York. Ills. maps. EX $30.00

GREELY, A.W. *Handbook of Arctic Discoveries.* 1897. maps. $10.00

GREELY, A.W. *Handbook of Polar Discoveries.* 1910. Boston. 5th ed. VG $20.00

GREEN, Ben K. *Horse Tradin'.* 1967. New York. 1st ed. dj. VG $10.00

GREEN, Ben K. *Wild Cow Tales.* 1969. New York. Knopf. 1st ed. dj. VG $10.00

GREEN, Charles. *Early Days in Kansas.* 1912. wrappers. G $40.00

GREEN, Doron. *History of Bristol, Pennsylvania.* 1911. Camden, NJ. McGrath. VG $30.00

GREEN, Floride. *Some Personal Recollections of Lillie Hitchcock.* 1935. San Francisco. Grabhorn. EX $70.00

GREEN, Gerald. *The Sword & the Sun.* 1953. Scribner. 1st ed. dj. VG $15.00

GREEN, Gil. *Cold War Fugitive; Personal Story McCarthy Years.* 1984. New York. International. 275 pp. $4.00

GREEN, Graham. *Nineteen Stories.* 1947. London. 1st ed. VG $30.00

GREEN, Henry. *Nothing.* 1950. Viking. 1st Am. ed. dj. VG $60.00

GREEN, Henry. *Nothing.* 1950. London. Hogarth Press. 1st ed. dj. $55.00

GREEN, Hugh. *Cosmopolitan Crimes.* 1977. New York. 1st ed. dj. EX $15.00

GREEN, J.C. & Niemi, G.J. *Birds of Superior National Forest.* 1980. photos. map. 79 pp. pb. EX $4.00

GREEN, J.D. *Birds of Britain.* 1967. New York. 1st ed. EX $22.50

GREEN, John P. *Fact Stranger than Fiction.* 1920. Cleveland, OH. 368 pp. index. $25.00

GREEN, John Richard. *England.* Collier. no date. 4 vol set. G $23.00

GREEN, Jonathan H. *The Arts & Miseries of Gambling.* 1843. Cincinnati. 1st ed. 360 pp. $1,150.00

GREEN, Joseph. *Forgotten Stars.* 1959. Golden Press. $3.00

GREEN, Julian. *The Closed Garden.* 1928. New York. Harper. 398 pp. $3.50

GREEN, Nathan. *Story of Spain & Cuba.* 1898. Baltimore. News & Book Co. 512 pp. $37.50

GREEN, Nelson Winch. *Fifteen Years Among the Mormons.* 1858. New York. 1st ed. 388 pp. G $95.00

GREEN, Nelson Winch. *The Mormons in the Valley of the Great Salt Lake.* 1856. VG $85.00

GREEN, Perry. *Kenneth Graham, a Biography.* 1859. World. 1st ed. ex-lib. dj. $4.50

GREEN, Roger Lancelyn. *A.E.W. Mason.* 1952. London. Parrish. 1st ed. dj. EX $30.00

GREEN, T. *World of Gold.* 1968. New York. dj. EX $7.00

GREEN, Thomas. *In Praise of Valor.* 1907. Cedar Rapids. Ltd. ed. 1/75. VG $15.00

GREEN, Vivien. *English Doll's Houses of 18th & 19th Centuries.* 1955. Batsford. 1st ed. dj. $20.00

GREEN, William Henry. *A Grammar of the Hebrew Language.* 1873. New York. Wiley & Son. 106 pp. $5.00

GREEN, William. *Augsburg Eagle, Story of the Messerschmitt 109.* 1971. Macdonald. 1st ed. EX $15.50

GREEN, Wm. & Pollinger, G. *The Aircraft of the World.* 1954. New York. Hanover House. 160 pp. VG $22.50

GREEN. *Journal of Texan Expedition Against Meir.* 1845. New York. 1st ed. $200.00

GREEN. *The Book of Good Manners.* 1923. Social Mentor Pub. $3.50

GREENAWALT, C. *Hummingbirds.* 1960. Doubleday. dj. VG $225.00

GREENAWAY, Kate. *A Apple Pie.* London. Warne. (ca.1920) VG $35.00

GREENAWAY, Kate. *A Day in a Child's Life.* 1881. London. 1st ed. VG $85.00

GREENAWAY, Kate. *Almanack for 1884.* 1884. London. VG $60.00

GREENAWAY, Kate. *Almanack for 1887* 1887. London. Routledge. $95.00

GREENAWAY, Kate. *April Baby's Book of Tunes.* 1900. New York. Macmillan. 1st ed. color pls. $35.00

GREENAWAY, Kate. *Kate Greenaway's Birthday Book.* Warne. reprint. dj. EX $27.50

GREENAWAY, Kate. *Language of Flowers.* London. no date. rebound. G $50.00

GREENAWAY, Kate. *Language of Flowers.* London. Routledge. VG $40.00

GREENAWAY, Kate. *Mother Goose or the Old Nursery Rhymes.* London. Warne. Ills. 1st ed. VG $125.00

GREENAWAY, Kate. *Mother Goose.* 1881. London. Routledge. 1st ed. $95.00

GREENAWAY, Kate. *Pied Piper of Hamelin.* London. Warne. Ills. VG $20.00

GREENAWAY, Kate. *Royal Progress of King Pepito.* 1889. London. 1st issue. $55.00

GREENAWAY, Kate. *Under the Window.* London. Ills. 1st ed. VG $125.00

GREENAWAY, Kate. *Under the Window.* 1878. New York. Routledge. Ills. 1st ed. $85.00

GREENAWAY, Kate. *16 Examples in Colour of the Artist's Work.* 1910. London. 1st ed. EX $120.00

GREENBERG, Alvin. *Going Nowhere.* 1971. New York. 1st ed. sgn. dj. VG $25.00

GREENBERG, Joanne. *Founder's Praise.* 1976. Holt. 1st ed. dj. VG $15.00

GREENBERG, Joanne. *High Crimes & Misdemeanors.* 1980. Holt. 1st ed. dj. EX $15.00

GREENBERG, Joanne. *In This Sign.* 1970. Holt. 1st ed. dj. VG $20.00

GREENBERG, Joanne. *The Far Side of Victory.* 1983. Holt. 1st ed. dj. VG $15.00

GREENBERG, Joanne. *The Search of Delight.* 1981. Holt. 1st ed. dj. VG $12.50

GREENBERG, M. *Journey to Infinity.* 1951. Gnome Press. 1st ed. sgn. dj. EX $20.00

GREENBIE. *Furs to Furrows.* 1939. 1st ed. dj. EX $20.00

GREENBIEW, Sydney & Barstow. *Hoof Beats to Heaven. Life of Peter Cartwright.* 1955. Penobscot, ME. Ills. 1st ed. 623 pp. $15.00

GREENBURG, Dan. *Scoring.* 1972. Doubleday. 1st ed. dj. VG $15.00

GREENE, Annie. *Bright River Trilogy.* 1984. proof copy. wrappers. VG $25.00

GREENE, Asa. *Travels in America by Geo. Fibbleton Esq.* 1833. New York. 216 pp. $65.00

GREENE, Graham & Greene, Hugh. *The Spy's Bedside Book.* 1957. London. Hart Davis. 1st ed. dj. EX $65.00

GREENE, Graham. *A Burnt Out Case.* 1961. London. 1st ed. dj. VG $27.00

GREENE, Graham. *A Burnt Out Case.* 1961. New York. Viking. 1st ed. dj. VG $25.00

GREENE, Graham. *A Hondrory Consul.* 1973. New York. Simon & Schuster. 1st ed. dj. $25.00

GREENE, Graham. *A Sense of Reality.* 1963. London. 1st ed. dj. VG $15.00

GREENE, Graham. *A Sort of a Life.* 1971. London. 1st ed. VG $35.00

GREENE, Graham. *Confidential Agent.* 1939. Armed Service ed. G $7.50

GREENE, Graham. *End of the Affair.* 1951. 1st Am. ed. dj. VG $55.00

GREENE, Graham. *End of the Affair.* London. 1st ed. dj. VG $35.00

GREENE, Graham. *Getting to Know the General.* 1984. Denny. 1st Canadian ed. dj. VG $17.50

GREENE, Graham. *Heart of the Matter.* 1948. Viking. 306 pp.. $12.50

GREENE, Graham. *In Search of a Character.* 1962. New York. Viking. 1st ed. dj. EX $25.00

GREENE, Graham. *In Search of a Character.* London. 1st ed. dj. VG $35.00

GREENE, Graham. *Lord Rochester's Monkey.* 1974. Viking. 1st Am. ed. dj. VG $20.00

GREENE, Graham. *May We Borrow Your Husband?* 1967. New York. Viking. 1st ed. dj. VG $30.00

GREENE, Graham. *May We Borrow Your Husband?* 1967. Bodley Head. 1st ed. dj. VG $35.00

GREENE, Graham. *Our Man in Havana.* 1958. London. 1st ed. $45.00

GREENE, Graham. *Stamboul Train.* 1932. London. 1st ed. VG $40.00

GREENE, Graham. *The Comedians.* 1966. London. 1st ed. dj. $40.00

GREENE, Graham. *The Comedians.* 1966. New York. 1st ed. dj. EX $15.00

GREENE, Graham. *The Complaisant Lover.* 1961. Viking Press. 1st Am. ed. dj. VG $30.00

GREENE, Graham. *The Human Factor.* 1978. Simon & Schuster. dj. VG $10.00

GREENE, Graham. *The Little Fire Engine.* 1973. London. Ills. E. Ardizzone. 1st ed. VG $45.00

GREENE, Graham. *The Little Steamroller.* New York. 1st ed. dj. $8.00

GREENE, Graham. *The Man Within.* 1929. New York. 1st Am. ed. $50.00

GREENE, Graham. *The Name of Action.* 1930. London. 1st Eng. ed. dj. $150.00

GREENE, Graham. *The Potting Shed.* 1957. New York. 1st ed. $10.00

GREENE, Graham. *The Quiet American.* 1956. New York. 1st ed. dj. VG $20.00

GREENE, Graham. *The Tenth Man.* London. 1st ed. $28.00

GREENE, Graham. *Travels with My Aunt.* 1970. New York. Viking. 1st ed. dj. VG $25.00

GREENE, Graham. *Travels with My Aunt.* 1969. Bodley Head. 1st ed. dj. VG $35.00

GREENE, Graham. *Ways of Escape.* 1980. Toronto. EX $35.00

GREENE, Graham. *Ways of Escape.* 1981. Simon & Schuster. proof copy. $50.00

GREENE, Graham. *Yes & Know.* London. Ltd. ed. 1/750. sgn. $75.00

GREENE, Homer. *Lincoln Conscript.* 1901. VG $17.50

GREENE, Hugh. *More Rivals of Sherlock Holmes.* 1971. London. Bodley Head. 1st ed. dj. VG $20.00

GREENE, Hugh. *The Rivals of Sherlock Holmes.* 1970. London. 1st ed. dj. EX $22.00

GREENE, N. *Fort Plain Nelliston History, 1580-1947.* 1947. Ills. maps. inscr. VG $25.00

GREENE, S. *Broken Seal, Morgan Abduction, & Murder.* 1870. Boston. $25.00

GREENE, Sarah P. McLean. *Power Lot.* 1906. New York. Ills. 396 pp. G $7.50

GREENE, Theodore. *The Arts & Art of Criticism.* 1940. Princeton. 1st ed. sgn. VG $35.00

GREENE. *Journey Without Maps.* 1936. 1st Am. ed. EX $35.00

GREENE. *Labrynthine Ways.* 1940. 1st Am. ed. VG $15.00

GREENE. *The Providence Plantations.* 1886. folio. VG $45.00

GREENEWALT, Crawford H. *Hummingbirds.* 1960. Garden City. Ills. 250 pp. 70 pls. dj. EX $225.00

GREENFIELD, K.R. *The Historian & the Army.* 1954. map. dj. VG $10.00

GREENLAW, Olga. *The Lady & the Tigers.* 1943. New York. 4th ed. 317 pp. $37.50

GREENLEAF, Benjamin. *A Key to the Introduction to National Arithmetic.* 1854. Boston. Davis. 141 pp. $7.50

GREENLEAF, Stephen. *Death Bed.* 1980. Dial Press. proof copy. wrappers. VG $85.00

GREENLEAF, Stephen. *State's Evidence.* 1983. London. 1st Eng. ed. dj. VG $15.00

GREENLEAF, Stephen. *The Ditto List.* 1985. New York. Villard Books. proof copy. EX $40.00

GREENLEE, Sam. *The Spook Who Sat by the Door.* 1969. New York. Baron. 1st ed. dj. EX $30.00

GREENWALD, Carol S. *Banks Are Dangerous to Your Wealth.* 1980. Prentice Hall. 1st ed. dj. VG $17.50

GREER, A. *The Sea Chase.* 1948. dj. G $8.00

GREER, Carl R. *The Buckeye Book of Direct Advertising.* 1925. Ohio. Ills. 222 pp. index. VG $12.50

GREER, Carlotta C. *A Text-Book of Cooking.* 1915. New York. 431 pp. $6.00

GREER, Gertrude. *Adventures in Weaving.* 1951. Peoria. Ills. 1st printing. index. $37.50

GREGG, C.T. *Tarawa.* 1984. Ills. map. dj. EX $20.00

GREGG, Cecil Freeman. *Accidental Murder.* 1952. London. Methuen. 1st ed. dj. VG $22.50

GREGG, Josiah. *Commerce of the Prairies.* 1954. U. of OK Press. 1st ed. dj. VG $30.00

GREGOROVIUS, Ferd. *Rome in the Middle Ages.* 1897. London. Ills. 11 vols. G $75.00

GREGORY, Charles. *Samuel F. Miller.* 1908. $5.00

GREGORY, Dick. *From the Back of the Bus.* 1962. Dutton. 1st ed. wrappers. EX $7.50

GREGORY, Dick. *The Shadow that Scares Me.* 1968. Doubleday. 1st ed. ex-lib. 210 pp. dj. $37.50

GREGORY, Horace. *The House on Jefferson Street.* 1971. Holt. 1st ed. dj. VG $15.00

GREGORY, W.K. & Raven, H.C. *In Quest of Gorillas.* 1937. Darwin. Ills. maps. 241 pp. EX $30.00

GREGORY. *Ace in the Hole.* Popular. pb. $3.00

GREGSON, W. *A Student's Guide to Wood Engraving.* 1953. London. Ills. 1st printing. dj. EX $15.00

GREIFFENHAGEN, Maurice. *Rubalyats of Omar Khayyam.* 1911. Lippincott. Ills. 1st ed. EX $15.00

GREINER, M. *Holland Kiddies.* 1926. Cupples & Leon.Ills. VG $4.50

GRENFELL, W.T. *A Labrador Doctor.* 1919. Boston. photos. VG $20.00

GRENFELL, W.T. *Life & Medical Work Among Fishermen of Labrador.* 1898. London. Ills. 240 pp. $18.50

GRENFELL, W.T. *Tales of the Labrador.* 1916. Boston. 1st ed. VG $10.00

GRENFELL, W.T. *The Harvest of the Sea.* 1905. $12.50

GRENSHAW, O. *Slave States in Presidential Election of 1860.* 1945. Baltimore. Johns Hopkins. inscr. sgn. VG $20.00

GRESHAM, W.L. *Monster Midway.* 1953. 1st Am. ed. dj. VG $25.00

GRESHAM, W.L. *Nighmare Alley.* 1946. New York. Rinehart. 1st ed. VG $20.00

GRETTON, Thomas. *Murders & Moralities.* 1980. London. Ills 1st ed. wrappers. $15.00

GREY, Katherine. *Rolling Wheels.* 1937. Boston. 209 pp. dj. VG $7.00

GREY, Owl. *The Men of the Last Frontier.* 1937. London. Country Life. photos. 253 pp. $27.50

GREY, Sidney. *A Tale of School Life.* 1859. New York. Carter. Ills. 358 pp. $10.00

GREY, Zane. *Adventures in Fishing.* 1952. Harper. 1st ed. dj. VG $50.00

GREY, Zane. *American Angler in Australia.* 1937. 2nd ed. $40.00

GREY, Zane. *Betty Zane.* 1903. New York. Ills. 1st ed. scarce. $300.00

GREY, Zane. *Desert Gold.* 1913. New York. 326 pp. VG $50.00

GREY, Zane. *Desert of Wheat.* 1919. $5.00

GREY, Zane. *Fighting Caravans.* 1929. New York. Grosset & Dunlap. 361 pp. $10.00

GREY, Zane. *Knights of the Range.* 1939. Harper. 1st ed. dj. VG $35.00

GREY, Zane. *Man of the Forest.* 1920. New York. Harper. 1st ed. VG $20.00

GREY, Zane. *Raiders of Spanish Peaks.* 1938. NY. Harper. 1st ed. dj. VG $110.00

GREY, Zane. *Redheaded Outfield.* 1948. Grosset & Dunlap. dj. VG $10.00

GREY, Zane. *Riders of the Purple Sage.* 1912. New York. Harper. Ills. 1st ed. $50.00

GREY, Zane. *Robbers Roost.* 1932. New York. 1st ed. $12.50

GREY, Zane. *Roping Lions in the Grand Canyon.* 1924. Grosset & Dunlap. EX $7.50

GREY, Zane. *Tales of Fishing Virgin Seas.* 1925. New York. Harper. 100 Ills. VG $60.00

GREY, Zane. *Tales of Fresh Water Fishing.* 1928. New York. Ills. 1st ed. 277 pp. VG $95.00

GREY, Zane. *Tales of Lonely Trails.* 1922. New York. Harper. dj. $10.00

GREY, Zane. *Tales of Southern Rivers.* 1924. Harper. 1st ed. VG $25.00

GREY, Zane. *Tales of Swordfish & Tuna.* 1927. Harper. 1st ed. EX $75.00

GREY, Zane. *Tappan's Burro.* 1923. New York. Harper. 1st ed. $27.50

GREY, Zane. *The Call of the Canyon.* 1924. New York. Harper. 1st ed. $10.00

GREY, Zane. *The Heritage of the Desert.* 1910. Grosset & Dunlap. Ills. $7.50

GREY, Zane. *The Last of the Plainsmen.* 1911. New York. Grosset & Dunlap. 314 pp. EX $4.50

GREY, Zane. *The Last of the Plainsmen.* 1936. Z. Grey. VG $12.50

GREY, Zane. *The Last Trail.* 1945. Triangle Books. EX $5.50

GREY, Zane. *The Light of Western Stars.* 1914. New York. Grosset & Dunlap. 389 pp. $4.50

GREY, Zane. *The Lost Wagon Train.* 1936. Collier. $6.50

GREY, Zane. *The Lost Wagon Train.* Grosset & Dunlap. Western ed. $8.50

GREY, Zane. *The Man of the Forest.* 1920. Harper. $8.50

GREY, Zane. *The Mysterious Rider.* 1929. New York. Grosset & Dunlap. 336 pp. dj. $4.50

GREY, Zane. *The Rainbow Trail.* dj. $7.00

GREY, Zane. *The Rainbow Trail.* 1915. 1st ed. VG $15.00

GREY, Zane. *The Shortstop.* 1937. New York. Grosset & Dunlop. 398 pp. $8.50

GREY, Zane. *The Trail Driver.* 1936. New York. Collier. 302 pp. VG $6.50

GREY, Zane. *The Vanishing American.* 1925. New York. 1st ed. dj. $8.00

GREY, Zane. *The Young Lion Hunter.* 1923. $7.50

GREY, Zane. *Thunder Mountain.* 1935. Collier. dj. $8.00

GREY, Zane. *Thunder Mountain.* 1935. Harper. 1st ed. dj. VG $27.50

GREY, Zane. *Tales of Lonely Trails.* 1922. New York. Blue Ribbon Books. VG $50.00

GREY, Zane. *Twin Sombreros.* 1940. 1st ed. dj. $15.00

GREY, Zane. *Under the Tonto Rim.* 1926. Harper. 1st ed. 281 pp. G $10.00

GREY, Zane. *Wanderer of the Wasteland.* 1923. Harper. 1st ed. VG $15.00

GREY, Zane. *West of the Pecos.* 1937. Collier. $6.50

GREY, Zane. *Western Union.* Grosset & Dunlap. dj. VG $12.50

GREY, Zane. *Wyoming.* 1953. New York. Harper. 1st ed. dj. VG $85.00

GRIDON, L.H. *The Phenomena of Plant Life.* 1867. Boston. rubbed. G $15.00

GRIER, Thomas Graham. *On the Canal Zone.* 1908. Chicago. Ills. map. 146 pp. $22.50

GRIER, Wm. H. & Cobbs, Price. *Black Rage.* 1968. New York. ex-lib. 213 pp. VG $6.00

GRIERSON, Francis. *The Valley of Shadows.* 1948. New York. Ills. 278 pp. dj. $7.50

GRIESHABER, Hap. *Woodcuts.* 1964. Germany. Arts Inc. Ills. wrappers. EX $45.00

GRIFFIN, E.F. *Westchester County & Its People.* 1946. New York. 3 vol set. EX $75.00

GRIFFIN, Gwyn. *A Last Lamp Burning.* 1965. Book Club. $2.50

GRIFFIN, Merv & Barsocchini. *From Where I Sit.* 1982. New York. Arbor House. 251 pp. dj. EX $5.00

GRIFFIN, Merv & Barsocchini. *Merv, an Autobiography.* 1980. New York. Simon & Schuster. 287 pp. dj. $5.00

GRIFFIN, Mrs. Ellen. *Moss Pitcher's Prophecies; or, American Sibyl.* 1895. Boston. wrappers. VG $15.00

GRIFFIN, R.B. & Little, A.D. *The Chemistry of Paper Making.* 1894. New York. Ills. G $45.00

GRIFFIS, William. *A Modern Pioneer in Korea.* 1912. photos. EX $30.00

GRIFFITH, Beatrice Fox. *Pennsylvania Doctor.* 1957. Harrisburg. Ills. 1st ed. 239 pp. $10.00

GRIFFITH, Bill. *Time for Franke Coolin.* 1982. Random House. 1st ed. dj. VG $15.00

GRIFFITH, D.W. *Barry, Iris. American Film Master.* 1940. New York. Film Lib. Series. 1st ed. $32.50

GRIFFITH, D.W. *The Birth of a Nation.* 1915. New York. Ills. 1st ed. wrappers. $95.00

GRIFFITH, D.W. *When the Movies Were Young.* 1925. Dutton. Ills. 1st ed. 256 pp. $50.00

GRIFFITH, G.W.E. *My 96 Years in the Great West.* 1929. 284 pp. $17.50

GRIFFITH, George. *Olga Romanoff, Syren of the Skies.* 1894. London. Tower. presentation copy. EX $225.00

GRIFFITH, Richard. *Anatomy of a Motion Picture.* 1959. New York. dj. VG $18.00

GRIFFITH, William H. *The Story of American Bank Note Company.* 1959. New York. dj. VG $85.00

GRIGGS, Edward. *A Boy Scouts Holiday.* 1921. $2.50

GRIGGS, Robert. *The Valley of Ten Thousand Smokes.* 1922. Washington. $40.00

GRIGORIEV. *Faces of Russia.* 1924. London. Ltd. ed. 30 pls. folio. $125.00

GRILLI, Elise. *Sharaku.* 1959. Elek. 36 plates. VG $26.00

GRIMBERT, LOPEZ & MEDINA. *Dreams in Stone.* 1976. U. Chicago. photos by authors. dj. EX $25.00

GRIMBLE, A. *Return to Islands, Life & Legends in the Gilberts.* 1957. Morrow. Ills. maps. 215 pp. dj. EX $10.00

GRIMBLE, A. *The Salmon Rivers of Ireland.* 1913. London. 2nd ed. fld maps. photos. VG $65.00

GRIMES, Edward Breene. *A Kettle of Coin.* 1901. Dayton, OH. 126 pp. $15.00

GRIMES, Martha. *Help the Poor Struggler.* 1985. Boston. 1st ed. inscr. sgn. dj. EX $35.00

GRIMES, Martha. *Jerusalem Inn.* 1984. Boston. 1st ed. inscr. sgn. dj. EX $45.00

GRIMES, Martha. *The Anodyne Necklace.* 1983. Boston. 1st ed. inscr. sgn. EX $60.00

GRIMM, Brothers. *King Grisly-Beard.* 1973. New York. Ills. Maurice Sendak. 1st ed. $15.00

GRIMM, Bruder. *Kinder und Hausmarchen.* Schneider. (ca. 1893) German text. EX $250.00

GRIMM, Jacob & Wilhelm. *Kinder und Hausmarchen.* 1898. Gutersloh. Ills. Menerheim. 311 pp. $35.00

GRIMM. *Grimm's Fairy Tales.* 1945. Grosset & Dunlap. Ills. VG $6.50

GRIMM. *Grimm's Fairy Tales.* 1945. Ills. Jr. Lib. & Kredel. VG $6.50

GRIMSLEY, W. *Football: Greatest Moments in S.W. Conference.* 1968. Ills. 1st ed. dj. VG $15.00

GRIMWODE, A. *The Queen's Silver.* 1953. London. Ills. 1st ed. 120 pp. $25.00

GRINNELL, G.B. *American Duck Shooting.* 1901. Ills. Sheppard. G $35.00

GRINNELL, G.B. *American Game Bird Shooting.* 1910. New York. 1st ed. EX $75.00

GRINNELL, G.B. *Pawnee Hero Stories & Folk Tales.* 1893. New York. Scribner. VG $22.00

GRINNELL, G.B. *Punishment of the Stingy & Other Indian Stories.* 1901. New York. pls. G $30.00

GRINNELL, G.B. *Two Great Scouts & Their Private Battalion.* 1928. Cleveland. Clark. VG $50.00

GRINNELL & SHELDON. *Hunting & Conservation.* 1925. VG $55.00

GRINSTEAD, J.E. *Hellfire Range.* 1st ed. ex-lib. $8.50

GRISBORNE, Maria & Williams E. *Shelley's Friends. Their Journals & Letters.* U. of OK Press.(ca1951) 1st ed. dj. EX $15.00

GRISMER, Karl H. *The Story of St. Petersburg.* 1948. St.Petersburg. inscr. 418 pp. $25.00

GRISWOLD, F. Gray. *Race Horses & Racing.* 1926. New York. Dutton. Ltd. ed. 1/500. VG $37.50

GRISWOLD, Frank. *Some Fish & Some Fishing.* 1921. Ills. 1st ed. VG $27.50

GRISWOLD, Morley. *The Covered Bridges of California.* 1938. Berkley. Ills. 1st ed. VG $25.00

GRITIN, Thomas. *Nothing But the Best.* 1959. New York. 1st ed. 273 pp. dj. EX $15.00

GROBER, Karl. *Kinder-Spielzeug, aus Alter Zeit.* 1928. Berlin. Ills. 12 color pls. $45.00

GROFF, Betty & Wilson, Jose. *Good Earth & Country Cooking.* 1974. Harrisburg, PA.Stackpole. Ills. 253 pp. $12.50

GROHMAN. *Sport in the Alps.* 1896. $22.50

GROLLMAN, Earl. *Judaism in Sigmund Freud's World.* 1965. Appleton. 1st ed. dj. $7.50

GRONEFELD, Gerhard. *Understanding Animals.* 1965. New York. Viking. Ills. 320 pp. $10.00

GRONNIOSAW, J.A.U. *Life of James Albert Ukawsaw Gronniosaw.* 1811. Leeds. G. Wilson. 48 pp. wrappers. $250.00

GROSBOIS, C. *Shunga Images Du Printemps.* 1965. Geneve. French text. Ills. $45.00

GROSLIER, BERNARD & ARTHAUD. *The Arts & Civilization of Angkor.* 1957. New York. 112 Ills. dj. VG $40.00

GROSS, Milt. *Nize Baby.* 1926. New York. Doran. Ills. G $7.50

GROSS, N.S. *History of the Birds of Kansas.* 1891. Topeka. Ills. 1st ed. 692 pp. VG $60.00

GROSS, Polly. *Western Motel.* 1985. Putnam. 1st ed. dj. VG $17.50

GROSS, S.D. *A Manual of General Anatomy.* 1828. Philadelphia. 1st Am. ed. 272 pp. $95.00

GROSSE, Edmund. *Nash's Unfortunate Traveller.* 1892. London. Chiswick Press. Ltd. ed. VG $20.00

GROSSMAN, Harold J. *Grossman's Guide to Wines, Spirits, & Beers.* 1964. New York. Scribner. 4th revised ed. dj. $10.00

GROSSMAN, Sid & Lampell, M. *Journey to the Cape.* 1959. New York. 1st ed. wrappers. EX $9.50

GROSSMAN, W. *Homer & Civil War.* Abrams. dj. EX $25.00

GROSSMAN, Wm. & Farrell, J.W. *The Heart of Jazz.* 1956. New York. NY U. Pr. dj. EX $25.00

GROSVENOR, D. *The Blue Whales.* 1977. Nat. Geog. Soc.Ills. 31 pp. EX $7.50

GROSVENOR, Edwin A. *Constantinople.* 1895. Boston. Roberts Bros. photos. maps. VG $50.00

GROSVENOR, G. & Wetmore, A. *The Book of Birds.* 1939. Nat. Geog. Soc.Ills. 2 vol set. EX $35.00

GROSVENOR. *Modern Backgammon.* 1928. New York. dj. VG $7.00

GROTE-HASENBALG, W. *Masterpieces of Oriental Rugs.* 1925. Berlin. 2nd ed. $10.00

GROTH, J. *John Groth's World of Sport.* 1970. New York. inscr. $10.00

GROTH, John. *Studio: Europe.* 1945. New York. Ills. 1st ed. sgn. 282 pp. VG $27.50

GROUEFF, S. *Manhattan Project.* 1967. Boston. 1st ed. VG $20.00

GROUNDS, Roger. *The Natural Garden.* 1976. New York. Stein & Day. $3.00

GROVE, George. *A Dictionary of Music & Musicians.* 1879-1890. London. 1st ed. 4 vol set. G $200.00

GROVE, Harriet Pyne. *The Girls of Greycliff.* 1923. A.L. Burt. 241 pp. dj. VG $4.50

GROVER, E.O. *Mother Goose.* 1971. Hubbard Press. Ills. dj. EX $25.00

GROVER, E.O. *Overall Boys.* 1924. Rand McNally. dj. VG $40.00

GROVER, E.O. *The Sunbonnet Babies Primer.* 2nd printing. VG $50.00

GROVER, P. *Henry James & the French Novel.* 1973. New York. 1st Am. ed. dj. EX $15.00

GROVES, C. *Horses, Asses, & Zebras in the Wild.* 1974. David Charles. photos. maps. 192 pp. dj. EX $20.00

GROZIER, E.A. *The Wreck of the Somerset.* 1886. Provincetown Advocate. 3rd ed. $20.00

GRUBAR. *William Rainey: Pioneer Painter of Early West.* 1962. Potter. dj. $20.00

GRUBB, Davis. *A Dream of Kings.* 1955. New York. 357 pp. dj. $10.00

GRUBB, Davis. *The Barefoot Man.* 1971. New York. 1st ed. dj. VG $6.00

GRUBB, Davis. *The Night of the Hunter.* 1953. New York. 1st ed. 273 pp. dj. $8.50

GRUBB, Davis. *The Watchman.* 1961. New York. 275 pp. dj. $10.00

GRUBB, Davis. *Twelve Tales of Suspense & the Supernatural.* 1964. New York. 1st ed. dj. EX $75.00

GRUBB, E.H. & Guilford, W.S. *The Potato, a Compilation of Information.* 1912. Doubleday Page.Ills. 1st ed. 545 pp. EX $20.00

GRUBB, Isabel. *Quaker Homespuns 1655-1833.* 1932. Allenson. 2nd printing. dj. $7.50

GRUBER, Frank. *Gunsight.* New York. 1st ed. $12.00

GRUBER, Frank. *Lonesome River.* New York. 1st ed. ex-lib. dj. $8.50

GRUBER, Frank. *The Honest Dealer.* 1947. New York. Rinehart. 1st ed. dj. VG $12.50

GRUBER, Frank. *The Limping Goose.* 1954. New York. Rinehart. 1st ed. dj. VG $10.00

GRUBER, Frank. *Zane Grey, a Biography.* 1969. New York. 1st ed. EX $20.00

GRUELLE, John B. *Nobody's Boy.* 1916. New York. Cupples & Leon. 1st ed. VG $20.00

GRUELLE, Johnny. *Cruise of Rickety-Robin. Adventures of Andy & Ann.*1931. Chicago. Ills. 16 pp. wrappers. VG $25.00

GRUELLE, Johnny. *Golden Book.* 1925. Donohue. Ills. 1st ed. 79 pp. $30.00

GRUELLE, Johnny. *Introducing Little Rag Brother of Raggedy Ann.* 1960. Indianapolis. Bobbs Merrill. Ills. VG $15.00

GRUELLE, Johnny. *Marcella Stories.* 1929. Joliet, IL. 94 pp. G $8.00

GRUELLE, Johnny. *Raggedy Andy Stories.* 1920. Chicago. Ills. VG $15.00

GRUELLE, Johnny. *Raggedy Andy Stories.* 1920. Joliet, IL. $8.00

GRUELLE, Johnny. *Raggedy Andy Stories.* 1960. Indianapolis. Bobbs Merrill. VG $3.50

GRUELLE, Johnny. *Raggedy Ann & Andy & Camel with Wrinkled Knees.* 1924. Chicago. Volland. Ills. $25.00

GRUELLE, Johnny. *Raggedy Ann in the Deep Woods.* 1930. Chicago. Ills. VG $20.00

GRUELLE, Johnny. *Raggedy Ann in the Magic Book.* 1939. Gruelle Co. Ills. Worth Gruelle. VG $15.00

GRUELLE, Johnny. *Raggedy Ann Stories.* 1961. Bobbs Merrill. 95 pp. VG $3.50

GRUELLE, Johnny. *Raggedy Ann's Magical Wishes.* 1928. Chicago. Donohue. Ills. 94 pp. $20.00

GRUELLE, Johnny. *Raggedy Anne's Wishing Pebble.* 1960. Bobbs Merrill. Ills. 96 pp. G $15.00

GRUELLE, Johnny. *The Little Brown Bear.* 1920. Chicago. Voland Co. Ills. VG $15.00

GRUMBACH, Doris. *The Ladies.* 1984. New York. Dutton. 1st ed. dj. EX $20.00

GRUNEWALD, Mattias. *Gemalde und Zeichungen V One.* (ca. 1890) 62 plts. $167.00

GRUSKIN. *Painting in the U.S.A.* 1946. New York City. $38.00

GRUTZNER, E. *King Henry IV.* 1886. 12 plates. $47.00

GRZIMEK, B. *He & I & the Elephants.* 1967. Hill Wang. Ills. 1st Am. ed. 208 pp. dj. $15.00

GRZIMEK, B. *Rhinos Belong to Everybody.* 1962. 1st ed. dj. EX $15.00

GUARRACINO, Beatrice. *The Book of Meals.* 1922. London. 4th ed. $18.00

GUBA, E.F. *Nantucket Odyssey.* 1951. Ills. dj. VG $10.00

GUEDALLA, P. *Supers & Supermen.* 1924. New York. ex-lib. 321 pp. VG $3.50

GUEDALLA, P. *Wellington. Biography of British Military Leader.* 1931. G $12.50

GUENON, Rene. *Man & His Becoming.* 1945. London. 1st ed. 187 pp. VG $37.50

GUEST, C.Z. *First Garden.* 1976. Putnam. 1st ed. dj. VG $25.00

GUEST, Edgar A. *A Heap of Living.* 1916. Reilly & Lee. 192 pp. EX $4.50

GUEST, Edgar A. *Harbor Lights of Home.* 1928. Reilly & Lee. 1st ed. $7.00

GUEST, Judith. *Ordinary People.* 1976. Viking Press. review copy. dj. VG $20.00

GUEVARA, Che. *Guerrilla Warfare.* 1985. Lincoln, NB. 440 pp. $10.00

GUGGENHEIM, Peggy. *Confessions of an Art Addict.* 1960. New York. 1st ed. dj. VG $10.00

GUGGISBERG, C. *Crocodiles.* 1972. Harrisburg. Stackpole. Ills. 1st ed. dj. $15.00

GUGGISBERG, C. *Wild Cats of the World.* 1975. London. Ills. 1st ed. 328 pp. dj. EX $22.50

GUGLIOTTA, B. *Pigboat 39. An American Sub Goes to War.* 1984. Ills. dj. EX $20.00

GUILES, F.L. *Marion Davies, a Biography.* 1972. New York. Ills. 419 pp. dj. $20.00

GUINEY, Louise Imogen. *Letters of Louise Imogen Guiney.* 1st ed. 2 vol set. VG $35.00

GUITERMAN & DOYLE. *An Undiscerning Critic Discerned.* 1968. Ltd. ed. 1/222. EX $20.00

GUITERMAN. *Ballads of Old New York.* 1920. New York. VG $5.00

GUITON, Paul. *Switzerland, Northern and Eastern.* London. Medici Society. Ills. VG $7.50

GUIZOT, Madame. *Popular Tales.* 1859. Boston. $25.00

GUIZOT. *Shakespeare & His Times.* 1852. London. 1st ed. $25.00

GULICK, B. *Snake River Country.* 1972. Caxton. Ills. map. 195 pp. dj. EX $20.00

GULL, Ranger. *The Air Pirate.* 1920. New York. Harcourt. 1st ed. G $10.00

GULL, William W. *A Collection of the Published Writings of Gull.* 1896. w/woodcuts & engravings. $155.00

GUMMERE, John. *A Treatise on Surveying.* 1840. Philadelphia. Kimber & Sharpless. G $25.00

GUMMERE, John. *A Treatise on Surveying.* 1860. Philadelphia. Ills. G $22.50

GUNDEL, Karoly. *Hungarian Cookery Book.* 1958. Budapest. 114 pp. dj. $47.50

GUNN, James. *The Dreamers.* 1980. New York. 1st ed. dj. VG $10.00

GUNN, James. *This Fortress World.* 1955. New York. Gnome. 1st ed. dj. VG $15.00

GUNN, Thomas. *Fighting Terms.* 1954. Fantasy Press. 1st ed. inscr. VG $20.00

GUNN, Thomas. *Sidewalks.* 1985. Albondocani Pr. Ills. Ltd. ed. sgn. wrappers. $35.00

GUNNIS, Robert. *Dictionary of British Sculptors 1660-1851.* London. no date. revised ed. dj. EX $15.00

GUNSTON, Bill. *Aircraft of WWII.* 1980. Octopus Books. 600 color Ills. EX $15.00

GUNSTON, Bill. *Flight Handbook.* 6th ed. $15.00

GUNTHER, John. *Behind the Curtain.* 1949. New York. Harper. 363 pp. $3.00

GUNTHER, John. *Inside Asia.* 1939. New York. Harper. 599 pp. dj. $4.00

GUNTHER, John. *Inside Europe Today.* 1961. New York. Harper. 357 pp. dj. EX $12.50

GUNTHER, John. *Inside Europe.* 1938. New York. Harper. 532 pp. $3.00

GUNTHER, John. *Inside Latin America.* 1941. New York. Harper. 498 pp. dj. $7.50

GUNTHER, John. *Inside Russia Today.* 1957. 550 pp. dj. EX $5.00

GUNTHER, John. *Inside U.S.A.* New York. 1st ed. dj. $6.50

GUNTHER, John. *Taken at the Flood: Story of Albert D. Lasker.* 1960. Harper. Kiplinger Book Club ed. dj. G $6.00

GUNTHER, John. *The Lost City.* 1964. New York. Harper & Row. 498 pp. $3.50

GUPPY. *Waiwai.* 1958. New York. 1st ed. dj. VG $25.00

GUPTILL, Arthur L. *Norman Rockwell Illustrator.* 1946. New York. 1st ed. VG $20.00

GURION, Itzhak. *Triumph on the Gallows.* 1950. Brooklyn, NY. 200 pp. dj. $5.00

GURN, J. *Commodore John Barry, Father of the American Navy.* 1933. Ills. VG $30.00

GURNEY, Edmund. *Phantasms of the Living.* 1970. 2 vol set. VG $15.00

GURNEY, Edmund. *Phantasms of the Living.* 1918. London. 2nd impression. 520 pp. VG $35.00

GURNEY, J.H. *Rambles of Naturalist in Egypt & Other Countries.* 1876. London. Jarrold. 307 pp. VG $45.00

GURNEY, J.J. *Memoirs of J.J. Gurney.* 1854. Philadelphia. 1st ed. 2 vol set. $65.00

GURNEY, J.J. *Observations Religious Peculiarities of Friends.* 1825. Philadelphia. 1st Am. ed. VG $45.00

GURNEY, Maj. Gene. *The War in the Air.* Bonanza Books. (ca.1962) dj. VG $10.00

GURUNG, K.K. *Heart of the Jungle, Wildlife of Chitwan, Nepal.* 1983. London. Deutsch. photos. 197 pp. dj. $20.00

GURY, Hilary Knight. *The Wonderful World of Aunt Tuddy.* 1958. Random House. Ills. 1st ed. dj. VG $20.00

GUSSOW, H.T. & Odell, W.S. *Mushrooms & Toadstools, Account of Edible Fungi.* 1927. Ottowa. Ills. inscr. pls. VG $40.00

GUSTAFSON, A.F. *Conservation in the United States.* 1949. New York. Comstock. TB. 534 pp. $4.00

GUTERMAN, Simeon. *Religious Toleration/Persecution in Ancient Rome.* 1951. Aiglon. 1st ed. dj. $12.50

GUTHE, Carl. *Manual for the Study of Food Habits.* 1945. Washington. 1st ed. stiff wrappers. $7.50

GUTHRIE, A.B., Jr. *Arfive.* 1970. Boston. 1st ed. dj. VG $20.00

GUTHRIE, A.B., Jr. *Fair Land, Fair Land.* 1982. Boston. Houghton Mifflin. 1st ed. dj. $20.00

GUTHRIE, A.B., Jr. *No Second Wind.* 1980. Boston. 1st ed. dj. VG $12.50

GUTHRIE, A.B., Jr. *The Genuine Article.* 1977. Boston. Houghton Mifflin. 1st ed. dj. $25.00

GUTHRIE, A.B., Jr. *The Way West.* 1949. New York. Wm. Sloane. 1st ed. dj. VG $30.00

GUTHRIE, A.B., Jr. *These Thousand Hills.* 1956. 1st ed. dj. EX $15.00

GUTHRIE, A.B., Jr. *Western Story. Recollections of Charley O'Kieffe.* 1960. Pioneer Heritage Series. dj. $12.50

GUY, Rosa. *A Measure of Time.* 1983. Holt. proof copy. wrappers. VG $35.00

GWATHMEY, J.H. *Love Affairs of Capt. John Smith.* 1935. 2nd ed. dj. G $10.00

GWYN, J. *The Enterprising Admiral.* 1974. Montreal. Ills. dj. EX $20.00

GZIMEK, B. & M. *Serengeti Shall Not Die.* 1960. Hamilton. 1st Eng. ed. 344 pp. dj. EX $20.00

GZOWSKI, Peter. *The Game of Our Lives.* 1981. 278 pp. dj. EX $12.50

H

HAAS, Irene. *The Maggie B.* 1975. New York. Ills. author. VG $15.00

HABBERTON, John. *The Jericho Road.* 1877. Chicago. 222 pp. $15.00

HABERLY, L. *Medieval English Pavingtitles.* 1937. Shakespeare Head Pr. Ltd. ed. $200.00

HABERLY, L. *Pursuit of Horizon.* 1948. New York. 1st ed. EX $17.50

HACKER, Marilyn. *Presentation Piece.* 1974. Viking Press. 1st ed. dj. VG $30.00

HACKETT, Francis. *Francis the First.* 1935. New York. Literary Guild. 448 pp. VG $5.00

HACKETT, Francis. *Henry VIII.* 1928. London. VG $30.00

HACKLE. *Fishless Days, Angling Nights.* 1971. 1st ed. dj. VG $10.00

HACKNEY, Louise. *Guide Posts to Chinese Painting.* 1929. Boston. $45.00

HACOX. *Chaffee of Roaring Horse.* Popular. pb. $3.00

HADDEN, J. Cuthbert. *The Operas of Wagner.* New York. Stokes. 24 color pls. dj. VG $25.00

HADDOCK, Jno. A. *The Picturesque St.Lawrence River.* 1896. exterior staining. $18.00

HADDON, Alfred C. *Magic & Fetishism.* 1906. London. 99 pp. G $30.00

HADDOW & GROSZ. *The German Giants: German R-Planes 1914-1918.* 1963. Putnam. 283 pp. scarce. dj. VG $55.00

HADER, B. & H. *Quack Quack.* 1962. Macmillan. 1st ed. VG $25.00

HADER, Berta & Elmer. *Pancho.* 1942. New York. Macmillan. Ills. 1st ed. $30.00

HADER, Berta & Elmer. *Reindeer Trail: Long Journey from Lapland to AK.* 1959. New York. Macmillan. Ills. 1st printing. $15.00

HADMAN, B. *As the Sailor Loves the Sea.* 1951. Harper. Ills. 1st ed. VG $10.00

HAFEN, L.R. *Broken Hand.* Old West Pub. reprint. dj. EX $32.50

HAFEN, L.R. *Ruxton of the Rockies.* 1950. Norman. 1st ed. 325 pp. index. dj. $22.50

HAFEN, L.R. *The Overland Mail, 1849-1869.* 1926. Clark. Ills. 1st ed. 362 pp. map. $115.00

HAFEN. *Handcarts to Zion (1856-1860).* 1960. dj. $15.00

HAFTMANN, HENTZEN & LIEBERMAN. *German Art of the 20th Century.* 1st ed. EX $40.00

HAGARTY, D.A. *Houdini Magical Hall of Fame.* no date. G $2.00

HAGEDORN, Hermann. *Edwin Arlington Robinson.* 1939. NY. Macmillan. 402 pp. $4.50

HAGEDORN, Hermann. *The Book of Courage.* 1930. Philadelphia. Ills. Godwin. maps. dj. $20.00

HAGEDORN, Ralph. *Benjamin Franklin & Chess in Early America.* 1958. U. of PA. 1st ed. dj. $8.50

HAGEMANN, Elizabeth Compton. *Navaho Trading Days.* 1963. U. of NM Press. 318 rare photos. 388 pp. $27.50

HAGEN, Walter. *The Walter Hagen Story.* 1956. Simon & Schuster. 1st ed. dj. $40.00

HAGER, Dorsey. *Practical Oil Geology.* 1919. New York. McGraw Hill. ex-lib. 253 pp. $4.00

HAGERBAUMER, D. & Lehman, S. *Selected American Gamebirds.* 1973. Caxton. 2nd ed. 26 color pls. EX $40.00

HAGGARD, H. Rider. *Allan & the Ice Gods.* 1927. 1st ed. VG $20.00

HAGGARD, H. Rider. *Ayesha.* 1905. Doubleday. Ills. 1st Am. ed. VG $35.00

HAGGARD, H. Rider. *Dr. Therne.* 1898. London. 1st ed. dj. $17.50

HAGGARD, H. Rider. *Lysbeth.* 1901. London. 1st ed. dj. VG $15.00

HAGGARD, H. Rider. *Montezuma's Daughter.* 1951. MacDonald. dj. VG $8.50

HAGGARD, H. Rider. *Regeneration.* 1910. London. 1st ed. G $15.00

HAGGARD, H. Rider. *She.* New York. 2nd ed. 382 pp. VG $5.00

HAGGARD, H. Rider. *Swallow.* 1899. 1st Eng. ed. VG $65.00

HAGGARD, H. Rider. *Wisdom's Daughter.* 1923. Doubleday Page. 1st ed. VG $60.00

HAGGERTY, Edward. *Guerrilla Padre in Mindanao.* 1946. New York. 257 pp. $4.50

HAGOPIAN, Richard. *The Dove Brings Peace.* 1944. New York. Ills. Tolegian. 210 pp. dj. VG $50.00

HAGUE, M. *Favourite Hans Christian Andersen Fairy Tales.* 1981. Holt. Ills. Ltd. 1st ed. sgn. boxed. $200.00

HAHN, Emily. *Africa to Me: Person to Person.* 1964. New York. Doubleday. dj. EX $10.00

HAHN, Emily. *Animal Gardens.* 1967. Doubleday. Ills. 1st ed. 403 pp. EX $15.00

HAHN, Emily. *China to Me.* 1944. Philadelphia. 429 pp. dj. $5.00

HAHN, Emily. *China to Me.* 1946. Garden City. $15.00

HAHN, Emily. *On the Side of the Apes.* 1971. Crowell. Ills. 239 pp. dj. EX $7.50

HAIIN, Emily. *The Soong Sisters.* 1944. New York. Doubleday Doran. 349 pp. $7.50

HAHN, Emily. *The Soong Sisters.* 1941. Garden City. Ills. dj. G $17.50

HAIBLUM, Isidore. *The Mutants Are Coming.* 1984. Garden City. review copy. dj. VG $10.00

HAIBLUM, Isidore. *Transfer to Yesterday.* 1981. Garden City. review copy. dj. VG $10.00

HAIG-BROWN. *Fisherman's Summer.* 1959. dj. VG $10.00

HAIG-BROWN. *Fisherman's Winter.* 1954. 1st ed. dj. EX $25.00

HAIG-BROWN. *Measure of the Year.* 1950. 1st ed. dj. VG $10.00

HAIG-BROWN. *Salt Water Summer.* 1948. 1st ed. VG $10.00

HAIGHT, Anne Lyon. *Portrait of Latin America as Seen by Print Makers.* 1946. New York. Ills. 1st ed. inscr. dj. VG $40.00

HAIGHT, Anne Lyon. *Banned Books.* 1955. London. 1st ed. dj. VG $20.00

HAILEY, Arthur. *Airport.* 1968. Doubleday. 1st ed. dj. VG $10.00

HAILEY, Arthur. *The Final Diagnosis.* 1959. Doubleday. 1st ed. dj. VG $15.00

HAILEY, Elizabeth Forsythe. *A Woman of Independent Means.* 1978. Viking. 1st ed. dj. VG $20.00

HAILEY, Elizabeth Forsythe. *Life Sentences.* 1982. Delacorte. 1st ed. dj. VG $15.00

HAINES, Edith. *Tried Temptations Old & New.* 1931. New York. 2nd ed. dj. $12.50

HAINES, Francis. *Appaloosa, the Spotted Horse in Art & History.* 1963. Austin. 103 pp. dj. VG $37.50

HAINES, Lynn. *The Lindberghs.* 1931. Vanguard. 1st ed. $10.00

HAINING, Peter. *Night Frights.* 1973. NY. Taplinger. 1st Am. ed. dj. EX $12.50

HAJEK, Lubor & Forman, W. *Japanese Woodcuts: Early Periods.* 1958. London. Ills. 175 pp. dj. EX $60.00

HAJEK, Lubor. *Contemporary Chinese Painting.* 1961. London. Ills. $45.00

HAJEK, Lubor. *Japanese Graphic Art.* 1976. 131 Ills. scarce. VG $45.00

HAJEK, Lubor. *The Osaka Woodcuts.* 1959. London. Ills. 99 pp. VG $65.00

HAJEK, Lubor. *Uamamro, Portraits in the Japanese Woodcut.* London. Ills. 143 pp. scarce. VG $60.00

HAKE, A.E. *The Story of Chinese Gordon.* 1884. London. Ills. 407 pp. VG $65.00

HAKE. *Button Book.* 1972. New York. 1st ed. dj. EX $27.50

HAKLUYT, R. *Navigations, Voyages, Traffiques, & Discoveries.* 1905. London. Maclehose & Sons. 12 vol set. VG $275.00

HALBERSTAM, D. *One Very Hot Day.* 1967. Boston. 371 pp. $5.00

HALBERSTAM, D. *The Making of a Quagmire.* 1965. New York. 1st ed. 323 pp. dj. VG $20.00

HALDANE, A. *How We Escaped from Pretoria.* 1977. African Books. Ills. fld map. . 231 pp. dj. EX $20.00

HALDANE, Charlotte. *The Last Great Empress of China.* 1965. VG $3.00

HALDEMAN, Joe. *All My Sins Remembered.* 1977. St.Martin. 1st ed. dj. EX $15.00

HALDEMAN, Joe. *Infinite Dreams.* 1978. New York. St.Martins. 1st ed. inscr. dj. $30.00

HALDEMAN, Joe. *Mindbridge.* 1976. New York. St.Martins. 1st ed. dj. EX $30.00

HALDEMAN, Joe. *War Year.* 1972. New York. Holt. 1st ed. dj. EX $35.00

HALDEMAN, Joe. *Worlds Apart.* 1983. New York. 1st ed. dj. EX $15.00

HALDEMAN, Joe. *Worlds Apart.* 1983. New York. review copy. dj. VG $20.00

HALDEMAN, Joe. *Worlds: Novel of the Near Future.* 1981. New York. Viking. 1st ed. dj. VG $15.00

HALE, John. *California as It Is.* Grabhorn Press.Ills. Ltd. ed. 1/150. EX $85.00

HALE, Sara J. *Love; or, Woman's Destiny.* 1870. Philadelphia. 1st ed. sgn. VG $30.00

HALE, Sarah J. *Northwood: Tale of New England.* 1827. Boston. 1st ed. 2 vol set. $150.00

HALE, Sarah J. *Woman's Record; Sketches of Distinguished Women.* 1855. New York. Ills. 912 pp. VG $25.00

HALE, Selma. *History of the United States.* 1837. Cooperstown. H. & E. Phinney. 298 pp. $15.00

HALE, Will. *24 Years a Cowboy & Ranchman in Texas & Mexico.* 1959. U. of OK Press.1st ed. VG $8.00

HALE, William H. *Horace Greeley, Voice of the People.* 1950. New York. 376 pp. dj. $10.00

HALE, William J. *Prosperity Beckons. Dawn of Alcohol Era.* 1936. Boston, Mass. presentation copy. 201 pp. dj. $10.00

HALE. *Vermeer of Delft.* 1913. Ills. 388 pp. VG $30.00

HALE-WHITE, William. *Keats as Doctor & Patient.* 1938. Oxford. dj. EX $17.50

HALEVY, Elie. *The Era of Tyrannies.* 1966. New York. NY U. Press. 324 pp. dj. VG $6.00

HALEY, Alex. *Roots.* 1976. Doubleday. 1st ed. dj. VG $20.00

HALEY, J. Evetts. *XIT Ranch of Texas.* 1929. Chicago. ex-lib. $150.00

HALEY, Nelson. *Whale Hunt.* 1948. New York. 1st ed. 304 pp. dj. $12.50

HALEY. *Rocketry & Space Exploration.* 1959. $12.50

HALIBRURTON, Thomas C. Esq. *Historical & Statistical Account of Nova Scotia.* 1829. Halifax. Howe. Ills. 1st ed. 2 vol set. VG $375.00

HALL, A. Oakley. *Old Whitey's Christmas Trot.* 1857. New York. Ills. Thwaites. 1st ed. $35.00

HALL, B. *The Great Polyglot Bibles.* San Francisco. Ltd. ed. 1/400. EX $300.00

HALL, B.H. *A Collection of College Words & Customs.* 1856. Cambridge. revised & enlarged. 508 pp. G $10.00

HALL, Basil. *Extracts of a Journal Written on Coasts of Chile.* 1824. Edinburgh. 3rd ed. 2 vol set. $75.00

HALL, Carl. *Drying Farm Crops.* 1957. Reynoldsburg. TB. 336 pp. VG $4.50

HALL, Donald. *Measure.* 1983. Ewert. Ltd. ed. 1/436. wrappers. $10.00

HALL, Donald. *Remembering Poets.* 1977. 1st ed. dj. $10.00

HALL, Donald. *String too Short to be Saved.* 1961. New York. Viking. 1st ed. VG $20.00

HALL, E.C. *Aunt Jane of Kentucky.* 1907. Boston. 1st ed. VG $15.00

HALL, E.G. *Book of Hand-Woven Coverlets.* 1927. Boston. Ills. $37.50

HALL, E.H. *Philipse Manor Hall.* 1912. Yonkers, NY. Ills. $15.00

HALL, E.R. & Kelson, K.R. *Mammals of North America.* 1959. Ronald Press. Ills. 2 vol set. VG $65.00

HALL, Edward H. *The Great West.* 1864. New York. 1st ed. 89 pp. fld map. VG $325.00

HALL, Edward H. *The Hudson-Fulton Celebration.* 1909. New York. Ills. maps. 2 vol set. VG $100.00

HALL, Eleanor. *Cuchulain, the Hound of Ulster.* 1909. London. Ills. Reid. 1st ed. 279 pp. VG $32.50

HALL, Frederic. *The Pedigree of the Devil.* 1883. Trubner. Ills. 1st ed. 256 pp. $75.00

HALL, Gordon Langley. *Vinnie Ream/Story of Girl Who Sculptured Lincoln.* 1963. 1st ed. 148 pp. dj. $52.50

HALL, Granville D. *Rending of Virginia.* 1902. Chicago. VG $22.00

HALL, Granville. *Lee's Invasion of Northwest Virginia in 1861.* 1911. sgn. VG $32.50

HALL, H.M. *A Full Creel.* 1946. Longman. 1st ed. dj. VG $20.00

HALL, H.M. *Woodcock Ways.* 1946. 1st ed. dj. VG $20.00

HALL, H.R. *Civilization of Greece in the Bronze Age.* 1928. London. 370 London. 302 pp. dj. $32.50

HALL, Henry Marion. *A Gathering of Shore Birds.* 1960. New York. Ills. 1st ed. 242 pp. dj. VG $37.50

HALL, Inez A.E. *Romance of Lake Conneaut or All's Well-Ends Well.*1932. Boston. 193 pp. $10.00

HALL, James N. *The Forgotten One & Other Tales of South Seas.* 1952. Boston. Little, Brown. 246 pp. G $2.50

HALL, James N. & Nordhoff, C. *Faery Lands of the South Seas.* 1921. New York. Garden City. 355 pp. VG $3.00

HALL, James. *Notes on the Western States.* 1838. Philadelphia. 304 pp. $85.00

HALL, Jason. *The Young Patriot. A Memorial.* 1862. Boston. 192 pp. 2 pls. G $12.50

HALL, Manly P. *Lectures on Ancient Philosophy.* 1929. Los Angeles. 1st ed. EX $35.00

HALL, Manly P. *Mystical Christ.* 1956. Los Angeles. 3rd ed. dj. VG $15.00

HALL, Manly P. *Old Testament Wisdom.* 1957. California. 1st ed. sgn. dj. VG $15.00

HALL, Manly P. *The Phoenix.* 1931. Ltd. 1st ed. 1/3000. 127 pp. $65.00

HALL, Marie. *Nine Days to Christmas.* 1959. 1st ed. VG $35.00

HALL, Mr. & Mrs. S.C. *The Book of the Thames.* 1859. London. Ills. EX $50.00

HALL, Mrs. Herman J. *Two Travelers in Europe.* 1898. Kuhlman & Co. Ills. $7.50

HALL, N.S. *Frank Luke, Balloon Buster.* 1928. 1st ed. VG $35.00

HALL, R. *Stanley, an Adventurer Explored.* 1975. Houghton Mifflin. 1st ed. dj. $20.00

HALL, Radclyffe. *Well of Loneliness.* 1928. New York. Ltd. 1st Am. ed. boxed. VG $35.00

HALL, Robert Lee. *Exit Sherlock Holmes.* 1977. London/NY. 1st ed. dj. EX $7.50

HALL, S.C. *The Book of British Ballads.* 1853. Bohn. $20.00

HALL, Walter Phelps. *Iron Out of Calvary.* 1946. New York. 1st ed. maps. 389 pp. $12.50

HALL. *Black's General Atlas.* 1840. Edinburgh. 50 maps. folio. VG $120.00

HALL. *Fragments of Voyages & Travels.* 1831. 3 vol set. $90.00

HALL. *The Main Trail.* 1971. Naylor. 193 pp. dj. EX $15.00

HALLAHAN, William. *Catch Me: Kill Me.* 1977. Indianapolis. 1st printing. wrappers. VG $25.00

HALLAHAN, William. *The Ross Forgery.* 1977. London. Gollancz. 1st Eng. ed. dj. VG $45.00

HALLAHAN, William. *The Search for Joseph Tully.* 1974. Indianapolis. advance copy. wrappers. VG $75.00

HALLAM, Henry. *Introduction to Literature of Europe Vol. I.* 1851. New York. Harper. ex-lib. 416 pp. $2.50

HALLAM, R. *Annals of St. James Church.* 1873. Hartford. VG $15.00

HALLAS, Richard. *You Play the Black & the Red Comes Up.* 1938. McBride. 1st ed. dj. VG $60.00

HALLE, Fannina. *Woman in Soviet Russia.* 1933. New York. Ills. 1st ed. VG $10.00

HALLE, L. *The Storm Petrel & the Owl of Athena.* 1970. Princeton. Ills. maps. 268 pp. dj. EX $10.00

HALLECK, Fitz Greene. *Fanny, with Other Poems.* 1839. New York. $25.00

HALLECK, Reuben P. *Psychology & Psychic Culture.* 1895. New York. 1st ed. 368 pp. VG $25.00

HALLENBECK, C. *Land of the Conquistadores.* 1950. Caldwell. 1st ed. dj. EX $32.50

HALLER, James. *The Blue Strawberry Cookbook.* 1976. Harvard. 150 pp. SftCvr. $2.50

HALLERAN, E.E. *Prairie Guns.* 1944. Philadelphia. Blakiston. 255 pp. dj. $3.50

HALLERAN. *Rustler's Canyon.* Pocketbooks. pb. $3.00

HALLET, J-P. *Animal Kitabu.* 1967. Random House. Ills. 1st printing. 292 pp. VG $10.00

HALLET, J-P. *Congo Kitabu.* 1967. Random House. photos. maps. 436 pp. dj. EX $15.00

HALLGREN, Mauritz. *Seeds of Revolt.* 1933. New York. Knopf. ex-lib. 273 pp. $4.50

HALLIBURTON, R. *Glorious Adventure.* 1927. sgn. dj. G $15.00

HALLIBURTON, R. *The Flying Carpet.* 1932. Ills. 352 pp. dj. VG $4.50

HALLIBURTON, R. *The Romantic World of Richard Halliburton.* 1961. Bobbs Merrill. Ills. 1st printing. dj. VG $15.00

HALLOCK, Charles. *Fishing Tourist.* 1873. 1st ed. VG $37.50

HALLOCK, Charles. *The Salmon Fisher.* 1890. New York. 1st ed. sgn. EX $100.00

HALLS, L.K. *White-Tailed Deer Ecology & Management.* 1984. Stackpole. Ills. maps. 870 pp. dj. EX $35.00

HALPER, Albert. *Atlantic Avenue.* 1956. New York. Dell. 1st ed. wrappers. VG $15.00

HALPER, Albert. *The Golden Watch.* 1953. New York. Holt. 1st ed. dj. EX $30.00

HALPERN, Daniel. *Life Among Others.* 1978. Viking. 1st ed. dj. VG $15.00

HALPERN, Daniel. *Seasonal Rights.* 1982. Viking. 1st ed. dj. VG $12.50

HALSEY, Elizabeth T. *Ladies' Home Journal Book of Interior Decoration.* 1957. Philadelphia. 256 pp. $5.00

HALSEY, R.T.H. & Tower, E. *The Homes of Our Ancestors.* 1935. Garden City. Doubleday Doran. pls. G $30.00

HALSMAN, Philippe. *Philippe Halsman's Jump Book.* 1959. 1st ed. $24.00

HALSMAN. *Dali's Mustache.* New York. 1st ed. $25.00

HALSTEAD, Murat. *Life & Achievements of Admiral Dewey.* 1899. 452 pp. $10.00

HALSTEAD, Murat. *Life & Distinguished Services of Wm. McKinley.* 1896. Edgewood Pub. 501 pp. $4.00

HALSTEAD, Murat. *Story of Cuba.* 1898. Chicago. $13.50

HALSTEAD, Murat. *Story of Philippines & Our New Possessions.* 1898. Ills. 512 pp. $12.50

HALSTEAD, Murat. *The Illustrious Life of William McKinley.* 1901. 464 pp. $5.00

HALSTEAD, Murat. *William McKinley. Memorial Edition.* 1901. 540 pp. $37.50

HAMBLIN, D.J. *Pots & Robbers.* 1970. New York. dj. VG $6.00

HAMBLIN, D.J. *That Was the Life.* 1977. New York. dj. EX $7.50

HAMBURG, Merrill. *Beginning to Fly: Book of Model Airplanes.* 1930. revised ed. G $20.00

HAMERTON, Philip G. *Etching & Etchers.* 1878. Boston. Roberts. Ills. VG $30.00

HAMERTON, Philip G. *Landscape.* 1885. 440 pp. $14.00

HAMILTON, Alastair. *A Study of Intellectuals & Fascism, 1919-1945.* 1971. London. Ills. 312 pp. dj. VG $6.00

HAMILTON, Alex. *Beam of Malice.* 1967. New York. 1st Am. ed. dj. VG $15.00

HAMILTON, Alex. *If You Don't Watch Out.* 1965. New York. McKay. 1st Am. ed. dj. VG $12.50

HAMILTON, Alexander. *The Federalist.* 1802. New York. 2nd ed. 318 pp. 2 vol set. EX $485.00

HAMILTON, C. *On the Trail of Stevenson.* 1916. New York. Ills. Walter Hale. G $10.00

HAMILTON, Charles. *Scribblers & Scoundrels.* 1968. Eriksson. dj. $37.50

HAMILTON, Elisabeth B. *Reginald Birch-His Book.* 1939. New York. Ills. Reginald Birch. 1st ed. $25.00

HAMILTON, Henrietta. *Answer in the Negative.* 1959. London. 1st ed. dj. VG $25.00

HAMILTON, Mary Agnes. *The Labour Party Today.* London. Labour Book Service. EX $20.00

HAMILTON, Peter J. *Mobile of the Five Flags.* 1913. Mobile. Ills. VG $45.00

HAMILTON, Schuyler. *History of the National Flag of the U.S.A.* 1852. Philadelphia. Ills. $10.00

HAMILTON, W.T. *My Sixty Years on the Plains.* 1905. New York. Ills. Russell/Forest/Stream. $100.00

HAMILTON. *Crusades.* 3rd ed. EX $6.00

HAMILTON. *Gene Autry & the Redwood Pirates.* 1946. Whitman. Ills. G $4.50

HAMILTON. *Gene Autry & the Thief River Outlaws.* 1944. Whitman. Ills. G $4.50

HAMILTON. *Longhorn Revenge.* Pyramid. pb. $3.00

HAMLEY, Edward. *The Operations of War Explained & Illustrated.* 1866. 1st ed. $22.50

HAMLIN, A.C. *Martyria; or, Andersonville Prison.* 1866. Boston. Ills. 1st ed. 256 pp. $50.00

HAMLIN, A.C. *The Tourmaline.* 1873. Boston. Ills. 107 pp. $30.00

HAMLIN, H. *Nine Mile Bridge, Three Years in the Maine Woods.* 1945. Norton. 233 pp. dj. EX $10.00

HAMMERTON, J.A. *Wonders of the Past.* 1952. Wise & Co. 2 vol set. VG $75.00

HAMMETT, Dashiell. *A Man Named Thin & Other Stories.* 1962. New York. Ferman. 1st ed. wrappers. $60.00

HAMMETT, Dashiell. *American Detective Stories.* 1943. London. Pilot Press. 1st ed. dj. VG $30.00

HAMMETT, Dashiell. *Modern Tales of Horror.* 1932. London. Gollancz. 1st Eng. ed. VG $25.00

HAMMETT, Dashiell. *Nightmare Town.* 1948. New York. 1st ed. wrappers. EX $45.00

HAMMETT, Dashiell. *The Big Knockover.* 1966. New York. Random House. 1st ed. dj. EX $45.00

HAMMETT, Dashiell. *The Glass Key.* 1931. New York. Knopf. 282 pp. $25.00

HAMMETT, Dashiell. *The Glass Key.* 1966. Penguin. 1st ed. wrappers. EX $18.00

HAMMETT, Dashiell. *The Maltese Falcon.* 1930. New York. Knopf. 1st ed. $250.00

HAMMETT, Dashiell. *The Maltese Falcon.* 1930. Maryland Lib. 1st ed. dj. VG $25.00

HAMMETT, Dashiell. *The Novels of Dashiell Hammett.* 1965. New York. Knopf. 726 pp. $4.00

HAMMOND, C.S. *Hammond's Handy Atlas of the World.* 1924. 160 pp. EX $4.50

HAMMOND, E. & L. *Elephants in the Living Room, Bears in the Canoe.* 1977. Delacorte. Ills. 1st printing. 244 pp. EX $7.50

HAMMOND, Geoffrey F. *Showdown at Newport.* 1974. 1st ed. dj. VG $12.50

HAMMOND, George P. *Treaty of Guadaloupe, February Second, 1848.* 1949. Berkeley. Grabhorn. Ills. 1st ed. 79 pp. $200.00

HAMMOND, J.M. *Winter Journeys in the South.* 1916. Philadelphia. 1st ed. sgn. 261 pp. $10.00

HAMMOND, J.W. *Men & Volts. Story of G.E.* 1941. New York. Ills. dj. VG $25.00

HAMMOND, O.C. *Hammond's Check List of New Hampshire History.* 1971. 129 pp. wrappers. $7.50

HAMMOND, Ralph. *Ante-Bellum Mansions of Alabama.* 1951. New York. reprint. dj. EX $10.00

HAMMOND, William A. *Military Medical & Surgical Essays.* 1864. Philadelphia. $150.00

HAMMOND & REY. *Narratives of Coronado Expedition.* 1940. U. of NM. 1st ed. sgns. EX $95.00

HAMNER, Earl, Jr. *The Homecoming.* 1970. New York. Random House. 1st ed. dj. VG $25.00

HAMNER, Laura V. *No-Gun Man of Texas: Century of Achievement.* 1935. Amarillo. Ills. 1st ed. 256 pp. $35.00

HAMPDEN, John. *The Book World.* 1935. London. Nelson. 1st ed. VG $30.00

HAMPSHIRE, A. Cecil. *Royal Sailors.* 1971. $8.50

HAMPTON, Benjamin B. *A History of the Movies.* 1932. London. Ills. 1st Eng. ed. VG $50.00

HAMPTON, Lou. *Ghosts of My Study.* 1927. Authors & Pub. Corp. 1st ed. $60.00

HAMSUN, Knut. *Dreamers.* 1921. New York. Knopf. 1st ed. EX $10.00

HANAFORD, P. *Daughters of America.* 1888. Augusta, ME 750 pp. $9.50

HANCOCK, A.R. *Reminiscences of Hancock, by His Wife.* 1887. New York. 1st ed. $25.00

HANCOCK, A.R. *Reminiscences of Winfield.* 1887. New York. Hancock. 1st ed. EX $15.00

HANCOCK, H. Irving. *Dave Darrin at Vera Cruz.* 1914. New York. 212 pp. dj. $3.50

HANCOCK, H. Irving. *The Young Engineers in Arizona.* 1912. Altemus. G $4.50

HANCOCK, H. Irving. *The Young Engineers in Colorado.* 1912. Altemus. G $4.50

HANCOCK, J. & Elliott, H. *Herons of the World.* 1978. Harper & Row. Ills. 1st Am. ed. 304 pp. dj. $60.00

HANDEL, Leo A. *Hollywood Looks at Its Audience.* 1950. IL U. Press. VG $9.00

HANDKE, Peter. *The Weight of the World.* 1984. New York. Farrar. proof copy. wrappers. $20.00

HANDKE, Peter. *The Weight of the World.* 1984. Seeker/Warburg.1st English ed. dj. VG $15.00

HANDLIN, O. *Al Smith & His America.* 1958. 1st ed. dj. $6.50

HANKINS, Maude McGehee. *Daddy Gander Rhymes.* 1916. New York. Ills. E. Walker. 1st ed. $25.00

HANKS, J. *The Struggle for Survival, the Elephant Problem.* 1979. Mayflower. Ills. 1st Am. ed. 176 pp. dj. $17.50

HANN, Enno. *Home Plumbing Guide.* 1957. G $3.00

HANNA, Alfred J. & Kathryn. *Napoleon III & Mexico.* 1971. sgn. $5.00

HANNA, ANDERSON & GRAY. *David's Friends at School.* 1935. Scott Foresman. Ills. 144 pp. $3.50

HANNA, Charles. *The Wilderness Trail.* 1911. London/NY. Ills. 2 vol set. VG $75.00

HANNAFORD. *Story of a Regiment.* 1868. Cincinnati. fld map. roster. VG $125.00

HANNAH, Barry. *Black Butterfly.* 1982. Palaemon. Ltd. ed. sgn. wrappers. EX $50.00

HANNAH, Barry. *Captain Maximus.* 1985. Knopf. proof copy. sgn. wrappers. EX $120.00

HANNAH, Barry. *Nightwatchmen.* 1973. Viking. 1st ed. sgn. dj. VG $40.00

HANNAH, Barry. *Power & Light.* 1983. Palaemon. 1st trade ed. sgn. EX $22.50

HANNAH, Barry. *Ray.* 1981. Penquin. 1st ed. sgn. wrappers. VG $10.00

HANNAH, Barry. *Ray.* 1980. Knopf. 1st ed. sgn. dj. VG $30.00

HANNAH, Barry. *The Tennis Handsome.* 1983. Knopf. 1st ed. sgn. dj. VG $25.00

HANNF, Helene. *Duchess of Bloomsbury Street.* 1973. Philadelphia. 1st ed. dj. EX $10.00

HANNUM, Alberta. *Paint the Wind.* 1958. New York. Ills. Beatien Yazz. 206 pp. VG $12.50

HANNUM, Hurst & Blumberg, R. *Brandies & Liqueurs of the World.* 1976. Garden City. Doubleday. Ills. 278 pp. dj. $8.50

HANRATTY, Peter. *Last Knight of Albion Blue Jay.* 1986. pb. EX $5.00

HANSCOM, Adelaide. *Rubaiyat of Omar Khayyam.* 1905. Dodge. Ills. 1st ed. VG $60.00

HANSEN, H.J. *Late Nineteenth Century Art.* 1972. New York. Ills. folio. dj. VG $32.50

HANSEN, Joseph. *Backtrack.* 1982. New York. Foul Play. 1st ed. dj. EX $20.00

HANSEN, Joseph. *Gravedigger.* 1982. New York. Holt. 1st ed. dj. EX $20.00

HANSEN, Joseph. *Nightwork.* New York. 1st ed. dj. EX $9.00

HANSEN, Kathryn. *Sarah.* 1984. Champaign. Ills. 1st ed. 171 pp. $50.00

HANSEN, Marcus Lee. *The Atlantic Migration 1607-1860.* 1941. Cambridge. ex-lib. 391 pp. VG $5.00

HANSEN, T. *Arabia Felix, the Danish Expedition of 1761-67.* 1964. Holt Rinehart. Ills. 1st ed. 381 pp. VG $15.00

HANSEN, Woodrow James, Ph.D. *Search for Authority in California.* 1960. Oakland. Ltd. 1st CA ed. 192 pp. EX $50.00

HANSEN. *Penn. Prints: Collection of J. O'Connor & Yeager.* 1980. Penn. State U. Press. $7.00

HANSON, Earl. *South from the Spanish Main.* 1967. 1st ed. 462 pp. dj. $50.00

HANSON, L. & E. *Golden Decade: Story of Impressionism.* 1961. London. 1st ed. dj. EX $10.00

HANSON, Lawrence & Elizabeth. *Chinese Gordon. The Story of a Hero.* 1954. New York. Funk & Wagnalls. G $15.00

HANSON, Lawrence & Elizabeth. *Noble Savage: Life of Paul Gauguin.* 1955. New York. Ills. 1st ed. dj. VG $22.50

HANSON, Ole. *Americanism Versus Bolshevism.* 1920. dj. $75.00

HAPGOOD, C.H. *The Path of the Pole.* 1970. New York. Ills. 413 pp. dj. $12.00

HAPGOOD, David. *The Screwing of the Average Man.* 1974. Doubleday. 1st ed. dj. $2.50

HAPPER, J.S. *Japanese Sketches & Japenese Prints.* 1934. Tokyo. Ills. very rare. $90.00

HARASZTI, Z. *John Adams & the Prophets of Progress.* 1952. Harvard. 1st ed. dj. EX $9.50

HARBESON, G. *American Needlework. Hist. of Decorative Stitchery.* 1938. Coward McCann. dj. slipcase. EX $45.00

HARBOURS, D. *Hunting the American Wild Turkey.* 1975. dj. EX $15.00

HARD, Walter. *Vermont, Salt & Vintage.* 1962. sgn. dj. VG $15.00

HARDACRE, F.C. *Atlas of Jasper County Illinois.* 1902. Vincennes, IN. $55.00

HARDEMAN, N.P. *Wilderness Calling in Am. Westward Movement.* 1977. TN. U. Press.1st ed. dj. EX $15.00

HARDEN. *Masterpieces of Glass.* 1969. Trustees of British Museum. $10.00

HARDIN, Alison. *Traditional Recipes for Christmas.* 1978. Melesina Press.Ltd. ed. 1/110. wrappers. EX $60.00

HARDIN, J.W. *Life of John Wesley Hardin.* 1896. Sequin, TX. 1st ed. wrappers. $80.00

HARDING, A.R. *Ferret Facts & Fancies.* 1915. Columbus, OH. Ills. VG $12.00

HARDING, A.R. *Ginseng & Other Medicinal Plants.* 1936. Columbus, OH. Harding. 367+3 pp. ads. $15.00

HARDING, Addie. *America Rides the Liners.* 1956. Coward McCann. 1st ed. dj. $10.00

HARDING, Emily J. *Slav Fairy Tales.* A.L. Burt. (ca.1900) Ills. EX $15.00

HARDING, John R. *One Hundred Years of Trinity Church. Utica, N.Y.* 1898. Utica, NY. photos. 151 pp. VG $5.00

HARDING. *3,001 Questions & Answers.* Harding Pub. $9.00

HARDMAN, Francis. *Frontier Life.* Philadelphia. (ca.1885) $35.00

HARDON, H.W. *Cole Family of Stark New Hampshire.* 1932. New York. inscr. 90 pp. $20.00

HARDWICK, E. *Bartley in Manhattan.* 1983. Random House. 1st ed. dj. VG $15.00

HARDWICK, E. *Sleepless Nights.* 1979. 1st ed. dj. EX $10.00

HARDWICK, Homer. *Winemaking at Home.* 1972. New York. 258 pp. $6.50

HARDWICK, Michael. *Private Life of Dr. Watson.* 1983. New York. 1st ed. dj. EX $7.50

HARDY, Lady Duffus. *Through Cities & Prairie Lands.* 1890. New York. 338 pp. G $10.00

HARDY, Mary Earle. *The Little King & the Princess True.* 1912. Chicago. Ills. 182 pp. $10.00

HARDY, Thomas. *Jude the Obscure.* 1896. London. Ills. H. Macbeth-Raeburn. map. $22.50

HARDY, Thomas. *Late Lyrics & Earlier.* 1922. London. 1st ed. 288 pp. $25.00

HARDY, Thomas. *Life & Art.* 1925. Greenburg. 1st ed. VG $75.00

HARDY, Thomas. *Life's Little Ironies.* 1894. New York. Harper. 1st Am. ed. VG $50.00

HARDY, Thomas. *Life's Little Ironies.* 1894. Leipzig. Tauchnitz. 1st ed. VG $20.00

HARDY, Thomas. *Selected Poems.* 1921. London/Boston. Ltd. ed. $70.00

HARDY, Thomas. *Selected Poems.* 1921. London. Medici Soc. Ltd. ed. 1/1025. $85.00

HARDY, Thomas. *The Famous Tragedy of the Queen of Cornwall.* 1923. London. 1st ed. VG $22.50

HARDY, Thomas. *The Return of the Native.* 1972. New York. Harper. 485 pp. VG $3.50

HARDY, Thomas. *The Three Wayfarers.* 1935. Dorchester. Ltd. 1st Eng. ed. 1/250. $60.00

HARDY, Thomas. *Thomas Hardy in Maine.* 1942. Portland. Ltd. ed. 1/425. VG $30.00

HARDY, Thomas. *Wessex & Other Verses.* 1898. London/NY. 30 Ills. $25.00

HARDY, Thomas. *Wessex Tales.* 1888. 1st Eng. ed. 2 vol set. VG $97.50

HARDY, Thomas. *Winter Words in Various Moods & Metres.* 1928. London. 1st ed. 202 pp. VG $30.00

HARDY, Thomas. *Winter Words in Various Moods & Metres.* 1928. New York. Ltd. ed. 1/500. VG $22.50

HARDY, Thomas. *Yuletide in a Younger World.* Ills. Rutherson. $8.00

HARDY, W.G. *Alberta, a Natural History.* 1967. Edmonton. Ills. maps. 343 pp. dj. VG $15.00

HARDY. *A Group of Noble Dames.* 1891. London. 1st ed. VG $40.00

HARE, Augustus J.C. *Cities of Northern & Central Italy.* 1876. New York. 1358 pp. 3 vol set. $25.00

HARE, Cyril. *Best Detective Stories of Cyril Hare.* 1959. London. Faber. 1st ed. dj. VG $25.00

HARE, Cyril. *He Should Have Died Hereafter.* 1958. London. Faber. 1st ed. dj. VG $25.00

HARE, Cyril. *With a Bare Bodkin.* 1946. London. 1st ed. dj. VG $25.00

HARE, Robert. *The Hand of the Chimpanzee.* 1934. New York. VG $30.00

HAREL, Isser. *The House on Garibaldi Street.* 1975. New York. Viking Press. 259 pp. dj. $5.00

HAREUZ, E. *Le Melange de Couleurs.* Paris. $15.00

HAREWOOD, Harry. *A Dictionary of Sports.* 1835. London. Ills. 1st ed. VG $65.00

HARGRAVE, C.P. *History of Playing Cards & Biblio. Cards & Gaming.* 1930. Boston. boxed. EX $350.00

HARGREAVES. *The Tropical Marine Aquarium.* 1978. McGraw Hill. Ills. dj. EX $5.50

HARING, C.H. *Spanish Empire in America.* 1947. Oxford. VG $18.00

HARING, H.A. *Our Catskill Mountains.* 1931. New York. photos. map. VG $10.00

HARINGTON, John. *A Tract on the Succession to the Crown.* 1880. London. rebound. VG $35.00

HARIOT, Theodore. *Brief & True Report of New Found Land of Virginia.* 1931. Ann Arbor. Ltd. ed. slipcase. $50.00

HARKEY, Dee. *Mean as Hell.* 1948. Albuquerque. 1st ed. dj. VG $10.00

HARKNESS, Marjory Gane. *The Tamworth Narrative.* 1958. Maine. Ills. dj. EX $15.00

HARKNESS, R. *Lady & the Panda.* 1938. New York. Ills. Carrick & Evans. G $25.00

HARLAN, J.R. & Speaker, E.B. *Iowa Fish & Fishing.* 1951. Ills. 1st ed. 238 pp. VG $12.50

HARLAN, Jacob W. *California, 1846-1888.* 1888. San Francisco. 242 pp. $100.00

HARLAND, Marion. *From My Youth Up.* 1874. New York. 1st ed. 397 pp. $10.00

HARLAND, Marion. *Under the Flag of the Orient.* 1897. Philadelphia. 2nd ed. EX $25.00

HARLOW, Alvin F. *The Serene Cincinnatians.* 1950. New York. Dutton. ex-lib. 442 pp. $10.00

HARLOW, F.P. *Making of a Sailor.* 1928. Salem Marine Research Soc. EX $55.00

HARLOW. *Modern Pueblo Pottery 1880-1960.* 1977. 1st ed. dj. EX $25.00

HARNER, M.J. *The Jivaro.* 1972. Ills. 1st ed. 233 pp. dj. VG $12.50

HARNESS, Charles J. *Flight into Yesterday.* 1953. New York. Bouregy. 1st ed. dj. EX $35.00

HARNESS, Charles L. *The Paradox Man.* 1984. 1st ed. dj. EX $20.00

HARNEY, W.E. *Life Among the Aborigines.* 1957. London. Ills. 219 pp. $10.00

HARNSBERGER, Caroline T. *Treasury of Presidential Quotations.* 1964. Chicago. 419 pp. dj. EX $10.00

HARNSBERGER, Caroline. *Lincoln Treasury.* 1950. Chicago. 1st ed. sgn. dj. EX $17.50

HAROLD, Anthony. *Aviation Photographs of Charles E. Brown.* 1983. England. Airlife Pub. $12.00

HARPER, F. *Birds of the Ungava Peninsula.* 1958. KS U. Pr. photos. maps. 171 pp. EX $10.00

HARPER, F. *Night Climb, Story of Skiing.* 1946. 1st ed. dj. VG $10.00

HARPER, Henry Howard. *The Devil's Nest.* 1923. Torch Press. Ltd. ed. 1/100. dj. EX $20.00

HARPER, Merritt W. *Animal Husbandry for Schools.* 1914. New York. Macmillan. TB. 409 pp. G $3.50

HARPER, Vincent. *The Mortgage on the Brain.* 1905. London. 1st Eng. ed. VG $30.00

HARPER PUBLISHERS. *Harper's Phrase Book, English, French, German.* 1895. EX $5.00

HARPER. *A Literary Man's London.* Great Britain. Ills. sgn. dj. EX $140.00

HARRARD, H.R. *The People of the Mist.* MacDonald. dj. VG $8.50

HARRER, H. *Seven Years in Tibet.* 1954. Dutton. Ills. 1st ed. 314 pp. dj. EX $12.50

HARRIER, H. *The White Spider.* 1968. London. dj. VG $20.00

HARRINGTON, Alan. *The Immortalist.* 1969. New York. Random House. 1st ed. dj. VG $30.00

HARRINGTON, Bob. *The Chaplain of Bourbon Street.* 1969. Doubleday. 1st ed. dj. $3.50

HARRINGTON, James. *Oceana.* 1771. London. $250.00

HARRINGTON, Michael. *Socialism.* 1972. New York. Saturday Review Press. 436 pp. $5.00

HARRIS, A.C. *Alaska & Klondike Gold Fields.* 1897. Washington. Ills. 566 pp. map. $75.00

HARRIS, Branson L. *Some Recollections of My Boyhood.* 1908. Indianapolis. 70 pp. $50.00

HARRIS, Frank. *Contemporary Portraits.* 1915. 1st ed. VG $17.50

HARRIS, Frank. *My Reminiscences as a Cowboy.* 1930. New York. Ills. 1st ed. 217 pp. VG $12.50

HARRIS, Frank. *My Secret Life.* 1966. Grove Press. 11 vols in 2. djs. slipcase. $20.00

HARRIS, Gideon & Assoc. *Audel's Automobile Guide.* 1915. New York. T. Audel & Co. 500 pp. $5.00

HARRIS, Hyde. *Kyd for Hire.* 1977. London. 1st ed. dj. EX $45.00

HARRIS, J.C. & Ortoli, F. *Evening Tales.* 1906. Scribner. 280 pp. EX $17.50

HARRIS, J.O. *Colonel Johnson of Johnson's Corners.* 1901. Chicago. Ills. Nendick. 1st ed. dj. VG $10.00

HARRIS, Joel Chandler. *Free Joe & Other Georgian Sketches.* 1887. New York. 1st ed. G $65.00

HARRIS, Joel Chandler. *On the Plantation.* 1892. New York. D. Appleton. 1st ed. 233 pp. $35.00

HARRIS, Joel Chandler. *Plantation Pageants.* 1899. Ills. E.B. Smith. 1st ed. G $50.00

HARRIS, Joel Chandler. *Tales of Home Folks in Peace & War.* 1898. Cambridge. Riverside Pr. 1st ed. 407 pp. $145.00

HARRIS, Joel Chandler. *The Chronicles of Aunt Minervy Ann.* 1899. Scribner. Ills. A.B. Frost. VG $27.50

HARRIS, Joel Chandler. *Uncle Remus & Brer Rabbit.* 1907. New York. Ills. 1st ed. VG $175.00

HARRIS, Joseph. *Harris on the Pig.* 1870. Ills. $37.50

HARRIS, Kilroy. *Kangaroo Land. Glimpses of Australia.* 1926. Cleveland. 71 Ills. sgn. 88 pp. map. VG $17.50

HARRIS, L. *Butterflies of Georgia.* 1972. OK U. Press. Ills. 1st ed. 326 pp. dj. EX $15.00

HARRIS, Laura. *Noah's Ark.* 1945. New York. Ills. Julian Wehr. dj. EX $75.00

HARRIS, M. *Field Guide to the Birds of the Galapagos.* 1982. London. Collins. Ills. revised ed. EX $25.00

HARRIS, Mark. *Mark the Glove Boy/Last Days of Richard Nixon.* 1964. Macmillan. 147 pp. dj. G $4.00

HARRIS, Nathaniel. *Rugs & Carpets of the Orient.* 1977. Hanlyn, NY. Ills. dj. VG $10.50

HARRIS, Richard. *Enemies.* 1979. Marek. 1st ed. dj. VG $12.50

HARRIS, Richard. *Honor Bound.* 1982. St.Martin. proof copy. wrappers. VG $20.00

HARRIS, Samuel. *Personal Reminiscences of Harris.* 1897. Chicago. Roberson Press. $20.00

HARRIS, Sidney. *On the Contrary.* 1964. 1st ed. dj. VG $10.00

HARRIS, T.M. *Sermon Preached After Jason Fairbanks' Execution.* 1801. Dedham. 25 pp. self wrappers. $100.00

HARRIS, Thomas. *Red Dragon.* 1981. Putnam. 1st ed. dj. VG $15.00

HARRIS, Timothy. *American Gigolo.* 1979. New York. Delacorte. 1st ed. dj. EX $25.00

HARRIS, Timothy. *Heat Wave.* 1979. New York. Dell. wrappers. EX $20.00

HARRIS, W.C. *Prison Life in Tobacco Warehouse at Richmond.* 1862. Philadelphia. scarce. EX $155.00

HARRIS, W.C. *Public Life of Zachariah Chandler 1851-1875.* 1917. Lansing. 152 pp. $12.50

HARRIS, Will. *The Bay Psalm Book Murder.* 1983. London. Hale. 1st ed. dj. $20.00

HARRIS. *Confessional.* 1930. Panurge Press. dj. VG $20.00

HARRIS. *Economics of American Medicine.* 1964. dj. $17.50

HARRIS. *Hatter Fox.* 1973. New York. dj. VG $5.00

HARRISON, Charles Yale. *There Are Victories.* 1937. New York. Covici Friede. 1st ed. dj. $25.00

HARRISON, Frank. *Step Softly on the Beaver.* 1971. New York. 248 pp. dj. $3.50

HARRISON, Gordon A. *Cross-Channel Attack.* 1951. Washington. 519 pp. photos. maps. charts. $27.50

HARRISON, H. *Queen Victoria's Revenge.* 1977. London. Severn. 1st ed. dj. EX $15.00

HARRISON, H.H. *American Birds in Color, Land Birds.* 1948. Wise. Ills. 486 pp. VG $10.00

HARRISON, Harry. *Astounding: John W. Campbell Memorial Anthology.* 1973. 1st ed. sgn. de Camp, Asimov, & Geo. Smith. $25.00

HARRISON, Harry. *Spaceship Medic.* 1970. Garden City. 1st Am. ed. review copy. dj. $12.50

HARRISON, Harry. *West of Eden.* 1984. New York. Bantam. 1st ed. dj. EX $15.00

HARRISON, Henry. *Battles of the Republic.* 1858. Ills. VG $30.00

HARRISON, Henry. *When I Come Back.* 1919. Boston/NY. Riverside Press. G $7.50

HARRISON, J. Houston. *Settlers by the Long Grey Trail.* 1983. Harrisonburg. reprint. Ills. 665 pp. $35.00

HARRISON, Jim. *A Good Day to Die.* 1973. New York. Simon & Schuster. 1st ed. VG $15.00

HARRISON, Jim. *Farmer.* 1976. New York. Viking. 1st ed. dj. VG $20.00

HARRISON, Jim. *Farmer.* 1976. New York. Viking. proof copy. VG $65.00

HARRISON, Jim. *Legends of the Fall.* 1979. Delacorte. proof copy. white wrappers. EX $175.00

HARRISON, Jim. *Legends of the Fall.* 1979. Delacorte. proof copy. red wrappers. EX $100.00

HARRISON, Jim. *Locations.* 1968. New York. Norton. 1st ed. VG $75.00

HARRISON, Jim. *Outlyer & Ghazals.* 1971. 1st ed. wrappers. VG $35.00

HARRISON, Jim. *Selected & New Poems.* 1982. Delacorte. Ltd. ed. sgn. slipcase. EX $80.00

HARRISON, Jim. *Sundog.* 1984. New York. Dutton. proof copy. wrappers. $65.00

HARRISON, Jim. *Sundog.* 1984. Dutton. Ltd. 1st ed. sgn. slipcase. EX $100.00

HARRISON, Jim. *Wolf.* 1971. New York. 1st ed. dj. VG $40.00

HARRISON, John M. *The Man Who Made Nasby, David Ross Locke.* 1969. Chapel Hill. U. Of NC Press. 335 pp. dj. $5.50

HARRISON, M.J. *In Viriconium.* 1982. London. 1st ed. dj. EX $20.00

HARRISON, M.J. *The Committed Men.* 1971. New York. Doubleday. 1st Am. ed. dj. EX $20.00

HARRISON, W.A. *Swordfish Special.* 1977. London. 1st ed. EX $14.50

HARRISON, William. *Africana.* 1977. New York. Morrow. 1st ed. dj. VG $25.00

HARRISON, William. *Savannah Blue.* 1981. New York. Marek. 1st ed. dj. EX $20.00

HARRISON, William. *Theophilus Walton; or, Majestry of Truth.* 1859. Nashville, TN. 408 pp. $12.50

HARRSEN. *Cursus Sanctae Mariane: A 13th Cent. Manuscript.* 1937. $10.00

HARSCH, J.C. *Pattern of Conquest.* 1941. Doubleday. G $15.00

HARSHBARGER, Gretchen. *McCall's Garden Book.* 1968. New York. Simon & Schuster. 1st ed. dj. $10.00

HARSHORN, J.E. *Politics & World Oil Economics.* 1962. New York. 364 pp. dj. VG $7.50

HARSTON, J.E. *Comanche Land.* 1963. Naylor Pub. 2nd ed. dj. EX $10.00

HART, Albert B. *Salmon Portland Chase.* 1899. Boston/NY. 465 pp. $10.00

HART, B.H. Liddell. *The Red Army.* 1956. Harcourt Brace.Ills. 1st Am. ed. 480 pp. dj. $15.00

HART, Frances Noyes. *Hide in the Dark.* 1929. Garden City. Doubleday. 1st ed. dj. $20.00

HART, Francis R. *The Disaster of Darien.* 1929. Boston. 1st ed. EX $125.00

HART, John S. *In School Room or Chapters in Philosophy of Ed.* 1868. Philadelphia. 276 pp. VG $20.00

HART, Mildred Y. *Morning Stands Up.* 1953. Salt Lake. Ills. Joyce Nicholes. $12.50

HART, Moss. *Act One. An Autobiography.* 1959. New York. Random House. 445 pp. dj. $12.50

HART, Moss. *Winged Victory: Army Air Force Play.* 1943. Random House. 1st printing. sgn. dj. $50.00

HART, V.E. & Stewart, George. *Farm Management & Marketing.* 1942. New York. Wiley. TB. 647 pp. VG $3.50

HART, William S. *Injun & Whitey Strike Out for Themselves.* 1921. New York. Grosset & Dunlap. $6.00

HART, William S. *My Life East & West.* 1929. Boston. Ills. 1st ed. sgn. VG $165.00

HART, William S. *Pinto Ben & Other Stories.* 1919. New York. 1st ed. VG $40.00

HART, William S. *Told Under a White Oak Tree.* 1922. Boston. Houghton Mifflin. Ills. Flagg. $40.00

HART & TOLLERIS. *Big Time Baseball.* 1950. Hart Pub. Ills. SftCvr. $6.50

HART. *The Violin; Its Famous Makers & Imitators.* 1885. London. 499 pp. $75.00

HARTE, Bret & Twain, Mark. *Sketches of the Sixties.* 1926. San Francisco. 1st trade ed. VG $30.00

HARTE, Bret & Twain, Mark. *Sketches of the Sixties.* 1926. San Francisco. Howell. Ltd. Deluxe ed. VG $125.00

HARTE, Bret. *Colonel Starbottle's Client & Some Other People.* 1892. Regent. VG $25.00

HARTE, Bret. *Complete Poetical Works.* Harrap. VG $20.00

HARTE, Bret. *Condensed Novels. 2nd Series. New Burlesques.* 1902. Boston. 1st ed. VG $40.00

HARTE, Bret. *Echoes of the Foot Hills.* 1875. Boston. 1st ed. VG $30.00

HARTE, Bret. *Gabriel Conroy.* 1876. Hartford. 1st ed. $75.00

HARTE, Bret. *Her Letter, His Answer & Her Last Letter.* 1905. Boston. Ills. Arthur I. Keller. VG $20.00

HARTE, Bret. *Luck of the Roaring Camp, etc.* 1894. Boston. G $7.50

HARTE, Bret. *Nine Sketches.* 1967. Ills. Ltd. ed. VG $25.00

HARTE, Bret. *Poems.* 1871. Boston. Osgood & Co. 1st ed. VG $17.50

HARTE, Bret. *Tales of the Argonauts & Other Sketches.* 1875. Boston. 1st ed. VG $40.00

HARTE, Bret. *The Heathen Chinee.* 1871. Boston. VG $90.00

HARTE, Bret. *The Queen of Pirate Isle.* 1955. London/NY. Ills. Greenaway. dj. EX $25.00

HARTE, Bret. *The Queen of Pirate Isle.* 1887. Boston. Ills. Greenaway. EX $125.00

HARTE, Bret. *Waif of the Plains.* 1890. Boston/NY. Ills. VG $95.00

HARTE, Bret. *Works of Bret Harte.* 1882. Riverside ed. 5 vol set. $35.00

HARTENSTEIN. *Charles Burchfield: Chas. Rand Penny Collection.* 1978. Smithsonian Institute. $5.00

HARTHAN, John. *The History of the Illustrated Book.* 1981. New York. Thames & Hudson. Ills. VG $50.00

HARTLAND, Michael. *Down Among the Dead Men.* 1983. Macmillan. proof copy. wrappers. VG $10.00

HARTLEY, L.P. *The Traveling Grave & Other Stories.* 1948. Sauk City. Arkham House. dj. $80.00

HARTLEY. *Spain Revisited.* Pott. Ills. $12.50

HARTLINE, David L. *Soldiers of Marion County Ohio, 1776-1900.* 1972. Marion, OH. 250 pp. wrappers. $10.00

HARTMAN, Frank. *Sunlight & Shadow.* 1934. Chicago. Ills. Levine. Ltd. ed. VG $20.00

HARTMAN, Franz. *Among the Gnomes.* 1896. Boston. Ills. 272 pp. G $65.00

HARTMAN, Joseph. *Facts & Mysteries of Spiritism.* 1885. Philadelphia. 1st ed. 378 pp. VG $45.00

HARTMAN, R. *Richard Strauss.* 1981. 1st Am. ed. boxed. $25.00

HARTMANN, Franz. *The Principles of Astrological Geomancy.* 1889. London. 1st ed. 136 pp. $20.00

HARTMANN, Franz. *The Talking Image of Urur.* 1890. New York. Lovell. VG $65.00

HARTSHORN, Caroline E. *You Know Whom; or, Our School at Pineville.* 1855. Boston. Ills. 144 pp. $7.50

HARTWIG, Franz. *Polar & Tropical Worlds.* 1874. 2 vol set. 811 pp. $13.50

HARVARD & THOMPSON. *Mountain of Storms.* 1974. 1st ed. dj. VG $10.00

HARVEY, Alexander. *Shelley's Elopement.* 1918. New York. Knopf. G $10.00

HARVEY, B. *Portfolio of New Zealand Birds.* 1970. Wellington. Ills. folio. 25 pls. dj. VG $75.00

HARVEY, D.C. *The French Regime in Prince Edward Island.* 1926. New Haven. 265 pp. $25.00

HARVEY, Henry. *History of the Shawnee Indians from 1681-1854.* 1855. Cincinnati. 1st ed. 1st issue. 316 pp. VG $300.00

HARVEY, Peter. *Reminiscences & Anecdotes of Daniel Webster.* 1901. Boston. VG $15.00

HARVEY, William. *Irish Life & Humor.* London. Ills. Erskine Nicol. VG $25.00

HARVEY-SMITH. *History of Wilkes Barre, Luzerne County PA.* 1909. private print. 6 vol set. VG $120.00

HARWELL, Richard B. *Confederate Music.* 1950. Chapel Hill. inscr. dj. VG $25.00

HASKELL, D.C. *Mormonism: an Address.* 1881. New York. 1st ed. 26 pp. pamphlet. $75.00

HASKELL, D.C. *The U.S. Exploring Expedition, 1838-1842.* 1942. New York. NY Public Lib. reprint. G $20.00

HASKELL, Frank. *Battle of Gettysburg.* 1908. Boston. 94 pp. wrappers. G $8.00

HASKELL, Henry C. & Fowler, R. *City of Future. Narrative History of Kansas City.* 1950. Kansas City. Roberts, Miller & Glen Pub. VG $21.50

HASKELL, John. *The Haskell Memoirs.* 1960. Putnam. 1st ed. dj. VG $12.50

HASKINS, S. *Cowboy Kate.* 1967. New York. Bantam. 1st ed. pb. EX $8.50

HASLAM, G.E. *Wise After the Event.* 1964. Manchester. Ltd. 1st ed. 1/500. wrappers. $80.00

HASLAM, W.E. *Style in Singing.* 1911. New York. VG $8.00

HASLEWOOD, Constance. *The Dear Old Nursery Rhymes*. London/NY. Warne. Ills. 8 pls. $65.00

HASLIP, Joan. *The Crown of Mexico*. 1971. New York. 531 pp. dj. $10.00

HASS, H. *Men & Sharks*. 1954. Doubleday. Ills. 1st Am. ed. dj. VG $10.00

HASSAL. *Treasures from Bodleian Library*. 1976. Columbia U. Press. $50.00

HASSAL. *Sixteen Portraits of People*. 1951. London. Ills. 1st ed. dj. VG $40.00

HASSELBLAND, Marva. *Lucky-Lucky*. 1966. New York. Ills. 1st ed. 220 pp. $12.50

HASSLER, Jon. *The Love Hunter*. 1981. Morrow. advance copy. wrappers. VG $15.00

HASSRICK, Royal B. *The Colorful Story of North American Indians*. 1974. London. Ills. 144 pp. dj. $12.00

HASTINGS, Robert. *A Nickel's Worth of Skim Milk*. 1972. Carbondale, IL. 149 pp. VG $3.50

HASTINGS, Robert. *How I Write. A Manual for Beginning Writers*. 1973. Springfield. sgn. 157 pp. wrappers. $12.50

HATCH, A. *General Ike*. 1944. Consolidated Book Pub. Ills. $4.50

HATCH, Alden & Keene, Foxhall. *Full Tilt*. 1938. Derrydale Pr. Ltd. ed. $75.00

HATCH, Alden. *American Express. A Century of Service*. 1950. Garden City. 1st ed. 287 pp. dj. EX $10.00

HATCH, Alden. *The Byrds of Virginia*. 1969. New York. 1st ed. dj. VG $15.00

HATCH, V.A. *Illustrated History of Bradford-McKean County PA*. 1901. Bradford. Ills. 261 pp. G $27.50

HATCHARD, Crary. *The Daughters of the Stars*. 1939. London. Ills. Dulac. 2 color pls. VG $25.00

HATCHER, Edmund N. *The Last Four Weeks of the War*. 1891. Columbus, OH. 1st ed. ex-lib. $35.00

HATCHER, H. & Walter, E. *A Pictorial History of the Great Lakes*. 1963. New York. 344 pp. $12.50

HATCHER, Harlan. *A Century of Iron & Men*. 1950. Indianapolis. Ills. 1st ed. 295 pp. $8.50

HATCHER, Harlan. *Lake Erie*. 1945. Indianapolis. Ills. 416 pp. dj. $12.50

HATCHER, Harlan. *The Western Reserve*. 1949. Indianapolis. 1st ed. 365 pp. sgn. $12.50

HATCHER, Julian. *Hatcher's Notebook*. 1947. Harrisburg. Military Service Pub. inscr. $35.00

HATCHER, Julian. *Pistols & Revolvers & Their Use*. 1927. Marshallton. Ills. 399 pp. VG $25.00

HATFIELD, Frank. *The Realm of Light*. 1908. Boston. Reid. 1st ed. dj. VG $60.00

HATTON, Joseph. *The White King of Manoa*. 1899. London. Hutchinson. 1st Eng. ed. VG $35.00

HAUN, Mildred. *The Hawks Done Gone*. 1940. Bobbs Merrill. dj. VG $20.00

HAUPT, Herman. *Reminiscences of General Herman Haupt*. 1901. Ltd. ed. sgn. 331 pp. $80.00

HAUPT, I.L. *An Introduction to Woodcuts of the 17th Century*. 1977. New York. Ills. 1st ed. $28.00

HAUSER, Gaylord. *Cook Book: Good Food, Good Health, Good Looks*. 1946. New York. Coward. 316 pp. $5.00

HAUSER, Gaylord. *Look Younger, Live Longer*. 1950. New York. Farrar. 383 pp. $4.00

HAUSER, Marianne. *Dark Dominion*. 1947. New York. 1st ed. inscr. sgn. dj. VG $27.50

HAUSER, Thomas. *Asworth & Palmer*. 1981. Morrow. advance copy. wrappers. VG $10.00

HAVEN, Charles T. & Belden, F. *A History of the Colt Revolver*. 1940. New York. 1st ed. dj. slipcase. EX $70.00

HAVERSTOCK, M. *An American Bestiary*. 1979. Abrams. Ills. 248 pp. dj. EX $17.50

HAVIGHURST, W. *The Heartland: Ohio, Indiana & Illinois*. 1962. Harpers. Ills. by G. Gordon. 400 pp. $3.50

HAVIGHURST, W. *Three Flags at the Strait*. 1966. dj. EX $7.50

HAVIGHURST, W. *Voices on the River*. 1964. Macmillan. Ills. 1st ed. 310 pp. dj. VG $20.00

HAVIGHURST, W. *Wilderness for Sale. Story 1st Western Land Rush*. 1956. 1st ed. VG $20.00

HAWEIS, Thomas. *The Evangelical Expositor*. 1831. London. Ills. 3 vol set. $150.00

HAWEIS. *Old Violins*. 1898. London. 293 pp. $40.00

HAWGOOD. *America's Western Frontiers*. 1967. Knopf. dj. VG $15.00

HAWKES, Clarence. *Shaggy Coat*. 1906. Philadelphia. Ills. Charles Copeland. EX $10.00

HAWKES, J. *The Passionate Artist*. Ltd. ed. 1/200. sgn. $65.00

HAWKES, Jacquetta. *Providence Island*. 1959. Random House. 1st ed. dj. EX $35.00

HAWKES, Jacquetta. *The World of the Past*. 1963. Knopf. Ills. 2 vol set. dj. boxed. EX $10.00

HAWKES, John. *Adventures in the Skin Trade*. 1985. Simon. proof copy. wrappers. VG $40.00

HAWKES. *The Innocent Party*. review copy. dj. VG $35.00

HAWKEYE, Harry. *Buffalo Bill, King of Scouts*. 1908. Chicago. Ills. 183 pp. SftCvr. $20.00

HAWKINS, N. *Indicator Catechism*. 1903. New York. G $125.00

HAWKINS, Q. *The Best Birthday*. 1954. Doubleday. Ills. Sotomayor. 1st ed. $10.00

HAWKINS, S.H. *Shakespeare's Sweetheart*. 1905. Philadelphia. Ills. G $6.00

HAWKINSON, Eric. *Images in Covenant Beginnings*. 1968. Chicago. Covenant Press. 168 pp. dj. $50.00

HAWKS, Ellison. *The Book of Remarkable Machinery*. 1928. London. 76 Ills. 40 pls. $12.50

HAWLEY, Estelle E. & Carden. *The Art & Science of Nutrition*. 1944. St.Louis, MO. 668 pp. $3.50

HAWLEY, W.A. *Oriental Rugs; Antique & Modern*. 1937. New York. 320 pp. 91 pls. slipcase. EX $75.00

HAWTHORNE, Nathaniel. *Blithedale Romance*. 1852. Boston. 1st ed. G $45.00

HAWTHORNE, Nathaniel. *Grandfather's Chair*. 1841. Boston. 1st ed. $125.00

HAWTHORNE, Nathaniel. *Hawthorne's Wonder Book*. New York. Doran. Ills. Rackham. $135.00

HAWTHORNE, Nathaniel. *Hawthorne's Works*. 1899. 25 vol set. EX $60.00

HAWTHORNE, Nathaniel. *Our Old Home*. 1863. 1st ed. VG $50.00

HAWTHORNE, Nathaniel. *Tanglewood Tales*. 1936. Ills. Milo Winter. G $7.50

HAWTHORNE, Nathaniel. *Tanglewood Tales*. 1921. New York. Hampton. Ills. Sterrett. $50.00

HAWTHORNE, Nathaniel. *Tanglewood Tales*. 1913. Windemere. Ills. Milo Winter. 1st ed. $22.50

HAWTHORNE, Nathaniel. *Tanglewood Tales*. Invicta Press. Ills. George Soper. EX $27.50

HAWTHORNE, Nathaniel. *The Great Stone Face*. 1889. Boston. Ills. VG $11.00

HAWTHORNE, Nathaniel. *The Scarlet Letter. A Romance*. 1850. Boston. 2nd ed. EX $300.00

HAWTHORNE, Nathaniel. *The Scarlet Letter. A Romance*. 1st ed. 1st issue. VG $500.00

HAWTHORNE, Nathaniel. *The Scarlet Letter. A Romance*. 1888. EX $150.00

HAWTHORNE, Nathaniel. *Twice-Told Tales*. 1895. Altemus. $4.00

HAWTHORNE, Nathaniel. *Twice-Told Tales*. 1893. Altemus. $5.00

HAWTHORNE, Nathaniel. *Twice-Told Tales.* 1893. Philadelphia. 529 pp. VG $5.00

HAWTHORNE, Nathaniel. *Wonder Book for Girls & Boys.* 1893. Boston. Ills. Walter Crane. $75.00

HAXTON, Brooks. *Dominion.* 1986. Knopf. proof copy. sgn. wrappers. VG $50.00

HAXTON, Brooks. *Dominion.* 1986. Knopf. 1st ed. sgn. dj. VG $25.00

HAY, Cecile & Mildred. *History of Derby, Vermont.* 1967. Ills. 240 pp. dj. VG $15.00

HAY, Henry. *Encyclopedia of Magic.* 1949. Philadelphia. McKay. VG $6.50

HAY, J. *In Defense of Nature.* 1969. Little, Brown. 1st ed. dj. EX $9.00

HAY, John. *Castilian Days.* 1871. Boston. 1st ed. 414 pp. $20.00

HAY & KAUFFMAN. *The Primal Alliance: Earth & Ocean.* 1971. San Francisco. 144 pp. folio. dj. VG $15.00

HAYCOX, Ernest. *Action by Nights.* Pocketbooks. pb. $3.00

HAYCOX, Ernest. *Bugles in the Afternoon.* 1944. Boston. $6.50

HAYCOX, Ernest. *Bugles in the Afternoon.* Signet. pb. $3.00

HAYCOX, Ernest. *Canyon Passage.* Signet. pb. $3.00

HAYCOX, Ernest. *Canyon Passage.* Pocketbooks. pb. $3.00

HAYCOX, Ernest. *Chaffee of Roaring Horse.* Warner. pb. $3.00

HAYCOX, Ernest. *Return of a Fighter.* Warner. pb. $3.00

HAYCOX, Ernest. *Riders West.* Popular. pb. $3.00

HAYCOX, Ernest. *Rim of the Desert.* Signet. pb. $3.00

HAYCOX, Ernest. *Saddle & Ride.* Signet. pb. $3.00

HAYCOX, Ernest. *Starlight Riders.* Popular. pb. $3.00

HAYCOX, Ernest. *The Silver Desert.* Popular. pb. $3.00

HAYCOX, Ernest. *Trouble Shooter.* Signet. pb. $3.00

HAYCOX, Ernest. *Wild Bunch.* Warner. pb. $3.00

HAYDEN, A. *Chats on English China.* 1920. London. 150 Ills. 4th ed. $12.50

HAYDEN, A. *Chats on English China.* 1904. London. Ills. 287 pp. $22.50

HAYDEN, A. *Chats on Old Prints.* 1906. New York. 110 Ills. EX $25.00

HAYDEN, A. *Furniture Designs of George Hepplewhite.* 1910. London. $30.00

HAYDEN, A. *Furniture Designs of Thomas Chippendale.* 1910. London. $30.00

HAYDEN, A. *Furniture Designs of Thomas Sheraton.* 1910. London. $30.00

HAYDEN, Horace. *Geological Essays.* 1820. Baltimore. 1st ed. VG $150.00

HAYES, Clair W. *The Boy Allies in the Trenches.* 1915. New York. A.L. Burt. 256 pp. $2.50

HAYES, Clair W. *The Boy Allies with Hiag in Flanders.* 1918. New York. A.L. Burt. 221 pp. $2.50

HAYES, Don. *Ice Hockey.* 1972. Dubuque. Wm. C. Brown. 64 pp. SftCvr. $2.00

HAYES, Helen & Loos, Anita. *Twice Over Lightly.* 1972. Harcourt Brace.1st ed. sgns. dj. VG $27.50

HAYES, Helen. *A Gift of Joy.* 1965. Lippincott. 1st ed. sgn. dj. $10.00

HAYES, Hiram. *The Peacemakers.* 1909. Boston. Rcid. 1st ed. VG $20.00

HAYES, I. *The Open Polar Sea.* 1867. New York. Ills. map. pls. VG $20.00

HAYES, John R. *Old Meeting Houses.* 1909. Philadelphia. Ills. G $8.50

HAYES, Johnson J. *The Land of Wilkes.* 1962. Wilkesboro, NC.Wilkes Co. Hist. Soc. sgn. $35.00

HAYES, Joseph. *No Escape.* 1982. Delacorte. proof copy. wrappers. EX $20.00

HAYES, M. Horace. *Veterinary Notes for Horse Owners.* 1968. 16th ed. 637 pp. $15.00

HAYES. *Hunting the Whitetailed Deer.* 1960. Barnes. 256 pp. $3.00

HAYES. *Riding on the Flat & Across Country.* 1891. London. Thacker. 3rd ed. EX $90.00

HAYMAKER, W. *The Founders of Neurology.* 1953. Thomas. Ills. 1st ed. dj. 480 pp. $55.00

HAYNES, B.C. *Meteorology for Pilots.* 1943. Washington. Ills. 246 pp. SftCvr. $4.50

HAYNES, B.D. & E. *The Grizzly Bear, Portraits from Life.* 1966. OK U. Press. Ills. 1st ed. 386 pp. dj. EX $20.00

HAYNES, F. Jay. *The Yellowstone National Park.* 1887. New York. Photogravure Co. 25 pls. $95.00

HAYNES, Fred Emory. *James Baird Weaver. Iowa Biography Series.* 1919. Iowa City. 494 pp. G $15.00

HAYNES, Roy A. *Prohibition Inside Out.* 1923. Garden City. 1st ed. VG $10.00

HAYNES, S. *Land of the Chimera. An Archaeological Excursion.* 1974. New York. Ills. 159 pp. index. $17.50

HAYNES, W. *Sandhills Sketches by W. Haynes.* 1916. New York. inscr. $10.00

HAYS, Arthur Garfield. *Let Freedom Ring.* 1937. New York. 475 pp. $4.00

HAYS, Helen & Funke, Lewis. *A Gift of Joy.* 1965. New York. M. Evans Co. 254 pp. dj. $4.50

HAYS, Rex. *Grand Prix & Sports Cars.* 1964. Arco. dj. EX $25.00

HAYS, Tom. *The Modern Hunting Rifle.* 1964. New York. 304 pp. dj. $3.50

HAYTER, Adrian. *Long Voyage.* 1959. New York. Harper. dj. $10.00

HAYWARD, J.F. *The Art of the Gunmaker.* 1965. 2nd ed. 2 vol set. djs. VG $35.00

HAYWARD, William Willis. *The History of Hanover, New Hampshire, 1764-1889.* 1889. Lowell, MA. Huse & Co. 1070 pp. rebound. $35.00

HAYWARD. *Practical Aeronautics.* 1912. Chicago. G $30.00

HAYWOOD, H.L. & Craig, J.E. *A History of Freemasonry.* London. Allen & Unwin. Ltd. ed. VG $15.00

HAYWOOD. *International Cookbook.* (ca.1920) $20.00

HAZARD, Bertha. *Three Years with the Poets.* 1904. New York. Houghton Mifflin. TB. 247 pp. $3.00

HAZARD, Caroline. *Songs in the Sun.* 1927. Boston. Ills. 1st ed. G $25.00

HAZARD, R.H. *The House on Stilts.* 1910. New York. Dillingham. 1st ed. VG $40.00

HAZEN, R.M. *North American Geology. Early Writings.* 1979. Hutchinson Ross. 356 pp. EX $20.00

HAZEN, William B. *General Hazen's Reply to the Second Comptroller.* 1886. Washington. 1st ed. 87 pp. $75.00

HAZEN. *A Bibliography of Horace Walpole.* 1973. London. Ills. 189 pp. dj. EX $35.00

HAZLITT, William. *Life of Napoleon.* London. Grolier Soc. Ltd. Deluxe ed. $175.00

HEAD, B.V. *Historia Numorum Manual of Greek Numismatics.* 1967. Chicago. dj. $50.00

HEAD, Matthew. *Another Man's Life.* 1953. New York. Simon & Schuster. 1st ed. dj. $25.00

HEAD, T.A. *Campaigns & Battles of 16th Reg't TN Volunteers.* 1961. McMinnville. Womack. 488 pp. VG $25.00

HEADLEY, C.P. *Life of Louis Kossuth.* 1852. Auburn. Derby & Miller. $12.50

HEADLEY, J.T. *Illustrated Life of Washington by J.T. Headley.* 1859. New York. 516 pp. $45.00

HEADLEY, J.T. *Letters from the Backwoods & the Adirondac.* 1850. New York. Taylor. 160 pp. $30.00

HEADLEY, J.T. *The Great Rebellie* 1898. 600 pp. 2 vol set. $16.50

HEADLEY & JOHNSON. *Stanley's Adventures in the Wilds of Africa.* 1890. Edgewood Pub. Ills. VG $7.50

HEADSTROM, R. *The Beetles of America.* 1977. Barnes. Ills. 488 pp. EX $15.00

HEADSTROM, R. *Your Reptile Pet.* 1978. McKay. Ills. 120 pp. dj. EX $12.50

HEAL, A. *London Furniture Makers 1660-1840.* 1953. London. $75.00

HEAL, Edith. *Robin Hood.* 1935. Chicago. Rand McNally. Ills. Content. $15.00

HEALY, Raymond J. *New Tales of Space & Time.* 1951. New York. Holt. dj. EX $25.00

HEANEY, Seamus. *Sweeney Ashtray.* 1984. Farrar. Ltd. 1st Am. ed. sgn. EX $60.00

HEAP, Gwimm Harris. *Central Route to the Pacific.* 1854. Lippincott. 1st ed. sgn. pls. map. VG $250.00

HEARD, Albert F. *The Russian Church & Russian Dissent.* 1887. New York. Harper. 1st ed. EX $45.00

HEARD, H.F. *The Notched Hairpin.* 1949. New York. 1st ed. dj. VG $35.00

HEARN, Lafcadio. *Chita: A Memory of Last Island.* 1889. New York. Harper. 1st ed. VG $90.00

HEARN, Lafcadio. *Gleanings in Buddha-Fields.* 1897. 1st ed. VG $35.00

HEARN, Lafcadio. *Glimpses of Unfamiliar Japan.* 1894. Boston. 1st ed. 1st printing. 2 vol set. $100.00

HEARN, Lafcadio. *Japan: Attempt at Interpretation.* 1904. 1st Am. ed. VG $15.00

HEARN, Lafcadio. *Kwaidan. Stories & Studies of Strange Things.* 1905. London. Ills. 2nd Eng. ed. $30.00

HEARN, Lafcadio. *Out of the East.* 1895. Boston/NY. 1st ed. 1st printing. G $55.00

HEARN, Lafcadio. *Two Years in the French West Indies.* 1890. Harper. Ills. 1st ed. VG $45.00

HEARN, Lafcadio. *Youma.* 1890. New York. Harper. G $60.00

HEARN, M.P. *The Annotated Huckleberry Finn.* New York. 1st ed. dj. EX $17.50

HEARN, M.P. *The Annotated Wizard of Oz.* 1973. New York. Ills. Denslow. 1st ed. dj. EX $15.00

HEARN & WATKIN. *Letters from Raven.* 1907. New York. Brentano. VG $65.00

HEARST, Patricia C. & Moscow. *Every Secret Thing.* 1982. New York. Doubleday. 466 pp. dj. $6.50

HEATH, Edward H. *The Country Kitchen Cook Book.* 1968. New York. Simon & Schuster. 238 pp. $7.50

HEATH, S. Burton. *Yankee Reporter.* 1940. New York. 1st ed. VG $10.00

HEATON, Nell & Simon, Andre. *A Calendar of Food & Wine.* London. Cresta Book. Ills. 270 pp. $5.00

HECHT, Ben. *Book of Miracles.* 1939. New York. 1st ed. 465 pp. dj. VG $30.00

HECHT, Ben. *Charlie.* 1957. New York. Harper. 1st ed. sgn. dj. EX $40.00

HECHT, Ben. *Gargoyles.* 1922. New York. 1st ed. G $20.00

HECHT, Ben. *The Florentine Dagger.* 1923. New York. Ills. Wallace Smith. 1st ed. G $10.00

HECHT, Ben. *A Jew in Love.* New York. Triangle Books. reprint. dj. $3.50

HECHT, Ben. *Gaily, Gaily; Memoirs of a Cub Reporter.* 1963. New York. Doubleday. 227 pp. dj. $4.50

HECHT, Ben. *The Kingdom of Evil.* 1924. New York. Pascal Covici. Ills. 1st ed. $37.50

HEDGECOE, J. *Book of Photography.* 1980. New York. dj. EX $12.50

HEDGES, David & Mayer, Fred. *Horses & Courses.* 1972. Viking Studio Book. dj. VG $15.00

HEDGES, Florence. *The Story of the Catacombs.* 1909. Cincinnati. Ills. pls. EX $20.00

HEDGPETH. *Bettina Portraying Life in Art.* 1978. Northland. $20.00

HEDGSON, R. *Poems.* 1918. 1st ed. dj. VG $75.00

HEDIGER, H. *Man & Animal in the Zoo.* 1969. Delacorte. photos. 303 pp. dj. EX $15.00

HEDIN, S. *Trans-Himalaya/Discoveries & Adventures in Tibet.* 1910-1913. London. 3 vol set. VG $175.00

HEDIN, Sven & Schmid, Toni. *The Eighty-Five Siddhas.* 1958. Stockholm. 171 pp. 18 pls. wrappers. $30.00

HEDIN, Sven. *A Conquest of Tibet.* 1934. New York. VG $35.00

HEDIN, Sven. *Jehol.* 1933. New York. Ills. 2nd ed. G $10.00

HEDIN, Sven. *My Life as an Explorer.* 1925. Garden City. Ills. G $20.00

HEDIN, Sven. *Through Asia.* 1899. 1st ed. 2 vol set. $50.00

HEDIN, Sven. *Trans-Himalaya/Discoveries & Adventures in Tibet.* 1909. Leipzig. Ills. 1st ed. maps. VG $60.00

HEDIN, Sven. *Wandering Lake.* 1940. New York. VG $25.00

HEDRICK, U.P. *A History of Agriculture in the State of New York.* 1933. New York. Hill & Wang. 465 pp. SftCvr. $7.50

HEDRICK, U.P. *The Land of the Crooked Tree.* 1948. New York. 3rd printing. VG $7.50

HEDRICK, U.P. *The Land of the Crooked Tree.* 1948. Oxford U. Press. 1st ed. dj. $18.00

HEDRICK, U.P. *The Pears of New York.* 1921. $40.00

HEDRICK, U.P. *The Small Fruits of New York.* 1925. VG $45.00

HEER, J. *World Events 1866-1966: 1st 100 Years of Nestle.* 1966. Switzerland. VG $20.00

HEFLIN, Alma. *Adventure Was the Compass.* 1942. Boston. Ills. 1st ed. 285 pp. $22.50

HEGAN, Alice. *Mrs. Wiggs of the Cabbage Patch.* 1902. Century. G $7.00

HEIDENRIECH, F.J. *Old Days & Old Ways in East New York.* 1948. 1st ed. sgn. VG $22.50

HEILNER, Van Campen. *Our American Game Birds.* 1941. New York. Ills. 1st ed. map. folio. $55.00

HEILNER, Van Campen. *Salt-Water Fishing.* 1937. Philadelphia. Ills. $25.00

HEILPRIN, Angelo. *The Tower of Pelee.* 1904. Lippincott. VG $37.50

HEIMANN, Robert. *Tobacco & Americans.* 1960. New York. 1st ed. dj. VG $20.00

HEINE, Heinrich. *Doctor Faust.* Ills. 1st Eng. ed. dj. EX $15.00

HEINISCH, O. *Seed Atlas of Most Important Forage Plants/Weeds.* 1955. Berlin. Ills. 122 pls. dj. $65.00

HEINLE. *Figure Studies.* 1954. VG $35.00

HEINLE. *Mexico.* 1945. VG $25.00

HEINLEIN, Robert A. *Assignment in Eternity.* Reading, PA. Fantasy Press. dj. $125.00

HEINLEIN, Robert A. *Farnham's Freehold.* 1964. New York. Putnam. 1st ed. scarce. EX $400.00

HEINLEIN, Robert A. *Friday.* 1982. New York. Holt. 1st ed. dj. VG $30.00

HEINLEIN, Robert A. *Have Space Suit Will Travel.* 1958. Scribner. 1st ed. custom bound. EX $175.00

HEINLEIN, Robert A. *Job, a Comedy of Justice.* 1984. New York. Del Rey. 1st ed. dj. EX $25.00

HEINLEIN, Robert A. *Job, a Comedy of Justice.* Ltd. ed. 1/750. sgn. slipcase. $100.00

HEINLEIN, Robert A. *Starman Jones.* 1953. Scribner. 1st ed. custom bound. EX $125.00

HEINLEIN, Robert A. *Starship Troopers.* 1959. New York. Putnam. 1st ed. G $225.00

HEINLEIN, Robert A. *The Cat Who Walks Through Walls.* Ltd. 1st ed. 1/350. sgn. $175.00

HEINLEIN, Robert A. *The Number of the Beast.* London. 1st ed. $45.00

HEINLEIN, Robert A. *Universe.* 1951. New York. Dell. 1st ed. G $40.00

HEINLEIN, Robert. *Citizen of the Galaxy.* 1957. 1st ed. dj. G $60.00

HEINLEIN, Robert. *Double Star.* 1958. 1st Eng. ed. dj. VG $150.00

HEINLEIN, Robert. *Farmer in the Sky.* 1950. New York. 1st ed. dj. EX $85.00

HEINLEIN, Robert. *I Will Fear No Evil.* 1970. 1st ed. dj. VG $50.00

HEINLEIN, Robert. *Sixth Column.* 1949. New York. 1st ed. dj. VG $125.00

HEINLEIN, Robert. *Space Cadet.* 1948. 2nd printing. dj. VG $20.00

HEINLEIN, Robert. *The Rolling Stones.* 1952. New York. dj. EX $20.00

HEINLEIN, Robert. *The Unpleasant Profession of Jonathan Hoag.* 1959. Hicksville. Gnome Press. 1st ed. dj. EX $75.00

HEINLEIN, Robert. *Time Enough for Love.* 1973. 1st ed. VG $40.00

HEINLEIN, Robert. *Waldo & Magic, Inc.* 1950. Garden City. 1st ed. dj. EX $40.00

HEINLEIN. *Sizieme Colone.* Paris. wrappers. VG $50.00

HEINTZELMAN, D.S. *Manual for Bird Watching in the Americas.* 1979. Universe. Ills. 254 pp. dj. EX $6.00

HEISENBERG, Werner. *The Physcial Principles of Quantum Theory.* 1930. Chicago. 1st ed. $75.00

HEISENFELT, Katheryn. *Betty Grable & the House of Cobwebs.* 1947. Racine, WI. Whitman. 250 pp. dj. $3.00

HEISENFELT, Katheryn. *Betty Grable & the House with the Iron Shutters.* 1943. Whitman. Ills. dj. EX $6.50

HEISENFELT, Katheryn. *Judy Garland & the Hoodoo Costume.* 1945. Racine, WI. Whitman. 248 pp. $3.00

HEISER, Victor. *An American Doctor's Odyssey.* 1937. Norton. $5.50

HEISER, Victor. *An American Doctor's Odyssey.* 1936. New York. Norton. 1st ed. 544 pp. dj. VG $32.50

HEITNER, Joseph. *Elements of Automotive Mechanics.* 1943. New York. Van Nostrand. TB. 395 pp. $3.50

HEIZER, R.F. & Whipple, M.A. *California Indians.* 1971. CA U. Press. 2nd revised ed. dj. VG $12.50

HELBURN, Theresa. *Enter the Hero.* 1918. New York. wrappers. EX $40.00

HELEY, J. Evetts. *Charles Goodnight: Cowman & Plainsman.* OK Press. 485 pp. dj. VG $20.00

HELINE, Corinne D. *Healing & Regeneration Through Music.* 1944. 3rd ed. sgn. 37 pp. VG $35.00

HELLER, Joseph & Vogel, Speed. *No Laughing Matter.* 1986. Putnam. 1st ed. sgns. dj. VG $40.00

HELLER, Joseph. *God Knows.* 1984. Knopf. Ltd. 1st ed. 1/350. sgn. dj. $50.00

HELLER, Joseph. *Good as Gold.* 1979. 1st ed. sgn. dj. EX $25.00

HELLER, Joseph. *We Bombed in New Haven.* 1968. Knopf. 1st ed. dj. VG $30.00

HELLER, Joseph. *We Bombed in New Haven.* 1968. presentation copy. sgn. VG $65.00

HELLMAN, G.T. *Mrs. D's Parties.* 1st ed. dj. EX $10.00

HELLMAN, Lillian. *An Unfinished Woman.* 1969. Little, Brown. 1st ed. $27.50

HELLMAN, Lillian. *Pentimento.* 1973. Little, Brown. 1st ed. dj. VG $20.00

HELLMAN, Lillian. *Scoundrel Time.* 1976. Little, Brown. 1st ed. dj. VG $15.00

HELLMAN, P. *Auschwitz Album.* 1981. New York. Random House. Ills. dj. EX $25.00

HELLMICH, W. *Reptiles & Amphibians of Europe.* 1962. London. Blanford. Ills. 1st Eng. ed. G $12.50

HELLMUTH, J. *A Wolf in the Family.* 1964. New Am. Lib. Ills. 1st printing. 186 pp. EX $9.00

HELM, J. *Pioneers of American Anthropology.* 1966. Washington. photos. dj. VG $12.50

HELM, T. *Dangerous Sea Creatures.* 1976. Funk Wagnalls. Ills. 278 pp. dj. EX $10.00

HELM, T. *Shark, Unpredictable Killer of the Sea.* 1965. Dodd Mead. Ills. 260 pp. EX $12.50

HELME, Eleanor E. *Four-Footed Helpers.* New York. Dodge. Ills. Briggs. $25.00

HELMERICKS, C. *Hunting in North America.* 1959. Stackpole. Ills. VG $7.50

HELMERICKS, C. & H. *We Live in Alaska.* 1949. VG $10.00

HELMERICKS, C. & H. *We Live in the Arctic.* 1947. Boston. Little, Brown. 329 pp. $3.50

HELPER, Hinton Rowan. *The Impending Crisis of the South: How to Meet It.* 1860. New York. 420 pp. $10.00

HELPRIN, Mark. *Ellis Island & Other Stories.* 1981. Delacorte. 1st ed. dj. VG $25.00

HELPRIN, Mark. *Refiner's Fire.* 1977. Knopf. 1st ed. dj. VG $30.00

HELPRIN, Mark. *Winter's Tale.* 1983. New York. Harcourt. 1st ed. dj. VG $25.00

HEMANS & WORDSWORTH. *Poems by Felicia Hemans & William Wadsworth.* 1875. New York. $40.00

HEMENWAY, Abby Maria. *Poets & Poetry of Vermont.* 1858. Rutland. Tuttle. 1st ed. $20.00

HEMENWAY, Robert. *The Girl Who Sang with the Beatles.* 1970. New York. Knopf. 1st ed. dj. VG $25.00

HEMING, J. *Red Gold, the Conquest of the Brazilian Indians.* 1978. Harvard. Ills. 677 pp. dj. EX $15.00

HEMINGWAY, Amanda. *Pzyche.* 1983. Arbor House. 1st ed. dj. VG $15.00

HEMINGWAY, Ernest. *A Farewell to Arms.* 1930. Tauchnitz. 1st ed. wrappers. $25.00

HEMINGWAY, Ernest. *A Farewell to Arms.* 1929. 4th printing. VG $25.00

HEMINGWAY, Ernest. *A Farewell to Arms.* 1948. Ills. Rasmusson. 1st ed. boxed. dj. $75.00

HEMINGWAY, Ernest. *A Moveable Feast.* 1964. Scribner. 1st ed. dj. VG $55.00

HEMINGWAY, Ernest. *Across the River into the Trees.* 1950. Scribner. 1st ed. dj. VG $35.00

HEMINGWAY, Ernest. *Collected Poems.* 1960. pirated ed. wrappers. G $20.00

HEMINGWAY, Ernest. *For Whom the Bell Tolls.* 1941. London. 1st Eng. ed. dj. $145.00

HEMINGWAY, Ernest. *For Whom the Bell Tolls.* 1940. Scribner. 1st ed. 2nd issue dj. VG $100.00

HEMINGWAY, Ernest. *For Whom the Bell Tolls.* 1940. Scribner. 1st ed. 1st issue dj. VG $125.00

HEMINGWAY, Ernest. *In Our Time.* 1926. 1st Eng. ed. dj. $825.00

HEMINGWAY, Ernest. *Islands in the Stream.* 1970. New York. Scribner. 1st ed. dj. VG $30.00

HEMINGWAY, Ernest. *Islands in the Stream.* 1970. Collins. 1st English ed. dj. VG $30.00

HEMINGWAY, Ernest. *Men at War/The Best War Stories of All Time.* 1942. New York. Crown. 1072 pp. VG $20.00

HEMINGWAY, Ernest. *Men Without Women.* 1927. New York. Scribner. 1st ed. dj. VG $40.00

HEMINGWAY, Ernest. *Men Without Women.* 1927. New York. 1st ed. 1st issue. G $35.00

HEMINGWAY, Ernest. *Men Without Women.* 1946. Ills. 1st ed. $50.00

HEMINGWAY, Ernest. *Old Man & the Sea.* 1984. New York. Scribner. Ills. EX $40.00

HEMINGWAY, Ernest. *Old Man & the Sea.* 1952. New York. 1st ed. 140 pp. dj. VG $75.00

HEMINGWAY, Ernest. *Old Man & the Sea.* 1952. London. 1st Eng. ed. dj. VG $35.00

HEMINGWAY, Ernest. *The Hemingway Reader.* 1953. New York. Scribner. 652 pp. VG $4.00

HEMINGWAY, Ernest. *The Spanish War.* 1935. 1st ed. wrappers. VG $85.00

HEMINGWAY, Ernest. *The Wild Years.* 1962. Dell. VG $10.00

HEMINGWAY, Ernest. *Winner Take Nothing.* 1933. Scribner. dj. VG $85.00

HEMMENWAY, Moses. *A Discourse to Children.* 1793. Boston. 2nd ed. 2 pls. wrappers. EX $100.00

HEMMING, J. *The Conquest of the Incas.* 1970. Harcourt Brace.Ills. 1st Am. ed. dj. EX $15.00

HEMPEL, Amy. *Reasons to Live.* 1985. Knopf. 1st ed. dj. VG $12.50

HEMRICKS, C. *Down the Wild River North.* 1968. Little, Brown. Ills. 1st ed. 501 pp. VG $10.00

HENDERSON, Daniel. *Golden Bees/Story of Betsy Patterson & Bonapartes.*1928. New York. 330 pp. dj. $10.00

HENDERSON, Daniel. *Yankee Ships in China Seas.* 1946. New York. 1st ed. $15.00

HENDERSON, G. *The Civil War, a Soldiers View.* 1958. Chicago. 1st ed. G. $15.00

HENDERSON, J. & Craig, E.L. *Economic Mammalogy.* 1932. Thomas. 397 pp. index. dj. VG $22.50

HENDERSON, James. *Firearms: Collecting for Amateurs.* 1966. Muller. 143 pp. dj. VG $6.50

HENDERSON, Mrs. M.F. *Practical Cooking & Dinner Giving.* 1881. New York. Harper. Ills. 376 pp. $25.00

HENDERSON, R.W. *Ball, Bat, & Bishop.* 1947. New York. 1st ed. VG $22.00

HENDERSON, Randall. *On Desert Trails.* 1961. Westernlore. 1st ed. dj. EX $15.00

HENDERSON. *Failure of a Mission, Berlin, 1937-1939.* 1940. New York. Putnam. 334 pp. EX $8.50

HENDRICK, B. *Lincoln's War Cabinet.* 1946. 1st ed. dj. VG $22.50

HENDRICK, B. *Statesmen of the Lost Cause.* 1939. Boston. 1st ed. sgn. dj. VG $25.00

HENDRICKS, Louie. *No Rules or Guidelines.* 1972. OK U. Press. Ills. sgn. 147 pp. VG $3.00

HENDRYX. *Gun Brand.* 1917. Ills. G $7.00

HENDY. *Art Treasures of National Gallery.* 1955. London. Abrams. 1st ed. dj. slipcase. $50.00

HENKIN, Harmon. *Fly Tackle, Guide to Tools of the Trade.* 1976. Ills. J. Johnson. 240 pp. $5.50

HENKLE, M.M. *The Life of Henry Bidleman Bascom.* 1854. Louisville. Morton & Griswold. 408 pp. $20.00

HENLEY, Beth. *Crimes of the Heart.* 1982. Viking. proof copy. sgn. wrappers. VG $55.00

HENLEY, W.E. *Poems.* 1898. London. inscr. VG $40.00

HENNESSY, Dorothy. *Civil War. The Years Asunder.* 1978. Ills. 208 pp. EX $7.50

HENRETTA, J. *Kane & the Upper Allegheny.* 1929. Ltd. ed. 1/600. EX $35.00

HENRI, Robert. *The Art Spirit.* 1930. Lippincott. dj. EX $20.00

HENRY, Frederick A. *Captain Henry of Geauga.* 1942. Cleveland. Ills. 1st ed. 735 pp. VG $55.00

HENRY, M. & Dennis, W. *Born to Trot.* 1950. 1st ed. VG $10.00

HENRY, M. & Dennis, W. *Justin Morgan Had a Horse.* 1954. sgns. dj. EX $15.00

HENRY, M. & Dennis, W. *King of Wind.* 1963. VG $9.00

HENRY, M. & Dennis, W. *Sea Star Orphan Chincoteague.* 1951. dj. VG $10.00

HENRY, M. & Dennis, W. *Stormy Misty's Foal.* 1963. 1st ed. sgns. dj. EX $15.00

HENRY, M. & Dennis, W. *Wagging Tails Album of Dogs.* 1955. 1st ed. sgns. dj. EX $15.00

HENRY, M. & Ward, Lynd. *Guadenzia, Pride of Palio.* 1960. 1st ed. sgns. dj. EX $20.00

HENRY, Marguerite. *Brighty of the Grand Canyon.* 1953. Chicago. Ills. Wesley Dennis. 1st ed. $15.00

HENRY, Marguerite. *Cinnabar, One O'Clock Fox.* 1956. New York. Ills. Dennis. 1st ed. 154 pp. $12.50

HENRY, Marguerite. *Geraldine Belinda.* 1942. New York. Ills. Gladys Rourke Blackwood. $12.50

HENRY, Marguerite. *Misty of Chincoteague.* 1947. Chicago. Rand McNally. dj. $10.50

HENRY, O. *Heart of the West.* 1913. New York. Doubleday Page. 313 pp. $4.00

HENRY, O. *The Hiding of Black Bill.* New York. (ca. 1913). rare. VG $75.00

HENRY, O. *The Voice of the City & Other Stories.* 1935. New York. Ltd. Ed. Club. Ills. Gross. VG $55.00

HENRY, O. *Waifs & Strays.* 1917. Ltd. ed. 1/200. G $20.00

HENRY, Robert Selph. *First with the Most Forrest.* 1969. Jackson. 1st ed. dj. EX $25.00

HENRY, Robert Selph. *The Story of the Confederacy.* 1936. 514 pp. VG $12.50

HENRY, Will. *Alias Butch Cassidy.* New York. 1st printing. dj. VG $15.00

HENRY, Will. *San Juan Hill.* 1962. New York. 276 pp. $10.00

HENRY. *Travels & Adventures in Canada & Indian Territory.*1809. New York. ex-lib. $275.00

HENSHALL, James. *Bass, Pike, Perch & Others.* 1903. Ills. 1st ed. VG $42.50

HENSLEE, Helen. *Pretty Redwing.* 1983. Holt. advance copy. dj. VG $15.00

HENTY, G.A. *A Final Reckoning.* London. no date. Ills. dj. VG $15.00

HENTY, G.A. *For Name & Fame.* New York. A.L. Burt. 385 pp. $3.50

HENTY, G.A. *Held Fast for England.* 1980. London. 1st ed. dj. VG $15.00

HENTY, G.A. *St. George for England.* New York. A.L. Burt. no date. 391 pp. $3.50

HENTY, G.A. *The Lion of the North.* Chicago. no date. 250 pp. $2.50

HENTY, G.A. *The Young Carthaginian.* New York. A.L. Burt. no date. 459 pp. $3.00

HENTY, G.A. *True to the Old Flag.* New York. (ca.1900) $3.50

HENTY, G.A. *Under Drake's Flag.* New York. no date. 352 pp. $3.00

HENTY, G.A. *With Clive in India.* 1897. Ills. 398 pp. VG $4.50

HENTY, G.A. *With Lee in Virginia.* 1890. London. 1st ed. EX $75.00

HENTY, G.A. *With the British Legion. Story of Carlist Wars.* 1902. Scribner. 1st Am. ed. VG $12.50

HEPBURN, James. *The Author's Empty Purse & Rise of Literary Agent.*1968. London. 1st ed. dj. VG $15.00

HEPNER, C.W. *Kurozumi Sect of Shinto.* 1935. Tokyo. Ills. $40.00

HEPWORTH. *Victorian & Edwardian Norfolk from Old Photos.* 1972. dj. EX $25.00

HERBERT, A.P. *The Water Gypsies.* 1930. Garden City. VG $6.00

HERBERT, F. *Nebula Winners Fifteen.* 1981. Harper & Row. 1st ed. dj. EX $10.00

HERBERT, F. *The White Plague.* 1982. New York. proof copy. $135.00

HERBERT, Frank & Brian. *Man of Two Worlds.* 1986. proof copy. VG $50.00

HERBERT, Frank & Ransom, Bill.*The Lazarus Effect.* 1983. Putnam. 1st ed. dj. VG $15.00

HERBERT, Frank. *Chapterhouse: Dune.* 1985. New York. Ltd. ed. 1/750. sgn. slipcase. $80.00

HERBERT, Frank. *Dosadi Experiment.* 1977. Berkley. dj. VG $20.00

HERBERT, Frank. *Dune Messiah.* 1969. New York. 1st ed. dj. EX $90.00

HERBERT, Frank. *God Emperor of Dune.* 1981. New York. Ltd. 1st ed. sgn. slipcase. VG $85.00

HERBERT, Frank. *God Emperor of Dune.* 1981. New York. Putnam. 1st trade ed. dj. EX $25.00

HERBERT, Frank. *Heretics of Dune.* 1984. Putnam. Ltd. 1st ed. sgn. slipcase. VG $75.00

HERBERT, Frank. *The Dragon in the Sea.* 1956. Doubleday. 1st ed. dj. $125.00

HERBERT, Frank. *The White Plague.* 1982. New York. Putnam. 1st ed. dj. EX $25.00

HERBERT, Frank. *The White Plague.* 1982. New York. 1st ed. review copy. dj. EX $20.00

HERBERT, George. *History of the Civil War.* 1885. New York. VG $20.00

HERBERT, George. *The Temple & Private Ejaculations.* 1927. London. Nonesuch Press. Ltd. ed. VG $175.00

HERBERT, H. *Herbert's Field Sports of the United States.* 1849. New York. 1st ed. 1st issue. $37.00

HERBERT, Henry William. *Frank Forester's Field Sports of U.S. & Provinces.* 1849. Stringer & Townsend. 2 vol set. $150.00

HERBERT, Henry William. *Frank Forester's Horse & Horsemanship of U.S.* 1857. New York. Ills. 1st ed. 2 vol set. EX $300.00

HERBERT, J. *Oriental Rugs.* 1978. New York. $18.00

HERBERT, James. *Moon.* London. 1st ed. sgn. $26.00

HERBERT, James. *The Magic Cottage.* London. 1st ed. sgn. $26.00

HERBERT, M. *The Snow People.* 1973. Putnam. Ills. 277 pp. dj. VG $10.00

HERBERT, Thomas. *Herbert's Memoirs of Charles I.* 1839. London. rebound. G $100.00

HERBERT. *Historical Catalogue of Printed Bibles.* 1968. New York. 1st ed. VG $25.00

HERBERT. *She-Shanties.* 1926. London. 1st ed. $13.00

HERCI. *Folk Toys, Les Jouets Populaires.* 1951. Prague. Eng text. 175 plates. $38.00

HERCULES, Frank. *Where the Hummingbird Flies.* 1st ed. dj. EX $7.50

HERD, Harold. *Seven Editors.* 1955. London. Allen & Unwin. 1st ed. 126 pp. $25.00

HEREFORD, Robert. *Old Man River.* 1942. Idaho. Caxton. Ills. inscr. $35.00

HERGESHEIMER, Joseph. *Quiet Cities.* 1928. $2.00

HERGESHEIMER, Joseph. *The Three Black Pennys.* 1923. New York. $5.50

HERGESHEIMER, Joseph. *Party Dress.* 1930. New York. 1st ed. sgn. dj. VG $50.00

HERING. *Memory.* 1913. Open Court Pub. 4th ed. EX $25.00

HERKOLTS, G.A.C. *The Birds of Trinidad & Tobago.* 1961. London. Collins. Ills. 1st ed. 287 pp. $20.00

HERLIHY, James Leo. *Midnight Cowboy.* 1965. New York. 1st ed. dj. EX $35.00

HERLIHY, James Leo. *The Season of the Witch.* 1971. New York. Simon & Schuster. 1st ed. dj. $20.00

HERMAN. *Work, Youth, & Unemployment.* 1968. dj. $17.50

HERMAN, Zvi. *Peoples, Seas, & Ships.* 1967. New York. Ills. 1st Am.. ed. fld pls. $17.50

HERNDON, B. *Berdorf's on the Plaza.* 1956. New York. 1st ed. dj. VG $20.00

HERNDON, Booton. *The Sweetest Music this Side of Heaven.* 1964. McGraw Hill. intro Guy Lombardo. 1st ed. $10.00

HERNDON, G.M. *William Tatham & Culture of Tobacco.* 1969. Miami U. Press. Ills. 506 pp. dj. EX $20.00

HERNDON, W.L. & Gibbon. *Exploration of the Valley of the Amazon.* 1854. Washington. Ills. G $45.00

HERNDON, William. *Herndon's Lincoln.* 1st ed. 3 vol set. rebound. VG $65.00

HERON & ALLEN. *Violin Making as It Was & Is.* 1901. Boston. Ills. G $65.00

HERON & ALLEN. *Violin Making as It Was & Is.* 1885. New York. $45.00

HERR, Michael. *Dispatches.* 1977. New York. Knopf. 1st ed. dj. EX $50.00

HERRESHOFF, L. Francis. *Capt. Nat Herreshoff.* 1953. New York. Sheridan House. 349 pp. VG $5.00

HERRICK, Christine T. *The Chafing Dish Supper.* 1895. G $10.00

HERRICK, Robert. *The Master of the Inn.* 1908. Scribner. 1st ed. dj. VG $12.50

HERRICK, Robert. *The Poetical Works of Robert Herrick.* 1908. London. Bell. 2 vol set. VG $30.00

HERRICK, Robert. *The Poetical Works of Robert Herrick.* 1928. London. Cresset Press. 4 vol set. EX $125.00

HERRING, Robert. *Hub.* 1981. Viking. 1st ed. sgn. dj. VG $25.00

HERRINGMAN, H. *The Works of Abraham Cowley.* 1700. G $100.00

HERRINGTON, Arthur. *The Chrysanthemum, Its Culture for Growers.* 1914. New York. Ills. 160 pp. EX $5.50

HERRIOT, James. *The Lord God Made Them All.* 1981. $10.00

HERRIOTT, F.I. *Iowa & Abraham Lincoln, 1856-1860.* Ames, IA. reprint. 189 pp. $30.00

HERRIOTT, William B. *Redwood County, MN: Its Advantages to Settlers.* 1879. St.Paul. Ills. 1st ed. 2 fld maps. $125.00

HERRLINGER, Robert. *History of Medical Illustration.* 1970. New York. boxed. VG $50.00

HERRMANN, Eva. *On Parade.* 1929. New York. Ills. 1st ed. dj. VG $25.00

HERSCHBERGER, Ruth. *A Way of Happening.* 1948. Pelligrini. 1st ed. dj. VG $7.50

HERSEY, Jean. *Care Free Gardening.* 1961. Princeton. Ills. 191 pp. VG $10.00

HERSEY, Jean. *The Shape of a Year.* 1967. New York. 243 pp. dj. EX $10.00

HERSEY, John. *A Bell for Adano.* 1945. Dial Press. $3.00

HERSEY, John. *Aspects of the Presidency.* 1980. Ticknor & Fields. 1st ed. dj. $15.00

HERSEY, John. *Here To Stay.* 1963. Knopf. 1st ed. dj. VG $20.00

HERSEY, John. *Hiroshima.* 1946. New York. Knopf. 118 pp. EX $4.00

HERSEY, John. *Letter to the Alumni.* 1970. Knopf. 1st ed. dj. VG $20.00

HERSEY, John. *Nothing So Strange.* 1947. Boston. 308 pp. $3.50

HERSEY, John. *The Algiers Motel Incident.* 1968. Knopf. 1st ed. dj. VG $20.00

HERSEY, John. *The Call.* 1985. Knopf. 1st trade ed. dj. VG $20.00

HERSEY, John. *The Child Buyer.* 1960. New York. Knopf. 258 pp. dj. VG $3.50

HERSEY, John. *The War Lover.* 1959. Knopf. 1st ed. dj. VG $10.00

HERSEY, John. *Too Far to Walk.* 1966. Knopf. 1st ed. dj. EX $20.00

HERSEY, John. *Under the Eye of the Storm.* 1967. Knopf. 1st ed. dj. VG $20.00

HERSEY, John. *White Lotus.* 1965. New York. Knopf. 1st ed. 683 pp. dj. VG $10.00

HERSH, B. *The Mellon Family.* 1978. Ills. $7.50

HERST, Herman. *Nassau Street.* 1960. Duell Sloan. 1st ed. 305 pp. index. dj. VG $20.00

HERTZ, L. *Handbook of Old American Toys.* 1947. Hartford. 1st ed. VG $22.50

HERTZ, L. *Making Your Model Railroad.* 1954. New York. $20.00

HERTZ, L. *New Roads to Adventure in Model Railroading.* 1952. $40.00

HERTZBERG, H.T.E. *Anthropometric Survey of Turkey, Greece & Italy.* 1963. New York. Macmillan. 1st ed. 302 pp. $15.00

HERTZLER, A.E. *Surgical Operations with Local Anesthesia.* 1916. New York. Ills. 2nd ed. 318 pp. VG $55.00

HERTZLER, A.E. *The Horse & Buggy Doctor.* 1938. New York. Harper. 322 pp. $5.00

HERTZOG. *Old Town Albuquerque.* 1964. Press of Territorian. SftCvr. $20.00

HERVEY, H. *Caravans by Night.* 1922. New York. Century. 1st ed. VG $10.00

HERVEY, Harry. *Ethan Quest His Saga.* 1925. New York. 334 pp. $7.50

HERVEY, J. *American Trotter.* 1947. New York. VG $15.00

HERVEY, J. *Meditations.* 1824. New York. 2 vols in 1. VG $40.00

HERVEY. *Sea Mosses.* 1882. Boston. Ills. inscr. $30.00

HERZOG, Arthur. *Earthsound.* 1975. Simon & Schuster. 1st ed. dj. $8.00

HERZOG, M.I. *The Yiddish Language in Northern Poland.* 1965. Bloomington. 350 pp. wrappers. $7.50

HERZOG & SERRAILLIER. *The Alps I Love.* 1962. New York. dj. VG $20.00

HESLER, L.R. & Smith, A.H. *North American Hygrophorus.* 1963. TN U. Press. 126 photos. 416 pp. EX $20.00

HESS, William N. *Thunderbolt at War.* 1976. New York. Doubleday. Book Club ed. dj. $8.00

HESSE, Herman C. *Engineering Tools & Processes.* 1941. New York. Van Nostrand. 627 pp. $3.50

HESSE, Hermann. *Autobiographical Writings.* 1972. New York. 1st Am. ed. 291 pp. dj. $16.00

HESSE, Hermann. *If the War Goes On.* 1971. Farrar. 1st Am. ed. dj. VG $25.00

HESSE, Hermann. *Journey to East.* 1st English ed. dj. VG $45.00

HESSE, Hermann. *Pictor's Metamorphoses.* 1982. Farrar. Ills. advance copy. dj. VG $25.00

HESSE, Hermann. *Rosshalde.* 1970. New York. 1st Am. ed. 213 pp. dj. $17.00

HESSE, Hermann. *Wandering.* 1972. Farrar. advance copy. dj. VG $25.00

HESTER, H.I. *Jewell Is Her Name. History of Jewell College.* 1967. Liberty, MO. Quality Press. Ills. 260 pp. $10.00

HETH, Edward H. *The Country Kitchen Cookbook.* 1968. New York. Simon & Schuster. 238 pp. $4.00

HETH, Edward H. *The Country Kitchen Cookbook.* 1968. New York. Farrar. 238 pp. $7.50

HEUSER, Ken. *The Whitetail Deer Guide.* 1972. New York. 1st ed. dj. $7.50

HEUSSER, Albert H. *George Washington's Map Maker, Robert Erskine.* 1966. New Brunswick. 268 pp. dj. $10.00

HEUVELMANS, Bernard. *In the Wake of Sea Serpents.* 1968. New York. Ills. 1st U.S. ed. maps. $25.00

HEUVELMANS, Bernard. *On the Track of Unknown Animals.* 1958. London. Hart Davis. Ills. 558 pp. VG $30.00

HEWETT, Edgar & Dutton, B. *The Pueblo Indian World.* 1945. Albuquerque. Ills. 1st ed. 176 pp. $35.00

HEWETT, Edgar & Mausy, Wayne. *Landmarks of New Mexico.* 1953. U. of NM Press.Ills. 3rd ed. 194 pp. dj. VG $35.00

HEWETT, Waterman T. *Cornell University. A History Vol. II.* 1905. New York. 417 pp. $7.50

HEWITT, C.G. *The Conservation of Wild Life in Canada.* 1921. Scribner. Ills. 344 pp. index. VG $17.50

HEWITT, Emma Churchman. *Karo Cook Book.* 1909. New York. 47 pp. wrappers. $8.50

HEWITT, William. *Visits to Remarkable Places.* 1854. Philadelphia. 3rd ed. G $25.00

HEWLETT, Maurice. *A Masque of Dead Florentines.* 1895. London. 1st ed. slipcase. VG $42.50

HEWSHALL, Jason A. *Camping & Cruising in Florida.* 1888. Cincinnati. gilt decor binding. VG $50.00

HEXAMER, F.M. *Asparagus.* 1918. New York. Ills. foxed. VG $10.00

HEYEN, William. *Depth of Field.* 1970. L.S.U. Press. 1st trade ed. inscr. dj. VG $50.00

HEYEN, William. *Erika: Poems of the Holocaust.* 1984. Vanguard. 1st ed. wrappers. EX $6.00

HEYEN, William. *Lord Dragonfly.* 1978. Scrimshaw. Ltd. ed. 1/450. sgn. VG $20.00

HEYEN, William. *The Trains.* 1981. Metacom. Ltd. ed. wrappers. EX $25.00

HEYEN, William. *William Heyen: Poet & Collector. An Exhibition.* 1982. no place. Ltd. ed. sgn. inscr. wrappers. $35.00

HEYER, Joseph. *The Herb Doctor & Medicine Man.* (ca.1920) Ills. 90 pp. $7.00

HEYERDAHL, T. *Aku-Aku, Secrets of Easter Island.* 1958. Rand McNally. Ills. map. 384 pp. VG $10.00

HEYERDAHL, T. *Fatu-Hiva.* 1974. 1st ed. dj. G $8.00

HEYERDAHL, T. *Kon-Tiki, Across the Pacific by Raft.* 1950. Rand McNally. photos. map. 304 pp. G $4.00

HEYERDAHL, T. *The Kon-Tiki Expedition.* 1950. Rand McNally. Ills. Palmquist. 1st Eng. ed. $12.50

HEYLYN, Peter. *Mikrokosmos: Description of the Great World.* 1631. Oxford. $65.00

HEYMAN, C.D. *The Last Power.* 1976. New York. 1st ed. $8.00

HEYMAN, K. *Willie.* 1963. New York. 1st ed. dj. EX $10.00

HEYMAN & CARPENTER. *They Became What They Beheld.* 1970. dj. EX $9.00

HEYWARD, Du Bose. *Porgy.* 1925. New York. 1st ed. dj. VG $20.00

HIBBARD, Addison. *The Lyric South. Anthology of Recent Poetry.* 1928. New York. 279 pp. VG $20.00

HIBBEN, F. *Hunting American Bears.* 1950. dj. EX $37.50

HIBBERT, Christopher. *Wolfe at Quebec.* 1959. Cleveland, OH. Ills. maps. 195 pp. dj. $12.00

HIBBETT, H. *The Floating World in Japanese Fiction.* 1959. Oxford U. Pr. Ills. dj. VG $10.00

HIBBON, Sheila. *American Regional Cookery.* 1963. Hearthside Pr. Book Club Ed. Ills. 318 pp. $6.50

HIBBON, Sheila. *American Regional Cookery.* 1946. Boston. Little, Brown. 354 pp. $7.50

HIBBS, R. *Straw Sculpture.* 1974. New York. EX $15.00

HICHENS, Robert. *The Garden of Allah.* 1904. New York. Grosset & Dunlap. 482 pp. $3.50

HICHENS, Robert. *The Near East.* 1913. New York. Ills. Guerin. 1st ed. 268 pp. $22.50

HICKEY. *Light of Other Days: Irish Life at Turn of Cent.* 1975. Godine. photos. $12.00

HICKMAN. *George Fiske, Yosemite Photographer.* 1980. 1st ed. photos. VG $20.00

HICKS, Granville. *Part of the Truth.* 1965. New York. 314 pp. $12.50

HICKS, Granville. *Proletarian Literature in the United States.* 1935. New York. 1st ed. dj. EX $50.00

HICKS, Wanda. *Seasons of Jessie Stuart.* 1976. dj. VG $20.00

HIEATT, Constance, retold by. *The Castle of Ladies.* 1973. New York. Ills. Laliberte. 1st printing. $10.00

HIEBERT, P.C. & Miller, O.O. *Feeding the Hungry-Russia Famine 1919-1925.* 1929. Scottsdale, PA. photos. 465 pp. EX $6.50

HIGBE, Kirby. *High Hard One.* 1967. 1st ed. dj. VG $7.50

HIGBY, Mary Jane. *Tune in Tomorrow.* 1968. G $4.00

HIGGINS, Alice. *Runaway Rhymes.* 1942. New York. Ills. Tom Lamb. $15.00

HIGGINS, Colin. *Harold & Maude.* 1971. Lippincott. 1st ed. dj. $15.00

HIGGINS, George V. *Style Verses Substance.* 1984. New York. Macmillan. 250 pp. $5.00

HIGGINS, George V. *The Judgement of Deke Hunter.* 1979. Boston. uncorrected proof. wrappers. $15.00

HIGGINS, George V. *The Patriot Game.* 1982. Knopf. 1st ed. dj. VG $12.50

HIGGINSON, E. *Alaska, the Greatest Country.* 1919. Macmillan. Ills. fld map. 583 pp. index. $17.50

HIGGINSON, Thomas W. *Army Life in a Black Regiment.* 1960. dj. VG $25.00

HIGGINSON, Thomas W. *The Monarch of Dreams.* 1887. Boston. Lee & Shepard. 1st ed. VG $45.00

HIGGINSON, Thomas W. *Women & Men.* 1888. New York. 326 pp. $15.00

HIGGINSON, Thomas. *Tales of the Enchanted Islands of the Atlantic.* 1898. New York. Ills. 259 pp. $5.00

HIGHAM, Charles. *Charles Laughton.* 1976. dj. $5.00

HIGHAM, Charles. *The Adventures of Conan Doyle.* 1976. New York. 1st ed. dj. VG $20.00

HIGHAM, R. & Siddal, A. *Flying Combat Aircraft of the USAAF-USAF.* 1975. Ames, IA. Ills. 1st ed. 154 pp. $12.50

HIGHSMITH, Patricia. *Little Tales of Misogyny.* 1977. London. Heinemann. 1st ed. dj. EX $15.00

HIGHSMITH, Patricia. *People Who Knock on the Door.* 1983. New York. Penzler. proof copy. wrappers. $15.00

HIGHSMITH, Patricia. *Ripley Underground.* 1970. New York. Doubleday. 1st ed. dj. EX $20.00

HIGHSMITH, Patricia. *The Boy Who Followed Ripley.* 1980. New York. Lippincott Crowell. 1st ed. EX $25.00

HIGHSMITH, Patricia. *The Tremor of Forgery.* 1969. London. Heinemann. 1st Eng. ed. dj. EX $20.00

HIGHSMITH, Patricia. *Those Who Walk Away.* 1967. New York. Doubleday. 1st ed. dj. EX $20.00

HIGHTOWER. *Pheasant Hunting.* 1946. Knopf. Ills. 1st ed. VG $20.00

HIGHWATER, Jamake. *The Sweet Grass Lives On.* 1980. Lippincott. Ills. 1st ed. dj. VG $25.00

HIGHWATER. *Song from the Earth. American Indian Painting.* 1976. New York. Graphic Society. 1st ed. dj. $30.00

HILBERT, David. *Foundations of Geometry.* 1910. Open Court Pub. dj. EX $30.00

HILBERT & COHN-VOSSEN. *Geometry & the Imagination.* 1952. $12.50

HILDEBRAND, Arthur Sturges. *Blue Water.* 1923. Harcourt Brace. 320 pp. $8.50

HILDEBRAND, Samuel S. *Autobiography of Hildebrand, Missouri Bushwacker.* 1870. State Times. 1st ed. rebound. VG $80.00

HILDRETH, James. *Dragoon Campaigns to Rocky Mountains, by Dragoon.* 1836. New York. 1st ed. ex-lib. $300.00

HILDRETH. *Harriet Beecher Stowe, a Bibliography.* 1976. 257 pp. dj. EX $17.50

HILL, A.F. *The White Rocks; or, The Robbers' Den.* 1900. Morgantown, WV. Ills. Swisher/Maxwell. 1st ed. $22.50

HILL, A.G. *Forty Years of Gardening.* 1938. New York. Ills. some foxing. VG $15.00

HILL, Alice Polk. *Tale of Colorado Pioneers.* 1884. Denver. Ills. Eugene Field. VG $95.00

HILL, Amelia. *The Complete Book of Table Setting.* 1949. New York. EX $4.50

HILL, Carol. *Let's Fall in Love.* 1974. Random House. 1st ed. dj. VG $20.00

HILL, Carol. *The Eleven Million Mile High Dancer.* 1985. Holt. 1st ed. dj. VG $17.50

HILL, D. *Bethel to Sharpsburg.* 1926. Raleigh. 1st ed. 2 vol set. VG $125.00

HILL, Frank. *To Meet William Shakespeare.* 1949. New York. Dodd Mead. Ills. 481 pp. $5.00

HILL, Frederick Trevor. *Lincoln the Lawyer.* 1906. New York. Ills. 1st ed. EX $20.00

HILL, George B. *Unpublished Letters of Dean Swift.* 1899. London. Ills. VG $30.00

HILL, Grace Livingston. *Ariel Custer.* 1925. Grosset & Dunlap. 336 pp. $4.50

HILL, Grace Livingston. *Bright Arrows.* 1946. 1st ed. $8.50

HILL, Grace Livingston. *Cloudy Jewel.* New York. Grosset & Dunlap. 351 pp. $4.00

HILL, Grace Livingston. *Where Two Ways Met.* 1947. Lippincott. 256 pp. dj. VG $5.50

HILL, H. *Wild Adventure.* 1954. Harrisburg. 1st ed. dj. EX $12.50

HILL, Helen. *George Mason, Constitutionalist.* 1938. Cambridge. Harvard U. Pr. 1st ed. 300 pp. $30.00

HILL, Henry C. *The Wonder Book of Knowledge.* 1925. Winston. Ills. 608 pp. VG $6.50

HILL, Henry W. *The Champlain Tercentenary Report.* 1911. Albany. VG $25.00

HILL, Herbert & Greenberg, J. *Citizen's Guide to Desegregation.* 1955. Boston. ex-lib. 185 pp. SftCvr. VG $4.50

HILL, Herbert. *Anger & Beyond.* 1966. New York. Harper. dj. EX $30.00

HILL, J.D. *Civil War Sketchbook of C. Stedman, Surgeon U.S.N.* 1976. Presido Pr. Ills. 79 pls. dj. EX $15.00

HILL, J.E. & Smith, J.D. *Bats, a Natural History.* 1984. TX U. Press. photos. maps. 243 pp. dj. EX $25.00

HILL, John Wesley. *Abraham Lincoln, Man of God.* 1927. 458 pp. G $12.50

HILL, Lucille E. *Athletics & Out-Door Sports for Women.* 1903. Ills. $8.00

HILL, R.N. *Yankee Kingdom.* 1960. New York. 338 pp. $5.00

HILL, R.T. *Physical Geography of Texas.* 1900. Ills. map. folio. VG $45.00

HILL, Ralph. *Sidewheeler Saga. Chronicle of Steamboating.* 1953. Rinehart. 1st ed. dj. $12.50

HILL, Rebecca. *Among Birches.* 1986. Morrow. 1st ed. sgn. dj. VG $30.00

HILL, Rebecca. *Blue Rise.* 1983. Morrow. 1st ed. sgn. dj. VG $30.00

HILL, Ruth Beebe. *Manta Yo: American Saga.* 1979. Doubleday. 1st ed. dj. EX $20.00

HILL, Sallie F. *The Progressive Farmer's Southern Cookbook.* 1961. New York. 470 pp. $7.50

HILL, Weldon. *The Iceman.* 1976. New York. 1st ed. $7.50

HILL. *Hunting the Hard Way.* 1953. Wilcox Follett. 1st ed. VG $47.50

HILL. *Materials of Aircraft Construction.* 1946. Pitman & Sons. Ills. EX $8.50

HILLARD & CAMPBELL. *The Third Franklin Reader.* 1873. Boston. Ills. T.B. 204 pp. $5.00

HILLARY, E. *High Adventure.* 1955. Ills. 1st ed. $7.50

HILLARY & DOIG. *High in the Thin Cold Air.* 1962. New York. dj. VG $8.50

HILLARY. *Nothing Venture, Nothing Win.* 1975. New York. 1st ed. dj. EX $12.50

HILLCOURT, William. *Handbook for Patrol Leaders.* 1942. New York. B.S.A. 14th printing 1945. VG $4.50

HILLCOURT, William. *Norman Rockwell's World of Scouting.* 1977. Fireside Book. 160 pp. SftCvr. $4.00

HILLCOURT. *Field Book of Nature Activities.* 1950. Putnam. Ills. 320 pp. EX $3.50

HILLEGAS, Oom. *Paul's People.* 1899. New York. Ills. 1st ed. EX $40.00

HILLEL, M. & Henry, Clarissa. *Of Pure Blood.* 1976. New York. McGraw Hill. Ills. EX $15.00

HILLEN, W. *Blackwater River.* 1972. Norton. Ills. 1st Am. ed. 169 pp. dj. $10.00

HILLER, Ernest. *Houseboat & River-Bottoms People.* 1939. U. of IL. 1st ed. stiff wrappers. $10.00

HILLERMAN, Tony. *Skinwalkers.* 1986. New York. Harper. proof copy. wrappers. $30.00

HILLERMAN, Tony. *The Blessing Way.* 1970. London. Macmillan. 1st Eng. ed. VG $30.00

HILLERMAN, Tony. *The Blessing Way.* 1970. New York. Harper. proof copy. VG $75.00

HILLES, Helen. *Farm Wanted.* 1951. New York. Messner. 236 pp. dj. G $3.00

HILLHOUSE, Margaret. *The White Rose Knight.* 1894. New York. Devinne Press. Ltd. ed. 1/200. $20.00

HILLIER, Jack Ronald & Smith. *Japanese Prints: 300 Years of Albums & Books.* 1980. London. Ills. 144 pp. dj. rare. EX $75.00

HILLIER, Jack Ronald. *Japanese Color Prints.* 1981. London. revised ed. Ills. dj. EX $40.00

HILLIER, Jack Ronald. *Japanese Masters of Colour Print; Heritage of Art.* 1954. London. Ills. 139 pp. VG Out of print. $160.00

HILLIER, Jack Ronald. *Suzuki Harunobu.* 1970. Philadelphia. Ills. 1st ed. $35.00

HILLIER, Jack Ronald. *The Art of Hokusai in Book Illustration.* 1980. 229 Ills. 288 pp. scarce. EX $145.00

HILLIER, Jack Ronald. *Utamaro: Colour Prints & Paintings.* 1961. Phaidon. Ills. 161 pp. scarce. VG $75.00

HILLIS, Marjorie. *Work Ends at Nightfall.* 1938. New York. Ills. ex-lib. 94 pp. G $3.00

HILLIS. *German Atrocities.* 1918. Ills. 160 pp. $12.50

HILLMAN, Libby. *Lessons in Gourmet Cooking.* 1946. Boston. Little, Brown. 354 pp. $7.50

HILLMAN, Libby. *Lessons in Gourmet Cooking.* 1963. New York. Hearthside. Ills. 318 pp. $6.50

HILLS, Margaret. *English Bible in America.* 1962. New York. 1st ed. VG $25.00

HILSCHER, Herbert H. *Alaska Now.* 1948. Boston. Ills. 1st ed. dj. EX $15.00

HILTON, James. *Goodbye Mr. Chips.* 1934. Hodder. 1st ed. dj. $15.00

HILTON, James. *Morning Journey.* 1951. Boston. 345 pp. VG $6.50

HILTON, James. *Nothing So Strange.* 1947. Atlantic Monthly. G $12.50

HILTON, James. *Random Harvest.* 1941. 1st ed. EX $45.00

HILTON, James. *Story of Dr. Wassell.* 1943. Boston. 1st ed. dj. $7.00

HILTON, James. *We Are Not Alone.* 1937. Boston. 231 pp. $3.50

HILZINGER, John G. *Treasure Land. A Story. Vol I.* 1897. Tuscon. Ills. 160 pp. wrappers. $175.00

HIMES, Chester. *The Quality of Hurt.* 1976. Garden City. Doubleday. 1st ed. dj. VG $25.00

HIMMELWRIGHT. *Pistol & Revolver Shooting.* 1933. Macmillan. Ills. 240 pp. $10.50

HINCKLEY, E.C. *Hinckley Heritage & History.* 1982. 3rd ed. 306 pp. wrappers. $10.00

HINCKLEY, F.L. *Directory of Antique Furniture.* 1953. 1st ed. dj. VG $25.00

HINCKLEY, Gordon B. *What of the Mormons? A Brief Study of the Church.* 1947. ex-lib. photos. 222 pp. $3.50

HINDEMITH, Paul. *Zeugnis in Bildern.* 1955. Mainz. Ills. VG $17.50

HINDUS, M. *To Sing with the Angels.* 1941. 1st ed. $6.50

HINDUS, Maurice. *Crisis in the Kremlin.* 1953. New York. Doubleday. 319 pp. $3.50

HINDWOOD, K. *Austrian Birds in Color.* 1966. Reed. Ills. 1st ed. 112 pp. dj. VG $10.00

HINE, Benjamin. *Miscellaneous Poetry; or, The Farmer's Muse.* 1835. New York. 273 pp. $20.00

HINE, Mrs. Walter. *New Flower Arrangements.* 1936. Scribner. Ills. VG $10.00

HINE, Mrs. Walter. *The Arrangement of Flowers.* 1933. Scribner. 1st ed. ex-lib. 147 pp. $17.50

HINE, Robert. *California's Utopian Colonies.* 1953. San Marino. Huntington Lib. 1st Am. ed. EX $30.00

HINES, Alan. *Square Dance.* 1984. Harper. proof copy. wrappers. VG $7.50

HINGSTON, R.W.G. *A Naturalist in Hindustan.* 1923. London. Witherby. Ills. 292 pp. VG $32.50

HINMAN. *Corporal Si Klegg & His Pard.* 1887. 193 Ills. 706 pp. $23-fb-.50

HINSDALE, W. *First People of Michigan.* 1930. VG $5.00

HIPKINS, A.J. *Musical Instruments Historic, Rare, & Unique.* 1921. London. Black. Ills. Ltd. ed. VG $75.00

HIPKINS, R. Thurston. *Horror Parade.* 1945. London. Mitre. wrappers. VG $25.00

HIRANO. *Color Atlas of the Nervous System.* 1980. Tokyo/New York.dj. VG $40.00

HIRSCHMANN, I.A. *Embers Still Burn.* 1949. New York. Simon & Schuster. G $15.00

HIRSCHY, Jean E. *Alger'n the Muck.* 1975. 240 pp. $15.00

HISCOCK *Around the World Wanderer III.* 1956. London. dj. $9.00

HISS, Philip H. *Bali.* 1941. New York. 1st ed. 112 pp. VG $25.00

HITCHCOCK, Enos. *Memoirs of the Bloomsgrove Family.* 1790. Boston. 1st ed. 2 vol set. $250.00

HITCHMAN, Janet. *Such a Strange Lady.* 1975. Harper. 1st ed. dj. VG $15.00

HITCHOCK. *Art of the World.* 1895. New York City. 2 vol set. w/50 pp. Expo photos. $150.00

HITLER, Adolf. *Fuhrer & Chancellor.* 1939. Berlin. 63 pp. wrappers. VG $15.00

HITLER, Adoloph. *Mein Kampf.* 1939. Reynal & Hitchcock. dj. G $20.00

HITLER, Adolph. *Mein Kampf.* 1939. New York. Book of Month. VG $12.50

HITLER, Adolph. *My New Order.* 1941. New York. dj. VG $15.00

HITT, Russell. *Cannibal Valley.* 1962. Harper. 253 pp. $27.50

HITTE, Kathryn. *Surprise for Susan.* 1950. VG $3.00

HITTI, P.K. *History of Syria.* 1961. New York. Ills. 749 pp. index. $27.50

HJORTSBERG, William. *Falling Angel.* 1978. Harcourt. 1st ed. dj. VG $20.00

HJORTSBERG, William. *Gray Matters.* 1971. 1st ed. dj. EX $25.00

HJORTSBERG, William. *Prize College Stories.* 1963. Random House. 1st ed. dj. VG $15.00

HJORTSBERG, William. *Symbiography.* 1973. Sumac. 1st ed. dj. VG $30.00

HJORTSBERG, William. *Tora! Tora! Tora!* 1974. Simon & Schuster. 1st ed. sgn. $25.00

HOAGLAND, E. *Walking the Dead Diamond River.* 1973. 1st ed. VG $30.00

HOARD, F.E. & Marlow, A.W. *The Cabinet Makers' Treasury.* 1952. New York. 1st ed. VG $20.00

HOBAN, Russell. *Kleinzeit.* 1974. Viking. 1st Am. ed. dj. VG $30.00

HOBBES, John O. *The Dream & the Business.* 1906. London. VG $12.50

HOBBES, John Oliver. *The Gods, Some Mortals, & Lord Wickenham.* 1895. $3.00

HOBBS, Captain James. *Wild Life in the Far West.* 1873. Hartford. 20 pls. 488 pp. G $250.00

HOBBS, E.W. *How to Make Clipper Ship Models.* 1927. Glasgow. $25.00

HOBBS, J.S. *The New British Channel Pilot.* 1844. London. VG $15.00

HOBHOUSE, Janet. *Everybody Who Was Anybody.* Putnam. Ills. 1st ed. dj. EX $15.00

HOBROCK, R.H. *On Recovery of A Strong Aluminum Alloy.* 1935. Akron. photos. charts. $3.50

HOBSON, H. *The Famous Cruise of the Kearsarge.* 1894. private print. VG $60.00

HOBSON, J.A. *John Ruskin. Social Reformer.* New York. (ca.1900) Ltd. ed. 1/1000. VG $12.50

HOBSON, Laura Z. *Gentleman's Agreement.* 1947. New York. Simon & Schuster. 275 pp. dj. $3.50

HOBSON, Laura Z. *The Tenth Month.* 1970. New York. Simon & Schuster. 277 pp. dj. $3.50

HOBSON, R.L. *Chinese Art.* 1927. New York. 100 color pls. VG $95.00

HOBSON, Richard P. *Nothing Too Good for a Cowboy.* 1955. 2nd printing, dj. $6.50

HOBSON, Richmond P. *Buck Jones at Annapolis.* 1907. New York. New York Book Co. 370 pp. $2.50

HOCHBAUM, H.A. *Travels & Traditions of Waterfowl.* 1956. MN U. Press. Ills. 301 pp. EX $17.50

HOCHMAN, Sandra. *Futures.* 1974. Viking Press. 1st ed. inscr. dj. VG $25.00

HOCIE, Jane L. *Suggestions for Hand Work in School & Home.* 1913. Springfield. Ills. Lewis Hine. $15.00

HOCKING, S. *Up the Rhine & Over the Alps.* Crombie. Ills. 2nd ed. VG $7.50

HOCKING, William E. *Freedom of the Press.* 1947. Chicago. U. of Chicago Press. 243 pp. $4.00

HODEL, Michael P. & Wright, S. *Enter the Lion.* 1980. London. 1st Eng. ed. dj. VG $15.00

HODGAM, Frank. *The Wandering Singer & His Songs & Other Poems.* 1899. Climax, MI. 203 pp. $12.50

HODGE, F.W. *Handbook of American Indians North of Mexico.* 1912. 2nd impression. VG $55.00

HODGE, F.W. *Handbook of American Indians North of Mexico.* 1907 & 1910. Ills. fld. map. 2 vol set. VG $85.00

HODGE, Gene Meany. *The Kachinas Are Coming. With Related Folk Tales.* 1936. Los Angeles. Ills. 1st ed. 18 pls. $300.00

HODGINS, Eric. *Mr. Blandings Builds His Dream House.* 1946. New York. Ills. Wm. Steig. 237 pp. $52.50

HODGKIN, Frank E. & Galvin, J. *Pen Pictures of Representative Men of Oregon.* 1882. Portland. Ills. 1st ed. wrappers. $150.00

HODGKIN, R.H. *6 Centuries of an Oxford College: Hist. of Queens.* 1949. Oxford. dj. VG $15.00

HODGKIN, T. *Lectures on Means of Promoting/Preserving Health.* 1835. London. G $125.00

HODGKINSON, Colin. *Best Foot Forward.* 1957. New York. Ills. 1st ed. 269 pp. $10.00

HODGSON, Adam. *Letters from America.* 1824. London. 1st Eng. ed. 405 pp. 2 vol set. $285.00

HODGSON, Fred T. *The Steel Square.* 1904. Chicago. 2 vol set. G $10.00

HODGSON, Moira. *Chinese Cooking with American Meals.* 1970. Garden City. Doubleday. Book Club Ed. $5.00

HODGSON, William Hope. *Boats of the Glen Carrig.* 1971. New York. Ballantine. 1st ed. pb. EX $17.50

HODGSON, William Hope. *Carnacki the Ghost Finder.* 1974. London. Sphere. 1st ed. pb. EX $15.00

HODGSON, William Hope. *Deep Waters.* 1967. Sauk City. Arkham House. 1st ed. dj. EX $75.00

HODGSON, William Hope. *Dream of X.* 1977. W. Kingston. Grant. Ills. Fabian. dj. EX $125.00

HODGSON, William Hope. *House on the Borderland.* New York. Ace. 1st ed. pb. EX $17.50

HODGSON, William Hope. *House on the Borderland.* 1946. Arkham House. G $30.00

HODGSON, William Hope. *Out of the Storm.* 1975. Kingston. Ills. Fabian. 1st ed. $75.00

HODGSON, William Hope. *Poems of the Sea.* 1977. London. Ferret. Ills. Ltd. ed. EX $67.50

HODGSON. *Builder's Architectural Drawing Self Taught.* 1903. Ills. 315 pp. VG $8.50

HOE, Robert. *A Lecture on Bookbinding as a Fine Art.* 1886. New York. 1st ed. 1/200. VG $250.00

HOEHLING, A.A. *Last Train from Atlanta.* 1958. New York. 2nd ed. dj. VG $10.00

HOELLER. *Toscanini, a Photobiography.* 1943. New York. review copy. wrappers. G $15.00

HOFFA, James R. & Fraley, O. *Hoffa, the Real Story.* 1975. New York. Stein & Day. 242 pp. dj. $6.00

HOFFER, Eric. *An American Odyssey.* 1968. New York. Dutton. 1st ed. 68 pp. VG $6.50

HOFFMAN, A. *Auto Soon Major Motion Picture.* 2nd ed. SftCvr. VG $9.00

HOFFMAN, Abbie. *Revolution for the Hell of It.* 1968. New York. Dial Press. dj. EX $12.00

HOFFMAN, Alice. *Angel Landing.* 1982. Severn House. 1st English ed. dj. VG $15.00

HOFFMAN, Frederick. *Race Traits & Tendencies of American Negro.* 1896. Am. Econ. Assoc. 1st ed. $20.00

HOFFMAN, H. *Hitler Was My Friend.* 1955. London. Ills. G $30.00

HOFFMAN, Hans. *By Wight.* 1957. Berkeley. inscr. $125.00

HOFFMAN, Henry. *Slovenly Peter.* Philadelphia. Porter & Coates. Ills. EX $50.00

HOFFMAN, Malvina. *Heads & Tales.* 1936. Scribner. Ills. 416 pp. VG $15.00

HOFFMAN, P. *O Vatican.* 1984. New York. Congdon & Weed. dj. EX $15.00

HOFFMAN, Professor. *Modern Magic.* Philadelphia. McKay. VG $40.00

HOFFMAN, W. *Camp, Court & Siege.* 1877. 1st ed. $45.00

HOFFMAN, William. *The Land that Drank the Rain.* 1982. Baton Rouge. 1st ed. dj. VG $35.00

HOFLAND, Barbara. *The Good Grandmother & Her Offspring.* 1817. New York. 1st Am. ed. EX $75.00

HOFLAND, Barbara. *The Son of a Genius.* 1814. 1st Am. ed. EX $75.00

HOFLAND, T.C. *British Angler's Manual; or, Art of Holfland.* 1848. London. $50.00

HOFSTDTER, Douglas. *Goedel, Escher, Bach: Eternal Golden Braid.* 1979. New York. 777 pp. $5.00

HOGAN, Clio. *Index of Stake Winners, 1865 to 1967.* Solvang, CA. 2 vol set. EX $125.00

HOGAN, Desmond. *A Curious Street.* 1984. Braziller. 1st Am. ed. dj. VG $12.50

HOGAN, J.P. *Code of the Lifemaker.* 1983. Del Rey. 1st ed. dj. EX $12.50

HOGAN, John Joseph. *On the Mission in Missouri 1857-1868.* 1892. Kansas City. 1st ed. 221 pp. $50.00

HOGAN. *Texas Republic, a Social & Economic History.* 1946. Norman. 1st ed. dj. $20.00

HOGARTH, Brendan. *Behan's Island.* 1962. 1st ed. dj. $16.00

HOGARTH, D.G. *The Nearer East.* 1902. London. 54 Ills. 296 pp. 5 maps. $15.00

HOGARTH, William. *Masters of Painting.* London. Ills. Reiach. VG $40.00

HOGBEN. *Thomas Cubitt Master Builder.* 1971. Universe Bks. $15.00

HOGG, G. *Cannibalism & Human Sacrifice.* 1958. London. Hale. 1st ed. 206 pp. dj. EX $27.50

HOGGSON, N.F. *Banking Through the Ages.* 1926. New York. 128 pp. $17.50

HOGMAN, Joseph. *Piano Playing with Piano Questions Answered.* 1920. Philadelphia. VG $12.00

HOGNER, D.C. *Conservation in America.* 1958. Lippincott. Ills. 1st ed. 240 pp. G $5.00

HOGNER, D.C. *Sea Mammals.* 1979. Crowell. Ills. 1st ed. dj. EX $7.50

HOGNER, Dorothy. *Navajo Winter Nights. Navajo Folk Tales & Myths.* 1935. New York. Nelson. 180 pp. $20.00

HOHMAN. *American Whaleman.* 1928. New York. 1st ed. VG $40.00

HOHN, P. & Peterman, J. *Curiosities of the Plant Kingdom.* 1980. Universe Books.Ills. 212 pp. dj. EX $15.00

HOHNE, H. *Order of Deaths Head.* 1969. London. 1st ed. dj. EX $45.00

HOIJER, Harry. *Language in Culture.* 1954. 1st ed. stiff wrappers. $10.00

HOKE. *Music Boxes.* 1957. New York. 1st ed. dj. EX $27.50

HOKLENBERG, J. *Soren Kierkengaard.* 1954. London. 321 pp. dj. VG $25.00

HOLBROOK, J. *Ten Years Among the Mail Bags.* 1874. Philadelphia. VG $15.00

HOLBROOK, Richard. *Portraits of Dante with Concise Iconography.* 1911. Boston. Ills. 263 pp. color pls. $45.00

HOLBROOK, Stewaret H. *Rocky Mountain Revolution.* 1956. 1st ed. dj. VG $10.00

HOLBROOK, Stewart H. *Holy Old Mackinaw.* 1938. New York. 1st ed. VG $20.00

HOLBROOK, Stewart H. *Little Annie Oakley & Other Rugged People.* 1948. New York. Ills. 1st printing. 238 pp. $12.50

HOLBROOK, Stewart H. *Machines of Plenty Pioneering in Am. Agriculture.* 1955. 1st ed. dj. EX $20.00

HOLBROOK, Stewart H. *The Golden Age of Quackery.* 1959. New York. Macmillan. 302 pp. $4.50

HOLBROOK, Stewart H. *The Swamp Fox.* 1959. New York. Random House. Ills. ex-lib. $5.00

HOLCIK, J. & Mihalik, J. *Fresh-Water Fishes.* 1972. Spring. 128 pp. 56 color pls. dj. EX $5.00

HOLDEN, Curry. *Hill of the Rooster.* 1956. New York. 1st ed. sgn. dj. $65.00

HOLDEN, G.P. *Streamcraft an Angling Man.* 1927. New York. Ills. G $15.00

HOLDEN, Ray. *Abe Lincoln. The Politician & the Man.* 1929. New York. Ills. $4.50

HOLDER, C.F. *Salt-Water Game Fishing.* 1923. New York. Ills. G $10.00

HOLDER, Charles F. *Big Game at Sea.* 1908. Ills. 1st ed. VG $25.00

HOLDER, Charles Frederick. *Recreations of a Sportsman on the Pacific Coast.* 1910. London/NY. Ills. 1st ed. 399 pp. $25.00

HOLDER, Charles. *Life in Open: Sport with Rod, Gun, Horse & Hound.* 1906. New York. 1st ed. 401 pp. EX $50.00

HOLDER. *Sweethearts & Valentines.* 1980. New York. 1st ed. dj. EX $12.50

HOLDER. *Treasure Divers.* 1898. Dodd Mead. $15.00

HOLDSTOCK, R. *Mythago Wood.* London. 1st ed. sgn. $85.00

HOLDSWORTH, J. *The Coyote & the Whirlwind.* 1973. Naylor. Ills. 205 pp. dj. VG $12.50

HOLE, Christine. *Witchcraft in England.* 1947. New York. Ills. M. Peake. 1st ed. dj. EX $32.50

HOLE, S.R. *Our Gardens.* 1899. London. Haddon Hall Library. $20.00

HOLISTER, U.S. *The Navajo & His Blanket.* 1903. Denver. sgn. slipcase. VG $275.00

HOLLAND, Annie. *Talitha Cumi.* 1904. Boston. 1st ed. VG $50.00

HOLLAND, C.F. *Morgan & His Raiders.* 1942. New York. 373 pp. $30.00

HOLLAND, Clive. *Old & New Japan.* 1907. London. Ills. M. Smyth. EX $55.00

HOLLAND, Dan. *The Upland Game Hunter's Bible.* 1961. New York. Doubleday. 1st ed. wrappers. $7.50

HOLLAND, J.G. *Authur Bonnicastle, an American Novel.* 1873. New York. 1st ed. 401 pp. G $17.50

HOLLAND, J.G. *The Life of Abraham Lincoln.* 1866. Springfield. Ills. 544 pp. $20.00

HOLLAND, Maurice. *Architects of Aviation.* 1951. 1st ed. ex-lib. 214 pp. VG $18.00

HOLLAND, R.S. *Historic Railroads.* 1927. Philadelphia. $18.00

HOLLAND, Ray. *Good Shot.* 1946. 1st ed. dj. EX $22.50

HOLLAND, Ray. *My Gun Dogs.* 1929. Houghton Mifflin. VG $25.00

HOLLAND, Ray. *Scattergunning.* 1951. Knopf. Ills. 1st ed. 379 pp. dj. VG $45.00

HOLLAND, Ray. *Shotgunning in the Uplands.* Ills. Hunt. Ltd. ed. 1/250. sgn. $250.00

HOLLAND, Rupert S. *Historic Airships.* 1928. Philadelphia. Ills. 343 pp. VG $32.50

HOLLAND, Rupert S. *Historic Railroads.* 1927. Philadelphia. Ills. VG $22.50

HOLLAND, Rupert S. *Sons of Seven Cities.* 1929. Philadelphia. 1st ed. VG $10.00

HOLLAND, W.J. *The Butterfly Book.* 1929. New York. G $8.50

HOLLAND, W.J. *The Moth Book.* 1916. Doubleday Page.Ills. 479 pp. VG $15.00

HOLLAND. *History of Parker Co. & Double Log Cabin.* 1936. Weatherford. 1st ed. $115.00

HOLLANDER, Eugene. *Die Medizin in der Klassischen Malerei, Stuttgart.*1903. 1st ed. $105.00

HOLLEY, Edward G. *Charles Evans: American Bibliographer.* 1963. U. of IL Press.343 pp. dj. $20.00

HOLLEY, I.B. *Ideas & Weapons.* 1953. New Haven. 1st ed. ex-lib. 222 pp. $10.00

HOLLIDAY, Fred. *Wildlife of Scotland.* 1979. London. Macmillan. Ills. 198 pp. dj. $12.50

HOLLIDAY, Robert Cortes. *Unmentionables.* 1933. New York. Long & Smith. Ills. 1st ed. VG $12.50

HOLLIDAY, Robert Kelvin. *Tests of Faith.* 1966. Oak Hill. Ills. 112 pp. dj. $7.50

HOLLING, C. *The Twins Who Flew Around the World.* 1931. New York. Platt & Munk. Ills. folio. VG $20.00

HOLLING, H.C. *Minn of the Mississippi.* 1951. Boston. Ills. 1st ed. dj. EX $20.00

HOLLING, H.C. *Paddle-to-Sea.* 1941. Boston. 1st ed. dj. EX $25.00

HOLLING, H.C. *The Book of Cowboys.* 1936. New York. Ills. 1st ed. maps. 125 pp. $11.00

HOLLING, H.C. *The Book of Indians.* 1935. New York. Ills. maps. 125 pp. $12.00

HOLLIS. *Frigate Constitution.* 1901. G $8.50

HOLLISTER, Josiah. *The Journal of Romanzo Norton Bunn.* 1928. 1st ed. wrappers. $8.50

HOLLOM, P.A.D. *Popular Handbook of British Birds.* 1955. London. Witherby. Ills. 428 pp. EX $17.50

HOLLON, W.E. *Frontier Violence, Another Look.* 1974. Oxford U. Pr. Ills. 1st ed. dj. VG $15.00

HOLLON, W.E. *The Southwest Old & New.* 1961. Knopf. dj. EX $15.00

HOLLOWAY, Laura C. *Adelaide Neilson.* 1885. New York. photos. $35.00

HOLLOWAY. *Ladies of the White House.* 1881. Ills. 1st ed. VG $12.50

HOLLY, J. *Encounter.* 1959. New York. dj. VG $15.00

HOLLY, J.H. *Mind Traders.* 1966. 1st ed. dj. EX $7.50

HOLM. *Edward S. Curtis in the Land of War Canoes.* 1980. U. of WA. $10.00

HOLMAN & PERSONS. *Buckskin & Homespun.* 1979. Wind River Pr. Ltd. ed. 1/450. dj. EX $200.00

HOLMAN. *Speedy.* 1928. Grossett & Dunlap. Ills. $4.50

HOLME, Bryan. *Heroshige. A Shoal of Fishes.* 1980. Viking. reprint of 1832 ed. scarce. EX $47.00

HOLME, C. Geoffrey, ed. *Children's Toys of Yesterday.* 1932. London. Studio. dj. VG $42.50

HOLMES, Abiel. *American Annals.* 1805. Cambridge. 1st ed. 2 vol set. $95.00

HOLMES, Burton. *Trip Around World Through Telebinocular.* 1930. Keystone View Co. $40.00

HOLMES, Charles E. *Birds of the West.* 1907. Hammond & Stephens. Ills. VG $20.00

HOLMES, Charles S. *The Clocks of Columbus.* 1972. New York. Atheneum. 1st ed. 360 pp. $10.00

HOLMES, Clay W. *The Elmira Prison Camp: History of Miltary Prison.* 1912. Putnam. $60.00

HOLMES, G.S. *Lenox China Story of Walter Scott Lenox.* 1924. private print. $25.00

HOLMES, Mabel Dodge. *The Ill-Starred Stewarts.* 1958. New York. 391 pp. $4.50

HOLMES, Mary J. *Aikenside.* 1909. $27.50

HOLMES, Mary J. *Dora Deane & Maggie Miller.* 1874. $30.00

HOLMES, Mary J. *Rose Mather.* 1874. $30.00

HOLMES, Mary J. *Rose Mather.* Hurst. undated. $4.00

HOLMES, Mary J. *The Cameron Pride.* 1868. $30.00

HOLMES, MARY J. *The Leighton Homestead.* 1856. $30.00

HOLMES, Mrs. Mary. *Mildred; or, Child of Adoption.* no date. $2.00

HOLMES, Oliver Wendell. *A Mortal Antipathy.* 1st ed. 2nd issue. sgn. $45.00

HOLMES, Oliver Wendell. *Autocrat of the Breakfast Table.* 1859. $15.00

HOLMES, Oliver Wendell. *Autocrat of the Breakfast Table.* 1907. Hurst & Co. Knickerbocker ed. 326 pp. $4.50

HOLMES, Oliver Wendell. *Poems.* 1836. Boston. 1st ed. 2nd issue. 163 pp. G $65.00

HOLMES, Oliver Wendell. *Poems.* 1848. Boston. Ticnor, Reed & Fields. $22.50

HOLMES, Oliver Wendell. *Professor at the Breakfast Table.* 1860. Boston. 1st ed. 8 vol set. $55.00

HOLMES, Oliver Wendell. *Professor at the Breakfast Table.* 1860. Boston. 1st ed. EX $50.00

HOLMES, Oliver Wendell. *The Iron Gate, & Other Poems.* 1880. Boston. 1st ed. $12.50

HOLMES. *Desert Trails.* Pocketbooks. $3.00

HOLMES. *Flame of Sunset.* Pocketbooks. pb. $3.00

HOLMES. *High Starlight.* Pennant. $3.00

HOLMSTROM, Ficlelson. *Tri-Lingual Dictionary Materials & Structures.* 1971. English/French/German text. $68.00

HOLROYD, Michael. *Lytton Strachey. A Critical Biography.* 1968. New York. 1st ed. 2 vol set. djs. boxed. $20.00

HOLST, Imogen. *Byrd. Great Composers Series.* 1972. New York. dj. EX $6.50

HOLSTEIN, H.L.V.D. *Memoirs of Simon Bolivar.* 1829. Boston. VG $20.00

HOLT, Felix. *The Gabriel Horn.* 1951. Dutton. 1st ed. $3.50

HOLT, Henry. *Garrulities of an Octogenarian Editor.* 1924. Boston. 2nd ed. VG $15.00

HOLT, R.B. *Rugs.* 1901. Chicago. $150.00

HOLT, Stephen. *Prairie Colt.* 1947. $3.00

HOLT, Victoria. *On the Night of the Seventh Moon.* 1972. New York. Doubleday. 352 pp. EX $3.50

HOLT, Victoria. *The King of the Castle.* 1967. New York. Doubleday. 253 pp. $3.50

HOLT. *Pioneering Southwest.* 1923. VG $20.00

HOLTHUSEN, Henry F. *James W. Wadsworth, Jr.* 1926. New York. Putnam. 243 pp. $6.00

HOLYOAKE, George J. *Among the Americans & a Stranger in America.* 1881. Chicago. 1st ed. dj. EX $95.00

HOLYOAKE, George J. *History Last Trial by Jury for Atheism in England.* 1851. London. 1st ed. $65.00

HOLZWORTH, John. *Wild Grizzlies of Alaska.* 1930. NY/London. Ills. 1st ed. 417 pp. VG $40.00

HOLZWORTH. *Wild Grizzlies of Alaska.* 1930. Putnam. Ills. 1st ed. 417 pp. index. $42.50

HOMANS, James. *Self-Propelled Vehicles.* 1911. Audel. Ills. 664 pp. EX $25.00

HOMANS, James. *Self-Propelled Vehicles.* 1905. New York. 2nd revised ed. $47.50

HOMANS, John. *Circulatory Diseases of the Extremities.* 1939. New York. Macmillan. 1st ed. 8 vol set. $45.00

HOME, Gordon. *Old London Bridge.* 1931. London. Ills. 382 pp. pls & fld. pls. $47.50

HOMER, H. *Wild Flowers.* 1974. Macmillan. Ills. 362 pp. dj. EX $30.00

HOMER. *Alfred Stieglitz & the Photo-Session.* 1983. dj. EX $37.50

HOMER. *The Iliad.* U. of Chicago. trans. Lattimore. 1st ed. EX $20.00

HOMEYE, E.F. *Orinthologische Briefe.* 1881. Berlin. 340 pp. $45.00

HOMSHER, Lola M. *South Pass, 1868. James Chisholm's Journal.* 1960. U. of NB Press. Pioneer Heritage Series. $14.00

HONCE, Charles. *A Vincent Starrett Library.* 1941. Mt. Vernon. Golden Eagle Pr. Ltd. ed. $125.00

HONE, Joseph. *W.B. Yeats. 1865-1939.* 1943. New York. Macmillan. Ills. 535 pp. $5.00

HONE, William. *The Everyday Book & Table Book.* 1839. London. Ills. 1st ed. 4 vol. set. VG $190.00

HONEY, W.B. *English Pottery & Porcelain.* 1947. London. 3rd ed. $20.00

HOOD, Hugh. *Strength Down Centre: Jean Beliveau Story.* 1970. Prentice Hall. Ills. 192 pp. VG $7.50

HOOD, J.B. *Advance & Retreat.* 1880. New Orleans. full leather. $60.00

HOOD, R.E. *Twelve at War: Great Photo Under Fire.* 1st ed. EX $12.50

HOOD, Samuel Stevens. *Archibald Henderson: The New Crichton.* 1949. New York. sgn. boxed. EX $70.00

HOOD, Thomas. *Tom Tucker & Little Bo-Peep.* 1891. London. Cassell. Ills. 14 pls. VG $35.00

HOOD. *Hood's Book of Home-Made Candies.* 1905. Lowell, Mass. 16 pp. wrappers. VG $10.00

HOOK, Sidney. *Academic Freedom & Academic Anarchy.* Boulder. (ca.1968) wrappers. EX $15.00

HOOKER, Alan. *Herb Cookery.* 1974. San Francisco. 192 pp. wrappers. $5.00

HOOKER, F.H. *Afternoons with Ceramics.* 1896. Syracuse. $7.00

HOOKER, Marion. *Farmhouses & Small Provincial Buildings in Italy.* 1925. New York. Ills. folio. dj. VG $40.00

HOOKER, Wm. F. *The Prairie Schooner.* 1918. Chicago. Saul Bros. 156 pp. 3 pls. $25.00

HOOLE, William Stanley. *Check & Finding List of Charleston Periodicals.* 1936. Durham, N.C. Duke U. Pr. 1st ed. 84 pp. $75.00

HOOPER, Robert. *The Physician's Vade-Mecum.* 1812. London. Murray. new ed. 334 pp. index. $45.00

HOOPER, S.K. *Rhymes of the Rockies.* 1887. Denver. Ills. 3rd ed. wrappers. VG $25.00

HOOPES, Townsend. *The Devil & John Forester Dulles.* 1973. Boston/Toronto. Ills. 1st ed. 562 pp. $7.50

HOOTEN, Earnest. *The Physical Anthropology of Ireland.* 1955. Peabody Museum. 1st ed. 2 vol set. wrappers. $20.00

HOOTON, Ted. *Spitfire Special, New Light on Historic Fighter.* 1972. London. 1st ed. EX $12.50

HOOVER, Herbert Clark. *A Remedy for Disappearing Game Fishes.* 1930. Ltd. 1st ed. $40.00

HOOVER, Herbert. *America's First Crusade.* 1942. 1st ed. inscr. sgn. VG $75.00

HOOVER, Herbert. *Boyhood in Iowa.* 1931. Aventine Press. Ltd. ed. 1/1000. slipcase. EX $30.00

HOOVER, Herbert. *Fishing for Fun.* 1963. Random House. Ills. 1st printing. VG $8.50

HOOVER, Herbert. *On Growing Up.* 1962. Morrow. presentation copy. $100.00

HOOVER, Herbert. *The Challenge to Liberty.* 1935. New York. Scribner. 212 pp. dj. $3.50

HOOVER, Herbert. *The Memoirs of Herbert Hoover.* 1952. New York. Macmillan. 6th ed. sgn. VG $15.00

HOPE, Anthony. *Double Harness.* 1903. $27.50

HOPE, Anthony. *Lucinda.* 1920. $27.50

HOPE, Anthony. *Phroso.* 1899. $30.00

HOPE, Anthony. *Prisoner of Zenda.* Briston/London.1st ed. 310 pp. VG $30.00

HOPE, Anthony. *Quisante.* 1900. $30.00

HOPE, Anthony. *Simon Dale.* 1897. $27.50

HOPE, Anthony. *Tales of Two People.* 1907. $27.50

HOPE, Anthony. *The Dolly Dialogs.* 1901. Ills. Christy. G $7.00

HOPE, Bob. *They Got Me Covered.* 1941. Hollywood. 1st ed. stiff wrappers. G $10.00

HOPE, Bob; & Martin, Pete.*The Last Christmas Show; Have Troupe, Will Fly.* 1974. New York. Doubleday. photos. 383 pp. EX $6.50

HOPE, Laura Lee. *Bunny Brown & Sister Sue at Christmas Tree Cove.* 1920. Grosset & Dunlap. VG $4.50

HOPE, Laura Lee. *Bunny Brown & His Sister Sue.* 1917. New York. Ills. F.E. Nosworthy. 246 pp. $3.00

HOPE, Laura Lee. *Bunny Brown & Sister Sue & Their Shetland Pony.* 1918. Grosset & Dunlap. Ills. VG $4.50

HOPE, Laura Lee. *Bunny Brown & Sister Sue at a Sugar Camp.* 1924. Grosset & Dunlap. VG $4.50

HOPE, Laura Lee. *Bunny Brown & Sister Sue on Grandpa's Farm.* 1916. Grosset & Dunlap. VG $4.50

HOPE, Laura Lee. *Camping Out.* 1923. Grosset & Dunlap. VG $8.50

HOPE, Laura Lee. *The Blythe Girls; Three on a Vacation.* 1925. New York. Grosset & Dunlap. 214 pp. $2.00

HOPE, Laura Lee. *The Blythe Girls: Helen, Margy, & Rose.* 1925. New York. Grosset & Dunlap. 214 pp. $3.00

HOPE, Laura Lee. *The Bobbsey Twins & Baby May.* 1924. Grosset & Dunlap. Ills. VG $4.50

HOPE, Laura Lee. *The Bobbsey Twins & Their Schoolmates.* 1928. New York. Grosset & Dunlap. 244 pp. $3.00

HOPE, Laura Lee. *The Bobbsey Twins at Cedar Camp.* 1921. Grosset & Dunlap. Ills. VG $4.50

HOPE, Laura Lee. *The Bobbsey Twins at Home.* 1916. New York. Grosset & Dunlap. 245 pp. $2.50

HOPE, Laura Lee. *The Bobbsey Twins at Lighthouse Point.* 1932. Grosset & Dunlap. EX $7.50

HOPE, Laura Lee. *The Bobbsey Twins at Meadow Brook.* 1915. New York. Grosset & Dunlap. 238 pp. dj. $3.50

HOPE, Laura Lee. *The Bobbsey Twins at School.* 1913. Grosset & Dunlap. dj. VG $6.50

HOPE, Laura Lee. *The Bobbsey Twins at Sugar Maple Hill.* 1946. New York. Grosset & Dunlap. 210 pp. $2.00

HOPE, Laura Lee. *The Bobbsey Twins at the Circus.* 1932. Grosset & Dunlap. Ills. VG $4.50

HOPE, Laura Lee. *The Bobbsey Twins at the County Fair.* 1922. Grosset & Dunlap. Ills. G $3.50

HOPE, Laura Lee. *The Bobbsey Twins at the Ice Carnival.* 1941. Grosset & Dunlap. Ills. G $3.50

HOPE, Laura Lee. *The Bobbsey Twins at the Seashore.* 1907. Grosset & Dunlap. Ills. G $3.50

HOPE, Laura Lee. *The Bobbsey Twins at the Snow Lodge.* 1913. Grosset & Dunlap. $6.50

HOPE, Laura Lee. *The Bobbsey Twins in the Country.* 1907. Grosset & Dunlap. G $4.50

HOPE, Laura Lee. *The Bobbsey Twins in the Country.* 1950. New York. Grosset & Dunlap. 179 pp. $3.00

HOPE, Laura Lee. *The Bobbsey Twins in Washington.* 1919. New York. Grosset & Dunlap. 244 pp. $2.00

HOPE, Laura Lee. *The Bobbsey Twins Keeping House.* 1925. Grosset & Dunlap. Ills. G $3.50

HOPE, Laura Lee. *The Bobbsey Twins on a Ranch.* 1935. New York. Grosset & Dunlap. 206 pp. dj. $3.50

HOPE, Laura Lee. *The Bobbsey Twins on the Deep Blue Sea.* 1918. Grosset & Dunlap. VG $6.50

HOPE, Laura Lee. *The Bobbsey Twins Solve a Mystery.* 1934. Grosset & Dunlap. Ills. G $3.50

HOPE, Laura Lee. *The Bobbsey Twins Treasure Hunting.* 1929. Grosset & Dunlap. Ills. VG $4.50

HOPE, Laura Lee. *The Bobbsey Twins Wonderful Secret.* 1921. Grosset & Dunlap. G $3.50

HOPE, Laura Lee. *The Bobbsey Twins Wonderful Secret.* 1932. Grosset & Dunlap. EX $7.50

HOPE, Laura Lee. *The Bobbsey Twins; Merry Days Indoors & Out.* 1950. Racine. Whitman. 216 pp. $2.50

HOPE, Laura Lee. *The Moving Picture Girls at Oak Farm.* 1914. World. Ills. G $3.50

HOPE, Laura Lee. *The Moving Picture Girls at Oak Farm.* 1914. New York. Grosset & Dunlap. 212 pp. $3.00

HOPE, Laura Lee. *The Outdoor Girls in a Motor Car.* 1913. Grosset & Dunlap. Ills. G $4.50

HOPE, Laura Lee. *The Outdoor Girls in Florida.* 1913. Grosset & Dunlap. 204 pp. G. $4.50

HOPE, Laura Lee. *The Outdoor Girls in the Air.* 1932. Racine. Whitman. 213 pp. $3.50

HOPKINS, Dr. J.C. *Report of Hopkins, Territorian Veterinarian.* 1887. Cheyenne. 25 pp. wrapppers. $150.00

HOPKINS, Everard. *Sentimental Journey Through France & Italy.* 1910. London. Ills. Ltd. ed. sgn. VG $60.00

HOPKINS, J. Castell. *World's Best Histories of Canada.* 1901. New York. Co-operative Pub. fair. $2.50

HOPKINS, R. Thurston. *Old Watermills & Windmills.* London. (ca.1930) Ills. 245 pp. pls. $37.50

HOPKINS, Tigbe. *Dungeons of Old Paris.* 1897. New York. Ills. 1st ed. VG $25.00

HOPKINS, Vira M. Darling. *Sunny Side Sketches for Young & Old.* 1887. Mennonite Pub. G $4.50

HOPKINS, Walter Lee. *Hopkins of Virginia & Related Families.* 1980. Harrisonburg. reprint. Ills. 405 pp. $32.50

HOPKINS. *The Kipling Country.* 1925. New York. 263 pp. VG $15.00

HOPKINSON, F. *Colonial Carter of Cartersville.* 1892. Houghton Mifflin.Ills. E.W. Kemble & author. $6.50

HOPPE, E.O. *Romantic America/Picturesque United States.* 1927. New York. 304 pp. photos. VG $40.00

HOPPE. *Fifth Continent.* 1931. London. VG $45.00

HOPPER, E.J. *Acropolis.* 1971. New York. 1st Am. ed. dj. EX $12.50

HOPPER, Hedda & Brough, James.*The Whole Truth & Nothing But.* 1963. New York. Doubleday, 331 pp. dj. $4.50

HOPPER, Mrs. R.P. *Old Time Primitive Methodism in Canada 1829-1884.* 1904. Toronto. G $12.50

HOPSON. *The Last Shoot-Out.* Prestige Books. pb. $3.00

HORA, B. *Encyclopedia of Trees of the World.* 1981. Oxford. Ills. maps. 288 pp. dj. EX $27.50

HORACE. *Odes & Epodes.* 1961. 2 vol set. boxed. $40.00

HORAN, James D. *Across the Cimarron.* 1956. 1st ed. dj. VG $40.00

HORAN, James D. *American Indians.* 1972. dj. $30.00

HORAN, James D. *Confederate Agent.* 1954. Ills. 1st ed. 326 pp. $12.50

HORAN, James D. *Desperate Men.* 1949. 1st ed. dj. VG $35.00

HORAN, James D. *Desperate Men. Revelations from Pinkerton Files.* 1962. New York. Ills. 391 pp. index. dj. VG $10.00

HORAN, James D. *McKenney-Hall Portrait Gallery of Amer. Indians.* Ltd. ed. 1/249. sgn. boxed. EX $75.00

HORAN, James D. *The Life & Art of Charles Schreyoogel.* 1969. New York. folio. dj. $58.00

HORAN, James D. *Timothy Sullivan/ America's Forgotten Photographer.* 1966. New York. 1st ed. dj. VG $25.00

HORANYI, Matyas. *The Magnificence of Esterhaza.* 1962. Budapest. Ills. VG $25.00

HORGAN, Paul. *A Distant Trumpet.* 1960. New York. Farrar, Straus & Cudahy. $3.50

HORGAN, Paul. *Citizen of New Salem.* 1961. New York. Ills. ex-lib. 89 pp. G $3.50

HORGAN, Paul. *Lamy of Santa Fe.* 1975. New York. Ltd. 1st ed. sgn. slipcase. EX $150.00

HORGAN, Paul. *Memories of the Future.* 1966. New York. 1st ed. dj. VG $35.00

HORGAN, Paul. *One Red Rose for Christmas.* 1952. Longman Green. 1st ed. dj. VG $20.00

HORGAN, Paul. *The Fault of Angels.* 1933. New York. Harper. 1st ed. dj. VG $45.00

HORGAN, Paul. *The Peach Stone.* 1967. New York. Farrar. 1st ed. dj. VG $40.00

HORGAN, Paul. *The Thin Mountain Air.* New York. 1st ed. sgn. dj. EX $30.00

HORGAN, Paul. *White Water.* 1970. New York. Farrar. 1st ed. dj. VG $35.00

HORGAN. *From Royal City.* New York. 1st ed. VG $25.00

HORGAN. *Peter Hurd: Portrait Sketch from Life.* 1971. Texas. $10.00

HORLER, Sydney. *The Curse of Boone.* 1930. New York. Mystery League. 1st Am. ed. $25.00

HORN, Madeline Darrough. *Farm on the Hill.* 1955. New York. Ills. Grant Wood. VG $15.00

HORN, S. *Invisible Empire. Story of the K.K.K.* 1939. Boston. 1st ed. dj. VG $35.00

HORN, Stanley F. *The Decisive Battle of Nashville.* 1956. Ills. 181 pp. VG $17.50

HORN, Tom. *Life of Tom Horn, Government Scout & Interpreter.* 1904. Denver. $75.00

HORN, Tom. *Life of Tom Horn, Government Scout & Interpreter.* 1964. U. of OK Press. 277 pp. dj. scarce. $15.00

HORNADAY, John. *The Book of Birmingham.* 1921. NY. Dodd Mead. VG $15.00

HORNADAY, William T. *Campfires in the Canadian Rockies.* 1906. New York. Ills. 1st ed. EX $65.00

HORNADAY, William T. *Campfires on Desert & Lava.* 1908. 1st ed. VG $20.00

HORNADAY, William T. *Campfires in the Canadian Rockies.* 1916. Ills. maps. VG $25.00

HORNADAY, William T. *Official Guide Book to New York Zoological Park.* 1931. NY Zoological Soc. photos. EX $4.00

HORNADAY, William T. *Official Guide to New York Zoological Park.* 1919. NY Zoological Soc. Ills. G $3.50

HORNADAY, William T. *Our Vanishing Wild Life.* 1913. 1st ed. VG $35.00

HORNADAY, William T. *Taxidermy & Zoological Collecting.* 1897. New York. Scribner. Ills. 5th ed. VG $32.50

HORNADAY, William T. *The American Natural History.* 1904. New York. 1st ed. G $25.00

HORNADAY, William T. *The Minds & Manners of Wild Animals.* 1923. Scribner. Ills. 328 pp. G $10.00

HORNADY. *Hornady Handbook of Cartridge Reloading.* 1967. Grand Island. 1st printing. 360 pp. VG $15.00

HORNE, Alex. *The York Legend in the Old Charges.* 1978. London. Lewis. 1st ed. 151 pp. dj. EX $12.50

HORNE, Charles. *Great Men & Famous Women. Pen & Pencil Sketches.* 1894. 8 vol set. $75.00

HORNE, H. Oliver. *History of Savings Banks.* 1947. Oxford. 1st ed. dj. $10.00

HORNE, Henry. *Strange Visitors.* 1869. New York. 1st ed. 249 pp. $22.50

HORNE, Herman H. *Shakespeare's Philosophy of Love.* 1945. Raleigh, NC. sgn. VG $10.00

HORNE, Thomas. *Introduction to Study of Biography.* 1814. London. 2 vol. rebound full leather. VG $250.00

HORNER, Harlan. *Lincoln & Greeley.* 1953. U. IL Press. 1st ed. dj. EX $10.00

HORNING. *Treasury of American Design.* 1976. Abrams. 2 vol set. VG $75.00

HORNUNG. *Book of the American West.* 1949. Simon & Schuster. Ills. dj. VG $20.00

HORWOOD, William. *Duncton Wood.* 1980. New York. McGraw Hill. 1st ed. dj. EX $30.00

HORWOOD, William. *The Stonor Eagle.* 1982. New York. Franklin Watts. 1st ed. dj. EX $25.00

HOSACK, David. *Lectures on the Theory & Practice of Physics.* 1838. Philadelphia. 700 pp. $35.00

HOSKING, Eric. *An Eye for a Bird.* 1973. 1st Am. ed. 301 pp. index. VG $10.00

HOSKINS, Katherine. *A Penetential Primer. Poems.* 1945. Cummington. Ltd. ed. wrappers. EX $65.00

HOSMER, James K. *Life of Young Sir Henry Vane.* 1888. New York. 1st ed. VG $22.50

HOSMER, James K. *The Color Guard.* 1864. Boston. 1st ed. 244 pp. G $27.50

HOSMER, James K. *Winthrop's Journal.* 1908. Ills. 2 vol set. G $22.50

HOSPITAL, Janette Turner. *The Ivory Swing.* 1982. Dutton. 1st Am. ed. dj. VG $15.00

HOTCHKIN, James H. *History of Purchase & Settlement of Western NY.* 1848. New York. Dodd. 1st ed. VG $50.00

HOTCHKISS. *Hummel Art.* 1978. Des Moines. Ltd. 1st ed. sgn. 400 photos. $75.00

HOTCHNER, E.A. *King of the Hill.* 1972. dj. EX $6.50

HOTCHNER. *Papa Hemingway.* 1955. 304 pp. dj. EX $7.00

HOTSON, Leslie. *Shelley's Lost Letters to Harriet.* 1930. Boston/London. Ltd. ed. 1/950. sgn. slipcase. $35.00

HOTTES, Alfred C. *The Book of Perennials.* 1933. New York. Ills. 272 pp. $5.00

HOTTON, N. *The Evidence of Evolution.* 1968. Am. Heritage. Ills. photos. 160 pp. dj. EX $10.00

HOUDIN, Robert. *Life of Houdin, King of the Conjurers.* Philadelphia. Coates. trans. MacKenzie. VG $17.50

HOUDIN, Robert. *Robert Houdin, the Great Wizard.* 1944. Minneapolis. Jones. trans. MacKenzie. VG $25.00

HOUDINI, Harry. *Houdini, a Magician Among the Spirits.* 1972. G $3.00

HOUDINI, Harry. *Miracle Mongers & Their Methods.* 1920. New York. Dutton. 1st ed. VG $50.00

HOUDINI, Harry. *Miracle Mongers & Their Methods.* 1929. New York. Ills. 2nd printing. 240 pp. EX $15.00

HOUDINI, Harry. *The Unmasking of Robert Houdin.* London. (ca.1920) inscr. dtd. 1923. $90.00

HOUGH, Emerson. *Law of the Land.* 1904. Ills. Keller. 1st ed. VG $20.00

HOUGH, Emerson. *North of 36.* 1923. 1st ed. VG $20.00

HOUGH, Emerson. *Out of Doors.* 1915. $27.50

HOUGH, Emerson. *The Covered Wagon.* 1922. Grosset & Dunlap. Ills. $5.50

HOUGH, Emerson. *The Girl at the Halfway House.* 1900. $28.00

HOUGH, Emerson. *The Mississippi Bubble.* 1902. Bowen Merrill. Ills. Henry Hutt. 1st ed. VG $20.00

HOUGH, Emerson. *The Purchase Price.* 1910. $27.50

HOUGH, Emerson. *The Ship of Souls.* 1925. $27.50

HOUGH, Emerson. *The Story of the Cowboy.* 1897. New York. Ills. C.M. Russell. 1st ed. EX $37.50

HOUGH, Emerson. *The Way of a Man.* 1907. $30.00

HOUGH, Emerson. *The Way of the West. Boone, Crockett, & Carson.* 1903. Bobbs Merrill. Ills. Remington. VG $25.00

HOUGH, Emerson. *The Way Out.* 1918. $27.50

HOUGH, Emerson. *Way of a Man.* 1907. New York. Grosset & Dunlap. 345 pp. dj. $3.00

HOUGH, Emerson. *54, 40 or Fight.* 1909. Bobbs Merrill. 1st ed. $15.00

HOUGH, Frank. *The Island War.* 1947. Lippincott. 1st ed. dj. VG $30.00

HOUGH, Franklin B. *Prize Essay on Medical & Vital Statistics.* 1867. Albany. Ills. 37 pp. $25.00

HOUGH, Henry Beetle. *Martha's Vineyard, 1835-1935.* 1936. Tuttle. Rutland. Ills. VG $30.00

HOUGH, Henry Beetle. *Thoreau of Walden. The Man & His Eventful Life.* 1956. New York. 1st printing. 275 pp. $10.00

HOUGH, Lynn Harold. *Twelve Merry Fishermen.* 1923. 1st ed. $8.50

HOUGH, Richard. *Edwina, Countess of Mountbatten of Burma.* 1984. Morrow. 1st Am. ed. dj. EX $25.00

HOUGH, Richard. *The Blind Horn's Hate.* 1971. Norton. Ills. 1st ed. dj. EX $15.00

HOUGH. *The Broken Gate.* 1917. 1st ed. VG $20.00

HOUGH. *The Web.* 1919. 1st ed. VG $20.00

HOUGHTON, Norris. *Moscow Rehearsals.* 1936. 1st ed. dj. $8.50

HOUGHTON, W. *British Fresh-Water Fishes.* 1981. London. Ills. 2nd ed. G $25.00

HOUGHTON, W. *British Fresh-Water Fishes.* 1984. London. Ills. Lydon. 256 pp. dj. $30.00

HOUGHTON, Walter. *History of American Politics.* 1883. Indianapolis. Ills. 550 pp. VG $25.00

HOUSE, Brant. *Death Torch Terror.* Corinth. pb. VG $7.50

HOUSE, Brant. *Secret Agent X. Servants of the Skull.* 1966. Corinth. pb. EX $8.50

HOUSE, Edward. *Hunters Campfires.* 1909. Ills. 1st ed. VG $48.00

HOUSE, Homer D. *Wild Flowers of New York.* 1918. Albany. 2 vol set. G $35.00

HOUSE, Homer D. *Wild Flowers.* 1934. New York. 1st ed. 364 Ills. EX $65.00

HOUSEHOLD, Geoffrey. *Arabesque.* 1948. Little, Brown. dj. $3.50

HOUSMAN, A.E. *A Shropshire Lad.* 1914. London. Warner. Ltd. ed. VG $225.00

HOUSMAN, A.E. *A Shropshire Lad.* 1986. London. Folio Society. Ills. 1st ed. $30.00

HOUSMAN, A.E. *Fifteen Letters to Walter Ashburner.* 1976. Edinburgh. Tragara Press. Ltd. 1st ed. $70.00

HOUSMAN, A.E. *More Poems.* 1936. New York. Knopf. 1st Am. ed. VG $10.00

HOUSMAN, A.E. *Name & Nature of Poetry.* 1933. New York. 1st ed. dj. VG $20.00

HOUSMAN, A.E. *The Collected Poems.* 1939. London. 1st collected ed. dj. VG $45.00

HOUSMAN, A.E. *The Confines of Criticism.* 1969. Cambridge. 1st unexpurgated printing. dj. $30.00

HOUSMAN, A.E. *The Name & Nature of Poetry.* 1933. New York. Macmillan. 50 pp. dj. VG $6.50

HOUSMAN, Clemence. *The Werewolf.* 1896. London/Chicago. Ills. 1st ed. VG $125.00

HOUSMAN, L. *A.E. Housman.* 1937. London. Cape. Ills. 1st ed. dj. VG $35.00

HOUSMAN, L. *Gracious Majesty.* 1942. New York. Ills. Shephard. 1st Am. ed. VG $15.00

HOUSMAN, L. *The Chinese Lantern.* 1908. 1st ed. VG $20.00

HOUSMAN, L. *The Queen's Progress.* 1932. 1st ed. VG $20.00

HOUSMAN. *Stories from the Arabian Nights.* 1907. Scribner. Ills. Dulac. EX $160.00

HOUSTON, David. *Eight Years with Wilson's Cabinet, 1913-1920.* 1926. New York. Ills. 2 vol set. EX $20.00

HOUSTON, J. *The White Dawn, an Eskimo Saga.* 1971. Harcourt Brace. Ills. 1st ed. 275 pp. dj. EX $6.00

HOVEY, H.C. *Mammoth Cave of Kentucky.* 1912. Louisville. revised ed. VG $25.00

HOVEY, R.B. *John Jay Chapman, an American Mind.* 1959. dj. VG $10.00

HOVING, Thomas. *King of the Confessors.* 1981. New York. Simon & Schuster. 365 pp. dj. $6.00

HOW, Louis. *The Other Don Juan.* 1932. New York. Ills. Steele Savage. VG $12.50

HOW, Robert. *Lecture on Bookbinding as a Fine Art.* 1886. New York. Grolier Club. Ltd. ed. $250.00

HOWARD, Elizabeth Metzger. *Before the Sun Goes Down.* 1946. New York. Doubleday. 378 pp. dj. $3.50

HOWARD, Joseph K. *Montana Margins, a State Anthology.* 1946. Yale U. Press. dj. G $15.00

HOWARD, Joseph K. *Strange Empire. Narrative of the Northwest.* 1952. New York. Ills. 601 pp. index. dj. $14.00

HOWARD, Keble. *The Peculiar Major.* 1919. New York. Doran. 1st ed. VG $15.00

HOWARD, L. *Birds as Individuals.* 1952. London. Collins. Ills. 223 pp. VG $5.00

HOWARD, L.O. *The Insect Book.* 1901. Doubleday. Ills. 1st ed. pls. VG $50.00

HOWARD, Louise E. *Sir Albert Howard in India.* 1954. Emmaus, PA. 272 pp. dj. EX $3.50

HOWARD, Maureen. *Grace Abounding.* 1982. Little, Brown. proof copy. wrappers. VG $25.00

HOWARD, Michael S. *Jonathan Cape, Publisher.* 1971. London. Cape. presentation copy. dj. $20.00

HOWARD, Patricia. *Gluck & the Birth of Modern Opera.* 1964. New York. 1st Am. ed. VG $20.00

HOWARD, R.W. *The Horse in America.* 1965. Follett. 89 photos. 289 pp. VG $10.00

HOWARD, Robert E. *Almuric.* 1975. Grant. 1st ed. dj. EX $25.00

HOWARD, Robert E. *Black Vulmea's Revenge.* 1976. 1st ed. dj. VG $15.00

HOWARD, Robert E. *Garden of Fear/Other Stories-Bizarre & Fantastic.* 1945. Crawford. wrappers. $20.00

HOWARD, Robert E. *Hour of the Dragon.* 1977. Putnam. 1st ed. dj. EX $15.00

HOWARD, Robert E. *King Conan.* 1953. New York. Gnome. 1st ed. dj. EX $75.00

HOWARD, Robert E. *Red Shadows.* 1968. 1st ed. dj. VG $75.00

HOWARD, Robert E. *Skull Face & Others.* 1946. Sauk City. Arkham House. 1st ed. EX $150.00

HOWARD, Robert E. *The Coming of Conan.* 1953. New York. Gnome. 1st ed. dj. VG $85.00

HOWARD, Robert E. *The Hour of the Dragon.* 1977. New York. Ills. 296 pp. dj. EX $25.00

HOWARD, Robert E. *The Sowers of the Thunder.* 1973. 1st ed. sgn. dj. EX $50.00

HOWARD, Robert E. *The Sword of Conan.* 1952. New York. Gnome. 1st ed. dj. VG $65.00

HOWARD, Robert E. *Tigers of the Sea.* 1974. Grant. 1st ed. dj. EX $15.00

HOWARD, Robert E. *Vultures Fictioneers.* 1975. 2nd ed. dj. EX $15.00

HOWARD, Vernon. *Power of Super Mind.* 1967. New York. sgn. dj. VG $8.00

HOWARD. *Dorothy's World/Childhood Sabine Bottom 1902-10.* 1977. 298 pp. dj. VG $15.00

HOWARD. *How to Solve Chess Problems.* 1945. Philadelphia. 1st ed. dj. VG $7.00

HOWARTH. *The Koh-I-Nor Diamond.* 1908. New York. 160 pp. dj. $20.00

HOWAT, John K. *The Hudson River & Its Painters.* New York. Studio Book. Ills. map. dj. $22.50

HOWE, Ellic. *The Magicians of the Golden Dawn.* 1972. London. 306 pp. dj. EX $22.50

HOWE, Gordon. *Hockey, Here's Howe!* 1963. Toronto. Ills. 89 pp. VG $5.00

HOWE, Helen. *The Gentle Americans, 1864-1960.* 1965. New York. Harper. Ills. 1st ed. 458 pp. $7.50

HOWE, Henry. *American Mechanics.* 1844. New York. 482 pp. $3.50

HOWE, Henry. *Historical Collection of the Great West.* 1857. New York. Tuttle. 2 vols in 1. 527 pp. $60.00

HOWE, Henry. *Historical Collections of Ohio, Vol. II.* 1907. Cincinnati. pub by State of Ohio. fair $45.00

HOWE, Henry. *Rivers of America. Salt-Rivers of Massachusetts.* 1951. Shore. $10.00

HOWE, Henry. *The Great West.* 1851. Cincinnati. rebound. G $20.00

HOWE, Julia W. *Later Lyrics.* 1866. Boston. Tilton. 1st ed. 1st issue. $30.00

HOWE, Julia Ward. *A Trip to Cuba.* 1860. Boston. 1st ed. $25.00

HOWE, Louise Kapp. *Moments on Maple Avenue.* 1984. New York. proof copy. wrappers. EX $30.00

HOWE, M.A. *The Boston Symphony Orchestra.* 1924. Boston. Ills. 1st ed. VG $15.00

HOWE, M.A. De Wolfe. *Who Lived Here?* 1952. Bramhall House.1st ed. photos. G $15.00

HOWE, Robin. *German Cooking.* 1957. London. Deutsch. 223 pp. $4.00

HOWE, Stuart. *Mosquito Portfolio.* 1984. London. 1st ed. EX $6.50

HOWE, W.H. *Here Lies. Collection of Epitaphs.* New York. 197 pp. dj. VG $6.00

HOWE CAVERNS, INC. *The Story of Howe Caverns.* New York. (ca.1930) Ills. Ltd. ed. $3.50

HOWELL, A.H. *Florida Bird Life.* 1932. Ills. Jaques. maps. 579 pp. EX $45.00

HOWELL, Barbara. *A Mere Formality.* 1981. Evans. proof copy. dj. VG $15.00

HOWELL, G.C. *The Case of Whiskey.* 1928. Altadena, CA. Howell. Ills. 238 pp. VG $10.00

HOWELL, John & Schroeder, H. *History of the Incandescent Lamp.* 1927. New York. Ills. 1st ed. 208 pp. $22.50

HOWELL, John. *The Life & Adventures of Alexander Selkirk.* 1829. Edinburgh. Oliver & Boyd. rebound. $100.00

HOWELL, W.W. *Cranial Variation in Man.* 1973. Peabody Museum.1st ed. stiff wrappers. $10.00

HOWELLS, W.D. *A Pair of Patient Lovers.* 1901. Harpers. 1st ed. G $20.00

HOWELLS, W.D. *An Imperative Duty.* 1892. New York. 150 pp. $15.00

HOWELLS, W.D. *Between the Dark & the Daylight.* 1907. London/NY. 184 pp. $12.50

HOWELLS, W.D. *Certain Delightful English Towns.* 1906. NY/London. Ills. 1st trade ed. 289 pp. $12.50

HOWELLS, W.D. *Impressions & Experiences.* 1896. New York. 281 pp. $17.50

HOWELLS, W.D. *Italian Journeys.* 1905. Boston. Ills. J. Pennell. VG $27.50

HOWELLS, W.D. *Literary Friends & Acquaintances.* 1901. London/NY. Ills. 287 pp. $15.00

HOWELLS, W.D. *Literature & Life Studies.* 1902. New York. VG $20.00

HOWELLS, W.D. *Questionable Shapes.* 1903. Harper. $9.00

HOWELLS, W.D. *The Coast of Bohemia. Biographical Edition.* 1899. NY/London. 340 pp. $15.00

HOWELLS, W.D. *The Knetons.* 1902. London/NY. 1st ed. $10.00

HOWELLS, W.D. *The Rise of Silas Lapham.* 1885. Boston. 1st ed. 2nd state. VG $45.00

HOWELLS, W.D. *The Sleeping Car.* 1899. Boston. Houghton Mifflin. 212 pp. $5.00

HOWELLS, W.D. *The Undiscovered Country.* 1880. Boston. 1st ed. 419 pp. $17.50

HOWELLS, W.D. *Their Silver Wedding.* 1899. New York. Harper. Ills. 2 vol set. G $15.00

HOWELLS, W.W. *Anthropometry of the Natives in Arnhem Land.* 1937. Peabody Museum.1st ed. stiff wrappers. $12.50

HOWELLS, William C. *Recollections of Life in Ohio 1813-1840.* 1895. Cincinnati. VG $100.00

HOWELLS. *A Boy's Town.* 1890. New York. 1st ed. VG $45.00

HOWES, P.G. *The Giant Cactus Forest & Its World.* 1954. Boston. Ills. 1st ed. $10.00

HOWITT, Mary. *Mabel on Midsummer Day.* 1881. Boston. Ills. Helen Hinds. $30.00

HOWLAND, Edward. *Grant as a Soldier & Statesman.* 1868. Hartford. Ills. 1st ed. EX $45.00

HOWLAND, Harry S. *America in Battle.* Paris. Ills. 1st ed. 615 pp. index. $15.00

HOWLAND, Joseph. *House Beautiful Book of Gardens & Outdoor Living.* 1958. Garden City. Doubleday. Ills. 376 pp. $15.00

HOWLETT, Thomas. *Anglo-Israel, the Jewish Problem, Ten Lost Tribes.*1894. Philadelphia. 158 pp. map. $20.00

HOYLE, F. & G. *Seven Steps to the Sun.* 1970. Harper & Row. 1st ed. dj. EX $15.00

HOYLE, Fred. *Ossian's Ride.* 1959. London. 1st ed. dj. VG $20.00

HOYT, Edwin P. *The Goulds.* 1969. ex-lib. G $2.50

HOYT, Edwin P. *The Mutiny on the Globe.* 1975. $7.50

HOYT, Edwin. *The Last Explorer, the Adventures of Admiral Byrd.*1968. John Day. photos. 380 pp. dj. EX $7.50

HOYT, R. *Siskiyou Two-Step.* 1983. Morrow. dj. EX $9.00

HOYT, R. *Trotsky's Run.* 1982. Morrow. dj. EX $8.50

HOYT, Richard. *Decoys.* 1980. New York. Evans. 1st ed. dj. EX $15.00

HOYT, Roy. *'We Can Take It.' Short Story of the C.C.C.* 1935. New York. American Book Co. Ills. Davis. $35.00

HSU, Francis. *Americans & Chinese.* Garden City. 492 pp. VG $7.00

HUARD, Frances W. *My Home in the Field of Mercy.* 1917. 269 pp. $6.00

HUBALA. *Baroque & Roccoco Art.* 1976. Universe Books. $5.00

HUBBARD, B. *Mush, You Malemutes.* 1938. America Press. photos. maps. 179 pp. G $12.50

HUBBARD, Bela. *Memorials of a Half-Century.* 1887. New York. Ills. 1st ed. 581 pp. $35.00

HUBBARD, E.H. *On Making & Collecting Etchings.* 1923. New York. 2nd ed. $20.00

HUBBARD, Elbert. *Elbert Hubbard Speaks.* 1934. Roycrofters. 142 pp. $12.50

HUBBARD, Elbert. *Health & Wealth.* 1908. Roycrofters. VG $20.00

HUBBARD, Elbert. *Little Journeys to the Homes of the Great.* 1926. New York. Wise. 203 pp. $75.00

HUBBARD, Elbert. *Little Journeys to the Homes of the Great.* 1913. memorial ed. 13 vol set. $30.00

HUBBARD, Elbert. *Man of Sorrows.* 1905. Roycrofters. Ills. 1st ed. VG $20.00

HUBBARD, Elbert. *The Notebook of Elbert Hubbard.* 1927. Wise & Co. Roycrofters. EX $12.50

HUBBARD, Elbert. *White Hyacinths.* 1907. East Aurora. EX $40.00

HUBBARD, L. Ron. *Black Genesis.* 1986. 1st ed. dj. EX $20.00

HUBBARD, L. Ron. *Dianetics*. 1950. Hermitage. 4th printing. dj. VG $45.00

HUBBARD, L. Ron. *Mission Earth*. 1985. Bridge Pub. uncorrected proof. wrappers. $65.00

HUBBARD, L. Ron. *Slaves of Sleep*. 1948. Chicago. Shasta. 1st ed. dj. VG $45.00

HUBBARD, L. Ron. *Typewriter in the Sky/Fear*. 1951. New York. Gnome. 1st ed. dj. VG $35.00

HUBBARD, Leonidas. *Woman's Way Through Labrador*. 1909. Doubleday. Ills. 2nd ed. $25.00

HUBBARD. *Merry Songs & Games for Kindergarten*. 1887. St.Louis. 2nd ed. 192 pp. $27.50

HUBBS, C.L. & Lagler, K.F. *Fishes of the Great Lakes Region*. 1947. Cranbrook Inst. Ills. 1st ed. 186 pp. VG $15.00

HUBERT *The Ohio River*. 1906. Ills. 378 pp. $12.50

HUBERT & PORCHER. *Carolingian Renaissance*. 1970. Braziller. dj. VG $50.00

HUBIN, Allen J. *Crime Fiction, 1749-1980*. 1984. New York. Garland. 2nd ed. EX $75.00

HUBLER, Richard G. *Straight Up*. 1961. New York. Ills. 1st ed. 340 pp. $12.50

HUC, M. *Travels in Tartary, Tibet & China*. London. (ca.1852?) 2 vol set. VG $65.00

HUDDLESTON, Sisley. *Back to Montparnasse*. 1931. Philadelphia. Lippincott. Ills. 1st ed. $10.00

HUDDLESTON, Sisley. *Europe in Zigzags*. 1929. Philadelphia. 1st ed. dj. VG $10.00

HUDLESTON, F.J. *Warriors in Undress*. 1926. Boston. Ills. 229 pp. VG $10.00

HUDSON, Alfred. *Kazak Social Structure*. 1938. Yale U. Press. 1st ed. stiff wrappers. $10.00

HUDSON, Derek. *Arthur Rackham, His Life & Work*. 1970. New York. 1st ed. dj. EX $45.00

HUDSON, Derek. *Arthur Rackham, His Life & Work*. 1973. Scribner. 67 color Ills. 181 pp. folio. $85.00

HUDSON, Derek. *Arthur Rackham, His Life & Work*. 1975. New York. 180 pp. dj. VG $25.00

HUDSON, G.E. *The Amphibians & Reptiles of Nebraska*. 1972. NB U. Press. Ills. 146 pp. EX $10.00

HUDSON, Helen. *Criminal Trespass*. 1985. New York. proof copy. wrappers. EX $25.00

HUDSON, Henry W. *The Story of Snag 56*. 1946. Cambridge. Ills. 110 pp. $6.00

HUDSON, W.H. *A Hind in Richmond Park*. 1923. Dutton. Ltd. 1st ed. VG $60.00

HUDSON, W.H. *A Hind in Richmond Park*. 1922. 1st ed. G $25.00

HUDSON, W.H. *A Little Boy Lost*. 1905. London. 1st ed. VG $50.00

HUDSON, W.H. *A Little Boy Lost*. 1923. New York. Knopf. 222 pp. EX $3.50

HUDSON, W.H. *Famous Missions of California*. 1901. New York. photos. sketches. VG $10.00

HUDSON, W.H. *Far Away & Long Ago*. 1918. London. 1st ed. EX $40.00

HUDSON, W.H. *Far Away & Long Ago*. 1918. New York. 1st ed. G $18.00

HUDSON, W.H. *Green Mansions*. 1944. Ills. E.M. Kauffer. $2.00

HUDSON, W.H. *Green Mansions*. 1943. New York. Knopf. Ills. Butler. VG $15.00

HUDSON, W.H. *Green Mansions*. 1925. Ltd. ed. VG $15.00

HUDSON, W.H. *Idle Days in Patagonia*. 1893. London. Chapman & Hall. Ltd. 1st ed. $85.00

HUDSON, W.H. *Men, Books, & Birds*. 1925. London. 1st ed. dj. VG $35.00

HUDSON, W.H. *Tales of the Gouchos*. 1946. Ills. H.C. Pitz. EX $30.00

HUDSON, W.H. *The Land's End*. 1908. Ills. 1st ed. VG $40.00

HUDSON & CLARKE. *Manhattan*. 1910. Roycrofters. Ills. VG $20.00

HUDSON & RAJCHMAN. *An Explanatary Atlas of the Far East*. London. 143 pp. maps. index. charts. $10.00

HUEBERT. *John Ford: Baroque English Dramatist*. 1977. $6.00

HUESTON, E. *Heaven & Vice Versa*. 1947. 1st ed. dj. EX $6.50

HUFF, Theodore. *Charlie Chaplin*. 1951. Schuman. 1st ed. dj. $20.00

HUFFARD, CARLISLE & FERRIS. *My Poetry Book*. 1934. Philadelphia. Ills. Willy Pogany. 1st ed. $30.00

HUFFARD, Grace Thompson. *My Poetry Book*. 1934. Chicago. Winston. Ills. Wm. Pogany. VG $25.00

HUGARD, Jean. *Card Manipulations*. New York. no date. Ills. $12.50

HUGHES *Tom Brown at Oxford*. World Syndicate. no date. G $4.50

HUGHES, Josiah. *Pioneer West Virginia*. 1932. Charleston. 186 pp. index. wrappers. $10.00

HUGHES, Langston. *An African Treasury*. 1960. New York. Crown. 1st ed. dj. EX $30.00

HUGHES, Langston. *Fields of Wonder*. 1947. New York. 1st ed. $12.00

HUGHES, Langston. *Freedom School Poetry*. 1965. Atlanta. 47 pp. wrappers. $4.00

HUGHES, Langston. *The Ways of White Folks*. 1947. Knopf. 4th ed. dj. VG $40.00

HUGHES, Rupert. *Clipped Wings*. 1914. $7.00

HUGHES, Rupert. *Don't Blame Me*. 1940. New York. 1st ed. dj. scarce $37.50

HUGHES, Rupert. *George Washington. The Human Being & the Hero*. 1926. New York. 2 vol set. EX $17.50

HUGHES, Rupert. *The Complete Detective, Life of Raymond Schindler*. 1950. New York. G $10.00

HUGHES, Sukey. *Washi: World of Japanese Paper*. 1978. Tokyo. Ltd. 1st ed. 1/1000. boxed. EX $250.00

HUGHES, Ted. *Cave Birds*. 1978. London. Ills. Baskin. Ltd 1st ed. sgn. $55.00

HUGHES, Ted. *Cave Birds*. 1978. Viking. Ltd. 1st Am. ed. dj. VG $15.00

HUGHES, Ted. *Crow*. 1971. Harper. 1st Am. ed. VG $6.00

HUGHES, Ted. *Moon-Bells*. 1978. London. 1st ed. $25.00

HUGHES, Ted. *New Selected Poems*. 1982. New York. Harper. 1st ed. dj. VG $25.00

HUGHES, Ted. *Poetry in the Making*. 1967. London. Faber. 1st ed. VG $35.00

HUGHES, Ted. *Scapegoats & Rabies*. 1967. London. Poet & Printer. 1st ed. sgn. $40.00

HUGHES, Ted. *The Earth-Owl & Other Moon-People*. 1963. Faber. Ills. Brandt. 1st ed. dj. VG $35.00

HUGHES, Ted. *Under the North Star*. 1981. London. Faber. 1st ed. sgn. dj. $40.00

HUGHES, Ted. *What is the Truth?* 1984. London. Faber. 1st ed. sgn. dj. EX $40.00

HUGHES, Thomas. *Tom Brown at Oxford*. Alden, IL. no date. VG $6.50

HUGHES, Thomas. *Tom Brown at Oxford*. U.S. Book Co. no date. VG $6.50

HUGHES, Thomas. *Tom Brown's School Days*. Hurst & Co. Arlington ed. Ills. G $4.50

HUGHES, Thomas. *Tom Brown's School Days*. Grosset & Dunlap. no date. VG $4.50

HUGHES, Thomas. *Tom Brown's School Days*. 1858. Tauchnitz. 1st ed. $50.00

HUGHS, Dom Anselm. *Early Medieval Music. Vol. II*. 1954. London. EX $15.00

HUGHS, Henry. *Immortal Sails*. 1969. $6.50

HUGHS. *The Boy Scout Afloat*. 1918. Barse & Hopkins. Ills. Wrenn. $3.50

HUGO, Madame. *Victor Hugo by a Witness of His Life*. 1863. New York. 1st ed. G $15.00

HUGO, Victor. *Les Miserables*. 1943. Book League. $3.00

HUGO, Victor. *Les Miserables*. 1888. New York. Routledge. Ills. 506 pp. $4.00

HUGO, Victor. *Notre-Dame de Paris*. 1955. Ltd. Ed. Club. trans. Haynes. Ills. Lamotte. $45.00

HUGO, Victor. *The Complete Works of Victor Hugo*. Paris. (ca.1896) 10 vol set. EX $125.00

HUGO, Victor. *The Toilers of the Sea*. 1866. New York. Harper. VG $40.00

HUGO, Victor. *The Toilers of the Sea*. 1878. New York. Ills. Dore. 1st ed. $40.00

HUIE, William Bradford. *From Omaha to Okinawa. Story of Seabees in WWII*. 1945. Dutton. Ills. 1st ed. $10.00

HUIE, William Bradford. *In the Hours of Night*. 1975. New York. Delacorte. 1st ed. dj. VG $20.00

HUIE, William Bradford. *The Case Against Admirals*. 1946. New York. Dutton. 1st ed. 216 pp. $52.50

HUIE, William Bradford. *The Execution of Private Slovik*. 1954. Boston/NY. 1st ed. dj. VG $10.00

HUIE, William Bradford. *The Klansman*. 1967. New York. Delacorte. 1st ed. dj. VG $25.00

HUISH, Marcus B. *The American Pilgrim's Way in England*. 1907. London. 375 pp. 43 pls Chettle. VG $85.00

HUISMAN & DORTU. *Lautrec by Lautrec*. Galahad. dj. EX $40.00

HULBERT, Archer B. *Forty-Niners. Chronicle of California Trail*. 1931. New York. Blue Ribbon Books. Ills. VG $6.50

HULBERT, Archer B. *Forty-Niners. Chronicle of California Trail*. 1931. Boston. Ills. 1st ed. 340 pp. VG $30.00

HULBERT, Archer B. *Washington & the West*. Century. G $30.00

HULBERT, Archer Butler. *Records of Original Proceedings of Ohio Company*. 1917. Marietta, OH. Ills. 2 vol set. $60.00

HULL, Arthur & Hale, S. *Coal Men of America*. 1918. Chicago. Ills. 506 pp. $20.00

HULL, Bobby. *Hockey is My Game*. 1967. Longman. Ills. 212 pp. dj. VG $7.50

HULL, Moses. *The Contrast*. 1873. Boston. 1st ed. 236 pp. VG $40.00

HULME, K. *Look a Lion in the Eye, on Safari Through Africa*. 1974. Little, Brown. Ills. 1st ed. 223 pp. dj. EX $10.00

HULME, S. *The Book of the Pig*. 1979. Saiga, England.Ills. 210 pp. dj. EX $10.00

HUME, Cyril. *Myself & the Young Bowman & Other Fantasies*. 1932. Garden City. Doubleday. Ltd. ed. sgn. EX $30.00

HUME, Fergus. *A Traitor in London*. 1900. New York. Buckles. 1st Am. ed. VG $8.50

HUME, Fergus. *The Disappearing Eye*. 1909. New York. Dillingham. 1st Am. ed. VG $10.00

HUME, Fergus. *The Harlequin Opal*. 1893. Chicago. Rand McNally. 1st ed. VG $25.00

HUME, M. *Histoire De La Maison De Stuart*. 1760. Alondres. 3 vol set. $50.00

HUMISTON, Fred. *Blue Water Men & Women*. 1965. $5.50

HUMPHREY, David. *Miscellaneous Works*. 1804. New York. VG $60.00

HUMPHREY, Maud. *Little Continentals*. 1900. Stokes. 6 color pls. rebound. VG $95.00

HUMPHREY, William. *Hostages to Fortune*. 1984. New York. Delacorte. 1st ed. dj. VG $20.00

HUMPHREY, William. *Proud Flesh*. 1973. New York. Knopf. 1st ed. dj. VG $25.00

HUMPHREY, William. *The Ordways*. 1965. New York. Knopf. 1st ed. dj. VG $20.00

HUMPHREY, William. *The Spawning Run*. 1970. Knopf. Ills. Wood. 2nd ed. dj. $7.50

HUMPHREYS, A.A. *Gettysburg to the Rapidon*. 1883. New York. 86 pp. $35.00

HUMPHREYS, David. *Life, Anecdotes, & Heroic Exploits of I.L. Putnam.*1849. Cleveland. Ills. 66 pp. wrappers. $35.00

HUMPHREYS, Frederick. *The Humphreys Family in America*. 1885. New York. Ills. 1115 pp. 2 vol set. VG $275.00

HUMPHREYS, J.R. *The Lost Towns & Roads of America*. 1961. New York. Doubleday. Photos. 194 pp. $10.00

HUMPHREYS, W.J. *Rain Making & Other Weather Vagaries*. 1926. Baltimore. Williams & Wilkins. 157 pp. G $6.00

HUNDERTWASSER. *Catalogue of the Exhibition of His Work*. 1975. 1st ed. $22.50

HUNEKER, James. *Painted Veils*. 1929. New York. Ills. Majecka. Ltd. ed. $30.00

HUNGERFORD, Edward. *Story of Waldorf-Astoria*. 1925. New York. Ills. 1st ed. VG $22.50

HUNGERFORD, Edward. *Wells Fargo. Advancing the American Frontier*. 1949. Random House. 1st ed. dj. G $12.50

HUNT, A.W. & Halkett, G.R. *Our Grandmothers Gowns*. London. color pls. $25.00

HUNT, B.W. *Indiancraft*. 1953. Milwaukee. Ills. 4th printing. 124 pp. $17.50

HUNT, Blanche S. *Little Brown Koko*. 1940. Ills. Wagstaff. 1st ed. VG $30.00

HUNT, E. Howard. *The Berlin Endings*. 1973. New York. dj. VG $7.50

HUNT, F. *MacArthur & War Against Japan*. 1944. New York. dj. VG $12.50

HUNT, Frazier. *Horses & Heroes/Story of Horse in America 450 Yrs.*1949. New York. 1st ed. dj. VG $15.00

HUNT, Frazier. *Untold Story of Douglas MacArthur*. 1954. New York. 1st ed. sgn. 533 pp. dj. G $12.50

HUNT, Helen. *Bits of Travel*. 1883. Boston. 304 pp. $7.50

HUNT, Jim. *The Men in the Nets*. 1972. McGraw Hill. Ills. Glen Hall. 145 pp. dj. $10.00

HUNT, John. *The Ascent of Everest*. 1954. London. Ills. 300 pp. $7.50

HUNT, L.F. *The International Book of Orchids*. 1984. London. Cavendish. Ills. 169 pp. dj. $20.00

HUNT, Leigh. *The Town; Its Remarkable Characters & Events*. 1848. London. Ills. 1st ed. 2 vol set. $195.00

HUNT, Percival. *If By Your Art*. 1948. Pittsburgh U. Press. 1st ed. $6.00

HUNT, R.C. *Salmon in Low Water*. 1950. New York. Ltd. ed. 1/500. EX $200.00

HUNT, Sir John. *Conquest Everest*. 1st Am. ed. dj. $11.00

HUNTER, Edward. *Brainwashing in Red China*. 1952. Tokyo. Tuttle. 311 pp. VG $15.00

HUNTER, Evan. *Last Summer*. 1968. Doubleday. 1st ed. dj. EX $15.00

HUNTER, George. *Practical Book of Tapestries*. 1925. Ills. EX $37.50

HUNTER, Geroge Leland. *Decorative Furniture*. 1923. Grand Rapids. Ills. folio. dj. VG $100.00

HUNTER, Henry. *Sacred Biography*. 1839. Philadelphia. Cross. G $35.00

HUNTER, Hiram. *Little Folk's Book of Nature*. 1922. New York. Ills. 63 pp. $3.00

HUNTER, J.A. *Hunter*. 1952. New York. Ills. 263 pp. dj. VG $3.50

HUNTER, J.H. *Adrift, Story of Twenty Days on a Raft*. 1943. Grand Rapids. 125 pp. dj. $3.00

HUNTER, John D. *Manners & Customs of Several Indian Tribes*. 1957. Minneapolis. Ltd. ed. 1/1500. 402 pp. $18.50

HUNTER, John D. *Memoirs of Captivity Among Indians of N. America.*1823. London. enlarged ed. $110.00

HUNTER, John. *Treatise on Blood, Inflammation & Gun Shot*. 1817. Philadelphia. Ills. 514 pp. $45.00

HUNTER, Kay. *Duet for a Life Time*. 1964. Ills. 1st Am. ed. dj. EX $12.50

HUNTER, M. *Canadian Wilds*. 1907. Harding. 277 pp. EX $15.00

HUNTER, Robert M.T. *Correspondence of Robert M.T. Hunter, 1826-1876*. 1918. Washington. 1st ed. 383 pp. $25.00

HUNTER, Sam. *American Art of 20th Century*. Abrams. Ills. folio. dj. VG $35.00

HUNTER, Stephen. *The Master Sniper*. 1980. New York. Morrow. 1st ed. dj. EX $25.00

HUNTER, Thomas. *Reflections on Letters of Earl of Chesterfield.* 1870. Boston. $40.00

HUNTER, W.L., M.D. *Jesus Christ Had Negro Blood in His Veins.* 1904. New York. $17.50

HUNTING, G. *The Vicarion.* 1927. Unity Press. 2nd ed. dj. VG $25.00

HUNTINGTON, D. *Our Big Game.* 1904. VG $45.00

HUNTINGTON, Dwight W. *Our Feathered Game. Handbook North Am. Game Birds.* 135 Ills. VG $12.50

HUNTINGTON, E. *Children's Kitchen Garden.* 1881. New York. 58 pp. G $10.00

HUNTINGTON, Ellsworth. *The Red Man's Continent.* 1919. New Haven. Yale U. Press. 183 pp. VG $3.75

HUNTINGTON, J. *On the Edge of Nowhere.* 1907. Crown. inscr. sgn. 183 pp. EX $10.00

HUNTLEY, Chet. *The Generous Years.* 1968. New York. Random House. 215 pp. dj. $6.00

HUNTLEY, Suxanne. *The Twelve Days of Christmas Cookbook.* 1965. Atheneum. Book Club Ed. 143 pp. $4.50

HURD, D.H. *History of Essex County, Mass.* 1888. Philadelphia. Ills. 3130 pp. 2 vol set. $75.00

HURD, Edith Thacher. *Nino & His Fish.* 1954. New York. Ills. Clement Hurd. 1st ed. VG $15.00

HURD, Louis. *Practical Poultry Farming.* 1929. New York. Macmillan. 405 pp. EX $4.50

HURD. *Story of Siegfried.* 1931. Scribner. 6 color pls. VG $14.00

HURLBUT, Gladys. *Next Week East Lynne!* 1950. New York. Dutton. 254 pp. dj. VG $4.50

HURLIMAN. *Germany.* 1961. dj. VG $35.00

HURST, Fannie. *Imitation of Life.* 1933. New York. Harper. 1st ed. $5.00

HURST, Jack. *Nashville's Grand Ole Opry.* 1975. New York. Abrams. Ills. dj. EX $45.00

HURST, John F. *Short History of the Church in the United States.* 1890. New York. 132 pp. $12.50

HURST, R. *The Smokejumpers.* 1966. Caxton. Ills. 284 pp. dj. EX $10.00

HURST & KLINEBURGER. *Big Game Hunting Around the World.* 1969. New York. Expo. Press. 1st ed. EX $17.50

HURSTON, Zora N. *Dust Tracks on a Road.* 1971. Philadelphia. 1st ed. dj. EX $12.50

HURT, Walter. *Scarlet Shadow/Story of Great Colorado Conspiracy.* 1907. Girard, KS. G $25.00

HURTZLER, Arthur E., M.D. *The Horse & Buggy Doctor.* 1938. $4.00

HURWITZ, Maximilian. *Workmen's Circle: History, Ideals, Organization.* 1936. New York. Workmen's Circle. 1st ed. VG $40.00

HUSBAND, Marjorie. *The Book of Marjorie.* 1920. Knopf. 1st ed. VG $10.00

HUSMAN, George. *American Grape Growing & Wine Making.* 1892. New York. VG $75.00

HUSSEIN, Taha. *An Egyptian Childhood.* 1932. London. 168 pp. $7.50

HUSTON, Cleburne. *The Story of the Houston-Huston Ancestors.* 1968. 198 pp. $25.00

HUTCHINGS, Jason M. *In the Heart of Sierras.* 1888. Oakland. Ills. 2nd ed. EX $80.00

HUTCHINS, Grace. *Labor & Silk.* 1929. New York. International. 1st ed. dj. EX $25.00

HUTCHINS, P. & C. *Houseboating on a Colonial Waterway.* 1910. Boston. 299 pp. $5.00

HUTCHINSON, A.S.M. *Once Aboard the Lugger.* 1908. Kennerley. 328 pp. $52.50

HUTCHINSON, Francis. *An Historical Essay Concerning Witchcraft.* 1718. London. 1st ed. 270 pp. EX $285.00

HUTCHINSON, Fredrick W. *The Men Who Found America.* 1909. Stern Press. Ills. Shrader & Moore. VG $15.00

HUTCHINSON, Ruth. *The New Pennsylvania Dutch Cook Book.* 1958. New York. Harper. Book Club Ed. 240 pp. $5.50

HUTCHINSON, Thomas. *History of Province of Massachusetts Bay.* 1828. London. VG $150.00

HUTCHINSON, William. *Cyrus Hall McCormick.* 1930. New York. Deluxe Ltd. ed. 2 vol set. VG $35.00

HUTCHINSON, Woods. *Preventable Diseases.* 1904. Boston. 435 pp. $8.50

HUTCHINSON. *Motoring in the Balkans.* 1909. Chicago. 1st ed. 118 photos. G $20.00

HUTCHINSON. *The Poetical Works of William Wordsworth.* 1920. Oxford U. Press. 986 pp. EX $6.50

HUTTON, Edward. *Brief History of the Kings Royal Rifle Corps.* 1917. Winchester. 2nd ed. maps. 84 pp. $35.00

HUTTON. *Course of Math.* 1806. London. 5th ed. 2 vol set. G $150.00

HUXLEY, Aldous. *After Many a Summer the Swan Dies.* 1939. New York. 1st ed. $15.00

HUXLEY, Aldous. *Along the Road.* 1925. 1st Am. ed. VG $15.00

HUXLEY, Aldous. *An Encyclopedia of Pacifism.* 1937. London. 1st ed. wrappers. VG. $20.00

HUXLEY, Aldous. *Antic Hay.* 1923. 1st Am. ed. VG $20.00

HUXLEY, Aldous. *Brave New World Revisited.* 1958. New York. 1st ed. dj. VG $15.00

HUXLEY, Aldous. *Brave New World.* 1932. New York. Dial Press. 311 pp. dj. $3.50

HUXLEY, Aldous. *Brave New World.* 1932. New York. 1st Am. ed. ex-lib. VG $20.00

HUXLEY, Aldous. *Crome Yellow.* 1921. London. 1st ed. dj. $45.00

HUXLEY, Aldous. *Do What You Will.* 1929. 1st ed. VG $20.00

HUXLEY, Aldous. *Eyeless in Gaza.* 1936. London. Chatto & Windus. 1st ed. dj. $75.00

HUXLEY, Aldous. *Island.* 1962. New York. Harper & Row. 333 pp. dj. $3.50

HUXLEY, Aldous. *Jesting Pilate.* Ills. 2nd printing. G $6.00

HUXLEY, Aldous. *Leda.* no date. 1st Am. ed. VG $22.50

HUXLEY, Aldous. *Little Mexican & Other Stories.* 1924. London. 1st ed. dj. VG $85.00

HUXLEY, Aldous. *Moksha.* 1977. $10.00

HUXLEY, Aldous. *Mortal Coils.* 1922. London. 1st ed. VG $40.00

HUXLEY, Aldous. *On the Margin.* 1st Eng. ed. dj. VG $85.00

HUXLEY, Aldous. *On the Margin.* 1923. New York. 1st Am. ed. G $15.00

HUXLEY, Aldous. *Point Counter Point.* 1928. New York. Doubleday Doran. 432 pp. $35.00

HUXLEY, Aldous. *The Complete Etchings of Goya.* 1943. New York. 266 Ills. dj. VG $45.00

HUXLEY, Aldous. *The Discovery.* 1924. London. Chatto & Windus. 1st ed. VG $35.00

HUXLEY, Aldous. *The Genius & the Goddess.* 1955. London. 1st ed. dj. VG $20.00

HUXLEY, Aldous. *The Gioconda Smile.* 1950. London. 1st ed. wrappers. VG $25.00

HUXLEY, Aldous. *The Olive Tree.* 1937. New York. Harper. 1st ed. $5.00

HUXLEY, Aldous. *Themes & Variations.* 1950. New York. Harper. 272 pp. dj. $3.00

HUXLEY, Aldous. *Time Must Have a Stop.* 1944. New York. Harper. 309 pp. dj. $4.00

HUXLEY, Aldous. *Two or Three Graces & Other Stories.* 1926. London. Chatto & Windus. 1st ed. dj. $65.00

HUXLEY, E. *Flame Trees of Thika.* 1959. London. Chatto & Windus. 280 pp. dj. $10.00

HUXLEY, E. *Scott of the Antarctic.* 1978. Atheneum. Ills. 1st Am. ed. 303 pp. VG $12.50

HUXLEY, E. *The Mottled Lizard.* 1982. London. Chatto & Windus. 311 pp. dj. $9.00

HUXLEY, E. *With Forks & Hope.* 1964. Morrow. 398 pp. dj. VG $9.00

HUXLEY, E. & Van Lawick, H. *Last Days in Eden.* 1984. Amaryllis Pr. Ills. 192 pp. dj. EX $15.00

HUXLEY, Francis. *The Raven & the Writing Desk.* 1976. New York. 1st ed. $7.50

HUXLEY, Julian. *Huxley's Diary of Voyage of H.M.S. Rattlesnake.* 1936. Doran. Ills. 1st ed. 301 pp. VG $25.00

HUXLEY, Juliette. *Wild Lives of Africa.* 1963. London. Collins. Ills. 1st ed. dj. VG $12.50

HUXLEY, Thomas H. *Collected Essays.* 1966. NY. Greenwood. reprint. EX $65.00

HUXLEY, Thomas H. *Science & the Christian Tradition.* 1898. New York. Appleton. VG $25.00

HUXLEY. *Arabia Infelix.* Ltd. 1st ed. 1/692. sgn. dj. $135.00

HUXLEY. *Brief Candles.* 1st English ed. VG $65.00

HUXLEY. *On the Origin of Species.* 1863. New York. Appleton. EX $80.00

HUXLEY. *Vulgarity in Literature.* 1st English ed. dj. VG $45.00

HUYGHE, Rene. *Art Treasures of the Louvre.* 1951. Abrams. VG $20.00

HUYSMANS, J.K. *Against the Grain.* 1931. Three Sirens Press. Ills. VG $17.50

HVASS, Hans. *Fishes of the World.* 1965. Dutton. Ills. Eigener. 1st Am. ed. dj. $10.00

HWELETT, Maurice. *A Masque of Dead Florentines.* 1895. 1st ed. VG $42.50

HYDE, Dayton O. *Yamsi: Journal of One Year on a Wilderness Ranch.* 1971. New York. Dial Press. photos. 318 pp. $4.00

HYDE, E.A. Watson. *Little Sisters to the Campfire Girls.* 1918. Chicago. Ills. Ella Dolbear Lee. dj. $10.00

HYDE, George E. *A History of the Oglala Sioux Indians.* 1937. Norman. 1st ed. EX $50.00

HYDE, George. *Pawnee Indians.* 1951. U. of Denver. 1st ed. dj. $17.50

HYDE, H. Montgomery. *Henry James at Home.* 1969. New York. 1st Am. ed. dj. EX $25.00

HYDE, Phillip. *Last Redwoods.* 1963. San Francisco. 1st ed. dj. VG $35.00

HYDE. *The Last Free Man.* 1973. 1st ed. dj. VG $15.00

HYMA, Albert. *The Dutch in the Far East.* 1942. Ann Arbor. Ills. 1st ed. inscr. 249 pp. $17.50

HYMAN, Mac. *No Time For Sergeants.* New York. 1st Am. ed. dj. VG $20.00

HYMAN, Mac. *No Time for Sergeants.* 1954. New York. Random House. 215 pp. dj. VG $3.50

HYMAN, Sidney. *The Lives of William Benton.* 1969. Chicago. 1st ed. dj. VG $10.00

HYMAN, Stanley Edgar. *The Tangled Bank.* 1962. New York. 1st ed. 492 pp. $7.50

HYMAN, Trina Schart. *Little Red Riding Hood.* 1983. Holiday House. dj. EX $15.00

HYMOFF, E. *1st Air Cavalry Division in Vietnam.* 1972. New York. $85.00

HYNEK, J.A. *UFO Experience.* 1972. 1st ed. sgn. dj. VG $10.00

HYNEMAN, Leon. *Freemasonry in England from 1567 to 1813.* 1877. New York. Worthington. 192 pp. G $20.00

IBANEZ, Blasco. *Blood & Sand.* 1919. 5th printing. VG $6.00

IBANEZ, Blasco. *Luna Benamor.* 1910. VG $6.00

IBANEZ, Blasco. *Mare Nostrum.* 1919. 10th printing. VG $9.00

IBANEZ, Blasco. *Reeds & Mud.* 1928. 289 pp. dj. VG $3.50

IBANEZ, Blasco. *The Four Horsemen of the Apocalypse.* 1921. $30.00

IBANEZ, Blasco. *The Four Horsemen of the Apocalypse.* 1918. VG $9.00

IBANEZ, Blasco. *The Shadow of the Cathedral.* 1919. 17th printing. VG $12.00

IBSEN, Henrik. *A Doll's House.* 1889. New York. 1st Am. ed. VG $25.00

IBSEN, Henrik. *A Doll's House.* 1889. London. Unwin. Ltd. ed. 1/115. sgn. VG $120.00

IBSEN, Henrik. *Arthur Miller's an Enemy of the People.* 1951. New York. Viking. 125 pp. $5.00

IBSEN, Henrik. *Peer Gynt.* 1936. Ills. Rackham. 1st Eng. trade ed. VG $50.00

IBSEN, Henrik. *Peer Gynt.* 1936. Philadelphia. Lippincott. Ills. Rackham. $150.00

IBSEN, Henrik. *Peer Gynt.* 1929. Garden City. Ills. MacKinstry. 1st ed. dj. $60.00

IBSEN, Henrik. *Peer Gynt.* 1955. Oslo. Ills. Per Krohg. 314 pp. VG $45.00

IBSEN, Henrik. *Plays.* 1946. Macmillan. $3.00

ICKIS, M. *The Standard Book of Quilt Making & Collecting.* 1949. Greystone Pr. 276 pp. dj. VG $17.50

IDELL, Albert E. *Centennial Summer.* 1943. New York. Holt. 426 pp. $3.00

ILES, Francis. *Before the Fact.* 1932. London. Gollancz. 1st ed. VG $85.00

ILES, Francis. *Malice Aforethought.* 1946. Stockholm. 1st ed. dj. wrappers. VG $15.00

ILES, G. *Flame, Electricity & the Camera.* 1900. New York. Doubleday & McClure. 398 pp. $20.00

ILIFF, Charles E. *Oculoplastic Surgery.* 1979. Philadelphia. Ills. $60.00

ILIN, M. *New Russia's Primer. The Story of 5-Year Plan.* 1931. 162 pp. $52.50

ILLINGWORTH, F. *Falcons & Falconry.* 1971. London House. Ills. 126 pp. dj. VG $10.00

IMLACH, Punch & Young, Scott. *Heaven & Hell in the N.H.L.* 1982. Ills. 216 pp. dj. EX $10.00

IMLACH, Punch & Young, Scott. *Hockey is a Battle.* 1969. Toronto. Ills. 203 pp. dj. VG $12.50

IMLAY. *Topographical Description Western North America.* 1793. London. Ills. map. $400.00

INCHFAWN, Fay. *Who Goes to the Woods.* 1942. Philadelphia. Winston. Ills. Thorne. $10.00

INGE, William. *Bus Stop.* 1955. Random House. 1st ed. dj. VG $40.00

INGE, William. *Good Luck, Miss Wyckoff.* 1970. Little, Brown. 1st ed. dj. VG $15.00

INGELOW, Jean. *Poems. Vol. I.* 1896. Boston. ex-lib. 513 pp. VG $3.00

INGERSOLL, Ernest. *Alaskan Bird Life.* 1914. Audubon Soc. Ills. Horsfall & Brooks. G $10.00

INGERSOLL, Ernest. *Crest of Continent: Summers Ramble in Mountains.* 1885. Chicago. 1st ed. 344 pp. EX $17.50

INGERSOLL, Ralph. *The Battle is the Payoff.* 1943. New York. 217 pp. dj. EX $4.00

INGERSOLL, Ralph. *Top Secret.* 1946. New York. 373 pp. $4.00

INGERSOLL, Robert G. *Crimes Against Criminals.* 1906. East Aurora. Ills. 1st ed. $10.00

INGLEHART, F.C. *Theodore Roosevelt, the Man as I Knew Him.* 1919. New York. 442 pp. $10.00

INGLIS, Fletcher. *Queen's Gift.* 1952. 382 pp. dj. VG $2.00

INGLIS, J.M. *History of Vegetation of Rio Grande Plain.* 1964. Texas Parks & Wildlife Dept. $10.00

INGLIS, Robert. *Shakespeare's Dramatic Works.* 1871. Gall & Inglis. 944 pp. 4 steel engravings. G $50.00

INGOLDSBY, Thomas. *Ingoldsby Legends.* 1846. New York. 1st ed. G $30.00

INGOLDSBY, Thomas. *The Ingoldsby Legends; or, Mirth & Marvels.* 1911. London. Ills. 546 pp. $15.00

INGPEN, Roger. *One Thousand Poems for Children.* 1923. Philadelphia. Ills. Ethel Franklin Betts. VG $30.00

INGRAHAM, J.H. *Fleming Field; or, The Young Artisan.* 1845. New York. 1st ed. $65.00

INGRAHAM, J.H. *The Prince of the House of David.* 1859. Philadelphia. Ills. EX $40.00

INGSTAD. *East of the Great Glacier.* 1937. New York. 1st Am. ed. VG $12.50

INMAN, Henry. *Buffalo Jones, Forty Years of Adventure.* 1899. Topeka. Ills. 1st ed. 469 pp. $160.00

INMAN, Henry. *The Old Santa Fe Trail.* 1897. Macmillan. Ills. Remington. 493 pp. VG $45.00

INMAN, Samuel G. *Inter-American Conferences 1826-1954.* 1965. Washington. University Press. 282 pp. dj. $3.00

INMAN & CODY. *The Great Salt Lake Trail.* 1899. Topeka. Ills. Clarke. $30.00

INMAN & CODY. *The Great Salt Lake Trail.* 1966. Haines. reprint. Ltd. ed. dj. EX $17.50

INN, Henry. *Hawaiian Types.* 1945. New York. 47 pls. dj. $22.00

INNES, H. *Blue Ice.* 1948. London. dj. VG $25.00

INNES, Hammond. *The Wreck of the Mary Deare.* 1956. Knopf. 211 pp. dj. EX $3.50

INNES, J.H. *New Amsterdam & Its People.* 1902. New York. Scribner. 365 pp. EX $30.00

INNES, Michael. *A Family Affair.* 1969. London. Gollancz. 1st ed. dj. VG $25.00

INNES, Michael. *Appleby's Answer.* 1973. London. Gollancz. 1st ed. sgn. dj. EX $45.00

INNES, Michael. *Appleby's End.* 1945. London. 1st ed. dj. VG $30.00

INNES, Michael. *Going It Alone.* 1980. Dodd Mead. 1st Am. ed. dj. VG $10.00

INNES, Michael. *The Ampersand Papers.* 1978. London. Gollancz. 1st ed. dj. EX $25.00

INNES, Michael. *The Gay Phoenix.* 1976. Dodd Mead. 1st Am. ed. dj. VG $15.00

INNES, Michael. *The Secret Vanguard.* 1941. New York. 1st ed. dj. VG $25.00

INNES, William T. *Exotic Aquarium Fishes.* 1966. 19th rev. ed. 500 Ills. 592 pp. 100 pls. $6.00

INNES, William T. *Exotic Aquarium Fishes.* 1955. Innes. Ills. 18th printing. 540 pp. $12.50

INVERSON, Marion. *The American Chair 1630-1890.* 1957. Hastings House. 1st ed. dj. $15.00

IONESCO, Eugene. *Story Number 1.* 1968. New York. Harlin Quist. dj. VG $15.00

IPCAR, Dahlov. *A Dark Horn Blowing.* 1978. Viking. 1st ed. VG $8.50

IPCAR, Dahlov. *The Warlock of the Night.* 1969. Viking. 1st ed. dj. EX $9.00

IRELAND, J. *Wall Street to Cashmere.* 1859. New York. Ills. 1st ed. dj. VG $50.00

IRISH, William. *Deadline at Dawn.* 1946. Tower. dj. VG $15.00

IRISH, William. *If I Should Die Before I Wake.* 1946. New York. Avon. pb. EX $35.00

IRISH, William. *Night Has a Thousand Eyes.* 1945. New York. 1st ed. dj. $12.00

IRISH, William. *The Dancing Detective.* 1938. Philadelphia. Lippincott. 1st ed. $12.50

IRVINE, Alexander. *From the Bottom Up.* 1910. New York. Ills. ex-lib. 304 pp. $4.00

IRVINE, Alexander. *My Lady of the Chimney Corner.* 1922. Santa Barbara. 221 pp. dj. VG $15.00

IRVING, Clifford. *The Story of Elmyr DeHory.* 1969. McGraw Hill. 1st ed. VG $15.00

IRVING, D. *Destruction of Dresden.* 1963. New York. 1st ed. $28.50

IRVING, Donald. *Sculpture, Material, & Process.* 1970. Van Nostrand. Ills. 1st ed. photos. dj. $4.50

IRVING, H.B. *Studies of French Criminals of the 19th Century.* 1901. Heinemann. 356 pp. G $10.00

IRVING, John. *Cider House Rules.* 1985. New York. 1st ed. sgn. dj. EX $20.00

IRVING, John. *The Hotel New Hampshire.* 1st ed. sgn. dj. EX $35.00

IRVING, John. *The Hotel New Hampshire.* 1981. Dutton. 1st trade ed. dj. VG $17.50

IRVING, John. *The World According to Garp.* 1978. Dutton. 1st ed. dj. VG $30.00

IRVING, John. *The 158-Pound Marriage.* 1974. Random House. 1st ed. dj. VG $60.00

IRVING, Laurence. *Henry Irving: Actor & His World.* 1952. Ills. 1st printing. 743 pp. VG $15.00

IRVING, R. *A History of British Mountaineering.* 1955. London. Ills. 1st ed. VG $20.00

IRVING, Washington. *Anecdotes of Enterprise Beyond Rocky Mountains.* 1868. Putnam. revised ed. complete 1 vol. VG $16.50

IRVING, Washington. *Astoria/Anecdotes of Enterprise Beyond Rocky Mnts.* 1836. Philadelphia. Ills. 1st ed. 2 vol set. $500.00

IRVING, Washington. *Child's Rip Van Winkle.* 1908. New York. Ills. Kirk. 1st ed. 12 pls. EX $30.00

IRVING, Washington. *History of Life & Voyages of Christopher Columbus.* 1831. New York. revised ed. ex-lib. 2 vol set. $22.50

IRVING, Washington. *History of Life & Voyages of Christopher Columbus.* 1850. New York. 3 vol set. VG $35.00

IRVING, Washington. *History of Life & Voyages of Christopher Columbus.* 1892. Putnam. Ills. Isabella ed. 3 vol set. $95.00

IRVING, Washington. *Journal 1803.* 1943. Oxford. 1st ed. dj. slipcase. EX $12.00

IRVING, Washington. *Knickerbocker's History of New York.* 1894. Putnam. Ills. Kemble. 1st ed. 2 vol set. $50.00

IRVING, Washington. *Old Christmas & Bracebridge Hall.* 1918. Constable. Ills. Baumer. VG $15.00

IRVING, Washington. *Old Christmas & Bracebridge Hall.* 1919. Boston/NY. Ills. Lewis Baumer. 1st ed. $25.00

IRVING, Washington. *Old Christmas at Bracebridge Hall.* 1906. New York. Ills. C.E. Brock. $18.00

IRVING, Washington. *Old Christmas.* 1947. Ltd. ed. 1/40. $20.00

IRVING, Washington. *Old Christmas.* 1876. Macmillan. Ills. R. Caldecott. 2nd ed. VG $15.00

IRVING, Washington. *Rip Van Winkle.* 1939. Garden City. Ills. Everett Shinn. VG $13.50

IRVING, Washington. *Sketch Book & Christmas.* Edinburgh. Ills. Duncan. 1st Eng. ed. VG $15.00

IRVING, Washington. *Tales of the Alhambra.* London. Ills. Dixon & Brock. VG $35.00

IRVING, Washington. *The Adventures of Captain Bonneville.* 1862. New York. Putnam. revised, complete ed. $10.00

IRVING, Washington. *The Alhambra.* 1895. Macmillan. Ills. Pennell. 1st ed. dj. VG $140.00

IRVING, Washington. *The Alhambra.* 1942. Macmillan. Ills. Goble. $30.00

IRVING, Washington. *The Angler.* 1931. Portland. Ltd. ed. 1/150. $50.00

IRVING, Washington. *The Crayon Miscellany.* 1849. New York. $35.00

IRVING, Washington. *The Legend of Sleepy Hollow.* Philadelphia. McKay. Ills. Rackham. 8 pls. $35.00

IRVING, Washington. *The Legend of Sleepy Hollow.* 1931. New York. Ills. Wall. Ltd. ed. 1/1200. $75.00

IRVING, Washington. *The Western Journals of U. of Oklahoma.* 1944. 1st ed. dj. $12.50

IRVING, Washington. *Voyages & Discoveries of Companions of Columbus.* 1929. New York. Ills. Ltd. ed. 1/374. VG $45.00

IRVING, Washington. *Voyages & Discoveries of Companions of Columbus.* 1831. Philadelphia. 1st ed. ex-lib. 350 pp. $37.50

IRVING, Washington. *Wolfert's Roost & Other Papers. Now 1st Collected.* 1855. New York. 1st Am. ed. 1st issue. 383 pp. $35.00

IRVING, Washington. *Works of G.P. Putnam.* 1891. revised ed. 21 vol set. G $125.00

IRVING, Washington. *Works of Washington Irving.* 1853. London. 10 vol set. EX $350.00

IRVING. *Tour of the Prairie.* 1967. Pantheon. dj. VG $15.00

IRWIN, Constance. *Fair Gods & Stone Faces.* 1963. New York. photos. 302 pp. dj. $4.00

IRWIN, Howard. *Roadside Flowers of Texas.* 1961. U. of Texas. Ills. Willis. dj. $20.00

IRWIN, J.A. *Hydrotherapy at Saratoga.* (ca.1892) G $18.00

IRWIN, John & Hall, Margaret. *Indian Embroideries.* 1973. Ahmedabad. Ills. dj. EX $35.00

IRWIN, Margaret. *Young Bess.* 1945. New York. 274 pp. $4.50

IRWIN, Will. *Herbert Hoover, a Reminiscent Biography.* 1928. New York. Century. photos. 315 pp. $5.00

ISAMAN, Sara White. *Sophisticating Uncle Hiram.* 1912. Chicago. 224 pp. VG $15.00

ISBELL, F.A. *1852-1870. Mining & Hunting in the Far West.* 1870. Stevenson, CT. J.S. Stewart. 1st ed. 41 pp. $600.00

ISHERMAN, Theodore R. *Industrial Peace & the Wagner Act.* 1947. New York. McGraw Hill. ex-lib. 91 pp. $3.50

ISHERWOOD, C. & Auden, W.H. *Journey to a War.* 1939. 1st Am. ed. inscr. VG $35.00

ISHERWOOD, Christopher. *C.I. & His Kind.* 3rd ed. dj. EX $10.00

ISHERWOOD, Christopher. *Down There on a Visit.* 1962. New York. 1st ed. dj. VG $30.00

ISHERWOOD, Christopher. *Down There on a Visit.* 1962. London. Methuen. 1st ed. dj. VG $35.00

ISHERWOOD, Christopher. *Exhumations.* 1966. Simon & Schuster. 1st ed. dj. $8.50

ISHERWOOD, Christopher. *Lions & Shadows.* 1947. Norfolk. 1st ed. dj. VG $50.00

ISHERWOOD, Christopher. *My Guru & His Disciples.* 1980. London. 1st Eng. ed. dj. EX $30.00

ISHERWOOD, Christopher. *Prater Violet.* 1946. London. Methuen. 1st Eng. ed. dj. VG $75.00

ISHERWOOD, Christopher. *The Memorial.* New York. 1st Am. ed. dj. VG $20.00

ISHERWOOD, Christopher. *The World in the Evening.* 1954. 1st Am. ed. dj. EX $32.50

ISHIDA, Mosaku. *Japanese Buddhist Prints.* 1964. 1st Eng. ed. Ills. folio. $120.00

ISHIKAWA, Masamochi. *The Magical Carpenter of Japan.* 1965. Tuttle. Ills. 260 pp. dj. rare. VG $65.00

IVES, J.C. *Memoir to Accompany a Military Map of Tampa Bay.* 1856. New York. Wynkoop. map. 42 pp. $350.00

IVES, J.C. *Report Colorado River of West, Explored in 1857-8.* 1861. Washington. VG $215.00

J.G. FERGUSON PUB. CO. *Alaska Book: Story of Our Northern Treasureland.* 1960. Chicago. Ills. photos. 320 pp. $10.00

JACK, Ellen. *The Fate of a Fairy or 27 Years in Far West.* 1910. Chicago. VG $40.00

JACKMAN. *Herbs & Medicinal Flowers.* 1973. Gallahad. Ills. Redoute/Daffinger. dj. $25.00

JACKS, L.P. *The Magic Formula.* 1927. Harper. 1st ed. VG $15.00

JACKS. *La Salle.* 1931. 1st ed. VG $15.00

JACKSON, Charles. *Captain Sazarac.* 1922. Indianapolis. 1st ed. 332 pp. dj. $8.00

JACKSON, Charles. *The Lost Weekend.* 1962. Time Books. pb. $1.50

JACKSON, Charles. *The Outer Edges.* 1948. Rinehart. 1st ed. VG $8.00

JACKSON, Crawford. *Near Nature's Heart. A Volume of Verse.* 1923. Atlanta. Ills. 96 pp. $7.50

JACKSON, Edward P. *A Demigod.* 1887. New York. Harper. 1st ed. VG $50.00

JACKSON, G. *The British Whaling Trade.* 1978. Archon. 1st ed. 310 pp. dj. EX $12.50

JACKSON, G.F. *Wyandotte Cave.* 1953. Ills. 1st ed. sgn. dj. VG $25.00

JACKSON, George A. *Jackson's Diary of '59.* 1929. Idaho Springs. Ills. 1st ed. 20 pp. wrappers. $125.00

JACKSON, Halliday. *Civilization of the Indian Natives.* 1830. Philadelphia. 1st ed. 120 pp. $125.00

JACKSON, Harry. *Lost Wax Bronze Casting.* 1972. Ltd. 1st ed. 1/100. $75.00

JACKSON, Helen Hunt. *A Century of Dishonor.* 1881. New York. Harper. 1st ed. VG $100.00

JACKSON, Helen Hunt. *A Century of Dishonor.* 1886. Boston. enlarged ed. VG $25.00

JACKSON, Helen Hunt. *A Century of Dishonor.* 1898. Boston. Little, Brown. 514 pp. $15.00

JACKSON, Helen Hunt. *Bits of Talk.* 1873. Boston. 1st ed. VG $20.00

JACKSON, Helen Hunt. *California & Its Missions.* 1902. Boston. Ills. 1st ed. EX $25.00

JACKSON, Helen Hunt. *Ramona.* 1900. Boston. Ills. Sandham. 618 pp. 2 vol set. $25.00

JACKSON, Helen Hunt. *Ramona.* 1926. Little, Brown. 308 pp. $3.50

JACKSON, Helen Hunt. *Verses.* 1870. Boston. 1st ed. $65.00

JACKSON, Herbert J. *European Hand Firearms of 16th & 18th Centuries.* New York. Bramhall House. Ills. 108 pp. $14.50

JACKSON, Holbrook. *Bookman's Holiday.* 1945. London. 1st ed. dj. VG $20.00

JACKSON, James S. & Margot Y. *At Home on the Hill.* 1983. Akron. Ills. 95 pp. wrappers. EX $6.00

JACKSON, James. *Memoir of James Jackson, Jr.* 1835. Boston. inscr. sgn. 444 pp. rebound. $85.00

JACKSON, John D., M.D. *The Black Arts in Medicine.* 1870. Cincinnati. 28 pp. wrappers. disbound. $25.00

JACKSON, Joseph H. *Western Gate: San Francisco Reader.* 1952. Farrar. $15.00

JACKSON, Joseph Henry. *Dickens' Children Stories.* 1929. Chicago. Donohue. Ills. 1st ed. VG $20.00

JACKSON, Joseph Henry. *Literary Landmarks of Philadelphia.* 1939. Philadelphia. Ills. Ltd. ed. 1/1050. EX $27.50

JACKSON, Joseph Henry. *Tintypes in Gold. Four Studies in Robbery.* 1939. Macmillan. VG $15.00

JACKSON, Kathryn. *The Santa Claus Book.* 1952. New York. Ills. 1st ed. VG $10.00

JACKSON, Leroy F. *The Peter Patter Book.* Rand McNally. Ills. Blanche Fisher Wright. $35.00

JACKSON, Robert B. *Here Comes Bobby Orr.* 1971. New York. Ills. 64 pp. VG $4.00

JACKSON, Robert. *Airships; Popular Hist. of Dirigibles, Zeppelins.* 1973. New York. Ills. 1st Am. ed. 277 pp. VG $17.50

JACKSON, Ronald V. *District of Columbia 1820 Census Index.* 1976. Bountiful, UT. VG $13.00

JACKSON, Ronald V. *Maryland 1800 Census Index.* 1974. Bountiful, UT. Accelerated Indexing Systems. $18.00

JACKSON, Ronald V. *Maryland 1830 Census Index.* 1976. Bountiful, UT. Accelerated Indexing Systems. $20.00

JACKSON, Ronald V. *Virginia 1810 Census Index.* 1975. Bountiful, UT. Accelerated Indexing Systems. $25.00

JACKSON, Shirley. *Hangsman.* 1951. Gollancz. 1st Eng. ed. dj. VG $30.00

JACKSON, Shirley. *Hangsman.* 1951. New York. 1st ed. dj. EX $25.00

JACKSON, Shirley. *Life Among Savages.* New York. 1st ed. dj. VG $22.00

JACKSON, Shirley. *The Bird's Nest.* 1954. New York. 1st ed. dj. EX $35.00

JACKSON, Shirley. *The Road Through the Wall.* 1948. dj. VG $95.00

JACKSON, Sir Charles J. *English Goldsmiths & Their Marks.* 1921. London. 2nd ed. folio. VG $175.00

JACKSON, Thomas. *A Letter to Rev. Edward B. Pusey.* 1843. New York. VG $25.00

JACKSON, William H. *Picture Maker of the Old West.* 1947. Scribner. 308 pp. EX $45.00

JACKSON, William H. *Time Exposure.* 1940. Putnam. Ills. 2nd ed. 341 pp. VG $32.50

JACKSON & Evans. *Marvel Book of American Ships.* 1917. 12 color pls. G $15.00

JACOB, Heinrich Eduard. *Felix Mendelssohn und Seine Zeit.* 1959. Frankfurt. dj. VG $8.50

JACOB, Heinrich Edward. *6,000 Years of Bread. Its Holy & Unholy History.* 1944. Doubleday. VG $30.00

JACOBI, Carl. *Disclosures in Scarlet.* 1972. Sauk City. 1st ed. 181 pp. dj. EX $12.50

JACOBI, Carl. *Revelations in Black.* 1947. Sauk City. Arkham House. $100.00

JACOBI. *Portraits in Moonlight.* 1964. Sauk City. Arkham House. dj. VG $35.00

JACOBIN, Lou. *Guide to Alaska.* (ca. 1972) wrappers. EX $7.50

JACOBS, Flora. *A History of Doll Houses.* 1965. New York. revised ed. 341 pp. dj. $15.00

JACOBS, Flora. *A History of Doll Houses.* 1954. Cassell. 1st Eng. ed. dj. $12.50

JACOBS, Flora. *A History of Doll Houses.* 1953. Scribner. 1st ed. dj. $15.00

JACOBS, Helen Hull. *Tennis.* 1941. A.S. Barnes. Ills. 77 pp. $4.50

JACOBS, Henry Eyster. *The Lutheran Movement in England.* 1890. Philadelphia. ex-lib. 376 pp. G $5.00

JACOBS, Lewis. *Rise of the American Film. A Critical History.* 1939. New York. $10.00

JACOBS, M. *Notes on Rebel Invasion of MD, PA, & Gettysburg.* 1864. Lippincott. 1st ed. G $15.00

JACOBS, Paul. *Is Curley Jewish?* 1965. New York. Atheneum. 339 pp. VG $7.00

JACOBS, Robert & Skelton, G. *Wagner Writes from Paris.* 1973. New York. dj. VG $8.00

JACOBS, W.W. *Snug Harbour.* 1931. Scribner. Ills. 1st ed. $12.50

JACOBS, W.W. *The Castaways.* 1917. New York. Scribner. 1st ed. 303 pp. G $20.00

JACOBS, W.W. *The Lady of the Barge.* 1902. New York. Ills. 1st ed. VG $25.00

JACOBS, Wilbur. *Diplomacy & Indian Gifts.* 1950. Stanford. 1st ed. dj. $12.50

JACOBSEN. *Sennacherib's Aqueduct at Jerwan.* 1935. U. of Chicago. Oriental Institute Pub. $10.00

JACOBSON, Pauline. *City Golden Fifties.* 1941. Berkeley. 1st ed. dj. VG $10.00

JACOBUS, X. *Untrodden Fields of Anthropology.* New York. 2 vols. in 1. G $25.00

JACOBY & CRAWFORD. *The Backgammon Book.* 1974. New York. Viking. SftCvr. EX $3.50

JACQUEMART, A. *History of the Ceramic Art.* 1877. VG $65.00

JAEGER, Edmund C. *Our Desert Neighbors.* 1950. Stanford. 1st ed. dj. EX $12.50

JAEGER, M. *The Question Mark.* 1926. New York. Macmillan. 1st ed. dj. $25.00

JAFFE, Irma B. *Joseph Stella.* 1970. Cambridge. Ills. 262 pp. dj. $15.00

JAFFEE, Al. *The Mad Book of Magic.* 1970. G $2.00

JAKEMAN, M. Wells, Ph.D. *The Origins & History of the Mayas.* 1945. Los Angeles. Ills. 203 pp. VG $25.00

JAKES, J. *Time.* 1972. 1st ed. dj. EX $15.00

JAMES, Edwin. *Narrative of Captivity & Adventure of John Tanner.* 1830. New York. 1st ed. $400.00

JAMES, George W. *In & Out of Old Missions. Pictorial Account.* 1905. Boston. Ills. 1st ed. EX $35.00

JAMES, George W. *In & Out of Old Missions. Pictorial Account.* 1927. Grosset & Dunlap. 392 pp. VG $12.50

JAMES, George W. *Indian Blankets & Their Makers.* 1914. Chicago. Ills. 1st ed. scarce. VG $300.00

JAMES, George W. *New Mexico, Land of the Delight Makers.* 1925. Boston. Ills. 469 pp. index. $35.00

JAMES, George W. *The Indian's Secret of Health.* 1917. Pasadena. EX $35.00

JAMES, George W. *The Old Franciscan Missions of California.* 1913. Boston. 1st ed. VG $35.00

JAMES, George W. *What the White Race May Learn from the Indians.* 1908. Chicago. many pls. EX $35.00

JAMES, George Wharton. *California Romantic & Beautiful.* 1919. Boston. $12.50

JAMES, Henry. *A Landscape Painter.* 1919. New York. Ltd. 1st ed. 1/250. VG $275.00

JAMES, Henry. *A Landscape Painter.* 1919. New York. Scott & Seltzer. 1st trade ed. $20.00

JAMES, Henry. *A Little Tour in France.* 1885. Boston. 1st ed. VG $47.50

JAMES, Henry. *A Most Unholy Trade.* 1923. Cambridge. Scarab Press. Ltd. 1st ed. VG $150.00

JAMES, Henry. *A Small Boy & Others.* 1913. New York. Scribner. 1st ed. VG $34.00

JAMES, Henry. *Autobiography: Small Boy & Others.* 1956. NY. Criterion. Ills. 1st 1 vol ed. dj. EX $32.50

JAMES, Henry. *Charles W. Eliot, President of Harvard University.* 1930. 393 pp. $5.00

JAMES, Henry. *Charles W. Eliot.* 1930. 2 vol set. VG $25.00

JAMES, Henry. *Complete Tales of Henry James.* 1962-64. Philadelphia. 12 vol set. EX $250.00

JAMES, Henry. *Daumier, Caricaturist.* 1954. London. Miniature Bks./Rodale. 1st ed. $37.50

JAMES, Henry. *Embarrassments.* 1896. London. 1st ed. VG $150.00

JAMES, Henry. *Embarrassments.* 1896. New York. 1st Am. ed. VG $75.00

JAMES, Henry. *English Hours.* 1905. Cambridge. Ltd. 1st Am. ed. 1/400. VG $150.00

JAMES, Henry. *French Poets & Novelists.* 1964. New York. 1st Am. ed. dj. EX $30.00

JAMES, Henry. *Henry James & Robert Louis Stevenson.* 1948. London. Hart Davis. 1st ed. dj. EX $37.50

JAMES, Henry. *In the Cage.* 1898. London. Duckworth. VG $150.00

JAMES, Henry. *Italian Hours.* 1968. NY. Horizon Pr.Ills. Pennell. 1st ed. dj. EX $17.50

JAMES, Henry. *Julia Bride.* 1909. New York. Harper. 1st ed. VG $50.00

JAMES, Henry. *Lady Barbarina & Other Tales.* 1961. New York. 1st ed. wrappers. VG $15.00

JAMES, Henry. *Master Eustace.* 1920. New York. 1st ed. EX $17.50

JAMES, Henry. *Notes & Reviews.* 1921. Cambridge. Dunster House. Ltd. ed. EX $50.00

JAMES, Henry. *Picture & Text.* 1893. New York. Harper. 1st ed. VG $70.00

JAMES, Henry. *Representative Selections.* 1941. New York. Am. Book Co. dj. VG $20.00

JAMES, Henry. *Siege of London/Pension Beaurepas & Point of View.* 1883. Boston. 1st ed. G $90.00

JAMES, Henry. *Tales of Three Cities.* 1884. Boston. Osgood. G $37.50

JAMES, Henry. *The Ambassadors.* 1903. New York. Harper. 1st Am. ed. dj. VG $175.00

JAMES, Henry. *The Ambassadors.* 1963. Ltd. Eds. Club.sgn. boxed. EX $50.00

JAMES, Henry. *The American Novels & Stories.* 1947. New York. Knopf. 1st ed. dj. EX $50.00

JAMES, Henry. *The American Scene.* 1967. Horizon Press. Ills. 1st ed. dj. EX $25.00

JAMES, Henry. *The American Scene.* 1907. 1st Eng. ed. EX $125.00

JAMES, Henry. *The American.* 1880. VG $100.00

JAMES, Henry. *The Better Sort.* 1903. New York. 1st Am. ed. G $110.00

JAMES, Henry. *The Heiress.* 1949. New York. United Book Guild. wrappers. $22.50

JAMES, Henry. *The House of Fiction.* 1957. London. Hart-Davis. dj. EX $15.00

JAMES, Henry. *The Letters of William James.* 1920. Boston. Atlantic Monthy. 1st ed. G $25.00

JAMES, Henry. *The Outcry.* 1911. New York. 1st ed. VG $35.00

JAMES, Henry. *The Portrait of a Lady.* 1967. Ltd. Eds. Club.sgn. boxed. EX $50.00

JAMES, Henry. *The Question of Our Speech.* 1905. Boston. 1st ed. $65.00

JAMES, Henry. *The Spoils of Poynton.* 1897. Boston/NY. 1st Am. ed. VG $125.00

JAMES, Henry. *The Wings of the Dove.* 1902. Westminister. 1st Eng. ed. VG $125.00

JAMES, Henry. *Theatre & Friendship.* 1932. Putnam. 1st Am. ed. dj. VG $37.50

JAMES, Henry. *View & Reviews.* 1908. Boston. Ltd. 1st ed. 1/160. VG $40.00

JAMES, Henry. *Within the Rim.* 1919. London. Collins. 1st ed. dj. EX $175.00

JAMES, Jessie, Jr. *Jessie James My Father.* 1906. G $15.00

JAMES, M.R. *The Five Jars.* 1922. 1st Eng. ed. dj. VG $180.00

JAMES, Marquis & Bess. *Biography of a Bank.* 1954. Harper. dj. VG $10.00

JAMES, Marquis. *Biography of Business.* 1942. Bobbs Merrill. Ills. 1st ed. dj. VG $12.50

JAMES, P.D. *A Taste for Death.* London. 1st ed. sgn. $38.00

JAMES, P.D. *An Unsuitable Job for a Woman.* 1972. London. Faber. 1st ed. dj. VG $45.00

JAMES, P.D. *Innocent Blood.* 1980. Scribner. 1st ed. inscr. dj. EX $40.00

JAMES, P.D. *Skull Beneath Skin.* 1982. 1st ed. sgn. EX $35.00

JAMES, Philip. *Children's Books of Yesterday.* 1933. London. Studio Pub. 1st ed. dj. VG $60.00

JAMES, R. *All About New York.* 1931. Ills. 1st ed. $7.50

JAMES, Sydney. *Three Visitors to Early Plymouth.* 1963. 1st ed. dj. EX $10.00

JAMES, Thomas. *Three Years Among the Indians & Mexicans.* 1916. St. Louis. Ltd. ed. 1/356. EX $135.00

JAMES, Thomas. *Three Years Among the Indians & Mexicans.* 1953. EX $25.00

JAMES, Will. *American Cowboy.* 1942. New York. 1st ed. VG $32.50

JAMES, Will. *Cow Country.* 1927. New York. Scribner. 1st ed. VG $20.00

JAMES, Will. *Cowboy Life in Texas.* 1895. Chicago. VG $25.00

JAMES, Will. *Cowboys North & South.* 1924. New York. Scribner. 1st ed. $30.00

JAMES, Will. *Lone Cowboy.* 1930. New York. Scribner. 1st ed. VG $15.00

JAMES, Will. *Rancho Bonita.* Western Novel of the Month. $4.00

JAMES, Will. *Scorpion. A Bad Horse.* 1936. New York. Scribner. Ills. 312 pp. $20.00

JAMES, Will. *Smoky the Cow Horse.* 1930. Scribner. VG $7.50

JAMES, Will. *Smoky the Cow Horse.* 1929. New York. Scribner. Ills. Classic ed. $27.50

JAMES, Will. *Uncle Bill.* 1932. New York. 1st ed. G $16.00

JAMES, William. *Talks to Teachers on Psychology.* 1899. New York. 1st ed. VG $65.00

JAMES & DAKAN. *Ohio & the Poultry Industry.* Ills. 180 pp. $5.00

JAMES. *Fifth Avenue.* 1971. dj. VG $27.50

JAMESON, A.B. *Winter Studies & Summer Rambles in Canada.* 1944. Toronto. Nelson. Ills. 276 pp. VG $10.00

JAMESON, Mrs. *Winter Studies & Summer Rambles in Canada. Vol. I.* 1839. New York. $12.50

JAMESON. *The History of Historical Writing in America.* 1969. reprint. EX $8.00

JAMISON, James. *With Walker in Nicaragua.* 1909. 181 pp. EX $95.00

JANE, F.T. *Blake of the Rattlesnake.* 1898. Ills. 1st ed. G $75.00

JANES, Don Carlos. *The Cedric Papers.* 1906. Cincinnati. 99 pp. $12.50

JANES, E.C. *Hunting Ducks & Geese.* 1954. dj. VG $20.00

JANEWAY, Elizabeth. *The Writer's World.* 1969. New York. McGraw Hill. 1st ed. 415 pp. $5.00

JANIN, Jules. *La Normandie.* 1844. Paris. Ills. EX $100.00

JANIS, Sidney. *They Taught Themselves.* 1942. New York. Ills. 1st ed. 236 pp. $20.00

JANSON, Charles W. *The Stranger in America.* 1807. London. Cundee. 1st ed. 500 pp. $675.00

JANSON, H.W. *History of Art.* 1966. Ills. TB. $10.00

JANVIER, Thomas A. *In the Sargasso Sea.* 1898. New York. Harper. VG $20.00

JAQUES, F.L. *Outdoor Life's Gallery of North American Game.* 1957. VG $25.00

JAQUES, F.P. *Snowshoe Country.* 1945. MN U. Press. Ills. 110 pp. dj. VG $15.00

JAQUES, F.P. *The Geese Fly High.* 1964. MN U. Press. Ills. 102 pp. dj. EX $17.50

JARDINE, Sir William. *The Naturalist's Library.* 1836. Edinburgh. 36 color pls. VG $125.00

JARES, Joe. *Whatever Happened to Gorgeous George?* 1974. Prentice Hall. 1st ed. photos. dj. EX $15.00

JARMAN, C. *Atlas of Animal Migration.* 1972. John Day. Ills. 123 pp. dj. EX $12.50

JARRELL, Randall & Durer, A. *Jerome: Biography of a Poem.* 1971. Grossman. Ills. Durer. 1st ed. dj. VG $20.00

JARRELL, Randall. *Blood for a Stranger.* 1942. New York. Harcourt. 1st ed. dj. EX $275.00

JARRELL, Randall. *Fly by Night.* 1976. Farrar. Ills. Sendak. 1st ed. dj. EX $17.50

JARRELL, Randall. *Little Friend, Little Friend.* 1945. Dial Press. 1st ed. dj. VG $20.00

JARRELL, Randall. *Pictures from an Institution.* 1954. Knopf. 1st ed. dj. VG $60.00

JARRELL, Randall. *Pictures from an Institution.* 1945. London. 1st Eng. ed. dj. VG $18.00

JARRELL, Randall. *Poetry & the Age.* New York. 1st ed. dj. EX $20.00

JARRELL, Randall. *The Bat Poet.* 1977. Collier. Ills. 1st ed. EX $7.00

JARRELL, Randall. *The Seven League Crutches.* 1951. New York. 1st ed. dj. EX $75.00

JARRELL, Randall. *The Third Book of Criticism.* 1969. Farrar. 1st ed. dj. VG $30.00

JARVES, James Jackson. *A Glimpse at the Art of Japan.* 1876. Hurd/Haughton. Ills. 216 pp. sl wear. rare. $70.00

JARVES, James Jackson. *History of the Hawaiian or Sandwich Islands.* 1843. Boston. Ills. 1st ed. fld map. 407 pp. $200.00

JARVES, James Jackson. *History of the Hawaiian or Sandwich Islands.* 1843. London. Moxon. 1st ed. 377 pp. $200.00

JARVIS, Edward, M.D. *Lecture on the Necessity of Physiology.* 1845. Boston. 55 pp. $40.00

JARVIS, Howard & Pack, Robert. *I'm Mad as Hell.* 1979. New York. Time Books. 310 pp. dj. $4.50

JASON, D. *P.G. Wodehouse, Portrait of a Master.* 1974. New York. Ills. 1st review copy. dj. G $35.00

JAUDON, Daniel. *Short System of Polite Learning.* 1809. Philadelphia. 2 pls. $75.00

JAWORSKI, Leon. *The Right & the Power.* 1976. New York. Reader's Digest Press. 305 pp. $5.00

JAY, William. *A Review of Causes & Consequences of Mexican War.* 1849. Boston. 333 pp. $22.50

JBABVALA, Ruth Prawer. *A Stronger Climate.* 1968. Norton. 1st Am. ed. dj. VG $17.50

JEAFFRESON, John. *A Book of Recollections.* 1894. Hurst & Blackett. 2 vol set. $17.50

JEAFFRESON, John. *The Real Shelley.* 1885. London. 1st ed. 2 vol set. VG $35.00

JEAN, Marcel. *History of Surrealist Painting.* 1967. New York. Grove Press. 2nd printing. dj. $32.50

JEAN-AUBREY, G. *Joseph Conrad, Life & Letters.* 1927. New York. Ills. 2 vol set. G $25.00

JEFFERIES, Richard. *Round About a Great Estate.* 1880. London. Smith, Elder. 1st ed. $45.00

JEFFERS, Lance. *My Blackness is the Beauty of This Land.* 1970. Detroit. 1st ed. wrappers. EX $10.00

JEFFERS, Le Roy. *The Call of the Mountains.* 1923. New York. 2nd printing. 282 pp. $10.00

JEFFERS, Robinson. *Roan Stallion, Tamar & Other Poems.* 1925. New York. 1st ed. VG $20.00

JEFFERS, Robinson. *The Women at Point Sur.* 1927. New York. VG $22.50

JEFFERS. *Dear Judas.* 1929. New York. Ltd. ed. 1/350. sgn. VG $85.00

JEFFERSON, Alan. *Operas of Richard Strauss in Britain 1910-1963.* 1963. London. 1st ed. dj. VG $22.00

JEFFERSON, Mark. *Peopling the Argentine Pampa.* 1926. New York. Am. Geographic Soc. 211 pp. EX $8.00

JEFFERSON, Thomas. *A Manual of Parliamentary Practice.* 1862. New York. VG $20.00

JEFFERSON, Wayland. *Cutchague Southhold's First Colony.* 1940. Ltd. 1st ed. sgn. VG $47.50

JEFFERSON. *Jefferson Reader.* 1953. Ills. 1st ed. dj. $52.50

JEFFREY. *Adobe & Iron. Story of Arizona Territorial Prison.* 1969. La Jolla. SftCvr. $15.00

JENCKS. *Inequality.* 1972. New York. dj. EX $7.50

JENISON, Madge. *Sunwise Turn.* 1923. Dutton. 1st ed. 2nd printing. 162 pp. $12.50

JENKINS, Alan C. *Introducing Pets.* London. Spring Books. Ills. dj. EX $10.00

JENKINS, Alan C. *The Naturalists.* 1978. Mayflower. Ills. 1st Am. ed. 200 pp. dj. $17.50

JENKINS, Burris. *Hand of Bronze.* 1933. Chicago. Willett Clark. 1st ed. dj. EX $40.00

JENKINS, Dan. *Semi-Tough.* 1972. 1st ed. dj. VG $7.50

JENKINS, Donald. *The Ledoux Heritage: Collecting Ukiyo-e Prints.* 1973. New York. Ills. 163 pp. dj. EX $45.00

JENKINS, Herbert. *Bindle Omnibus.* 1932. London. 1st printing. VG $40.00

JENKINS, J.S. *History of the War Between U.S. & Mexico, etc.* 1851. Auburn. Derby & Miller. Ills. $12.50

JENKINS, J.T. *Whales & Modern Whaling.* 1932. London. 1st ed. $28.50

JENKINS. *Audubon & Other Capers.* 1976. dj. VG $15.00

JENKINS. *Button Gwinnett.* 1926. 1st ed. 291 pp. $32.50

JENKS, Tudor. *World Fair Book for Boys & Girls.* 1893. Century. $15.00

JENNESS, Diamond. *Dawn in Arctic Alaska.* 1957. Minneapolis. Ills. ex-lib. 222 pp. dj. $2.50

JENNEWEIN. *Calamity Jane of Western Trails.* 1965. Mitchell. 3rd ed. 71 pp. wrappers. $10.00

JENNINGS, Dana Close. *Cattle on a Thousand Hills.* 1968. Aberdeen, SD. 2nd ed. 96 pp. dj. $50.00

JENNINGS, Isaac. *Medical Reform: Treatise on Man's Physical Being.* 1847. Oberlin. Fitch & Jennings. 375 pp. $60.00

JENNINGS, J.B. *Feeding, Digestion, & Assimilation in Animals.* 1972. Macmillan. Ills. 244 pp. dj. EX $15.00

JENNINGS, John. *Next to Valour.* 1939. New York. Macmillan. 820 pp. VG $5.50

JENNINGS, N.A. *A Texas Ranger.* 1899. New York. 1st ed. G $95.00

JENNINGS, N.A. *A Texas Ranger.* 1959. Scribner. reprint. EX $25.00

JENNINGS, Preston. *A Book of Trout Flies.* 1972. 5th printing. VG $9.00

JENNINGS. *Instinct Shooting.* 1968. dj. EX $10.00

JENNINGS. *Instinct Shooting.* 1959. VG $6.00

JENNISON, Keith. *The Humorous Mr. Lincoln.* 1965. New York. reprint. dj. EX $7.00

JENSEN, Dean. *The Biggest, Smallest, Longest, Shortest.* 1975. 1st ed. photos. dj. VG $20.00

JEPSEN. *Horned Shepherd.* 1927. Ills. Wilfried Jones. Ltd. ed. $20.00

JERITZA, Maria. *Sunlight & Song.* 1929. New York. Ills. VG $35.00

JERNIGAN, C.B. *From Prairie Schooner in Texas to City Flat in NY.* 1926. Brooklyn. 140 pp. scarce. $17.50

JERNINGHAM, Edward. *The Fall of Mexico, a Poem.* 1775. London. 1st ed. 59 pp. $150.00

JEROME, Chauncey. *History of American Clock Business, Past 60 Years.* 1860. 1st ed. ex-lib. 144 pp. G $42.00

JEROME, Jerome K. *Three Men in a Boat.* 1890. New York. 1st Am. ed. VG $50.00

JEROME, V.J. *Social Democracy & the War.* 1940. New York. Workers Library. wrappers. EX $20.00

JEROME, V.J. *The Negro in Hollywood Films.* 1950. New York. Masses & Mainstream. wrappers. $25.00

JERROLD, B. *Life of Gustave Dore.* 1891. London. Ills. Dore. 415 pp. VG $65.00

JERROLD, Douglas. *Whimsical Tales.* 1948. Allentown, PA. Ills. Lewis Daniel. 168 pp. $10.00

JESCHKE, Wolfgang. *The Last Day of Creation.* 1984. New York. 1st Am. ed. review copy. dj. $15.00

JESEPHSON, Matthew. *The Robber Barons.* 1934. New York. 1st ed. 474 pp. G $10.00

JESSE, John H. *Memoirs of Court of England, London & Celebrities.* Boston. Ltd. ed. 1/50. $200.00

JESSE, John H. *Memoirs of Pretenders & Their Adherents.* 1845. London. 2 vol set. VG $60.00

JETER, Goetze. *The Strikers.* 1937. New York. Stokes. advance copy. EX $40.00

JEWETT, John Howard. *Friends of the Hunted.* 1909. New York. Ills. C.W. Cancoast. VG $10.00

JEWETT, Sarah Orne. *The Tory Lover.* 1901. Boston. 1st ed. later printing. VG $145.00

JEWRY, Mary. *Warne's Model Cookery & Housekeeping Book.* London. Ills. $35.00

JHABALA, Ruth Prawer. *An Experience of India.* 1972. New York. 1st ed. dj. EX $10.00

JHABVALA, Ruth Prawer. *How I Became a Holy Mother.* 1976. Harper. 1st Am. ed. dj. VG $15.00

JHABVALA, Ruth Prawer. *Like Birds, Like Fishes.* 1964. Norton. 1st Am. ed. dj. VG $20.00

JHABVALA, Ruth Prawer. *Travelers.* 1973. Harper. 1st Am. ed. dj. VG $15.00

JOAQUIN, Murrietta. *California Outlaw.* 1925. Chicago. Ltd. ed. 1/975. VG $50.00

JOB, H. *Propagation of Wild Birds.* 1923. Doubleday Page. Ills. 308 pp. index. VG $30.00

JOERG, W.L.G. *Pioneer Settlement.* 1932. New York. Am. Geographical Soc. 473 pp. $8.00

JOHANNES, Wilhelm. *Heinrich Boll: Teller of Tales.* 1969. Ungar. 1st Am. ed. dj. VG $15.00

JOHANSEN, D. *Empire of Columbia: History of Pacific North West.* 1957. New York. 19 maps. 70 pls. VG $12.50

JOHN, B. *Tabb on Emily Dickinson.* 1950. New York. Ltd. ed. 1/500. scarce. $30.00

JOHNES, Meredith. *The Boy's Book of Modern Travel & Adventure.* 1871. New York. 333 pp. $10.00

JOHNS, C.A. *The Forest Trees of Britain.* London. (ca.1860) Ills. 2 vol set. $37.50

JOHNSGARD, P.A. *Cranes of the World.* 1983. London. Croom Helm. 1st Eng. ed. dj. $55.00

JOHNSGARD, P.A. *Ducks, Geese, & Swans of the World.* 1978. NB U. Press. Ills. 404 pp. dj. EX $35.00

JOHNSGARD, P.A. *Grouse & Quails of North America.* 1973. NB U. Press. 1st ed. 553 pp. dj. VG $35.00

JOHNSGARD, P.A. *The Plovers, Sandpipers, & Snipes of the World.* 1981. NB U. Press. Ills. 493 pp. dj. EX $45.00

JOHNSON, A.F. *Selected Essays on Books & Printing.* 1970. Amsterdam. dj. EX $100.00

JOHNSON, Amandus. *Journal & Biography of Nicholas Collin 1741-1831.* 1936. Philadelphia. Ills. 1st ed. 368 pp. boxed. $25.00

JOHNSON, Burgess. *Beastly Rhymes.* 1906. New York. Ills. Blaisdell. 1st ed. VG $30.00

JOHNSON, Charles S. & Assoc. *Into the Main Stream.* 1947. New York. ex-lib. 355 pp. VG $5.00

JOHNSON, Clifton. *Highways & Byways of the Mississippi Valley.* 1906. New York. Ills. $12.00

JOHNSON, Clifton. *Highways & Byways of the Pacific Coast.* 1908. New York. Ills. 323 pp. $10.00

JOHNSON, Clifton. *Highways & Byways of the South.* 1904. New York. Ills. 362 pp. $12.50

JOHNSON, Clifton. *The New England Country.* 1893. Boston. Ills. 121 pp. $12.50

JOHNSON, Crisfield. *History of Cuyahoga County, Ohio.* 1879. Cleveland. 534 pp. $60.00

JOHNSON, Denis. *Angels.* 1983. New York. Knopf. 1st ed. dj. EX $20.00

JOHNSON, Dorothy M. *The Hanging Tree.* 1st ed. ex-lib. $10.00

JOHNSON, Edgar. *Charles Dickens. His Tragedy & Triumph.* 1952. Ills. 2 vol set. $18.00

JOHNSON, Embree & Alexander. *The Collapse of Cotton Tenancy.* 1935. Chapel Hill. U. of NC Press. ex-lib. 81 pp. $3.50

JOHNSON, Eric & Peterson, C.F. *Svenskarne I Illinois: Historiska Anteckningar.* 1880. Chicago. Ills. 1st ed. 471 pp. $60.00

JOHNSON, Evelyn. *Kennedy & Johnson.* 1968. 1st ed. 207 pp. $50.00

JOHNSON, G. *Ship Model Building.* 1961. Cambridge. Ills. 301 pp. index. dj. VG $20.00

JOHNSON, G.R. *Peru from the Air.* 1930. Am. Geog. Soc. 1st ed. VG $20.00

JOHNSON, G.W. *Andrew Jackson.* 1927. New York. 1st ed. VG $25.00

JOHNSON, George Clayton. *Writing for the Twilight Zone.* 1980. Outre House. Ltd. 1st ed. 1/100. sgn. EX $35.00

JOHNSON, H. *Gutenberg & the Book of Books.* 1932. New York. Rudge. Ltd. ed. 1/750. boxed. $75.00

JOHNSON, Harold E. *Jean Sibelius.* 1959. New York. 1st ed. dj. VG $12.50

JOHNSON, Irving & Electa. *Yankee's People & Places.* 1955. 1st ed. sgns. dj. VG $30.00

JOHNSON, Irving. *The Peking Battles Cape Horn.* 1977. $9.00

JOHNSON, Isaac Thorne. *Young People's Natural History.* 1901. Ills. 434 pp. $12.50

JOHNSON, J.A. *His Letters, Travels & Addresses.* 1908. Fargo, ND. private print. 263 pp. VG $20.00

JOHNSON, J.W. *Homeopathic Veterinary Handbook for Farmers.* 1879. Cleveland. 130 pp. $15.00

JOHNSON, James Weldon. *Black Thought.* 1930. New York. Ills. 1st ed. VG $15.00

JOHNSON, John. *The Defense of Charleston Harbor, 1863-5.* 1890. Charleston. Ills. maps. plans. VG $150.00

JOHNSON, John. *Typographia or the Printer's Instructor.* 1966. London. reprint. 2 vol set. EX $22.50

JOIINSON, L.F. *Famous Kentucky Tragedies & Trials.* 1916. Louisville. 1st ed. VG $30.00

JOHNSON, Lady Bird. *A White House Diary.* 1970. New York. 806 pp. dj. $6.50

JOHNSON, Lyndon. *The Vantage Point.* 1971. 1st ed. photos. 636 pp. dj. $125.00

JOHNSON, Martin. *Lion, African Adventure with the King of Beasts.* 1929. Putnam. Ills. 281 pp. $15.00

JOHNSON, Martin. *Lion Hunter.* 1929. New York. Putnam. Ills. VG $7.50

JOHNSON, Martin. *Safari, a Saga of Africa & Adventure.* 1928. Ills. 294 pp. dj. VG $17.50

JOHNSON, Mary. *Cease Firing.* 1912. Ills. 1st ed. 457 pp. $13.50

JOHNSON, Merle. *High Spots of American Literature.* 1929. New York. Ltd. ed. 1/750. VG $65.00

JOHNSON, Osa. *Four Years in Paradise.* 1941. London. 1st ed. sgn. VG $37.50

JOHNSON, Osa. *I Married Adventure.* 1940. New York. Lippincott. 376 pp. dj. $5.00

JOHNSON, Osa. *Lives & Adventures of Marin & Osa Johnson.* 1942. Halcyon House. Ills. dj. VG $10.00

JOHNSON, Owen. *The Wasted Generation.* 1921. Boston. 343 pp. $4.00

JOHNSON, P. *Parker, America's Finest Shotgun.* 1963. EX $27.50

JOHNSON, Pamela Hansford. *Corkstreet, Next to the Hatters.* 1965. Scribner. 1st ed. dj. VG $35.00

JOHNSON, Pamela Hansford. *Night & Silence, Who is Here?* 1963. 1st ed. dj. VG $20.00

JOHNSON, Pamela Hansford. *The Survival of the Fittest.* 1968. New York. Scribner. 1st ed. dj. VG $30.00

JOHNSON, R. *Battles & Leaders of the Civil War.* 1884-7. 4 vol set. $50.00

JOHNSON, R. *Battles & Leaders of the Civil War.* 1956. reprint ed. 4 vol set. boxed. $36.00

JOHNSON, Robert Underwood. *Poems of War & Peace.* 1917. $8.50

JOHNSON, Rossiter. *Campfires & Battlefields.* 1967. New York. 532 pp.+index. dj. EX $15.00

JOHNSON, Samuel. *A Journey to Western Island of Scotland.* 1810. Baltimore. 1st Am. ed. $175.00

JOHNSON, Samuel. *Poetical Works.* 1785. London. 3rd collected ed. VG $85.00

JOHNSON, Samuel. *Rasselas, a Tale.* 1827. Hartford. VG $40.00

JOHNSON, Samuel. *Rasselas, a Tale.* 1817. London. Booth. 1st ed. 222 pp. $40.00

JOHNSON, Samuel. *The History of Rasselas, Prince of Abyssinia.* 1816. London. G $30.00

JOHNSON, Samuel. *The Idler.* 1761. London. Newbery. 2 vol set. rebound. $150.00

JOHNSON, Samuel. *The Lives of the Most Eminent English Poets.* 1793. London. new ed. $100.00

JOHNSON, Samuel. *The Poetical Works of Samuel Johnson.* 1785. London. new ed. VG $85.00

JOHNSON, W. Fletcher. *Life of Sitting Bull & History of the Indian War.* 1891. Edgewood Pub. Ills. 544 pp. $17.50

JOHNSON, W. Fletcher. *Life of William Tecumseh Sherman.* 1891. Edgewood Pub. 607 pp. $4.50

JOHNSON, W.B. *Folktales of Brittany.* 1927. London. 156 pp. EX $17.00

JOHNSON, Walter. *How We Drafted Adlai Stevenson.* 1955. New York. Knopf. ex-lib. 172 pp. dj. $3.50

JOHNSON, Warren B. *From Pacific to Atlantic. Journey Overland.* 1887. Webster. 1st ed. G $45.00

JOHNSON, William A. *Christopher Polem: Father of Swedish Technology.* 1963. Hartford. Ltd. ed. EX $30.00

JOHNSON, William J. *Abraham Lincoln the Christian.* 1913. New York. 228 pp. $5.00

JOHNSON. *Ballads of Farm & Home.* 1902. Mennonite Pub. VG $20.00

JOHNSON. *Dictionary of the English Language.* 1805. Philadelphia. EX $110.00

JOHNSON. *History of the Yorubas.* 1921. London. $35.00

JOHNSON. *Johnson's Dictionary of English Language.* 1822. London. 19th ed. 284 pp. VG $55.00

JOHNSON. *Legends of Vancouver.* 1920. Mclelland. new ed. wrappers. VG $15.00

JOHNSON. *The Bloody Boseman.* 1971. 1st ed. dj. EX $20.00

JOHNSTON, A.K. *Handy Royal Atlas.* 1868. London. 98 pp. index. $97.50

JOHNSTON, Annie Fellows. *Asa Holmes.* 1903. $30.00

JOHNSTON, Annie Fellows. *Georgina of the Rainbows.* 1916. New York. Ills. Jackson. 348 pp. VG $7.50

JOHNSTON, Annie Fellows. *The Land of the Little Colonel.* 1929. Boston. 1st ed. ex-lib. VG $25.00

JOHNSTON, Annie Fellows. *The Little Colonel at Boarding School.* 1920. Page Co. Ills. Bridgman. $3.00

JOHNSTON, Annie Fellows. *The Little Colonel's Knight Comes Riding.* 1907. 1st Am. ed. VG $12.50

JOHNSTON, Annie Fellows. *The Road of the Loving Heart.* 1922. Boston. Ills. Bromhall. 1st ed. VG $30.00

JOHNSTON, Elizabeth B. *Visitor's Guide to Mount Vernon.* 1891. Washington. 17th ed. 80 pp. wrappers. $12.50

JOHNSTON, Hank. *Death Valley Scotty: Fastest Con in the West.* 1974. Ills. 1st ed. inscr. folio. $25.00

JOHNSTON, Harry. *The Story of My Life.* 1923. Bobbs Merrill. Ills. photos. 504 pp. index. $20.00

JOHNSTON, Henry P. *Yale & Her Honor Roll in American Revolution.* 1888. New York. private print. Ills. G $20.00

JOHNSTON, J.E. *Reports, Routes from San Antonio to El Paso.* 1850. Washington. ex-lib. fld mps. pls. $235.00

JOHNSTON, Mary. *Lewis Rand.* 1908. New York. 510 pp. $3.00

JOHNSTON, Mary. *The Long Roll.* 1911. Ills. 681 pp. $13.50

JOHNSTON, Mary. *To Have & to Hold.* 1900. Boston. G $6.50

JOHNSTON, Mary. *1492.* 1923. 315 pp. $3.00

JOHNSTON, R.F. *The Chinese Drama.* 1921. Shanghai. Ills. folio. G $85.00

JOHNSTON, Ralph. *Buffalo Bill.* 1938. New York. Allyn & Bacon. 180 pp. $11.00

JOHNSTON, Stanley. *Queen of the Flat Tops.* 1942. 1st ed. inscr. VG $15.00

JOHNSTON, Verna. *Sierra Nevada.* 1970. Boston. 1st ed. dj. EX $10.00

JOHNSTON. *The Chemistry of Common Life.* 1855. New York. 3rd ed. 2 vol set. $40.00

JOHNSTONE, Edward. *Writing, Illuminating, & Lettering.* New York. (ca.1906) 499 pp. $7.50

JOHNSTONE, H.W. *Truth of War Conspiracy.* 1861. Curryville, GA. 1st ed. 40 pp. wrappers. $50.00

JOHNSTONE, J.H.S. *Horse Book.* 1912. photos. VG $25.00

JOKELSON, Paul. *Sulphides: Art of Cameo Incrustation.* 1968. Galahad, NY. Ills. dj. VG $7.50

JOLAS, Eugene. *Mots-Deluge.* 1933. Paris. Ltd. ed. 1/589. VG $65.00

JOLAS, Eugene. *Transition Workshop.* 1949. New York. Vanguard. 413 pp. $15.00

JOLINE. *Meditations of an Autograph Collector.* 1902. $15.00

JONES, A.D. *Illinois & the West.* 1838. Boston. Ltd. ed. 1/500. 255 pp. $10.00

JONES, B. *Habits & Haunts of the Moose.* 1901. private print. Ltd. ed. VG $50.00

JONES, Bobby. *Golf Is My Game.* 1960. Doubleday. dj. EX $17.50

JONES, Bobby. *The Basic Golf Swing.* 1969. Doubleday. 1st ed. dj. EX $30.00

JONES, Bradley. *Aviation.* 1931. New York. Ills. ex-lib. 314 pp. $10.00

JONES, C.L. *Caribbean Backgrounds & Prospects.* 1931. Ills. 1st ed. $7.50

JONES, Charles C., Jr. *The Dead Towns of Georgia.* 1878. Savannah. Ills. Ltd. 1st ed. 263 pp. $125.00

JONES, Daniel. *Forty Years Among the Indians.* 1890. Salt Lake City. $75.00

JONES, Daniel. *40 Yrs. Among Indians. True & Thrilling Narrative.* 1960. Westernlore. reprint ed. 378 pp. dj. VG $25.00

JONES, David. *Journal: Visit Indian Nations West of Ohio River.* 1865. New York. Ltd ed. 1/250. $250.00

JONES, Douglas C. *The Barefoot Brigade.* 1982. Holt. 1st ed. dj. VG $15.00

JONES, E. Alfred. *Old Silver of Europe & America.* 1928. Lippincott. 96 pls. VG $45.00

JONES, Elizabeth Orton. *Maminka's Children.* 1940. New York. 1st ed. sgn. dj. EX $45.00

JONES, Elizabeth Orton. *Maminka's Children.* 1967. New York. Ills. dj. $12.50

JONES, Enid H. *Mrs. Humphry Ward.* 1973. New York. 1st ed. dj. VG $7.50

JONES, H. *Samuel Butler, a Memoir.* 1910. London. 2 vol set. VG $17.50

JONES, Isabel Morse. *Hollywood Bowl.* 1936. New York. Ills. VG $18.00

JONES, J. *Oration of General Washington.* 1825. London. 2nd ed. rebound. $20.00

JONES, J. *World War II.* 1975. Ills. G $27.50

JONES, J. McHenry. *Hearts of Gold. A Novel.* 1896. Wheeling. 299 pp. $22.50

JONES, J. Wm. *Christ in Camp or Religion in Confederate Army.* 1904. Atlanta. Martin & Hoyt. Ills. 612 pp. $35.00

JONES, James O. *West Virginians: Work of Biography.* 1928. Ills. 494 pp. index. VG $25.00

JONES, James. *A Touch of Danger.* 1973. Doubleday. 1st ed. dj. VG $20.00

JONES, James. *From Here to Eternity.* 1951. Scribner. 1st ed. VG $120.00

JONES, James. *Go to the Widow-Maker.* 1967. Delacorte. 1st ed. dj. VG $20.00

JONES, James. *Some Came Running.* 1957. New York. 1st ed. VG $20.00

JONES, James. *The Merry Month of May.* 1971. Delacorte. 1st ed. dj. VG $20.00

JONES, James. *The Pistol.* 1958. Scribner. 1st ed. dj. VG $40.00

JONES, James. *Thin Red Line.* 1962. 1st ed. dj. $27.50

JONES, James. *Whistle.* 1978. Delacorte. 1st trade ed. dj. VG $15.00

JONES, James. *Whistle.* 1978. New York. Delacorte. 1st ed. dj. VG $25.00

JONES, Jessie & Elizabeth. *Small Rain.* 1943. Viking. 1st ed. inscr. sgn. VG $50.00

JONES, Jessie Orton. *Secrets.* 1945. Viking. Ills. E.O. Jones. 1st ed. VG $25.00

JONES, John. *Stories of Great American Scouts.* 1924. Whitman. Ills. $5.00

JONES, John. *Stories of Great Explorers.* 1924. Whitman. Ills. 61 pp. $5.00

JONES, Johnny. *Now Let Me Tell You.* 1950. Columbus, OH. 212 pp. $8.00

JONES, K.M. *Heroines of Dixie.* 1955. 1st ed. 430 pp. $26.00

JONES, Kenneth & Gwyn. *A Prospect of Wales.* 1948. King Penguin. Ills. Rowntree. VG $20.00

JONES, LeRoi. *The System of Dante's Hell.* 1965. Grove Press. 1st ed. dj. VG $30.00

JONES, M.E. *Folktales of Ireland.* 1949. Oxford. Ills. 180 pp. dj. $14.00

JONES, M.W. *George Cruikshank. His Life & London.* 1978. London. 1st ed. Ills. dj. $20.00

JONES, Max & Chilton, John. *Louis: Louis Armstrong Story.* 1971. Boston. Little, Brown. 1st Am. ed. dj. $15.00

JONES, N.E. *The Squirrel Hunters of Ohio.* 1898. Cincinnati. 1st ed. sgn. EX $80.00

JONES, Nard. *Marcus Whitman.* 1968. Harper. 1st ed. dj. EX $10.00

JONES, Paul. *Flora Magnifica.* 1975. London. Ills. boxed. EX $650.00

JONES, Penelope R. *Story of the Pennsylvania Turnpike.* 1950. photos. $5.00

JONES, Pomeroy. *Annals & Recollections of Oneida County.* 1851. Rome/NY. 893 pp. VG $75.00

JONES, Preston. *Latin America.* 1942. New York. Odyssey Press. 1st ed. 850 pp. $4.50

JONES, Raymond F. *Renaissance.* 1951. New York. Gnome. 1st ed. dj. EX $17.50

JONES, Raymond F. *The Cybernetic Brains.* 1962. New York. Avalon. 1st ed. dj. VG $17.50

JONES, Raymond F. *The Toymaker.* 1951. Los Angeles. 1st ed. dj. VG $20.00

JONES, Robert. *The Civil War in the Northwest.* 1960. U. of OK. 1st ed. dj. $10.00

JONES, Samuel. *The Siege of Charleston.* 1911. Neal. EX $125.00

JONES, Sheridan R. *Fishing Facts.* 1935. 90 pp. $5.00

JONES, T. *Heart of Oak.* 1984. dj. VG $7.50

JONES, T.C. *The Ways of Game Fish.* 1972. Ferguson. Ills. 1st ed. 326 pp. dj. EX $25.00

JONES, Terry. *The Great Gretzky.* 1980. General Pub. Ills. 94 pp. pb. EX $7.50

JONES, Thomas. *A Diary with Letters 1931-1950.* 1954. London. dj. VG $10.00

JONES, Tristan. *Adrift.* 1980. Macmillan. 1st ed. VG $15.00

JONES, Tristan. *Ice.* 1978. 1st ed. VG $15.00

JONES, V.C. *Ranger Mosby.* 1944. Chapel Hill. Ills. 2nd printing. 347 pp. VG $20.00

JONES, William D. *Mirror of Modern Democracy.* 1864. New York. 270 pp. VG $20.00

JONES. *Stanley Morison Displayed.* 1976. London. 1st ed. dj. EX $35.00

JONES. *Theatre in the Round.* 1951. $10.00

JONG, Erica. *Loveroot.* 1975. Holt. 1st ed. dj. VG $12.50

JORAN, Ralph W. *Oons.* 1915. St. Paul. 1st ed. VG $15.00

JORDAN, Mildred. *Asylum for the Queen.* 1948. New York. Knopf. 409 pp. VG $3.50

JORDAN. *Elephants & Ivory.* 1956. 1st ed. dj. $30.00

JORDON, E.L. *Hammond's Nature Atlas of America.* 1952. VG $6.50

JORDON, J. & Marberry, M.M. *Fool's Gold.* 1966. Ills. dj. VG $7.50

JORDON, June. *Things That I Do in the Dark.* 1977. New York. Random House. dj. EX $25.00

JORDON, Neil. *The Past.* London. 1st ed. VG $25.00

JORGENSEN, P. *Dressing Flies for Fresh & Salt Water.* 1973. 1st ed. dj. EX $12.50

JOSCELYN, Archie. *Ambush on Satan's Hill.* Paperback Library. $3.00

JOSCELYN, Archie. *Bad Hombre.* Star Books. pb. $4.00

JOSCELYN, Archie. *Gunhand's Pay.* Pyramid. pb. $3.00

JOSCELYN, Archie. *Trapper's Rendezvous.* 1st ed. ex-lib. dj. $6.00

JOSCELYN, Archie. *Wyoming Outlaw.* Paperback Library. $3.00

JOSEPH, Samantha. *Advances.* 1983. Macmillan. proof copy. wrappers. VG $10.00

JOSEPHSON, E. *Your Life is Their Toy.* 1940. New York. 1st ed. sgn. inscr. 449 pp. VG $20.00

JOSEPHSON, Matthew. *Edison, a Biography.* 1959. New York. McGraw Hill. 511 pp. dj. $4.50

JOSEPHSON, Matthew. *The Robber Barons.* 1934. $7.50

JOSEPHY, Alvin. *American Heritage Book of Indians.* 1961. Ills. 424 pp. dj. $24.00

JOSEPHY, Alvin M. *Patriot Chiefs/Chronicle of Am. Indian Leadership.* 1961. New York. 1st ed. dj. VG $20.00

JOSEPHY, Alvin M., Jr. *Black Hills, White Sky.* 1978. New York. Time Books. 220 pp. EX $12.50

JOSEPHY, Alvin M., Jr. *Nez Perce Indians & Opening of Northwest.* 1965. Yale. dj. EX $27.50

JOSEPHY, Alvin M., Jr. *The Congress of the United States.* 1975. Ills. 416 pp. dj. EX $7.00

JOSEPHY, Alvin M., Jr. *The Horizon History of Africa.* 1971. Ills. 2 vols in 1. EX $18.00

JOSEPHY, Alvin M., Jr. *The Indian Heritage of America.* 1968. New York. Ills. 1st ed. 384 pp. dj. $15.00

JOSLIN, Eliot P. *Treatment of Diabetes Mellitus.* 1916. Philadelphia. Ills. 8 vol set. 410 pp. $40.00

JOUTEL, Henri. *Journal of La Salle's Last Voyage.* 1896. Chicago. Caxton. Ills. Ltd. ed. 231 pp. $200.00

JOUTEL, Henri. *Journal: Last Voyage by Mon. de La Salle.* 1714. London. 1st Eng. ed. 205 pp. fld map. $850.00

JOYCE, J. *Collected Poems of James.* Ltd. ed. 1/800. $200.00

JOYCE, James. *Finnegans' Wake.* 1947. New York. VG $10.00

JOYCE, James. *Finnegans' Wake.* 1939. London. 1st ed. dj. EX $275.00

JOYCE, James. *Giacomo Joyce.* 1968. Viking. Ltd. ed. slipcase. EX $50.00

JOYCE, James. *Levin.* 1941. New Directions. $10.00

JOYCE, James. *My Impossible Health.* 1977. London. 2nd revised ed. wrappers. $15.00

JOYCE, James. *Portrait.* 1921. Egoist Press. 3rd Eng. ed. $40.00

JOYCE, James. *Portrait.* 1917. Huebsch. 2nd Am. ed. VG $75.00

JOYCE, James. *Portrait.* 1965. Folio Society. VG $15.00

JOYCE, James. *Portrait.* Huebsch. 1st ed. VG $200.00

JOYCE, James. *The Cat & the Devil.* 1964. New York. Ills. Richard Erdoes. 1st ed. $17.50

JOYCE, James. *Two Tales of Shem & Shaun.* 1932. London. 1st ed. VG $40.00

JOYCE, James. *Ulysses.* 1934. Random House. 1st Am. ed. EX $75.00

JOYCE, James. *Ulysses.* 1932. Hamsburg. Odyssey Press. 1st printing. $285.00

JOYCE, James. *Ulysses.* 1924. Paris. 5th printing. $35.00

JOYCE, James. *Ulysses.* 1927. Shakespeare Co. 9th printing. $45.00

JOYCE, James. *Ulysses.* 1936. John Lane. 1st Eng. ed. 1/100. EX $400.00

JOYCE, James. *Ulysses.* 1924. Shakespeare Co. 4th printing. $110.00

JOYCE. *Atlas & History of Ireland.* 1899. New York. EX $35.00

JOYCE. *Letters.* 1957. New York. 1st ed. dj. EX $25.00

JUDD, Laura Fish. *Sketches of Life in Hawaiian Islands. 1828-1861.* 1966. Chicago. Ills. 379 pp. index. EX $12.50

JUDD, Neil M. *Two Chaco Canyon Pit Houses.* 1924. Washington. wrappers. VG $12.50

JUDKINS, Henry & Merrill, M. *Principles of Dairying Testing & Manufacturing.* 1941. New York. Wiley. 315 pp. VG $4.50

JUDSON, Helena. *Light Entertaining. Book of Dainty Recipes.* 1910. New York. VG $20.00

JUDSON, Helena. *The Butterick Cookbook.* 1911. New York. Butterick Pub. 359 pp. $5.00

JUDSON, K. *Myths & Legends of the Pacific North West.* 1910. Ills. 1st ed. dj. VG $60.00

JUDSON. *Mary Jane in Scotland.* 1929. Grosset & Dunlap. Ills. Wrenn. $4.50

JUDY, I.M. *The Red Fox.* 1947. Petersburg, WV. anti-drinking pamphlet. EX $7.00

JUDY, Will. *Dog Encyclopedia.* 1936. Chicago. Ills. w/supplements. VG $20.00

JULIAN, Philip. *The Triumph of Art Nouveau, Paris Exhibition 1900.* 1974. New York. dj. VG $17.50

JULITTE, P. *Block 26: Sabotage at Buchenwald.* 1971. Doubleday. G $10.00

JUNIUS. *Stat Nominus.* 1812. London. Ills. VG $55.00

JURMAN, S. *From Trunk to Tail, Elephants Legendary & Real.* 1978. Harcourt Brace. Ills. 1st ed. 88 pp. dj. EX $12.50

JUSTI, H.D. & Son. *Ills. Catalog & Price List of Dental Supplies.* 1901. Philadelphia. Ills. 410 pp. $25.00

JUSTICE, William. *A Man, Woman, & God. Love Sonnets.* 1939. Pikeville, KY. 56 pp. $6.00

KABOTIE, Fred. *Hopi Indian Artist.* 1977. Arizona. AZ Musuem. 1st ed. dj. VG $30.00

KAEMPFFERT, Waldemar. *The New Art of Flying.* 1911. New York. Ills. 280 pp. index. VG $100.00

KAFKA, Franz. *The Basic Kafka.* 1979. New York. Pocket Books. wrappers. EX $22.50

KAFKA, Franz. *The Great Wall of China.* 1946. Schocken. 1st Am. ed. inscr. dj. VG $20.00

KAFKA, Franz. *The Penal Colony.* 1948. Schocken. 1st Am. ed. EX $12.50

KAGANOVICH, A.L. *Splendours of Leningrad.* 1969. Cowles Book Co.Ills. Deluxe ed. dj. EX $35.00

KAGIN, D.H. *Private Gold Coins & Patterns of the United States.* 1981. 406 pp. $17.50

KAHANE, Melanie. *There's a Decorator in Your Doll House.* 1969. Atheneum. 2nd printing. dj. $10.00

KAHN, Arthur. *Brownstone.* 1953. New York. Independence. Ltd. ed. dj. EX $35.00

KAHN, D. *Code Breakers.* 1967. London. Weidenfeld & Nicholas. dj. G $15.00

KAHN, E.J. *About the New Yorker & Me.* 1979. New York. 453 pp. dj. $10.00

KAHN, E.J. *The Voice. Story of American Phenomenon. Sinatra.* 1947. New York. Ills. 1st ed. 125 pp. dj. $20.00

KAHN, Roger. *The Boys of Summer.* 1972. New York. Harper & Row. 439 pp. dj. EX $6.50

KAHN & WISMER. *The 1955 Mutual Baseball Almanac.* New York. 1st ed. VG $7.50

KAHN. *On Thermonuclear War.* 1961. 2nd ed. index. $15.00

KAIN, A. *Budapest.* 1910. photos. 400 pp. $47.00

KAINEN. *John Baptist Jackson.* 1962. $30.00

KAINS, M.G. *Making Horticulture Pay.* 1909. New York. Judd Co. 276 pp. EX $5.50

KAINS, M.G. *Plant Propagation.* 1916. New York. Judd Co. ex-lib. 322 pp. VG $4.00

KAISER, A. Faber. *Jesus Died in Kashmir.* 1977. London. $28.50

KAISER, Estella. *The Victorious Knight.* 1930. 1st ed. dj. $8.50

KALASHNIKOFF, Nicholas. *Jumper, Life of a Siberian Horse.* 1945. Scribner. 224 pp. $37.50

KALASHNIKOFF, Nicholas. *They That Take the Sword.* 1939. New York. Harper. ex-lib. 717 pp. $3.00

KALETSKI, Alexander. *Metro: Novel of the Moscow Underground.* 1985. Viking. proof copy. wrappers. VG $20.00

KALLAWAY, Wm. *Philharmonic: Music Makers Since 1932.* 1972. Hampshire. Ills. dj. VG $11.00

KALLEN, Horace. *Art & Freedom.* 1942. 1st ed. 2 vol set. VG $18.00

KALLET, Arthur & Schlink, F.J. *100,000,000 Guinea Pigs.* 1933. New York. 312 pp. $3.50

KALNOKY, I. *Guest House.* Indianapolis. Bobbs Merrill. $15.00

KAMINSKY, Stuart. *Bullet for a Star.* 1981. London. 1st Eng. ed. dj. EX $20.00

KAMINSKY, Stuart. *Never Cross a Vampire.* 1980. New York. St.Martins. 1st ed. dj. VG $25.00

KANDER, Mrs. Simon. *The Settlement Cookbook.* 1938. Milwaukee. 22nd ed. 623 pp. VG $5.00

KANE, Annie. *The Golden Sunset, or the Homeless Blind Girl.* 1864. Baltimore. 235 pp. dj. $12.50

KANE, Elisha Kent. *Arctic Explorations in Years 1853, '54, '55.* 1856. Philadelphia. Childs/Peterson. 2 vol set. VG $150.00

KANE, Harnett T. *Bride of Fortune.* 1948. New York. Doubleday. 301 pp. dj. $5.50

KANE, Harnett T. *New Orleans Woman.* 1947. Doubleday. $5.50

KANE, Harnett T. *The Golden Coast.* 1959. New York. Ills. 1st ed. 212 pp. index. $6.00

KANE, Harnett T. *The Lady of Arlington.* 1954. New York. Doubleday. 288 pp. $3.50

KANE, Harnett T. *The Smiling Rebel.* 1955. New York. Doubleday. 313 pp. $3.50

KANE, Harnett T. & Henry, I. *Miracle in the Mountains.* 1956. New York. Doubleday. $5.00

KANE, S., ed. *A Memorial to the Jewish Community of Ripin.* 1962. Tel Aviv. Hebrew/Eng. text. 942 pp. $22.50

KANER, H. *The Sun Queen.* 1946. London. Kaner Pub. 1st ed. dj. VG $30.00

KANTOR, MacKinlay. *Andersonville.* 1955. New York. World. 767 pp. $10.00

KANTOR, MacKinlay. *But Look, the Morn.* 1947. Coward. 1st presentation copy. $12.50

KANTOR, MacKinlay. *Cuba Libre.* 1940. New York. 136 pp. $2.50

KANTOR, MacKinlay. *Midnight Lace.* 1948. New York. VG $5.00

KANTOR, MacKinlay. *Spirit Lake.* 1961. World Pub. 1st ed. dj. VG $17.50

KANTOR, MacKinlay. *The Noise of Their Wings.* 1938. New York. Ills. VG $7.50

KANTOR, MacKinlay. *The Romance of Rosy Ridge.* 1937. New York. Ills. VG $7.50

KANTOR, MacKinlay. *The Voice of Bugle Ann.* 1935. New York. Coward McCann. 128 pp. dj. VG $3.50

KANTOR, MacKinlay. *Turkey in the Straw.* 1935. New York. Ills. VG $7.50

KANTOR, MacKinlay. *Valedictory.* 1939. New York. 92 pp. $2.50

KANTOR, MacKinlay. *The Children Sing.* 1973. Hawthorn Press.1st ed. dj. VG $20.00

KAPLAN, Bert. *A Study of Rorschach Responses in Four Cultures.* 1954. Peabody Museum.1st ed. stiff wrappers. $10.00

KAPLAN, M.N. *Big Game Angler's Paradise.* 1937. New York. 1st ed. dj. VG $50.00

KAPPA KAPPA GAMMA. *Kappa Kappa Gamma Cookbook.* 1926. Denver. soiled. $10.00

KAPPLER. *Indian Affairs: Law & Treaties.* 1904. Washington. 2nd ed. 7 vol set. $50.00

KAPS, Dr. Johannes. *The Tragedy of Silesia 1945-1946.* 1953. Munich. $15.00

KAPSNER, O.L. *Catholic Subject Headings.* 1953. Minneapolis. 612 pp. VG $30.00

KARASZ, Ilonka. *The Twelve Days of Christmas.* 1949. New York. Harper & Row. Ills. 1st ed. VG $17.50

KARDINER, A. & Preble. *They Studied Man.* 1961. 1st ed. photos. dj. EX $15.00

KARLINSKY, S. *The Nabokov-Wilson Letters, 1940-71.* 1979. New York. 1st ed. EX $12.50

KARLOFF, Boris. *Tales of Terror.* 1943. World. dj. VG $12.50

KARMALI, J. *Birds of Africa.* 1980. Viking. Ills. 1st ed. 191 pp. dj. EX $22.50

KARNES, T.L. William. *Gilpin Western Nationalist.* 1970. Texas U. Press.dj. EX $10.00

KAROLEVITZ, Robert F. *This Was Trucking.* 1966. Seattle. Ills. 1st ed. 192 pp. dj. VG $27.50

KARPEL. *Arts in American: A Bibliography.* 1980. Smithsonian. 4 vol set. $100.00

KARR, Charles L. & Robbins, C. *Remington Handguns.* 1956. Harrisburg. Ills. 3rd ed. 152 pp. dj. $18.50

KARSH. *Portraits of Greatness.* 1960. $39.00

KARSNER, David. *Silver Dollar. Story of the Tabors.* 1932. New York. 354 pp. G $10.00

KASCO. *Dog Owners Guide.* 1953. Ills. 137 pp. SftCvr. $4.50

KASSAY. *The Book of Shaker Furniture.* 1980. U. of MA. Press. $15.00

KASTNER, Erich. *Annaluise & Anton.* 1933. New York. Ills. Walter Trier. 1st ed. EX $30.00

KATCHADOURIAN, Sarkis. *Rubaiyat of Omar Khayyam.* 1946. New York. dj. VG $15.00

KATCHER, L. *Post Mortem.* 1968. London. Hamish Hamilton. G $20.00

KATZ, William L. *The Black West.* 1971. New York. Ills. 336 pp. biblio. dj. $30.00

KATZENBACH, John. *In the Heat of the Summer.* 1982. New York. Atheneum. 1st ed. dj. VG $25.00

KATZENBACH, Maria. *The Grab.* 1978. New York. Morrow. 1st ed. dj. VG $30.00

KAUFFELD, C. *Snakes & Snake Hunting.* 1957. Hanover House. Ills. 266 pp. index. dj. EX $25.00

KAUFFMAN, Henry. *Pennsylvania Dutch American Folk Art.* 1946. dj. EX $20.00

KAUFFMAN, Reginald Wright. *Seventy-Six!* 1926. Philadelphia. Ills. Clyde O. DeLand. VG $15.00

KAUFFMAN, Reginald Wright. *Spanish Dollars.* 1925. Philadelphia. Ills. Manning de V. Lee. $25.00

KAUFMAN, Pamela. *Shield of Three Lions.* 1983. Crown. advance copy. wrappers. VG $10.00

KAUFMAN, Paul & Farver, W.E. *Indian Lore of the Muskingham Headwaters of Ohio.* 1973. no place. Ills. 216 pp. VG $12.50

KAUFMAN & HENNESSEY. *The Letters of Alexander Woolcott.* 1st ed. VG $6.00

KAUFMANN, Myron. *Thy Daughter's Nakedness.* 1968. 1st ed. dj. VG $15.00

KAUS, Gina. *Catherine, the Portrait of an Empress.* 1935. New York. Literary Guild. 384 pp. $4.50

KAVAN, Anna. *Ice.* 1970. Garden City. Doubleday. 1st ed. dj. EX $40.00

KAVANAUGH, James. *The Celibates.* 1985. Harper. proof copy. wrappers. VG $15.00

KAWAKATSU, Kenichi. *Kimono: Japanese Dress.* 1947. Japan Travel Bureau. Ills. pb. $6.00

KAY, Ernest. *The World Who's Who of Women.* 1978. Cambridge. Ills. 4th ed. 1302 pp. VG $10.00

KAY, Gertrude Alice. *Adventures in Geography.* 1941. New York. Ills. Kay. $15.00

KAY, Gertrude Alice. *Adventures in Geography.* 1930. Volland. Ills. Kay. 1st ed. VG $20.00

KAY, Gertrude Alice. *Friends of Jimmy.* 1926. New York. Volland. Ills. unpp. EX $12.50

KAY, Gertrude Alice. *The Jolly Old Shadow Man.* 1920. Sunny Book Series. Ills. $18.00

KAY, Terry. *After Eli.* 1981. Boston. 1st ed. dj. VG $15.00

KAYE, Barbara. *The Company We Kept.* 1986. Blakeney. Ills. 1st ed. sgn. EX $30.00

KAYE, Ivan. *Good Clean Violence.* 1973. New York. Lippincott. Illls. 288 pp. dj. $3.50

KAYE, Marvin & Godwin, Parke. *Wintermind.* 1982. Garden City. 1st ed. dj. VG $12.50

KAYE, Marvin. *The Possession of Immanuel Wolf & Other Tales.* 1981. Garden City. 1st ed. dj. VG $8.00

KAYE-SMITH, Sheila. *Ember Lane.* 1940. London. Cassell. 1st ed. G $15.00

KAYE-SMITH, Sheila. *Gallybird.* 1934. New York. Harper. 375 pp. $3.00

KAYE-SMITH, Sheila. *Sussex Gorse. The Story of a Fight.* 1933. New York. Knopf. 462 pp. $2.50

KAYE-SMITH, Sheila. *The End of the House of Alard.* 1923. New York. 353 pp. $2.50

KAYE-SMITH, Sheila. *Superstition Corner.* 1934. Harper. 1st ed. VG $10.00

KAZAN, E. *The Understudy.* 1st English ed. dj. $8.00

KAZAN, Elia. *The Arrangement.* 1967. New York. Stein & Day. 544 pp. $4.00

KAZANTAZAKIS, Kikos. *Serpent & Lilly.* 1980. U. of CA. 1st ed. dj. VG $20.00

KAZANTKAKIS, N. *Le Christ Recrucifie.* 1955. Paris. 1st French ed. $300.00

KEARNEY, B. *A Slave Holder's Daughter.* 1900. VG $25.00

KEARNEY, Patrick J. *The Private Case.* 1981. London. Ltd. 1st ed. 1/1000. dj. EX $80.00

KEARNS, Doris. *Lyndon Johnson & the American Dream.* 1976. New York. Harper & Row. 1st ed. 432 pp. $4.00

KEARTON, C. *My Dog Simba.* 1926. London. Arrowsmith. 1st ed. 127 pp. VG $12.50

KEARTON, C. *The Island of Penguins.* 1930. London. Longman. Ills. map. 223 pp. VG $12.50

KEARY, A. & E. *The Heroes of Asgard.* 1979. Ills. 1st ed. EX $50.00

KEATING, B. *The Gulf of Mexico.* 1981. Viking Press. Ills. 75 pp. EX $10.00

KEATING, H.R.F. *Inspector Ghote Hunts the Peacock.* 1968. London. 1st ed. dj. VG $15.00

KEATING, H.R.F. *Whodunit?* 1982. New York. Van Nostrand. 1st ed. dj. EX $35.00

KEATING. *The Gentlemen from Colorado. A Memoir.* 1964. Saga Books. 522 pp. dj. VG $10.00

KEATON, Buster. *My Wonderful World of Slapstick.* 1960. Doubleday. 1st ed. dj. VG $20.00

KEATS, John. *Isabella; or, The Pot of Basil.* Philadelphia. no date. Ills. Jessie M. King. $15.00

KEATS, John. *Letters of John Keats to Fanny Brawne.* 1878. New York. 128 pp. EX $95.00

KEATS, John. *Poems Published in 1820.* 1909. Oxford. Clarendon Press. reprint ed. $25.00

KEATS, John. *Poetical Works of John Keats. Vol. I.* 1899. Boston. Houghton Mifflin. VG $20.00

KEATS, John. *The Odes of Keats.* 1897. Oxford. Clarendon Press. VG $25.00

KEATS, John. *Walter Jackson Bate.* 1963. Cambridge. Harvard U. Pr. Ills. 732 pp. $35.00

KECKLEY, Elizabeth. *Behind the Scenes; or, 30 Years a Slave.* 1868. New York. 371 pp. $65.00

KEELER, C. *San Francisco & Thereabout.* 1902. not 1st ed. $7.50

KEELER, Edward Elmer. *Here's How Health Happens.* 1912. Syracuse, NY. Good Health Clinic. G $5.00

KEELER, Harry. *Case of the Beans.* 1944. Phoenix. ex-lib. dj. $25.00

KEELER. *The Box from Japan.* 1932. New York. 1st ed. VG $20.00

KEEN, Benjamin. *Aztec Image in Western Thought.* 1971. New Brunswick. Ills. 667 pp. dj. $30.00

KEENE, Carolyn. *Nancy Drew & the Bungalow Mystery.* 1930. New York. Grosset & Dunlap. dj. VG $3.50

KEENE, Carolyn. *Nancy Drew & the Clue of the Black Keys.* 1951. New York. Grosset & Dunlap. dj. VG $3.50

KEENE, Carolyn. *Nancy Drew & the Mystery of Lilac Inn.* 1930. New York. Grosset & Dunlap. dj. VG $3.50

KEENE, Carolyn. *Nancy Drew & the Password to Larkspur Lake.* 1933. New York. Grosset & Dunlap. dj. VG $3.50

KEENE, Carolyn. *Nancy Drew & the Ringmaster's Secret.* 1953. New York. Grosset & Dunlap. dj. VG $3.50

KEENE, Carolyn. *Nancy Drew & the Secret of the Golden Pavilion.* 1959. New York. Grosset & Dunlap. dj. VG $3.50

KEENE, Carolyn. *Nancy Drew & the Sign of the Twisted Candle.* 1933. New York. Grosset & Dunlap. VG $3.50

KEENE, Carolyn. *The Clue in the Diary.* 1962. EX $3.00

KEENE, Carolyn. *The Invisible Intruder.* New York. Grosset & Dunlap. VG $7.50

KEENE, Carolyn. *The Mysterious Manne-quin.* New York. Grosset & Dunlap. VG $7.50

KEENE, Carolyn. *The Nancy Drew Cookbook.* 1973. New York. Grosset & Dunlap. 159 pp. $3.50

KEENE, Day. *Seed of Doubt.* 1961. New York. Simon & Schuster. 1st ed. $6.00

KEENE, John H. *Boys Own Guide to Fishing.* 1894. Boston. VG $45.00

KEENLYSIDE. *Peaks & Pioneers.* 1975. London. 1st ed. dj. EX $30.00

KEESING. *The European Communities: Establishment & Growth.* 1975. New York. Scribner. 208 pp. dj. $3.00

KEIFER. *American Children Through Their Books, 1700-1835.* 1948. New York. 1st ed. dj. EX $17.50

KEIGHTLEY, Thomas. *World Guide to Gnomes, Fairies, Elves, & Others.* 1975. Avenel Books. Ills. 1st printing. VG $20.00

KEILIG, W. *Die Generale des Heeres.* 1983. Friedberg. dj. EX $20.00

KEILIG, W. *Rangliste des Deutschen Heeres 1944-1945.* 1984. Friedberg. $25.00

KEINEN, Imao. *Keinen Album, Birds & Flowers.* 1979. 4 vol set. wrappers. $90.00

KEISER. *God Returns to the Vuelta Aba-jo.* 1936. New York. Scott. dj. VG $25.00

KEITH, Agnes. *Three Came Home.* 1947. Boston. 2nd ed. 317 pp. $37.50

KEITH, Carlton. *The Diamond Studded Typewriter.* 1958. New York. Macmillan. 1st ed. dj. VG $15.00

KEITH, Elmer. *Big Game Rifles & Car-tridges.* 1946. South Carolina. sgn. dj. VG $195.00

KEITH, Elmer. *Elmer Keith's Big Game Hunting.* 1954. Boston. Ills. Bob Kuhn. sgn. dj. VG $115.00

KELEHER, Wm. A. *Maxwell Land Grant, a New Mexico Item.* 1942. Santa Fe. 1st ed. inscr. $160.00

KELEHER, Wm. A. *The Fabulous Fron-tier.* 1962. U. NM Press. Ills. dj. EX $25.00

KELEHER, Wm. A. *Turmoil in New Mex-ico.* 1952. Rydal Press. 1st ed. dj. VG $62.50

KELLAND, Clarence B. *Merchant of Valor.* 1947. $25.00

KELLAND, Clarence B. *Miracle.* 1925. $27.50

KELLAND, Clarence B. *The Key Man.* 1952. $25.00

KELLAND, Clarence. *Dreamland.* 1935. $27.50

KELLAND, Clarence. *Land of the Tor-reones.* 1945. 1st ed. dj. VG $12.50

KELLAND. *Mark Tidd, Manufacturer.* 1918. Grosset & Dunlap. G $4.50

KELLAND. *Mark Tidd in the Backwoods.* 1914. Grosset & Dunlap. G $4.50

KELLAND. *Mark Tidd.* 1913. Grosset & Dunlap. G $4.50

KELLAND. *Mark Tidd: Citadel.* 1916. Grosset & Dunlap. G $4.50

KELLEHER, D.L. *Anthology of Christmas Prose & Verse.* 1928. Cresset Press. VG $30.00

KELLER, David H. *Fan News Mag No. 340, Defense of Dr. David Keller.* Fargo, ND. Dunkelberger. 11 pp. wrappers. $5.00

KELLER, David H. *La Guerre Du Lierre. Traduction de Regis Messac.* 1936. Seine, France. 196 pp. sgn. rare $175.00

KELLER, David H. *Tales from Underwood.* 1952. New York. Pellegrini. 1st ed. dj. EX $35.00

KELLER, David H. *The Devil & the Doc-tor.* 1940. New York. Simon & Schuster. 1st ed. EX $50.00

KELLER, David H. *The Homunculus.* 1949. Philadelphia. Prime Press. inscr. dj. EX $150.00

KELLER, David H. *The Signs of the Bur-ning Heart.* 1938. Saint-Lo. Ltd. ed. 1/100. sgn. rare. $250.00

KELLER, David H. *The Solitary Hunters & the Abyss.* 1948. New Era Pub. 1st ed. sgn. dj. $55.00

KELLER, David H. *The Thing in the Cellar.* Millheim, PA. reprint. 32 pp. sgn. VG $30.00

KELLER, Francis Ruth. *The Contented Little Pussy Cat.* 1949. New York. Ills. Adele Werber & D. Laslo. $15.00

KELLER, Harry Stephen. *Thieves' Night.* 1930. London. 1st ed. inscr. dj. EX $45.00

KELLER, Helen. *Out of the Dark.* 1913. Doubleday Page. 1st ed. VG $15.00

KELLER, Hermann. *The Organ Works of Bach.* 1967. New York. trans. Helen Hewitt. EX $12.50

KELLER, Werner. *Diaspora. Post-Biblical History of Jews.* 1966. New York. 522 pp. $7.00

KELLEY, K. *Elizabeth Taylor, Last Star.* 1981. New York. Ills. 448 pp. dj. VG $6.00

KELLEY, Robert F. *American Rowing.* 1932. New York. Ills. EX $20.00

KELLEY, William Kelley. *A Drop of Pa-tience.* 1965. Garden City. Doubleday. 1st ed. dj. EX $20.00

KELLEY, William Melvin. *Dancers on the Shore.* 1965. London. Hutchinson. 1st Eng. ed. VG $20.00

KELLEY, William Melvin. *Dunfords Travels Everywheres.* 1970. Garden City. Doubleday. 1st ed. dj. $15.00

KELLEY. *Blood-Drenched Altars: Mexican Study & Comment.* 1935. Bruce. 1st ed. 502 pp. VG $15.00

KELLOGG, Elijah. *The Young Ship Builders of Elm Island.* 1898. Boston. Lee & Shepard. Ills. 304 pp. $10.00

KELLOGG, John. *Capture & Escape.* 1908. 1st ed. 201 pp. $28.50

KELLOGG, Louise P. *Frontier Advance on the Upper Ohio, 1778-1779.* 1916. Madison. Ills. Ltd. 1st ed. 509 pp. $45.00

KELLY, Charles. *Outlaw Trail. Story of Butch Cassidy 'Wild Bunch.'* 1954. New York. Ills. maps. 374 pp. dj. $10.00

KELLY, Eric P. *The Trumpeter of Krakow.* 1933. New York. Ills. Angela Pruszynaska. EX $15.00

KELLY, Fanny. *Narrative of My Captivi-ty Among Sioux Indians.* 1872. Hartford. 285 pp. 10 pls. G $45.00

KELLY, Fred C. *The Permanent Ade. Liv-ing Writings of George Ade.* 1947. In-dianapolis. Bobbs Merrill. 347 pp. dj. $7.50

KELLY, Hall Jackson. *Settlement on the Oregon River.* 1828. Washington. 1st ed. wrappers. $350.00

KELLY, Howard. *Some American Medical Botanists.* 1914. Tory, New York. Ills. 215 pp. dj. VG $45.00

KELLY, Joanne M. *Cuna.* 1966. NY/Lon-don. 440 pp. dj. $15.00

KELLY, Lawrence. *Navaho Roundup. Kit Carson's Expedition 1863-65.* 1970. Boulder, CO. Ills. 1st ed. 192 pp. maps. EX $20.00

KELLY, Michael. *Reminiscences of King's Theatre & Drury Lane.* 1826. New York. 1st ed. VG $65.00

KELLY, Walt. *Pogo a la Sundae.* 1961. 1st ed. wrappers. EX $20.00

KELLY, Walt. *Pogo a la Sundae.* 1961. 1st ed. dj. EX $20.00

KELLY, Walt. *Pogo Papers.* 1st Am. ed. pb. VG $10.00

KELLY, Walt. *Pogo Sunday Book.* 1956. 1st ed. dj. VG $20.00

KELLY, Walt. *Pogo.* 1st Am. ed. pb. VG $15.00

KELLY, Walt. *Pogo's Sunday Punch.* 1957. 1st ed. dj. VG $20.00

KELLY, Walt. *The Pogo Stepmother Goose.* 1954. New York. wrappers. EX $15.00

KELLY, Walt. *The Pogo Sunday Parade.* 1958. New York. 1st printing. SftCvr. VG $20.00

KELLY, Wm. J. *Presswork. A Practical Handbook.* 1898. Chicago. 85 pp. $10.00

KELLY. *Etchings-Drawings of Hawaiians.* 1943. $39.00

KEMBLE, Frances A. *Journal of a Residence on a Georgian Plantation.* 1863. New York. $20.00

KEMELMAN, Harry. *The Nine Mile Walk.* 1967. New York. Putnam. 1st ed. dj. EX $30.00

KEMP, E. *How to Lay Out a Garden.* 1860. 2nd ed. G $30.00

KEMP, P. *History of the Royal Navy.* 1969. Ills. maps. dj. EX $25.00

KEMPSTER, Aquila. *The Way of the Gods.* 1901. New York. Quail. 1st ed. EX $17.50

KENDALL, B.J. *The Doctor at Home.* 1887. Enosburgh Falls. Ills. 95 pp. $12.50

KENDALL, Ezra. *The Vinegar Buyer's Sharp Sayings of Sharp People.*1909. Cleveland. Ills. 188 pp. $7.50

KENDALL, Ezra. *Top Soil.* 1909. J.B. Savage Co.Ills. 200 pp. G $12.50

KENDALL, G.W. *Narrative of Texan Santa Fe Expedition.* 1844. London. Ills. fld map. 2 vol set. $375.00

KENDALL, G.W. *Narrative of Texan Santa Fe Expedition.* 1844. New York. 1st ed. fld map. 2 vol set. $200.00

KENDRICK, Baynard. *The Flames of Time.* 1948. New York. Scribner. 1st ed. 374 pp. dj. $4.50

KENDRICK & ARNETT. *South Looks at Its Past.* 1935. Chapel Hill. 1st ed. VG $15.00

KENEALLY. *A Dutiful Daughter.* 1971. 1st Am. ed. dj. EX $15.00

KENEALLY. *Bring Larks & Heroes.* 1977. 1st Am. ed. dj. EX $25.00

KENEALLY. *The Place at Whitton.* 1964. New York. 1st Am. ed. dj. VG $35.00

KENEALLY. *Victim of the Aurora.* 1978. 1st Am. ed. dj. EX $12.50

KENNAN, George. *Memoirs.* 1967. Book of Month Club. dj. EX $8.00

KENNAN, George. *Siberia & Exile System.* 1891. 1st English ed. 2 vol set. $25.00

KENNAN, George. *Tent Life in Siberia: Adventure Among Koraks.* 1910. New York. VG $35.00

KENNARD, E. *Hopi Kachinas.* 1938. New York. 1st ed. 29 color pls. VG $125.00

KENNEDY, Adam. *Debt of Honor.* 1981. Delacorte. proof copy. wrappers. EX $15.00

KENNEDY, Adam. *In a Far Country.* 1983. Delacorte. 1st ed. dj. VG $12.50

KENNEDY, Howard Angus. *The Red Man's Wonder Book.* 1931. Dutton. Ills. 1st ed. VG $10.00

KENNEDY, John F. *Profiles in Courage.* 1956. New York. 1st ed. dj. EX $25.00

KENNEDY, John F. *The Strategy of Peace.* 1960. New York. Harper. 1st ed. sgn. VG $30.00

KENNEDY, Mary. *A Surprise to the Children.* 1933. New York. Ills. J.H. Dowd. 88 pp. dj. EX $30.00

KENNEDY, Raymond. *Columbine.* 1980. New York. Farrar. proof copy. wrappers. $20.00

KENNEDY, Robert F. *The Enemy Within.* 1960. New York. 1st ed. dj. VG $35.00

KENNEDY, Robert F. *Thirteen Days.* 1971. New York. 184 pp. SftCvr. $2.50

KENNEDY, Robert F. *Thirteen Days.* 1969. New York. 1st ed. dj. EX $6.50

KENNEDY, Robert. *German Campaign in Poland.* 1956. Washington. Ills. 141 pp. 11 fld maps. VG $37.50

KENNEDY, W. *Billy Phelan's Greatest Game.* 1978. New York. 1st ed. dj. EX $25.00

KENNEDY, W. *Hurrah for the Life of a Sailor.* 1900. Edinburgh. Ills. G $27.50

KENNEDY, W. Sloane. *Henry W. Longfellow: Biography, Criticism.* 1882. Cambridge. Ills. 3rd ed. VG $25.00

KENNEDY, William. *Ironweed.* 1983. New York. Viking. 1st ed. dj. $40.00

KENNEDY, William. *Legs.* 1975. New York. Coward. 1st ed. dj. EX $50.00

KENNEDY, William. *The Ink Truck.* 1969. New York. Dial Press. 1st ed. VG $90.00

KENNEDY. *John Woodward. A Memoir.* 1897. Brooklyn. private printed. VG $25.00

KENNEDY. *Rise, Progress, & Prospects of Republic of Texas.* 1925. Fort Worth. Ltd. ed. $65.00

KENNERLY, Wm. C. *Persimmon Hill.* 1949. U. of OK Press. 273 pp. pls. dj. VG $12.50

KENNETH, Roberts. *I Wanted to Write.* 1949. 1st ed. dj. EX $20.00

KENNY, Nick. *How to Write, Sing, & Sell Popular Songs.* 1946. New York. dj. VG $14.00

KENRICK, Vivienne. *Horses in Japan.* 1964. Hokuseido Press. Ills. 196 pp. $60.00

KENSETT, P.F. *The Amulet of Tarv.* 1925. Burrow. 1st ed. dj. VG $25.00

KENT, Frank Richardson. *Story of Maryland Politics.* 1911. Baltimore. Ills. 393 pp. $12.50

KENT, Louise Andrews. *Mrs. Appleyard & I.* 1968. Boston. Houghton Mifflin. 414 pp. $10.00

KENT, Louise Andrews. *The Summer Kitchen.* 1957. Houghton Mifflin. 1st ed. dj. $15.00

KENT, Louise Andrews. *Village Greens of New England.* 1948. New York. Barrows. 1st ed. 280 pp. $12.50

KENT, Rockwell. *A Northern Christmas.* 1941. New York. Am. Artists Group. 1st ed. dj. $35.00

KENT, Rockwell. *Candide.* 1929. New York. Literary Guild. 112 pp. $7.50

KENT, Rockwell. *Famous Paintings.* 1939. Wise. $22.50

KENT, Rockwell. *Hans the Eskimo.* 1934. Boston. VG $15.00

KENT, Rockwell. *Leaves of Grass.* Whitman. Heritage Press. dj. VG $22.50

KENT, Rockwell. *Memoirs of Jacques Casanova de Seingalt.* 1925. Aventuros. Ltd. ed. EX $195.00

KENT, Rockwell. *Moby Dick.* 1930. Random House. Ills. 1st ed. dj. VG $45.00

KENT, Rockwell. *N By E.* 1930. Chicago. Literary Guild. Ills. 281 pp. $5.00

KENT, Rockwell. *N by E.* 1933. Blue Ribbon. 5th printing. VG $15.00

KENT, Rockwell. *N by E.* 1930. NY Literary Guild. 1st ed. dj. $20.00

KENT, Rockwell. *Rockwellkentiana.* 1933. Harcourt Brace.1st ed. dj. VG $75.00

KENT, Rockwell. *The Saga of Gisli, Son of Sour.* 1936. New York. Ills. 1st ed. VG $40.00

KENT, Rockwell. *This is My Own.* 1945. Duell Sloan. Ills. 1st ed. 393 pp. dj. VG $45.00

KENT, Rockwell. *This is My Own.* 1940. New York. 1st ed. VG $50.00

KENT, Rockwell. *Voyaging Southward from Strait of Magellan.* 1924. Putnam. dj. EX $17.50

KENT, Rockwell. *Voyaging Southward from Strait of Magellan.* 1924. New York. 4th printing. 184 pp. VG $55.00

KENT, Rockwell. *Wilderness: Journal of Quiet Adventure in Alaska.* 1937. New York. Ills. 5th printing. VG $40.00

KENT, Rockwell. *World Famous Paintings.* 1939. New York. Ills. VG $20.00

KENT, William K. *Rare Hooked Rugs.* 1948. Ills. dj. EX $7.50

KENTFIELD, Calvin. *The Great Green: Memoirs of a Merchant Mariner.* 1974. New York. 256 pp. dj. $5.50

KENWORTHY, J.D. *Fisherman's Philosophy.* 1933. 1st color ills ed. VG $20.00

KEONIGSWALD, G.H.R. *Jahre Neanderthaler Neanderthal Centenary.* 1958. 1st ed. $20.00

KEPES, Gyorgy. *The Nature & Art of Motion.* 1965. 3rd ed. 1975 pp. dj. $50.00

KEPES, Gyorgy. *The Visual Arts Today.* 1963. Middletown, CT. EX $22.00

KEPHART, Horace. *Book of Camping & Woodcraft.* 1906. 1st ed. VG $15.00

KEPHART, Horace. *Camping & Woodcraft, Vol. I.* 1922. Macmillan. 405 pp. $6.50

KEPHART, Horace. *Captives Among the Indians, First Hand Narratives.*1915. Oyster Bay, NY. Ills. end papers. 240 pp. $17.50

KEPHART. *Our Southern Highlanders.* 1926. New York. $17.50

KEPPEL, Capt. H. *Expedition to Borneo of H.M.S. Dido.* 1846. New York. 413 pp. G $50.00

KERBY, Robert L. *Kirby Smith's Confederacy.* 1972. Columbia U. Pr.1st ed. 529 pp. dj. VG $22.50

KERCHEVAL. *Lorin Mooruck & Other Indian Stories.* 1888. Boston. 1st ed. $25.00

KERENYI. *Dionysos: Archetypal Image of Indestructible Life.* 1976. Princeton U. Press. $20.00

KERIHER, Harry C. *Who's Who in Hockey.* 1973. Arlington House. EX $10.00

KERNAHAN, Coulson. *Captain Shannon.* 1896. New York. Dodd. 1st Am. ed. VG $17.50

KERNAHAN, Coulson. *Captain Shannon.* 1897. London. Ward Lock. 1st ed. G $30.00

KEROUAC, Jack. *Dharma Bums.* 1958. Viking. 1st ed. dj. VG $50.00

KEROUAC, Jack. *Maggie Cassidy.* New York. 1st ed. wrappers. VG $15.00

KEROUAC, Jack. *On the Road.* 1957. New York. 1st ed. 310 pp. $195.00

KEROUAC, Jack. *Pic.* 1971. New York. Grove/Zebra. 1st ed. wrappers. $10.00

KEROUAC, Jack. *Town & the City.* 1950. New York. VG $45.00

KEROUAC, Jack. *Tristessa.* 1st Am. ed. pb. EX $25.00

KEROUAC, Jan. *Baby Driver.* 1981. St.Martins. 1st ed. dj. VG $12.50

KEROUAC. *Rimbaud.* New York. 2nd ed. EX $30.00

KERR, Alvah M. *Two Young Inventors.* 1904. Boston. Lee & Shepard. Ills. $12.50

KERR, Graham. *The Graham Kerr Cookbook.* 1969. Garden City. Doubleday. Ills. 284 pp. $7.50

KERR, J.G. *A Naturalist in the Gran Chaco.* 1968. Greenwood. Ills. maps. 235 pp. EX $25.00

KERR, J.L. *Wilfred Grenfell, His Life & Work.* 1959. Dodd Mead. Ills. dj. VG $10.00

KERR, R.S. *Land, Wood, & Water.* 1960. Fleet. 380 pp. dj. VG $5.00

KERR, Walter. *Thirty Plays Hath November.* 1969. New York. 1st ed. dj. $4.00

KERSH, Gerald. *Faces in a Dusty Picture.* 1944. London. Heinemann. 1st ed. dj. VG $40.00

KERSH, Gerald. *Men Without Bones.* 1962. New York. 1st ed. ex-lib. wrappers. $6.50

KERSH, Gerald. *The Dead Look On.* 1943. London. 1st ed. sgn. dj. VG $40.00

KERSTING, R. *The White World.* 1902. New York. VG $65.00

KERTESZ, Andre. *Of New York.* 1976. New York. sgn. dj. EX $175.00

KERTESZ, Andre. *Portraits; Landscapes; Birds; American.* 1979. New York. 1st pb. ed. wrappers. $17.50

KERTESZ, Andre. *Sixty Years of Photography 1912-1972.* 1972. Grossman. sgn. dj. EX $175.00

KESEY, Ken. *Cuckoo's Nest.* London. 1st ed. dj. VG $85.00

KESEY. *Sometimes a Great Notion.* 2nd printing. dj. EX $25.00

KESSEL, Joseph. *The Lion.* 1959. Knopf. 1st Am. ed. 244 pp. $37.50

KESSLER, D. *Alaska's Salt-Water Fishes & Other Sea Life.* 1985. Alaska. Ills. 358 pp. $20.00

KESSLER, Harry. *In the Twenties. The Diaries of Harry Kessler.* 1971. New York. 1st ed. dj. VG $10.00

KESTING, Ted. *Trout Fishing.* 1962. Ills. dj. VG $12.50

KETCHAM, Hank. *Dennis the Menace Rides Again.* 1955. Ills. $3.00

KEYES, Frances Parkinson. *All This Is Louisiana.* 1950. photos. VG $20.00

KEYES, Frances Parkinson. *Blue Camellia.* 1957. New York. 432 pp. $5.00

KEYES, Frances Parkinson. *Came a Cavalier.* 1947. New York. 435 pp. $3.50

KEYES, Frances Parkinson. *Dinner at Antione's.* 1948. New York. 422 pp. $3.00

KEYES, Frances Parkinson. *I, the King.* 1966. New York. McGraw Hill. 365 pp. dj. $5.00

KEYES, Frances Parkinson. *Madame Castel's Lover.* 1962. New York. 471 pp. dj. VG $6.00

KEYES, Frances Parkinson. *Station Wagon in Spain.* 1959. New York. 224 pp. $6.00

KEYES, Frances Parkinson. *Steamboat Gothic.* 1952. New York. Messner. 1st ed. inscr. dj. VG $60.00

KEYES, Frances Parkinson. *The Chess Players.* 1960. New York. 508 pp. $3.50

KEYES, Frances Parkinson. *The Heritage.* 1968. New York. McGraw Hill. 330 pp. dj. $7.00

KEYES, Frances Parkinson. *The River Road.* 1945. New York. 622 pp. $7.00

KEYES, Frances Parkinson. *The Royal Box.* 1954. New York. 303 pp. $7.00

KEYES, Frances Parkinson. *Victorine.* 1958. New York. 288 pp. $6.00

KEYES, Frances Parkinson. *Joy Street.* 1950. New York. Messner. 422 pp. $7.50

KEYES, Geoffrey. *Ten Sermons of John Donne.* Nonsuch Press. Ltd. ed. 1/725. VG $35.00

KEYES, Nelson B. *Ben Franklin/An Affectionate Portrait.* 1956. New York. Hanover House. 318 pp. dj. $4.50

KEYES, Roger S. *The Theatrical World of Osaka Prints.* 1973. Philadelphia. Ills. 336 pp. EX $75.00

KEYES, Roger. *Surimono: Privately Published Japanese Prints.* 1984. 268 Ills. 200 pp. dj. EX $60.00

KEYNES, G. *Henry James in Cambridge.* 1967. Cambridge. Ltd. 1st ed. 1/1000. dj. EX $35.00

KEYNES, John Maynard. *Die Wirtschaftlichen Folgen des Friedensvertrages.* 1920. Munich/Leipzig.2 vol set. rare. $65.00

KEYZER, Frances. *French Household Cooking.* 1928. London. VG $15.00

KHAN, Mohammad Ayub. *Friends Not Masters.* 1967. New York. Oxford U. Press. ex-lib. dj. $5.00

KHOSLA. *Himalayan Circuit.* 1956. London. 1st ed. dj. EX $10.00

KIBBE, Pauline R. *Latin Americans in Texas.* 1946. Albuquerque. 1st ed. dj. VG $30.00

KIBBY, G. *Mushrooms & Toadstools, a Field Guide.* 1979. Oxford U. Pr. Ills. 1st ed. 256 pp. dj. EX $25.00

KIDD, John. *On Adaptation of External Nature to Physical Man.* 1833. Philadelphia. $10.00

KIDD, Robert. *Vocal Culture & Elocution: Exercises in Reading.* 1857. Cincinnati. 480 pp. $10.00

KIDDER, Al. *Archaeological Exploration in North-East Arizona.* 1919. Washington. Ills. 1st ed. VG $20.00

KIDDER, Charles H. *Burley's U.S. Centennial Gazetteer & Guide.* 1876. Philadelphia. 892 pp. $30.00

KIDDER, Tracy. *House.* 1983. Boston. Houghton Mifflin. proof copy. $20.00

KIEJE, Nicolas. *Japanese Grotesqueries.* 1973. Tuttle. 1st printing. Ills. 245 pp. EX $38.00

KIEPERT, Henry. *Atlas Antiquus.* Berlin/NY. (ca.1892) Ills. map. index. $35.00

KIERAN, J. *An Introduction to Birds.* 1950. Garden City. Ills. Eckelberry. 1st ed. dj. $7.50

KIERAN, J. *Treasury of Great Nature Writings.* 1957. Hanover House. 640 pp. VG $10.00

KIERKEGAARD, S. *The Point of View.* 1939. Oxford. dj. VG $12.50

KIESLING, Barrett C. *Talking Pictures. How They Are Made.* 1937. ex-lib. $27.50

KIKUCHI, Sadao. *Treasury of Japanese Wood Block Prints.* 1969. Ukiyo. Crown. dj. VG $75.00

KILBOURNE, Frederick. *Chronicle of the White Mountains.* 1916. Boston. Ills. G $17.50

KILBOURNE, S.A. & Goode, G.B. *Game Fishes of the United States.* 1972. Winchester. Ills. Ltd. ed. 1/1000. folio. $75.00

KILE, Orville Merton. *The Farm Bureau Through Three Decades.* 1948. Baltimore, MD. 416 pp. index. $8.00

KILGORE, William H. *Journal of Overland Journey to California in 1850.* 1949. New York. Ltd. ed. 1/1000. 63 pp. $12.50

KILGORE. *Ranger Legacy.* Ills. Madrona. 1st ed. dj. EX $25.00

KILLEBREW, J.B. *Introduction to Resources of Tennessee.* 1874. Nashville. 1200 pp. fld maps. G $50.00

KILLEBREW, J.B. & Myrick, H. *Tobacco, Culture, Cure, Marketing, Manufacture.* 1897. New York. Ills. VG $45.00

KILLITS, John M. *Toledo & Lucas County Ohio, 1623-1923.* 1923. Chicago/Toledo. Ills. 3 vol set. G $52.50

KILMAN, Ed & Wright, Theon. *Hugh Roy Cullen, a Story of American Opportunity.* 1954. New York. 376 pp. dj. $5.00

KILMER, Annie K. *Leaves from My Life.* 1925. New York. sgn. $30.00

KILMER, Joyce. *Poems, Essays, & Letters.* 1918. New York. 2 vol set. dj. slipcase. EX $20.00

KILMER, Joyce. *Poems & Essays. Vol. II.* 1918. VG $5.00

KIMBALL, Caleb. *The Young Christian Directed.* 1847. Boston. 180 pp. $3.00

KIMBALL, M. *Thomas Jefferson's Cook Book.* 1949. 1st ed. G $15.00

KIMBALL, Richard B. *Romance of Student Life Abroad.* New York. Putnam. 3rd ed. 261 pp. VG $12.50

KIMBALL, Richard. *In the Tropics. By a Settler in Santo Domingo.* 1863. New York. VG $17.50

KIMBROUGH, Emily. *Floating Island.* 1968. Harper & Row. sgn. 243 pp. dj. $50.00

KIMMEL, Stanley. *Mad Booths of Maryland.* 1940. Bobbs Merrill. Ills. 1st ed. 400 pp. dj. VG $45.00

KINARD, M. & Blanchard, M. *The Kitchen Scholar.* 1967. New York. Citadel Press. 240 pp. $10.00

KINCAID, Jamaica. *Annie John.* Farrar. proof copy. wrappers. EX $30.00

KINCAID, Robert L. *The Wilderness Road.* 1947. Indianapolis. Ills. 1st ed. 392 pp. index. $10.00

KINDERLEHRER, Jane. *Confessions of a Sneaky Cook.* 1971. Rodale. 245 pp. $7.50

KINDERSLEY, David. *Eric Gill, Further Thoughts by an Apprentice.* 1982. wrappers. $10.00

KINERT, Reed. *America's Fighting Planes in Action.* 1943. New York. Ills. 142 pp. $12.50

KING, Alexander. *May This House be Safe from Tigers.* 1960. New York. Simon & Schuster. 1st ed. dj. $30.00

KING, Alfred Castner. *Mt. Idylls & Other Poems.* 1901. Chicago. Ills. dj. VG $10.00

KING, Alfred Castner. *Passing of the Storm.* 1907. G $8.00

KING, B. & Dickinson, E.C. *Field Guide to Birds of Southeast Asia.* 1983. London. Collins. Ills. 480 pp. EX $20.00

KING, Ben. *Jane Jones & Some Others.* 1909. Ills. J.A. Williams. 94 pp. $6.50

KING, Beulah. *Ruffs & Pompons.* 1924. Boston. Ills. Maurice Day. 1st ed. EX $20.00

KING, Charles. *A Night of Columbia.* 1904. Ills. 1st ed. G $5.00

KING, Charles. *A War-Time Wooing.* 1900. $5.00

KING, Charles. *An Army Wife.* 1896. New York. 278 pp. $3.50

KING, Charles. *Daughter of the Sioux.* 1903. NY. Hobart. Ills. Deming & Remington. G $17.50

KING, Clarence. *Mountaineering in Sierra Nevada.* 1963. 1st ed. VG $12.50

KING, Constance E. *The Encyclopedia of Toys.* 1986. Secaucus. Chartwell. Ills. dj. VG $15.00

KING, E.J. *U.S. Navy at War 1941-45.* 1946. Washington. Ills. 305 pp. fld map. $17.50

KING, Ernest. *Main Line, 50 Years Railroading with So. Pacific.* 1948. dj. VG $17.50

KING, F.H. *Farmers of 40 Centuries or Permanent Ag. in China.* 1911. Madison, WS. Ills. VG $35.00

KING, Harold. *Paradigm Red.* 1975. Bobbs Merrill. 1st printing. sgn. dj. VG $35.00

KING, Jessie. *Glasgow, City of the West.* 1911. 1st ed. dj. $85.00

KING, John W. *Illinois Historical & Douglas Co. Biographical.* 1910. Munsell Pub. 1 vol. rebound. $60.00

KING, L.W. & Hall, H.R. *Egypt/Western Asia in Light of Recent Discoveries.* 1907. London. Ills. VG $40.00

KING, Larry & Yoffe, Emily. *Larry King.* 1982. New York. Simon & Schuster. 207 pp. dj. $5.00

KING, Larry L. *Confessions of a White Racist.* 1971. New York. Viking. 1st ed. dj. EX $15.00

KING, Martin Luther, Jr. *Letter from Birmingham Jail.* 1968. Stamford. Ltd. ed. 1/600. wrappers. $30.00

KING, Moses. *King's Pocket Book of Providence, RI.* 1882. Subscr. ed. Ltd. ed. 1/1000. 124 pp. $25.00

KING, Moses. *Notable New Yorkers of 1896-1899.* 1899. New York. G $30.00

KING, Rufus. *Malice in Wonderland.* 1958. Garden City. 1st ed. dj. EX $40.00

KING, Rufus. *Murder by the Clock.* 1929. Doubleday. 1st ed. 288 pp. $37.50

KING, Stephen & Straub, Peter. *The Talisman.* 1984. New York. Viking. 1st ed. dj. EX $25.00

KING, Stephen & Straub, Peter. *The Talisman.* 1st Eng. ed. dj. EX $35.00

KING, Stephen & Straub, Peter. *The Talisman.* 1984. West Kingston. Grant. 2 vol set. sgns. boxed. $350.00

KING, Stephen. *Christine.* 1983. New York. Viking. 1st ed. dj. VG $35.00

KING, Stephen. *Christine.* 1983. New York. proof copy. tan wrappers. EX $235.00

KING, Stephen. *Christine.* 1st trade ed. $25.00

KING, Stephen. *Cujo.* 1984. Denmark. 1st ed. wrappers. EX $30.00

KING, Stephen. *Cujo.* 1st trade ed. dj. VG $10.00

KING, Stephen. *Cujo.* 1981. New York. Viking Press. 1st ed. EX $30.00

KING, Stephen. *Cujo.* 1981. New York. proof copy. grey wrappers. EX $285.00

KING, Stephen. *Cujo.* 1981. Mysterious Pr. Ltd. 1st ed. sgn. boxed. EX $350.00

KING, Stephen. *Cycle of the Werewolf.* 1983. Westland. Ltd. ed. 1/7500. dj. EX $75.00

KING, Stephen. *Cycle of the Werewolf.* 1983. New York. 1st ed. dj. EX $80.00

KING, Stephen. *Dark Tower.* 2nd ed. $75.00

KING, Stephen. *Dark Tower.* Ltd. 1st ed. 1/500. sgn. $500.00

KING, Stephen. *Dark Tower.* 1982. 1st ed. dj. $125.00

KING, Stephen. *Different Seasons.* 1982. New York. Viking Press. 1st ed. EX $35.00

KING, Stephen. *Eye of the Dragon.* New York. proof copy. $225.00

KING, Stephen. *Eye of the Dragon.* 1984. Philtrum. Ltd. ed. 1/1250. sgn. $550.00

KING, Stephen. *Firestarter.* 1980. Phantasia Pr. Ltd. ed. sgn. dj. slipcase. EX $300.00

KING, Stephen. *Firestarter.* 1980. New York. Viking. proof copy. wrappers. $225.00

KING, Stephen. *It.* proof copy. $135.00

KING, Stephen. *Night Shift.* 1979. Signet. 1st ed. sgn. VG $45.00

KING, Stephen. *Night Shift.* 1978. New York. dj. VG $22.50

KING, Stephen. *Pet Sematary.* 1983. New York. Doubleday. 1st ed. dj. VG $30.00

KING, Stephen. *Pet Sematary.* 1983. Hall. 1st large print issue. dj. VG $25.00

KING, Stephen. *Skeleton Crew.* 1985. Putnam. 1st ed. dj. EX $50.00

KING, Stephen. *Skeleton Crew.* proof copy. $160.00

KING, Stephen. *Skeleton Crew.* 1985. Scream Press. Ltd. ed. sgn. slipcase. Mint. $330.00

KING, Stephen. *The Dead Zone.* 1970. New York. 1st ed. dj. EX $45.00

KING, Stephen. *The Running Man.* 1981. 1st Am. ed. wrappers. EX $50.00

KING, Stephen. *The Shining.* 1977. New York. 1st ed. dj. VG $125.00

KING, Stephen. *The Stand.* 1978. New York. 1st ed. dj. EX $90.00

King, Stephen. *The Tailsman.* 1st ed. dj. EX $40.00

KING, Stephen. *Whispers 17018.* 1982. Ltd. ed. sgn. $100.00

KING, Thomas Starr. *The White Hills, Their Legend, Landscape, Poetry.* 1960. Boston. 60 Ills. VG $35.00

KING, Thomas. *California, Wonder of the Age.* 1850. New York. $85.00

KING, William. *The World's Progress.* 1896. Cincinnati. 701 pp. $5.00

KING & DERBY *Campfire Sketches & Battlefield Echoes* 1886. 1st edition. 624 pp. $21.00

KING. *Mountaineering in Sierra Nevada.* 1872. Boston. 1st Am. ed. VG $200.00

KING. *Nina & Skeezix & the Problem of the Lost Ring.* 1942. Whitman. Ills. G $4.50

KINGMAN, Dong. *San Francisco: City on Golden Hill.* 1967. Garden City. 1st ed. dj. VG $30.00

KINGSBURY, Benjamin. *Mass. Townsman; or, Laws for Regulation of Towns.* 1856. Boston. 408 pp. $10.00

KINGSFORD, Anna. *Clothes with the Sun.* 1937. London. 3rd ed. 210 pp. dj. G $35.00

KINGSFORD-SMITH, C.E. & Ulm. *Flight of the Southern Cross.* 1929. New York. Ills. 1st Am. ed. 295 pp. G $9.50

KINGSLEY, Charles. *The Water Babies.* 1917. Philadelphia. Ills. Maria Kirk. VG $25.00

KINGSLEY, Charles. *The Water Babies.* 1916. New York. Dodd Mead. Ills. J.W. Smith. $110.00

KINGSLEY, Charles. *The Water Babies.* 1937. 4 color pls. G $20.00

KINGSLEY, Charles. *Westward Ho!* 1935. New York. Ills. N.C. Wyeth. $30.00

KINGSLEY, Charles. *Westward Ho!* 1923. London/NY. Ills. E.A. Cox. 1st ed. VG $30.00

KINGSLEY, Charles. *Westward Ho!* 1947. boxed. VG $30.00

KINGSLEY, Charles. *Westward Ho!* 1936. Scribner. Ills. N.C. Wyeth. VG $15.00

KINGSLEY, Florence M. *Stephen, a Soldier of the Cross.* 1896. New York. Christian Pub. 369 pp. $3.50

KINGSTON, W.H.G. *Adventures Among the Indians.* 1888. New York. Butler Bros. Ills. 252 pp. $10.00

KINGSTON. *The Missing Ship/Notes from Log of Ouzel Galley.* NY/London. Ills. Murray. $12.50

KINKEAD, E. *Wilderness Is All Around Us.* 1978. Dutton. 1st ed. 178 pp. dj. EX $7.50

KINKLE, Roger D. *The Complete Encyclopedia of Popular Music & Jazz.* 1974. New Rochelle. 4 vol set. djs. VG $47.50

KINNARD, C. *This Must Not Happen Again!* 1945. New York. Pilot Pr. Ills. G $35.00

KINNEARD, Lawrence. *The Frontiers of New Spain.* 1958. Berkeley. Quivira Soc. Ltd. ed. 1/400. G $50.00

KINNELL, Galway. *Black Light.* 1966. Houghton. 1st ed. dj. VG $35.00

KINNELL, Galway. *Mortal Acts Mortal Words.* 1980. Boston. Houghton Mifflin. 1st ed. sgn. $20.00

KINNELL, Galway. *Remarks.* 1984. Ewert. Ltd. ed. 1/115. sgn. wrappers. $50.00

KINNELL, Galway. *The Fundamental Project of Technology.* 1983. Ewert. Ills. G. Tyler. Ltd. ed. EX $45.00

KINNELL, Galway. *What a Kingdom It Was.* 1960. Boston. Houghton Mifflin. 1st ed. sgn. $60.00

KINNEY, Coates. *Lyrics of the Ideal & the Real.* 1887. 140 pp. $15.00

KINNEY, Jean & Cle. *21 Kinds of American Folk Art & How to Make Each.* 1972. Atheneum. 121 pp. dj. EX $3.50

KINNISON, William A. *Building Sullivant's Pyramid.* 1970. Columbus. 225 pp. dj. EX $12.50

KINROSS, Albert. *The Fearsome Island.* Duffield reprint. VG $15.00

KINROSS, Albert. *The Fearsome Island.* 1896. Chicago. Stone & Kimball. 1st Am. ed. $50.00

KINROSS, Lord. *Ataturk.* 1964. London. 542 pp. $12.50

KINROSS, Lord. *Turkey.* 1959. Viking. Ills. dj. EX $50.00

KINSBURN, Emart. *Tong Men & a Million.* 1927. 1st ed. $10.00

KINSELLA, W.P. *Shoeless Joe.* 1982. Boston. Houghton Mifflin. 1st ed. VG $20.00

KINSELLA, W.P. *The Iowa Baseball Confederacy.* 1986. Boston. 1st ed. sgn. dj. EX $25.00

KINZIE, John H. *Wau-bun, the Early Day in the North-West.* 1856. New York. Ills. 1st ed. $175.00

KIP, Leonard. *Hannibal's Man.* 1878. Albany. 1st ed. G $50.00

KIPLING, Rudyard. *Actions & Reactions.* 1909. New York. 1st Am. ed. VG $15.00

KIPLING, Rudyard. *Around the World with Kipling.* 1926. New York. Doubleday. 1st ed. 121 pp. $5.00

KIPLING, Rudyard. *Captains Courageous.* 1897. London. Macmillan. 1st ed. VG $75.00

KIPLING, Rudyard. *Captains Courageous.* 1897. Tauchnitz. 1st ed. VG $35.00

KIPLING, Rudyard. *Collected Verse of Kipling.* 1907. New York. 1st ed. 1st issue. VG $25.00

KIPLING, Rudyard. *How the Rhinoceros Got His Skin.* 1942. Garden City. Ills. Feodor Rojankovsky. VG $15.00

KIPLING, Rudyard. *Just So Stories.* 1956. Garden City. Ills. Gleeson & author. VG $15.00

KIPLING, Rudyard. *Just So Stories.* 1902. New York. Macmillan. Ills. 1st ed. G $90.00

KIPLING, Rudyard. *Just So Stories.* 1912. Doubleday Page. Ills. Gleeson. $10.00

KIPLING, Rudyard. *Kim.* 1907. 1st ed. 2nd issue. dj. VG $12.50

KIPLING, Rudyard. *Kipling's Stories of India.* 1939. Rand McNally. Ills. Paul Strayer. VG $7.50

KIPLING, Rudyard. *Kiplings Stories for Boys.* 1931. Cupples & Leon. Ills. Hastings. dj. VG $6.50

KIPLING, Rudyard. *Puck of Pook's Hill.* 1906. New York. Ills. Rackham. 1st ed. EX $50.00

KIPLING, Rudyard. *Rewards & Fairies.* 1910. 1st Am. ed. $10.00

KIPLING, Rudyard. *Something of Myself.* 1937. 1st ed. dj. $5.50

KIPLING, Rudyard. *Song of the English.* London. Ills. Heath. 1st ed. 30 pls. $135.00

KIPLING, Rudyard. *Stalky & Co.* 1899. New York. 1st Am. ed. EX $40.00

KIPLING, Rudyard. *Tales of India.* 1937. Rand McNally. Ills. Strayer. G $7.50

KIPLING, Rudyard. *Tales of India.* 1936. Chicago. Ills. Paul Strayer. VG $15.00

KIPLING, Rudyard. *The Day's Work.* 1898. New York. Doubleday. 1st ed. 431 pp. $20.00

KIPLING, Rudyard. *The Five Nations.* 1903. 1st Am. ed. $10.00

KIPLING, Rudyard. *The Light that Failed.* 1911. Doubleday Page. $4.50

KIPLING, Rudyard. *The Second Jungle Book.* 1903. New York. Century. 1st ed. $40.00

KIPLING, Rudyard. *The Second Jungle Book.* 1895. London. 1st ed. VG $100.00

KIPLING, Rudyard. *The Years Between.* 1919. London. dj. $27.50

KIPLING, Rudyard. *They.* 1906. New York. Ills. VG $15.00

KIPLING, Rudyard. *Traffics & Discoveries.* 1904. New York. 1st Am. ed. dj. VG $15.00

KIPLING, Rudyard. *Under the Deodars.* 1888. 1st ed. 1st issue. $75.00

KIPLING, Rudyard. *Wee Willie Winkie.* Racine. Ills. Frobisher. $15.00

KIPLING, Rudyard. *With the Night Mail.* 1909. New York. Ills. 1st ed. VG $35.00

KIPLING, Rudyard. *Works of Kipling.* New York. (ca.1910) 10 vol set. EX $60.00

KIPPIS, A. *Narrative of Voyages Round World by Capt. Cook.* 1832. Philadelphia. 2 vol set. rebound. VG $30.00

KIRBY, W.E. *Butterflies & Moths of the United Kingdom.* London. Routledge. Ills. 463 pp. VG $65.00

KIRCHHOFF, H. *Boliva en Accion.* 1949. Buenos Aires. Ltd. ed. 1/3000. photos. VG $38.00

KIRK, Irina. *Born with the Dead.* 1963. 1st ed. dj. $8.50

KIRK, Mary Wallace. *Locust Hill.* 1972. U. of AL. 142 pp. dj. VG $4.50

KIRK, R. *Lord of the Hollow Dark.* 1979. St.Martins. 1st ed. dj. EX $20.00

KIRK. *Adventures of a Brownie.* 1922. Lippincott. 14 color pls. $40.00

KIRK. *John Randolph of Roanoke Regnancy.* 1964. dj. VG $15.00

KIRKE, Edmond. *Among the Pines: or, South in Secession-Time.* 1862. New York. 310 pp. $23.00

KIRKE, Edmond. *Down in Tennessee & Back by Way of Richmond.* 1864. 1st ed. $27.50

KIRKER, Harold & Kirker, J. *Bulfinch's Boston.* 1964. New York. 1st ed. $35.00

KIRKLAND, Joseph. *The McVeys.* 1888. VG $15.00

KIRKLAND. *Book of Home Beauty.* 1852. New York. $25.00

KIRKMAN, Marshall. *The Romance of Gilbert Holmes.* 1900. Chicago. 425 pp. $10.00

KIRKMAN, Marshall. *Westinghouse Air Brake/New York Air Brake.* 1903. World Railway. 102 pp. 60 fld pls. $275.00

KIRKPATRICK, C. *Nazi Germany: Its Women & Family Life.* 1938. Bobbs Merrill. 1st ed. 353 pp. dj. EX $15.00

KIRKPATRICK, I. *Mussolini: Study in Power.* 1964. Ills. dj. G $12.50

KIRKPATRICK, T.W. *Insect Life in the Tropics.* 1957. London. Ills. 1st ed. 311 pp. EX $15.00

KIRKUP, James. *A Beswick Bestiary.* 1971. Washington. Ills. 1st ed. 43 pp. VG $20.00

KIRKWOOD, Edith Brown. *Animal Children.* 1913. New York. Ills. M.T. Ross. $25.00

KIRKWOOD, James. *Hit Me with a Rainbow.* 1985. Delacorte. proof copy. EX $25.00

KIRKWOOD, James. *P.S. Your Cat is Dead.* 1972. New York. 2nd ed. VG $10.00

KIRKWOOD. *Some Kind of Hero.* proof copy. VG $60.00

KIRMSE, M. *Dogs in the Field.* Derrydale Pr. Ltd. ed. 1/685. EX $500.00

KIRPATRICK, Jeanne J. *Strategy of Deception: Study Communist Tactics.* 1963. New York. 1st ed. 444 pp. dj. G $7.00

KIRPATRICK, Ralph. *Domenico Scarlatti.* 1953. Princeton U. dj. EX $22.50

KIRSCH & MURPHY. *West of the West.* 1967. 1st ed. $7.00

KIRSCHNER, Martin, M.D. *Operative Surgery, Abdomen & Rectum.* 1933. Lippincott. Ills. $25.00

KIRST, H.H. *The Night of the Generals.* 1963. dj. VG $6.00

KIRST, H.H. *The Revolt of Gunner Asch.* 1956. dj. VG $6.00

KIRSTEL, M.R. *Pas De Deux.* 1969. New York. dj. EX $32.50

KISER. *Trends & Variations in Fertility in U.S.* 1968. dj. $17.50

KITCHENER, William. *The Cook's Oracle, & Housekeeper's Manual.* 1830. New York. G $100.00

KITCHIN, C.H.B. *Book of Life.* 1960. 1st English ed. dj. EX $10.00

KITCHIN, C.H.B. *Jumping Joan.* 1954. 1st English ed. dj. EX $15.00

KITCHIN, C.H.B. *Secret River.* 1956. 1st English ed. dj. EX $15.00

KITCHIN, C.H.B. *Short Walk in Williams Park.* 1971. 1st English ed. dj. EX $10.00

KITCHIN, C.H.B. *Ten Pollitt Place.* 1957. 1st English ed. $10.00

KITTEL, Mary. *Japanese Flower Arrangement.* 1960. New York. Viking. 1st ed. dj. $5.00

KITTO. *An Illustrated History of the Holy Bible.* 1870. Henry Bill Pub. Ills. 735 pp. VG $25.00

KITTON, Frederic. *The Dickens Country.* 1911. London. Ills. 235 pp. $5.00

KITTREDGE, George L. *The Old Farmer & His Almanac.* 1920. Harvard Press. $15.00

KLAPTHOR, Margaret Brown. *The First Ladies Cookbook.* 1969. New York. Parents' Magazine Press. Ills. $8.00

KLAPTHOR, Margaret Brown. *The First Ladies.* White House Hist. Assoc. Ills. $3.50

KLAUBER, Laurence M. *Rattlesnakes: Habits/Life Hist./Influence on Man.* 1972. Berkeley/L.A. Ills. 2nd ed. 2 vol set. $90.00

KLAUSER, Karl. *Universal Library of Music.* 1913. Boston. Ills. 7 vol set. $35.00

KLAUSNITZER, B. *Beetles.* 1983. Exeter. Ills. 1st Am. ed. 214 pp. dj. $27.50

KLEEFELD, Carolyn. *Climates of the Mind.* 1979. Los Angeles. Ltd. ed. 1/500. sgn. EX $15.00

KLEIN, A. *Colour Music, Art of Light.* 1930. London. Ills. 2nd ed. $95.00

KLEIN, Carole. *Aline.* 1979. New York. Ills. 1st ed. 352 pp. dj. $17.50

KLEIN, H. *Lucky Bwana.* 1953. dj. EX $80.00

KLEIN, M. *For the Love of Animals.* 1979. Morrow. Ills. 1st Am. ed. 316 pp. dj. $12.50

KLEIN, Norma. *Wives & Other Women.* 1982. St. Martin. 1st ed. dj. VG $12.50

KLEIN, T.E.D. *The Ceremonies.* 1984. New York. advance copy. wrappers. EX $75.00

KLEIN. *Surfing.* 1965. Philadelphia. dj. VG $6.00

KLIGERMAN, J. *The Birds from John Burroughs.* 1976. Hawthorn. Ills. Fuertes. 1st ed. dj. EX $12.50

KLINE, Otis A. *Call of the Savage.* 1937. New York. 1st ed. VG $20.00

KLINE, Otis A. *The Port of Peril.* 1949. Providence. Ills. St. John. 1st ed. dj. VG $40.00

KLINGBERG, Frank J. *Old Sherry, Portrait of a Virginia Family.* 1938. Richmond. Ills. 1st ed. 218 pp. VG $17.50

KLINGEL. *The Bay.* 1951. 1st ed. $15.00

KLINGENDER, Francis. *Art & the Industrial Revolution.* 1947. Royble. 1st ed. dj. $15.00

KLINK. *Mighty Cortez Fish Trap.* 1974. 1st ed. dj. EX $10.00

KLOTS, A.B. *Field Guide to Butterflies East of Great Plains.* 1960. Houghton Mifflin. 349 pp. dj. $7.50

KLUCKHOHN, Clyde. *To the Foot of the Rainbow.* 1928. London. Ills. 1st Eng. ed. 242 pp. VG $15.00

KLUTE, Jeanette. *Woodland Portraits.* 1954. Boston. 50 pls. $45.00

KNAPP, Joseph G. *Seeds that Grew.* 1960. Hinsdale, NY. Anderson House. 535 pp. dj. $7.00

KNAPPEN, Theodore. *Wings of War.* 1920. Putnam. Ills. 1st ed. 289 pp. VG $40.00

KNAPTON, E. *Empress Josephine.* 1963. Harvard. 1st ed. dj. EX $8.50

KNEALE. *Indian Agent.* 1950. Caxton Press. Ills. 1st ed. 429 pp. VG $25.00

KNEBEL, Fletcher. *Crossing in Berlin.* 1981. Doubleday. 1st ed. dj. EX $15.00

KNEBEL, Fletcher. *Dave Sulkin Cares!* 1978. Doubleday. 1st ed. dj. VG $10.00

KNEBEL, Fletcher. *Night of Camp David.* 1965. New York. Harper. 1st ed. dj. VG $40.00

KNEBEL, Fletcher. *Vanished.* 1968. dj. EX $4.00

KNEE, Ernest. *Santa Fe New Mexico.* 1942. Ills. 102 pp. $15.00

KNEELAND, F.N. & Bryant, L.P. *Northampton (Massachusetts) the Meadow City.* 1894. Northampton. 108 pp. 250 photos. $25.00

KNIGHT, C.W.R. *The Book of the Golden Eagle.* 1939. London. Hodder Stoughton. 224 pp. dj. $17.50

KNIGHT, Damon. *Orbit 12.* 1973. New York. Putnam. 1st ed. dj. EX $10.00

KNIGHT, Damon. *The Clarion Awards.* 1984. Garden City. 1st ed. dj. VG $10.00

KNIGHT, Damon. *CV Tor.* 1985. dj. EX $10.00

KNIGHT, Damon. *Hell's Pavement.* 1955. Lion Lib #13. pb. EX $17.50

KNIGHT, Damon. *Orbit 6.* 1970. New York. review copy. dj. VG $20.00

KNIGHT, Damon. *The World & Thorinn.* 1981. New York. 1st ed. review copy. dj. EX $20.00

KNIGHT, E. *Lassie Come Home.* 1940. Philadelphia. Ills. M. Kirmse. VG $15.00

KNIGHT, Eric. *Song on Your Bugles.* 1937. New York. 1st ed. sgn. inscr. dj. VG $25.00

KNIGHT, Eric. *This Above All.* 1941. New York. Grosset & Dunlap. 473 pp. VG $3.50

KNIGHT, James. *Improvement of Health.* 1875. New York. 406 pp. VG $35.00

KNIGHT, James. *Observations on Assiento Trade by South Sea Co.* 1728. London. 1st ed. $250.00

KNIGHT, John Alden. *Fresh-Water Tackle.* 1949. 1st ed. dj. VG $8.50

KNIGHT, John Alden. *Ruffed Grouse.* 1947. Knopf. Ills. 1st ed. 271 pp. dj. VG $37.50

KNIGHT, Lucian Lamar. *Tracking Sunset/Shrines of History Around World.* 1925. Atlanta. Ills. 628 pp. index. $15.00

KNIGHT, Lucian Lamar. *Woodrow Wilson, the Dreamer & the Dream.* 1924. $6.00

KNIGHT, R.P. *An Account of the Remains of Worship of Priapus.* 1786. London. folio. G $95.00

KNIGHT & DURHAM. *Hitch Your Wagon. Story of Bernt Balchen.* 1950. Drexel Hill. inscr. $20.00

KNIGHT. *War Birds Diary of an Unknown Aviator.* 1926. New York. $25.00

KNOKE, Heinz. *I Flew for the Fuhrer.* 3rd printing. VG $20.00

KNOOP, Douglas & Jones, G.P. *The Genesis of Freemasonry.* 1978. London. 334 pp. EX $27.50

KNOPF, Alfred A. *Sixty Photographs.* 1975. New York. Knopf. 1st ed. wrappers. EX $25.00

KNOPF, Richard C. *Anthony Wayne, a Name in Arms.* 1960. Pittsburgh. Ills. 1st ed. 566 pp. dj. VG $32.50

KNORR, E.R. *Papers on Eastern & Northern Extensions of Gulf.* 1871. Washington. 2 fld maps. VG $25.00

KNOTT, Leonard L. *The Children's Book of the Saguenay.* 1945. Montreal. Ills. Jacques Gagnier. 1st ed. $10.00

KNOWLES, J. *Phineas 6 Stories.* 1968. 1st ed. VG $10.00

KNOWLES, James. *King Arthur & His Knights.* 1923. New York. Ills. Rhead. 383 pp. VG $12.00

KNOWLES, John. *The Life & Writings of Henry Fuseli.* 1881. London. 1st ed. 3 vol set. $100.00

KNOWLES & WHEELWRIGHT. *Travels in New England.* 1977. Barre, Mass. Ills. 1st ed. 317 pp. dj. $17.50

KNOWLES. *A Kipling Primer.* 1899. 1st ed. $20.00

KNOWLTON, Charles. *Fruits of Philosophy.* 1937. Peter Pauper. Ltd ed. 1/450. $18.00

KNOWLTON, Frank H. *Birds of the World.* 1909. New York. 236 Ills. 16 pls. 873 pp. $25.00

KNOX, Eunice. *An Indian Swimming Pageant.* 1933. New York. Woman's Press. wrappers. VG $15.00

KNOX, Ronald A. *Essays in Satire.* 1928. London. 1st ed. VG $22.50

KNOX, Ronald. *The Three Taps.* 1927. New York. Simon & Schuster. 1st ed. VG $40.00

KNOX, Thomas W. *Boy Travelers in Northern Europe.* 1892. New York. VG $15.00

KNOX, Thomas W. *Boy Travellers in the Far East.* 1879. New York. G $10.00

KNOX, Thomas W. *Decisive Battles Since Waterloo.* 1888. Ills. 490 pp. $21.00

KNOX, Thomas W. *The Lost Army.* 1899. Akron. Ills. $22.50

KNOX, William. *The Present State of the Nation.* 1768. London. 100 pp. wrappers. $90.00

KNUTTEL, Gerard. *The Letter as a Work of Art.* 1951. Ills. 1st ed. VG $40.00

KOBAYASHI, Tadashi. *Utamaro.* 1982. Kodansha. Ills. 1st ed. folio. dj. EX $38.00

KOBER, Arthur. *Bella, Bella, Kissed a Fella.* 1951. New York. 1st ed. $4.00

KOBLER, John. *Damned in Paradise: Life of John Barrymore.* 1977. VG $4.00

KOCH, A. *Farbige Wohnraume Der Neuzeit.* 1926. $30.00

KOCH, M. *The Shay Locomotive. Titan of Timber.* 1971. Denver. Ltd. ed. sgn. EX $125.00

KOCH, Robert. *Louis C. Tiffany, Rebel in Glass.* 1964. Crown. 1st ed. $35.00

KOCH. *California, Our Western Wonderland.* 1921. Chicago. Ills. 222 pp. $10.00

KOEGLER. *Urs Graf.* 1947. 100 pls. $58.00

KOEHLER-BROMAN, Mela. *When Grandma was a Little Girl.* New York. 9 color pls. VG $20.00

KOENIG, Laird. *The Little Girl Who Lives Down the Lane.* 1974. Coward, McCann, & Geoghegan. $3.00

KOENIG, Louis W. *Bryan.* 1971. Putnam. 736 pp. $4.50

KOERNER, James D. *The Parsons College Bubble.* 1970. New York. 1st ed. dj. $8.50

KOESTLER, Arthur. *Act of Creation.* 1964. dj. VG $15.00

KOESTLER, Arthur. *Scum of the Earth.* 1946. New York. Macmillan. 287 pp. $4.00

KOESTLER, Arthur. *The Age of Longing.* 1951. Macmillan. 1st ed. dj. VG $15.00

KOESTLER, Arthur. *The Call Girls.* 1973. New York. Random House. dj. VG $12.50

KOHLER, W. *Intelligenzprufungen an Menschenaffein.* 1921. Berlin. Ills. 1st ed. $90.00

KOIKE, Shigeru. *Gissing East & West.* 1970. London. Ltd. 1st ed. 1/300. dj. EX $25.00

KOIZUMI, Kazuo Hearn. *Re-Echo.* 1957. Caxton. Ills. Lafcadio Hearn. EX $30.00

KOKE. *Accomplice in Treason.* 1973. New York Ills. 325 pp. $12.50

KOLB, E.L. *Through the Grand Canyon from Wyoming to Mexico.* 1914. Macmillan. Ills. 344 pp. $12.50

KOLB, E.L. *Through the Grand Canyon from Wyoming to Mexico.* 1946. New York. Ills. 344 pp. $10.00

KOLB, E.L. *Through the Grand Canyon from Wyoming to Mexico.* 1952. Macmillan. photos. maps. 344 pp. $15.00

KOLB, John, H. & Brunner, E. *A Study of Rural Society.* 1946. Boston. Ills. TB. 532 pp. EX $4.50

KOLBE, H. *Ornamental Waterfowl.* 1979. Leipzig. Ills. maps. 258 pp. dj. EX $20.00

KOLDIN, Leonard C. *The Welfare Crisis.* 1971. New York. Exposition Press. 235 pp. $3.50

KOLLER, L.R. *Handguns.* New York. 1st ed. VG $10.00

KOLLER, L.R. *How to Shoot.* 1964. VG $5.50

KOLLER, L.R. *Shots at Whitetails.* 1970. Knopf. Ills. 360 pp. $6.50

KOLLER, L.R. *Taking Larger Trout.* 1950. 1st ed. sgn. dj. VG $45.00

KOLLER, L.R. *Treasury of Angling.* 1963. Golden Press. 252 pp. $6.50

KOLLER, L.R. *Treasury of Angling.* 1963. 1st ed. dj. EX $17.50

KOLLOCK, Henry. *Sermons on Various Subjects.* 1811. Savannah. 1st ed. 282 pp. $125.00

KOLLOCK, J. *These Gentle Hills.* 1976. Copple House. inscr. dj. VG $25.00

KOLLWITZ, Kaethe. *Diaries & Letters.* 1955. Chicago. 1st ed. dj. VG $40.00

KOLODIN, Irving. *Story of the Metropolitan Opera.* 1953. New York. 1st ed. EX $27.50

KOMISARJEVSKY & SIMONSON. *Settings & Costumes of the Modern Stage.* 1933. Studio. EX $110.00

KONDO, Ichitaro. *Japanese Genre Painting.* 1961. Tuttle. Ills. 148 pp. folio. scarce. $105.00

KONDO, Ichitaro. *The Fifty-Three Stages of Takaido By Hirochige.* 1960. Japan. Ills. rare. $60.00

KONDO, Ichitaro. *The Thirty-Six Views of Mount Fuji by Hokusai.* 1968. Heibonsha Ltd. 46 pls. rare. $65.00

KONVITZ, Milton. *The Recognition of Ralph Waldo Emerson.* 1972. U. MI Press. 224 pp. dj. EX $6.50

KONYOT. *The White Rider.* 1961. Ills. 1st ed. dj. VG $20.00

KOO, T.S.Y. *Studies of Alaska Red Salmon.* 1962. WA U. Press. Ills. maps. 449 pp. VG $20.00

KOONTX, Dean. *Twilight Eyes.* Ltd. 1st ed. 1/200. sgn. $75.00

KOONTZ, Dean. *A Darkness in My Soul.* 1972. pb. EX $7.50

KOONTZ, Dean. *Dark of the Woods/Soft Come the Dragons.* 1970. Ace Double. 1st ed. pb. EX $7.50

KOONTZ, Dean. *Hanging On.* 1973. New York. Evans. 1st ed. dj. EX $45.00

KOONTZ, Dean. *Night Chills.* 1976. advance copy. wrappers. EX $25.00

KOONTZ, Dean. *Night Chills.* 1976. Atheneum. 1st ed. dj. EX $15.00

KORN, B.W. *American Jewry & the Civil War.* 1951. Philadelphia. Ills. 331 pp. index. $12.50

KORNBLUTH, Cyril M. *Takeoff.* 1952. Garden City. 1st ed. dj. EX $20.00

KORNBLUTH, J. *Rebel Voices: An I.W.W. Anthology.* 1964. Ann Arbor. Ills. 416 pp. $20.00

KORRIG, Walt. *Battle Report.* 1944. 383 pp. $4.00

KORSAKOFF, Rimsky. *My Musical Life.* 1925. Knopf. Ills. 2nd revised ed. VG $20.00

KORSAKOFF, Rimsky. *My Musical Life.* 2nd ed. VG $8.00

KORTRIGHT, F. *The Ducks, Geese, & Swans of North America.* 1943. Wildlife Inst. Ills. maps. 476 pp. VG $15.00

KORTYKOV, Alexei. *It's Hard to be a Russian Spy.* 1985. New York. Long Shadow. proof copy. VG $25.00

KOSINSKI, Jerzy. *Blind Date.* 1977. Boston. Houghton Mifflin. 1st ed. dj. $15.00

KOSINSKI, Jerzy. *Cockpit.* 1st ed. dj. $7.00

KOSINSKI, Jerzy. *Passion Play.* 1979. St.Martins. Ltd. ed. sgn. dj. VG $60.00

KOSINSKI, Jerzy. *Passion Play.* 1979. New York. 1st ed. dj. G $7.00

KOSINSKI, Jerzy. *Pinball.* 1982. Bantam. 1st ed. dj. EX $15.00

KOSINSKI, Jerzy. *The Devil Tree.* 1973. Harcourt. 1st ed. dj. VG $25.00

KOSINSKI, Jerzy. *The Painted Bird.* 1966. London. Allen. 1st Eng. ed. VG $75.00

KOSLOW, Jules. *The Green & the Red, Sean O'Casey, Man & Plays.* 1949. Golden Griffin.1st ed. dj. $10.00

KOTZEBUE, Otton von. *Neue Reise um die Welt, in den Jahre 1823.* 1st German ed. fld maps. $400.00

KOTZWINKLE, William. *Doctor Rat.* 1976. Knopf. 1st ed. dj. EX $25.00

KOTZWINKLE, William. *Great World Circus.* 1983. 1st ed. dj. EX $12.00

KOTZWINKLE, William. *Jack in the Box.* 1980. Putnam. 1st ed. dj. VG $12.50

KOTZWINKLE, William. *Seduction in Berlin.* 1985. Putnam. Ills. 1st ed. dj. VG $15.00

KOUES, Helen. *American Woman's New Encyclopedia of Decorating.* 1954. $20.00

KOUFAX, Sandy. *Koufax.* 1966. Viking. 1st ed. sgn. dj. VG $20.00

KOURDAKOV, Sergei. *The Persecutor.* 1973. 254 pp. dj. EX $2.00

KOUVACH. *City of Vancouver.* 1976. Douglas. Ltd. ed. $12.00

KOUWENHOVEN, John A. *The Columbia Historical Portrait of New York.* 1953. New York. Doubleday. Ills. 1st ed. VG $30.00

KOUWENHOVEN. *Adventures of America 1857-1900.* 1938. Harper. EX $75.00

KOVACS, Ernie. *Zoomar.* 1957. Garden City. Doubleday. 1st ed. dj. $85.00

KOWADA, Gonpei. *Biography of Benjamin Smith Lyman.* 1937. 1st ed. ex-lib. 104 pp. VG $12.00

KOZLOVSKY, Eugene. *Ukrainian Self-Taught.* Winnipeg. (ca.1900) 119 pp. $10.00

KRAEMER, Heddy. *More Time Than Money.* 1963. sgn. $5.00

KRAFT, Barbara S. *The Peace Ship.* 1978. $6.50

KRAFT, Irma. *Plays, Players, Playhouses.* 1928. Ills. 363 pp. $12.00

KRAFT, Ken. *Garden to Order.* 1963. New York. Doubleday. dj. $6.00

KRAFT-EBING, R. Von. *Psychopathia Sexualis.* 1965. New York. 1st unexpurgated Eng. ed. G $22.00

KRAIG, W. *Don't Tread on Me.* 1954. dj. VG $12.50

KRAMER, Aaron. *The Golden Trumpet.* 1949. New York. International. wrappers. EX $15.00

KRAMER, Aaron. *Thunder of the Grass.* 1948. New York. International. wrappers. EX $15.00

KRAMER, Jack. *Natural Gardens, Gardening with Native Plants.* 1973. Scribner. Ills. Valdex & Heoppner. $3.50

KRAMER, Kathryn. *A Handbook for Visitors from Outer Space.* 1984. New York. 1st ed. review copy. dj. VG $15.00

KRAMER. *Magical Mimics in Oz.* 1946. Snow, Rielly & Lee. dj. $45.00

KRAMER. *Shaggy Man of Oz.* Reilly & Lee. $30.00

KRANTZ, Judith. *Mistral's Daughter.* 1982. Crown. proof copy. wrappers. $10.00

KRANTZ, Judith. *Princess Daisy.* 1980. dj. VG $4.00

KRANZLER, D. *Japanese, Nazis & Jews.* 1976. New York. 644 pp. index. $16.00

KRASILSCHIK, S. *WWII; Dispatches from the Soviet Front.* 1985. New York. Sphinx Press. 372 pp. $9.00

KRASKEL, D. *Season of the Elk.* 1976. Lowell Press. Ills. 1st ed. 117 pp. dj. EX $12.50

KRAUSS, Ruth. *A Hole Is to Dig.* 1952. New York. Harper. Ills. dj. $15.00

KRAUSS, Ruth. *The Bundle Book.* 1951. Harper. Ills. Helen Stone. EX $7.50

KRAUTHEIMER. *Studies Early Christian Medieval Renaissance Art.* 1969. 86 pls. $27.00

KREDEL, Fritz. *Grimm's Fairy Tales.* 1945. New York. Grosset & Dunlap. 1st ed. $10.00

KREIDER, Claude. *Bamboo Rod & How to Build It.* 1951. Macmillan. Ills. 1st ed. dj. 140 pp. VG $27.50

KREIDER, Claude. *Steelhead.* 1948. Putnam. Ills. 1st ed. 182 pp. dj. VG $15.00

KREIDOLF, Ernest. *Servants of the Spring.* 1979. Ills. Kreidolf. EX $10.00

KREIG, Margaret. *Green Medicine. Search for Plants that Heal.* 1964. Chicago. 1st ed. dj. VG $15.00

KREMENTZ. *A Very Young Dancer.* 1976. Knopf. Ills. 1st ed. dj. VG $15.00

KREPPS, Robert. *El Cid.* 1961. Gold Medal. 1st printing. $2.50

KREPS. *The Science of Trapping.* 1944. Harding Pub. 229 pp. $4.50

KREYMBORG, Albert. *Less Lonely.* 1923. New York. Harcourt. inscr. dj. EX $35.00

KREYMBORG, Alfred. *Funnybone Alley.* 1927. Macaulay. Ills. Artzybasheff. 1st ed. VG $15.00

KREYMBORG, Alfred. *Poetic Drama.* 1941. New York. Modern Age. 855 pp. $10.00

KREYMBORG, Alfred. *Puppet Plays.* 1923. 1st ed. $8.50

KREYMBORG, Alfred. *Selected Poems: 1912-1944.* 1945. New York. 1st ed. slipcase. $10.00

KREYMBORG, Alfred. *An Anthology of American Poetry 1630-1941.* 1941. New York. 673 pp. VG $5.00

KRIEG, Shirley Kresan. *The History of Zeta Tau Alpha. 1898-1928.* 1939. no place. Ills. 4th printing. 2 vol set. $20.00

KRIEGER, J.L. & Icanberry, G. *Valley Division Vignettes. Story of Santa Fe R.R.* 1983. Valley Rail Pr. dj. VG $35.00

KRIG, Merton. *Duboy, a Wilderness Saga.* 1946. Appleton. Ills. 335 pp. $12.50

KRIM, Seymour. *The Beats.* 1960. Greenwich. Gold Medal. wrappers. EX $12.50

KRISTELLER, Paul Oskar. *Eight Philosophers of Italian Renaissance.* 1966. Stanford. 194 pp. EX $10.00

KRISTELLER, Paul Oskar. *Latin Manuscript Books Before 1600.* 1960. New York. VG $30.00

KRISTELLER, Paul Oskar. *The Philosophy of Marsilio Ficino.* 1964. Gloucester. Smith. 2nd impression. 441 pp. $10.00

KRISTOFFERSEN, Eva M. *The Merry Matchmakers.* 1940. Chicago. Ills. Hedvig Collin. 1st ed. $20.00

KROEBER, A.L. *Configurations of Cultural Growth.* 1944. U. of CA. 1st ed. dj. $15.00

KROEBER, A.L. *Cultural & Natural Areas of Native North America.* 1947. CA U. Press. Ills. maps. 241 pp. dj. VG $22.50

KROEBER, Theodora. *Alfred Kroeber: Personal Configuration.* 1970. Berkeley. 1st ed. dj. EX $10.00

KROH, Patricia. *Design with Flowers Unlimited.* 1959. Doubleday. Ills. 1st ed. dj. $4.50

KRON, Karl. *Ten Thousand Miles on a Bicycle.* 1887. Kron. $35.00

KRONENBERGER, Louis. *Atlantic Brief Lives.* 1971. Boston. Little, Brown. 2nd ed. $7.50

KRONENBERGER, Louis. *Cavalcade of Comedy.* 1953. New York. 1st ed. 715 pp. $10.00

KROOK, D. *Ordeal of Consciousness in Henry James.* 1962. Cambridge. 1st ed. dj. EX $42.50

KROPOTKIN, P.A. *The Great French Revolution 1789-1793.* 1909. New York. Putnam. 1st ed. dj. VG $65.00

KROTT, P. *Bears in the Family.* 1963. Dutton. Ills. 1st Am. ed. 144 pp. VG $9.00

KROTT, P. *Tupu-Tupu-Tupu.* 1958. London. Hutchinson. Ills. 1st Eng. ed. $17.50

KRUCKMAN, Herb. *Hol' Up Yo' Head.* 1936. New York. Ills. Ltd. ed. wrappers. VG $50.00

KRUEGER, Glee. *A Gallery of American Samplers.* 1984. New York. Bonanza Books. Ills. dj. VG $10.00

KRUEGER, Karl. *The Way of the Conductor.* 1958. New York. review copy. EX $12.50

KRUG, M.E. *DuBay: Son-in-Law of Oshkosh.* 1946. Appleton, WI. 335 pp. $10.00

KRUG, M.E. *DuBay: Son-in-Law of Oshkosh.* 1946. Ills. Ltd. ed. 1/500. sgn. dj. VG $10.00

KRUMMEL, D.W. *English Music Printing 1553-1700.* 1975. Oxford U. Pr. folio. EX $35.00

KRUTCH, J.W. *Great American Nature Writings.* 1950. Sloane. 396 pp. dj. VG $10.00

KRUUK, H. *Spotted Hyena, Study Predation & Social Behavior.* 1974. Chicago. Ills. maps. 335 pp. dj. EX $25.00

KTAFT, Victor. *The Vienna Circle.* 1953. Philadelphia Lib. 1st ed. dj. $7.50

KUBIZEK, A. *The Young Hitler I Knew.* 1955. 1st Am. ed. VG $15.00

KUCK, Loraine & Tongg, R. *The Tropical Garden.* 1936. New York. Macmillan. ex-lib. 378 pp. $4.00

KUECHLER, O. *Cooning With Cooners.* 1924. Columbus, Ohio. Ills. 217 pp. EX $35.00

KUGLER, F. *History of Germany During Frederick the Great.* 1845. 450 Ills. Adolph Menzerl. G $25.00

KUHNERT, Wilhelm. *Im Lande Meiner Modelle.* 1918. Leipzig. Ills. VG $50.00

KUHNS, Oscar. *German-Swiss Settlements of Colonial Pennsylvania.* 1901. New York. 1st ed. 268 pp. $20.00

KULLMAN, Harry. *The Battle Horse.* 1981. Bradbury Press. proof copy. wrappers. EX $40.00

KULSKI, W.W. *The Soviet Regime. Communism in Practice.* 1954. Syracuse U. 1st ed. dj. $15.00

KUMIN, Maxine. *Halfway.* 1961. Holt. 1st ed. dj. EX $35.00

KUMIN, Maxine. *The Passions of Uxport.* 1968. Harper. 1st ed. dj. VG $20.00

KUMIN, Maxine. *Up Country.* 1972. Harper. Ills. B. Swan. 1st ed. dj. VG $35.00

KUNG, H. *On Being Christian.* 1976. dj. $6.00

KUNZ, G.F. *Gems & Precious Stones of North America.* 1890. EX $60.00

KUNZ, G.F. *Ivory & the Elephant.* 1916. Garden City. Doubleday. Ills. G $175.00

KUNZ, G.F. *Shakespeare & Precious Stones.* 1916. Lippincott. 1st ed. sgn. $35.00

KUNZ, G.F. *The Book of the Pearl.* 1908. New York. Ills. $125.00

KUNZ, G.F. *The Curious Lore of Precious Stones.* 1913. Philadelphia/London. Ills. VG $100.00

KUNZ, G.F. *The Magic of Jewels & Charms.* 1915. Philadelphia. Ills. 1st ed. EX $80.00

KUPFERBERG, Tuli. *Selected Fruits & Nuts.* 1959. New York. Birth Press. wrappers. VG $12.50

KURSH, H. *Cobras in His Garden.* 1965. Harvey House. Ills. 192 pp. dj. EX $12.50

KURTH, Julius. *Sharaku.* 1922. Munchen. dj. VG $50.00

KURTZ, B. *Experimental Religion, One Thing Needful.* 1863. Baltimore. 14 pp. wrappers. $15.00

KURZ, Otto. *Fakes.* 1967. G $4.00

KUTTNER, Henry & Moore, C.L. *Mutant.* 1953. New York. Gnome. 1st ed. dj. VG $35.00

KUTTNER, Henry. *Ahead of Time.* 1953. New York. Ballantine. 1st ed. dj. $50.00

KUTTNER, Henry. *Fury.* 1950. New York. Grosset & Dunlap. 1st ed. dj. $15.00

KUTTNER, Henry. *The Murder of a Mistress.* 1956. New York. Perma. 1st ed. pb. EX $15.00

KUTTNER, Henry. *The Murder of Eleanor Pope.* 1956. New York. Perma. 1st ed. pb. EX $15.00

KWITNEY. *Vicious Circles.* 1979. Norton. 1st ed. dj. VG $17.50

KYLE, Sefton. *The Durand Case.* 1936. London. Jenkins. 1st ed. dj. EX $115.00

KYLE, Sefton. *The Girl Known as D13.* 1940. London. 1st ed. VG $20.00

KYNE, Peter B. *Cappy Ricks or the Sub-jugation of Matt Peasley.* 1916. Grosset & Dunlap. 349 pp. $4.50

KYNE, Peter B. *Cappy Ricks Retires.* 1922. $30.00

KYNE, Peter B. *Cappy Ricks.* 1943. $30.00

KYNE, Peter B. *Captain Scraggs.* 1919. $25.00

KYNE, Peter B. *Kindred of the Dust.* 1920. New York. Grosset & Dunlap. 376 pp. $7.00

KYNE, Peter B. *Money to Burn.* 1928. $25.00

KYNE, Peter B. *Never the Twain Shall Meet.* 1923. $25.00

KYNE, Peter B. *The Enchanted Hill.* 1924. $25.00

KYNE, Peter B. *The Long Chance.* 1914. $25.00

KYNE, Peter B. *They Also Serve.* 1927. $25.00

KYNE, Peter B. *Tide of Emprie.* 1926. New York. Ills. Broadhead. EX $27.50

KYTLE, Elizabeth. *Willie Mae.* 1959. Knopf. dj. $7.50

L

L'AMOUR, Louis. *Frontier*. 1984. 1st ed. photos. dj. VG $20.00

L'AMOUR, Louis. *The Hills of Homicide*. 1938. VG $15.00

L'ENGLE, Madeleine. *A Severed Wasp*. 1982. Farrar. proof copy. wrappers. VG $20.00

L'ENGLE, Madeleine. *Ladder of Angels*. 1979. Seabury. Ills. 1st ed. dj. EX $14.00

L'ENGLE, Madeleine. *The Other Side of the Sun*. 1971. New York. revised copy. dj. EX $25.00

L'ERMITE, Pierre. *The Mighty Friend*. 1913. New York. Benziger Bros. 1st ed. dj. EX $75.00

L'HEUREUX, Bill. *Hockey for Boys*. 1962. Chicago. Follett Pub. Ills. 96 pp. EX $7.00

L'HOMMEDIEU, D.K. *Nipper, the Little Bull Pup*. Ills. Marguerite Kirmse. dj. $15.00

LA BASTILLE, A. *Assignment Wildlife*. 1980. Dutton. Ills. 1st ed. 243 pp. dj. EX $10.00

LA BRANCHE, Corporal Ernest E. *American Battery in France*. 1923. Worcester. ex-lib. 237 pp. $25.00

LA CROIX, Paul. *The Arts in the Middle Ages & the Renaissance*. 1964. New York. dj. VG $16.00

LA FARGE, Christopher. *Each to the Other, a Novel in Verse*. 1939. New York. Coward McCann. 422 pp. VG $3.00

LA FARGE, John. *An Artist's Letters from Japan*. 1970. Capo Press. Ills. 293 pp. $40.00

LA FARGE, Oliver. *Santa Eulalia. Religion of Cuchumatan Indian Town*. 1947. U. Chicago Pr. Ills. 211 pp. dj. $15.00

LA FARGE, Oliver. *The American Indian*. 1960. New York. Ills. Young Readers ed. dj. $15.00

LA FARGE, Oliver. *The Cooper Pot*. 1942. Houghton Mifflin. dj. G $17.50

LA FARGE, Oliver. *The Pictorial History of the American Indian*. 1956. New York. Ills. 270 pp. dj. $24.00

LA FLESCHE, Francis. *A Dictionary of the Osage Language*. 1975. Phoenix, AZ. 406 pp. $35.00

LA MONT. *Little Black Sambo*. 1959. Whitman Pub. 28 pp. G $3.50

LA MONTE, Ellen N. *The Ethics of Opium*. 1924. NY. Century Press. 1st ed. EX $20.00

LA MONTE, F. & Welch, M.H. *Vanishing Wilderness*. 1949. Liveright. 340 pp. EX $7.50

LA PEROUSE, Jean F.G. de. *Voyage Round the World in Years 1785-1788*. 1798. London. Johnson. 1st Eng. ed. 3 vol set. $1,150.00

LA SPINA. *Invaders from the Dark*. Arkham House. 1st ed. dj. EX $50.00

LA TORRE, Ronald. *Sexual Identity*. 1979. Welson-Hall. $3.00

LA VARRE, W. *Gold, Diamonds & Orchids*. 1935. Revell. Ills. map. 298 pp. VG $12.50

LABRIE. *Amateur Taxidermist*. 1972. 1st ed. dj. EX $10.00

LACEY, P. *History of the Nude in Photography*. 1964. New York. 1st ed. pb. EX $9.00

LACEY, Peter. *The Wedding*. 1969. Ridge Press. Ills. 282 pp. $4.50

LADD, Anna C. *Hieronymus Rides*. 1912. London. Macmillan. $8.00

LADD, Horatio. *The Origin & History of Grace Church, Jamaica, NY*. 1914. New York. 441 pp. VG $20.00

LAENNEC. *On the Chest*. 1823. damaged. $10.00

LAGERLOF, Selma. *The Miracles of Antichrist*. 1899. Boston. 1st ed. VG $20.00

LAGLER, K.F. *Fresh-Water Fishery Biology*. 1969. Brown. Ills. 421 pp. VG $10.00

LAGUARDIA, F.H. *Fiorello H. LaGuardia*. 1948. $7.50

LAHM, R.S. *Balloon Terms, Definitions, & French Equivalents*. 1918. Washington. 30 pp. wrappers. G $22.50

LAIDLER, L. *Otters in Britain*. 1982. David & Charles. Ills. 200 pp. $20.00

LAIDLER. *Chem Kinetics*. 1950. $12.50

LAIGHTON, Oscar. *Ninety Years at the Isle of Shoals*. 1929. Andover, MA. Ills. 1st ed. sgn. dj. VG $25.00

LAING, A. *Clipper Ships & Their Makers*. 1966. Ills. VG $8.00

LAING, Alexander. *Clipper Ship Men*. 1944. $15.00

LAING, John & Son. *Serving a Nation at War*. 1946. London. photos. 124 pp. $22.50

LAIRD, Charlton. *And Gladly Teche*. 1970. 217 pp. dj. $6.50

LAIRD, Corobeth. *Encounter with an Angry God*. 1975. 1st ed. dj. VG $12.50

LAKE, A. *Hunter's Choice*. 1954. dj. VG $27.50

LAKE, Stuart W. *Wyatt Earp Frontier Marshall*. 1931. Boston. Ills. 391 pp. $30.00

LAMAR, E. *Notes on Paper Napkin*. 1980. Caldwell, NJ. 1st ed. dj. EX $7.00

LAMB, Charles & Mary. *Mrs. Liecester's School*. 1880. London. Ills. Greenaway. VG $45.00

LAMB, Charles & Mary. *Tales from Shakespeare*. 1918. New York. Ills. Louis Rhead. VG $20.00

LAMB, Charles & Mary. *Tales from Shakespeare*. Stoughton. Ills. Dulac, Rackham & others. $25.00

LAMB, Charles & Mary. *Tales from Shakespeare*. London. Ills. A.E. Jackson. VG $25.00

LAMB, Charles & Mary. *Tales from Shakespeare*. 1878. London. Ills. VG $45.00

LAMB, Charles & Mary. *Tales from Shakespeare*. Scribner. Ills. Norman Price. 20 pls. EX $22.50

LAMB, Charles & Mary. *Tales from Shakespeare*. Hurst & Co. no date. 402 pp. VG $12.50

LAMB, Charles & Mary. *Tales From Shakespeare*. 1922. Philadelphia. Ills. E.S. Green Elliott. $75.00

LAMB, Charles. *The Book of Ranks & Dignities of British Society*. 1924. London. Ills. 1st ed. VG $25.00

LAMB, Charles. *The Living Phantom*. 1934. Omaha. Ltd. ed. 1/100. wrappers. EX $50.00

LAMB, Charles. *Works of Charles Lamb*. 1865. Boston. Ltd. ed. 1/100. $100.00

LAMB, D. *Enchanted Vagabonds*. 1938. 1st ed. dj. EX $20.00

LAMB, Harold. *The Crusades*. 1930. New York. 368 pp. $6.00

LAMB, Harold. *The March of the Barbarians*. 1940. $6.50

LAMB. *The Adventures of Ulysses*. 1928. Platt & Munk. Ills. Squire/Mars. VG $12.50

LAMBERT, Bernard J. *Shepherd of the Wilderness*. 1967. L'Anse, MI. Ills. sgn. 255 pp. dj. $10.00

LAMBERT, Clara. *The Story of Alaska*. 1940. New York. Ills. 1st ed. $15.00

LAMBERT, R.S. *Adventure in Polar Sea*. 1950. Bobbs Merrill. 1st ed. dj. VG $10.00

LAMBERT. S.M. *A Yankee Doctor in Paradise*. 1941. Ills. map. 393 pp. VG $15.00

LAMBIE, Thomas. *Boot & Saddle in Africa*. 1943. Philadelphia. VG $7.50

LAMERS, William. *The Edge of Glory*. 1961. Harcourt Brace.1st ed. 499 pp. index. VG $30.00

LAMPE, David. *The Tunnel*. 1963. London. Harrat. 1st ed. 219 pp. dj. $15.50

LAMPEN, C.D. *Mirango the Man Eater*. 1899. London. Ills. 1st ed. $50.00

LAMPLOUGH & FRANCIS. *Cairo & Its Environs*. 1909. London. Ills. 191 pp. VG $20.00

LAMPMAN, Ben Hur. *A Leaf from French Eddy*. 1965. Touchstone Press. Ltd. ed. dj. $50.00

LAMPORT, F. *Scrap Iron*. 1961. Ills. Gorey. 1st ed. dj. VG $18.00

LAMPORT, Felicia. *Cultural Slag.* 1966. Ills. Gorey. 1st ed. dj. $14.50

LAMSA, George. *Man from Galilee.* 1970. New York. 1st ed. sgn. dj. VG $12.50

LAMSON, P.D. *The Heart Rhythms.* 1921. Baltimore. Williams & Wilkins. 100 pp. $10.00

LANCASTER, Bruce. *For Us the Living.* 1940. New York. 556 pp. $3.50

LANCASTER, Bruce. *The Secret Road.* 1952. New York. 259 pp. dj. $3.50

LANCASTER, C. *Illustrated Treatise on Art of Shooting.* 1892. G $25.00

LANCIANI, Rodolfo. *Ancient Rome in Light of Recent Discoveries.* 1892. New York. G $12.50

LAND, Hugh. *Birds of Guatemala.* 1970. Livingston. Ills. 1st ed. 381 pp. EX $30.00

LAND, Myrick. *The Fine Art of Literary Mayhem.* 1963. London. Hamilton. 1st Eng. ed. dj. EX $20.00

LANDAU, R. *Islam & the Arabs.* 1959. New York. 299 pp. index. $12.50

LANDAY, J.M. *Silent Cities, Sacred Stones.* 1971. New York. Ills. 272 pp. $15.00

LANDCASTOR. *Jet Propulsion Engines.* 1959. 800 pp. $12.50

LANDER, S. *Our Own School Arithmetic.* 1863. Greensboro. VG $175.00

LANDON, Edward. *Picture Framing.* 1945. VG $5.00

LANDON, M. *Never Dies the Dream.* 1949. 1st ed. $6.50

LANDOR, Walter Savage. *Imaginary Conversations.* 1891. London. 6 vol set. VG $75.00

LANDRUM, Carl. *Quincy in the Civil War.* 1966. Quincy, IL. 127 pp. sgn. wrappers. $37.50

LANDRUM, Grace W. *Charlotte.* 1919. New York. 1st ed. VG $10.00

LANDSMAN, Anne C. *Needlework Designs from the American Indians.* 1977. Barnes. Ills. 1st ed. dj. VG $17.50

LANDSTROM, B. *Columbus.* 1967. New York. Ills. $22.50

LANDSTROM, B. *The Ship, an Illustrated History.* 1961. Ills. dj. VG $30.00

LANE, Ex-Sheriff Samuel A. *Fifty Years & Over of Akron & Summit County.* 1893. Akron. Ills. 1187 pp. VG $87.50

LANE, F.C. *The Story of Trees.* 1953. Doubleday. 384 pp. VG $6.00

LANE, M. *Life with Ionides.* 1963. London. Hamilton. Ills. 1st ed. dj. VG $20.00

LANE, Margaret. *The Tale of Beatrix Potter.* 1946. Ills. 1st ed. $10.00

LANE, Mark. *A Citizen's Dissent.* 1968. 1st ed. dj. VG $17.50

LANE, Mills. *The People of Georgia: Illustrated Social History.* 1975. Savannah. Ills. 350 pp. slipcase. $25.00

LANE, Richard Douglas. *Images from the Floating World.* 1978. New York. Putnam. Ills. EX $40.00

LANE, Richard Douglas. *Images from the Floating World.* 1978. 900 Ills. folio. dj. EX $70.00

LANE, William A. *Homer: Its Pioneers & Its Business Men of Today.* 1888. Homer, MI. Ills. 1st ed. 146 pp. $50.00

LANE. *Arabian Night's Entertainment.* Philadelphia. McKay. Ills. $30.00

LANE. *Chinese Rugs.* 1975. dj. EX $12.00

LANE. *Rugs & Wall Hangings.* 1976. dj. EX $14.00

LANES. *The Art of Maurice Sendak.* 1980. Abrams. 1st ed. plastic cvr. EX $50.00

LANES. *The Art of Maurice Sendak.* 1980. New York. sgn. Lanes/Sendak. EX $150.00

LANESS, Halldor. *Independent People.* 1946. Knopf. trans. Thompson. dj. VG $100.00

LANFFORD, Gerald. *The Richard Harding Davis Years.* 1961. Holt. Ills. 1st ed. 336 pp. $5.00

LANG, Andrew. *Books & Bookman.* 1887. London. Ills. 1st Eng. ed. VG $35.00

LANG, Andrew. *Helen of Troy.* 1882. London. 1st ed. presentation copy. VG $25.00

LANG, Andrew. *Lilac Fairy Book.* 1910. New York. Longman. Ills. Ford. 1st ed. $25.00

LANG, Andrew. *Prince Charles Edward.* 1900. Paris. Joyant & Co. Ltd. ed. pls. VG $350.00

LANG, Andrew. *The Blue Fairy Book.* 1929. Hale & Co. Ills. Ford & Hood. ex-lib. $4.00

LANG, Andrew. *The Blue Fairy Book.* 1905. Stitt Pub. Ills. Ford & Hood. $3.00

LANG, Andrew. *The Blue Fairy Book.* 1921. Philadelphia. McKay. Ills. Godwin. dj. VG $20.00

LANG, Andrew. *The Blue Fairy Book.* 1930. Philadelphia. Winston. Ills. Richardson. dj. $15.00

LANG, Andrew. *The Brown Fairy Book.* 1904. London. Ills. Ford. 1st ed. VG $65.00

LANG, Andrew. *The Green Fairy Book.* Grosset & Dunlap. Ills. Ford. $6.00

LANG, Andrew. *The Green Fairy Book.* Hurst. Ills. Ford. $8.00

LANG, Andrew. *The Olive Fairy Book.* 1907. London. Ills. Ford. 1st ed. VG $70.00

LANG, Andrew. *The Orange Fairy Book.* 1906. London. Ills. Ford. 1st ed. VG $55.00

LANG, Andrew. *The Orange Fairy Book.* 1968. Dover, NY. Ills. H.J. Ford. EX $60.00

LANG, Andrew. *The Puzzle of Dickens' Last Plot.* 1905. London. Chapman. 1st ed. VG $30.00

LANG, Andrew. *The Red Book of Heroes.* 1909. NY/London. Ills. Wallis Mills. EX $75.00

LANG, Andrew. *The Red Book of Romance.* 1905. London. Ills. 1st ed. VG $25.00

LANG, Andrew. *The Red Fairy Book.* 1923. Ills. Ford & Speed. $7.50

LANG, Andrew. *The Red Fairy Book.* Grosset & Dunlap. $6.00

LANG, Andrew. *The Red Fairy Book.* Caldwell. no date. Ills. Ford & Speed. $6.00

LANG, Andrew. *The Red Fairy Book.* Saalfield. no date. Ills. Ford & Speed. $6.00

LANG, Andrew. *The Rose Fairy Book.* 1948. New York. Longman. Ills. Bock. 1st ed. $7.50

LANG, Andrew. *The Yellow Fairy Book.* Grosset & Dunlap. Ills. Ford. $4.00

LANG, H.J. *The Wit & Wisdom of Abraham Lincoln.* 1942. Cleveland. 1st ed. dj. EX $7.00

LANG, John & Taylor, Samuel. *Report of a Visit to Some Tribes of Indians.* 1843. New York. 1st ed. 34 pp. wrappers. EX $85.00

LANG, Lincoln A. *Ranching with Teddy Roosevelt.* 1926. Philadelphia. 1st ed. dj. VG $37.50

LANG, Mrs. *Princes & Princesses.* 1908. Ills. Ford. 8 color pls. EX $45.00

LANG, William W. *Summary of TX State as Field for Immigration.* 1881. New York. 62 pp. wrappers. $75.00

LANGERLOF, Selma. *The Story of Gosta Berling.* 1899. Boston. 1st ed. VG $20.00

LANGERLOF. *Wonderful Adventures of Nils.* 1913. New York. Ills. Frye. 1st ed. 24 pls. EX $25.00

LANGEWIESCHE, W. *Lightplane Flying.* 1939. New York. Pitman. Ills. dj. VG $15.00

LANGFORD. *Discovery of Yellowstone Park.* 1870. 1st ed. EX $50.00

LANGLEY, Harold D. *Utah with Dragoons, & Glimpses of Life in AZ & CA.* 1974. Salt Lake City. Ills. 1st ed. 230 pp. dj. $25.00

LANGSTAFF, J.B. *Dr. Bard of Hyde Park.* 1942. Dutton. inscr. dj. VG $15.00

LANGSTROM. *Columbus.* 1966. Macmillan. slipcase. VG $20.00

LANGTON, Mary B. *How to Know Oriental Rugs.* 1905. New York. 20 full pp. Ills. $11.00

LANGWORTHY. *Scenery, Plains, Mountains, Mines, California.* 1855. Ogdensburgh. 1st ed. 324 pp. $200.00

LANHAM, Edwin. *Thunder in the Earth.* 1941. Harcourt Brace. $3.50

LANHAM, V. *The Bone Hunters.* 1973. 1st ed. dj. EX $17.50

LANIER, Sidney. *The Boy's Froissart/Sir J. Froissart's Chronicles.* 1879. New York. Scribner. Ills. Knappe. $15.00

LANIER, Sterling. *The Unforsaken Hero.* 1983. New York. 1st ed. dj. VG $10.00

LANIER, Sydney. *Hymns of the Marshes.* 1907. Scribner. Ills. Troth. 1st ed. EX $35.00

LANING. *The Sea Witch.* 1933. $6.00

LANKESTER. *Diversions of a Naturalist.* 1915. Macmillan. Ills. VG $6.50

LANMAN, Charles R. *A Sanskrit Reader with Vocabulary & Notes.* 1898. Boston. 1st ed. 2nd issue. 405 pp. G $20.00

LANMAN, Charles. *The Japanese in America.* 1872. New York. 1st ed. 352 pp. VG $45.00

LANNING, J. Frank. *My Trip to South Africa.* 1905. Richmon. Ills. 123 pp. $10.00

LANSDELL, H. *Through Siberia.* 1882. Houghton Mifflin. 2 vol set. G $45.00

LANSING, A. *Endurance, Shakleton's Incredible Voyage.* 1959. McGraw Hill. Ills. 1st ed. 282 pp. dj. EX $15.00

LANTIS, M. *Alaskan Eskimo Ceremonialism.* 1947. Am. Ethnological Soc. 127 pp. $30.00

LANZA, M.C. & Harvey, J.C. *Scarabaeus.* 1892. Cassell. 1st Eng. ed. VG $40.00

LAPHAM, Alice Gertrude. *Planters of Beverly in MA & 1000 Acre Grant 1635.* 1930. Cambridge. 1st printing. VG $30.00

LAPHAM, Edward A. *Stony Brook Secrets.* 1942. New York. 1st ed. dj. VG $20.00

LAPHAM, W.B. *History of Woodstock, Maine, with Family Sketches.* 1882. Portland. Ills. 315 pp. $40.00

LAPINER. *Pre-Columbian Art of South America.* 1976. Abrams. 1st ed. dj. $75.00

LAPPE, Frances M. *Diet for a Small Planet.* 1982. Ills. 496 pp. $3.50

LAQUEUR, W. *The Israel/Arab Reader.* 1969. New York. 371 pp. $12.50

LARBAUD, Valery. *Poems of a Multi-Millionaire.* 1955. Grove. review copy. dj. VG $17.50

LARDNER, John. *Strong Cigars & Lovely Women.* 1951. New York. Funk & Wagnall. Ills. Kelly. $15.00

LARDNER, Ring. *Bib Ballads.* 1915. New York. Volland. 1st ed. $85.00

LARDNER, Ring. *How to Write Short Stories.* 1924. New York. 1st ed. VG $25.00

LARDNER, Ring. *Round Up.* 1929. New York. 1st ed. $30.00

LARDNER, Ring. *Symptoms of Being 35.* 1921. Indianapolis. 1st ed. VG $22.00

LARDNER, Ring. *The Portable Ring Lardner.* 1946. New York. 1st ed. dj. VG $10.00

LARDNER, Ring. *What of It?* 1925. New York. 1st ed. VG $30.00

LARIVIERE & BOURNIVAL. *The Right Start.* 1973. Toronto. Holt Rinehart. revised ed. pb. $2.50

LARKIN, David. *The Unknown Paintings of Kay Nielsen.* 1977. Toronto. Peacock Press. Ills. 1st ed. $25.00

LARKIN, Oliver. *Samuel F.B. Morse & American Democratic Art.* 1954. Little, Brown. 1st ed. $8.50

LARKIN, Stillman Carter. *The Pioneer History of Meigs County.* 1908. Columbus, OH. Ills. 1st ed. 208 pp. $50.00

LAROCHELLE, Claude. *Guy Lafleur, Hockey's #1.* 1976. Quebec. Lotographie Inc. 251 pp. dj. $7.50

LARRABEE, E. & Vignelli, M. *Knoll Design.* 1981. Abrams. Ills. folio. dj. VG $60.00

LARSEN, Ernest. *Not a Through Street.* 1981. Random House. review copy. dj. VG $12.50

LARSEN, T. *The World of the Polar Bear.* 1978. Hamlyn. Ills. map. 96 pp. dj. VG $15.00

LARSON, P. & M. *All About Ants.* 1976. Crowell. Ills. 219 pp. VG $6.00

LARWOOD, J. & Hutton, J.C. *English Inn Signs.* 1951. London. Ills. folio. dj. VG $25.00

LASCELLES, G. *The Art of Falconry.* 1985. London. Spearman. Ills. 163 pp. dj. EX $12.50

LASKER, Rudolph. *Bloody Herrin.* 1925. Washington. Ills. 48 pp. wrappers. $15.00

LASKI, Marghanita. *The Tower.* 1974. Tacoma. Lanthorne Pr. Ltd. ed. EX $7.50

LASKIER, Frank. *Log Book.* 1943. $5.00

LASKY. *J.F.K.: Man & the Myth.* 1963. 11th printing. dj. EX $10.00

LASKY. *The Ugly Russian.* 1965. 1st ed. $6.50

LASSERRE, Henri. *Our Lady of Lourdes.* 1885. New York. 497 pp. $3.50

LASSWELL, M. *Rags & Hope. Recollections of Val C. Giles.* 1961. Coward McCann. 280 pp. dj. VG $22.50

LASSWELL, Mary. *High Time.* 1944. Houghton Mifflin. 1st ed. dj. $3.50

LASSWELL, Mary. *I'll Take Texas.* 1958. Boston. 1st ed. dj. VG $12.50

LASSWELL, Mary. *One on the House.* 1949. Boston. VG $8.00

LASSWELL, Mary. *Suds in Your Eye.* 1949. Houghton Mifflin. Ills. Price. $3.00

LASSWELL, Mary. *Tio Pepe.* 1963. Boston. 1st printing. dj. VG $12.50

LATHAM, Aaron. *Crazy Sundays, F. Scott Fitzgerald in Hollywood.* 1st ed. sgn. dj. EX $15.00

LATHAM, Robert E. *Marine Engines & Equipment.* (ca. 1960). 3rd ed. 460 pp. $4.00

LATHAN, E. *Green Grow the Dollars.* 1982. Simon & Schuster. dj. EX $7.50

LATHAN, E. *Inexpected Developments.* 1984. St.Martins. dj. EX $8.00

LATHBURY, Mary A. *Idyls of the Months. Poems & Drawings.* 1885. London. Ills. $45.00

LATHEN, Emma. *Murder to Go.* 1969. New York. 1st ed. dj. EX $25.00

LATHEN, Emma. *Murder Without Icing.* 1972. New York. Simon & Schuster. 1st ed. dj. $15.00

LATHROP, D.W. *The Upper Amazon.* 1970. Praeger. Ills. 256 pp. dj. VG $17.50

LATHROP, Dorothy. *Colt from Moon Mountain.* 1941. Macmillan. 1st ed. dj. EX $75.00

LATHROP, Dorothy. *Hide & Go Seek.* 1938. 1st ed. VG $30.00

LATHROP, Dorothy. *Hitty, Her First Hundred Years.* 1939. New York. dj. VG $16.00

LATHROP, Dorothy. *Hitty.* 1955. Macmillan. 22 Ills. $10.00

LATHROP, Dorothy. *Mr. Bumps & His Monkey.* Winston. Ills. G $15.00

LATHROP, Dorothy. *Presents for Lupe.* 1940. New York. Ills. 1st ed. $30.00

LATHROP, Dorothy. *The Dog in the Tapestry Garden.* 1962. Macmillan. Ills. 1st ed. inscr. dj. $45.00

LATHROP, Dorothy. *The Long Island.* 1929. Boston. Ills. 1st ed. $12.00

LATHROP, Dorothy. *The Skittle Skattle Monkey.* 1945. Macmillan. 1st ed. dj. VG $18.00

LATHROP, Elise. *Early American Inns & Taverns.* 1946. New York. 365 pp. VG $12.00

LATHROP, Elise. *Early American Inns & Taverns.* 1935. New York. Ills. 249 pp. dj. VG $20.00

LATHROP, Elise. *Historic Houses of Early America.* 1927. Tudor, NY. Ills. dj. VG $32.50

LATHROP, S.K. *Pre-Columbian Art of Robert W. Bliss Collection.* 1959. London. Ills. 2nd revised ed. 292 pp. $115.00

LATHROP. *The Grateful Elephant.* 1923. Yale U. 10 Ills. 1st ed. $25.00

LATHROP. *Whispering Rails.* 1930. Goldsmith Pub. dj. VG $4.50

LATIMER, Jonathan. *Sinners & Shrouds.* 1955. New York. Simon & Schuster. 1st ed. dj. $25.00

LATON, Frank. *Lomai of Lenake.* 1903. Revell. VG $15.00

LATROBE, Charles Joseph. *The Rambler in Mexico.* 1836. New York. 1st Am. ed. G $95.00

LATTIMORE, O. *Inner Asian Frontiers of China.* 1940. Am. Geog. Soc. maps. 585 pp. index. VG $40.00

LATTIMORE, O. *Ordeal by Slander.* 1950. Boston. Atlantic Monthly. G $10.00

LAU-LAVIE, Naphtali. *Moshe Dayan, a Biography.* 1968. New York. ex-lib. dj. EX $6.00

LAUBENFELS, M.W. de. *The Sponges of the West-Central Pacific.* 1954. 1st ed. wrappers. $10.00

LAUBIN, Reginald & Gladys. *The Indian Tipi: Its Hist., Construction & Use.* 1957. U. of OK Press. Ills. 208 pp. index. dj. $25.00

LAUDAN, Stanley. *The White Baton.* 1957. London. 1st ed. dj. VG $15.00

LAUDE. *African Art of the Dogon: Myths of Cliff Dwellers.* 1973. Brooklyn Museum/Viking Press. $5.00

LAUDER, Harry. *A Minstrel in France.* 1918. Hearst. Ills. 338 pp. Vg $6.50

LAUGHLIN, C. *So You're Going South.* 1940. Ills. 1st ed. $10.00

LAUGHLIN, C. *So You're Seeing New England.* 1940. Ills. 1st ed. $7.50

LAUGHLIN, James. *New Directions in Prose & Poetry.* 1939. Norforlk. Ills. 390 pp. VG $30.00

LAUGHLIN, James. *New Directions. Number 10.* 1948. 512 pp. $15.00

LAUGHLIN, James. *New Directions. Number 14.* 1953. New York. 408 pp. $15.00

LAUGHLIN, James. *New Directions. Number 8.* 1944. Norfolk. 407 pp. $25.00

LAUGHLIN, James. *New Directions. Number 9.* 1946. Norfolk. 415 pp. $20.00

LAUMER, Keith. *Time Trap.* 1970. New York. review copy. dj. VG $20.00

LAUNER, J. *The Enemies' Fighting Ships.* 1944. Ills. VG $40.00

LAUREL, Alicia Bay. *Living on the Earth.* 1970. Bookworks. Ills. $2.50

LAURENCE, John. *A History of Capital Punishment.* 1960. 230 pp. $6.00

LAURENCE, Margaret. *The Fire Dwellers.* 1969. New York. 1st ed. dj. EX $12.50

LAURENCIN, Marie. *Camille.* 1937. London. Ills. slipcase. VG $150.00

LAURIE, Joe, Jr. *Vaudeville, from the Honkytonks to the Palace.* 1953. New York. Holt. 1st ed. 525 pp. dj. $20.00

LAURIE. *Rise & Early Constitution of Universities.* 1886. $25.00

LAUT, Agnes C. *Overland Trail. Epic Path of Pioneers to Oregon.* 1929. New York. Ills. 1st ed. 358 pp. index. $17.50

LAUT, Agnes C. *The Fur Trade of America.* 1921. 1st ed. VG $35.00

LAUTREC, Toulouse. *Elles.* 1952. Ills. VG $50.00

LAVELL, Edith. *The Girl Scouts' Captain.* 1925. New York. A.L. Burt. 242 pp. $2.00

LAVENDER, David. *Bent's Fort.* 1954. Garden City. Doubleday. 1st ed. dj. VG $40.00

LAVENDER, David. *The Fist in the Wilderness.* 1964. Garden City. Doubleday. 1st ed. dj. VG $35.00

LAVENDER, David. *The Rockies.* 1968. New York. Harper. 1st ed. dj. VG $35.00

LAVER, James. *A Stitch in Time.* 1927. Nonesuch. Ltd. ed. 1/1525. $30.00

LAVER, James. *Ladies' Mistakes.* 1933. London. Nonesuch Press. Ltd. ed. VG $35.00

LAVIGNAC, Albert. *Music Dramas of Richard Wagner & Festive Theatre.* 1906. New York. Ills. VG $22.50

LAVIGNAC, Albert. *The Music Dramas of Richard Wagner.* 1898. Dodd Mead. trans. Singleton. Ills. $4.50

LAVIN, Mary. *A Memory & Other Stories.* 1973. Boston. 1st ed. dj. EX $12.50

LAVIN, Mary. *Selected Stories.* 1959. New York. 1st ed. dj. VG $15.00

LAVONDA, Marsha. *The Mask of Satan.* 1954. New York. Exposition Pr. 1st ed. 389 pp. $52.50

LAWES, L.E. *Life & Death in Sing Sing.* 1928. Ills. 1st ed. 267 pp. $12.50

LAWES, L.E. *Twenty Thousand Years in Sing Sing.* 1932. New York. photos. 412 pp. $3.00

LAWFORD, Valentine. *Vogue's Book of Houses, Gardens, People.* 1968. New York. Viking Press. Ills. 195 pp. $20.00

LAWLER, James J. *Lawler's American Sanitary Plumbing.* 1896. New York. revised ed. 313 pp. $35.00

LAWRENCE, D.H. *A Modern Lover.* 1934. dj. EX $70.00

LAWRENCE, D.H. *A Plea for Better Manners.* 1924. EX $45.00

LAWRENCE, D.H. *Aaron's Rod.* 1922. London. VG $27.50

LAWRENCE, D.H. *Birds, Beasts, & Flowers.* 1923. New York. Seltzer. 1st ed. dj. VG $150.00

LAWRENCE, D.H. *Etruscan Places.* 1932. London. Secker. 1st ed. dj. scarce. VG $110.00

LAWRENCE, D.H. *Lady Chatterley's Lover.* 1928. Florence. Ltd. ed. 1/1000. $750.00

LAWRENCE, D.H. *Lady Chatterley's Lover.* 1959. Grove. 1st ed. dj. VG $25.00

LAWRENCE, D.H. *Lady Chatterley's Lover.* no date. 1st Am. ed. VG $20.00

LAWRENCE, D.H. *Love Among the Haystacks.* 1930. London. Ltd. ed. 1/1600. dj. $100.00

LAWRENCE, D.H. *Mornings in Mexico.* 1931. Knopf. VG $10.00

LAWRENCE, D.H. *Pansies.* 1929. London. Secker. 1st trade ed. dj. VG $90.00

LAWRENCE, D.H. *Rawdon's Roof.* 1928. Woburn Books. Ltd. ed. sgn. VG $125.00

LAWRENCE, D.H. *St. Mawr.* 1925. 1st Am. ed. VG $40.00

LAWRENCE, D.H. *The Boy in the Bush.* 1924. New York. Seltzer. 1st ed. VG $22.50

LAWRENCE, D.H. *The Escaped Cock.* 1973. Ltd. ed. 1/750. dj. EX $20.00

LAWRENCE, D.H. *The Ladybird.* 1923. 1st ed. VG $45.00

LAWRENCE, D.H. *The Lost Girl.* 1921. 1st Am. ed. G $25.00

LAWRENCE, D.H. *The Lost Girl.* 1920. London. 1st ed. 2nd issue. VG $22.50

LAWRENCE, D.H. *The Prussian Officer & Other Stories.* 1917. New York. VG $25.00

LAWRENCE, D.H. *We Need One Another.* 1933. Equinox. Ills. John P. Heins. 68 pp. VG $25.00

LAWRENCE, David. *Beyond the New Deal.* 1934. New York. McGraw Hill. 317 pp. $3.50

LAWRENCE, E.A. *Clover Passage.* 1954. Caxton. Ills. 260 pp. dj. EX $10.00

LAWRENCE, Freida. *Not I But the Wind.* 1934. 1st trade ed. inscr. dj. $10.00

LAWRENCE, Frieda. *Not I But the Wind.* 1934. Rydal Press. Ltd. ed. 1/100. sgn. VG $85.00

LAWRENCE, Frieda. *The Memoirs & Correspondence.* 1964. Knopf. 1st ed. dj. $10.00

LAWRENCE, Joseph. *Years Are So Long.* 1934. 1st ed. $6.50

LAWRENCE, Lars. *Morning, Noon, & Night.* 1954. New York. Putnam. 1st ed. dj. EX $20.00

LAWRENCE, Lars. *Old Father Antic.* 1961. New York. International. 1st ed. dj. EX $35.00

LAWRENCE, Lars. *Out of the Dust.* 1956. New York. Putnam. 1st ed. dj. VG $20.00

LAWRENCE, R. *Charles Napier Friend & Fighter 1782-1853.* 1952. London. Murray. Ills. dj. EX $15.00

LAWRENCE, R.D. *In Praise of Wolves.* 1986. Holt. photos. 245 pp. dj. EX $15.00

LAWRENCE, T.E. *Men in Print.* 1940. Golden Cockrell. Ltd. ed. EX $375.00

LAWRENCE, T.E. *Revolt in the Desert.* 1927. New York. Ills. 1st Am. ed. G $17.50

LAWRENCE, T.E. *Seven Pillars of Wisdom, a Triumph.* 1935. Doubleday. Ills. dj. VG $15.00

LAWRENCE, T.E. *Seven Pillars of Wisdom, a Triumph.* 1936. New York. Doubleday. 672 pp. dj. VG $7.50

LAWRENCE, T.E. *The Home Letters of T.E. Lawrence & His Brothers.* 1954. Macmillan. 1st ed. $22.50

LAWRENCE. *Complete Farrier & British Sportsman.* 1816. $600.00

LAWSON, Lizzie. *Old Proverbs with New Pictures.* London. (ca.1890) Ills. VG $25.00

LAWSON, Lizzie. *Old Proverbs with New Pictures.* London. Cassell, Peter, Galpin. EX $25.00

LAWSON, R. *The Fabulous Fight.* 1949. 1st ed. dj. VG $35.00

LAWSON, Robert. *Ben & Me.* 1939. Ills. 4th printing. dj. VG $15.00

LAWSON, Robert. *Country Colic.* 1944. Boston. Ills. 1st ed. 2nd printing. VG $10.00

LAWSON, Robert. *From the Horn of the Moon.* 1937. Garden City. Ills. dj. VG $25.00

LAWSON, Robert. *Monroe Leaf.* 1938. Viking. Ills. 1st ed. dj. EX $45.00

LAWSON, Robert. *Mr. Revere & I.* 1953. Boston. Ills. Lawson. 1st ed. dj. VG $25.00

LAWSON, Robert. *Mr. Wilbur.* 1945. Boston. 1st ed. dj. VG $15.00

LAWSON, Robert. *Rabbit Hill.* 1944. Viking. Ills. 128 pp. dj. VG $6.50

LAWSON, Robert. *Robbut.* 1948. New York. 1st ed. sgn. dj. EX $65.00

LAWSON, Robert. *Smeller Martin.* 1950. Viking. 1st ed. dj. EX $15.00

LAWSON, Ted W. *Thirty Seconds Over Tokyo.* 1944. New York. 215 pp. VG $4.00

LAWSON, Ted W. *Thirty Seconds Over Tokyo.* 1943. Random House. 221 pp. dj. EX $6.50

LAWSON, Thomas. *Frenzied Finance. Vol. I.* 1905. New York. 1st ed. VG $50.00

LAWSON, William. *A New Orchard & Garden.* 1927. London. Cresset Pr. Ltd. ed. inscr. VG $50.00

LAWSON. *Aesop's Fables.* 1941. Heritage House. $10.00

LAWTON, Mary. *Queen of Cooks & Some Kings. Story of Rosa Lewis.* 1925. New York. VG $15.00

LAWTON, Wilbur. *The Boy Aviators in Africa.* 1910. Hurst. G $5.50

LAWTON, Wilbur. *The Boy Aviators Treasure Quest.* 1910. Hurst. G $5.50

LAWTON, Wilbur. *The Dreadnought Boys on the Submarine.* 1911. Hurst. G $3.50

LAYARD, Austen H. *Nineveh & Its Remains.* 1849. New York. Ills. 1st ed. VG $175.00

LAYCOCK, G. *Autumn of the Eagle.* 1973. Scribner. Ills. 239 pp. EX $12.50

LAYCOCK, G. *The Alien Animals, Story of Imported Wildlife.* 1966. Ills. 1st ed. 240 pp. dj. EX $10.00

LAYLANDER, O.J. *Whittlings.* 1928. Torch Press. Ills. VG $12.50

LAYNE, Bobby. *Always on Sunday.* 1962. New Jersey. Ills. dj. VG $10.00

LAYTON, I. *Gucci Bag.* Ltd. ed. 1/429. sgn. $30.00

LAZAREV, V. *Old Russian Murals & Mosaics XI-XVI Centuries.* 1966. Phaidon. Ills. folio. $37.50

LAZARSFIELD, Safie. *Woman's Experience of the Male.* 1967. Encyclopedia Press. $3.50

LAZELL, Bathsheba Anna. *Glimpses of Sundry Places in Europe.* 1932. no pub. listed. 155 pp. $5.50

LE ARTI. *Che Vanno Per Via Nella Citta Di Venezia.* 1803. Ills. folio. $175.00

LE BLAC, Georgette. *The Blue Bird for Children.* 1914. Boston. Ills. $15.00

LE BLANC, Maurice. *Man of Miracles.* 1931. New York. Macaulay. 1st ed. dj. VG $12.50

LE CARRE, John. *A Perfect Spy.* 1986. proof copy. $80.00

LE CARRE, John. *A Perfect Spy.* 1986. London. Ltd. ed. 1/250. sgn. EX $45.00

LE CARRE, John. *Call for the Dead.* 1962. New York. Walker. 1st ed. dj. EX $65.00

LE CARRE, John. *Honourable Schoolboy.* 1977. London. dj. EX $30.00

LE CARRE, John. *Smiley's People.* 1980. Knopf. 1st trade ed. dj. VG $15.00

LE CARRE, John. *Smiley's People.* 1980. review copy. dj. EX $60.00

LE CARRE, John. *The Little Drummer Girl.* 1983. Knopf. 1st Am. ed. dj. EX $15.00

LE CARRE, John. *The Looking Glass War.* 1965. London. dj. EX $25.00

LE CARRE, John. *The Looking Glass War.* 1965. New York. Coward McCann. 320 pp. $3.50

LE CARRE, John. *The Spy Who Came in from the Cold.* 1964. New York. 1st Am. ed. dj. VG $30.00

LE CONTE. *Ramblings Through the High Sierra.* 1900. Sierra Club. Ills. G $45.00

LE CORBUSIER. *The Radiant City.* 1967. New York. 1st ed. EX $40.00

LE FANU, J. Sheridan. *Green Tea & Other Ghost Stories.* 1945. Sauk City. Arkham House. dj. $150.00

LE FANU, Sheridan. *Uncle Silas.* 1947. London. 1st Eng. ed. dj. EX $40.00

LE GALLIENNE, R. *An Old Country House.* 1905. Ills. Eliz. Shippen Green. VG $25.00

LE GALLIENNE, R. *Painted Shadows.* 1904. $10.00

LE GALLIENNE, R. *Romantic '90s.* 1925. $10.00

LE GALLIENNE, R. *The Romance of Perfume.* 1928. NY/Paris. Ills. George Barbier. EX $35.00

LE GALLIENNE, R. *The Romance of Zion Chapel.* 1898. NY/London. Bradley. 1st ed. EX $20.00

LE GALLIENNE, R. *Young Lives.* 1899. $10.00

LE GARE, Robert. *The Coonhound.* 1924. Columbus, OH. Ills. VG $20.00

LE GETTE, Blythe. *Marshall Ney: a Dual Life.* Stackpole. 1st ed. VG $20.00

LE GORBEAU, Adrien. *The Forest Giant.* 1924. New York. 1st ed. dj. $15.00

LE GUIN, Ursula K. *From Elfland to Poughkeepsie.* 1975. Portland. 2nd ed. wrappers. VG $15.00

LE GUIN, Ursula K. *From Elfland to Poughkeepsie.* 1973. Portland. Pendragon Press. Ltd. ed. $75.00

LE GUIN, Ursula K. *Malafrena.* 1979. 1st ed. dj. EX $15.00

LE GUIN, Ursula K. *The Beginning Place.* 1980. New York. proof copy. sgn. VG $60.00

LE GUIN, Ursula K. *The Beginning Place.* 1980. 1st Am. ed. dj. EX $20.00

LE GUIN, Ursula K. *The Compass Rose.* 1982. New York. 1st ed. dj. VG $12.50

LE GUIN, Ursula K. *The Compass Rose.* 1982. Ltd. ed. 1/550. sgn. EX $65.00

LE GUIN, Ursula K. *The Eye of the Heron, in Millenial Women.* 1978. 1st ed. dj. EX $30.00

LE GUIN, Ursula K. *The Farthest Shore.* 1972. 1st Am. ed. dj. VG $90.00

LE GUIN, Ursula K. *Very Far Away from Anywhere Else.* 1978. 1st ed. dj. EX $30.00

LE GUIN. *The Left Hand of Darkness.* 1969. Walker. VG $125.00

LE MAIR, H. Willebeek. *Grannie's Little Rhyme Book.* McKay. dj. VG $45.00

LE MASSENA, C.E. *Galli-Curci's Life of Song.* 1945. New York. Ills. Wartime ed. dj. VG $30.00

LE MAY & KANTOR. *Mission with LeMay. My Story.* Ills. dj. G $15.00

LE MOYNE. *Country Houses in Europe & America.* 1908. folio. VG $50.00

LE PAGE DU PRATZ, Antoines. *History of Louisiana.* 1763. London. Becket & Hondt. 1st Eng. ed. $850.00

LE QUEUX, William. *Devil's Dice.* 1897. Chicago. VG $110.00

LE QUEUX, William. *Secrets of Monte Carlo.* 1900. Dillingham. $4.50

LE QUEUX, William. *The Closed Book.* 1904. London/NY. Smart Set Pub. 1st ed. $25.00

LE QUEUX, William. *Zoraida.* 1895. London. Tower. Ills. 1st ed. $12.50

LE SAGE, Laurent. *The New French Novel.* 1962. PA State U. 150 pp. $5.00

LE VIEN, Jack & Lord, John. *Winston Churchill. The Valiant Years.* 1962. New York. 411 pp. dj. EX $4.50

LEA, Henry C. *History Sacerdotal Celibacy in Christian Church.* 1907. London. 3rd ed. 2 vol set. G $75.00

LEA, Homer. *The Day of the Saxon.* 1912. Harper. 1st ed. VG $32.50

LEA, M. Carey. *Manual of Photography.* 1871. Philadelphia. 2nd ed. VG $80.00

LEA, Tom. *Bibliography of Writings & Illustrations.* 1971. El Paso. Ltd. ed. sgn. dj. VG $50.00

LEA, Tom. *Old Mount Franklin.* 1968. El Paso. Ltd. ed. 1/450. VG $165.00

LEA, Tom. *Randado.* 1941. Hertzog. Ills. Ltd. ed. 1/100. sgn. VG $80.00

LEA, Tom. *The Brave Bulls.* 1949. Boston. Ills. Lea. 1st ed. 270 pp. $15.00

LEA, Tom. *The King Ranch.* 1905. Boston. 1st trade ed. 2 vol set. EX $85.00

LEA, Tom. *The King Ranch.* 1957. Boston. Little, Brown. 2 vol set. boxed. $75.00

LEA, Tom. *The Wonderful Country.* 1952. Boston. 1st ed. dj. VG $15.00

LEACH, B. *Beyond East & West.* 1978. New York. Ills. dj. VG $10.00

LEACH, Bernard. *Potter in Japan.* 1967. Faber. 2nd impression. dj. VG $10.00

LEACH, J.A. *An Australian Bird Book.* 1911. Melboune. Ills. 200 pp. G $10.00

LEACH, Paul R. *The Man Dawes.* 1930. Chicago. Ills. 349 pp. index. $18.50

LEACOCK. *Nonsense Novels.* 1921. 8 color pls. dj. VG $12.50

LEAF, Munro. *Ferdinandus Taurus.* 1962. New York. Ills. Robert Lawson. EX $17.50

LEAF, Munro. *Noodle.* 1937. New York. Ills. Ludwig Bemelmans. $35.00

LEAHY, John Martin. *Drome.* 1952. Los Angeles. Fantasy Press. dj. $50.00

LEAKEY, L.S.B. *Animals of East Africa.* 1973. Nat. Geog. Soc. Ills. map. 199 pp. EX $15.00

LEAKEY, L.S.B. *By the Evidence, Memoirs of Leakey 1932-1951.* 1974. Harcourt Brace. 1st ed. 276 pp. dj. EX $15.00

LEAKEY. *Animals of East Africa.* 1969. dj. EX $10.00

LEAMING, Mary M. *The Book of Home Ecomomics.* 1942. New York. New Home Library. 507 pp. VG $4.00

LEAR, D. *Book of Nonsense.* 1895. 30th ed. $35.00

LEAR, D. *Old Steamboat Days on Hudson.* 1907. New York. Grafton Press. Ills. 1st ed. $25.00

LEAR, Edward & Nash, Ogden. *The Scroobious Pip.* 1968. Harper & Row. Ills. Burkert. 1st ed. dj. EX $40.00

LEAR, Edward. *Nonsense Books.* 1946. Boston. Ills. dj. EX $20.00

LEAR, Edward. *The Collected Nonsense Songs.* 1947. London. Grey Walls Press. 1st ed. dj. $20.00

LEAR, Edward. *The Nutcracker & the Sugar Tongs.* 1978. Boston. Ills. Marcia Sewall. 1st ed. $10.00

LEARY, Timothy. *Confessions of a Dope Fiend.* 1973. New York. Bantam. advance copy. pb. EX $20.00

LEARY, Timothy. *Psychedelic Prayers.* 1966. Kerhonkson. Poets Press. 1st ed. wrappers. $35.00

LEASCARBOURA, Austin C. *Radio for Everybody.* 1922. New York. Ills. 334 pp. $7.50

LEASOR, James. *Passport to Oblivion.* 1964. London. Heinemann. 1st ed. dj. VG $25.00

LEATHERBEE, A.T. *Knocking About.* 1924. Yale. Ills. 1st ed. 176 pp. $27.50

LEAVENS, John. *The Catboat Book.* 1973. Camden, Maine. 1st ed. dj. $150.00

LEAVENS, R.F. & Lord, A.H. *Dr. Tuckers Dartmouth.* 1965. Dartmouth. Ills. 1st ed. 273 pp. dj. EX $10.00

LEAVITT, David. *Family Dancing.* 1984. Knopf. 1st ed. dj. VG $20.00

LEBLANC, Henri. *Catalogue de L'Oeuvre Complet de Gustave Dore.* 1931. Paris. Ills. G $25.00

LEBOWITZ, Fran. *Social Studies.* 1981. Random House. 1st ed. dj. VG $10.00

LEBRUN, Rico. *Reco Lebrun Drawings.* 1961. Berkeley. Ills. 1st ed. dj. EX $25.00

LECKY. *Poems.* 1891. New York. Appleton. EX $145.00

LEDERER, Wm. J. *Timothy's Song.* New York. Ills. Ardizzone. 1st ed. dj. $25.00

LEDOUX, Louis Vernon. *An Essay on Japanese Prints.* 1938. New York. Ills. Ltd. ed. 1/1000. rare. $90.00

LEDROUX, M. *Ice Making Machines.* 1902. 5th ed. VG $30.00

LEE, B. *Death Valley.* 1930. New York. 1st ed. VG $25.00

LEE, Brian North. *The Bookplate Designs of Rex Whistler.* 1973. Pinner. 1st ed. $40.00

LEE, C. *They Call It Pacific.* 1943. G $7.50

LEE, E.B. *Naomi: Boston 200 Years Ago.* 1848. Boston. 1st ed. G $20.00

LEE, Elizabeth. *Ouida: a Memoir.* 1914. London. Ills. VG $25.00

LEE, F. *Cuba's Struggle Against Spain.* 1899. New York. photos. 676 pp. VG $8.00

LEE, Francis Bazley. *New Jersey as a Colony & as a State.* 1902. New York. 4 vol set. VG $35.00

LEE, Gypsy Rose. *G-String Murders.* Tower. 1st ed. $7.00

LEE, Harper. *To Kill a Mockingbird.* 1960. London. Hienemann. 1st Eng. ed. dj. EX $75.00

LEE, Henry. *Sir & Brother.* 1948. New York. Appleton. 1st ed. dj. EX $25.00

LEE, John D. *Mormonism Unveiled.* 1891. St. Louis. Ills. 413 pp. $40.00

LEE, John. *Fighter Facts & Fallacies.* 1942. New York. Ills. 63 pp. dj. $15.00

LEE, Kenneth Fuller. *Big Game Hunting & Marksmanship.* 1941. Samworth. 217 pp. dj. $7.00

LEE, Mabel Barbee. *Cripple Creek Days.* 1958. New York. Ills. 270 pp. dj. $15.00

LEE, Robert E. *Recollections & Letters of Gen. Robert E. Lee.* 1924. 471 pp. $12.50

LEE, Robert E. *Recollections & Letters of Gen. Robert E. Lee.* 1909. 461 pp. $18.50

LEE, Ruth Webb. *History of Valentines.* 1952. New York. Ills. 1st ed. 239 pp. $32.50

LEE, Ruth Webb. *19th Century Art Glass.* 1952. $20.00

LEE, Sherman E. *The Sketchbooks of Hiroshige.* 1984. 2 vols in 1. Ills. scarce. EX $55.00

LEE, Sir Sidney. *A Life of William Shakespeare.* 1923. New York. Macmillan. ex-lib. 758 pp. VG $6.00

LEE, Tere. *Guidebook to the Tokaido.* 1983. U. of KS. Ills. wrappers. scarce. $20.00

LEE, Umphrey. *Hist. Backgrounds of Early Methodist Enthusiasm.* 1931. Columbia. 1st ed. $12.50

LEE, W. Storrs. *Great California Deserts.* 1963. New York. Putnam. 1st ed. dj. EX $12.50

LEE, W. Storrs. *The Yankees of Connecticut.* 1957. Holt. 1st ed. dj. $8.50

LEE. *Scotty Philip, the Man Who Saved the Buffalo.* 1972. 1st ed. VG $15.00

LEE. *The World of the Whitetailed Deer.* 1962. Lippincott. 149 pp. dj. VG $4.00

LEE. *Uncle William, the Man Who was Shif'less.* 1906. A.L. Burt. $4.50

LEECH, Margaret. *In the Days of McKinley.* 1959. Harper. 1st ed. sgn. dj. VG $35.00

LEECH, Margaret. *Reveille in Washington.* NY/London. Harper. Ills. 483 pp. $10.00

LEECH & MC KENNA. *Hide & Seek Riddle Book.* 1943. Grosset & Dunlap. Ills. dj. VG $5.50

LEECH. *Little Tour in Ireland.* 1859. London. $75.00

LEECHMAN, Douglas. *The Hiker's Handbook.* 1944. Norton. 1st ed. 220 pp. dj. $75.00

LEEKLEY. *The World of Manabozho Tales of Chippewa Indians.* 1965. 1st ed. dj. EX $15.00

LEEMING, G. *Who's Who in Henry James.* 1976. New York. dj. EX $10.00

LEES-MINE, J. *The Last Stuarts: British Royalty in Exile.* 1983. New York. $18.50

LEESE, O. *Cacti.* 1973. London. Triune. Ills. 144 pp. dj. EX $22.50

LEFFINGWELL, William B. *Wild Fowl Shooting.* 1888. Chicago. VG $30.00

LEGENDRE-HARTMANN. *Domenikos Theotoko-Poulos, Called El Greco.* 1937. $29.00

LEGMAN, C. *Rationale of Dirty Joke. Analysis of Sexual Humor.* 1968. New York. 811 pp. index. dj. VG $15.00

LEGOUVE, Ernest. *Maria Malibran.* Paris. French text. ex-lib. wrappers. $20.00

LEHANE, Brendan. *The Complete Flea.* 1969. New York. 1st ed. dj. EX $12.50

LEHMAN, Irving. *Benjamin Nathan Cardozo.* 1928. Stamford. Ltd. ed. 1/350. VG $15.00

LEHMAN, Milton. *This High Man, Life of Robert H. Goddard.* 1963. New York. 1st ed. $15.00

LEHMAN. *Law of the .45.* Star Books. $4.00

LEHMAN-HAUPT. *Fifty Books About Bookmaking.* 1934. EX $20.00

LEHMANN, Ernst. *The Zeppelins.* 1927. New York. Ills. 1st ed. VG $80.00

LEHMANN, John. *New Writing in England.* 1939. New York. 1st ed. wrappers. VG $45.00

LEHMANN. *Australian Primitive Painters.* 1977. U. of Queensland Press. $10.00

LEHMANN-HAUPT. *The Gottingen Model Book.* 1972. U. of MO. $15.00

LEHNER, E. & J. *Folklore & Symbolism of Flowers, Plants, & Trees.* 1960. Tudor. Ills. 120 pp. EX $10.00

LEIBER, Fritz. *A Specter is Haunting Texas.* 1968. New York. Walker. 1st ed. dj. EX $20.00

LEIBER, Fritz. *Bazaar of the Bizarre.* 1978. sgn. dj. VG $25.00

LEIBER, Fritz. *Gather Darkness.* 1950. 1st ed. dj. VG $35.00

LEIBER, Fritz. *Night's Black Agents.* 1947. Sauk City. Arkham House. 1st ed. inscr. $70.00

LEIBER, Fritz. *Rime Island Whispers Press.* 1977. dj. EX $25.00

LEIBLING. *The Sweet Science.* 1956. Viking. 1st ed. dj. $12.50

LEIGH, W.R. *Forgotten Waters/Adventures in Gulf of California.* 1941. 1st ed. dj. EX $15.00

LEIGH, W.R. *Frontiers of Enchantment.* 1938. New York. 2nd printing. VG $25.00

LEIGH, W.R. *Frontiers of Enchantment.* 1940. dj. VG $12.50

LEIGHTON, Claire. *Wood Engraving & Woodcuts.* 1932. London. Studio. Ills. 2nd printing. VG $35.00

LEIGHTON, Claire. *Wood Engraving of 1930's.* 1936. London. Studio. 192 pp. wrappers. VG $25.00

LEIGHTON, Clara. *Give Us This Day.* 1943. Ills. 1st ed. dj. EX $30.00

LEIGHTON, Clare. *Country Matters.* 1937. New York. Ills. Leighton. 1st Am. ed. $22.50

LEIGHTON, Clare. *Four Hedges: A Gardener's Chronicle.* 1935. New York. Macmillan. Ills. sgn. $25.00

LEIGHTON, Clare. *Sometime-Never.* 1939. New York. Ills. 1st Am. ed. 178 pp. $15.00

LEIGHTON, Clare. *Southern Harvest.* 1942. Macmillan. 1st ed. dj. VG $20.00

LEIMBACH, Patricia Penton. *All My Meadows.* 1977. Englewood Cliffs. 235 pp. $7.50

LEINSTER, Murray. *Colonial Survey.* 1957. Gnome. 1st ed. dj. VG $15.00

LEINSTER, Murray. *Forgotten Planet.* 1954. New York. Gnome. 1st ed. dj. VG $20.00

LEINSTER, Murray. *Operation Outer Space.* 1954. Fantasy Press. 1st trade ed. dj. VG $20.00

LEINSTER, Murray. *Sidewise in Time.* 1950. Chicago. Shasta. sgn. dj. EX $80.00

LEITCH. *Chinese Rugs.* 1926. New York. Ills. 1st ed. dj. VG $22.50

LEITH, Prue. *The Cook's Handbook.* 1981. New York. dj. VG $7.50

LEITHAUSER, Brad. *Equal Distance.* 1985. Knopf. 1st ed. dj. VG $17.50

LEKACHMAN, Robert. *Greed Is Not Enough, Reaganomics.* 1982. New York. 213 pp. dj. $3.00

LEM, Stanislaw. *A Perfect Vacuum.* 1979. Harcourt. 1st Am. ed. dj. VG $20.00

LEM, Stanislaw. *His Master's Voice.* 1983. New York. Harcourt. 1st ed. dj. VG $15.00

LEM, Stanislaw. *Imaginary Magnitude.* 1984. Harcourt. review copy. dj. VG $20.00

LEM, Stanislaw. *More Tales of Pirx the Pilot.* 1982. New York. 1st ed. review copy. dj. EX $10.00

LEM, Stanislaw. *Return from the Stars.* 1980. New York. Harcourt. 1st ed. dj. VG $20.00

LEM, Stanislaw. *The Invincible.* 1973. Seabury. 1st Am. ed. dj. EX $20.00

LEM, Stanislaw. *The Star Diaries.* 1971. New York. 1st ed. dj. VG $20.00

LEMMON, R.S. & Sherman, C.L. *Flowers of the World.* 1958. Hanover House. Ills. 280 pp. dj. EX $10.00

LEMMON, Robert S. *Our Amazing Birds.* 1952. Garden Guild. Ills. Eckelberry. dj. EX $4.50

LEMMON, Robert S. & Johnson. *Wildflowers of North America in Color.* 1961. Garden City. 280 pp. $10.00

LEMPRIERE, J. *Classical Dictionary.* 1801. 1st Am. ed. G $60.00

LENGYEL, E. *Siberia.* 1943. Random House. Ills. 1st printing. dj. EX $12.50

LENGYEL, O. *Five Chimneys.* 1947. New York. Ziff-Davis. G $20.00

LENHOFF. *Freemasons: History, Nature, Development, Secret.* 1978. London. 1st ed. 375 pp. $12.50

LENK, Torsten. *The Flintlock: Its Origin & Development.* New York. Bramhall House. reprint. dj. $17.50

LENNOX, Wm. G. & Cobb, S. *Epilepsy. Medical Monograph.* 1927. 1st ed. 197 pp. $55.00

LENOTRE, G. *Last Days of Marie Antoinette.* 1908. London. Ills. 2nd impression. VG $12.50

LENSKI, Lois. *Blueberry Corners.* 1940. Philadelphia. sgn. 209 pp. $12.50

LENSKI, Lois. *Deer Valley Girl.* 1968. Philadelphia. Ills. 1st ed. $15.00

LENSKI, Lois. *Down Town, a Betsy Tacy Story.* 1943. New York. 1st ed. 180 pp. VG $10.00

LENSKI, Lois. *Ocean-Born Mary.* 1939. New York. 388 pp. dj. $5.00

LENZ, Sidney S. *Lenz on Bridge.* 1926. New York. Simon & Schuster. 371 pp. $3.50

LEONARD, E.J. & Goodman, J. C. *Buffalo Bill, King of the Wild West.* 1955. New York. Ills. 320 pp. dj. $10.00

LEONARD, Elmore. *Cat Chaser.* 1982. New York. Arbor House. 1st ed. 283 pp. $12.50

LEONARD, Elmore. *City Primeval*. 1981. London. Allen. 1st Eng. ed. dj. EX $30.00

LEONARD, Elmore. *City Primeval*. 1980. 1st Am. ed. sgn. dj. EX $40.00

LEONARD, Elmore. *Dutch Treat*. Mysterious Pr. Ltd. 1st ed. 1/350. sgn. dj. $50.00

LEONARD, Elmore. *Forty Lashes Less One*. 1972. New York. Bantam. pb. EX $30.00

LEONARD, Elmore. *Glitz*. 1985. Mysterious Pr. Ltd. ed. sgn. slipcase. $60.00

LEONARD, Elmore. *La Brava*. 1983. New York. Arbor House. 1st ed. dj. VG $25.00

LEONARD, Elmore. *Split Images*. 1981. New York. Arbor House. 1st ed. dj. VG $40.00

LEONARD, Elmore. *Stick*. 1983. New York. Arbor House. 1st ed. dj. EX $30.00

LEONARD, Irving, trans. *Spanish Approach to Pensacola, 1689-1693*. 1939. Albuquerque. Ills. Ltd. ed. 323 pp. $200.00

LEONARD, John Lynn. *The Care & Handling of Dogs*. 1928. Garden City. $3.00

LEONARD, Jon & Taylor, Elaine. *Live Longer Now Cookbook for Joyful Health & Life*. 1977. New York. 368 pp. $7.50

LEONARD, Jonathan & Time Life. *American Cooking: Great West*. 1971. New York. Time Life. Ills. 208 pp. $10.00

LEONARD. *Swag*. 1976. 1st Am. ed. sgn. dj. EX $60.00

LEONARD. *52 Pickup*. 1st ed. sgn. pb. wrappers. EX $10.00

LEONE, Gene. *Leone's Italian Cookbook*. 1967. New York. Harper. Ills. 244 pp. $5.00

LEONHARDT. *New Orleans Drawn & Quartered*. 1938. Ltd. ed. $47.00

LEOPOLD, Aldo. *A Sand County Almanac & Sketches Here & There*. 1968. Oxford U. Pr. Ills. 226 pp. EX $7.50

LEOPOLD, Aldo. *A Sand County Almanac Illustrated*. 1977. Tamarack Press. Ills. Algire. 152 pp. dj. EX $20.00

LEOPOLD, Nathan F., Jr. *Life Plus 99 Years*. 1958. New York. 1st ed. 381 pp. dj. VG $12.50

LEOPOLD. *Game Management*. 1947. Scribner. Ills. 480 pp. Vg $9.50

LEQUIN, U.K. *Eye of the Heron*. 1978. Harper & Row. 1st ed. dj. EX $25.00

LERMAN, Rhoda. *Call Me Ishtar*. 1973. Doubleday. 1st ed. dj. VG $25.00

LERMAN, Rhoda. *The Book of the Night*. 1984. Holt. review copy. dj. VG $20.00

LERNER. *Gregory Gillespie*. 1977. Smithsonian Institute Press. $6.00

LEROI-GOURHAN. *Treasures of Pre-Historic Art*. 1967. New York City. $47.00

LEROUX, Gaston. *Bride of the Sun*. 1915. New York. McBride. 1st ed. VG $25.00

LEROUX, Gaston. *Phantom of the Opera*. 1911. Bobbs Merrill. Ills. Andre Castaigne. 1st ed. $25.00

LEROUX, Gaston. *Secret of the Night*. 1914. New York. Macaulay. 1st ed. EX $10.00

LEROUX, Gaston. *The Machine to Kill*. 1935. New York. Macaulay. G $12.50

LERRIGO. *The Boy Scout Treasure Hunters*. 1917. Barse & Hopkins. Ills. G $3.50

LESCARBOURA, Austin C. *Radio for Everybody*. 1923. New York. 354 pp. $12.50

LESESNE, Thomas Petigru. *Landmarks of Charleston*. 1932. Richmond. Garrett & Massie. Ills. maps. $20.00

LESLIE, Frank. *Leslie's Ills. Famous Leaders & Battle Scenes*. 1896. folio. VG $150.00

LESLIE, Lawrence J. *The Rivals of the Trail*. 1913. New York. 116 pp. $3.50

LESLIE, Miss. *75 Receipts for Pastry, Cakes, & Sweetmeats*. 1835. Boston. G $85.00

LESLIE, P. *The Liberation of the Riviera*. 1980. London. Ills. dj. EX $15.00

LESLIE, R.F. *Wild Pets*. 1970. Crown. Ills. 240 pp. dj. EX $6.00

LESLIE, Shane. *A Ghost in the Isle of Wight*. 1929. London. Ltd. ed. 1/530. sgn. dj. VG $25.00

LESLIE, Shane. *Shane Leslie's Ghost Book*. 1955. London. Hollis & Carter. 1st ed. dj. $25.00

LESLIE, Shane. *Twenty-Five Poems*. 1959. Dublin. Ltd. ed. 1/120. dj. EX $35.00

LESLIE. *Afloat on the Flood*. 1915. New York Book Co. EX $5.50

LESLIE. *Stranger in Boots*. Pyramid. pb. $3.00

LESLIE. *With Trapper Jim in the North Woods*. 1913. New York Book Co. $5.50

LESLIE-MELVILLE, B. & J. *There's a Rhino in the Rosebed, Mother*. 1973. Doubleday. 1st ed. 253 pp. dj. EX $7.00

LESSING, Doris. *Conopus in Argos. The Sirian Experiment*. 1981. Knopf. 1st ed. 288 pp. $6.50

LESSING, Doris. *Shikasta*. 1979. New York. Knopf. 1st ed. dj. VG $20.00

LESSING, Doris. *Temptation of Jack Orkney*. 1972. New York. 1st ed. dj. EX $12.50

LESSING, Doris. *The Good Terrorist*. 1985. Knopf. proof copy. wrappers. VG $60.00

LESSING, Doris. *The Good Terrorist*. Ltd. ed. 1/250. sgn. $65.00

LESSING, Doris. *The Grass is Singing*. 1950. 1st Eng. ed. dj. VG $75.00

LESSING, Doris. *The Making of the Representative for Planet 8*. 1982. New York. Knopf. 1st ed. dj. VG $20.00

LESSING, Doris. *The Making of the Representative from Planet 6*. 1982. Knopf. 1st Am. ed. dj. VG $12.50

LESSING, Doris. *The Marriages Between Three, Four, & Five*. 1980. New York. Knopf. 1st ed. dj. VG $20.00

LESSING, Doris. *The Memoirs of a Survivor*. 1975. General Pub. 1st Canadian ed. dj. VG $15.00

LESSING, Doris. *The Sentimental Agents*. 1983. New York. Knopf. 1st ed. dj. VG $20.00

LESSING, Doris. *The Summer Before the Dark*. 1973. New York. 1st ed. dj. EX $12.50

LESSING, Doris. *This Was the Old Chief's Country*. 1951. Joseph. 1st ed. dj. VG $60.00

LESTER, Francis E. *My Friend the Rose*. 1942. Harrisburg. dj. EX $15.00

LESTER, John E. *The Yo-Semite; History, Scenery, Development*. 1873. Providence. 1st ed. wrappers. $125.00

LESTER. *Historic Costume*. 1933. dj. $15.00

LESUEUR, Meridel. *Annunciation*. 1935. Los Angeles. Platen Pr. inscr. wrappers. $125.00

LESUEUR, Meridel. *Corn Village*. 1970. Sauk City. Stanton & Lee. 1st ed. sgn. EX $15.00

LESUEUR, Meridel. *Crusaders*. 1955. New York. Blue Heron. 1st ed. inscr. EX $35.00

LESY, Michael. *Wisconsin Death Trip*. 1973. Pantheon. dj. EX $35.00

LETAROUILLY, Paul. *Edifices De Rome Moderne*. 1928. London. Tiranti. 6 vol set. $55.00

LETHBRIDGE, A. *Halfway to Yesterday*. 1974. EX $7.50

LETHBRIDGE, A. *Well Do I Remember*. 1976. EX $6.00

LETTER PRESS *Kinston, Whitehall, & Goldsboro*. 1890. 1st ed. 92 pp. $23.50

LETTY, Cythna. *Trees of South Africa*. 1975. Cape Town. Ills. 1st ed. dj. EX $10.00

LEUPP, Francis E. *In Red Man's Land*. 1914. New York. 161 pp. $10.00

LEUTSCHER, A. *Keeping Reptiles & Amphibians as Pets*. 1976. Scribner. Ills. 164 pp. dj. VG $10.00

LEUTWILER, O.A. *Elements of Machine Design*. 1917. 1st ed. 5th impression. 607 pp. $75.00

LEVAI. *Black Book on the Martyrdom of Hungarian Jewry*. 1848. Zurich. Ills. 1st ed. dj. VG $90.00

LEVANT, Oscar. *A Smattering of Ignorance.* 1942. Garden City. 267 pp. dj. $10.00

LEVERMORE, Charles Herbert. *Forerunner & Competitors of Pilgrims & Puritans.* 1912. Brooklyn. 852 pp. 2 vol set. $22.50

LEVERTOV, Denise. *Conversation in Moscow.* 1973. Hovey Street Pr. Ltd. ed. 1/1000. wrappers. VG $20.00

LEVERTOV, Denise. *Two Poems.* 1983. Ewert. Ltd. ed. sgn. handbound. $85.00

LEVERTOV, Denise. *With Eyes at the Back of Our Heads.* 1959. New Directions.1st ed. dj. VG $45.00

LEVEY, D.A. *Suburban Monastery Death Poem.* 1968. Cleveland. Zero Eds. inscr. wrappers. VG $40.00

LEVI, Eliphas. *The History of Magic.* 1922. London. trans. Waite. 2nd ed. 20 pls. $75.00

LEVICK, G. Murray. *Antarctic Penguins.* 1914. Heinemann. 2nd printing. $17.50

LEVIN, Ira. *Rosemary's Baby.* 1967. Random House. dj. EX $12.50

LEVIN, Meyer. *The Obsession.* 1973. New York. 1st ed. dj. $10.00

LEVIN, N. *Holocaust: Destruction of European Jewry 1933-45.* 1973. New York. Stocken Books. SftCvr. G $15.00

LEVIN & LURIE. *American Indian Today.* 1970. Penguin. Ills. 352 pp. map. SftCvr. $6.50

LEVINE, Isaac Don. *Stalin.* 1931. New York. Cosmopolitan. 421 pp. G $6.00

LEVY, D.A. *No Parking.* 1972. Madison. 1st ed. wrappers. EX $15.00

LEVY, D.A. *Stone Sarcophagus.* Madison. Radical America. wrappers. VG $15.00

LEVY, D.A. *The Beginning of Sunny Dawn & Red Lady.* 1969. San Francisco. Ltd. ed. 1/500. EX $20.00

LEVY, H. *Chinese Footbinding.* 1966. New York. Ills. dj. EX $12.50

LEVY, Harriet. *920 Farrell Street.* 1947. Doubleday. Ills. VG $10.00

LEW, Robert L. *The Parties & the Men.* 1898. 546 pp. VG $10.00

LEWES, George H. *On Actors & the Art of Acting.* 1892. New York. 237 pp. $12.50

LEWIN, Michael Z. *Ask the Right Question.* 1972. London. Hamish Hamilton. 1st ed. dj. $40.00

LEWIN, Michael Z. *Night Cover.* 1976. London. Hamish Hamilton. 1st ed. dj. $35.00

LEWIN, Michael Z. *Outside In.* 1980. Knopf. dj. EX $17.50

LEWIN, Michael Z. *The Enemies Within.* 1974. New York. Knopf. 1st ed. dj. EX $25.00

LEWIN, Michael Z. *The Way We Die Now.* 1973. New York. Putnam. 1st ed. dj. EX $40.00

LEWINSHON, R. *Animals, Men, & Myths.* 1954. Harper. Ills. 1st ed. 422 pp. dj. EX $10.00

LEWINSOHN, Dr. Richard. *Basil Zaharoff Munitions King.* 1934. London. Lippincott. ex-lib 241 pp. G $4.50

LEWIS, A.W. *Basic Bookbinding.* 1957. VG $2.00

LEWIS, Alfred A. *The Mountain Artisans Quilting Book.* 1974. Ills. 4th ed. VG $18.00

LEWIS, Andrew. *Orderly Book of Army Stationed at Williamsburg.* 1860. Richmond. Ltd. 1st ed. 1/100. $225.00

LEWIS, B.R. *The Shakespeare Documents.* 1940. Stanford. 2 vol set. VG $75.00

LEWIS, Benjamin. *Riding.* 1939. Garden City. 141 pp. 185 photos. dj. $52.50

LEWIS, C. *Noah & Waters.* 1st English ed. dj. VG $50.00

LEWIS, C. Day. *Christmas Eve.* 1954. London. 1st ed. $10.00

LEWIS, C.L. *David Glasgow Farragut.* 1941. 372pp. $12.50

LEWIS, C.S. *Abolition of Man.* 1947. Macmillan. 1st ed. dj. EX $20.00

LEWIS, C.S. *The Case for Christianity.* 1943. Macmillan. 1st Am. ed. dj. VG $45.00

LEWIS, C.S. *The Four Loves.* 1960. London. 1st ed. dj. VG $10.00

LEWIS, C.S. *The Problem of Pain.* 1943. Macmillan. 1st Am. ed. dj. EX $45.00

LEWIS, C.S. *The World's Last Night.* 1960. Harcourt. 1st Am. ed. dj. VG $30.00

LEWIS, C.S. *Till We Have Faces.* 1956. Bles. 1st ed. dj. VG $75.00

LEWIS, E.W. *Motor Memories.* 1947. Detroit. sgn. $12.50

LEWIS. *Trader Horn.* 1927. Garden City. 302 pp. $6.50

LEWIS, Flora. *Red Dawn: Story of Noel Field.* 1965. Garden City. Doubleday. 283 pp. VG $10.00

LEWIS, Franklin. *The Cleveland Indians.* 1949. Putnam. Ills. 276 pp. EX $6.50

LEWIS, G.W. *The Ape I Knew.* 1961. Caxton. Ills. 263 pp. VG $16.00

LEWIS, Harry R. *Poultry Keeping.* 1915. Philadelphia. Lippincott. TB. 365 pp. VG $4.50

LEWIS, Henry. *The Valley of the Mississippi Illustrated.* 1967. St.Paul. Ltd. ed. 1/2000. color pls. $75.00

LEWIS, Hunter & Allison, D. *The Real World War.* 1982. New York. 276 pp. dj. $4.50

LEWIS, John F. *The Redemption of the Lower.* 1924. Philadelphia. Ills. sgn. 171 pp. EX $50.00

LEWIS, L. Sherman. *Fighting Prophet.* 1932. New York. Harcourt Brace. Ills. 1st ed. $10.00

LEWIS, Matthew Gregory. *Journal of West India Proprietor.* 1834. London. 1st ed. VG $125.00

LEWIS, Matthew Gregory. *The Monk.* 1913. London. Ills. R.C. Armour. sole ed. VG $60.00

LEWIS, Michael. *Armada Guns: Comparative Study of Eng. & Spanish.* 1961. Allen & Unwin. 1st printing. 243 pp. dj. $22.50

LEWIS, Michael. *The History of the British Navy.* 1959. dj. G $12.50

LEWIS, Noland. *Pyromania Pathological Firesetting.* 1951. 1st ed. dj. $17.50

LEWIS, Oscar & Hall, Carroll. *Bonanza Inn.* 1939. New York. Ills. 1st ed. dj. VG $20.00

LEWIS, Oscar & Hall, Carroll. *Bonanza Inn. America's First Luxury Hotel.* 1940. New York. $10.00

LEWIS, Oscar. *Silver Kings.* 1947. New York. 1st ed. 286 pp. $12.50

LEWIS, Oscar. *The Children of Sanchez.* 1961. Random House. 1st ed. dj. $4.50

LEWIS, R.W.B. *Edith Wharton, a Biography.* 1975. New York. Harper. Ills. 1st ed. 592 pp. $10.00

LEWIS, Roy Harley. *Antiquarian Books.* 1978. London. David & Charles. 1st ed. dj. $15.00

LEWIS, Sinclair. *Ann Vickers.* 1933. New York. Doubleday Doran. 562 pp. $27.50

LEWIS, Sinclair. *Arrowsmith.* 1925. New York. Grosset & Dunlap. 448 pp. $27.50

LEWIS, Sinclair. *Babbitt.* 1922. New York. $27.50

LEWIS, Sinclair. *Cass Timberlane.* 1945. New York. Random House. 390 pp. dj. $25.00

LEWIS, Sinclair. *Cheap & Contented Labor.* 1929. Scripps-Howard. 1st ed. 2nd state. scarce. VG $60.00

LEWIS, Sinclair. *Dodsworth.* 1929. New York. Harcourt Brace. 377 pp. $27.50

LEWIS, Sinclair. *Gideon Planish.* 1943. New York. World. 438 pp. $25.00

LEWIS, Sinclair. *God Seeker.* 1949. Random House. 1st ed. dj. VG $17.50

LEWIS, Sinclair. *It Can't Happen Here.* 1935. New York. 1st ed. VG $10.00

LEWIS, Sinclair. *Kingsblood Royal.* 1947. New York. 1st ed. $25.00

LEWIS, Sinclair. *Selected Stories of Sinclair Lewis.* 1937. Garden City. Doubleday. 426 pp. $5.00

LEWIS, Sinclair. *The Prodigal Parents.* 1938. $27.50

LEWIS, Sinclair. *Trail of the Hawk.* 1915. Harper. Rockwell frontispiece. G $25.00

LEWIS, Sinclair. *Work of Art.* 1934. New York. Doubleday Doran. 452 pp. $30.00

LEWIS, Sinclair. *Work of Art.* 1934. 1st ed. dj. EX $35.00

LEWIS, Thomas M.V. & Kneberg. *Tribes That Slumber.* 1958. Knoxville, TN. Ills. Kneberg. 1st ed. 196 pp. $15.00

LEWIS, W. *Human Age.* 1st Eng. ed. dj. VG $45.00

LEWIS, W. *Wild Body.* Ltd. ed. 1/276. $35.00

LEWIS, William Draper. *The Life of Theodore Roosevelt.* 1919. 544 pp. $10.00

LEWIS, William S. *Reminiscences of Joseph H. Boyd.* 1924. Seattle. Ills. Ltd. 1st ed. wrappers. $100.00

LEWIS, Wilmarth. *Collector's Progress.* 1951. New York. 1st ed. dj. VG $12.50

LEWIS, Wilmarth. *Collector's Progress.* 1952. London. Constable. 1st Eng. ed. dj. VG $20.00

LEWIS, Wilmarth. *The Yale Collections.* 1946. New Haven. Yale U. Pr. 54 pp. VG $20.00

LEWIS, Wyndham. *The Stuffed Owl.* 1930. London. Ills. 1st ed. VG $35.00

LEWIS & CLARK. *History of Expedition to Sources of Missouri.* 1814. Philadelphia. Ills. 1st ed. 2 vol set. VG $2,250.00

LEWIS & CLARK. *Journals of Lewis & Clark.* 1962. Heritage Press. 2 vol set. boxed. VG $42.50

LEWIS & CLARK. *Travels in the Interior of America.* 1807. London. 1st Eng. ed. EX $575.00

LEWIS & CLARK. *Travels to the Source of the Mississippi River.* 1814. London. 1st Eng. ed. 663 pp. fld map. $1,875.00

LEWIS & CLARK. *Travels to the Source of the Missouri River.* 1815. London. Ills. 6 maps. 3 vol set. $1,100.00

LEWISOHN, Ludwig. *Expression in America.* 1932. New York. Harper. 624 pp. $4.00

LEWISOHN, Ludwig. *Upstream: An American Chronicle.* 1926. Modern Library. G $7.50

LEY, W. *Dawn of Zoology.* 1968. Prentice Hall. Ills. 280 pp. VG $6.00

LEY, W. *Salamanders & Other Wonders.* 1955. Viking. Ills. 293 pp. dj. VG $7.50

LEY. *Dragons in Amber.* 1951. New York. 328 pp. dj. $15.00

LEYENDECKER, Hilary M. *Problems & Policy in Public Assistance.* 1955. New York. Harper. 400 pp. dj. $4.50

LHEVINNE, Isadore. *The Enchanted Jungle.* 1933. Ills. 1st ed. $12.50

LHOTE. *Search for the Tassili Frescoes.* 1959. Dutton. VG $15.00

LI CHIH-CHANG. *The Travels of an Alchemist.* 1963. London. trans. Arthur Waley. 166 pp. $45.00

LIANG-YU, Lin. *Chinese Enamel Ware, Its History, Authentication.* 1978. Taipei. Ills. 1st ed. sgn. EX $26.00

LIANG-YU, Lin. *Great Age of Western Philosophy.* 1957. New York. 6 vol set. slipcase. EX $48.00

LIBBY, Bill. *Pro Hockey Heroes of Today.* 1974. Random House. Ills. EX $10.00

LIBERMAN, A. *Artist in His Studio.* 1960. New York. inscr. dj. $100.00

LIBRARY OF CONGRESS *Correspondence of G. Washington with Congress.* 1906. Washington Ills. 741 pp. $27.50

LICHTENBERG, Jacqueline. *Mahogany Trinrose.* 1981. Garden City. review copy. dj. EX $12.50

LICHTENSTEIN, Grace. *A Long Way Baby.* 1974. dj. $5.50

LIDDELL, T.H. *China; Its Marvel & Mystery.* 1909. London. 40 color pls. $47.50

LIDE, Alice & Johansen, M.A. *Thord Firetooth.* 1937. Boston/NY. Ills. 1st ed. $15.00

LIEB, Frederick G. *The Boston Red Sox.* 1947. Putnam. Ills. 257 pp. $6.50

LIEBER, Francis. *On Civil Liberty & Self-Government.* 1859. Philadelphia. enlarged 1 vol ed. 629 pp. $15.00

LIEBERMAN, William S. *Pablo Picasso: Blue & Rose Periods.* 1969. New York. Abrams. color pls. dj. $10.00

LIEBERSON. *J.F.K. as We Knew Him.* 1965. $28.00

LIEGEG, J. *Animal Chemistry.* 1845. Philadelphia. 111 pp. $45.00

LIERS, E.E. *An Otter's Story.* 1953. Jr. Literary Guild. Ills. 191 pp. VG $6.00

LIGGETT, Walter. *Pioneers of Justice.* 1930. New York. Macaulay. ex-lib. 249 pp. $27.50

LIGHT, R.U. *Focus on Africa.* 1944. reprint. VG $35.00

LILIENTHAL, David. *This I Do Believe, an American Credo.* 1949. New York. Harper. 208 pp. dj. $3.50

LILLIE, Lucy C. *A Family Dilemma.* 1894. Philadelphia. 314 pp. $3.50

LILLINGSTON, Luke. *Reflection on Mr. Burchet's Memoirs.* 1704. London. 1st ed. 171 pp. VG $275.00

LILLISH. *Stained Glass of Saint-Pere de Chartes.* 1978. Wesleyan. $15.00

LILLY, J.C. *Man & Dolphin.* 1961. Doubleday. Ills. 1st ed. 312 pp. dj. EX $7.00

LIMA, Almeida P. *Cerebral Angiography.* 1950. Oxford Press. Ills. 1st ed. $110.00

LIMBOUR, Georges. *Tableau Bon Levain a Vous de Cuire La Pate.* 1953. Paris. Ltd. ed. 1/1000. VG $45.00

LIN, Tsuifeng. *Secrets of Chinese Cooking.* New York. Bonanza Books. VG $5.00

LINCOLN, A, & Stein, M. *Abe Lincoln's Jokes.* 1943. Chicago. 159 pp. VG $4.00

LINCOLN, Almira. *Familiar Lectures on Botany.* 1832. Hartford. Huntington Pub. Ills. G $15.00

LINCOLN, Joseph C. *All Alongshore Cape Cod Characters.* 1941. New York. Blue Ribbon Books. dj. VG $20.00

LINCOLN, Joseph C. *C.Y. Whittaker's Place.* 1908. New York. Grosset & Dunlap. 403 pp. $8.00

LINCOLN, Joseph C. *Cape Cod Ballads & Other Verse.* 1902. Trenton. 1st ed. 198 pp. VG $70.00

LINCOLN, Joseph C. *Cape Cod Ballads.* 1902. Brandt. 1st ed. $65.00

LINCOLN, Joseph C. *Captain Dan's Daughter.* 1914. New York. $30.00

LINCOLN, Joseph C. *Captain Eri. A Story of the Coast.* 1904. New York. Harper. Ills. 1st ed. 379 pp. $85.00

LINCOLN, Joseph C. *Captain Eri. A Story of the Coast.* 1904. New York. Barnes. Ills. 1st ed. 397 pp. $85.00

LINCOLN, Joseph C. *Kent Knowles: Quahaug.* 1914. New York. 451 pp. $7.50

LINCOLN, Joseph C. *Keziah Coffin.* 1909. New York. Grosset & Dunlap. 387 pp. $20.00

LINCOLN, Joseph C. *Mr. Pratt.* 1911. New York. $30.00

LINCOLN, Joseph C. *Mr. Pratt's Patients.* 1913. New York. A.L. Burt. 345 pp. $10.00

LINCOLN, Joseph C. *Our Village.* 1909. New York. Appleton. Ills. 1st ed. VG $65.00

LINCOLN, Joseph C. *Queer Dudson.* 1925. New York. A.L. Burt. 362 pp. VG $3.50

LINCOLN, Joseph C. *Rugged Water.* 1924. New York. 1st ed. $30.00

LINCOLN, Joseph C. *Shavings.* 1918. New York. $27.50

LINCOLN, Joseph C. *Silas Bradford's Boy.* 1928. New York. Appleton. 1st ed. G $12.50

LINCOLN, Joseph C. *The 'Old Home House.'* 1907. New York. Barnes. Ills. 1st ed. 291 pp. $30.00

LINCOLN, Joseph C. *The 'Old Home House.'* 1907. New York. Barnes. 1st ed. 3rd printing. $30.00

LINCOLN, Joseph C. *The Bradshaws of Harniss.* 1943. New York. 1st ed. 379 pp. $30.00

LINCOLN, Joseph C. *The Postmaster.* 1912. New York. $30.00

LINCOLN, Joseph C. *The Woman-Haters.* 1911. New York. $30.00

LINCOLN, Mrs. D.A. *Mrs. Lincoln's Boston Cook Book.* 1889. Boston. $25.00

LINCOLN, William E. *John Larkin Lincoln, 1817-1891.* 1983. New York. 1st ed. $25.00

LINCOLN ELECTRIC CO. *New Lessons in Arc Welding.* 1951. 312 pp. $3.00

LINCOLN. *Boston Cookbook.* 1915. scarce. $15.00

LINCOLN. *Collected Works of Abraham Lincoln.* 1953. Rutgers U. Press. 9 vol set. $100.00

LINDAUER, Gottfried. *Pictures of Old New Zealand.* 1930. Auckland. Ills. 214 pp. $25.00

LINDBERGH, Anne Morrow. *Listen! The Wind.* 1938. New York. 1st ed. 275 pp. dj. $12.50

LINDBERGH, Anne Morrow. *North to the Orient.* 1935. New York. maps by Charles Lindbergh. $25.00

LINDBERGH, Anne Morrow. *North to the Orient.* 1935. New York. 1st ed. dj. VG $25.00

LINDBERGH, Anne. *Gift from the Sea.* 1955. Pantheon. Ills. 120 pp. VG $7.00

LINDBERGH, Charles A. *Of Flight & Life.* 1948. New York. 1st ed. 56 pp. dj. $20.00

LINDBERGH, Charles A. *The Spirit of St. Louis.* 1953. New York. Scribner. photos. 562 pp. dj. $6.50

LINDBERGH, Charles A. *Wartime Journals of Charles A. Lindbergh.* 1970. New York. Ills. map. 1038 pp. dj. $7.50

LINDBERGH, Charles A. *We.* 1927. New York. 1st ed. sgn. dj. VG $100.00

LINDBLAD, J. *Journey to the Red Birds.* 1969. Hill Wang. Ills. 176 pp. dj. EX $15.00

LINDEN, Margaret. *Pasha the Persian.* 1936. Kendall. Ills. Milt Gross. 1st ed. VG $45.00

LINDERMAN, Frank B. *American. Life Story of a Great Indian.* 1930. New York. EX $25.00

LINDERMAN, Frank B. *Indian Why Stories.* 1915. New York. Ills. Charles Russell. 1st ed. $75.00

LINDERMAN. *American: Life Story of a Great Indian.* 1930. Ills. Stoops Day. EX $27.50

LINDGREN, Ernest. *The Art of the Film.* 1948. London. VG $9.00

LINDLEY, K. *Graves & Graveyards.* 1972. London. dj. EX $15.00

LINDNER, Robert. *Explorations in Psychoanalysis/Tribute to T. Reik.* 1953. Julian Press. 1st ed. dj. $8.50

LINDSAY, Howard & Crouse, R. *Life with Father.* 1940. New York. Knopf. Ills. 1st ed. 208 pp. $7.50

LINDSAY, Jack. *Aristophanes: Ecclesiazusai/Women in Parliament.* 1929. London. Ills. Ltd. ed. sgn. VG $175.00

LINDSAY, Jack. *Helen Comes of Age.* 1928. Fanfrolico Pr. Ltd. ed. 1/500. sgn. VG $60.00

LINDSAY, Jack. *J.M.W. Turner, His Life & Work.* 1966. New York. 1st ed. dj. VG $10.00

LINDSAY, Norman. *Madam Lifes' Lover.* Fanfrolico Press. VG $45.00

LINDSAY, Vachel. *Candle in the Cabin.* 1926. New York. Appleton. dj. VG $65.00

LINDSAY, Vachel. *Daniel Jazz & Other Poems.* 1920. London. 1st ed. $30.00

LINDSAY, Vachel. *Every Soul Is a Circus.* 1929. Macmillan. 1st ed. G $20.00

LINDSAY, Vachel. *General William Booth.* 1921. New York. sgn. VG $50.00

LINDSAY, Vachel. *The Golden Book of Springfield.* 1920. New York. 1st ed. dj. EX $95.00

LINDSAY. *Inveraray & the Dukes of Argyll.* 1973. Edinburgh. $20.00

LINDSAY. *The Story Teller.* 1915. Lathrop, Lee & Shephard. Ills. $4.50

LINDSEY, Merrill. *100 Great Guns; Illustrated History of Firearms.* Ills. 379 pp. sgn. dj. $50.00

LINDSEY, T.J. *Ohio at Shiloh.* 1903. Cincinnati. 1st ed. map. EX $35.00

LINDUSKA, J.P. *Waterfowl Tomorrow.* 1964. Ills. 770 pp. EX $20.00

LINE, L. & Ricciuti, E.R. *The Audubon Society Book of Wild Cats.* 1985. Abrams. Ills. 256 pp. dj. EX $45.00

LINE, L. & Russell, F. *The Audubon Society Book of Wild Birds.* 1976. Abrams. Ills. 292 pp. dj. EX $22.50

LINEWEAVER, T.H. & Backus, R. *The Natural History of Sharks.* 1975. Lippincott. Ills. 256 pp. dj. VG $12.50

LINGEMAN, Richard R. *Don't You Know There's a War On?* 1970. New York. Putnam. 415 pp. dj. EX $4.00

LINGENFELTER, R.E. *Presses of the Pacific Islands.* 1967. Los Angeles. Plantin Press. Ills. 1st ed. $75.00

LINGLE, Robert & Linford, D. *The Pecos River Commission of New Mexico & Texas.* 1961. Santa Fe. presentation copy. 284 pp. $10.00

LINGLEY, C.R. *Since the Civil War.* 1926. Century. Ills. maps. 730 pp. $8.50

LINK, Suzuki, & Keyes. *Primitive Ukiyoe from J.A. Michener Collection.* 1980. Hawaii. Ills. 322 pp. dj. EX $45.00

LINKLATER. *The Wind on the Moon.* 1944. New York. 1st ed. dj. VG $10.00

LINKLETTER, Art. *The Secret World of Kids.* 1959. 1st ed. 287 pp. dj. $20.00

LINN, John J. *Reminiscences of Fifty Years in Texas.* 1883. New York. 1st ed. $125.00

LINSDALE, Jean. *A Herd of Mule Deer.* 1953. U. of CA. 1st ed. dj. $12.50

LINSKILL, W.T. *Golf.* 1895. London. 3rd ed. VG $75.00

LINSLEY, Leslie. *America's Favorite Quilts.* 1983. New York. Delacorte. Ills. 1st printing. $10.50

LINZEY, A.V. & D.W. *Mammals of the Great Smoky National Park.* 1971. TN U. Press. Ills. 1st ed. 114 pp. $6.00

LIONNI, Leo. *Mouse Days.* 1981. New York. Ills. Lionni. 1st ed. dj. EX $15.00

LIPMAN, Michael. *The Chatterlings in Wordland.* 1935. New York. Ills. Lipman. EX $15.00

LIPMAN, Michael. *The Chatterlings.* 1928. Volland. Ills. 96 pp. boxed. EX $20.00

LIPMAN, Michael. *The Chatterlings.* 1928. Volland. Ills. 3rd printing. VG $20.00

LIPMAN & WINCHESTER. *The Flowering of American Folk Art 1776-1876.* 1974. New York. Ills. 288 pp. $25.00

LIPPINCOTT, Joseph Wharton. *Persimmon Jim the 'Possum.* 1924. Philadelphia. Ills. author. 1st ed. EX $10.00

LIPPINCOTT, William. *Poultry Production.* 1916. New York. Febiger. TB. 517 pp. G $3.50

LIPPMAN, W. *A Preface to Morals.* 1929. 1st ed. $6.50

LIPPMAN, Walter. *The Public Philosophy.* 1955. Boston. 189 pp. dj. VG $6.00

LIPPMAN, Walter. *U.S. Foreign Policy.* 1943. Boston. 344 pp. dj. $30.00

LIPPMAN, Walter. *U.S. Foreign Policy: Shield of the Republic.* 1943. Boston. Little, Brown. 177 pp. $3.50

LIPS. *Savage Hits Back.* 1937. New Haven. VG $20.00

LIPTON, L. *The Holy Barbarians.* 1959. New York. Messner. Ills. 320 pp. VG $12.00

LISH, Gordon. *Peru.* 1986. Dutton. proof copy. wrappers. EX $45.00

LISTER, R.P. *Allotments.* 1985. Andoversford. Whittington Press. Ills. sgn. $45.00

LISTER, Raymond. *The Loyal Blacksmith.* 1957. Cambridge. Ltd. 1st ed. 1/90. sgn. EX $45.00

LISTER. *Earl Morris & Southwestern Archaeology.* 1968. U. of NM Press. 1st ed. VG $15.00

LISTON, Robert. *Great Detectives.* 1966. Platt & Munk. 270 pp. $50.00

LITTAUER, V.S. *Jumping the Horse.* 1931. New York. Derrydale Pr. Ltd. ed. dj. EX $45.00

LITTAUER, V.S. & Kournakoff. *The Defense of the Jump.* 1934. New York. Ills. 1st ed. 142 pp. VG $30.00

LITTELL, Robert. *The Debriefing.* 1979. Harper. 1st ed. dj. VG $12.50

LITTLEJOHN, Bruce. *Laugh with the Judge.* 1974. Lexington, SC. 1st ed. 146 pp. dj. $6.00

LITTLETON, M.W. *Will of the People.* 1914. St.Louis. $8.00

LITVINOFF, B. *A Peculiar People* 1969. New York. EX $10.00

LIU, F.F. *A Military History of Modern China 1924-1949.* 1956. Princeton. 1st ed. 310 pp. dj. EX $15.00

LIVERMORE, Abiel A. *The War with Mexico Reviewed.* 1850. Boston. 298 pp. scarce. $65.00

LIVINGSTONE, David. *Interior of Africa.* 1872. Philadelphia. Ills. VG $25.00

LIVINGSTONE, David. *Last Journals of David Livingstone.* 1875. Harper. VG $25.00

LIVINGSTONE, David. *Missionary Travels & Researches in South Africa.* 1858. New York. 1st Am. ed. 732 pp. $55.00

LIVINGSTONE, David. *Travels & Researches in South Africa.* Philadelphia. Potter. 1st ed. 398 pp. $75.00

LIVINGSTON, Don. *Film & the Director.* 1953. Ills. 1st ed. VG $10.00

LIVINGSTON, Edward. *Project of New Penal Code for State of Louisiana.* 1824. London. 1st Eng. ed. 146 pp. G $275.00

LIVINGSTONE, W.P. *Mary Slessor of Calabar.* 1906. Hodder Stoughton. 347 pp. VG $20.00

LIVINGSTONE-LEARMONTH, David. *The Horse in Art.* 1958. Studio. 1st ed. dj. $15.00

LLEWELLYN, Mervyn. *Initiation & Magic.* 1965. London. 169 pp. dj. $35.00

LLOSA, Mario Vargas. *Aunt Julia & the Scriptwriter.* 1982. New York. Farrar. 1st ed. dj. EX $30.00

LLOSA, Mario Vargas. *Captain Pantoja & the Special Service.* 1978. Cape. 1st English ed. dj. VG $20.00

LLOSA, Mario Vargas. *Conversation in the Cathedral.* 1975. Harper. 1st Am. ed. dj. VG $25.00

LLOSA, Mario Vargas. *The Time of the Hero.* 1966. Grove Press. 1st Am. ed. dj. VG $35.00

LLOSA, Mario Vargas. *The War of the End of the World.* 1984. Farrar. 1st Am. ed. sgn. VG $85.00

LLOYD, Henry D. *A Sovereign People. Study of Swiss Democracy.* 1907. New York. 1st Am. ed. VG $15.00

LLOYD, John. *Productive Vegetable Growing.* 1915. Philadelphia. Lippincott. ex-lib. 339 pp. VG $4.00

LLOYD, John. *Right Side of the Car.* 1897. Ills. VG $35.00

LLOYD, John. *Stringtown on the Pike.* 1900. New York. 1st ed. photos. $25.00

LLOYD, Nelson. *Soldier of the Valley.* 1904. Scribner. Ills. A.B. Frost. G $25.00

LLOYD. *Twin Rivers.* 2nd ed. VG $7.50

LLYWELYN, Morgan. *The Wind from Hastings.* 1978. Boston. Houghton Mifflin. 1st ed. dj. $30.00

LO BELLO, Nino. *The Vatican Empire.* 1968. New York. 1st ed. dj. VG $10.00

LOBEL, Arnold. *Mouse Tales.* 1972. New York. Ills. 1st ed. dj. $15.00

LOBENSTINE, Bell. *Extracts from the Diary of Wm. C. Lobenstine.* 1851. private print. VG $35.00

LOBSTEIN, John Fred. *A Treatise on the Human Sympathetic Nerve.* 1831. Philadelphia. 6 pls. G $45.00

LOCHE, William J. *The Wonderful Year.* 1941. John Lane Co. $5.00

LOCHER, A. *With Star & Crescent.* 1981. Philadelphia. Ills. 634 pp. VG $30.00

LOCHNER, Louis P. *The Goebbels Diaries.* 1948. New York. 1st ed. dj. VG $10.00

LOCHTE, Dick. *Sleeping Dog.* 1985. New York. Arbor House. 1st ed. dj. EX $20.00

LOCKE, J.C. *Englishman in India.* 1930. London. Routledge. Ills. 1st ed. G $15.00

LOCKE, William J. *The Tale of Triona.* 1922. New York. Dodd Mead. 1st ed. 379 pp. EX $25.00

LOCKE. *Guidance Principles of Guided Missile Design.* 1955. 2nd printing. $12.50

LOCKHART, D.G. *Life of Napoleon Bonaparte.* 1897. London. Ills. EX $25.00

LOCKHART, J. *The Men of Cajamarca.* 1972. U. of TX. 496 pp. maps. tables. dj. VG $12.00

LOCKHART, J.G. *Curses, Lucks, & Talismans.* 1938. London. 184 pp. index. G $45.00

LOCKRIDGE, Frances & Richard. *The Judge is Reversed.* 1960. Lippincott. 1st ed. ex-lib. dj. $3.00

LOCKRIDGE, Norman. *Waggish Tales of the Czechs.* 1947. Candide Press. 1st ed. VG $20.00

LOCKRIDGE, Ross Jr. *Raintree County.* 1948. Boston. Houghton Mifflin. 1st ed. dj. $45.00

LOCKWOOD, C. *Tragedy at Honda.* 1960. 1st ed. dj. EX $17.50

LOCKWOOD, Frank C. *Pioneer Days in Arizona.* 1932. New York. Ills. 1st ed. EX $45.00

LOCKWOOD, Frank. *The Law & Lawyers of Pickwick.* 1894. London. Roxburghe Press. 1st ed. $50.00

LOCKWOOD, George B. *The New Harmony Movement.* 1905. New York. Ills. 1st ed. 404 pp. $25.00

LOCKWOOD, L.V. *Colonial Furniture in America.* 1957. New York. Scribner. 2 vol set. $20.00

LOCKWOOD. *Pioneer Days in Arizona.* 1932. New York. 1st ed. VG $65.00

LODGE, Henry Cabot. *Theodore Roosevelt.* 1919. Boston/NY. Ltd. ed. 1/575. sgn. $25.00

LODGE, John. *Descriptive & Ills. Catalog of Chinese Bronzes.* 1946. Smithsonian Institute. 1st ed. $20.00

LODGE, Oliver. *Raymond or Life After Death.* 1916. New York. 404 pp. VG $25.00

LOEDERER, Richard. *Voodoo Fire in Haiti.* Ills. 274 pp. VG $10.00

LOEDHAS, Sorche Nic. *By Loch & by Lin: Tales from Scottish Ballads.* 1969. New York. Ills. Vera Bock. 1st ed. dj. $12.00

LOEHR, A.R.V. *Wiener Medailleure 1899.* 1899. Wien. 1st ed. pls. folio. $45.00

LOENING, Grover C. *Takeoff into Greatness.* 1968. New York. $5.00

LOEWEN, Gertrude. *Crusader for Freedom.* 1969. Nashville, TN. Southern Pub. 227 pp. dj. EX $4.50

LOFTING, H. *The Twilight of Magic.* 1930. London. 1st Eng. ed. $30.00

LOFTING, Hugh. *Doctor Dolittle & the Secret Lake.* 1948. Lippincott. Ills. EX $40.00

LOFTING, Hugh. *Doctor Dolittle in the Moon.* 1928. Stokes. Ills. EX $40.00

LOFTING, Hugh. *Doctor Dolittle in the Moon.* 1928. Lippincott. Ills. 13th impression. EX $20.00

LOFTING, Hugh. *Doctor Dolittle in the Moon.* 1929. London. 1st Eng. ed. 71 pls. $30.00

LOFTING, Hugh. *Doctor Dolittle's Circus.* 1924. New York. Ills. Lofting. 2nd ed. VG $20.00

LOFTING, Hugh. *Doctor Dolittle's Circus.* 1924. Boston. Ills. 18th impression. VG $18.00

LOFTING, Hugh. *Doctor Dolittle's Return.* 1933. New York. Ills. 1st ed. 273 pp. G $12.50

LOFTING, Hugh. *Doctor Dolittle's Caravan.* Stokes. 1st ed. EX $50.00

LOFTING, Hugh. *Gub Gub's Book.* 1932. Stokes. Ills. 1st ed. EX $20.00

LOFTING, Hugh. *Porridge Poetry.* 1924. Stokes. Ills. 95 pp. G $5.50

LOFTING, Hugh. *The Story of Doctor Dolittle.* 1922. New York. Ills. $10.00

LOFTING, Hugh. *The Story of Doctor Dolittle.* 1920. New York. Stokes. 1st ed. VG $40.00

LOFTS, Norah. *Crown of Aloes.* 1974. New York. Doubleday. 317 pp. dj. $3.50

LOFTS, Norah. *The Claw.* 1981. Doubleday. 1st Am. ed. dj. VG $12.50

LOFTS, Norah. *The Concubine.* 1963. New York. Doubleday. 310 pp. $3.50

LOGAN, Harry B. *A Traveler's Guide to North American Gardens.* 1974. New York. Scribner. Ills. 253 pp. dj. $10.00

LOGAN, John A. *The Great Conspiracy: Origin & History.* 1886. Ills. ex-lib. maps. G $25.00

LOGAN, Rayford W. *What the Negro Wants.* 1944. Chapel Hill. ex-lib. 352 pp. VG $6.50

LOGAN, Sheridan A. *Old Saint Jo. Gateway to the West.* 1979. dj. VG $15.00

LOGAN, W.E. *Remarks on Mining Region of Lake Superior.* 1847. Montreal. 31 pp. wrappers. $65.00

LOGIER, E.B.S. *The Reptiles of Ontario.* 1939. Ontario. 63 pp. wrappers. EX $12.50

LOGSDON, Gene. *Small Scale Grain Raising.* 1977. Emmaus, PA. Rodale Press. 305 pp. SftCvr. $3.50

LOGUE, Christopher. *The Weekdream Sonnets.* 1955. Jack Straw. Ills. Tajiri. Ltd. ed. 1/200. $20.00

LOGUE, Christopher. *Wand & Quadrant.* 1954. Ltd. ed. 1/300. wrappers. EX $25.00

LOKHEN, Roscoe L. *Iowa Public Land Disposal.* 1942. Iowa City. $25.00

LOMAS, Steve. *Fishing Fleet Boy.* 1962. $5.00

LOMASK, Milton. *Aaron Burr.* 1979. Farrar & Straus. 1st printing. $8.50

LOMAX, Alan. *The Rainbow Sign.* 1959. New York. 1st ed. dj. EX $20.00

LOMAX, Elizabeth L. *Leaves from an Old Washington Diary 1854-1863.* 1943. Dutton. 1st ed. dj. $5.50

LOMAX, John A. *Songs of Cattle Trail & Cow Camp.* 1927. New York. G $15.00

LOMAX, John A. *The Adventures of a Ballad Hunter.* 1947. New York. 1st ed. dj. VG $35.00

LOMAX. *Fight for Sweetwater.* Pocketbook. pb. $3.00

LOMEN, Carl J. *Fifty Years in Alaska.* 1954. McKay. dj. VG $22.50

LONDON, Hannah R. *Miniatures of Early American Jews.* 1953. Springfield. Ltd. ed. sgn. EX $150.00

LONDON, Hannah R. *Shades of My Forefathers.* 1941. Springfield. Ltd. ed. sgn. EX $135.00

LONDON, Jack. *A Cry for Justice: Anthological Social Protest.* Sinclair. wrappers. VG $15.00

LONDON, Jack. *Adventure.* 1st Eng. ed. VG $125.00

LONDON, Jack. *Before Adam.* 1907. New York. 1st ed. VG $35.00

LONDON, Jack. *Best Short Stories.* 1949. $20.00

LONDON, Jack. *His Best Short Stories.* 1945. Dial Press. 1st collected ed. dj. VG $12.50

LONDON, Jack. *Jerry of the Islands.* 1917. New York. Macmillan. 1st ed. VG $95.00

LONDON, Jack. *John Barleycorn.* 1913. Century. 1st ed. dj. VG $50.00

LONDON, Jack. *Love of Life & Other Stories.* 1907. New York. Macmillan. 1st ed. 265 pp. VG $55.00

LONDON, Jack. *Love of Life.* 1915. $30.00

LONDON, Jack. *Moon Face.* 1906. Macmillan. 1st ed. VG $145.00

LONDON, Jack. *Smoke Bellew.* 1953. New York. $30.00

LONDON, Jack. *Smoke Bellew.* 1912. New York. Ills. 1st ed. 385 pp. $50.00

LONDON, Jack. *South Sea Tales.* 1946. New York. G $7.00

LONDON, Jack. *The Call of the Wild.* 1914. New York. $28.00

LONDON, Jack. *The Call of the Wild.* 1960. Racine. Whitman. 219 pp. $7.50

LONDON, Jack. *The Call of the Wild.* 1903. New York. 1st ed. VG $45.00

LONDON, Jack. *The Faith of Men.* 1904. New York. $30.00

LONDON, Jack. *The Game.* 1905. New York. 1st ed. 1st issue. VG $20.00

LONDON, Jack. *The Iron Heel.* 1932. London. Mills & Boon. Ltd. ed. 292 pp. $45.00

LONDON, Jack. *The Sea Wolf.* 1st ed. white lettering. G $25.00

LONDON, Jack. *The Sea Wolf.* 1st ed. gilt decor. $85.00

LONDON, Jack. *The Son of the Wolf.* Grosset & Dunlap. 251 pp. EX $6.50

LONDON, Jack. *The Son of the Wolf.* 1900. Boston. 1st ed. grey cloth. G $175.00

LONDON, Jack. *The Star Rover.* 1917. New York. dj. G $25.00

LONDON, Jack. *Valley of the Moon.* 1913. New York. Macmillan. 1st ed. EX $175.00

LONDON, Jack. *War of the Classes.* 1912. $30.00

LONDON, Jack. *White Fang.* 1933. $30.00

LONDON, Jack. *White Fang.* 1906. Macmillan. Ills. Chas. L. Bull. 1st ed. $50.00

LONDON, Jack. *White Fang.* 1907. London. 1st Eng. ed. VG $120.00

LONDON, Joan. *Jack London & His Times.* 1939. New York. Book League. 1st ed. VG $10.00

LONDON MUSEUM. *Costume.* 1935. London. Ills. G $10.00

LONG, Daniel. *Pittsburgh Memoranda.* 1935. Santa Fe. Ltd. ed. 1/1000. sgn. 87 pp. $45.00

LONG, Dennis. *Growth & Development Pennsylvania R.R. 1846-1926.* 1927. $17.50

LONG, Erica. *Fanny.* 1980. dj. EX $5.00

LONG, Frank Belknap. *In Mayan Splendor.* 1977. Sauk City. 1st ed. 66 pp. dj. EX $10.00

LONG, Frank Belknap. *John Carstairs: Space Detective.* 1949. New York. 1st ed. dj. EX $25.00

LONG, Frank Belknap. *The Horror from the Hills.* 1963. Sauk City. Arkham House. dj. $60.00

LONG, Frank Belknap. *The Hounds of Tindalos.* 1946. Sauk City. Arkham House. $125.00

LONG, Frank Belknap. *The Hounds of Tindalos.* Arkham House. 1st ed. dj. VG $75.00

LONG, Huey P. *Every Man a King.* 1933. 1st ed. $10.00

LONG, John. *Voyages & Travels of Indian Intrepreter & Trader.* 1791. London. 1st ed. 295 pp. fld map. EX $985.00

LONG, Katherine W. *Yuma from Hell-Hole to Heaven.* 1950. Yuma. Ills. 61 pp. SftCvr. $10.00

LONG, Margaret. *Shadow of the Arrow.* 1950. Caldwell. Caxton. 2nd ed. dj. EX $12.50

LONG, Mason. *The Life of Mason Long, the Converted Gambler.* 1878. Chicago. Donnelley, Loyd & Co. 256 pp. $35.00

LONG, Mason. *The Life of Mason Long, the Converted Gambler.* 1883. VG $15.00

LONG, Ray. *My Favorite Story.* 1928. New York. 290 pp. $3.00

LONG, William. *School of the Woods: Studies of Animal Instincts.* 1903. Boston. Ginn. Ills. Copeland. VG $17.50

LONG, William. *Wilderness Ways.* 1901. Boston. Ginn. Ills. Copeland. $5.00

LONGFELLOW, Henry Wadsworth. *Best Loved Poems by Henry Wadsworth Longfellow.* 1949. Chicago. Peoples Book Club. 372 pp. dj. $4.00

LONGFELLOW, Henry Wadsworth. *Favorite Poems of Henry Wadsworth Longfellow.* 1947. New York. Doubleday. Ills. Wilson. dj. $4.00

LONGFELLOW, Henry Wadsworth. *Keramos & Other Poems.* 1878. Boston. 1st ed. VG $40.00

LONGFELLOW, Henry Wadsworth. *Longfellow's Works.* 1866. Houghton Mifflin. 14 vol set. $55.00

LONGFELLOW, Henry Wadsworth. *Tales of a Wayside Inn.* 1863. Boston. 1st ed. G $22.00

LONGFELLOW, Henry Wadsworth. *The Complete Poetical Works.* Boston. (ca.1893) 5 vol set. EX $40.00

LONGFELLOW, Henry Wadsworth. *The Courtship of Miles Standish & Other Poems.* 1858. Ticknor & Fields. 1st Am. ed. $50.00

LONGFELLOW, Henry Wadsworth. *The Courtship of Miles Standish.* London. 1st English ed. VG $225.00

LONGFELLOW, Henry Wadsworth. *The Divine Tragedy.* 1871. Boston. 1st ed. VG $35.00

LONGFELLOW, Henry Wadsworth. *The New England Tragedies.* 1868. Boston. 1st ed. VG $25.00

LONGFELLOW, Henry Wadsworth. *The New England Tragedies.* 1868. Boston. 1st ed. 1st issue. EX $50.00

LONGFELLOW, Henry Wadsworth. *The Poetical Works of Longfellow.* 1865. Boston. Ills. sgn. EX $285.00

LONGFELLOW, Henry Wadsworth. *The Seaside & the Fireside.* 1850. Boston. 1st ed. VG $80.00

LONGFELLOW, Henry Wadsworth. *The Song of Hiawatha.* 1899. New York. Ills. Merrill & Copeland. VG $20.00

LONGFELLOW, Henry Wadsworth. *The Song of Hiawatha.* 1911. Boston/NY. Ills. Parrish/Remington/Wyeth. $50.00

LONGFELLOW, Henry Wadsworth. *The Song of Hiawatha.* 1909. Chicago. Ills. John R. Neill. 208 pp. $75.00

LONGFELLOW, Henry Wadsworth. *The Story of Evangeline.* 1913. New York. Ills. Maria Kirk & G. Hood. VG $45.00

LONGFELLOW, Henry Wadsworth. *The Story of Evangeline.* 1905. Bobbs Merrill. Ills. Christy. $17.50

LONGHURST, Henry. *My Life & Soft Times.* 1971. London. 1st ed. dj. EX $45.00

LONGMATE, N. *Air Raid. The Bombing of Coventry. 1940.* 1978. Ills. dj. EX $15.00

LONGRIDGE. *Cutty Shark.* 1973. 2 vol in 1. 5 pls. VG $15.00

LONGSTAFF, T. *This is My Voyage.* 1950. Scribner. Ills. maps. 324 pp. dj. VG $20.00

LONGSTREET, J. *From Manassas to Appomattox.* 1960. Indianapolis. 1st ed. $25.00

LONGSTREET, Stephen & Ethel. *The Joys of Jewish Cooking.* 1978. New York. Weathervane. 1st ed. dj. VG $7.50

LONGSTREET, Stephen & Ethel. *Yoshiwara: City of the Senses.* 1970. Ills. 224 pp. dj. sl wear. $44.00

LONGSTREET, Stephen. *A Century on Wheels. Story of Studebaker.* 1952. New York. Ills. $30.00

LONGSTREET, Stephen. *The Drawings of Hokusai.* 1969. Borden. Ills 1st ed. $25.00

LONGSTREET, Stephen. *The Wilder Shore.* 1968. Doubleday. Ills. 1st ed. dj. VG $7.50

LONGSTREET, Stephen. *War Cries on Horseback.* 1970. New York. Ills. 335 pp. dj. $10.00

LONGSTREET, Stephen. *We All Went to Paris.* 1972. New York. Macmillan. 1st printing. $25.00

LONGSTRETH, T.M. *Quebec Montreal & Ottawa.* 1933. New York. 1st printing. photos. maps. VG $18.00

LONGSTRETH, T.M. *The Adirondacks.* 1917. 1st ed. $5.00

LOOK. *Look at America.* Boston. Houghton Mifflin. 344 pp. $5.00

LOOK. *Story of the FBI, Official Picture History.* 1947. New York. Ills. 1st ed. sgn. Hoover. G $27.50

LOOK. *The Far West: Handbook in Pictures, Maps & Text.* 1948. Boston. Houghton Mifflin. 402 pp. $2.50

LOOKER, Earle. *The White House Gang.* 1929. New York. presentation copy. sgn. VG $15.00

LOOKER, Earle. *The White House Gang.* 1929. New York. Revell. Ills. J.M. Flagg. $12.50

LOOMIS, Alfred F. *The Great Blue-Water Yacht Races 1866-1935.* 1967. New York. Ills. reprint. dj. $20.00

LOOMIS, Alfred F. *Yachts Under Sail.* 1933. 1st ed. photos. VG $14.00

LOOMIS, Andrew. *Drawing on the Head & Hands.* 1956. Viking. 1st ed. 154 pp. dj. VG $35.00

LOOMIS, C.P. & Beegle, J.A. *Rural Sociology & the Strategy of Change.* 1957. Eng. Cliffs. Prentis Hall. TB. 488 pp. VG $4.00

LOOMIS, Leander. *A Journal of the Birmingham Emigrating Co.* 1928. $35.00

LOOMIS, N.M. *Wells Fargo.* 1968. Ills. 1st ed. dj. G $10.00

LOOMIS. *West to the Sun.* Gold Medal. pb. $3.00

LOOMS, George. *John No-Brawn.* 1925. New York. Doubleday. 1st ed. 320 pp. EX $37.50

LOOS, Anita. *A Mouse is Born.* 1951. New York. Doubleday. 1st ed. dj. 214 pp. $17.50

LOOS, Anita. *Gentlemen Prefer Blondes.* 1925. Boni & Liveright. Ills. $4.50

LOOS, Anita. *Kiss Hollywood Good-Bye.* 1974. New York. 1st ed. $6.50

LOOTENS, J.G. *Photo Enlarging & Print Quality.* 1945. dj. VG $12.50

LOPEZ, B. *Of Wolves & Men.* 1978. Scribner. Ills. 309 pp. dj. EX $20.00

LOPEZ, Barry. *Arctic Dreams.* Book Club ed. dj. VG $10.00

LOPEZ, Claude-Anne. *Mon Cher Papa. Franklin & the Ladies of Paris.* 1966. Yale U. Press. $10.00

LOPEZ. *Three Ages of the Italian Renaissance.* 1970. U. of VA. $6.00

LOPEZ-RAY, Manuel. *Crime, an Analytical Appraisal.* 1970. New York. 277 pp. dj. $10.00

LOPUKHIN, I.V. *Some Characteristics of the Interior Church.* 1912. London. trans. Nicholson. 1st ed. VG $35.00

LORAC, E.C.R. *Murder by Matchlight.* 1945. London. Collins. 1st ed. dj. VG $20.00

LORAND, Arnold, M.D. *Old Age Deferred.* 1911. Philadelphia. 3rd ed. 480 pp. VG $15.00

LORANGER, Phil. *If They Played Hockey in Heaven.* 1976. Marjoguyhen Pub. SftCvr. EX $8.50

LORANT, Stefan. *Lincoln. Life in Photographs.* 1941. 1st ed. dj. EX $17.50

LORANT, Stefan. *The New World: First Pictures of America.* 1946. New York. 1st ed. dj. VG $40.00

LORD, Beman. *Rough Ice.* 1963. New York. 64 pp. juvenile fiction. EX $3.00

LORD, Esabel Ely. *The Household Cookbook.* 1936. New York. 1st ed. VG $12.00

LORD, Frances A. *Civil War Collector's Encyclopedia.* 1965. 358 pp. $4.50

LORD, John, L.L.D. *Beacon Lights of History. Vol. 5, Great Women.* 1887. New York. w/gilt decor. VG $4.00

LORD, Russell. *The Wallaces of Iowa.* 1947. Boston. $25.00

LORD, W. *The Fremantle Diary.* 1954. 1st ed. $10.00

LORD, Walter. *A Night to Remember.* 1955. New York. 1st ed. dj. $15.00

LORD, Walter. *Day of Infamy.* 1957. New York. Holt. photos. 243 pp. dj. $5.00

LORD, Walter. *Incredible Victory.* 1967. New York. Harper & Row. 331 pp. VG $7.50

LORD & FOLEY. *The Folk Arts & Crafts of New England.* 1965. New York. Ills. 1st ed. sgns. $25.00

LORD. *Lonely Vigil. Coastwatchers of the Solomons.* 1977. Ills. dj. VG $9.00

LORENTE, Sebastian. *Historia Antigua del Peru.* 1860. Lima. 341 pp. $45.00

LORENZ, J.D. *Jerry Brown, Man on the White Horse.* 1978. Boston. 267 pp. dj. EX $6.00

LORENZ, K.Z. *The Year of the Greylag Goose.* 1978. Harcourt Brace. Ills. 1st ed. 199 pp. dj. EX $10.00

LORIE. *Memoirs of Rev. Walter M. Lorie, Missionary.* 1854. Presbyterian Board Pub. $12.50

LORIMER, George H. *The False Gods.* 1906. New York. Appleton. 1st ed. dj. EX $25.00

LORING, E. *Contraverted Elections of Massachusetts Assembly.* 1886. Boston. 1st ed 550 pp. $25.00

LORRAIN, Alfred. *The Square Rigged Cruiser or Sea Sermons.* 1852. Thompson. $10.00

LOSSING, Benson J. *Biography of James A. Garfield.* 1882. New York. 1st ed. VG $20.00

LOSSING, Benson J. *Pictorial Field Book of the Revolution, Vol. I.* 1850. Harper. Ills. 576 pp. G $47.50

LOSSING, Benson J. *Pictorial Field Book of the Revolution.* 1855. New York. 2nd ed. 2 vol set. $110.00

LOSSING, Benson J. *The Home of Washington.* 1871. New York. G $15.00

LOSSING, Benson J. *Washington & Mount Vernon.* 1859. New York. Ills. 1st ed. VG $50.00

LOTH, David. *The Erotic in Literature.* 1961. London. Secker & Warburg. 1st ed. dj. $25.00

LOTHE, Ada. *The Best from Midwest Kitchens.* New York. Gramercy. 284 pp. $4.00

LOTHROP, S.K. & Mahler, Joy. *Late Nazca Burials in Chavina Peru.* 1957. Peabody Museum. 1st ed. wrappers. $10.00

LOTHROP. *Treasures of Ancient America.* 1964. $59.00

LOTI, Pierre. *The Iceland Fisherman.* New York. Stokes. no date. VG $25.00

LOTZ, W. *Champagne Spy/Israel's Master Spy Tells His Story.* 1972. Ills. dj. VG $7.50

LOUGHBOROUGH, J. *Pacific Telegraph & Railway.* 1849. ex-lib. 2 fld maps. rare. $100.00

LOUNSBERRY, Alice. *A Guide to the Wild Flowers.* 1899. New York. Stokes. Ills. ex-lib. 347 pp. $50.00

LOUYS, Pierre. *Aphrodite Fair.* 1932. New York. Ills. Buttera. 1st ed. 247 pp. $12.50

LOUYS, Pierre. *Aphrodite.* New York. Falstaff Press. Ills. Ltd. ed. $35.00

LOUYS, Pierre. *Aphrodite. Ancient Manners.* 1932. New York. Ills. Buttera. 251 pp. $12.50

LOUYS, Pierre. *Aphrodite. Ancient Manners.* 1928. New York. Ltd ed. 1/100. 284 pp. $7.50

LOUYS, Pierre. *The Collected Tales of Pierre Louys.* 1930. Chicago. Ills. Austen. 293 pp. VG $20.00

LOVE, Donald M. *Henry Churchill King of Oberlin.* 1956. New Haven. 300 pp. dj. $10.00

LOVE, E. *History of First African Baptist Church 1788-1888.* 1888. Savannah. VG $75.00

LOVE, Edmund. *The Situation in Flushing.* 1965. New York. 1st ed. dj. VG $12.00

LOVECHILD, Lawrence. *Aladdin; or, Wonderful Lamp.* 1846. Philadelphia. Ills. 118 pp. VG $25.00

LOVECHILD, Mrs. *Talk About Indians.* Concord. (ca.1850) Ills. wrappers. $35.00

LOVECRAFT, H.P. *At the Mountains of Madness.* 1968. Sauk City. Arkham House. dj. EX $22.50

LOVECRAFT, H.P. *Best Supernatural Stories of H.P. Lovecraft.* 1945. Cleveland. World. 2nd printing. VG $50.00

LOVECRAFT, H.P. *Dagon & Other Macabre Tales.* 1965. Sauk City. Arkham House. 1st ed. dj. EX $50.00

LOVECRAFT, H.P. *Something About Cats & Other Pieces.* 1949. Sauk City. Arkham House. dj. $125.00

LOVECRAFT, H.P. *Supernatural Horror in Literature.* 1945. Abramson. dj. scarce $85.00

LOVECRAFT, H.P. *The Dream Quest of Unknown Kadath.* 1955. Shroud Pub. Ltd. 1st ed. 1/1500. dj. $100.00

LOVECRAFT, H.P. *The Dunwich Horror & Others.* 1963. Sauk City. Arkham. 2nd printing. dj. EX $20.00

LOVECRAFT, H.P. *The Shuttered Room.* 1959. Sauk City. 1st ed. dj. EX $75.00

LOVECRAFT, H.P. *The Weird Shadow over Innsmouth.* 1944. New York. Bart House. wrappers. EX $75.00

LOVECRAFT, H.P. & Derleth, A. *The Lurker at the Threshold.* 1945. Sauk City. Arkham House. 1st ed. dj. $80.00

LOVECRAFT, H.P. & Derleth, A. *The Survivor & Others.* 1957. Sauk City. Arkham House. 1st ed. dj. EX $100.00

LOVECRAFT & DERLETH. *The Lurker at the Threshold.* 1st Am. ed. dj. EX $50.00

LOVELACE, Maud H. *Down Town, a Betsy-Tacy Story.* 1943. New York. Ills. Lois Lenski. 1st ed. VG $10.00

LOVELL, Ernest J. *His Very Self & Voice.* 1954. 1st ed. dj. $8.50

LOVELL, Harold W. *Hope & Help for the Alcoholic.* 1956. Doubleday. $3.00

LOVERIDGE, A. *Reptiles of the Pacific World.* 1946. Macmillan. 259 pp. dj. G $15.00

LOVERIDGE. *Twins in Twain.* 1909. dj. EX $6.50

LOVESEY, P. *The False Inspector.* 1982. Pantheon. 1st Am. ed. dj. EX $7.50

LOVESEY, Peter. *A Case of Spirits.* 1975. London. Macmillan. 1st ed. dj. EX $15.00

LOVESTONE, Jay. *The Government Strikebreaker.* 1923. New York. Workers Party of America. EX $40.00

LOVETT, J. *Old Boston Boys & the Games They Played.* 1906. Boston. Ltd. ed. 1/250. 241 pp. VG $30.00

LOVING, Amory. *The Mountains of Longing.* 1971. San Francisco. photos Philip Evans. dj. EX $30.00

LOVING, J.C. *The Loving Brand Book.* 1965. Austin. Pemberton Press. Ills. 118 pp. $50.00

LOW, Rachael & Manvell, R. *History of the British Film. 1896-1906.* 1948. London. 1st ed. VG $12.50

LOW. *Fishing Is for Me.* 1963. 1st ed. dj. EX $10.00

LOWANCE. *Massachusetts Broadsides of American Revolution.* 1978. MA U. Press. 1st ed. dj. EX $35.00

LOWDERER, R. *Voodoo Fire in Haiti.* 1935. Literary Guild. Ills. 1st ed. 274 pp. VG $15.00

LOWDES, Mrs. Belloc. *The Lodger.* 1913. London. Metheun. 1st ed. G $45.00

LOWE, Belle. *Experimental Cookery.* 1937. Wiley. $4.00

LOWE, Jaques. *Portrait. The Emergence of John F. Kennedy.* 1961. New York. McGraw Hill. 224 pp. dj. VG $6.00

LOWELL, Amy. *John Keats.* Boston/NY. 3rd printing. 2 vol set. dj. $40.00

LOWELL, Amy. *John Keats.* 1925. Boston/NY. Ills. 1st ed. 2 vol set. VG $50.00

LOWELL, Amy. *Pictures of the Floating World.* 1919. New York. 1st ed. sgn. VG $40.00

LOWELL, Amy. *Sword Blades & Poppy Seed.* 1914. New York. Houghton Mifflin. 246 pp. VG $3.00

LOWELL, J.R. *Heartsease & Rue.* 1888. Boston/NY. 1st ed. $65.00

LOWELL, James Russell. *My Study Windows.* 1871. 1st ed. G $30.00

LOWELL, James Russell. *Poems of James Russell Lowell.* 1900. New York. A.L. Burt. 447 pp. G $4.00

LOWELL, James Russell. *Poems.* Altemus. no date. 246 pp. $3.50

LOWELL, R. *For the Union Dead.* 1964. 1st ed. dj. VG $22.50

LOWELL, R. *Life Studies.* 1959. 1st ed. VG $25.00

LOWELL, R. *Notebook: 1967-68.* 1969. Farrar. 1st ed. dj. VG $25.00

LOWELL, R. *Selected Poems.* 1976. New York. Farrar. 1st printing. 243 pp. $15.00

LOWELL, Robert. *The Oresteia of Aeschylus.* 1979. Faber. 1st English ed. dj. VG $20.00

LOWENFELS, W. & McCord, H. *The Life of Fraenkel's Death.* WA State U. 1st ed. wrappers. EX $15.00

LOWENTHAL, M. *A World Passed By.* 1938. New York. 500 pp. index. $12.50

LOWERY, G.H. *Louisiana Birds.* 1974. LA State U. Ills. 651 pp. dj. EX $25.00

LOWERY, G.H. *Louisiana Birds.* 1955. LA State U. Ills. 1st ed. sgn. dj. VG $25.00

LOWES. *Road to Xanadu.* 1931. London. $12.50

LOWIE, R. *Indians of the Plains.* 1954. New York. Ills. 2nd printing. 222 pp. $15.00

LOWIE, Robert. *Culture & Ethnology.* 1917. McMurtrie. 1st ed. $20.00

LOWMAN, Al. *Printing Arts in Texas.* 1975. Ltd. ed. 1/395. EX $165.00

LOWNDES, Marie B. *The Lodger.* 1935. $10.00

LOWNDES, Robert W. *Mystery of the Third Mine.* 1953. Philadelphia. 1st ed. dj. EX $20.00

LOWREY, Carolyn. *The First One Hundred Men & Women of the Screen.* 1920. New York. 100 Ills. 1st ed. 210 pp. $65.00

LOWREY, Malcolm. *Dark as the Grave Wherein My Friend Is Laid.* 1968. 1st ed. dj. VG $27.50

LOWREY, Malcolm. *Hear Us O Lord from Heaven Thy Dwelling Place.* 1961. 1st ed. dj. VG $35.00

LOWREY, Malcolm. *Lunar Caustic.* 1977. Cape. 1st ed. dj. VG $10.00

LOWREY, Malcolm. *October Ferry to Gabriola.* 1970. New York. 1st ed. dj. VG $20.00

LOWREY, Malcolm. *Under the Volcano.* 1947. New York. Reynal & Hitchcock. 1st ed. $25.00

LOWRY, Beverly. *Daddy's Girl.* 1981. Viking. 1st Am. ed. dj. VG $15.00

LOWRY, Robert. *Casualty.* 1946. New Directions.1st ed. dj. EX $45.00

LOWTHER, Minnie Kendall. *Blennerhassett Island in Romance & Tragedy.* 1936. Rutland. Ills. sgn. 200 pp. index. $32.50

LOXTON, H. *The Beauty of Big Cats.* 1973. London. Triune. Ills. 144 pp. dj. EX $15.00

LUBBOCK, John. *Scenery of Switzerland & Causes Which It Is Due.* 1896. New York. Ills. 1st Am. ed. fld map. VG $20.00

LUBIN, Gilbert. *The Promised Land.* 1930. Boston. Christopher Pub. 1st ed. dj. $35.00

LUBKE, Wilhelm. *Grund der Kunts.* 1908. $79.00

LUCAS, E.V. *A Wanderer in Venice.* 1914. Macmillan. G $95.00

LUCAS, E.V. *Adventures & Enthusiasms.* 1920. New York. 329 pp. $2.50

LUCAS, E.V. *Cloud & Silver.* 1916. 189 pp. $3.00

LUCAS, E.V. *Only the Other Day/A Volume of Essays.* Philadelphia. Lippincott. 211 pp. $5.00

LUCAS, F. *Animals of the Past.* 1913. Ills. 266 pp. EX $15.00

LUCAS, G. *Star Wars.* 1976. Ballantine. 1st ed. pb. VG $12.50

LUCAS, Harriet & Ward, Herman. *Prose & Poetry of England.* 1950. Singer. $2.00

LUCAS, Jeremy. *Whale.* 1981. Summit. 1st ed. dj. VG $10.00

LUCE. *Seamanship Compiled from Various Sources.* 1873. New York. 5th ed. 87 pls. G $20.00

LUCIE-SMITH, E. *World of the Makers. Today's Master Craftsmen.* 1975. New York. $6.50

LUDLOW, Fitz-Hugh. *The Hasheesh Eater.* 1903. New York. Rains. VG $15.00

LUDLUM, Robert. *Rhinemann Exchange.* 1974. New York. 1st printing. dj. $25.00

LUDLUM, Robert. *The Aquitaine Progression.* 1984. New York. Random House. 1st ed. dj. VG $25.00

LUDLUM, Robert. *The Aquitaine Progression.* 1984. London. Granada. 1st ed. dj. VG $35.00

LUDLUM, Robert. *The Bourne Identity.* 1980. Marek. 1st ed. dj. VG $12.50

LUDLUM, Robert. *The Bourne Supremacy.* 1986. Random House. 1st ed. dj. VG $20.00

LUDLUM, Robert. *The Gemini Contenders.* 1976. Dial Press. 1st ed. dj. VG $17.50

LUDLUM, Robert. *The Holcroft Covenant.* 1978. New York. Marek. 1st ed. dj. VG $35.00

LUDLUM, Robert. *The Materese Circle.* 1979. Marek. 1st ed. dj. VG $15.00

LUDLUM, Robert. *The Parsifal Mosaic.* 1982. New York. Random House. 1st ed. dj. VG $25.00

LUDLUM, Robert. *The Road to Gondolfo.* 1975. Dial Press. 1st ed. dj. VG $15.00

LUDLUM, Robert. *The Scarlatti Inheritance.* 1971. New York. 1st ed. dj. VG $37.50

LUDWIG, C. *Maxfield Parrish.* 1975. $15.00

LUDWIG, Emil. *Cleopatra, Story of a Queen.* 1937. New York. Viking Press. 221 pp. dj. $5.00

LUDWIG, Emil. *Lincoln.* 1930. Boston. dj. VG $7.50

LUDWIG, Emil. *The Nile, the Life Story of a River.* 1937. Viking. Ills. fld map. 619 pp. G $12.50

LUDY, R.B. *Historic Churches of the World.* 1926. Boston. Stratford Co. photos. 325 pp. $20.00

LUHAN, Mabel D. *European Experiences.* 1935. New York. 1st ed. $12.50

LUHAN, Mabel D. *Intimate Memories.* 1933. New York. 1st ed. $12.50

LUHAN, Mabel D. *Movers & Shakers.* 1936. New York. 1st ed. dj. VG $15.00

LUI, G. *Inside Los Angeles Chinatown.* 1948. photos. VG $15.00

LUIDWIG, Emil. *Napoleon.* 1924. Modern Library. ex-lib. $3.00

LUISI, Billie. *Practical Guide to Small-Scale Goatkeeping.* 1979. Emmaus, PA. Rodale Press. 208 pp. dj. EX $4.00

LUKE, L.D. *Travels/Adventures: New Wonderland & Yellowstone.* 1886. Utica. $100.00

LULLIES, Reinhard. *Greek Sculpture.* 1957. Abrams. $20.00

LUMBRERAS, L. *The Peoples & Cultures of Ancient Peru.* 1974. Smithsonian. Ills. 248 pp. VG $20.00

LUMMIS, Charles F. *Land of Poco Tiempo.* 1921. New York. VG $17.50

LUMMIS, Charles F. *Land of Poco Tiempo.* 1913. Scribner. Ills. VG $20.00

LUMMIS, Charles F. *The Land of Poco Tiempo.* 1925. New York. Ills. 310 pp. $18.50

LUMMIS, Charles F. *The Spanish Pioneers.* 1893. VG $15.00

LUMPKIN, Grace. *The Wedding.* 1939. New York. 1st ed. VG $20.00

LUMSDEN, Alec. *Wellington Special.* 1974. London. 1st ed. EX $12.50

LUNDBERG, Ferdinand. *Imperial Hearst.* 1936. New York. Ills. 407 pp. dj. $20.00

LUNDGREN, William. *Across the High Frontier.* 1955. New York. Ills. 288 pp. dj. $4.50

LUNN, Arnold. *The Mountains of Youth.* 1925. Oxford. presentation copy. sgn. EX $45.00

LUNN, Charles E. *Pilot to the Sky.* 1947. New York. Hobson Book Press. 149 pp. $4.00

LUNT, George. *Origin of the Late War.* 1866. 1st ed. $23.50

LUPOFF, Richard. *Sword of the Demon.* 1977. Harper. 1st ed. dj. VG $12.50

LURIE, Alison. *Only Children.* 1979. New York. Random House. 1st ed. 257 pp. $7.50

LURIE, Alison. *Real People.* 1969. New York. Random House. 1st printing. $7.50

LURIE, Alison. *The Heavenly Zoo.* 1979. New York. Ills. Monika Beisner. dj. VG $15.00

LURIE, E. *Louis Agazziz, a Life in Science.* 1960. Chicago. Ills. 1st ed. 449 pp. dj. EX $17.50

LURIE, Leonard. *The Running of Richard Nixon.* 1972. New York. 409 pp. VG $4.00

LURIE, Rose G. *The Great March/Post Biblical Jewish Stories.* 1931. New York. Ills. Todros Geller. G $5.00

LUSCOMB, S.C. *Collectors Encyclopedia of Buttons.* 1967. New York. EX $24.50

LUSTBADER, Eric Van. *Beneath an Opal Moon.* 1980. Garden City. 1st ed. dj. VG $10.00

LUTES, Della T. *The Country Kitchen.* 1938. Boston. VG $10.00

LUTZ, W. *The News of Detroit.* 1973. Boston. 2nd printing. VG $5.00

LUTZ. *Relentless Gun.* Gold Medal. pb. $3.00

LUTZ. *To Hell & Texas.* Gold Medal. $3.00

LUVAAS, Jay. *The Military Legacy of the Civil War.* 1959. U. of Chicago. 1st ed. dj. $10.00

LYALL, Edna. *The Autobiography of a Slander.* 1894. Ills. L. Speed. $40.00

LYALL, Gavin. *The Most Dangerous Game.* 1964. London. Hodder & Stoughton. 1st ed. VG $15.00

LYALL, Gavin. *The War in the Air. Royal Air Force in WWII.* 1969. Ills. 1st Am. ed. VG $10.00

LYALL, Gavin. *The War in the Air. Royal Air Force in WWII.* 1970. Ills. pb. VG $3.00

LYDEKKER, R. *Mostly Mammals.* 1903. London. Hutchinson. Ills. 383 pp. VG $55.00

LYDEKKER, R. *Reptiles, Amphibia, Fishes, & Lower Chordata.* 1979. New Delhi. A.J. Reprints. Ills. 510 pp. $60.00

LYDENBERG & ARCHER. *The Care & Repair of Books.* 1931. New York. dj. VG $15.00

LYDIS, Mariette. *B. Aires.* 1945. Ltd. ed. $36.00

LYDIS, Mariette. *Beggar's Opera.* 1937. Paris. lithos. slipcase. VG $45.00

LYDON, A.F. *English Lake Scenery.* 1880. London. Ills. gilt decor. VG $60.00

LYELL, Charles. *A Second Visit to United States of North America.* 1849. Harper. Ills. 2 vol set. VG $80.00

LYELL, Charles. *Principles of Geology.* 1835. London. Ills. 4th ed. map. fld pls. $50.00

LYELL, Charles. *The Geological Evidences of Antiquity of Man.* 1873. London. 4th ed. 572 pp. index. VG $100.00

LYELL, Charles. *Travels in North America in Years 1841-1842.* 1845. New York. Ills. 2 vols in 1. VG $95.00

LYLE, Mel. *The Mystery of the Burning Ocean.* 1965. Racine. Whitman. 210 pp. $2.50

LYMAN, G. *John Marsch Pioneer; Life Story of a Trailblazer.* 1931. Chautauqua. VG $12.50

LYMAN, Henry M. *Hawaiian Yesterdays.* 1906. Chicago. Ills. 1st ed. 281 pp. $45.00

LYMAN, Horace S. *History of Oregon.* 1903. Ills. 4 vol set. VG $180.00

LYMAN GUN SIGHT CORP. *Lyman Reloading Handbook 43rd Edition.* 1964. Middlefield. 222 pp. SftCvr. $2.50

LYMAN. *Striped Bass Fishing.* 1954. 1st ed. dj. EX $15.00

LYNCH, Bohun. *Max Beerbohm in Perspective.* 1921. London. Ills. 1st ed. $65.00

LYNCH, Jeremiah. *Three Years in the Klondike.* 1967. Chicago. Ills. $8.50

LYNCH. *Shadowed by Three.* 1883. 1st ed. $25.00

LYNCH. *Trails to Successful Trapping.* 1935. Harding Pub. 170 pp. $5.50

LYND, Robert S. & Merrell, H. *Middletown in Transition-A Study in Conflict.* 1937. New York. 604 pp. $7.50

LYNN, W. Gardner & Grant, C. *The Herpetology of Jamaica.* 1940. Inst. Jamaica. 1st ed. stiff wrappers. $22.50

LYNN-ALLEN. *Shotgun & Sunlight: Game Birds of East Africa.* 1951. Ills. Dugmore. dj. $30.00

LYON, P.J. *Native South Americans.* 1974. Boston. 1st printing. 433 pp. EX $14.00

LYON, W. Parker. *Episodes in the Life of Hollywood.* 1940. Putnam. Ills. 1st ed. photos. $20.00

LYONS, Eugene. *Assignment in Utopia.* 1937. New York. Harcourt. 658 pp. $6.00

LYONS, Eugene. *Our Unknown Ex-President, Portrait of Hoover.* 1948. Doubleday. 337 pp. G $4.50

LYONS, Louis M. *Newspaper Story, 100 Years of the Boston Globe.* 1971. Cambridge. Globe. Ltd. ed. dj. $25.00

LYONS, Nathan. *Photography on Photography.* 1966. New York. 1st ed. EX $35.00

LYTLE, Andrew. *Alchemy.* 1979. Palaemon Press. Ltd. ed. sgn. $35.00

LYTLE, Andrew. *A Novel, a Novella, & Four Stories.* 1958. New York. McDowell. 1st ed. 327 pp. $10.00

LYTLE, Andrew. *Alchemy.* 1979. Palaemon. Ltd. 1st ed. 1/300. VG $20.00

LYTLE, Andrew. *Hero with Private Parts.* 1966. Baton Rouge. 1st ed. dj. VG $37.50

LYTTON, Earl of. *The Desert & the Green.* 1957. London. Ills. 1st ed. 350 pp. $12.50

LYTTON, Edward B. *The Last Days of Pompeii.* 1891. Alden. $4.50

M'MURTRIE. *Sketches of Louisville & Environs.* 1819. Louisville. 1st ed. 3 fld maps. fld pl. $700.00

MA, Nancy Chih. *Mrs. Ma's Chinese Cookbook.* 1968. Rutland. Tuttle. 12th printing. 178 pp. $9.50

MAAS, D. & Hill, G. *A Gallery of Waterfowl & Upland Birds.* 1978. Peterson. Ills. 120 pp. dj. EX $45.00

MAAS, Peter. *The Valachi Papers.* 1968. New York. Putnam. 286 pp. G $6.00

MABEE, Jack. *Sourdough Jack's Cookery.* 1965. 48 pp. $4.00

MABERLY, J. *The Print Collector.* 1880. New York. Ills. VG $150.00

MABIE, Chester W. *The Mystic Chord, Collection of Masonic Odes.* 1897. New York. 11th ed. 112 pp. index. G $10.00

MABIE, Hamilton Wright. *Fairy Tales Every Child Should Know.* 1923. Garden City. Ills. Mary Hamilton Frye. dj. $22.00

MABIE, Hamilton Wright. *My Study Fire.* 1899. New York. Ills. Alice & Cowles. VG $20.00

MABIE, Hamilton Wright. *The Great World.* 1911. Dodd Mead. 2nd ed. VG $9.00

MABIE, Mary Louise. *The Long Knives Walked.* 1932. Indianapolis. 1st ed. 304 pp. $12.50

MABON, Mary Frost. *A B C of America's Wines.* 1942. New York Knopf. 233 pp. $3.50

MABY, J. Cecil. *Physical Principles of Radiesthesia.* 1966. Birmingham. presentation copy. sgn. $60.00

MAC ARTHUR, Douglas. *Reminiscences.* 1964. Ills. $7.50

MAC ARTHUR, Douglas. *Revitalizing a Nation.* 1952. Chicago. Heritage. 96 pp. photos. dj. $65.00

MAC ASKILL. *Out of Halifax.* Derrydale Pr. Ltd. ed. 1/450. boxed. $250.00

MAC BETH, R.G. *The Romance of Western Canada.* 1918. Toronto. 1st ed. G $25.00

MAC CURDY, Edward. *The Notebooks of Leonardo da Vinci.* New York. 1st Am. ed. 2 vol set. VG $45.00

MAC DEVITT, D. *The Naval History of Treasure Island.* 1946. 2 vol set. folio. VG $45.00

MAC DONALD, Betty. *The Egg & I.* 1943. New York. Lippincott. 287 pp. $3.50

MAC DONALD, Duncan. *Estate Management.* 1868. London. 1014 pp. $22.50

MAC DONALD, Dwight. *Parodies/Anthology from Chaucer to Beerbohm.* 1960. Random House. 1st ed. dj. EX $10.00

MAC DONALD, E.J. & Nelson, H. *Castles of England & Wales.* New York. Ills. $12.00

MAC DONALD, George. *At the Back of the North Wind.* 1924. New York. Ills. Charles Mozley. $14.00

MAC DONALD, George. *At the Back of the North Wind.* 1909. Philadelphia. Ills. Maria L. Kirk. dj. $17.00

MAC DONALD, George. *The Golden Key.* 1961. Yale. dj. $20.00

MAC DONALD, George. *The Light Princess & Other Fairy Tales.* Putnam. Ills. Maud Humphrey. G $30.00

MAC DONALD, George. *The Princess & the Goblin.* 1927. Saalfield. Ills. Brundage. 1st ed. VG $22.50

MAC DONALD, Greville. *Count Billy.* 1928. New York. Ills. Mears. 1st ed. 246 pp. $6.00

MAC DONALD, J. *Condominium.* 1977. Lippincott. 1st ed. dj. VG $7.50

MAC DONALD, J. *No Deadly Drug.* 1968. New York. Doubleday. 1st ed. 656 pp. VG $5.00

MAC DONALD, J. *The End of the Night.* 1960. Simon & Schuster. 1st ed. dj. $55.00

MAC DONALD, J. *The Last One Left.* 1967. New York. McGee. 1st ed. G $8.00

MAC DONALD, J.D. *Cinnamon Skin.* 1982. Harper. dj. VG $7.50

MAC DONALD, J.D. *Free Fall in Crimson.* 1981. Harper. dj. VG $6.50

MAC DONALD, J.D. *One More Sunday.* 1984. Knopf. dj. VG $6.00

MAC DONALD, Jessica North. *History of Alpha Delta Pi.* 1930. Ames, IA. Ills. 389 pp. $9.00

MAC DONALD, John D. *The Ballroom of the Skies.* 1952. New York. 1st ed. dj. VG $20.00

MAC DONALD, John Ross. *Find a Victim.* 1954. New York. Knopf. 1st ed. dj. VG $75.00

MAC DONALD, John Ross. *Meet Me at the Morgue.* 1953. New York. Knopf. 1st ed. dj. VG $50.00

MAC DONALD, John Ross. *The Barbarous Coast.* 1957. London. Cassell. 1st Eng. ed. EX $100.00

MAC DONALD, John Ross. *The Chill.* 1964. New York. Knopf. 1st ed. dj. $60.00

MAC DONALD, John Ross. *The Doomsters.* 1st Eng. ed. dj. $40.00

MAC DONALD, John Ross. *The Instant Enemy.* 1968. New York. Knopf. 1st ed. dj. EX $40.00

MAC DONALD, John. *Quill Gordon.* 1972. New York. 1st ed. dj. VG $14.00

MAC DONALD, John. *Strategy in Poker, Business & War.* 1950. New York. Ills. Osborn. 1st ed. VG $12.50

MAC DONALD, Malcolm. *Angkor.* 1958. London. 112 photos. 158 pp. $12.50

MAC DONALD, Philip. *Death & Chicanery.* 1962. Crime Club. 1st ed. dj. VG $20.00

MAC DONALD, R. *Archer in Jeopardy.* 1979. review copy. dj. EX $75.00

MAC DONALD, R. *Inward Journey.* 1984. Cordelia. Ltd. ed. 1/1000. sgn. dj. VG $40.00

MAC DONALD, R. *Pucinni, King of Verismo.* 1973. New York. 1st ed. dj. VG $11.00

MAC DONALD, R. *Self-Portrait.* 1981. Santa Barbara. 1st ed. dj. EX $15.00

MAC DONALD, R. *Sleeping Beauty.* 1973. New York. Knopf. 1st ed. dj. $12.50

MAC DONALD, Raymond Alden. *Why the Chimes Rang.* 1909. Bobbs Merrill. $17.50

MAC DONALD, W. *Annihilation of Wicked Scripturally Considered.* 1872. NY/Cincinnati. 99 pp. $12.50

MAC DONALD, William Colt. *Riders of the Whistling Skull.* 1934. New York. 1st ed. dj. VG $25.00

MAC DONALD, William Colt. *Sleepy Horse Range.* Triangle. $5.50

MAC DONALD. *Jewels & Gems.* 1940. New York. 288 pp. dj. $12.50

MAC DONOUGH, Nancy. *Garden Sass: Catalog of Arkansas Folkways.* 1975. New York. photos. 319 pp. dj. VG $7.50

MAC DOUGALL, Allen Ross. *The Gourmet's Almanac.* 1931. London. Ills. 1st ed. dj. VG $37.50

MAC DOUGALL, Arthur. *Trout Fisherman's Bedside Book.* 1963. Ills. 1st ed. VG $17.50

MAC DOUGALL, Arthur. *Under a Willow Tree.* 1946. Coward McCann. Ills. 1st ed. 200 pp. dj. VG $22.50

MAC DOWELL, Sylvia. *Western Trout.* 1948. Knopf. Ills. 1st ed. 261 pp. index. $27.50

MAC EWAN. *John Ware's Cow Country.* 1967. 3rd printing. dj. VG $20.00

MAC FADDEN, Bernarr. *Hair Culture.* 1925. New York. Macfadden Pub. dj. G $10.00

MAC FADDEN, Bernarr. *Muscular Power & Beauty.* 1906. Spotswood, NJ. photos. 200 pp. SftCvr. $3.00

MAC FADDEN, Bernarr. *Physical Culture Cookbook.* 1924. New York. 1st ed. $12.00

MAC FADDEN, C.H. *A Bibliography of Pacific Area Maps.* 1941. San Francisco. 1st ed. 107 pp. dj. VG $15.00

MAC FADDEN, Harry. *Rambles in the Far West.* 1906. $50.00

MAC FALL, Haldane. *History of Painting.* 1900. $57.00

MAC FARLAN, A. & P. *Knotcraft, the Art of Knot Tying.* 1967. New York. Ills. 186 pp. dj. $5.00

MAC FIE, Harry. *Wasa Wasa.* 1951. New York. 1st ed. dj. VG $20.00

MAC GAHAN, J.A. *Campaigning on the Oxus & the Fall of Kiva.* 1874. New York. Harper. $50.00

MAC GOWAN, Michael. *The Hard Road to Klondike.* 1962. London. Ills. 150 pp. dj. $10.00

MAC GOWAN & ROSSE. *Masks & Demons.* 1923. New York. Ills. $27.50

MAC GRATH, Harold. *Hearts & Masks.* 1905. Bobbs Merrill. Ills. Harrison Fisher. EX $10.50

MAC GRATH, Harold. *The Best Man.* 1907. $30.00

MAC GRATH, Harold. *The Goose Girl.* 1909. $27.50

MAC GRATH, Harold. *The Grey Cloak.* 1903. $27.50

MAC GRATH, Harold. *The Man on the Box.* 1904. $30.00

MAC GRATH, Harold. *The World Outside.* 1923. 1st ed. $30.00

MAC GREGOR, G. *Warriors Without Weapons.* 1946. U. of Chicago. 228 pp. pls. dj. $15.00

MAC GREGOR, Mary. *The Story of France.* 1920. New York. Ills. William Rainey. $17.50

MAC GREGOR, Morris J., Jr. *Integration of the Armed Forces, 1940-1965.* 1981. Washington. 1st ed. inscr. 647 pp. photos. $32.50

MAC HESEY, K.J. *Panzer Division.* 1972. $3.50

MAC HETANZ, Sara. *Where Else But Alaska?* 1954. New York. Ills. Machetanz. 214 pp. dj. $6.00

MAC INNES, Helen. *Above Suspicion.* 1961. Horizon. $25.00

MAC INNES, Helen. *Assignment in Brittany.* 1943. New York. Dial Press. 373 pp. $35.00

MAC INNES, Helen. *Friends & Lovers.* 1947. Boston. 367 pp. $25.00

MAC INNES, Helen. *I & My True Love.* 1953. Harcourt. 1st Am. ed. inscr. dj. VG $45.00

MAC INNES, Helen. *Pray for a Brave Heart.* 1955. $25.00

MAC INNES, Helen. *Rest & Be Thankful.* 1949. $25.00

MAC INNES, Helen. *The Deadly Decisions.* 1960. New York. 2 novels in 1. 728 pp. dj. $4.00

MAC INNES, Helen. *The Salzburg Connection.* 1968. $25.00

MAC INNES, Helen. *The Snare of the Hunter.* 1974. $25.00

MAC INTOSH, J. *Principles of Pathology & Practice of Physic.* 1836. Philadelphia. Key & Biddle. 2 vol set. $65.00

MAC INTYRE, D. *The Naval War Against Hitler.* 1971. Book Club ed. Ills. maps. dj. G $12.50

MAC ISAAC, Fred. *The Hothouse World.* 1965. 1st ed. dj. EX $8.50

MAC IVER, R.M. *Great Expressions of Human Rights.* 1950. New York. Harper. ex-lib. 321 pp. $3.50

MAC KANESS, G. *The Life of Vice-Admiral Bligh.* New York. (ca. 1931) Ills. 2 vol set. VG $25.00

MAC KAY, Andrew. *The Complete Navigator.* 1807. Philadelphia. Ills. 1st Am. ed. $175.00

MAC KAY, Margaret. *The Poetic Parrot.* 1951. New York. Ills. Kurt Wiese. 1st ed. VG $10.00

MAC KAYE, Harold S. *The Panchronicon.* 1904. New York. Scribner. 1st ed. VG $25.00

MAC KELLER, Thomas. *Tam's Fortnight Ramble & Other Poems.* 1847. Philadelphia. presentation copy. $25.00

MAC KELLER, Thomas. *The American Printer.* 1882. Philadelphia. 383 pp. VG $30.00

MAC KENZIE, Alexander. *Life of Commodore Oliver Hazard Perry.* 1840. New York. 2 vol set. $15.00

MAC KENZIE, Alexander. *Voyages from Montreal on the River St.Laurence.* 1802. Philadelphia. 2 vol set. fld maps. $750.00

MAC KENZIE, Alexander. *Voyages from Montreal on the River St.Laurence.* 1801. London. 1st ed. 412 pp. 3 fld maps. $1,750.00

MAC KENZIE, Alexander. *Voyages from Montreal on the River St.Laurence.* 1927. reprint. 498 pp. $30.00

MAC KENZIE, David. *The Lion of Tashkent.* 1974. Georgia. 1st ed. dj. EX $10.00

MAC KENZIE, George S.B. *Travel in the Islands of Iceland.* 1811. Edinburgh. 1st ed. 492 pp. 3 maps. $4.50

MAC KENZIE, Henry. *The Mirror, a Periodical Paper.* 1787. London. 7th ed. 3 vol set. $45.00

MAC KENZIE, Jean Kenyon. *African Adventures.* 1977. Mass. Missionary Pub. Ills. 119 pp. $5.00

MAC KENZIE, W. Douglas. *South Africa. Its History, Heroes, & Wars.* 1899. Chicago. Ills. VG $50.00

MAC KENZIE, W. Roy. *Ballads & Sea Songs from Nova Scotia.* 1928. Cambridge. Harvard Press. 1st ed. dj. VG $70.00

MAC KILLOP, J. *Letters to Young Sportsmen on Hunting; Angling.* 1930. Scribner. Ills. L. Edwards. revised ed. $50.00

MAC LAVERTY, B. *Cal.* London. proof copy. $75.00

MAC LEAN, Alistair. *Bear Island.* 1971. $20.00

MAC LEAN, Alistair. *Breakheart Pass.* 1974. Doubleday. 1st Am. ed. dj. VG $7.50

MAC LEAN, Alistair. *Caravan to Vaccares.* 1970. $25.00

MAC LEAN, Alistair. *Circus.* 1975. Doubleday. 1st Am. ed. dj. VG $5.00

MAC LEAN, Alistair. *Floodgate.* 1984. Doubleday. review copy. dj. VG $20.00

MAC LEAN, Alistair. *Force 10 from Navarone.* 1968. Doubleday. 1st Am. ed. dj. VG $15.00

MAC LEAN, Alistair. *H.M.S. Ulysses.* 1956. Doubleday. 1st Am. ed. dj. VG $15.00

MAC LEAN, Alistair. *Ice Station Zebra.* 1963. Doubleday. 1st Am. ed. dj. VG $15.00

MAC LEAN, Alistair. *South by Java Head.* 1958. $25.00

MAC LEAN, Alistair. *The Golden Gate.* 1976. $25.00

MAC LEAN, Alistair. *The Guns of Navarone.* 1957. $25.00

MAC LEAN, Alistair. *The Way to Dusty Death.* 1973. Doubleday. 1st Am. ed. dj. VG $10.00

MAC LEAN, Katherine. *Missing Man.* 1973. New York. Putnam. 1st ed. dj. EX $12.50

MAC LEISH, Archibald. *A Continuing Journey.* 1967. Boston. 3rd printing. 374 pp. dj. $4.00

MAC LEISH, Archibald. *America Was Promises.* 1939. New York. 1st ed. sgn. dj. VG $65.00

MAC LEISH, Archibald. *Collected Poems. 1917-1976.* Ltd. ed. 1/500. sgn. slipcase. $25.00

MAC LEISH, Archibald. *J.B., a Play in Verse.* 1958. New York. Houghton Mifflin. 153 pp. dj. $3.50

MAC LEISH, Archibald. *Land of the Free.* 1938. London. Boriswood Pub. VG $50.00

MAC LEISH, Archibald. *Poems 1924-1933.* 1933. Boston. Houghton Mifflin. sgn. dj. VG $35.00

MAC LEISH, Archibald. *The Fall of the City.* 1937. New York. 1st ed. VG $35.00

MAC LEOD, Fiona. *The Mountain Lovers.* 1895. Boston. Roberts. VG $15.00

MAC LEOD, Grace & Taylor, C.M. *Rose's Foundations of Nutrition.* 1944. New York. Macmillan. TB. 549 pp. $3.00

MAC LEOD, Mary. *The Book of King Arthur & His Noble Knights.* New York. no date. Ills. A.G. Walker. EX $25.00

MAC MICHAEL, W.F. *The Oxford & Cambridge Boat Races, 1829-1869.* 1870. Cambridge. 1st ed. fld pls. $40.00

MAC MILLAN, Harold. *The Blast of War: 1939-1945.* 1968. New York. EX $12.50

MAC MILLAN, Michael. *Globe Trotter in India.* 1895. London. VG $12.50

MAC MILLAN, Miriam. *Green Seas & White Ice.* 1948. Dodd Mead. Ills. 287 pp. VG $10.00

MAC NAIR, J. *Livingstone's Travels.* 1954. Macmillan. Ills. maps. 429 pp. VG $17.50

MAC PHERSON, David. *History of European Commerce with India.* 1812. London. 1st ed. VG $125.00

MAC QUARRIE, Hector. *Tahiti Days.* 1920. New York. Ills. 266 pp. $7.50

MAC QUOID, P. & Edwards, R. *Dictionary of English Furniture.* 1924. London/NY. Country Life/Scribner. 3 vol set. $450.00

MAC RAY, W. *Manual of British Historians.* 1845. London. ex-lib. 109 pp. VG $25.00

MAC SWINEY, M. *Six Came Flying.* 1971. London. Joseph. Ills. 190 pp. $7.50

MACAFFREY, Anne. *The White Dragon.* 1978. New York. Ballantine. 1st ed. dj. EX $25.00

MACAN, T.T. & Worthington, E. *Life in Lakes & Rivers.* 1974. London. Collins. Ills. 320 pp. dj. EX $9.00

MACARTNEY, William N. *Fifty Years a Country Doctor.* 1941. New York. Dutton. 584 pp. VG $5.00

MACAULAY, Rose & Beny, Roloff. *Pleasure of Ruins.* 1966. Ills. 2nd impression. dj. EX $27.50

MACAULAY, Rose. *Crocodile Trader.* 1960. London. Adventurers Club. Ills. dj. VG $25.00

MACAULAY, Rose. *Life Among the English.* 1942. Collins. Ills. 49 pp. $3.50

MACAULAY, Rose. *The Towers of Trebizond.* 1950. London. Book Society. dj. EX $7.50

MACAULAY, Rose. *Told by an Idiot.* 1923. New York. 340 pp. $3.00

MACAULAY, Thomas B. *The History of England.* 1899. London/NY. 2 vol set. $55.00

MACAULAY, Thomas. *Lays of Ancient Rome.* London. Ills. G $50.00

MACAULAY. *The Works of Macaulay.* 1871. London. 8 vol set. VG $160.00

MACAULAY, Thomas B. *History of England.* 1861. Mershon. 5 vol set. VG $25.00

MACH, Ernst. *Analysis of the Sensations.* 1910. Open Court Pub. dj. EX $40.00

MACH, Ernst. *Popular Scientific Lectures.* 1910. Open Court Pub. Ills. EX $25.00

MACHEN, Arthur. *Autobiography.* 1951. London. Richards. 1st ed. dj. EX $22.50

MACHEN, Arthur. *Hill of Dreams.* 1954. London. Richards. 1st printing. dj. EX $17.50

MACHEN, Arthur. *Tales of Horror & the Supernatural.* 1948. New York. Knopf. dj. VG $12.50

MACHEN, Arthur. *The Bowmen.* 1915. London. Simpkin. 1st ed. VG $25.00

MACHEN, Arthur. *The Chronicle of Clemendy.* 1923. Carbonnek. Ltd. ed. 1/1050. sgn. G $35.00

MACHEN, Arthur. *The Terror.* 1965. New York. Norton. 1st printing. dj. EX $15.00

MACHEN, Arthur. *The Three Imposters.* 1972. New York. Ballantine. 1st ed. pb. EX $7.50

MACHEN, Arthur. *The Three Imposters.* 1895. London. Roberts. 1st ed. VG $125.00

MACHEN, Authur. *Dreads & Drolls.* 1926. London. dj. $30.00

MACHIAVELLI. *History of Florence.* 1901. New York. Ills. VG $10.00

MACHOL, Libby. *Giana.* 1967. 1st ed. sgn. dj. VG $10.00

MACKEY, Albert G. *Encyclopedia of Freemasonry & Kindred Sciences.* 1921. Chicago/NY. 2 vol set. VG $25.00

MACKEY, Albert G. *History of Freemasonry.* 1898. New York. Masonic Pub. 7 vol set. VG $100.00

MACKEY & SINGLETON. *History of Freemasonry.* 1906. New York. Ills. 7 vol set. EX $75.00

MACKLEY, George. *Wood Engraving, Its History & Technique.* 1948. London. Ills. 1st ed. 144 pp. dj. EX $20.00

MACKSEY, K. *The German Invasion of England.* 1940. Ills. maps. dj. EX $17.50

MACLAURIN, C. *Post Mortem, Historical & Medical.* 1922. $6.50

MACLAY. *History of American Privateers.* 1899. 1st ed. 519 pp. G $50.00

MACLEOD, Fiona. *The Silence of Amor.* Duffield Uniform ed. $10.00

MACMILLAN CO. *Audubon's Birds of America, Popular Edition.* 1950. New York. 320 pp. dj. EX $5.00

MACQUOID, Percy & Edwards, R. *The Dictionary of English Furniture.* 1924-1927 London. 1st ed. 3 vol set. folio. $250.00

MACQUOID, Percy. *History of English Furniture.* 1904-1924. London. 4 vol set. folio. $250.00

MACY, John. *Socialism in America.* 1916. 247 pp. $37.50

MADDEN, David. *Bijou, a Novel.* 1974. New York. Crown. 500 pp. dj. $7.50

MADDEN, David. *The Beautiful Greed.* 1961. New York. Random House. 1st Am. ed. VG $15.00

MADDEN, David. *The Poetical Image in Six Genres.* 1969. IL U. Press. sgn. 241 pp. $10.00

MADDEN, Edwin C. *The U.S. Government's Shame.* 1908. Detroit. National Book Co. 2nd ed. VG $15.00

MADER, Friedrich. *Distant Worlds.* 1932. New York. Scribner. 1st ed. VG $15.00

MADIS, George. *The Winchester Book.* 1971. Lancaster, TX. Art & Reference House. 1st ed. $62.50

MADISON, C.A. *The Owl Among the Colophons.* Holt. dj. EX $10.00

MADISON, Lucy. *Washington.* 1927. Philadelphia. Schoonover. Ills. EX $25.00

MAETERLINCK, Maurice. *Life of the White Ant.* 1927. 1st ed. $6.50

MAETERLINCK, Maurice. *Mountain Path.* 1919. 1st ed. $6.50

MAETERLINCK, Maurice. *News of Spring & Other Nature Studies.* 1913. New York. Ills. 213 pp. VG $50.00

MAETERLINCK, Maurice. *The Blue Bird.* 1911. New York. Ills. F.C. Robinson. 1st ed. $75.00

MAETERLINCK, Maurice. *The Intelligence of the Flowers.* 1907. Dodd Mead. 1st ed. Coburn photo pls. VG $120.00

MAFFITT, E.M. *The Life & Services of John Newland Maffitt.* 1906. New York. Neale. 1st ed. VG $200.00

MAGEE, David. *The Golden Cave.* 1973. San Francisco. Bohemian Club. 1st ed. dj. $45.00

MAGEE. *Infinite Riches.* 1973. VG $10.00

MAGER, Henri. *Water Diviners & Their Methods.* 1931. London. Bell. Ills. 1st Eng. ed. $75.00

MAGILL, Frank N. *Contemporary Literature Scene II.* 1979. Salem Press. dj. VG $25.00

MAGILL, Frank N. *Masterpieces of World Literatue in Digest Form.* 1955. New York. Harper. 1171 pp. dj. $10.00

MAGINLEY, C.J. *America in Miniatures: How to Make Model Houses.* 1975. New York. Ills. dj. VG $10.50

MAGRUDER, Jeb Stuart. *An American Life.* 1974. New York. 370 pp. dj. $4.00

MAGRUDER, Julia. *Struan.* 1899. Boston. 1st ed. VG $15.00

MAHAFFY, J.P. *The Greek World Under Roman Sway.* 1890. London. 1st ed. EX $60.00

MAHOLICH, Frank. *Ice Hockey.* 1964. London. Pelham. Ills. 69 pp. dj. EX $5.00

MAHOLY-NAGY, L. *Vision in Motion.* 1947. Chicago. Thebald. ex-lib. 371 pp. $12.50

MAIER, Pauline. *The Old Revolutionaries.* 1980. New York. Knopf. proof copy. wrappers. $30.00

MAILER, Norman. *Advertisements for Myself.* 1959. Putnam. 1st ed. 1st issue. dj. EX $20.00

MAILER, Norman. *An American Dream.* 1965. Dial Press. 1st ed. dj. VG $30.00

MAILER, Norman. *Ancient Evenings.* 1983. Boston. 3rd ed. sgn. dj. VG $25.00

MAILER, Norman. *Barbary Shore.* 1951. New York. 1st ed. dj. VG $25.00

MAILER, Norman. *Barbary Shore.* 1952. London. 1st Eng. ed. dj. EX $50.00

MAILER, Norman. *Existential Errands.* 1972. Little, Brown. 1st ed. dj. VG $20.00

MAILER, Norman. *Genius & Lust.* 1976. Grove Press. 1st ed. sgn. dj. VG $50.00

MAILER, Norman. *Marilyn.* 1973. Grosset & Dunlap. Ltd. 1st ed. $150.00

MAILER, Norman. *Marilyn.* 1969. 1st ed. folio. dj. EX $30.00

MAILER, Norman. *Of a Fire on the Moon.* 1970. $10.00

MAILER, Norman. *The Deer Park.* 1955. Putnam. 1st ed. dj. VG $50.00

MAILER, Norman. *The Executioner's Song.* 1979. Little, Brown. dj. EX $10.00

MAILER, Norman. *The Fight.* 1975. Little, Brown. 1st ed. dj. VG $17.50

MAILER, Norman. *The Naked & the Dead.* 1948. New York. Rhinehart. 721 pp. $4.00

MAILER, Norman. *The Presidential Paper.* 1063. Putnam. 1st ed. dj. VG $35.00

MAILER, Norman. *The Prisoner of Sex.* 1971. Little, Brown. 1st ed. dj. VG $20.00

MAILER, Norman. *Tough Guys Don't Dance.* 1984. New York. Random House. 1st ed. sgn. VG $15.00

MAILING, Arthur. *Rheingold Route.* 1979. New York. 1st ed. dj. VG $10.00

MAIN, J.T. *Social Structure of Revolutionary America.* 1965. 1st ed. dj. EX $40.00

MAINE, C.E. *He Owned the World.* 1960. New York. Avalon. 1st ed. dj. EX $15.00

MAINWARING, Marion. *Murder in Pastiche.* 1954. New York. Macmillan. 1st ed. G $12.50

MAIRS, Thomas I. *Some Pennsylvania Pioneers in Agriculture Science.* 1928. 1st ed. ex-lib. VG $12.00

MAISON. *Faumier.* 1960. New York. EX $35.00

MAITLAND, Frederic William. *Domesday Book & Beyond.* 1897. Cambridge. 527 pp. $25.00

MAJDALANY, Fred. *Account of Battle to Take Monte Cassino in WWII.* 1946. London. G $7.50

MAJOR, Harlan. *Fishing Behind the Eight Ball.* 1952. Harrisburg. Stackpole, Ills. Boorhies. VG $10.00

MAJOR, J. Russell. *The Western World.* 1966. Philadelphia. Lippincott. G $8.00

MAJOR, William Montgomery. *The Entertainment Speaker.* 1927. Chicago. Whitman. 256 pp. VG $3.50

MAJUMDAR, D.N. *Himalayan Polyandry.* 1963. Bombay. Asia Publishing House. Ills. $30.00

MAKEMSON, Maud Worcester. *The Book of the Jaguar Priest.* 1951. New York. Ills. 238 pp. index. dj. $20.00

MALAMUD, Bernard. *A New Life.* 1961. Farrar. 1st ed. dj. VG $12.50

MALAMUD, Bernard. *God's Grace.* 1982. Farrar. Ltd. 1st ed. 1/300. sgn. dj. $75.00

MALAMUD, Bernard. *Pictures of Fidelman.* 1969. New York. Farrar. dj. VG $15.00

MALAMUD, Bernard. *Rembrandt's Hat.* 1973. Farrar. 1st ed. dj. VG $20.00

MALAMUD, Bernard. *The Magic Barrel.* 1960. Eyre. 1st English ed. dj. VG $50.00

MALAMUD, Bernard. *The Magic Barrel.* 1958. Farrar. 1st ed. dj. VG $20.00

MALAMUD, Bernard. *The Natural.* 1952. Harcourt. 1st ed. VG $15.00

MALAMUD, Bernard. *The Stories of Bernard Malamud.* 1983. Farrar. 1st ed. dj. VG $12.50

MALAMUD, Bernard. *The Tenants.* 1971. New York. Farrar. 1st ed. VG $15.00

MALAURIE, Jean. *The Last Kings of Thule.* 1982. Dutton. Ills. maps. dj. EX $20.00

MALCOLM, Arthur. *Robin Hood.* 1927. Sears. Ills. M. Geiszel. $3.50

MALCOLM-SMITH, George. *The Grass is Always Greener.* 1947. New York. Doubleday. 1st ed. dj. EX $15.00

MALENGREAU, M. Auguste. *Voyage en Espagne.* 1866. Bruxelles. Ills. VG $40.00

MALGAIGNE, J.F. *Surgery & Ambrose Pare.* 1965. OK U. Press. 1st ed. 435 pp. dj. VG $20.00

MALILLOL, Aristide. *Woodcuts of Malillol.* 1951. New York. Pantheon. dj. EX $35.00

MALIS, Gene. *The Great Movie Quiz.* 1980. New York. 1st ed. photos. pb. EX $3.00

MALLEA, Eduardo. *The Bay of Silence.* 1944. New York. Knopf. 1st ed. EX $40.00

MALLESON, G.B. *The Indian Mutiny of 1857.* 1891. New York. Ills. VG $30.00

MALLETT, Theirry. *Glimpses of Barren Lands.* 1930. New York. Ills. 1st ed. VG $20.00

MALLETT, Thierry. *Plain Tales of the North.* 1925. private print. VG $35.00

MALLETT, M. *A White Woman Among the Masai.* 1923. Dutton. 1st ed. 288 pp. dj. VG $50.00

MALLETT, Theirry. *Glimpses of Barren Lands.* 1930. Revillon Freres. Ills. 142 pp. $20.00

MALLINSON, J. *Okavango Adventure.* 1973. Norton. Ills. 1st ed. 208 pp. dj. VG $12.50

MALLIS, A. *American Entomologists.* 1971. Rutgers. Ills. 549 pp. dj. EX $25.00

MALLOCH, Douglas. *Come on Home.* 1923. New York. 222 pp. G $5.00

MALLORY, Tom. *King Arthur & Knights of the Round Table.* 1950. New York. Ills. Florian. 280 pp. $8.50

MALLORY. *Life & Speeches of Henry Clay.* 1843. New York. 2 vol set. $16.00

MALONE, Bill C. *Country Music U.S.A.: Fifty Year History.* 1968. Austin. 422 pp. $12.50

MALONE, Dumas. *Jefferson & Ordeal of Liberty.* 1962. 1st ed. dj. VG $10.00

MALONE, Dumas. *Jefferson & Rights of Man.* 1951. Boston. 1st ed. dj. VG $12.50

MALONE, Michael. *Dingley Falls.* 1980. Harcourt. dj. VG $10.00

MALONE, Michael. *Handling Sin.* 1986. Boston. Little, Brown. advance copy. $30.00

MALONE, Michael. *Uncivil Seasons.* 1983. Delacorte. revised ed. dj. VG $17.50

MALONEY, Tom. *U.S. Camera.* 1962. dj. VG $15.00

MALONEY, William E. *The Illustrated Cat.* 1976. New York. Harmony. 72 pp. $3.50

MALOT, Hector. *Adventures of Remi.* 1925. Rand. Ills. by M. Schaeffer. $5.00

MALOY, Lois & Dagliesh. *Wooden Shoes in America.* 1940. New York. dj. $10.00

MALRAUX, Andre. *Le Musee Imaginaire de la Sculpture Mondiale.* 1952. Paris. Ills. 1st ed. 700+ pls. VG $35.00

MALRAUX, Andre. *The Conquerers.* 1976. Holt. 1st Am. ed. dj. VG $15.00

MALRAUX, Andre. *The Metamorphosis of the Gods.* 1960. Doubleday. trans. Gilbert. 1st Am. ed. EX $15.00

MALRAUX, Andre. *The Voices of Silence: Man & His Art.* 1953. Doubleday. 1st ed. dj. $22.50

MALTZ, Albert. *The Underground Stream.* 1940. Boston. Little, Brown. 1st ed. dj. VG $60.00

MALZBERG, Barry. *Beyond Apollo.* 1974. Faber. 1st English ed. dj. VG $12.50

MAMOULIAN, Rouben. *Abigayil: Story of Cat at the Manger.* 1964. New York. Ills. Marshall Goodman. dj. VG $20.00

MANAS, John H. *Divination, Ancient & Modern.* 1947. New York. 1st ed. 298 pp. dj. EX $35.00

MANCHESTER, Raymond. *The Saturday Letters.* 1942. Cuyahoga Falls. 266 pp. $15.00

MANCHESTER, William. *Portrait of a President.* 1967. Boston. 266 pp. dj. $5.00

MANCHESTER, William. *The Death of a President.* 1967. New York. Harper & Row. 710 pp. dj. $7.50

MANDAHL-BARTH, G. & Anthon, H. *Cage Birds in Color.* 1959. Barrows. Ills. 1st Am. ed. 149 pp. dj. $9.00

MANDELSTAM, Nadezhda. *Hope Abandoned.* 1974. New York. 1st ed. dj. EX $15.00

MANES, Stephen. *Pictures of Motion & Pictures that Move.* 1982. New York. Ills. 1st printing. dj. EX $10.00

MANFORD, Erasmus. *Twenty-Five Years in the West.* 1875. Chicago. revised ed. 375 pp. VG $22.50

MANKIEWICZ, Frank. *Perfectly Clear, Nixon from Whittier to Watergate.* 1973. New York. Times Books. 239 pp. dj. $4.00

MANLEY, A. *Rushion & His Times in American Conoeing.* 1977. Syracuse U. Ills. 203 pp. EX $9.00

MANLEY, William Lewis. *Death Valley in '49.* 1894. San Jose. Ills. 1st ed. 498 pp. $100.00

MANLEY, William Lewis. *Death Valley in '49.* 1949. Century. 1st ed. dj. EX $22.50

MANLY, G.B. *Aircraft Electrical & Ignition Systems.* 1942. Chicago. Drake. 280 pp. dj. $125.00

MANN, A.R. *Beginnings in Agriculture.* 1914. New York. Macmillan. TB. 341 pp. VG $4.00

MANN, Albert W. *Walks & Talks About Historic Boston.* 1917. Boston. Ills. 1st ed. 586 pp. $25.00

MANN, Arthur. *The Jackie Robinson Story.* 1950. New York. Grosset & Dunlap. 224 pp. dj. $4.00

MANN, Kathleen. *Peasant Costumes in Europe.* 1935 & 1936. London. Ills. 2 vol set. dj. G $25.00

MANN, L. *From Jungle to Zoo, Adventures of Naturalist Wife.* 1934. Jr. Lit. Guild. Ills. 246 pp. G $12.50

MANN, Thomas. *Confessions of Felix Krull, Confidence Man.* 1955. Knopf. 1st Am. ed. dj. VG $15.00

MANN, Thomas. *Der Erwahlte.* 1951. Frankfurt. 1st ed. VG $30.00

MANN, Thomas. *Die Forderung des Tages.* 1930. Berlin. 1st ed. EX $40.00

MANN, Thomas. *Joseph in Egypt.* 1938. Knopf. 1st ed. 2 vol set. boxed. $36.50

MANN, Thomas. *Stories of Three Decades.* 1936. New York. Knopf. 567 pp. $4.00

MANN, Thomas. *The Holy Sinner.* 1951. New York. 1st Am. ed. dj. VG $20.00

MANN, Thomas. *The Transposed Heads.* 1941. New York. Knopf. dj. VG $15.00

MANN, William M. *Ant Hill Odyssey.* 1948. Ills. $7.50

MANNERHEIM, Marshall. *Memoirs of Marshall Mannerheim.* 1954. New York. 1st ed. dj. EX $27.50

MANNES, Marya. *Message from a Stranger.* 1948. New York. dj. VG $12.50

MANNING, William Ray. *The Nootka Sound Controversy.* 1966. $5.50

MANNING. *Bull Hunter's Romance, a Western Story.* 1924. Chelsea House. $4.50

MANNING. *Renegade Ranch.* Pocketbooks. pb. $3.00

MANNIX, D.P. *Adventure Happy.* 1954. 1st printing. 276 pp. dj. G $10.00

MANNIX, D.P. *All Creatures Great & Small.* 1963. McGraw Hill. Ills. 1st ed. 241 pp. dj. VG $10.00

MANNIX, D.P. *More Back-Yard Zoo.* 1936. Coward McCann. Ills. 252 pp. VG $10.00

MANNON, M.M. *Murder on the Program.* 1944. Indianapolis. Bobbs Merrill. 1st ed. G $12.50

MANO, D. Keith. *Take Five.* 1982. Doubleday. 1st ed. dj. VG $25.00

MANO, D. Keith. *The Death & Life of Harry Goth.* 1971. Knopf. 1st ed. dj. VG $15.00

MANSFIELD, Katherine. *Novels & Novelists.* 1930. New York. 1st ed. 321 pp. $12.50

MANSFIELD, Katherine. *Poems.* 1923. London. 1st ed. dj. VG $60.00

MANSFIELD, Katherine. *Something Childish & Other Stories.* 1924. London. 1st ed. 2nd issue. dj. EX $95.00

MANSFIELD, Katherine. *The Dove's Nest.* 1923. New York. 1st ed. G $10.00

MANTEGAZZA, P. *Sexual Relations of Mankind.* 1932. Ltd. ed. 1/1500. VG $18.00

MANTLE, Mickey. *The Quality of Courage.* 1964. New York. Doubleday. 185 pp. dj. $5.00

MANTLE. *The Best Plays of 1932-1933.* 1933. Dodd Mead. Ills. $6.50

MANVELL, R. *Goring.* 1972. New York. Ballentine. Ills. SftCvr. $5.00

MANVELL, Roger. *A Seat at the Cinema.* 1951. dj. VG $8.00

MANWARING, Charles W. *Early Connecticut Probate Records 1635-1750.* 1904. Hartford. Ltd. ed. 3 vol set. EX $150.00

MANWARING, G.E. *The Diary of Henry Teonge.* 1927. $7.50

MANZANO, J.M. *Invorporacion De Las Indias La Corona De Castilla.* 1948. Madrid. 356 pp. EX $46.00

MAO, S.H. *Turtles of Taiwan.* 1971. Taiwan, Ills. 128 pp. VG $30.00

MAPEI, Camillo. *Italy Classical History & Picturesque.* 1847. Glasgow. 62 pls. folio. $300.00

MAPIE. *La Cuisine De France.* 1964. Orion Pub. 1st ed. VG $25.00

MAPLE, T.L. & Hoff, M.P. *Gorilla Behavior.* 1982. Van Nostrand. Ills. 290 pp. EX $17.50

MARACHE, N. *Marache's Manual of Chess.* 1866. New York. Ills. 1st ed. VG $35.00

MARAN, Rene. *Batouala.* 1932. Ltd. Editons. Ills. Covarrubias. 1st ed. VG $15.00

MARBERRY, M.M. *Splendid Poseur Joaquin. Miller, American Poet.* 1953. dj. VG $10.00

MARBOE, Ernest. *The Book of Austria.* 1948. Vienna. Ills. 544 pp. index. dj. $10.00

MARCEAU, Marcel. *The Story of Bip.* 1976. Harper & Row. Ills. 1st ed. dj. VG $25.00

MARCH, Francis. *A History of the World War.* 1919. Canada/Chicago. ex-lib. 800 pp. VG $7.00

MARCH, Francis. *A History of the World War.* 1918. Universal Book & Bible Pub. $3.00

MARCH, Francis. *March's Thesaurus Dictionary.* 1958. New York. Doubleday. 1240 pp. $8.00

MARCH, Joseph Moncure. *Fifteen Lyrics.* 1929. New York. Fountain Press. Ltd. ed. sgn. $25.00

MARCH, Ngaio. *Black Beech & Honeydew, an Autobiography.* 1965. Boston. Ills. 1st Am. ed. 343 pp. dj. $12.50

MARCH, Peyton C. *The Nation at War.* 1932. Garden City. 407 pp. $12.50

MARCH, W. *Come in at the Door.* 1934. 1st ed. VG $25.00

MARCH, W. *Company K.* 1933. G $12.50

MARCH, William. *October Island.* 1952. Little, Brown. 1st ed. dj. VG $7.50

MARCH, William. *The Bad Seed.* 1954. Rinehart. 1st ed. dj. VG $12.50

MARCH, William. *The Looking Glass.* 1943. Little, Brown. 1st ed. G $5.00

MARCH, William. *Trial Balance. Collected Short Stories.* 1945. New York. 1st ed. 506 pp. VG $12.50

MARCOSSON, Isaac F. *Anaconda.* 1957. New York. Dodd Mead. Ills. 370 pp. dj. $7.50

MARCOSSON, Issac F. *The Story of Revere Copper & Brass Inc.* 1955. New York. Dodd Mead. 254 pp. dj. G $6.00

MARCOU, Jules. *American Geological Classification & Nomenclature.* 1888. Cambridge. 1st ed. 75 pp. $50.00

MARCOU, Jules. *Barrande & the Taconic System.* 1889. presentation copy. inscr. $50.00

MARCOU, Jules. *Cours de Geologie Palentologique.* 1856. Zurich. 1st ed. 16 pp. wrappers. $50.00

MARCOU, Jules. *Taconic System, Position in Stratigraphic Geology.* 1885. Cambridge. presentation copy. wrappers. $75.00

MARCUS, Adrianne. *The Chocolate Bible.* 1979. Putnam. dj. VG $15.00

MARCUS, G.J. *A Naval History of England.* 1962. maps. dj. VG $22.50

MARCUS, Stanley. *Quest for the Best.* 1979. Viking. 1st ed. dj. VG $11.50

MARCUS. *Rise & Destiny of German Jews.* 1934. Cincinnati. 417 pp. VG $22.50

MARCY, Randolph. *The Prairie Traveler.* 1859. New York. Ills. 1st ed. fld map. $210.00

MARDEN, Orison Swett. *Every Man a King.* 1906. Crowell. 240 pp. $3.50

MARDEN, Orison Swett. *Little Visits with Great Americans.* 1905. New York. VG $15.00

MARDEN. *Greece & Aegean Islands.* 1907. Boston. inscr. $20.00

MARE, Walter de la. *Desert Islands & Robinson Crusoe.* 1930. Faber. Ltd. 1st Deluxe ed. sgn. $25.00

MAREVNA. *Life with the Painters of LaRuche.* 1974. EX $4.00

MARGARET. *Great Horse.* 1937. Farrar. Ltd. ed. 1/1000. sgn. VG $20.00

MARGULIES, Leo. *Cactus & Sagebrush.* 1945. New York. 360 pp. $10.00

MARGULIES, Leo. *Flying Wildcats.* 1943. New York. Hampton Pr. 1st ed. 347 pp. G $17.50

MARIANA. *P'sich.* Far Gallery. Ills. Ltd. ed. 1/500. EX $225.00

MARIE, Duchess of Russia. *Education of a Princess, a Memoir.* 1931. New York. Viking. 388 pp. $6.00

MARIE, Joseph. *Medical Vocabulary.* 1939. Philadelphia. 389 pp. VG $20.00

MARIE, Queen of Romania. *The Lost Princess.* New York. Ills. Mabel Attwell. VG $40.00

MARILLIER, H.C. *Christie's 1766 to 1925.* 1926. London. Ills. 311 pp. $47.50

MARINGER, J. & Bandi, H.G. *Art in the Ice Age.* 1952. Praeger. Ills. folio. dj. VG $25.00

MARINI, F. *Meeting with Japan.* 1960. New York. Ills. dj. G $15.00

MARION, Frederick. *In My Mind's Eye.* 1950. New York. dj. EX $10.00

MARKEY, Richard. *The Aircraft Propeller.* 1943. Pitman. Ills. 3rd ed. 161 pp. $125.00

MARKHAM, Christopher A. *The New Pewter Marks & the Old Pewter Wares.* 1928. Reeves & Turner. $45.00

MARKHAM, Christopher A. *The New Pewter Marks & the Old Pewter Wares.* 1909. London. Reeves & Turner. Ills. G $125.00

MARKHAM, Edwin. *California the Wonderful.* 1914. New York. Hearst. Ills. 400 pp. index. $16.00

MARKHAM, Edwin. *Campbell Meeker.* 1925. Ltd. ed. 1/147. sgn. VG $50.00

MARKHAM, Edwin. *Gates of Paradise & Other Poems.* 1920. Doubleday Page. Country Life Press. VG $12.50

MARKHAM, Virgil. *Death in the Dusk.* 1928. New York. Knopf. 1st ed. dj. EX $45.00

MARKINO, Yoshio. *Japanese Artist in London.* 1910. Jacobs. 1st ed. $12.50

MARKS, Edward B. *They All Sang.* 1934. New York. Ills. presentation copy. G $18.00

MARKS, Geoffrey & Beatty, W. *The Precious Metals of Medicine.* 1975. New York. 294 pp. index. dj. EX $25.00

MARKS, Jeanette. *The Children in the Wood Stories.* 1919. Springfield. Ills. Clara M. Burd. 1st ed. $15.00

MARKS, Marilla. *Memoirs of the Life of David Marks, Minister.* 1846. Dover, NH. Free Will Baptist Pub. 516 pp. $100.00

MARKS, Richard & Morgan, N. *Golden Age of English Manuscript Painting.* 1982. London. Ills. 1st ed. wrappers. $20.00

MARKUS, Julia. *American Rose.* 1981. Houghton. 1st ed. dj. VG $12.50

MARKUS, Julia. *Friends Along the Way.* 1985. Houghton. 1st ed. dj. VG $15.00

MARKUS, Julia. *Uncle.* 1978. Houghton. 1st ed. dj. VG $15.00

MARLOWE, Christopher. *Edward II.* 1929. Kensington. Aquila Press. Ltd. ed. 1/500. $100.00

MARLOWE, George F. *Coaching Roads of Old New England.* 1945. New York. 200 pp. dj. $10.00

MARNE, Patricia. *Crime & Sex in Handwriting.* 1981. VG $4.00

MARQUAND, John P. *Point of No Return.* 1949. $25.00

MARQUAND, John P. *Sincerely Willis Wayde.* 1955. Boston. Little, Brown. 1st ed. $5.00

MARQUAND, John P. *So Little Time.* 1946. $25.00

MARQUAND, John P. *Thank You Mr. Moto.* 1938. $30.00

MARQUAND, John P. *The Late George Apley.* 1937. $25.00

MARQUAND, John P. *Thirty Years.* 1954. 1st ed. $30.00

MARQUAND, John P. *Women & Thomas Harrow.* 1958. $25.00

MARQUEZ, Gabriel Garcia. *Chronicles of Death Foretold.* 1982. Knopf. trans. Rabassa. 1st Am. ed. VG $15.00

MARQUEZ, Gabriel Garcia. *Evil Hour.* 1979. Harper. 1st Am. ed. dj. EX $25.00

MARQUEZ, Gabriel Garcia. *Innocent Erendira.* 1978. Harper. 1st Am. ed. dj. VG $30.00

MARQUEZ. *One Hundred Years of Solitude.* 1970. Harper. 1st ed. ex-lib. dj. VG $50.00

MARQUIS, Don. *Almost Perfect State.* 1927. 1st ed. VG $20.00

MARQUIS, Don. *Archy & Mehitable.* 1927. 1st ed. dj. VG $25.00

MARQUIS, Don. *Archy's Life of Mehitable.* 1933. Garden City. 1st ed. dj. EX $20.00

MARQUIS, Don. *Out of the Sea.* 1927. 1st ed. VG $20.00

MARQUIS, Don. *Revolt of the Oyster.* 1922. 1st ed. VG $20.00

MARQUIS, Don. *The Lives & Times of Archy & Mehitabel.* 1935. Garden City. Ills. Herriman. 477 pp. $10.00

MARQUIS, Don. *The Old Soak & Hail & Farewell.* 1921. Doubleday. 141 pp. $6.50

MARQUIS, James. *The Raven, Bibliography of Sam Houston.* 1929. New York. 489 pp. $15.00

MARQUIS, James. *They Had Their Hour.* 1934. Indianapolis. index. dj. EX $10.00

MARRIOTT, Alice. *Hell on Horses & Women.* 1953. U. of OK Press. Ills. Lefranc. 2nd ed. VG $11.00

MARRIOTT, Alice. *Plains Indian Mythology.* 1975. 1st ed. dj. EX $15.00

MARRIOTT, Alice. *The Ten Grandmothers.* 1945. Norman. 1st ed. dj. $15.00

MARRIOTT, Alice. *These Are the People. Notes on South West Indians.* 1949. Santa Fe. 1st ed. sgn. wrappers. $12.50

MARRYAT, Frank. *Mountains & Mole Hills.* 1855. New York. 1st Am. ed. 393 pp. $165.00

MARRYAT, Frederick. *A Diary in America.* 1839. New York 1st ed. 263 pp. $45.00

MARRYAT, Frederick. *Mr. Midshipman Easy.* 1909. London. Dent. Ills. Downing. 6 vol set. $12.50

MARRYAT, Frederick. *Peter Simple.* 1929. London. Ills. Ltd. ed. $60.00

MARRYAT, Frederick. *Stories of the Sea.* 1836. Harpers. $20.00

MARRYAT, Frederick. *The Children of the New Forest.* 1927. New York. Ills. Stafford Good. 1st ed. $30.00

MARSH, J.B.T. *Story of Jubilee Singers, with Their Songs.* 1880. Boston. revised ed. G $40.00

MARSH, John. *Lyman, George D.* 1931. New York. $15.00

MARSH, Ngaio & R.M. *Burden. New Zealand.* 1942. London. Collins. 1st ed. 48 pp. dj. VG $25.00

MARSH, Ngaio. *Black Beech & Honeydew.* 1966. London. Collins. 1st ed. dj. EX $55.00

MARSH, Ngaio. *Colour Scheme.* 1943. London. Collins. 1st ed. dj. VG $75.00

MARSH, Ngaio. *Final Curtain.* 1947. London. Collins. 1st ed. dj. VG $55.00

MARSH, Ngaio. *Hand in Glove.* 1962. Little, Brown. 1st Am. ed. dj. VG $25.00

MARSH, Ngaio. *Off with His Head.* 1957. London. Collins. 1st ed. VG $30.00

MARSH, Ngaio. *Overture to Death.* 1939. New York. 1st ed. ex-lib. G $10.00

MARSH, Ngaio. *When in Rome.* 1971. Boston. 1st ed. dj. EX $10.00

MARSH, Richard. *The Beetle.* Putnam reprint. VG $8.50

MARSH & EHRE. *Thirty Years of Best Sports Stories.* 1975. Dutton. 318 pp. dj. $4.50

MARSHALL, Archibald. *Pippin.* 1923. New York. Dodd Mead. 3rd ed. 376 pp. $37.50

MARSHALL, Catherine. *A Man Called Peter.* 1951. New York. McGraw Hill. 342 pp. dj. EX $4.50

MARSHALL, Catherine. *Adventures in Prayer.* 1975. dj. EX $3.00

MARSHALL, Catherine. *To Live Again.* 1957. New York. McGraw Hill. 335 pp. $4.50

MARSHALL, Catherine. *Together.* 1946. 310 pp. $4.00

MARSHALL, David. *Grand Central.* 1946. Whittlesey House. 2nd ptg. dj. $8.50

MARSHALL, Edison. *Castle in the Swamp.* 1948. $25.00

MARSHALL, Edison. *Child of the Wild.* 1926. $30.00

MARSHALL, Edison. *Gypsy Sixpence.* 1949. $25.00

MARSHALL, Edison. *Heart of the Hunter.* 1956. dj. EX $20.00

MARSHALL, Edison. *The Infinite Woman.* 1950. $25.00

MARSHALL, Edison. *The Light in the Jungle.* 1933. $25.00

MARSHALL, Edison. *The Strength of the Pines.* 1921. $30.00

MARSHALL, Edison. *Yankee Pasha.* 1947. $25.00

MARSHALL, H.E. *An Island Story.* New York. Stokes. no date. 1st printing. $25.00

MARSHALL, John. *The Life of George Washington.* 1926. Fredricksburg. Ltd. ed. 5 vol set. VG $50.00

MARSHALL, John. *The Life of George Washington.* 1807. London. Ills. 1st Eng. ed. VG $300.00

MARSHALL, John. *The Life of George Washington.* 1807. Philadelphia. 1st ed. $475.00

MARSHALL, Logan. *Sinking of the Titanic.* 1912. Ills. 350 pp. $5.00

MARSHALL, Logan. *Life of Theodore Roosevelt, Story of African Trip.* 1910. 424 pp. $10.00

MARSHALL, Logan. *The Panama Canal.* 1913. Ills. 286 pp. $4.00

MARSHALL, Logan. *The True Story of Our National Calamity.* 1913. photos. 352 pp. $4.50

MARSHALL, Louis. *Selected Papers & Addresses.* 1957. Philadelphia. 2 vol set. boxed. VG $10.00

MARSHALL, Paule. *The Chosen Place, the Timeless People.* 1970. London. Longmans. 1st Eng. ed. VG $35.00

MARSHALL, S.L.A. *American Heritage History of World War I.* 1964. no place. Ills. 384 pp. maps. dj. VG $17.50

MARSHALL, S.L.A. *Battles in Monsoon.* 1967. New York. 1st ed. EX $20.00

MARSHALL, S.L.A. *Crimsoned Prairie.* 1972. New York. Ills. maps. 268 pp. dj. $12.50

MARSHALL, S.L.A. *Pork Chop Hill.* 1956. Morrow. 1st ed. sgn. dj. VG $22.50

MARSHALL, T.B. & Evans, G.C. *They Found It in Natchez.* 1939. sgn. VG $22.50

MARSHALL, T.H. *Exotic Fish Keeping, Breeding the Egg Layers.* 1953. Saturn. Ills. 40 pp. G $6.00

MARSHALL, Thomas F. *Speeches & Writings of Hon. Thomas F. Marshall.* 1858. Cincinnati. 462 pp. $15.00

MARSHALL & WOLLMAN. *Festival! Book of American Musical Celebrations.* 1970. New York. 1st ed. wrappers. EX $8.50

MARSHALL. *Bullets at Clearwater.* Popular. pb. $3.00

MARSHALL. *Kitty.* 1946. World Pub. photos. $4.50

MARTELLI, G. *Livingstone's River/ History of Zambesi Expedition.* 1969. Ills. 1st Am. ed. map. dj. EX $17.50

MARTEN & CROSS. *The Doctor Looks at Murder.* 1937. Garden City. Ills. 1st ed. 325 pp. VG $35.00

MARTI-IBANEZ, Felix. *All the Wonders We Seek.* 1963. New York. Potter. 1st ed. VG $20.00

MARTIGNON, Margaret. *The Illustrated Treasury of Children's Literature.* 1955. Grosset & Dunlap. G $8.50

MARTIN, A.E. *After the White House.* 1951. dj. VG $10.00

MARTIN, Aime. *Langage des Fleurs.* 1835. Paris. French text. Ills. $130.00

MARTIN, B.P. *Sporting Birds of the British Isles.* 1984. David Charles. Ills. maps. pls. 256 pp. dj. $30.00

MARTIN, Douglas D. *Lamp in the Desert.* 1960. Ills. dj. VG $10.00

MARTIN, Douglas D. *The Earps of Tombstone.* Tombstone. 2nd ed. stiff wrappers. VG $12.50

MARTIN, Douglas D. *Tombstone's Epitaph.* 1951. Mexico Press. Ills. maps. 272 pp. $22.50

MARTIN, E.G. *Cruising & Ocean Racing.* 1948. London. Ills. photos. EX $25.00

MARTIN, Edward W. *The Secrets of the Great City.* 1868. Philadelphia. Jones Bros. Ills. 551 pp. $15.00

MARTIN, George & Tuttle, Lisa. *Windhaven.* 1981. New York. 1st ed. inscr. sgn. dj. EX $20.00

MARTIN, George. *Big Bend Basket Maker.* 1933. San Antonio. 1st ed. wrappers. $10.00

MARTIN, George. *Dying of the Light.* 1978. 1st Am. ed. dj. EX $20.00

MARTIN, George. *Verdi: His Music, Life, & Times.* 1963. New York. Ills. dj. VG $28.00

MARTIN, H. Newell. *Human Body.* 1898. 5th revised ed. 408 pp. $6.50

MARTIN, John A. *Addresses of Martin, Delivered in Kansas.* 1888. Topeka. 1st ed. 248 pp. $125.00

MARTIN, John Bartlow. *Call It North Country.* 1949. New York. 5th printing. G $6.00

MARTIN, John Bartlow. *Indiana: An Interpretation.* 1947. New York. 1st ed. dj. VG $12.50

MARTIN, Kay. *All the Gods & Goddesses.* 1963. New York. Putnam. 180 pp. $3.50

MARTIN, M.F. *Trout Lore.* 1942. New York. 1st ed. photos. VG $17.00

MARTIN, Malachi. *Hostage to the Devil.* 1976. New York. Reader's Digest Press. 477 pp. $4.50

MARTIN, Martha Evans. *The Friendly Stars.* 1907. Harper. 1st ed. $2.50

MARTIN, Nettie Parish. *A Pilgrim's Progress in Other Worlds.* 1908. Boston. Mayhew. 1st ed. VG $60.00

MARTIN, Percy. *Mexico's Treasure-House.* 1906. New York. Ills. maps. EX $35.00

MARTIN, Pete. *Will Acting Spoil Marilyn Monroe?* 1956. Doubleday. 1st ed. dj. VG $20.00

MARTIN, Rex. *Commercial Aviation* 1931. 3 vols. wrappers. $105.00

MARTIN, Sidney Walter. *Florida's Flagler.* 1949. Athens, GA. 1st ed. dj. VG $25.00

MARTIN, William. *Peter Parley's Tales About Boy Banditti.* London. (ca.1848) $20.00

MARTIN. *Behind the Scenes in Washington.* 1873. EX $25.00

MARTIN. *Boots & the Mystery of the Unlucky Vase.* 1943. Whitman. Ills. dj. EX $6.50

MARTINDALE, Thomas. *Sport Royal, I Warrant You!* 1897. Philadelphia. private print. inscr. 148 pp. $35.00

MARTINEAU, Harriet. *Feats on the Fiord.* 1924. Macmillan. Ills. 304 pp. $40.00

MARTINEAU, Harriet. *Retrospect of Western Travel.* 1838. London/NY. 2 vol set. 276; 239 pp. $125.00

MARTINET, Giles. *Marxism of Our Time.* 1964. New York. 1st ed. dj. EX $7.50

MARTINI, Helen. *My Zoo Family.* 1955. Harper. Ills. 208 pp. EX $10.00

MARTZOLFF, Clement L. *History of Perry County, Ohio.* 1902. Columbus, OH. Ills. 195 pp. $40.00

MARVEL, J.K. *Reveries of a Bachelor.* 1894. Altemus. $5.00

MARVIN, Charles. *Training the Trotter.* 1890. New York. 2nd ed. $20.00

MARVIN, E.M. *Lectures on Transubstantiation & Papacy.* 1878. St. Louis. 2nd ed. 592 pp. $12.50

MARX, Arthur. *Life with Groucho.* 1954. $5.00

MARX, Carl. *Capital.* 1906-1909. 1st ed. 3 vol set. $150.00

MARX, Groucho. *Groucho Letters. Letters to & from Groucho Marx.* 1967. New York. Simon & Schuster. 319 pp. VG $8.00

MARX, Groucho. *Memoirs of Mangy Lover.* 1963. Geis. 1st ed. dj. VG $22.50

MARX, Harpo. *Harpo Speaks.* 1961. Geis. 1st ed. dj. VG $40.00

MARX, Karl. *Letters to Dr. Kugelmann.* 1943. Moscow. VG $25.00

MARX, R.F. *Buried Treasure of U.S. Bonanza.* 1980. 401 pp. EX $22.50

MARX, Samuel. *Mayer & Thalberg, Make Believe Saints.* 1975. New York. Ills. 1st ed. EX $15.00

MASEFIELD, John & Seago, Ed. *The Country Scene.* 1937. London. Ills. Seago. VG $65.00

MASEFIELD, John. *John M. Synge: Few Personal Recollections.* 1915. Churchtown. Cuala Pr. Ltd. ed. 1/350. VG $75.00

MASEFIELD, John. *Philip the King & Other Poems.* 1914. London. 1st ed. slipcase. EX $65.00

MASEFIELD, John. *Reynard the Fox.* 1921. Ills. G.C. Armour. Ltd. sgn. $175.00

MASEFIELD, John. *Right Royal.* 1922. London. Ills. Ltd ed. 1/375. sgn. $135.00

MASEFIELD, John. *Salt-Water Poems & Ballads.* 1916. Macmillan. Ills. 163 pp. VG $35.00

MASEFIELD, John. *Salt-Water Poems & Ballads.* 1924. New York. 12 color pls. G $10.00

MASEFIELD, John. *The Midnight Fox.* 1932. New York. Ills. Rowland Hilder. 1st ed. $40.00

MASEFIELD, John. *The Nine Days Wonder.* 1941. Macmillan. 1st ed. $75.00

MASEFIELD, John. *The Story of a Round House.* 1916. New York. Macmillan. new & revised ed. $4.00

MASEFIELD, John. *The Wanderer of Liverpool.* 1930. $12.50

MASKELL, Alfred. *Ivories.* 1966. Rutland, VT. Tuttle. 1st ed. 551 pp. dj. EX $25.00

MASKELYNE, John N. *Sharps & Flats: Secrets of Cheating.* 1894. Longmans. Ills. EX $50.00

MASKELYNE, Nevil. *Maskelyne on the Performance of Magic.* 1976. VG $2.00

MASON, A.E. *Running Water.* 1907. $30.00

MASON, A.E. *The Winding Stair.* 1923. $27.50

MASON, Arthur. *Wee Men of Ballywooden.* 1931. London. Ills. Lawson. 1st English ed. $20.00

MASON, Bernard S. *Drums, Tomtoms, & Rattles.* 1938. New York. Ills. 1st ed. 208 pp. dj. VG $20.00

MASON, Bernard S. *Roping.* 1940. Willis & Goodin. dj. $4.00

MASON, Bobbie Ann & Stiles, M. *Landscapes.* 1984. Ltd. ed. sgns. wrappers. VG $30.00

MASON, Bobbie Ann. *In Country.* 1985. Harper. advance copy. wrappers. EX $50.00

MASON, Bobbie Ann. *In Country.* 1985. Harper. 1st ed. sgn. dj. VG $35.00

MASON, E.L. *Hiero-Salem.* 1889. Boston. Cupples & Leon. VG $15.00

MASON, Emily V. *The Southern Poems of the War.* 1867. Baltimore. $35.00

MASON, F. Van Wyck. *Castle Island Case.* 1938. London. Ills. VG $20.00

MASON, F. Van Wyck. *Proud New Flags.* 1951. New York. Lippincott. 493 pp. VG $4.50

MASON, F. Van Wyck. *Rivers of Glory.* 1942. Lippincott. dj. $3.50

MASON, F. Van Wyck. *The Hong Kong Airbase Murders.* 1937. New York. Doubleday. 1st ed. dj. VG $10.00

MASON, F. Van Wyck. *Three Harbours.* 1938. New York. 694 pp. $3.50

MASON, Frances. *John Norton & Sons, Merchants of London/Virginia.* 1937. Richmond. 1st ed. 573 pp. $35.00

MASON, Frances. *John Norton & Sons, Merchants of London/Virginia.* 1968. London. 573 pp. index. dj. EX $17.50

MASON, Francis K. *Aces of the Air.* 1981. New York. 1st ed. EX $12.50

MASON, Francis K. *The Hawker Hurricane.* 1962. London. Macdonald. 1st ed. EX $17.50

MASON, George. *Colonial Churches of Tidewater.* 1945. Richmond. Whittet & Shepperson. 381 pp. $20.00

MASON, H.M. *Lafayette Escadrille.* 1964. New York. dj. $20.00

MASON, James. *The Principles of Chess in Theory & Practice.* Philadelphia. 4th ed. revised & enlarged. $15.00

MASON, K. *Abode of Snow: Hist. of Himalayan Mountaineering.* 1955. New York. Ills. maps. VG $15.00

MASON, Miriam E. *Little Jonathan.* 1944. New York. Ills. George & Doris Hauman. $15.00

MASON, Mrs. *Ellegiac (sic) Poems, Sacred to Friendship.* 1803. Greenwich. Simon & Schuster. 1st ed. $45.00

MASON, Otis T. *Aboriginal American Basketry: Textile Art.* 1902. 377 pp. 248 pls. $25.00

MASON, R.O. *Telepathy & the Subliminal Self.* 1899. New York. 343 pp. index. $7.50

MASON, Revil. *Prehistory of the Transvaal.* Johannesburg. 1st ed. $22.50

MASON, Richard Lee. *Narrative of Mason in Pioneer West, 1819.* 1915. New York. Heartman. Ills. 1st ed. $150.00

MASON, Stuart. *Bibliography of Oscar Wilde.* 1941. London. 1st ed. index. dj. VG $150.00

MASON, Walt. *The Poet Philosopher.* 1910. Chicago. Ills. sgn. 189 pp. $7.50

MASON & DIXON. *Journal of Charles Mason & Jeremiah Dixon.* 1961. Philadelphia. trans from National Archives. $18.50

MASON & WEAVER. *The Electromagnetic Field.* 1932. $12.50

MASPERO. *Art in Egypt.* 1921. London. Ills. 1st ed. VG $18.00

MASSEY, Mary. *Bonnet Brigades. American Women & the Civil War.* 1966. Knopf. 1st ed. dj. $10.00

MASSEY, Ruth. *The Crime in the Boulevard Raspail.* 1932. London. Nelson. 1st ed. VG $12.50

MASSON, Flora. *Victorians All.* 1970. Kennikat. EX $17.50

MASSON, Tom. *The Von Blumers.* 1906. New York. Moffat Yard. Ills. B. Jones. $27.50

MASTERMAN, W. *The Borderland.* New York. Dutton. 1st ed. dj. VG $25.00

MASTERS, Brian. *The Dukes.* 1977. London. 1st ed. inscr. dj. EX $12.50

MASTERS, E. *Domesday Book.* 1920. New York. Macmillan. 1st ed. 396 pp. VG $15.00

MASTERS, E. *Spoon River Anthology.* 1915. New York. 1st ed. $125.00

MASTERS, E. *The Sangamon.* 1942. Ills. Lynd Ward. 1st ed. VG $10.00

MASTERS, John. *Bhowani Junction.* 1954. New York. Viking. 394 pp. dj. $3.50

MASTERS, John. *Bugles & a Tiger.* 1956. Viking. Ills. 314 pp. VG $10.00

MASTERS & JOHNSON. *Human Sexual Response.* 1966. Boston. 1st ed. 2nd printing. $47.50

MASTERSON, Bat. *Famous Gunfighters of the Western Frontier.* 1957. Frontier Press.VG $25.00

MASTERTON, Elsie. *Off My Toes!* 1961. Boston. Little, Brown. $7.50

MASTIN, John. *Through the Sun in an Airship.* 1909. London. Griffin. 2nd binding. VG $25.00

MATEJCEK. *Gothic Mural Painting Bohemia, Moravia.* 1964. English text. $36.00

MATEJCEK. *Gothic Painting in Bohemia 1350-1450.* 1938. Prague. original Czech ed. $88.00

MATES, Julian. *The American Musical Stage Before 1800.* 1962. dj. VG $9.00

MATES, R.E. *Photographing Art.* 1966. New York. dj. EX $15.00

MATHER, Increase. *Remarkable Providences.* 1890. London. 262 pp. $10.00

MATHERS, E. Powys. *The Book of the Thousand Nights & One Night.* 1923. London. Casanova Society. Ltd. ed. EX $80.00

MATHERS, James & Houts, M. *From Gun to Gavel.* 1954. New York. 1st ed. 246 pp. $8.50

MATHERS, Michael. *Riding the Rails.* 1973. Gambit. 1st printing. $17.50

MATHERS, S.L. MacGregor. *The Sacred Magic of Abra-Melin, the Mage.* 1948. Chicago. 3rd ed. G $45.00

MATHESON, Geo. *The Representative Men of the Bible.* Hodder. 369 pp. $3.00

MATHESON, Richard. *Born of Man & Woman.* 1954. 1st Am. ed. dj. EX $145.00

MATHESON, Richard. *Hell House.* 1971. New York. Viking. 1st ed. dj. EX $75.00

MATHESON, Richard. *I Am Legend.* 1954. 1st ed. pb. VG $45.00

MATHESON, Richard. *The Beardless Warriors.* 1960. 1st ed. dj. EX $100.00

MATHESON, Richard. *The Shrinking Man.* 1st ed. pb. VG $12.00

MATHESON, Richard. *What Dreams May Come.* 1978. New York. Putnam. 1st ed. dj. VG $25.00

MATHEWS, Ed. *Boy Scouts Courageous, Stories of Scout Valor.* 1918. Harcourt Brace. dj. $6.50

MATHEWS, F.S. *Field Book of Wild Birds & Their Music.* 1936. Putnam. Ills. 325 pp. VG $17.50

MATHEWS, John J. *The Osages Children of the Middle Waters.* 1961. U. of OK Press. 1st ed. dj. $15.00

MATHEWS, John J. *Wah'Kon-Tah. Osage & the White Man's Road.* 1932. U. Of OK Press.Ills. Aaron. 1st ed. 359 pp. $20.00

MATHISON, Volney. *The Radio Buster.* 1924. New York. Stokes. 1st ed. EX $20.00

MATSON, Ruth. *Cooking by the Garden Calendar.* 1955. Doubleday. 1st ed. inscr. dj. VG $3.00

MATSUKI, Heikichi. *Kodomo No Asobi: Children at Play.* 1907. Tokyo. Ills. rare. $750.00

MATTERN. *Handloading Ammunition.* 1926. VG $15.00

MATTHEWS, Brander. *Poems of American Patriotism.* 1922. New York. Ills. N.C. Weyth. 1st ed. VG $65.00

MATTHEWS, Greg. *Further Adventures of Huckleberry Finn.* 1983. Crown. 1st Am. ed. dj. VG $15.00

MATTHEWS, Herbert L. *The Cuban Story.* 1961. Braziller. 1st ed. dj. VG $10.00

MATTHEWS, J.H. *Surrealism & the Novel.* 1969. U. MI Press. 2nd printing. 189 pp. dj. EX $5.00

MATTHEWS, Jack. *Bitter Knowledge.* 1st Am. ed. dj. EX $10.00

MATTHEWS, Jack. *Dubious Persuasions.* 1981. John Hopkins. U. Pr. 155 pp. $7.50

MATTHEWS, Leonard H. *The Natural History of the Whale.* 1978. Columbia U. Ills. 219 pp. dj. EX $20.00

MATTHEWS, Leonard H. *The Natural History of the Whale.* 1968. Ills. 287 pp. dj. VG $25.00

MATTHEWS, S.K. *Photography in Archaeology & Art.* 1968. New York. dj. EX $15.00

MATTHEWS, T.S. *Under the Influence.* 1979. London. 354 pp. dj. EX $10.00

MATTHEWS & HUTTON. *The Life & Art of Edwin Booth.* 1906. Ills. 317 pp. $13.50

MATTHEWS. *Flying High: Book of Aviation & Model Airplanes.* 1930. Grosset & Dunlap. G $15.00

MATTHEWS. *Harry Bradford's Crusade.* 1883. Cassell. Ills. fair. $8.50

MATTHIESSEN, P. & Porter, E. *The Tree Where Man Was Born: African Experience.* 1972. New York. Dutton. 1st ed. dj. VG $15.00

MATTHIESSEN, Peter. *Blue Meridian, Search for the Great White Shark.* 1971. Random House. Ills. 204 pp. dj. VG $15.00

MATTHIESSEN, Peter. *Cloud Forest. Chronicle of South Am. Wilderness.* 1961. Viking. Ills. 280 pp. dj. VG $15.00

MATTHIESSEN, Peter. *Far Tortuga.* 1975. New York. 1st Am. ed. dj. VG $20.00

MATTHIESSEN, Peter. *Race Rock.* 1954. Harper. 1st ed. dj. VG $80.00

MATTHIESSEN, Peter. *Under the Mountain Wall, New Guinea.* 1962. New York. dj. VG $15.00

MATTHIESSEN, Peter. *Wildlife in America.* 1959. New York. Viking. 1st ed. dj. VG $37.50

MATTHIESSEN & MURDOCK. *The Notebooks of Henry James.* 1947. Oxford U. Pr. 1st ed. dj. $15.00

MATTINGLY, Garrett. *Catherine of Aragon.* 1941. ex-lib. VG $3.50

MATTISON, H. *Spirit-Rapping Unveiled!* 1855. New York. Ills. 240 pp. G $12.00

MATTISON, H. & Ballou, R. *William James on Psychical Research.* 1960. New York. Viking Press. 1st ed. 339 pp. $55.00

MATTOCKS, Brewer. *Minnesota as a Home for Invalids.* 1871. Philadelphia. 1st ed. 206 pp. $75.00

MATUNAS, E. *American Ammunitions & Ballistics.* 1979. dj. EX $12.50

MATZ, B.W. *Inns & Taverns of Pickwick.* 1921. New York. Ills. 1st ed. VG $15.00

MAUD, Alfred. *The Untouchables.* Ills. Ben Shahn. wrappers. VG $10.00

MAUDE, John. *Visit to the Falls of Niagara, in 1800.* 1826. London. Ills. Ltd. 1st ed. $500.00

MAUGHAM, R. *The Slaves of Timbuktu.* 1961. London. Longman. Ills. 1st ed. dj. VG $15.00

MAUGHAM, W. Somerset. *Ashenden or the British Agent.* 1941. New York. sgn. dj. VG $40.00

MAUGHAM, W. Somerset. *Cakes & Ale.* 1930. London. Heinemann. 1st ed. dj. EX $50.00

MAUGHAM, W. Somerset. *Catalina.* 1948. Doubleday. 275 pp. $3.50

MAUGHAM, W. Somerset. *Don Fernando.* 1935. 1st Am. ed. dj. VG $30.00

MAUGHAM, W. Somerset. *France at War.* 1940. London. 1st ed. ex-lib. VG $18.00

MAUGHAM, W. Somerset. *Liza of Lambeth.* 1947. London. Jubilee ed. G $75.00

MAUGHAM, W. Somerset. *Of Human Bondage.* 1936. Doubleday. 565 pp. $3.50

MAUGHAM, W. Somerset. *Rain.* Dell. SftCvr. EX $10.00

MAUGHAM, W. Somerset. *Strictly Personal.* Ltd. ed. 1/515. sgn. dj. VG $185.00

MAUGHAM, W. Somerset. *The Land of the Blessed Virgin.* 1905. London. Heinemann. 1st ed. VG $65.00

MAUGHAM, W. Somerset. *The Moon & Sixpence.* 1919. London. 1st ed. 1st issue. $65.00

MAUGHAM, W. Somerset. *The Narrow Corner.* 1st Eng. ed. VG $10.00

MAUGHAM, W. Somerset. *The Painted Veil.* 1925. New York. Ltd. ed. 1/250. sgn. G $100.00

MAUGHAM, W. Somerset. *The Razor's Edge.* 1944. Philadelphia. 250 pp. dj. $7.50

MAUGHAM, W. Somerset. *The Summing Up.* 1938. New York. Literary Guild. 310 pp. $7.50

MAUGHAM, W. Somerset. *The Summing Up.* 1938. Doubleday. 1st ed. $12.50

MAUGHAM, W. Somerset. *The Travel Books.* 1955. London. 1st ed. dj. $9.00

MAUGHAM, W. Somerset. *Then & Now.* 1946. Doubleday. 278 pp. $7.50

MAUGHAM, W. Somerset. *Up at the Villa.* 1941. London. 1st ed. dj. VG $40.00

MAUGHAM, W. Somerset. *Writer's Notebook.* 1949. 1st Am. ed. VG $80.00

MAULDIN, Bill. *Back Home.* 1947. Sloane. Ills. dj. EX $6.50

MAULDIN, Bill. *This Damn Tree Leaks.* 1945. 1st ed. wrappers. EX $22.50

MAULDIN, Bill. *Up Front.* 1945. Holt. photos. 228 pp. VG $4.50

MAUPASSANT, Guy de. *A Woman's Life.* 1942. Nonesuch & Heritage. boxed. EX $8.50

MAURIAC, Francois. *The Desert of Love.* 1951. New York. 1st Am. ed. VG $25.00

MAURICE, A.B. *Fifth Avenue.* 1918. New York. Ills. A.G. Cram. 1st ed. dj. $25.00

MAURICE, A.B. *New York in Fiction.* 1901. $21.00

MAURIER, Daphne du. *Modern Classics of Suspense.* 1938. Readers Digest. $3.50

MAUROIS, Andre. *Ariel. Life of Shelley.* 1925. New York. VG $15.00

MAUROIS, Andre. *Chelsea Way.* 1930. London. Ltd. ed. 1/530. sgn. dj. EX $80.00

MAUROIS, Andre. *Fattypuffs & Thinifers.* 1968. Bodley Head. Ills. Wegner. 1st ed. dj. VG $10.00

MAUROIS, Andre. *Le Pays de Trente-Six Mille Volontes.* 1929. Lib. Hachette. Ills. D'Andrienne Segur. sgn. $80.00

MAUROIS, Andre. *Lelia. The Life of George Sand.* 1958. New York. Harper. 482 pp. VG $7.00

MAUROIS, Andre. *Lelia. The Life of George Sand.* 1954. Harper. 482 pp. $4.00

MAUROIS, Andre. *Ni Ange, Ni Bete.* 1927. Paris. Ills. Pierre Gandon. sgn. EX $75.00

MAUROIS, Andre. *Prometheus. The Life of Balzac.* 1965. New York. Harper. Ills. 573 pp. dj. $7.50

MAUROIS, Andre. *The Thought Reading Machine.* 1938. New York. Harper. 1st ed. dj. EX $20.00

MAURY, M.F. *The Physical Geography of the Sea.* 1855. New York. Ills. 5th ed. 287 pp. $25.00

MAURY, R. *War of the Godly.* 1928. Ills. 1st ed. VG $10.00

MAURY. *Folk Origins of Indian Art.* 1969. Columbia U. Press. $10.00

MAUS, Cynthia P. *Pictures & Poetry.* 1947. Caxton. dj. EX $15.00

MAVOR, William. *Elements of Knowledge.* 1817 & 1819. New York. 2 vol set. $75.00

MAVOR, William. *Historical Account of Celebrated Voyages.* 1797. London. Ills. 1st ed. 20 vol set. $485.00

MAWHINNEY, A.H. *The Messenger of the Black Prince.* Philadelphia. 299 pp. $37.50

MAXON, P.B. *The Waltz of Death.* 1941. New York. Mystery House. 1st ed. VG $15.00

MAXWELL, Aymer. *Pheasants & Covert Shooting.* 1913. London. 332 pp. 16 pls. VG $20.00

MAXWELL, Elsa. *How to Do It.* 1957. Boston. 1st ed. dj. $12.50

MAXWELL, G. *Raven Seek Thy Brother.* 1969. Dutton. Ills. 1st ed. dj. VG $10.00

MAXWELL, G. *Ring of Bright Water.* 1961. Dutton. Ills. 1st ed. 211 pp. dj. VG $10.00

MAXWELL, G. *The Rocks Remain.* 1963. Dutton. Ills. 1st ed. 209 pp. dj. EX $10.00

MAXWELL, H. *History of Tucker County, West Virginia.* 1884. Kingwood, WV. Ills. 574 pp. $85.00

MAXWELL, Haymond, Sr. *The Story of Sycamore.* 1938. Ills. presentation copy. $25.00

MAXWELL, Herbert. *Rainy Days in a Library.* 1896. London. 1st ed. G $15.00

MAXWELL, William. *The Warner Letters.* 1982. London. Chatto & Windus. proof copy. $50.00

MAXWELL, William. *The Writer as Illusionist.* 1955. wrappers. EX $50.00

MAXWELL, William. *They Came Like Swallows.* 1937. 1st ed. VG $45.00

MAXWELL. *Lords of the Atlas.* 1966. New York. 1st ed. dj. EX $15.00

MAY, Earl Chapin. *The Canning Clan: Pageant of Pioneering Americans.* 1937. Macmillan. 1st printing. 487 pp. G $5.00

MAY, John Birchard. *The Hawks of North America.* 1935. New York. Ills. Brooks/Peterson. 140 pp. $35.00

MAY, Julian. *The Adversary.* 1984. Boston. 1st ed. dj. VG $10.00

MAY, Julian. *The Golden Torch.* 1982. Boston. 1st ed. review copy. dj. VG $20.00

MAY, Julian. *The Many Colored Land.* 1981. Boston. 1st ed. dj. EX $15.00

MAY, Julian. *The Many Colored Land.* 1981. 1st ed. proof copy. VG $30.00

MAY, Julian. *The Nonborn King.* 1983. Boston. 1st ed. dj. EX $15.00

MAY, Julian. *The Stanley Cup Playoffs.* 1975. Mankato, MN. Ills. 47 pp. juvenile. VG $5.00

MAY, Sophie. *Little Prudy Stories.* 1893. Boston. Ills. Davidson. 6 vol set. VG $50.00

MAY, Sophie. *Little Prudy's Cousin Grace.* 1899. Boston. Ills. Bertah Davidson. 1st ed. $15.00

MAYAKOVSKII, Vladimir. *Mayakovsky & His Poetry.* 1942. London. 151 pp. $8.00

MAYER, A.M. *Sport with Guns & Rod in American Woods & Waters.* 1883. Ills. 1st ed. VG $55.00

MAYER, Arthur. *Merely Colossal.* 1953. New York. Ills. Price. 1st printing. VG $9.00

MAYER, Charles. *Trapping Wild Animals in the Malay Jungle.* 1921. Garden City. Ills. 207 pp. dj. EX $20.00

MAYHAR, Ardath. *Exile on Vlahil.* 1984. Garden City. 1st ed. dj. VG $8.00

MAYHEW, Athol. *A Jorum of 'Punch.'* 1895. London. 1st ed. VG $20.00

MAYHEW, Edward. *Dogs.* 1854. Routledge. 1st ed. $22.50

MAYHEW, Ralph & Johnson, B. *The Happy-Go-Lucky Bubble Book.* 1919. New York. Ills. Chase. w/3 records. $40.00

MAYNARD, Joyce. *Baby Love.* 1981. Knopf. 1st ed. dj. VG $10.00

MAYNARD, Joyce. *Looking Back.* 1973. Doubleday. 1st ed. dj. VG $25.00

MAYNARD, W.B. *Genealogy of Maynard, Maurer & Related Families.* 1984. Baltimore. 2 vol set. $30.00

MAYO, Charles. *The Story of My Family & My Career.* 1968. Doubleday. 351 pp. $37.50

MAYR, Ernst. *Systematics & Origin of Species.* 1942. New York. Columbia U. Press. 1st ed. $110.00

MAZZOTI, Giuseppe. *Venetian Villas.* 1957. Rome. Photos. VG $35.00

MC ADAM, Roger W. *Commonwealth Giantess of the Sound.* 1959. $12.50

MC ADAM, Roger W. *Priscilla of Fall River.* 1947. $15.00

MC ADOO, William G. *Crowded Years, an Autobiography.* 1931. ex-lib. 542 pp. $12.00

MC AFEE, Robert B. *History of the Late War in Western Country.* 1919. Bowling Green. Ltd. ed. 1/300. VG $100.00

MC ALEENAN, Joseph. *Grand Canyon Trails.* 1924. New York. inscr. sgn. rare. $250.00

MC ALEER, John & Dickson, B. *Unit Pride.* 1981. New York. 1st ed. sgn. 515 pp. dj. $15.00

MC ALEER, John. *Rex Stout, a Biography.* 1977. Boston. Ills. 1st ed. 621 pp. dj. EX $10.00

MC ALISTER, Hugh. *The Mystery at Roaring Greek Farm.* 1931. Saalfield. $2.50

MC ALLISTER, Anna. *Ellen Ewing Wife of General Sherman.* 1936. 379 pp. $12.50

MC ARDLE, Kenneth, ed. *A Cavalcade of Collier's.* 1959. $5.00

MC ATEE, W.L. *The Ring-Necked Pheasant & Its Management.* 1945. Ills. ex-lib. $7.50

MC BAIN, E. *Heat.* 1981. New York. Viking Press. wrappers. $30.00

MC BAIN, E. *Snow White & Rose Red.* 1985. Holt. 1st ed. dj. VG $15.00

MC BETH, Kate C. *The Nez Perces Since Lewis & Clark.* 1908. New York. 272 pp. $35.00

MC BRIDE, Bill. *Pocket Guide to Identification of First Editions.* 1985. McBride. 3rd revised ed. wrappers. EX $6.00

MC BRIDE, J.C. *Past & Present Christian Co. Illinois.* 1904. Chicago. Clarke. G $75.00

MC BRIDE, Sarah. *Fabrics & Clothing.* 1931. New York. Ills. 1st ed. VG $10.00

MC BRIDE. *The White Lions of Timbavati.* 1977. Paddington Press. 220 pp. dj. $6.50

MC CABE, J.D. *Lights & Shadows of New York Life.* 1872. Philadelphia. $32.50

MC CAFFREY, A. *The Year of Lucy.* proof copy. $35.00

MC CAFFREY, Anne. *Dragon Drums.* 1979. 1st Eng. ed. inscr. EX $20.00

MC CAFFREY, Anne. *Moreta, Dragonlady of Pern.* 1983. New York. Ballantine. 1st ed. dj. $37.50

MC CAFFREY, Anne. *Moreta, Dragonlady of Pern.* 1983. London. 1st Eng. ed. sgn. dj. $30.00

MC CAFFREY, Anne. *The White Dragon.* London. 1st ed. sgn. $40.00

MC CALL, Dan. *Beecher.* 1979. Dutton. proof copy. dj. VG $15.00

MC CALL, Dan. *Bluebird Canyon.* 1983. dj. VG $15.00

MC CALL, Dan. *Bluebird Canyon.* 1982. Congdon. proof copy. wrappers. EX $10.00

MC CALLAN. *Life on Old St.David's Bermuda.* 1948. Hamilton. G $12.50

MC CAMMON, Robert R. *Mystery Walk.* 1983. 1st Am. ed. dj. EX $15.00

MC CANDLISH, Edward. *Daddy Turtle & the Well Sweep.* 1926. New York. Ills. Mc Candlish. VG $10.00

MC CANDLISH, Edward. *Little Miss Ducky Daddles.* 1926. New York. Ills. McCandlish. VG $10.00

MC CANN, C. *100 Beautiful Trees of India.* 1959. Bombay. Taraporevala. Ills. 168 pp. VG $15.00

MC CANN, E.A. *Ship Model Making. Vol. II.* 1931. New York. dj. G $10.00

MC CANN, Edson. *Preferred Risk.* 1955. New York. 1st ed. dj. EX $50.00

MC CANN. *Complete Cheerful Cherub, 1001 Verses.* Convici-Friede Pub. Ills. dj. $6.50

MC CARTHY, Albert. *Dance Band Era. Dancing Decades Ragtime to Swing.* 1971. Chilton. Ills. 1st ed. 176 pp. dj. VG $25.00

MC CARTHY, Jerome. *Basic Marketing: A Managerial Approach.* 1968. VG $5.00

MC CARTHY, Justin Huntley. *If I Were King.* 1901. Grosset & Dunlap. $5.00

MC CARTHY, Justin. *The Story of Gladstone's Life.* 1898. New York. Macmillan. 2nd ed. 516 pp. $6.00

MC CARTHY, Mary. *Birds of America.* 1971. Harcourt. 1st ed. dj. EX $15.00

MC CARTHY, Mary. *Hanoi.* 1968. Weidenfeld. 1st English ed. dj. VG $20.00

MC CARTHY, Mary. *Memories of a Catholic Girlhood.* 1957. New York. 1st ed. dj. EX $17.50

MC CARTHY, Mary. *On the Contrary. Articles of Belief, 1946-1961.* 1961. Farrar. 1st ed. dj. VG $15.00

MC CARTHY, Mary. *The Group.* 1963. Harcourt. 1st ed. dj. VG $15.00

MC CARTNEY, Linda. *Linda's Pictures: Collection of Photographs.* 1976. New York. 1st Am. ed. dj. EX $25.00

MC CARTY, John L. *Maverick Town, Story of Old Tascosa.* 1968. U. of OK. Ills. dj. VG $22.50

MC CAUGHEY, H. *Marco Polo Sheep Hunt.* 1962. private print. inscr. wrappers. EX $25.00

MC CAUSLAND, Elizabeth. *George Innes 1825-1894.* 1946. New York. Ills. 87 pp. $25.00

MC CLANAHAN, Ed. *Famous People I Have Known.* 1985. Farrar. 1st ed. dj. VG $15.00

MC CLANAHAN, Ed. *The Natural Man.* 1983. Farrar. 1st ed. dj. VG $15.00

MC CLANE, A.J. *The Practical Fly Fisherman.* 1975. Prentice Hall. dj. $3.50

MC CLEERY & GLICK. *Curtain Going Up.* 1939. Ills. 407 pp. dj. VG $15.00

MC CLELLAN, George. *Organization of the Army on the Potomac.* 1864. 242pp. $21.00

MC CLELLAN, George. *Reported Organization & Campaigns Army of Potomac.* 1864. New York. 1st ed. fld map. $35.00

MC CLELLAN, Isaac. *Haunts of Wild Game.* 1896. 1st ed. 300 pp. VG $32.50

MC CLELLAND, Doug. *Golden Age of B Movies.* 1981. reprint. dj. $6.00

MC CLELLAND, H. *How to Tie Flies for Trout.* 1931. VG $27.50

MC CLELLAND, Nancy. *Duncan Phyfe & English Regency 1795-1830.* 1939. William Scott. Ltd. 1st ed. 1/350. sgn. VG $100.00

MC CLINTOCK. *The Old North Trail.* 1910. London. Macmillan. Ills. photos. maps. $50.00

MC CLOSKEY, Robert. *Make Way for Ducklings.* 1952. New York. Viking. $5.00

MC CLOSKEY, Robert. *Time of Wonder.* 1957. folio. dj. VG $10.00

MC CLURE, Alexander K. *The Authentic Life of William McKinley.* 1901. W.E. Schull. Ills. 504 pp. $12.50

MC CLURE, J.B. *'Abe' Lincoln's Yarns & Stories.* 1901. Ills. 512 pp. VG $12.50

MC CLURE, J.B. *Stories & Sketches of General Garfield.* 1880. Chicago. 158 pp. $37.50

MC CLURE, Michael. *Gorf.* 1976. New Directions.1st ed. dj. VG $10.00

MC CLURE. *Man of Moderation.* Ltd. 1st ed. 1/500. wrappers. $10.00

MC COAN, J.C. *Egypt as It Is.* 1877. New York. fld map. EX $25.00

MC COMICK, Edgar L. *Creatures Here Below.* 1972. Kent, OH. sgn. 67 pp. EX $10.00

MC COMICK, Edgar L. *Home Place & Other Poems.* 1981. Kent, OH. sgn. 80 pp. EX $7.50

MC COMSEY & EDWARDS. *The Soldier & the Law.* Harrisburg. Ills. 401 pp. VG $18.00

MC CONKEY, Harriet E. *Dakota War Whoop. Indian Massacres & War in MN.* 1970. 429 pp. $12.00

MC CONKEY, Harriet E. *Dakota War Whoop. Indian Massacres & War in MN.* 1965. Chicago. Ills. 395 pp. $12.50

MC CONKLE, John. *Three Years with Quantrell.* Armstrong, MO. (ca.1914) 1st ed. 157 pp. $300.00

MC CONNELL, James R. *Flying for France with Am. Escadrille at Verdun.* 1919. New York. G $20.00

MC CONNELL, James R. *Flying for France.* 1917. New York. Doubleday. Ills. 157 pp. VG $5.00

MC CONNELL, James. *Understanding Human Behavior.* 1977. Holt, Rinehart & Winston. $2.00

MC CONNELL, W.J. *Early History of Idaho.* 1913. Caldwell. Ills. 1st ed. 420 pp. $85.00

MC COOK, Henry Christopher. *Nature's Craftsmen.* 1907. New York. Ills. 1st ed. 316 pp. $20.00

MC CORD, David. *The Star in the Pail.* 1975. Boston. Ills. Marc Simont. 1st ed. VG $15.00

MC CORD, Howard. *Peach Mountain Smoke Out.* 1977. Salt Works. Ltd. ed. wrappers. EX $5.00

MC CORD, William B. *History of Columbiana County, Ohio.* 1905. Chicago. Ills. 848 pp. $75.00

MC CORMICK, John B. *The Square Circle or Stories of the Prize Ring.* 1897. New York. Continental Pub. 274 pp. $40.00

MC COSKER, M.J. *Hist. Collection of Insurance Co. North America.* 1945. Philadelphia. Ills. VG $15.00

MC COUGALL, W. *Abnormal Psychology.* 1926. $20.00

MC COUGALL & BAGGLEY. *Plants of Yellowstone National Park.* 1936. 160 pp. SftCvr. $20.00

MC COWAN, Dan. *Animals of the Canadian Rockies.* 1938. Toronto. Macmillan. Ills. sgn. 302 pp. VG $10.00

MC COY, Horace. *I Should Have Stayed Home.* 1938. New York. 1st ed. G $25.00

MC COY, Melvin & Mellnik. *Ten Escape from Tojo.* 1944. New York. Ills. 106 pp. $12.50

MC COY, Raymond. *The Massacre of Old Fort Mackinac.* 1940. Bay City, MI. Ills. 167 pp. wrappers. $20.00

MC COY, Samuel Duff. *Nor Death Dismay.* 1944. $7.50

MC CRACKAN, W.D. *The Rise of the Swiss Republic.* 1892. Boston. VG $15.00

MC CRACKEN, Harold. *Frederic Remington's Own West.* 1960. New York. Dial Press. 1st ed. 254 pp. VG $22.50

MC CRACKEN, Harold. *George Catlin & the Old Frontier.* 1954. New York. Ills. 216 pp. folio. dj. $45.00

MC CRACKEN, Harold. *Nicolai Fechin.* 1961. New York. $80.00

MC CRACKEN, Harold. *Portrait of the Old West.* 1952. New York. Ills. 1st ed. 232 pp. dj. VG $35.00

MC CRACKEN, Harold. *The American Cowboy.* 1973. Garden City. 1st ed. 196 pp. dj. EX $25.00

MC CRACKEN, Harold. *The American Cowboy.* 1973. Garden City. Ltd. ed. sgn. $200.00

MC CRACKEN, Harold. *The Charles M. Russell Book.* 1957. New York. dj. EX $50.00

MC CRACKEN, Harold. *The Frank Tenney Johnson Book.* 1974. New York. 207 pp. folio. dj. $55.00

MC CRACKEN, Harold. *The Frederic Remington Book.* 1966. Garden City. Ltd. 1st ed. sgn. boxed. $150.00

MC CRAE, Thomas. *Osler's Principles & Practice of Medicine.* 1931. Appleton. revised 11th ed. VG $25.00

MC CRONE, Guy. *Red Plush* 1946. $3.00

MC CUE, James Westaway. *Joe Lincoln of Cape Cod.* 1949. Mass. 2 djs. $20.00

MC CULLERS, Carson. *Ballad of the Sad Cafe.* 1951. Boston. 1st ed. dj. VG $40.00

MC CULLERS, Carson. *Clock Without Hands.* 1961. 1st ed. VG $50.00

MC CULLERS, Carson. *Reflections in a Golden Eye.* 1941. Boston. 1st ed. dj. VG $85.00

MC CULLERS, Carson. *The Member of the Wedding.* 1946. Houghton. 1st ed. VG $15.00

MC CULLOCH, J.R. *Dictionary of Commerce & Commercial Navigation.* 1845. Philadelphia. 2 vol set. G $20.00

MC CULLOUGH, C. *The Thorn Birds.* 1977. Harper & Row. 1st ed. VG $30.00

MC CULLOUGH, David G. *The Johnstown Flood.* 1968. New York. Ills. 302 pp. VG $10.00

MC CURDY, Michael. *American Decorative Papermakers.* 1983. Boston. Busyhaus Pub. Ills. Ltd. ed. $60.00

MC CURDY, Michael. *Giono, the Man Who Planted Trees.* 1985. Chelsea. Ills. 1st printing. dj. EX $10.00

MC CUTCHEON, George Barr. *A Fool & His Money.* 1913. New York. Ills. A.I. Keller. 373 pp. G $30.00

MC CUTCHEON, George Barr. *Beverly of Graustark.* 1904. Dodd Mead. Ills. Harrison Fisher. $10.50

MC CUTCHEON, George Barr. *Black Is White.* 1914. $30.00

MC CUTCHEON, George Barr. *Castle Craneycrow.* 1902. New York. Grosset & Dunlap. 391 pp. $30.00

MC CUTCHEON, George Barr. *Castle Craneycrow.* 1902. Chicago. Stone. 1st ed. 1st issue. $20.00

MC CUTCHEON, George Barr. *Graustark.* 1901. New York. Grosset & Dunlap. 399 pp. G $10.00

MC CUTCHEON, George Barr. *Jane Cable.* 1906. New York. 336 pp. $10.00

MC CUTCHEON, George Barr. *Mr. Bingle.* 1915. $30.00

MC CUTCHEON, George Barr. *The City of Masks.* 1918. $30.00

MC CUTCHEON, George Barr. *The Daughter of Anderson Crow.* 1907. Dodd Mead. Ills. B. Martin Justice. $8.50

MC CUTCHEON, George Barr. *The Merivales.* 1929. $27.50

MC CUTCHEON, George Barr. *The Sherrods.* 1903. New York. Dodd Mead. 343 pp. $37.50

MC CUTCHEON, George Barr. *Truxton King.* 1000. New York. 769 pp. $10.00

MC CUTCHEON, George Barr. *Viola Gwyn.* 1922. $30.00

MC CUTCHEON, George G. *Brewster's Millions.* 1902. New York. Grosset & Dunlap. Ills. $10.00

MC DADE, M. Thomas. *The Annals of Murder.* 1961. OK Press. 1st ed. 360 pp. index. dj. VG $21.50

MC DANIEL, Ruel. *Vinegarroon; or, Saga of Judge Roy Bean.* 1936. Kingsport, TN. 142 pp. $12.00

MC DANIEL. *The Desert. God's Crucible.* 1926. Boston. 1st ed. dj. VG $15.00

MC DERMAND, Charles. *Waters of the Golden Trout Country.* 1946. Ills. VG $25.00

MC DERMOTT, J. *Audubon in the West.* 1965. OK U. Press. Ills. 1st ed. 131 pp. dj. EX $15.00

MC DERMOTT, J.F. *Travelers on the Western Frontier.* 1970. Ills. dj. VG $12.50

MC DONALD, Arthur N. *Checklist of Bookplates by Mc Donald.* 1914. Princeton. private print. Ltd. ed. 1/250. $85.00

MC DONALD, Edward D. *The Posthumous Papers of D.H. Lawrence.* 1936. New York. Viking. 1st ed. dj. VG $75.00

MC DOUGAL, Henry C. *Recollections, 1884-1909.* 1910. Kansas City. dj. VG $40.00

MC DOWALL, Roddy. *Double Exposure.* 1966. Delacorte. 1st ed. dj. EX $20.00

MC DOWELL, Robert Emmett. *City of Conflict.* 1962. Louisville. Ills. 1st ed. sgn. 259 pp. dj. $20.00

MC DOWELL, Tremaine. *American Sketchbook.* 1938. Macmillan. Ills. Rockwell Kent. 706 pp. $6.50

MC ELHONES. *Magical Mysteries.* 1929. New York. dj. VG $6.00

MC ELROY, J. *Hind's Kidnap.* 1969. 1st ed. VG $45.00

MC ELROY, J. *Ship Rock.* 1980. Ewart. Ltd. ed. 1/226. sgn. VG $45.00

MC ELROY, John. *Andersonville: Story of Rebel Military Prisons.* 1879. Toledo. Ills. 1st ed. 654 pp. $40.00

MC ELROY, T.P. *Handbook of Attracting Birds.* 1951. Knopf. Ills. 163 pp. dj. VG $7.50

MC ELROY, T.P. *The Habitat Guide to Birding.* 1974. Knopf. Ills. 257 pp. EX $10.00

MC ELROY. *Ancient History.* revised copy. dj. VG $45.00

MC EWAN, Ian. *The Cement Garden.* 1978. Simon & Schuster. 1st Am. ed. $17.50

MC EWAN, Ian. *The Comfort of Strangers.* 1981. Simon & Schuster. 1st Am. ed. $10.00

MC FARLAND, J. Horace. *American Rose Annual.* 1918. Harrisburg. VG $10.00

MC FARLANE, Brian. *Hockey Quiz.* 1974. Pagurian Press.Ills. 191 pp. dj. EX $7.50

MC FARLANE, Brian. *Stanley Cup Fever.* 1978. Pagurian Press.Ills. 253 pp. dj. EX $8.50

MC FARLING, Lloyd. *Exploring the Northern Plains 1804-1876.* 1955. Caxton Press. 1st ed. dj. EX $17.50

MC FEE, Inez. *The Story of Idylls of the King.* 1912. New York. Ills. Kirk & Hood. 1st ed. $50.00

MC FEE, William. *North of Suez.* 1930. Garden City. Ltd. ed. 1/350. sgn. VG $45.00

MC FEE, William. *The Life of Sir Martin Frobisher.* 1928. Harper. Ills. 1st ed. 276 pp. VG $37.50

MC FERRIN, John Berry. *Caldwell & Company.* 1939. Chapel Hill. 1st ed. G $15.00

MC GAW, James F. *Philip Seymour; or, Pioneer Life in Richland Co.* 1902. Mansfield, OH. 3rd ed. 432+7 pp. ads. $20.00

MC GEE, J.E. *Glories of Ireland.* 1876. New York. Ills. 4 vols in 1. 152 pp. VG $37.50

MC GEE, Leo & Boone, R. *The Black Rural Landowner.* 1979. 1st ed. $6.50

MC GILL, Ralph. *The South & the Southerner.* 1963. 1st ed. VG $10.00

MC GILL, William M. *Caverns of Virginia.* 1933. VG $30.00

MC GILLYCUDDY, Julia B. *McGillycuddy Agent: Biography of Dr. Valentine.* 1941. Stanford. Ills. 1st ed. 291 pp. $50.00

MC GINLEY, Patrick. *Bogmail.* 1981. New York. Ticknor & Fields. 1st ed. EX $35.00

MC GINLEY, Patrick. *Foggage.* 1983. New York. St. Martins. 1st ed. dj. EX $25.00

MC GINLEY, Patrick. *Goosefoot.* 1982. New York. Dutton. 1st ed. dj. EX $25.00

MC GINLEY, Patrick. *The Trick of the Ga Bolga.* 1985. New York. St. Martins. 1st ed. dj. EX $20.00

MC GINLEY, Phillis. *Merry Christmas, Happy New Year.* 1958. sgn. $6.00

MC GINLEY, Phyllis. *A Short Walk from the Station.* 1951. New York. Viking. Ills. MacDonald. EX $15.00

MC GINLEY, Phyllis. *The Horse Who Lived Upstairs.* 1944. Philadelphia. Ills. Helen Stone. 1st ed. $25.00

MC GLASHAN, Charles F. *History of the Donner Party.* 1880. San Francisco. 3rd ed. $160.00

MC GLUNG, R. *Lost Wild Worlds.* 1976. Morrow. Ills. Hines. 1st ed. dj. VG $15.00

MC GOVERN, James. *Life & Life Work of Pope Leo XII.* 1903. 535 pp. $37.50

MC GOVERN, John. *The Golden Censer.* 1883. Chicago. 448 pp. $5.50

MC GOVERN, William M. *Jungle Paths & Inca Ruins.* 1927. New York. Ills. 526 pp. EX $18.00

MC GOVERN, William M. *Jungle Paths & Inca Ruins. Record of Expedition.* 1928. London. fld map. photos. $22.50

MC GOVERN, William Montgomery.*The Early Empires of Central Asia.* 1939. U. of NC Press.Ills. 529 pp. $5.50

MC GOWN, Pearl L. *You Can Hook Rugs.* 1953. dj. VG $7.50

MC GRAW, Eloise Jarvis. *Master Cornhill.* 1973. New York. Ills. 1st ed. dj. EX $10.00

MC GRAW, Jim. *Making Money on the Trotters.* 1952. New York. inscr. dj. EX $10.00

MC GRAW, Lisa. *Rex Brasher's Treasury of Bird Paintings.* 1967. New York. folio. 162 full pp color pls. $100.00

MC GRAW & WAGNER. *Merry Go Round in Oz.* 1963. Chicago. 1st ed. 2nd issue. ex-lib. $75.00

MC GROARTY, John Steven. *Just California & Other Poems.* 1933. Los Angeles. Times Mirror Press. 203 pp. VG $15.00

MC GUANE, Thomas. *Missouri Breaks.* 1976. 1st Am. ed. wrappers. EX $15.00

MC GUANE, Thomas. *Ninety Two in the Shade.* 1973. 1st Am. ed. dj. EX $30.00

MC GUANE, Thomas. *Panama.* 1978. Farrar. 1st ed. sgn. dj. VG $30.00

MC GUANE, Thomas. *Something to Be Desired.* 1984. Random House. 1st ed. sgn. dj. VG $30.00

MC GUANE, Thomas. *The Bushwacked Piano.* 1971. New York. Simon & Schuster. 1st ed. VG $30.00

MC GUANE, Thomas. *The Sporting Club.* 1968. Simon & Schuster. 1st ed. dj. $50.00

MC GUFFEY, William H. *McGuffey's Eclectic Fourth Reader.* 1848. New York. Clark, Austin & Smith. 336 pp. $5.00

MC GUFFEY, William H. *McGuffey's New Eclectic Second Reader.* 1865. Cincinnati. 162 pp. $10.00

MC GUFFEY, William H. *McGuffey's Newly Revised Eclectic Second Reader.* Cincinnati. (ca.1853) 224 pp. $20.00

MC HENRY, Beth & Myers, F.N. *Home is the Sailor.* 1948. New York. 1st ed. wrappers. VG $15.00

MC HUGH, Hugh. *Skiddoo.* 1906. Dillingham Co. Ills. G. Grant. 112 pp. EX $4.50

MC HUGH, Tom. *The Time of the Buffalo.* 1972. New York. Ills. 350 pp. biblio. dj. $15.00

MC ILWAINE, Shields. *Memphis Down in Dixie.* 1948. New York. Dutton. 2nd printing. 400 pp. $10.00

MC INERNEY, Jay. *Bright Lights, Big City.* London. 1st hardcover ed. VG $40.00

MC INERNEY, Jay. *Bright Lights, Big City.* 1985. London. Cape. 1st Eng. ed. cloth binding. VG $25.00

MC INTOSH, Christopher. *Astrologers & Their Creed: Historical Outline.* 1969. London. Hutchinson. 1st ed. 146 pp. EX $15.00

MC INTYRE, Vonda N. *Dreamsnake.* 1978. Boston. Houghton Mifflin. 1st ed. VG $60.00

MC INTYRE, Vonda N. *Superluminal.* 1983. Ltd. ed. 1/300. sgn. boxed. VG $25.00

MC INTYRE, Vonda N. *Superluminal.* 1983. Boston. review copy. dj. EX $15.00

MC ISAAC. *The Mental Marvel.* 1930. G $3.50

MC KAY, Donald. *Some Famous Sailing Ships & Their Builders.* 1928. New York. Ills. EX $30.00

MC KAY, Richard. *South Street, a Maritime History of New York.* 1934. New York. Ills. 1st ed. dj. VG $25.00

MC KEAN, Thomas J. *Report of Engineer of the Iowa Western Railroad.* 1851. 20 pp. wrappers. $400.00

MC KEARIN, George S. *American Glass.* 1944. New York. $12.50

MC KEE, Lanier. *The Land of Nome.* 1902. New York. VG $20.00

MC KEE. *Great Lakes Country.* 1966. 2nd ed. dj. EX $10.00

MC KEE. *Havasupai Baskets & Their Makers 1930-1940.* 1975. 1st ed. dj. EX $15.00

MC KELVEY, B. *Rochester on the Genesee.* 1973. Syracuse U. Pr.1st ed. dj. VG $10.00

MC KELWAY, St. Clair. *The Edinburgh Plot.* 1962. New York. Holt. 1st ed. sgn. 190 pp. dj. $5.00

MC KENNA, Dolores. *Hootie-the-Owl.* 1921. Stokes. Ills. Ruth Bennett. 34 pp. $3.00

MC KENNA, Joseph. *Union Pacific Railroad Company.* 1897. Washington. 1st ed. 90 pp. $75.00

MC KENNEY, H.D. & Anderson, W. *Music in History.* 1940. Am. Book Co. Ills. 904 pp. EX $15.50

MC KENNEY & HALL. *History of Indian Tribes of North America.* 1848. Philadelphia. 1st ed. color pls. $900.00

MC KENNEY. *Loud Red.* 1947. 1st ed. dj. VG $9.00

MC KENNY, M. *Birds in the Garden & How to Attract Them.* 1939. Hitchcock. Ills. 349 pp. VG $12.50

MC KENNY, M. *Wildlife in the Pacific Northwest.* 1954. Binfords Mort. Ills. 299 pp. dj. EX $7.50

MC KEOWN, Bonni. *Peaceful Patriot: Story of Tom Bennett.* 1980. Charleston, WV. Ills. 1st ed. 224 pp. $5.00

MC KIE, Ronald. *The Survivors.* 1953. $8.50

MC KIERNAN, Dennis. *Shadows of Doom.* 1984. Garden City. 1st ed. dj. $10.00

MC KILLIP, P.A. *The Chronicles of Morgon.* 1979. London. Sidgwick. 1st ed. EX $25.00

MC KIM, R.H. *General J.E.B. Stuart in Gettysburg Campaign.* 1909. Richmond. 24 pp. wrappers. VG $15.00

MC KINLEY, Ashley C. *Applied Aerial Photography.* 1929. New York. Ills. 1st ed. 341 pp. $12.50

MC KINLEY, W.L. *Karluk, Great Untold Story of Arctic Exploration.* 1976. St.Martins. Ills. 170 pp. dj. VG $17.50

MC KUEN, Rod. *And to Each Season.* 1972. New York. Ltd. ed. 1/1000. inscr. sgn. $20.00

MC KUEN, Rod. *Fields of Wonder.* 1971. New York. inscr. sgn. VG $20.00

MC KUEN, Rod. *In Someone's Shadow.* 1969. 3rd printing. dj. EX $7.00

MC KUEN, Rod. *Lonesome Cities.* 1967. New York. 1st ed. inscr. sgn. dj. VG $20.00

MC KUEN, Rod. *Moment to Moment.* 1974. Simon & Schuster. dj. VG $3.00

MC KUSICK, M. *Men of Ancient Iowa.* 1964. IA. State U. Press. dj. VG $35.00

MC LANATHAN, Richard. *The Art of Marguerite Stix.* 1977. New York. pls. dj. EX $45.00

MC LANE, L. *A Piney Paradise in Monterey Bay.* 1952. 1st ed. sgn. VG $15.00

MC LAUGHLIN, J. Fairfax. *Matthew Lyon. Hampden of Congress.* 1900. New York. Ills. 1st ed. 531 pp. $35.00

MC LAUGHLIN, James. *My Friend the Indian.* 1926. Boston/NY. Ills. 417 pp. $30.00

MC LAUGHLIN, Robert. *The Heartland; IL, IN, MI, OH, WI.* 1967. New York. Time Life Library. 192 pp. $8.50

MC LAUGHLIN, Terence. *The Gilded Lily.* 1972. London. Cassell. 188 pp. dj. VG $4.00

MC LAURIN, J. *Sketches in Crude Oil.* 1896. Ills. 1st ed. G $50.00

MC LEAN, Beth Bailey. *Modern Homemaker's Cookbook.* 1950. New York. Barrows. 311 pp. $6.50

MC LEAN, Olive. *Flowers of Hawaii.* 1938. Dodd. 1st ed. 30 color pls. boxed. $35.00

MC LEAVE, Hugh. *Rogues in the Art Gallery.* 1981. VG $3.00

MC LENNAN, J.S. *Louisbourg from Foundation to Fall, 1713-1758.* 1969. Sydney. Ills. 328 pp. $25.00

MC LEOD, Alex. *The Ecclesiastical Catechism.* 1806. New York. Hopkins & Seymour. 129 pp. $7.00

MC LOUGHLIN, D. *Wild & Woolly. Encyclopedia of the Old West.* 1975. Doubleday. 1st ed. VG $12.50

MC LOUGHLIN. *Santa Claus & His Doings.* 1901. VG $20.00

MC MAHAN, Anne. *With Shelley in Italy 1818-1822.* 1905. Chicago. McClure. Ills. 1st ed. EX $45.00

MC MAHAYN, Thomas. *McKay's Bees.* 1979. Harper. 1st ed. dj. VG $15.00

MC MILLAN, George. *The Old Breed/History 1st Marine Division in WWII.* 1949. Washington. Ills. 1st ed. 483 pp. G $47.50

MC MILLAN, Harold. *Winds of Change.* 1966. New York. 1st ed. $10.00

MC MILLAN, Prisilla. *Marina & Lee.* 1977. New York. 1st ed. wrappers. EX $40.00

MC MURRICH, J.P. *Leonardo Da Vinci, the Anatomist (1452-1519).* 1930. Baltimore. Carnegie Inst. Ills. 264 pp. $22.50

MC MURTRY, Larry. *Cadillac Jack.* Ltd. ed. sgn. slipcase. EX $27.50

MC MURTRY, Larry. *Last Picture Show.* 1966. New York. 1st ed. dj. EX $50.00

MC MURTRY, Larry. *Moving On.* 1970. 1st ed. dj. EX $20.00

MC MURTRY, Larry. *Somebody's Darling.* 1978. 1st ed. ex-lib. dj. VG $17.50

MC MURTRY, Larry. *Terms of Endearment.* 1975. New York. Simon & Schuster. 1st ed. VG $25.00

MC MURTRY, Larry. *The Desert Rose.* London. Allen. 1st Eng. ed. dj. EX $25.00

MC MURTRY, R. Gerald. *Let's Talk of Lincoln.* 1938. sgn. VG $15.00

MC MURTRY. *All My Friends Are Going to be Strangers.* 1972. New York. 1st ed. dj. EX $22.50

MC NAB, Allan. *The Picture-Book of Rivers.* 1932. New York. Ills. 1st ed. VG $25.00

MC NAB, Tom. *Flanagan's Run.* 1982. Morrow. advance copy. wrappers. VG $10.00

MC NAIR, Ralph J. *Square Dancing.* 1951. Ills. 188 pp. $5.00

MC NEAL, T. *When Kansas Was Young.* 1940. Topeka. Capper Pub. dj. VG $15.00

MC NEER, M. *John Wesley.* 1951. Ills. Lynd Ward. 1st ed. $30.00

MC NEER, M. *Tales from the Crescent Moon.* 1930. Farrar & Rinehart. 1st ed. VG $35.00

MC NEER, Max. *Martin Luther.* 1953. Ills. Ward. 1st ed. dj. $12.50

MC NEER, May. *America's Abraham Lincoln.* 1957. Boston. Ills. Lynd Ward. 1st ed. $20.00

MC NEER, May. *The Golden Flash.* 1947. New York. 1st ed. dj. VG $30.00

MC NEILL, F. Marian. *Scots Kitchen.* 1930. G $10.00

MC NEILL, W.A. *Cabellian Harmonics.* 1928. Ltd. ed. 1/1500. VG $25.00

MC NEILL, William H. *Pursuit of Power.* 1982. Chicago. Ills. 1st ed. 405 pp. dj. EX $10.00

MC NEILLY, Mildred Masterson. *Each Bright River, a Novel of the Oregon Country.* 1950. Morrow. $37.50

MC NICOL, Donald M. *Amerindians from Acuera/Sitting Bull/Big Bear.* 1937. New York. 1st ed. 341 pp. index. dj. $18.50

MC NULTY, F. *The Whooping Crane, Birds that Defie Extinction.* 1966. Dutton. Ills. 1st ed. 190 pp. dj. EX $10.00

MC NULTY, Faith & Keiffer, E. *Whooly Cats.* 1962. Bobbs Merrill. Ills. 1st ed. dj. VG $20.00

MC PHEE, John. *Coming Into the Country.* 1977. Farrar. Ills. 438 pp. dj. $10.00

MC PHEE, John. *Giving Good Weight.* 1979. New York. Farrar. dj. EX $15.00

MC PHEE, John. *Oranges.* 1967. New York. 1st ed. dj. EX $35.00

MC PHEE, John. *The Deltoid Pumpkin Seed.* 1973. Farrar. 1st ed. dj. VG $20.00

MC PHEE, John. *The Headmaster.* 1966. Farrar. 1st ed. dj. VG $55.00

MC PHEE, John. *The Survival of the Bark Canoe.* 1975. 1st ed. dj. $25.00

MC PHERSON, James Lowell. *Goodbye Rosie.* 1965. New York. Knopf. 1st ed. dj. VG $45.00

MC RAE, Earl. *Requiem for Reggie.* 1977. Chimo Pub. 159 pp. dj. EX $7.00

MC SPADDEN, J. Walker. *Illinois. A Romantic Story for Young People.* 1926. New York. Ills. Hasting. 128 pp. $7.50

MC SPADDEN, J. Walker. *Stories from Great Operas.* 1923. New York. Crowell. Ills. 1st ed. $20.00

MC VAUGHN, Rogers. *Edward Palmer, Plant Explorer of the West.* 1956. OK U. Press. Ills. 1st ed. 430 pp. dj. VG $22.50

MC VICKER, Mary Louise. *The Writings of J. Frank Dobie: a Bibliography.* 1968. Ltd. ed. 1/500. sgn. boxed. $75.00

MC VICKER, Mary Louise. *The Writings of J. Frank Dobie: a Bibliography.* 1968. Lawton. dj. VG $50.00

MC WHIRTER, Norris & Ross. *Guinness Book of World Records.* 75th ed. 687 pp. $5.00

MC WHORTER, Lucullus V. *Border Settlers of Northwestern Virginia 1768-95.* 1915. Hamilton, OH. Ills. VG $65.00

MC WILLIAMS, Carey. *Southern California Country.* 1946. 1st ed. dj. EX $20.00

MEAD, Albert. *Giant African Snail Problem in Econ. Malacology.* 1961. U. of Chicago. 1st ed. dj. $8.50

MEAD, David. *Yankee Eloquence in the Middle West.* 1951. MI State U. 1st ed. dj. $12.50

MEAD, F.B. *Heroic Statues in Bronze of Abraham Lincoln.* 1932. Fort Wayne. Ills. Ltd. ed. 1/300. G $30.00

MEAD, G.R.S. *Some Mystical Adventures.* 1910. London. 1st ed. 303 pp. G $45.00

MEAD, G.R.S. *The Doctrine of the Subtle Body.* 1919. London. Watkins. 1st ed. G $45.00

MEAD, M. & Heyman, K. *Family.* 1965. New York. dj. EX $10.00

MEAD, Margaret. *Culture & Commitment.* 1970. Natural Hist. Press/Doubleday. $3.50

MEAD, Margaret. *New Lives for Old.* 1956. New York. 548 pp. dj. EX $6.50

MEAD, William. *Family Prayers.* 1834. Alexandria. 120 pp. $25.00

MEADE, L.T. *A Little Mother to the Others.* 1905. $30.00

MEADE, L.T. *A Madcap.* 1904. Mershon Co. Ills. H. Copping. 261 pp. VG $5.50

MEADE, L.T. *A World of Girls.* 1910. $20.00

MEADE, L.T. *Betty, a Schoolgirl.* 1894. $25.00

MEADE, L.T. *Dr. Rumsey's Patient, a Strange Story.* 1896. $30.00

MEADE, L.T. *Sue a Little Heroine.* 1910. $30.00

MEADE, L.T. *The Gold Star Line.* 1899. London. Ward & Lock. 1st ed. VG $125.00

MEADE, L.T. *The Princess of the Revels.* 1910. $30.00

MEADE, L.T. *The Rebellion of Lil Carrington.* 1898. $30.00

MEADE, L.T. *The Temptation of Olive Latimer.* 1899. $30.00

MEADE, Mrs. L.T. *A Young Mutineer.* 1893. Grosset & Dunlap. VG $4.50

MEADOWCROFT, Enid. *The Story of Crazy Horse.* 1954. New York. Ills. Wm. Reussiwg. 181 pp. $7.00

MEADOWS, Don. *Historic Place Names in Orange County.* 1966. Paisano Press. 1st ed. inscr. sgn. dj. $10.00

MEAGHER, M.M. *The Bison of Yellowstone National Park.* 1973. Ills. 161 pp. VG $7.50

MEAGHER, Maude. *Fantastic Traveller.* 1931. Boston. Houghton Mifflin. sgn. dj. VG $35.00

MEAN, M. *Der Begnabe ein Schriftendeckt.* 1830. Selims-Grove. 192 pp. $15.00

MEANS, P. *Newport Tower.* 1942. New York. 344 pp. VG $25.00

MEANS. *Ancient Civilizations of the Andes.* 1931. Scribner. Ills. 1st ed. 586 pp. VG $35.00

MEANY, Tom. *Babe Ruth/The Big Moments of the Big Fellow.* 1951. New York. Grosset & Dunlap. 249 pp. $2.50

MEARNS, David C. *The Lincoln Papers.* 1947. 1st ed. 2 vol set. slipcase. $45.00

MEARNS, David C. *The Lincoln Papers.* 1948. Garden City. 1st ed. 2 vol set. djs. boxed. $20.00

MEARSON, Lyon. *Footsteps in the Dark.* 1927. NY. Macaulay. 1st ed. VG $15.00

MECHANICUS, P. *Year of Fear.* 1964. New York. Hawthorn Books. EX $25.00

MECKAUER, Walter. *The Books of the Emperor Wu Ti.* 1931. New York. Minton. 1st ed. dj. EX $20.00

MEDIAVEAL. *Codex Diplomatarius, St. Michael's 1427.* 1845. P.A. Munch, ed. Ills. rare. $50.00

MEDILIN, F. *Centuries of Owls.* 1967. Silvermine. Ills. 1st Am. ed. 93 pp. dj. $15.00

MEDWAY, Lord. *Wild Mammals of Malay & Singapore.* 1978. Oxford. Ills. 2nd revised ed. 128 pp. $35.00

MEDWIN, Thomas. *Journal of Conversations of Lord Byron 1821-1822.* 1824. New York. 1st Am. ed. VG $45.00

MEE, Charles L., Jr. *The Ohio Gang. World of Warren G. Harding.* 1981. New York. 1st ed. 248 pp. dj. $12.50

MEEKER, Arthur. *Prairie Avenue.* 1949. New York. Knopf. 380 pp. $27.00

MEEKER, E. *The Busy Life of Eighty-Five Years.* 1916. Seattle. 1st ed. VG $20.00

MEEKER, Ezra. *Kate Mulhall.* 1926. New York. private print. Ills. 287 pp. $6.50

MEEKER, Ezra. *The Ox Team on Old Oregon Trail 1852-1906.* 1906. VG $15.00

MEES, C.E.K. *Dry Plates to Ektachrome.* 1961. New York. 1st ed. dj. EX $7.50

MEHL. *The Kansas City Athletics.* 1956. 1st ed. dj. VG $10.00

MEIGS, Cornelia. *Clear Weather.* 1928. Boston. 1st ed. ex-lib. sgn. G $4.50

MEIGS, Cornelia. *Mounted Messenger.* 1943. New York. Macmillan. 1st ed. EX $15.00

MEIGS, Cornelia. *Wind in the Chimney.* 1935. New York. Macmillan. Ills. Mansfield. $3.50

MEIGS, Cornelia. *Wind in the Chimney.* 1943. New York. Macmillan. Ills. Mansfield. $12.50

MEIKLE, R.S. & M.R. *After Big Game.* London. (ca.1915) $50.00

MEILACH, Dana. *Weaving Off Loom.* 1973. Chicago. Ills. 202 pp. dj. $10.00

MEINERTZHAGEN, R. *Kenya Diary.* 1957. Edinburgh. scarce. EX $160.00

MEISSNER, Kurt. *Japanese Woodblock Prints in Miniature.* 1970. Tuttle. Ills. 2nd ed. 143 pp. $120.00

MELCHIOR, M. *A Rabbi Remembers.* 1968. New York. Lyle Stuart. 2nd ed. dj. EX $12.50

MELDOLA, R. *The Chemistry of Photography.* 1889. London. $36.00

MELE, Pietro. *Tibet.* 1957. London. 80 pls. VG $18.00

MELINE, James F. *Two Thousand Miles on Horseback.* 1873. New York. 4th ed. 317 pp. fld map. VG $40.00

MELISH, John. *Military & Topographical Atlas of United States.* 1813. Philadelphia. Ills. 1st ed. G $375.00

MELLANBY, K. *The Mole.* 1971. London. Collins. Ills. 1st ed. 159 pp. $10.00

MELLAND, F. *Elephants in Africa.* 1938. London. Country Life. Ills. 1st ed. VG $40.00

MELLEN, Ida. *Natural History of the Pig.* 1952. Exposition Books. 1st ed. dj. $8.50

MELLEN, Kathleen D. *In a Hawaiian Valley.* 1947. Hastings. Ills. 126 pp. dj. $15.00

MELLQUIST, Jerome & Wiese, L. *Paul Rosenfeld, Voyager in the Arts.* 1948. New York. Creative Age Pr. 284 pp. $15.00

MELROSE, Millicent. *Color & Harmony Design in Dress.* 1922. New York. Mentor. 62 pp. wrappers. $5.00

MELVIL, James. *The Memoires of Melvil.* 1683. London. 1st ed. folio. $85.00

MELVILLE, Herman. *Journal of a Visit.* 1948. New York. 1st ed. dj. EX $35.00

MELVILLE, Herman. *Journal Up Straits.* New York. Ltd. ed. 1/600. VG $100.00

MELVILLE, Herman. *Melville Log.* New York. 1st ed. 2 vol set. boxed. EX $75.00

MELVILLE, Herman. *Moby Dick, or the White Whale.* 1949. $20.00

MELVILLE, Herman. *Moby Dick, or the White Whale.* 1934. Dodd Mead. Ills. Mead Schaeffer. VG $7.50

MELVILLE, Herman. *Moby Dick, or the White Whale.* 1930. Random House. Ills. Rockwell Kent. 822 pp. $17.50

MELVILLE, Herman. *Romances of Melville.* 1931. New York. Tudor. 1660 pp. $15.00

MELVILLE, Herman. *The Piazza Tales.* 1856. New York. Dix & Edwards. 1st issue. $450.00

MELVILLE, Herman. *Typee.* 1962. VG $20.00

MENABONI, Athos & Sara. *Menaboni's Birds.* 1984. Potter. Ills. 1st revised ed. dj. VG $25.00

MENCKEN, & LaMonte, R.R. *Men vs. the Man.* 1910. Holt. 1st ed. VG $40.00

MENCKEN, H.L. *American Language. Supplement One.* 1945. 1st ed. dj. VG $25.00

MENCKEN, H.L. *Christmas Story.* 1946. New York. Ills. Bill Crawford. VG $12.50

MENCKEN, H.L. *Happy Days.* 1940. New York. 2nd ed. dj. $10.00

MENCKEN, H.L. *Heathen Days.* 1943. New York. 1st ed. dj. VG $35.00

MENCKEN, H.L. *Newspaper Days 1899-1906.* 1942. London. 1st Eng. ed. G $45.00

MENCKEN, H.L. *On Pants-Pressers, Publishers, & Editors.* 1980. U. West FL. Ltd. 1st ed. wrappers. EX $20.00

MENCKEN, H.L. *The American Language.* 1919. New York. Ltd. ed. 1/1500. $45.00

MENCKEN, H.L. *The American Language.* 1936. New York. 4th ed. 769 pp. $15.00

MENCKEN, H.L. *The Bathtub Hoax.* 1958. New York. 1st ed. dj. VG $12.50

MENCKEN, H.L. *The Philosophy of Friedrich Nietzche.* 1908. Boston. Luce. VG $150.00

MENCKEN, H.L. *Three Years. 1924-1927.* 1927. New York. Knopf. Ltd. ed. 1/600. sgn. $85.00

MENCKEN. *Notes on Democracy.* 1926. $20.00

MENDEL. *Chuck Coonie & Lady Rabbit.* 1917. Whitman. Ills. Carsey. $5.50

MENDELEEF. *A Chemical Conception of the Ether.* 1904. $50.00

MENDOZA, George. *Norman Rockwell's Americana ABC.* 1975. New York. dj. VG $10.00

MENEN, Aubrey. *The Backward Bride.* 1950. Scribner. 1st ed. $27.50

MENKE, Frank G. *Sports Tales & Anecdotes.* 1953. New York. 308 pp. dj. EX $3.50

MENNINGER, E. *Fantastic Trees.* 1967. Viking. Ills. 1st ed. dj. VG $17.50

MENPES, M. & D. *Japan: Record in Colour.* 1905. England. 75 color pls. EX $75.00

MENUHIN, Yehudi. *Unfinished Journey.* 1977. Knopf. 394 pp. dj. VG $12.00

MENZHAUSEN, Joachim. *The Green Vaults.* 1968. Leipzig. $20.00

MERA, H.P. *Indian Silverwork Bridles of the Southwest Ills.* 1944. Santa Fe. 12 pls. wrappers. EX $25.00

MERCEIN, T.R. *Serenata.* 1929. Ltd. ed. 1/100. VG $15.00

MERCHANT, Elizabeth. *King Arthur & His Knights.* 1927. Winston. Ills. Frank Godwin. $4.00

MEREDITH, George. *An Essay on Comedy.* 1897. Westminister. 1st ed. EX $20.00

MEREDITH, George. *Letters of George Meredith to Alice Meynell.* Nonsuch Press. Ltd. ed. 1/850. VG $35.00

MEREDITH, George. *One of Our Conquerors.* 1891. London. 1st ed. 3 vol set. $95.00

MEREDITH, Owen. *Lucille.* 1889. Stokes Co. Ills. Gregory. $5.00

MEREDITH, Owen. *The Poetical Works of Owen Meredith.* New York. (ca.1880) 480 pp. VG $3.00

MEREDITH, Roy. *Face of Robert E. Lee.* 1947. Ills. 1st ed. VG $25.00

MEREDITH, Roy. *Mr. Lincoln's General.* 1959. Dutton. Ills. 1st ed. dj. $12.50

MEREDITH, Roy. *This Was Andersonville.* 1957. New York. 1st ed. VG $20.00

MEREDITH. *Diana of the Crossways.* 1885. London. 1st ed. 3 vol set. VG $65.00

MEREJKOWSKI, Dmitri. *The Romance of Leonardo Da Vinci.* 1928. New York. Random House. 573 pp. VG $6.00

MEREJKOWSKI, Dmitri. *The Romance of Leonardo Da Vinci.* 1931. New York. Random House. 2nd ed. 375 pp. $37.50

MERELE, Robert. *The Day of the Dolphin.* 1969. New York. Simon & Schuster. 1st ed. dj. $25.00

MERENESS, Newton D. *Maryland as a Proprietary Province.* 1901. New York. 1st ed. $50.00

MERFIELD, Fred. *Gorilla Hunter.* 1956. Farrar. Ills. 1st ed. dj. VG $25.00

MERFIELD, Fred. *Gorillas Were My Neighbors.* 1957. London. Companion Book Club. dj. G $7.50

MERIDETH, William. *The Cheer: Poems.* 1980. New York. Knopf. dj. EX $15.00

MERILLAT, Herbert C. *Sculpture West & East, Two Traditions.* 1973. New York. dj. EX $7.50

MERIMEE, P. *Carmen.* London. (ca.1926) 16 color pls. EX $95.00

MERK, Frederick. *The Oregon Question.* 1967. Cambridge. 427 pp. dj. $12.50

MERKIN, Robert. *Zombie Jamboree.* 1986. New York. Morrow. proof copy. wrappers. $25.00

MERRIAM, F.A. *Birds Through an Opera Glass.* 1889. New York. Chautauqua Press. 225 pp. $10.00

MERRIAM, J.C. *Published Papers & Addresses of J.C. Merriam.* 1938. Washington. 4 vol set. wrappers. $47.50

MERRICK, Leonard. *Cynthia, Daughter of the Philistines.* 1896. London. 1st ed. sgn. VG $25.00

MERRICK, Pliny. *A Letter on Speculative Free Masonry.* 1829. Worcester, Dorr & Howland. VG $35.00

MERRIL, Judith. *Shadow on the Hearth.* 1950. 1st Am. ed. dj. EX $20.00

MERRIL, Judith. *The Best of the Best.* 1967. New York. Delacorte. 1st ed. dj. EX $15.00

MERRILL, Albert Adams. *The Great Awakening.* 1899. Boston. George Book Co. sgn. EX $135.00

MERRILL, Arch. *Pioneer Profiles.* 1957. New York. Stratford Press. Ills. 215 pp. $4.00

MERRILL, Arch. *River Ramble: Saga of the Genesee Valley.* 1943. Rochester. sgn. Vol I. dj. VG $15.00

MERRILL, Frances & Mason. *Among the Nudists.* 1931. New York. Knopf. Ills. 1st ed. G $20.00

MERRILL, James M. *Spurs to Glory. Story of U.S. Cavalry.* 1967. Chicago. Ills. dj. VG $15.00

MERRILL, James. *Recitative.* 1986. Berkeley. proof copy. wrappers. EX $30.00

MERRILL & DAVIS. *How to be an Aviator.* 1939. McBride. 192 pp. G $4.50

MERRIMAN. *In Kedar's Tents.* 1897. London. 1st ed. $14.00

MERRITT, A. *Dwellers in the Mirage.* Providence. Grandon. dj. VG $20.00

MERRITT, A. *The Face in the Abyss.* 1931. New York. Liveright. 1st ed. VG $40.00

MERRITT, A. *The Fox Woman.* 1977. Avon. pb. VG $20.00

MERRITT, A. *The Ship of Ishtar.* 1949. Ills. Finlay. Borden Pub. memorial ed. dj. $25.00

MERRITT, A. *The Story Behind the Story.* 1942. 1st Am. ed. inscr. sgn. VG $75.00

MERRITT, A. *Through the Dragon Glass.* 1932. Jamaica, NY. 1st ed. wrappers. VG $75.00

MERRLEES, Hope. *Lud-in-the-Mist.* 1927. New York. Knopf. 1st ed. dj. VG $25.00

MERRYMAN, Richard. *Andrew Wyeth.* 1968. Boston. 1st ed. dj. VG $125.00

MERRYMAN, Richard. *Andrew Wyeth.* 1968. Boston. 1st ed. dj. EX $150.00

MERRYWEATHER, F. Somner. *Bibliomania in the Middle Ages.* 1900. New York. Ltd. ed. 1/500. 322 pp. $35.00

MERSHON, Stephen L. *The Power of the Crown in Valley of the Hudson.* 1925. Montclair. Ills. maps. VG $25.00

MERTON, Holmes W. *Discipline Mentality from the Head, Face & Hand.* 1899. Philadelphia. Ills. 219 pp. $12.00

MERTON, Thomas *The Living Bread.* 1956. 1st Am. ed. dj. EX $17.50

MERTON, Thomas. *Bread in Wilderness.* 1953. 1st Am. ed. dj. EX $30.00

MERTON, Thomas. *Disputed Questions.* 1960. New York. 1st ed. dj. $15.00

MERTON, Thomas. *Last of the Fathers.* 1954. 1st Am. ed. dj. VG $17.50

MERTON, Thomas. *Sign of Jonas.* 1953. 1st Am. ed. dj. EX $20.00

MERTON, Thomas. *Thomas Merton on Peace.* 1971. New York. dj. VG $10.00

MERTON, Thomas. *Waters of Siloe.* 1949. New York. 1st ed. dj. VG $15.00

MERWIN, W.S. *Animae.* 1969. Kayak Press. Ills. Schroeder. Ltd. ed. dj. $20.00

MERWIN, W.S. *Carriers of Ladders.* 1970. New York. 1st ed. sgn. wrappers. $30.00

MERWIN, W.S. *The Miner's Pale Children.* 1970. New York. Atheneum. 1st ed. $5.00

MERWIN, W.S. *The Satires of Persius.* 1961. IN U. Pr. 1st trade ed. dj. VG $10.00

MERWIN, W.S. *The Satires of Persius.* 1961. IN U. Pr. 1st ed. dj. VG $20.00

MERWIN, W.S., trans. *Some Spanish Ballads.* 1961. London. Abelard-Schuman. dj. EX $25.00

MESERVE, F. & Sandburg, C. *The Photographs of Abraham Lincoln.* 1944. New York. 1st ed. dj. VG $27.50

MESPOULET, M. *Creators of Wonderland.* 1934. Arrown Ed. Pub. Ltd. 1st ed. VG $35.00

MESSURIER, A.L. *Game, Shore, & Water Birds of India.* 1904. London. Thacher. Ills. 323 pp. VG $95.00

METCALF, R.L. *The Real Bryan.* 1908. Des Moines. 320 pp. VG $20.00

METCALFE, Henry. *Course in Instruction in Ordinance & Gunnery.* 1894. New York. Ills. 3rd ed. $65.00

METCALFE, John. *The Feasting Dead.* 1954. Sauk City. Arkham House. VG $125.00

METCALFE, Willie Adele. *Our Growing English.* 1932. Auburn, AL. Prather Pub. TB. 130 pp. EX $3.50

METER, Sondra van. *Marion Co. Kansas; Past & Present.* 1972. Hillsboro, KS. 344 pp. VG $26.00

METRAUX, Alfred. *Voodoo by Metraux.* New York. 1st ed. dj. $15.00

METZ. *Prairie, Pines, & People.* 1976. 1st ed. EX $25.00

MEYER, Franz. *Marc Chagall.* Abrams. Ills. 53 color pls. dj. EX $60.00

MEYER, Lynn. *Paperback Thriller.* 1975. New York. Random House. 1st ed. dj. EX $20.00

MEYER, Michael. *Ibsen.* 1971. Garden City. Doubleday. Ills. 865 pp. $10.00

MEYER, Nicholas. *The West End Horror.* 1976. New York. Dutton. 1st ed. dj. $5.00

MEYER, Susan E. *America's Great Illustrators.* 1978. Ills. folio. dj. scarce. EX $35.00

MEYER. *James Montgomery Flagg: Most Popular Illustrator.* 1974. 1st ed. dj. EX $45.00

MEYERS, Jeffrey. *Hemingway, a Biography.* 1985. Harper. proof copy. green wrappers. EX $32.50

MEYERS, Jeffrey. *Katherine Mansfield.* 1980. New York. New Directions. 2nd printing. $5.00

MEYNELL, Alice. *Poems.* 1923. Scribner. 1st ed. dj. $17.50

MEYNELL, Alice. *Poems.* 1913. New York. 1st collected ed. VG $15.00

MEYNELL, Francis. *English Printed Books.* 1946. London. Collins. 1st ed. dj. VG $20.00

MICHAEL, Paul. *The Academy Awards: A Pictorial History.* 1972. New York. Crown. 2nd ed. 374 pp. dj. $7.50

MICHAELIS, Richard. *Looking Further Forward.* 1890. Chicago. Rand McNally. 1st ed. $12.50

MICHAELS, K.W. & O.E. *Alfred Krupp, His Life & Work.* 1888. 1st ed. ex-lib. 72 pp. VG $17.00

MICHAELS, Leonard. *The Men's Club.* 1981. Farrar. advance copy. wrappers. EX $20.00

MICHAELS, Marguerite. *Showing the Flag.* 1982. New York. Simon & Schuster. 282 pp. dj. $4.50

MICHAUX, Francois. *Travels to Westward of the Allegheny Mountains.* 1805. London. Phillips. 96 pp. fld map. $150.00

MICHAUX, Henri. *L'Infini Turbulant.* 1957. Paris. Ltd. 3rd ed. VG $20.00

MICHAUX, Henri. *Miserable Miracle.* 1963. City Lights. trans. Varese. wrappers. VG $12.50

MICHAUX, Henri. *Miserable Miracle.* 1956. Monaco. Ltd. 1st ed. folio. wrappers. $17.50

MICHAUX, Henri. *Nouvelles de L'Etranger.* 1952. Paris. Ltd. 1st ed. wrappers. VG $20.00

MICHAUX, Henri. *Paix Dams les Brisements.* 1959. Paris. Ills. Ltd. 1st ed. wrappers. $20.00

MICHEAUX, Oscar. *The Case of Mrs. Wingate.* 1945. New York. inscr. VG $45.00

MICHEL, Emile. *Rubens: His Life, Work, & Times.* 1899. Scribner. Ills. 2 vol set. VG $50.00

MICHELL, E.B. *The Art & Practice of Hawking.* 1976. London. Holland. Ills. 291 pp. dj. EX $15.00

MICHELSON, Miriam. *In the Bishop's Carriage.* 1904. Ills. H. Fisher. EX $5.00

MICHENER, James A. *About Centennial.* Ltd. ed. 1/3200. dj. VG $25.00

MICHENER, James A. *Caravans.* 1963. New York. Random House. 341 pp. dj. $3.50

MICHENER, James A. *Chesapeake.* 1978. New York. Random House. 1st ed. dj. VG $35.00

MICHENER, James A. *Hawaii.* 1960. London. Secker & Warburg. 1st ed. dj. $80.00

MICHENER, James A. *Hawaii.* 1959. New York. Random House. 1st ed. dj. EX $55.00

MICHENER, James A. *Iberia.* 1968. New York. 1st ed. dj. VG $50.00

MICHENER, James A. *Japanese Prints from Early Masters to Modern.* 1975. Tuttle. Ills. 287 pp. dj. Mint. $120.00

MICHENER, James A. *Poland.* 1983. Random House. proof copy. wrappers. EX $35.00

MICHENER, James A. *Poland.* 1983. Random House. 1st trade ed. dj. VG $17.50

MICHENER, James A. *Rascals in Paradise.* 1957. London. 1st ed. dj. VG $25.00

MICHENER, James A. *Return to Paradise.* 1951. New York. Random House. 437 pp. $3.50

MICHENER, James A. *Space.* 1982. New York. Random House. 1st ed. dj. VG $30.00

MICHENER, James A. *Space.* 1982. review copy. dj. EX $35.00

MICHENER, James A. *Tales of the South Pacific.* 1948. Macmillan. $3.50

MICHENER, James A. *Texas.* Ltd. ed. 1/1000. sgn. boxed. $120.00

MICHENER, James A. *The Bridges at Andau.* 1957. New York. 1st ed. VG $20.00

MICHENER, James A. *The Covenant Vol I.* 1980. New York. Random House. 456 pp. dj. $3.50

MICHENER, James A. *The Covenant Vol. II.* 1980. New York. 972 pp. $3.50

MICHENER, James A. *The Covenant.* 1980. Random House. 1st trade ed. dj. VG $15.00

MICHENER, James A. *The Drifters.* 1971. New York. Random House. 751 pp. $3.50

MICHENER, James A. *The Floating World.* 1954. Random House. 65 Ills. 403 pp. $80.00

MICHENER, James A. *The Hokusai Sketchbooks.* 1958. Rutland/Tokyo. Ills. 1st ed. 285 pp. dj. $95.00

MICHENER, James A. *The Hokusai Sketchbooks.* 1959. 3rd printing. dj. EX $22.50

MICHENER, James A. *The Quality of Life.* 1970. Girard. Ltd. ed. slipcase. EX $40.00

MICHENER, James A. *The Source.* 1965. Random House. 1st ed. dj. VG $25.00

MICHENER, James A. *The Voice of Asia.* 1951. New York. Random House. 245 pp. dj. VG $3.50

MICHIE, Allan A. *Air Offensive Against Germany.* 1943. New York. $15.00

MIDDLEMANS, Keith. *Antique Colored Glass.* 1979. New York. Exeter. Ills. dj. VG $15.50

MIDDLETON, C.H. & Heath, A. *From Garden to Kitchen.* 1937. London. 1st ed. VG $15.00

MIDDLETON, D. *Baker of the Nile.* 1949. Falcon. Ills. 1st ed. 280 pp. dj. EX $20.00

MIDDLETON, Don. *Roy Rogers & the Gopher Creek Gunman.* 1945. Racine. Whitman. 248 pp. $3.00

MIDDLETON, Drew. *Submarine, the Ultimate Naval Weapon.* 1976. Chicago. Ills. 1st ed. 256 pp. dj. VG $12.50

MIDDLETON, Drew. *The Supreme Choice.* 1963. New York. Knopf. 292 pp. dj. $3.00

MIDDLETON. *Railways of Thirty Nations.* 1937. New York. VG $10.00

MIDDLETON. *Tobacco Coast.* 1953. Newport. 1st ed. VG $250.00

MIDWOOD, Barton. *Phantoms.* 1970. New York. review copy. dj. EX $10.00

MIERS, Earl Schenck. *The American Story/Age of Exploration to Atom Age.* 1956. New York. 352 pp. $5.50

MIERS, Earl Schenck. *Last Campaign.* 1972. 1st ed. $10.00

MIERS, Earl Schenck. *Rainbow Book of American History.* 1955. World. Ills. Daugherty. 2nd printing. $15.00

MIGDALSKI, E.C. *Fresh-Water & Salt-Water Fishes of the World.* 1976. Knopf. Ills. 1st ed. 316 pp. dj. EX $25.00

MIGEL, Parmenia. *Titania.* 1967. dj. EX $12.00

MIJATICH, C. *Servia of the Servians.* 1915. New York. 234 pp. index. $10.00

MIKITA, Stan. *Inside Hockey.* 1971. Chicago. Contemporary Books. SftCvr. VG $6.00

MILANICH, J. & Proctor, S. *Essays on Indians of FL & Southeastern GA.* 1978. U. of FL. 1st ed. 219 pp. maps. charts. $22.50

MILBURN, Lucy McDowell. *The Child of the Nations.* 1914. Chicago. Ltd. ed. 1/300. sgn. G $12.50

MILBURN, William Henry. *Ten Years of Preacher Life.* 1859. New York. 1st ed. 363 pp. $25.00

MILES, A. Graham. *A Fisherman's Breeze, the Log of Ruth M. Martin.* 1924. New York. Ills. 102 pp. $12.50

MILES, Charles. *Indian & Eskimo Artifacts.* 1963. New York. Ills. 243 pp. folio. dj. $15.00

MILES, E.B. *Spirit of the Mountains.* 1975. TN U. Press. dj. VG $10.00

MILFORD, Louis Leclerc de. *Milford's Memoir.* 1956. EX $25.00

MILFORD, Nancy. *Zelda. A Biography.* 1970. New York. Harper. $7.50

MILI, Gjon. *Picasso's Third Dimension.* 1970. Triton. Ills. 1st ed. dj. VG $35.00

MILINOWSKI, Marta. *Teresa Carreno: By the Grace of God.* 1940. New Haven. inscr. VG $35.00

MILLAIS, J.G. *Newfoundland & Its Untrodden Ways.* 1967. reprint. Ills. 340 pp. dj. EX $25.00

MILLAR, C.E., Turk & Foth. *Fundamentals of Soil Science.* 1958. New York. Wiley. TB. 526 pp. VG $4.50

MILLAR, George. *Orellana.* 1954. Heinemann. 1st ed. dj. $8.50

MILLAR, Margaret. *The Fiend.* 1964. Random House. 1st ed. sgn. dj. EX $40.00

MILLAR, Margaret. *The Listening Walls.* 1959. Random House. 1st ed. dj. VG $15.00

MILLAR, Margaret. *The Murder of Miranda.* 1979. New York. Random House. 1st ed. dj. VG $25.00

MILLAR. *Measured Drawings of Colonial & Georgian Houses.* New York City. (ca. 1920) $49.00

MILLARD, David. *Journal of Travels in Egypt, Arabia, Petraea.* 1848. New York. Ills. G $27.50

MILLAY, Edna St. Vincent. *Fatal Interview. Sonnets.* 1931. New York. 1st ed. $7.50

MILLAY, Edna St. Vincent. *King's Henchman.* 1927. New York. Ltd. Artist ed. 1/500. sgn. $45.00

MILLAY, Edna St. Vincent. *Make Bright the Arrows.* 1940. New York. 1st ed. dj. EX $55.00

MILLAY, Edna St. Vincent. *Poems Selected for Young People.* 1921. Harper. Ltd. ed. 1/1050. boxed. EX $35.00

MILLAY, Edna St. Vincent. *Renaissance & Other Poems.* 1917. New York. 1st ed. 1st issue. $60.00

MILLAY, Norma. *Collected Poems of Edna St. Vincent Millay.* 1956. New York. Harper. 738 pp. dj. $4.00

MILLER, Alice Duer. *Come Out of the Kitchen.* 1916. $25.00

MILLER, Alice Duer. *Five Little Heiresses.* 1936. $25.00

MILLER, Alice Duer. *Gowns by Roberta.* 1934. $25.00

MILLER, Alice Duer. *Green Isle.* 1930. $25.00

MILLER, Alice Duer. *Manslaughter.* 1921. $20.00

MILLER, Alice Duer. *The White Cliffs.* 1941. Coward McCann. Deluxe ed. VG $20.00

MILLER, Arthur. *Arthur Miller's Collected Plays.* 1957. New York. Viking. 439 pp. dj. $5.50

MILLER, Arthur. *Death of a Salesman.* 1949. Viking. 1st ed. dj. G $12.00

MILLER, Arthur. *Death of a Salesman.* 1949. Viking. 2nd ed. dj. VG $5.00

MILLER, Caroline. *Lamb in His Bosom.* 1933. $27.50

MILLER, Caroline. *Lebanon.* 1944. $20.00

MILLER, D. *You Can't Do Business with Hitler.* 1941. Boston. Little, Brown. G $10.00

MILLER, E.T. *Financial History of Texas.* 1916. Austin. 1st ed. ex-lib. $35.00

MILLER, Emily Huntington. *The Royal Road to Fortune.* 1869. Chicago/Boston. 333 pp. $10.00

MILLER, F. Houghton. *The Great Lecture.* 1872. Pittsburgh. 2nd ed. 56 pp. $10.00

MILLER, Francis Travelyan. *History of Civil War.* 1957. 10 vols in 5. VG $87.50

MILLER, Francis Trevelyan. *History of World War II.* 1945. Iowa Falls. Armed Services Memorial ed. $8.00

MILLER, Francis Trevelyan. *Photographic History of Civil War.* 1911. Ills. Brady. 10 vol set. $150.00

MILLER, Francis Trevelyan. *The World of the Air.* 1200 Ills. 2 vol set. $25.00

MILLER, Francis Trevelyan. *Thomas A. Edison. Benefactor of Mankind.* 1931. Philadelphia. Winston. Ills. 320 pp. G $15.00

MILLER, Francis Trevelyan. *World in the Air, Story of Flying in Pictures.* 1930. New York. Ills. 2 vol set. $95.00

MILLER, Francis. *Hero Tales from American Life.* 1909. New York. 454 pp. $7.50

MILLER, Heather Ross. *A Spiritual Divorce.* 1974. Blair. 1st ed. dj. VG $20.00

MILLER, Heather Ross. *Gone a Hundred Miles.* 1968. Harcourt. 1st ed. dj. VG $25.00

MILLER, Helen. *After the Glory.* 1958. $20.00

MILLER, Helen. *Blue Marigolds.* 1934. $22.50

MILLER, Helen. *Cameo.* 1951. 1st ed. $27.50

MILLER, Helen. *Christmas at Mount Vernon.* 1957. 1st ed. 58 pp. dj. $50.00

MILLER, Helen. *Christmas at Sagamore Hill with T. Roosevelt.* 1960. New York. Longman Green. 56 pp. $4.00

MILLER, Helen. *Christmas for Tad at Hermitage.* New York. 1st ed. dj. VG $7.50

MILLER, Helen. *Nightshade.* 1960. 1st ed. $25.00

MILLER, Helen. *Sing One Song.* 1956. $27.50

MILLER, Helen. *Slow Dies the Thunder.* 1955. $22.50

MILLER, Helen. *Song After Midnight.* 1944. $22.50

MILLER, Helen. *The Mulberry Bush.* 1940. $22.50

MILLER, Helen. *The Sound of Chariots.* 1947. $20.00

MILLER, Henry. *An Open Letter to Stroker.* 1978. Ills. Miller. 1st ed. sgn. VG $25.00

MILLER, Henry. *Insomnia or Devil at Large.* 1974. Ills. sgn. dj. VG $50.00

MILLER, Henry. *Love Between the Sexes.* 1978. Greenwich Books. Ltd. ed. sgn. $45.00

MILLER, Henry. *Mother China & the World Beyond.* 1977. Capra Press. Ltd. ed. sgn. dj. VG $45.00

MILLER, Henry. *Murder the Murderer.* 1944. wrappers. VG $22.50

MILLER, Henry. *My Bike & Other Friends.* 1978. Capra Press. Ltd. ed. sgn. dj. EX $50.00

MILLER, Henry. *My Life & Times.* 1975. Playboy. 1st trade ed. dj. VG $35.00

MILLER, Henry. *Of, By, & About Henry Miller.* 1947. Yonkers, NY. Ltd. ed. wrappers. VG $20.00

MILLER, Henry. *On Turning Eighty.* 1972. Capra Press. Ills. Nash. Ltd. ed. sgn. EX $35.00

MILLER, Henry. *Opus Pistorum.* 1983. Grove Press. 1st ed. dj. VG $12.50

MILLER, Henry. *Order & Chaos Chez Hans Reichel.* 1966. Loujon Press. 1st ed. dj. boxed. EX $60.00

MILLER, Henry. *Plexus. The Rosy Crucifixion. Book II.* 1962. Olympia Press. 1st ed. dj. VG $25.00

MILLER, Henry. *Plexus: The Rosy Crucifixion. Book II.* 1976. Grove Press. 1st ed. dj. VG $20.00

MILLER, Henry. *Reflections on the Mauizius Case.* 1974. Capra Press. Ltd. ed. sgn. EX $60.00

MILLER, Henry. *Sunday After War.* 1944. New York. 1st ed. dj. VG $75.00

MILLER, Henry. *The Air-Conditioned Nightmare.* 1945. New Direction. Ills. 1st ed. 292 pp. $35.00

MILLER, Henry. *The Cosmological Eye.* 1939. New Direction. 1st ed. $30.00

MILLER, Henry. *The Happy Rock.* 1947. Porter. dj. VG $20.00

MILLER, Henry. *The Red Notebook.* Jargon. 1st ed. wrappers. EX $40.00

MILLER, Henry. *To Paint Is to Love Again.* 1968. Grossman Pub. 1st ed. ed. VG $25.00

MILLER, Henry. *Tropic of Cancer.* 1939. Paris. Obelisk Press. 5th printing. $25.00

MILLER, Henry. *Tropic of Capricorn.* 1939. Obelisk. wrappers. $300.00

MILLER, Henry. *Wisdom of the Heart.* 1941. New York. 1st ed. dj. VG $125.00

MILLER, Joaquin. *Building of the City Beautiful.* 1893. Chicago. Stone & Kimball. 1st ed. VG $35.00

MILLER, Joaquin. *True Bear Stories.* 1900. Chicago. Ills. 1st ed. 1st issue. VG $55.00

MILLER, John, Jr. *Cartwheel: Reduction of Rabaul.* 1959. Washington. 418 pp. photos. maps. charts. $10.00

MILLER, Joseph. *Arizona Story.* 1952. New York. Ills. Ross Santee. EX $12.50

MILLER, Lee G. *An Ernie Pyle Album.* 1946. New York. 1st ed. dj. VG $15.00

MILLER, Lewis B. *Saddles & Lariats.* 1912. Boston. inscr. scarce. VG $100.00

MILLER, Lewis. *The Virginia Journal of Lewis Miller 1856-57.* 1951. New York. Ltd. ed. 1/750. $35.00

MILLER, M.R. *The Brook Book.* 1902. Doubleday Page. Ills. 241 pp. G $7.50

MILLER, Max. *The Great Trek.* 1935. Ills. 1st ed. 224 pp. VG $22.50

MILLER, Merle. *Lyndon, an Oral Biography.* 1980. New York. Putnam. 645 pp. dj. $6.00

MILLER, Merle. *Plain Speaking, an Oral Biography of Harry Truman.* 1974. New York. 448 pp. dj. EX $6.00

MILLER, Olive Beaupre. *A Picturesque Tale of Progress.* 1949. 9 vol set. VG $55.00

MILLER, Olive Beaupre. *Engines & Brass Bands.* 1933. New York. Ills. 1st ed. dj. EX $15.00

MILLER, Olive Beaupre. *Little Pictures of Japan.* 1950. Ills. Sturges. dj. VG $17.50

MILLER, Olive Beaupre. *My Bookhouse.* 1925. 5 vol set. VG $75.00

MILLER, Olive Beaupre. *Nursery Friends From France.* 1927. Chicago. Ills. Maud & Miska Petersham. $25.00

MILLER, Olive Beaupre. *Tales Told in Holland.* 1948. Chicago. Ills. Maud & Miska Petersham. $30.00

MILLER, Olive Beaupre. *Tales Told in Holland.* 1926. Chicago. Illus. Petersham. 1st ed. $25.00

MILLER, Olive Beaupre. *Tales Told in Holland.* 1952. Book House Pub. Ills. Petersham. G $17.50

MILLER, Olive Thorne. *Little Folks in Feathers & Fur & Others.* 1883. New York. Ills. VG $35.00

MILLER, P. Schuyler. *The Titan, a Tale of the Red Planet.* 1952 Reading, PA. Fantasy Press. dj. $75.00.

MILLER, Perry. *The Life of the Mind in America.* 1965. New York. 338 pp. $5.00.

MILLER, Richard. *Snail.* 1984. New York. review copy. dj. VG $20.00

MILLER, Thomas. *Common Wayside Flowers.* 1860. London. 185 pls. $70.00.

MHLLER, Townsend. *Letter from Texas.* 1939. Dallas. Ltd. ed. 1/450. VG $200.00

MILLER, Walter M. *A Canticle for Leibowitz.* 1960. Philadelphia. 1st ed. ex-lib. dj. VG $45.00

MILLER, Walter M. *Beyond Armageddon.* 1985. 1st Am. ed. dj. EX $15.00

MILLER, William. *Catalogue of a Pickwick Exhibition.* 1936. London. Dickens Fellowship. 1st ed. VG $55.00.

MILLER & FIELD. *Caldecott Medal Books 1938-1957.* 1957. Boston. ex-lib. dj. VG $15.00

MILLER & RUTTER. *Child Artists of the Australian Bush.* 1952. London. Ills. dj. VG $15.00.

MILLER. *Memorial Album of Revolutionary War Soldiers.* 1958. Ills. 406 pp. $13.50

MILLER. *Plain Speaking.* 1974. 448 pp. dj. EX $7.50

MILLER. *Roy Rogers & the Gopher Creek Gunman.* Whitman, Ills. VG $4.50

MILLER. *Roy Rogers & the Outlaws of Sundown Valley.* 1950. Whitman. Ills. VG $4.50

MILLER. *Roy Rogers & the Raiders of Sawtooth Ridge.* 1946. Whitman. Ills. G $3.50

MILLER. *Roy Rogers & the Rimrod Renegades.* 1952. Whitman. Ills. VG $4.50

MILLER. *Saddles & Lariats.* 1912, VG $60.00

MILLER. *The Colfax Book Plate.* 1926. $10.00

MILLER. *The Home Beautiful.* 1921. Westminster Press. $3.50

MILLER. *The Negro in America.* 1968. 3rd printing. dj. EX $10.00

MILLER. *The Old Red Sandstone.* 1882. New York. EX $15.00

MILLIGAN, David. *All Color Photo Book of Wine.* 1974. Octopus Books. Ills. 72 pp. dj. $10.00

MILLIGAN, Spike. *Puckoon.* 1963. London. 1st ed. dj. VG $20.00

MILLIKEN, Henry. *Hunting in Maine.* 1947. Freeport. Ills. 1st ed. VG $12.50

MILLIS, Walter. *The Martial Spirit.* 1931. Ills. 427 pp. $3.00

MILLS, Alfred. *Pictures of English History in Miniature.* London. Darton & Harbey. 2 vol set. VG $250.00

MILLS, Enos A. *Bird Memories of Rockies.* 1931. Houghton Mifflin. 1st ed. dj. $30.00

MILLS, Enos A. *Rocky Mountain Wonderland.* 1915. Boston/NY. Ills. 362 pp. $20.00

MILLS, Enos A. *The Spell of the Rockies.* 1911. Boston. 1st ed. sgn EX $16.50

MILLS, Enos A. *Waiting in the Wilderness.* 1921. Doubleday. $8.50

MILLS, Enos A. *Wild Life on the Rockies.* 1909. Boston/NY. Ills. 1st ed. 262 pp. $25.00

MILLS, Enos A. *Wild Life on the Rockies.* 1924. Boston. Houghton Mifflin. 263 pp. G $5.00

MILLS, Enos A. *Your National Parks.* 1917. Houghton Mifflin. 1st ed. $20.00

MILLS, J. *A Mountain Boyhood.* 1926. Sears. Ills. 286 pp. VG $5.00

MILLS, John. *The Sportsman's Library.* 1845. Edinburgh. VG $55.00

MILLS, Winifred & Dunn, L.M. *Shadow Plays & How to Produce Them.* 1941. Doubleday. VG $15.00

MILLS. *Avesta Eschatology.* 1908. Open Court Pub. EX $25.00

MILNE, A.A. *Autobiography.* 1939. New York. 1st ed. ex-lib. 315 pp. VG $12.00

MILNE, A.A. *By Way of Introduction.* 1929. New York. Ltd. ed. 1/166. sgn. slipcase. $90.00

MILNE, A.A. *By Way of Introduction.* 1929. London. Methuen. 1st ed. dj. $30.00

MILNE, A.A. *Four Days of Wonder.* 1933. New York. Dutton. 1st ed. dj. VG $15.00

MILNE, A.A. *Fourteen Songs From When We Were Very Young.* 1927. New York. Ills. E.H. Shephard. VG $25.00

MILNE, A.A. *Now We Are Six.* 1950. New York. Dutton. Ills. reprint. 102 pp. $3.00

MILNE, A.A. *Now We are Six.* London. 1st ed. gilt decor. VG $60.00

MILNE, A.A. *Now We Are Six.* New York. Dutton. new uniform ed. VG $7.50

MILNE, A.A. *Now We Are Six.* 1927. London. Methuen. 1st ed. $120.00

MILNE, A.A. *Now We Are Six.* London. 1st trade ed. VG $17.50

MILNE, A.A. *Now We are Six.* 1927. Dutton. Ills. Shepard. 1st Am. ed. VG $20.00

MILNE, A.A. *Once on a Time.* 1912. Ills. $55.00

MILNE, A.A. *Once Upon a Time.* 1962. New York. Ills. Susan Perl. 1st ed. $10.00

MILNE, A.A. *Once Upon a Time.* London. Ills. Robinson. VG $22.50

MILNE, A.A. *Songs From Now We Are Six.* 1927. New York. Dutton. Ills. Shepard. 1st ed. $55.00

MILNE, A.A. *The Christopher Robin Story Book.* 1929. Dutton. Ills. Shepard. 1st ed. VG $15.00

MILNE, A.A. *When We Were Very Young.* 1950. New York. Dutton. Ills. reprint. 100 pp. $3.00

MILNE, A.A. *Winnie the Pooh.* 1971. New York. Ills. dj. slipcase. VG $25.00

MILNE, A.A. *Winnie the Pooh.* 1961. New York. Dutton. 1st ed. dj. $10.00

MILNE, A.A. *Winnie the Pooh; House at Pooh Corner.* 1950. New York. Ills. reprint. 178 pp. $3.00

MILNE, A.A. *Winnie the Pooh; House at Pooh Corner.* 1929. 2 vol. gift set. VG $300.00

MILNE, A.A. *Winnie the Pooh; House at Pooh Corner.* 1928. London. Methuen. 1st trade ed. $110.00

MILNE, A.A. *Year In, Year Out.* 1953. New York. Dutton. 215 pp. dj. EX $47.50

MILNE, Christopher. *The Path Through the Trees.* 1979. Dutton. 1st Am. ed. dj. VG $10.00

MILNE, L. & M. *Paths Across the Earth.* 1958. Harper. Ills. 216 pp. dj. EX $4.00

MILNE, L. & M. *The Nature of Life.* 1972. Crown. Ills. 360 pp. VG $6.00

MILNE; Hoff, Benjamin. *The Tao of Pooh.* 1982. New York. Ills. E.H. Shepard. 1st ed. EX $7.50

MILNER, J. *The Cruise of H.M.S. Galatea 1867-68.* 1869. London. Ills. 487 pp. $25.00

MILOSZ, Czeslaw. *The Land of Ulro.* 1984. Farrar. proof copy. wrappers. EX $25.00

MILOSZ, Czeslaw. *Visions from San Francisco Bay.* 1982. New York. advance copy. wrappers. EX $25.00

MILROY, M.E.W. *Guide to Lace Making.* 1934. Ills. 69 pp. VG $12.50

MILTON, Charles J. *Landmarks of Old Wheeling & Surrounding Country.* 1943. Wheeling. photos. 99 pp. $17.50

MILTON, G. *Abraham Lincoln & the 5th Column.* 1942. New York. 1st ed. $20.00

MILTON, John. *Comus.* London. Ills. Rackham. 24 pls. $195.00

MILTON, John. *Paradise Lost.* 1764. $50.00

MILTON, John. *Paradise Lost.* 1730. 12 pls. $100.00

MILTON, John. *The Masque of Comus & the Airs by Henry Lawes.* 1953. Heritage Press. Ills. Dulac. EX $60.00

MILTOUN, Francis. *The Spell of Normandy.* 1925. Boston. Ills. Mcmanus. new ed. G $8.50

MILTS, M.H. *Only a Gringo Would Die for an Anteater.* 1979. Norton. Ills. 1st ed. 225 pp. dj. VG $7.50

MINARIK, Else H. *Father Bear Comes Home.* 1959. New York. Harper & Row. Ills. dj. VG $9.00

MINARIK, Else H. *Little Bear.* 1957. Harper. Ills. dj. EX $10.00

MINARIK, Else H. *Little Bear's Friend.* 1960. New York. Harper. Ills. dj. VG $9.00

MINARIK, Else H. *No Fighting, No Biting!* 1958. New York. Harper. Ills. VG $10.00

MINER, Charles. *History of Wyoming.* 1845. Philadelphia. Ills. 488 pp. $42.50

MINGTAO. *Roof of the World.* 1982. Abrams. dj. EX $25.00

MINNIGH, L.W. *Gettysburg.* 1924. no place. Ills. 168 pp. wrappers. G $22.50

MINOR, W. *Footprints in the Trail.* 1950. Bellevue. Ills. 232 pp. G $6.00

MINTON, S. & M. *Giant Reptiles.* 1973. Scribner. Ills. 1st ed. 345 pp. dj. VG $20.00

MINTON, S. & M. *Venomous Reptiles.* 1969. Scribner. Ills. 274 pp. dj. VG $20.00

MIRACLE, L. & Decker, M.H. *Complete Book of Camping.* 1961. Outdoor Life. Ills. 594 pp. $3.00

MIRHBEAU, Octave. *Torture Garden.* 1931. New York. Kendall. 1st ed. EX $20.00

MIRSKY, Jeannett. *Great Chinese Travelers.* 1964. New York. Pantheon. dj. G $15.00

MIRSKY, Jeannette. *Elisha Kent Kane & the Seafaring Frontier.* 1954. Little, Brown. 1st ed. $8.50

MIRSKY, Jeannette. *Westward Crossings.* 1946. New York. Ills. 1st ed. fld map. dj. EX $6.50

MIRSKY & NEVINS. *The World of Ely Whitney.* 1st ed. dj. VG $9.00

MIRZA, Youel B. *The Rug that Went to Mecca.* 1939. New York. Ills. Artzybasheff. 1st ed. $25.00

MISHIMA, Yukio. *Five Modern No Plays.* 1957. New York. Knopf. dj. VG $15.00

MISHIMA, Yukio. *Forbidden Colors.* 1968. New York. Knopf. 1st Am. ed. dj. EX $30.00

MISHIMA, Yukio. *Spring Snow.* 1972. Knopf. trans. 1st Am. ed. dj. VG $30.00

MISHIMA, Yukio. *The Decay of the Angel.* 1975. Secker Warburg.1st English ed. dj. EX $25.00

MISHIMA, Yukio. *The Sailor Who Fell from Grace with the Sea.* 1965. Knopf. 1st Am. ed. dj. VG $40.00

MISHIMA, Yukio. *The Temple of the Golden Pavilion.* 1959. Knopf. 1st Am. ed. dj. VG $50.00

MISHIMA, Yukio. *Thirst for Love.* 1969. New York. Knopf. dj. VG $15.00

MISHIMA, Yukio. *Young Samurai: Bodybuilders of Japan.* 1966. Tokyo. photos. dj. VG $12.50

MITCHELL, Austin. *The Half-Gallon Quarter-Acre Pavlova Paradise.* New Zealand. Christchurch. 184 pp. $3.50

MITCHELL, Benjamin Wiestling. *Trail Life in the Canadian Rockies.* 1924. Macmillan. 1st ed. dj. $12.50

MITCHELL, C. Bradford. *Touching the Adventures & Perils.* 1970. $6.50

MITCHELL, Carleton. *Isles of the Caribbees.* 1966. Washington. Ills. 208 pp. index. dj. $7.50

MITCHELL, Charles. *A Book of Ships.* 1941. 1st King Penguin ed. Ills. VG $18.00

MITCHELL, Curtis. *God in the Garden.* 1957. New York. Doubleday. photos. dj. $3.50

MITCHELL, Donald G. *Dream Life.* 1899. Altemus. Ills. 296 pp. VG $4.50

MITCHELL, Donald G. *English Lands, Letters, & Kings.* 1897. New York. 1st ed. VG $20.00

MITCHELL, Edward P. *Memoirs of an Editor.* 1924. New York. VG $15.00

MITCHELL, Edwin Valentine. *Morocco Bound.* 1929. VG $10.00

MITCHELL, Edwin Valentine. *The Steamer Book.* 1925. $12.50

MITCHELL, Ewing Young. *Kicked In & Kicked Out/President's Little Cabinet.* 1936. Washington. 1st ed. 371 pp. $10.00

MITCHELL, Horace. *Raising Game Birds.* 1945. Knopf. Ills. 315 pp. dj. VG $15.00

MITCHELL, J.W.S. *The History of Freemasonry & Masonic Digest.* 1866. 2 vol set. $125.00

MITCHELL, Joseph. *Armies & Leaders in Revolutionary War.* 17 maps. 223 pp. dj. $10.00

MITCHELL, Joseph. *Joe Gould's Secret.* 1965. New York. 1st ed. dj. $15.00

MITCHELL, Joseph. *McSorley's Wonderful Saloon.* 1943. New York. presentation copy. 253 pp. $20.00

MITCHELL, Joseph. *Old Mister Flood.* 1948. New York. 1st ed. dj. EX $18.00

MITCHELL, Kate L. *Japan's Industrial Strength.* 1942. New York. Knopf. ex-lib. 140 pp. $4.00

MITCHELL, Langdon Elwynn. *Poems.* 1894. Cambridge. Riverside Pr. 1st ed. 92 pp. $67.50

MITCHELL, Leonard Jan. *Luchow's German Cookbook.* 1958. $8.00

MITCHELL, Leonard Jan. *Luchow's German Cookbook.* 1952. Garden City. Book Club ed. 224 pp. $4.50

MITCHELL, Lucy. *Here & Now Story Book.* 1948. Dutton. Ills. Van Loon/Price. dj. VG $15.00

MITCHELL, Margaret J. *The Fireless Cookbook.* 1911. Garden City. Doubleday. 315 pp. $7.50

MITCHELL, Margaret. *Gone with the Wind.* 1964. $27.50

MITCHELL, Margaret. *Gone with the Wind.* 1936. $30.00

MITCHELL, Margaret. *Gone with the Wind.* 1939. New York. movie ed. wrappers. EX $32.50

MITCHELL, Margaret. *Gone with the Wind.* 1961. New York. Ills. Stahl. Anniversary ed. $45.00

MITCHELL, Margaret. *Gone with the Wind.* 1936. New York. 1st ed. 1st issue. EX $150.00

MITCHELL, O.M. *The Orbs of Heaven.* 1860. London. Ills. $22.00

MITCHELL, Paige. *A Wilderness of Monkeys.* 1965. Dutton. 1st ed. dj. VG $15.00

MITCHELL, Paige. *The Covenant.* 1973. Atheneum. 1st ed. dj. VG $15.00

MITCHELL, S. Augustus. *A System of Modern Geography.* 1868. Philadelphia. Butler. Ills. $10.00

MITCHELL, S. Augustus. *The Primary Geography.* 1881. Philadelphia. Butler. Ills. maps. 114 pp. $6.00

MITCHELL, S. Weir. *The Hill of Stone & Other Poems.* 1883. 1st ed. $35.00

MITCHELL, Silus Weir. *Characteristics.* 1892. 1st ed. $15.00

MITCHELL, Silus Weir. *Circumstance.* 1901. $2.00

MITCHELL, Silus Weir. *Hugh Wynne Free Quaker. Vol. II.* 1899. New York. Century. 261 pp. VG $4.50

MITCHELL, Silus Weir. *Little Stories.* 1903. 1st ed. $25.00

MITCHELL, Silus Weir. *The Mother & Other Poems.* 1893. 1st ed. $25.00

MITCHELL, Silus Weir. *When all the Wood Are Green.* 1894. New York. 1st ed. $35.00

MITCHELL, William. *Winged Defense.* 1925. New York. ex-lib. VG $12.50

MITCHELL. *Corn Palace City of the World & Davison Co. S.D.* photos. gilt wrappers. $10.00

MITCHISON, Naomi. *Barbarian Stories.* 1929. New York. Harcourt. 1st ed. VG $15.00

MITFORD, Jessica. *A Fine Old Conflict.* 1977. London. 1st ed. dj. EX $25.00

MITFORD, Jessica. *The American Way of Death.* 1963. New York. 6th printing. dj. VG $10.00

MITFORD, Mary Russell. *Our Village: Sketches of Rural Character/Scenery.* 1876. London. Bell & Sons. ex-lib. 536 pp. G $3.00

MITFORD, Nancy. *Frederick the Great.* 1970. London. Ills. 1st ed. dj. VG $22.00

MITFORD, Nancy. *Madame De Pompadour.* 1968. Harper. Ills. 304 pp. dj. $6.50

MITFORD, Nancy. *Noblesse Oblige.* 1956. London. 1st ed. dj. VG $20.00

MITFORD, Nancy. *The Blessing.* 1951. New York. 1st printing. $10.00

MITFORD, William. *The History of Greece.* 1814. London. 8 vol set. VG $125.00

MITFORD, William. *The History of Greece.* 1838. London. 8 vol set. VG $130.00

MITSCHELICH, A. & Mielke, F. *Doctors of Infamy.* 1949. New York. Ills. Henry Schuman. G $50.00

MITTELMAN, Capt. Joseph B. *Eight Stars to Victory.* 1948. Washington. Ills. maps. 406 pp. $45.00

MIURA. *Man Who Skied Down Everest.* 1978. 1st ed. dj. EX $7.50

MIX, Gladys. *Combined Atlas of Columbiana County OH 1841-1906.* 1983. Salem. 78 pp. wrappers. VG $15.00

MIYAMOTO, Y. *Fingerprints.* 1963. Japan. trans. Ills. 64 pp. charts. VG $8.00

MIZNER, Arthur. *This Side of Paradise.* 1951. Boston. Houghton Mifflin. 362 pp. dj. $7.50

MOBERLY, Henry & Cameron, Wm. *When Fur Was King.* 1929. New York. fld map. 7 pls. 237 pp. VG $15.00

MOCHI, Ugo. *African Shadows.* 1933. Jr. Literary Guild. dj. VG $20.00

MODY, N.H.N. *Collection of Nagasaki Colour Prints & Paintings.* 1969. Tuttle. reprint. Ills. folio. rare. $105.00

MOE, Alfred K. *Honduras Geographical Sketch.* 1904. Washington. Ills. 252 pp. map. $25.00

MOE, V. *Animal Inn.* 1946. Ills. Winter. 174 pp. G $5.00

MOELLER, Philip. *The Blind Beggars & One Less Blind.* 1918. New York. wrappers. VG $40.00

MOFFATT. *Missionary Labours & Scenes in South Africa.* 1847. New York. G $40.00

MOFFIT, Ella B. *The Cocker Spaniel.* 1947. New York. Judd Pub. photos. 282 pp. $5.00

MOGELEVER, Jacob. *Death to Traitors, Story of Gen. Lafayette Baker.* 1960. New York. Ills. 1st ed. dj. VG $20.00

MOHOLY-NAGY, Laszlo. *Vision in Motion.* 1947. 1st ed. dj. EX $135.00

MOHR, C.E. & Sloane, H.N. *Celebrated American Caves.* 1955. Rutgers. Ills. photos. 339 pp. VG $7.50

MOHR, Francis & Redwood, T. *Practical Pharmacy.* 1849. Philadelphia. Lea/Blanchard. 1st ed. 558 pp. $75.00

MOIR, Jane. *A Lady's Letters from Central Africa.* 1891. Glasgow. $15.00

MOJTABAI, A.G. *Autumn.* 1982. Boston. 1st ed. dj. VG $15.00

MOJTABAI, A.G. *Mundome.* 1974. Simon & Schuster. 1st ed. dj. $35.00

MOKIERE. *The Dramatic Works of Moliere.* Philadelphia. Barrie. 3 vol set. VG $35.00

MOLER. *The Manual of Beauty Culture.* 1911. 179 pp. $3.50

MOLES, H.R. *Model Specifications.* 1948. Columbus. 92 pp. wrappers. $15.00

MOLESWORTH, Mary Louisa. *Stories.* 1922. New York. Ills. Edna Cooke. dj. $25.00

MOLESWORTH, Mrs. *Carrots: Just a Little Boy.* 1934. London. Ills. Walter Crane. EX $12.50

MOLESWORTH, Mrs. *Four Winds Farm.* 1910. Macmillan. Ills. Walter Crane. G $25.00

MOLESWORTH, Mrs. *Grandmother Dear.* 1898. Hurst. 239 pp. fair $3.50

MOLESWORTH, Mrs. *Miss Mouse & Her Boys.* 1900. London/NY. Ills. L. Leslie Brooke. VG $12.50

MOLESWORTH, Mrs. *My New Home.* 1901. London. Ills. L. Leslie Brooke. VG $12.50

MOLESWORTH, Mrs. *The Cuckoo Clock.* 1947. New York. Macmillan. Ills. Walter Crane. $10.00

MOLESWORTH, Mrs. *The House that Grew.* 1902. London/NY. Ills. Alice B. Woodward. VG $12.50

MOLESWORTH, Mrs. *Two Little Waifs.* 1920. London. Ills. Walter Crane. VG $12.50

MOLIERE, Jean. *Oeuvres Completes.* Paris. (ca. 1850) 10 color pls. VG $50.00

MOLINARD. *Paris Insolite.* 1954. Ills. Ltd. ed. 1/5500. dj. VG $20.00

MOLLHAUSEN, Baldwin. *Diary of Journey from Mississippi to Pacific.* 1858. London. 1st Eng. ed. 2 vols in 1. $750.00

MOLLINS & THICKENS. *Ramblings in CA: Adventures of Henry Cerruti.* 1954. Berkeley. Ltd. ed. 1/500. VG $12.50

MOLLOY, Anne. *The Pigeoneers.* 1947. Boston. Ills. E. Converse. 1st ed. $15.00

MOLLOY, Paul. *A Pennant for the Kremlin.* 1964. Garden City. Doubleday. dj. $20.00

MOLNAR, Ferenc. *The Plays of Ferenc Molnar.* 1929. New York. Ltd. ed. 1/300. 822 pp. $75.00

MOLYNEAUX. *Romantic Story of Texas.* 1936. Cordova Press. sgn. VG $25.00

MOMMSEN, Theodore. *The History of Rome.* 1868. London. 4 vol set. VG $135.00

MONACHESI, Nicola. *A Manual for China Painters.* 1907. Boston. revised. ed. dj. VG $24.00

MONAGAN, Frank. *World War II, an Illustrated History.* 1943. EX $50.00

MONAGHAN, Elizabeth. *What to Eat & How to Prepare It.* 1922. New York. VG $10.00

MONAGHAN, Jay. *The Book of the American West.* 1963. New York. 1st ed. VG $15.00

MONAGHAN, Jay. *Diplomat in Carpet Slippers.* 1945. Indianapolis. 1st ed. 505 pp. dj. index. EX $10.00

MONAGHAN, Jay. *Great Rascal, Life & Adventure of Ned Buntline.* 1952. Little, Brown. Ills. VG $15.00

MONAGHAN, Jay. *Lincoln Bibliography.* 1943. 2 vol set. EX $60.00

MONAGHAN, Jay. *Man Who Elected Lincoln.* 1956. 1st ed. dj. VG $17.50

MONCRIEFF, A.R.H. *Romance & Legend of Chivalry.* 1978. Bell Pub. Ills. 439 pp. dj. EX $5.50

MONCRIEFF, Perrine. *New Zealand Birds & How to Identify Them.* 1961. Whitcombe Tombs. Ills. 151 pp. $15.00

MONDEY, David. *Aircraft, All Color Story of Modern Flight.* 1973. New York. Octopus Books. 1st ed. EX $10.00

MONDEY, David. *Hamlyn Concise Guide to British Aircraft of WWII.* 1982. London. Hamlyn/Aerospace. 1st ed. EX $14.00

MONDOT, Armand. *Histoire des Indiens des Etats-Utis.* 1858. Paris. 176 pp. $125.00

MONETTE, John W. *History of Discovery & Settlement of MS. Valley.* 1846. New York. Ills. rebound. VG $275.00

MONKHOUSE & WILKINSON. *Maps & Diagrams.* 1958. London/NY. 199 Ills. 330 pp. dj. $15.00

MONROE, Harriet. *Valeria & Other Poems.* 1891. Chicago. Ltd. ed. sgn. $200.00

MONROE, Harriet. *You & I.* 1914. New York. Macmillan. sgn. EX $65.00

MONROE, Marilyn. *My Story.* 1974. New York. 1st ed. dj. VG $15.00

MONROE. *Monroe's New Third Reader.* 1885. Cowperthwait. $10.00

MONSARRAT, Nicholas. *The Cruel Sea.* 1953. London. Cassell. 416 pp. dj. $3.50

MONSARRAT, Nicholas. *The Tribe that Lost Its Head.* 1956. New York. Sloan. ex-lib. 598 pp. $3.50

MONSMA, John C. *The Evidence of God in an Expanding Universe.* 1958. New York. Putnam. 250 pp. VG $7.00

MONSON, G. & Sumner, L. *Desert Bighorn Life History, Ecology, Management.* 1980. AZ U. Press. Ills. 370 pp. dj. EX $25.00

MONTAGUE, Margaret Prescott. *The Poet, Miss Kate, & I.* 1905. New York. Baker & Taylor. Ills. Hood. VG $35.00

MONTAGUE, R. *Oceans, Poles, & Airmen.* 1971. New York. dj. $15.00

MONTALE, Eugenio. *It Depends: a Poet's Notebook.* 1980. New Directions.1st Am. ed. dj. VG $15.00

MONTALE, Eugenio. *The Butterfly of Dinard.* 1971. U. Press KY. 1st Am. ed. dj. VG $20.00

MONTBARD, G. *Among the Moors.* 1894. New York. Ills. EX $50.00

MONTE, George. *Shooter's Bible: Pistol & Revolver Guide.* 1967. Chicago. Follett. wrappers. VG $7.50

MONTEFIORE, Brice A. *David Livingstone.* London. (ca.1900) 160 pp. G $15.00

MONTEITH. *First Lessons in Geography.* 1864. New York. 67 pp. 12 colored maps. $125.00

MONTELEONE, Thomas. *Ozymandias.* 1981. Garden City. 1st ed. dj. VG $8.00

MONTESSORI, Maria. *Pedagogical Anthropology.* 1913. Stokes. 1st ed. $22.50

MONTGOMERY, BAUER & GRAY. *Happy Days with Our Friends.* 1948. Scott Foresman. Ills. Steed. $3.50

MONTGOMERY, D.H. *The Leading Facts of American History.* 1896. Boston. Ginn. G $6.00

MONTGOMERY, E.G. *Productive Farm Crops.* 1916. Philadelphia. Lippincott. ex-lib. 501 pp. VG $3.50

MONTGOMERY, Frances Trego. *Billy Whiskers at the Fair.* 1937. Akron. Ills. Arthur DeBebain. VG $12.50

MONTGOMERY, Frances Trego. *Billy Whiskers' Frolics.* 1923. Saalfield Pub. Ills. Paul Hawthorne. 6 pls. $12.50

MONTGOMERY, Frances Trego. *Billy Whiskers' Kids.* 1931. Akron. Ills. W.H. Fry. popular ed. VG $12.50

MONTGOMERY, Frances Trego. *Billy Whiskers' Kids; or, Day & Night.* 1903. Saalfield. Ills. W.H. Fry. 134 pp. EX $15.00

MONTGOMERY, Frances Trego. *Billy Whiskers' Twins.* 1939. Akron. Saalfield. Ills. Pairpoint. $12.50

MONTGOMERY, Frances Trego. *On a Lark to the Planets.* 1904. 1st ed. sgn. VG $60.00

MONTGOMERY, L.M. *Anne of Avonlea.* 1909. $30.00

MONTGOMERY, L.M. *Anne of Green Gables.* 1962. $25.00

MONTGOMERY, L.M. *Anne of Green Gables.* 1920. $30.00

MONTGOMERY, L.M. *Anne of Windy Poplars.* 1939. $30.00

MONTGOMERY, L.M. *Anne's House of Dreams.* 1917. Stokes. Ills. VG $35.00

MONTGOMERY, L.M. *Emily's Quest.* 1927. Stokes. 1st ed. dj. VG $40.00

MONTGOMERY, L.M. *Further Chronicles of Avonlea.* 1970. $30.00

MONTGOMERY, R. *The Living Wilderness.* 1964. Dodd Mead. Ills. 294 pp. VG $7.50

MONTGOMERY, Richard G. *'Pecheck' Lorne Knight's Adventures in the Arctic.* 1932. New York. ex-lib. 291 pp. $4.00

MONTGOMERY & KANE. *American Art: 1750-1800, Towards Independence.* 1976. Boston. Ills. 320 pp. dj. $25.00

MONTGOMERY. *Stan Ball of the Rangers.* 1941. McKay. Ills. Abbott. VG $3.50

MONTHAN, R.G. *Gorman: The Lithographs.* 1978. Northland. 1st ed. 2nd printing. $20.00

MONTHAN. *Art & Indian Individualists.* 1975. Northland. 1st ed. $20.00

MONTULE, Edouard de. *Voyage to North America & West Indies in 1817.* 1821. London. Ills. 102 pp. EX $325.00

MOODY, D.L. *Life & Labors of D.L. Moody.* 1899. Philadelphia. Northrup. Ills. G $10.00

MOODY, D.W. *Life of a Rover.* 1926. Chicago. 116 pp. wrappers. VG $22.50

MOODY, Margarite A. *Moody's Household Advisor & Cookbook.* 1884. Chicago. 1st ed. VG $36.00

MOODY, Mrs. Wm. Vaughn. *Cookbook.* 1931. New York. Scribner. 475 pp. G $12.50

MOODY, Ralph. *Horse of a Different Color.* 1968. $27.50

MOODY, Ralph. *Little Britches.* 1950. $27.50

MOODY, Ralph. *Man of the Family.* 1951. $27.50

MOODY, W.R. *Life of D.L. Moody.* 1900. Revell. 1st ed. 116 photos. VG $12.50

MOODY & SANKEY. *Lives & Labors of J. Potts.* 1876. Toronto. 1st ed. G $10.00

MOODY. *Edwin Forrest.* 1960. dj. VG $17.50

MOON, Bucklin, ed. *Primer for White Folks.* 1945. New York. Doubleday. 491 pp. $5.00

MOON, Grace. *Magic Trail.* 1929. Jr. Literary Guild. G $12.00

MOON. *Chi Wee.* Doubleday Doran. dj. EX $8.00

MOON. *Nadita.* 1946. Doubleday. Ills. dj. EX $10.00

MOONEY, James & Thomas, Cyrus. *Miami Indians.* 1952. pamphlet. Ft. Wayne Lib. 8 pp. wrappers. $3.00

MOONEY, Ted. *Easy Travel to Other Planets.* 1981. New York. Farrar. proof copy. wrappers. $35.00

MOORCOCK, M. *Hollow Lands.* 1974. Harper. 1st ed. dj. EX $10.00

MOORCOCK, M. *The City in the Autumn Stars.* London. 1st ed. sgn. $22.00

MOORCOCK, Michael. *A Cure for Cancer.* 1971. New York. Holt. dj. EX $12.50

MOORCOCK, Michael. *Byzantium Endures.* 1981. New York. Random House. 1st ed. dj. EX $35.00

MOORCOCK, Michael. *Stormbringer.* 1964. London. 1st ed. dj. VG $50.00

MOORCOCK, Michael. *The Black Corridor.* 1969. Ace Pub. 1st Am. ed. pb. EX $8.50

MOORCOCK, Michael. *The Eternal Champion.* 1978. New York. 1st hardcover ed. dj. VG $15.00

MOORCOCK, Michael. *The Laughter of Carthage.* 1984. New York. Random House. 1st ed. dj. VG $30.00

MOORCOCK, Michael. *The Stealer of Souls.* 1963. London. 1st ed. dj. VG $60.00

MOORCOCK, Michael. *The Vanishing Tower.* 1981. Cambridge. Archival Press. 1st Am. ed. EX $30.00

MOORCOCK, Michael. *The War Hound & the World's Pain.* 1981. New York. 1st ed. dj. VG $12.50

MOORE, Albert B. *Conscription & Conflict in Confederacy.* 1924. New York. 1st ed. 367 pp. $50.00

MOORE, Amos. *Gunsmoke at Clarion.* Triangle. $4.00

MOORE, Anne Carroll. *Century of Kate Greenaway.* 1946. London/NY. Ills. 15 pp. wrappers. $15.00

MOORE, Anon. *John Harvey, a Novel of the Twentieth Century.* 1897. Chicago. Kerr. 1st ed. dj. EX $75.00

MOORE, Brian. *Fergus.* 1970. Holt. 1st ed. dj. VG $20.00

MOORE, Brian. *I Am Mary Dunne.* 1968. Viking. 1st ed. dj. VG $25.00

MOORE, Brian. *The Luck of Ginger Coffey.* 1960. London. Deutsch. 1st ed. dj. EX $30.00

MOORE, Brian. *The Mangan Inheritance.* 1979. Farrar. proof copy. dj. VG $20.00

MOORE, C.L. *Judgement Night.* 1952. New York. Gnome. 1st ed. 344 pp. $30.00

MOORE, C.L. *Scarlet Dream.* 1981. D.M. Grant. Ills. Austin. Ltd. ed. 1/220. $45.00

MOORE, C.L. *Shambleau.* 1953. New York. Gnome. 1st ed. dj. EX $45.00

MOORE, Charles W. *The New Masonic Trestle-Board.* 1850. Boston. Moore. 1st ed. 2 vols in 1. VG $25.00

MOORE, Charles. *The Life & Times of Charles Follen McKim.* 1929. Houghton. 1st ed. $15.00

MOORE, Clarence B. *The Book of Wild Pets.* 1954. Branford. Ills. 553 pp. EX $10.00

MOORE, Clement C. *Poems.* 1844. New York. 1st ed. inscr. 216 pp. $400.00

MOORE, Clement C. *The Night Before Christmas.* Philadelphia. Ills. Rackham. reprint ed. $6.50

MOORE, Clement C. *The Night Before Christmas.* 1944. New York. Crown. Ills. Wohlberg. 1st ed. $20.00

MOORE, Clement C. *The Night Before Christmas.* Crown. reprint. Ills. Rackham. $12.50

MOORE, Clement C. *The Night Before Christmas.* 1931. Philadelphia. Ills. Rackham. dj. $125.00

MOORE, Clement C. *The Night Before Christmas.* 1949. New York. Ills. Weisgard. $25.00

MOORE, Clement C. *The Night Before Christmas.* 1931. Philadelphia. Lippincott. Ills. Rackham. EX $95.00

MOORE, Clement C. *The Night Before Christmas.* 1961. Ills. Grandma Moses. folio. VG $15.00

MOORE, Cornelius. *Ancient Charges & Regulations of Freemasonry.* 1855. Cincinnati. $15.00

MOORE, Cornelius. *Craftsman & Freemason's Guide.* 1857. Cincinnati. Ernst. 11th ed. 319 pp. G $27.50

MOORE, E.W. *Natchez Under the Hill.* 1958. 1st ed. sgn. dj. G $12.50

MOORE, Frank. *Rebel Rhymes & Rhapsodies Collected & Edited.* 1864. New York. 1st ed. 299 pp. $100.00

MOORE, George E. *A Banner in the Hills. West Virginia's Statehood.* 1963. New York. Ills. 256 pp. index. $10.00

MOORE, George M. *Final Notes on Witchcraft in Massachusetts.* 1885. New York. 120 pp. VG $25.00

MOORE, George. *A Communication to My Friends.* 1933. Nonesuch. Ltd. ed. 1/1000. VG $20.00

MOORE, George. *A Story Teller's Holiday.* 1918. New York. private print. Ltd. ed. $15.00

MOORE, George. *A Story Teller's Holiday.* 1928. New York. Ltd. ed. sgn. 2 vol set. VG $35.00

MOORE, George. *Aphrodite in Aulis.* 1930. London. Ltd. 1st ed. sgn. $50.00

MOORE, George. *Pure Poetry.* Nonesuch Press.Ltd. ed. 1/1250. VG $40.00

MOORE, George. *Works of George Moore.* 1922-24. NY. Ltd. ed. sgn. 21 vol set. EX $250.00

MOORE, Hortense. *Bread Loaf Book of Plays.* 1941. Middlebury College Pr. 199 pp. $10.00

MOORE, Ida Cecil. *Lucky Orphan.* 1947. New York. Ills. Primrose. 1st ed. sgn. $10.00

MOORE, John Trotwood. *A Summer Hymnal.* 1925. Nashville. Cockesbury Pr. inscr. 332 pp. $22.50

MOORE, Joseph West. *Picturesque Washington.* 1887. Ills. 308 pp. $13.50

MOORE, Joseph West. *Picturesque Washington.* 1889. Providence. Ills. VG $18.00

MOORE, Joseph West. *Picturesque Washington.* 1888. Washington. Ills. maps. 308 pp. VG $30.00

MOORE, Judge Charles Forrest. *One Thing & Another.* 1924. New York. Rudge. VG $15.00

MOORE, Keiko Hiratsuka. *Moku-Hanga: How to Make Japanese Wood Block Print.* 1973. Acropolis. wrappers. G $15.00

MOORE, Langdon W. *Langdon W. Moore, His Story of His Eventful Life.* 1893. Boston. 659 pp. $10.00

MOORE, M.B. *The Dixie Speller.* 1864. Raleigh, NC. Branson & Farrar. 120 pp. G $75.00

MOORE, Marianne. *Collected Poems.* 1964. New York. 11th printing. sgn. dj. VG $60.00

MOORE, Marianne. *Like a Bulwark.* 1956. 1st ed. VG $40.00

MOORE, Marianne. *Nevertheless.* 1944. New York. 1st ed. dj. EX $45.00

MOORE, Marianne. *O to Be a Dragon.* 1959. 1st ed. VG $35.00

MOORE, Marianne. *Poems.* 1921. London. sgn. $600.00

MOORE, Marianne. *Selected Poems.* 1935. New York. 1st ed. VG $27.50

MOORE, Marianne. *Tell Me, Tell Me.* 1966. Viking. 1st ed. dj. VG $35.00

MOORE, Marianne. *The Complete Poems of Moore.* 1967. New York. Macmillian/Viking. 1st ed. dj. $12.50

MOORE, Marianne. *What Are Years.* 1941. New York. 1st ed. VG $22.50

MOORE, Merrill. *War Diary of an Army Psychiatrist.* 1955. 1st ed. dj. VG $20.00

MOORE, Mrs. Augustus. *Without Sin, a Novel.* 1896. Chicago. Stone. 1st Am. ed. EX $35.00

MOORE, N. Hudson. *The Collector's Manual.* 1906. New York. Tudor Publishing. 329 pp. VG $5.00

MOORE, P.H. *Gun & Rod in Canada.* 1922. VG $27.50

MOORE, Robert K. *Stone Tools & Relics of the American Indian.* 1971. Ills. 19 pp. $3.00

MOORE, T. Sturge. *Roderigo of Bivar.* 1925. New York. Rogers. Ltd. ed. VG $25.00

MOORE, Thomas. *Lalla Rookh, an Oriental Romance.* 1869. London. Ills. ex-lib. 303 pp. $15.00

MOORE, Thomas. *Lalla Rookh.* 1887. Boston. Estes & Lauriat. Ills. VG $45.00

MOORE, Thomas. *Life of Lord Byron.* 1854. London. new ed. VG $240.00

MOORE, Thomas. *The Poetical Works of Thomas Moore.* 1840. $7.50

MOORE, Ward. *Bring the Jubilee.* 1953. New York. dj. $50.00

MOORE, Ward. *Greener than You Think.* 1947. New York. Sloane. 1st ed. dj. VG $20.00

MOORE, Warren. *Weapons of American Revolution & Accouterments.* New York. Promontory Pr. Ills. 224 pp. $25.00

MOOREHEAD, A. *Cooper's Creek.* 1963. Harper. Ills. 1st ed. 222 pp. dj. EX $20.00

MOOREHEAD, A. *Darwin & the Beagle.* 1970. Harper. Ills. 280 pp. dj. EX $20.00

MOOREHEAD, A. *Russian Revolution.* 1958. Harper. 1st ed. 301 pp. dj. $17.00

MOOREHEAD, A. *The Blue Nile.* 1962. Harper. Ills. 1st ed. dj. EX $15.00

MOOREHEAD, A. *The White Nile.* 1960. Harper. Ills. 358 pp. dj. VG $7.50

MOOREHEAD, Elizabeth. *These Too Were Here, Louise Homer & Willa Cather.* 1950. Pittsburgh U. 1st ed. dj. $8.50

MOOREHEAD, M. & L. *New Mexico's Royal Road.* 1958. U. of OK Press.dj. EX $15.00

MOORGAT, A. *Tammuz.* 1949. Berlin. $40.00

MOORHOUSE, Geoffrey. *Fearful Void.* 1974. Lippincott. 288 pp. dj. VG $10.00

MOOS, Malcolm & Hess, Stephen. *Hats in the Ring.* 1960. New York. 194 pp. dj. $10.00

MOOSDORF, J. *Next Door.* 1964. New York. VG $15.00

MORA, Jo. *Californios.* 1949. New York. Doubleday. Ills. Mora. $30.00

MORA, Jo. *Year of Hopi: J. Mora Paintings & Photos 1904-6.* 1979. Smithsonian Institute. $5.00

MORAIN, Alfred. *The Underworked of Paris.* 1931. New York. ex-lib. 320 pp. $3.50

MORAN, Benjamin. *The Journal of 1857-1865.* 1948. U. of Chicago. 1st ed. djs. 2 vol set. $15.00

MORAN, C. *Money.* 1863. New York. 228 pp. $20.00

MORAND, Paul. *East India & Co.* 1927. New York. Boni. 1st ed. VG $8.50

MORANTE, Elsa. *History of a Novel.* 1977. New York. 1st trade ed. dj. EX $10.00

MORAVIA, Alberto. *Time of Desecration.* 1980. Farrar. 1st ed. dj. EX $12.50

MORAVIA, Alberto. *Time of Desecration.* 1978. 1st ed. VG $25.00

MORAVIA, Alberto. *Two Women.* 1st English ed. dj. VG $10.00

MORAVIA, Alberto. *Two Women.* 1972. New York. Farrar. 1st ed. dj. EX $35.00

MORAVIA, Alberto. *1934.* 1983. New York. Farrar. 1st ed. dj. EX $20.00

MORDAUNT, Elinor. *The Dark Fire.* 1927. New York. Century. 1st Am. ed. VG $12.00

MORDECAI, Alfred. *Military Commission to Europe in 1855-56.* 1861. Washington. fld pls. VG $40.00

MORDECAI, Samuel. *Richmond in Bygone Days.* 1946. Richmond. 362 pp. $15.00

MORDELL, A. *Discovery of Genius/Wm. D. Howells & Henry James.* 1961. New York. 1st ed. dj. EX $25.00

MORDELL, A. *Literary Reviews & Essays.* 1957. New York. Twayne. 1st printing. dj. EX $25.00

MORDEN, W.J. *Across Asia's Snows & Deserts.* 1927. New York. Ills. 415 pp. $15.00

MORE, Anthony. *Puzzle Box.* 1946. Trover Hall. 1st ed. dj. VG $65.00

MORE, Hannah. *Memoirs of Life & Correspondence of Hannah More.* 1835. New York. 1st ed. 2 vol set. VG $40.00

MORE, Hannah. *Search After Happiness.* 1797. Worcester. Thomas. $35.00

MORE, T.H. *Utopia.* 1878. Boston. Roberts. Ltd. ed. sgn. VG $75.00

MOREAU, F. Frederic. *Aux Etats-Unis: Notes de Voyage.* 1888. Paris. Ills. 1st ed. 263 pp. $125.00

MOREHOUSE, Ward. *George M. Cohan: Prince of American Theatre.* 1943. $10.00

MORELL, P. *Lillian Russell.* 1943. Garden City. Ills. $4.50

MORENO, G.R. *Estudios De Literatura Boliviana.* 1955-56. Bolivia. 2 vol set. VG $30.00

MORFI, Juan Agustin. *History of Texas, 1673-1779.* 1935. Albuquerque. Quivera Soc. 2 vol set. $500.00

MORGAN, Alfred. *Woodworking Tools & How to Use Them.* 1948. Gramercy. Ills. $3.00

MORGAN, B. *Summer's Children.* 1961. Scarsdale. 1st ed. dj. VG $25.00

MORGAN, Barbara. *Martha Graham Sixteen Dances in Photographs.* 1980. New York. Ills. 1st revised ed. dj. VG $15.00

MORGAN, Charles. *Sparkenbroke.* 1936. London. 1st ed. $15.00

MORGAN, Clifford T. & King, R. *Introduction to Psychology.* 1971. 4th ed. 784 pp. $7.50

MORGAN, Dale. *The Humboldt.* 1943. Rinehart. 1st ed. dj. VG $20.00

MORGAN, Edmund S. *Virginians at Home, Family Life in 18th Century.* 1952. Williamsburg. 2nd printing. dj. $10.00

MORGAN, Edward & Woods, Henry. *God's Loaded Dice. Alaska 1897-1930.* 1948. Caxton. Ltd. ed. 1/1000. sgn. dj. EX $40.00

MORGAN, James Morris. *Recollections of a Rebel Reefer.* 1917. Boston/NY. 1st ed. VG $55.00

MORGAN, James. *Abraham Lincoln: Boy & Man.* 1908. New York. Ills. 1st ed. VG $8.50

MORGAN, John G. *Charleston, 175.* 1970. Charleston. Ills. 112 pp. VG $5.00

MORGAN, M. *The Last Wilderness.* 1956. Viking. Ills. 275 pp. dj. EX $12.50

MORGAN, Willard D. *Complete Photographer.* 1942. New York. 10 vol set. djs. VG $47.50

MORGAN, Willard D. *1001 Ways to Improve Your Photographs.* 1945. New York. 385 pp. EX $4.50

MORGAN, Willard D. *The Encyclopedia of Photography.* 1949. New York. Ills. 11 vol set. EX $60.00

MORGANSTERN, G. *The Story of the Secret War: Pearl Harbor.* 1947. New York. 2nd ed. 425 pp. dj. VG $20.00

MORGENSTERN, S. *The Silent Gondoliers.* 1st Am. ed. dj. EX $12.50

MORGENTHAU, Henry. *Ambassador Morgenthau's Story.* 1918. New York. Doubleday Page. 407 pp. $3.50

MORGENTHAU, R.S. *Political Parties in French-Speaking West Africa.* 1964. London. dj. VG $7.50

MORHART, Hilda Dischinger. *Zoar Story.* 1967. Dover, Ohio. Ills. sgn. 137 pp. wrappers. $12.50

MORIER, James. *Hajji Babba of Ispahan.* 1937. New York. Ills. Baldridge. 402 pp. dj. $50.00

MORIN, Relman. *Dwight D. Eisenhower, a Gauge of Greatness.* 1965. Assoc. Press. 256 pp. $75.00

MORISON, S. & Commager, H. *The Growth of the American Republic.* 1942. New York. 2 vol set. $10.00

MORISON, S.E. *History of U.S. Naval Operations in WWII. Vol. 6.* 1950. Ills. maps. G $17.50

MORISON, S.E. *Oxford History of the American People.* 1965. Oxford U. Press. 1150 pp. $15.00

MORISON, S.E. *The Development of Harvard University 1869-1929.* Ills. dj. $17.50

MORISON, S.E. *The European Discovery of America.* 1974. Oxford U. Pr. 1st ed. dj. VG $10.00

MORISON, S.E. *The Invasion of France & Germany 1944-1945.* 1957. 1st ed. dj. $12.50

MORISON, Stanley. *Brief Survey of Printing.* 1923. New York. 1st ed. dj. VG $30.00

MORISON, Stanley. *First Principles of Typography.* 1936. Cambridge. 1st ed. dj. VG $25.00

MORISON, Stanley. *Four Centuries of Fine Printing.* 1960. New York. new ed. 254 pp. dj. VG $22.50

MORISON, Stanley. *The Typographic Book. 1450-1935.* 1963. 1st Am. ed. boxed. $95.00

MORLEY, Christoper. *Blue & Gray; or, War is Hell.* 1930. New York. 1st ed. sgn. dj. VG $65.00

MORLEY, Christopher. *Christopher Morley's Briefcase.* 1936. New York. 1st ed. wrappers. $15.00

MORLEY, Christopher. *Ex-Libris Carissimis.* 1936. Philadelphia. Lippincott. 75 pp. dj. G $7.50

MORLEY, Christopher. *Ex-Libris Carissimis.* 1932. Philadelphia. U. of PA. 134 pp. $10.00

MORLEY, Christopher. *Haunted Bookshop.* Grosset & Dunlap. dj. VG $7.50

MORLEY, Christopher. *Human Being.* 1934. New York. 350 pp. $3.50

MORLEY, Christopher. *Letter to Lenora.* 1928. Marshall Field. sgn. wrappers. VG $50.00

MORLEY, Christopher. *Old Loopy.* 1935. Ills. Ederkeimer. $25.00

MORLEY, Christopher. *Parnassus on Wheels.* 1917. Doubleday. 1st ed. VG $45.00

MORLEY, Christopher. *Parnassus on Wheels.* 1918. Garden City. Doubleday. 2nd ed. VG $15.00

MORLEY, Christopher. *Poems.* 1929. New York. 1st ed. dj. $15.00

MORLEY, Christopher. *Powder of Sympathy.* 1923. New York. 1st ed. dj. VG $10.00

MORLEY, Christopher. *The Arrow.* 1927. New York. 1st ed. sgn. dj. VG $25.00

MORLEY, Christopher. *The Ballad of New York, New York.* 1950. New York. Doubleday. 93 pp. EX $3.00

MORLEY, Christopher. *The Goldfish Under Ice.* 1932. New York. 1st ed. dj. $10.00

MORLEY, Christopher. *The Goldfish Under Ice.* 1929. London. Ltd. ed. sgn. dj. EX $50.00

MORLEY, Christopher. *The Haunted Bookshop.* 1919. 1st ed. 1st issue. $90.00

MORLEY, Christopher. *The Haunted Bookshop.* reprint ed. 289 pp. VG $10.00

MORLEY, Christopher. *The Man Who Made Friends with Himself.* 1949. New York. 1st ed. dj. VG $12.50

MORLEY, Christopher. *The Trojan Horse.* 1937. Lippincott. 1st ed. sgn. dj. VG $25.00

MORLEY, Christopher. *The Worst Christmas Story.* 1928. New York. Ills. Jones. Ltd. ed. sgns. $28.00

MORLEY, Christopher. *Thunder on the Left.* 1925. New York. 1st ed. dj. VG $10.00

MORLEY, Christopher. *Travels in Philadelphia.* 1920. McKay. 1st ed. sgn. dj. VG $125.00

MORLEY, Christopher. *Where the Blue Begins.* 1922. London/NY. Ills. Arthur Rackham. VG $85.00

MORLEY, Edith J. *Henry Crabb Robinson on Books & Their Writers.* 1938. London. 1st ed. 3 vol set. VG $45.00

MORLEY, F.V. & Hodgson, J.S. *Whaling North & South.* 1926. New York. Ills. 1st ed. 235 pp. dj. VG $22.50

MORLEY, S.G. *The Ancient Maya.* 1946. Stanford. Ills. 1st ed. 520 pp. dj. VG $36.00

MORLEY. *Edmund Burke: a Historical Study.* 1867. Macmillan. EX $75.00

MORLEY-FLETCHER, H. *Investing in Pottery & Porcelain.* 1968. London. Ills. 1st ed. $15.00

MORRAH, Herbert A. *Highways & Hedges.* 1911. London. Black. 20 mounted color pls. $37.50

MORRAY, J.P. *The Second Revolution in Cuba.* 1962. New York. 1st ed. dj. EX $7.50

MORRELL, Benjamin. *Narrative of Four Voyages to South Sea, 1822-31.* 1832. New York. 492 pp. $150.00

MORRILL, Milo True. *History of Christian Domination in America.* 1912. Dayton, Ohio. 407 pp. $15.00

MORRIS, Brian. *John Cleveland (1613-1658). Bibliography of Poems.* 1967. London. 62 pp. $15.00

MORRIS, D. *Animal Days.* 1980. Morrow. 1st Am. ed. 304 pp. dj. EX $10.00

MORRIS, D. *The Naked Ape/A Zoologist's Study of Human Animal.* 1967. McGraw Hill. 1st Am. ed. VG $6.00

MORRIS, Desmond. *The Mammals, a Guide to the Living Species.* 1965. Harper. 448 pp. VG $4.50

MORRIS, Donald R. *Washing of the Spears.* 1965. New York. dj. VG $22.50

MORRIS, E. *The Russian Navy. Myth & Reality.* 1977. dj. VG $10.00

MORRIS, E.B. *Sultan in Oman.* 1957. Munich. Ills. dj. $7.50

MORRIS, F. *Birds of Prey of Australia.* 1976. Landsowne. Ills. 124 pp. dj. EX $30.00

MORRIS, Gouverneur. *If You Touch Them, They Vanish.* 1913. New York. Scribner. 1st ed. EX $15.00

MORRIS, Gouverneur. *The Voice in the Rice.* 1910. New York. Dodd. 1st ed. dj. VG $20.00

MORRIS, Henry C. *History of the First National Bank of Chicago.* 1902. 1st ed. 210 pp. $20.00

MORRIS, Henry O. *Waiting for the Signal.* 1897. Chicago. Schulte. VG $40.00

MORRIS, J. *Path of the Dragon.* 1980. London. 1st ed. dj. EX $10.00

MORRIS, James. *The Road to Huddersfield.* 1963. New York. photos. 235 pp. dj. $4.00

MORRIS, Janet. *Earth Dreams.* 1982. New York. 1st ed. dj. VG $10.00

MORRIS, Kay. *Western Cookery.* 1936. Culinary Arts Press. 48 pp. $4.50

MORRIS, Kenneth. *The Fates of the Princess Dyfed.* 1978. Newcastle. pb. EX $10.00

MORRIS, Lucille. *Bald Knobbers.* 1939. Caxton. 1st ed. dj. VG $50.00

MORRIS, May. *William Morris: Artist, Writer, Socialist.* 1966. 2 vol set. EX $55.00

MORRIS, Paul. *American Sailing Coasters of North Atlantic.* 1973. Chardon, Ohio. 1st ed. dj. $20.00

MORRIS, R. & D. *Men & Snakes.* 1965. McGraw Hill. Ills. 224 pp. VG $10.00

MORRIS, Ralph. *The Life & Astonishing Adventures of John Daniel.* 1926. London. Holden. reprint. VG $40.00

MORRIS, Robert. *Freemasonry in the Holy Land.* 1876. New York. Masonic Pub. 610 pp. $75.00

MORRIS, Tyler Seymour. *Record of Gilbert Ruggles & Evelina Tucker.* 1901. Chicago. $40.00

MORRIS, William. *News from Nowhere.* 1890. Boston. Roberts. 1st unauthorized ed. $125.00

MORRIS, Willie. *The Last of the Southern Girls.* 1973. Knopf. 1st ed. sgn. dj. VG $35.00

MORRIS, Wright. *Fire Sermon.* 1971. Harper. 1st ed. dj. VG $20.00

MORRIS, Wright. *My Uncle Dudley.* 1942. New York. Harcourt. 1st ed. dj. EX $450.00

MORRIS, Wright. *Real Losses, Imaginary Gains.* 1976. Harper. 1st ed. dj. VG $15.00

MORRIS, Wright. *The Deep Sleep.* 1953. New York. Scribner. dj. $40.00

MORRIS, Wright. *The Fork River Space Project.* 1977. Harper. 1st ed. dj. VG $15.00

MORRIS, Wright. *The Huge Season.* 1954. New York. Viking. 1st ed. dj. $35.00

MORRIS, Wright. *The Inhabitants.* 1946. New York. press copy. dj. $200.00

MORRIS, Wright. *The Works of Love.* 1952. New York. Knopf. 1st ed. VG $25.00

MORRIS, Wright. *Will's Boy.* 1981. New York. Harper. 1st ed. dj. EX $20.00

MORRIS. *British Violin Makers.* 1920. London. 318 pp. $40.00

MORRIS. *Circle of the Century, Achievements of 100 Years.* 1900. International Pub. 646 pp. $9.50

MORRIS. *Finding the North Pole.* 1909. Ills. W.E. Scull. $28.00

MORRIS. *Good Old Boy.* 1971. Harper. 1st ed. dj. VG $40.00

MORRIS. *Sailing for America's Cup.* 1964. 1st ed. Ills. Rosenfeld. G $10.00

MORRISON, Adele Sarpy. *Memoirs of Adele Sarpy Morrison.* 1911. St.Louis. Ltd. 1st ed. 1/100. 206 pp. $5.00

MORRISON, Alex. *A New Way to Better Golf.* 1935. New York. dj. VG $10.00

MORRISON, Arthur. *Exhibition of Japanese Prints: Ills. Catalogue.* 1910. London. Ills. 58 pp. extremely rare. $75.00

MORRISON, Arthur. *The Green Diamond.* 1904. Boston. Page. 1st Am. ed. VG $15.00

MORRISON, Arthur. *The Hole in the Wall.* 1902. New York. McClure. 1st Am. ed. VG $25.00

MORRISON, F.B. *Feeds & Feeding.* 1945. Ithaca, NY. Morrison Pub. 20th ed. 105 pp. $7.00

MORRISON, H. *Preliminary Check List of Am. Almanacs 1639-1800.* 1907. Washington. EX $60.00

MORRISON, H.R. & Lee, C.E. *America's Atlantic Islands.* 1981. Nat. Geog. Soc. Ills. 199 pp. dj. EX $12.50

MORRISON, John. *History of American Steam Navigation.* 1958. Stephen Daye Press. 1st ed. $12.50

MORRISON, Kathleen. *Robert Frost.* 1974. New York. Holt. Ills. 1st ed. 133 pp. $10.00

MORRISON, Mrs. Clifford Davis. *The Country Art of Blueberry Cookery.* 1972. Middletown, NY. 119 pp. wrappers. $4.00

MORRISON, Neil F. *Garden Gateway to Canada.* 1954. Toronto. Ills. 1st ed. 344 pp. $35.00

MORRISON, S.A. *Middle East Survey: Political, Social, Religious.* 1954. London. dj. G $7.50

MORRISON, S.E. *Old Bruin, Commodore Matthew Calbraith Perry.* 1967. Boston. Atlantic Monthly. Ills. dj. G $20.00

MORRISON, Toni. *Tar Baby.* 1981. New York. Knopf. 1st ed. dj. EX $35.00

MORRISON, W.H. *Hellbirds. Story of B-29s in Combat.* 1960. Ills. dj. G $6.50

MORRISON, William. *Mel Oliver & Space Rover on Mars.* 1954. Gnome. 1st ed. dj. EX $20.00

MORRISON & JARVIS. *Morrison's Strangers Guide for Washington City.* 1876. lg fld map. 52 pp. SftCvr. VG $5.50

MORROW, Donald. *Where Shakespeare Stood.* 1935. Milwaukee. Casanova Pr. 1st ed. dj. VG $25.00

MORROW, J.E. *Fresh-Water Fishes of Alaska.* 1980. Alaska. Ills. photos. maps. EX $25.00

MORROW, L.H. *Atlantis.* 1902. Boston. Eastern Pub. Co. 1st ed. EX $75.00

MORROW, W.C. *The Ape, the Idiot, & Other People.* 1897. Philadelphia. Lippincott. 1st ed. boxed. EX $200.00

MORSE, A. Reynolds. *The Works of M.P. Shiel.* 1948. Los Angeles. Fantasy Pub. dj. $50.00

MORSE, A.D. *While Six Million Died/Chronicle American Apathy.* 1968. New York. 435 pp. index. $7.50

MORSE, Abner. *History of the Towns of Sherborn & Holliston.* 1856. Boston. Damrell & Moore. 340 pp. $35.00

MORSE, E.W. *The Vanguard of American Volunteers.* 1919. Ills. G $7.50

MORSE, Frances C. *Furniture of Olden Time.* 1940. Ills. new ed. VG $12.50

MORSE, Jedidiah. *American Gazetteer.* 1797. 1st ed. maps. VG $85.00

MORSE, Jedidiah. *Geography Made Easy.* 1812. 1st ed. maps. G $25.00

MORSE, Jedidiah. *Universal Geography.* 1812. Boston. dj. G $18.00

MORSE, Lucy G. *Breezes.* 1921. Ills. Morse. 5 p. forward Amy Lowell. VG $12.50

MORSE & GREEN. *The Old Pike: Ills. Narrative of National Road.* 1971. dj. VG $10.00

MORTENSEN, Otto. *Jens Olsen's Clock, Technical Description.* 1957. Copenhagen. 1st ed. $15.00

MORTENSEN, W. *Outdoor Portraiture.* 1943. San Francisco. dj. VG $12.50

MORTENSEN. *Monsters & Madonnas.* 1936. 2nd ed. G $90.00

MORTENSEN. *New Projection Control.* 3rd ed. $20.00

MORTENSEN. *Pictorial Lighting.* 8th printing. $15.00

MORTENSEN. *Print Finishing.* 2nd printing. $12.50

MORTIMER, Charles. *Racing a Sports Car.* 1951. London. Ills. ex-lib. 138 pp. G $7.50

MORTON, Frederick. *The Rothschilds, a Family Portrait.* 1962. New York. 305 pp. $6.00

MORTON, H.V. *In Search of Scotland.* 1930. London. Methuen. Ills. 288 pp. VG $10.00

MORTON, H.V. *In Search of Wales.* 1932. New York. ex-lib. photos. 345 pp. $4.00

MORTON, Nathaniel. *New England's Memorial.* 1826. Boston. 5th ed. 482 pp. $40.00

MORTON, O.P. *Reconstruction.* 1868. VG $15.00

MORTON, Oren F. *A History of Pendleton County, West Virginia.* 1910. Dayton, VA. Ills. 493 pp. $75.00

MOSBY, John S. *Causes & Cures of Crime.* 1913. Mosby Co. Ills. 354 pp. VG $4.50

MOSCHELES, Ignace. *The Life of Beethoven.* 1841. Ditson. 390 pp. $125.00

MOSELEY, Edwin Lincoln. *Milk Sickness Caused by White Snakeroot.* 1941. Bowling Green. 171 pp. wrappers. $8.50

MOSES, Bernard. *Federal Government of Switzerland.* 1889. Oakland. 1st ed. G $20.00

MOSES & BROWN. *American Theatre as Seen by Critics.* 1934. 2nd ed. $12.50

MOSES. *Ring Up the Curtain.* 1932. Little, Brown. Ills. Janet Scott. 1st ed. VG $25.00

MOSGROVE, George. *Kentucky Cavaliers.* 1957. Jackson, TN. sgn. dj. EX $10.00

MOSHER, Edith R. *From Indian Legends to Modern Book Shelf.* 1931. Ann Arbor. 395 pp. $12.50

MOSHER, Thomas B. *The Bibelot.* 1895. New York. Ltd. ed. 21 vol set. 400 pp. ea. $55.00

MOSHER. *A Little Garland of Christmas Verse.* 1908. Portland. Ltd. 3rd ed. 1/950. $10.00

MOSKOWITZ, Sam, ed. *The Man Who Called Himself Poe.* 1976. 1st Am. ed. dj. EX $25.00

MOSKOWITZ, Sam. *Under the Moon of Mars.* 1970. New York. 1st ed. dj. EX $22.50

MOSLEY, L. *Backs to the Wall.* 1971. Ills. dj. VG $10.00

MOSLEY, L. *Hirohito Emperor of Japan.* 1966. Prentice Hall. Ills. dj. $15.00

MOSLEY, L. *Lindbergh, a Biography.* 1976. Ills. dj. VG $8.00

MOSLEY, L. *On Borrowed Time.* 1969. New York. Random House. 509 pp. dj. G $4.00

MOSLEY, L. *Power Play. Oil in the Mideast.* 1973. Ills. dj. VG $15.00

MOSS, Howard. *Notes from the Castle.* 1979. Atheneum. Ltd. ed. 1/750. dj. VG $25.00

MOSS, J.E. *Textiles & Fabrics, Care & Preservation.* 1961. New York. $7.50

MOSSA. *Gulliver's Travels.* Hodder & Stoughton. 12 pls. $55.00

MOSTOVETS, N. *Henry Winston; Profile of a U.S. Communist.* 1983. Moscow. 133 pp. $6.00

MOTHER GOOSE. *Mother Goose: Her Best Known Rhymes.* 1933. Akron. Ills. Fern Bisel Peat. VG $30.00

MOTLEY, Willard. *Knock on Any Door.* 1947. Appleton Century. 1st ed. $3.00

MOTLEY, Willard. *We Fished All Night.* 1951. New York. Appleton. 1st ed. dj. VG $20.00

MOTT, Abigail & Wood, M.S. *Narratives of Colored Americas.* 1875. New York. Wood. 1st ed. EX $60.00

MOTT, Lawrence. *The White Darkness.* 1907. New York. Outing Pub. Ills. 1st ed. VG $20.00

MOTT, Mrs. D.W. *Legends & Lore of the Long Ago.* 1929. Los Angeles. Ills. 232 pp. dj. $18.50

MOTTON, Celeste. *L'Ecole Des Meilleures Cuisinieres Bourgeoises.* 1870. Paris. Ills. $25.00

MOTTRAM, Eric. *William Burroughs.* 1971. Intrepid Press.sgns. EX $30.00

MOTTRAM, V.H. *Food & the Family.* 1926. London. VG $18.00

MOULTON, Forest Ray. *An Introduction to Astronomy.* 1919. New York. Macmillan. Ills. maps. $4.50

MOULTON, Harold G. & Mario, L.*The Control of Germany & Japan.* 1944. Washington. Brookings Institute. 116 pp. $3.00

MOULTON. *Portland by the Sea.* 1926. EX $11.00

MOUNTEVANS, Adm. Lord. *Man Against the Desolate Antarctic.* 1951. New York. Ills. 1st ed. 172 pp. $12.50

MOUNTFORT, G. *Saving the Tiger.* 1981. Viking. Ills. 120 pp. dj. EX $12.50

MOUNTFORT, G. *Tigers.* 1973. Crescent. Ills. 96 pp. dj. EX $10.00

MOUNTFORT, G. *Wild Paradise, Story of Coto Danana Expeditions.* 1958. Houghton Mifflin. 1st ed. dj. $10.00

MOURLOT, Fernand. *Art in Posters.* 1959. New York. Ills. dj. VG $100.00

MOURLOT, Fernand. *Prints from the Mourlot Press.* 1964. Paris. Ltd. ed. wrappers. $200.00

MOUROIS, Andre. *Picture of a Victorian Age.* 1964. Time-Life. $5.00

MOWAT, Farley. *A Whale for the Killing.* 1972. Little, Brown. Ills. 1st ed. 239 pp. dj. G $5.00

MOWAT, Farley. *Ancient Norse in Greenland & North America.* 1965. Little, Brown. Ills. 1st ed. 240 pp. dj. VG $17.50

MOWAT, Farley. *People of the Deer.* 1952. Little, Brown. Ills. 344 pp. VG $10.00

MOWAT. *This Rock Within the Sea.* 1968. dj. VG $15.00

MOWERY, Wm. A. *Recollections of a New England Educator 1838-1908.* 1908. New York. 292 pp. $3.50

MOYER, J. *Practical Taxidermy.* 1953. Ronald. Ills. 126 pp. dj. EX $10.00

MOYER, Willard. *The Witchery of Sleep.* 1903. New York. EX $25.00

MOYERS, William & Cooke, D. *Famous Indian Tribes.* 1954. New York. Ills. Moyers. 64 pp. $7.50

MOYES, Philip J.R. *Bomber Squadrons of the R.A.F. & Their Aircraft.* 1971. London. MacDonald. 3rd printing. EX $25.00

MOYES, Philip J.R. *R.A.F. Bombers of WWII, Vols. 1 & 2.* 1968. London. Ills. Goulding. 1st ed. EX $15.00

MOYES, Philip J.R. *R.A.F. Jet Fighter Flypast.* 1972. London. 1st ed. EX $10.00

MOYNAHAN, J.M. & Tromp, Andy. *The West of Sandy Ingersoll.* 1974. Cheney, WA. Ltd. ed. 1/100. boxed. $150.00

MUCH, Peter. *Sociology of Tristan Da Cunha.* 1945. Oslo. 1st ed. wrappers. $15.00

MUELLER, Chester & Olson, J. *Small Arms Lexicon & Concise Encyclopedia.* 1968. Hackensack. Ills. 1st ed. 309 pp. dj. VG $17.50

MUELLER, Hans Alexander. *Woodcuts & Wood Engravings: How I Make Them.* 1939. New York. Pynson Printers. Ltd. ed. EX $60.00

MUENCH, Joseph. *Salt Lake City. A Pictorial Study.* 1947. dj. $5.50

MUENSCHER, W.C. *Keys to Woody Plants.* 1950. Ithaca, NY. 108 pp. VG $3.50

MUGON, M.D. *A New Graded Method in English Grammar.* 1888. St.Louis. Ingerson. 64 pp. $3.50

MUIR, John. *My First Summer in the Sierra.* 1911. Cambridge. Ills. 1st ed. EX $45.00

MUIR, John. *My First Summer in the Sierra.* 1911. Boston. Ills. 1st ed. VG $40.00

MUIR, John. *Our National Parks.* 1901. Cambridge. Riverside Press. 1st ed. $75.00

MUIR, John. *Stickeen.* 1910. Boston/NY. 8th impression. VG $15.00

MUIR, John. *Stickeen.* 1915. G $20.00

MUIR, John. *Stickeen.* 1909. Houghton Mifflin. 74 pp. G $7.50

MUIR, John. *The Cruise of the Corwin.* 1917. Boston/NY. EX $50.00

MUIR, John. *The Mountains of California.* 1901. New York. VG $40.00

MUIR, John. *The Story of My Boyhood & Youth.* 1913. Boston/NY. VG $45.00

MUIR, John. *Thousand Mile Walk to the Gulf.* 1916. Boston. Ills. Ltd. ed. 220 pp. dj. VG $110.00

MUIR, John. *Travels in Alaska.* 1916. Boston/NY. 6th impression. VG $40.00

MUIR, Percy. *Victorian Illustrated Books.* 1971. London. Ills. 1st ed. dj. VG $55.00

MUIRHEAD. *Normandy.* 1921. Paris. 1st ed. 60 maps. $12.00

MUIRHEAD. *Northeastern France.* 1922. London. 55 maps & plans. VG $10.00

MUKERJI, Dhan Gopal. *Face of Silence.* 1926. New York. VG $20.00

MUKERJI, Dhan Gopal. *Fierce-Face.* 1936. New York. Ills. Lathrop. 1st ed. $40.00

MUKERJI, Dhan Gopal. *Gay-Neck.* 1940. New York. Ills. Artzybasheff. VG $10.00

MULDER, Arnold. *Americans from Holland.* 1947. Philadelpha. Lippincott. ex-lib. 320 pp. VG $5.50

MULFORD, Clarence. *Black Buttes.* 1923. $30.00

MULFORD, Clarence. *Hopalong Cassidy Saddle Mate.* Popular. pb. $3.00

MULFORD, Clarence. *Hopalong Cassidy Returns.* 1924. $30.00

MULFORD, Clarence. *Hopalong Cassidy Returns.* 1943. Triangle. dj. VG $12.50

MULFORD, Clarence. *Hopalong Cassidy Takes Cards.* Triangle. $5.00

MULFORD, Clarence. *Hopalong Cassidy's Protege.* 1926. $30.00

MULFORD, Clarence. *Rustler's Valley.* Thrilling Novels. pb. $4.00

MULFORD, Clarence. *Tex.* Graphic. pb. $3.00

MULFORD, Clarence. *The Man from Bar-20.* 1918. $30.00

MULFORD, Prentice. *Prentice Mulford's Story.* 1953. Oakland. Ills. Remington. Ltd. ed. VG $32.50

MULHOLLAND, John. *Beware of Familiar Spirits.* 1979. pb. VG $4.00

MULHOLLAND. *Quicker Than the Eye. Magic & Magicians of World.* 1932. Indiana. Ills. 1st ed. ex-lib. G $5.00

MULLAN, John. *Miners & Traveler's Guide to OR, WA, & CO.* 1865. New York. 1st ed. 153 pp. $285.00

MULLER, Dan. *My Life with Buffalo Bill.* 1948. Chicago. Reilly. Ills. 1st ed. dj. EX $15.00

MULLER, F. Max. *Auld Lang Syne.* 1898. Scribner. 1st ed. 325 pp. index. VG $10.50

MULLER, F. Max. *Theosophy or Psychological Religion.* 1911. London. 585 pp. VG $40.00

MULLER, J.W. *The Invasion of America.* 1916. New York. Dutton. Ills. 1st ed. VG $35.00

MULLER, Marcia. *The Cheshire Cat's Eyes.* 1983. New York. 1st ed. sgn. dj. EX $25.00

MULLER, Marcia. *The Cheshire Cat's Eyes.* 1983. New York. proof copy. sgn. wrappers. EX $30.00

MULLER, Max. *India: What Can It Teach Us?* 1883. New York. 1st Am. ed. wrappers. EX $30.00

MULLINS, John. *The Divining Rod: History, Truthfulness & Utility.* 1927. Bath. Ills. 1st ed. 97 pp. $45.00

MULOCK, Miss. *The Adventures of a Brownie.* 1934. New York. Ills. J. DuBois. dj. $5.00

MULOCK, Miss. *The Little Lame Prince.* 1928. New York. Sears. Ills. Eva Noe. $25.00

MULOCK, Miss. *The Little Lame Prince.* Grosset & Dunlap. Ills. G $4.50

MULVEY, Timothy. *These Are Your Sons.* 1952. New York. 278 pp. dj. VG $10.00

MUMFORD, John K. *Oriental Rugs.* 1900. New York. Ills. 1st ed. maps. 278 pp. $35.00

MUMFORD. Lewis. *Herman Melville.* 1929. New York. Lit. Guild. 1st ed. 377 pp. $10.00

MUNARI, Bruno. *Who's There? Open the Door!* 1957. NY/Cleveland. VG $30.00

MUNBY, A.N.L. *Philipps Studies.* 1951-1960. Cambridge. 1st ed. 5 vol set. VG $185.00

MUNBY, A.N.L. *The Alabaster Hand.* 1949. London. Dobson. 1st ed. dj. VG $40.00

MUNDY, Talbot & King, Bradley. *The Bubble Reputation.* 1923. London. Hutchinson. 1st ed. dj. VG $45.00

MUNDY, Talbot. *C.I.D.* 1932. Century. 1st ed. dj. $200.00

MUNDY, Talbot. *East & West.* 1937. New York. Appleton. 1st ed. 310 pp. G $30.00

MUNDY, Talbot. *Full Moon.* 1935. Appleton. 2nd printing. sgn. $75.00

MUNDY, Talbot. *Guns of the Gods.* 1921. A.L. Burt. dj. G $10.50

MUNDY, Talbot. *Her Reputation.* photoplay ed. VG $17.50

MUNDY, Talbot. *Jimgrim & Allah's Peace.* 1936. Appleton. 1st ed. dj. $200.00

MUNDY, Talbot. *King of the Khyber Rifles.* McKinlay reprint. VG $6.50

MUNDY, Talbot. *Mystery of Khufu's Tomb.* 1935. Appleton. 1st ed. dj. $175.00

MUNDY, Talbot. *Om.* 1924. Indianapolis. Bobbs Merrill. 1st ed. VG $20.00

MUNDY, Talbot. *The Devil's Guard.* 1945. Philadelphia. Oriental Club. dj. VG $15.00

MUNDY, Talbot. *The Eye of Zeitoon.* McKinlay. reprint. VG $6.50

MUNDY, Talbot. *The Gunga Sahib.* 1934. 1st ed. dj. VG $20.00

MUNDY, Talbot. *The Gunga Sahib.* 1934. Appleton. 2nd ed. VG $10.00

MUNDY, Talbot. *The Hundred Days & the Woman Ayisha.* Century. no date. dj. $125.00

MUNDY, Talbot. *The Ivory Trail.* 1919. Indianapolis. Bobbs Merrill. 1st ed. VG $25.00

MUNDY, Talbot. *The King in Check.* 1934. New York. Appleton. 1st Am. ed. VG $25.00

MUNDY, Talbot. *The Marriage of Meldrum Strange.* Hutchinson reprint. G $8.00

MUNDY, Talbot. *The Purple Pirate.* 1959. New York. Gnome. reprint. dj. EX $20.00

MUNDY, Talbot. *The Thunder Dragon Gate.* 1937. Appleton. 1st ed. dj. $125.00

MUNDY, Talbot. *Tros of Samothrace.* 1958. Gnome reprint. dj. EX $20.00

MUNELES, Otto. *Biographical Survey of Jewish Prague.* 1952. Ills. 563 pp. index. $17.50

MUNFORD, Lewis. *Herman Melville.* 1931. New York. 377 pp. dj. $12.50

MUNK, Joseph A. *Arizona Sketches.* 1905. Gafton. Ills. 230 pp. G $25.00

MUNKITTRICK, Richard K. *The Moon Prince.* 1893. New York. Harper. 1st ed. VG $30.00

MUNN, Charles Clark. *The Girl from Tim's Place.* 1906. Ills. F.T. Merrill. EX $5.00

MUNRO, A. *Progress of Love.* Toronto. 1st ed. sgn. $25.00

MUNRO, Alice. *Something I've Been Meaning to Tell You.* 1974. Toronto. McGraw Hill. 1st ed. VG $65.00

MUNRO, Alice. *The Moons of Jupiter.* 1982. New York. Knopf. 1st Am. ed. dj. EX $15.00

MUNRO, Alice. *The Moons of Jupiter.* 1982. Toronto. Macmillan. 1st ed. VG $40.00

MUNRO, G.C. *Birds of Hawaii.* 1976. Tuttle. Ills. 192 pp. dj. EX $15.00

MUNRO, H.H. *Beasts & Superbeasts.* 1914. London. 1st ed. VG $35.00

MUNROE, D.H. *The Grand National 1839-1930.* 1930. New York. Huntington. Ltd. ed. 1/501. $30.00

MUNROE, Kirk. *Through Swamp & Glade.* 1896. New York. $20.00

MUNSEY, C. *Guide to Collecting of Coca Cola.* 1967. New York. $35.00

MUNSEY. *Tragedy of Errors.* 1889. New York. 1st ed. $20.00

MUNSON, Kenneth. *Bombers 1939-1945, Patrol & Transport Aircraft.* 1975. Macmillan. 2nd Am. ed. EX $7.00

MUNSTERBERG, Hugo. *The Japanese Print.* 1982. Weatherhill. Ills. 220 pp. dj. Mint. $35.00

MUNSTERBERG, Hugo. *The War in America.* 1914. G $5.00

MUNTHE, Axel. *Memories & Vagaries.* 1930. New York. 1st Am. ed. dj. VG $20.00

MURBARGER, Nell. *Ghosts of the Glory Trail.* 1965. Los Angeles. Ills. 6th printing. sgn. dj. $12.50

MURBARGER, Nell. *Ghosts of the Glory Trail.* 1956. Desert Mag. Pr.Ills. 1st ed. dj. EX $20.00

MURCHIE, Guy. *Men on the Horizon.* 1932. Houghton Mifflin. 1st ed. sgn. $10.00

MURCHIE, Guy. *Song of the Sky. Exploration of Ocean of the Air.* 1954. Boston. Ills. dj. G $7.50

MURCHISON, Carl. *The Case for & Against Psychical Belief.* 1927. Worcester. Clark. 1st ed. 365 pp. $60.00

MURDOCH, Iris. *A Word Child.* 1975. Viking. 1st Am. ed. dj. VG $15.00

MURDOCH, Iris. *A Word Child.* 1st English proof. VG $50.00

MURDOCH, Iris. *An Address.* 1981. London. Ltd. 1st ed. 1/750. wrappers. $30.00

MURDOCH, Iris. *Bruno's Dream.* 1969. London. 1st ed. dj. EX $25.00

MURDOCH, Iris. *Sartre, Romantic Rationalist.* 1953. Cambridge. Bowes & Bowes. 1st ed. dj. EX $100.00

MURDOCH, Iris. *The Black Prince.* 1973. London. Chatto & Windus. 1st ed. dj. $25.00

MURDOCH, Iris. *The Black Prince.* 1973. New York. 1st ed. dj. VG $15.00

MURDOCH, Iris. *The Good Apprentice.* 1985. Hogarth Press. Ltd. 1st ed. sgn. VG $75.00

MURDOCH, Iris. *The Italian Girl.* 1964. Viking. 1st Am. ed. dj. VG $20.00

MURDOCH, Iris. *The Philosopher's Pupil.* 1983. Viking. advance copy. wrappers. EX $60.00

MURDOCH, Iris. *The Sea. The Sea.* 1978. New York City. $10.00

MURDOCH, Iris. *The Sea. The Sea.* 1978. London. $10.00

MURDOCH, Iris. *The Time of the Angels.* 1966. $10.00

MURDOCH, Iris. *The Unicorn.* 1963. Viking. 1st Am. ed. dj. EX $20.00

MURDOCH, Iris. *The Unicorn.* 1963. London. 1st ed. dj. EX $30.00

MURDOCK, Harold. *Earl Percy's Dinner-Table.* 1907. Boston. Riverside Press. Ltd. ed. VG $45.00

MURGER, Henry. *Scenes de la Vie de Boheme.* 1902. Paris. Ltd. ed. 1/300. EX $250.00

MURGUAND, John P. *Point of No Return.* 1949. Boston. 557 pp. dj. $3.50

MURIE, Adolph. *A Naturalist in Alaska.* 1961. Devin Adair. Ills. photos. 302 pp. dj. VG $17.50

MURIE, Adolph. *Birds of Mount McKinley National Park, Alaska.* 1963. Ills. photos. maps. EX $10.00

MURIE, Adolph. *The Wolves of Mount McKinley.* 1971. Ills. maps. EX $12.50

MURIE, M.E. *Two in the Far North.* 1983. Alaska. Ills. 385 pp. EX $7.50

MURPHY, Arthur. *The Gray's Inn Journal.* 1756. 2 vol set. $250.00

MURPHY, B. *Revealing Eye.* 1967. New York. 1st ed. dj. EX $32.50

MURPHY, Dennis. *Doomed Race.* 1949. New York. Ills. inscr. 1st ed. 95 pp. G $12.50

MURPHY, Mrs. Donald. *1955 Murphytown's 100th Anniversary.* Ills. 16 pp. wrappers. $10.00

MURPHY, R.C. *Logbook for Grace.* 1947. New York. Ills. reprint. dj. VG $10.00

MURPHY, Robert. *The Trumai Indians of Central Brazil.* 1955. Augustin. 1st ed. $12.50

MURPHY, W.H.H. *Laylight Land.* 1888. Boston. VG $35.00

MURPHY & SHAIFER. *A Son of Poland.* 1978. New York. 1st ed. $12.00

MURQUAND, John P. *H.M. Pulham, Esquire.* 1941. Boston. 431 pp. VG $3.50

MURRAY, A.M. *Letters from the U.S., Cuba, & Canada.* 1856. New York. Putnam. 402 pp. VG $25.00

MURRAY, Albert. *Trainwhistle Guitar.* 1974. New York. McGraw Hill. proof copy. EX $40.00

MURRAY, Charles A. *Travels in North America in Years 1834-1836.* London. 473 pp. 2 vol set. $175.00

MURRAY, G.W. *Dare Me to the Desert.* 1968. Barnes. Ills. 1st Am. ed. maps. dj. EX $10.00

MURRAY, Henry. *Lands of the Slave & the Free.* 1855. London. 2 vol set. VG $17.50

MURRAY, Henry. *The Art of Portrait Painting on Oil Colours.* Middlesex, Eng.Winsor & Newton. Ills. VG $5.00

MURRAY, John Middleton. *Journal of Katherine Mansfield.* 1927. Knopf. Ills. 1st ed. 3rd printing. VG $15.00

MURRAY, Lindley. *Sequel to the English Reader.* 1814. Baltimore. G $7.50

MURRAY, Michael. *The Mystery of the Hollywood Horse.* 1964. Racine. Whitman. 280 pp. $2.00

MURRAY, N. *Revealing Eye.* 1967. New York. 1st ed. dj. EX $32.50

MURRAY, N. *The Love of Elephants.* 1976. Octopus. Ills. 96 pp. dj. EX $15.00

MURRAY, Robert K. *The 103rd Ballot.* 1976. New York. Harper & Row. 336 pp. dj. $4.50

MURRAY, W.H.H. *Adirondack Adventures.* 1869. Boston. EX $20.00

MURRAY, W.H.H. *Adirondack Tales.* 1877. Boston. 1st ed. VG $15.00

MURRAY, W.H.H. *Adventures in Wilderness/Camp Life in Adirondacks.* 1869. Boston. Ills. 1st ed. 236 pp. $30.00

MURRAY, W.H.H. *Adventures in Wilderness/Camp Life in Adirondacks.* 1970. Syracuse U. Ills. 311 pp. dj. EX $15.00

MURRAY, W.H.H. *Lake Champlain & Its Shores.* 1890. $24.00

MURRAY, W.W. *The Epic of Vimy.* 1936. Ottawa. Ills. G $42.50

MURRAY. *Ballads & Songs of Scotland.* 1874. London. G $8.00

MURRILL, Howard Agassiz. *Mountain & Stream Songs of the Virginias.* 1918. Nashville. presentation copy. 91 pp. VG $9.00

MURROW, Edward R. *In Search of Light: Broadcasts of E.R. Murrow.* 1967. 1st ed. dj. VG $10.00

MURRY, John Middleton. *Poems & Verses of John Keats. Vols. I & II.* 1930. London. King's Printers. Ltd. ed. VG $65.00

MURRY, John Middleton. *Reminiscences of D.H. Lawrence.* 1933. New York. Holt. 1st printing. 279 pp. G $9.50

MUSCATINE, Doris. *A Cook's Tour of San Francisco.* 1963. New York. Scribner. 370 pp. $5.00

MUSICK, John. *Hawaii, Our New Possessions.* 1898. New York. Ills. fld map. EX $50.00

MUSMANNO, M. *Ten Days to Die.* 1951. Doubleday. Ills. G $15.00

MUSSER, J.W. *The New & Everlasting Covenant of Marriage.* no date. 87 pp. wrappers. VG $20.00

MUSSEY, Barrows. *Old New England.* 1946. New York. Ills. 128 pp. $12.50

MUSSOLINI, Benito. *Parlo Con Bruno.* 1942. Ills. SftCvr. G $20.00

MUSSOLINI, Benito. *Storia di un Anno.* 1944. 2nd ed. SftCvr. VG $20.00

MUTHER, Richard. *History of Modern Painting.* 1896. New York. Ills. 3 vol set. $57.50

MUTSCHMANN, H. & Wentersdorf. *Shakespeare & Catholicism.* 1952. New York. dj. VG $10.00

MYER, Anton. *Once an Eagle.* 1968. Holt. 1st ed. dj. VG $25.00

MYERS, Denys P. *Manual of Collections of & to Treaties.* 1922. Cambridge. Harvard U. Pr. 1st ed. 685 pp. $75.00

MYERS, Ephraim E. *True Story of the Civil War Veteran.* York, PA. (ca.1910?) Ills. 1st ed. $85.00

MYERS, John. *San Francisco's Reign of Terror.* 1966. Doubleday. 1st ed. dj. VG $7.50

MYERS, John. *Silverlock.* 1949. New York. Dutton. 1st ed. sgn. dj. EX $65.00

MYERS, John. *The Harp & the Blade.* 1944. New York. Dutton. 1st ed. dj. VG $20.00

MYERS, John. *The Moon's Fire Eating Daughter.* Ltd. ed. 1/250. sgn. EX $35.00

MYERS, John. *The Wild Yazoo.* 1947. New York. 1st ed. 378 pp. $10.00

MYERS, Robert. *The Cross of Frankenstein.* 1975. Lippincott. 1st ed. dj. EX $8.50

MYERS, Robert. *The Slave of Frankenstein.* 1976. Lippincott. 1st ed. dj. EX $8.50

MYERS, William W. *Hotep: Dream of the Nile.* 1905. Cincinnati. Clarke. 1st ed. VG $12.50

MYKLEBOST, T. *They Came as Friends, Nazi Occupation of Norway.* 1943. London. G $7.50

MYRICK, Herbert. *Chache la Poudre.* 1905. Ltd. ed. 1/500. $150.00

MYTINGER, Caroline. *Headhunting in Solomon Islands.* 1942. New York. Macmillan. Ills. 416 pp. VG $5.50

N.A.S.A. *Earth Photographs.* 1968. Washington. 327 pp. EX $6.00

NABOKOV, Vladimir. *Ada.* 1969. London. 1st ed. dj. VG $25.00

NABOKOV, Vladimir. *Conclusive Evidence.* 1951. New York. Harper. 1st ed. dj. EX $150.00

NABOKOV, Vladimir. *Defense.* New York. 1st ed. dj. EX $20.00

NABOKOV, Vladimir. *Despair.* New York. 1st ed. dj. VG $30.00

NABOKOV, Vladimir. *Invitation to Beheading.* 1959. dj. VG $20.00

NABOKOV, Vladimir. *King, Queen, Knave.* 1968. McGraw Hill. 1st Am. ed. dj. VG $30.00

NABOKOV, Vladimir. *Laughter in the Dark.* 1960. New Direction. dj. VG $25.00

NABOKOV, Vladimir. *Lectures on Don Quixote.* 1983. Harcourt. 1st Am. ed. dj. EX $17.50

NABOKOV, Vladimir. *Lolita.* 1st Eng. ed. dj. VG $50.00

NABOKOV, Vladimir. *Lolita: a Screenplay.* 1974. McGraw Hill. 1st Am. ed. dj. VG $20.00

NABOKOV, Vladimir. *Mary.* 1970. McGraw Hill. 1st Am. ed. dj. VG $30.00

NABOKOV, Vladimir. *Nabokov's Congeries.* 1968. New York. Viking. advance copy. EX $150.00

NABOKOV, Vladimir. *Nabokov's Quartet.* New York. 1st ed. dj. EX $20.00

NABOKOV, Vladimir. *Nikolai Gogol.* London. 1st ed. $65.00

NABOKOV, Vladimir. *Pnin.* 1957. Doubleday. 1st ed. dj. VG $30.00

NABOKOV, Vladimir. *Speak, Memory, an Autobiography Revisited.* 1966. New York. Putnam. photos. 316 pp. dj. $4.50

NABOKOV, Vladimir. *The Eye.* 1965. Phaedra. 1st Am. ed. dj. VG $85.00

NABOKOV, Vladimir. *The Eye.* 1965. New York. Grossman. dj. VG $18.50

NABOKOV, Vladimir. *The Gift.* New York. 1st ed. dj. VG $20.00

NABOKOV, Vladimir. *The Tee.* New York. 1st ed. dj. VG $50.00

NABOKOV, Vladimir. *Transparent Things.* 1972. 1st Am. ed. dj. EX $15.00

NABOKOV, Vladimir. *Tyrants Destroyed.* 1975. McGraw Hill. 1st Am. ed. dj. VG $20.00

NABOKOV, Vladimir. *Waltz Invention.* New York. 1st ed. dj. EX $20.00

NADAILLAC, Marquis de. *Pre-Historic America.* 1895. New York. Putnam. 219 Ills. VG $15.00

NAETHER, C. *Soft-Billed Birds.* 1955. All Pet. Ills. 64 pp. VG $7.00

NAGEL. *The Drawings of Kathe Kollowitz.* 1972. Crown. Ills. folio. VG $85.00

NAIPAUL, V.S. *A Flag on the Island.* 1967. Macmillan. 1st Am. ed. dj. VG $35.00

NAIPAUL, V.S. *Finding the Center.* 1984. Knopf. 1st Am. ed. dj. VG $15.00

NAIPAUL, V.S. *Guerillas.* 1975. Knopf. 1st Am. ed. dj. VG $15.00

NAIPAUL, V.S. *Guerillas.* 1975. London. 1st ed. dj. $45.00

NAIPAUL, V.S. *The Loss of El Dorado.* 1970. 1st ed. VG $35.00

NAIPAUL, V.S. *The Mimic Men.* 1967. London. Deutsch. 1st ed. VG $40.00

NAIPAUL, V.S. *The Mystic Masseur.* 1959. Vanguard. 1st ed. dj. EX $75.00

NAKAMURA. *Onna (Women).* 1965. Tokyo. EX $42.50

NAKASHIAN, Dr. A. *Man Who Found a Country.* 1940. New York. Crowell. Ills. dj. EX $55.00

NAMATH, J. *Can't Wait Until Tomorrow.* 1969. 1st ed. sgn. dj. VG $12.00

NANCE, R. Morton. *Sailing Ship Models.* 1924. Ltd. ed. 1/1750. VG $110.00

NANSEN, Fridjof. *Eskimo Life.* 1894. London. 2nd ed. gilt decor. scarce. EX $100.00

NANSEN, Fridjof. *Farthest North; Voyage of Exploration of the Fram.* 1897. New York. Harper. 1st ed. 2 vol set. $95.00

NANSEN, Fridjof. *Farthest North; Voyage of Exploration of the Fram.* 1897. Westminister. 1st ed. maps. VG $125.00

NANSEN, Fridjof. *In Nacht Und Eis.* 1897. Leipzig. 2 vol set. G $22.50

NANSEN, O. *From Day to Day.* 1949. New York. Putnam. Ills. G $25.00

NAPIER, J. *Bigfoot, Yetti, & Sasquatch in Myth & Reality.* 1973. Dutton. Ills. 1st ed. 240 pp. EX $15.00

NARAZAKI, M. & Mitchell, C.H. *The Japanese Print: Its Evolution & Essence.* 1970. Ills. Folio. 274 pp. $110.00

NARAZAKI, Muneshige. *Sharaku. The Enigmatic Ukiyo-e Master.* 1983. Kodansha. Ills. 1st ed. 48 pp. Folio. EX $35.00

NASH, J.M. *Age of Rembrandt & Vermeer.* 1972. Phaidon. dj. VG $30.00

NASH, Joseph. *Mansions of England in the Olden Time.* 1874. London. Ills. folio. VG $60.00

NASH, Manning. *Machine Age Maya.* 1958. 1st ed. wrappers. $10.00

NASH, Ogden. *Four Prominent So & So's.* 1934. New York. Dutch Treat Club. $15.00

NASH, Ogden. *Good Intentions.* 1942. 1st reprint. inscr. sgn. $50.00

NASH, Ogden. *Hard Lines.* 1932. London. 1st ed. dj. VG $15.00

NASH, Ogden. *Hard Lines.* 1931. New York. Ills. 1st ed. VG $10.00

NASH, Ogden. *I'm a Stranger Here Myself.* 1938. 283 pp. $6.00

NASH, Ogden. *I'm a Stranger Here Myself.* Little, Brown. no date. G $6.00

NASH, Ogden. *Parents Keep Out.* 1949. 137 pp. $6.00

NASH, Ogden. *The Bad Parent's Garden of Verse.* 1936. New York. Ills. R. Birch. dj. VG $75.00

NASH. *John Nash.* 1925. London. Ills. 1st ed. VG $30.00

NASMITH, G. *Canada's Sons & Great Britain in WWI.* 1919. Ills. G $17.50

NASSAU, Robert Hamill. *Fetishism in West Africa.* 1904. New York. 1st ed. 389 pp. 12 pls. VG $32.50

NAST, Thomas. *Swinging Round the Circle.* 1867. Boston. Ills. Nast. 1st ed. 299 pp. $20.00

NATHAN, G.J. *Mr. George Jean Nathan Presents.* 1917. New York. Knopf. 1st ed. 310 pp. $10.00

NATHAN, G.J. *The Bachelor Life.* 1941. New York. sgn. dj. $12.50

NATHAN. *Tapiola's Brave Regiment.* 1941. Knopf. Ills. Kurt Wiese. 1st ed. dj. $12.50

NATIONAL GEOGRAPHIC SOCIETY. *Book of Wild Flowers.* 1933. Washington. 250 col pls. VG $12.50

NATIONAL GEOGRAPHIC SOCIETY. *The Book of Birds.* 1918. Fuertes, IL. VG $20.00

NATIONAL GEOGRAPHIC SOCIETY. *The Book of Birds. Birds of Town & Country.* 1925. Washington. 94 Ills. 215 pp. index. dj. $20.00

NATIONAL GEOGRAPHIC SOCIETY. *Wild Animals of North America.* 1971. Ills. dj. $12.50

NAUMANN, Emil. *The History of Music Traced by F. Praeger.* 1885. London. special ed. Ills. 5 vol set. $50.00

NAVE. *Topical Bible.* 1903. 1450 pp. $40.00

NAYLOR, Gloria. *Linden Hills.* 1985. New York. advance copy. wrappers. EX $25.00

NAYLOR, Gloria. *Linden Hills.* 1985. Ticknor & Fields. 1st ed. dj. $17.50

NAYLOR, Gloria. *The Women of Brewster Place.* 1982. Viking. proof copy. wrappers. VG $35.00

NAYLOR, James Ball. *Old Home Week.* 1907. Boston. Ills. 86 pp. VG $10.00

NAYLOR, James Ball. *Sign of the Prophet.* 1901. Akron. 1st ed. 416 pp. $17.50

NEAGOE, Peter. *Storm.* 1932. Paris. New Review Pub. wrappers. $20.00

NEAGOE, Peter. *What is Surrealism?* Paris. New Review Pub. Ills. 23 pp. $12.50

NEAL, Daniel. *The History of New England.* 1747. London. 2nd ed. fld map. 2 vol set. $250.00

NEAL, R.M. *High Green & the Bark Peelers.* 1950. New York. ex-lib. VG $15.00

NEAL, W. Keith & Black, D.H.L. *Forsyth & Co. Patent Gunmakers.* 1969. Bell & Sons. Ills. 280 pp. dj. VG $22.50

NEALE, Dennis. *Memoirs of the Life of Dennis Neale.* 1754. London. $36.00

NEARING, Scott. *Educational Frontiers.* 1925. New York. Seltzer. 1st ed. scarce. $40.00

NEARING, Scott. *Reducing the Cost of Living.* 1914. Philadelphia. Jacobs. 1st ed. $35.00

NEAVE, Airey. *Escape Room.* photos. VG $7.50

NEBEL, Gustave. *Daisy Miller.* 1969. Ltd. Eds. Club. Ills. 1/1500. sgn. boxed. EX $75.00

NEBHARD, Mabel. *Fantasies.* 1896. London. 1st ed. EX $37.50

NEBLETTE, Brehm, & Priest. *Elementary Photography for Club & Home Use.* 1937. New York. Macmillan. 253 pp. $2.50

NECKER, Clare. *Four Centuries of Cat Books.* 1973. Scarecrow Press. EX $15.00

NECKER, Clare. *The Cat's Got Our Tongue.* 1973. Scarecrow Press. EX $15.00

NEEDHAM, Henry B. *Divorcing Lady Nicotine.* 1913. Chicago. 70 pp. $10.00

NEEDHAM, J. *Science & Civilization in China.* 1971. Cambridge. Ills. photos. maps. dj. EX $50.00

NEESE. *Prison Exposures. Photographs Inside Prison.* 1959. Philadelphia. 1st ed. $15.00

NEFF, Mark. *Personal Memoirs of H.P. Blavatsky.* 1937. Dutton. 1st ed. dj. $17.50

NEHRU. *Mahatma Ghandi.* 1949. Calcutta. Ills. 169 pp. $3.00

NEIDER, Charles. *The Complete Humorous Sketches & Tales of Twain.* 1961. Hanover House. 720 pp. $4.50

NEIDER, Charles. *The Great West.* 1958. Bonanza Books. dj. $18.50

NEIDER, Charles. *Great Shipwrecks & Castaways.* 1952. Harper. 1st ed. 238 pp. $8.00

NEIDER, Charles. *The Complete Short Stories of Mark Twain.* 1957. New York. Hanover House. 676 pp. $5.00

NEIHARDT, J.G. *Life Story of a Holy Man of the Ogalala Sioux.* 1932. New York. Ills. Standing Bear. $40.00

NEIHARDT, John. *Bundle of Myrrh.* 1907. 1st ed. VG $45.00

NEIHARDT, John. *Eagle Voice.* 1953. 1st Eng. ed. dj. $10.00

NEIHARDT, John. *Sender of Words.* 1984. dj. EX $12.50

NEIHARDT, John. *When the Tree Flowered.* 1951. New York. review copy. dj. VG $20.00

NEIHART, John G. *The River & I.* 1910. Putnam. VG $20.00

NEIL, Marion Harris. *A Calendar of Dinners with 615 Recipes.* 1921. Cincinnati. VG $10.00

NEIL, Marion Harris. *Ryzon Baking Book.* 1916. New York. VG $15.00

NEILL, John R. *Children's Stories that Never Grow Old.* 1908. Reilly & Britton. 1st ed. pls. $30.00

NEILL, John R. *Cowardly Lion of Oz.* 1923. Reilly & Lee. 2nd printing. $48.00

NEILL, John R. *Hungry Tiger of Oz.* 1926. Reilly & Lee. 1st ed. VG $95.00

NEILL, John R. *Jack Pumpkinhead of Oz.* 1929. Reilly & Lee. 1st ed. VG $95.00

NEILL, John R. *Lucky Bucky in Oz.* 1942. Reilly & Lee. 1st ed. VG $75.00

NEILL, John R. *Magic of Oz.* Reilly & Lee. reprint. $42.00

NEILL, John R. *Tin Woodsman of Oz.* 1918. Reilly & Britton. 1st ed. $105.00

NEILSEN. *East of the Sun & West of the Moon.* Garden City. 8 pls. $75.00

NEIMAN, LeRoy. *Winners, My Thirty Years in Sports.* 1983. New York. photos. sgn. VG $30.00

NEL, Elizabeth. *Mr Churchill's Secretary: Recollections, 1941-'45.* 1958. London. $10.00

NELSON, Bruce. *Land of the Dacotahs.* 1946. 1st ed. G $15.00

NELSON, E.W. *Wild Animals of North America.* 1930. Nat. Geog. Soc. Ills. Fueretes & Seton. EX $25.00

NELSON, George. *Tomorrow's House.* 1954. 3rd ed. VG $25.00

NELSON, R.K. *Hunters of the Northern Ice.* 1969. Chicago. Ills. 429 pp. dj. EX $17.50

NELSON, Senator Gaylord. *America's Last Chance.* 1970. dj. $27.50

NEQUATEWA. *Truth of a Hopi, Stories Relating to Origin.* 1967. Flagstaff. 136 pp. SftCvr. $12.50

NERO, R.W. *Great Gray Owl, Phantom of the Northern Forest.* 1980. Smithsonian. Ills. 1st ed. dj. EX $20.00

NERUDA, Pablo. *Passions & Impressions.* 1982. Farrar. advance copy. wrappers. EX $30.00

NESBIT, E. *Royal Children of English History.* London. Tuck. no date. Ills. Brundage. $50.00

NESBIT, E. *The Bastable Children.* 1929. Coward McCann. Ills. VG $20.00

NESBIT, E. *The Children's Shakespeare.* 1900. Altemus. Ills. 1st ed. G $90.00

NESBIT, E. *The Phoenix & the Carpet.* New York. Ills. J.S. Goodall. VG $7.50

NESBIT, E. *The Story of the Treasure Seekers.* 1903. London. Ills. G. Browne & L. Baumer. $17.00

NESBIT, Troy. *Mystery at Rustler's Fort.* 1964. Racine. Whitman. 282 pp. $2.50

NESBIT, Troy. *The Indian Mummy Mystery.* 1964. Racine. Whitman. 280 pp. $2.50

NESBIT, Wilbur D. *As Children Do.* 1929. Joliet. Ills. Ellery Friend. 1st ed. $20.00

NESBITT, M.L. *Grammar-Land.* 1878. New York. Holt. Ills. 120 pp. VG $15.00

NESS, Eliot. *The Untouchables.* 1957. 1st ed. dj. VG $10.00

NESS. *Practical Dope & the Big Bores.* 1952. EX $30.00

NESTLE CO. *Nestle's Cookbook.* 184 pp. $3.50

NESTLER, Al. *Al Nestler's Southwest.* 1970. Northland. Ltd. ed. 1/1700. $20.00

NETBOY, A. *Salmon, World's Most Harassed Fish.* 1980. Winchester. Ills. dj. EX $12.50

NETHERCOT, Arthur. *First Five Lives of Annie Besant.* 1960. dj. VG $25.00

NETZER, Corinne. *Brand Name Calorie Counter.* 1969. dj. EX $3.00

NEUBAUER, R. *Packaging: Contemporary Media.* 1973. 1st ed. dj. EX $15.00

NEUBERGER, Richard L. *Adventures in Politica, We Go to Legislature.* 1954. New York. Oxford U. Press. G $6.00

NEUER, Roni & Lebertson, H. *Ukiyo-e: 250 Years of Japanese Art.* 1978. Ills. 337 pp. dj. Mint. $48.00

NEUMANN, E. *Functional Graphic Design in the 20's.* 1967. Reinhold. dj. VG $17.50

NEUMANN, George C. *History of Weapons of the American Revolution.* 1967. New York. Ills. 373 pp. dj. $25.00

NEVILL, Ralph. *Old English Sporting Prints & Their History.* 1923. London. Ltd. ed. 1/1500. $125.00

NEVINS, Allan & Hill, Frank E. *Ford: Expansion & Challenge, 1915-1933.* 1957. New York. Ills. 1st ed. 714+ pp. $35.00

NEVINS, Allan. *Fremont, the West's Greatest Adventurer.* 1928. NY/London. Ills. 1st ed. 2 vol set. $40.00

NEVINS, Allan. *John D. Rockefeller.* 1940. New York. 1st ed. 2 vol set. boxed. $16.00

NEVINS, Allan. *Ordeal of the Union.* 1947. New York. Ills. 1st ed. 2 vol set. $22.50

NEVINS, Allan. *The War for the Union.* (ca.1945) Ills. 1st ed. dj. EX $15.00

NEVINS, Allan. *The War for the Union.* Scribner. 4 vol set. $45.00

NEVINS, Winfield S. *Witchcraft in Salem Village in 1692.* 1892. Salem. Ills. 1st ed. VG $100.00

NEVINS. *Civil War Books: Critical Bibliography.* 1969. Baton Rouge. 2 vol set. dj. VG $50.00

NEVIUS, Blake. *Edith Wharton.* 1953. U. of CA. 1st ed. dj. $10.00

NEWBERRY, J.S. *The First Oil Well.* 1890. Harper. 7 pp. sgn. wrappers. $5.00

NEWBERRY, John. *Newtonian System of Philosophy.* 1798. London. new, improved ed. 5 pls. $75.00

NEWBY, E. *Great Ascents.* 1977. dj. EX $20.00

NEWBY, E. *Slowly Down the Ganges.* 1967. London. dj. VG $15.00

NEWBY, Eric. *The Last Grain Race.* 1956. $8.50

NEWCOMB, Ethel. *Leschetizky as I Knew Him.* 1967. New York. Da Capo. dj. VG $20.00

NEWCOMB, R. *Mission Churches & Historic Houses of California.* 1925. Philadelphia. Ills. 1st ed. rebound. EX $50.00

NEWCOMB, W.W. *Indians of Texas from Prehistoric to Modern Times.* 1961. U. of TX. 1st ed. dj. $10.00

NEWELL, B. *Time in New England.* 1950. Oxford U. Pr. 1st ed. dj. EX $85.00

NEWELL, G.R. *Ships of the Inland Sea.* 1960. Ills. dj. EX $12.50

NEWELL, George. *Girl Scout Song Book.* 1929. revised ed. 130+ pp. VG $7.50

NEWELL, Peter. *Pictures & Rhymes.* 1900. New York. Ills. $20.00

NEWELL, Peter. *Slant Book.* 1967. Tuttle. reprint ed. VG $20.00

NEWELL, Peter. *The Rocket Book.* 1912. New York. 1st ed. 22 pls. EX $75.00

NEWELL, William Wells. *Games & Songs of American Children.* 1883. New York. 254 pp. $37.50

NEWELL. *Mother Goose for Grown-Ups, by Carryl.* Ills. 1st ed. dj. VG $15.00

NEWELL. *Sounding Rockets.* 1959. $10.00

NEWELL. *The Fishing & Hunting Answer Book.* 1949. Newell. Ills. Lyne Bogue. $2.50

NEWGASS, Edgar. *An Outline of Anglo American Bible History.* 1958. Batsford. 1st ed. dj. $10.00

NEWHALL, B. *Daguerrotype in America.* 1961. Duell. 1st ed. dj. EX $32.50

NEWHALL, B. *History of Photography.* 1964. revised, enlarged ed. VG $30.00

NEWHALL, B. *Photography: Essays & Images.* 1980. New York. 1st ed. EX $35.00

NEWHALL, B. *The History of Photography from 1839 to Present.* 1949. 1st ed. dj. VG $145.00

NEWHALL, N. *Edward Weston.* 1946. New York. 1st ed. dj. VG $30.00

NEWHOUSE, J. *The Sporty Game, Making & Selling of Airliners.* 1982. dj. EX $12.50

NEWHOUSE, S. *The Trapper's Guide.* 1867. Oneida. 2nd ed. VG $40.00

NEWLAND, H. *Forest Scenes in Norway & Sweden.* 1855. London. 2nd ed. VG $45.00

NEWLANDS. *Carpenters & Joiners Assistant.* (ca. 1899) $87.00

NEWLON, Clarke. *L.B.J. The Man from Johnson City.* 1965. London. Muller. 197 pp. dj. $65.00

NEWMAN, A. *Brave Stravinsky.* 1980. Cleveland. 1st ed. EX $12.50

NEWMAN, Francis. *The Hard-Boiled Virgin.* Boni & Liveright. 4th ed. VG $12.50

NEWMAN, Isidora. *Fairy Flowers.* 1926. Holt. Ills. Pogany. 1st ed. 196 pp. $45.00

NEWMAN, Sharan. *Guinevere.* 1981. New York. St.Martins. dj. EX $15.00

NEWMAN, Sharan. *The Chessboard Queen.* 1983. New York. 1st ed. review copy. dj. EX $15.00

NEWQUIST, Roy. *Counterpoint.* 1964. Chicago. Rand McNally. 2nd printing. $7.50

NEWSOME. *Button Collecting & Crafting.* 1976. New York. dj. EX $12.50

NEWTON, A. Edward. *Amenities of Book Collecting.* 1935. New York. Modern Library. 1st ed. VG $10.00

NEWTON, A. Edward. *Derby Day & Other Adventures.* 1934. Boston. Ltd. 1st ed. sgn. VG $50.00

NEWTON, A. Edward. *Doctor Johnson, a Play.* 1923. Atlantic Monthly Press. $12.50

NEWTON, A. Edward. *On Books & Business.* 1930. Apellicon Pr. Ills. 1st ed. sgn. VG $50.00

NEWTON, A. Edward. *The Greatest Book in the World & Other Papers.* Boston. (ca.1926) 1st ed. sgn. VG $50.00

NEWTON, A. Edward. *This Book Collecting Game.* 1930. London. Ills. 1st Eng. ed. dj. $12.50

NEWTON, C.T. *Travels & Discoveries in Levant.* 1865. London. Ills. 2 vol set. EX $275.00

NEWTON, Joseph Fort. *The Builders, Study & Story of Masonry.* 1916. Torch Press. 317 pp. $35.00

NEWTON, R. *The Characters of Theopharastus.* 1754. Oxford. 1st ed. VG $50.00

NEWTON, T.M. *Pen Pictures & Bio Sketches of Old Settlers.* 1886. St.Paul, MN. G $37.00

NEWTON. *A Magnificent Farce.* 1921. $12.00

NICHOL. *Natural Vegetation of Arizona.* 1937. U. of AZ. 41 pp. 22 pls. SftCvr. $10.00

NICHOL. *Phenomena & Order of the Solar System.* 1843. $35.00

NICHOLAS, Anna. *An Idyll of the Wabash & Other Indiana Stories.* 1898. Indianapolis. Ills. 1st ed. 256 pp. $10.00

NICHOLAS, George. *A Letter to His Friend in Virginia.* 1799. Philadelphia. J. Carey. 39 pp. wrappers. $225.00

NICHOLS, A.H. *Woodland Romance.* 1923. wrappers. G $25.00

NICHOLS, Alice. *Bleeding Kansas.* 1954. New York. 2nd printing, 307 pp. $12.50

NICHOLS, Beverly. *Book of Old Ballads.* 1934. London. Ills. 279 pp. folio. $50.00

NICHOLS, Beverly. *The Art of Flower Arrangement.* 1967. Viking. 1st Am. ed. dj. VG $25.00

NICHOLS, Beverly. *The Sweet & Twenties.* 1958. London. Ills. dj. VG $20.00

NICHOLS, Beverly. *Young Man's Candid Recollections of Elders.* New York. Doran. 256 pp. $12.50

NICHOLS, Eugene. *Science of Higher Sense Perception.* 1972. 1st ed. 214 pp. dj. $8.00

NICHOLS, George W. *Story of Great March from Diary of Staff Officer.* 1865. New York. 16th ed. map. VG $30.00

NICHOLS, Henry C. *The Voice At Sea.* 1948. $10.00

NICHOLS, J. *The Sterile Cuckoo.* Arkham House. 1st ed. dj. VG $50.00

NICHOLS, J. *The Sterile Cuckoo.* 1965. New York. advance copy. wrappers. $65.00

NICHOLS, John. *The Milagro Beanfield War.* 1967. London. Deutsch. 1st Eng. ed. VG $65.00

NICHOLS, John. *The Wizard of Loneliness.* 1966. New York. Putnam. 1st ed. dj. VG $15.00

NICHOLS, Nell B. *Farm Journal's Homemade Snacks.* 1976. Doubleday. 210 pp. dj. EX $5.00

NICHOLS, Nell B. *Informal Entertaining Country Style.* 1973. Garden City. Doubleday. 1st ed. 277 pp. dj. $9.50

NICHOLS, Roy Franklin. *The Disruption of American Democracy.* 1948. New York. 1st ed. 612 pp. dj. $10.00

NICHOLS, Rudge & Poole, C.N. *Peter Powers Pioneer; 1st Settler in Hollis, NH.* 1930. Concord. Ills. Ltd. 1st ed. sgn. Poole. $50.00

NICHOLSON, Meredith. *A Hoosier Chronicle.* 1912. Boston. 1st ed. VG $20.00

NICHOLSON, Meredith. *Otherwise Phyllis.* Ills. C. Dana Gibson. 1st ed. $7.50

NICHOLSON, Meredith. *Rosalind at Redgate.* 1907. $27.50

NICHOLSON, Meredith. *Style & the Man.* 1911. Indianapolis. 55 pp. scarce. $15.00

NICHOLSON, Meredith. *The Cavalier of Tennessee.* 1928. $27.50

NICHOLSON, Meredith. *The House of a Thousand Candles.* 1905. Ills. H.C. Christy. 1st ed. $6.50

NICHOLSON, Meredith. *The Little Brown Jug at Kildare.* 1908. Indianapolis. Bobbs Merrill. Ills. Flagg. $4.50

NICHOLSON, Meredith. *The Main Chance.* 1903. $27.50

NICHOLSON, Meredith. *The Proof of the Pudding.* 1916. $27.50

NICHOLSON, Peter. *Nicholson's Carpenter's Guide for Workmen.* 1825. London. Jones & Co. 1st improved ed. $65.00

NICHOLSON, William. *An Almanac of Twelve Sports.* New York. 28 full pp. color Ills. $60.00

NICHOLSON, William. *Words by R. Kipling.* 1898. New York. folio. rare. VG $325.00

NICKLES, Eliz. & Ashcraft, L. *The Coming Matriarchy.* 1981. New York. Play Boy Press. proof copy. $30.00

NICKLIN, J. Bernard. *Divine Time-Measures.* 1933. London. 1st ed. 206 pp. dj. G $25.00

NICOL, C.W. *From the Roof of the Africa.* 1972. Knopf. Ills. 1st ed. dj. EX $12.50

NICOL, Eric & More, Dave. *The Joy of Hockey.* 1978. Hurtig Pub. Ills. 158 pp. dj. EX $8.50

NICOL & WHALLEY. *Russia, Anyone?* 1963. Harper. 1st ed. $8.50

NICOLAY, H. *Personal Traits of Abraham Lincoln.* 1912. New York. 1st ed. VG $12.50

NICOLAY & HAY. *Abraham Lincoln, a History.* 1890. New York. 10 vol set. VG $55.00

NICOLAY. *The Outbreak of the Rebellion* (ca. 1864). 220 pp. $13.50

NICOLL, M.J. *Three Voyages of a Naturalist.* 1908. London. Witherby. Ills. 246 pp. VG $37.50

NICOLL, W. R. & Wise, T. *Literary Anecdotes of the Nineteenth Century.* 1895. London. 1st ed. $35.00

NICOLSON, J.U. *Fingers of Fear.* 1937. NY. Covici. sgn. inscr. dtd. VG $50.00

NICOLSON, N. *Portrait of a Marriage.* 1973. Ills. $7.50

NIEDIECK, Paul. *Cruising in the Bering Sea.* 1909. London. Ills. map. VG $25.00

NIELSEN, Kay. *East of the Sun & West of the Moon.* 1914. New York. Doran. 25 color pls. VG $125.00

NIELSEN, Kay. *East of the Sun & West of the Moon.* 1930. Doran. 25 color pls. $150.00

NIELSEN, Kay. *Fairy Tales by Andersen.* 1932. Garden City. 8 color plates. $75.00

NIELSEN, Kay. *Kay Nielsen.* 1975. London. Ills. VG $25.00

NIELSEN, Kay. *Twelve Dancing Princesses.* 1923. New York. 1st ed. 16 mounted color pls. $125.00

NIEMOELLER. *Dachau Sermons.* 1946. sgn. dj. VG $22.50

NIEMOELLER. *Hero of the Concentration Camp.* 1942. dj. VG $10.00

NIGEN, L. *Integral Trees.* 1983. Del Ray. 1st ed. sgn. dj. EX $25.00

NIGHTINGALE, Florence. *Notes on Nursing.* 1859. London. 1st ed. boxed. $485.00

NIJINSKY, Romola. *Nijinsky.* 1934. New York. Simon & Schuster. 446 pp. dj. $4.50

NILES, John Jacob. *Singing Soldiers.* 1927. New York. Scribner. 1st ed. dj. VG $65.00

NIMOY, Leonard. *Come Be with Me.* 1978. 1st ed. EX $10.00

NIMOY, Leonard. *We Are All Searching for Love.* 1977. 1st ed. EX $10.00

NIMOY, Leonard. *Will I Think of You.* 1974. 1st ed. VG $10.00

NIMOY, Leonard. *You & I.* 1973. 2nd ed. VG $7.50

NIN, Anais. *A Spy in the House of Love.* 1954. Paris/NY. 1st ed. dj. EX $40.00

NIN, Anais. *Cities of the Interior.* 1959. Swallow. 800 pp. wrappers. VG $20.00

NIN, Anais. *D.H. Lawrence, an Unprofessional Study.* 1932. Paris. 1st ed. dj. EX $40.00

NIN, Anais. *Delta of Venus.* 1977. 250pp. $37.50

NIN, Anais. *Diary of A. Nin.* 1966. Harcourt Brace. Swallow Press. EX $55.00

NIN, Anais. *Henry & June.* 1986. New York. advance copy. wrappers. EX $35.00

NIN, Anais. *Letters to Henry Miller.* 1986. proof copy. VG $50.00

NIRENSTEIN, A. *Tower from the Enemy.* 1959. New York. Orion. Ills. G $30.00

NISSENSON, Hugh. *The Tree of Life.* 1985. New York. Harper. Ills. wrappers. EX $15.00

NITCHIE, Elizabeth. *Advanced Lessons in Lip-Reading.* 1923. New York. 313 pp. VG $18.00

NITCHIE, Elizabeth. *Mary Shelley.* 1953. Rutgers U. Pr. dj. VG $15.00

NIVEN, John. *Connecticut for the Union.* 1965. Yale Press. $20.00

NIVEN, L. & Barnes, S. *Dream Park.* 1981. Phantasia Pr. Ltd. ed. 1/600. sgn. boxed. EX $100.00

NIVEN, L. & Pournelle, J. *Oath of Fealty.* 1981. Phantasia Pr. Ltd. ed. 1/750. sgn. boxed. EX $150.00

NIVEN, Larry. *A Gift from Earth.* 1970. New York. Walker. 1st Am. ed. dj. EX $30.00

NIVEN, Larry. *A World Out of Time.* 1976. New York. Holt. 1st ed. dj. EX $20.00

NIVEN, Larry. *Ringworld Engineers.* 1979. Phantasia Pr. Ltd. ed. 1/500. sgn. boxed. EX $175.00

NIVEN, Larry. *Ringworld.* 1977. New York. Holt. 1st Am. ed. dj. $35.00

NIVEN, Larry. *The Integral Trees.* 1984. New York. 1st ed. dj. VG $10.00

NIVEN & POURNELLE. *Lucifer's Hammer.* 1977. Playboy Press. 1st ed. dj. EX $15.00

NIX, E.D. *Oklahombres. Former U.S. Marshall of OK Territory.* 1929. 1st ed. dj. VG $35.00

NIXON, H.K. *Psychology for the Writer.* 1928. Harper 6th ed. index. 330 pp. $4.00

NIXON, Howard. *Five Centuries of English Bookbinding.* 1978. London. dj. EX $25.00

NIXON, L. *The Canal Tolls & American Shipping.* 1914. G $10.00

NIXON, Richard. *Memoirs.* 1978. Grosset & Dunlap. 1st ed. sgn. dj. VG $95.00

NIXON, Richard. *Six Crises.* 1962. New York. Doubleday. 1st ed. sgn. dj. EX $30.00

NIZER, L. *What to Do with Germany.* 1941. Chicago. G $15.00

NIZER, Louis. *My Life in Court.* 1961. New York. Doubleday. 524 pp. dj. $6.00

NOAKES, Aubrey. *Sportsmen in a Landscape.* 1954. London. Ills. VG $15.00

NOBBS, Percy E. *Design, Treatise on Discovery of Form.* 1937. London. dj. VG $8.00

NOBLE, H. *Woman with a Sword.* 1948. G $7.50

NOBLE, J. Ashcroft. *Impressions & Memories.* 1893. London/NY. 173 pp. $12.50

NOBLE, Peter. *Hollywood Scapegoat, Biog. of Erich von Stroheim.* 1950. London. VG $12.00

NODLAND, Gerald. *Gaston Lachaise.* 1974. New York. 1st ed. dj. VG $20.00

NOEL, John. *Story of Everest.* 1931. Blue Ribbon Books. Ills. G $10.00

NOEL, John. *Story of Everest*. 1931. New York. VG $7.50

NOEL, Mary. *Villains Galore*. 1954. Macmillan. 1st ed. dj. $8.50

NOEL, S. *I Killed Stalin*. 1952. pb. G $3.00

NOEL, T. *A Campaign from Santa Fe to the Mississippi*. 1961. Houston. Ltd. ed. 1/700. dj. $85.00

NOGUCHI, Yone. *Hiroshige with 19 Ills. & Colored Frontispiece*. 1921. New York. Ills. Ltd. ed. 1/750. G $125.00

NOGUCHI, Yone. *The Ukiyo-e Primitives*. 1933. Ills. Ltd ed. 1/1000. folio. $270.00

NOICE, H. *Back of the Beyond*. 1939. Putnam. Ills. map. 247 pp. VG $15.00

NOLAN, J. Bennett. *George Washington & the Town of Reading*. 1931. sgn. VG $27.50

NOLAN, Jeanette C. *Getting to Know the Ohio River*. 1973. New York. Ills. 72 pp. dj. $5.00

NOLAN, Jeanette C. *James Whitcomb Riley, Hoosier Poet*. 1941. $10.00

NOLAN, K.W. *Battle for Hue. Tet 1968*. 1984. Ills. map. EX $15.00

NOLAN, William A. *Communism Versus the Negro*. 1951. Chicago. ex-lib. 276 pp. $5.00

NOLAN, William F. *Dashiell Hammett; a Casebook*. 1969. 1st ed. dj. EX $20.00

NOLAN, William F. *The Pseudo-People*. 1965. Sherbourne. 1st ed. dj. VG $10.00

NOLTE, Vincent. *Fifty Years in Both Hemispheres*. 1854. New York. 1st Am. ed. G $65.00

NONIS, U. *Mushrooms & Toadstools*. 1982. Hippocrene. Ills. 229 pp. EX $12.50

NORBYE, Jan P. *The Wankel Engine*. 1971. Chilton. Ills. 1st ed. 518 pp. $10.00

NORCROSS, C. & Quinn, James. *How to Do Aircraft Sheetmetal Work*. 1942. McGraw Hill. Ills. 285 pp. fld blueprint. $125.00

NORDHOFF, C. *California for Health, Pleasure & Residence*. 1882. Harper. new ed. VG $35.00

NORDHOFF, Charles & Hall, J.N. *Botany Bay*. 1941. Boston. 1st ed. dj. VG $60.00

NORDHOFF, Charles & Hall, J.N. *Faery Lands of the South Seas*. 1911. 354 pp. VG $18.00

NORDHOFF, Charles & Hall, J.N. *Men Against the Sea*. 1934. Boston. 1st ed. VG $12.00

NORDHOFF, Charles & Hall, J.N. *Mutiny on the Bounty*. 1935. Boston. 379+ pp. $4.00

NORDHOFF, Charles & Hall, J.N. *Pitcairn's Island*. 1934. Boston. 1st ed. VG $10.00

NORDHOFF, Charles & Hall, J.N. *The Bounty Trilogy*. 1948. Ills. Wyeth. $12.50

NORDHOFF, Charles & Hall, J.N. *The Dark River*. 1938. New York. World. 336 pp. $4.00

NORDHOFF, Charles & Hall, J.N. *The High Barbaree*. 1945. Boston. 230 pp. $10.00

NORDHOFF, Charles & Hall, J.N. *Pitcairn's Island*. 1939. Boston. 333 pp. $5.00

NORDHOFF, Charles. *In Yankee Windjammers*. 1940. $10.00

NORDHOFF, Charles. *The Communistic Societies of the United States*. 1875. New York. VG $50.00

NORDYKE, Lewis. *Cattle Empire. Story of 3,000,000 Acre XIT*. 1949. New York. Ills. 1st ed. map. 273 pp. VG $10.00

NORDYKE, Lewis. *Great Roundup, Story of TX & Southwestern Cowmen*. 1955. New York. Morrow. Ills. 288 pp. dj. EX $17.50

NORDYKE, Lewis. *John Wesley Hardin, Texas Gunman*. 1957. New York. Ills. 1st ed. dj. VG $20.00

NOREN, C.H. *Camera of My Family*. 1976. New York. 1st ed. dj. EX $17.50

NORMAN, Charles. *Poets & People*. 1972. Indianapolis. Bobbs Merrill. Ills. 320 pp. $5.00

NORMAN, D. *Alfred Stieglitz*. 1973. New York. 1st ed. dj. EX $47.50

NORMAN, J.R. *History of Fishes*. 1948. Ills. 1st Am. ed. dj. VG $15.00

NORMAN, J.R. & Fraser, F.C. *Giant Fishes, Whales, & Dolphins*. 1938. Norton. Ills. 1st ed. VG $10.00

NORRIS, Frank. *A Deal in Wheat*. 1903. New York. Doubleday. Ills. 1st ed. VG $35.00

NORRIS, Frank. *Complete Works of Frank Norris*. 1903. Doubleday Page. Golden Gate ed. 7 vol set. VG $200.00

NORRIS, Frank. *Vandover & the Brute*. 1914. New York. Doubleday. 1st ed. VG $25.00

NORRIS, Gloria. *Three Stories*. 1986. Turnipseed Pr. Ltd. ed. 1/300. sgn. wrappers. $12.50

NORRIS, Kathleen. *Barberry Bush*. 1927. New York. 366 pp. $3.50

NORRIS, Kathleen. *Beauty's Daughter*. 1935. New York. 354 pp. $3.50

NORRIS, Kathleen. *Little Ships*. 1925. New York. 427 pp. $3.50

NORRIS, Kathleen. *Margaret Yorke*. 1930. New York. 313 pp. $3.50

NORRIS, Kathleen. *Mother*. 1911. New York. Ills. F.C. Yohn. 198 pp. $3.50

NORRIS, Kathleen. *Second Hand Wife*. 1931. New York. 351 pp. $3.50

NORRIS, Kathleen. *The Foolish Virgin*. 1928. Philadelphia. 356 pp. $3.50

NORRIS, Kathleen. *The Sea Gull*. 1929. New York. Doubleday. 540 pp. $3.50

NORRIS, Kathleen. *Three Men & Diana*. 1934. New York. 343 pp. $3.50

NORRIS. *Eastern Upland Shooting*. New York. 1st ed. dj. EX $25.00

NORTH, Grace May. *Meg of Mystery Mountain*. 1926. New York. 310 pp. $2.00

NORTH, Grace May. *Sisters*. 1928. New York. A.L. Burt. 320 pp. $3.00

NORTH, Joseph. *Behind the Florida Bombings*. 1952. New York. Century. 1st ed. wrappers. $20.00

NORTH, S.D. & R.H. *Hist. of 1st Pistol Manufacturer U.S. Government*. 1913. 18 pls. VG $40.00

NORTH, Sterling. *Midnight & Jeremiah*. 1943. Philadelphia. Ills. Kurt Wiese. VG $20.00

NORTH, Sterling. *Rascal*. 1963. Dutton. Ills. 189 pp. dj. EX $7.50

NORTH. *Camp & Camino in Lower California*. 1910. 1st ed. photos. VG $40.00

NORTHCOTE, James. *Fables, Original Selected by Late J. Northcote*. 1833. London. Ills. Wood. $65.00

NORTHEND, M.H. *We Visit Old Inns*. 1926. Boston. 2nd printing. 176 pp. $12.50

NORTHERN STATES MISSION. *The Book of Mormon*. 1907. Chicago. 623 pp. VG $5.00

NORTHROP, H.D. *The World's Fair as Seen in One Hundred Days*. 1893. New York. Union Publishing House. $5.00

NORTHROP, H.D. *World's Greatest Calamities*. 1904. no place. Ills. 474 pp. $15.00

NORTHROP, N.B. *Pioneer History of Medina County*. 1861. Medina, OH. 224 pp. $100.00

NORTON, A.B. *The Great Revolution of 1840*. 1888. Dallas. $25.00

NORTON, Andre. *Breed to Come*. 1972. Viking. 1st ed. dj. EX $35.00

NORTON, Andre. *Catseye*. 1961. New York. Harcourt. 1st ed. dj. EX $40.00

NORTON, Andre. *Dread Companion*. 1970. New York. Harcourt. 1st ed. dj. EX $20.00

NORTON, Andre. *Fur Magic*. 1968. Cleveland. World. 1st ed. dj. EX $40.00

NORTON, Andre. *Ice Crown*. 1970. New York. Viking. 1st ed. dj. EX $35.00

NORTON, Andre. *Jargoon Park*. 1974. Atheneum. 1st ed. dj. EX $25.00

NORTON, Andre. *Judgement on Janus*. 1963. New York. Harcourt. 1st ed. dj. EX $65.00

NORTON, Andre. *Night of Masks.* 1964. New York. Harcourt. 1st ed. sgn. dj. EX $85.00

NORTON, Andre. *Plague Ship.* 1956. New York. Gnome. 1st ed. dj. VG $15.00

NORTON, Andre. *Quag Keep.* 1983. Atheneum. 1st ed. dj. EX $25.00

NORTON, Andre. *Quest Crosstime.* 1965. New York. Viking. 1st ed. dj. EX $40.00

NORTON, Andre. *Ralestone Luck.* 1938. New York. Appleton Century. 1st ed. VG $85.00

NORTON, Andre. *Sargasso of Space.* 1955. New York. Gnome. 1st ed. dj. VG $15.00

NORTON, Andre. *Scarface.* Comet. pb. EX $12.50

NORTON, Andre. *Space Service.* 1953. Cleveland/NY. 1st ed. dj. EX $15.00

NORTON, Andre. *The Defiant Agents.* 1962. Cleveland. World. 1st ed. dj. EX $60.00

NORTON, Andre. *The Iron Cage.* 1974. New York. Viking. 1st ed. dj. VG $20.00

NORTON, Andre. *The Opal-Eyed Fan.* 1977. Dutton. wrappers. EX $65.00

NORTON, Andre. *The Time Traders.* 1958. Cleveland. World. 1st ed. dj. EX $65.00

NORTON, Andre. *The Zero Stone.* 1968. New York. Viking. 1st ed. dj. EX $50.00

NORTON, Andre. *Ware Hawk.* 1983. Atheneum. 1st ed. dj. EX $17.50

NORTON, H. *Record of Facts Concerning Persecutions.* 1849. New York. 1st ed. 228 pp. $15.00

NORTON, Oliver Willcox. *Attack & Defense of Little Round Top, Gettysburg.* 1913. ex-lib. 350 pp. scarce. $65.00

NORTON, R. *Bernini & Other Studies in the History of Art.* 1914. New York. 69 pls. EX $27.50

NORTON, R. *The Toll of the Sea.* 1909. New York. Appleton. 1st ed. VG $40.00

NORTON, Thomas Elliot. *Fur Trade in Colonial New York.* 1974. Madison. 1st ed. 243 pp. index. EX $15.00

NORTON, Vera. *Some Descendants of Samuel Hinckley.* 1976. Ills. Ltd ed. 1/100. 92 pp. $25.00

NORWOOD, Edwin P. *The Adventures of Diggeldy Dan.* 1922. Boston. Ills. A.C. Peyton. 1st ed. $30.00

NORWOOD, Thomas M. *TX Pacific R.R. Contrasted with So. Pacific R.R.* 1878. Ills. fld. map. 20 pp. wrappers. $350.00

NOSS, Christopher. *Tohoku the Scotland of Japan.* 1918. Philadelphia. Ills. 2 fld maps. VG $20.00

NOTESTEIN, Lucy L. *Wooster of the Middle West.* 1937. New Haven. 333 pp. dj. $12.50

NOTT, D. *Into the Lost World.* 1975. Prentice Hall. Ills. 1st ed. 186 pp. dj. EX $10.00

NOTT, Stanley Charles. *Chinese Jade Throughout the Ages.* 1937. Scribner. Ills. 192 pp. index. VG $45.00

NOURSE, A. *RX for Tomorrow.* 1971. New York. McKay. 1st ed. dj. VG $15.00

NOURSE, A. *Scavengers in Space.* 1959. New York. McKay. 1st ed. dj. EX $10.00

NOURSE, J.E. *American Exploration in the Ice Zones.* 1884. Boston. Ills. maps. VG $45.00

NOVA, Craig. *The Good Son.* 1982. Dial Press. advance copy. wrappers. EX $35.00

NOVA, Craig. *Turkey Hash.* 1972. New York. Harper. 1st ed. VG $25.00

NOVAK. *The Future is Ours.* 1960. Comrad. 1st Am. ed. dj. VG $85.00

NOWARRA, Heinz J. *Messerschmitt 109, Famous German Fighter.* 1966. London. enlarged revised ed. 200 pp. $15.00

NOWELL-SMITH, S. *Legend of the Master.* 1948. New York. 1st ed. dj. VG $25.00

NOWLAN, Philip Francis. *Armageddon 2419 A.D.* 1962. New York. 1st ed. dj. EX $20.00

NOYES, Alfred. *A Book of Princeton Verse.* 1916. 1st ed. $16.50

NOYES, Alfred. *Collected Poems, Vol. I.* 1913. New York. 426 pp. $3.00

NOYES, Alfred. *Forty Singing Seamen & Other Poems.* 1930. New York. Ills. MacKinstry. VG $25.00

NOYES, J. *History of American Socialisms.* 1961. New York. Ltd. ed. 1/500. $20.00

NUCKEL, Otto. *Destiny, a Novel in Pictures.* 1930. New York. 1st Am. ed. dj. EX $35.00

NUNIS, Boyce B., Jr. *Frontier Fighter, Autobiography of George W. Coe.* 1984. Chicago. Ills. 384 pp. index. VG $12.50

NUNIS, D.B. *The California Diary of Faxon Dean Atherton.* 1964. Ritchie Press. Ltd. ed. map. dj. EX $32.50

NUTT, Charles. *History of Worchester & Its People.* 1919. New York. VG $55.00

NUTTALL, Thomas. *Journal of Travels Arkansas Territory.* 1821. Philadelphia. exlib. fld map. $325.00

NUTTING, Anthony. *Lawrence of Arabia.* 1961. London. $7.50

NUTTING, Wallace. *England Beautiful.* 1936. New York. Ills. 284 pp. $12.50

NUTTING, Wallace. *Furniture Treasury.* 1954. Macmillan. Ills. 2 vols in 1. dj. EX $25.00

NUTTING, Wallace. *Ireland Beautiful.* 1925. 1st ed. $11.00

NUTTING, Wallace. *Ireland Beautiful.* 1925. Farmingham, MA. Ills. 302 pp. EX $20.00

NUTTING, Wallace. *Massachusetts Beautiful.* Bonanza Books. 304 Ills. 301 pp. dj. $125.00

NUTTING, Wallace. *Pennsylvania Beautiful.* 1924. Framingham. 1st ed. 302 pp. index. $15.00

NUTTING, Wallace. *Pennsylvania Beautiful.* 1935. Garden City. Ills. VG $25.00

NUTTING, Wallace. *Vermont Beautiful.* 1936. dj. VG $20.00

NUTTING, Wallace. *Virginia Beautiful.* 1935. New York. Ills. dj. VG $25.00

NYCE, Vera. *A Jolly Christmas at the Patterprints.* 1971. New York. Parent's Mag. Pr. Ills. $10.00

NYE, Bill. *Bill Nye's Remarks.* 1896. Ills. 504 pp. fair $10.50

NYE, Bill. *Remarks.* Thompson & Thomas. no date. $12.50

NYE, W.S. *Carbine & Lance. Story of Old Fort Sill.* 1938. U. of OK Press. 2nd ed. $17.50

NYE, W.S. *Carbine & Lance. Story of Old Fort Sill.* 1943. Norman. 1st ed. EX $55.00

NYE. *Desert of the Damned.* Popular. pb. $3.00

NYE. *The Lonely Grass.* Pocketbooks. pb. $3.00

O

O'BEIRNE, F. *Johns: Outhouse Beautiful.* 1952. Chicago. Ills. dj. VG $10.00

O'BRIAN, John L. *National Security & Individual Freedom.* 1955. Cambridge. Harvard Press. ex-lib. 84 pp. $3.00

O'BRIAN, Patrick. *H.M.S. Surprise.* 1973. London. Collins. 1st ed. dj. $60.00

O'BRIAN, Patrick. *The Fortune of War.* 1979. London. Collins. 1st ed. dj. $45.00

O'BRIAN, Patrick. *The Ionian Mission.* 1981. London. 1st ed. dj. EX $22.00

O'BRIEN, Andy & Plante, J. *The Jacques Plante Story.* 1972. McGraw Hill. Ills. 162 pp. dj. EX $10.00

O'BRIEN, Andy. *Superstars.* 1973. McGraw Hill. Ills. dj. EX $10.00

O'BRIEN, Edward J. *The Best Short Stories of 1917.* 1918. Boston. Small, Maynard. 600 pp. $12.50

O'BRIEN, Edward J. *The Best Short Stories of 1928.* 1929. $10.00

O'BRIEN, Fitz-James. *The Diamond Lens.* 1932. New York. Ltd. 1st ed. dj. EX $50.00

O'BRIEN, Frederick. *Mystic Isles of the South Seas.* 1921. 1st ed. $8.50

O'BRIEN, Frederick. *White Shadows in the South Seas.* 1920. New York. Century. Ills. G $20.00

O'BRIEN, Frederick. *White Shadows in the South Seas.* 1919. Grosset & Dunlap. 450 pp. $6.50

O'BRIEN, George. *New York Times Book of Interior Design & Decor.* 1965. New York. Farrar. Ills. dj. VG $10.00

O'BRIEN, Jack. *Silver Chief, Dog of the North.* Chicago. Winston. Ills. Wiese. 218 pp. $14.00

O'BRIEN, Pat. *The Wind at My Back.* 1964. Doubleday. $3.50

O'BRIEN, Seumas. *Blind.* 1918. New York. wrappers. EX $40.00

O'BRIEN, Tim. *Northern Lights.* 1975. New York. Delacorte. 1st ed. dj. EX $30.00

O'BRIEN, Tim. *The Nuclear Age.* 1985. 1st ed. dj. VG $17.50

O'BRIEN, Tim. *The Nuclear Age.* 1985. proof copy. $35.00

O'BRIEN. *Outwitting the Hun.* 1918. New York. sgn. $30.00

O'BRIEN. *Pioneer Irish in New England.* 1937. New York. 1st ed. VG $12.50

O'CASEY, Sean. *Oak Leaves & Lavender, or World on Wallpaper.* 1946. London. 1st ed. VG $30.00

O'CASEY, Sean. *The Plough & the Stars.* 1926. New York. 1st Am. ed. EX $15.00

O'CONNER, John. *Canals, Barges, & People.* 1950. London. Art & Technics. 1st ed. EX $20.00

O'CONNOR, Edwin. *The Last Hurrah.* 1956. New York. Little, Brown. 427 pp. VG $4.00

O'CONNOR, Flannery. *A Good Man is Hard to Find.* 1955. New York. Harcourt. 1st ed. dj. $250.00

O'CONNOR, Flannery. *A Good Man is Hard to Find.* 1955. Farrar. 1st ed. dj. VG $125.00

O'CONNOR, Flannery. *The Habit of Being.* 1979. New York. 1st ed. $15.00

O'CONNOR, Flannery. *The Violent Bear It Away.* 1960. Farrar. 1st ed. dj. EX $190.00

O'CONNOR, Flannery. *Wise Blood.* 1952. New York. 1st ed. VG $100.00

O'CONNOR, Frank. *The Lonely Voice.* 1963. Cleveland. World. 1st ed. dj. $7.50

O'CONNOR, Frank. *The Midnight Court.* 1945. trans. dj. VG $25.00

O'CONNOR, Jack. *Big Game Animals of North America.* 1961. New York. Dutton. 20 pls. dj. VG $20.00

O'CONNOR, Jack. *Big Game Hunts.* 1964. Ills. dj. EX $35.00

O'CONNOR, Jack. *Complete Book of Shooting.* 1972. New York. Harper. 385 pp. dj. VG $8.50

O'CONNOR, Jack. *Horse & Buggy West.* 1969. New York. scarce. dj. EX $225.00

O'CONNOR, Jack. *Hunting in the South West.* 1945. New York. VG $145.00

O'CONNOR, Jack. *The Rifle Book: New Edition of Shooter's Classic.* 1964. Knopf. Ills. 2nd revised ed. dj. $7.50

O'CONNOR, Richard. *Bat Masterson.* 1957. dj. VG $10.00

O'CONNOR, Richard. *Heywood Broun.* 1975. New York. Putnam. ex-lib. VG $4.00

O'CONNOR, Richard. *Pat Garett, Biography of Famous Marshall.* 1960. New York. 1st ed. dj. $17.50

O'CONNOR, Richard. *The German-Americans.* 1968. 1st ed. dj. EX $15.00

O'CONNOR, Richard. *Wild Bill Hickock.* Ace. pb. $3.00

O'DONNELL, Elliot. *Ghosts of London.* 1933. Dutton. 1st ed. G $8.00

O'DONNELL, Elliott. *For Satan's Sake.* Benman reprint. G $10.00

O'DONNELL, Elliott. *The Dead Riders.* 1952. London. 1st ed. dj. EX $35.00

O'DONNELL, Peter. *Sabre-Tooth.* 1966. London. Souvenir Press. 1st ed. dj. VG $25.00

O'DONNELL, T.C. *Snubbing Posts: Black River Canal.* 1949. Boonville. 1st ed. sgn. dj. VG $30.00

O'DONNELL. *History of Life Insurance.* 1936. $9.00

O'DONOGHUE, M. & Springer, F. *Adventures of Phoebe Zeitgeist.* 1968. 1st Am. ed. dj. EX $35.00

O'FAOLAIN, Sean. *Come Back to Erin.* 1940. Viking. 1st Am. ed. dj. VG $50.00

O'FAOLAIN, Sean. *Midsummer Night Madness.* 1932. 1st Eng. ed. dj. VG $135.00

O'FAOLAIN, Sean. *The Man Who Invented Sin.* 1948. Devin Adair. 1st Am. ed. dj. VG $40.00

O'FLAHERTY, Liam. *The Ecstasy of Angus.* 1931. London. Ltd. ed. sgn. VG $30.00

O'FLAHERTY, Liam. *The Informer.* 1935. Penguin #17. 1st ed. pb. $15.00

O'FLAHERTY, Patrick. *The Rock Observed.* 1979. U. Toronto Pr. Ills. 222 pp. dj. $10.00

O'FLYNN, Thomas F. *Story of Worcester Massachusetts.* 1910. Ills. 1st ed. $10.00

O'GARA, W.H. *In All Its Fury, History of Blizzard of 1888.* 1947. private print. $40.00

O'GORMAN, Ned. *The Night of the Hammer.* 1959. Harcourt. 1st ed. dj. EX $20.00

O'HANLON. *Irish American History of the United States.* 1907. Murphy. 2 vol set. G $75.00

O'HARA, Frank. *In Memory of My Feelings, a Selection of Poems.* 1967. New York. slipcase. VG $175.00

O'HARA, Frank. *Love Poems.* 1965. Tibor de Nagy. Ltd. ed. wrappers. VG $30.00

O'HARA, J. *And Other Stories.* 1968. $10.00

O'HARA, J. *From the Terrace.* 1958. Random House. 1st ed. dj. EX $30.00

O'HARA, J. *Ourselves to Know.* 1960. $10.00

O'HARA, J. *Pal Joey.* 1940. Duell. 1st ed. dj. VG $85.00

O'HARA, J. *Sermons & Soda Water.* 1960. Random House. 1st ed. 3 vol set. slipcase. $30.00

O'HARA, J. *Sermons & Soda Water.* 1961. Cresset. 1st Eng. ed. dj. EX $20.00

O'HARA, J. *The Big Laugh.* 1962. Random House. 1st ed. dj. VG $20.00

O'HARA, J. *The Horse Knows the Way.* 1964. New York. Random House. 1st printing. $5.00

O'HARA, J. *The Instrument.* 1967. New York. Random House. 308 pp. dj. $10.00

O'HARA, J. *The Lockwood Concern.* 1965. $10.00

O'HARA, John. *Appointment in Samarra.* 1934. New York. 1st ed. VG $35.00

O'HARA, Mary. *Flicka's Friend, an Autobiography of Mary O'Hara.* 1982. New York. Putnam. photos. 284 pp. dj. $5.00

O'HARA, Mary. *Green Grass of Wyoming.* 1946. 1st ed. VG $17.50

O'HARA, Mary. *My Friend Flicka.* 1941. Philadelphia. Lippincott. dj. VG $10.00

O'HARA, Mary. *My Friend Flicka.* 1941. New York. Ills. Don Sibley. 282 pp. $3.50

O'HARA, Mary. *The Son of Adam Wyngate.* 1952. New York. 440 pp. $3.50

O'HARA, Mary. *Thunder Head.* 1943. $22.50

O'HARA, Mary. *Wyoming.* 1946. 1st ed. dj. VG $10.00

O'HARA. *Canvassing, a Tale by the O'Hara Family.* 1835. Philadelphia. 237 pp. $10.00

O'HENRY. *Gentle Grafter.* New York. McLure. 1st ed. VG $45.00

O'HENRY. *Henryianna.* 1920. New York. Ltd. ed. VG $75.00

O'HENRY. *Roads of Destiny.* 1909. 1st ed. 1st issue. $15.00

O'HIGGINS. *A Grand Army Man.* 1908. Century. Ills. M. Justice. $7.50

O'KANE, Walter Collins. *Intimate Desert.* 1969. Tucson. 1st ed. sgn. dj. EX $15.00

O'KEEFE, John. *Recollections of the Life of John O'Keefe.* 1827. Philadelphia. 2 vols in 1. VG $25.00

O'MALLEY, F. *The Best Go First.* 1950. 1st ed. dj. VG $7.00

O'MEARA, James. *The Vigilance Committee of 1856.* 1890. San Francisco. 57 pp. orig. wrappers. EX $65.00

O'MEARA, W. *Guns of Vengeance.* Popular. pb. $3.00

O'NEIL, Rose. *The Goblin Woman.* 1930. New York. 1st ed. dj. VG $25.00

O'NEILL, Eugene. *A Touch of the Poet.* 1957. Yale. 1st ed. 1st printing. dj. $15.00

O'NEILL, Eugene. *Ah, Wilderness.* 1933. Random House. 1st ed. dj. VG $40.00

O'NEILL, Eugene. *Days Without End.* 1934. Random House. 1st ed. dj. VG $50.00

O'NEILL, Eugene. *Dynamo.* 1929. New York. Ltd. ed. sgn. wrappers. boxed. $250.00

O'NEILL, Eugene. *Dynamo.* 1929. Liveright. dj. VG $40.00

O'NEILL, Eugene. *Emperor Jones, Different, the Straw.* 1921. New York. 1st ed. 285 pp. $25.00

O'NEILL, Eugene. *Emperor Jones.* 1928. New York. Ills. King. Ltd. ed. sgn. dj. $150.00

O'NEILL, Eugene. *Lazarus Laughed.* 1927. New York. Ltd. ed. sgn. wrappers. boxed. $175.00

O'NEILL, Eugene. *Long Day's Journey into Night.* 1956. New York. dj. $10.00

O'NEILL, Eugene. *Lost Plays of Eugene O'Neill.* Citadel Press. 1st ed. VG $30.00

O'NEILL, Eugene. *Mourning Becomes Electra.* 1931. New York. 1st ed. dj. VG $30.00

O'NEILL, Eugene. *Mourning Becomes Electra.* 1931. Liveright. Ltd. 1st Am. ed. 1/500. sgn. $200.00

O'NEILL, Eugene. *Mourning Becomes Electra.* 1931. Liveright. 1st Am. trade ed. VG $75.00

O'NEILL, Eugene. *Plays of Eugene O'Neill.* 1934. Scribner. Ltd. ed. 12 vol set. EX $600.00

O'NEILL, Eugene. *Strange Interlude.* 1928. New York. Boni. 1st ed. dj. EX $65.00

O'NEILL, Eugene. *Ten Lost Plays.* 1964. Random House. 1st ed. dj. EX $25.00

O'NEILL, Eugene. *The Complete Works of Eugene O'Neill.* 1924. Boni/Liveright. Ltd. ed. 1/1200. sgn. 2 vol set. $200.00

O'NEILL, Eugene. *The Emperor Jones.* 1928. New York. Ltd. ed. sgn. wrappers. boxed. $250.00

O'NEILL, Eugene. *The Hairy Age.* 1929. New York. Ltd. ed. sgn. dj. boxed. EX $250.00

O'NEILL, George. *Special Hunger. The Tragedy of Keats.* 1931. New York. 329 pp. dj. EX $15.00

O'NEILL, John. *New/Easy System of Geography & Popular Astronomy.* 1808. Baltimore. maps. G $57.50

O'NEILL, John. *Prodigal Genius Nilola Tesla.* 1944. Ives Washburn Pub. 1st ed. VG $17.50

O'NEILL, Michael. *Yes & No.* 1984. San Francisco. Light House Books. dj. EX $45.00

O'NEILL, Rose. *Boss of Little Arcady.* 1905. Boston. VG $5.00

O'NEILL, Rose. *Irving Caesar's Sing a Song of Safety.* 1937. Ills. 1st ed. scarce. VG $85.00

O'NEILL. *A Moon for the Misbegotten.* 1st ed. dj. VG $25.00

O'REILLY, Bernard. *Greenland.* 1818. New York. 1st Am. ed. 251 pp. EX $200.00

O'REILLY, Harrington. *Fifty Years on the Trail.* 1889. London. Chatto & Windus. Ills. 1st ed. $150.00

O'REILLY, T. *Purser's Progress. Adventures Seagoing Office Boy.* 1944. Ills. G $5.00

O'ROURKE, G.G. *The F-4 Phantom II. Famous Aircraft Series.* 1969. Ills. 64 pp. VG $5.00

O'SHAE. *Spain & Portugal.* 1905. London. Black. maps. charts. $10.00

O'SULLIVAN, Vincent. *A Book of Bargains.* 1896. London. 1st ed. VG $95.00

O'TOOLE, G.J. *Poor Richard's Game.* 1982. Delacorte. proof copy. wrappers. EX $15.00

OAKEY. *From Attic to Cellar, Book for Young Housekeepers.* 1879. Putnam. 155 pp. $4.50

OAKLEY, Violet. *Samuel F.B. Morse. A Dramatic Outline.* 1939. Philadelphia. Ills. Special ed. sgn. dj. VG $35.00

OATES, Bob. *A Game of Passion.* 1975. forward by Ray Bradbury. VG $15.00

OATES, Joyce Carol. *A Bloodsmoor Romance.* 1982. Dutton. 1st ed. dj. VG $17.50

OATES, Joyce Carol. *A Sentimental Education.* 1980. New York. Dutton. 1st ed. dj. VG $25.00

OATES, Joyce Carol. *Angel of Light.* 1981. Cape. 1st Eng. proof copy. wrappers. $80.00

OATES, Joyce Carol. *Bellefleur.* 1981. New York. 1st ed. dj. EX $10.00

OATES, Joyce Carol. *Bellefleur.* 1980. Dutton. 1st trade ed. dj. VG $15.00

OATES, Joyce Carol. *Childwold.* 1976. Vanguard. 1st ed. dj. VG $15.00

OATES, Joyce Carol. *Crossing the Border.* 1976. Vanguard. 1st ed. dj. VG $15.00

OATES, Joyce Carol. *Do With Me What You Will.* 1973. New York. Vanguard. 1st ed. dj. VG $30.00

OATES, Joyce Carol. *Love & Its Derangements.* 1970. L.S.U. Press. 1st ed. dj. VG $25.00

OATES, Joyce Carol. *Marriages & Infidelities.* 1972. Vanguard. 1st ed. dj. VG $25.00

OATES, Joyce Carol. *Marya.* 1986. proof copy. $25.00

OATES, Joyce Carol. *Miracle Play.* 1974. Black Sparrow. 1st ed. wrappers. VG $10.00

OATES, Joyce Carol. *Night-Side.* 1977. New York. Vanguard. 1st ed. dj. VG $25.00

OATES, Joyce Carol. *Queen of the Night.* Ltd. 1st ed. 1/300. sgn. $50.00

OATES, Joyce Carol. *Son of the Morning.* 1978. Vanguard. 1st ed. dj. VG $15.00

OATES, Joyce Carol. *The Goddess & Other Women.* 1974. Vanguard. 1st ed. dj. VG $15.00

OATES, Joyce Carol. *The Poisoned Kiss.* 1975. Vanguard. 1st ed. dj. VG $15.00

OATES, Joyce Carol. *The Seduction & Other Stories.* 1975. Los Angeles. Ltd. ed. sgn. dj. EX $40.00

OATES, Joyce Carol. *Them.* 1969. Vanguard. 1st ed. dj. VG $35.00

OATES, Joyce Carol. *Unholy Loves.* proof copy. sgn. $55.00

OATES, Joyce Carol. *Upon Sweeping Flood.* 1966. 1st Am. ed. dj. EX $30.00

OATES, Joyce Carol. *Upon Sweeping Flood.* 1979. Tale Blazer. 1st ed. wrappers. VG $10.00

OATES, Joyce Carol. *Where Are You Going, Where Have You Been?* 1979. Tale Blazer. 1st ed. wrappers. VG $10.00

OATES, Joyce Carol. *Wild Nights.* 1985. Croissant. Ltd. ed. 1/300. sgn. dj. VG $45.00

OATES, Joyce Carol. *Wonderland.* 1971. Vanguard. 1st ed. dj. VG $30.00

OATES, Joyce. *The Girl.* Ltd. 1st ed. 1/300. sgn. VG $30.00

OATES. *Expensive People.* 1968. 1st Am. ed. dj. EX $17.50

OBERDORFER, D. *Tet!* 1971. New York. 1st ed. $15.00

OBERHOLSER, Harry C. *The Bird Life of Texas.* 1974. Austin. U. of Texas. Ills. Fuertes. $52.50

OBERJOHANN, H. *Wild Elephant Chase/Adventure in Lake Chad Region.* 1953. London. Dobson. Ills. 189 pp. dj. VG $15.00

OBERNDORF, C.P. *The Psychiatric Novels of Oliver Wendell Holmes.* 1943. Columbia. 1st ed. dj. VG $15.00

OBERT, Karl. *This is California.* 1958. Menlo Park, CA. 2nd ed. 216 photos. VG $20.00

OBODIAC, Stan. *Red Kelly.* 1971. Clarke Irwin. Ills. 70 pp. EX $6.00

OBODIAC, Stan. *The Toronto Maple Leafs 1979-1980.* 1979. McClelland & Stewart. 175 pp. $15.00

OBOLER, Arch. *House on Fire.* 1969. Bartholomew House. 1st ed. $25.00

OBOLER, Arch. *Oboler Onmibus.* 1945. New York. 3rd printing. 309 pp. $4.50

OBOLER, Arch. *Plays for Americans.* 1942. New York. Farrar. 1st ed. 271 pp. $7.50

OBOOKIAH, Henry. *Memoirs of Henry Obookiah. Native of Owhyhee.* 1819. New Haven. G $50.00

OBRUCHEV, V.A. *Plutonia, an Adventure Through Pre-History.* 1957. London. 1st English ed. dj. VG $15.00

OCHSNER, A.J., M.D. *Handbook of Appendicitis.* 1902. Chicago. 1st ed. 182 pp. index. VG $10.00

ODD, Gilbert. *Boxing, the Great Champions.* 1974. 1st ed. dj. EX $15.00

OEHSNER. *United States, Encyclopedia of History.* 1967. Philadelphia. Ills. 16 vol set. $44.00

OEMLER, Marie C. *Johnny Reb.* 1929. 1st ed. dj. VG $25.00

OFFENBACH, Jacques. *La Vie Parisienne.* 1869. New York. 44 pp. wrappers. VG $80.00

OFFICER, H.R. *Australian Flycatchers & Their Allies.* 1974. Melbourne. Bird Obs. Club. Ills. 111 pp. $17.50

OFFICIAL RECORD. *French & English Military Technical Dictionary* 1917. 565 pp. $8.50

OFFICIAL RECORD. *Report on Invasion of the City of Washington.* 1814. Washington. 370 pp. $65.00

OFFICIAL RECORD. *The Carolina Campaign.* 1865. Vol XLI. 1st ed. 1236 pp. $12.50

OFFICIAL RECORD. *The Kansas Constitution.* 1858. Washington 1st ed. 263 pp. $32.50

OFFICIAL RECORD. *The Trans-Mississippi.* 1864. Vol. XLI. 1128 pp. $12.50

OFFICIAL RECORD. *The United States Conscription Act.* 1863. Concord, NH. 1st ed. $15.00

OFFICIAL RECORD. *Trial Of Andrew Johnson.* 1868. Washington 3 vol set. $47.50

OGAN, Lew. *History of Vinton County, Ohio.* 1954. McArthur. Ills. 314 pp. $18.50

OGBURN, C. *The Marauders.* 1959. dj. VG $12.50

OGBURN, Charleton, Jr. *The Winter Beach.* 1966. New York. Ills. 321 pp. index. $12.50

OGDEN, George W. *The Trail Rider.* 1924. Grosset & Dunlap. $4.50

OGDEN, Samuel. *Step by Step Organic Vegetable Gardening.* 1971. Rodale Press. 1st ed. dj. $3.50

OGG, Frederic A. *Opening of Mississippi: Struggle for Supremacy.* 1904. New York. Ills. 1st ed. 5 maps. $75.00

OGIER, Thomas Lowes. *A Memorial to James Bowen Everhart.* 1889. NY/London. 156 pp. $10.00

OGILBY, C.S. *Successful Yacht Racing.* 1951. Ills. G $7.50

OGILVIE, Wm. *Early Days on the Yukon & Story of Its Gold Finds.* 1913. New York. Ills. 1st ed. ex-lib. 306 pp. $25.00

OGLANBY, E. *Gage.* 1975. Ills. Cranston. $15.00

OKA, Isaburo. *Hiroshige.* 1982. Kodansha. Ills. 1st ed. scarce. EX $38.00

OKELLO, John. *Revolution in Zanzibar.* 1967. Nairobi. Ills. 1st ed. wrappers. EX $15.00

OKUDAIRA, Hideo. *Japanese Picture Scrolls.* 1962. EX $20.00

OLCOTT, Anthony. *Murder at the Red October.* 1981. Chicago. Academy. proof copy. wrappers. $20.00

OLDBOY. *A Tour Around New York.* 1893. New York. Harper. Ills. EX $22.50

OLDER, Mrs. Fremont. *California Missions & Their Romances.* 1945. New York. Ills. 314 pp. dj. $5.00

OLDER, Mrs. Fremont. *William Randolph Hearst, American.* 1936. New York. Ills. 581 pp. $20.00

OLDHAM, John. *The Works of Oldham, with His Remains.* 1698. London. $50.00

OLDMIXON, John. *The British Empire in America.* 1741. London. 2nd ed. 8 fld maps. 2 vol set. $1,075.00

OLDRIN, John. *The Round Meadow.* 1951. Haler Co. Ills. Kurt Weise. $3.50

OLIPHANT, Mrs. *William Blackwood & His Sons.* 1897. New York. 1st Am. ed. $40.00

OLIVANT, Alfred. *Bob, Son of Battle.* 1898. New York. 1st ed. EX $65.00

OLIVANT, Alfred. *Redcoat Captain, Story of that Country.* 1907. New York. 1st ed. 2nd printing. $12.00

OLIVER, Anthony. *Victorian Staffordshire Figure.* 1971. London. Ills. 1st ed. sgn. $17.00

OLIVER, Basis. *The Cottages of England.* 1929. New York. Ills. 1st Am. ed. 91 pp. $20.00

OLIVER, Douglas L. *The Pacific Islands.* 1951. Cambridge. Harvard U. Press. 313 pp. $3.50

OLIVER, F.S. *Ordeal by Battle, Causes of War.* 1916. G $6.00

OLIVER, H. *Gold & Cattle Country.* 1962. 2nd ed. dj. VG $12.50

OLIVER, P. *Shelter, Sign, & Symbol.* 1977. Overlook. Ills. 1st Am. ed. 228 pp. dj. $12.50

OLIVER, Peter. *New Chronicle of the Complete Angler.* 1936. Ills. VG $75.00

OLIVER. *Stalkers of Pestilence.* 1930. G $10.00

OLIVIER, Lawrence. *On Acting.* London. Ltd. ed. 1/300. sgn. $85.00

OLMSTEAD, Fred L. *Forty Years of Landscape Architecture.* 1922. New York. 1st ed. 2 vol set. $100.00

OLMSTEAD. *Journey in Seaboard Slave States.* 1856. New York. G $35.00

OLSCHAK, Blanche. *Mystic Art of Ancient Tibet.* 1973. New York. 224 pp. 514 pls. dj. $65.00

OLSEN, J. *Aphrodite. Desperate Mission.* 1970. Ills. dj. G $10.00

OLSEN, J. *Night of the Grizzlies.* 1969. Putnam. Ills. 254 pp. dj. VG $15.00

OLSEN, J. *Silence on Monte Sole.* 1968. Book Club ed. dj. VG $10.00

OLSEN, Olaf Reed. *Two Eggs on My Plate.* 1952. Chicago. Ills. 365 pp. dj. $10.00

OLSEN, T. *Tell Me a Riddle.* 1961. New York. 1st ed. dj. EX $50.00

OLSEN, T. *Yonnondio, from the Thirties.* 1974. New York. 2nd printing. dj. EX $10.00

OLSEN. *Preparing the Manuscript.* 1961. Boston. $5.00

OLSON, James C. *History of Nebraska.* 1955. Lincoln, NB. Ills. 372 pp. index. EX $15.00

OLSON, L. *Japan in Post-War Asia.* 1970. dj. VG $8.00

OLSON, Lorraine. *Old Buttons & Their Values.* 1940. Chicago. Ills. 1st ed. 109 pp. VG $15.00

OLSON, Robert. *A Short Introduction to Philosophy.* 1976. Harcourt, Brace & World. $2.00

OLSON, S.E. *Prospectus. Reliance Gold Mining Co. Deadwood, SD.* 1905. Minneapolis. Ills. 36 pp. maps. wrappers. $50.00

OLSON, S.F. *Open Horizons.* 1969. Knopf. Ills. 1st ed. 229 pp. dj. EX $8.00

OLSON, S.F. *Runes of the North.* 1963. Knopf. Ills. Hines. 1st ed. 255 pp. $12.50

OLSON, S.F. *Sigurd Olson's Wilderness Days.* 1972. Knopf. Ills. Jaques. 1st ed. dj. EX $15.00

OLSON, S.F. *The Lonely Land.* 1961. Knopf. Ills. Jaques. 273 pp. VG $10.00

OLSON, S.F. *The Singing Wilderness.* 1956. Knopf. 1st ed. dj. VG $35.00

OLSON, S.F. *Wilderness Days.* 1972. Ills. Ltd. ed. 1/350. sgn. $40.00

OLSON. *Exciter Fishing.* 1978. Winchester Press. 270 pp. $3.50

OLSSON, N.W. *A Pioneer in North-West America 1841-1858.* U. MN Press. 1st ed. 2 vol set. VG $40.00

OMAN, R. & Adam, Charles M. *Doctors Aweigh.* 1943. New York. Doubleday. 231 pp. G $5.00

OMMANNEY, F.D. *Lost Leviathan.* 1971. Dodd Mead. Ills. 1st Am. ed. 280 pp. dj. $17.50

ONASSIS. *The Firebird.* 1978. New York. dj. EX $18.00

ONASSIS-BOUVIER, Jacqueline. *One Special Summer.* Delacorte. 1st ed. $35.00

ONDAATJE, Michael. *The Man with Seven Toes.* 1969. Coach House. Ltd. ed. inscr. dj. EX $125.00

ONIONS, Oliver. *The Tower of Oblivion.* 1921. New York. Macmillan. 1st Am. ed. dj. VG $12.50

ONO, Yoko. *Grapefruit.* 1964. New York. 1st ed. dj. VG $15.00

OPLER, Morris E. *Myths & Legends of the Lipan Apache Indians.* 1940. New York. 1st ed. 296 pp. $45.00

OPPE. *The Watercolor Drawings of John Sell Cotman.* 1923. London. 24 pls. wrappers. $60.00

OPPENHEIM, E. Phillips. *A Daughter of Astrea.* 1912. New York. Newton. reprint. VG $15.00

OPPENHEIM, E. Phillips. *Clowns & Criminals.* 1931. Omnibus. Little, Brown. $12.00

OPPENHEIM, E. Phillips. *Exit a Dictator.* 1939. London. 1st ed. dj. VG $35.00

OPPENHEIM, E. Phillips. *Matorni's Vineyard.* 1928. Boston. 1st ed. VG $18.00

OPPENHEIM, E. Phillips. *Miss Brown of X.Y.O.* 1927. Little, Brown. $3.50

OPPENHEIM, E. Phillips. *Slane's Long Shots.* 1930. London. 1st Eng. ed. dj. VG $30.00

OPPENHEIM, E. Phillips. *The Colossus of Arcadia.* 1938. Boston. Little, Brown. 1st ed. dj. VG $30.00

OPPENHEIM, E. Phillips. *The Dumb Gods Speak.* 1937. London. 1st ed. dj. VG $55.00

OPPENHEIM, E. Phillips. *The Dumb Gods Speak.* 1937. Boston. 1st Am. ed. dj. VG $20.00

OPPENHEIM, E. Phillips. *The Illustrious Prince.* 1910. London. 1st ed. VG $35.00

OPPENHEIM, E. Phillips. *The Man from Sing Sing.* 1932. Boston. 1st ed. 306 pp. dj. VG $17.50

OPPENHEIM, E. Phillips. *The Milan Grill Room.* 1940. London. 1st ed. dj. VG $40.00

OPPENHEIM, E. Phillips. *The Quest for Winter Sunshine.* 1927. Ills. 1st ed. $7.50

OPPENHEIM, James. *Night.* 1918. New York. wrappers. $60.00

OPPENHEIMER, George. *The Passionate Playgoer.* 1958. New York. Viking. 1st ed. 623 pp. VG $15.00

OPPER, F. *Aesop's Fables.* 1916. Philadelphia. 100 Ills. 320 pp. VG $45.00

OPTIC, Oliver. *At the Front.* 1897. 1st ed. VG $12.00

OPTIC, Oliver. *Four Young Explorers of Sight-Seeing in Tropics.* 1896. Lee & Shephard. 357 pp. VG $9.50

OPTIC, Oliver. *Northern Lands; or, Young America in Russia.* 1872. Lee & Shephard. G. $7.50

OPTIC, Oliver. *The Boat Club; or, The Bunkers of Rippleton.* 1855. Boston. 1st ed. $25.00

OPTIC, Oliver. *The Soldier Boy.* Hurst. no date. VG $6.50

OPTIC, Oliver. *Try Again; or, Trails & Triumphs of Harry West.* Donahue. no date. $3.50

ORCUTT, William Dana. *Good Old Dorchester.* 1908. Cambridge. 2nd ed. inscr. sgn. G $60.00

ORCUTT, William Dana. *In Quest of the Perfect Book.* 1926. Boston. Little, Brown. Ills. G $23.00

ORCUTT, William Dana. *Mary Baker Eddy & Her Books.* 1950. Boston. Christian Science Pub. 198 pp. $4.50

ORCUTT, William Dana. *The Flower of Destiny.* 1905. Chicago. Ils. Charlotte Weber. 1st ed. $125.00

ORCUTT, William Dana. *The Writer's Desk Book.* 1913. $10.00

ORCZY, Baroness. *The Heart of a Woman.* 1911. $30.00

ORCZY, Baroness. *The Man in Grey.* 1918. $27.50

ORCZY, Baroness. *The Scarlet Pimpernel.* 1927. $27.50

ORGIGNY, A.D. *Voyage Pittoresque Dans Les Deux Ameriques.* 1836. Paris. 1st ed. fld maps. VG $250.00

ORGILL, Doug. *T-34.* 1972. $3.50

ORLOV, Uri. *The Lead Soldiers.* 1980. New York. Taplinger. advance copy. EX $30.00

ORMOND, Clyde. *Hunting in the Northwest.* 1948. VG $27.50

ORMOND, Clyde. *The Complete Book of Hunting.* 1962. Outdoor Life. Ills. 467 pp. $4.50

ORMOND, Clyde. *The Complete Book of Hunting.* 1972. Outdoor Life. Ills. 432 pp. $4.00

ORMSBEE, T. *Care & Repair of Antiques.* 1959. dj. VG $3.00

ORMSBEE, T.C. *English China & Its Marks.* 1962. London. revised ed. 200 pp. dj. $25.00

ORNDOFF, Don. *Sketches of Tom Phillips.* 1971. Kansas City. Ltd. 1st ed. 1/2750. $60.00

ORNITZ, D. *Living Photography.* 1966. wrappers. VG $7.50

ORPERN, William. *The Outline of Art.* 1927. New York. Putnam. Ills. 722 pp. 2 vol set. $14.00

ORPERN, William. *The Outline of Art.* 1926. New York. Crown Pub. Ills. VG $25.00

ORPHEUS, C. *Kerr Papers.* 1862. New York. 1st ed. VG $20.00

ORR, Frank. *Great Goalies of Pro Hockey.* 1973. Random House. Ills. 153 pp. EX $5.00

ORR, Frank. *Hockey Scrapbook.* 1969. Longman. Ills. SftCvr. EX $5.00

ORR, Robert T. *Animals in Migration.* 1970. Macmillan. Ills. review copy. 303 pp. dj. $12.50

ORR, Robert T. *The Animal Kingdom.* 1965. New York. Macmillan. photos. 380 pp. EX $6.50

ORR, William S. *The Flower Garden.* 1838. London. 10 pls. G $33.00

ORTON, Helen Fuller. *The Twin Lambs.* 1931. New York. Ills. Flack. 106 pp. dj. VG $8.00

ORTON, James. *The Andes & the Amazon.* 1871. New York. Ills. G $50.00

ORTZEN, L. *Guns at Sea, the World's Great Naval Battles.* 1976. Ills. G $15.00

ORWELL, George. *Animal Farm.* 1946. New York. Harcourt Brace. 1st Am. ed. $10.00

ORWELL, George. *England Your England.* 1954. London. 224 pp. dj. $3.50

ORWELL, George. *Nineteen Eighty Four.* 1949. London. Seever & Warburg. 1st ed. VG $60.00

ORWELL, George. *Nineteen Eighty Four.* New York. 1st Am. ed. 1st issue dj. EX $100.00

ORWELL. *Collection of Essays.* Harcourt Brace. 4 vol set. dj. EX $70.00

OSBORN, C.S. *The Andean Land.* 1909. McClurg. Ills. 1st ed. 2 vol set. VG $45.00

OSBORN, H.F. *Impressions of Great Naturalists.* 1924. Scribner. Ills. 216 pp. VG $10.00

OSBORNE, Bryon L. *Malone Story, Dream of Two Quaker Young People.* 1970. Newton. 359 pp. sgn. dj. $10.00

OSBORNE, D. *Danger is My Destiny.* 1955. dj. VG $7.50

OSBORNE, D. *Master of the Girl Pat.* 1949. dj. G $10.00

OSBORNE, H. *South American Mythology.* 1968. Hamlyn. 1st ed. pls. dj. EX $18.00

OSBORNE, J. *The Entertainer.* 1957. London. 1st ed. dj. EX $30.00

OSBORNE, John & Creighton, A. *Epitaph for George Dillon.* 1958. Faber. 1st Am. ed. dj. VG $30.00

OSBORNE, John. *A Patriot for Me.* 1966. Faber. 1st ed. dj. VG $25.00

OSBORNE, Philip B. *The War that Business Must Win.* 1970. New York. McGraw Hill. 117 pp. dj. $3.50

OSBOURNE, Lloyd. *The Adventurer.* 1907. New York. Appleton. 1st ed. VG $20.00

OSGOOD, F. *Poetry of Flowers.* 1941. New York. Ills. $100.00

OSGOOD, Samuel. *The Tenents of Freemasonry. Ills in Sermon.* 1822. 15 pp. wrappers. VG $10.00

OSKI, Vera. *Historia De Indias.* 1958. Buenos Aires. Ills. 124 pp. VG $24.00

OSLER, William. *Acute Nephritis in Typhoid Fever.* 1890. Baltimore. John Hopkins. wrappers. $55.00

OSLER, William. *Science & Immortality.* 1904. Boston. 1st ed. EX $50.00

OSLER, William. *The Principles & Practice of Medicine.* 1892. New York. Appleton. 1079 pp. $550.00

OSSA, H. *They Saved Our Birds.* 1973. Hippocrene. Ills. 287 pp. dj. EX $10.00

OSSENDOWSKI, F. *Beasts, Men, & Gods.* 1925. Dutton. map. VG $10.00

OSSMAN, David. *The Sullen Art.* 1963. New York. Corinth. wrappers. EX $15.00

OSSOLI, Margret Fuller. *Memoirs of Margret Fuller Ossoli.* 1852. Boston. EX $15.00

OSTER, G.F. & Wilson, E.O. *Caste & Ecology in the Social Insects.* Princeton. Ills. 352 pp. dj. EX $10.00

OSTERWEIS, R. *Three Centuries of New Haven, 1638-1938.* 1953. New Haven. 1st ed. 541 pp. $25.00

OSTRANDER, Gilman M. *Nevada the Great Rotten Borough.* 1966. New York. 1st ed. dj. VG $7.50

OSWALD, A. *The History & Practice of Falconry.* 1982. London. Spearman. 1st ed. 119 pp. dj. $10.00

OSWALD, J. *Printing in the Americas.* 1968. New York. EX $40.00

OTIS, James. *The Boy Spies with the Swamp Fox.* 1899. A.L. Burt. G $4.50

OTIS, James. *The Boys of 1745.* 1895. Boston. Estes & Lauriat. Ills. VG $17.50

OTIS, James. *The Navy Boys Cruise with Paul Jones.* 1899. A.L. Burt. VG $6.50

OTIS, James. *The Search for the Silver City.* 1893. New York. A.L. Burt. 1st ed. VG $12.50

OTIS, James. *Toby Tyler; or, Ten Weeks with a Circus.* 1930. New York. Harper. 252 pp. $3.50

OTIS, James. *Toby Tyler; or, Ten Weeks with a Circus.* 1923. New York. Harper. Ills. Rogers & Brehm. $12.50

OTIS, Jason. *The Life Savers/Story of U.S. Life Saving Service.* 1899. New York. Ills. 1st ed. dj. VG $25.00

OTIS, P.A. *The Chicago Symphony Orchestra, 1891-1924.* 1924. Chicago. presentation copy. VG $27.50

OTT, John. *My Ivory Cellar.* 1958. 20th Century Press. 1st ed. $20.00

OTT, W. *Sharks & Little Fish.* 1958. G $7.50

OTTERO, M.A. *My Life on the Frontier.* 1935. New York. 1st ed. EX $40.00

OTTLEY, Roi. *New World A-Coming.* 1943. Houghton Mifflin. dj. $10.00

OUIDA. *A Dog of Flanders, a Christmas Story.* 1901. L.C. Page. Ills. VG $15.00

OUIDA. *An Altruist.* 1897. $30.00

OURSLER, Fulton. *Behold this Dreamer!* 1964. Boston. Little, Brown. 1st ed. 501 pp. $3.50

OUSLEY & RUSSELL. *The Little White House.* 1948. Ginn. Ills. Steed & Segner. 160 pp. $2.50

OUTCAULT, R.F. *Buster Brown Abroad.* 1904. Stokes. Ills. 1st ed. dj. VG $75.00

OUTDOOR LIFE BOOKS. *Secrets of Successful Fresh-Water Fishing.* 1952. New York. Popular Science Pub. 250 pp. $5.00

OUTDOOR LIFE BOOKS. *Story of American Hunting & Firearms.* 1976. Ills. 168 pp. $8.50

OUTERBRIDGE, Paul. *Photographing in Color.* 1940. New York. Random House. 1st ed. 204 pp. $45.00

OUTHWAITE, Leonard. *The Atlantic, History of an Ocean.* 1957. Coward McCann. Ills. maps. 479 pp. VG $8.00

OUTHWAITE, Leonard. *Unrollin' the Map, Story of Exploration.* 1935. John Day. Ills. maps. 351 pp. VG $20.00

OVENDEN, G. *Hill & Adamson.* 1973. New York. 1st ed. dj. EX $17.50

OVERSTREET, H.A. *The Enduring Quest.* 1931. 283 pp. $5.00

OVERTON, Grant. *American Nights Entertainment.* 1923. New York. 1st ed. dj. VG $12.00

OVERTON, Grant. *When Winter Comes to Main Street.* 1922. New York. Doran. G $7.50

OVERTON, Mark. *Jack Winters' Ice-Boat Wonder.* 1919. New York. 188 pp. $2.00

OVERY, R.J. *The Air War 1939-1945.* 1980. Book Club. Ills. EX $10.00

OVIATT, Edwin. *The Beginnings of Yale 1701-1726.* 1916. New Haven. Ills. Diedricksen. 456 pp. $25.00

OVID. *Metamorphoseon.* 1751. Varorum ed. by D. Chrispinus. $35.00

OVITT, Mable. *Golden Treasure.* 1952. Dillon, MT. Ills. Ltd. ed. 1/1000. 252 pp. $35.00

OWEN, Frank. *The Porcelain Magician.* 1948. Gnome Press. 1st ed. dj. VG $15.00

OWEN, Frank. *The Wind that Tramps the World.* 1929. New York. Lantern Press. 1st ed. EX $20.00

OWEN, Guy. *The Flim-Flam Man & the Apprentice Drifter.* 1972. 1st ed. dj. EX $30.00

OWEN, Robert. *Footfalls on the Boundary of Another World.* Philadelphia. Lippincott. VG $30.00

OWEN, Robert. *Robert Owen und der Sozialismus*. 1919. Berlin. 1st ed. 134 pp. wrappers. $35.00

OWEN, Ruth Bryan. *Leaves from a Greenland Diary*. 1935. New York. Ills. inscr. sgn. dj. VG $20.00

OWENS, Bill. *Documentary Photography*. 1978. 1st ed. wrappers. VG $25.00

OWENS, Hamilton. *Baltimore on the Chesapeake*. 1941. Garden City. Ills. 1st ed. 342 pp. dj. $8.50

OWENS, William. *Slave Mutiny: Story of the Schooner Amistad*. 1953. London. 280 pp. $8.00

OWENS. *Hope Diamond Refuses*. uncorrected proof copy. $10.00

OXENHAM, John. *The Man Who Would Save the World*. 1935. London. Longman. new ed. VG $10.00

OXFORD & ASQUITH. *Memories & Reflections, 1852-1927*. 1928. Boston. Ills. 1st Am. ed. 2 vol set. $20.00

OZ, Amos. *The Hills of Evil Counsel*. 1978. Harcourt. 1st Am. ed. dj. VG $12.50

OZ, Amos. *Touch the Water, Touch the Wind*. 1973. Harcourt. 1st Am. ed. dj. VG $15.00

OZ, Amos. *Unto Death*. 1975. Harcourt. 1st Am. ed. dj. VG $12.50

OZ, Amos. *Unto Death*. 1976. Chatto/Windus. 1st English ed. dj. VG $15.00

OZAKI, Y.T. *Japanese Fairy Tales*. 1903. A.L. Burt. Ills. EX $15.00

OZANAM. Monsieur Jacques. *Recreations Mathematical & Physical*. 1708. London. Ills. 530 pp. $300.00

OZICK, Cynthia. *Art & Ardor*. 1983. New York. Knopf. 1st ed. dj. EX $25.00

OZICK, Cynthia. *Bloodshed & Three Novellas*. 1976. Knopf. 1st ed. dj. VG $20.00

OZICK, Cynthia. *The Cannibal Galaxy*. 1983. New York. Knopf. 1st ed. dj. VG $20.00

PAAR, J.P.S. *Jack Paar.* 1983. $7.50

PACE. *Golden Gulch, Story of Montana's Ader Gulch.* 1962. Virginia City. sgn. Sft Cvr. $20.00

PACH, Walter. *The Art Museum in America.* 1948. Pantheon. 1st ed. dj. $12.50

PACK, Charles Lathrop. *War Garden Victorious.* 1919. Philadelphia. Ills. 179 pp. $22.50

PACK, S.W.C. *Operation Husky, Allied Invasion of Sicily.* 1977. Ills. maps. dj. EX $10.00

PACKARD, Aubigne Lermond. *A Town that Went to Sea.* 1950. $15.00

PACKARD, Frank L. *The Miracle Man.* 1914. New York. 300 pp. $3.00

PACKARD, Mrs. E.P.W. *Modern Persecution; or, Insane Asylums Unveiled.* 1874. Hartford. Ills. gilt decor. 2 vol set. $150.00

PACKARD, REYNOLDS & ELANOR. *Balcony Empire. Fascist Italy at War.* 1942. G $7.50

PACKARD, Vance. *The Sexual Wilderness.* 1968. 1st ed. $15.00

PACKER, C.E. *Manual for Chevrolet Owners.* 1952. 304 pp. dj. $50.00

PACKER, William. *Fashion Drawing in VOGUE.* 1983. New York. Ills. dj. VG $20.00

PADDACK, W.C. *Life on the Ocean.* 1893. $15.00

PADDLEFORD, Clementine. *How America Eats.* 1960. Scribner. 1st ed. dj. VG $40.00

PADGETT, Lewis. *Mutant.* 1953. New York. Gnome Press. dj. $60.00

PADGETT, Lewis. *Robots Have No Tails.* 1952. 1st Am. ed. dj. $50.00

PADGETT, Lewis. *The Brass Ring.* 1946. New York. Duell Sloane. 1st ed. VG $20.00

PADILLA, Herberto. *Heroes Are Grazing in My Garden.* 1984. Farrar. trans. Hurley. 1st ed. dj. VG $17.50

PAGE, Elizabeth. *The Tree of Liberty.* 1939. New York. Ltd. 1st ed. 1/500. dj. VG $15.00

PAGE, Elizabeth. *Wild Horses & Gold from Wyoming to the Yukon.* 1932. New York. 1st ed. 362 pp. $50.00

PAGE, Harry S. *Between Flags, Recollections of Gentlemen Rider.* 1929. New York. Ltd. ed. 1/850. EX $65.00

PAGE, Kirby. *A New Economic Order.* 1930. New York. ex-lib. 387 pp. $3.50

PAGE, LEITCH & KNIGHTLEY. *The Philby Conspiracy.* 1968. Ills. dj. VG $7.50

PAGE, Marco. *The Shadowy Third.* 1946. 228 pp. dj. $37.50

PAGE, Thomas Nelson. *A Captured Santa Claus.* 1902. Scribner. Ills. by W.L. Jacobs. $8.00

PAGE, Thomas Nelson. *Gordon Keith.* 1903. $30.00

PAGE, Thomas Nelson. *Modern Air Craft.* 1928. Ills. 858 pp. $25.00

PAGE, Thomas Nelson. *Red Rock.* 1909. $27.50

PAGE, Thomas Nelson. *Red Rock.* 1899. $30.00

PAGE, Thomas Nelson. *Social Life in Virginia Before the War.* 1898. Cowles. VG $10.00

PAGE, Thomas Nelson. *The Old Gentleman of the Black Stock.* 1901. $30.00

PAGE, Victor W. *Aviation Engines: Design/Construction/Operation.* 1917. New York. Ills. 589 pp. G $17.50

PAGE. *History & Preservation of Mount Vernon.* 1910. New York. VG $10.00

PAGE. *The Civilization of the American Indians.* 1979. 1st ed. photos. dj. EX $20.00

PAGEANT BOOKS, INC. *The Confederate Soldier in the Civil War.* 1959. Ills. 480 pp. $21.00

PAGET, Violet. *Supernatural Tales.* 1955. London. 1st ed. dj. VG $40.00

PAHER, S. *Nevada Ghost Towns & Mining Camps.* 1970. Berkeley. Ills. 3rd ed. dj. EX $20.00

PAIN, Barry. *Collected Tales. Vol. I.* 1916. New York. Stokes. 1st Am. ed. VG $40.00

PAINE, Albert Bigelow. *Captain Bill McDonald, Texas Ranger.* 1909. New York. 448 pp. $175.00

PAINE, Albert Bigelow. *Joan of Arc.* 1925. New York. 1st ed. $35.00

PAINE, Albert Bigelow. *Mark Twain, a Biography.* 1912. New York. 1st ed. sgn. 4 vol set. G $75.00

PAINE, Albert Bigelow. *Tent Dwellers.* 1908. Outing. $12.50

PAINE, Albert Bigelow. *The Arkansas Bear.* 1929. Philadelphia. Altemus. Ills. Frank Ver Beck. $15.00

PAINE, Albert Bigelow. *The Arkansas Bear.* 1902. Philadelphia. Altemus. Ills. Frank Ver Beck. $10.00

PAINE, Albert Bigelow. *The Great White Way.* 1901. New York. Taylor. 1st ed. VG $40.00

PAINE, Albert Bigelow. *Theodore Nast, His Period & His Pictures.* 1904. New York. Ills. 1st ed. VG $40.00

PAINE, L. *Gentleman Johnny: Life of Gen. J. Burgoyne.* 1973. London. $6.00

PAINE, Ralph D. *Ships Across the Sea.* 1920. $10.00

PAINE, Ralph. *The Ships & Sailors of Old Salem.* 1927. Boston. Ills. EX $30.00

PAINE, Thomas. *The Political Works of Thomas Paine.* Chicago. (ca.1900?) 448 pp. $10.00

PALEY, Grace. *The Little Disturbances of Man.* 1959. Doubleday. 1st ed. dj. VG $60.00

PALFREY. *A History of New England.* 1865. Boston. Little, Brown. 3 vol set. EX $110.00

PALLIS, Marco. *The Way & the Mountain.* 1961. London. 216 pp. 17 pls. VG $25.00

PALMER, A.J. *Riding High: Story of the Bicycle.* 1956. New York. Ills. 1st ed. 191 pp. dj. VG $20.00

PALMER, B. *They Shall Not Pass.* 1977. dj. VG $7.50

PALMER, Charles. *Adventures of a Slum Fighter.* 1955. Atlanta. 271 pp. inscr. dj. $75.00

PALMER, F. *America in France.* 1918. VG $15.00

PALMER, F. *Our Gallant Madness.* 1937. G $10.00

PALMER, Frank R. & Luerssen. *Tool Steel Simplified.* 1948. Reading, PA. revised ed. 564 pp. $5.00

PALMER, Frederick. *With Kuroki in Manchuria.* 1904. New York. Ills. James H. Hare. 362 pp. $65.00

PALMER, George Thomas. *A Conscientious Turncoat.* 1941. New Haven, CT. Yale U. Press. ex-lib. 297 pp. $6.00

PALMER, H.R. *This Was Air Travel.* 1960. dj. G $12.50

PALMER, J. *Moliere.* 1930. 494 pp. $12.50

PALMER, Rose A. *Account of American Indians North of Mexico.* 1943. Smithsonian. Scientific Series Vol. 4. $12.50

PALMER, Stuart. *The Green Ace.* 1950. New York. Morrow. 1st ed. dj. EX $20.00

PALMER, Thomas. *A Serious Address to Unbaptized Christians.* 1750. York. $25.00

PALMER, W.J. *Report, Survey Across the Continent.* 1869. Philadelphia. 2 fld maps. $200.00

PALMER. *Jade.* 1967. London. 54 pp. $15.00

PALTOCK, Robert. *The Life & Adventures of Peter Wilkins.* 1884. London. 2 vol set. $62.00

PANCAKE, Breece D'J. *The Stories of Breece D'J Pancake.* 1983. Boston. Little, Brown. 1st ed. dj. EX $35.00

PANDOSY, M.C. *Grammar & Dictionary of Yakama Language.* 1862. New York. Cramoisy Pr. 1st ed. 59 pp. $150.00

PANETTI, Charles. *The Pleasure of Rory Malone.* 1982. St.Martin. 1st ed. dj. VG $10.00

PANGBORN, Edgar. *The Trial of Callista Blake.* New York. St.Martins. dj. EX $20.00

PANKHURST, C. *Plain Facts About a Great Evil.* 1913. New York. 157 pp. $15.00

PANKHURST, R. *Sylvia Pankhurst, Artist & Crusader.* 1979. Ills. dj. EX $20.00

PANKHURST. *Ethiopia & Eritrea.* 1953. Essex. dj. VG $22.50

PANOFSY. *Idea: Concept on Art Theory.* 1968. U. SC. $6.00

PANSHIN, Alexis. *Transmutations, Book of Personal Alchemy.* 1982. Dublin. PA. Ltd. 1st ed. inscr. EX $50.00

PANSON, M. *Vision of Misery Hill, Legend of Sierra Nevada.* 1891. Putnam. Ills. VG $12.50

PANSY, Isabella Alden. *A Sevenfold Trouble.* 1889. Boston. Ills. L.J. Bridgman. 1st ed. $20.00

PANSY, Isabella Alden. *Four Girls at Chautauqua.* 1904. $30.00

PANSY, Isabella Alden. *Four Girls at Chautauqua.* 1876. Boston. Lothrop. Ills. 1st ed. G $20.00

PANSY. *Her Associate Members.* 1891. $30.00

PANSY. *Tip Lewis & His Lamp.* 1895. $30.00

PAPANDREOU, A. *Democracy at Gunpoint.* 1970. dj. EX $10.00

PAPANIKOLAS, H. *Peoples of Utah.* 1976. UT Hist. Soc.1st ed. dj. VG $12.50

PAPE. *At the Sign of the Reine Pedaque.* 1922. 12 Ills. VG $16.00

PAPE. *Figures of Earth.* 1925. McBride. 12 Ills. VG $17.00

PAPE. *Mother of Pearl.* 1929. France. Bodley Head. 12 Ills. $18.00

PAPE. *Penguin Island.* 1929. France. Dodd Mead. 12 Ills. $17.00

PAPE. *Works of Rabelais.* Abbey. Ills. 730 pp. $17.00

PARDEE, Harold E.B. *Clinical Aspects of the Electrocardiogram.* 1925. New York. 8 vol set. 224 pp. $50.00

PARDOE, F.L. *The Kings Royal Rifle Corps Chronicle.* 1940. Winchester. 197 pp. $20.00

PARET, J.P. *The Lawn Tennis Library.* 1927. New York. 3 vol set. Ills. $30.00

PARETO, Vilfredo. *The Mind & Society.* 1942. New York. 4 vol set. dj. VG $18.00

PARGETER, C.J. *'Hipper' Class Heavy Cruisers.* 1982. London. Ills. maps. EX $10.00

PARIS, Ayrton John. *Pharmacologia: History of Medical Substances.* 1822. New York. 428 pp. $65.00

PARK, M. *The Life & Travels of Mungo Park.* 1944. New York. ex-lib. 248 pp. $4.00

PARKER, Barbara & Wheeler, A. *John Singleton Copley: American Portraits.* 1938. Boston. Museum of Fine Arts. 130 pls. $50.00

PARKER, Bertha M. *Golden Treasury of Natural History.* 1952. New York. Ills. 1st ed. index. VG $12.50

PARKER, David B. *Chautauqua Boy in '61 & Afterward.* 1912. Boston. Ills. 1st ed. 388 pp. $40.00

PARKER, Don. *Local History & How to Gather It.* 1944. New York. wrappers. $5.00

PARKER, Don. *Recollections of Philander Prescott: Frontiersman.*1966. U. of NB. dj. EX $22.50

PARKER, Dorothy. *Collection of Her Stories & Poems.* 544 pp. VG $8.50

PARKER, Dorothy. *Enough Rope.* 1926. New York. 1st ed. 110 pp. $25.00

PARKER, Dorothy. *Not So Deep as a Well.* 1936. New York. dj. VG $25.00

PARKER, Dorothy. *Sunset Gun.* 1928. New York. Boni. 1st ed. 75 pp. $7.50

PARKER, Eric. *An Angler's Garland.* 1920. Philip Allan & Co. VG $75.00

PARKER, Eric. *Fine Angling for Coarse Fish.* (ca.1903) Ills. VG $22.50

PARKER, Eric. *The Lonsdale Anthology of Sporting Prose & Verse.* Philadelphia. no date. Ills. dj. $25.00

PARKER, Foxhall A. *Squadron Tactics Under Steam.* 1864. New York. Ills. 1st ed. VG $150.00

PARKER, Gilbert & Bryan, C. *Old Quebec, the Fortress of New France.* 1904. Macmillan. Ills. 486 pp. $20.00

PARKER, Gilbert & Bryan, C. *Old Quebec, the Fortress of New France.* 1903. Macmillan. 1st ed. G $25.00

PARKER, Gilbert. *The Right of Way.* 1901. Ills. A.I. Keller. $4.00

PARKER, H.W. *Snakes.* 1963. London. Hale. 1st ed. 191 pp. dj. EX $20.00

PARKER, Maria H. *Auntie's Elfin Land.* 1890. Boston. Cupples. 1st ed. VG $20.00

PARKER, Mrs. E. *The Popular Pomeranian.* London. Popular Dogs Pub. 148 pp. G $3.50

PARKER, N. Howe. *Iowa As It Is in 1855.* 1855. Chicago. Ills. VG $40.00

PARKER, R. *Scholastical Discourse Against Symbolizing .* 1607. Amsterdam. 2 parts in 1 vol. $100.00

PARKER, Robert & Joan. *Three Weeks in Spring.* 1978. Boston. 1st ed. dj. EX $40.00

PARKER, Robert A. *Illustrated Franklin.* C. Potter Pub. (ca.1970) 1st ed. wrappers. VG $10.00

PARKER, Robert A. *The Transatlantic Smith.* 1959. Random House. 1st ed. 237 pp. $5.00

PARKER, Robert B. *A Savage Place.* 1981. 1st ed. sgn. dj. EX $35.00

PARKER, Robert B. *Early Autumn.* 1981. New York. Delacorte. 1st ed. dj. EX $25.00

PARKER, Robert B. *God Save the Child.* 1974. Boston. 1st ed. dj. $50.00

PARKER, Robert B. *Judas Goat.* 1978. Houghton Mifflin. sgn. dj. VG $27.50

PARKER, Robert B. *The Widening Gyre.* 1983. New York. Delacorte. 1st ed. dj. EX $25.00

PARKER, Samuel. *Journal, Exploring Tour Beyond Rocky Mountains.* 1838. Ithaca. 1st ed. fld map. $350.00

PARKER, T. *Trial of T. Parker for Speech Against Kidnapping.* 1855. Boston. ex-lib. 221 pp. $12.50

PARKER, Thomas V. *Cherokee Indians.* 1907. Grafton Pr. 116 pp. VG $20.00

PARKER, Thomas W. *The Knights Templars in England.* 1963. Tucson. VG $15.00

PARKER. *Wilderness.* 1979. 1st Am. ed. dj. VG $45.00

PARKES, J. *The Story of Jerusalem.* 1949. London. maps. dj. G $7.50

PARKES, O. *Ships of the Royal Navies.* 1934. London. Ills. G $17.50

PARKHAM, Francis. *La Salle & the Discovery of the Great West.* 1907. Boston. Little, Brown. map. G $7.50

PARKHURST, G. *A King in the Making.* 1925. New York. Ills. $10.00

PARKINSON, C. Northcote. *Big Business.* Boston. Ills. 263 pp. index. $15.00

PARKINSON, C. Northcote. *Devil to Pay.* 1973. London. Murray. 1st ed. dj. EX $35.00

PARKINSON, C. Northcote. *Fireship, Novel of Lt. Richard Delancey.* 1975. dj. EX $10.00

PARKINSON, C. Northcote. *Jeeves.* 1979. New York. St. Martins. 1st ed. dj. EX $25.00

PARKINSON, C. Northcote. *The Law & the Profits.* 1960. Ills. 3rd printing. dj. VG $8.50

PARKINSON, C. Northcote. *The Law & the Profits.* 1960. London. Murray. Ills. 1st ed. $20.00

PARKINSON, C. Northcote. *The Law of Delay.* 1970. London. Murray. 1st ed. dj. VG $20.00

PARKINSON, Edward. *The Practical Country Gentleman*. 1911. Chicago, IL. Ills. 189 pp. $3.50

PARKINSON, Hank. *Winning Your Campaign: Nuts & Bolts Guide*. 1970. 270 pp. dj. $27.50

PARKINSON, J., Jr. *Yarns for Davy Jones*. 1966. private print. Ills. VG $12.50

PARKMAN, Francis. *La Salle & the Discovery of the Great West*. 1885. 446 pp. $15.00

PARKMAN, Francis. *Montcalm & Wolfe*. 1902. maps. 2 vol set. $25.00

PARKMAN, Francis. *Oregon Trail Sketches of Prairie & Mountain Life*. 1925. Ills. Remington. G $75.00

PARKMAN, Francis. *Oregon Trail Sketches of Prairie & Mountain Life*. 1946. Doubleday. Ills. Benton. EX $35.00

PARKMAN, Francis. *Oregon Trail Sketches of Prairie & Mountain Life*. 1892. Boston. Ills. Remington. 1st ed. VG $190.00

PARKMAN, Francis. *Oregon Trail Sketches of Prairie & Mountain Life*. 1943. Heritage. Ills. Dixon. 1st ed. boxed. EX $35.00

PARKMAN, Francis. *Oregon Trail Sketches of Prairie & Mountain Life*. 1925. Little, Brown. Ills. Wyeth. Ltd. ed. EX $100.00

PARKMAN, Francis. *The California & Oregon Trail*. 1849. New York. 448 pp. $385.00

PARKMAN, Francis. *The Old Regime in Canada*. 1874. Boston. 1st ed. maps. 448 pp. $30.00

PARKMAN, Francis. *Works of Francis Parkman*. 1915. 17 vol set. VG $60.00

PARKMAN. *History of Buckeye Canal*. 1957. Pheonix. 37 pp. wrappers. $12.50

PARKS, E. *The World of the Bison*. 1969. Lippincott. Ills. 1st ed. 161 pp. dj. VG $12.50

PARKS, Gordon. *A Poet & His Camera*. 1968. $5.00

PARKS, Gordon. *Camera Portraits*. 1948. VG $35.00

PARKS & LEIGHTON. *The Roosevelts, a Family in Turmoil*. 1981. Prentice-Hall. 1st ed. $12.50

PARLEY, Peter. *Story of the Faithful Dog*. 1829. SftCvr. $35.00

PARLIN, S.W. *The American Trotter*. 1905. Boston. 1st ed. G $45.00

PARLOA, Maria. *Home Ecomomics*. 1898. Century. Ills. VG $17.50

PARMALEE, P.W. *Amphibians of Illinois*. 1954. State Museum. Ills. 38 pp. EX $10.00

PARMALEE, P.W. & Loomis, F.D. *Decoys & Decoy Carvers of Illinois*. 1969. U. N. IL Pr. 506 pp. EX $150.00

PARMELEE, M. *Blockade & Sea Power. Blockade 1914-1919*. 1924. VG $15.00

PARRACK, J. *The Naturalist in Majorca*. 1973. David & Charles. 224 pp. dj. $17.50

PARRATT, G. *The Royal Navy, the Sure Shield of the Empire*. 1930. London. Ills. G $12.50

PARRINDER, Geoffrey. *African Mythology*. 1967. London. Ills. 139 pp. dj. $12.50

PARRINGTON, Vernon L. *Main Currents of American Thoughts*. 1930. New York. Harcourt. 3 vol set. $12.50

PARRISH, Anne & Dillwyn. *Lustres*. 1924. New York. 1st ed. G $20.00

PARRISH, Anne. *The Perennial Bachelor*. 1925. New York. 338 pp. $3.50

PARRISH, Anne. *The Story of Appleby Capple*. 1950. Harper. Ills. 1st ed. 184 pp. dj. $25.00

PARRISH, L. *Slave Songs of the Georgia Sea Islands*. 1942. New York. 1st ed. dj. VG $60.00

PARRISH, Maxfield. *Arabian Nights*. 1944. NY/London. Scribner. G $16.00

PARRISH, Maxfield. *Arabian Nights*. 1935. Ills. $20.00

PARRISH, Maxfield. *Poems of Childhood*. 1904. Scribner. 1st ed. 9 color pls. EX $75.00

PARRISH, Maxfield. *Reading Aloud*. 1937. New York. Nelson & Sons. 401 pp. $3.50

PARRISH, Maxfield. *The Arabian Nights*. 1925. Scribner. 9 color pls. VG $40.00

PARRISH, Maxfield. *The Arabian Nights*. 1945. Scribner. 9 color pls. $34.00

PARRISH, Randall. *Keith of the Border*. 1910. New York. 362 pp. $3.50

PARRISH, Randall. *Maid of the Forest, Romance of St. Clair's Defeat*. 1913. McClurg. Ills. Schoonover. 1st ed. VG $8.50

PARRISH. *A Wonder Book & Tanglewood Tales*. 1920. Duffield. 10 color pls. VG $50.00

PARRISH. *The Golden Age*. 1900. Bodley Head. 18 Ills. G $30.00

PARROT, A. *Ziggurats et Tour de Babel*. 1949. Paris. Ills. 237 pp. wrappers. VG $35.00

PARROTT, A. *Queer & Rare Fishes of New Zealand*. 1960. London. Hodder Stoughton. 1st ed. dj. $22.50

PARRY, A. *Whistler's Father*. 1939. 1st ed. sgn. dj. EX $8.00

PARRY, David M. *The Scarlet Empire*. 1906. Indianapolis. Bobbs Merrill. 1st ed. EX $45.00

PARRY, Edwin S. *Betsy Ross, Quaker Rebel*. 1930. Chicago/Phila. Ills. 252 pp. boxed. $18.50

PARRY, Edwin S. *Betsy Ross, Quaker Rebel*. 1930. Philadelphia. Ills. Ltd. ed. 1/285. inscr. $20.00

PARRY, G. & Putnam, R. *Birds of Prey*. 1979. London. Country Life. 120 pp. dj. EX $45.00

PARRY, J.H. *The Discovery of South America*. 1979. New York. Ills. 1st ed. 320 pp. dj. VG $22.00

PARRY, W. *Butter-Scotia*. 1896. VG $25.00

PARRY & SHERLOCK. *Short History of West Indies*. 1960. London. dj. EX $10.00

PARRY. *Don Quixote of la Mancha*. 1900. Ills. Walter Crane. 243 pp. $50.00

PARRY. *Katawampus*. 1895. VG $25.00

PARSONS, E.C. *Isleta Paintings*. 1962. Washington. 140 full pp. paintings. dj. $20.00

PARSONS, F.A. *Interior Decorating Principles & Practice*. 1916. New York. Ills. VG $17.50

PARSONS, J. *Wildlife Painting*. 1984. London. Batsford. 1st ed. dj. EX $10.00

PARSONS, J.E. *Henry Deringer's Pocket Pistol*. 1952. New York. 1st ed. VG $45.00

PARSONS, J.E. *The Peacemaker & Its Rivals*. 1950. 1st ed. VG $15.00

PARSONS, P. Allen. *Complete Book of Fresh-Water Fishing*. 1966. New York. Outdoor Life/Harper. EX $8.50

PARSONS, P. Allen. *Complete Book of Fresh-Water Fishing*. 1963. Outdoor Life. Ills. 332 pp. $5.50

PARSONS, Sam. *Parsons on the Rose, Treatise on Propagation, Etc.* 1869. New York. Ills. revised ed. pls. VG $12.50

PARTINGTON, Wilfred. *Forging Ahead: True Story of Thomas James Wise*. 1939. New York. Putnam. 1st ed. dj. EX $40.00

PARTINGTON, Wilfred. *Thomas J. Wise in the Original Cloth*. 1946. London. Hale. Ills. 1st ed. dj. VG $40.00

PARTON, James. *General Butler in New Orleans*. 1864. New York. 4th ed. 647 pp. $28.00

PARTON, James. *The Life of Horace Greeley*. 1855. New York. 1st ed. VG $15.00

PARTRIDGE, Bellamy. *Country Lawyer*. 1939. $30.00

PARTRIDGE, Bellamy. *Excuse My Dust*. 1943. New York. McGraw Hill. 359 pp. $27.50

PARTRIDGE, Bellamy. *January Thaw*. 1945. $30.00

PARTRIDGE, Bellamy. *The Old Oaken Bucket*. 1949. $30.00

PASCHAL, George W. *U.S. Constitution Defined & Carefully Annotated*. 1868. Washington. 1st ed. scarce. VG $50.00

PASKINS & DOCKRILL. *The Ethics of War.* 1979. London. sgn. VG $15.00

PASSANT, E.J. *A Short History of Germany 1815-1945.* 1966. maps. dj. VG $12.50

PASSINGHAM, W.J. *London's Markets; Their Origin & History.* London. Ills. 1st ed. 302 pp. $22.50

PASTEN, Linda. *Even as We Sleep.* 1980. Croissant. Ltd. ed. 1/100. sgn. wrappers. $15.00

PASTERNAK, B. *Essay in Autobiography.* 1st English ed. dj. $10.00

PASTEUR, Louis. *Studies on Fermentation; Diseases of Beer.* 1879. London. 1st Eng. ed. VG $45.00

PASTON, George. *Old Colored Books.* 1905. London. 1st ed. color pls. VG $18.00

PATCH, Edith M. *Holiday Pond.* 1934. New York. Macmillan. Ills. Bronson. $10.00

PATCHEN, Kenneth. *Aflame & Afun of Walking Faces.* 1970. New Directions. 1st ed. wrappers. VG $15.00

PATCHEN, Kenneth. *See You in the Morning.* 1947. Padell. 1st ed. dj. $15.00

PATCHEN, Kenneth. *The Love Poems of Kenneth Patchen.* 1964. City Lights. 1st ed. wrappers. VG $10.00

PATCHEN. *First Will & Testament.* Ltd. ed. 1/800. VG $40.00

PATCHIN, Frank G. *The Battleship Boys at Sea.* 1910. Saalfield. Ills. fair. $3.50

PATCHIN, Frank G. *The Pony Rider Boys in New Mexico.* 1910. Saalfield. Ills. VG $6.50

PATCHIN, Frank G. *The Pony Rider Boys in Texas.* 1910. Altemus. Ills. G $5.50

PATCIIIN, Frank G. *The Pony Rider Boys in the Alkali.* 1910. Saalfield. Ills. G $5.50

PATCHIN, Frank G. *The Pony Rider Boys in the Rockies.* 1909. Saalfield. Ills. dj. EX $8.50

PATCHIN, Frank G. *The Pony Rider Boys on the Blue Ridge.* 1924. Saalfield. Ills. VG $6.50

PATCHIN, Frank G. *The Pony Rider Boys with the Texas Rangers.* 1920. Saalfield. Ills. VG $6.50

PATCHIN, Frank G. *The Pony Rider Stories.* 1920. Saalfield. Ills. G $9.50

PATCHIN, Frank G. *The Range & Grange Hustlers on the Ranch.* 1912. Philadelphia. 250 pp. $2.50

PATEL, Harshad. *Vanishing Herds.* 1973. New York. photos. dj. EX $35.00

PATER, Roger. *Mystic Voices.* 1923. London. Burnes. 1st ed. dj. VG $95.00

PATER, Walter. *Coleridge's Writings.* 1910. London. Gowans & Gray. $20.00

PATER, Walter. *Uncollected Essays.* 1903. Portland. Ltd. ed. 1/50. dj. VG $17.50

PATERSON, A. *Birds of the Bahamas.* 1972. Durrell. Ills. 1st ed. 180 pp. dj. EX $15.00

PATERSON, Wilma. *Country Wines & Cordials.* 1980. Hertfordshire. Omega Books. Ills. 88 pp. $7.50

PATHERICK. *Joseph Guanerius.* 1906. London. 220 pp. $30.00

PATKIN. *The Dunera Internees.* 1979. Cassell. Ills. 1st ed. dj. EX $15.00

PATON, Alan. *Cry, the Beloved Country.* 1948. New York. Scribner. 277 pp. $3.50

PATON, Alan. *South Africa & Her People.* 1958. London. Ills. 140 pp. EX $3.50

PATON, Alan. *Tales from a Troubled Land.* 1961. Scribner. 1st Am. ed. dj. VG $25.00

PATON, Alan. *Too Late the Phalarope.* 1953. $10.00

PATON, James. *Thirty Years Among South Sea Cannibals.* 1902. A.L. Burt. $3.00

PATON. *Water Babies.* 1869. Boston. VG $30.00

PATRI, Angelo. *A Schoolmaster of the Great City.* 1917. New York. 1st ed. VG $10.00

PATRIC, John. *Yankee Hobo in the Orient.* 1945. Oregon. Ills. 8th ed. inscr. sgn. VG $15.00

PATRICK, Ed & Spitzer, Silas. *Great Restaurants of America.* New York. Bramhall House. Ills. 383 pp. $7.50

PATRICK, Lynn & Moahan, L. *Let's Play Hockey!* 1957. Toronto. Ills. 79 pp. scarce. VG $9.00

PATRICK, Marsena. *Inside Lincoln's Army Diary of Patrick.* 1964. Yoseloff. 1st ed. dj. $8.50

PATRICK, Mary. *Sappho & the Island of Lesbos.* 1912. Houghton Mifflin. 1st ed. $8.50

PATTEE, Fred Lewis. *A History of American Literature Since 1870.* 1915. New York. ex-lib. 449 pp. VG $3.00

PATTEE, Fred Lewis. *The New American Literature 1890-1930.* 1930. New York. ex-lib. 507 pp. VG $3.50

PATTEN, C. *A Tennessee Chronicle.* 1953. 1st ed. sgn. $20.00

PATTEN, Lewis B. *Gene Autry & Arapaho War Drums.* 1957. Racine. Whitman. 282 pp. $3.50

PATTEN, Matthew. *The Diary of Matthew Patten of Bedford, NH.* 1903. 545 pp. $45.00

PATTENGILL, H. *Primer of Michigan History.* 1909. G $4.00

PATTERN, Marguerite. *Book of Savoury Cooking.* 1961. London. Ills. 1st ed. 594 pp. dj. $7.50

PATTERN, Marguerite. *Family Cookbook in Color.* 1973. London. Ills. 349 pp. dj. $10.00

PATTERSON, A. *American Homes of Today.* 1924. New York. 1st ed. EX $75.00

PATTERSON, Calvin. *Patterson's Common School Speller.* 1874. New York. 160 pp. $10.00

PATTERSON, G. *Journey with Loshay, Adventure in Tibet.* 1954. New York. 1st ed. $10.00

PATTERSON, Gerry. *Behind the Superstars.* 1978. Prentice Hall. Ills. 173 pp. EX $6.50

PATTERSON, J. *The Jericho Commandment.* 1979. dj. EX $6.00

PATTERSON, J.B. *Black Hawk's Autobiography.* 1912. Rock Island. 3 maps. 164 pp. 8 pls. VG $12.00

PATTERSON, J.H. *The Man Eaters of Tsavo.* 1926. London. G $20.00

PATTERSON, J.H. *The Man Eaters of Tsavo.* 1986. St. Martins. Ills. 346 pp. dj. EX $17.50

PATTERSON, J.H. *The Man Eaters of Tsavo.* 1927. New York. Ills. 1st ed. 401 pp. EX $50.00

PATTERSON, James Medill. *A Little Brother of the Rich.* 1908. Chicago. Reilly & Britton. 1st ed. dj. $65.00

PATTERSON, James Medill. *Rebellion.* 1911. Chicago. Reilly & Britton. 1st ed. VG $30.00

PATTERSON, R.M. *The Buffalo Head.* 1961. Sloane. Ills. 273 pp. dj. $3.00

PATTERSON, R.M. *Trail to the Interior.* 1966. New York. 255 pp. dj. EX $10.00

PATTERSON, Robert. *Fables of Infidelity & Facts of Faith.* 1864. Cincinnati. $15.00

PATTERSON, S.W. *Old Chelsea & St. Peter's Church.* 1935. New York. VG $25.00

PATTERSON, Samuel. *Narrative of Adventures & Suffering of Patterson.* 1817. Palmer. 1st ed. 144 pp. $375.00

PATTERSON, Samuel. *Narrative of Adventures & Suffering of Patterson.* 1825. Providence. 2nd ed. 164 pp. VG $275.00

PATTERSON, W. *Ogilvie's How To Play Checkers.* New York. Ogilvie. 2nd ed. 61 pp. G $12.50

PATTERSON, Wilma. *Country Wines & Cordials.* 1980. Hertfordshire. Omega Books. Ills. 88 pp. $7.50

PATTON, George S. *War as I Knew It.* 1947. Boston. 425 pp. maps. index. VG $15.00

PATTON, H. *Riding Down.* 1932. dj. G $5.00

PATTON, H. *Young Eagles.* 1932. Chicago. Goldsmith. 123 pp. $3.00

PAUCHARD, A. *The Other World.* 1952. 1st Am. ed. VG $25.00

PAUL, E. *Mayhem in B-Flat.* 1940. 1st ed. dj. VG $8.00

PAUL, Elliot. *Linden on the Saugus Branch.* 1948. London. 1st Eng. ed. $9.00

PAUL, Elliot. *Springtime in Paris.* 1951. London. 1st Eng. ed. dj. VG $30.00

PAUL, Elliot. *The Life & Death of a Spanish Town.* 1937. New York. Random House. 427 pp. dj. $5.00

PAUL, Elliot. *Waylaid in Boston.* 1953. New York. Random House. 1st ed. dj. EX $25.00

PAUL, R.A. *American Military Commitments Abroad.* 1973. Ills. dj. VG $10.00

PAUL, Raymond. *The Thomas Street Horror.* 1982. Viking. 1st ed. dj. VG $12.50

PAUL. *Harry Callahan.* 1967. VG $15.00

PAULING & WILSON. *Introduction to Quantum Mechanics.* 1935. $15.00

PAULL. *Ruby & Ruthy.* 1917. Cupples & Leon. G $4.50

PAULL. *Ruby's Ups & Downs.* 1917. Cupples & Leon. G $4.50

PAULLIN, C. *Atlas of the Historical Geography of U.S.* 1932. Carnegie Institute. VG $100.00

PAULLIN, C.O. *Commodore John Rodgers.* 1967. Ills. dj. EX $17.50

PAULSON, Arvid & Edwards, C. *The Story of Don Quixote.* 1922. New York. Ills. Choate & Curtis. VG $25.00

PAVITT, W.T. *The Book of Talismans, Amulets, & Zodiacal Gems.* 1914. London. 3rd revised ed. 292 pp. G $45.00

PAVLOV, P. *Lectures on Conditioned Reflexes.* 1928. New York. 8 vol set. $65.00

PAWLET. *St. John. Fourteen Sermons.* 1737. London. $25.00

PAXSON, Frederic L. *History of the American Frontier 1763-1893.* 1924. Boston/NY. TB. 598 pp. index. $15.00

PAXTON, J.G. *The Coast Guard.* 1958. Ills. G $7.50

PAYETTE, B.C. *Oregon Country Under the Union Jack.* 1962. Montreal. 682 pp. VG $20.00

PAYNE, A.G. *Common Sense Papers on Cookery.* London. (ca.1920) VG $30.00

PAYNE, Alma & Callahan, D. *The Low Sodium, Fat-Controlled Cookbook.* 1960. Little, Brown. ex-lib. inscr. $3.00

PAYNE, Arthur F. *Art Metal Work with Inexpensive Equipment.* 1929. Peoria, IL. Ills. 176 pp. $7.50

PAYNE, H. *Archaic Marble Sculpture from the Acropolis.* Morrow. photos. EX $175.00

PAYNE, J. *Beauties of Nature & Art Displayed in World Tour.* 1763. London. 100 pls. maps. 14 vol set. VG $150.00

PAYNE, J.H. *Home! Sweet Home!* 1890. Boston. Prang. wrappers. EX $27.50

PAYNE, Jack. *Modoc Renegade.* 1958. Portland. 259 pp. VG $17.50

PAYNE, R. *The Life & Death of Adolf Hitler.* 1973. Ills. maps. VG $17.50

PAYNE, William. *Contributions to the Science of Education.* 1886. New York. Harper. 358 pp. $125.00

PAYNE. *Cleveland.* 1876. Ills. $10.00

PAYSON, Howard. *The Boy Scouts Badge of Courage.* 1917. A.L. Burt. dj. EX $7.50

PAYSON, Howard. *The Boy Scouts Mountain Camp.* 1912. $3.50

PAYSON, Howard. *The Boy Scouts of the Eagle Patrol.* 1911. A.L. Burt. VG $5.50

PAYSON, Howard. *The Boy Scouts with the Allies in France.* 1915. New York. A.L. Burt. 309 pp. $2.50

PEABODY. *Log of the Grand Turks.* 1926. 1st ed. VG $20.00

PEAKE, H. & Fleure, H.J. *The Way of the Sea.* 1929. Yale U. Press. Ills. 168 pp. VG $10.00

PEAKE. *Titus Groan.* New York. 1st ed. G $20.00

PEALE, Norman Vincent. *Imaging: The Powerful Way to Change Your Life.* 1982. Carmel, NY. Guidepost Assoc. 187 pp. dj. $3.00

PEALE, Norman Vincent. *The Power of Positive Thinking.* 1952. Prentice Hall. 274 pp. $4.00

PEALE, Norman Vincent. *You Can if You Think You Can.* 1974. Carmel, NY. Guidepost Assoc. 321 pp. dj. $4.50

PEARCE, G.F. *The U.S. Navy in Pensacola.* 1980. Ills. dj. G $17.50

PEARCY, Arthur. *Dakota at War.* 1982. London. Allan. 1st ed. $15.00

PEARE, Catherine Owens. *John Keats, a Portrait in Words.* 1960. New York. Ills. dj. EX $15.00

PEARL. *Gems, Minerals, Crystals, & Ores.* 1964. New York. 320 pp. $10.00

PEARSE, Eleanor. *Florida's Vanishing Era.* 1954. reprint. 75 pp. dj. $10.00

PEARSE, James. *Narrative of the Life of James Pearse.* 1825. Rutland. 1st ed. 144 pp. $350.00

PEARSE, S.B. & Ackroyd, W. *Mother Goose Fun.* New York. Stokes. (ca.1920) Ills. VG $25.00

PEARSON, Drew. *Diaries 1949-1959.* 1974. New York. 592 pp. $4.00

PEARSON, E.L. *Books in Black or Red.* 1924. New York. dj. VG $15.00

PEARSON. *Shaker Image.* 1974. New York. dj. EX $22.50

PEARSON, Edmund. *Autobiography of Criminal Henry Tufts.* 1930. New York. 357 pp. dj. $9.00

PEARSON, Edmund. *The Secret Book.* 1914. New York. Macmillan. G $25.00

PEARSON, H.S. *Success on the Small Farm.* 1946. New York. McGraw Hill. 285 pp. G $5.00

PEARSON, Lester. *The Four Faces of Peace.* 1964. New York. ex-lib. 267 pp. dj. VG $4.00

PEARSON, M. *Tears of Glory, the Heroes of Vercors.* 1978. Book Club ed. Ills. maps. dj. G $10.00

PEARSON, Norman. *Some Problems of Existence.* 1907. Arnold. 1st ed. $20.00

PEARSON, T. Gilbert. *Birds of America.* 1936. New York. Ills. L.A. Fuertes. 289 pp. $35.00

PEARSON. *Early Churches of Washington State.* 1980. U. of WA. $12.00

PEARY, Josephine. *The Snow Baby.* 1901. Stokes. Ills. 8th ed. VG $15.00

PEARY, Mrs. *My Arctic Journal, Year Among Ice Fields & Eskimos.* 1893. Philadelphia. VG $50.00

PEARY, Robert E. *Nearest the Pole.* 1907. New York. 1st ed. VG $55.00

PEARY, Robert E. *Northward Over the Great Ice.* 1898. New York. Stokes. Ills. 1st ed. $90.00

PEASE, A.E. *The Badger.* 1898. London. Ills. 120 pp. VG $17.50

PEASE, Eleanor Fairchild. *Brave Tales of Real Dogs.* 1952. Ills. VG $4.50

PEASE, Eleanor Fairchild. *Brave Tales of Real Dogs.* 1934. Chicago. 10th printing. 160 pp. $5.00

PEASE, Eleanor Fairchild. *Heroes All.* 1940. Chicago. Whitman. Ills. Orloff. 1st ed. $15.00

PEASE, Howard. *Border Ghost Stories.* 1919. London. MacDonald. 1st ed. VG $35.00

PEASE, T.C. *Story of Illinois.* 1949. U. of Chicago. 1st ed. 284 pp. $15.00

PEASE, T.C. & Ernesting, J. *Illinois on the Eve of Seven Year's War.* 1940. Springfield. 977 pp. $20.00

PEASE, T.C. & Werner, R.C. *The French Foundations 1680-1693.* 1934. Springfield. 426 pp. $20.00

PEAT, Fern Bisel. *A Children's Garden of Verses.* 1940. Saalfield. Deluxe 1st ed. VG $45.00

PEAT, Fern Bisel. *Christmas Carols.* 1937. Saafield. Ills. 1st ed. VG $35.00

PEAT, Fern Bisel. *Little Black Sambo.* 1943. Am. Crayon Co. Ills. VG $40.00

PEAT, Fern Bisel. *Peter Rabbit.* 1931. Am. Crayon Co. Ills. wrappers. VG $30.00

PEAT. *Private Peat.* 1917. Indianapolis. Bobbs Merrill. Ills. $6.00

PEATTIE, Donald C. *A Book of Hours.* 1937. Putnam. Ills. Lynd Ward. dj. VG $20.00

PEATTIE, Donald C. *A Natural History of Western Trees.* 1953. Boston. Ills. Paul Landacre. $20.00

PEATTIE, Donald C. *A Natural History of Western Trees.* 1953. Bonanza. Ills. 751 pp. VG $20.00

PEATTIE, Donald C. *A Prairie Grove.* 1938. Literary Guild.Ills. 289 pp. VG $6.00

PEATTIE, Donald C. *Audubon's America.* 1940. 1st ed. EX $30.00

PEATTIE, Donald C. *Flowering Earth.* 1939. Putnam. Ills. 260 pp. VG $5.00

PEATTIE, Donald C. *Green Laurels.* 1936. New York. Literary Guild. Ills. 1st ed. $10.00

PEATTIE, Donald C. *Singing in the Wilderness, Salute to Audubon.* 1935. Putnam. Ills. 245 pp. G $5.00

PEATTIE, Donald C. *Sportsman's Country.* 1952. Ills. Kane. 180 pp. dj. VG $10.00

PEATTIE, R. *Look to New Frontiers, Geography for Peace Tables.*1970. maps. diagrams. EX $10.00

PEATTIE, Rod. *Invented Mountains, Canyons of the West.* 1948. New York. photos. dj. VG $9.00

PECK, Bradford. *The World of a Department Store.* 1900. Lewiston. 1st ed. dj. EX $45.00

PECK, George W. *Peck's Bad Boy Abroad.* 1905. Chicago. Thompson & Thomas. Ills. VG $22.50

PECK, George W. *Peck's Uncle Ike & the Redheaded Boy.* 1889. Chicago. G $6.50

PECK, George W. *Sunbeams.* 1900. New York. Ills. Ike Morgan. 220 pp. $7.50

PECK, Richard. *New York Time.* 1981. Delacorte. 1st ed. dj. VG $10.00

PECK, W.H. & Ross, J.G. *Egyptian Drawings.* 1978. Dutton. folio. dj. VG $20.00

PECK, Walter Edwin. *Shelley, His Life & Work.* 1927. Cambridge. Ills. Ltd. ed. sgn. 2 vol set. $75.00

PECK. *Peck's Condominium of Fun.* 1883. VG $40.00

PECK. *The Art of Fine Baking.* 1961. Simon & Schuster. 320 pp. G $4.50

PECKHAM, Howard. *Narratives of Colonial America, 1704-1765.* 1971. Chicago. Ills. $8.50

PEDEN, Rachel. *Rural Free/A Farmwife's Almanac of Country Living.*1961. New York. Knopf. 382 pp. dj. EX $4.00

PEDEN, Rachel. *Speak to the Earth/Pages from Farm Wife's Journal.*1974. Knopf. Ills. 1st ed. 240 pp. dj. EX $10.00

PEDLER, Margaret. *Distant Dawn.* 1934. $25.00

PEDLER, Margaret. *Kindled Flame.* 1931. $25.00

PEDLER, Margaret. *Not Heaven Itself.* 1941. 1st ed. $25.00

PEDLER, Margaret. *Red Ashes.* 1925. $25.00

PEDLER, Margaret. *The Guarded Halo.* 1929. $25.00

PEDLER, Margaret. *The Hermit of Far End.* 1920. $20.00

PEDLER, Margaret. *The House of Dreams Come True.* 1919. $25.00

PEDLER, Margaret. *The Lamp of Fate.* 1921. $2.00

PEDLER, Margaret. *The Moon Out of Reach.* 1921. $25.00

PEDLER, Margaret. *The Shining Cloud.* 1940. $25.00

PEDLER, Margaret. *The Splendid Folly.* 1921. $25.00

PEDLER, Margaret. *The Vision of Desire.* 1922. $25.00

PEDLER, Margaret. *Tomorrow's Tangle.* 1926. $25.00

PEDLER, Margaret. *Waves of Destiny.* 1924. $25.00

PEDLEY, Katherine Greenleaf. *Moriarty in the Stacks.* 1966. Berkley. Peacock Pr. 1st ed. wrappers. $35.00

PEEBLES, J.M. *Jesus, Myth, Man, or God.* 1870. London. sgn. 108 pp. G $32.00

PEEL, Alfreda Marion. *Witch in the Mill.* 1947. Richmond. Ills. 118 pp. dj. EX $10.00

PEEL, Dorothy C. *My Own Cookery Book.* 1923. London. VG $20.00

PEERS & BRELIS. *Behind the Burma Road.* 1963. Ills. dj. G $7.50

PEERY, Paul. *Chimes & Electronic Carillons.* 1948. EX $45.00

PEFYREFITTE, R. *The Jews.* 1965. London. $10.00

PEGLER, Westbrook. *T'aint Right.* 1936. New York. 1st ed. presentation copy. $15.00

PEIRCE, Benjamin. *A History of Harvard University.* 1833. Cambridge. 159 pp. $45.00

PEIRCE, E.W. *Indian History, Biography & Genealogy.* 1878. N. Abington. G $22.00

PEISSEL. *Great Himalayan Passage.* 1975. 1st ed. dj. EX $12.50

PEISSEL. *Mustang, Forbidden Kingdom.* 1967. New York. 1st ed. dj. VG $20.00

PELLAPRAT, Henry-Paul. *Modern French Culinary Art.* 1966. World Pub. Ills. 1st ed. dj. VG $25.00

PELLEGRINI, Angelo. *The Food-Lovers Garden.* 1970. New York. Knopf. Ills. 2nd printing. $5.00

PELLETIER, A. *Mirage III/5/50.* 1982. Paris. Ills. EX $10.00

PELLETT, Frank. *How to Attract Birds.* 1947. New York. Ills. 156 pp. $2.50

PELLEW, John C. *Acrylic Landscape Painting.* 1968. New York. Ills. 1st Am. ed. dj. EX $10.00

PELLOW, George. *John Jay, American Statesman.* 1900. Boston. Houghton Mifflin. $5.00

PELTZ, George A. *Grandpa's Stories or Home Talks from Wonder Book.* Philadelphia. Hubbard Bros. VG $25.00

PELTZ, Mary Ellis. *Behind the Golden Curtain. Met Opera 1883-1950.* 1950. $10.00

PEMBER, G.H. *Earth's Earliest Ages.* London. (ca.1885) 14th ed. 494 pp. VG $37.50

PEMBERTON, Max. *The Giant's Gate.* 1901. New York. Stokes. 1st ed. VG $12.50

PEMBERTON, Max. *The Phantom Army.* 1898. New York. Appleton. 1st ed. dj. VG $8.50

PENBERTON, Robert L. *A History of Pleasants County, West Virginia.* 1929. St. Marys, WV. 272 pp. $65.00

PENDERGAST, J. *The Origin of Maple Sugar.* 1982. Nat. Mus. Canada. Ills. 79 pp. $6.00

PENDEXTER, Hugh. *Harry Idaho.* 1926. A.L. Burt. 315 pp. VG $4.50

PENDLETON, L. *Alexander H. Stephens.* 1908. 406 pp. $12.50

PENDLETON. *Outlaw Justice.* Graphic. pb. $3.00

PENFIELD, Edward. *Holland Sketches.* 1907. New York. 1st ed. 147 pp. VG $25.00

PENFIELD, Edward. *Spanish Sketches.* 1911. New York. Scribner. Ills. Penfield. VG $35.00

PENFIELD, Wilder & Erickson. *Epilepsy & Cerebral Localization.* 1941. Springfield. 1st ed. 623 pp. $210.00

PENGELLY, J.B. *Blue Book of Style.* 1949. Chicago. inscr. EX $20.00

PENHALLOW, Samuel. *History of Wars of New England & Eastern Indians.* 1969. reprint of 1859 ed. $10.00

PENINGTON, Isaac. *The Works of Isaac Penington.* 1784. London. 3rd ed. 3 vol set. G $50.00

PENKOVSKY, Oleg. *Papers.* 1965. New York. 1st ed. $12.50

PENLAKE, R. *Book of Modern Palestine.* no date. (ca.1915) EX $15.00

PENMAN, Sharon Kay. *The Sunne in Splendour.* 1982. Holt. review copy. dj. VG $20.00

PENNELL, Elizabeth Robins. *Mary Wollstonecraft. Eminent Women Series.* 1885. London. G $25.00

PENNELL, Joseph & Robins, E. *Two Pilgrim's Progress.* 1887. Boston. 18 Ills. 1818 pp. appendix. $22.50

PENNELL, Joseph. *Adventures of an Illustrator.* 1925. Little, Brown. 1st trade ed. VG $45.00

PENNELL, Joseph. *The Graphic Arts.* 1921. Chicago Press. VG $30.00

PENNELL, Mary E. *Good Times with Beverly.* 1933. Ginn. Ills. M. Davis. 178 pp. $3.50

PENNY, M. *Birds of Seychelles & the Outlying Islands.* 1982. London. Collins. Ills.. 160 pp. EX $20.00

PENROSE, Edgar H. *Descriptive Catalogue of Collection of Firearms.* 1949. Melbourne. G $20.00

PENROSE, Evelyn. *Adventure Unlimited, Diviner Travels the World.* 1958. London. Ills. Boissevain. 208 pp. dj. $15.00

PENROSE, H. *Wings Across the World.* 1980. London. Ills. dj. VG $17.50

PENROSE. *The Motor Girls at Camp Surprise.* 1916. Goldsmith. VG $4.50

PENROSE. *The Motor Girls in the Mountains.* 1917. Ills. G $3.50

PENROSE. *The Motor Maids by Palm & Pine.* 1911. Stokes, Donahue. G $3.50

PENTECOST, Hugh. *With Intent to Kill.* 1982. Dodd Mead. 1st ed. dj. VG $10.00

PENZER, N.M. *Nala & Damayanti.* 1926. London. $50.00

PENZER, N.M. *The Harem.* 1965. Philadelphia. Lippincott. dj. VG $20.00

PEOPLE WEEKLY. *The Best of People Weekly, the First Decade.* 1984. Fawcett Columbine. 255 pp. dj. $4.50

PEPITONE, Lena & Stadiem, Wm. *Marilyn Monroe Confidential.* 1979. New York. 1st ed. photos. dj. VG $15.00

PEPLE, Edward. *The Littlest Rebel.* 1935. Dodd Mead. Ills. VG $10.00

PEPLER, Douglas. *The Devil's Devices.* 1915. Ills. Eric Gill. 1st Eng. ed. $225.00

PEPLOW, B. & Peplow, Ed. *Roundup Recipes.* 1951. New York. World. 278 pp. dj. VG $4.00

PEPPER, Charles M. *Everyday Life in Washington.* 1900. New York. Ills. 1st ed. 416 pp. VG $15.00

PERCEVAL. *A Navajo Sketch Book.* 1974. Northland. $10.00

PERCY, Bishop. *Percy's Folio Manuscript, Ballads & Romances.* 1867-8. London. 3 vol set. rebound. VG $65.00

PERCY, Walker. *Lancelot.* 1977. Farrar. 1st ed. dj. VG $20.00

PERCY, Walker. *Lost in the Cosmos.* 1983. New York. Farrar. proof copy. wrappers. $75.00

PERCY, Walker. *Lost in the Cosmos.* 1983. Farrar. Ltd. 1st ed. sgn. slipcase. EX $60.00

PERCY, Walker. *Love in the Ruins.* 1971. Farrar. 1st ed. dj. EX $65.00

PERCY, Walker. *The Last Gentleman.* 1967. London. 1st Eng. ed. dj. VG $75.00

PERCY, Walker. *The Message in the Bottle.* 1975. Farrar. 1st ed. 2nd issue. dj. VG $60.00

PERCY, Walker. *The Movie-Goer.* 1963. London. 1st Eng. ed. dj. VG $95.00

PERCY, Walker. *The Second Coming.* 1980. Farrar. 1st trade ed. dj. VG $25.00

PERCY, Walker. *The Second Coming.* 1980. Franklin Lib. 1st ed. sgn. EX $75.00

PERCY, Walker. *The Second Coming.* 1980. Farrar. Ltd. 1st ed. sgn. slipcase. EX $100.00

PEREIRA, Jonathan, M.D. *Selecta Praescriptis.* 1881. London. 17th ed. revised. VG $25.00

PERELMAN, S.J. *Acres & Pains.* 1947. New York. Reynal. 1st ed. dj. VG $20.00

PERELMAN, S.J. *Listen to the Mockingbird.* 1949. New York. Ills. Hirschfeld. 1st ed. $17.50

PERELMAN, S.J. *Strictly from Hunger.* 1937. Random House. reprint. dj. VG $5.00

PERELMAN, S.J. *The Ill-Tempered Clavichord.* 1953. London. Reinhardt. 1st Eng. ed. dj. $25.00

PERELMAN, S.J. *The Rising Gorge.* 1961. New York. 1st ed. 287 pp. $17.50

PERELMAN, S.J. *The Swiss Family Perelman.* 1950. Simon & Schuster. 1st ed. dj. $25.00

PERGLER, Charles. *Czechoslovak State.* Ltd. ed. 1/500. VG $15.00

PERKERSON, Medora F. *White Columns in Georgia.* 1952. New York. Bonanza. Ills. dj. VG $10.50

PERKIN, R.L. *1st 100 Years, Informal Hist. Denver & Mountains.* 1959. 1st ed. sgn. dj. EX $25.00

PERKINS, Charles Elliott. *The Pinto Horse.* 1960. New York. Ills. Edward Borein. dj. EX $10.00

PERKINS, D.A.W. *History of O'Brien County, Iowa.* 1897. Sioux Falls. Ills. 1st ed. $100.00

PERKINS, Edna Brush. *The White Heart of Mojave.* 1922. New York. Ills. ex-lib. G $15.00

PERKINS, Eleanor Ellis. *Eve Along the Puritans.* 1956. Boston. 1st ed. sgn. dj. VG $16.00

PERKINS, Howard Cecil. *Northern Editorials on Secession.* 1942. New York. 1st ed. 2 vol set. djs. $50.00

PERKINS, Lucy Fitch. *The French Twins.* 1918. Boston. Ills. dj. $10.00

PERKINS, Lucy Fitch. *The Irish Twins.* 1917. Boston. Ills. 1st ed. VG $15.00

PERKINS, Marlin. *My Wild Kingdom, an Autobiography.* 1982. Dutton. Ills. 1st ed. 263 pp. dj. EX $10.00

PERKINS, Maxwell E. *Editor to the Author.* 1979. Scribner. Book of Month Club. 315 pp. $5.00

PERKINS, Samuel. *The World as It Is.* 1839. Belknap. Ills. 5th ed. $25.00

PERKINS & GAREY. *The Mellon Chansonnier.* 1979. New Haven. 2 vol set. EX $60.00

PERKINS & HAGE. *Airplane Performance Stability & Control.* 1960. $8.50

PERKINS. *Annals of the West: Embracing Principle Events.* 1850. St.Louis. 2nd ed. 808 pp. $50.00

PERKINS. *Cowboys of the High Sierra.* 1980. 1st ed. dj. EX $20.00

PERL. *Hunter's Stew & Hangtown Fry/What Pioneer Am. Ate.* 1977. 1st ed. ex-lib. dj. EX $12.50

PERLES, Alfred. *My Friend Henry Miller.* 1956. New York. John Day. 255 pp. dj. VG $15.00

PERLES, Alfred. *Reunion in Big Sur.* 1959. Scorpion Press.Ltd. ed. sgn. dj. VG $75.00

PERLEY, S. *Indian Land Titles of Essex County Massachusetts.* 1912. Salem. Essex Book & Print Club. EX $75.00

PERLMUTTER, A. *Guide to Marine Fishes.* 1961. Bramhall. Ills. 431 pp. dj. EX $15.00

PERMUTT, Cyril. *Collecting Old Cameras.* 1976. DaCapo Press. Ills. 1st ed. VG $20.00

PEROTTI, V.A. *Important Firsts in Missouri Imprints 1808-1858.* 1967. Kansas City. Ltd. ed. 1/500. 21 pls. dj. EX $20.00

PEROWNE, Barry. *Raffles Revisited.* 1974. New York. Harper. 1st ed. dj. EX $35.00

PEROWNE, Barry. *Rogue's Island.* 1950. New York. Morrow. 1st ed. dj. VG $2.00

PERRAULT, Charles. *Tales of Passed Times.* 1922. Ltd. ed. 1/200. sgn. EX $150.00

PERRINS, C. *Birds, Their Life, Their Ways, Their World.* 1976. Abrams. Ills. Cameron. 160 pp. dj. EX $15.00

PERRY, Bela. *Treatment on Human Hair & Its Diseases.* 1859. New Bedford. VG $20.00

PERRY, Bliss. *Emerson Today.* 1931. Princeton U. Press. $10.00

PERRY, Bliss. *Fishing with a Worm.* 1916. 1st ed. sgn. $40.00

PERRY, Bliss. *Pools & Ripples.* 1927. Little, Brown. 1st ed. VG $25.00

PERRY, C. *New England's Buried Treasure.* 1946. New York. Ills. 348 pp. dj. VG $25.00

PERRY, George & Aldridge, A. *The Penguin Book of Comics*. 1967. G $7.00

PERRY, George & Mason, N. *The Victorians, a World Built to Last*. 1974. VG $8.00

PERRY, George Session. *My Granny Van*. 1949. McGraw Hill. 1st ed. sgn. dj. VG $25.00

PERRY, H.D. *Libby Holman: Body & Soul*. 1983. 1st ed. $15.00

PERRY, Hex McCall. *Letters from My Father to My Mother*. 1889. Philadelphia. 1st ed. 147 pp. scarce. $85.00

PERRY, Lawrence. *Our Navy in the War*. 1918. New York. Scribner. Ills. 279 pp. $3.50

PERRY, Paul. *Chines & Electronic Carillons*. 1948. 1st ed. dj. EX $12.00

PERRY, R. *Mountain Wildlife*. 1981. Stackpole. Ills. 1st ed. 179 pp. dj. EX $10.00

PERRY, R. *The Polar Worlds*. 1973. Taplinger. Ills. 1st ed. 316 pp. dj. EX $15.00

PERRY, R. *The World of the Jaguar*. 1970. London. David & Charles. Ills. 168 pp. $25.00

PERRY, R. *Watching Sea Birds*. 1975. Taplinger. Ills. 230 pp. VG $10.00

PERRY & BIAB. *The Binding of Books*. 1940. Peoria. dj. VG $10.00

PERSHING, J.J. *My Experiences in the World War*. 1931. Ills. VG $25.00

PERTWEE, Roland. *Hell's Loose*. 1929. Boston. Houghton Mifflin. 1st ed. dj. $15.00

PERUTZ, Leo. *From Nine to Nine*. 1926. New York. Viking. 1st ed. VG $15.00

PERUTZ, Leo. *The Marquis of Bolibar*. 1927. New York. Viking. 1st ed. dj. EX $25.00

PERUTZ, Leo. *The Master of the Day of Judgement*. 1930. New York. Boni. VG $15.00

PESCE, G. *And No Quarter: Italian Partisans in WW II*. 1972. OH U. Press. 1st Am. ed. dj. VG $10.00

PETAIA, Emil. *As Dream & Shadow*. 1972. Ills. Ltd. ed. 1/1000. dj. EX $45.00

PETERKIN, George W. *Protestant Episcopal Church in West Virginia*. 1902. Ills. 856 pp. $20.00

PETERKIN, Julia. *A Plantation Christmas*. 1934. $6.50

PETERKIN, Julia. *Bright Skin*. 1932. Indianapolis. Bobbs Merrill. 1st ed. dj. EX $40.00

PETERS, A. *Feathers Preferred*. 1951. dj. VG $17.50

PETERS, Dewill C. *The Life & Adventures of Kit Carson*. 1859. New York. Ills. VG $75.00

PETERS, Elizabeth. *Borrower of the Night*. 1974. London. Cassell. 1st Eng. ed. dj. VG $20.00

PETERS, Ellis. *Dead Man's Ransom*. 1984. London. Macmillan. 1st ed. dj. sgn. EX $30.00

PETERS, Ellis. *Devil's Novice*. London. 1st ed. sgn. $25.00

PETERS, Ellis. *Monk's Head*. 1981. Morrow. 1st Am. ed. dj. EX $12.50

PETERS, Ellis. *The Pilgrim of Hate*. 1984. London. Macmillan. 1st ed. sgn. dj. EX $30.00

PETERS, Ellis. *Virgin in the Ice*. 1983. Morrow. 2nd printing. dj. EX $5.00

PETERS, Frazier Forman. *Houses of Stone*. 1936. New York. Ills. 180 pp. sgn. $45.00

PETERS, Fred J. *Clipper Ship Prints by Currier & Ives*. 1930. Antique Bulletin Co. 109 pp. $40.00

PETERS, Fred J. *Sporting Prints by Currier & Ives*. 1930. Antique Bulletin Co. 204 pp. $40.00

PETERS, Harry T. *California on Stone*. 1935. Ltd. 1st ed. 1/501. dj. $325.00

PETERS, Harry T. *California on Stone*. 1976. New York. Arno reprint ed. $100.00

PETERS, Harry T. *Currier & Ives: Printmakers to American People*. 1942. New York. 1st ed. dj. VG $18.00

PETERS, R. *Dance of the Wolves*. 1985. McGraw Hill. Ills. 221 pp. dj. EX $17.50

PETERS, Ralph. *Bravo Romeo*. 1981. Marek. review copy. dj. VG $10.00

PETERS, Stephen. *The Park is Mine*. 1981. Doubleday. 1st ed. dj. VG $10.00

PETERS, Thomas & Waterman, R. *In Search of Excellence*. 1982. VG $2.00

PETERSEN, K. *The Saga of Norwegian Shipping*. 1955. Oslo. Ills. VG $47.50

PETERSEN, William F. *Lincoln-Douglas: Weather as Destiny*. 1943. Springfield. Ills. 1st ed. sgn. EX $12.50

PETERSEN, William J. *Iowa History Reference Guide*. 1952. 192 pp. VG $20.00

PETERSEN, William J. *Steamboating on the Upper Mississippi*. 1937. Iowa. 1st ed. VG $75.00

PETERSEN, William J. *Steamboating on the Upper Mississippi*. 1968. Ills. 1st ed. 576 pp. dj. EX $30.00

PETERSEN. *The Fur Traders & Fur Bearing Animals*. 1914. 1st ed. EX $40.00

PETERSHAM, Maud & Miska. *America's Stamps*. 1947. Macmillan. Ills. 1st ed. dj. VG $25.00

PETERSHAM, Maud & Miska. *Story Book of Gold*. 1935. Philadelphia. Winston. Ills. 1st ed. $10.00

PETERSHAM, Maud & Miska. *The Silver Mace*. 1956. Macmillan. Ills. 1st ed. VG $10.00

PETERSON, Frank Loris. *The Hope of the Race*. 1934. Nashville. 333 pp. $12.50

PETERSON, Harold. *Pageant of the Gun*. 1966. New York. Doubleday. Ills. dj. $6.00

PETERSON, Harold. *Remington Historical Treasury of American Guns*. 1966. New York. Ills. 157 pp. wrappers. VG $5.00

PETERSON, Harold. *The Last of the Mountain Men*. 1969. New York. Scribner. photos. 160 pp. dj. $3.50

PETERSON, M. *Thomas Jefferson: a Profile*. 1968. New York. 3rd ed. $6.50

PETERSON, R.O. *Wolf Ecology & Prey Relationships on Isle Royal*. 1977. Ills. maps. 210 pp. EX $12.50

PETERSON, R.T. *A Field Guide to the Birds*. 1947. $10.00

PETERSON, R.T. *A Field Guide to Western Birds*. 1941. Boston. 1st ed. 240 pp. dj. $18.00

PETERSON, R.T. *Field Guide to Birds of the American West*. 1984. Easton. Ills. maps. 309 pp. EX $25.00

PETERSON, R.T. *Penguins*. 1979. Houghton Mifflin. 238 pp. dj. $20.00

PETERSON, R.T. *The Birds*. 1963. Time Life. Ills. VG $7.50

PETERSON, R.T. *The Junior Book of Birds*. 1939. Boston. Houghton Mifflin. Ills. VG $7.50

PETERSON, R.T. *World Atlas of Birds*. 1974. New York. Ills. 1st ed. dj. EX $25.00

PETERSON, R.T. & Fisher, J. *Wild America*. 1956. Houghton Mifflin. 434 pp. $8.50

PETERSON, R.T. & Fisher, J. *Wild America*. 1955. Houghton Mifflin. 1st ed. $15.00

PETERSON, Robert. *Leaving Taos*. 1981. Harper. 1st ed. dj. VG $10.00

PETERSON. *Guide to U.S. Navy Insignia, Flags, & Decorations*. 1942. Whitman. VG $10.00

PETERSON. *Round Shot & Rammers*. Bonanza. dj. $15.00

PETHERICK. *The Repairing & Restoration of Violins*. 1903. London. 199 pp. $40.00

PETIEVICH, Gerald. *Money Men & One-Shot Deal*. 1981. Harcourt. 1st ed. dj. VG $20.00

PETIEVICH, Gerald. *The Quality of the Informant*. 1985. New York. Arbor House. 1st ed. dj. EX $15.00

PETIEVICH, Gerald. *To Die in Beverly Hills*. 1983. New York. Arbor House. 1st ed. dj. EX $25.00

PETIT, Gaston, & Arboleda, A. *Evolving Techniques in Japanese Woodblock Prints.* 1977. Kodansha. Ills. 175 pp. 1st ed. scarce. $38.00

PETITE, I. *Mister B.* 1963. Doubleday. Ills. 167 pp. dj. VG $6.00

PETRIE, Flinders. *Social Life in Ancient Egypt.* 1923. London. 1st ed. dj. VG $35.00

PETRIE, M. & Hill, R. *Australian Birds.* 1972. Sydney. Golden Press. 1st ed. 109 pp. $7.50

PETRIE, Sidney. *Martinis & Whipped Cream.* 1971. Parker. 268 pp. dj. $7.00

PETRUCCI, Raphael. *Chinese Painters.* 1920. New York. $17.00

PETRY, Ann. *Country Place.* 1947. Boston. 1st ed. dj. EX $20.00

PETTEE, F.M. *The Palgrave Mummy.* 1929. New York. Payson. 1st ed. VG $15.00

PETTENGILL, Samuel B. *Smoke-Screen.* 1940. New York. Southern Pub. 126 pp. EX $30.00

PETTIGREW, Thomas F. *A Profile of the Negro American.* 1964. Princeton, NJ. 250 pp. dj. EX $4.00

PETTINGILL, O.S. & Whitney, N. *Birds of the Black Hills.* 1965. Cornell U. Ills. 139 pp. VG $10.00

PETTUS, Daisy Caden. *The Rosalie Evans Letters from Mexico.* 1926. Indianapolis. Ills. 472 pp. $12.50

PETTY, Lee. *Punch His Ticket.* 1968. Minneapolis. 67 pp. dj. $17.50

PETZAL, D. *Upland Bird & Waterfowl Hunting.* 1975. VG $12.50

PEYTON, Green. *The Face of Texas.* 1961. dj. VG $6.50

PEZET, A. Washington. *Aristokia.* 1919. New York. Century. VG $15.00

PFAFFENBERGER, Clarence J. *Training Your Spaniel.* 1963. New York. photos. 207 pp. EX $5.00

PFEFFER, P. *Asia, a Natural History.* 1968. Random House. Ills. 298 pp. VG $17.50

PFEIFFER, I. *Visit to Iceland & the Scandinavian North.* 1852. London. Ills. 354 pp. $45.00

PFEIFFER, Ida. *A Woman's Journey Around the World.* 1856. London. color pls. VG $25.00

PFEIFFER, J. *The Search for Early Man.* 1963. Am. Heritage. Ills. 1st ed. 151 pp. EX $10.00

PFISTER, Guenter. *Beginning German, a Way to Self-Awareness.* 1985. Stipes. 383 pp. $37.50

PFLIEGER, W. *A Distributional Study of Missouri Fishes.* 1971. KS U. Press. maps. EX $12.50

PHELPS, Elizabeth Stuart. *Chapters from a Life.* 1897. Boston. EX $12.50

PHELPS, Elizabeth Stuart. *Gates Ajar.* 1870. Boston. Ills. VG $20.00

PHELPS, Elizabeth Stuart. *Hedge In.* 1870. Boston. Fields, Osgood. $12.50

PHELPS, Elizabeth Stuart. *The Oath of Allegiance.* 1909. Boston. Houghton Mifflin. 1st ed. dj. $12.50

PHELPS, Lyon William. *Robert Browning, How to Know Him.* 1915. $5.50

PHELPS, R. *Newgate of Connecticut, Its Origins & Early Hist.* 1876. Hartford. EX $27.50

PHELPS, Robert. *Belles Saisons: Collette Scrapbook.* 1978. Farrar. 1st ed. dj. EX $7.50

PHELPS, Robert. *Collette: Earthy Paradise. An Autobiography.* 1966. Farrar. 1st Am. ed. dj. VG $7.50

PHELPS. *Holy Land.* 1864. Ills. G $20.00

PHILBRICK, Herbert A. *I Led Three Lives.* 1952. New York. Grosset & Dunlap. 323 pp. dj. $4.00

PHILIPS, Edith. *The Good Quaker.* 1932. Philadelphia. Ills. ex-lib. 235 pp. VG $3.00

PHILLIP, Allen S. *The Adventures of Remi.* 1935. Rand McNally. Windemere Series. Ills. $11.00

PHILLIPS, Allan. *The Birds of Arizona.* 1964. Tucson. 1st ed. dj. VG $30.00

PHILLIPS, Brad. *The History of Atlas, West Virginia & Vicinity.* 1984. Parsons, WV. Ills. 119 pp. wrappers. EX $8.50

PHILLIPS, C. *Steichen at War.* 1981. Ills. EX $37.50

PHILLIPS, Catherine Coffin. *Cornelius Cole.* 1929. San Francisco. Ills. Ltd. 1st ed. 1/250. $22.50

PHILLIPS, Ethel Calvert. *Peter Peppercorn.* 1939. Boston. Ills. Bischoff. 1st ed. dj. VG $12.50

PHILLIPS, Everett F. *Beekeeping.* 1928. New York. Macmillan. TB. 490 pp. EX $6.00

PHILLIPS, H.I. *Private Purkey in Love & War.* 1942. Ills. G $7.50

PHILLIPS, J. *American Waterfowl.* 1930. G $37.50

PHILLIPS, Jayne Anne. *Fast Lanes.* Ltd. ed. 1/2000. wrappers. VG $20.00

PHILLIPS, Jayne Anne. *Machine Dreams.* 1984. New York. Dutton. 1st ed. dj. EX $25.00

PHILLIPS, John C. *George Washington, Sportsman.* 1928. private print. VG $95.00

PHILLIPS, Josephine E. *Wagons Away! A Social Studies Reader.* 1951. New York. Ills. 182 pp. EX $8.00

PHILLIPS, L. *Story of Iron Horse & Some of Roads It Travelled.* 1965. New York. folio. dj. $20.00

PHILLIPS, LeRoy. *Bibliography of the Writings of Henry James.* 1968. New York. EX $15.00

PHILLIPS, LeRoy. *Bibliography of the Writings of Henry James.* 1930. New York. Coward McCann. Ltd. ed. sgn. $175.00

PHILLIPS, LeRoy. *Bibliography of the Writings of Henry James.* 1906. Boston/NY. Ltd. 1st ed. 1/250. VG $125.00

PHILLIPS, Michael Joseph. *Four Major Visual Poets.* 1980. Indianapolis. Free U. Pr. wrappers. EX $10.00

PHILLIPS, Michael Joseph. *Concrete Poetry.* 1972. Brooklyn. Print Center. wrappers. EX $10.00

PHILLIPS, R. Hart. *The Cuban Dilemma.* 1962. New York. 1st ed. dj. VG $10.00

PHILLIPS, Roland. *Golden Isle.* 1925. New York. Chelsea House. 1st ed. dj. VG $15.00

PHILLIPS, U.B. & Glunt, J.D. *FL Plantation Records from Papers of George Jones.* 1971. New York. reprint 1927 ed. 596 pp. $30.00

PHILLIPS, Ulrich. *Life & Labor in the Old South.* 1929. Boston. Ills. 375 pp. fld map. VG $20.00

PHILLIPS, Van & Owen, Thomas. *The Travelers' Book of Colour Photography.* 1966. London. 256 pp. dj. $7.50

PHILLIPS, W. *Qataban & Sheba: Exploring Ancient Kingdoms.* 1955. England. VG $12.50

PHILLIPS. *Water Babies.* 1900. Rand McNally. VG $32.00

PHILLIPS-BIRT, D. *Fore & Aft Sailing Craft.* 1962. London. Ills. dj. EX $10.00

PHILLPOTTS, Eden & Bennett, A. *Doubloons.* New York. McClure. G $8.50

PHILLPOTTS, Eden. *A Dish of Apples.* London. Hodder & Stoughton. 1st ed. $47.50

PHILLPOTTS, Eden. *Black, White & Brindled.* 1923. New York. Macmillan. 1st ed. VG $30.00

PHILLPOTTS, Eden. *From the Angle of 88.* 1951. London. Hutchinson. 1st ed. dj. EX $15.00

PHILLPOTTS, Eden. *My Devon Year.* 1903. 1st ed. $7.50

PHILLPOTTS, Eden. *The Girl & the Faun.* 1917. Philadelphia. Ills. folio. dj. VG $20.00

PHILPOTT, Gordon M. *Daring Venture/Life Story of Wm. H. Danforth.* 1960. Random House. 1st ed. sgn. dj. VG $8.00

PHIPSON, T.L. *Famous Violinists & Fine Violins.* 1903. London. new ed. $20.00

PHOMEROY, Charles A. *Traditional Crafts of Japan.* 1968. Weatherhill. Ills. 1st ed. dj. rare. EX $75.00

PHYSIOLOGUS. *Ancient Book of Beasts, Plants, & Stones.* 1953. San Francisco. Ills. Ltd. ed. 1/325. dj. $200.00

PIAF, Edith. *The Wheel of Fortune.* 1965. Philadelphia. dj. VG $15.00

PIATT, John James. *The Poems of George D. Prentice.* 1883. Cincinnati. 240 pp. $12.50

PICASSO, Pablo. *Guernica.* 1947. New York. Valentin. 128 pp. 104 pls. $65.00

PICASSO, Pablo. *Lithographs 1945-1948.* 1948. New York. colored frontis. 66 pls. $25.00

PICHON, Baron Jerome. *The Life of Charles Henry Count Hoym.* 1899. Grolier Club. Ills. VG $70.00

PICKER, Martin. *The Chanson Albums of Marguerite of Austria.* 1965. Berkeley. dj. EX $50.00

PICKETT, La Salle Corbell. *What Happened to Me.* 1917. Brentano. Ills. 1st ed. 366 pp. VG $10.00

PICKETT, S. *American National Red Cross.* 1924. New York. EX $10.00

PICKMAN, D.L. *Some Mountain Views.* 1933. Boston. Ills. Ltd. ed. 94 pp. dj. VG $10.00

PICKNEY, Josephine. *Three O'Clock Dinner.* 1945. New York. 1st ed. VG $8.00

PIECZENICK, Steve R. *The Mind Palace.* 1985. New York. Simon & Schuster. proof copy. $40.00

PIECZENICK, Steve R. *The Mind Palace.* 1985. New York. Simon & Schuster. 1st ed. dj. $20.00

PIERCE, Josephine H. *Fire on the Hearth.* 1951. Springfield. Ills. 1st ed. 254 pp. dj. VG $32.50

PIERCE & SCHUON. *John H. Glenn, Astronaut.* 1962. New York. 1st ed. dj. VG $10.00

PIERCE. *Turkey & Armenia.* 1896. VG $12.50

PIERCY, Marge. *To Be of Use.* 1973. Garden City. Doubleday. 1st ed. dj. EX $15.00

PIERCY, Marge. *Vida.* 1979. Summit. 1st ed. ex-lib. dj. EX $12.50

PIERCY, Marge. *Women on the Edge of Time.* 1976. Knopf. 1st ed. dj. VG $20.00

PIERIK, M. *Dramatic & Symbolic Elements in Gregorian Chant.* 1963. New York. dj. EX $10.00

PIERSALL & HIRSHBERG. *Fear Strikes Out.* 1957. Bantam. pb. $2.50

PIERSON, A.T. *Plain Sermons for the People.* 1883. Indianapolis. 257 pp. $15.00

PIGGOTT, Juliet. *Japanese Mythology.* 1983. revised new ed. Ills. dj. EX $50.00

PIJL, L. & Dodson, C.H. *Orchid Flowers, Their Pollination & Evolution.* 1969. Miami U. Press. Ills. 214 pp. dj. VG $17.50

PIKE, D.W. *Secret Societies.* 1939. London. Ills. 152 pp. G $35.00

PIKE, D.W. *The Barren Ground of Northern Canada.* 1917. Dutton. G $45.00

PIKE, D.W. *The Barren Ground of Northern Canada.* 1967. reprint. 300 pp. dj. EX $20.00

PIKE, James. *The New Puritan, Life of Robert Pike.* 1879. New York. inscr. $20.00

PIKE, S.N. *Illustrated Water Divining.* 1946. Toronto. 43 pp. wrappers. $18.00

PIKE, S.N. *Water Divining, Book of Practical Instruction.* 1945. London. Ills. 1st ed. 40 pp. $40.00

PIKE, Z.M. *Pike's Explorations to Sources of the Mississippi.* 1867. 572 pp. G $22.50

PIKROVSKY & GRIGOROVICH. *The Bolshoi.* 1979. New York. VG $26.00

PILCER, Sonia. *Maiden Rites.* 1982. Viking. review copy. dj. VG $15.00

PILKINGTON, A. *A Mirror for the Female Sex.* 1799. $140.00

PINCHOT, G. *Breaking New Ground.* 1947. Harcourt Brace. Ills. 1st ed. 522 pp. dj. VG $20.00

PINCHOT, Gifford. *The Adirondack Spruce.* 1898. New York. 1st ed. VG $30.00

PINCKNEY, Josephine. *My Son & Foe.* 1952. New York. 1st ed. dj. VG $10.00

PINCKNEY, Pauline A. *American Figureheads & Their Carvers.* 1940. New York. Ills. 1st ed. $50.00

PINKERTON, Alan. *Spy of the Rebellion.* 1883. Chicago. Ills. 688 pp. $40.00

PINKERTON, Allan. *Claude Melnotte as a Detective & Other Stories.* 1875. Chicago. Ills. 282 pp. $20.00

PINKERTON, Allan. *Model Town & Detectives.* 1876. 1st ed. VG $75.00

PINKERTON, Frank. *Jim Cummings; or, the Great Adams Express Robbery.* 1887. Chicago. Ills. 162 pp. $20.00

PINKERTON, Katherine. *Cooking Afloat.* 1959. New York. Barrows. Ills. 279 pp. $6.50

PINKERTON, R.E. *The Canoe: Its Selection, Care & Use.* 1959. dj. VG $6.00

PINKEVITCH, Albert P. *The New Education in the Soviet Republic.* 1929. New York. 403 pp. $12.50

PINNEY, Roy. *Wild Animal Pets.* 1959. New York. Golden Press. Ills. G $10.00

PINS, Jacob. *The Japanese Pillar Print.* 1982. Ills. folio. EX $120.00

PIPER, H. Beam. *A Planet for Texans.* Ace. pb. VG $12.50

PIPER, Watty. *Eight Fairy Tales.* 1938. New York. Ills. Eulalie. VG $15.00

PIPER, Watty. *Famous Fairy Tales.* 1933. New York. Ills. Eulalie. VG $30.00

PIPER, Watty. *Stories that Never Grow Old.* 1938. New York. Ills. Hauman. Star ed. VG $35.00

PIPER, Watty. *The Bumper Book.* 1946. Ills. Eulalie. 2nd ed. VG $35.00

PIPER, Watty. *The Little Engine That Could.* 1930. New York. Platt & Munk. Ills. L. Lenski. $5.00

PIPER, Watty. *The Road in Storyland.* 1932. New York. Ills. Holling. Star ed. $35.00

PIPP, E.G. *Men Who Have Made Michigan.* 1938. VG $18.00

PIQUION, Rene. *Manuel de Negritude.* Port Au Prince. 338 pp. wrappers. VG $20.00

PIRANDELLO, Luigi. *Naked Truth.* 1934. New York. Dutton. Ltd. ed. 1/200. VG $22.50

PIRONE, P. *What's New in Gardening.* New York. Hanover House. 254 pp. dj. VG $3.50

PIRTLE. *Life & Times of the American Cowboy.* 1975. Birmingham. 1st ed. color pls. dj. VG $40.00

PITHA WALLA, Maneck. *The Light of Ancient Persia.* 1923. India. 257 pp. VG $25.00

PITMAN, B. *Manual of Phonography.* 1860. Cincinnati. 144 pp. $45.00

PITMAN, Isaac. *The Pilgrim's Progress in Shorthand.* 1876. London. wrappers. scarce. VG $40.00

PITMAN. *A Chinese Wonder Book.* 1919. New York. 12 color pls. VG $20.00

PITOU, Eugene. *Un Hiver en Egypte.* Tours: Mame et Cie. 1860. Ills. $40.00

PITT-TAYLOR, Nora. *All About Dutchie Van Deal.* New York. Cupples & Leon. no date. Ills. $10.00

PITTENGER, William. *Daring & Suffering.* 1864. Philadelphia. Ills. 288 pp. $45.00

PITZ, Henry. *A Treasury of American Book Illustration.* 1947. American Studio. 1st ed. dj. $20.00

PITZ, Henry. *Howard Pyle.* 1974. New York. Bramhall House. VG $20.00

PITZ, Henry. *Illustrating Children's Books.* 1963. New York. Ills. 200 pp. dj. EX $20.00

PITZ, Henry. *The Brandywine Tradition.* 1969. Houghton Mifflin. 1st ed. dj. $30.00

PITZER, Sara. *Whole Grains.* 1981. Charlotte, VT. Garden Way. Ills. 169 pp. $5.00

PIZER, V. *The United States Army.* 1969. Ills. dj. VG $10.00

PIZZEY, G. *A Field Guide to the Birds of Australia.* 1981. Sydney. Collins. Ills. 460 pp. EX $35.00

PLAIDY, Jean. *Beyond the Blue Mountains.* 1947. Appleton Century. 1st ed. $10.00

PLANTE, David. *Difficult Women.* 1983. Gollancz. 1st English ed. dj. VG $15.00

PLANTE, David. *The Family.* NY. Farrar. proof copy. wrappers. EX $30.00

PLANTE, Jaques. *Goaltending.* 1973. Collier. Ills. 110 pp. EX $4.00

PLATH, Iona. *The Decorative Arts of Sweden.* 1948. Scribner. maps. $25.00

PLATH, Sylvia. *Johnny Panic & the Bible of Dreams: Short Stories.* 1979. 1st Am. ed. dj. VG $10.00

PLATH, Sylvia. *Letters Home.* 1975. New York. dj. EX $15.00

PLATH, Sylvia. *The Bell Jar.* 1963. 1st Eng. ed. VG $50.00

PLATH, Sylvia. *The Bell Jar.* 1971. Harper. 1st Am. ed. dj. EX $30.00

PLATH. *Colossus.* New York. 1st ed. dj. EX $55.00

PLATT, Isaac Hull. *Bacon Cryptogram's in Shakespeare & Other Studies.* 1905. Boston. 1st ed. 122 pp. $10.00

PLAUSZEWSKI. *Burgeons at Fleurs en Phototype.* 1898. Paris. 60 pls. folio. $100.00

PLAYER, I. *The White Rhino Saga.* 1973. Stein Day. Ills. 1st Am. ed. 254 pp. dj. $17.50

PLENN, J.H. *Saddle in the Sky, the Lone Star State.* 1940. Indianapolis. 1st ed. VG $25.00

PLIMPTON, George. *The Bogey Man.* 1968. 1st ed. $25.00

PLIMPTON, George. *The Education of Shakespeare.* 1933. London. Oxford U. Pr. Ills. 140 pp. $10.00

PLOMER, William. *A Message in Code, Diary of Richard Rumbold.* 1964. London. dj. VG $10.00

PLOMER, William. *The Case is Altered.* 1932. London. 1st ed. $35.00

PLOTZ, Helen. *Imagination's Other Place-Poems of Science & Math.* 1955. New York. Crowell. Ills. dj. EX $15.00

PLUMB, J.H. *The Horizon Book of the Renaissance.* 1961. Ills. 431 pp. Ex $12.00

PLUMMER, Frank Everett. *Garcia: Social Tragedy.* 1900. Chicago. Ills. VG $50.00

PLUNKET, Robert. *My Search for Warren Harding.* 1983. New York. Knopf. 1st ed. dj. VG $30.00

PLUTARCHUS. *The Lives of the Noble Grecians & Romans.* 1612. London. trans. Knighthead. folio. $550.00

POBLETE, E.O. *Plantas Medicinales De Boliva.* 1969. La Paz. 1st ed. 90 pls. 525 pp. VG $24.00

POCHE, E. *Bohemian Porcelain.* Artia. 1st ed. dj. boxed. $27.50

POCOCK. *Robinson Crusoe.* Garden City. 8 color pls. VG $12.00

PODACH, E.F. *The Madness of Nietzsche.* 1931. London. Ills. 1st English ed. 237 pp. $22.50

POE, Edgar Allan. *Complete Works of Edgar Allan Poe.* 1908. Akron, OH. 10 vol set. VG $45.00

POE, Edgar Allan. *Edgar Allan Poe Letters Till Now Unpublished.* 1925. Ltd. ed. 1/1550. $40.00

POE, Edgar Allan. *Edgar Allan Poe Letters Till Now Unpublished.* 1925. 1st Am. ed. dj. VG $40.00

POE, Edgar Allan. *Edgar Allen Poe's Works in 5 Vols.* 1903. Collier. Raven ed. VG $20.00

POE, Edgar Allan. *Journal of Julius Rodman.* 1947. San Francisco. Colt Press. folio. EX $35.00

POE, Edgar Allan. *Poe.* 1986. New Jersey. Ills. Hildebrandt. 161 pp. EX $17.00

POE, Edgar Allan. *Sonnet to My Mother in Leaflets of Memory.* 1850. Philadelphia. gilt decor. VG $50.00

POE, Edgar Allan. *Tales of Edgar Allan Poe.* 1944. New York. Random House. Ills. 562 pp. EX $5.00

POE, Edgar Allan. *Tales of Mystery & Imagination.* 1933. Tudor. Ills. G $45.00

POE, Edgar Allan. *Tales of Mystery & Imagination.* London/NY. no date. Ills. Ltd. ed. $50.00

POE, Edgar Allan. *Tales of Mystery & Imagination.* 1936. New York. Tudor. Ills. Clarke. 412 pp. $85.00

POE, Edgar Allan. *Tales of Mystery & Immagination.* New York. Brentano. Ills. dj. EX $115.00

POE, Edgar Allan. *Tales of Mystery & Imagination.* 1941. Heritage. Ills. Sharp. $20.00

POE, Edgar Allan. *The Raven.* 1884. Harper. Ills. Dore. 1st ed. VG $195.00

POGANY, Willy. *Adventures of Odysseus & Tale of Troy.* 1918. Macmillan. 1st ed. 254 pp. VG $35.00

POGANY, Willy. *Fairy Flowers.* 1926. Holt. Ills. 1st ed. 196 pp. 15 pls. $45.00

POGANY, Willy. *Parsifal.* 1912. Crowell. 1st ed. 16 color pls. VG $150.00

POGANY, Willy. *Rime of Ancient Mariner.* New York. Doran. (ca.1920) 20 pls. dj. $125.00

POGANY, Willy. *Rubaiyat of Omar Khayyam.* New York. Crowell. no date. 95 pp. EX $40.00

POGANY, Willy. *Rubaiyat of Omar Khayyam.* London. Harrap. no date. $20.00

POGANY, Willy. *Rubaiyat of Omar Khayyam.* 1920. New York. 126 color pls. gilt decor. dj. $85.00

POGANY, Willy. *Rubaiyat of Omar Khayyam.* Crowell. (ca.1935) Ills. dj. VG $15.00

POGANY, Willy. *The Art of Drawing.* 1946. dj. VG $15.00

POGANY, Willy. *Willy Pogany's Mother Goose.* 1928. New York. Nelson. 4th printing. dj. EX $110.00

POGANY, Willy. *Willy Pogany's Oil Painting Lessons.* 1954. New York. Ills. 63 pp. dj. VG $25.00

POGUE, F.C. *George C. Marshall, Education of a General.* 1963. dj. VG $12.50

POHL, F. *Beyond the Blue Event.* 1980. Horizon. 1st ed. dj. EX $15.00

POHL, F. *Early Phol.* 1976. Doubleday. 1st ed. dj. EX $12.50

POHL, F. *Gateway.* 1977. New York. St. Martins. 1st ed. dj. EX $35.00

POHL, F. *Man Plus.* 1976. New York. Random House. 1st ed. dj. EX $50.00

POHL, F. *Midas World.* 1985. Del Rey. 1st ed. sgn. dj. EX $25.00

POHL, F. *Starburst.* 1982. 1st ed. sgn. dj. EX $25.00

POHL, F. & Kornbluth, C.M. *The Space Merchants.* 1953. New York. 1st ed. dj. VG $45.00

POHL, Frederick & Williamson. *Undersea City.* 1958. Hicksville. Gnome. 1st ed. dj. VG $20.00

POHL, Frederick. *Dunkard's Walk.* 1960. New York. Gnome. 1st ed. dj. EX $17.50

POHL, Frederick. *Slave Ship.* 1957. 1st Am. ed. dj. G $20.00

POHL, Frederick. *The Age of the Pussyfoot.* 1969. New York. Trident. 1st ed. dj. EX $25.00

POHL, Frederick. *The Cool War.* 1981. New York. 1st ed. review copy. dj. EX $15.00

POHL, Frederick. *The Cool War.* 1979. Del Ray. 1st ed. dj. EX $15.00

POHL, Frederick. *Uncovering Track of Vikings in America.* 1952. Ills. 1st ed. $7.50

POINSETT, J.R. *Execution of Treaty with the Winnebagoes.* 1839. Washington. 1st ed. 112 pp. $75.00

POINSETT, J.R. *Report from the Secretary of War.* 1838. Washington. Ills. 1st ed. 2 fld maps. $200.00

POITIER, Sidney. *This Life.* 1980. New York. Knopf. 371 pp. dj. EX $6.00

POKROVSKII, M.N. *Russia in World History, Selected Essays.* 1975. dj. EX $10.00

POLEVOI, B. *The Final Reckoning. The Nuremburg Diaries.* 1978. Moscow. Ills. dj. EX $12.50

POLI, F. *Sharks Are Caught at Night.* 1958. Regnery. Ills. 158 pp. dj. EX $10.00

POLIAKOFF, V. *The Tragic Bride.* 1927. Appleton. Ills. 1st ed. 300 pp. $17.50

POLIAKOV, A. *White Mammoths: Russian Tanks in Action.* 1943. New York. Ills. 1st ed. dj. VG $15.00

POLIAKOV, L. *Aryan Myth, Hist. of Racist & Nationalist Ideas.* 1974. New York. 388 pp. $12.50

POLIAKOV, L. *History of Anti-Semitism.* 1973-1976. New York. 3 vol set. $37.50

POLIAKOV, L. & Wulf, J. *El Tercer Reich y Los Judios.* 1960. Barcelona. Spanish text. Ills. G $30.00

POLITI, Leo. *A Boat for Peppe.* 1950. New York. Ills. Politi. 1st ed. dj. VG $20.00

POLITI, Leo. *Mission Bell.* 1953. Scribner. Ills. 1st ed. folio. dj. EX $30.00

POLITI, Leo. *Pedro, the Angel of Olvera Street.* 1946. New York. Scribner. Ills. sgn. $20.00

POLITI, Leo. *Song of the Swallows.* 1949. Scribner. Ills. 1st ed. $35.00

POLK, James K. *Compensation to Generals Cass & Taylor.* 1848. Washington. 1st ed. 233 pp. $40.00

POLK, James K. *Correspondence Between Sec. War & Gen. Scott.* 1848. Washington. 1st ed. 63 pp. $25.00

POLK, Ralph W. *The Practice of Printing.* 1937. Peoria. Ills. G $10.00

POLKINGHORNE, R.K. & M.I.R. *Toy Making in School & Home.* 1921. London. Ills. 299 pp. $22.50

POLLACK, Jack Harrison. *Croiset the Clairvoyant.* 1964. $2.00

POLLARD, A.F. *Factors in American History.* 1925. New York. Macmillan. exlib. $8.00

POLLARD, A.F. *Henry VIII.* 1902. Ills. Foupil & others. folio. $250.00

POLLARD, Alfred W. *Fine Books.* 1964. Cooper Square Pub. $25.00

POLLARD, Edward A. *Life of Jefferson Davis; History of Confederacy.* 1869. National Publishing Co. VG $32.50

POLLARD, Edward A. *Second Year of the War.* 1864. New York Ills. 1st ed. 386 pp. $42.50

POLLARD, Edward A. *Southern History of the Civil War.* 1864. Ills. maps. G $25.00

POLLARD, Edward A. *The Lost Cause. History of War of Confederates.* 1890. Ills. 778 pp. $27.50

POLLARD, Edward A. *The Lost Cause. History of War of Confederates.* 1866. New York. 1st ed. 752 pp. G $40.00

POLLARD, F.E. *War & Human Values. Essay on Immorality of War.* 1953. London. G $6.00

POLLARD, Josephine. *The Boston Tea Party. December, 1773.* 1882. New York. Ills. H.W. McVockar. VG $25.00

POLLARD, Josephine. *The Decorative Sisters.* 1881. New York. Randolph. Ills. Satterlee. VG $18.50

POLLEN, Arthur H. *The British Navy in Battle.* 1919. $10.00

POLLER, W. *Medical Block Buchenwald.* 1965. New York. Ills. $35.00

POLLER, W. *Medical Block Buchenwald.* 1961. New York. Lyle Stuart. Ills. dj. EX $30.00

POLLOK, Robert. *The Course of Time.* 1841. Hartford. Belknap & Hameisley. $40.00

POLMAR, N. *The Ships & Aircraft of the U.S. Fleet.* 1981. Ills. 12th ed. dj. VG $20.00

POLMAR & ALLEN. *Rickover. Controversy & Genius.* 1982. Ills. dj. VG $20.00

POLMAR & FRIEDMAN. *Warships. An Illustrated History.* 1981. EX $12.50

POMEROY, Earl. *In Search of the Golden West.* 1957. Knopf. Ills. 1st ed. 232 pp. dj. VG $10.00

POMEROY, Seth. *The Journals & Papers of Seth Pomeroy.* 1926. New Haven. Ills. 1st ed. $25.00

POMFRET, John E. *California Gold Rush Voyages 1848-1849.* 1954. San Morino, CA. 246 pp. index. $18.50

POMODORO, Giovanni. *Geometria Pattica.* 1903. Rome. 51 full pp pls. VG $425.00

POND, Enoch. *A History of God's Church.* 1875. Hartford, CT. Ills. 1066 pp. $17.50

POND, H. *Salerno, Account of the WWII Battle.* 1974. London. Ills. dj. EX $10.00

POND, William C. *Gospel Pioneering.* 1921. 191 pp. VG $32.50

PONGE, Francis. *Braque, Le Reconciliateur.* 1948. French text. VG $40.00

PONSELLE, Rosa & Drake, James. *Ponselle, a Singer's Life.* 1982. New York. 1st ed. VG $7.50

POOLMAN, Kenneth. *Guns Off Cape Ann.* 1961. Ills. G $15.00

POOLMAN, Kenneth. *Periscope Depth.* 1981. London. Ills. dj. EX $20.00

POOR, Charles Lane. *Men Against the Rule.* 1937. New York. Derrydale Pr. Ltd. ed. EX $100.00

POOR, Henry V. *You & the Law.* 1971. Reader's Digest Book. 863 pp. $5.00

POORE, Ben. *Perley's Reminiscences of 60 Years in Metropolis.* 1886. Philadelphia. 2 vol set. $25.00

POORE, Perley. *Congressional Directory, 42nd Congress 1872.* 1870. Washington. Ills. 1st ed. 128 pp. G $6.50

POOTMAN, F.J. *Secrets of the Animal World.* 1962. Fleet. Ills. 1st Am. ed. 287 pp. VG $4.00

POPE, Alexander. *Pastorals.* 1930. Chelsea. Ltd. ed. 1/100. VG $30.00

POPE, Alexander. *The Dunciad.* 1928. Oxford. Ltd. ed. 1/500. $17.50

POPE, Alexander. *The Rape of the Lock.* 1968. Ills. Beardsley. pb. VG $3.00

POPE, Dudley. *Ramage & the Drum Beat.* 1967. London. 1st ed. dj. VG $25.00

POPE, Frank L. *Modern Practice of the Electric Telegraph.* 1888. New York. Van Nostrand. 160 pp. $3.50

POPE, Franklin. *Evolution of the Electric Incandescent Lamp.* 1889. Elizabeth, NY. Ills. 91 pp. VG $22.50

POPE, Katherine. *Hawaii, Rainbow Land.* 1924. New York. photos. map. VG $15.00

POPE & OTIS. *Elements of Aeronautics.* 1941. Ills. dj. EX $20.00

POPE-HENNESSEY, John. *Essays on Italian Sculpture.* 1968. London. $15.00

POPE-HENNESSEY, John. *Sins of the Fathers.* 1968. Knopf. 1st ed. dj. EX $15.00

POPENOE, Joshua. *Inside Summerhill.* New York. Hart.photos. 112 pp. wrappers. $37.50

PORCHE, Francois. *Charles Baudelaire.* 1928. New York. Ills. 253 pp. dj. VG $10.00

PORTA. *Natural Magick.* 1957. slipcase. VG $25.00

PORTER, Bern. *Happy Rock.* 1945. private print. Ltd. ed. dj. $25.00

PORTER, Eleanor H. *Dawn.* 1919. $20.00

PORTER, Eleanor H. *Just David.* 1916. $20.00

PORTER, Eleanor H. *Miss Billy, Married.* 1918. $25.00

PORTER, Eleanor H. *Oh, Money! Money!* 1918. $20.00

PORTER, Eleanor H. *Pollyanna, the Glad Book.* 1940. Grosset & Dunlap. 310 pp. VG $4.50

PORTER, Eleanor H. *Pollyanna, the Glad Book.* 1943. New York. Grosset & Dunlap. 308 pp. $5.00

PORTER, Eleanor H. *Pollyanna, the Glad Book.* 1913. $25.00

PORTER, Eleanor H. *The Road to Understanding.* 1917. $20.00

PORTER, Eleanor H. *The Story of Margo.* 1911. $25.00

PORTER, Eleanor H. *The Tangled Threads.* 1919. $25.00

PORTER, Eliot & Matthiessen. *Tree Where Man Was Born.* 1972. Dutton. dj. EX $17.50

PORTER, Eliot. *All Under Heaven, the Chinese World.* 1983. 1st ed. $35.00

PORTER, Eliot. *Forever Wild, the Adirondacks.* folio. color photos. $20.00

PORTER, Eliot. *Galapagos.* 1966. Sierra Club. 2 vol set. boxed. EX $95.00

PORTER, Eliot. *In Wilderness Is the Preservation of the World.* 1962. Sierra Club. folio. dj. EX $25.00

PORTER, Eliot. *In Wildness Is Preservation.* 1962. San Francisco. dj. EX $25.00

PORTER, Eliot. *Moments of Discovery, Adventures with Am. Birds.* 1977. Dutton. 1st ed. dj. EX $32.50

PORTER, Eliot. *Summer Island Penobscot.* 1966. Sierra Club. 1st ed. dj. VG $45.00

PORTER, G. *The World of the Frog & Toad.* 1967. Lippincott. Ills. 1st ed. dj. VG $15.00

PORTER, Gene Stratton. *A Daughter of the Land.* 1918. $25.00

PORTER, Gene Stratton. *A Girl of the Limberlost.* 1909. $25.00

PORTER, Gene Stratton. *Freckles.* 1965. $15.00

PORTER, Gene Stratton. *Freckles.* 1904. $25.00

PORTER, Gene Stratton. *Her Father's Daughter.* 1921. Doubleday. VG $20.00

PORTER, Gene Stratton. *Laddie.* 1913. Ills. 1st ed. $12.50

PORTER, Gene Stratton. *Music of the Wild.* 1910. Doubleday Page.1st ed. VG $90.00

PORTER, Gene Stratton. *The Harvester.* 1911. Doubleday. VG $20.00

PORTER, Gene Stratton. *The Harvester.* 1912. $25.00

PORTER, Gene Stratton. *The Keeper of the Bees.* 1925. Doubleday. VG $20.00

PORTER, Horace. *Campaigning with Grant.* 1897. New York. 1st ed. 546 pp. VG $42.50

PORTER, J. *Dover Two.* 1965. New York. 1st ed. dj. EX $12.50

PORTER, Jane. *The Scottish Chiefs.* 1930. New York. Scribner. Ills. Wyeth. 503 pp. $37.50

PORTER, Jane. *The Scottish Chiefs.* 1941. Ills. N.C. Wyeth. G $25.00

PORTER, John Addison. *Sketches of Yale Life.* 1886. Washington. 288 pp. $18.50

PORTER, K. *John Jacob Astor.* 1931. Cambridge. 1st ed. 2 vol set. VG $40.00

PORTER, Katherine Anne. *A Christmas Story.* 1967. Delacorte. Ills. Shahn. 1st ed. dj. VG $17.50

PORTER, Katherine Anne. *A Defense of Circe.* 1954. New York. Ltd. ed. VG $20.00

PORTER, Katherine Anne. *Flowering Judas.* 1930. Harcourt. Ltd. 1st ed. 1/600. VG $100.00

PORTER, Katherine Anne. *Flowering Judas.* 1935. Harcourt. 1st expanded ed. 1st issue. VG $20.00

PORTER, Katherine Anne. *Hacienda.* 1934. Harrison of Paris. 1st ed. EX $125.00

PORTER, Katherine Anne. *Leaning Tower & Other Stories.* 1st ed. EX $65.00

PORTER, Katherine Anne. *Ship of Fools.* 1962. Little, Brown. 1st ed. dj. VG $25.00

PORTER, Katherine Anne. *The Days Before.* 1952. Harcourt. 1st ed. dj. VG $25.00

PORTER, Katherine Anne. *The Leaning Tower.* 1944. New York. Harcourt Brace. dj. VG $25.00

PORTER, Katherine Anne. *The Leaning Tower.* 1944. Harcourt. 1st ed. dj. EX $45.00

PORTER, Katherine Anne. *The Never Ending Wrong.* 1977. Little, Brown. 1st ed. dj. VG $15.00

PORTER, N. *Hist. Discourse Before Citizens of Farmington.* 1841. Hartford. 99 pp. $25.00

PORTER, Robert K. *Travelling Sketches in Russia & Sweden 1805-1808.* 1809. Philadelphia. VG $45.00

PORTER. *The Negro in the United States.* 1970. Ltd. ed. ex-lib. VG $15.00

PORTIS, Charles. *True Grit.* 1968. Simon & Schuster. 1st ed. dj. $10.00

PORTIS, Charles. *True Grit.* 1968. New York. advance copy. wrappers. EX $35.00

PORTLOCK, Nathaniel. *Voyage to North-West Coast of America.* 1789. London. Ills. 1st ed. 6 fld maps. VG $1,000.00

POST, Emily. *Etiquette 'Blue Book of Social Usage.'* 1937. New York. Funk & Wagnalls. photos. 877 pp. $4.00

POST, Emily. *Etiquette 'Blue Book of Social Usage.'* 1960. New York. Funk & Wagnalls. Ills. 671 pp. $5.00

POST, Melville D. *Dwellers in the Hills.* 1901. New York. Putnam. 1st ed. dj. VG $30.00

POST, Melville D. *The Mountain School Teacher.* 1922. New York. Appleton. 1st ed. VG $30.00

POSTGATE, R.W. *The Devil Wilkes.* 1929. New York. 275 pp. index. dj. $10.00

POSTON. *Building a State in Apache Land.* 1963. Aztec Press. 174 pp. EX $4.50

POTOCKI. *Snobbery with Violence.* 1932. London. 1st ed. VG $45.00

POTOK, Chaim. *Davita's Harp.* 1985. Knopf. 1st ed. dj. EX $15.00

POTOK, Chaim. *In the Beginning.* 1975. New York. Knopf. 1st ed. dj. VG $25.00

POTOK, Chaim. *My Name Is Asher Lev.* 1972. New York. Knopf. 1st ed. dj. VG $25.00

POTOK, Chaim. *The Book of Lights.* 1981. New York. Knopf. 1st ed. dj. VG $20.00

POTOK, Chaim. *The Chosen.* 1967. New York. Simon & Schuster. 1st ed. dj. $60.00

POTOK, Chaim. *The Promise.* 1969. proof copy. VG $65.00

POTOK, Chaim. *The Promise.* 1969. New York. Knopf. 1st ed. dj. VG $35.00

POTTER, Beatrix. *Beatrix Potter 1866-1943.* 1966. London. Ills. Centenary Catalog. VG $35.00

POTTER, Beatrix. *Ginger & Pickles.* 1909. London. Ills. 1st ed. 1st issue. $110.00

POTTER, Beatrix. *Letters to Children.* 1966. New York. facsimile Potter vignette. $35.00

POTTER, Beatrix. *Peter Rabbit & the Little Boy.* 1935. New York. Ills. dj. EX $17.50

POTTER, Beatrix. *The Fairy Caravan.* 1929. McKay. Ills. VG $55.00

POTTER, Beatrix. *The Peter Rabbit Story Book.* 1935. New York. Ills. Bess Goe Willis. EX $35.00

POTTER, Beatrix. *The Tale of Benjamin Bunny.* 1904. London. 1st issue color Ills. VG $135.00

POTTER, Beatrix. *The Tale of Jemima Puddle-Duck.* 1908. London. Warne. 1st ed. $100.00

POTTER, Beatrix. *The Tale of Mr. Tod.* 1912. London. Ills. 1st ed. VG $135.00

POTTER, Beatrix. *The Tale of Mrs. Tittlemouse.* 1938. London. Warne. Ills. G $8.50

POTTER, Beatrix. *The Tale of Peter Rabbit.* New York. Ills. $8.50

POTTER, Beatrix. *The Tale of Pigling Bland.* 1913. London. Ills. 1st ed. VG $125.00

POTTER, Beatrix. *The Tale of Tom Kitten.* 1907. London. Ills. 1st ed. VG $95.00

POTTER, Elisha R. *Memoir Concerning French Settlement & Settlers RI.* 1879. Providence. 1st ed. 81 pp. wrappers. $25.00

POTTER, Jeremy. *The Dance of Death.* 1968. New York. Walker. 1st ed. dj. EX $20.00

POTTER, John Deane. *Admiral of the Pacific.* 1965. London. Heinemann. 1st ed. dj. VG $20.00

POTTER, Margaret. *Istar of Babylon.* 1902. New York. 1st ed. VG $30.00

POTTER, Olave Muriel. *The Color of Rome.* 1925. London. Ills. Yoshio Markino. 261 pp. $35.00

POTTLE, Frederick. *Boswell in Holland 1763-1764.* 1952. New York. 1st ed. EX $15.00

POTTLE, Frederick. *Boswell's London Journal 1762-1763.* 1950. McGraw Hill. 1st ed. 370 pp. $12.50

POUCHOT, Francois. *Memoir Upon Late War in North America, 1755-60.* 1866. Roxbury, MA. Ltd. 1st & only in Eng. ed. $600.00

POUGH, R.H. *Audubon Bird Guide, Eastern Land Birds.* 1946. Doubleday. Ills. 1st ed. 312 pp. VG $10.00

POUGH, R.H. *Audubon Water Bird Guide.* 1951. Doubleday. Ills. 352 pp. dj. EX $10.00

POULENC, Francis. *My Friends & Myself.* 1978. London. Ills. 1st Eng. ed. dj. VG $15.00

POULSSON, Emilie. *Finger Plays for Nursery & Kindergarten.* 1893. Boston. Ills. L.J. Bridgman. G $25.00

POUND, Arthur. *Lake Ontario.* 1945. Indianapolis. Ills. 1st ed. 384 pp. dj. $12.50

POUND, Ezra. *A Selection of Poems.* 1940. London. 1st ed. VG $18.00

POUND, Ezra. *Cathay.* 1915. 1st Eng. ed. wrappers. VG $300.00

POUND, Ezra. *Cinco Poesias De Ezra Pound.* 1952. Miami. Ltd. ed. 1/225. wrappers. VG $45.00

POUND, Ezra. *Ezra Pound at Seventy.* 1955. Norfolk. New Directions. pamphlet. EX $35.00

POUND, Ezra. *Ezra Pound in Italy.* 1978. New York. 1st ed. dj. VG $12.50

POURNELL, J. *King David's Space Ship.* 1980. 1st ed. dj. EX $15.00

POUTY, Olive Higgins. *The Star in the Window.* 1918. $25.00

POWDERMAKER, Hortense. *Hollywood, Dream Factory.* 1950. Boston. 1st ed. VG $7.00

POWEL & AYMAR. *The Deck Chair Reader, Anthology for Travellers.* 1947. G $7.50

POWELL, Anthony. *From a View to a Death.* Boston. 1st Am. ed. dj. VG $10.00

POWELL, Anthony. *Hearing Secret Harmonies.* 1975. Little, Brown. 1st Am. ed. dj. EX $15.00

POWELL, Anthony. *Soldier's Art.* 1st Eng. ed. dj. VG $25.00

POWELL, Anthony. *Temporary Kings.* 1973. London. Heinemann. 1st ed. dj. $25.00

POWELL, Anthony. *The Military Philosphers.* 1968. Boston. 1st Am. ed. dj. VG $10.00

POWELL, E. Alexander. *End of the Trail Far West, NM to British Columbia.* 1914. New York. Ills. 1st ed. map. G $20.00

POWELL, E. Alexander. *The Last Home of Mystery.* 1929. Garden City. Ills. $6.00

POWELL, E.A. *Italy at War, & the Allies in the West.* 1919. Ills. G $6.00

POWELL, E.E. *Spinoza & Religion.* 1906. Chicago. 344 pp. index. $7.50

POWELL, G. *The Green Howards, Famous Regiment Series.* 1968. London. Ills. dj. EX $12.50

POWELL, H.M.T. *The Santa Fe Trail to California 1849-1852.* 1981. New York. reprint. Ills. 272 pp. $245.00

POWELL, Hickman. *The Last Paradise.* 1930. New York. 1st ed. G $30.00

POWELL, Horace B. *The Original Has This Signature, W.W. Kellogg.* 1956. Englewood Cliffs, NJ. 358 pp. $6.00

POWELL, John Hare. *Reply to Col. Pickering's Attack on Penn. Farmer.* 1825. Philadelphia. 1st ed. 24 pp. $50.00

POWELL, John Wesley. *Down in Colorado.* 1969. 1st ed. photos. dj. EX $45.00

POWELL, John Wesley. *Report Lands of Arid Region.* 1879. Washington. 2nd ed. wrappers. VG $50.00

POWELL, John Wesley. *5th Annual Report U.S. Geological Survey 1883-84.* 1885. Ills. VG $45.00

POWELL, Lawrence Clark. *Robinson Jeffers.* 1940. Pasadena. San Pasqual Pr. Ltd. ed. VG $20.00

POWELL, Lyman. *Historic Towns of the Western States.* 1901. New York. Putnam. Ills. 1st ed. 702 pp. $20.00

POWELL, Nicholas. *The Drawings of Henry Fuseli.* 1960. London. Faber & Faber. 115 pp. VG $15.00

POWELL, Padgett. *Edisto.* 1983. NY. Farrar. proof copy. wrappers. EX $60.00

POWELL, Padgett. *Edisto.* 1983. NY. Farrar. advance copy. orange wrappers. $60.00

POWELL, Scott. *History of Marshall County from Forest to Field.* 1925. Mounsville, WV. Ills. 334 pp. $60.00

POWELL. *Bookmans Progress.* New York. 1st ed. dj. EX $12.50

POWER, John. *A Handy Book About Books.* 1870. London. 1st ed. $55.00

POWERS, Alfred. *Redwood Country.* 1949. New York. Duell, Sloan & Pearce. 1st ed. $7.00

POWERS, Amos H. *The Powers Family. General Historical Record.* 1884. Chicago. Ills. 199 pp. VG $25.00

POWERS, Grant. *Historical Sketches of Discovery of Coos Country.* 1880. Haverhill, NH. G $40.00

POWERS, J.F. *Prince of Darkness.* 1947. Doubleday. 1st ed. VG $5.00

POWERS, Ron. *Toot-Toot-Tootsie-Good-Bye.* 1981. New York. Delacorte. proof copy. VG $30.00

POWERS, Tim. *Anubis Gates.* London. proof copy. $400.00

POWERS, Tim. *Dinner at Deviant's Palace.* London. 1st ed. $75.00

POWERS, Tim. *Dinner at Deviant's Palace.* London. proof copy. $325.00

POWERS, Tim. *Night Moves.* Ltd. 1st ed. 1/300. Intro Blylock. sgns. $25.00

POWLEY, E.B. *The Naval Side of King William's War 1688-1690.* 1972. Ills. dj. VG $17.50

POWNALL, H. *Some Particulars Relating to the History of Epsom.* 1825. 6 pls. VG $100.00

POWNALL, T. *A Topographical Description of Dominations of U.S.* 1949. Pittsburgh. revised ed. maps. 235 pp. $45.00

POWYS, J.C. *A Glastonbury Romance.* 1932. New York. Ltd. ed. sgn. EX $45.00

POWYS, J.C. *Atlantis.* 1st Eng. ed. dj. EX $65.00

POWYS, Llewelyn. *An Hour on Christianity.* 1930. Philadelphia. 1st ed. $10.00

POWYS, T.E. *Mr. Tasker's Gods.* 1925. London. Chatto & Windus. 1st ed. VG $75.00

POWYS, T.F. *Two Stories.* 1967. Hastings. Ltd. 1st ed. 1/525. $30.00

PRAGNELL, Festus. *The Green Man of Graypec.* 1950. Greenberg Pub. dj. VG $25.00

PRANGE, G.W. *At Dawn We Slept. Untold Story of Pearl Harbor.* 1981. Ills. Maps. VG $20.00

PRANGE, G.W. *Miracle at Midway.* 1982. Ills. maps. EX $17.50

PRASSEL. *Western Peace Officer.* 1972. OK U. Press. dj. VG $15.00

PRATER, S.H. *The Book of Indian Animals.* 1980. Bombay. Ills. 324 pp. dj. EX $35.00

PRATT, A. *The Lore of the Lyrebird.* 1938. Melbourne. Robertson Mullens. revised ed. $20.00

PRATT, Charles. *Here on the Island.* 1974. $7.50

PRATT, Dorothy & Richard. *A Guide to Early American Homes: North & South.* 1956. New York. Bonanza. reprint. 249 pp. $12.50

PRATT, Dorothy & Richard. *A Guide to Early American Homes: North & South.* New York. Bonanza. Ills. 2 vol set. $8.50

PRATT, F. *Civil War in Pictures.* 1955. New York. Ills. each pp. dj. EX $8.00

PRATT, F. *Double in Space.* 1951. Garden City. 1st ed. dj. EX $25.00

PRATT, F. *Studies in American Command.* 1949. 1st ed. dj. VG $15.00

PRATT, F. *The Compact History of the U.S. Navy.* 1967. Ills. 3rd ed. maps. dj. G $10.00

PRATT, F. *The Navy, a History. Story of a Service in Action.* 1941. Ills. G $7.50

PRATT, F. *The Navy's War.* 1944. Ills. maps. G $12.50

PRATT, F. *The U.S. Army. Guide to Its Men & Equipment.* 1942. Ills. David Pattee. G $7.50

PRATT, F. *The Undying Fire.* 1953. New York. 1st ed. dj. EX $15.00

PRATT, F. *The Well of the Unicorn.* 1948. New York. 1st ed. dj. VG $30.00

PRATT, F. & de Camp, L.S. *Land of Unreason.* 1942. New York. 1st ed. dj. VG $65.00

PRATT, Guy A. *Let's Bind a Book.* 1940. Milwaukee. VG $7.50

PRATT, H. *Personal Finances of Abraham Lincoln.* 1943. 198 pp. EX $25.00

PRATT, Julius W. *America's Colonial Experiment.* 1951. New York. 460 pp. $6.00

PRATT, Parley P. *Key to the Science of Theology.* 1891. VG $25.00

PRATT, Richard. *A Treasury of Early American Homes.* 1949. New York. Ills. 136 pp. $12.50

PRATT, Richard. *Houses, History, & People.* 1965. New York. Evans. Ills. 240 pp. dj. $12.50

PRATT, W.M. *The Burning of Chelsea.* 1908. Boston. Ills. 1st ed. 149 pp. $20.00

PRATT, Waldo. *History Music.* 1935. Schirmer. Ills. VG $15.00

PRATT, William A. *The Yachtman & Coaster's Book of Reference.* 1880. Hartford. 110 pp. G $20.00

PRAY, L. *Taxidermy.* 1943. 1st ed. VG $27.50

PREBBLE, John. *Spanish Stirrup & Other Stories.* 1973. dj. $5.50

PREECE, Harold. *Lone Star Man, Ira Aten, Last of Texas Rangers.* 1960. New York. Ills. 256 pp. dj. EX $12.50

PREININGER, Margaret. *Japanese Flower Arrangement for Modern Homes.* 1936. Boston. Ills. dj. VG $75.00

PRENTICE, Harry. *Captured by Apes.* 1888. New York. 1st ed. VG $40.00

PRENTISS, Augustin M. *Civil Air Defense.* 1941. New York. McGraw Hill. 334 pp. $7.50

PRESCOTT, Brad. *Coastal Maine. As I See It.* 1970. Ills. Ltd. ed. sgn. dj. slipcase. VG $40.00

PRESCOTT, Jerome. *Our Favorite Recipes.* (ca.1930) 64 pp. $7.50

PRESCOTT, William H. *A Bibliography of Bookplate Literature.* 1914. Am. Bookplate Soc. Ltd. ed. $85.00

PRESCOTT, William H. *Biographical & Critical Miscellanies.* 1867. Philadelphia. $15.00

PRESCOTT, William H. *Complete Works of William H. Prescott.* Croxley. Ltd. ed. 1/1000. 4 vol set. VG $20.00

PRESCOTT, William H. *Historical Works.* 1904. Philadelphia. Ltd. ed. 1/1000. 22 vol set. $250.00

PRESCOTT, William H. *History of the Conquest of Peru.* 1847. New York. 1st ed. 2 vol set. VG $100.00

PRESCOTT, William H. *History of the Conquest of Peru.* 1848. London. Bentley. 3rd ed. 2 vol set. VG $30.00

PRESSER, J. *Destruction of the Dutch Jews.* 1969. New York. Dutton. Ills. dj. VG $30.00

PRESSLAND. *The Art of the Tin Toy.* 1979. boxed. VG $22.50

PRESTON, A. *Cruisers. An Illustrated History, 1880-1980.* 1980. Ills. maps. dj. EX $17.50

PRESTON, A. *Decisive Battles of the Pacific War.* 1979. Ills. maps. dj. G $17.50

PRESTON, George. *Thomas Wolfe Bibliography.* 1943. New York. 1st ed. 127 pp. index. $75.00

PRESTON, M. *Aunt Dorothy.* 1890. New York. 1st ed. G $10.00

PRESTON, William. *Illustrated Masonry/1st American Improved Edition.* 1804. Portsmouth. 400 pp. $65.00

PREVIN, Dory. *Bog Trotter.* 1st ed. $7.50

PREYER, David C. *Art of the Berlin Galleries.* 1912. Boston. Ills. 1st ed. VG $17.50

PRICE, A. Grenfell. *White Settlers in the Tropics.* 1939. New York. Am. Geographical Soc. 311 pp. $8.00

PRICE, Alfred. *Focke Wulf 190 at War.* 1977. London. Allan. 1st ed. EX $15.00

PRICE, Alfred. *Spitfire at War.* 1974. London. 1st ed. $15.00

PRICE, B. *Into the Unknown.* 1968. Platt Munk. Ills. 306 pp. dj. EX $5.00

PRICE, Carl F. *Wesleyan's First Century.* 1932. Middleton. VG $15.00

PRICE, E. Hoffman. *Far Lands, Other Days.* 1975. Chapel Hill. Carcosa. Ills. G. Evans. sgn. $75.00

PRICE, Eugenia. *Don Juan McQueen.* 1974. Philadelphia. 1st ed. 384 pp. dj. $7.50

PRICE, Frederic Newlin. *The Etchings & Lithos of Arthur B. Davies.* 1929. Mitchell. 1st ed. EX $65.00

PRICE, George F. *Across the Continent with the Fifth Cavalry.* 1883. inscr. $125.00

PRICE, George. *Good Humor Man.* 1940. New York. Farrar & Rinehart. 1st ed. $80.00

PRICE, Irving. *Buying Country Property.* 1972. New York. Harper. Ills. 173 pp. $4.50

PRICE, Margaret Evans. *A Child's Book of Myths.* 1924. Rand McNally. VG $45.00

PRICE, Margaret Evans. *Enchantment Tales for Children.* 1926. Rand McNally. VG $45.00

PRICE, Margaret Evans. *The Betty Fairy Book.* 1915. Rochester. Ills. 1st ed. wrappers. VG $40.00

PRICE, Margaret Evans. *The Land of Nod.* 1916. Rochester. Ills. 1st ed. scarce. VG $40.00

PRICE, Margaret Evans. *The Windy Shore.* 1930. New York. Ills. dj. EX $40.00

PRICE, Reynolds. *A Generous Man.* 1966. Atheneum. 1st ed. dj. $15.00

PRICE, Reynolds. *A Long & Happy Life.* 1962. New York. 1st ed. dj. $90.00

PRICE, Reynolds. *A Palpable God.* New York. 1st Am. ed. dj. EX $10.00

PRICE, Reynolds. *Kate Vaiden.* 1986. NY. Atheneum. proof copy. wrappers. VG $15.00

PRICE, Reynolds. *Lessons Learned.* 1977. Albondocani. Ltd. ed. 1/300. sgn. wrappers. $40.00

PRICE, Reynolds. *Love & Work.* 1968. Atheneum. 1st ed. dj. VG $25.00

PRICE, Reynolds. *Permanent Errors.* 1970. Atheneum. 1st ed. dj. VG $25.00

PRICE, Reynolds. *The Annual Heron.* 1980. Albondocani. Ltd. ed. 1/300. sgn. VG $35.00

PRICE, Reynolds. *The Surface of Earth.* 1975. Atheneum. 1st ed. dj. VG $20.00

PRICE, Richard. *Ladies' Man.* 1978. Boston. 1st ed. sgn. dj. EX $35.00

PRICE, Richard. *The Breaks.* 1983. Simon & Schuster. 1st ed. EX $20.00

PRICE, W.H. *Civil War Handbook.* 1961. Ills. 72 pp. wrappers. G $6.50

PRICE, William B. *Mound Builders, Indians, & Pioneers.* 1956. Parkersburg. Ills. 296 pp. dj. $30.00

PRICHARD, H. Hesketh. *Through the Heart of Patagonia.* 1902. New York. Ills. 346 pp. fld maps. VG $135.00

PRICHARD, Mari & Carpenter, H. *A Thames Companion.* 1975. Oxford. 1st ed. dj. EX $10.00

PRICHARD, Mari & Carpenter, H. *The Last Paradise.* 1930. New York. 1st ed. G $30.00

PRIDEQUX, W.F. *Bibliography of Works of Robert Louis Stevenson.* 1917. London. Hollings. new/revised ed. VG $35.00

PRIEST, C. *Indoctrinaire.* 1970. New York. Harper. 1st Am. ed. dj. EX $20.00

PRIEST, C. *The Affirmation.* 1981. New York. 1st Am. ed. review copy. dj. $15.00

PRIEST, C. *The Glamour.* London. 1st ed. sgn. $22.00

PRIEST, C. *The Space Machine.* London. 1st ed. sgn. $25.00

PRIESTLY, A.F. *Japanese Color Prints.* 1927. 1st ed. 78 pp. dj. $48.00

PRIESTLY, J.B. *Literature & Western Man.* 1960. New York. Book of Month Club. 512 pp. $5.00

PRIESTLY, J.B. *Lost Empires.* 1965. Boston. 364 pp. $3.50

PRIESTLY, J.B. *Margin Released.* 1962. Harper & Row. 1st ed. 236 pp. dj. $52.50

PRIESTMAN, Mabel T. *Handicrafts in the Home.* 1910. London. 75 Ills. G $32.50

PRIME, W.C. *I Go A-Fishing.* 1913. 3rd ed. VG $17.50

PRINCE, J.H. *How Animals Hunt.* 1980. Nelson. Ills. 1st ed. 128 pp. dj. EX $7.50

PRITCHETT, V.S. *Blind Love & Other Stories.* 1969. New York. Random House. 1st ed. $5.00

PRITCHETT, V.S. *New York Proclaimed.* 1965. EX $45.00

PRITTIE. *Story of a Bad Boy.* 1927. Winston. 14 color pls. $10.00

PROBEST, Thomas. *Lost Mines/Buried Treasures of West Bibliography.* 1977. 593 pp. dj. EX $25.00

PROCTER, George. *The Fisherman's Memorial & Record Book.* 1873. Gloucester. Ills. 1st ed. VG $45.00

PROCTOR, A.P. *Sculptor in Buckskin.* 1971. U. of OK Press. 1st ed. boxed. EX $25.00

PROCTOR, P. & Castieau, Wm. *The Modern Dictionary of Arts & Sciences.* (ca. 1780) 4 vol set. G $50.00

PROCTOR. *The Iron Division.* 1919. dj. VG $10.00

PROFIT, Nicholas. *Gardens of Stone.* 1983. Carroll & Graf. review copy. dj. VG $17.50

PROGRESSO. *A Taste of Italy.* 1984. Milwaukee. Ills. dj. VG $5.50

PROKOSCH, Frederic. *Age of Thunder.* 1945. New York. 311 pp. dj. $10.00

PROKOSCH, Frederic. *America, My Wilderness.* 1972. New York. Farrar. 1st ed. dj. VG $25.00

PROKOSCH, Frederic. *The Conspirators.* 1943. Harper. 1st ed. dj. VG $35.00

PROKOSCH, Frederic. *The Seven Sisters.* 1962. New York. Farrar. 1st ed. dj. VG $30.00

PROKOSCH, Frederic. *The Wreck of the Cassandra.* 1966. Farrar. 1st ed. dj. VG $20.00

PROKOSCH, Frederic. *Voices.* 1982. NY. Farrar. proof copy. wrappers. EX $20.00

PRONZINI, Bill. *Blowback.* 1977. New York. Random House. 1st ed. dj. EX $15.00

PRONZINI, Bill. *Masques.* 1981. Arbor House. 1st ed. dj. VG $12.50

PRONZINI. *Bindlestiff.* 1983. 1st Am. ed. dj. VG $15.00

PRONZINI. *Nightshades.* 1984. 1st Am. ed. dj. VG $12.50

PROPERT, J.L. *A History of Miniature Art.* 1887. Macmillan. ex-lib. rebound. $50.00

PROSKE, B.G. *Castilian Sculpture.* 1951. New York. VG $20.00

PROUST, Marcel. *Letters to Antoine Bibesco.* 1953. London. Ltd. 1st ed. 1/500. EX $50.00

PROUST, Marcel. *Remembrance of Things Past.* 1934. New York. Random House. 4 vol set. VG $20.00

PROUT, Ebenezer. *The Orchestra.* 1897. London. Augener. 2 vol set. $100.00

PROUT, William. *An Inquiry of Nature & Treatment of Diabetes, etc.* 1826. Philadelphia. 308 pp. $25.00

PROUTY, Lorenzo. *Fish: Their Habits & Haunts.* 1883. VG $30.00

PROUTY, Olive Higgins. *Bobbie, General Manager.* 1913. EX $10.00

PROUTY, Olive Higgins. *Conflict.* 1927. $25.00

PROUTY, Olive Higgins. *Home Port.* 1947. Boston. Houghton Mifflin. 284 pp. $10.00

PROUTY, Olive Higgins. *Stella Dallas.* 1923. $22.50

PROVENSEN, Alice & Martin. *Golden Treasury of Myths & Legends.* 1959. Golden Press. Ills. 1st ed. 164 pp. dj. VG $20.00

PROVENSEN, Alice & Martin. *The Golden Bible for Children: New Testament.* 1953. New York. Ills. 1st ed. folio. EX $15.50

PROZESKY, O.P.M. *Field Guide to the Birds of Southern Africa.* 1980. London. Collins. Ills. 350 pp. EX $20.00

PRUCHA, F.P. *American Indian Policy in Crisis.* 1976. U. OK Press. 1st ed. dj. EX $10.00

PRUDDEN. *On the Great American Plateau.* 1906. Ills. 1st ed. VG $25.00

PRYDE, Duncan. *Nunaga: Ten Years of Eskimo Life.* 1971. New York. photos. 285 pp. dj. $3.50

PSYCHIC MAGAZINE. *Psychics.* 1972. New York. Harper. 1st ed. 148 pp. dj. EX $10.00

PUCKETT. *Folk Beliefs of the Southern Negro.* 1926. Chapel Hill. Ills. 1st ed. 644 pp. index. $40.00

PUIG, Manuel. *The Buenos Aires Affair.* 1976. Dutton. 1st Am. ed. dj. VG $15.00

PUIG, Manuel. *The Kiss of the Spider Woman.* 1979. Knopf. 1st Am. ed. ex-lib. dj. VG $15.00

PULBROOK, Susan & Gould, R. *The Gracious Art of Flower Arrangement.* 1969. Garden City. Doubleday. Ills. 118 pp. dj. $12.50

PULLEN, J.J. *The 20th Maine, Volunteer Regiment in Civil War.* 1957. Lippincott. Ills. 1st ed. 338 pp. $15.00

PULLEY, K. *Marine Fishes of Australian Waters.* 1974. Melbourne. Lansdowne. Ills. 1st ed. dj. E $17.50

PULLIAM, Eugene. *This Is Arizona.* 1962. Pheonix. Ills. 560 pp. folio. wrappers. $20.00

PULLING, Edward. *Random Reminiscences.* 1973. Oyster Bay. inscr. VG $10.00

PULSE, Charles K. *A Novel of the Ohio River Valley 1818-1862.* 1952. Chicago. 436 pp. rebound. $6.00

PULVER. *Dictionary of Old English Music & Instruments.* 1923. London. Ills. VG $25.00

PUMPELLY, Raphael. *Across America & Asia.* 1870. New York. 2nd ed. EX $50.00

PUNCH. *Punch's History of the Great War.* 1919. Stokes. EX $120.00

PUNSHON, E.R. *Dark is the Clue.* 1955. London. Gollancz. 1st ed. dj. VG $15.00

PUNSHON, E.R. *Helen Passes By.* 1947. London. Gollancz. 1st ed. dj. VG $20.00

PUNSHON, E.R. *Night's Cloak.* 1944. London. Gollancz. 1st ed. dj. VG $20.00

PURCHAS, Samuel. *Purchas/His Pilgrimage; or, Relation of the World.* 1617. London. 3rd ed. 1144 pp. $750.00

PURCHASE, S. *Hakluytus Postmus.* 1905. Maclehose & Sons. 20 vol set. VG $310.00

PURDY, James. *Cabot Wright Begins.* 1964. Farrar. 1st ed. sgn. dj. EX $50.00

PURDY, James. *Dream Places.* 1980. New York. Viking. 1st ed. dj. VG $30.00

PURDY, James. *In a Shallow Grave.* 1975. 1st Am. ed. dj. EX $12.50

PURDY, James. *Mourners Below.* 1981. New York. Viking. 1st ed. dj. VG $25.00

PURDY, James. *Narrow Rooms.* 1978. New York. 1st ed. sgn. dj. EX $50.00

PURDY, James. *Narrow Rooms.* 1980. Black Sheep. 1st Eng. ed. dj. VG $15.00

PURDY, James. *On Glory's Course.* 1984. New York. Viking. 1st ed. dj. VG $20.00

PURDY, James. *The Nephew.* 1960. Farrar. review copy. dj. VG $35.00

PURDY, James. *63: Dream Palace.* 1957. Gollancz. 1st Eng. ed. dj. VG $15.00

PURKAYASTHA, R.P. & Chandra. *Manual of Indian Edible Mushrooms.* 1985. New Delhi. Ills. 1st ed. 267 pp. dj. EX $40.00

PURNELL. *Walt Disney's Bambi.* 1944. Ills. Disney Studio. 1st ed. $20.00

PURRINGTON, B.A. *Saul.* 1940. Bohemian Club. Ills. Camille. Ltd. ed. VG $20.00

PURSER, FAGET & SMITH. *Manned Spacecraft.* 1964. Ills. 500 pp. $22.50

PURVIANCE, Robert. *Narrative of Events Occurring in American Revolution.* 1849. Baltimore. $35.00

PUTNAM, A. *Madami.* 1954. Prentice Hall. Ills. 303 pp. dj. VG $7.50

PUTNAM, Allen. *Biography of Mrs. J.H. Contant.* 1873. Boston. 2nd ed. 322 pp. G $45.00

PUTNAM, Allen. *Witchcraft of New England.* 1880. Boston. 1st ed. 428 pp. $22.50

PUTNAM, G.B. *North Dakota Singing: Anthology of ND Poetry.* 1936. New York. Paebar Co. dj. VG $10.00

PUTNAM, G.H. *A Prisoner of War in Virginia.* 1912. New York. $30.00

PUTNAM, G.H. *Books & Their Makers During the Middle Ages.* 1896 & 1897. Putnam. 2 vol set. $45.00

PUTNAM, George P. *Andree, the Record of a Tragic Adventure.* 1930. New York. $10.00

PUTNAM, George P. *Death Valley & Its Country.* 1946. New York. Duell, Sloan & Pearce. 2nd ed. $10.00

PUTNAM, George P. *Death Valley Handbook.* 1947. New York. 1st ed. map. EX $15.00

PUTNAM, Mary Lowell. *Tragedy of Errors.* 1862. Boston. 1st ed. $15.00

PUTNAM, Samuel P. *400 Years of Freethought.* 1894. New York. Truth Seeker. Ills. 800 pp. VG $75.00

PUTNAM. *Last Flight of Amelia Earhart.* 1937. New York. dj. $15.00

PUZO, Mario. *The Godfather.* 1969. New York. Putman. 448 pp. $4.00

PYLE, Ernie. *Brave Men.* 1944. New York. 466 pp. $5.00

PYLE, Ernie. *Here Is Your War.* 1943. New York. World. 246 pp. VG $4.00

PYLE, Ernie. *Home Country.* 1947. $5.00

PYLE, Ernie. *Home Country.* 1940. New York. Duell Sloane. 472 pp. VG $5.00

PYLE, Ernie. *Last Chapter.* 1946. New York. Holt. 1st ed. 150 pp. VG $10.00

PYLE, Howard & Katherine. *The Wonder Clock.* 1922. New York. $17.50

PYLE, Howard. *Captain Ravenshaw.* 1901. Boston. L.C. Page. Ills. VG $17.50

PYLE, Howard. *Howard Pyle's Book of Pirates.* 1921. Harper. Ills. VG $60.00

PYLE, Howard. *Howard Pyle's Book of the American Spirit.* 1923. NY/London. Ills. Pyle. 1st ed. VG $100.00

PYLE, Howard. *Jack Ballister's Fortunes.* 1942. Ills. Pyle. VG $6.00

PYLE, Howard. *Jack Ballister's Fortunes.* 1895. Century. 14 Ills. 1st ed. scarce $40.00

PYLE, Howard. *Ruby of Kishmoor.* 1908. Harper. 10 color pls. 1st ed. EX $40.00

PYLE, Howard. *The Garden Behind the Moon.* 1895. New York. Scribner. Ills. 1st ed. $100.00

PYLE, Howard. *The Merry Adventures of Robin Hood.* 1929. Scribner. 42 Ills. VG $32.00

PYLE, Howard. *The Merry Adventures of Robin Hood.* 1924. New York. $17.50

PYLE, Howard. *The Story of King Arthur & His Knights.* 1913. Scribner. EX $35.00

PYLE, Howard. *The Story of King Arthur & His Knights.* 1933. Scribner. 44 Ills. Brandywine ed. EX $32.00

PYLE, Howard. *The Story of King Arthur & His Knights.* 1929. New York. Scribner. Ills. $20.00

PYLE, Howard. *The Story of King Arthur & His Knights.* 1904. New York. VG $30.00

PYLE, Howard. *The Story of Lancelot & His Companions.* 1907. New York. 1st ed. VG $50.00

PYLE, Howard. *The Story of Siegfried.* 1911. Scribner. Ills. EX $17.50

PYLE, Howard. *The Story of the Champions of the Round Table.* 1905. New York. Ills. Pyle. 1st ed. VG $85.00

PYLE, Howard. *The Story of the Champions of the Round Table.* 1935. Scribner. 328 Ills. Brandywine ed. VG $40.00

PYLE, Howard. *The Story of the Champions of the Round Table.* 1920. Scribner. VG $30.00

PYLE & WYETH. *The Brandywine Heritage.* 1971. Greenwich, CT. Ills. Pyle & Wyeth. 121 pp. $25.00

PYLE. *Book of the American Spirit.* 1923. Harper. 1st ed. $120.00

PYLE. *Line of Love.* 1905. Harper. 1st ed. 10 color pls. VG $35.00

PYLE. *The Island of Enchantment.* 1905. Harper. 4 color pls. 1st ed. VG $26.00

PYLE. *The Parasite.* 1895. Harper. 4 Ills. 1st ed. EX $35.00

PYM, Barbara. *Crampton Hodnet.* 1985. NY. Dutton. proof copy. wrappers. EX $35.00

PYNCHON, T. *Gravity's Rainbow.* 1973. 1st ed. VG $125.00

PYNCHON, T. *Slow Learner.* 1985. London. Cape. 1st Eng. ed. dj. $25.00

PYNCHON, T. *The Crying of Lot 49.* 1966. Philadelphia. Lippincott. inscr. dj. EX $125.00

PYNCHON, T. *V.* 1966. NY. Modern Lib. 1st ed. dj. EX $25.00

PYNE, W. *On Rustic Figures in Imitation of Chalk.* 1817. London. Ills. G $100.00

PYNE, W.H. *The History of the Royal Residences.* 1819. London. Ills. 3 vol set. G $60.00

PYRNELLE, L. *Miss Li'l Tweety.* 1917. New York. 1st ed. VG $20.00

PYRNELLE. *Diddle, Dumps & Tot.* 1910. New York. VG $20.00

Q

QUAD, M. *Field, Fort, & Fleet.* 1885. Detroit, MI. Ills. 520 pp. $55.00

QUAIFE, M.M. *Absalom Grimes, Confederate Mail Runner.* 1926. Yale U. Press. $32.50

QUAIFE, M.M. *Chicago & the Old North West. 1673-1835.* 1913. 1st ed. 480 pp. $75.00

QUAIFE, M.M. *Kingdom of Saint James.* 1930. Yale U. Press. 1st ed. VG $75.00

QUARLES, B. *The Negro in the Civil War.* 1953. 1st ed. $15.00

QUAYLE, Eric. *Ballantyne the Brave.* 1967. London. Hart Davis. Ills. 1st ed. dj. $15.00

QUAYLE, Eric. *Collector's Book of Books.* New York. 1st ed. dj. $25.00

QUAYLE, Eric. *Collector's Book of Children's Books.* New York. 1st ed. dj. VG $40.00

QUAYLE, Eric. *Collector's Book of Detective Fiction.* 1972. London. Studio Vista. 1st ed. dj. VG $85.00

QUAYLE, W.A. *In God's Out of Doors.* 1902. Cincinnati/NY. 232 pp. VG $15.00

QUAYLE, William A. *The Prairie & the Sea.* 1905. Ills. G $7.50

QUEEN, Ellery. *Cheechako.* 1941. New York. 1st ed. EX $90.00

QUEEN, Ellery. *In the Queen's Parlour.* 1957. London. Gollancz. 1st ed. dj. EX $40.00

QUEEN, Ellery. *Inspector Queen's Own Case.* 1956. New York. Simon & Schuster. 1st ed. dj. $15.00

QUEEN, Ellery. *Japanese Golden Dozen.* 1978. 1st ed. dj. VG $15.00

QUEEN, Ellery. *Napoleons of Mystery.* 1978. 1st ed. dj. EX $12.00

QUEEN, Ellery. *Ten Days' Wonder.* 1948. 1st ed. dj. VG $20.00

QUEEN, Ellery. *The American Gum Mystery.* 1933. New York. 1st ed. G $18.00

QUEEN, Ellery. *The Misadventures of Sherlock Holmes.* 1944. Boston. Little, Brown. 1st ed. dj. EX $25.00

QUEEN, Ellery. *The Player on the Other Side.* 1963. 1st ed. dj. EX $20.00

QUEEN, Ellery. *The Roman Hat Mystery.* 1979. New York. Mysterious Pr. Ltd. ed. dj. EX $85.00

QUEEN, Ellery. *The Scarlet Letters.* 1953. 1st ed. dj. VG $20.00

QUEEN, Ellery. *To the Queen's Taste.* 1946. Little, Brown. 1st ed. dj. $15.00

QUEEN, Ellery. *20th Anniversary Annual.* 1965. New York. Random House. 1st ed. $52.50

QUEEN VICTORIA. *Leaves from Journal of Our Life in the Highlands.* 1868. London. Ills. inscr. folio. $700.00

QUEENY, Edgar M. *Prairie Wings.* 1946. Philadelphia. 1st ed. G $200.00

QUEENY, Edgar M. *Prairie Wings.* 1947. Philadelphia. 2nd ed. EX $235.00

QUEENY, Edgar M. *Prairie Wings.* 1947. Philadelphia. 1st trade ed. VG $115.00

QUEENY, Edgar M. *Prairie Wings.* 1946. Ducks Unlimited. Ills. 256 pp. $85.00

QUEENY, Edgar M. *Prairie Wings.* 1979. Schiffer. Ills. 256 pp. EX $40.00

QUESTER, G.H. *Deterrence Before Hiroshima.* 1966. VG $12.50

QUIARANTE, Jacinto. *Mexican American Artists.* 1973. Austin. sgn. dj. $15.00

QUICK, Herbert. *The Fairview Idea.* 1919. Indianapolis. Bobbs Merrill. 285 pp. $5.00

QUICK, Herbert. *Virginia of the Air Lanes.* 1909. Indianapolis. Bobbs Merrill. 1st ed. dj. VG $30.00

QUIGLEY, Martin, Jr. *Magic Shadows. Story of Origin Motion Pictures.* 1948. GA U. $9.00

QUILLER-COUCH, A. *Adventures in Criticism.* 1925. New York. 1st ed. VG $10.00

QUILLER-COUCH, A. *Lady Good for Nothing.* 1910. London. 1st ed. VG $20.00

QUILLER-COUCH, A. *Lady Good for Nothing.* 1910. London. presentation copy. $20.00

QUILLER-COUCH, A. *The Splendid Spur.* 1927. New York. Doubleday. Ills. VG $3.50

QUINBY, M. *Mysteries of Bee Keeping Explained.* 1865. New York. Judd Co. 348 pp. VG $8.00

QUINCEY, Thomas de. *Confessions of an English Opium Eater.* 1932. Three Sirens Pr. Ills. Chaves. $25.00

QUINCY, J.P. *The Peckster Professorship.* 1888. Boston. Houghton. VG $25.00

QUINN, Edward. *Picasso at Work, an Intimate Photographic Study.* Garden City. folio. dj. VG $50.00

QUINN, Seabury. *Roads.* 1948. Arkham House. Ills. dj. VG $50.00

QUINN, Seabury. *The Phantom Fighter.* 1966. Sauk City. 1st ed. 263 pp. dj. EX $37.50

QUINT, Alonzo. *The Potomac & the Rapidan.* 1864. 1st ed. 407 pp. $37.50

QUINTANILLA, Luis. *All the Brave.* 1939. New York. Modern Age. wrappers. VG $40.00

QUINTON, Robert. *The Strange Adventures of Captain Quinton.* 1912. New York. Christian Herald. 486 pp. $10.00

R

RABINOVITZ, Rubin. *Iris Murdoch.* 1968. Columbia U. review copy. wrappers. VG $10.00

RABY, Peter. *The Stratford Scene 1958-1968.* 1968. Toronto. dj. VG $15.00

RACINE, Louis. *La Religion, Poeme.* 1743. Paris. 1st ed. EX $100.00

RACKHAM, Arthur. *A Christmas Carol.* Lippincott. 1st Am. ed. 12 color pls. VG $125.00

RACKHAM, Arthur. *A Christmas Carol.* 1915. Philadelphia. Lippincott. VG $55.00

RACKHAM, Arthur. *Aesop's Fables.* 1912. Doubleday. 1st Am. ed. 13 color pls. VG $95.00

RACKHAM, Arthur. *Aesop's Fables.* 1912. London. Ills. 1st ed. VG $60.00

RACKHAM, Arthur. *Alice's Adventures in Wonderland.* 1907. Heinemann. 13 color pls. $95.00

RACKHAM, Arthur. *Arthur Rackham's Book of Pictures.* 1927. Heinemann. 44 color pls. EX $195.00

RACKHAM, Arthur. *Compleat Angler.* McKay. 12 color pls. dj. $150.00

RACKHAM, Arthur. *Compleat Angler.* 1931. London. VG $52.00

RACKHAM, Arthur. *Grimm's Fairy Tales.* 1909. London. Ltd. ed. 1/750. sgn. VG $860.00

RACKHAM, Arthur. *Grimm's Fairy Tales.* 1909. Doubleday. 1st Am. ed. 55 color pls. VG $295.00

RACKHAM, Arthur. *Gulliver's Travels.* 1909. Dutton. 1st Am. ed. 12 color pls. $125.00

RACKHAM, Arthur. *Midsummer Night's Dream.* 1908. 1st ed. 40 color pls. $275.00

RACKHAM, Arthur. *Midsummer Night's Dream.* Doubleday. 16 color pls. VG $75.00

RACKHAM, Arthur. *Peer Gynt.* Philadelphia. no date. 1st Am. ed. dj. $115.00

RACKHAM, Arthur. *Peter Pan in Kensington Gardens.* 1929. Scribner. Ills. 126 pp. dj. EX $75.00

RACKHAM, Arthur. *Peter Pan in Kensington Gardens.* 1919. Scribner. 16 color pls. VG $65.00

RACKHAM, Arthur. *Peter Pan in Kensington Gardens.* 1906. London. 1st trade ed. EX $375.00

RACKHAM, Arthur. *Princess Mary's Gift Book.* London. Ills. Dulac/Rackham/others. EX $35.00

RACKHAM, Arthur. *Rhinegold & the Valkyrie.* 1910. Heinemann. 1st ed. 34 color pls. EX $195.00

RACKHAM, Arthur. *Rhinegold & the Valkyrie.* 1910. Doubleday. 34 color pls. VG $150.00

RACKHAM, Arthur. *Rhinegold & the Valkyrie.* 1910. London. Ills. 2nd impression. VG $125.00

RACKHAM, Arthur. *Ring of the Niblung.* 1939. Garden City. 48 color pls. dj. $135.00

RACKHAM, Arthur. *Romance of King Arthur.* 1917. Ills. $20.00

RACKHAM, Arthur. *Siegfried & the Twilight of the Gods.* Ltd. 1st ed. 1/1150. sgn. $600.00

RACKHAM, Arthur. *Siegfried & the Twilight of the Gods.* 1911. 1st ed. 30 color pls. EX $195.00

RACKHAM, Arthur. *Tales from Shakespeare.* 1909. Dent. 12 color pls. VG $145.00

RACKHAM, Arthur. *The Arthur Rackham Fairy Book.* Philadelphia. Lippincott. no date. Ills. $85.00

RACKHAM, Arthur. *The Ingoldsby Legends, Mirth & Marvels.* 1920. London. Heinemann. Ills. 36 pls. $77.50

RACKHAM, Arthur. *The Ingoldsby Legends, Mirth & Marvels.* 1907. New York. 1st Am. trade ed. VG $195.00

RACKHAM, Arthur. *The Sleeping Beauty.* Lippincott. Ltd. ed. 1/625. sgn. EX $475.00

RACKHAM, Arthur. *The Sleeping Beauty.* 1920. Heinemann. VG $75.00

RACKHAM, Arthur. *The Tempest.* 1926. Heinemann. Ltd. ed. sgn. 21 color pls. VG $750.00

RACKHAM, Arthur. *The Wind in the Willows.* 1954. New York. Ills. 12 color pls. dj. VG $25.00

RACKHAM, Arthur. *The Wind in the Willows.* 1940. New York. Ltd. Ed. Club. $600.00

RACKHAM, Arthur. *The Wind in the Willows.* 1940. Heritage House. Ills. 1st ed. slipcase. VG $45.00

RACKHAM, Arthur. *Undine.* 1920. Doubleday. 15 color pls. VG $115.00

RACKHAM, Arthur. *Where the Blue Begins.* 1924. Doubleday. 4 color pls. EX $75.00

RADCLIFF, William. *Fishing from the Earliest Times.* 1921. New York. 478 pp. VG $50.00

RADCLIFFE, Ann. *The Mysteries of Udolpho.* 1803. London. 5th ed. 4 vol set. VG $50.00

RADCLIFFE, Garnett. *The Flower Gang.* 1930. Boston. Houghton Mifflin. 1st ed. dj. $10.00

RADCLIFFE-BROWN, A.R. *The Andaman Islanders.* 1948. Free Press. Ills. 1st Am. ed. 510 pp. VG $22.50

RADDIN, George Gates, Jr. *Caritat & the Genet Episode.* 1953. Dover, N.J. Ltd. 1st ed. 51 pp. $35.00

RADER, Dotson. *Blood Dues.* 1973. Knopf. 1st ed. dj. VG $15.00

RADIN, P. *Indians of South America.* 1942. New York. Ills. 1st ed. 324 pp. dj. VG $25.00

RADIN, P. *Story of the American Indian.* 1937. Murray. VG $12.50

RADOSH, Ronald & Milton, J. *The Rosenberg File: Search for the Truth.* 1983. Holt. proof copy. wrappers. VG $20.00

RADZINOWICZ, Leon. *History of English Criminal Law & Administration.* 1948. Macmillan. 1st ed. 853 pp. dj. $17.50

RADZIWILL, Catherine. *The Last Tzarina.* 1928. Dial Press. Ills. 1st ed. 325 pp. $17.50

RAE, John. *Granny Goose!* 1926. Volland. boxed. VG $22.00

RAE, John. *New Adventures of Alice.* 1917. Volland. 12 color pls. G $30.00

RAEMAKERS, Louis. *America in the War.* 1918. New York. folio. VG $22.50

RAEMAKERS, Louis. *Kultur in Cartoons.* 1917. New York. folio. VG $20.00

RAHT, C.G. *Romance of Davis Mountains & Big Bend County.* 1919. El Paso. 1st ed. map. VG $100.00

RAINE, K. *The Lost Country.* 1st English ed. dj. EX $12.50

RAINE, Kathleen. *David Jones & the Actually Loved & Known.* 1978. Ipswich. Golgonooza Press. 1st ed. sgn. $45.00

RAINES, Howell. *Whiskey Man.* 1977. Viking. proof copy. wrappers. VG $12.50

RAINES, W.M. *A Daughter of the Dons.* 1914. Ills. Hutchison. 320 pp. $4.50

RAINES, W.M. *A Gun for Tom Falcon.* Popular. pb. $3.00

RAINES, W.M. *Gunsight Pass.* 1946. Triangle. dj. $6.50

RAINES, W.M. *Judge Colt.* 1927. New York. Grosset & Dunlap. 268 pp. $6.50

RAINES, W.M. *River Bend Feud.* Popular. pb. $3.00

RAINES, W.M. *The Highgrader.* 1915. Grosset & Dunlap. Ills. $4.50

RAINES, W.M. *The Trail of Danger.* Triangle. dj. $5.00

RAINES, W.M. *The Yukon Trail.* 1917. Houghton Mifflin. Ills. Wolfe. $4.50

RAINES, W.M. *45 Caliber Law.* 1941. Way of Life Series. VG $7.00

RAINSFORD, W. *Land of the Lion*. 1909. G $65.00

RAINWATER, D. *American Silverplate*. 1968. 480 pp. $37.50

RAKOSI, Carl. *Droles de Journal*. 1981. Ltd. ed. 1/150. sgn. EX $50.00

RALEIGH, A.S. *Philosophia Hermetica*. 1916. 1st ed. 127 pp. VG $45.00

RALPH, Julian. *A Prince of Georgia & Other Tales*. 1899. $4.00

RALPH, Julian. *Our Great West*. 1893. New York. Ills. EX $25.00

RALPHSON, G. Harvey. *Boy Scouts Beyond the Arctic Circle*. 1913. $3.00

RALPHSON, G. Harvey. *Boy Scouts in an Airship*. 1912. $3.00

RALPHSON, G. Harvey. *Boy Scouts in Death Valley*. 1914. Donahue. G $4.50

RALPHSON, G. Harvey. *Boy Scouts in the North Sea*. 1914. Donahue. G $3.50

RALPHSON, G. Harvey. *Boy Scouts with the Cossacks*. 1916. Donahue. VG $4.50

RAMADAN, Said. *Islamic Law, Its Scope & Equity*. 1970. no place. 2nd ed. 184 pp. index. $10.00

RAMALEY, R. *Colorado Plant Life*. 1927. CO U. Press. Ills. VG $17.50

RAMBAUD, Alfred. *World's Best Histories Russia, Vol. II*. New York. no date. G $3.00

RAMEE, Louisa de la & Ruskin. *A Dog of Flanders*. 1927. Saalfield. Ills. Burndage. VG $3.50

RAMSAY, David. *History of the Revolution of South Carolina*. 1785. Trenton. 1st ed. 5 fld maps. 2 vol set. $1,175.00

RAMSAY, David. *Life of George Washington*. 1807. VG $75.00

RAMSAY, Dean. *Reminiscences of Scottish Life & Character*. no date. Ills. H. Kerr. VG $35.00

RAMSAY. *American Potters & Pottery*. 1939. $9.00

RAMSBOTTOM, J. *Mushrooms & Toadstools*. 1959. London. Collins. Ills. 306 pp. G $12.50

RAMSDEN, Lewis. *The Temple of Fire*. London. Collins. 1st ed. VG $40.00

RAMSEY, Alexander. *Message of Govenor of MN to Legislative Assembly*. 1851. St.Paul. 1st ed. 15 pp. $150.00

RAMSEY, Frederic, Jr. *Been Here & Gone*. 1960. Rutgers. 1st ed. sgn. dj. EX $20.00

RAMSEY, L.G. *The Complete Encyclopedia of Antiques*. 1952. dj. VG $15.00

RAND, A. *Atlas Shrugged*. 1957. New York. 1st ed. 1168 pp. VG $35.00

RAND, Austin L. *American Water & Game Birds*. 1956. Dutton. Ills. 1st ed. 239 pp. EX $15.00

RAND, E.S. *Bulbs*. 1866. Ills. 1st ed. 306 pp. $15.00

RAND, Frank Prentice. *Wordsworth's Mariner Brother*. 1966. $9.50

RANDALL, Bob. *The Calling*. 1981. Simon & Schuster. review copy. $10.00

RANDALL, Bruce. *The Barbell Way to Physical Fitness*. 1970. Doubleday. 147 pp. G $37.50

RANDALL, D.A. *Handwriting of God in Egypt, Sinai, & Holy Land*. 1867. Philadelphia. Ills. 355 pp. VG $32.50

RANDALL, Homer. *Army Boys in the Big Drive*. 1919. $4.00

RANDALL, John. *Landscape & the Looking Glass/W. Cather's Search*. 1960. Houghton Mifflin. 1st ed. dj. $10.00

RANDALL, Randolph C. *James Hall, Spokesman for the New West*. 1964. Ohio State Pr. dj. VG $11.00

RANDALL, Ruth P. *Mary Lincoln: Biography of a Marriage*. 1953. Boston. Little, Brown. 399 pp. EX $4.00

RANDALPH, J. *Texas Brags*. 1950. 1st ed. VG $7.00

RANDEL, William Pierce. *Centennial: American Life in 1876*. 1969. dj. EX $10.00

RANDOLPH, Edmund. *Hell Among the Yearlings*. 1955. New York. 1st ed. dj. VG $15.00

RANDOLPH, Edmund. *Hell Among the Yearlings*. 1978. Chicago. Lakeside Classic. EX $10.00

RANDOLPH, J. *Marsmen in Burma*. 1946. Huston. Ltd. 1st ed. sgn. VG $95.00

RANDOLPH, John W. *The World of 'Wood, Field, & Stream.'* 1962. New York. 177 pp. dj. EX $4.00

RANDOLPH, Mary. *The Virginia Housewife*. 1836. Baltimore. $125.00

RANDOLPH, Paschal Beverly. *After Death, Disembodiment of Man*. 1866. 4th revised ed. 260 pp. VG $55.00

RANDOLPH, Paschal Beverly. *Eulis, History of Love*. 1906. 4th ed. 221 pp. G $65.00

RANDOLPH, Vance. *Ozark Mountain Folks*. 1932. Vanguard. Ltd. ed. 1/250. sgn. dj. $25.00

RANDOLPH, Vance. *Sticks in the Knapsack & Other Ozark Folk Tales*. 1958. Columbia U. Pr. Ills. Glen Rounds. dj. VG $16.00

RANDOLPH. *British Travellers Among the Southern Indians*. 1973. OK U. Press. dj. VG $20.00

RANDOM HOUSE, INC. *A Treasury of Stephen Foster*. 1946. New York. Random House. Ills. 222 pp. VG $3.50

RANHOFER, Charles. *The Epicurean*. 1920. Chicago. G $95.00

RANKIN, Claire. *The Tall Voyagers*. 1965. $7.50

RANKIN, Hugh F. *Narratives of the American Revolution*. 1976. Chicago. Ills. $8.50

RANSOM, Arthur. *Big Six*. 1941. Ills. 1st ed. VG $12.50

RANSOM, Arthur. *Missee Lee*. 1942. Ills. 1st ed. VG $12.50

RANSOM, Arthur. *Secret Water*. 1940. Ills. 1st ed. VG $12.50

RANSOM, Elmer. *Fishing's Just Luck*. 1945. 1st ed. VG $12.50

RANSOM, J.C. *The World's Body*. 1938. New York. 1st ed. dj. EX $50.00

RANSOM, John Crowe. *Chills & Fever*. 1924. New York. 1st ed. dj. VG $100.00

RANSOME, Arthur. *Aladdin in Rhyme*. Ills. Mackenzie. 1st trade ed. $125.00

RAPER, A.F. *Tragedy of Lynching*. 1933. Chapel Hill. 1st ed. $20.00

RAPHAEL, A. *Goethe & the Philosophers Stone*. 1965. New York. 273 pp. 9 pls. dj. $17.00

RAPOPORT, A. *The Navy League of the United States, a History*. 1962. VG $12.50

RAPPORT, Leonard & Northwood. *Rendezvous with Destiny/History of 101st Airborne*. 1948. Washington. Ills. 1st ed. 810 pp. VG $20.00

RAPPORT & SCHARTLE. *America Remembers*. 1956. New York. Hanover House. 669 pp. $5.00

RASCOE, B. & Conklin, G. *The Smart Set Anthology*. 1934. New York. Reynal & Hitchcock. 844 pp. $10.00

RASCOE, B. & Conklin, G. *We Were Interrupted*. 1947. Doubleday. 342 pp. $4.00

RASCOE, Burton. *An American Reader*. 1938. Chicago. 1029 pp. dj. VG $20.00

RASCOE, Burton. *Belle Starr*. 1941. 1st ed. 340 pp. $13.50

RASCOE, ed. *The Treasure Album of Pancho Villa*. 1962. Toyahvale, TX. 126 pp. 90 photos. SftCvr. $25.00

RASHLEIGH, Ralph. *Adventures of Ralph Rashleigh*. 1929. London. Ills. 349 pp. $27.50

RASKIN, Saul. *Genesis*. 1944. 1st ed. VG $25.00

RASKIN, Saul. *Haggadah*. 1941. 1st ed. VG $25.00

RASKIN, Saul. *Pirka Aboth*. 1940. 1st ed. $25.00

RASMUSSEN, Knud. *Across Arctic America*. 1927. New York. 1st ed. VG $75.00

RASOR, E.L. *Reform in Royal Navy, Social Hist. of Lower Deck*. 1976. EX $17.50

RASTELL, John. *The Four Elements.* 1971. Cambridge. Ltd. ed. 1/500. EX $25.00

RATAJ, K. & Zukal, R. *Aquarium Fishes & Plants.* 1971. Spring. Ills. 132 pp. dj. EX $5.00

RATCHFORD, Fannie E. *A Review of Reviews.* 1946. U. of Texas. Ills. 1st ed. sgn. wrappers. $60.00

RATCHFORD, Fannie E. *Certain Nineteenth Century Forgeries.* 1946. U. of Texas. 57 pp. wrappers. VG $40.00

RATCHFORD, Fannie E. *Letters of Thomas J. Wise to John Henry Wrenn.* 1944. New York. Knopf. Ills. 1st ed. VG $35.00

RATCLIFF, Rosemary. *Refurbishing Antiques.* 1971. dj. VG $4.00

RATCLIFFE, Dorothy Una. *South African Summer.* London. (ca.1920's) Ills. map. dj. VG $20.00

RATH, E.J. *The Sixth Speed.* 1908. New York. Moffat. 1st ed. VG $10.00

RATHBONE, Basil. *In & Out of Character.* 1962. Doubleday. 1st ed. dj. VG $32.50

RATHBONE, St. George. *A Goddess of Africa.* 1897. New York. Hobart. VG $25.00

RATHBONE, St. George. *The House Boat Boys.* 1912. Donahue. VG $4.50

RATHBONE & TARPLEY. *Fabrics & Dress.* 1931. Houghton Mifflin. 430 pp. $4.50

RATHBONE. *The Young Fur Takers.* 1912. Donahue. EX $6.50

RATHBUN, M.J. *Crustaceans.* 1910. Smithsonian. Ills. 337 pp. EX $45.00

RATHBUN, M.J. *The Oxystomatous & Allied Crabs of America.* 1937. Smithsonian. Ills. 278 pp. VG $25.00

RATIGAN, W. *Great Lakes Shipwrecks & Survivals.* 1974. revised ed. dj. EX $10.00

RATTRAY, Mrs. M.E. *Sweetmeat Making at Home.* 1908. London. 3rd ed. VG $20.00

RAUCH, Earl. *Dirty Pictures from the Prom.* 1969. Doubleday. 1st ed. dj. $2.50

RAUCH, John H. *Intramural Interment in Polulous Cities.* 1866. Chicago. 68 pp. $75.00

RAULET, Sylvie. *Art Deco Jewelry.* 1985. 1st ed. photos. dj. EX $85.00

RAUSA, R. *The Blue Angels.* 1979. Ills. EX $12.50

RAUSHENBUSH, S. & J. *War Madness. Anti-War Essay.* 1937. G $6.00

RAVEN, Anthony. *The Occult Lovecraft.* 1975. Saddle River. Ltd. ed. 1/900. EX $175.00

RAVEN, Simon. *Boys Will Be Boys.* 1963. London. 1st ed. dj. VG $20.00

RAVENAL, E.C. *Peace with China? U.S. Decisions for Asia.* 1971. dj. EX $7.50

RAVITZ, Abe. *Clarence Darrow & the American Literary Tradition.* 1962. Western Reserve U. 1st ed. dj. $10.00

RAVOUX, Monsignor Augustin. *Reminiscences, Memoirs, & Lectures of Ravoux.* 1890. St. Paul. 1st ed. 223 pp. $150.00

RAWLINGS, Alfred & Hogg, W. *A Book of Sundials.* 1922. London. Foulis Pub. new ed. EX $35.00

RAWLINGS, J. *Fighter Squadrons of the R.A.F. & Their Aircraft.* 1969. London. MacDonald. 1st ed. EX $25.00

RAWLINGS, J. *Pictorial History of Fleet Air Arm.* 1974. London. Allan. 2nd ed. EX $10.00

RAWLINGS, J. *100 Studies of Figure.* 1951. New York. dj. EX $12.50

RAWLINGS, Marjorie K. *Cross Creek Cookery.* 1942. New York. Scribner. Ills. Camp. VG $15.00

RAWLINGS, Marjorie K. *The Yearling.* 1938. New York. Scribner. 428 pp. dj. $7.50

RAWLINSON, George. *History of Ancient Egypt.* 1882. 2 vol set. $25.00

RAWNSLEY & WRIGHT. *Night Fighter.* 1957. pb. G $3.00

RAWSON, Philip. *Erotic Art of the East.* 1968. Prometheus. dj. EX $20.00

RAWSON. *Candleday Art.* 1938. New York. 1st ed. dj. EX $27.50

RAY, C. & Ciampi, E. *Underwater Guide to Marine Life.* 1956. Barnes. Ills. 338 pp. dj. VG $10.00

RAY, Dorothy. *Eskimo Art/Tradition & Innovation in North Alaska.* 1977. U. of Washington. $12.00

RAY, Ginger. *The Bending Cross.* 1949. Rutgers. VG $10.00

RAY, Gordon N. *The Letters & Private Papers of Wm. M. Thackeray.* 1945. Harvard. Ills. 4 vol set. $55.00

RAY, Joseph. *Key to Ray's Algebra.* 1852. New York. Hinkle. 343 pp. $6.50

RAY, M. *Self-Portrait.* 1963. Boston. Ills. 1st ed. 402 pp. $55.00

RAY, Michele. *Two Shores of Hell.* 1968. New York. Ills. 217 pp. dj. VG $15.00

RAYMOND, Alex. *Flash Gordon in the Caverns of Mongo.* 1936. New York. Grosset & Dunlap. 1st ed. dj. $125.00

RAYMOND, Edward. *Sights & Scenes of World, Photographic Portfolio.* 1894. Chicago. 328 pp. G $125.00

RAYMOND, Harry. *The Ingrams Shall Not Die!* 1948. New York. Daily Worker. Ills. wrappers. $15.00

RAYMOND, J. *Power at the Pentagon.* 1964. G $10.00

RAYMOND, James F. *The Lost Colony.* 1891. Philadelphia. Petersen. 1st ed. VG $40.00

RAYMOND, P.E. *Prehistoric Life.* 1939. Harvard. Ills. 324 pp. VG $17.50

RAYMOND. *Stephen Crane.* 1923. Ltd. ed. 1/250. $50.00

RAYNAL, Abbe. *Philosophical & Political History of East Indies.* London. Cadell. 1st ed. 4 vol set. $200.00

RAYNAL, Abbe. *The Revolution in America.* 1792. New York. original leather. G $30.00

RAYNAL. *History of Modern Painting: Picasso to Surrealism.* 1950. Albert Skira. boxed. $50.00

RAYNAL. *Peintres du XX Siecle.* 1947. $44.00

READ, D. *Barefoot over the Serengetti.* 1979. London. Cassell. Ills. 1st ed. dj. EX $12.50

READ, George H. *The Last Cruise of the Saginaw.* 1912. Boston. Ltd. ed. 1/150. VG $30.00

READ, Herbert. *Art Now.* 1936. London. Ills. revised ed. EX $15.00

READ, Herbert. *The Art of Sculpture.* 1956. New York. dj. $12.50

READ, K. *The High Valley.* 1965. Scribner. Ills. 266 pp. dj. EX $12.50

READ, Miss. *Village Christmas.* 2nd ed. VG $12.00

READ, Piers Paul. *Alive, the Story of the Andes Survivors.* 1974. New York. Lippincott. photos. 352 pp. $4.00

READ, Susannah. *Needleworkers Constant Companion.* 1978. New York. Ills. VG $30.00

READ, Thomas Buchanan. *The Wagoner of the Alleghenies.* 1863. Philadelphia. 276 pp. $12.50

READE, B. *Aubrey Beardsley.* 1967. New York. Viking. $25.00

READE, Charles. *The Cloister & the Hearth.* 1893. Ills. Johnson Harper. 2 vol set. $12.50

READE, Charles. *The Cloister & the Hearth.* 1926. London. Harrap. Ills. E. Paul. 706 pp. $5.00

READE, T.B. *Female Poets of America.* 1864. Butler & Co. VG $40.00

READER'S DIGEST BOOKS. *Great Events of the 20th Century.* 1977. Ills. 543 pp. $5.00

READER'S DIGEST BOOKS. *Great True Stories of Crime, Mystery, & Detection.* 1965. 576 pp. $4.50

READER'S DIGEST BOOKS. *Strange Stories, Amazing Facts.* 1976. Ills. 608 pp. dj. $5.00

REAGAN, Ronald. *Where's the Rest of Me.* 1962. Pearce. 1st ed. dj. VG $17.50

REAGAN. *Notes on the Indians of Fort Apache Region.* 1930. 64 pp. SftCvr. $10.00

REAGE, Pauline. *Return to the Chateau.* 1971. Grove, NY. 1st ed. 100 pp. dj. $50.00

REAMY, Tom. *Blind Voices.* 1979. 1st Am. ed. dj. EX $25.00

REAMY, Tom. *San Diego Lightfoot Sue.* 1979. 1st ed. dj. EX $30.00

REARDON, M. & M. *Zululand, a Wildlife Heritage.* 1984. Cape Town. Struik. 1st ed. 159 pp. dj. EX $20.00

REARDON-ANDERSON, J. *Yenan & the Great Powers.* 1980. $12.50

REATH, Nancy & Sachs, Eleanor. *Persian Textiles.* 1937. New Haven. Ltd. ed. 1/500. 133 pp. VG $37.50

REAVES. *Air Pilots Register 1935.* 1935. New York. wrappers $25.00

REAVIS, Logan Uriah. *St. Louis: Future Great City of the World.* 1875. St. Louis. Ills. $75.00

REBOLD, Emmanuel. *A General History of Freemasonry in Europe.* 1868. Cincinnati. Am. Masonry Pub. 432 pp. G $20.00

REBOUX, Michel. *Sputnik: Exploration De I'Infini.* 1957. Paris. 1st ed. photos. wrappers. EX $15.00

RECHY, John. *The Sexual Outlaw.* 1977. Grove. 1st ed. dj. VG $15.00

RECLUS, Armand. *Panama & Darien: Voyages d'Exploration.* 1881. Paris. Ills. 1st ed. map. wrappers. $75.00

RECLUSE, E. *The Earth & Its Inhabitants-Southwestern Asia.* 1891. Appleton. Ills. maps. 504 pp. VG $30.00

RECTOR, George. *A la Rector.* 1933. New York. 1st ed. sgn. VG $15.00

RECTOR, George. *The Girls from Rectors.* 1927. $10.00

RED FOX. *The Memoirs of the Chief Red Fox.* 1971. New York. Ills. 176 pp. $3.00

REDDING, J. Saunders. *No Day of Triumph.* 1942. New York. Harper. 716 pp. $3.50

REDDING, J.M. & Leyshon, H.I. *Skyways to Berlin.* 1943. Indianapolis. $20.00

REDDING, M. Wolcott. *Masonic Antiquities of the Orient Unveiled.* 1878. New York. Ills. 403 pp. $20.00

REDDING, M. Wolcott. *Scarlet Book of Free Masonry.* 1888. New York. Redding. 1st ed. 458 pp. G $35.00

REDEMANN, H. *Die Fliegenden Verbande der Lufwaffe 1856-1982.* 1983. Stuttgart. Ills. dj. EX $27.50

REDFORD, P. *Raccoons & Eagles, Two Views of American Wildlife.* 1965. Dutton. Ills. 1st ed. 254 pp. dj. EX $7.50

REDGROVE, H.S. *Alchemy, Ancient & Modern.* 1922. 2nd revised ed. $15.00

REDPATH, James. *The Public Life of Capt. John Brown.* 1860. Boston. G $25.00

REDWAY, J & Winman, R. *Natural Elementary Geography.* 1915. Ills. 140 pp. $4.50

REECE, Maynard. *The Waterfowl Art of Maynard Reece.* 1985. Abrams. Ills. 179 pp. dj. EX $45.00

REED, A. *C-130 Hercules, Modern Combat Aircraft.* 1984. London. Ills. dj. EX $12.50

REED, A. *F-14 Tomcat, History of a Modern Fighter Plane.* 1978. Ills. dj. VG $10.00

REED, Alma. *The Mexican Muralists.* 1960. Crown. 1st ed. dj. $20.00

REED, Andrew. *Rolls Plumbe: Authentic Memoir of a Child.* Am. Tract Soc. (ca.1857) VG $10.00

REED, Arthur & Beamont, R. *Typhoon & Tempest at War.* 1974. London. Allan. 1st ed. EX $15.00

REED, C.K. & Reed, C.A. *Guide to Taxidermy.* 1914. VG $27.50

REED, C.K. & Reed, C.A. *Guide to Taxidermy.* 1908. Doubleday Page. Ills. 304 pp. G $10.00

REED, Chester A. *Bird Guide/Land Birds East of the Rockies.* 1916. New York. Doubleday. 229 pp. $5.00

REED, Earl H. *Silver Arrow & Other Romances of Dune Country.* 1926. Chicago. 1st ed. sgn. VG $25.00

REED, Earl H. *Sketches in Duneland.* 1918. Ills. 1st ed. 281 pp. $25.00

REED, Earl H. *Sketches in Jacobia.* 1919. private printed. G $40.00

REED, Earl H. *The Voice of the Dunes & Other Etchings.* 1913. 1st ed. inscr. G $85.00

REED, Ishmael. *Flight to Canada.* 1976. New York. Random House. 1st ed. dj. EX $30.00

REED, Ishmael. *The Last Days of Louisiana Red.* 1974. Random House. 1st ed. dj. VG $17.50

REED, Ishmael. *The Terrible Twos.* New York. 1st Am. ed. dj. EX $10.00

REED, Ishmael. *Yellow Back Radio Broke Down.* 1969. Doubleday. 1st ed. dj. VG $25.00

REED, Kit. *Fort Privilege.* 1985. Garden City. 1st ed. dj. VG $8.00

REED, Louis. *Burning Springs.* 1985. Huntington, WV. Ills. 275 pp. wrappers. EX $10.00

REED, Myrtle. *Flowers of the Dusk.* 1910. Putnam. 341 pp. $27.00

REED, Opie. *An Arkansas Planter.* 1896. Rand McNally. $25.00

REED, Parker McCobb. *History of the Lower Kennebec, 1602-1889.* 1889. Bath. 1st ed. 72 pp. wrappers. $35.00

REED, Stanley. *All Color Book of Oriental Carpets & Rugs.* 1972. Octopus Books. 72 pp. color pls. $125.00

REED, Walt. *Great American Illustrators.* 1979. New York. Ills. 159 pp. EX $17.50

REED, Walt. *Harold Von Schmidt: Draws & Paints the Old West.* 1972. Northland. 1st ed. dj. $20.00

REED, Walt. *John Clymer: Artist's Rendevous with Frontier West.* 1976. Northland. $25.00

REED, William *Hospital Life in the Army of the Potomac.* 1866. 1st ed. $27.50

REED, William. *Olaf Wieghorst.* 1976. Northland. $15.00

REEDER, Red & Campion N. *The West Point Story.* 1956. New York. Ramdom House. photos. dj. $3.00

REEDY, George. *The Twilight of the Presidency.* 1970. 2nd ed. dj. $27.50

REEP, T.P. *Lincoln at New Salem.* 1927. 147 pp. $30.00

REES, J. Rogers. *Brotherhood of Letters.* 1889. New York. 1st Am. ed. 271 pp. $10.00

REGAMEY, Feliz. *Japan in Art & Industry.* 1892. Putnam. ex-lib. Ills. 349 pp. EX $110.00

REGARDIE, Israel. *A Garden of Pomegranates: Outline of the Oabalah.* 1971. St.Paul. Llewellyn Pub. 3rd ed. dj. EX $10.00

REGARDIE, Israel. *Golden Dawn: Account Teachings, Rites, Ceremonies.* 1971. St.Paul. Llewellyn Pub. 4th ed. 2 vol set. $45.00

REGARDIE, Israel. *The Middle Pillar.* 1945. Chicago. Aries Press. 154 pp. EX $20.00

REGARDIE, Israel. *The Philosopher's Stone.* 1938. London. 1st ed. 204 pp. VG $30.00

REGARDIE, Israel. *The Philosopher's Stone.* 1970. 2nd ed. 204 pp. dj. VG $35.00

REGINALD, John. *Footwear Evidence.* 1964. Springfield. 1st ed. dj. EX $20.00

REGLER, Gustave. *The Great Crusade.* 1940. New York. 1st ed. 448 pp. dj. $25.00

REGLI, Adolph C. *Rubber's Goodyear. Story of Man's Perseverance.* 1954. Messner. Ills. Annand. 6th printing VG $7.50

REICH. *John Marin Drawings 1886-1951.* 1969. U. of Utah Press. $6.00

REICHART & KEASEY. *Modern Methods in Archery.* 1936. New York. Ills. 1st ed. VG $12.50

REID, A. *Discovery & Exploration.* 1983. Jupiter. Ills. 328 pp. index. dj. EX $15.00

REID, Agnes Just. *Letters of Long Ago.* 1936. Caxton. 2nd ed. sgn. 138 pp. dj. $15.00

REID, B.L. *The Man from New York.* 1968. Oxford U. Pr. dj. VG $12.50

REID, Capt. *The Rifle Rangers.* 1899. Federal Book Co. Ills. $17.50

REID, Edith G. *The Great Physician: Short Life of William Osler.* 1931. London. Oxford U. Press. VG $25.00

REID, Forrest. *Illustrators of the Sixties.* 1928. Faber & Gwyer. 1st ed. dj. $100.00

REID, G.K. *Ecology of Inland Waters & Estuaries.* 1965. Reinhold. Ills. 375 pp. VG $10.00

REID, J. *The Life of Christ in Woodcuts.* 1930. New York. 77 Ills. 1st ed. slipcase. EX $25.00

REID, J.C. *Bucks & Bruisers; Pierce Egan & Regency England.* 1971. London. Ills. VG $25.00

REID, Mayne. *The Cliff Climbers or Lone Home in the Himalayas.* 1882. New York. VG $20.00

REID, P.R. *Escape from Colditz.* 1953. New York. Lippincott. Ills. 622 pp. dj. $5.00

REID, V.S. *New Day, a Novel of Jamaica.* 1949. New York. Knopf. 1st ed. VG $25.00

REID, W.M. *Old Fort Johnson.* 1906. New York. Knickerbocker Press. Ills. VG $20.00

REID. *Ace Reid's Cowpokes Ride Again.* 1974. San Antonio. SftCvr. $6.00

REID. *Boy Hunters.* Hurst. no date. VG $4.50

REIGART, J. Franklin. *The Life of Robert Fulton.* 1856. Ills. 297 pp. rebound. VG $65.00

REIGER, George. *Profiles in Salt-Water Angling/A History of Sport.* 1973. Ills. Roy Grinnell. $20.00

REILLY, Robin. *Rest to Fortune, Life of Maj. Gen. James Wolfe.* 1960. London. Ills. 367 pp. $35.00

REILLY & RAE. *Physico-Chemical Methods.* 1953. 5th ed. 2 vol set. $45.00

REILY, Catherine W. *English Poetry of the First World War.* 1978. London. 402 pp. $17.50

REIMANN, L.C. *Between the Iron & the Pine.* 1951. sgn. dj. VG $15.00

REIMANN, L.C. *Incredible Seney.* 1953. dj. VG $15.00

REIMANN, L.C. *When Pine Was King.* 1952. sgn. dj. VG $20.00

REIN, David. *S. Weir Mitchell as a Phychiatric Novelist.* 1952. 1st ed. dj. $10.00

REINHARDT, Ed & Rogers, Hal. *How to Make Your Own Picture Frames.* 1968. VG $5.00

REINHARDT, Hans. *Holbein.* 1938. Paris. Hyperion Press. Ills. dj. EX $45.00

REIS, Jacob S. *The Battle with the Slum.* 1902. New York. Macmillan. 465 pp. VG $15.00

REISCHAUER, E. *Ennin's Diary: Record of Pilgrimage to China.* 1955. New York. 454 pp. map. EX $35.00

REISS, C. *Self-Betrayed.* 1942. New York. G $17.50

REITELL, Charles. *Let's Go Fishing.* 1931. Ills. 1st ed. VG $25.00

REITTER, Ewald. *Beetles.* 1960. Putnam. Ills. 205 pp. dj. EX $30.00

REMARQUE, Erich Maria. *A Time to Love & a Time to Die.* 1954. Harcourt. 1st Am. ed. dj. VG $20.00

REMARQUE, Erich Maria. *All Quiet on the Western Front.* 1929. Boston. 1st Am. ed. dj. EX $40.00

REMARQUE, Erich Maria. *Arch of Triumph.* 1945. New York. 455 pp. $3.00

REMARQUE, Erich Maria. *The Night in Lisbon.* 1964. Harcourt. 1st Am. ed. dj. VG $15.00

REMARQUE, Erich Maria. *The Night in Lisbon.* 1964. NY. Harcourt. advance copy. dj. EX $30.00

REMINGTON, Frederic. *Crooked Trails.* 1923. Ills. $12.00

REMINGTON, Frederic. *Done in the Open.* 1902. New York. Ills. 2nd issue. $75.00

REMINGTON, Frederic. *Frederic Remington's Own West.* 1960. New York. Dial Press. Ills. 1st ed. VG $17.50

REMINGTON, Frederic. *John Erskine of Yellowstone.* 1902. New York. Ills. 1st ed. VG $35.00

REMINGTON, Frederic. *Men with the Bark On.* 1890. New York. VG $60.00

REMINGTON, Frederic. *Pony Tracks.* 1923. New York. VG $40.00

REMINGTON, Frederic. *Prentice Mulford's Story.* 1953. Oakland. Ills. 1st CA ed. 1/500. EX $75.00

REMINGTON, Frederic. *Remington's Frontier Sketches.* 1898. Chicago. Werner. 1st ed. slipcase. $600.00

REMMINGTON & RUSSELL. *Fireside Book of Guns.* 1959. color pls. VG $10.00

REMY, Jules & Brenchley, J. *A Journey to Great-Salt-Lake-City.* 1861. London. Ills. 1st ed. fld map. 2 vol set. $175.00

RENARD, Jules. *Bucoliques.* 1898. Paris. inscr. VG $37.50

RENARD, Maurice. *The Hands of Orlac.* 1929. New York. Dutton. 1st ed. dj. EX $75.00

RENAULT, Mary. *Fire from Heaven.* 1969. New York. 1st ed. dj. VG $10.00

RENAULT, Mary. *The Mask of Apollo.* 1966. New York. Pantheon. 1st ed. dj. VG $35.00

RENAULT, Mary. *The Praise Singer.* 1978. New York. Pantheon. 1st ed. dj. EX $25.00

RENDELL, Ruth. *An Unkindness of Ravens.* 1985. New York. 1st Am. ed. dj. EX $7.50

RENDELL, Ruth. *Live Flesh.* London. 1st ed. sgn. $28.00

RENDELL, Ruth. *Speaker of Mandarin.* 1983. Pantheon. 1st Am. ed. dj. VG $12.50

RENDELL, Ruth. *The Fever Tree.* 1982. Pantheon. 1st Am. ed. dj. VG $12.50

RENDELL, Ruth. *The Killing Doll.* 1984. Pantheon. 1st Am. ed. dj. VG $12.50

RENDER. *The Mountains & the Sky.* 1974. Glenbow-Alberta Institute. $20.00

RENEK, Morris. *Las Vegas Strip.* 1st ed. dj. EX $7.00

RENIERS, Perceval. *Roses from the South.* 1959. New York. 1st ed. 383 pp. VG $7.50

RENIERS, Percival. *Springs of VA: Life, Love, & Death at Waters.* 1941. Chapel Hill. 1st ed. dj. VG $25.00

RENISE, Jac. *The Golden Age of Toys.* 586 Ills. 252 pp. dj. boxed. $55.00

RENOIR, Jean. *Renoir, My Father.* 1962. Toronto. 1st ed. dj. VG $18.00

RENOIR, Jean. *Renoir, My Father.* 1962. Boston. Little, Brown. photos. EX $6.00

RENOLDS, Charles B. *Washington Standard Guide.* 1917. Reynolds Co. Ills. SftCvr. $6.50

RENSELAER, Eleanor van. *Decorating with Seed Mosaics.* 1960. Van Nostrand. Ills. 1st ed. $3.50

RENWICK, Helen Goodwin. *Heaven's Own Mosaic & Other Poems.* 1929. Los Angeles. inscr. 95 pp. $32.50

REPPLIER, Agnes. *To Think of Tea!* 1932. Boston. 208 pp. dj. VG $12.50

RESNICK, M. *Eros at Zenith.* 1984. Phantasia. Ltd. ed. 1/300. sgn. boxed. EX $40.00

REUSS, Harry S. *Revenue Sharing: Crutch or Catalyst.* 1970. New York. ex-lib. 170 pp. dj. EX $4.50

REVERE, Joseph Warren. *A Tour of Duty in California.* 1849. New York. 1st ed. $135.00

REVERE, Joseph Warren. *Naval Duty in California.* 1947. Oakland. Ltd. ed. 1/1000. EX $45.00

REWALD, John. *The History of Impressionism.* 1961. Ills. dj. $18.00

REXROTH, Kenneth. *In What Hour.* 1940. New York. 1st ed. dj. EX $85.00

REXROTH, Kenneth. *100 Poems from the Chinese.* New Directions. 1st ed. EX $25.00

REY, C.F. *In the Country of the Blue Nile.* 1927. London. Duckworth. 1st ed. 296 pp. VG $30.00

REY, H.A. *Find the Constellations.* 1954. Boston. Houghton Mifflin. Ills. index. $22.50

REYNAUD, Mala. *The Stove Top Cookbook.* 1960. Gramercy. inscr. $3.00

REYNOLD, D.A. *Wolverton; or, the Modern Arena.* 1891. Chicago/NY. Rand McNally. 391 pp. $20.00

REYNOLDS, F.C. *115th Infantry in the World War.* 1920. 241 pp. VG $15.00

REYNOLDS, James. *Gallery of Ghosts.* 1965. Intro by Lon Chaney, Jr. $10.00

REYNOLDS, James. *Panorama of Austria.* 1956. Putnam. Ills. $14.50

REYNOLDS, Mack. *The Case of the Little Green Men.* 1951. New York. 1st ed. dj. VG $20.00

REYNOLDS, Myra. *The Poems of Anne, Countess of Winchilsea.* 1903. U. Chicago Pr. 436 pp. $20.00

REYNOLDS, Quentin. *Dress Rehearsal.* 1943. Blue Ribbon. Ills. dj. $10.00

REYNOLDS, Quentin. *Minister of Death.* 1960. Viking. 1st ed. photos. dj. EX $20.00

REYNOLDS, Quentin. *The Curtain Rises.* 1944. New York. Random House. 353 pp. dj. $4.00

REYNOLDS, Quentin. *The F.B.I.* 1954. New York. Random House. 180 pp. EX $3.50

REYNOLDS, Quentin. *The Fiction Factory.* 1955. Random House. Ills. 1st ed. 283 pp. $3.50

REYNOLDS, Quentin. *70,000 to 1.* 1946. 1st ed. dj. $7.00

REYNOLDS, Reginald. *Beds: Lying On, Under, & About Them.* 1952. London. 1st ed. dj. VG $12.50

REYNOLDS & CHURCHILL. *World War Events.* 1919. Collier. 3 vol set. $10.50

REZANOV, N.P. *The Rezanov, Voyage to Nueva, California in 1806.* 1926. San Francisco. Russell. Ltd. ed. sgn. $120.00

RHEAD, Louis. *American Trout Stream Insects.* 1916. New York. Stokes. Ills. 177 pp. G $25.00

RHEAD, Louis. *Arabian Nights Entertainments.* 1916. NY/London. Harper. Ills. Rhead. VG $20.00

RHEAD, Louis. *Book of Fish & Fishing.* 1908. New York. 1st ed. VG $20.00

RHEIMS. *Flowering of Art Nouveau.* Abrams. no date. EX $110.00

RHINE, J.B. *New Frontiers of Mind.* 1937. New York. 1st ed. dj. VG $15.00

RHINEHART, Mary Roberts. *The Breaking Point.* 1922. New York. 356 pp. $3.50

RHINEHART, Mary Roberts. *The Wall.* 1938. New York. Farrar & Rhinehart. 338 pp. $3.50

RHODE, John. *Death at the Dance.* 1952. London. 1st ed. dj. VG. $35.00

RHODE, John. *Death Invades the Meeting.* 1944. London. Collins. 1st ed. dj. VG $35.00

RHODE, John. *Death of an Author.* 1947. London. 1st ed. dj. VG $40.00

RHODE, John. *Murder at Derivale.* 1958. London. 1st ed. dj. VG $35.00

RHODE, John. *Peril at Cranbury Hill.* 1930. London. 1st ed. dj. $35.00

RHODE, John. *The Lake House.* 1946. London. 1st ed. dj. G. $30.00

RHODE, John. *The Venner Crime.* 1933. London. Odhams. 1st ed. dj. VG $30.00

RHODES, Daniel P. *Pleasure Book of Grindelwald.* 1903. New York. Ills. fld map. VG $15.00

RHODES, James Ford. *Historical Essays.* 1909. New York. 1st ed. VG $15.00

RHODES, Laura & Freeman, Lucy. *Chastize Me with Scorpions.* 1964. Putnam. sgn. dj. VG $20.00

RHODES, W.H. *The Case of Summerfield.* 1907. Elder. 1st ed. dj. slipcase. EX $50.00

RHODES. *Hypnosis: Theory, Practice, & Application.* 1950. New York. dj. VG $20.00

RHYNER, P. & Mannix, D.P. *The Wildest Game.* 1958. Lippincott. Ills. 1st ed. 320 pp. dj. EX $15.00

RHYS, E. *Captain Cook's Voyages of Discovery.* 1906. London. 479 pp. $13.50

RHYS, Jean. *Smile Please.* 1975. New York. dj. EX $12.50

RHYS, Jean. *Tigers Are Better Looking.* 1947. New York. 1st ed. dj. EX $12.50

RIBOT, T. *Diseases of Personality.* 1906. Open Court Pub. 4th ed. EX $25.00

RIBOT, T. *Diseases of the Will.* 1903. Open Court Pub. 3rd ed. EX $25.00

RIBOT, T. *Essay on the Creative Imagination.* 1906. Open Court Pub. dj. EX $30.00

RIBOT, T. *Psychology of Attention.* 1911. Open Court Pub. EX $25.00

RICCI, A. *Travels of Marco Polo.* 1931. New York. Ills. G $12.50

RICCIUTI, E. *The Wild Cats.* 1979. Ridge Press. Ills. 238 pp. dj. EX $17.50

RICE, Alice H. *A Romance of Billy-Goat Hill.* 1912. New York. Century. Ills. Geo. Wright. $4.50

RICE, Allen T. *Reminiscences of A. Lincoln by Men of His Time.* 1909. new revised ed. VG $15.00

RICE, Anne. *Cry to Heaven.* 1982. Knopf. 1st ed. dj. VG $15.00

RICE, Anne. *Exit to Eden.* 1985. Arbor House. 1st ed. dj. VG $17.50

RICE, Anne. *The Feast of All Snakes.* 1979. Simon & Schuster. 1st ed. dj. $15.00

RICE, Craig. *My Kingdom for a Hearse.* 1957. 1st ed. dj. VG $7.00

RICE, D.G. *Rockingham Pottery & Porcelain.* 1971. London. Barrie & Jenkins. VG $35.00

RICE, E.G. & Compton, R.H. *Wild Flowers of the Cape of Good Hope.* 1957. 250 pls. dj. EX $25.00

RICE, Elmer. *Counsellor-at-Law.* 1931. New York. 1st ed. dj. $35.00

RICE, Elmer. *The Left Bank.* 1931. New York. 1st ed. dj. $30.00

RICE, Elmer. *The Living Theatre.* 1959. New York. Harper. 1st ed. 306 pp. $3.50

RICE, Frances & Wallace. *Belles & Beaux. Book of Society.* 1913. Donohue. $10.00

RICE, Harold. *Within the Ropes.* 1946. New York. ex-lib. G $3.00

RICE, J.E. & Botsford, H.E. *Practical Poultry Management.* 1925. New York. Wiley & Sons. TB. 506 pp. VG $4.50

RICE, James & Hall, G. *Judging Poultry for Production.* 1930. Wiley & Sons. $3.00

RICE, Tamara. *Russian Icons.* New York. 48 color pls. VG $22.50

RICE, Victor A. *Breeding & Improvement of Farm Animals.* 1957. New York. McGraw Hill. TB. 537 pp. VG $4.50

RICE. *National Standard Squab Book.* 1905. $5.00

RICH, George E. *Artistic Horseshoeing.* 1895. New York. Ills. 153 pp. $15.00

RICH, J. *The Face of South America, an Aerial Traverse.* 1942. Am. Geog. Soc. Ills. 299 pp. VG $27.50

RICH, Louise D. *Mindy.* 1959. Lippincott. 1st ed. dj. $3.00

RICH, Louise D. *We Took to the Woods.* 1942. New York. Lippincott. 322 pp. dj. $4.50

RICH, Walter. *Feathered Game of North East.* 1907. Ills. 1st ed. VG $45.00

RICHARD, T.A. *T.A. Richard. Retrospesct, an Autobiography.* 1937. 1st ed. ex-lib. 402 pp. $10.00

RICHARD, T.A. *The Romance of Mining.* 1945. Macmillan. Ills. dj. VG $10.00

RICHARDS, Carmen. *Minnesota Skyline.* 1944. Minnesota. 10th ed. 143 pp. dj. $52.50

RICHARDS, Colin. *Bowler Hats & Stetsons.* 1966. New York. Ills. 214 pp. dj. $7.50

RICHARDS, Eva. *Arctic Mood.* 1949. Caxton. Ills. 282 pp. dj. VG $7.50

RICHARDS, Grant. *Author Hunting by an Old Literary Sportsman.* 1934. New York. Ills. 1st ed. VG $25.00

RICHARDS, J.M. *The Bombed Buildings of Britain.* 1942. Aberdeen. 140 pp. photos. $10.00

RICHARDS, J.M. *With John Bull & Jonathan.* 1906. New York. 1st ed. 307 pp. $17.50

RICHARDS, Joe. *Princess in New York.* 1956. 1st ed. dj. $10.00

RICHARDS, Laura E. *Hildegarde's Harvest.* 1897. Estes & Lauriat. Ills. $17.50

RICHARDS, Laura E. *Honor Bright.* 1920. Boston. Ills. Merrill. 327 pp. VG $7.50

RICHARDS, Laura E. *Snow White.* 1900. Boston. 1st ed. inscr. VG $25.00

RICHARDS, Laura E. *Star Bright.* 1927. Boston. Ills. Merrill. 1st ed. 194 pp. $7.50

RICHARDS, Laura E. *Stepping Westward.* 1931. New York. Appleton. 1st ed. 406 pp. $10.00

RICHARDS, Laura E. *The Golden Windows.* 1936. Boston. Ills. Julia Ward Richards. EX $12.50

RICHARDS, Mrs. Waldo. *High Tide.* 1919. Houghton Mifflin. VG $20.00

RICHARDS, Mrs. Waldo. *The Melody of Earth.* 1918. Houghton Mifflin. VG $20.00

RICHARDS, Robert. *California Crusoe; or, The Lost Treasure Island.* 1854. London. 1st ed. 162 pp. $300.00

RICHARDS, William C. *The Last Billionaire.* 1948. NY/London. 1st ed. 422 pp. index. $8.50

RICHARDSON, Albert D. *A Personal History Of Ulysses S. Grant.* 1868. Ills. 560 pp. $17.50

RICHARDSON, Albert D. *Beyond the Mississippi.* 1869. Hartford. new ed. 216 engravings. EX $17.50

RICHARDSON, Albert D. *Beyond the Mississippi.* 1867. Hartford, CT. 1st ed. $27.50

RICHARDSON, Albert D. *The Secret Service.* 1865. Ills. 511 pp. $18.50

RICHARDSON, B. *Strangers Devour the Land.* 1976. Knopf. Ills. 342 pp. EX $5.00

RICHARDSON, Darrell. *Max Brand, the Man & His Work.* 1952. Los Angeles. 198 pp. VG $12.50

RICHARDSON, E.P. *American Romantic Painting.* 1944. New York. $20.00

RICHARDSON, Frederick. *Old, Old Tales Retold.* 1923. Chicago. Volland. EX $75.00

RICHARDSON, Frederick. *The White Elephant.* 1929. Faulkner. Ills. 1st ed. $30.00

RICHARDSON, James D. *Compilation of Messages & Papers of Presidents.* 1902. 10 vol set. $25.00

RICHARDSON, Joan. *Fanny Brawne, a Biography.* 1952. New York. Ills. dj. EX $12.50

RICHARDSON, Joan. *Wallace Stevens.* 1986. New York. proof copy. wrappers. EX $15.00

RICHARDSON, M. *The Fascination of Reptiles.* 1972. Hill Wang. Ills. 240 pp. dj. EX $17.50

RICHARDSON, N.S. *Historical Sketch of Watertown, 1741-1858.* 1858. Waterbury. 72 pp. $25.00

RICHARDSON. *Adventures of Pinocchio.* 1930. Winston. 8 color pls. VG $12.50

RICHARDSON. *Charles Miner, a Pennsylvania Pioneer.* 1916. Wilkes-Barre. G $30.00

RICHER, Conrad. *A Country of Strangers.* 1966. New York. 1st ed. dj. EX $10.00

RICHEY, P. *Fighter Pilot.* 1941. New York. dj. $10.00

RICHIE, W.A. *The Archaeology of Martha's Vineyard.* 1969. 253 pp. 56 pls. $15.00

RICHLER, Mordecai. *Home Sweet Home: My Canadian Album.* 1984. Knopf. 1st ed. dj. VG $17.00

RICHLER, Mordecai. *St. Urbain's Horseman.* 1971. Knopf. 1st ed. dj. VG $12.50

RICHLER, Mordecai. *The Best of Modern Humor.* 1983. New York. Book of Month Club. dj. $5.00

RICHMAN, Irving B. *Ioway to Iowa.* 1931. Iowa City. Ills. G $25.00

RICHMOND, Grace. *Cherry Square.* 1926. 1st ed. dj. VG $5.00

RICHMOND, Grace. *On Christmas Day in the Evening.* 1910. Ills. Chas. M. Relyea. $8.00

RICHTER, Conrad. *The Aristocrat.* 1968. Knopf. 1st ed. dj. VG $15.00

RICHTER, Conrad. *The Lady.* 1957. Knopf. 1st ed. dj. VG $15.00

RICHTER, Hans. *Dreams that Money Can Buy.* 1947. Films International. wrappers. $7.00

RICKENBACKER, Edward V. *Fighting the Flying Circus.* 1965. New York. Doubleday. 296 pp. dj. $6.00

RICKENBACKER, Edward V. *Rickenbacker.* 1967. Englewood. dj. $7.00

RICKENBACKER, Edward V. *Seven Came Through.* 1943. New York. Doubleday. 118 pp. dj. $5.00

RICKETT, H.W. *Wild Flowers of America.* 1975. New York. 12th printing. $25.00

RICKETT, Richard. *A Brief Survey of Austrian History.* 1975. 5th ed. Ills. VG $8.00

RICKETTS, Charles. *Charles Ricketts R.A.* 1933. London. 65 Ills. 1st ed. dj. EX $120.00

RICKETTS, Charles. *Self-Portrait Taken from Letters & Journals.* 1939. London. Ills. Ricketts. VG $45.00

RIDDLE, A.G. *The Life of Benjamin F. Wade.* 1886. Cleveland. 310 pp. $17.50

RIDE, W.D.L. *A Guide to the Native Mammals of Australia.* 1970. Oxford. Ills. 264 pp. dj. EX $47.50

RIDELL, J. *The Ski Runs of Switzerland.* 1957. London. Ills. 1st ed. 28 maps. VG $12.50

RIDER, Fremont. *Rider's New York City.* 1916. New York. 506 pp. 16 maps. 18 plans. $22.50

RIDER. *The Circle C Carries On.* Pocketbooks. pb. $3.00

RIDGER, A. Loton. *A Wanderer's Trail.* 1914. 60 photos. $12.50

RIDGEWAY, Matthew. *The Korean War.* 1967. Doubleday. Ills. 1st ed. 291 pp. index. $15.00

RIDGWAY, Robert. *The Hummingbirds.* 1890. 130 pp. 46 pls. $8.00

RIDING, Laura. *Anarchism Is Not Enough.* 1928. New York. 1st Am. ed. dj. VG $20.00

RIDING, Laura. *Contemporaries & Snobs.* 1928. New York. 1st Am. ed. dj. VG $22.50

RIDINGS, Samuel P. *The Chisholm Trail.* 1936. Guthrie. Ills. 1st ed. 591 pp. $225.00

RIDPATH, J.C. *Beyond Sierras: Tour of 60 Days in CA Valleys.* 1963. Oakland. Ltd. 1st CA ed. 1/650. EX $50.00

RIDPATH, J.C. *History of the United States.* 1906. 1st ed. G $18.00

RIEFENSTAHLI, L. *Coral Gardens.* 1978. Harper. Ills. 1st Am. ed. 223 pp. dj. $25.00

RIEMAN, Margo. *Quick Gourmet Dinners.* 1972. New York. Harper. 141 pp. $6.50

RIEMSCHNEIDER, Margarete. *Die Welt der Hethiter.* 1954. Stuttgart. 259 pp. fld map. 108 pls. $25.00

RIENHART, S.C. *With the Tibetan in Tent & Temple.* 1901. Revell & Co. $25.00

RIFKIN, Jeremy. *Entropy.* 1980. 1st ed. inscr. dj. EX $10.00

RIFKIND. *Main Street: Face of Urban America.* 1977. Harper. $10.00

RIGER, R. *Man in Sport.* 1967. Baltimore Museum. wrappers. EX $7.50

RIGG, W.P. *Astrology of the Mysteries.* 1959. London. 1st ed. 179 pp. dj. $30.00

RIGGS, S.R. & Williamson, J.P. *Dakota Odowan. Hymns in the Dakota Language.* 1865. New York. Am. Tract Soc. 162 pp. $150.00

RIGGS, Stephen R. *A Dakota English Dictionary.* 1890. Washington. 1st ed. VG $30.00

RIGGS, Stephen R. *Mary & I. Forty Years with the Sioux.* 1880. Chicago. 1st ed. 388 pp. $50.00

RIHA, J. & Subik, R. *Cacti & Other Succulents.* 1981. Octopus. Ills. 1st Eng. ed. 352 pp. dj. $17.50

RIIS, J. *Battle with Slum.* 1902. $12.50

RIIS, J. *Making of an American.* 1902. New York. $15.00

RIIS, J. *Making of an American.* 1901. New York. $35.00

RIIS, J.A. *Neighbors.* 1914. Macmillan. 1st ed. EX $20.00

RILEY, James Whitcomb. *A Hoosier Romance.* 1912. Bobbs Merrill. Ills. John Walcott. G $15.00

RILEY, James Whitcomb. *A Host of Children.* 1920. Indianapolis. Ills. Betts. 16 color pls. VG $50.00

RILEY, James Whitcomb. *Afterwhiles.* 1891. Bowen Merrill. inscr. $40.00

RILEY, James Whitcomb. *An Old Sweetheart of Mine.* 1902. Bobbs Merrill. Ills. Christy. $50.00

RILEY, James Whitcomb. *Armazindy.* 1894. 1st ed. $25.00

RILEY, James Whitcomb. *Best Loved Poems of James Whitcomb Riley.* New York. Blue Ribbon. Ills. Betts. $35.00

RILEY, James Whitcomb. *Child Rhymes.* 1905. Indianapolis. Bobbs Merrill. EX $20.00

RILEY, James Whitcomb. *Child Rhymes.* 1898. Bowen Merrill. Ills. $10.50

RILEY, James Whitcomb. *Farm Rhymes.* 1905. Indianapolis. Bobbs Merrill. EX $20.00

RILEY, James Whitcomb. *Flying Islands of the Night.* 1892. Bowen Merrill. VG $90.00

RILEY, James Whitcomb. *Flying Islands of the Night.* 1913. Ills. Booth. $40.00

RILEY, James Whitcomb. *Good-Bye, Jim.* 1913. Bobbs Merrill. Ills. Christy. VG $12.50

RILEY, James Whitcomb. *Green Field & Running Brooks.* Bobbs Merrill. ex-lib. 224 pp. $50.00

RILEY, James Whitcomb. *Love Lyrics.* 1888. Bobbs Merrill. Ills. Dyer. VG $15.00

RILEY, James Whitcomb. *Morning, the Poems & Prose.* 1917. Scribner. $8.50

RILEY, James Whitcomb. *Orphant Annie Book.* 1908. Bobbs Merrill. 8 color pls. G $20.00

RILEY, James Whitcomb. *Pipes O'Pan at Zekesbury.* 1892. Bowen Merrill. inscr. $40.00

RILEY, James Whitcomb. *Rhymes of Childhood.* 1891. inscr. $40.00

RILEY, James Whitcomb. *Riley Songs of Summer.* 1908. Ills. Will Vawter. $9.50

RILEY, James Whitcomb. *Rubaiyat of Doc Sifers.* 1897. New York. Century. Ills. Relyea. 1st ed. $12.50

RILEY, James Whitcomb. *Songs O'Cheer.* 1905. Ills. Will Vawter. $8.50

RILEY, James Whitcomb. *Songs of Summer.* 1909. Indianapolis. Bobbs Merrill. EX $20.00

RILEY, James Whitcomb. *The Runaway Boy.* 1906. Indianapolis. Ills. Betts. 8 color pls. G $20.00

RILEY, Norman. *Butterflies & Moths.* 1970. Viking. Ills. revised ed. dj. VG $25.00

RILEY, Robert. *The Fashion Makers: Photographic Record.* 1968. New York. Crown. Ills. dj. G $10.50

RILKE, Rainer Maria. *Later Poems.* Hogarth. Ltd. 1st Eng. ed. 1/1020. $22.50

RILKE, Rainer Maria. *Lay of Love & Death of Cornet Cristopher Rilke.* 1983. San Francisco. Arion Press. Ills. Chappell. $75.00

RILKE, Rainer Maria. *Letters to a Young Poet.* 1934. Norton. trans. 1st Am. ed. dj. VG $30.00

RIMBAUD. *Prose Poems from the Illuminations.* 1946. New Directions.1st ed. inscr. dj. VG $5.00

RIMINGTON, C. *Fighting Fleets.* 1943. New York. Dodd Mead. Ills. 312 pp. VG $15.00

RINALDI, A. & Tyndale, V. *The Complete Book of Mushrooms.* 1974. Crown. Ills. 1st Am. ed. dj. EX $30.00

RINEHART, Luke. *Long Voyage Back.* 1983. 1st ed. dj. EX $8.50

RINEHART, Mary Roberts. *The Album.* 1933. New York. 1st ed. VG $12.50

RINEHART, Mary Roberts. *The Circular Staircase.* 1908. Indianapolis. Ills. Lester Ralph. 1st ed. EX $75.00

RINEHART, Mary Roberts. *Tish.* 1916. Boston. 1st ed. VG $20.00

RINEHART, Mary Roberts. *When a Man Marries.* 1909. Bobbs Merrill. Ills. Fisher. 1st ed. VG $12.50

RINGWALT, J. Luther. *American Encyclopedia of Printing.* 1871. Philadelphia. VG $25.00

RIODAIN, Sean. *Antiquities of the Irish Countryside.* 1943. Cork Press. 60 pp. 47 pls. wrappers. $12.00

RIPLEY, L. *Sporting Etchings.* 1970. dj. EX $27.50

RIPLEY, Mary. *The Chinese Rug Book.* 1927. Stokes. 1st ed. $15.00

RIPLEY, Roswell S. *The War with Mexico.* 1849. New York. 1st ed. 2 vol set. $150.00

RIPLEY, Roswell S. *The War with Mexico.* 1970. New York. reprint. 2 vol set. $35.00

RIPLEY, S.D. *Rails of the World.* 1977. Boston. Ills. Landsdowne. folio. EX $140.00

RIPLEY, S.D. *The Land & Wildlife of Tropical Asia.* 1964. Life Nature Lib. Ills. 200 pp. $12.50

RIPLEY, T.E. *Green Timber.* 1968. Am. West Pub. Ills. dj. VG $10.00

RIPLEY, W.Z. *Main Street & Wall Street.* 1927. Boston. VG $8.00

RIPLEY. *Oriental Rug Book.* 1936. Tudor. EX $35.00

RIPSTRA, J.H. *Lincoln Group Papers.* 1945. Torch Press. dj. VG $12.50

RITSON, Joseph. *Essay: Abstinence from Animal Food as Moral Duty.* 1802. London. VG $90.00

RITSON, Joseph. *Robin Hood, a Collection of All the Ancient Poems.* 1887. London. 2 vol set. VG $45.00

RITSON, Joseph. *The Romance of Primitive Methodism.* 1909. London. 312 pp. $9.00

RITTER, William. *The California Woodpecker & I.* 1938. U. of CA. 1st ed. $10.00

RITTLINGER, H. *Photography & Nude.* 1961. London. dj. EX $17.50

RIVERA, Diego & Wolfe, B. *Portrait of America.* 1934. New York. Ills. 1st ed. 232 pp. photos. $57.50

RIVERA, Diego & Wolfe, B. *Portrait of Mexico.* 1937. New York. Ills. 1st ed. photos. 249 pls. $37.50

RIVERA, Diego & Wolfe, B. *The Fabulous Life of Diego Rivera.* 1963. New York. dj. EX $25.00

RIVERAIN, J. *Concise Encyclopedia of Explorations.* 1966. Collins Follett. Ills. 279 pp. $15.00

RIVERS, Hallie Ermine. *Complete Book of Etiquette.* 1934. Philadelphia. J.C. Winston Co. 514 pp. dj. $4.00

RIVOLIER, J. *Emperor Penguins.* 1958. Speller. Ills. 1st ed. 131 pp. dj. EX $12.50

ROARK, Garland. *Should the Wind Be Fair.* 1960. Garden City. Doubleday. 1st ed. dj. VG $25.00

ROBACKER, E. *Pennsylvania Dutch Stuff.* Ills. 5th ed. 163 pp. dj. $12.50

ROBB, Wilfred. *The Price of Our Heritage.* 1919. Des Moines. 420 pp. $25.00

ROBBINS, Ann Roe. *Treadway Inns Cook Book.* 1958. Boston. Little, Brown. 1st ed. sgn. $10.00

ROBBINS, C.H. *The Gam, Being a Group of Whaling Stories.* 1899. New Bedford. VG $15.00

ROBBINS, Chandler. *History of Second Church; or, Old North in Boston.*1852. Boston. G $15.00

ROBBINS, G.E.S. *Quail, Their Breeding & Management.* 1981. World Pheasant Assn. 108 pp. $17.50

ROBBINS, Harold. *The Carpet Baggers.* 1961. New York. Knopf. 1st ed. dj. VG $40.00

ROBBINS, Harold. *The Dream Merchants.* 1949. New York. Knopf. 1st ed. 2nd printing. $20.00

ROBBINS, Harold. *79 Park Avenue.* 1955. New York. Knopf. 1st ed. dj. VG $30.00

ROBBINS, M. *A Refrain of Roses.* 1965. Denver. Alan Swallow. inscr. dj. $15.00

ROBBINS, Tom. *Even Cowgirls Get the Blues.* 1976. Houghton. 1st ed. dj. VG $70.00

ROBBINS, Tom. *Jitterbug Perfume.* 1984. Bantam. 1st ed. dj. VG $15.00

ROBERTON, William. *The History of Discovery & Settlement of America.* 1845. Edinburgh. G $25.00

ROBERTS, Charles G.D. *The Haunters of the Silences.* 1907. Boston. Ills. Livingston. 1st ed. G $25.00

ROBERTS, Elder B.H. *Joseph Smith.* 1927. Salt Lake City. 2nd ed. 84 pp. $15.00

ROBERTS, Elizabeth Madox. *A Buried Treasure.* 1931. New York. 1st ed. dj. VG $20.00

ROBERTS, Guy & Burt, Frank H. *Mt. Washington, Its Past & Present.* 1927. Whitefield, NH. Ills. 56 pp. wrappers. $5.00

ROBERTS, Guy. *The Willey Slide, Its History, Legend, & Romance.* 1925. Ills. 10th ed. 44 pp. $5.00

ROBERTS, J. *My Congo Adventure.* 1963. London. Jarrolds. Ills. 1st ed. dj. VG $20.00

ROBERTS, James. *New York in the Revolution.* 1898. Ills. 2nd ed. $45.00

ROBERTS, Job. *Pennsylvania Farmer.* 1804. Philadelphia. A. Bertram. 224 pp. $100.00

ROBERTS, John. *Life & Explorations of David Livingstone.* 1874. Boston. G $20.00

ROBERTS, K. *Florida Loafing.* 1925. Indianapolis. 1st ed. VG $15.00

ROBERTS, K. & Tarkington, B. *Antiquamania/Collected Papers of Milton Kilgaller.* 1928. New York. Ills. 1st ed. inscrs. sgns. VG $45.00

ROBERTS, Kenneth & Anna. *Moreau de St.Mery's American Journey 1793-1798.* 1947. New York. Doubleday. 394 pp. $7.00

ROBERTS, Kenneth. *Boon Island.* 1956. $10.00

ROBERTS, Kenneth. *Don't Say that About Maine.* 1986. Portland. Ltd. ed. 1/1500. wrappers. VG $8.00

ROBERTS, Kenneth. *Good Maine Food.* 1947. Doubleday. dj. VG $17.50

ROBERTS, Kenneth. *Henry Gross & His Dowsing Rod.* 1951. New York. Doubleday. 1st ed. 308 pp. dj. $17.50

ROBERTS, Kenneth. *Kenneth Roberts' Reader.* 1945. Garden City. Doubleday. 1st ed. $7.50

ROBERTS, Kenneth. *Kiteworld.* London. 1st ed. sgn. $24.00

ROBERTS, Kenneth. *Lively Lady.* 1931. 1st ed. inscr. dj. VG $20.00

ROBERTS, Kenneth. *Lydia Bailey.* Ltd. 1st ed. 1/1050. sgn. $195.00

ROBERTS, Kenneth. *Lydia Bailey.* 1947. inscr. dj. VG $15.00

ROBERTS, Kenneth. *Northwest Passage.* 1937. Doubleday. 709 pp. $6.50

ROBERTS, Kenneth. *Northwest Passage.* 1937. 1st ed. sgn. dj. VG $35.00

ROBERTS, Kenneth. *Oliver Wiswell.* 1940. Doubleday Doran. Ltd. ed. sgn. $100.00

ROBERTS, Kenneth. *Oliver Wiswell.* 1940. New York. Doubleday. 1st trade ed. $12.50

ROBERTS, Kenneth. *Seventh Sense/Sequel to Henry Gross & Dowsing Rod.* 1953. New York. Doubleday. Ills. 1st ed. dj. $17.50

ROBERTS, Kenneth. *The Battle of Cowpens: Great Morale-Builder.* 1958. New York. Ills. 1st ed. index. VG $12.50

ROBERTS, Kenneth. *Trending into Maine.* 1938. Boston. Ills. Wyeth. 1st ed. dj. VG $50.00

ROBERTS, Kenneth. *Water Unlimited.* 1957. New York. Doubleday. 1st ed. dj. $17.50

ROBERTS, Leslie. *There Shall be Wings.* 1960. London. Ills. 1st Eng. ed. 290 pp. dj. $27.50

ROBERTS, M. *Watchers of the Trails.* 1906. Wessels. G $35.00

ROBERTS, O. *Lincoln in Illinois.* 1918. Boston/NY. Ills. Hornby. 1st ed. 120 pp. $20.00

ROBERTS, Oliver Ayer. *History of Ancient & Honorable Artillery of MA.* 1897. 479 pp. $10.00

ROBERTS, Oliver Ayer. *History of Military Company of Massachusetts.* 1895. Boston. 4 vol set. $75.00

ROBERTS, Oral. *The Fourth Man.* 1951. 139 pp. dj. $27.50

ROBERTS, Peter. *Veteran & Vintage Cars.* 1974. Octopus Books. Ills. 128 pp. dj. VG $4.00

ROBERTS, R.N. *The Halifax File.* 1982. London. wrappers. EX $15.00

ROBERTS, S.C. *A Picture Book of British History.* 1931. Cambridge. 3 vol set. $20.00

ROBERTS, S.C. *Holmes & Watson.* 1953. London. 1st ed. dj. EX $35.00

ROBERTS, W. *Book Verses, Anthology of Poems.* New York. no date. 213 pp. $17.50

ROBERTS, W.A. *Lake Pontchartrain.* 1946. Bobbs Merrill. Ills. 376 pp. dj. VG $15.00

ROBERTS, William. *The Book Hunter in London.* 1895. Chicago. VG $45.00

ROBERTS. *Hoof Prints on Forest Ranges.* 1963. Naylor Co. VG $10.00

ROBERTS. *Who's Got the Button?* 1962. New York. 1st ed. dj. EX $12.50

ROBERTSON, Bruce. *Beaufort Special.* 1976. London. Allan. 1st ed. EX $12.50

ROBERTSON, Bruce. *Lancaster, Story of a Famous Bomber.* 1964. London. Harleyford Pub. Ltd. 2nd ed. $15.00

ROBERTSON, Bruce. *Lysander Special.* 1977. London. Allan. 1st ed. EX $12.00

ROBERTSON, C.F. *Attempts to Separate the West from American Union.* St. Louis. (ca.1884) 1st ed. wrappers. $125.00

ROBERTSON, Don. *Miss Margaret Ridpath & Dismantling of Universe.* 1977. New York. Putnam. review copy. dj. VG $25.00

ROBERTSON, G. *An Account of the Discovery of Tahiti.* 1955. London. Folio Soc. Ills. 127 pp. VG $17.50

ROBERTSON, John. *Michigan in the War.* 1882. Lansing. revised ed. 1039 pp. $45.00

ROBERTSON, Morgan. *The Three Laws & the Golden Rule.* 1898. McClure. 1st ed. VG $12.50

ROBERTSON, R.B. *Of Whales & Men.* 1954. Knopf. Ills. 300 pp. VG $7.50

ROBERTSON, Robert S. *Valley of the Upper Maumee River.* 1889. Madison. 498 pp. $75.00

ROBERTSON, Stephen L. *The Shropshire Racket.* 1937. London. Ills. Derrick. 1st ed. dj. VG $30.00

ROBERTSON, William. *Historical Disquisition, Knowledge of India.* 1794. London. 2nd ed. fld maps. 441 pp. VG $100.00

ROBERTSON, William. *The History of America.* 1821. Philadelphia. 2nd ed. 2 vol set. G $75.00

ROBERTSON & ROBERTSON. *The Chafing Dish Cookbook.* 1950. New York. 238 pp. $3.00

ROBESON, Eslanda Goode. *African Journey.* 1945. New York. 154 pp. photos. dj. $8.00

ROBESON, K. *Quest of the Spider.* 1933. Street & Smith. 1st ed, VG $35.00

ROBESON, Kenneth. *The Man of Bronze.* 1983. 1st Am. ed. dj. G $35.00

ROBESON, Mrs. Paul. *What Do the People of Africa Want?* 1945. Paris. 1st ed. sgn. wrappers. EX $35.00

ROBESON, Paul. *Here I Stand.* 1958. New York. sgn. dj. $35.00

ROBINS, E. *Secret Eden, Africa's Enchanted Wilderness.* 1980. London. Elm Tree. Ills. 128 pp. dj. EX $20.00

ROBINS, Elizabeth. *Camilla.* 1918. Ills. C. Allen Gilbert. EX $4.00

ROBINS, John D. *Incomplete Angler.* 1944. dj. VG $20.00

ROBINSON, A. Mary. *Emily Bronte.* 1893. Oston. 1st ed. EX $15.00

ROBINSON, A.G. *The Philippines, the War & the People.* 1901. New York. 1st ed. VG $15.00

ROBINSON, Alfred. *Life in California.* 1947. Oakland. Ills. $47.50

ROBINSON, Basil William. *Japanese Landscape Prints of Nineteenth Century.* 1957. Faber & Faber. Ills. hard-to-find. VG $40.00

ROBINSON, Basil William. *Kuniyoshi. The Warrior Prints.* 1982. Cornell U. Ills. 208 pp. dj. EX $65.00

ROBINSON, Ben C. *Woodland Field & Waterfowl Hunting.* 1946. Philadelphia. Ills. dj. VG $12.00

ROBINSON, Bill. *A Berth to Bermuda.* 1961. Princeton. Ills. dj. VG $8.00

ROBINSON, C.N. *Celebrities of the Army.* 1902. London. 71 color pls. folio. $37.50

ROBINSON, C.N. *The British Tar in Fact & Fiction.* 1909. London. Ills. VG $15.00

ROBINSON, Charles. *Rubaiyat of Omar Khayyam.* 1928. London. Ills. 1st ed. VG $90.00

ROBINSON, D.H. *The Dangerous Sky, a History of Aviation Medicine.* 1973. London. Ills. dj. EX $15.00

ROBINSON, Dan M. *The Carter House Focus of the Battle of Franklin.* 1963. Ills. wrappers. VG $35.00

ROBINSON, Douglas & Keller, C. *Up Ship!* 1982. Annapolis. photos. new in dj. $30.00

ROBINSON, Douglas H. *Giants in the Sky.* 1979. Seattle. 3rd printing. photos. 376 pp. $20.00

ROBINSON, E.A. *King Jasper.* Ltd. 1st ed. 1/250. sgn. VG $37.50

ROBINSON, E.A. *Roman Bartholow.* 1923. New York. Ltd. 1st ed. 1/750. sgn. VG $35.00

ROBINSON, E.A. *Sonnets.* 1927. New York. Crosby Gaige. Ltd. ed. sgn. VG $30.00

ROBINSON, E.A. *The Glory of the Nightingales.* 1930. New York. Merrymount Pr. Ltd. 1st ed. VG $30.00

ROBINSON, E.A. *The Man Who Died Twice.* 1924. New York. Ltd. 1st ed. sgn. boxed. VG $30.00

ROBINSON, E.F. & T.P. *Houses in America.* 1936. New York. Ills. 1st ed. 240 pp. $7.50

ROBINSON, Edwin A. *Amaranth.* 1934. Macmillan. 1st ed. dj. VG $25.00

ROBINSON, Edwin A. *Cavender's House.* 1929. Macmillan. 1st ed. dj. VG $25.00

ROBINSON, Edwin A. *Tilbury Town.* 1960. Macmillan. 3rd printing. 144 pp. $5.00

ROBINSON, Edwin A. *Tristram.* 1943. Macmillan. 210 pp. dj. $37.50

ROBINSON, F. Cayley. *The Bluebird.* 1920. Dodd Mead. Ills. 16 color pls. VG $35.00

ROBINSON, Harriet. *Massachusetts in Woman Suffrage Movement.* 1881. Boston. Roberts. 1st ed. $75.00

ROBINSON, Henry C. *Diary.* 1870. Boston. 1st ed. 2 vol set. $15.00

ROBINSON, Henry Morton. *The Great Snow.* 1947. New York. 277 pp. $3.00

ROBINSON, Jackie & Duckett, A. *I Never Had It Made.* 1972. New York. Putnam. 287 pp. dj. EX $5.00

ROBINSON, James Harvey. *Medieval & Modern Times.* 1919. New York. Ginn & Co. Ills. maps. photos. $5.00

ROBINSON, James Harvey. *Outlines of European History, Part I.* 1914. New York. Ginn & Co. Ills. & maps. G $4.00

ROBINSON, Jerry. *Comics, Illustrated History of Comic Strip Art.* 1974. Ills. 1st ed. dj. EX $15.00

ROBINSON, Jill. *Dr. Rocksinger & the Age of Longing.* 1982. Knopf. review copy. dj. VG $20.00

ROBINSON, Jill. *Perdido.* 1978. Knopf. 1st ed. ex-lib. dj. VG $10.00

ROBINSON, Julian. *Fashion in the 30's.* London. reprint ed. Ills. dj. VG $10.50

ROBINSON, Kim S. *The Wild Shore.* London. 1st ed. sgn. $45.00

ROBINSON, Kim S. *The Wild Shore.* proof copy. $35.00

ROBINSON, L. *Further Letters of John Butler Yeats.* 1920. Dundrum. Cuala Press. Ltd. ed. 81 pp. $65.00

ROBINSON, L. *Lady Gregory's Journals. 1916-1930.* 1947. New York. Macmillan. 1st ed. dj. VG $10.00

ROBINSON, Lennox. *A Little Anthology of Modern Irish Verse.* 1928. Dublin. Cuala Press. Ltd. ed. VG $85.00

ROBINSON, Lewis G. *The Making of a Man, an Autobiography.* 1970. Cleveland. Ills. 1st ed. 213 pp. dj. $12.50

ROBINSON, Luther E. *Hist. & Biogr. Record of Monmouth & Warren Co.* 1927. Munsell Pub. 2 vol set. G $85.00

ROBINSON, Mabel L. *Robin & Tito.* 1930. New York. Macmillan. Ills. Burns. $15.00

ROBINSON, Marilynne. *Housekeeping.* 1980. Farrar. 1st ed. dj. VG $20.00

ROBINSON, Mary. *An Amateur's Guide to the Night.* 1983. New York. Knopf. 1st ed. dj. EX $20.00

ROBINSON, Mary. *Days.* 1979. New York. Knopf. 1st ed. VG $15.00

ROBINSON, Mary. *Oh!* 1981. New York. Knopf. 1st ed. dj. EX $30.00

ROBINSON, Rowland. *Hunting Without a Gun & Other Papers.* 1905. New York. 1st ed. 381 pp. $25.00

ROBINSON, Rowland. *In the Green Wood.* 1899. Burlington, VT. 1st ed. inscr. 163 pp. $75.00

ROBINSON, Rowland. *Uncle Lish's Outing.* 1897. New York. 308 pp. $25.00

ROBINSON, Spider & Jeanne. *Stardance.* 1979. 1st Am. ed. dj. EX $25.00

ROBINSON, Spider. *Mindkiller.* 1982. 1st Am. ed. dj. EX $15.00

ROBINSON, Spider. *Telempath.* 1976. New York. Berkley. 1st ed. dj. EX $20.00

ROBINSON, Tacred. *An Account of Several Late Voyages & Discoveries.* 1711. London. Ills. 3 fld maps. 223 pp. $950.00

ROBINSON, W.H. *A Midsummer Night's Dream.* 1914. Holt. Ills. 12 color pls. VG $45.00

ROBINSON, W.H. *Water Babies.* 1915. Houghton Mifflin. Ills. VG $28.00

ROBINSON, W.H. *Works of Rabelais.* London. private print. Ills. $30.00

ROBINSON, W.W. *Panorama, Picture History of Southern California.* 1953. Los Angeles. Ills. SftCvr. $10.00

ROBINSON, William F. *A Certain Slant of Light.* 1980. Boston. Ills. 1st ed. dj. EX $10.00

ROBINSON, William Morrison. *The Confederate Privateers.* 1928. New Haven. Yale U. Press. Ills. 1st ed. $20.00

ROBINSON. *Excavations at Olynthus, Part X.* 1941. Johns Hopkins Press. VG $20.00

ROBISON, James. *Rumor & Other Stories.* 1985. Summit. 1st ed. dj. VG $15.00

ROBOTTI, Frances. *Chronicles of Old Salem.* 1948. Salem. 1st ed. dj. $8.50

ROBSON, R.W. *The Pacific Islands Handbook.* 1946. Macmillan. Ills. 371 pp. VG $10.00

ROBY, Kinley E. *A Writer at War, Arnold Bennett 1914-1918.* 1972. Baton Rouge. dj. VG $10.00

ROCH, Philip. *Circles of Time.* 1981. Seaview. review copy. dj. EX $12.50

ROCHELEAU, W.F. *Products of the Soil.* 1902. New York. Flanagan. TB. 178 pp. VG $3.50

ROCK, James A. *Who Goes There/Biblio. of Pseudonymous Literature.* 1979. Bloomington. 1st ed. dj. VG $30.00

ROCKWELL, Carey. *Tom Corbett Stand by for Mars.* 1958. Grosset & Dunlap. VG $7.50

ROCKWELL, Norman. *My Adventures as an Illustrator.* 1960. Garden City. Ills. dj. slipcase. EX $20.00

ROCKWELL, R.H. *My Way of Becoming a Hunter.* 1955. Norton. Ills. 1st ed. 285 pp. dj. VG $25.00

ROCKWELL & Grayson, Esther. *The Complete Book of Flower Arrangement.* 1955. Doubleday. Ills. dj. $6.50

ROCKWOOD, Roy. *Bomba the Jungle Boy & the Lost Explorers.* 1930. Cupples & Leon. VG $4.50

ROCKWOOD, Roy. *Bomba the Jungle Boy Among the Pygmies.* 1931. Cupples & Leon. G $3.50

ROCKWOOD, Roy. *Bomba the Jungle Boy Among the Slaves.* 1929. Cupples & Leon. VG $4.50

ROCKWOOD, Roy. *Bomba the Jungle Boy at the Giant Cataract.* 1926. Cupples & Leon. G $3.50

ROCKWOOD, Roy. *Bomba the Jungle Boy at the Moving Mountain.* Cupples & Leon. G $3.50

ROCKWOOD, Roy. *Bomba the Jungle Boy in a Strange Land.* 1931. Cupples & Leon. G $3.50

ROCKWOOD, Roy. *Bomba the Jungle Boy in the Abandoned·City.* 1927. Cupples & Leon. G $3.50

ROCKWOOD, Roy. *Bomba the Jungle Boy in the Swamp of Death.* 1929. Cupples & Leon. VG $4.50

ROCKWOOD, Roy. *Bomba the Jungle Boy on Jaguar Island.* 1927. Cupples & Leon. G $3.50

ROCKWOOD, Roy. *Bomba the Jungle Boy on Terror Trail.* 1928. Cupples & Leon. G $3.50

ROCKWOOD, Roy. *Bomba the Jungle Boy on the Underground River.* 1930. Cupples & Leon. VG $4.50

ROCKWOOD, Roy. *The Wizard of the Sea.* 1900. New York. A.L. Burt. dj. EX $20.00

ROCKWOOD. *The Speedwell Boys in a Submarine.* 1913. Cupples & Leon. Ills. G $4.50

ROCQ. *California Local History, a Bibliography.* 1970. 2nd revised ed. 611 pp. EX $80.00

RODALE, Robert. *Sane Living in a Mad World.* 1972. Rodale Press. 1st ed. dj. $3.00

RODELL, Marie. *Mystery Fiction Theory & Technique.* 1943. Duell. 1st ed. dj. $12.50

RODELL. *Woe Unto You Lawyers.* 1939. Hitchcock. 1st ed. dj. VG $15.00

RODERICH, N. *Altai-Himalaya.* 1929. New York. 407 pp. $10.00

RODGERS, W.L. *Naval Warfare Under Oars.* 1983. Ills. maps. EX $15.00

RODIN, A. *A La Venus De Milo.* 1945. Paris. Ltd. ed. 1/2500. wrappers. $90.00

RODIN, A. *Phaillon Ed.* 1939. Oxford U. Press. dj. $30.00

RODKINSON, Michael. *History of Amulets, Charms, & Talismans.* 1893. New York. 93 pp. VG $65.00

RODKINSON, Michael. *The History of the Talmund.* 1918. Boston. 2 vols in 1. 2 pls. $27.50

RODMAN, O.H.P. *The Salt-Water Fisherman's Favorite Four.* 1948. New York. Ills. VG $18.00

RODMAN, Seldon. *Mortal Triumph & Other Poems.* 1932. New York. 1st ed. dj. VG $17.50

RODMAN, Seldon. *The Insiders.* 1960. Louisiana U. 1st ed. dj. $15.00

RODMAN, Seldon. *Popular Artists of Brazil.* 1977. $10.00

RODMAN, Seldon. *The Revolutionists, a Tragedy in Three Acts.* 1942. New York. Ills. 1st ed. 193 pp. $7.50

ROE, Clifford G. *The Great War on White Slavery.* 1911. photos. 448 pp. $5.00

ROE, E.P. *The Gray & the Blue.* 1887. Chicago. Rand McNally. 292 pp. $17.50

ROE, J.E. *Mortal Moon; or, Bacon & His Masks.* 1891. New York. inscr. 605 pp. $15.00

ROEDIGER, Virginia. *Ceremonial Costumes of Pueblo Indians.* 1941. U. CA Press. Ills. 1st ed. dj. scarce. VG $165.00

ROEHL, L.M. *Fitting Farm Tools.* 1940. Milwaukee. Bruce. Ills. ex-lib. VG $4.00

ROGERS, Agnes. *Women Are Here to Stay.* 1949. New York. Ills. dj. $7.50

ROGERS, Andrew. *Bernhard Eduard Fernow: Story of N. Am. Forestry.* 1951. Princeton. sgn. $30.00

ROGERS, Aurelia. *Life Sketches of Orson Spence & Others.* 1898. 333 pp. G $75.00

ROGERS, B. *Essays of Montaigne.* 1904. Boston. Ltd. ed. 1/265. 3 vol set. $600.00

ROGERS, B. *Will Rogers/Story of His Life Told by His Wife.* 1941. New York. Garden City. photos. 312 pp. $4.00

ROGERS, C. *Trodden Glory, Story of California Poppy.* 1949. Santa Barbara. Hibberd. Ills. VG $10.00

ROGERS, Camerson. *Col. Bob Ingersoll.* 1927. New York. VG $15.00

ROGERS, Clara Kathleen. *Memories of a Musical Career.* 1919. Boston. Ills. 1st ed. inscr. G $45.00

ROGERS, D. *The House in My Head.* 1967. New York. 1st ed. dj. VG $15.00

ROGERS, Dale Evans. *Grandparents Can.* 1983. Old Tappan, NJ. 128 pp. dj. EX $3.50

ROGERS, Dale Evans. *My Spiritual Diary.* 1955. Old Tappan, NJ. 144 pp. dj. EX $3.50

ROGERS, Fred. *The Architect's Guide, Textbook of Information.* 1877. London. Ills. 384 pp. $27.50

ROGERS, George. *History Georgetown Co. South Carolina.* U. SC Press. 2nd ed. dj. VG $12.50

ROGERS, Glendon J. *Stories Along the Kern.* 1958. San Francisco. Ills. sgn. 103 pp. $12.50

ROGERS, J. *Old Public Schools of England.* 1938. London. 1st ed. VG $10.00

ROGERS, John William. *Finding Literature on the Texas Plains.* 1931. Dallas. Southwest Press. 57 pp. EX $75.00

ROGERS, Julia Ellen. *Trees.* 1922. New York. Ills. EX $12.50

ROGERS, Julia Ellen. *Trees.* 1926. New York. 291 pp. dj. $5.00

ROGERS, Lebbeaus Harding. *The Kite Trust.* 4th ed. VG $10.00

ROGERS, Lebbeaus Harding. *The Kite Trust.* 1900. New York. Kite Trust Pub. 1st ed. VG $25.00

ROGERS, Lela E. *Ginger Rogers & the Riddle of the Scarlet Cloak.* 1942. Racine. Whitman. 248 pp. dj. $3.00

ROGERS, Mondel. *Old Ranches of Texas Plains: Paintings by Rogers.* 1976. Texas A. & M. Press. $15.00

ROGERS, Robert. *A History of Babylonia & Assyria.* 1901. New York. 2nd ed. 2 vol set. G $65.00

ROGERS, Robert. *Concise Account of North America.* 1765. London. ex-lib. $425.00

ROGERS, S. *The Atlantic, History of the Ocean.* 1930. London. Ills. G $10.00

ROGERS, Samuel. *Human Life, a Poem.* 1819. London. 1st ed. $20.00

ROGERS, Samuel. *Pleasures of Memory & Other Poems.* 1808. New York. Duyckinck. Ills. VG $35.00

ROGERS, Samuel. *Poems.* 1834. London. Ills. Stothard. EX $75.00

ROGERS, Samuel. *Poems.* 1812. London. VG $180.00

ROGERS, Samuel. *The Poetical Works of Samuel Rogers.* 1869. Routledge. Ills. VG $30.00

ROGERS, W. *Cruising Voyage Around the World.* 1928. Ills. VG $10.00

ROGERS, Will. *How We Elect Our Presidents.* 1952. Boston. 1st ed. 175 pp. $50.00

ROGERS, Will. *Letters of a Self-Made Diplomat to His President.* 1926. Boni. Ills. Johnson. 1st ed. VG $30.00

ROGERS, Will. *There's Not a Bathing Suit in Russia & Bare Facts.* 1927. Boni. Ills. Herb Roth. 1st ed. VG $30.00

ROGERS, William. *Pumps & Hydraulics.* 1905. Audel. Ills. 2 vol set. $150.00

ROGERS & HAMMERSTEIN. *Pipe Dream.* 1956. New York. Viking. 1st ed. dj. $15.00

ROGERS. *5,000 Years of Gems & Jewelry.* 1964. New York. 309 pp. $17.50

ROGET, Peter M. *Thesaurus of English Words.* 1854. Boston. 1st Am. ed. VG $85.00

ROHAN, Michael Scott. *The Anvil of Ice.* London. 1st ed. sgn. $25.00

ROHAN, Michael Scott. *The Anvil of Ice.* 1986. New York. Morrow. proof copy. wrappers. $20.00

ROHMER, Sax. *Bat Wing.* 1921. New York. Ills. 1st ed. EX $30.00

ROHMER, Sax. *Brood of the Witch Queen.* A.L. Burt. dj. EX $30.00

ROHMER, Sax. *Daughter of Fu Manchu.* 1931. Doubleday Doran. 1st ed. dj. $175.00

ROHMER, Sax. *Day the World Ended.* 1930. Doubleday Doran. 1st ed. dj. $75.00

ROHMER, Sax. *Day the World Ended.* 1930. New York. Crime Club. 1st ed. dj. EX $75.00

ROHMER, Sax. *Dope.* 1920. New York. 4th printing. EX $25.00

ROHMER, Sax. *Fire Tongue.* 1922. New York. Ills. 1st ed. EX $20.00

ROHMER, Sax. *Fu Manchu's Bride.* 1933. Collier. Orient ed. $4.50

ROHMER, Sax. *Quest of the Sacred Slipper.* 1919. New York. Doubleday. 1st Am. ed. VG $25.00

ROHMER, Sax. *Return of Sumuru.* Gold Medal. pb. VG $15.00

ROHMER, Sax. *Seven Sins.* 1943. McBride. 1st ed. dj. $125.00

ROHMER, Sax. *Sinister Madonna.* Gold Medal. pb. VG $15.00

ROHMER, Sax. *Sumuru.* Gold Medal. pb. VG $17.00

ROHMER, Sax. *The Devil Doctor.* 1916. London. Methuen. 1st ed. VG $55.00

ROHMER, Sax. *The Fire Goddess.* Gold Medal. pb. VG $15.00

ROHMER, Sax. *The Golden Scorpion.* 1920. New York. 1st ed. VG $20.00

ROHMER, Sax. *The Green Eyes of Bast.* 1920. New York. 1st ed. EX $20.00

ROHMER, Sax. *The Insidious Dr. Fu Manchu.* 1913. A.L. Burt. $7.50

ROHMER, Sax. *The Mask of Fu Manchu.* 1932. Doubleday Doran. 1st ed. dj. $18.50

ROHMER, Sax. *The Romance of Sorcery.* 1914. London. Ills. 1st ed. press copy. $80.00

ROHMER, Sax. *The Si-Fan Mysteries.* 1917. London. Methuen. 1st ed. VG $40.00

ROHMER, Sax. *The Sins of Sumuru.* 1950. London. 1st ed. dj. VG $55.00

ROHMER, Sax. *Trail of Fu Manchu.* 1934. Collier. Orient ed. $4.50

ROHMER, Sax. *Trail of Fu Manchu.* 1936. London. 2nd ed. dj. G $18.00

ROJANKOVSKY. *Daniel Boone.* 1931. Paris. Domino Press. 1st ed. EX $100.00

ROJO, Richardo. *My Friend Che.* 1968. Dial Press. trans. 1st ed. dj. $10.00

ROLFE, Edwin. *The Lincoln Battalion.* 1939. New York. $20.00

ROLFE, France. *Tarcissus: Boy Martyr of Rome.* 1972. London. reprint. $15.00

ROLFE, William J. *Shakespeare the Boy.* 1897. London. Ills. Rockwell Kent. VG $12.50

ROLFE. *I Walked by Night.* 1948. London. dj. VG $15.00

ROLLAND, Romain. *Tolstoy.* 1911. New York. Dutton. 321 pp. G $4.00

ROLLE, A.F. *Lost Cause, Confederate Exodus to Mexico.* 1966. $20.00

ROLLIN, Charles. *The Ancient History, Vol. II.* 1848. Cincinnati. George Conclin Pub. VG $18.00

ROLLINS, William, Jr. *The Obelisk.* 1930. New York. Brewer & Warren. 1st ed. dj. $35.00

ROLLINS, William, Jr. *The Wall of Men.* 1938. New York. Modern Age. 1st ed. VG $35.00

ROLLINSON, John K. *Pony Trails in Wyoming.* 1944. Caxton. dj. VG $25.00

ROLLINSON, John K. *Wyoming Cattle Trails.* 1948. Caldwell. Ills. 1st ed. VG $40.00

ROLLINSON, John K. *Wyoming Cattle Trails.* 1948. Ltd. 1st ed. 1/1000. sgn. EX $75.00

ROLPH, J. Alexander. *Dylan Thomas.* 1956. London. Dent. Ills. 1st ed. 16 pls. VG $115.00

ROLT-WHEELER. *Boy with the U.S. Indians.* 1913. Boston. 36 Ills. 410 pp. VG $10.00

ROLVAG, O.E. *Giants in the Earth, a Saga of the Prairie.* 1927. Harper. 1st ed. VG $18.00

ROMAGNOLI, M. & Franco, G. *The Romagnolis' Meatless Cookbook.* 1976. Boston. Little, Brown. 272 pp. $7.50

ROMAINE, Lawrence. *The Weathercock Crows.* 1955. N. Middleboro. Weathercock House. 102 pp. $6.00

ROMAINS, J. *The Prelude to Battle.* 1939. G $7.50

ROMAINS, J. *Verdun.* 1939. New York. Knopf. 500 pp. $4.00

ROMAN, A. *Military Operations of Gen. Beauregard.* 1884. New York. Harper. 2 vol set. VG $75.00

ROMANES, George J. *Darwin, & After Darwin.* 1910. Open Court Pub. 3 vol set. EX $50.00

ROMBAUER & BECKER. *Joy of Cooking.* 1946. VG $15.00

ROMBAUER & BECKER. *Joy of Cooking.* 1953. Bobbs Merrill. 1013 pp. $4.50

ROME, C. *An Owl Who Came to Stay.* 1980. Crown. Ills. 144 pp. dj. EX $7.50

ROMER, Alfred. *Osteology of Reptiles.* 1968. Chicago. Ills. 772 pp. VG $30.00

ROMERO, Matias. *Coffee & India-Rubber Culture in Mexico.* 1898. NY/London. 417 pp. $35.00

ROMNEY. *Two Little Crusoes.* Blackie & Son. Ills. 48 pp. VG $3.50

ROMULO, Carlos P. *I Saw the Fall of the Philippines.* 1946. Ills. G $7.50

ROMULO, Carlos P. *I Saw the Fall of the Philippines.* 1942. Sydney. Ills. 288 pp. $5.00

RONALDSHAY, Earl. *Sport & Politics Under an Eastern Sky.* 1902. London. $60.00

RONAN, P. *Historical Sketch of Flathead Indian Nation.* Haines. reprint. dj. EX $10.00

RONBERG, Gary. *The Violent Game.* 1975. Prentice Hall. Ills. 192 pp. dj. EX $8.50

RONDELLE, L. *Foil & Sabre, a Grammar of Fencing.* 1892. Boston. 1st ed. 218 pp. VG $20.00

RONDOT, P. *The Changing Patterns of the Middle East 1919-58.* 1961. London. dj. G $7.50

RONNE, Finn. *Antarctic Conquest, Story of Ronne Expedition.* 1949. New York. Ills. 1st ed. $20.00

ROOD. *Wisconsin at Vicksburg.* 1914. Madison. Ills. 501 pp. VG $35.00

ROOF. *William Smith & His Lady.* 1929. Ills. 347 pp. $12.50

ROOKE, Leon. *Shakespeare's Dog.* 1983. Knopf. 1st Am. ed. dj. VG $10.00

ROOKS, Cecil. *Light Horses.* 1946. 2nd ed. dj. $37.50

ROOME, W.J.W. *Tramping Through Africa.* 1930. Macmillan. Ills. 325 pp. dj. VG $47.50

ROONEY, Andrew A. *And More by Andy Rooney.* 1982. Atheneum. 242 pp. dj. EX $3.50

ROONEY, Andrew A. *Fortunes of War.* 1962. Boston. Ills. 241 pp. dj. VG $12.50

ROOSEVELT, Anne E. *Hunting Big Game in the Eighties.* 1933. 1st ed. dj. VG $27.50

ROOSEVELT, Capt. Wyn. *Frontier Boys in the Rockies.* 1909. New York. 245 pp. $3.50

ROOSEVELT, Capt. Wyn. *Frontier Boys in Frisco.* 1911. Platt & Peck. Ills. Mencl. G $4.50

ROOSEVELT, Eleanor. *This I Remember.* Book Club. 1st ed. $5.50

ROOSEVELT, Eleanor. *This I Remember.* 1949. Ills. $7.50

ROOSEVELT, Eleanor. *Tomorrow is Now.* 1963. New York. Harper. 1st ed. 139 pp. $6.50

ROOSEVELT, Eleanor. *If You Ask Me.* 1946. Curtis. 156 pp. dj. EX $4.50

ROOSEVELT, Franklin D. *The Future of the Great Plains.* 1937. Washington. Ills. 1st ed. 194 pp. $85.00

ROOSEVELT, Franklin D. *The Public Papers & Addresses of Roosevelt.* 1938. Random House. 5 vol set. djs. slipcase. VG $50.00

ROOSEVELT, Kermit. *A Sentimental Safari.* 1963. 1st ed. dj. VG $12.50

ROOSEVELT, Kermit. *The Long Trail.* 1921. New York. 79 pp. $10.00

ROOSEVELT, Robert B. *Game Fish of Northern States & British Provinces.* 1884. New York. Ills. 1st ed. VG $45.00

ROOSEVELT, T. & Grinnel, G.B. *Hunting in Many Lands.* 1895. New York. Ills. 1st ed. 477 pp. VG $17.50

ROOSEVELT, Theodore & Kermit. *East of the Sun & West of the Moon.* 1926. Blue Ribbon Books. 284 pp. $7.50

ROOSEVELT, Theodore. *African Game Trails.* Syndicate Pub. (ca.1910) Ills. photos. VG $60.00

ROOSEVELT, Theodore. *American Bears.* 1983. CO U. Press. Ills. 193 pp. EX $10.00

ROOSEVELT, Theodore. *An Autobiography.* 1923. New York. Scribner. Ills. VG $8.50

ROOSEVELT, Theodore. *An Autobiography.* 1913. Ills. 1st ed. VG $25.00

ROOSEVELT, Theodore. *Big Game Hunting.* Ltd. ed. 1/1000. sgn. $300.00

ROOSEVELT, Theodore. *Fear God & Take Your Own Part.* 1916. Doubleday. 414 pp. $4.50

ROOSEVELT, Theodore. *Outdoor Pastimes of an American Hunter.* 1905. Longmans. 1st Eng. ed. Ills. 369 pp. G $22.50

ROOSEVELT, Theodore. *Outdoor Pastimes of an American Hunter.* 1908. Scribner. Ills. 2nd ed. 420 pp. $17.50

ROOSEVELT, Theodore. *Outdoor Pastimes of an American Hunter.* 1905. NY. Scribner. 1st trade ed. 369 pp. VG $65.00

ROOSEVELT, Theodore. *Ranch Life & the Hunting Trail.* 1888. New York. Ills. Remington. 1st ed. VG $285.00

ROOSEVELT, Theodore. *Ranch Life & the Hunting Trail.* 1896. Century. Ills. Remington. VG $15.00

ROOSEVELT, Theodore. *Stories from the Winning of the West.* 1920. New York. 291 pp. VG $15.00

ROOSEVELT, Theodore. *The Deer Family.* 1902. New York. Ills. Carl Rungus. 1st ed. EX $45.00

ROOSEVELT, Theodore. *The Rough Riders.* 1899. New York. 1st ed. dj. VG $75.00

ROOSEVELT, Theodore. *The Winning of the West.* 1900. Putnam. Alleghany ed. 4 vol set. VG $50.00

ROOSEVELT, Theodore. *Through the Brazilian Wilderness.* 1914. New York. Ills w/photos by K. Roosevelt. $50.00

ROOSEVELT, Theodore. *Through the Brazilian Wilderness.* 1919. VG $25.00

ROOSEVELT, Theodore. *Through the Brazilian Wilderness.* 1922. Ills. $15.00

ROOSEVELT, Theodore. *Wilderness Hunter. Big Game in U.S. & Its Chase.* 1893. New York. Putnam. Ills. 1st ed. 472 pp. $35.00

ROOSEVELT, Theodore. *Works of Theodore Roosevelt.* 1910. New York. Homeward Bound ed. 20 vol set. $35.00

ROOT, A.I. *ABC of Bee Culture.* 1891. Medina, OH. Ills. gilt decor. VG $25.00

ROOT, A.I. & E.R. *The ABC & XYZ of Bee Culture.* 1919. Ohio. 856 pp. G $16.00

ROOT, A.I. & E.R. *The ABC & XYZ of Bee Culture.* 1940. $15.00

ROOT, A.I. & E.R. *The ABC & XYZ of Bee Culture.* 1929. Root. Ills. 815 pp. VG $15.00

ROOT, Frank A. & Connelley, W. *The Overland Stage to California.* reprint. College Book Co. dj. VG $25.00

ROOT, Frank A. & Connelley, W. *The Overland Stage to California.* 1950. Columbus, OH. Ills. 630 pp. $55.00

ROOT, Frank A. & Connelley, W. *The Overland Stage to California.* 1901. Topeka. 1st ed. $130.00

ROOT, George. *The Bugle Call.* 1863. Root & Cady. 60 pp. $18.00

ROOTEN, Luis d'Antin van. *Van Rooten's Book of Improbable Saints.* 1975. Grossman Pub., Viking Press. $3.50

ROOTHAM, Jasper. *Verses 1928-1972.* 1972. Cambridge. Ltd. ed. 1/500. VG $15.00

ROPES, John. *The Story of the Civil War Manuscripts.* 1965. Indianapolis. wrappers. VG $20.00

ROSALITA, Sister M. *No Greater Service.* 1948. Detroit. $12.50

ROSAMOND, Robert. *Crusade for Peace.* 1962. New York. Lexington Pub. 243 pp. dj. $4.00

ROSCOE, T. *On the Seas & in the Skies.* 1970. Ills. G $15.00

ROSCOE, T. *Sub Operations in WWII.* 1950. $27.50

ROSCOE, T. *U.S. Destroyer Operations in WWII.* 1957. U.S. Naval Institute. EX $27.50

ROSCOE, T. *Wanderings in North Wales.* 1836. London. Ills. EX $110.00

ROSE, Grace Norton. *Williamsburg: Today & Yesterday.* 1940. New York. Putnam. Ills. Jack Manly Rose. $6.50

ROSE, R. *Living Magic.* 1956. Rand McNally. Ills. 1st ed. 240 pp. VG $10.00

ROSE, Robert R. *Advocates & Adversaries.* 1977. Chicago. $8.50

ROSE, William G. *Cleveland, the Making of a City.* 1950. Cleveland. World Pub. photos. 1272 pp. $20.00

ROSE. *Maryland Hunt Cup.* 1931. New York. 1st ed. VG $25.00

ROSE. *Wine, Women, & Words.* 1948. Ills. Dali. pb. $35.00

ROSEBERRY, Lord. *The Last Phase.* 1900. London. 261 pp. $12.50

ROSEN, Barbara & Barry. *The Destined Hour.* 1982. New York. Doubleday. 328 pp. dj. $4.50

ROSEN, E. *Fran Kap Til Alexandria.* 1912. Swedish text. VG $50.00

ROSENBACH, A.S.W. *Book Hunter's Holiday.* 1936. Boston. Ltd. ed. boxed. EX $125.00

ROSENBACH, A.S.W. *Books & Bidders* 1927. Boston. Ltd. ed. 1/785. sgn. EX $100.00

ROSENBACH, A.S.W. *Books & Bidders* 1927. Boston. 1st ed. sgn. $55.00

ROSENBACH, A.S.W. *The Unpublishable Memoirs.* 1917. New York. Kennerley. 1st ed. inscr. sgn. $150.00

ROSENBACH, A.S.W. *The Unpublishable Memoirs.* 1924. London. 1st ed. VG $30.00

ROSENBACH. *A Biography of Wolf & Fleming.* 1961. London. 1st Eng. ed. review copy. VG $45.00

ROSENBAUM, Jeanette. *Myer, Myers, Goldsmith 1723-1795.* 1954. 1st ed. $10.00

ROSENBERG, C.G. *The Man of the People.* 1843. Winchester. 60 pp. wrappers. $45.00

ROSENBERG. *The Age of Louis XV: French Painting 1710-1774.* Toledo Museum of Art. pb. $5.00

ROSENBLUM, L.A. & Cooper, R.W. *The Squirrel Monkey.* 1968. Academic Press. Ills. 451 pp. dj. EX $10.00

ROSENFELD, A. *A Thomason Sketchbook.* 1969. Texas U. Press. dj. EX $30.00

ROSENFELD, Morris. *Under Full Sail.* 1957. sgn. $9.00

ROSENFELD, Paul. *Men Seen.* 1925. New York. Dial Press. 1st ed. 380 pp. $5.00

ROSENGARTEN, Frank. *The Italian Anti-Fascist Press (1919-1945).* 1968. Cleveland. 263 pp. dj. EX $12.50

ROSENNE, S. *6,000,000 Accusers/Israel's Case Against Eichmann.* 1961. Jerusalem. Ills. dj. EX $20.00

ROSENTHAL, Irving. *Sheeper.* 1967. New York. Grove Press. 1st ed. $4.00

ROSENTHAL, Leonard. *Kingdom of the Pearl.* New York. Ills. Dulac. Ltd. ed. 1/675. $250.00

ROSENTHAL, Philip. *Sein Leben und Sein Porzellan.* 1929. Leipzig. Ills. Ltd. ed. folio. VG $42.50

ROSS, A. & Emerson, W.K. *Wonders of Barnacles.* 1974. Dodd Mead. Ills. 78 pp. dj. EX $5.00

ROSS, Annette & Disney, Jean. *The Art of Making Good Cookies, Plain & Fancy.* 1963. Garden City. Doubleday. 252 pp. $5.00

ROSS, Barnaby. *The Tragedy of Z.* 1933. New York. Viking. 1st ed. dj. VG $45.00

ROSS, Christian K. *Father's Story of Charley Ross: Kidnapped Child.* 1876. Philadelphia. 431 pp. G $2.50

ROSS, Harvey. *Lincoln's First Years in Illinois.* 1946. reprint. Ltd. ed. 1/500. VG $15.00

ROSS, I. *The General's Wife/Life of Mrs. Ulysses S. Grant.* 1959. New York. photos. 372 pp. $4.50

ROSS, Lillian. *Picture, a Story About Hollywood.* 1952. New York. dj. VG $8.00

ROSS, Stanley. *Pictorial History of Aircraft.* 1975. Norwalk. Longmeadow Pr. 1st Am. ed. EX $12.00

ROSS, W.S. *The Last Hero: Charles A. Lindbergh, a Biography.* 1968. Ills. G $10.00

ROSS. *Theory of Pure Design.* 1933. Peter Smith. $10.00

ROSSELL. *Tracks & Trails.* 1928. Boy Scout Pub. VG $15.00

ROSSET, Barney. *Evergreen Review Reader, a Ten Year Anthology.* 1968. New York. Grove Press. 1st ed. $25.00

ROSSETTI, Christina. *Goblin Markets.* 1933. Ills. Rackham. 1st Am. trade ed. VG $40.00

ROSSETTI, Dante Gabriel. *Ballads & Sonnets.* 1903. Portland. Ltd. ed. 1/450. 334 pp. $35.00

ROSSETTI, Dante Gabriel. *New Life of Dante Alighieri.* 1901. New York. Ills. 115 pp. $25.00

ROSSETTI, William Michael. *Life of John Keats.* 1887. London. 1st ed. G $45.00

ROSSI. *Italian Jeweled Arts.* 1954. New York. 233 pp. dj. $50.00

ROSSITER, C. & Lare, J. *The Essential Lippmann.* 1963. New York. Random House. 552 pp. dj. $4.00

ROSSITER. *William Blake: Paradise Lost.* 1947. New York. Ills. folio portfolio. $45.00

ROSSMAN, E. *Black Sunlight, a Log of the Arctic.* 1926. Oxford. Ills. inscr. 231 pp. G $7.50

ROSSMAN, Kenneth. *Thomas Mifflin & Politics of American Revolution.* 1952. Chapel Hill. 1st ed. dj. $10.00

ROSSNER, Judith. *Any Minute I Can Split.* 1972. McGraw Hill. 1st ed. dj. VG $15.00

ROSSNER, Judith. *Looking for Mr. Goodbar.* 1975. Simon & Schuster. 1st ed. dj. $15.00

ROSTAND, Edmond. *Cyrano de Bergerac.* 1901. Paris. EX $50.00

ROSTEN, Leo C. *Hollywood: The Movie Colony, the Movie Makers.* 1941. New York. G $5.00

ROSTENBERG & STERN. *Old & Rare.* 1974. sgn. dj. VG $15.00

ROSTRON, Arthur. *Home from the Sea.* 1931. New York. $12.50

ROTERS, E. *Painters of the Bauhaus.* 1965. Praeger. 1st ed. dj. $20.00

ROTH, C. *Earl of Deaconsfield.* 1952. New York. 1st ed. $10.00

ROTH, C. *Venice.* 1930. Philadelphia. Ills. 380 pp. index. $7.50

ROTH, Henry. *Nature's First Green.* 1979. Targ. Ltd. 1st ed. sgn. dj. VG $35.00

ROTH, Philip. *My Life as a Man.* 1974. Holt. 1st ed. dj. VG $15.00

ROTH, Philip. *Our Gang.* 1971. New York. Random House. 1st ed. dj. VG $25.00

ROTH, Philip. *Portnoy's Complaint.* 1969. Random House. 1st trade ed. dj. VG $30.00

ROTH, Philip. *Portnoy's Complaint.* 1969. Cape. 1st English ed. dj. VG $30.00

ROTH, Philip. *Professor of Desire.* New York. 1st Am. ed. dj. EX $10.00

ROTH, Philip. *Reading Myself & Others.* 1975. Farrar. 1st ed. dj. EX $15.00

ROTH, Philip. *The Anatomy Lesson.* 1983. New York. Farrar. proof copy. wrappers. $50.00

ROTH, Philip. *The Beast.* 1973. Cape. 1st English ed. dj. VG $15.00

ROTH, Philip. *The Beast.* 1972. New York. 1st ed. dj. EX $15.00

ROTH, Philip. *The Great American Novel.* 1973. New York. Holt. 1st ed. dj. VG $30.00

ROTH, Philip. *When She Was Good.* 1967. New York. Random House. 1st ed. dj. VG $40.00

ROTH, W.E. *Study of Arts, Crafts, Customs of Guiana Indians.* 1929. ex-lib. 110 pp. 34 pls. $10.00

ROTH & WHITING. *History of Kappa Kappa Gamma Fraternity 1870-1930.* 1932. Westerman. Ills. 887 pp. G $12.50

ROTH. *Letting Go.* 1st Am. ed. dj. VG $20.00

ROTHA, Paul & Manvell, Roger. *Movie Parade 1888-1949, Survey of the Cinema.* 1950. London. 157 pp. VG $16.00

ROTHA, Paul. *Documentary Film.* 1936. London. Ills. 1st ed. 252 pp. $27.50

ROTHENBERG, G.E. *Anatomy of Israeli Army, Defense Force 1948-1978.* 1979. Ills. dj. EX $17.50

ROTHENSTEIN, William. *Augustus John.* 1945. London. Phaidon. Ltd. ed. $20.00

ROTHENSTEIN, William. *Twenty-Four Portraits.* 1920. New York. Ltd. ed. 1/2000. EX $35.00

ROTHERY, Agnes. *Houses Virginians Have Loved.* 1954. Bonanza. reprint. dj. VG $15.00

ROTHSCHILD, Lincoln. *Sculpture Through the Ages.* 1942. NY/London. Ills. folio. VG $32.50

ROTTSOLK. *Pines, Mines & Lakes, Story of Itasca County.* 1960. 1st ed. dj. EX $25.00

ROUDYBUSH, Alexandra. *Blood Ties.* 1st ed. dj. $8.00

ROUECHE, Berton. *Curiosities of Medicine.* 1963. Boston. 1st ed. 338 pp. dj. VG $25.00

ROUECHE, Berton. *The Greener Grass & Some People Who Found It.* 1948. NY. Harper. 1st ed. dj. EX $30.00

ROUFF. *Passionate Epicure.* 1962. $8.00

ROUGHLEY, T.C. *Fish & Fisheries of Australia.* 1951. Robertson. Ills. revised ed. 343 pp. EX $45.00

ROULE, L. *Fishes, Their Journeys & Migrations.* 1933. Norton. Ills. 1st Am. ed. 270 pp. G $10.00

ROUNDTREE, J.G.R. *The Hereditary Register of the U.S.A.* 1972. Washington. 474 pp. $20.00

ROURKE, Constance. *Audubon.* 1936. Harcourt Brace.Ills. 342 pp. VG $10.00

ROURKE, Constance. *Troupers of Gold Coast; or, Rise of Lotta Crabtree.* 1928. New York. Ills. 262 pp. index. dj. $15.00

ROUSE, B. *Letters of Ellen Glasgow.* 1958. New York. 1st ed. dj. VG $20.00

ROUSSET, David. *The Legacy of the Bolshevik Revolution.* 1982. London. Allison & Busby. 333 pp. $8.00

ROUSSY DE SALES, Raoud de. *The Making of Tomorrow.* 1942. dj. $5.50

ROVERE, R.H. & Schlesinger, A. *The General & the President.* 1951. New York. 1st ed. dj. VG $10.00

ROVERE, Richard H. *Affairs of State, the Eisenhower Years.* 1956. New York. Farrar, Straus & Cudahey. dj. $4.50

ROWAN, Mrs. Lelia M. *Trailing Arbutus.* 1902. Lansing. Ills. 183 pp. $12.50

ROWAN, R. *The Four Days of Mayaguez.* 1975. Ills. dj. EX $10.00

ROWE, H. *Tercentenary History of Newton, 1630-1930.* 1930. VG $25.00

ROWE. *Friendship in Death: Letters from Dead to Living.* 1797. London. G $200.00

ROWE. *Sergeant Dick of the Royal Mounted Police.* 1929. Cupples & Leon. VG $4.50

ROWELL, Earle Albert & Robert. *On the Trail of Marijuana, Weed of Madness.* 1939. Mountain View. Ills. 96 pp. wrappers. VG $35.00

ROWELL, Earle Albert. *Dope Adventures of David Dare.* 1937. Nashville. Southern Pub. wrappers. EX $25.00

ROWES, Barbara. *Grace Slick.* 1980. Garden City. Ills. 1st ed. dj. VG $10.00

ROWLAND, K.T. *Steam at Sea.* 1970. Ills. dj. EX $10.00

ROWLANDS, J.J. *Cache Lake Country.* 1959. Norton. Ills. H.B. Kane. 272 pp. VG $6.00

ROWSE, A.L. *William Shakespeare.* 1963. Harper & Row. 1st ed. $15.00

ROWSE. *West Country Stories.* 1945. London. 1st ed. $9.00

ROXBOROUGH, Henry. *The Stanley Cup Story.* 1964. Toronto. 2nd ed. VG $7.50

ROXON, Lillian. *Lillian Roxon's Rock Encyclopedia.* 1969. New York. Ills. photos. dj. VG $18.00

ROY, Andrew. *History of the Coal Miners of the United States.* 1906. Colorado. $25.00

ROY, Ewell Paul. *Contract Farming, U.S.A.* 1963. 572 pp. $3.00

ROY, J. *The Trial of Marshal Petain.* 1968. dj. G $7.50

ROY, Lillian Elizabeth. *Polly in New York.* 1922. Grosset & Dunlap. Ills. $3.50

ROY, Lillian Elizabeth. *Woodraft Boys in the Rockies.* 1928. New York. Grosset & Dunlap. 252 pp. $2.00

ROYALL, Anne. *Sketches of Scenery & Manners in the U.S.* 1829. Ills. 188 pp. $45.00

ROYCE, Sarah. *Frontier Lady: Recollections of Gold Rush & CA.* 1932. Yale U. Press. 1st ed. dj. VG $15.00

ROYE. *Nude Ego.* 1958. London. 1st ed. dj. EX $7.50

ROYKO, Mike. *Boss.* 1971. book plate. G $2.00

ROYS, Willis E. *Flame Eternal.* 1936. New York. 1st ed. dj. EX $40.00

RUANE, J.W. *Beginnings of Society of the St. Supice in U.S.* 1935. Baltimore. 266 pp. $10.00

RUARK, Robert. *Grenadine Etching.* 1947. Doubleday. 1st ed. sgn. dj. VG $35.00

RUARK, Robert. *Old Man's Boy Grows Older.* 1961. Holt. 1st ed. dj. VG $37.50

RUARK, Robert. *Something of Value.* 1955. Garden City. Doubleday. Ills Schwartz. G $12.50

RUARK, Robert. *The Old Man & the Boy.* 1957. New York. 1st ed. dj. EX $45.00

RUARK, Robert. *Use Enough Gun.* 1966. New Am. Lib. Ills. 1st ed. 333 pp. dj. $20.00

RUARK, Robert. *Use Enough Gun.* 1966. New York. 1st ed. dj. EX $30.00

RUARK, Robert. *Women.* 1967. New York. 1st ed. G $35.00

RUARK. *Honey Badger.* 1965. 1st Am. ed. dj. EX $30.00

RUARK. *Horn of the Hunter.* 1953. New York. dj. EX $35.00

RUAS, Charles. *Conversations with American Writers.* 1985. Knopf. 1st ed. dj. VG $17.50

RUBENS, Alfred. *History of Jewish Costume.* 1967. Funk. 1st ed. dj. $15.00

RUBENSTEIN, Arthur. *My Many Years.* 1980. New York. 1st ed. 626 pp. dj. EX $7.50

RUBENSTEIN, Arthur. *My Young Years.* Knopf. Ills. 1st ed. dj. VG $10.00

RUBIN, Theodore. *Through My Own Eyes.* 1982. Macmillan. dj. $3.00

RUBIN, W.B. *The Toiler in Europe.* 1916. Cincinnati. sgn. VG $12.50

RUBIN. *Bibliographical Guide to Study Southern Literature.* 1969. 1st ed. 368 pp. EX $30.00

RUBY, R. & Brown, J.A. *Myron Eells & Puget Sound Indians.* 1976. 1st ed. dj. VG $12.50

RUD, Anthony. *The Devil's Heirloom.* 1924. New York. 1st ed. wrappers. $15.00

RUDLOE, J. *The Sea Brings Forth.* 1968. Knopf. Ills. 1st ed. 261 pp. dj. EX $5.00

RUE, L.L. *Furbearing Animals of North America.* 1981. Crown. Ills. 1st ed. 343 pp. dj. EX $17.50

RUE, L.L. *Game Birds of North America.* 1976. Outdoor Life. Ills. 490 pp. dj. VG $12.50

RUE, L.L. *Pictorial Guide to the Birds of America.* 1970. Crowell. Ills. 1st ed. 368 pp. dj. EX $15.00

RUE, L.L. *Sportsman's Guide to Game Animals.* 1971. Outdoor Life. Ills. 655 pp. G $7.50

RUE, L.L. *The Deer of North America.* 1981. Outdoor Life. Ills. 463 pp. dj. EX $15.00

RUE, L.L. *World of the White-Tailed Deer.* 1962. Lippincott. Ills. 134 pp. dj. EX $10.00

RUEGAMER, Lana. *A History of Indiana Historical Society 1830-1980.* 1980. Indianapolis. 383 pp. $12.50

RUESCH, Jurgen & Kees, Weldon. *Nonverbal Communication.* 1956. Berkeley. U. CA Pr. 1st ed. dj. EX $30.00

RUESCH. *Back to the Top of the World.* 1973. 1st ed. dj. EX $7.50

RUGG, Henry W. *History of Freemasonry in Rhode Island.* 1895. Providence. Freeman & Con. 1st ed. 869 pp. $27.50

RUGGLES, C.L. *Stresses in Wire Wrapped Guns & Carriages.* 1916. Ills. G $25.00

RUGGLES, Eleanor. *Prince of Players, Edwin Booth.* 1953. New York. Norton. photos. 401 pp. $4.50

RUKAVINA, K.S. *Jungle Pathfinder.* 1951. London. Hutchinson. Ills. 1st ed. VG $17.50

RUKEYSER, Muriel. *Body of Waking.* 1958. New York. Harper. 1st ed. dj. EX $25.00

RUKEYSER, Muriel. *The Orgy.* 1965. New York. Coward. 1st ed. dj. EX $25.00

RUKEYSER, Muriel. *Theory of Flight.* 1935. Yale U. Press. dj. EX $95.00

RUKEYSER, Muriel. *Wake Island.* 1942. Doubleday. 1st ed. wrappers. VG $30.00

RUKEYSER, Muriel. *Wilard Gibbs.* 1942. $7.50

RULE, Ann. *Possession.* 1983. Norton. proof copy. wrappers. VG $20.00

RULE, Christopher. *Grimm's Fairy Tales.* 1926. New York. Sears & Co. Ills. VG $12.50

RUMBELOW, Donald. *The Complete Jack the Ripper.* 1975. dj. $10.00

RUNDALL, L.B. *The Ibex of Sha-Ping & Other Himalayan Studies.* 1915. London. Macmillan. Ills. 152 pp. VG $60.00

RUNYON, Damon. *Runyon from First to Last.* 1954. London. 1st ed. VG $20.00

RUOTOTO, Lucio. *Six Existential Heroes, the Politics of Faith.* 1973. Harvard U. Press. 161 pp. $5.00

RUSE, Gary A. *Gods of Cerus Major.* 1982. Garden City. 1st ed. dj. VG $8.00

RUSH, Benjamin. *Medical Inquiries & Observations.* 1818. Philadelphia. 4 vols in 2. 5th ed. $95.00

RUSH, Richard. *Land District-South of Tennessee.* 1828. Washington. 1st ed. 22 pp. $25.00

RUSHBROOKE. *Introduction to Statistical Mechanics.* 1949. $20.00

RUSHDIE, Salman. *Grimus.* 1st ed. dj. VG $35.00

RUSHING, Jane Gilmore. *The Raincrow.* 1977. Doubleday. proof copy. wrappers. EX $25.00

RUSHING, Lilith & Voss, Ruth. *The Cake Cookbook.* 1965. NY/Philadelphia. Chilton. dj. $6.50

RUSKAY, Sophie. *Horsecars & Cobblestones.* 1948. Beechurst Pr. Ills. Cecil B. Ruskay. 240 pp. $7.00

RUSKIN, John. *Lectures on Architecture & Painting.* 1853. New York. Wiley. Ills. 1st Am. ed. $65.00

RUSKIN, John. *Modern Painters.* 1892. London. Ills. 5 vol set. $175.00

RUSKIN, John. *Pantheon Story of Art for Young People.* 1964. Pantheon. 1st ed. dj. $10.00

RUSKIN, John. *Seven Lamps of Architecture.* 1849. London. Ills. 14 pls. $55.00

RUSKIN, John. *The Stones of Venice.* 1886. England. Ills. 4th ed. 3 vol set. $135.00

RUSKIN, John. *The Works of John Ruskin.* 6 vols in 2. 1079 pp. VG $110.00

RUSS, Joanna. *The Two of Them.* 1978. New York. Berkeley. 1st ed. dj. EX $10.00

RUSS, Martin. *The Last Parallel.* 1957. NY/Toronto. Ills. 333 pp. $10.00

RUSSELL, Andy. *Adventures with Wild Animals.* 1978. Knopf. Ills. 1st ed. 176 pp. VG $10.00

RUSSELL, Andy. *Grizzly Country.* 1967. Knopf. Ills. 302 pp. dj. EX $17.50

RUSSELL, Anna. *I'm Not Making This Up, You Know.* 1985. New York. 1st ed. $10.00

RUSSELL, Anna. *The Power of Being a Positive Stinker.* 1956. Citadel Press. 57 pp. EX $8.50

RUSSELL, Bertrand. *History of Western Philosophy.* 1947. London. 2nd ed. inscr. dj. VG $45.00

RUSSELL, Bertrand. *Satan in the Suburbs.* 1953. New York. Simon & Schuster. 1st ed. dj. $20.00

RUSSELL, Bertrand. *The Basic Writings of Bertrand Russell, 1903-59.* 1961. New York. Simon & Schuster. 736 pp. $7.50

RUSSELL, Bertrand. *The Prospects of Industrial Civilization.* 1923. New York. 1st ed. dj. VG $20.00

RUSSELL, Carl. *Guns on the Early Frontiers.* 1957. Berkely. 1st ed. dj. $15.00

RUSSELL, Charles Edward. *A Rafting on the Mississippi.* 1928. New York. Ills. 1st ed. 357 pp. VG $50.00

RUSSELL, Charles Edward. *Lawless Wealth.* 1908. New York. 1st ed. $12.50

RUSSELL, Charles M. *Back-Trailing on the Old Frontier.* 1922. Great Falls. Ills. 1st ed. sgn. wrappers. $150.00

RUSSELL, Charles M. *Good Medicine.* 1930. Garden City. Ills. author. 162 pp. $28.00

RUSSELL, Charles M. *More Rawhides.* 1925. Great Falls. Ills. 1st ed. orig. wrappers. $475.00

RUSSELL, Charles M. *Paper Talk.* 1962. Fort Worth. $25.00

RUSSELL, Charles M. *Trails Plowed Under.* 1927. New York. Ills. author & Borein. 1st ed. $500.00

RUSSELL, Don. *103 Fights & Scrimmages, Story of Reuben Bernard.* 1936. Ills. 173 pp. maps. SftCvr. $45.00

RUSSELL, Dorothy & Rubenstein. *Pathology of Tumors of the Nervous System.* 1959. London. 1st ed. many photos. 318 pp. $95.00

RUSSELL, Eric F. *Next of Kin.* 1959. London. Dennis Dobson. 1st ed. dj. VG $15.00

RUSSELL, Eric F. *Sentinels from Space.* 1953. New York. Bouregy. 1st ed. dj. VG $45.00

RUSSELL, F. *Mountains of America from Alaska to Great Smokies.* 1951. Bonanza. Ills. 224 pp. VG $17.50

RUSSELL, F. *Season on the Plain.* 1974. Readers Digest. 1st ed. 313 pp. VG $10.00

RUSSELL, F. *The Secret Islands, an Exploration.* 1965. Norton. Ills. 1st ed. 238 pp. dj. EX $10.00

RUSSELL, F. *The Shadow of Blooming Grove.* 1968. 1st ed. $10.00

RUSSELL, F.E. & Scharffenberg. *Bibliography of Snake Venoms & Venomous Snakes.* 1964. Bibliog. Assoc. 220 pp. VG $30.00

RUSSELL, George. *Vale & Other Poems.* 1931. New York. 1st ed. 50 pp. VG $7.50

RUSSELL, Howard S. *A Long, Deep Furrow: Three Centuries of Farming.* 1976. Hanover, NH. 1st ed. 672 pp. EX $20.00

RUSSELL, I.C. *Geological Reconnaissance of Southern Oregon.* 1884. U.S. Geol. Survey 4th Annual Report. $10.00

RUSSELL, Isaac. *Hidden Heroes of the Rockies.* 1927. New York. 294 pp. $16.00

RUSSELL, J. *Nelson & the Hamiltons.* 1970. Ills. G $12.50

RUSSELL, J. & R. *On the Loose.* 1967. Sierra Club. Ills. 121 pp. dj. VG $10.00

RUSSELL, John & Brown, Ashley. *Satire, a Critical Anthology.* 1967. Cleveland. 420 pp. $4.00

RUSSELL, John. *Aubrey Beardsley: Selected Drawings.* 1967. New York. 1st ed. dj. $27.00

RUSSELL, Lester F. *Profile of a Black Heritage.* 1977. sgn. $18.00

RUSSELL, M. *Nubia & Abyssinia.* 1845. New York. Harper's Family Lib. 331 pp. $12.50

RUSSELL, Mary LaFatra. *Nursery Songs.* 1916. New York. Gabriel Sons. Ills. 31 pp. $16.00

RUSSELL, P. *John Paul Jones: Man of Action.* 1927. New York. Ills. Underwood. 314 pp. VG $27.00

RUSSELL, P.F. *Keys to the Anopheline Mosquitos of the World.* 1943. Am. Entom. Soc. Ills. 152 pp. $7.50

RUSSELL, Ray. *The Bishop's Daughter.* 1981. Houghton. review copy. dj. VG $15.00

RUSSELL, Ross. *Bird Lives.* 1973. Charterhouse. 1st ed. dj. G $35.00

RUSSELL, Thomas H. *America's Greatest Flood & Tornado Calamity.* 1913. 320 pp $4.00

RUSSELL, W. Clark. *The Wreck of the Grosvenor.* 1909. New York. $10.00

RUSSELL, William Howard. *My Diary North & South.* 1863. Boston. 1st ed. 602 pp. $47.50

RUSSELL, William Howard. *My Diary North & South.* 1863. London. 1st ed. 2 vol set. $45.00

RUSSELL, William. *Pilgrim Memorials & Guide to Plymouth.* 1864. Crosby & Nichols. $35.00

RUSSELL, William. *Scientific Horseshoeing.* 1895. Cincinnati. Ills. VG $40.00

RUSSELL. *Education & Good Life.* 1954. dj. EX $10.00

RUSSELL. *100 Years in Yosemite.* 1947. revised ed. dj. VG $30.00

RUSSO, Dorothy & Sullivan. *Bibliography of Booth Tarkington.* 1949. $17.50

RUST, Art, Jr. *Get that Nigger Off the Field.* 2nd printing. G $25.00

RUST, Z. *Teddy Bare Western Island.* 1971. 1st ed. SftCvr. $7.00

RUSTRUM, C. *Chips from a Wilderness Log.* 1982. Scarborough. Ills. 243 pp. EX $6.00

RUTH. *Touring the Old West.* 1971. 1st ed. dj. EX $10.00

RUTHERFORD, Ward. *Kasserine.* 1972. $3.00

RUTLEDGE, Archibald. *Home by the River.* 1941. New York. photos. 167 pp. $7.50

RUTLEDGE, Archibald. *Home by the River.* 1941. Indianapolis. Ills. dj. $10.00

RUTLEDGE, Archibald. *Old Plantation Days.* 1921. Stokes. Ills. Bull. 1st ed. VG $20.00

RUTLEDGE, Archibald. *Peace in the Heart.* 1930. Garden City. 1st ed. 316 pp. VG $10.00

RUTLEDGE, Archibald. *Plantation Game Trials.* 1921. Boston. Houghton Mifflin. 300 pp. $25.00

RUTLEDGE, Brett. *The Death of Lord Haw Haw.* 1940. New York. Book League. 306 pp. dj. $7.00

RUTSTRUM, C. *Chips from a Wilderness Log.* 1982. Scarborough. Ills. 243 pp. EX $6.00

RUTTER, Owen. *The Monster of Mu.* 1932. London. 1st ed. wrappers. VG $20.00

RYAN, A. *Cast a Cold Eye.* 1984. Dark Harvest. Ltd. ed. 1/200. sgn. boxed. EX $75.00

RYAN, Cornelius. *A Bridge Too Far.* 1977. New York. Ills. $3.00

RYAN, Cornelius. *A Bridge Too Far.* 1974. New York. Simon & Schuster. 1st ed. dj. $25.00

RYAN, L.W. *French Travelers in Southeastern United States.* 1939. Bloomington. Principia Press. 107 pp. $17.50

RYAN, Marah Ellis. *Indian Love Letters.* 1907. Chicago. Ills. 122 pp. $7.50

RYAN, Marah Ellis. *That Girl Montana.* 1901. Grosset & Dunlap. 357 pp. $5.50

RYAN, Marah Ellis. *The Flute of the Gods.* 1909. New York. 1st ed. 2nd issue. 338 pp. VG $15.00

RYAN, Marah Ellis. *Told in the Hills.* 1905. New York. 362 pp. $3.00

RYAN. *The Last Battle.* 1966. 571 pp. $8.50

RYBACK, E. & T. *The Ultimate Journey.* 1973. Chronicle. Ills. 203 pp. dj. EX $5.00

RYDBERG, P.A. *Flora of the Rocky Mountains & Adjacent Plains.* 1969. Haffner. reprint. 1144 pp. dj. EX $65.00

RYDER, James. *Voigtlander & I.* 1902. Cleveland. Ills. 1st ed. sgn. 251 pp. $75.00

RYERSON, Rev. John. *Hudson's Bay, a Missionary Tour.* 1855. Toronto. Sanderson. 1st ed. 190 pp. $100.00

RYVES, T.E. *Bandersnatch.* 1950. 1st ed. dj. $60.00

SAARINEN, Aline. *The Proud Possessors.* 1958. Random House. sgn. dj. VG $15.00

SABARTES. *Paintings & Drawings of Picasso.* 1946. New York. Tudor Pub. $10.00

SABATINI, Rafael. *Saint Martin's Summer.* New York. 331 pp. $3.50

SABATINI, Rafael. *Scaramouche.* 1921. New York. 392 pp. $3.50

SABATINI, Rafael. *The Banner of the Bull.* New York. 254 pp. $3.50

SABATINI, Rafael. *The Strolling Saint.* 1924. New York. 442 pp. $3.50

SABER, Clifford. *Desert Rat Sketch Book.* 1959. New York. 1st ed. folio. slipcase. EX $100.00

SABIN, Edwin L. *General Crook & the Fighting Apaches.* 1918. Lippincott. EX $75.00

SABIN, Edwin L. *In the Ranks of Old Hickory.* 1927. Lippincott. Ills. Eltonhead. VG $6.50

SABIN, Edwin L. *Into Mexico with General Scott.* 1920. Lippincott. Ills. Chas. Stephens. 317 pp. $7.50

SABIN, Edwin L. *Wild Men of the Wild West.* 1929. New York. Ills. 363 pp. VG $65.00

SABIN, Edwin L. *With Sam Houston in Texas.* 1916. Phila./London. Ills. 1st ed. maps. 319 pp. $15.00

SABINE, Ellen S. *American Folk Art.* 1958. New York. Bonanza. Ills. dj. VG $10.50

SABINE, Lorenzo. *Notes on Duels & Dueling.* 1855. Boston. 1st ed. VG $45.00

SABINE, W. *Collected Papers on Acoustics.* 1922. Harvard U. Pr. $30.00

SACHEHEIM, Eric. *Silent Firefly: Japanese Songs of Love & Things.* 1963. Kodansha. Ills. 203 pp. VG $35.00

SACHS, Emanie. *'The Terrible Siren' The Victoria Woodhull 1838-1927.* 1928. New York. Ills. 1st ed. dj. VG $10.00

SACHS, Wulf. *Black Hamlet.* 1947. Boston. 1st ed. 324 pp. dj. VG $15.00

SACHSE, Julius F. *German Pietists of Provincial Penn., 1694-1708.* 1895. Philadelphia. Ills. Ltd. 1st ed. 1/500. EX $175.00

SACK, John. *Lt. Calley, His Own Story.* 1971. New York. 1st ed. $8.50

SACKETT, Frances Robertson. *Dick Dowling.* 1937. Houston. EX $50.00

SACKVILLE-WEST, V. *Daughter of France.* 1959. Doubleday. 1st Am. ed. dj. EX $15.00

SACKVILLE-WEST, V. *Knole & the Sackevilles.* 1926. London. VG $45.00

SACKVILLE-WEST, V. *Saint Joan of Arc.* 1936. New York. Literary Guild. 395 pp. VG $4.50

SACKVILLE-WEST, V. *The Garden.* 1946. London. Joseph. dj. VG $25.00

SACKVILLE-WEST, V. *The Garden.* 1946. Garden City. Doubleday. 1st Am. ed. dj. EX $20.00

SACKVILLE-WEST, V. *Twelve Days.* 1928. 1st Eng. ed. VG $75.00

SADLEIR, Michael. *Authors & Publishers.* 1933. London. 1st ed. dj. VG $60.00

SADLEIR, Michael. *Things Past.* 1944. London. 1st ed. dj. VG $30.00

SAFFORD, J.M. & Killebrew, J. *The Elements of the Geology of Tennessee.* 1900. Foster Webb. Ills. 264 pp. VG $20.00

SAGAN, Francoise. *A Certain Smile.* 1956. Dutton. dj. VG $6.00

SAGAN, Francoise. *Those Without Shadows.* 1957. New York. Dutton. 1st ed. 125 pp. dj. $52.50

SAGE, Dean. *Salmon & Trout.* 1902. Am. Sportsman Lib. Ills. VG $42.50

SAGE, Leland L. *William Boyd Allison.* 1956. Iowa City. 334 pp. $25.00

SAGE, Rufus. *Scenes in the Rocky Mountains.* 1854. Philadelphia. Ills. 2nd ed. revised. $275.00

SAGLIO, A. *French Furniture.* 1913. London. 59 pls. 194 pp. $17.50

SAIKAKU, Ihara. *The Life of an Amorous Woman & Other Writings.* 1963. New Directions.Ills. 403 pp. dj. G $55.00

SAINSBURY, John S. *Dictionary of Musicians: from the Earliest Times.* 1966. New York. reprint. 2 vol set. VG $35.00

SAINSBURY, Noel. *Bill Bolton & the Hidden Danger.* 1933. Goldsmith Pub. 251 pp. dj. VG $4.50

SAINT, L.B. & Arnold, H. *Stained Glass of Middle Ages in England & France.* 1913. London. Black. pls. folio. VG $20.00

SAINT FRANCIS of ASSISI. *Song of the Sun.* 1952. New York. Ills. E. Orton Jones. $25.00

SAINT-EXUPERY, Antoine de. *Airman's Odyssey.* 1942. Reynal & Hitchcock. G $3.50

SAINT-EXUPERY, Antoine de. *Der Kleine Prinz.* 1965. Dusseldorf. Rauch. Ills. dj. $10.00

SAINT-EXUPERY, Antoine de. *The Wisdom of the Sands.* 1950. New York. 350 pp. dj. $12.00

SAINTSBURY, George. *A Saintsbury Miscellany.* 1947. Oxford U. Pr. 1st Am. ed. inscr. dj. VG $10.00

SAINZ, Gustavo. *Gazapo!* 1968. Farrar. 1st Am. ed. dj. VG $15.00

SALE, Edith T. *Historic Gardens of Virginia.* 1923. Richmond. Ills. 2nd ed. 355 pp. $25.00

SALE, Roger. *On Not Being Good Enough.* 1979. Oxford U. Pr. 218 pp. $5.00

SALINGER, J.D. *Franny & Zooey.* 1961. Heinemann. 1st Eng. ed. dj. $55.00

SALINGER, J.D. *Raise High the Roof Beam, Carpenters & Seymour.* 1959. Little, Brown. 1st ed. 2nd issue. dj. EX $20.00

SALINGER, J.D. *The Catcher in the Rye.* 1951. Boston. Book Club ed. EX $75.00

SALINGER, J.D. *The Catcher in the Rye.* 1951. Little, Brown. 1st ed. dj. VG $150.00

SALINGER, Pierre. *American Held Hostage.* 1981. Ills. dj. VG $9.00

SALINGER, Pierre. *With Kennedy.* 1966. New York. Doubleday. 391 pp. dj. $4.50

SALISBURY, Albert & Jane. *Here Rolled the Covered Wagons.* 1948. Seattle. 1st ed. sgns. $15.00

SALISBURY, H.E. *The 900 Days: Siege of Leningrad.* 1969. New York. dj. VG $15.00

SALISBURY, Harrison. *Orbit of China.* 1967. New York. 1st ed. sgn. dj. VG $10.00

SALISBURY, Harrison. *Russia on the Way.* 1946. Macmillan. 1st printing. $37.50

SALISBURY, William. *The American Emperor.* 1913. New York. Tabard. 1st ed. VG $25.00

SALMI. *Complete Works Raphael.* 1969. VG $56.00

SALMIERI, S. *Stonetone Portfolio.* New York. 6 pls. EX $25.00

SALMONSON, Jessica. *Tales by Moonlight.* 1983. Garcia. Ltd. 1st ed. 1/1200. sgn. $15.00

SALOMON, Julian Harris. *The Book of Indian Crafts & Indian Lore.* 1928. London/NY. Ills. 418 pp. index. $25.00

SALOUTOS, Theodore. *The Greeks in the United States.* 1964. Cambridge. Harvard. Ills. 1st ed. 445 pp. $25.00

SALT, H.S. *Richard Jefferies, His Life & His Ideals.* 1905. London. G $7.50

SALT, Sydney. *Christopher Columbus & Other Poems.* 1937. Boston. 1st ed. inscr. sgn. dj. VG $17.50

SALTA. *The Pleasures of Italian Cooking.* 1962. Macmillan. 239 pp. dj. VG $4.50

SALTEN, Felix. *Bambi.* 1928. New York. Ills. Wiese. 1st Am. ed. VG $20.00

SALTER, James. *A Sport & a Pastime.* 1967. Garden City. Doubleday. 1st ed. sgn. VG $35.00

SALTER, James. *The Hunters*. 1956. New York. Harper. 1st ed. VG $50.00

SALTER, William. *Memoirs of Joseph W. Pickett*. 1880. Burlington, IA.1st ed. 150 pp. $45.00

SALTUS, Edgar. *The Anatomy of Negation*. 1886. London. 1st ed. VG $20.00

SALVATO, Sharon. *The Fires of July*. 1983. Dell. proof copy. wrappers. VG $5.00

SALVIN, F.H. & Brodrick, W. *Falconry in the British Isles*. 1973. Thames Valley. reprint. Ills. 147 pp. dj. EX $35.00

SAMBOURNE. *Water Babies*. 1886. Macmillan. 100 Ills. G $30.00

SAMBOURNE. *Water Babies*. 1912. New York. 100 Ills. G $20.00

SAMMIS, Edward R. *Last Stand at Stalingrad*. 1966. New York. Macmillan. Ills. 96 pp. dj. $4.50

SAMPSON, A. *The Arms Bazaar, from Lebanon to Lockheed*. 1977. dj. EX $10.00

SAMPSON, A. *The Seven Sisters, Great Oil Companies & World*. 1975. maps. dj. VG $12.50

SAMPSON, Emma Speed. *Miss Minerva's Cookbook*. 1931. Reilly & Lee. 1st ed. dj. VG $65.00

SAMPSON, Marmaduke B. *Central America & Transit Between Oceans*. 1850. New York. 1st ed. 28 pp. $50.00

SAMPSON, Mowery & Kugler. *Farm Shop Skills in Mechanized Agriculture*. 1955. Chicago. Ills. 395 pp. VG $4.50

SAMS, R. & Sytsma, J. *Ahrens-Fox*. no place. no date. Ills. G $12.50

SAMSON, Harold E. *Tug Hill Country Tales*. 1971. Lakemont. photos. 227 pp. dj. EX $4.00

SAMSON, J. *Modern Falconry*. 1984. Stackpole. Ills. 160 pp. EX $12.50

SAMUEL, H.B. *Unholy Memories of the Holy Land*. 1930. London. Hogarth Press. Ills. G $10.00

SAMUEL, Maurice. *The Second Crucifixion*. 1960. 1st ed. dj. VG $15.00

SAMUELS, Ernest. *Henry Adams, the Middle Years*. 1958. Cambridge. dj. $10.00

SAMUELS, Peggy & Harold. *Encyclopedia of Artists of the American West*. 1976. New York. 1st ed. dj. EX $35.00

SANBORN, Edwin D. *History of New Hampshire*. 1875. 1st ed. 422 pp. $20.00

SANBORN, F.B. *The Personality of Thoreau*. 1901. Boston. ex-lib. 71 pp. $4.00

SANBORN, Mary Farley. *Sweet & Twenty*. 1891. Boston. 310 pp. $3.50

SANBORN, Ralph & Clark, B. *A Bibliography of Works of Eugene O'Neill*. 1931. Random House. Ltd. ed. inscr. Clark. VG $75.00

SANCHEZ, Ramon Diaz. *Cumboto*. 1969. Austin. 273 pp. $7.00

SAND, George. *The Master Mosaic Workers*. London. J.M. Dent. 232 pp. G $4.50

SANDBORN, Kate. *Truthful Woman in Southern California*. 1893. New York. $12.50

SANDBURG, Carl. *Abraham Lincoln*. New York. Harcourt. 6 vol set. VG $60.00

SANDBURG, Carl. *Abraham Lincoln: Prairie Years & War Years*. 1954. New York. Ills. 1st ed. dj. EX $17.50

SANDBURG, Carl. *Abraham Lincoln: The Prairie Years*. 1926. 2 vol set. Ills. boxed. VG $20.00

SANDBURG, Carl. *Abraham Lincoln: The War Years*. 1950. New York. 4 vol set. $45.00

SANDBURG, Carl. *Abraham Lincoln: The War Years*. 1939. New York. Ills. 4 vol set. $75.00

SANDBURG, Carl. *Always the Young Strangers*. 1953. Ltd. ed. 1/600. sgn. EX $90.00

SANDBURG, Carl. *Chicago Poems*. 1916. New York. 1st ed. dj. VG $80.00

SANDBURG, Carl. *Home Front Memo*. 1943. New York. Ills. Steichen. 1st ed. dj. EX $22.50

SANDBURG, Carl. *Lincoln Collector; Story of O. Barrett Collection*.1949. New York. Ltd. ed. sgn. slipcase. EX $100.00

SANDBURG, Carl. *Slabos of the Sunburnt West*. 1922. 1st ed. dj. $12.50

SANDBURG, Carl. *Storm Over the Land: Profile of Civil War*. 1942. New York. Ills. 1st ed. dj. EX $12.50

SANDBURG, Carl. *The American Songbag*. 1927. inscr. sgn. $75.00

SANDBURG, Carl. *The People, Yes*. 1936. New York. 3rd ed. sgn. $25.00

SANDBURG, Steichen. *The Photographer*. 1929. New York. Ltd. ed. sgns. folio. EX $300.00

SANDERS, Alvin H. *At the Sign of the Stock Yard Inn*. 1915. Chicago. Breeders Gazette. Ills. EX $25.00

SANDERS, Charles W. *The School Reader, Fifth Book*. 1860. Chicago. 456 pp. $4.00

SANDERS, Charles W. *The School Reader, Third Book*. 1870. Taylor & Co. Ills. 264 pp. G $4.50

SANDERS, Ed. *The Family: Story of Charles Manson*. 1971. New York. 383 pp. EX $3.50

SANDERS, J.H. *Breeds of Life Stock & Principles of Heredity*. 1887. Chicago. Sanders. Ills. 480 pp. EX $75.00

SANDERS, Jacquin. *A Night Before Christmas*. 1963. Putnam. 1st ed. dj. EX $35.00

SANDERS, Lawrence. *Caper*. 1980. New York. Putnam. 1st ed. dj. VG $40.00

SANDERS, Lawrence. *The Case of Lucy Binding*. 1982. Putnam. review copy. dj. VG $15.00

SANDERS, Lawrence. *The Marlow Chronicles*. 1977. New York. Putnam. 1st ed. dj. EX $35.00

SANDERS, Lawrence. *The Sixth Commandment*. 1979. Putnam. 1st ed. dj. EX $10.00

SANDERSON, Derek & Fischler. *Hockey for the Coach, the Player, & the Fan*. 1979. New York. Simon & Schuster. 384 pp. dj. $12.50

SANDERSON, I.T. *Animal Treasure*. 1937. Viking. Ills. 1st ed. 325 pp. VG $8.00

SANDERSON, I.T. *Caribbean Treasure*. 1939. Viking. Ills. 1st ed. VG $9.00

SANDERSON, I.T. *John & Juan in the Jungle*. 1953. New York. Dodd Mead. Ills. Covarrubias. $25.00

SANDERSON, I.T. *Living Treasure*. 1941. Viking. Ills. 1st ed. G $9.00

SANDERSON, I.T. *The Dynasty of Abu*. 1962. Knopf. Ills. 376 pp. dj. EX $15.00

SANDERSON, I.T. & Loth, D. *Book of the Great Jungles*. 1965. Messner. Ills. 480 pp. dj. VG $15.00

SANDERSON, James G. *Cornell Stories*. 1908. New York. Scribner. 251 pp. $5.00

SANDOZ, Mari. *Buffalo Hunters*. 1954. Hastings House.dj. VG $15.00

SANDOZ, Mari. *Crazy Horse*. 1942. New York. 1st ed. dj. VG $65.00

SANDOZ, Mari. *Old Jules*. 1955. reprint. inscr. dj. VG $30.00

SANDOZ, Maurice. *Fantastic Memories*. 1945. New York. Ills. Dali. VG $22.50

SANDS, Frederick & Broman, S. *The Divine Garbo*. 1979. New York. Ills. 1st ed. 243 pp. dj. VG $12.50

SANDS, George. *Mazelli & Other Poems*. 1849. presentation copy. inscr. $35.00

SANDS, George. *The Countess of Rudolstadt*. Avon ed. $35.00

SANDS, Ledyard. *The Bird, the Gun, & the Dog*. 1939. New York. Ltd. ed. 1/100. sgn. VG $65.00

SANDYS. *The History of the Violin*. 1864. London. 390 pp. $40.00

SANFORD, J. *The Black Hills Souvenir*. 1902. Denver. Ills. 1st ed. VG $50.00

SANFORD. *Paleolithic Man & Nile-Faiyum Divide*. 1929. U. of Chicago. Oriental Institute. $10.00

SANFORD. *The Water Fowl Family*. 1903. $10.00

SANGER, M.B. *World of the Great White Heron*. 1967. Devin Adair. Ills. 144 pp. dj. EX $5.00

SANGER, William. *The History of Prostitution.* 1939. New York. Eugenics. 708 pp. $75.00

SANKHALA, K. *Tiger! Story of the Indian Tiger.* 1977. Simon & Schuster. 220 pp. dj. $12.50

SANN, Paul. *The Lawless Decade.* 1957. Crown. 233 pp. $7.00

SANSOM, William. *A Book of Christmas.* 1968. New York. dj. VG $12.50

SANTAYANA, George. *Lucifer or the Heavenly Truce.* 1924. Cambridge. Southworth Press. Ltd. ed. $42.50

SANTAYANA, George. *Persons & Places.* 1944. Scribner. 266 pp. dj. $52.50

SANTEE, Ross. *Men & Horses.* 1926. New York. 100 Ills. $35.00

SANTEE, Ross. *The Rummy Kid Goes Home & Other Stories.* 1965. 1st ed. dj. EX $20.00

SAPONARO, M. *Fishers of Men.* 1962. New York. $10.00

SARA, Dorothy. *The New American Garden Book.* 1954. New York. 810 pp. dj. G $5.00

SARETT, Lew. *Slow Smoke.* 1925. New York. Holt. 1st ed. 104 pp. $7.50

SARG, Tony. *Tony Sarg's Savings Book.* 1946. Cleveland. Ills. 1st ed. dj. $50.00

SARGEAUNT & WEST. *Grand Strategy. Search for Victory.* 1943. London. Book Club ed. G $7.50

SARGENT, Elizabeth. *Love Poems of Elizabeth Sargent.* 1966. New York. Ltd. ed. 1/750. sgn. $5.00

SARGENT, Epes. *Arctic Adventure by Sea & Land.* 1858. Boston. Ills. map. VG $45.00

SARGENT, P. *War & Education.* 1944. private print. G $7.50

SARGENT, Pamela. *Alien Upstairs.* 1983. Garden City. 1st ed. dj. EX $8.00

SARGENT, Pamela. *Golden Space.* 1982. New York. review copy. dj. VG $15.00

SARGO, John. *The Marx He Knew.* 1909. Chicago. Kerr. 1st ed. EX $15.00

SAROLEA, C. *How Belgium Saved Europe.* 1915. G $7.50

SAROYAN, Aram. *Genesis Angels: Lew Welch & Beat Generation.* 1979. New York. 1st ed. $10.00

SAROYAN, William. *Chance Meetings, a Memoir.* 1958. New York. Norton. 1st ed. $7.50

SAROYAN, William. *Dear Baby.* 1945. London. 1st Eng ed. $10.00

SAROYAN, William. *I Used to Believe I Had Forever, Now I'm Not Sure.* 1968. New York. Cowles. 1st ed. 234 pp. dj. $12.50

SAROYAN, William. *Jim Dandy.* 1947. New York. 1st ed. dj. VG $10.00

SAROYAN, William. *Laughing Matter.* 1953. New York. 1st ed. VG $25.00

SAROYAN, William. *Letters from 74 Rue Tailbout.* 1969. 1st ed. dj. EX $15.00

SAROYAN, William. *My Name Is Aram.* 1940. New York. Ills. Don Freeman. 1st ed. dj. $15.00

SAROYAN, William. *Not Dying.* 1963. New York. 1st ed. dj. $15.00

SAROYAN, William. *Papa, You're Crazy.* 1957. Boston. Little, Brown. 1st ed. dj. $12.50

SAROYAN, William. *Places Where I've Done Time.* 1972. New York. Praeger. 1st ed. dj. $7.50

SAROYAN, William. *Short Drive, Sweet Chariot.* 1966. 1st ed. sgn. dj. EX $10.00

SAROYAN, William. *Sons Come & Go, Mothers Hang in Forever.* 1976. McGraw Hill. 1st ed. $12.00

SAROYAN, William. *The Cave Dwellers.* 1958. New York. Putnam. 1st ed. $10.00

SAROYAN, William. *The Human Comedy.* 1943. London. 1st Eng. ed. dj. VG $18.00

SAROYAN, William. *The Time of Your Life.* 1939. New York. Harcourt. 1st ed. 247 pp. dj. $25.00

SAROYAN, William. *The William Saroyan Reader.* 1958. New York. Braziller. 1st ed. 498 pp. $10.00

SARRANTONIA, Al. *Worms.* 1985. 1st ed. dj. $15.00

SARRAUTE, Nathalie. *Martereau.* 1959. New York. Braziller. 250 pp. dj. $5.00

SARTON, Mary. *Plant Dreaming Deep.* 1968. New York. 1st ed. dj. EX $20.00

SARTON, May. *A Reckoning.* 1978. New York. Norton. 1st ed. dj. $10.00

SARTON, May. *Crucial Conversations.* 1975. Norton. 1st ed. dj. VG $20.00

SARTON, May. *Kinds of Love.* 1970. New York. Norton. 1st ed. 464 pp. dj. $15.00

SARTON, May. *Miss Pickthorn & Mr. Hare.* 1966. New York. 1st ed. dj. VG $10.00

SARTON, May. *The House by the Sea.* 1977. New York. Norton. Ills. 1st ed. dj. $12.50

SARTON, May. *The Magnificent Spinster, a Novel.* 1985. New York. Norton. 1st ed. 384 pp. dj. $7.50

SARTRE, J.P. *The Words.* 1964. New York. Braziller. 255 pp. $11.50

SARTRE, J.P. *Troubled Sleep.* 1951. New York. Knopf. dj. VG $12.00

SASEK, Miroslav. *This Is San Francisco.* 1968. Macmillan. Ills. dj. VG $10.00

SASSON, V. *Catalogue of Sasson Chinese Ivories.* 1950. London/NY. Ltd ed. 1/250. 3 vol set. $650.00

SASSOON, Siegfried. *Memoirs of a Fox Hunting Man.* 1929. London. Ills. Nicholson. 1st ed. sgn. $37.50

SASSOON, Siegfried. *The Heart's Journey.* 1928. London. 1st ed. VG $15.00

SASSOON, Siegfried. *The Road to Ruin.* 1933. London. 23 pp. $32.00

SATURDAY EVENING POST. *Saturday Evening Post Treasury.* 1954. 1st ed. EX $10.00

SAUER, Martin. *A Geographical & Astronomical Expedition.* 1802. London. 1st ed. fld map. 332 pp. $950.00

SAUL, John. *The God Project.* 1982. Bantam. 1st ed. dj. VG $10.00

SAUNDERS, Frederick. *Story of Some Famous Books.* 1887. New York. 1st Am. ed. 208 pp. $15.00

SAUNDERS, John Monk. *Wings.* 1927. Grosset & Dunlap. 249 pp. $5.50

SAUNDERS, L. *Act of War.* 1982. dj. EX $8.50

SAUNDERS, Marshall. *Beautiful Joe, Autobiography of a Dog.* 1955. Racine. Whitman. 283 pp. $3.00

SAUNDERS, Marshall. *Beautiful Joe, Autobiography of a Dog.* 1894. Philadelphia. Ills. 1st ed. 1st issue. VG $60.00

SAUNDERS, Marshall. *Beautiful Joe, Autobiography of a Dog.* 1907. London. Ills. 303 pp. G $7.50

SAUNDERS, William. *Through the Light Continent, or U.S. in 1877-8.* 1879. London. 2nd ed. 409 pp. $15.00

SAURI, M. *Institutions Mathematiques.* 1772. Paris. 2nd ed. $35.00

SAUVIN, Georges. *Autour de Chicago: Notes dur les Etats-Unis.* 1893. Paris. 1st ed. 263 pp. wrappers. $125.00

SAVAGE, B. *Rip Foster Rides the Gray Planet.* 1952. Whitman. 1st ed. dj. EX $8.50

SAVAGE, C.C. *The World-Geographical, Historical & Statistical.* 1853. Ills. maps. 496 pp. $10.00

SAVAGE, D.S. *The Withered Branch.* New York. Pellegrini. $5.00

SAVAGE, Elie. *The Little Gypsie.* 1865. Boston. Ills. Lorenz Frolich. G $10.00

SAVAGE, James W. *The Discovery of Nebraska.* 1880. Omaha, NB. 1st ed. 42 pp. wrappers. rare. $150.00

SAVAGE, Mildred. *In Vivo.* 1964. Simon & Schuster. $2.50

SAVAGE, Sarah. *The Two Birth-Days, a Moral Tale.* 1826. Boston. 1st ed. VG $125.00

SAVAGE. *Doctor at Coffin Gap.* Pocketbook. pb. $3.00

SAVILLE, Malcolm. *Susan, Bill, & the Golden Clock.* 1955. London. Nelson. Ills. Shepherd. dj. $10.00

SAWYER, C.W. *Our Rifles*. 1946. Boston. Ills. 412 pp. VG $15.00

SAWYER, L. *Way Sketches, Travels Across the Plains*. 1926. Ltd. ed. 1/385. $110.00

SAWYER, R. *The Christmas Ann Angel*. 1944. Ills Kate Seredy. 1st ed. dj. $35.00

SAWYER, Roland D. *Cal Coolidge, President*. 1924. Boston. Ills. 128 pp. $12.50

SAWYER, Ruth. *Roller Skates*. 1936. New York. Viking. Ills. Angelo. 1st ed. $40.00

SAWYER & MITCHELL. *The Liberty Ships*. 1985. Ills. 2nd ed. dj. EX $40.00

SAXE, John G. *John G. Saxe's Poems*. 1892. Boston. Household ed. VG $7.50

SAXE, John G. *Rhyme By Rail*. 1873. New York. Lacy. 16 pp. wrappers. $50.00

SAXON, L. *Fabulous New Orleans*. 1950. New Orleans. Ills. Suydan. dj. VG $10.00

SAXON, TALLANT & DREYER. *Gumbo-Ya-Ya, a Collection of Louisiana Folk Tales*.1965. Bonanza Books. Ills. VG $25.00

SAXTON, Harry. *Domestic Mink*. private print. 26 pp. $2.50

SAXTON, Josephine. *Group Feast*. 1971. 1st Am. ed. dj. EX $20.00

SAXTON, Mark. *The Islar: Islandia Today*. 1969. Boston. Houghton Mifflin. dj. EX $10.00

SAYCE, R.U. *Primitive Arts & Crafts*. 1933. Cambridge. Ills. 219 pp. dj. VG $30.00

SAYER, Dorothy. *Unpopular Opinions*. 1st Eng. ed. dj. VG $30.00

SAYERS, Dorothy L. *Even the Parrot*. 1944. London. Methuen. 1st ed. 55 pp. dj. $65.00

SAYERS, Dorothy L. *Gaudy Night*. 1936. 1st ed. dj. $90.00

SAYERS, Dorothy L. *Murder Must Advertise*. 1933. London. Gollancz. 1st ed. VG $75.00

SAYERS, Dorothy L. *The Dragon's Head*. 1951. Munich. 1st separate ed. wrappers. VG $75.00

SAYERS, Dorothy L. *The Nine Tailors*. 1934. London. Gollancz. 1st ed. VG $75.00

SAYERS, Frances Clarke. *Bluebonnets for Lucinda*. 1934. New York. Ills. Helen Sewell. 1st ed. VG $20.00

SAYERS & BYRNE. *Busman's Honeymoon*. 1937. London. Gollancz. 1st ed. wrappers. VG $85.00

SAYLES, John. *Union Dues*. 1977. Boston. dj. EX $15.00

SAYLES. *Fantasies of Gold. Legends of Treasures*. 1968. Tucson. 1st ed. dj. $15.00

SCADUTO, Tony. *Mick Jagger-Everybody's Lucifer*. 1974. New York. Ills. dj. VG $18.00

SCAMMELL, G.V. *World Encompassed, 1st European Maritime Empires*. 1981. CA U. Press. Ills. 1st ed. dj. EX $45.00

SCARBOROUGH, D. *A Song Catcher in Southern Mountains*. 1937. New York. 1st ed. VG $45.00

SCARBOROUGH, D. *On the Trail of Negro Folk Songs*. 1925. Cambridge. 289 pp. VG $75.00

SCARTH. *Twelve Years in China, by a British Resident*. 1860. ex-lib. 8 color pls. $30.00

SCHAAP. *An Illustrated History of the Olympics*. 1963. Knopf. dj. VG $15.00

SCHAEFER, Jack. *Shane*. 1949. Houghton Mifflin. 1st ed. dj. $45.00

SCHAEFER, Jack. *Shane*. 1954. Boston. Ills. 214 pp. dj. VG $7.50

SCHAEFER. *Stubby Pringle's Christmas*. 1964. 1st ed. dj. VG $15.00

SCHAEFFER, R.G. *Red, White, & Blue*. 1917. dj. G $6.00

SCHAFER, Joseph. *Carl Shurz, Militant Liberal*. 1930. Wisconsin. State Hist. Soc. Ills. 270 pp. $10.00

SCHAFER, Kermit. *All Time Great Bloopers*. 1972. Avenel Books. Ills. Doug Anderson. 113 pp. $3.50

SCHAFFNER, I.K. *Turkeys in Texas*. 1954. Naylor. Ills. 67 pp. EX $15.00

SCHALDACH, W. *Path to Enchantment, an Artist in Sonoran Desert*. 1963. Macmillan. 1st ed. dj. $15.00

SCHALDACH, W. *Wind on Your Cheek*. 1972. dj. EX $15.00

SCHALDACH. *Currents & Eddies-Chips from Log of Artist Angler*.1946. Barnes. Ills. Schaldach. 1st ed. VG $20.00

SCHALETTS. *Old Nameless, Epic of a U.S. Battlewagon in WWII*. 1943. G $12.50

SCHALLER, G.B. *Mountain Monarchs, Wild Sheep & Goats of Himalaya*.1982. Chicago. Ills. 425 pp. EX $15.00

SCHALLER, G.B. *Serengeti, a Kingdom of Predators*. 1972. Knopf. Ills. review copy. 114 pp. dj. $30.00

SCHALLER, G.B. *Serengeti Lion, Study of Predator-Prey Relations*. 1980. Chicago. Ills. 479 pp. EX $15.00

SCHALLER, G.B. *Stones of Silence, Journeys in the Himalayas*. 1980. Viking. Ills. 1st ed. 292 pp. dj. EX $20.00

SCHALLER, G.B. *The Deer & the Tiger, Study of Wildlife in India*. 1967. Chicago. Ills. 370 pp. dj. EX $25.00

SCHALLER, G.B. *The Year of the Gorilla*. 1964. Chicago. Ills. 260 pp. dj. EX $15.00

SCHAPERA, I. *The Bantu-Speaking Tribes of South Africa*. 1937. Maskew Miller. 1st ed. $25.00

SCHARDT. *Paris 1900: Masterworks of French Poster Art*. 1970. Putnam. VG $40.00

SCHARFF, Robert. *Complete Book of Wood Finishing*. 1956. G $4.00

SCHARFFER, Susan Fromberg. *The Thymes & Runes of the Toad*. 1975. New York. Macmillan. Ills. Flueret. $10.00

SCHARY, Dore. *Case History of the Movie*. 1950. New York. G $10.00

SCHEAHAN, James W. & Upton, G.*Great Conflagration Chicago-Past, Present, Future*.1871. Chicago. Ills. maps. 458 pp. $25.00

SCHEEL, Jorgen. *Riviluns of the Old World*. 1968. New York. Ills. 473 pp. EX $15.00

SCHEFFER, V.B. *The Amazing Sea Otter*. 1981. Scribner. Ills. 144 pp. dj. EX $17.50

SCHEIKEVITCH, Marie. *Time Past: Memories of Proust & Others*. 1935. Boston/NY. Ills. 1st ed. 321 pp. VG $15.00

SCHEINFIELD, Anran. *You & Heredity*. 1939. New York. F. Stokes. 434 pp. $4.00

SCHEITHAUER, W. *Hummingbirds*. 1967. Crowell. Ills. 1st Am. ed. 176 pp. dj. $17.50

SCHELL, Orville. *Brown*. 1978. New York. Random House. 307 pp. dj. EX $6.00

SCHELLIE. *The Tucson Citizen, Century of Arizona Journalism*.1970. Tucson. Ills. 96 pp. SftCvr. $17.50

SCHERER, James A.B. *The First Forty-Niner & Story of Golden Tea Caddy*.1925. New York. 1st ed. G $30.00

SCHERMAN, K. *Spring on an Arctic Island*. 1956. Little, Brown. Ills. 331 pp. dj. VG $7.50

SCHERMERHORN. *Schermerhorn's Stories*. 1928. Sully & Co. 397 pp. $7.50

SCHETZER & KUETHE. *Foundations of Aerodynamics*. 1950. $8.50

SCHICKEL, Richard. *D.W. Griffith, an American Life*. 1984. New York. Ills. 1st ed. 672 pp. dj. EX $12.50

SCHICKEL, Richard. *His Picture in the Paper*. 1974. New York. Ills. 1st ed. 2nd printing. VG $10.00

SCHIEFNER, F. Anton von. *Tibetan Tales Derived from Indian Sources*. 1920. London. 368 pp. VG $45.00

SCHIELE, Egon. *Oeuvre Catalog*. 1961. 561pp. $118.00

SCHIFF, Bessie. *The Traveling Gallery*. 1936. Chicago. Ills. Emma Brock. 1st ed. $15.00

SCHIFF, Stuart David. *Whispers IV*. 1983. 1st Am. ed. dj. EX $15.00

SCHILLINGER. *J. Schillinger, a Memoir by His Wife*. 1949. New York. 9 Ills. Ltd. ed. sgn. $35.00

SCHINDLER, S. *A Sequel to Looking Backward.* 1894. Boston. 1st ed. $36.50

SCHISGALL, Oscar. *Eyes on Tomorrow: Evolution of Procter & Gamble.* 1981. Chicago. 295+ pp. dj. VG $6.00

SCHLEE, Ann. *The Proprietor.* 1983. Holt. 1st Am. ed. dj. VG $15.00

SCHLEIDEN, M.J. *Poetry of the Vegetable World.* 1853. Cincinnati. 1st Am. ed. VG $60.00

SCHLESINGER, Arthur M. *A Thousand Days.* 1965. Boston. 1087 pp. dj. EX $7.00

SCHLESINGER, Arthur M. *History of U.S. Political Parties.* 1973. Chelsea House. 4 vol set. VG $125.00

SCHLESINGER, Arthur M. *Political & Social History of the U.S. 1829-1925.* 1929. New York. $4.00

SCHLESINGER, Arthur M. *The Age of Jackson.* 1950. G $8.50

SCHLESINGER, Arthur M. *The Best & the Last of Edwin O'Connor.* 1970. Boston. Little, Brown. 1st ed. 465 pp. $4.50

SCHLESINGER, Arthur M. *The Colonial Merchants & American Revolution.* 1966. New York. dj. VG $10.00

SCHLESINGER, Arthur M. *The Coming of the New Deal.* 1959. Boston. 669 pp. VG $5.00

SCHLESINGER, Arthur M. *The Crisis of the Old Order 1919-1933.* 1957. Boston. 557 pp. VG $5.00

SCHLESINGER, Arthur M. *The Imperial Presidency.* 1973. Boston. 505 pp. dj. EX $4.50

SCHLIEMANN. *Narrative of Researches & Discoveries at Mycenae.* 1878. New York. Armstrong. Ills. VG $100.00

SCHLIEPHAKE, H. *The Birth of the Luftwaffe.* 1971. London. Ills. dj. VG $20.00

SCHMALENBACH, W. *African Art.* New York. 131 Ills. 16 color pls. $15.00

SCHMALHAUSEN, I.I. *The Origin of Terrestrial Vertebrates.* 1968. Academic Press. Ills. 314 pp. EX $17.50

SCHMIDLY, D. *Texas Mammals East of the Balcones Fault Zone.* 1983. Austin. Ills. 1st ed. 400 pp. $12.50

SCHMIDT, D.A. *Yemen, the Unknown War.* 1968. Ills. maps. dj. VG $8.50

SCHMIDT, Erich F. *Flights over Ancient Cities of Iran.* 1940. Chicago. Ills. maps. EX $300.00

SCHMIDT, Erich F. *Persepolis II, Contents of Treasury & Discoveries.* 1957. Chicago. 89 pls. dj. VG $90.00

SCHMIDT, Karl Patterson. *Homes & Habits of Wild Animals.* 1934. Chicago. Donohue. Ills. Weber. sgn. EX $35.00

SCHMIDT, Max. *Primitive Races of Mankind, Study of Ethnology.* 1926. Boston. Ills. 360 pp. index. $20.00

SCHMIDT, Stanley. *Aliens from Analog.* 1983. New York. review copy. dj. VG $10.00

SCHMIDT, Stanley. *War & Peace: Possible Futures from Analog.* 1983. New York. 1st ed. dj. VG $8.00

SCHMIDT. *The Alishar Huyuk: Seasons of 1928-1929.* 1932. U. Chicago Press. $12.00

SCHMIDT. *100 Jahre Osterriche Glaskunst 1823-1923.* 1925. $53.00

SCHMIDT. *400 Outstanding Women of World & Costumology.* 1931. Ills. sgn. 583 pp. dj. G $12.50

SCHMIDT-GORG, J. & Schmidt. *Ludwig Von Beethoven.* 1970. New York. Ills. 275 pp. $47.50

SCHMITT, Martin F. *Fighting Indians of the West.* 1948. Ills. 1st ed. 362 pp. $16.50

SCHMUCKER, Samuel M. *A History of the Four Georges, Kings of England.* 1893. New York. 438 pp. P $3.00

SCHNABEL, A. *Reflections on Music.* 1934. New York. VG $15.00

SCHNECKEBIAR, Lawrence. *Government Publications & Their Use.* 404 pp. VG $6.00

SCHNEIDER, Duane. *An Interview with Anais Nin.* 1970. Schneider. Ltd. 1st ed. 1/176. wrappers. $70.00

SCHNEIDER, Isadore. *Comrade Mister.* 1934. New York. Equinox Co-op Pr. Ltd. ed. VG $35.00

SCHNEIDER, Isidor. *The World of Love.* New York. 1st ed. 2 vol set. VG $22.50

SCHNEIDER, Norris F. *Moskingham County Men & Women in WWII.* 1947. Zanesville, OH. Ills. 511 pp. $37.50

SCHNEIDERMAN, William. *Dissent on Trial: Story of Political Life.* 1983. Minneapolis. 250 pp. $6.00

SCHNITTKIND, Henry T. *The Story of Eugene Debs.* 1929. Boston. presentation copy. inscr. EX $40.00

SCHNITZLER, Arthur. *Casanova's Homecoming.* 1947. New York. Ills. Rockwell. Ltd. ed. $50.00

SCHOENBERG, Arnold. *Berliner Tagebuch.* 1974. Frankfurt. German text. EX $15.00

SCHOENBERG, Wilfred. *Jesuits in Montana 1840-1960.* 1960. 129 pp. wrappers. $12.50

SCHOENER, Allan. *Portal to America Lower East Side 1870-1925.* 1967. Ills. 1st ed. 104 pp. dj. VG $25.00

SCHOFIELD, John & Colin, J. *Finishing of Wool Goods.* 1935. Huddersfield. Ills. 800 pp. G $22.00

SCHOLEM, Gershom G. *Major Trends in Jewish Mysticism.* 1961. New York. Schocken Books. 460 pp. VG $7.50

SCHOLEM, Gershom G. *On the Kabbalah & Its Symbolism.* 1960. New York. Schocken. 1st ed. 216 pp. $22.50

SCHOLL, Frank B. *The Automobile Owner's Guide.* 1920. NY/London. 338 pp. $10.00

SCHOLL-LATOUR, P. *Death in Rice Fields/Eyewitness Account of Vietnam.* 1979. EX $12.50

SCHONBERG, Harold. *The Great Conductors.* 1967. Simon & Schuster. 384 pp. dj. $6.50

SCHOONOVER, Frank. *Frank Schoonover, Illustrator of N. Am. Frontier.* 1976. Guptil. 1st ed. 208 pp. dj. EX $40.00

SCHOONOVER. *With Cortez the Conqueror.* Hampton. 7 color pls. EX $16.00

SCHOONOVER. *Yankee Ships in Pirate Water.* 1931. Garden City. Ills. 1st ed. VG $25.00

SCHOPFLIN, G. *The Soviet Union & Eastern Europe, a Handbook.* 1970. dj. EX $20.00

SCHORGER, A.W. *Passenger Pigeon/Its Natural History & Extinction.* 1973. OK U. Press. Ills. 424 pp. dj. EX $22.50

SCHORGER, A.W. *The Wild Turkey, Its History & Domestication.* 1966. OK U. Press. Ills. 1st ed. 625 pp. dj. EX $55.00

SCHORSCH, Anita. *American Clocks.* 1981. EX $8.00

SCHOTT, W. *Chinesische Sprachlehre.* 1857. Berlin. ex-lib. 169 pp. rebound. $15.00

SCHOULER, James. *Ideals of the Republic.* 1908. Boston. $5.00

SCHREIDER, H. & F. *Exploring the Amazon.* 1970. Nat. Geog. Soc. Ills. 207 pp. dj. VG $12.50

SCHREINER, Olive. *Dream Life & Real Life.* 1893. Boston. Roberts Bros. 1st Am. ed. VG $30.00

SCHREINER, Olive. *Stories, Dreams, Allegories.* 1923. New York. 1st ed. VG $12.50

SCHREINER, Olive. *Trooper Peter Halket of Mashonaland.* 1897. Boston. 1st ed. VG $17.50

SCHREINER, Olive. *Trooper Peter Halket of Mashonaland.* 1974. reprint. VG $7.00

SCHRENKEISEN, Ray. *Fishing for Salmon & Trout.* 1940. Ills. VG $12.50

SCHREVELLI, Cornelii. *Lexicon Greek/Latin.* 1781. London. VG $40.00

SCHRIFGIESSER, Karl. *Oscar of the Waldorf.* 1943. New York. Ills. 1st ed. sgn. dj. VG $25.00

SCHROEDER, Doris. *Annette & the Desert Inn Mystery.* 1961. Whitman. 210 pp. $3.50

SCHROEDER, Doris. *Patty Duke & Mystery Mansion.* 1964. Racine. Whitman. 212 pp. $2.50

SCHROEDER, Doris. *The Beverly Hillbillies/The Saga of Wildcat Creek.* 1963. cine. Whitman. 212 pp. $2.50

SCHROEDER, Doris. *The Lennon Sis... The Secret of Holiday Island.* 1960. Whitman. $2.50

SCHROEDER, ... *...to Carve Wildfowl.* 1984. Stackpole. ...st ed. 255 pp. $30.00

SCHUBERT, H. *Mathematical Essays.* 1910. Open Court Pub. EX $25.00

SCHUBERT, P. *Sea Power in Conflict.* 1942. maps. G $7.50

SCHULBERG, Bud. *The Disenchanted.* 1950. Random House. 1st ed. dj. VG $20.00

SCHULMAN, L.M. *Come Out of the Wilderness.* 1965. New York. Popular Library. wrappers. $20.00

SCHULMAN, Max. *The Zebra Derby.* 1946. New York. Ills. Bill Crawford. 1st ed. $15.00

SCHULTE, George. *Words for Wizards.* 1924. Chicago. VG $9.00

SCHULTHESS, Emil. *Africa.* 1960. Collins. 1st ed. EX $50.00

SCHULTHESS, Emil. *Antarctica.* 1960. New York. 1st ed. dj. VG $25.00

SCHULTZ, James W. & Donaldson. *The Sun God's Children.* 1930. Boston/NY. Ills. Reiss. 1st ed. 254 pp. $35.00

SCHULTZ, James Willard. *Blackfeet Tales of Glacier National Park.* 1916. Boston. Ills. 1st ed. 242 pp. $50.00

SCHULTZE. *Bunny's Red Book.* 1912. New York. Ills. 1st ed. scarce. $225.00

SCHULZ, Charles M. *A Charlie Brown Christmas.* 1977. New York. Scholastic Books. Ills. EX $8.00

SCHULZ, Charles M. *Christmas is Together Time.* 1964. San Francisco. Ills. 1st ed. dj. VG $5.00

SCHULZ, E.D. *Texas Wild Flowers.* 1928. Laidlow. Ills. 505 pp. VG $25.00

SCHUMACH, Murray. *The Face on the Cutting Room Floor.* 1964. New York. dj. VG $9.00

SCHUMACHER, E.F. *Good Work.* 1979. Harper & Row. 1st ed. dj. $3.00

SCHUMAKER, E. *The Last Paradises.* 1967. Doubleday. Ills. 315 pp. dj. EX $15.00

SCHUMAN, F.L. *The Cold War, Retrospect & Prospect.* 1962. dj. EX $7.50

SCHURMAN, J. Gould. *The Balkan Wars 1912-1913.* 1914. Princeton. 1st ed. map. VG $10.00

SCHURMANN, T. *Australian Water Birds.* 1982. Rigby. Ills. 88 pp. dj. EX $15.00

SCHUTZE, Martin. *Goethe Centenary Papers 1831-1931.* 1933. Chicago. 1st ed. VG $15.00

SCHUYLER, George. *Black & Conservative.* 1966. 362 pp. $4.00

SCHUYLER, K. *Archery from Golds to Big Game.* 1970. dj. EX $20.00

SCHUYLER, M. *American Architecture Studies.* 1892. New York. Harper. Ills. sgn. 211 pp. $25.00

SCHWAB. *James Gibbons Huneker.* 1963. dj. $15.00

SCHWARTZ, Alvin. *The Blowtop.* 1948. New York. Dial Press. 1st ed. EX $15.00

SCHWARTZ, C.W. & E.R. *The Game Birds of Hawaii.* 1949. HI Fish & Game. Ills. 168 pp. $25.00

SCHWARTZ, Harry. *Russia's Soviet Economy.* 1950. New York. ex-lib. 592 pp. $4.00

SCHWARTZ, Harry. *This Book Collecting Racket.* 1937. Chicago. sgn. dj. $15.00

SCHWARTZ, Howard. *Imperial Messages.* 1976. New York. Avon. proof copy. wrappers. EX $20.00

SCHWARTZ, Jacob. *1100 Obscure Points.* 1931. London. 2nd impression. inscr. sgn. VG $45.00

SCHWARTZ, L.W. *Memoirs of My People.* 1963. New York. Schocken Books. G $10.00

SCHWARTZ, Stephen. *The Perfect Peach.* 1977. Boston. Ills. L.B. Lubin. 1st ed. VG $12.50

SCHWARTZ & WOLF. *History of American Art Porcelain.* 1967. New York. 1st ed. pls. EX $20.00

SCHWARTZ. *The Prairie Chicken in Missouri.* 1944. 84 photos. dj. $60.00

SCHWARZ, Ted. *The Hillside Strangler.* 1981. Doubleday. 1st ed. dj. VG $10.00

SCHWATKA, F. *Along Alaska's Great River.* 1885. New York. Ills. 1st ed. maps. pls. VG $37.50

SCHWATKA, F. *Along Alaska's Great River.* 1983. Alaska. Ills. 95 pp. $7.00

SCHWATKA, F. *In the Land of Cave & Cliff Dwellers.* 1893. New York. $10.00

SCHWEINFURTH, George. *In the Heart of Africa.* 1874. New York. 1st Am. ed. 2 vol set. VG $100.00

SCHWEITZER, Albert. *Aus Meinem Leben un Denken.* 1932. Leipzig. Ills. 1st ed. 211 pp. EX $75.00

SCHWENDINGER, H. & J. *Sociologists of the Chair.* 1974. New York. 1st ed. VG $15.00

SCHWIMMER, Rosika. *Tisza Tales.* 1928. Garden City. Ills. Willy Pogany. 1st ed. $60.00

SCOBEE, Barry. *Old Fort Davis.* 1947. San Antonio. 1st ed. sgn. dj. VG $25.00

SCORTIA, Thomas N. *Strange Bedfellows.* 1972. New York. 1st ed. dj. EX $10.00

SCORTIA, Thomas N. *The Best of Thomas N. Scortia.* 1981. Garden City. review copy. dj. EX $10.00

SCOTT, Cyril. *An Outline of Modern Occultism.* 1935. New York. 1st ed. 239 pp. dj. VG $20.00

SCOTT, David. *John Sloan, Paintings, Prints, & Drawings.* 1975. New York. 1st ed. dj. VG $45.00

SCOTT, Eugene. *The Tennis Experience.* 1979. Larrouse. Ills. DiGiacomo. dj. EX $17.50

SCOTT, George R. *Phallic Worship.* 1952. New York. Ills. 1st ed. dj. EX $15.00

SCOTT, J. *Defense of Graechus Babeuf.* 1967. MA U. Press. dj. VG $10.00

SCOTT, J. *Normandie Triangle.* 1981. dj. EX $8.50

SCOTT, J.D. *City of Birds & Beasts.* 1978. Putnam. Ills. 119 pp. dj. EX $7.00

SCOTT, J.D. & Sweet, O. *Moose.* 1981. Putnam. Ills. 64 pp. dj. EX $7.00

SCOTT, Janet Laura. *Children Across the Sea.* 1931. Saalfield. Ills. 1st ed. VG $20.00

SCOTT, Jock. *Spinning Up to Date.* London. (ca.1920) 2nd ed. VG $15.00

SCOTT, John. *Behind the Urals.* 1942. Cambridge. 279 pp. $5.00

SCOTT, Joseph. *A Geographical Description of Pennsylvania.* 1806. Philadelphia. 147 pp. fair $40.00

SCOTT, Leonora Cranch. *Life & Letters of Christopher Pearse Cranch.* 1917. NY/Boston. Ills. 395 pp. $20.00

SCOTT, Leroy. *The Walking Delegate.* 1905. New York. Doubleday. 1st ed. $45.00

SCOTT, Michael. *Cruise of the Midge.* 1894. Gibbings & Co. Ills. Ltd. 1st ed. 2 vol set. $20.00

SCOTT, Michael. *Tom Cringle's Log.* 1927. New York. Ills. Schaeffer. 1st ed. $45.00

SCOTT, Mrs. A.M. *Day Dawn in Africa; or, Progress of Protest.* 1858. New York. 314 pp. pls. G $25.00

SCOTT, Orland. *Pioneer Days on the Shadowy St. Joe.* 1968. Coeur d'Alene. 2nd ed. dj. VG $30.00

SCOTT, Paul. *On Writing & the Novel.* 1987. New York. Morrow. proof copy. wrappers. $35.00

SCOTT, Peter. *Morning Flight, a Book of Wildfowl.* 1949. London. Ills. VG $15.00

SCOTT, Peter. *Observations on Wildlife.* 1980. Cornell U. Pr. Ills. 1st ed. 112 pp. dj. EX $15.00

SCOTT, Robert L. *Damned to Glory.* 1945. New York. G $17.50

SCOTT, Robert L. *Damned to Glory.* 1944. New York. $15.00

SCOTT, Robert L. *Flying Tiger: Chennault of China.* 1959. New York. Doubleday. ex-lib. 285 pp. G $4.50

SCOTT, Robert L. *God is My Co-Pilot.* 1944. $4.00

SCOTT, Temple. *Goudy, an Address at Meeting of A.I.G.A.* 1923. Rudge. Ltd. ed. 1/400. EX $15.00

SCOTT, V.E. *Cavity Nesting Birds of North America Forests.* 1977. Ills. 112 pp. $6.00

SCOTT, W. *Gems of Modern German Art.* 1873. London. Ills. gilt decor. VG $20.00

SCOTT, Walter. *Complete Poetical Works of Sir Walter Scott.* 1894. Ills. 770 pp. VG $20.00

SCOTT, Walter. *Ivanhoe.* 1913. Boston. Ills. E. Boyd Smith. dj. $30.00

SCOTT, Walter. *Ivanhoe.* 1918. Chicago. Ills. Milo Winter. 1st ed. VG $40.00

SCOTT, Walter. *Kenilworth.* Philadelphia. McKay. no date. Ills. Ford. $25.00

SCOTT, Walter. *Lady of the Lake.* Cromwell $85.00

SCOTT, Walter. *Letters on Demonology & Witchcraft.* 1842. New York. 338 pp. G $75.00

SCOTT, Walter. *Minstrelsy of the Scottish Border.* New York. Crowell. Ills. VG $40.00

SCOTT, Walter. *New Shelley Letters.* 1949. New Haven. Ills. dj. EX $20.00

SCOTT, Walter. *The Antiquary.* 1816. London. 1st ed. 3 vol set. VG $75.00

SCOTT, Walter. *Waverley Novels.* 1893. Boston. Ills. Ltd. ed. 1/24 sets. EX $650.00

SCOTT, Walter. *Waverley Novels.* 1868. Edinburgh. Ills. 4 vol set. EX $225.00

SCOTT, Walter. *Waverly Novels.* 1883. Edinburg. Centenary ed. 12 vol set. VG $135.00

SCOTT, Winifred. *Jefferson Hogg, Portrait of Shelley's Biographer.* 1961. London. dj. EX $25.00

SCOTT & SCOTT. *The Armed Forces of the U.S.S.R.* 1979. Ills. dj. VG $20.00

SCOTT. *Bullet Brand.* Pyramid. pb. $3.00

SCOTT. *Chronicles of the Canongate.* 1827. Philadelphia. 1st ed. 2 vol set. $25.00

SCOTT. *Death in the Saddle.* Pyramid. pb. $3.00

SCOTT. *Death on the Rimrock.* Pyramid. pb. $3.00

SCOTT. *Lessons in Elocution.* 1806. Hartford. G $75.00

SCOTT. *Raiders of the Rio Grande.* Pyramid. pb. $3.00

SCOTT. *Ranger's Revenge.* Pyramid. pb. $3.00

SCOTT. *Rider of the Mesquite Trail.* Pyramid. pb. $3.00

SCOTT. *Romance of Highways of California.* 1947. 1st ed. inscr. dj. EX $20.00

SCOTT. *Scott's Last Expedition.* 1913. New York. 1st ed. 2 vol set. VG $75.00

SCOVELL, J. Boardman. *A Short History of the Niagara Portage.* 1951. Niagara Falls. Ills. wrappers. VG $10.00

SCOVILLE, Warren C. *Revolution in Glassmaking.* 1848. Cambridge. Ills. 1st ed. 398 pp. dj. VG $25.00

SCOYEN & TAYLOR. *Rainbow Canyons.* 1931. Stanford. VG $15.00

SCUDAMORE. *Treatise on Nature & Cure of Gout & Rheumatism.* 1819. Philadelphia. 1st Am. ed. VG $75.00

SCUDDER, A. *The Grey Studio.* 1934. Boston. Hill. 1st ed. dj. EX $15.00

SCUDDER, Horace E. *James Russell Lowell.* 1901. Boston. Houghton Mifflin. 2 vol set. $12.50

SCUDDER. *Brief Guide to the Commoner Butterflies.* 1893. New York. VG $10.00

SCULLY, William C. *The White Hecatomb.* 1897. New York. Holt. 1st ed. VG $10.00

SCWAB, George. *Tribes of the Liberian Hinterland.* 1947. Peabody Museum. 1st ed. wrappers. $20.00

SEABROOK, William. *Adventures in Arabia.* 1927. New York. Ills. 346 pp. index. dj. $15.00

SEABROOK, William. *Jungle Ways.* 1931. Blue Ribbon. Ills. 308 pp. G $5.00

SEABROOK, William. *No Hiding Place.* 1942. Philadelphia. 1st ed. dj. G $10.00

SEABROOK, William. *The Magic Island.* 1929. New York. Harcourt Brace. Ills. King. VG $17.50

SEABROOK, William. *These Foreigners.* 1938. New York. ex-lib. 358 pp. $7.50

SEABROOK, William. *Witchcraft: Its Power in the World Today.* 1940. New York. 1st ed. dj. VG $20.00

SEABURY, George J. *Shall Pharmacists Become Tradesmen?* 1899. New York. 3rd ed. 241 pp. $17.50

SEAGER, R. *Explorations in the Island of Mochlos.* 1912. Boston. Ills. 1st ed. VG $65.00

SEAGRAVE, Gordon S. *Burma Surgeon.* 1943. Peoples Book Club. Ills. dj. $5.50

SEAMAN, N.G. *Indian Relics of the Pacific Northwest.* 1946. Portland. Ills. 157 pp. index. dj. $15.00

SEARLE, Ronald. *More Cats.* 1975. Ills. 1st Am. ed. $12.50

SEARS, Fred C. *Productive Orcharding.* 1917. Philadelphia. Lippincott. ex-lib. 315 pp. VG $4.50

SEARS, Hugh. *Mechanizing Our Army. Close-Ups of Equipment.* 1941. Grosset & Dunlap. Ills. 61 pp. $6.50

SEARS, Hugh. *What's New in the Air Corps.* 1941. New York. Grosset & Dunlap. dj. VG $8.00

SEARS, P. *Deserts on the March.* 1937. OK U. Press. 231 pp. G $6.00

SEARS, P. *Lands Beyond the Forest.* 1969. Prentice Hall. Ills. 206 pp. dj. EX $9.00

SEARS, Stephens. *The American Heritage.* 1974. Ills. 400 pp. VG $25.00

SEATON, Ethel. *Sir Richard Roos Lancastrian Poet.* 1961. Hart Davis. 1st ed. dj. $12.50

SEAVER, George. *Edward Wilson of the Antartic.* 1937. 1st ed. ex-lib. 301 pp. VG $22.00

SEAVER, J. Montogomery. *Brooks Family Records.* Philadelphia. no date. 29 pp. $12.00

SEAVER, J. Montogomery. *Cook Family Records.* Philadelphia. no date. 29 pp. $12.00

SEAVER, J. Montogomery. *Henderson Family Records.* Philadelphia. $12.00

SECATARY, Hawkins. *Incuba Cazanova Treasure.* 1921. Cincinnati. 1st ed. VG $25.00

SECKEL, Helmut. *Bird-Headed Dwarfs.* 1960. Thomas. 1st ed. $17.50

SECKEL. *Stability & Control of Airplanes & Helicopters.* 1964. $10.00

SEDGES, John. *The Townsman.* 1945. New York. 384 pp. $3.50

SEDGMAN, Frank. *Frank Sedgman's Winning Tennis.* 1954. New York. Ills. 132 pp. $5.00

SEDGWICK, Miss. *The Poor Rich Man, & the Rich Poor Man.* 1839. New York. Harper. TB. 186 pp. $5.00

SEDGWICK, N.M. *The Young Shot.* 1940. London. Ills. VG $25.00

SEE, R.R.M. *English Pastels 1750-1830.* 1911. G. Bell. 1st ed. ex-lib. $35.00

SEEBER. *George Elburt Burr 1859-1939.* 1971. Northland Press. $15.00

SEEGER, Alan. *Poems.* 1916. New York. Ltd. 1st ed. boxed. VG $45.00

SEESE, Mildred Parker. *Old Orange Houses.* 1941. 1st ed. sgn. 2 vol set. $125.00

SEFI, A.J. *An Introduction to Advanced Philately.* 1932. London. dj. G $50.00

SEGAL, Erich. *Oliver's Story.* 1977. Harper & Row. dj. $2.50

SEGAL, Lore. *Lucinella.* 1976. New York. Farrar. 1st ed. dj. EX $20.00

SEGAL, M. *Painted Ladies: Models of the Great Artists.* 1972. New York. $8.50

SEGAR. *Thimble Theatre Starring Popeye.* 1935. Racine. VG $12.50

SEGHERS, Anna. *Revolt of the Fishermen.* 1930. New York. 1st ed. dj. EX $37.50

SEIDL, Anton. *Anton Seidl, a Memorial by His Friends.* 1889. Scribner. Ltd. 1st ed. 1/1000. $20.00

SEIDLITZ, Woldemar von. *A History of Japanese Colour Prints.* 1910. London. Ills. 207 pp. VG rare. $155.00

SEIFERT, Elizabeth. *Hospital Zone.* 1948. New York. 361 pp. dj. $3.50

SEIFERT, Elizabeth. *Love Calls the Doctor.* 1958. New York. 281 pp. dj. $4.00

SEIFERT, Elizabeth. *The Doctor's Bride.* 1960. New York. 275 pp. $3.50

SEIGER, H.F. *The Complete German Short Haired Pointer.* 1951. VG $35.00

SEIGMEISTER, E. *Music Lover's Hand Book.* 1943. Morrow. dj. VG $14.50

SEITZ, D.C. *Braxton Bragg, General of the Confederacy.* 1924. VG $65.00

SEITZ, William. *Hans Hoffmann.* 1963. Ills. pb. VG $20.00

SEITZ, William. *The Art of Assemblage.* 1962. dj. EX $10.00

SEITZ. *Famous American Duels.* 1st ed. VG $35.00

SEITZ. *Famous American Duels.* 1966. reprint. VG $17.50

SELBY, Hubert, Jr. *Last Exit to Brooklyn.* 1964. Grove. 1st ed. dj. VG $30.00

SELBY, Hubert, Jr. *The Demon.* 1976. Playboy Press. 1st ed. dj. VG $15.00

SELDES, Gilbert. *Movies Came from America.* 1937. London/NY. Ills. 120 pp. dj. VG $17.50

SELF, Margaret. *Irish Adventure.* 1954. 1st ed. VG $14.00

SELFRIDGE-FIELD, Eleanor. *Venetian Instruments Music: Gabrieli to Vivaldi.* 1975. Oxford. Ills. dj. VG $22.00

SELIGSON, Marcia. *The Eternal Bliss Machine.* 1973. VG $3.00

SELINKO, Annemarie. *Desiree.* 1953. New York. Morrow. 539 pp. VG $3.50

SELL, Henry B. & Weybright, V. *Buffalo Bill & the Wild West.* 1955. New York. 278 pp. $17.50

SELLE, E.A. *Donald of China, Story of William Henry Donald.* 1948. G $6.00

SELLE, Ralph A. *Texas Grapefruit.* 1933. Houston. phamphlet. scarce. $17.50

SELLER, W.C. & Yeatman R.J. *1066 & All That.* 1931. EX $5.00

SELOUS, Percy. *Travel & Big Game.* 1897. New York. Ills. 195 pp. VG $40.00

SELSAM, M. *Land of the Giant Tortoise/Story of the Galapagos.* 1977. Four Winds. Ills. 1st ed. 55 pp. dj. EX $7.50

SELTSAM, William H. *Metropolitan Opera Annals.* 1947. New York. 1st ed. inscr. VG $42.50

SELTZER, C.A. *Coming of the Law.* 1912. New York. 1st ed. dj. $15.00

SELTZER, Louis B. *The Years Were Good.* 1956. NY/Cleveland. Ills. 1st ed. 317 pp. $10.00

SELTZER. *Arizona Jim.* Popular. pb. $3.00

SELTZER. *Double Cross Ranch.* Popular. pb. $3.00

SELWYN-BROWN, Arthur. *Physician Throughout the Ages.* 1938. 2 vol set. VG $75.00

SEMPLE, Daisy. *Tommy & Jane & the Birds.* 1929. Akron. Saalfield. Ills. Fern B. Peat. $30.00

SENDAK, Maurice. *In the Night Kitchen.* 1970. New York. Ills. dj. EX $10.00

SENDAK, Maurice. *King Grisly Beard.* 1973. 1st ed. sgn. $30.00

SENDAK, Maurice. *Seven Little Monsters.* 1st Eng. ed. $20.00

SENDAK, Maurice. *The Love for Three Oranges.* 1984. Ltd. ed. 1/200. sgn. slipcase. $12.50

SENDAK, Maurice. *Where the Wild Things Are.* 1963. New York. Harper & Row. Ills. dj. EX $12.50

SENDREY, Alfred. *Music in Ancient Israel.* 1969. New York. Ills. dj. VG $37.00

SENEFELDER, Alois. *The Invention of Lithography.* 1911. New York. VG $30.00

SENNETT, Mack. *King of Comedy.* 1954. New York. 1st ed. VG $7.50

SENNETT, Richard. *An Evening of Brahms.* 1984. New York. Knopf. 1st ed. dj. EX $20.00

SENNETT, Richard. *The Frog Who Dared Croak.* 1982. New York. 1st ed. dj. EX $25.00

SERANNE, Ann & Gaden, Eileen. *The Blender Cookbook.* 1961. Garden City. Doubleday. Ills. 288 pp. $6.50

SERANNE, Ann & Wilson, Joan. *The Copco Pots & Pans Cookbook.* 1968. Garden City. Doubleday. 276 pp. $5.00

SERANNE, Ann. *America Cooks.* 1967. New York. Putnam. 796 pp. $12.50

SERANNE, Ann. *The General Federation of Women's Clubs Cookbook.* 1967. New York. Putnam. 796 pp. $12.50

SEREDY, Kate. *Listening.* 1936. New York. Viking. Ills. 1st ed. $30.00

SEREDY, Kate. *Philomena.* 1955. 1st ed. dj. EX $20.00

SEREDY, Kate. *The Chestry Oak.* 1948. New York. 1st ed. sgn. dj. EX $25.00

SEREDY, Kate. *The Singing Tree.* 1946. New York. Viking. Ills. dj. $10.00

SEREDY, Kate. *The White Stag.* 1937. Viking. 1st ed. sgn. dj. EX $30.00

SERLE, W. & Morel, G.J. *A Field Guide to the Birds of West Africa.* 1983. London. Collins. Ills. 351 pp. EX $20.00

SERLING, R.J. *Ceiling Unlimited/Story of North Central Airlines.* 1973. Ills. VG $15.00

SERRES, D. & J.T. *Liber Nauticus.* 1979. London. Ills. 108 pp. dj. EX $80.00

SERT, Misia. *Misia & the Muses.* 1953. New York. dj. EX $10.00

SERVENTY, V. *The Singing Land.* 1972. Scribner. Ills. 1st ed. 96 pp. dj. EX $12.50

SERVICE, E.R. *A Profile of Primitive Culture.* 1958. Harper. Ills. 474 pp. G $15.00

SERVICE, Robert W. *Ballads of a Bohemian.* 1921. Barse & Hopkins. 220 pp. VG $7.50

SERVICE, Robert W. *Harper of Heaven.* 1948. Dodd Mead. 1st ed. dj. VG $22.50

SERVICE, Robert W. *Master of the Microbe.* 1926. New York. Barse & Hopkins. 1st ed. VG $30.00

SERVICE, Robert W. *The Spell of the Yukon & Other Verses.* 1907. Barse & Hopkins. 126 pp. VG $5.50

SERVICE, Robert W. *The Trail of Ninety-Eight.* 1910. New York. 514 pp. $4.00

SERVICE, Robert W. *Why Not Grow Young?* 1928. New York. VG $20.00

SERVICE, Robert. *Rhymes of Red Cross Man.* 1916. $12.00

SERVICE, W. *Owl.* 1969. Knopf. Ills. 93 pp. dj. EX $4.00

SERVISS, Garrett P. *A Columbus of Space.* 1911. New York. Appleton. 1st ed. VG $125.00

SERVISS, Garrett P. *Astronomy with an Opera Glass.* 1896. $20.00

SERVISS, Garrett P. *The Moon Metal.* 1900. New York. Harper. 1st ed. VG $60.00

SESSIONS, Francis C. *In Western Levant.* 1890. New York. Ills. Hall. 1st ed. VG $15.00

SETH, R. *Unmasked! Story of Soviet Espionage.* 1965. Ills. dj. VG $15.00

SETH-SMITH, D. *Small Parrots.* 1979. Ills. revised ed. EX $10.00

SETON, Anna. *Pulse of the Pueblo.* 1939. Santa Fe. 1st ed. $22.00

SETON, Anya. *Dragonwyck.* 1944. Boston. 316 pp. $4.00

SETON, Anya. *Green Darkness.* 1972. Boston. Book Club ed. 627 pp. dj. $4.00

SETON, Anya. *The Turquoise.* 1946. 1st ed. dj. $8.50

SETON, Anya. *The Winthrop Woman.* 1958. Boston. Houghton Mifflin. 586 pp. G $4.50

SETON, Cynthia. *A Private Life.* 1982. Norton. proof copy. wrappers. VG $10.00

SETON, E.T. *Animal Heroes.* 1905. New York. Scribner. 1st ed. $50.00

SETON, E.T. *Library of Pioneering & Woodcraft.* 1926. Doubleday Page.Ills. 5 vol set. VG $55.00

SETON, E.T. *Lives of the Hunted.* 1901. New York. Scribner. 1st ed. VG $45.00

SETON, E.T. *Lives of the Hunted.* 1967. Schocken. Ills. 350 pp. dj. EX $10.00

SETON, E.T. *Rolf in the Woods.* 1911. Grosset & Dunlap. 437 pp. $20.00

SETON, E.T. *The Biography of a Grizzly.* 1927. New York. Grosset & Dunlap. 167 pp. dj. $6.00

SETON, E.T. *The Book of Woodcraft.* 1921. Garden City. Ills. 590 pp. $10.00

SETON, E.T. *The Nature Library Animals.* 1926. Doubleday. Ills. Tadhunter. 295 pp. $4.50

SETON, E.T. *The Preacher of Cedar Mountain.* 1917. Garden City. 1st ed. 428 pp. dj. VG $20.00

SETON, E.T. *The Trail of the Sandhill Stag.* 1899. New York. Scribners. 1st ed. sgn. VG $100.00

SETON, E.T. *Wild Animals I Have Known.* 1926. Ills. 358 pp. G $5.00

SETON, E.T. *Wild Animals Ways.* 1922. Doubleday Page.Ills. 243 pp. $5.00

SETON-WATSON, R.W. *Britain & the Dictators.* 1938. Cambridge. 460 pp. $6.00

SETTLE, Mary & Raymond. *Empire on Wheels.* 1949. Stanford Press.Ills. 1st ed. VG $15.00

SETTLE, Mary Lee. *Blood Tie.* 1977. Boston. 1st ed. dj. EX $25.00

SETTLE, Mary Lee. *O Beulah Land.* 1956. 1st Am. ed. dj. VG $25.00

SETTLE, Mary Lee. *Prisons.* 1973. New York. Putnam. 1st ed. dj. EX $25.00

SETTLE, Mary Lee. *Prisons.* 1973. 1st Am. ed. dj. EX $10.00

SETTLE, Mary Lee. *The Killing Ground.* 1982. New York. Farrar. 1st ed. dj. VG $25.00

SETTLE, Mary Lee. *The Killing Ground.* 1982. New York. advance copy. wrappers. EX $40.00

SETTLE, Mary Lee. *The Killing Ground.* 1982. Farrar. proof copy. wrappers. VG $20.00

SETTLE, Mary Lee. *The Killing Ground.* 1982. Farrar. Ltd. 1st ed. sgn. slipcase. EX $60.00

SETTLE, Mary Lee. *The Scapegoat.* 1980. New York. Random House. 1st ed. dj. VG $30.00

SETTLE, Raymond & Mary L. *Saddles & Spurs, the Pony Express Age.* 1955. Harrisburg, PA.Ills. 1st ed. 217 pp. dj. $15.00

SEUSS, Dr. *I Had Trouble in Getting to Solla Sollew.* 1965. Rand McNally. dj. VG $16.00

SEUSS, Dr. *The Omnibus Boners.* 1931. Blue Ribbon Books. Ills. VG $5.50

SEUSS, Dr. *The 500 Hats of Bartholomew Cubbins.* 1938. New York. Ills. Seuss. 1st ed. EX $100.00

SEUSS, Dr. *Thidwick the Big-Hearted Moose.* 1948. Rand McNally. VG $20.00

SEVAREID, Eric. *Candidates of 1960 Behind the Headlines.* 1959. New York. ex-lib. 369 pp. dj. VG $4.00

SEVAREID, Eric. *Not So Wild a Dream.* 1946. $7.50

SEVERENCE, Frank H. *Studies of the Niagara Frontier.* 1911. Buffalo. 1st ed. EX $25.00

SEVERINGHAUS & BLACKSHAW. *A New Guide to the Birds of Taiwan.* 1976. Taiwan. Mei Ya. Ills. 222 pp. EX $17.50

SEVERN, James. *The Collecting of Guns.* 1964. no place. Ills. 272 pp. dj. VG $20.00

SEVERN, James. *The Collecting of Guns.* New York. Bonanza. Ills. 272 pp. dj. VG $15.00

SEVRUK, V. *How Wars End, Accounts of Fall of Berlin.* 1974. Moscow. Ills. Eng. text. dj. EX $12.50

SEWALL, R.K. *Sketches of St.Augustine.* 1848. New York. G $75.00

SEWARD, Olive Risley. *William H. Seward's World Travels.* 1873. New York. Appleton. Ills. 780 pp. $5.00

SEWELL, Anna. *Black Beauty, His Grooms, & Companions.* Hurst. no date. 243 pp. $4.00

SEWELL, Anna. *Black Beauty.* 1890. Ills. Am. Humane ed. VG $175.00

SEWELL, Anna. *Black Beauty.* 1926. New York. Ills. J. McMann. 244 pp. VG $8.00

SEWELL, Anna. *Black Beauty.* 1946. Ills. Dennis. World Rainbow ed. EX $12.50

SEXTON, Anne. *Selected Poems.* 1964. Oxford U. Pr. 1st ed. dj. VG $40.00

SEXTON, Anne. *Self-Portrait in Letters.* 1977. Boston. 1st ed. dj. EX $15.00

SEXTON, Anne. *The Book of Folly.* 1972. Boston. 1st ed. dj. EX $20.00

SEXTON, Anne. *The Book of Folly.* 1972. Ltd. ed. 1/500. sgn. VG $25.00

SEXTON, Anne. *The Death Note Books.* 1974. Boston. 1st ed. dj. VG $20.00

SEXTON, Anne. *To Bedlam & Part Way Back.* 1960. Boston. 1st printing. $25.00

SEXTON, Anne. *Transformations.* 1971. Boston. Ills. B. Swan. 1st ed. dj. EX $30.00

SEXTON, Anne. *Transformations.* 1971. Ltd. ed. 1/500. sgn. VG $25.00

SEXTON, Anne. *Words for Dr. Y.* 1978. Boston. 1st ed. dj. EX $15.00

SEYBERT, Adam. *Annales Statistiques des Etats-Unis.* 1820. Paris. Ills. 1st French ed. 455 pp. $100.00

SEYMOUR, C. *American Diplomacy During the World War.* 1964. EX $17.50

SEYMOUR, C. *The Intimate Papers of Colonel House.* 1926. Ills. 2 vol set. G $15.00

SEYMOUR, E.L. *The Garden Encyclopedia.* 1939. New York. Wise & Co. 1300 pp. VG $5.50

SEYMOUR, Flora Warren. *The Indians Today.* 1927. Chicago. Ills. 235 pp. $6.50

SEYMOUR, Flora Warren. *The Story of the Red Man.* 1929. New York. 1st ed. $25.00

SEYMOUR, Flora Warren. *We Called Them Indians.* 1940. London/NY. Ills. 1st ed. 280 pp. index. $17.50

SEYMOUR, G. *Capt. Nathan Hale & Major John P. Wyllys.* 1933. New Haven. Ltd. ed. 1/1000. 296 pp. $25.00

SEYMOUR. *A Jackdaw in Georgia.* 1923. London. 1st ed. $15.00

SEYMOUR. *Favorite Flowers in Color.* 1949. Wise. 300 photos. dj. $37.50

SEYTON, Walter. *A Story of Rural Life in Virginia.* 1859. Boston. Ills. $12.00

SEZNAC, Jean. *Survival of the Pagan Gods.* 1953. New York. Bollingen Foundation. 1st ed. $30.00

SGARATO, N. *Soviet Aircraft of Today.* 1978. Ills. 80 pp. VG $7.50

SGARATO, N. *U.S.A.F. Aircraft of Today.* 1978. Ills. 103 pp. wrappers. VG $7.50

SHACHTMAN, T. *The Phony War 1939-1940.* 1982. dj. EX $15.00

SHACKELTON, Robert. *Book of Boston.* 1923. Philadelphia. VG $25.00

SHACKLETON, E. *South, Story of Shackleton's Last Expedition.* 1920. Macmillan. Ills. 374 pp. VG $45.00

SHADBOLT, M. & Ruhen, O. *Isles of the South Pacific.* 1971. Nat. Geog. Soc.Ills. 211 pp. dj. VG $10.00

SHAFFER, E. *Caroline Gardens.* 1939. New York. 1st ed. $20.00

SHAFFER, Mary T.S. *Old Indian Trails of the Canadian Rockies.* 1911. Putnam. $22.50

SHAFFER, Peter. *The Private Ear/The Public Eye.* 1964. New York. Stein & Day. 1st Am. ed. dj. $30.00

SHAH, Sayed Indries. *The Secret Lore of Magic, Books of Sorcerers.* 1958. New York. dj. VG $8.50

SHAHN, Ben. *Ecclesiastes.* 1971. New York. Grossman. dj. VG $18.50

SHAHN, Ben. *Hamlet.* 1959. New York. Ills. VG $25.00

SHAKESPEARE, William. *As You Like It, a Comedy.* 1903. New York. Roycroft. 1st ed. VG $25.00

SHAKESPEARE, William. *Dramatic Works.* Gall & Ingis. no date. 4 engravings. $3.00

SHAKESPEARE, William. *The Tempest.* London/NY. Heinemann. Ills. Rackham. VG $50.00

SHAKESPEARE, William. *The Tempest.* 1908. London. Ills. Woodroffe. folio. VG $50.00

SHAKESPEARE, William. *Tragedy of Macbeth.* 1880. Ginn. $20.00

SHAKLETON, Robert & Elizabeth.*The Book of Antiques.* 1938. Philadelphia. Penn Pub. Ills. 284 pp. G $3.00

SHAKSPEAR, John. *A Grammar of the Hindustani Language.* 1818. London. 2nd ed. VG $100.00

SHALETT. *Old Nameless.* 1943. Appleton. Ills. 1st ed. sgn. 177 pp. VG $20.00

SHALIMAR. *True Tales of Sail & Steam.* London. (ca. 1943) Ills. F. Mason. G $10.00

SHAMBAUGH, Benjamin F. *The Old Stone Capitol Remembers.* 1935. Iowa City. 435 pp. $15.00

SHAMBURGER. *Tracks Across the Sky, Pioneers of U.S. Air Mail.* 1964. Philadelphia. $10.00

SHANGE, Ntozake. *A Daughter's Geography.* 1983. New York. 1st ed. dj. EX $15.00

SHANHOLTZER, Wesley Albert. *Timberline.* 1929. 198 pp. dj. $50.00

SHANKLAND, P. *Byron of the Wager.* 1976. Ills. EX $10.00

SHANLY, C.D. *A Jolly Bear & His Friends.* 1867. New York. Ills. Stephens. 1st ed. EX $75.00

SHANN, Renee. *Twenty-Four Hours Leave.* 1943. Philadelphia. 271 pp. dj. $3.50

SHANNON, Dell. *Appearances of Death.* 1977. Morrow. 1st ed. dj. VG $12.50

SHANNON, Dell. *Crime File.* 1974. New York. Morrow. 1st ed. dj. EX $17.50

SHANNON, Dell. *Death by Inches.* 1967. London. Gollancz. 1st Eng. ed. dj. VG $15.00

SHANNON, Dell. *Felony at Random.* 1979. Morrow. 1st ed. dj. VG $12.50

SHANNON, H.J. *The Book of the Seashore, Naturalist on the Beach.*1935. New York. Ills. VG $25.00

SHANNON, Monica. *Tawnymore.* 1931. Garden City. Ills. Jean Charlot. 1st ed. VG $25.00

SHANOR, D.R. *Soviet Europe.* 1975. dj. EX $8.50

SHAPIRO, H.L. *Physical Characters of the Society Islanders.* 1930. Bishop Museum. 1st ed. folio. wrappers. $15.00

SHAPIRO, I. *John Henry & the Double-Jointed Steam Drill.* 1945. New York. Ills. James Daugherty. EX $10.00

SHAPIRO, I. *The Story of Yankee Whaling.* 1959. Am. Heritage. Ills. 153 pp. VG $7.50

SHAPIRO, Karl. *Adult Bookstore.* 1976. Random House. 1st ed. dj. VG $15.00

SHAPIRO, Karl. *To Abolish Children.* 1968. Quadrangle. 1st ed. dj. VG $20.00

SHAPIRO, Karl. *V-Letter & Other Poems.* 1944. Reynal & Hitchcock. 1st ed. VG $60.00

SHAPIRO, Nat & Hentoff, N. *The Jazz Makers.* 1957. New York. Rinehart. dj. VG $40.00

SHAPIRO, S. *Our Changing Fisheries.* 1971. Ills. 534 pp. VG $14.00

SHAREFF, Victory. *Garbage Can Cat.* 1970. Westminster Pr. Ills. Watson. $10.00

SHARELL, R. *The Tuatara, Lizards & Frogs of New Zealand.* 1966. London. Collins. Ills. 94 pp. dj. $42.00

SHARF, A. *British Press & Jews Under Nazi Rule.* 1964. London. $15.00

SHARP, Ann Pearsall. *Little Garden People & What They Do.* 1938. Akron. Ills. Marion Bryson. $16.00

SHARP, Capt. Bartholomew. *Voyages & Adventures of Capt. Sharp & Others.* 1684. London. 1st ed. 172 pp. $2,250.00

SHARP, Dallas Lore. *Spirit of the Hive.* 1925. NY/London. 1st ed. 240 pp. G $12.50

SHARP, Dallas Lore. *Watcher in the Woods.* 1915. New York. Century. TB. 127 pp. G $3.00

SHARP, Margery. *Cluny Brown.* 1944. Boston. 270 pp. $3.50

SHARP, Margery.*Martha, Eric, & George.* 1964. Boston. Little, Brown. 1st ed. $10.00

SHARP, Margery. *Miss Bianca in the Antarctic.* 1971. Boston. Ills. Erik Blegvad. VG $25.00

SHARP, Margery. *The Gypsy in the Parlour.* 1953. Boston. 249 pp. $3.50

SHARP, Margery. *The Turret.* 1963. Boston. Ills. Garth Williams. 1st ed. $40.00

SHARP, Roland Hall. *South America Uncensored.* 1945. New York. Longman Green. 363 pp. $3.00

SHARP, William. *Life of Percy Bysshe Shelley.* 1887. London. EX $25.00

SHARPE, L.W. *How to Draw Merchant Ships.* 1945. London. Ills. dj. G $6.50

SHARPE, Tom. *Vintage Stuff.* 1982. London. Secker & Warburg. 1st ed. dj. $20.00

SHARPE, Tom. *Wilt on High.* 1984. London. 1st ed. sgn. dj. EX $30.00

SHARPMAM, Edward. *Cupids Whirligig.* Golden Cockerel. Ltd. ed. VG $35.00

SHASTID, Thomas Hall. *Tramping to Failure.* 1937. Ann Arbor, MI. Ills. 1st ed. 503 pp. dj. $20.00

SHAVER, Richard J. *I Remember Lemuria & Return of Sathanas.* 1948. Evanston. Venture books. 1st ed. VG $35.00

SHAVER. *Furniture Boys Like to Build.* 1931. Bruce Pub. Ills. 216 pp. VG $8.50

SHAW, A.H. *The Plain Dealer, 100 Years in Cleveland.* 1942. Knopf. dj. EX $8.00

SHAW, Albert. *Abraham Lincoln-Year of His Election Cartoon Hist.*1929. 2 vol set. VG $50.00

SHAW, E. *Rural Architecture.* 1843. Boston. 108 pp. 52 pls. VG $135.00

SHAW, E.P. & W.P. *Rambling Round Cape Cod.* 1948. Ills. 64 pp. wrappers. $3.00

SHAW, G. Bernard. *Adventures of the Black Girl in Search for God.* 1933. New York. Ills. Farleigh. 75 pp. $12.50

SHAW, G. Bernard. *Complete Plays with Prefaces.* 1963. Dodd Mead. 6 vol set. VG $60.00

SHAW, G. Bernard. *Geneva, a Fancied Page of History in Three Acts.* 1939. London. Ills. Topolski. 113 pp. $9.00

SHAW, G. Bernard. *Intelligent Woman's Guide to Socialism/Capitalism.*1928. 1st printing. dj. VG $35.00

SHAW, G. Bernard. *Nine Plays.* 1942. New York. Dodd Mead. 1147 pp. $6.00

SHAW, G. Bernard. *Perfect Wagnerite: Commentary on Ring of Niblungs.*1898. London. 1st ed. G $20.00

SHAW, G. Bernard. *Ruskin's Politics.* 1921. VG $25.00

SHAW, G. Bernard. *Selected Plays with Prefaces.* 1948. New York. 898 pp. VG $4.50

SHAW, G. Bernard. *Socialism & Individualism.* 1908. Fabian Socialist Series No.3. $25.00

SHAW, G. Bernard. *Wreath of Stars.* London. 1st ed. sgn. $15.00

SHAW, G.B. *How to Settle the Irish Question.* 1917. Dublin/London. 32 pp. $25.00

SHAW, George C. *Chinnook Jargon & How to Use It.* 1909. Seattle. 1st ed. wrappers. VG $45.00

SHAW, I. *Act of Faith & Other Stories.* Random House. 1st ed. VG $15.00

SHAW, I. *Beggar-Man, Thief.* 1977. New York. 372 pp. dj. EX $4.00

SHAW, I. *Bread Upon the Waters.* 1981. Delacorte. Ltd. ed. sgn. slipcase. $50.00

SHAW, I. *In the Company of Dolphins.* 1964. dj. G $6.50

SHAW, J. *Red Army Resurgent. WWII Series.* 1979. Time Life. Ills. VG $15.00

SHAW, J. *The Hard-Boiled Omnibus.* 1946. New York. Simon & Schuster. 367 pp. $52.50

SHAW, L. *Cowboy Dances.* 1949. Caxton. Ills. VG $16.00

SHAW, L. *Cowboy Dances.* 1940. Caxton. $10.00

SHAW, L. *True History of Some of the Pioneers of Colorado.* 1909. Denver. 1st ed. 12 pls. wrappers. VG $50.00

SHAW, Mark. *The John F. Kennedys, a Family Album.* 1964. New York. 4th ed. 160 pp. $37.50

SHAW, R.C. *Across the Plains in Forty-Nine.* 1896. W.C. West, Pub. 200 pp. $225.00

SHAW, Samuel. *Narrative of Travels of Jame Bruce to Abyssinia.* 1790. London. 1st ed. rebound. G $65.00

SHAW, Thomas. *Clovers & How to Grow Them.* 1906. Orange Judd. 1st ed. $10.00

SHAW, Thomas. *Weeds & How to Eradicate Them.* 1893. Toronto. $10.00

SHAW. *Historial Origins & Historical Critiques.* 1892. $25.00

SHAWCROSS, John. *Shelley's Literary & Philosophical Criticism.* 1909. London. Frowde. EX $25.00

SHAY, Felix. *Elbert Hubbard of East Aurora.* 1926. New York. Ills. Denslow. 1st ed. 553 pp. $20.00

SHAYLOR, Joseph. *The Fascination of Books.* 1912. London. 1st ed. VG $40.00

SHEA, James. *It's All in the Game.* 1960. New York. Ills. 1st ed. dj. VG $30.00

SHEA, John G. *The Pennsylvania Dutch & Their Furniture.* 1980. New York. Nostrand. Ills. dj. VG $10.50

SHEA, John Gilmary. *Early Voyages Up & Down the Mississippi.* 1861. Albany. Munsell. Ltd./only ed. 1/100. $225.00

SHEA, John Gilmary. *The Fallen Brave.* 1861. Ills. 1st ed. $32.50

SHEALY, Ann. *The Ravaged Garden.* 1985. Pompano Beach. 1st ed. sgn. 86 pp. dj. EX $15.00

SHEEAN, V. *Not Peace But a Sword.* 1939. 1st ed. $6.50

SHEEAN, Vincent. *Indigo Bunting, Memoir of Edna St. Vincent Millay.* 1951. New York. dj. VG $10.00

SHEEAN, Vincent. *Oscar Hammerstein I.* 1956. New York. Ills. 1st ed. dj. VG $12.50

SHEEHAN, Perley Poore. *Abyss of Wonders.* 1953. Polaris Press. Ltd. 1st ed. 1/1500. dj. $35.00

SHEERAN, James. *Confederate Chaplain in a War Journal.* 1960. Bruce. 1st ed. dj. $7.50

SHEIL, M.P. *How the Old Woman Got Home.* 1928. New York. VG $6.00

SHELDON, C. *Wilderness of Denali, Explorations in Northern AL.* 1960. New York. new ed. 412 pp. dj. EX $12.50

SHELDON, Charles. *The Wilderness of the North Pacific Coast Islands.* 1912. Scribner. Ills. 1st ed. 246 pp. VG $17.50

SHELDON, George. *History Deerfield, Massachusetts.* 1895. Deerfield. 1st ed. 2 vol set. VG $125.00

SHELDON, H.P. *Tranquility.* 1936. New York. Derrydale. Ltd. ed. EX $125.00

SHELDON, H.P. *Tranquility.* 1945. Ills. Arthur Fuller. 1st ed. $25.00

SHELDON, J.P. *To Canada & Through It with British Association.* 1885. Ottawa. 32 pp. fld map. wrappers. VG $35.00

SHELDON, Luke. *Doomed Planet.* 1967. 1st ed. dj. EX $7.50

SHELDON, Sidney. *Stranger in the Mirror.* New York. dj. VG $5.00

SHELDON, W.G. *The Wilderness of the Giant Panda.* 1975. MA U. Press. Ills. 196 pp. dj. EX $20.00

SHELDRICK, D. *Animal Kingdom, Story of Tsavo African Game Park.* 1973. Bobbs Merrill. Ills. 1st Am. ed. dj. EX $10.00

SHELLABARGER, Samuel. *Lord Vanity.* 1953. Boston. 473 pp. $3.50

SHELLEY, E.M. *Hunting Big Game with Dogs in Africa.* 1924. sgn. scarce. VG $85.00

SHELLEY, Mary W. *Frankenstein; or, The Modern Prometheus.* 1984. Berkeley. U. of CA Press. Ills. Moser. $30.00

SHELLEY, Mary W. *Journal.* 1947. U. of OK. 1st ed. dj. $20.00

SHELLEY, Mary W. *Letters of Mary Shelley.* 1918. Bibliophile Soc. Ltd. 1st ed. $35.00

SHELLEY, Mary W. *Letters of Mary Shelley.* 1918. Harper. Ltd. ed. 1/448. VG $17.50

SHELLEY, Percy B. & Elizabeth. *Original Poetry by Victor & Cazire.* 1898. London. VG $60.00

SHELLEY, Percy Bysshe. *A Defense of Poetry.* 1904. Bobbs Merrill. Ltd. ed. 1/500. EX $30.00

SHELLEY, Percy Bysshe. *Adonais.* 1927. London. glassine dj. VG $25.00

SHELLEY, Percy Bysshe. *Complete Poetical Works of Percy Bysshe Shelley.* 1934. London. Oxford. EX $45.00

SHELLEY, Percy Bysshe. *Complete Poetical Works of Percy Bysshe Shelley.* 1948. London. Oxford. EX $30.00

SHELLEY, Percy Bysshe. *Poems & Lyrics.* Mt. Vernon. Peter Pauper Press. EX $15.00

SHELLEY, Percy Bysshe. *Shelley's Prose of the Trumpet of a Prophecy.* 1954. Albuquerque. U. of NM Pr. 1st ed. VG $22.50

SHELLEY, Percy Bysshe. *The Esdaile Notebook, a Volume of Early Poems.* 1964. New York. Knopf. dj. EX $25.00

SHELLEY, Percy Bysshe. *The Poetical Works of Percy Bysshe Shelley.* 1839. London. Moxon. 4 vol set. EX $150.00

SHELLEY, Percy Bysshe. *Zastrozzi.* 1955. London. Ltd. ed. 1/200. boxed. dj. VG $85.00

SHELTON, William. *Totem Legends of Northwest Coast Country.* Washington. (ca.1900) Ills. wrappers. VG $25.00

SHELTONS, Louise. *Beautiful Gardens of America.* 1916. $9.00

SHEN, T.S. & Liu. *S.C. Tibet & the Tibetans.* 1973. New York. Ills. 2nd ed. G $10.00

SHENSTONE, W. *Men & Manners.* 1927. Boston. Gibbings. Ltd. ed. 1/500. VG $95.00

SHENSTONE, W. *Pastorial Ballard.* High House Pr. Ltd. ed. 1/120. VG $35.00

SHEPARD, Ernest. *Ben & Brock.* 1966. New York. Ills. Shepard. VG $20.00

SHEPARD, Lucius. *Green Eyes.* London. 1st ed. $60.00

SHEPARD, M. *Mary Poppins in the Park.* 1952. 1st Am. ed. VG $10.00

SHEPARD. *The Wind in the Willows.* 1954. Scribner. Ills. dj. VG $25.00

SHEPHARD, Esther. *Paul Bunyan.* 1924. New York. Ills. Rockwell Kent. 1st ed. $25.00

SHEPHARD, William. *Prairie Experiences in Handling Cattle & Sheep.* 1885. New York. Ills. 1st Am. ed. 215 pp. $150.00

SHEPHERD, A. *Flight of the Unicorns.* 1965. London. Elek. Ills. 1st ed. dj. VG $15.00

SHEPHERD, Christopher. *German Aircraft of WWII.* 1975. London. Sidgewick & Jackson. 1st ed. $15.00

SHEPHERD, Grant. *Silver Magnet, 50 Years in a Mexican Silver Mine.* 1938. 1st ed. ex-lib. VG $10.00

SHEPHERD, J.R. *History of Oberlin-Wellington Rescue.* 1859. Boston. VG $55.00

SHEPHERD, Jack. *Adams Chronicles.* 1975. 1st ed. $15.00

SHEPHERD, M. *The Road to Gandolfo.* 1975. dj. VG $6.50

SHEPP, Jason W. *Shepp's World's Fair Photographed.* 1893. Chicago. Ills. 529 pp. $30.00

SHEPPARD, Mubin. *Taman Indera, Malay Decorative Arts & Pastimes.* 1972. Oxford. dj. EX $25.00

SHEPPARD, Nathan. *The Essays of George Eliot. Complete.* 1883. New York. 1st ed. wrappers. scarce. EX $125.00

SHEPPARD, Thomas F. *Lourmarin in 18th Century/Study of French Village.* 1971. Baltimore. 262 pp. $20.00

SHERBOURNE, James. *Death's Gray Angel.* 1981. Houghton. review copy. dj. VG $10.00

SHERIDAN, P.H. *Personal Memoirs of P.H. Sheridan, Gen. U.S. Army.* 1888. New York. Ills. 1st ed. 2 vol set. VG $35.00

SHERIDAN. *Rasamuri, Tarahumasa Colonial Chronicle 1607-1791.* 1979. wrappers. $8.00

SHERMAN, A. *Rape of the Ape.* 1973. Playboy Press. dj. VG $12.50

SHERMAN, Allan. *I Can't Dance.* 1964. Harper. Ills. Hoff. 1st ed. dj. $10.00

SHERMAN, Edgar J. *Recollections of a Long Life.* 1908. Ills. inscr. 320 pp. $11.50

SHERMAN, Edgar J. *Recollections. Salem.* 1908. some Sherman genealogy. $20.00

SHERMAN, Harold M. *Goal to Go!* 1931. New York. Grosset & Dunlap. 240 pp. dj. $3.00

SHERMAN, Loren A. *Science of the Soul.* 1895. 1st ed. 414 pp. $30.00

SHERMAN. *Boy Scouts with Joffre; or, Trenches in Belgium.* Donahue. dj. EX $6.50

SHERO, Fred & Kothare, Vijay. *Shero: Man Behind the System.* 138 pp. pb. EX $3.00

SHERRILL, Robert. *The Oil Follies of 1970-1980.* 1983. New York. 1st ed. 590 pp. index. dj. $12.50

SHERROD, Robert. *History of Marine Corps Aviation in World War II.* 1952. Washington. Ills. 1st ed. 496 pp. dj. VG $32.50

SHERROD, Robert. *Tarawa, Story of a Battle.* 1944. Duell Sloan. 1st ed. 183 pp. dj. VG $15.00

SHERWELL, Samuel. *Old Recollections of an Old Boy.* 1923. New York. Ills. 1st ed. 271 pp. $100.00

SHERWIN, Oscar. *Uncorking Old Sherry: Life & Times R.B. Sheridan.* 1960. 352 pp. dj. EX $10.00

SHERWOOD, M. *Big Game in Alaska.* 1981. Yale U. Press. Ills. 200 pp. dj. EX $30.00

SHERWOOD, Mary. *The Happy Choice.* Philidelphia. (ca.1825) $45.00

SHERWOOD, Mary. *The Wishing Cap.* 1833. New York. Day. $35.00

SHERWOOD, Robert E. *Roosevelt & Hopkins.* 1948. New York. Harper. Ills. 979 pp. VG $6.00

SHERWOOD, Robert E. *There Shall Be No Night.* 1940. New York. 1st ed. dj. VG $15.00

SHEVILLE, John & Gould, J.L. *Guide to the Royal Arch Chapter.* New York. Ills. 272 pp. EX $17.50

SHEW. *2nd Companion to Murder.* 1962. Knopf. 1st ed. dj. VG $25.00

SHIBER, Eita. *Paris, Underground.* 1943. New York. Scribner. 1st ed. 392 pp. $17.50

SHICK, Alice. *Serengeti Cats.* 1977. Lippincott. Ills. Joel Schick. dj. VG $15.00

SHIEL, M.P. *How the Old Woman Got Home.* 1928. New York. Macy. 1st ed. EX $17.50

SHIEL, M.P. *Lord of the Sea.* 1901. New York. Stokes. 1st ed. 1st issue. G $20.00

SHIEL, M.P. *Prince Zaleski & Cummings King Monk.* 1977. Sauk City. 1st ed. 220 pp. dj. EX $12.50

SHIEL, M.P. *The Yellow Danger.* 1899. New York. Fenno. 1st ed. VG $20.00

SHIEL, M.P. *The Young Men Are Coming.* 1937. New York. Vanguard. 1st ed. dj. $25.00

SHIELDS, G.O. *The Big Game of North America.* 1890. Chicago. 1st ed. VG $17.00

SHIELDS, Sophie K. *Edwin Markham, a Bibliography.* 1952. 2 vols. $30.00

SHILLABER, B.P. *Rhymes with Reason & Without.* 1853. VG $35.00

SHIMER, J.A. *This Sculptured Earth, the Landscape of America.* 1959. Columbia U. Pr. Ills. 255 pp. VG $12.50

SHIMER. *Index Fossils of North America.* Cambridge. 837 pp. $50.00

SHINN, Everett. *The Christ Story.* 1943. Phila./Toronto.Ills. 1st ed. VG $25.00

SHINN, Josiah H. *History of Education in Arkansas.* 1900. Washington. Ills. 1st ed. 131 pp. $35.00

SHIOYA, Sakae. *Chushingura, an Exposition.* 1940. Hokuseido Press. 230 pp. rare. $40.00

SHIPLEY, Joseph T. *The Art of Eugene O'Neill.* 1928. U. Washington. 1st ed. wrappers. $30.00

SHIPTON, E. *Men Against Everest.* 1955. New York. VG $10.00

SHIRAS, G. *Hunting Wild Life With Camera & Flashlight.* 1935. Nat. Geog. Soc.Ills. 2 vol set. EX $25.00

SHIRER, William L. *Berlin Diary, Journal of a Foreign Correspondent.* 1941. New York. Knopf. 605 pp. $6.00

SHIRER, William L. *Rise & Fall of Third Reich.* 1960. 6th printing. dj. EX $10.00

SHIRER, William L. *The Consul's Wife.* 1956. Little, Brown. 1st ed. dj. VG $20.00

SHIRK, George H. *Oklahoma Place Names.* 1966. Norman. sgn. 233 pp. dj. EX $15.00

SHIRLEY, H.A. *Forestry & Its Career Opportunities.* 1952. New York. McGraw Hill. 492 pp. VG $3.50

SHIVELL, Paul. *Ashes of Roses.* 1898. Dayton, Ohio. 192 pp. scarce. $10.00

SHIVERS, Louise. *Here to Get My Baby Out of Jail.* 1983. New York. Random House. 1st ed. dj. EX $10.00

SHOBERL, Frederic. *Forget Me Not.* 1830. London. 14 pls. 422 pp. $25.00

SHOEFIELD, A.H. *The Joy Peddler.* 1927. New York. Ltd. 1st ed. 1/1250. sgn. $10.00

SHOEMAKER, Charles C. *Choice Dialect.* 1915. Philadelphia. ex-lib. 200 pp. $5.50

SHOEMAKER, J.S. & Teskey, B.J.*Tree Fruit Production.* 1959. Wiley. Ills. 456 pp. dj. EX $15.00

SHOEMAKER, M. *Fresh-Water Fishing.* 1945. dj. VG $10.00

SHOEMAKER, Sam. *I Stand by the Door.* 1967. 4th printing. dj. EX $9.00

SHOEMAKER, Vaughn. *'41 & '42 A.D. Cartoons by Vaughn Shoemaker.* 1942. Chicago. Ills. Ltd. ed. sgn. $20.00

SHOMETTE, D.G. *Pirates on the Chesapeake, a History of Pirates.* 1985. dj. EX $17.50

SHOMETTE, D.G. *Shipwrecks on the Chesapeake.* 1982. Ills. dj. EX $17.50

SHOR, J. *After You, Marco Polo.* 1955. McGraw Hill. Ills. 294 pp. dj. VG $7.50

SHORE, Wendy. *Ukiyo-e.* 1980. Woodbine Books. 30 pp. EX $12.00

SHORES, Christopher F. *Fighter Aces.* 1975. London. Hamlyn. 1st ed. EX $20.00

SHORES, Christopher F. *Ground Attack Aircraft of WWII.* 1977. London. Ills. dj. VG $12.50

SHORES, Christopher F. *2nd Tactical Air Force.* 1970. London. Osprey. 1st ed. EX $25.00

SHORPE, Dinah. *My Horse, My Love.* 1892. New York. 155 pp. $12.00

SHORT, Luke. *Vengeance Valley.* 1950. Boston. Houghton Mifflin. 219 pp. $4.00

SHORT, W. *The Cheechakoes.* 1964. Random House. Ills. 1st ed. 244 pp. dj. EX $10.00

SHORTER, Clement. *Complete Poems of Charlotte Bronte.* 1923. New York. 1st ed. VG $22.50

SHORTT. *Sports Afield Collection Waterfowl Color Plates.* 1948. Minneapolis. scarce. EX $95.00

SHOSKES, H. *No Traveller Returns.* 1945. Doubleday. dj. G $12.50

SHOTEN, K. *Pictorial Encyclopedia of Oriental Arts.* 1969. New York. Ills. 4 vols. $50.00

SHOTWELL, J.T. & Laseron, Max. *Poland & Russia 1919-1945.* 1945. New York. Crown. 114 pp. $3.00

SHOTWELL, Louisa R. *The Harvesters.* 1961. New York. Doubleday. ex-lib. 242 pp. $3.50

SHOUP, Paul. *Sidetracks from the Main Line.* 1924. San Francisco. EX $37.50

SHOWALTER, Elaine. *A Literature of Their Own.* 1977. Princeton U. Press. 378 pp. $10.00

SHRYOCK, D. *The Golden Key to Musical Truths.* 1872. Cincinnati. John Church & Co. TB. 63 pp. $10.00

SHTERNFELD, Ari. *Soviet Space Science.* 1959. New York. photos. 360 pp. $5.00

SHUBE, A. *An Empire Loses Hope, Return of Stalin's Ghost.* 1970. Ills. VG $12.50

SHUCK, Oscar. *The California Scrapbook.* 1869. San Francisco. 704 pp. $75.00

SHUFELDT. *Studies Human Form.* 1908. $57.00

SHULL, A.F. *Principles of Animal Biology.* 1946. McGraw Hill. Ills. 425 pp. VG $7.50

SHULLMAN, Irving. *Valentino.* 1967. New York. Ills. 2nd ed. 499 pp. $12.50

SHULMAN, Alix Kates. *On the Stroll.* 1981. Knopf. 1st ed. dj. VG $10.00

SHULMAN, Max. *The Many Loves of Dobie Gillis.* 1951. Doubleday. 1st ed. VG $4.00

SHULMAN, Max. *The Zebra Derby.* 1946. New York. Doubleday. Ills. 1st ed. dj. $15.00

SHUMAKER, Arthur W. *A History of Indiana Literature.* 1962. Indianapolis. 611 pp. $15.00

SHURLEFF, N. *Records of Colony of New Plymouth in New England.* 1855. Boston. 4 vols in 2. Ltd. ed. 1/800. $65.00

SHUTE, Nevil. *A Town Like Alice.* 1950. London. 1st ed. dj. VG $25.00

SHUTE, Nevil. *Kindling.* 1938. 1st ed. dj. EX $50.00

SHUTE, Nevil. *On the Beach.* 1957. Heinemann. 1st ed. dj. VG $20.00

SHUTE, Nevil. *Pastoral.* 1944. New York. 246 pp. $3.50

SHUTE, Nevil. *Requiem for a Wren.* 1955. London. Heinemann. 1st ed. dj. VG $30.00

SHUTE, Nevil. *Round the Bend.* 1951. New York. 341 pp. dj. $3.50

SHUTE, Nevil. *Stephen Morris.* 1961. London. 1st ed. dj. VG $20.00

SHUTE, Nevil. *The Chequer Board.* 1947. London. 1st ed. dj. VG $25.00

SHUTE, Nevil. *Trustee from Toolroom.* 1960. London. 1st ed. dj. VG $70.00

SHUTE, Nevil. *Vinland the Good.* 1946. London. Heinemann. 1st ed. dj. VG $45.00

SHUTES, Milton. *Lincoln & the Doctors.* 1933. New York. 1st ed. EX $25.00

SHUTTLEWORTH, D.E. *Wildlife of South America.* 1974. Hastings House. Ills. 120 pp. dj. EX $5.00

SIBBET, Robert Lowery. *Siege of Paris by an American Eye Witness.* 1892. Harrisburg. 1st ed. 580 pp. VG $35.00

SIBLEY, Brian. *A.A. Milne.* 1976. Sidcup, Kent. Ltd. 1st ed. 1/200. wrappers. $20.00

SIBLEY, Roger. *Rommel.* 1972. $3.50

SIBSON, Francis H. *Unthinkable.* 1933. New York. Harrison Smith. 1st Am. ed. VG $45.00

SICHEL, Allan. *A Guide to Good Wine.* 1970. London. Abbey Lib. Ills. revised ed. $7.50

SICKELS, Daniel. *The General Ahiman Rezon & Freemason's Guide.* 1865. New York. Macoy Pub. 408 pp. VG $27.50

SIDEMAN, B.B. *Europe Looks at the Civil War.* 1960. New York. Orion. 1st printing. dj. VG $12.50

SIDGWICK, Frank. *Diary & Other Material Relating to A.H. Bullen.* 1975. Oxford. Ltd. ed. 1/1000. dj. $25.00

SIDNEY, Margaret. *Five Little Peppers & How They Grew.* 1948. Grosset & Dunlap. Ills. VG $5.50

SIDNEY, Margaret. *Five Little Peppers & How They Grew.* 1909. Boston. Ills. Hermann Hyer. $12.50

SIDNEY, Margaret. *Five Little Peppers & How They Grew.* 1881. Boston. Lathrop Pub. Ills. G $50.00

SIDNEY, Margaret. *Five Little Peppers Midway.* 1918. New York. Grosset & Dunlap. 426 pp. dj. $3.50

SIDNEY, Margaret. *The Adventures of Joel Pepper.* 1900. Boston. Ills. Sears Gallagher. VG $10.00

SIDNEY, Margaret. *The Stories Polly Pepper Told.* 1899. Boston. Ills. Etheldred Barry. VG $10.00

SIDNEY, Philip. *History of Gunpowder Plot: Conspiracy & Agents.* 1904. London. 313 pp. 16 pls. $15.00

SIDNEY, Samuel. *The Three Colonies of Australia.* 1854. 1st Am. ed. 408 pp. scarce. VG $175.00

SIDWORTHY, J. *Snakes of the World.* 1978. Ills. revised ed. 160 pp. EX $7.50

SIEDENTOPF, A.R. *The Last Stronghold of Big Game.* 1946. McBride. Ills. 202 pp. dj. VG $17.50

SIEGEL, Curt. *Structure & Form in Modern Architecture.* 1962. New York. dj. VG $20.00

SIEGEL, Eli. *Hot Afternoons Have Been in Montana: Poems.* 1957. Definition. 1st pb ed. wrappers. EX $5.00

SIEGEL, Max. *Portrait of Barbara.* 1937. Chicago. Clark. sgn. VG $20.00

SIEGFRIED, Andre. *Canada, an International Power.* New York. trans. Hemming. dj. VG $10.00

SIEMEL, S. & E. *Jungle Wife.* 1949. Doubleday. Ills. 308 pp. G $6.00

SIEPEN, Edith. *Continental Cookery for the English Table.* 1915. London. 1st ed. VG $22.50

SIGAL, Clancy. *Going Away.* 1961. Houghton. 1st ed. dj. EX $10.00

SIGOURNEY, Mrs. G.H. *Scenes in My Native Land.* 1845. Boston. $25.00

SIGOURNEY. *Noble Deeds of American Women.* NY/Auburn. G $10.00

SIKORSKI, Gen. W. *Modern Warfare. Its Character & Problems.* London. (ca.1942) G $7.50

SIKORSKY, Igor. *Story of the Winged-S.* 1958. New York. inscr. dj. $20.00

SIKORSKY, Igor. *Story of the Winged-S.* 1942. New York. presentation copy. dj. EX $35.00

SILBERBERG, R. & Garrett, R. *The Dawning Light.* 1959. New York. Gnome. 1st ed. dj. EX $25.00

SILERER, Herbert. *Viertausend Kilomeyter im Ballon.* Leipzig. Ills. ex-lib. VG $40.00

SILLIMAN, Benjamin. *The American Journal of Science & Arts. Vol. XVII.* 1830. New Haven. Ills. ex-lib. 420 pp. $35.00

SILLITOE, Alan. *A Start in Life.* 1970. New York. Scribner. 1st ed. dj. EX $25.00

SILLITOE, Alan. *A Tree on Fire.* 1968. Doubleday. 1st Am. ed. dj. VG $20.00

SILLITOE, Alan. *Barbarians & Other Poems.* 1973. Turret. Ltd. ed. 1/500. dj. VG $25.00

SILLITOE, Alan. *Ragman's Daughter.* 1964. New York. 1st Am. ed. dj. EX $15.00

SILLITOE, Alan. *Raw Material.* 1972. Scribner. 1st Am. ed. dj. VG $17.00

SILLITOE, Alan. *Shaman & Other Poems.* 1968. Turret. Ltd. ed. dj. VG $30.00

SILLITOE, Alan. *The Second Chance & Other Stories.* 1981. London. 1st ed. sgn. dj. EX $25.00

SILLITOE, Alan. *The Second Chance & Other Stories.* 1981. Simon & Schuster. 1st Am. ed. $15.00

SILLITOE, Alan. *The Storyteller.* 1979. New York. Simon & Schuster. 1st ed. dj. $25.00

SILLITOE, Alan. *The Widower's Son.* 1977. New York. Harper & Row. 1st ed. dj. EX $20.00

SILONE, Ignazio. *A Handful of Blackberries.* 1953. Harper. 1st Am. ed. dj. VG $15.00

SILONE, Ignazio. *Bread & Wine.* 1937. Harper. 1st Am. ed. dj. VG $20.00

SILVERBERG, Robert. *Collision Course.* 1961. New York. Avalon. 1st ed. dj. EX $35.00

SILVERBERG, Robert. *Dying Inside.* 1972. New York. 1st ed. dj. VG $12.50

SILVERBERG, Robert. *Lord of Darkness.* 1983. New York. 1st ed. dj. VG $10.00

SILVERBERG, Robert. *Lord of Darkness.* 1983. Arbor. 1st ed. dj. EX $15.00

SILVERBERG, Robert. *Lord Valentine's Castle.* 1980. New York. 1st ed. dj. VG $10.00

SILVERBERG, Robert. *Lord Valentine's Castle.* 1980. New York. proof copy. wrappers. EX $40.00

SILVERBERG, Robert. *Lord Valentine's Castle.* 1980. New York. Ltd. ed. 1/250. sgn. slipcase. $60.00

SILVERBERG, Robert. *Lost Cities & Vanished Civilizations.* 1962. New York. 177 pp. dj. EX $3.50

SILVERBERG, Robert. *Sailing to Byzantium.* 1985. Ltd. ed. 1/250. sgn. boxed. EX $40.00

SILVERBERG, Robert. *Sunrise on Mercury.* 1975. New York. Nelson. sgn. dj. VG $12.50

SILVERBERG, Robert. *The Book of Skulls.* 1971. New York. 1st ed. dj. EX $20.00

SILVERBERG, Robert. *Unfamiliar Territory.* 1973. New York. 1st ed. dj. EX $12.50

SILVERBERG, Robert. *Valentine Pontifex.* 1983. New York. 1st ed. review copy. dj. EX $20.00

SILVERBERG, Robert. *Valentine Pontifex.* 1983. Arbor House. 1st ed. dj. VG $15.00

SILVERBERG, Robert. *World of a Thousand Colors.* 1982. New York. 1st ed. dj. EX $10.00

SILVERMAN, William. *The Violin Hunter.* 1972. London. dj. VG $12.50

SILVERSTONE. *U.S. Warships of WWII.* 1965. New York. $22.50

SIMAK, Clifford D. *A Choice of Gods.* 1972. New York. 1st ed. dj. VG $15.00

SIMAK, Clifford D. *Cosmic Engineers.* 1950. New York. Gnome. 1st ed. dj. $40.00

SIMAK, Clifford D. *Empire.* 1951. Galaxy. 1st ed. wrappers. VG $8.50

SIMAK, Clifford D. *Enchanted Pilgrimage.* 1975. New York. 1st ed. dj. VG $12.50

SIMAK, Clifford D. *Fellowship of the Talisman.* 1978. New York. 1st ed. dj. EX $12.50

SIMAK, Clifford D. *Fellowship of the Talisman.* 1980. London. 1st ed. dj. EX $20.00

SIMAK, Clifford D. *Mastodonia.* 1978. New York. 1st ed. dj. VG $12.50

SIMAK, Clifford D. *Our Children's Children.* 1974. New York. 1st ed. dj. VG $10.00

SIMAK, Clifford D. *Project Pope.* 1981. New York. 1st ed. dj. VG $10.00

SIMAK, Clifford D. *Skirmish.* 1977. New York. 1st ed. sgn. dj. EX $25.00

SIMAK, Clifford D. *Special Deliverance.* 1982. New York. 1st ed. dj. EX $15.00

SIMAK, Clifford D. *Strangers in the Universe.* 1956. New York. 1st ed. dj. EX $25.00

SIMAK, Clifford D. *The Creator.* 1946. Los Angeles. Crawford. 1st ed. EX $50.00

SIMAK, Clifford D. *The Visitors.* 1980. New York. 1st ed. dj. VG $12.50

SIMAK, Clifford D. *The Worlds of Clifford Simak.* 1960. New York. 1st ed. dj. EX $20.00

SIMENON, George. *Bells of Bicetre.* 1964. New York. 1st Am. ed. dj. VG $7.50

SIMENON, George. *Disappearance of Odile.* 1971. New York. dj. EX $7.50

SIMENON, George. *In Case of Emergency.* 1958. Doubleday. 1st Am. ed. dj. VG $20.00

SIMENON, George. *Maigret & the Apparition.* 1976. New York. 1st Am. ed. dj. VG $6.00

SIMENON, George. *Maigret's Boyhood Friend.* 1968. Book Club. $2.50

SIMENON, George. *November.* 1970. Harcourt. 1st Am. ed. dj. VG $15.00

SIMENON, George. *The Hatter's Phantoms.* 1976. New York. 1st ed. dj. $8.50

SIMENON, George. *The Innocents.* 1973. NY. Harcourt. proof copy. wrappers. EX $25.00

SIMENON, George. *The Iron Staircase.* 1977. New York. 1st Am. ed. dj. $7.50

SIMENON, George. *The Man Who Watched the Trains Go By.* 1946. New York. Reynal & Hitchcock. 1st ed. EX $30.00

SIMENON, George. *The Premier: the Train.* 1966. New York. 1st Am. ed. $7.50

SIMENON, George. *The Shadow Falls.* 1945. New York. 1st Am. ed. dj. VG $15.00

SIMENON, George. *Tidal Wave.* 1954. Garden City. Doubleday. 1st ed. dj. EX $15.00

SIMENON, George. *When I Was Old.* 1971. Harcourt. Ills. 1st ed. 343 pp. dj. $12.50

SIMKHOVITCH, Natasha. *Merry Christmas.* 1943. New York. Knopf. Ills. folio. $20.00

SIMKINS, F.B. *Pitchfork Ben Tillman.* 1944. 1st ed. VG $15.00

SIMMONDS, W.H. *The Practical Grocer; Manual & Guide for Grocer.* 1909. London. 4 vol set. $45.00

SIMMONITE, W.F. *Horary Astrology.* 1896. London. 6th ed. 240 pp. VG $60.00

SIMMONS, A.D. *Wing Shots.* 1936. New York. Derrydale. Ltd. ed. VG $50.00

SIMMONS, Amelia. *American Cookery.* 1937. Hartford. Prospect Pr. Ltd. ed. VG $50.00

SIMMONS, Amelia. *American Cookery.* 1963. WV Pulp & Paper. Ltd. ed. VG $12.50

SIMMONS, Clifford. *A Tendency to Deprave & Corrupt?* 1972. London. 1st ed. 39 pp. wrappers. VG $10.00

SIMMONS, Gurdon. *This is Your America. Vol I.* 1943. EX $10.00

SIMMONS, James Raymond. *The Historic Trees of Massachusetts.* 1919. Boston. 140 pp. VG $22.50

SIMMONS, Leo W. *Sun Chief: Autobiography of a Hopi Indian.* 1942. New Haven. Yale U. Pr. Ills. 1st ed. dj. $50.00

SIMMONS, V. *Air Piloting. Manual of Flight Instruction.* 1941. Ills. revised ed. G $7.50

SIMMONS, William. *History of National Association of Naval Veterans.* 1895. Philadelphia. Ills. 161 pp. G $25.00

SIMMS, W. Gilmore. *Life of Francis Marion.* 1860. New York. 347 pp. $15.00

SIMON, Andre. *Encyclopedia of Gastronomy.* 1952. Harcourt Brace. 1st ed. dj. VG $15.00

SIMON, Andre. *In the Twilight.* 1969. London. dj. EX $15.00

SIMON, Andre. *The Wines, Vineyards, & Vignerons of Australia.* 1967. Hamlyn Pub. maps, photos. dj. VG $15.00

SIMON, Andre. *Wines of World.* 1968. McGraw Hill. Ills. 700 pp. $18.00

SIMON, Bill. *Effective Card Magic.* 1952. New York. VG $10.00

SIMON, Claude. *The Wind.* 1959. New York. Braziller. 254 pp. $5.00

SIMON, H. *Chameleons & Other Quick Change Artists.* 1973. Dodd Mead. Ills. 157 pp. dj. EX $12.50

SIMON, H. *The Date Palm, Bread of the Desert.* 1978. Dodd Mead. Ills. 1st ed. dj. EX $15.00

SIMON, Maron J. *Your Solar House.* 1947. New York. Ills. dj. VG $25.00

SIMON, Oliver. *Introduction to Typography.* 1945. London. 1st ed. dj. VG $20.00

SIMON, Philip J. *Log of the Mayflower.* 1956. $10.00

SIMON. *Your Solar House.* 1947. VG $38.00

SIMOND, L. *A Tour in Italy & Sicily.* 1828. London. G $40.00

SIMONDS, Frank H. *History of the World War.* 1917. New York. Doubleday. 5 vol set. VG $30.00

SIMONDS, Frank. *Can Europe Keep the Peace.* 1934. G $5.00

SIMONDS, Williams. *Edison. His Life, His Work, His Genius.* 1934. 1st ed. ex-lib. 364 pp. VG $25.00

SIMONDS. *Starr King in California.* 1917. Elder. 2 Ills. 105 pp. VG $10.00

SIMONS, A.M. *Social Forces in American History.* 1929. New York. Book League. 325 pp. $7.00

SIMONT, Marc. *Opera Souffle, Sixty Pictures in Bravura.* 1950. New York. 1st ed. inscr. dj. VG $20.00

SIMPSON, C. *The Lusitania.* 1973. dj. VG $15.00

SIMPSON, Charles. *Life in the Mines.* 1905. Chicago. Ills. H.S. DeLay. 343 pp. $10.00

SIMPSON, Colin. *Plumes & Arrows.* Sydney. Halstead Press. 415 pp. $17.50

SIMPSON, E. *Treatise on Ordnance & Naval Gunnery.* 1871. New York. Van Nostrand. 5th ed. 493 pp. $15.00

SIMPSON, Eileen. *The Maze.* 1st ed. sgn. dj. EX $22.50

SIMPSON, G.G. *Penguins, Past & Present, Here & There.* 1976. Yale. Ills. 150 pp. dj. EX $6.00

SIMPSON, Harriette. *Mountain Path.* 1936. Covici Friede. 1st ed. G $70.00

SIMPSON, Thomas. *Narrative of Discoveries North Coast of America.* 1843. London. 1st ed. maps. 419 pp. $390.00

SIMPSON. *Narrative of Journey Around the World, 1841-1842.* 1868. Cincinnati. 1st ed. 2 vol set. VG $250.00

SIMS, A.E. *The Witching Weed.* London. Harrap. 207 pp. dj. $25.00

SIMS, George. *Coat of Arms.* 1984. London. Macmillan. 1st ed. dj. EX $15.00

SIMS, George. *Hunter's Point.* 1973. London. 1st ed. dj. VG $20.00

SIMS, George. *The Last Best Friend.* 1968. New York. Stein & Day. dj. VG $10.00

SIMS & TWINING. *American Aces in Great Fighter Battles of WWII.* 1958. New York. $7.00

SIMSON, F. *Letters on Sport in Eastern Nepal.* 1886. London. $110.00

SINCLAIR, A.R.E. *African Buffalo, Study of Resource Limitations.* 1977. Chicago. Ills. 355 pp. dj. EX $25.00

SINCLAIR, Bertrand W. *Big Timber.* 1916. 321 pp. VG $4.00

SINCLAIR, D.W. *New Zealand Birds & Flowers.* 1963. Wellington. Ills. 32 pp. paper cover. $3.00

SINCLAIR, H. *The Port of New Orleans.* 1942. Doubleday. 1st ed. 335 pp. dj. VG $12.50

SINCLAIR, Jo. *Wasteland.* 1946. New York. 1st ed. dj. VG $12.50

SINCLAIR, May. *The Intercessor.* 1931. New York. 1st Am. ed. VG $30.00

SINCLAIR, May. *Uncanny Stories.* 1923. Macmillan. Ills. Bosschere. 1st ed. $15.00

SINCLAIR, Upton. *A Captain of Industry.* 1906. Girard. 1st ed. $60.00

SINCLAIR, Upton. *A Drama of O. Henry in Prison.* 1925. Pasadena, CA. private print. 58 pp. $20.00

SINCLAIR, Upton. *A Personal Jesus.* 1952. Evans Pub. 1st ed. dj. $7.50

SINCLAIR, Upton. *A World to Win.* 1946. New York. Viking. 581 pp. dj. $6.00

SINCLAIR, Upton. *Affectionately, Eve.* 1961. Twayne. 1st ed. dj. EX $15.00

SINCLAIR, Upton. *Another Pamela.* 1950. Viking. 1st ed. dj. VG $10.00

SINCLAIR, Upton. *Between Two Worlds.* 1941. New York. Viking. 859 pp. $6.00

SINCLAIR, Upton. *Cry for Justice.* 1915. Winston. 1st ed. VG $45.00

SINCLAIR, Upton. *Jimmy Higgins, a Story.* 1919. Racine. 282 pp. $3.50

SINCLAIR, Upton. *Limbo on the Loose.* 1948. Girard. Haldeman-Julius. wrappers. EX $15.00

SINCLAIR, Upton. *Mannassas.* 1904. New York. Macmillan. 1st ed. VG $25.00

SINCLAIR, Upton. *Money Writes.* 1927. New York. Boni. 1st ed. 227 pp. G $10.00

SINCLAIR, Upton. *Overman.* 1907. $55.00

SINCLAIR, Upton. *Profits of Religion.* 1918. Pasadena. Sinclair. 1st ed. VG $15.00

SINCLAIR, Upton. *Samuel the Seeker.* 1923. Pasadena. Sinclair. 2nd ed. dj. $15.00

SINCLAIR, Upton. *The Goslings.* 1924. G $20.00

SINCLAIR, Upton. *The Jungle.* 1906. Doubleday. 1st ed. 413 pp. VG $25.00

SINCLAIR, Upton. *The Metropolis.* 1908. New York. Moffat. 1st ed. VG $20.00

SINCLAIR, Upton. *The Return of Lanny Budd.* 1953. Viking. 1st ed. dj. EX $15.00

SINCLAIR, Upton. *Upton Sinclair Anthology.* 1947. Culver City. Murray & Gee. 1st ed. dj. $35.00

SINCLAIR, Upton. *Wide is the Gate.* 1943. Viking. 1st ed. dj. VG $20.00

SINCLAIR, Upton. *World's End.* 1940. New York. 740 pp $6.00

SINCLAIR, Upton. *100%/The Story of a Patriot.* 1920. Pasadena. Sinclair. 1st ed. wrappers. EX $20.00

SINCLAIR-STEVENSON, C. *Blood Royal, the Illustrious House of Hanover.* 1980. Ills. EX $10.00

SINDEN, Harry. *Hockey Showdown.* 1972. Doubleday. Ills. 126 pp. dj. VG $8.50

SINGER, C. *A History of Technology.* 1958. Oxford U. Press. 5 vol set. $100.00

SINGER, Caroline & Baldridge. *White Africans & Black.* 1929. New York. Ills. Baldridge. EX $30.00

SINGER, Dorothea Waley. *Giordano Bruno, His Life & Thought.* 1950. New York. Ills. 389 pp. index. dj. $12.50

SINGER, Isaac Bashevis. *A Day of Pleasure.* 1969. Farrar. 1st ed. photos. dj. VG $25.00

SINGER, Isaac Bashevis. *A Friend of Kafka.* 1970. Farrar. 1st ed. dj. VG $25.00

SINGER, Isaac Bashevis. *Enemies, a Love Story.* 1972. New York. Farrar. 1st ed. dj. VG $25.00

SINGER, Isaac Bashevis. *Love & Exile.* 1985. Cape. 1st English ed. dj. VG $20.00

SINGER, Isaac Bashevis. *Mazel & Shlimazel.* 1979. Cape. Ills. Zemach. 1st Eng. ed. dj. $20.00

SINGER, Isaac Bashevis. *Nobel Lecture.* 1979. Farrar. 1st ed. dj. VG $15.00

SINGER, Isaac Bashevis. *Old Love.* 1979. New York. 1st ed. $15.00

SINGER, Isaac Bashevis. *Old Love.* 1980. Cape. 1st English ed. dj. VG $30.00

SINGER, Isaac Bashevis. *Old Love.* 1979. Farrar. proof copy. wrappers. VG $85.00

SINGER, Isaac Bashevis. *One Day of Happiness.* 1982. New York. Ltd. ed. 1/155. sgn. $40.00

SINGER, Isaac Bashevis. *Reaches of Heaven.* 1980. New York. Farrar. 1st ed. dj. EX $25.00

SINGER, Isaac Bashevis. *Reaches of Heaven.* 1980. Farrar. Ills. Moskowitz. 1st trade ed. $15.00

SINGER, Isaac Bashevis. *Short Friday.* 1964. Farrar. 1st ed. dj. VG $35.00

SINGER, Isaac Bashevis. *Shosha.* New York. Farrar. 1st ed. dj. VG $20.00

SINGER, Isaac Bashevis. *Stories for Children.* 1984. Farrar. Ltd. 1st ed. sgn. slipcase. EX $50.00

SINGER, Isaac Bashevis. *The Collected Stories of Isaac B. Singer.* 1982. New York. 610 pp. dj. VG $5.00

SINGER, Isaac Bashevis. *The Estate.* 1969. New York. Farrar. 1st ed. dj. VG $40.00

SINGER, Isaac Bashevis. *The Family Moskat.* 1950. Knopf. 1st ed. dj. VG $50.00

SINGER, Isaac Bashevis. *The Fearsome Inn.* 1967. Scribner. 1st trade ed. dj. VG $30.00

SINGER, Isaac Bashevis. *The Fearsome Inn.* 1967. Scribner. Ills. Hogrogian. 1st ed. dj. $30.00

SINGER, Isaac Bashevis. *The Fools of Chelm.* 1973. Farrar. Ills. Shulevitz. 1st ed. dj. $20.00

SINGER, Isaac Bashevis. *The Golem.* 1982. Farrar. proof copy. wrappers. EX $75.00

SINGER, Isaac Bashevis. *The Golem.* 1982. Farrar. Ltd. 1st ed. sgn. slipcase. EX $65.00

SINGER, Isaac Bashevis. *The Image.* 1985. Farrar. proof copy. wrappers. EX $75.00

SINGER, Isaac Bashevis. *The Manor.* 1967. New York. Farrar. 1st ed. dj. VG $40.00

SINGER, Isaac Bashevis. *The Penitent.* 1983. New York. Farrar. proof copy. wrappers. $35.00

SINGER, Isaac Bashevis. *The Slave.* 1962. Farrar. 1st ed. dj. VG $40.00

SINGER, Isaac Bashevis. *Yentl the Yeshiva Boy.* 1983. Farrar. Ltd. 1st ed. sgn. slipcase. EX $60.00

SINGER, Janet. *Cheer Leader.* 1934. Chicago. Goldsmith. 251 pp. dj. $3.00

SINGH, A. *Tiger Haven.* 1973. London. Macmillan. Ills. 1st ed. dj. $25.00

SINGLETON, Esther. *Historic Buildings* 1903. New York. photos. 340 pp. VG $4.00

SINGLETON, Esther. *Social New York Under the Georges.* 1902. New York. 1st ed. $25.00

SINGLETON, Esther. *Story of the Universe, Vol. II, Earth, Land, Sea.* 1905. Collier. $2.50

SINGLETON. *Love in Literature & Art.* Dodd Mead. Ills. old masters. 1st ed. $25.00

SINGMASTER, Elsie. *Pennsylvania's Susquehanna.* 1950. Harrisburg. photos. dj. EX $15.00

SIODMAK, C. *City in the Sky.* 1974. Putnam. 1st ed. dj. EX $12.50

SIODMAK, C. *Donavan's Brain.* 1943. New York. Knopf. 1st ed. dj. VG $25.00

SIRINGO, Charles A. *A Cowboy Detective.* 1912. Chicago. scarce. G $100.00

SIRINGO, Charles A. *Lone Star Cowboy.* 1919. Santa Fe. 1st ed. $85.00

SIRINGO, Charles A. *Riata & Spurs.* 1927. $75.00

SISKIND, Aaron. *Photographs.* 1959. 1st ed. dj. EX $90.00

SISSON, D. *American Revolution of 1800.* 1974. dj. VG $10.00

SITWELL, Edith. *A Poet's Notebook.* 1950. Boston. 1st ed. inscr. sgn. dj. VG $35.00

SITWELL, Edith. *Alexander Pope.* 1930. London. Ills. Whistler. 1st ed. sgn. $35.00

SITWELL, Edith. *Children's Tales from the Russian Ballet.* 1920. London. Ills. Lockyear. 1st ed. VG $35.00

SITWELL, Edith. *Collected Poems.* 1957. Macmillan. 1st ed. dj. VG $35.00

SITWELL, Edith. *Five Poems.* 1928. London. Ltd. ed. sgn. wrappers. VG $75.00

SITWELL, Edith. *Green Song.* 1944. Macmillan. 1st ed. dj. EX $40.00

SITWELL, Edith. *Taken Care Of.* 1965. New York. 2nd ed. dj. EX $8.50

SITWELL, Edith. *The Atlantic Book of British & American Poetry.* 1958. Boston. 1st ed. sgn. dj. VG $32.50

SITWELL, Edith. *The Last Years of a Rebel.* 1967. Boston. 1st Am. ed. dj. VG $15.00

SITWELL, Edith. *The Song of the Cold.* 1948. Vanguard. 1st Am. ed. dj. VG $15.00

SITWELL, H.O.W. *Crown Jewels & Other Regalia.* 1953. London. 116 pp. $65.00

SITWELL, N. *Wildlife '74, World Conservation Yearbook.* 1974. Danbury. Ills. maps. 143 pp. VG $12.50

SITWELL, Osbert & Sacheverell. *All at Sea.* 1927. London. 1st ed. VG $25.00

SITWELL, Osbert. *Argonaut & Juggernaut.* 1919. London. 1st ed. dj. VG $22.50

SITWELL, Osbert. *Discursions.* 1925. London. Ills. 1st ed. VG $25.00

SITWELL, Osbert. *Laughter in the Next Room.* 1948. 1st Am. ed. dj. VG $10.00

SITWELL, Osbert. *Penny Foolish.* 1935. Macmillan. Ills. Farleigh. 1st ed. dj. VG $45.00

SITWELL, Osbert. *Pound Wise.* 1st Am. ed. dj. VG $15.00

SITWELL, Osbert. *Selected Poems.* 1943. London. 1st ed. dj. EX $20.00

SITWELL, Osbert. *The Death of a God.* 1949. Macmillan. 1st ed. dj. VG $35.00

SITWELL, Sacheverell. *German Baroque Art.* 1927. London. Ills. 1st ed. VG $30.00

SITWELL, Sacheverell. *Great Houses of Europe.* 1970. London. $20.00

SITWELL, Sacheverell. *The Hunters & the Hunted.* 1948. Macmillan. 1st Am. ed. dj. VG $25.00

SITWELL. *Great Flower Books: 1700-1900.* Ltd. ed. 1/295. sgn. $875.00

SIZER, N. *Heads & Faces, & How to Study Them.* 1888. New York. Fowler & Wells. Ills. 199 pp. $15.00

SJOWALL, M. & Wahloo, P. *Murder at the Savoy.* 1972. London. Gollancz. 1st Eng. ed. dj. EX $25.00

SJOWALL, M. & Wahloo, P. *Roseanna.* 1968. London. Gollancz. 1st ed. dj. VG $45.00

SJOWALL, M. & Wahloo, P. *The Abominable Man.* 1973. London. Gollancz. 1st ed. dj. EX $25.00

SJOWALL, M. & Wahloo, P. *The Locked Room.* 1973. London. Gollancz. 1st Eng. ed. dj. VG $25.00

SJOWALL, M. & Wahloo, P. *Murder at the Savoy.* 1971. New York. Pantheon. 1st ed. dj. EX $25.00

SJOWALL, M. & Wahloo, P. *The Terrorists.* 1977. London. Macmillan. 1st ed. dj. EX $20.00

SKELTON, John. *Charles I.* 1898. Goupil & Co. Ills. Jean Boussod. folio. $250.00

SKELTON, John. *Turning of Elynour Rumming.* 1928. Fanfrolico Pr. Ills. Binder. Ltd. ed. 1/500. $60.00

SKIDMORE, Hubert. *Hawk's Nest.* 1941. Doubleday. 1st ed. dj. VG $27.50

SKIDMORE, Hubert. *I Will Lift Up My Eyes.* 1936. Doubleday. 1st ed. dj. VG $35.00

SKILLINGS, Helen Wieland. *We're Standing on Iron!* 1972. Duluth. 69 pp. $10.00

SKINNER, Constance Lindsay. *Roy Roy, the Frontier Twins.* 1934. New York. Ills. 218 pp. EX $7.50

SKINNER, Cornelia Otis. *Madame Sarah.* 1966. Boston. Houghton Mifflin. 356 pp. $6.00

SKINNER, Joseph. *The Present State of Peru.* 1805. London. Phillips. 1st ed. 487 pp. $985.00

SKINNER, M. *The Birds of Yellowstone National Park.* 1925. Ills. 181 pp. VG $12.50

SKINNER, Otis & Kimbrough, E. *Our Hearts Were Young & Gay.* 1942. $3.00

SKINNER, Otis. *Footlights & Spotlights.* 1924. $18.00

SKLAR, George. *The Two Worlds of Johnny Truro.* 1947. Little, Brown. 1st ed. sgn. VG $30.00

SKUES, G.E.M. *Minor Tactics of the Chalk Stream.* 1924. London. Black. 3rd ed. VG $20.00

SKUTCH, A.F. *A Bird Watcher's Adventures in Tropical America.* 1977. Texas U. Press. Ills. Gardner. 327 pp. dj. EX $20.00

SKUTCH, A.F. *Birds of Tropical America.* 1983. Texas U. Press. Ills. 1st ed. dj. EX $30.00

SKUTCH, A.F. *Parent Birds & Their Young*. 1976. Texas U. Press. 503 pp. 116 pls. dj. VG $22.50

SLATER, J.H. *How to Collect Books*. 1905. London. Chiswick Press. 1st ed. VG $35.00

SLATER, P. *Rare & Vanishing Australian Birds*. 1980. Rigby. Ills. 96 pp. dj. EX $20.00

SLAUGHTER, Frank G. *In a Dark Garden*. 1946. New York. Doubleday. 435 pp. $3.50

SLAUSON, H.W. *Everyman's Guide to Motor Efficiency*. 1924. EX $15.00

SLAVITT, David R. *Vital Signs*. 1975. Doubleday. 1st ed. dj. VG $15.00

SLEATH, Frederick. *The Red Vulture*. 1923. Boston. Houghton Mifflin. 1st ed. EX $12.50

SLEEMAN. *Torpedoes & Torpedo Warfare, a Complete Account*. 1889. Portsmith. 83 plates. G $25.00

SLESAR, Henry. *Grey Flannel Shroud*. 1959. Random House. $3.00

SLESINGER, Tess. *Time: The Present*. 1935. Simon & Schuster. 1st ed. $20.00

SLESSOR, John. *The Central Blue*. 1956. London. Ills. 1st ed. 709 pp. $25.00

SLEZAK, Walter. *What Time's the Next Swan?* 1962. 1st ed. 227 pp. dj. $27.50

SLINEY, Eleanor Mathews. *Forward Ho*. 1960. NY/Washington. Ills 1st ed. 332 pp. dj. $6.00

SLOAN, Alfred P. *My Years with General Motors*. 1964. Garden City. Book Club ed. 471 pp. dj. G $5.00

SLOAN, Donald. *The Shadow Catcher*. 1940. New York. 1st ed. dj. VG $15.00

SLOAN, Eric. *Weather Book*. 1955. Ills. 3rd ed. VG $20.00

SLOANE, Eric. *Your Body in Flight*. 1943. Dayton, Ohio. Ills. wrappers. VG $50.00

SLOANE. *Classic Guitar Construction*. Dutton. 1st ed. $55.00

SLOBODKIN, L. *One Is Good But Two Are Better*. 1956. Vanguard. 1st ed. VG $20.00

SLOBODKIN, L. *The Late Cuckoo*. 1962. New York. Vanguard. Ills. 1st ed. dj. $15.00

SLOBODKIN, L. *The Polka-Dot Goat*. 1964. Macmillan. Ills. 1st ed. VG $15.00

SLOCUM, Eugene. *Ye Gods & Little Fishes*. 1927. 1st ed. VG $20.00

SLOCUM, Joshua. *Sailing Alone Around the World 1895-1898*. 1969. Westavco Pub. Ills. 263 pp. VG $12.50

SLUD, P. *The Birds of Costa Rica*. 1966. Am. Mus. Nat. Hist. 430 pp. VG $40.00

SMALL, A. *The Birds of California*. 1974. Winchester. Ills. 310 pp. dj. EX $15.00

SMALL, Sidney H. *The Lord of Thundergate*. 1923. Indianapolis. Bobbs Merrill. 1st ed. dj. EX $10.00

SMARIDGE, Norah. *Graymoor's Treasury of Meatless Recipes*. 1965. New York. Graymoor Pr. 72 pp. $3.50

SMART, Charles Allen. *R.F.D.* 1938. New York. Norton. 256 pp. VG $3.00

SMART, Christopher. *A Portion of Jubilate Agno*. 1957. Fogg Museum. Ills. Shahn. 1st ed. wrappers. $7.50

SMART, Paul. *The International Butterfly Book*. 1975. Crowell. Ills 275 pp. dj. EX $30.00

SMEDLEY, Agnes. *Battle Hymn of China*. 1943. New York. Book Find Club. dj. VG $10.00

SMEDLEY, Agnes. *China Fights Back*. 1938. London. Gollancz. Book Club ed. VG $20.00

SMEDLEY, Agnes. *China's Red Army Marches*. 1934. New York. Vanguard. 1st ed. VG $40.00

SMEDLEY, Agnes. *Daughter of Earth*. 1929. New York. Coward. 1st ed. VG $25.00

SMEDLEY, W. *Life & Character, Drawings*. 1899. New York. Ills. folio. $30.00

SMELTZER, Wallace Guy, D.D. *Historical Records Methodism in West PA 1784-1968*. 1969. New York. VG $15.00

SMILES, Samuel. *Life of a Scotch Naturalist: Thomas Edward*. 1877. New York. Ills. George Reid. $30.00

SMILES, Samuel. *Memories & Correspondence of John Murray*. 1891. London. 2nd ed. 2 vol set. VG $38.00

SMILES, Samuel. *The Life of George Stephenson, Railway Engineer*. 1859. ex-lib. 513 pp. VG $62.00

SMILES, Samuel. *The Life of George Stephenson & His Son Robert*. 1868. New York. 1st ed. EX $50.00

SMILES, Samuel. *Thrift; or, How to Get On in the World*. 1881. Chicago. Belford, Clarke & Co. 307 pp. $10.00

SMILEY, Jane. *At Paradise's Gate*. 1981. Simon & Schuster. proof copy. $10.00

SMILTZER, Wallace Guy. *Methodism on the Headwaters of the Ohio*. 1951. Nashville. Ills. sgn. 448 pp. index. dj. $12.50

SMITH, A. *Jambo, African Balloon Safari*. 1963. Dutton. Ills. 272 pp. dj. EX $12.50

SMITH, A.D.H. *Fighting the Turk in the Balkans*. 1908. Ills. G $20.00

SMITH, A.M. *On to Alaska with Buchanan, Building Citizenship*. 1937. Los Angeles. Ward Ritchie Press. 124 pp. $10.00

SMITH, Adam. *Inquiry into Nature & Causes of Wealth of Nations.* London. 3 vol set. G $90.00

SMITH, Albert. *Struggles & Adventures of Christopher Tadpole*. 1897. Downe & Co. Ills. John Leech. $20.00

SMITH, Amanda. *Amanda Smith's Own Story*. 1893. G $25.00

SMITH, Anthony. *The Seasons*. 1970. Ills. 318 pp. dj. EX $4.00

SMITH, B.F. *Road to Nuremburg*. 1981. New York. G $15.00

SMITH, Benjamin T. *Private Smith's Journal*. 1963. Chicago. $8.50

SMITH, Betty. *A Tree Grows in Brooklyn*. 1943. 1st ed. VG $35.00

SMITH, Betty. *Joy in the Morning*. 1963. Harper. 1st ed. sgn. dj. VG $25.00

SMITH, Bill. *The Vaudevillians*. 1976. New York. Ills. 1st ed. dj. VG $10.00

SMITH, Bradley. *Mexico: History in Art*. 1968. Abrams. folio. $25.00

SMITH, C. Fox. *There Was a Ship*. 1929. $6.50

SMITH, C.B.A. *Scallion Stone*. 1980. Whispers Press.Ltd. ed. 1/250. sgn. boxed. EX $30.00

SMITH, C.W. *Aircraft Turbine Engines*. 1956. $7.50

SMITH, Calvin J. *Handbook for Travellers Through the U.S.* 1849. New York. Ills. 233 pp. $165.00

SMITH, Charles F. *Games & Recreational Methods*. 1947. New York. 704 pp. $5.00

SMITH, Clark Ashton. *Genius Loci & Other Tales*. 1948. 1st ed. dj. EX $60.00

SMITH, Clark Ashton. *Genius Loci*. Arkham House. 1st ed. dj. EX $75.00

SMITH, Clark Ashton. *Lost Worlds*. 1944. Arkham House. 1st ed. dj. $50.00

SMITH, Clark Ashton. *Selected Poems*. 1971. 1st ed. dj. EX $45.00

SMITH, Clark Ashton. *Tales of Science & Sorcery*. 1964. Sauk City. Arkham House. dj. $80.00

SMITH, Clark Ashton. *Tales of Science & Sorcery*. 1964. 1st ed. dj. VG $40.00

SMITH, Clark Ashton. *The Double Shadow & Other Fantasies*. 1933. 1st Am. ed. sgn. wrappers. G $125.00

SMITH, Daniel. *Stedman's Wanderings in Interior of South Africa*. 1856. New York. VG $20.00

SMITH, Dave. *Onliness*. 1984. Baton Rouge. proof copy. wrappers. EX $20.00

SMITH, Dave. *Southern Delights*. 1984. Croissant. Ltd. ed. 1/100. sgn. dj. VG $30.00

SMITH, David. *Walks & Talks in Numberland*. 1929. Boston. Ills. TB. $3.00

SMITH, De Cost. *Martyrs of the Oblong & Little Nine*. 1948. Caxton. Ltd. 1st ed. 1/000. EX $20.00

SMITH, Dodie. *I Capture the Castle*. 1948. Boston. 1st ed. dj. VG $8.50

SMITH, E. *Geology of the Coastal Plain of Alabama.* 1894. Montgomery. Ills. 759 pp. $25.00

SMITH, E. Boyd. *Fun in the Radio World.* 1923. New York. Ills. 1st ed. $42.50

SMITH, E. Boyd. *Story of Noah's Ark.* 1905. Boston. 1st ed. EX $35.00

SMITH, E. Boyd. *The Farm Book.* 1982. Boston. Houghton Mifflin. 1st ed. dj. $12.00

SMITH, E.E. *Children of the Lens.* 1954. Reading. Fantasy. 1st trade ed. dj. VG $25.00

SMITH, E.E. *Hellflower.* 1953. New York. 1st ed. dj. EX $15.00

SMITH, E.E. *Lost in Space.* 1959. New York. Avalon. 1st ed. dj. EX $15.00

SMITH, E.E. *Nomad.* 1950. Philadelphia. Prime Press. 1st ed. dj. EX $15.00

SMITH, E.E. *Pattern for Conquest.* 1949. New York. Gnome. 1st ed. dj. EX $25.00

SMITH, E.E. *The Gray Lensman.* 1951. Reading. Fantasy. 1st trade ed. dj. EX $30.00

SMITH, E.E. *The Gray Lensman.* 1951. New York. Gnome. 306 pp. dj. EX $15.00

SMITH, E.E. *The Skylark of Space.* 1947. Providence. Hadley. 2nd ed. sgn. inscr. VG $35.00

SMITH, E.E. *The Skylark of Valeron.* 1949. Reading. Fantasy. 1st trade ed. sgn. $45.00

SMITH, E.E. *The Vortex Blaster.* 1960. Hicksville. Gnome. 1st issue. dj. EX $30.00

SMITH, E.E. *Triplanetary.* 1948. Reading. Fantasy. 1st trade ed. dj. $20.00

SMITH, E.E. *Troubled Star.* 1957. New York. Avalon. 1st ed. dj. EX $15.00

SMITH, E.E. *Venus Equilateral.* 1949. Philadelphia. Prime Press. 2nd printing. dj. $10.00

SMITH, Edgar W. *Profile by Gaslight.* 1944. New York. Simon & Schuster. dj. VG $35.00

SMITH, Edmund Ware. *Further Adventures of a One-Eyed Poacher.* 1947. Crown. Ills. Ripley. 1st ed. 219 pp. $30.00

SMITH, Edward. *The Frogs Who Wanted a King.* 1977. New York. Ills. Margot Zemach. $20.00

SMITH, Edward G. *The Real Theodore Roosevelt.* 1910. London. 205 pp. $12.50

SMITH, Elbert H. *Ma-Ka-Tai; or, Black Hawk & Scenes in the West.* 1849. New York. 299 pp. VG $20.00

SMITH, F. Hopkinson. *A Day at Laguerre's & Other Days.* 1892. Boston. 1st trade ed. 190 pp. G $12.50

SMITH, F. Hopkinson. *Charcoals of New & Old New York.* 1912. Doubleday Page. G $30.00

SMITH, F. Hopkinson. *Colonel Carter of Cartersville.* 1891. Boston. 1st ed. VG $50.00

SMITH, F. Hopkinson. *Colonel Carter's Christmas.* 1903. New York. Ills. F.C. John. $45.00

SMITH, F. Hopkinson. *Gondola Days.* 1897. Houghton Mifflin. 205 pp. $10.00

SMITH, F. Hopkinson. *In Dicken's London.* 1914. Scribner. Ills. 2nd ed. 127 pp. VG $20.00

SMITH, F. Hopkinson. *Kennedy Square.* 1911. Ills. A.I. Keller. VG $12.50

SMITH, F. Hopkinson. *Old Fashioned Folk.* 1907. Boston. Ltd. 1st ed. 1/750. 52 pp. G $15.00

SMITH, F. Hopkinson. *The Tides of Barnegat.* 1906. Ills. Geo. Wright. VG $9.00

SMITH, F. Hopkinson. *The Wood Fire in No. 3.* 1905. Scribner. Ills. Alonzo Kimball. 298 pp. $52.50

SMITH, Frank & Warren, Audrey. *Mississippians All.* 1968. Pelican. 1st ed. sgn. Smith. dj. VG $15.00

SMITH, Fredrika Shumway. *The Magic City.* 1949. Boston. dj. EX $10.00

SMITH, G. Barnett. *Ferdinand DeLesseps, His Life & Enterprises.* 1895. 2nd ed. exlib. 448 pp. G $24.00

SMITH, G. Wayne. *Nathan Goff, Jr., a Biography.* 1959. Charleston. 375 pp. $12.50

SMITH, G.E. *Elephants & Ethnologists.* 1924. London. Ills. 135 pp. 52 pls. $25.00

SMITH, George Adam. *Historical Geography of the Holy Land.* 1907. New York. 713 pp. 6 maps. $35.00

SMITH, George H. *Druid's World.* 1967. 1st ed. dj. EX $8.50

SMITH, George O. *Fire in the Heavens.* 1958. New York. Avalon. 1st ed. dj. EX $12.50

SMITH, George O. *Nomad.* 1950. Prime Press. 286 pp. dj. $18.00

SMITH, Gipsy. *Gipsy Smith.* 1908. New York. 330 pp. VG $6.50

SMITH, H. *Dreams of Natural Places.* 1981. Down East. Ills. 102 pp. dj. EX $10.00

SMITH, H. Allen. *A Short History of Fingers & Other State Papers.* 1963. Boston. Ills. Hershfield. 1st ed. dj. $17.50

SMITH, H. Allen. *Don't Get Personal with a Chicken.* 1959. Boston. 1st ed. 132 pp. dj. $15.00

SMITH, H. Allen. *Lost in the Horse Latitudes.* 1944. Doubleday Doran. Ills. dj. $4.50

SMITH, H. Allen. *Low Man on a Totem Pole.* 1941. New York. Doubleday. 1st ed. 295 pp. $25.00

SMITH, H. Allen. *The Life & Legend of Gene Fowler.* 1977. New York. Ills. 1st ed. 320 pp. $10.00

SMITH, H. Allen. *The Pig in the Barber Shop.* 1958. Little, Brown. 1st ed. dj. VG $15.00

SMITH, H.B. *First Nights & First Editions.* 1931. Boston. Ills. 1st ed. 325 pp. VG $12.50

SMITH, H.L. *Pollyanna of the Orange Blossoms.* 1924. Boston. Ills. 1st ed. 313 pp. VG $8.00

SMITH, H.L. *Tale of Grunty Pig.* 1921. Grosset & Dunlap. 4 color pls. $10.00

SMITH, H.L. *Tale of Master Meadow Mouse.* 1921. Grosset & Dunlap. 6 pls. $10.00

SMITH, H.M. *Snakes as Pets.* 1977. Ills. 160 pp. VG $10.00

SMITH, H.N. *Mark Twain of the Enterprise.* 1957. Berkley. 1st ed. dj. VG $15.00

SMITH, H.P. *Farm Machinery & Equipment.* 1948. New York. McGraw Hill. TB. 520 pp. EX $5.50

SMITH, Harriet L. *The Uncertain Glory.* 1926. Boston. Ills. H.W. Taylor. 305 pp. $3.50

SMITH, Harry W. *Life & Sport in Aiken.* 1935. Derrydale. Ltd. ed. 1/950. EX $90.00

SMITH, Harvey. *The Gang's All Here.* 1941. Princeton. 325 pp. G $50.00

SMITH, Holland M. *Coral & Brass.* 1949. New York. 289 pp. dj. VG $20.00

SMITH, Hugh. *The Fresh-Water Fishes of Siam or Thailand.* 1946. Smith Inst. Ills. 620 pp. VG $35.00

SMITH, Ira L. & Smith, H.A. *Low & Inside, a Book of Baseball Anecdotes.* 1949. New York. Doubleday. ex-lib. 243 pp. $3.50

SMITH, J. *Narrative of Major Andre.* 1809. New York. G $50.00

SMITH, J. & Fey, Charles. *History of Freemasonry in Michigan.* 1963. 1st ed. 232 pp. VG $17.50

SMITH, J. Frazier. *White Pillars: Architecture of the South.* 1941. Bramhall House. Ills. dj. VG $45.00

SMITH, J. Russell. *The Ocean Carrier.* 1908. $12.50

SMITH, J.E. *Germany Beyond Wall/People, Politics & Prosperity.* 1969. dj. VG $12.50

SMITH, J.R. *Tree Crops, a Permanent Agriculture.* 1953. Devin Adair. Ills. 408 pp. VG $22.50

SMITH, Jay H. *Hockey's Legend Bobby Orr.* 1977. Ills. 30 pp. hardbound. EX $4.00

SMITH, Jessica Wilcox. *A Child's Garden of Verses.* 1924. Scribner. 9 color pls. EX $35.00

SMITH, Jessica Wilcox. *A Child's Garden of Verses.* 1905. Scribner. 1st ed. 12 color pls. VG $65.00

SMITH, Jessica Wilcox. *An Old-Fashioned Girl.* 1907. 12 Ills. dj. VG $25.00

SMITH, Jessica Wilcox. *At Back of the North Wind.* McKay. 8 color pls. VG $65.00

SMITH, Jessica Wilcox. *Children of Dickens.* 1945. 10 color pls. VG $15.00

SMITH, Jessica Wilcox. *Children's Garden of Verses.* 1905. London. 1st ed. 12 color pls. VG $125.00

SMITH, Jessica Wilcox. *Heidi.* 1922. McKay. 1st ed. color pls. VG $75.00

SMITH, Jessica Wilcox. *Little Women.* 1922. 8 color pls. VG $30.00

SMITH, Jessica Wilcox. *The Children of Dickens.* 1926. Scribner. 10 color pls. VG $30.00

SMITH, Jessica Wilcox. *Twas the Night Before Christmas.* 1912. Houghton Mifflin. 1st ed. G $95.00

SMITH, Jessica Wilcox. *Water Babies.* 1937. New York. 4 color pls. VG $25.00

SMITH, Jessie Wilcox. *A Child's Book of Modern Stories.* 1935. Dial Press. reprint. Ills. EX $50.00

SMITH, Jessie Wilcox. *Boys & Girls of Bookland.* 1923. Cosmopolitan Pub. VG $120.00

SMITH, Jessie Wilcox. *Dickens' Children.* 1912. Scribner. Ills. 1st ed. VG $30.00

SMITH, Jessie Wilcox. *In the Closed Room.* 1904. New York. Ills. 1st ed. $25.00

SMITH, John Corson. *History of Freemasonry in Illinois, 1804-1829.* 1905. Chicago. Rogers/Smith. 2nd ed. 165 pp. $25.00

SMITH, Joseph. *The Book of Mormon.* 1874. Lamoni, IA. 3rd Am. ed. 545 pp. $50.00

SMITH, Joseph. *The Book of Mormon.* 1869. New York. 1st ed. 116 pp. $75.00

SMITH, Kate. *Upon My Lips a Song.* 1960. New York. Ills. dj. VG $15.00

SMITH, Kay Nolte. *Elegy for a Soprano.* 1985. Villard. 1st ed. dj. VG $15.00

SMITH, Kay Nolte. *The Watcher.* 1980. New York. Coward McCann. 1st ed. dj. EX $45.00

SMITH, L. *American Game Preserve Shooting.* 1937. dj. VG $27.50

SMITH, L.B. *Elizabeth Tudor.* 1975. $10.00

SMITH, L.H. *Bermuda's Oldest Inhabitants: Tales of Plant Life.* 1963. Ills. May Middleton. 3rd ed. $15.00

SMITH, L.L. & Doughty, R.W. *The Amazing Armadillo, Geography of a Folk Critter.* 1984. Texas U. Press. Ills. 1st ed. dj. EX $15.00

SMITH, Lawrence B. *The Sunlight Kid & Other Western Verses.* 1935. New York. 1st ed. photos. 120 pp. $17.50

SMITH, Lee. *Black Mountain Breakdown.* 1980. New York. Putnam. 1st ed. dj. EX $25.00

SMITH, Lee. *Cakewalk.* 1981. New York. Putnam. 1st ed. sgn. dj. EX $35.00

SMITH, Lee. *Oral History.* 1983. New York. Putnam. 1st ed. dj. EX $20.00

SMITH, Lee. *Something in the Wind.* 1971. NY. Harper. 1st ed. sgn. dj. EX $65.00

SMITH, Lillian. *Killers of the Dream.* 1949. Norton. 1st ed. inscr. dj. VG $20.00

SMITH, Lillian. *The Journey.* 1954. World. 1st ed. dj. VG $20.00

SMITH, Logan Pearsall. *Afterthoughts.* 1931. London. Ltd. ed. 1/100. VG $15.00

SMITH, Louisa. *Sevenoaks.* 1934. England. 1st ed. $10.00

SMITH, M.J., Jr. *Keystone Battlewagon. U.S.S. Pennsylvania.* 1983. Ills. 44 pp. wrappers. EX $5.00

SMITH, Mark. *Doctor Blues.* 1983. Morrow. 1st ed. dj. VG $15.00

SMITH, Martin Cruz. *Gorky Park.* 1981. Random House. 1st ed. dj. VG $17.50

SMITH, Martin Cruz. *Gypsy in Amber.* 1971. Putnam. 1st ed. dj. VG $30.00

SMITH, Martin Cruz. *Nightwing.* 1977. Norton. 1st ed. dj. EX $10.00

SMITH, Mrs. E. Oakes. *Woman & Her Needs.* 1851. New York. Fowler & Wells. 120 pp. $25.00

SMITH, Mrs. J. *Notes of Travel in Mexico & California.* 1886. St. Albans. sgn. EX $30.00

SMITH, N. *Golden Doorway to Tibet.* 1949. Bobbs Merrill. dj. EX $15.00

SMITH, O. Warren. *Musings of an Angler.* 1942. VG $15.00

SMITH, O.H. *Early Indiana Trails & Sketches.* 1858. Cincinnati. 640 pp. $35.00

SMITH, Patrick. *The Beginning.* 1967. Exposition. proof copy. dj. VG $15.00

SMITH, Paul C. *Personal File.* 1964. Appleton/Century. 1st ed. VG $6.00

SMITH, R.C. *A Manual of Astrology.* 1828. London. 1st ed. 256 pp. rebound. $100.00

SMITH, R.G. *Sailing Made Easy.* 1952. Ills. revised ed. G $6.00

SMITH, R.L. *Venomous Animals of Arizona.* 1982. AZ U. Press. Ills. 134 pp. EX $12.50

SMITH, R.P. *Animal Tracks & Signs of North America.* 1982. Stackpole. Ills. 271 pp. EX $12.50

SMITH, R.T. *Instrument Flying Guide, Modern Aircraft Series.* 1967. Ills. VG $4.00

SMITH, Red. *Out of the Red.* 1950. Knopf. Ills. Mullin. 1st ed. 294 pp. $25.00

SMITH, Rex Alan. *Moon of Popping Tree.* 1975. New York. 1st ed. dj. VG $10.00

SMITH, Richard K. *The Airships Akron & Macon.* 1965. Annapolis. Ills. 4th ed. 228 pp. $22.00

SMITH, Robert. *Modern Writing.* 1955. New York. Arrowhead. 275 pp. $4.00

SMITH, Robert. *Where Did You Go? Out. What Did You Do? Nothing.* 1957. New York. Norton. Ills. Spanfeller. $10.00

SMITH, S. & Hosking, E. *Birds Fighting.* 1955. London. Faber. Ills. 1st ed. dj. VG $10.00

SMITH, Seba. *The Western Captive; or, Times of Tecumseh.* 1842. New York. 48 pp. wrappers. $100.00

SMITH, Senex. *His Notes & Notions as They Appeared in Herald.* 1890. Cincinnati. 400 pp. VG $15.00

SMITH, Thorne. *Did She Fall?* Grosset & Dunlap. G $5.00

SMITH, Thorne. *Night Life of the Gods.* 1947. Pocket PB. #428. 4th printing. VG $6.00

SMITH, Thorne. *Stray Lamb.* Grosset & Dunlap. G $5.00

SMITH, Thorne. *The Glorious Pool.* 1947. Pocket PB. #409. 8th printing. VG $6.00

SMITH, Thorne. *The Passionate Witch.* 1942. Dial Press. dj. VG $10.00

SMITH, Thorne. *The Passionate Witch.* 1941. Garden City. 1st ed. dj. EX $25.00

SMITH, W. Eugene. *His Photographs & Notes.* 1969. New York. 1st ed. dj. EX $47.50

SMITH, W. Eugene. *Minamata.* 1975. New York. 1st ed. dj. EX $42.50

SMITH, W. Letterman. *William Updick: His Philosophy.* 1908. NY/Washington. Neale Pub. 111 pp. VG $12.50

SMITH, W.A. *The Anson Guard.* 1914. Charlotte. 1st ed. sgn. VG $250.00

SMITH, W.B. *Eisenhower's Six Great Decisions.* 1956. dj. G $10.00

SMITH, W.B. *Moscow Mission 1946-49.* 1950. London. G $15.00

SMITH, W.C. *Bibliography of John Walsh, 1695-1720.* 1948. London. Oxford U. Press. Ills. 1st ed. $40.00

SMITH, W.H.B. & Smith, Joseph. *Small Arms of the World.* 1969. Harrisburg. Stackpole. Ills. 768 pp. dj. $15.00

SMITH, Wilbur. *Before I Forget.* 1971. Chicago. Moody Press. dj. $5.00

SMITH, Wilbur. *Cry Wolf.* 1977. Doubleday. 1st Am. ed. dj. VG $20.00

SMITH, William. *A Green Place.* 1982. Delacorte. Ills. Hnizdovsky. 1st ed. dj. $17.50

SMITH, William. *Journal of a Voyage in the Missionary Ship Duff.* 1813. New York. 1st ed. 288 pp. $290.00

SMITH, William. *Old English Drinking Songs.* 1903. Cincinnati. Byway Pr. Ltd. ed. 63 pp. EX $10.00

SMITH & TAYLOR. *United States Service Symbols.* 1942. Ills. G $15.00

SMITH. *A Dictionary of Greek & Roman Antiquities, Vol II.* 1891. Ills. 1072 pp. $6.50

SMITH. *Ancient Egypt Represented in Museum of Fine Arts.* 1942. Boston. Museum of Fine Arts. 175 pp. $6.50

SMITH. *Brazil, the Amazon, & the Coast.* 1879. Scribner. $25.00

SMITH. *Carthage & the Carthaginians.* 1908. London. VG $5.00

SMITH. *Datelines & By-Lines. Presbyterian Growth in AZ.* 1969. Phoenix. Ills. 90 pp. SftCvr. $10.00

SMITH. *Lost Worlds.* Arkham House. 1st ed. dj. VG $125.00

SMITH. *Pictorial History of Architecture in America.* 1976. Norton. 2 vol boxed. $20.00

SMITH. *Red Ryder & the Secret of the Lucky Mine.* 1947. Whitman. Ills. G. $3.50

SMITH. *Springs & Wells of Manhattan & the Bronx.* 1938. New York. VG $12.50

SMITH. *The Classics in Translations.* 1966. New York. reprint. EX $12.50

SMOLLETT, Tobias. *Gil Blas of Santillane.* 1853. 20 steel engravings. EX $40.00

SMOLLETT, Tobias. *The Adventures of Peregrine Pickle.* 1929. New York. Ills. Ltd. ed. 2 vol set. EX $75.00

SMOLLETT, Tobias. *The Adventures of Roderick Random.* 1815. London. Walker. 568 pp. $40.00

SMOLLETT, Tobias. *The Expedition of Humphrey Clinker.* 1785. London. 2 vol set. VG $115.00

SMTHE, H. *Historical Sketch of Parker Co. & Weatherford, TX.* 1973. Waco, TX. reprint. Ltd. ed. 476 pp. $50.00

SMUCKER. *The Life & Times of Thomas Jefferson.* 1857. Evans. 400 pp. $10.50

SMYTH, W. & Lowe, F. *Narrative of Journey from Lima to Para by Rivers.* 1836. Ills, some foxing. $200.00

SMYTH, Henry DeWolf. *Atomic Energy for Military Purposes.* 1945. Princeton. Ills. 1st ed. 264 pp. VG $45.00

SMYTHE, J. Henry. *The Amazing Benjamin Franklin.* 1929. New York. VG $7.50

SMYTHE. *Behold the Mountains.* 1949. 1st ed. dj. VG $25.00

SMYTHE. *British Mountaineers.* 1932. Collins. EX $40.00

SMYTHE. *Valley of Flowers.* 1949. New York. 1st Am. ed. VG $15.00

SNELL, Edmund. *Kontrol.* 1928. Philadelphia. Lippincott. 1st ed. dj. $25.00

SNELL, Edmund. *The Z Ray.* 1932. Philadelphia. 1st ed. dj. VG $25.00

SNELL, George. *The Shapers of American Fiction, 1798-1947.* 1947. Dutton. 1st ed. dj. VG $35.00

SNELL, Peter & Gilmour, G. *No Bugles No Drums.* 1965. New Zealand. Photos. 240 pp. dj. EX $2.50

SNELL, Roy J. *The Secret Mark.* 1923. Reilly & Lee. sgn. VG $4.50

SNELL. *Jane Withers & the Phantom Violin.* 1943. Whitman. Ills. VG $4.50

SNELLING, O.F. *Double O Seven. James Bond.* 1964. London. Holland Press. 1st ed. dj. EX $35.00

SNELLING, W.J. *Tales of the Northwest.* 1971. Haines. reprint ed. dj. EX $10.00

SNODGRASS, W.D. *Bryde Callyng Jennie Wrenn.* 1984. Ewert. Ltd. ed. 1/136. sgn. wrappers. $35.00

SNODGRASS, W.D. *Heart's Needle.* 1966. New York. reprint ed. inscr. $30.00

SNODGRASS, W.D. *In Radical Pursuit.* 1975. Harper. 1st ed. dj. VG $20.00

SNOW, Alice Rowe. *Log of a Sea Captain's Daughter.* 1944. Boston. 2nd ed. sgn. dj. VG $12.50

SNOW, C.P. *Death Under Sail.* 1931. London. Heinemann. 1st ed. dj. VG $450.00

SNOW, C.P. *Homecoming.* 1956. $10.00

SNOW, C.P. *The Malcontents.* 1972. $10.00

SNOW, C.P. *The Two Cultures & a Second Look.* 1964. 2nd ed. dj. $37.50

SNOW, Dorothea. *Honey Bear.* 1964. Lowe Co. Ills. Turn-a-Dial. SftCvr. VG $2.50

SNOW, Dorothea. *Lassie & the Mystery at Blackberry Bog.* 1956. Racine. Whitman. 282 pp. $3.50

SNOW, Edgar. *People on Our Side.* 1944. New York. World Pub. Ills. 324 pp. $2.50

SNOW, Edgar. *Red China Today.* 1970. Ills. dj. EX $17.50

SNOW, Edgar. *Red Star Over China/Inside Account of Mao's China.* 1978. pb. VG $3.50

SNOW, Edgar. *Red Star Over China/Inside Account of Mao's China.* 1938. New York. Ills. 1st ed. 474 pp. EX $35.00

SNOW, Edward Rowe. *Famous Lighthouse of America.* 1945. New York. 1st ed. sgn. dj. EX $25.00

SNOW, Edward Rowe. *Fantastic, Folklore & Fact, New England Tales.* 1968. New York. 270 pp. 16 pls. index. $7.50

SNOW, Edward Rowe. *Ghosts, Gales, & Gold.* 1972. Dodd Mead. 5th printing. dj. VG $6.50

SNOW, Edward Rowe. *Great Gales & Dire Disasters.* 1952. Dodd Mead. dj. VG $10.00

SNOW, Edward Rowe. *Legends of the Northeast Coast.* 1957. Dodd Mead. sgn. dj. VG $15.00

SNOW, Edward Rowe. *Northeast Sea Drama.* 1953. sgn. dj. VG $12.50

SNOW, Edward Rowe. *Piracy, Mutiny, & Murder.* 1959. Ills. dj. VG $12.50

SNOW, Edward Rowe. *Romance of Casco Bay.* 1975. Dodd Mead. inscr. dj. VG $20.00

SNOW, Edward Rowe. *Secrets of the North Atlantic Islands.* 1950. Dodd Mead. inscr. dj. VG $12.50

SNOW, Edward Rowe. *Storms & Shipwrecks of the Northeast.* 1943. Yankee Pub. 1st ed. VG $10.00

SNOW, Edward Rowe. *The Romance of Boston Bay.* 1944. Boston. Ills. 1st ed. 319 pp. $15.00

SNOW, Edward Rowe. *The Story of Minot's Light.* 1955. West Hanover. Ills. 2nd ed. $25.00

SNOW, Glenna. *Glenna Snow's Cookbook.* 1938. Akron. 1st ed. 396 pp. $20.00

SNOW, Jack. *Dark Music & Other Spectral Tales.* 1947. New York. 1st ed. dj. EX $30.00

SNOW, Jack. *The Shaggy Man of Oz.* 1949. Chicago. Reilly & Lee. Ills. F. Kramer. $130.00

SNOW, Marshall S. *Higher Education in Missouri.* 1898. Washington. Ills. 1st ed. wrappers. $35.00

SNOW, Thad. *From Missouri.* 1954. Boston. 1st ed. dj. $7.50

SNYDER, Carl. *Capitalism the Creator.* 1940. New York. Macmillan. ex-lib. 473 pp. G $4.00

SNYDER, Frank. *Life Under Sail.* 1964. New York. Ills. 1st ed. VG $12.50

SNYDER, Gary. *Earth House Hold.* 1969. New Directions. dj. VG $15.00

SNYDER, Gerald S. *The Royal Oak Disaster.* 1976. $7.50

SNYDER, Gerald S. *The Royal Oak Disaster.* 1978. Book Club ed. Ills. dj. G $15.00

SNYDER, Harry Snyder. *Snyder's Book of Big Game Hunting.* 1950. Greenburg. Ills. Ltd. ed. 302 pp. index. $32.50

SNYDER, John Francis. *Selected Writings.* 1962. Springfield. IL State Hist. Soc. 329 pp. $52.50

SNYDER, L.L. *The War, a Concise History 1939-1945.* 1961. Ills. maps. G $12.50

SNYDER, Laurence H. *The Principals of Heredity, 2nd Edition.* 1940. New York. T.B. 452 pp. $3.00

SNYDER, H. *The Chemistry of Plant & Animal Life.* 1907. Macmillan. TB. 406 pp. VG $3.50

SOBEL, L.A. *Palestinian Impasse.* 1977. VG $12.50

SOBY, J.T. *After Picasso.* 1935. Hartford. 126 pp. 60 pls. $17.50

SOBY, J.T. *Ben Shahan Paintings.* New York. 2nd printing. $15.00

SOFTLY, Barbara. *Magic People Around the World.* 1970. New York. Ills. Vera Bock. 1st ed. EX $7.50

SOHL, Jerry. *Altered Ego.* 1964. New York. dj. VG $20.00

SOHL, Jerry. *Night Slaves.* 1965. Greenwich. Fawcett. 1st ed. pb. EX $9.50

SOLIS, Don Antonio de. *History of the Conquest of Mexico by Spaniards.* 1724. London. 1st Eng. ed. 6 fld maps. $465.00

SOLLAS, W.J. *Ancient Hunters & Their Modern Representatives.* 1924. New York. Ills. 3rd ed. 689 pp. fld pls. $12.00

SOLLEYSER, Jacques & Cherry. *The Art of Shoeing Horses: Notes on His Practice.* 1842. London. Ills. VG $85.00

SOLOMON, D.E. *Diseases of the Horse.* 1890. Washington. Ills. $13.50

SOLONOMSKY, Nicolas. *Music of Latin America.* 1945. New York. VG $18.00

SOLOVYOV, B. *The Turning Point of World War II.* 1982. Moscow. Ills. Eng. text. maps. dj. EX $12.50

SOLZHENITSYN, Aleksandr. *August 1914.* 1972. Farrar. 1st Am. ed. dj. VG $25.00

SOLZHENITSYN, Aleksandr. *Lenin in Zurich.* 1976. New York. 1st ed. dj. VG $10.00

SOLZHENITSYN, Aleksandr. *Letter to the Soviet Leaders.* 1974. dj. VG $6.00

SOLZHENITSYN, Aleksandr. *One Day in the Life of Ivan Denisovich.* 1963. New York. Dutton. 1st ed. 160 pp. $25.00

SOLZHENITSYN, Aleksandr. *The Cancer Ward.* Taiwan piracy. dj. VG $30.00

SOLZHENITSYN, Aleksandr. *The Cancer Ward.* 1968. Bodley Head. 1st English ed. dj. VG $40.00

SOLZHENITSYN, Aleksandr. *The Love Girl & the Innocent, a Play.* 1969. 1st ed. VG $25.00

SOLZHENITSYN, Aleksandr. *The Oak & the Calf.* 1980. Harper. 1st trade ed. dj. VG $15.00

SOMERS, A.N. *History of Lancaster, New Hampshire.* 1899. Concord. 652 pp. EX $32.50

SOMERS, John. *The Brethern of the Axe.* 1927. New York. Dutton. 1st ed. VG $10.00

SOMERSET, Somers. *Land of the Muskeg.* 1895. London. photos. maps. VG $50.00

SOMERVELL, D.C. *The Reign of King George.* 1935. New York. $8.00

SOMERVILLE, A. *Shikar Near Calcutta.* 1924. Calcutta. 1st ed. VG $20.00

SOMERVILLE, E. *The States Through Irish Eyes.* 1930. Boston. Ltd. ed. 1/375. sgn. boxed. $150.00

SOMERVILLE, William. *The Chase.* 1802. London. Ills. Bewick. VG $45.00

SOMERVILLE & ROSS. *In Mr. Knox's Country.* 1915. London. VG $10.00

SOMMER, Elyse. *Career Opportunities in Crafts.* 1977. Crown. pb. $2.00

SONNECK, Oscar. *A Bibliography of Early Secular American Music.* 1967. New York. Da Capo reprint. dj. $15.00

SONNECK, Oscar. *The Star Spangled Banner.* 1914. Washington. revised ed. 25 pls. VG $25.00

SONNICHSEN, & MORRISON. *Alias Billy the Kid.* 1955. Albuquerque. Ills. 1st ed. 136 pp. index. $25.00

SONNICHSEN, C.L. *Billy King's Tombstone.* 1951. Caxton. Ills. dj. VG $15.00

SONNICHSEN, C.L. *Cowboys & Cattle Kings.* 1950. $10.00

SONTAG, Susan. *A Susan Sontag Reader.* 1982. Farrar. 1st trade ed. dj. VG $17.50

SONTAG, Susan. *Death Kit.* 1976. Farrar. 1st ed. dj. VG $15.00

SONTAG, Susan. *Etcetera.* 1978. Farrar. 1st ed. dj. VG $15.00

SONTAG, Susan. *Illness as Metaphor.* Farrar. 1st ed. sgn. dj. EX $25.00

SONTAG, Susan. *On Photography.* 1977. Farrar. 1st ed. dj. VG $15.00

SONTAG, Susan. *Styles of Radical Will.* 1969. Farrar. 1st ed. dj. VG $30.00

SONTAG, Susan. *The Benefactor.* 1963. Farrar. 1st ed. dj. VG $35.00

SONTAG, Susan. *Under the Sign of Saturn.* 1980. Farrar. 1st ed. dj. VG $15.00

SOOTHILL, E. & Whitehead, P. *Wildfowl of the World.* 1978. Peerage. Ills. 297 pp. dj. EX $25.00

SOPER, M.F. *New Zealand Bird Portraits.* 1963. Whitcome Tombs. Ills. 1st ed. 104 pp. dj. EX $17.50

SORANO. *Sacrum Martyrologium Romanum.* 1610. Cologne. $100.00

SORELL. *Other Face: Mask in Arts.* 1973. New York. 1st ed. dj. EX $27.50

SORENSEN, Theodore. *Kennedy.* 1965. New York. Harper & Row. 783 pp. dj. VG $7.50

SORIA. *Perceptions & Evocations: Art of Elihu Vedder.* 1979. Smithsonian Inst. 1st ed. $10.00

SORRENTINO, Gilbert. *Splendide Hotel.* 1973. New Directions. Ltd. ed. sgn. dj. EX $35.00

SORRENTINO, Gilbert. *The Sky Changes.* 1966. New York. Hill & Wang. 1st ed. dj. EX $35.00

SOULE, Bihon & Nisbet. *Annals of San Francisco.* 1855. New York. Ills. 1st ed. 824 pp. VG $55.00

SOULE, G. *Mystery Monsters of the Deep.* 1981. Watts. Ills. 134 pp. dj. EX $10.00

SOULE, S.H. *Rand McNally Guide to the Great Northwest.* 1903. Ills. maps. VG $15.00

SOUSA, John Philip. *The Fifth String.* 1902. Indianapolis. Bowen-Merrill. 125 pp. $10.00

SOUSA, John Phillip. *Marching Along, Recollections of Men-Women-Music.* 1928. Ills. Hale, Cushman & Flint. $6.50

SOUTH, R. *Butterflies of the British Isles.* 1928. London. Warne. 210 pp. 125 pls. VG $40.00

SOUTH, R. *Moths of the British Isles.* 1933. London. Warne. revised ed. 2 vol set. $110.00

SOUTHARD, Charles. *Treatise on Trout for the Progressive Angler.* 1931. 1st ed. VG $22.50

SOUTHERLAND, Edwin H. *Principles of Criminology.* 1947. Philadelphia. revised ed. 643 pp. $10.00

SOUTHERN, Terry & Hoffenberg. *Candy.* 1964. New York. VG $7.50

SOUTHERN, Terry. *Blue Movie.* 1970. World. 1st ed. dj. VG $15.00

SOUTHERN, Terry. *Red Dirt Marijuana.* 1967. 1st ed. dj. EX $20.00

SOUTHEY, R. *A Vision of Judgement.* 1821. London. 1st ed. dj. VG $60.00

SOUTHEY, R. *Life Admiral Horatio Nelson.* 1902. Ills. G $12.50

SOUTHWOLD, Stephen. *The Seventh Bowl.* 1930. London. Partridge. Ltd. ed. dj. EX $60.00

SOUTHWORTH, Alvan S. *Four Thousand Miles of African Travel.* 1875. New York. Ills. maps. 381 pp. G $5.00

SOUTHWORTH, Mrs. E.D. *Gypsy's Prophesy.* Donohue. no date. 274 pp. $4.00

SOWERBY, A. *A Sportsman's Miscellany.* 1917. Tiensin. Ills. VG $395.00

SOWERBY, G. *A Conchological Manual.* 1852. London. Ills. 4th ed. $45.00

SOWERBY, Mill & Githa. *Childhood.* 1907. Duffield. Ills. EX $85.00

SOWLS, L.K. *The Peccaries.* 1984. AZ U. Press. Ills. 251 pp. dj. EX $25.00

SOYINKO, Wole. *Madmen & Specialists.* 1971. New York. Hill & Wang. dj. EX $30.00

SPACKMAN, W.M. *An Armful of Warm Girl.* 1978. Knopf. 1st ed. dj. VG $15.00

SPAETH, Sigmund. *A History of Popular Music in America.* 1962. New York. Random House. 729 pp. $10.00

SPAETH, Sigmund. *Weep Some More, My Lady.* 1927. EX $10.00

SPALDING, Charles C. *Annals of the City of Kansas.* 1858. Kansas City. Van Horn & Abeel. 1st ed. $1,250.00

SPANTON, A.I. *Fifty Years of Buchtel.* 1922. Akron. Ills. sgn. G $25.00

SPARGO, John. *Applied Socialism.* 1912. New York. Huebsch. 1st ed. dj. $40.00

SPARGO, John. *Bennington Battle Monument.* 1925. Tuttle. Ills. 1st ed. VG $10.00

SPARK, M. & Stanford, D. *My Best Mary. Selected Letters of Mary Shelley.* 1953. London. dj. EX $15.00

SPARK, Muriel. *Collected Poems I.* 1967. Macmillan. 1st ed. dj. EX $10.00

SPARK, Muriel. *Collected Poems.* 2nd ed. dj. EX $6.00

SPARK, Muriel. *Girls of Slender Means.* 1963. New York. 1st ed. dj. VG $10.00

SPARK, Muriel. *Loitering with Intent.* 1981. Coward McCann. 1st Am. ed. dj. VG $12.50

SPARK, Muriel. *Not to Disturb.* 1972. Viking. 1st Am. ed. dj. VG $15.00

SPARK, Muriel. *The Abyss of Crewe.* 1974. Viking. 1st Am. ed. dj. VG $15.00

SPARK, Muriel. *The Driver's Seat.* 1970. Knopf. 1st Am. ed. dj. VG $15.00

SPARK, Muriel. *The Hothouse by the East River.* 1973. Macmillan. 1st ed. dj. VG $20.00

SPARK, Muriel. *The Prime of Miss Jean Brodie.* 1961. London. Barker. 1st ed. dj. VG $45.00

SPARK, Muriel. *The Public Image.* 1968. Knopf. 1st Am. ed. dj. VG $20.00

SPARK, Muriel. *The Stories of Muriel Spark.* 1985. Dutton. proof copy. wrappers. EX $35.00

SPARK, Muriel. *The Takeover.* 1976. Viking. 1st Am. ed. dj. VG $15.00

SPARKS, Fred. *Jackie & Ari's 1st Year.* 1970. 240 pp. dj. $5.00

SPARKS, J. & Soper, T. *Owls, Their Natural & Unnatural History.* 1970. Taplinger. Ills. Gillmor. 1st ed. dj. EX $12.50

SPARROW, Gerald. *The Great Forgers.* 1963. London. 1st ed. dj. VG $20.00

SPARROW, Gerald. *Vintage Victorian Murder.* 1971. London. Barker. 1st ed. sgn. dj. VG $20.00

SPARROW, J. *Line Upon Line.* 1967. Cambridge. Ltd. 1st ed. 1/500. VG $80.00

SPARROW, John. *Lapidaria Octava.* 1981. Cambridge. Ltd ed. 1/200. wrappers. $25.00

SPARROW, John. *Poems of Bishop Henry King.* Nonsuch Press. Ltd. ed. 1/900. VG $35.00

SPARROW, W.S. *Angling in British Art.* 1923. London. EX $195.00

SPAULDING, Phebe Estelle. *Tahquitch Maiden: Tale of San Jacintos.* 1911. San Francisco. P. Elder & Co. Ills. 26 pp. $20.00

SPAVIN. *Chippewa Dawn Legends of an Indian People.* 1977. 1st ed. dj. EX $15.00

SPAWLS, S. *Sun, Sand, & Snakes.* 1979. London. Collins. Ills. 254 pp. dj. EX $17.50

SPAYTHE, Jacob A. *History of Hancock County, Ohio.* 1903. Toledo, Ohio. Ills. 312 pp. $40.00

SPEAKMAN, Harold. *Mostly Mississippi.* 1927. New York. Ills. 360 pp. $10.00

SPEAR. *American Watch Papers.* 1952. Am. Antiquarian Soc. wrappers. $15.00

SPEAR. *Uncle Billy Reminiscences.* 1940. Phoenix. $12.50

SPEARE, Eva. *New Hampshire Folk Tales.* 1964. revised ed. dj. VG $10.00

SPEARE, Eva. *Stories of New Hampshire.* 1977. 2nd printing. wrappers. EX $10.00

SPEARMAN, Frank H. *Nan of Music Mountain.* 1916. New York. Ills. Wyeth. 430 pp. $10.00

SPEARMAN, Frank H. *Whispering Smith.* 1906. New York. Scribner. Ills. Wyeth. 1st ed. $35.00

SPEARS, John R. *Ills. Sketches of Death Valley & Other Deserts.* 1892. New York. 1st ed. 226 pp. wrappers. $100.00

SPEARS, John R. *Story of the New England Whalers.* 1922. New York. Ills. 418 pp. $12.50

SPEARS, John R. *The Story of the American Merchant Marine.* 1910. $15.00

SPEATH, Sigmund. *Read 'Em & Weep.* 1926. New York. Ills. 1st ed. $15.00

SPEED, Harold *The Practice & Science of Drawing.* 1920. London Ills. $40.00

SPEER, A. *Infiltration.* 1981. New York. Macmillan. 384 pp. dj. $7.00

SPEER, A. *Inside the Third Reich.* 1970. New York. 1st printing. dj. VG $12.50

SPEER, A. *Spandau: Secret Diaries.* 1976. Ills. Book Club ed. dj. VG $10.00

SPEER, Emory. *Lincoln, Lee, Grant/Other Biographical Addresses.* 1909. New York. Ills. 1st ed. 269 pp. G $35.00

SPEER, INC. *Speer Manual for Reloading Ammunition.* 1964. Lewiston, ID. 334 pp. SftCvr. VG $2.50

SPEIGHT, E.E. & Nance, R.M. *Britain's Sea Story.* 1912. $7.50

SPEISER, E.A. *The United States & the Near East.* 1947. dj. G $7.50

SPEKE, J.H. *Journal of Discovery of the Source of the Nile.* 1969. Greenwood. reprint. 658 pp. EX $30.00

SPEKKE, Arnolds. *Ancient Amber Routes & Discovery of E. Baltic.* 1957. Stockholm. Ills. 1st Eng. text ed. maps. $20.00

SPELL, L. & H. *Forgotten Men of Cripple Creek.* 1959. Denver. Ills. 1st ed. sgn. dj. VG $20.00

SPELLMAN, A.B. *Four Lives in the Bebop Business.* 1967. London. 1st Eng. ed. dj. VG $14.00

SPELMAN, John. *The Life of Alfred the Great.* 1709. Oxford. 1st ed. 238 pp. $135.00

SPEMANN, W. *The Golden Book of Music.* 1900. Berlin. Ills. VG $30.00

SPENCE, B. *Harpooned, the Story of Whaling.* 1980. Greenwich. Ills. dj. EX $17.50

SPENCE, J. *The Gate of Heavenly Peace.* 1981. Ills. dj. EX $17.50

SPENCER, Claire. *Gallows Orchard.* 1930. 1st Am. ed. dj. EX $7.50

SPENCER, D.A. *Colour Photography in Practice.* 1952. New York. 3rd ed. VG $12.50

SPENCER, D.A. *Photography Today.* 1936. Oxford U. Press. $15.00

SPENCER, David. *The New Professional Hockey Almanac.* 1978. Paqurian Press. Ills. 192 pp. EX $5.00

SPENCER, Elizabeth. *Marilee.* 1981. U. Press MS. 1st trade ed. sgn. wrappers. $10.00

SPENCER, Elizabeth. *Marilee.* 1981. U. Press MS. Ltd. 1st ed. sgn. dj. EX $35.00

SPENCER, Elizabeth. *No Place for an Angel.* 1967. McGraw Hill. 1st ed. dj. VG $30.00

SPENCER, Elizabeth. *Ship Island & Other Stories.* 1968. McGraw Hill. 1st ed. sgn. dj. VG $40.00

SPENCER, Elizabeth. *The Mules.* 1982. Palaemon. Ltd. 1st ed. 1/150. sgn. EX $30.00

SPENCER, Elizabeth. *The Voice at the Back Door.* 1956. McGraw Hill. 1st ed. sgn. dj. VG $60.00

SPENCER, Elizabeth. *This Crooked Way.* 1952. McGraw Hill. 1st ed. dj. VG $60.00

SPENCER, J.A. *History of the United States.* New York. Johnson & Fry. wrappers. VG $150.00

SPENCER, William Loring. *Salt Lake City, a Latter Day Romance.* 1884. Boston. 1st ed. 328 pp. $35.00

SPENCER. *The Native Americans.* 1965. 1st ed. VG $10.00

SPENDER, Kristol & Lasky. *Encounters.* 1963. Basic Books. 1st Am. ed. dj. VG $20.00

SPENDER, Stephen. *Poems.* 1933. Faber. 1st ed. VG $50.00

SPENDER, Stephen. *Ruins & Visions.* 1942. Random House. 1st Am. ed. dj. VG $35.00

SPENDER, Stephen. *The Edge of Being.* 1949. London. 1st ed. VG $20.00

SPENDER, Stephen. *Trial of a Judge.* 1938. Random House. 1st Am. ed. sgn. dj. VG $35.00

SPERLING. *Catalog of a Loan Exhibition of French Primitives.* 1927. New York. $15.00

SPERRY, Armstrong. *Bamboo, the Grass Tree.* 1942. New York. Macmillan. Ills. 1st ed. dj. $15.00

SPERRY, Armstrong. *River of the West, Story of the Boston Men.* 1967. Ills. Henry C. Pitz. dj. VG $5.00

SPERRY, Armstrong. *Wagons Westward.* 1936. Winston. 1st ed. VG $20.00

SPICER, Stanley T. *Masters of Sail.* 1968. $8.50

SPIELMANN & LAYARD. *Greenaway.* 1905. London. 2nd printing. $50.00

SPILLANE, Mickey. *The Deep.* 1961. London. 1st ed. dj. EX $12.50

SPILLANE, Mickey. *Tomorrow I Die.* Ltd. 1st ed. 1/250. sgn. $70.00

SPILLANE, Mickey. *Tomorrow I Die.* proof copy. $45.00

SPINAGE, C.A. *The Book of the Giraffe.* 1968. London. Collins. Ills. 191 pp. dj. EX $22.50

SPINDEN, H. *Ancient Civilizations of Mexico & Central America.* 1948. Ills. photos. fld map. 270 pp. $17.50

SPINKA, Matthew. *Nicolas Berdyaev: Captive of Freedom.* 1950. Westminster. 1st ed, dj. $8.50

SPINRAD, Norman. *Bug Jack Barron.* 1969. 1st Am. ed. dj. EX $50.00

SPINRAD, Norman. *Songs from the Stars.* 1980. 1st Am. ed. dj. EX $15.00

SPIRES, Elizabeth. *Boardwalk.* 1980. Bits. 1st trade ed. wrappers. EX $5.00

SPIVAK, John L. *Plotting America's Pogroms.* 1934. New York. New Masses. 1st ed. wrappers. $12.50

SPLINT, Sara Field. *The Art of Cooking & Serving.* 1926. Cincinnati. VG $10.00

SPOCK, L.E. *Guide to the Study of Rocks.* 1962. Harper. Ills. 298 pp. dj. VG $7.50

SPOFFORD, A.R. *Library of Historical Characters.* 10 vol set. EX $50.00

SPORTS AFIELD. *Guns & Game.* 1979. 112 pp. $3.00

SPORTS ILLUSTRATED. *Sports Illustrated Book of Wet-Fly Fishing.* 1961. NY. Lippincott. ex-lib. 89 pp. VG $3.50

SPOTTISWOODE, Raymond. *A Grammar of the Film.* 1950. U. of California. G $6.00

SPOTTS, David L. *Campaigning with Custer.* 1965. New York. VG $22.50

SPRAGUE, Kurth. *The Promise Kept.* 1975. Austin. Ills. Groth. Ltd. ed. sgns. EX $65.00

SPRAGUE, M. *Massacre.* Little, Brown. dj. EX $17.50

SPRAGUE, M. *Newport in the Rockies* Sage. 1961. dj. EX $10.00

SPRECHER, Samuel. *Apostolic Method Realizing True Ideal of Church.* 1866. Baltimore. 44 pp. Wrappers. $12.50

SPRENGER. *Malleus Maleficarum.* Folio Society. VG $17.50

SPRIGGE, Elizabeth & Kihm, J. *Jean Cocteau: the Man & the Mirror.* 1968. New York. Ills. 1st Am. ed. 268 pp. dj. $8.50

SPRING, Agnes Wright. *Caspar Collins: Life Exploits of Indian Fighter.* 1927. Columbia U. Pr. EX $35.00

SPRING, James W. *Boston & the Parker House.* 1927. Boston. private print. Ills. VG $25.00

SPRINGER, John. *Forest Life & Forest Trees.* 1851. New York. Ills. 1st ed. 259 pp. $125.00

SPRINGER, S. *Revision of the Catsharks, Family Scyliorhinidae.* 1979. Ills. 152 pp. EX $10.00

SPROAT, Eleanor M. *Daily Cookery from Breakfast to Supper.* 1923. London. VG $10.00

SPROUT, H. & M. *The Rise of American Naval Power, 1776-1918.* 1939. Ills. VG $17.50

SPROUT, H. & M. *Toward a New Order of Sea Power.* 1943. VG $12.50

SPRUILL, Steven. *The Imperator Plot.* 1983. Garden City. review copy. dj. VG $12.50

SPRUNGMAN, Ormal I. *Photography Afield.* 1951. 1st ed. index. dj. VG $15.00

SPRUNT, Alex & Chamberlain, E. *South Carolina Bird Life.* 1949. Columbia. Ills. dj. boxed. EX $52.50

SPRUNT, Alex. *Florida Bird Life.* 1954. Coward McCann. 1st ed. VG $47.50

SPRUNT, Alex. *North American Birds of Prey.* 1955. 1st ed dj. $40.00

SPRUNT, Alex. *South Carolina Bird Life.* 1970. Columbia, SC. 655 pp. dj. $65.00

SPUILL, Steven G. *The Psychopath Plague.* 1978. Garden City. Doubleday. 1st ed. dj. EX $20.00

SPURLING, R. Glen. *Practical Neurological Diagnosis.* 1940. Ills. dj. EX $45.00

SPYRI, Johanna. *Cornelli.* 1920. New York. A.L. Burt. 275 pp. $4.50

SPYRI, Johanna. *Dora.* 1924. New York. Blue Ribbon. 215 pp. $2.00

SPYRI, Johanna. *Grotli's Children, a Story of Switzerland.* 1924. New York. Blue Ribbon. 265 pp. $3.50

SPYRI, Johanna. *Heidi.* 1922. McKay. Ills. Jessie Wilcox Smith. G $12.50

SPYRI, Johanna. *Heidi.* 1945. New York. Grosset & Dunlap. Ills. Sharp. $4.00

SPYRI, Johanna. *Maxa's Children.* 1926. New York. 244 pp. $3.50

SPYRI, Johanna. *Mazli, a Story of the Swiss Valleys.* 1921. New York. Blue Ribbon. 265 pp. $3.50

SQUIER. *Children of Twilight, Folk Tales of Indian Tribes.* 1926. Cosmopolitan. 257 pp. VG $22.50

SQUIRE, Lorene. *Wildfowling with a Camera.* 1938. 1st ed. $20.00

ST. BARTHOLOMEW'S CHURCH. *St. Bart's Cookbook.* Norwich, NY. (ca.1960) 202 pp. VG $5.00

ST. DENIS, Ruth. *An Unfinished Life.* 1929. Harper. 1st ed. 391 pp. index. dj. $25.00

ST. DENIS, Ruth. *Lotus Light. Poems by Ruth St. Denis.* 1932. Houghton Mifflin. 1st ed. $35.00

ST. GEORGE, Eleanor. *Dolls of Three Centuries.* 1951. G $4.00

ST. GEORGE, Eleanor. *Old Dolls.* 1950. G $4.00

ST. JOHN, Bruce. *John Sloan's New York Scene.* 1965. Ills. drawings. photos. $15.00

ST. JOHN, Charles. *A Scottish Naturalist 1809-1856.* 1982. London. Ills. 191 pp. folio. dj. $11.00

ST. JOHN, Charles. *Wild Sports & Natural History of the Highlands.* 1927. London. Ills. Armour & Alexander. VG $45.00

ST. JOHN, Elizabeth. *Sammy the White House Mouse.* 1976. Handel Pub. Ills. Quiram. 1st ed. VG $12.50

ST. JOHN, J. Allen. *The Face in the Pool.* 1905. McClurg. Ills. 1st ed. VG $125.00

ST. JOHN, Mrs. Horace. *Audubon, Naturalist of the New World.* 1862. Boston. 311 pp. $10.00

ST. JOHN, Mrs. Horace. *Boy's Life of Audubon, Naturalist of New World.* 1869. New York. Ills. J.W. Orr. G $12.50

ST. JOHN, Percy B. *The Arctic Crusoe.* Boston/NY. Ills. $15.00

ST. JOHN, Philip. *Rocket Jockey.* 1952. Philadelphia. 1st ed. dj. VG $15.00

ST. JOHN, Robert. *From the Land of Silent People.* 1942. New York. 352 pp. dj. G $5.00

ST. JOHN, Stevas. *The Right to Life.* 1963. London. 128 pp. VG $60.00

ST. JOHNS, Adela Rogers. *The Honeycomb: An Autobiography.* 1969. Garden City. dj. G $8.00

ST. JOHNS, Adela. *Field of Honor.* 1938. Dutton. 1st ed. dj. $8.50

STABLES, Gordon. *In the Great White Land: Tale of Antarctic Ocean.* London. Blackie. (ca.1910) G $24.00

STACKPOLE, E.A. *Smugglers Luck.* 1931. New York. Ills. Rogers. 1st ed. 310 pp. $7.50

STACKPOLE, E.A. *The Sea Hunters, Great Age of Whaling.* 1953. Ills. dj. G $15.00

STACKPOLE BOOKS. *Scrimshaw at Mystic Seaport.* 1958. 1st ed. wrappers. VG $10.00

STACKPOLE BOOKS. *The New Hunters Encyclopedia.* 1966. Stackpole. 1131 pp. dj. $20.00

STACKPOOLE, H. de Vere. *Drums of War.* 1910. London. Murray. 1st ed. 336 pp. G $22.50

STAENDER. *Adventures with Arctic Wildlife.* 1970. Caxton. Ills. 360 pp. dj. $3.00

STAFFORD, E.P. *The Big E.* 1962. Random House. Ills. 1st ed. 500 pp. dj. VG $22.50

STAFFORD, Jean. *Boston Adventure.* 1944. New York. Harcourt. 1st ed. dj. EX $25.00

STAFFORD, Jean. *Children Are Bored on Sunday.* 1953. Harcourt. 1st ed. dj. VG $30.00

STAFFORD, Jean. *The Collected Stories of Jean Stafford.* 1969. $10.00

STAFFORD, Jean. *The Mountain Lion.* 1947. Harcourt. 1st ed. dj. VG $20.00

STALEY. *Guilds of Florence.* 1906. $50.00

STALLINGS, Laurence. *The Doughboys; Story of the AEF, 1917-1918.* 1963. New York. Ills. 1st ed. maps. 404 pp. $12.50

STAMM, FISCHLER & FRIEDMAN. *Power Skating the Hockey Way.* 1977. Hawthorn Books.Ills. EX $6.00

STAMM, Sara D.B. *Yankee Magazine's Favorite New England Recipes.* 1972. Dublin. Ills. 303 pp. $10.50

STANARD, M.N. *The Story of Virginia's 1st Century.* 1928. Philadelphia. 1st ed. VG $20.00

STANDLEY. *Plants of Glacier National Park.* 1926. 110 pp. 5 color pls. SftCvr. $15.00

STANEK, V.J. *Pictorial Encyclopedia of Insects.* 1972. London. Ills. 544 pp. dj. VG $15.00

STANEK, V.J. *Pictorial Encyclopedia of the Animal Kingdom.* 1970. London. Hamlyn. Ills. dj. EX $15.00

STANISLAVSKI, C. *An Actor Prepares.* 1936. New York. trans. 1st Eng. ed. 295 pp. $35.00

STANISLAVSKY. *My Life in Art.* Moscow. dj. $8.50

STANLEY, Arthur P. *Historical Memorials of Westminster Abbey.* New York. (ca.1882) Ills. ed. 2 vol set. $20.00

STANLEY, Clark. *Life & Adventure of the American Cowboy.* 1897. Providence. wrappers. scarce. VG $150.00

STANLEY. *James Joyce Today.* 1979. Greenwood. reprint. EX $10.00

STANLEY, Father. *E.V. Sumner, Maj. Gen., U.S. Army 1797-1863.* 1969. Borger, TX. 1st ed. inscr. 382 pp. dj. VG $40.00

STANLEY, Father. *Giant in Lilliput, Story of Donaciano Vigil.* 1963. Pampa, TX. inscr. VG $30.00

STANLEY, Father. *The Clovis, New Mexico Story.* 1966. Pampa, TX. Ltd. 1st ed. 1/500. sgn. dj. $45.00

STANLEY, Father. *The Yankee New Mexico Story.* 1964. Ltd. ed. sgn. SftCvr. $7.50

STANLEY, Henry. *How I Found Livingstone.* 1872. Scribner. VG $20.00

STANLEY, Henry. *In Darkest Africa.* 1891. New York. Ills. 2nd Am. ed. 2 vol set. $35.00

STANLEY, Henry. *In Darkest Africa.* 1890. New York. 1st ed. 2 vol set. VG $47.50

STANLEY, Henry. *Through the Dark Continent.* 1878. New York. 2 maps. VG $80.00

STANLEY, Louis. *How to Be a Better Woman Golfer.* 1952. New York. Ills. 127 pp. dj. $4.50

STANLEY, Mrs. H. M. *London Street Arabs.* 1890. London. Ills. $15.00

STANLEY, R.M. *Prelude to Pearl Harbor. War in China, 1937-1941.* 1982. Ills. maps. EX $20.00

STANLEY, William. *Surveying & Leveling Instruments.* 1914. London. Stanley Co. 4th ed. 603 pp. G $35.00

STANLEY & PEARTON. *The International Trade in Arms.* 1972. dj. VG $10.00

STANLEY & SCOTT. *Cattle Feeding in AZ.* 1925. U. of AZ. Ills. 41 pp. SftCvr. $10.00

STANSBURY, Howard. *Exploration & Survey, Great Salt Lake.* 1852. 2 vol set. $200.00

STANTON, Blair Hughes. *Pitcher, V. The Searcher.* 1929. London. Ills. Stanton. Ltd. ed. dj. VG $15.00

STANTON, Edward. *Dreams of the Dead.* 1892. Boston. Lee & Shepard. 1st ed. VG $40.00

STANTON, George S. *Path of Flight.* 1946. Washington. 32 pp. SftCvr. $3.50

STANTON, Shelby L. *Order of Battle.* 1984. Novato, CA. Ills. 620 pp. dj. EX $60.00

STANTON, Shelby L. *Rise & Fall of an American Army.* 1985. Novato, CA. 411 pp. maps. dj. EX $22.50

STANTON, Shelby L. *Vietnam Order of Battle.* 1986. New York. Ills. 396 pp. dj. VG $42.50

STANTON, W. *The Great U.S. Exploring Expedition of 1838-1842.* 1975. Ills. dj. EX $20.00

STANTON. *By Middle Seas.* 1927. photos. VG $45.00

STANTON. *Encyclopedia of Face & Form Reading.* 1919. Philadelphia. Ills. 5th ed. 1203 pp. VG $48.00

STAPLEDON, Olaf. *Last & First Men.* 1931. New York. VG $10.00

STAPLEDON, Olaf. *Star Maker.* 1937. Methuen. 1st ed. VG $35.00

STAPLEDON, Olaf. *To the End of Time.* 1953. VG $12.50

STAPLETON, Marjorie. *Make Things Sailors Made.* 1975. $5.00

STAPLETON, Ruth Carter. *Brother Billy.* 1978. Harper & Row. 1st ed. dj. EX $7.50

STARBUCK, Alexander. *History of Nantucket County, Island, & Town.* 1924. Boston. Ills. 871 pp. index. VG $65.00

STARK, James. *Stark's History & Guide to Bahama Islands.* 1891. Boston. 1st ed. $20.00

STARK, Richard. *The Hunter.* 1st Am. ed. pb. EX $10.00

STARK & ROITER. *Gateways & Caravans.* 1971. New York. 1st ed. dj. EX $12.50

STARKIE, W. *Don Gypsy.* 1936. Murray. Ills. Rackham. 1st ed. dj. VG $20.00

STAROKADOMSKIY, L.M. *Charting the Russian Northern Sea Route.* 1976. Montreal. Ills. dj. EX $15.00

STARR, John. *Lincoln & the Railroads.* 1927. New York. Ills. Ltd. ed. sgn. EX $45.00

STARR, S. Frederick. *Red & Hot: Fate of Jazz in Soviet Union 1917-80.* 1983. New York. 1st ed. dj. G $14.00

STARR. *Decoys of the Atlantic Flyway.* 1974. Ills. 308 pp. dj. EX $35.00

STARRETT, Vincent. *Centaur Bibliography of Stephen Crane.* 1923. New York. Ltd. 1st ed. dj. $50.00

STARRETT, Vincent. *Dead Man Inside.* 1931. New York. 1st ed. dj. VG $27.50

STARRETT, Vincent. *Flame & Dust.* 1924. Chicago. Ltd. 1st ed. $40.00

STARRETT, Vincent. *Murder in Peking.* 1946. New York. 1st ed. sgn. dj. VG $30.00

STARRETT, Vincent. *Seaports in the Moon.* 1928. Doubleday Doran. 1st ed. dj. $50.00

STARRETT, Vincent. *The End of Mr. Garment.* 1932. New York. 1st ed. dj. VG $27.50

STARRETT, Vincent. *The Glorious Mystery.* 1924. Chicago. Covici-McGee. 1st ed. VG $20.00

STARRETT, Vincent. *The Quick & the Dead.* 1965. Sauk City. 1st ed. 145 pp. dj. EX $37.50

STARRETT. *Born in a Bookshop.* 1965. 1st ed. VG $25.00

STARRETT. *Through 150 Years. University of Pittsburgh.* 1937. U. of Pittsburgh. Ltd. 1st ed. $30.00

STATE STREET BANK *The Town Seals of Massachusetts.* 1950. Ills. 2 vol set. $6.50

STATLER, Oliver. *Japanese Inn, a Reconstruction of the Past.* 1961. New York. Ills. dj. VG $25.00

STAUFFER, Frank H. *The Queer, the Quaint, & the Quizzical.* 1882. Philadelphia. $8.50

STAVELEY, G. *Broken Waters Sing.* 1971. Little, Brown. Ills. 283 pp. EX $10.00

STAVRIANOS, L.S. *The Balkans Since 1453.* 1963. New York. Ills. 970 pp. maps. index. $10.00

STAWELL. *Fairies I Have Met.* 1920. London. Ills. Dulac. VG $60.00

STEAD, Christina. *Dark Places of the Heart.* 1966. New York. 1st ed. dj. EX $15.00

STEAD, Christina. *The Puzzleheaded Girl.* 1967. Holt. 1st ed. dj. VG $20.00

STEADMAN, William. *La Tierra Encantada.* 1969. Tucson. dj. VG $15.00

STEARNS, Winfred A. *Labrador, a Sketch of Its People, Indians, Etc.* 1884. Labrador. 1st ed. $10.00

STEBBING, E.P. *The Diary of a Sportsman Naturalist in India.* 1920. London. Lane. Ills. 298 pp. VG $40.00

STEBBINS, Emma. *Charlotte Cushman/Letters & Memories of Her Life.* 1878. Boston. Ills. 1st ed. 308 pp. index. $5.00

STEBBINS, Henry M. *Rifles, a Modern Encyclopedia.* 1958. Harrisburg. Stackpole. Ills. 376 pp. $17.50

STEBBINS. *Selected Oil Sketches by Frederich E. Church.* 1978. Smithsonian Institute Press. $10.00

STECH, V.V. *Rembrandt Etchings & Drawings.* Hamlyn. 2nd ed. 55 pls. dj. VG $45.00

STEDMAN, Charles. *Origin, Progress, & Termination of American War.* 1794. London. 1st ed. 11 fld maps. 2 vol set. $1,250.00

STEEDMAN, Amy. *When They Were Children.* New York. Nelson. Ills. Skelton. $12.50

STEEGMULLER, Francis. *Maupassant, a Lion in the Path.* 1949. New York. Random House. 1st printing. $7.50

STEEL, F.A. *English Fairy Tales.* 1918. New York. Ills. Rackham. 1st Am. ed. VG $60.00

STEELE, James. *The Conveyor.* 1935. New York. International. dj. $45.00

STEELE, John. *Across the Plains in 1850.* 1930. Chicago. Caxton Club. Ltd. ed. 1/350. $80.00

STEELE. *New Descriptive Astronomy.* 1884. Barnes. Ills. EX $5.50

STEELL, W. *Benjamin Franklin of Paris: 1776-1785.* 1928. New York. 1st ed. $10.00

STEEN, Marguerite. *The Sun is My Undoing.* 1942. Philadelphia. 1176 pp. VG $4.00

STEEN, Ralph. *Texas, Story of Progress.* 1942. Steck. $5.50

STEFANSSON, V. *Great Adventures & Explorations.* 1952. New York. revised ed. 788 pp. maps. dj. $12.50

STEFANSSON, V. *Hunters of the Great North.* 1922. Harcourt Brace. Ills. 301 pp. VG $12.50

STEFANSSON, V. *Not By Bread Alone.* 1946. Macmillan. 1st ed. dj. VG $22.50

STEFANSSON, Vilhjalmur. *My Life with the Eskimo.* 1919. New York. Macmillan. 2nd ed. sgn. VG $30.00

STEGNER, W. *One Nation.* 1945. Boston. Look. photos. 340 pp. $5.00

STEGNER, W. *Wolf Willow.* 1963. New York. 2nd ed. dj. VG $15.00

STEGNER, Wallace. *A Shooting Star.* 1961. Viking. 1st ed. dj. VG $15.00

STEGNER, Wallace. *Sound of Mountain Water.* 1969. New York. 1st ed. 286 pp. dj. $25.00

STEGNER, Wallace. *The Big Rock Candy Mountain.* 1943. 1st ed. dj. G $30.00

STEICHEN, Dana. *Beethoven's Beloved.* 1959. Garden City. 1st ed. 4 vol set. dj. EX $125.00

STEICHEN, E. *Sandburg.* 1966. New York. 1st ed. dj. EX $12.50

STEICHEN, E. *The Blue Ghost.* 1947. New York. Harcourt Brace. Ills. 1st ed. $62.50

STEICHEN, E. *The Family of Man.* 1955. New York. 503 photos. dj. VG $6.00

STEICHEN, E. *The Family of Man.* 1955. New York. Deluxe 1st ed. dj. EX $25.00

STEICHEN. *A Life in Photoplay.* 1963. Doubleday. dj. VG $40.00

STEICHEN. *Bitter Years, 1935-1941.* 1962. 27 photo pls. VG $20.00

STEICHEN. *Gardens in Color.* 1944. dj. VG $20.00

STEIG, William. *About People.* 1939. Duell. VG $5.00

STEIG, William. *Agony in the Kindergarten.* 1950. Duell. 1st ed. dj. EX $25.00

STEIG, William. *All Embarrassed.* 1944. Duell. 1st ed. VG $10.00

STEIG, William. *The Lonely Ones.* 1942. Duell. 1st ed. VG $12.50

STEIG, William. *The Rejected Lovers.* 1951. New York. 1st ed. EX $15.00

STEIG, William. *Till Death Do Us Part.* 1947. Duell. 1st ed. inscr. VG $12.50

STEIN, Gertrude. *Brewsie & Willie.* 1946. New York. 1st ed. VG $20.00

STEIN, Gertrude. *First Reader.* 1946. dj. $50.00

STEIN, Gertrude. *Four Saints in Three Acts.* 1946. New York. 1st ed. $25.00

STEIN, Gertrude. *Four Saints.* 1934. Folio Society. 1st ed. VG $25.00

STEIN, Gertrude. *Geography & Plays.* 1922. Boston. 1st ed. 1st issue. $75.00

STEIN, Gertrude. *How to Write.* 1931. Paris. Plain Editions. inscr. $5.50

STEIN, Gertrude. *Ida.* 1941. Random House. 1st ed. $12.50

STEIN, Gertrude. *Lectures in America.* 1935. New York. Random House. 1st ed. $17.50

STEIN, Gertrude. *Portraits & Prayers.* 1934. New York. 1st ed. VG $30.00

STEIN, Gertrude. *The Autobiography of Alice B. Toklas.* 1933. Harcourt. 2nd ed. dj. VG $5.00

STEIN, Gertrude. *Three Lives.* New Directions. dj. VG $15.00

STEIN, Gertrude. *Transition, an Elucidation.* 1927. 16 pp. wrappers. VG $50.00

STEIN, Herman & Cloward, R. *Social Perspectives on Behavior.* 1967. Free Press. $2.00

STEINBECK, J. & Rickets, E.F. *Sea of Cortez.* 1941. Viking. 1st ed. dj. VG $175.00

STEINBECK, John. *A Russian Journal.* 1948. Viking. 1st ed. dj. VG $20.00

STEINBECK, John. *America & Americans.* Ills. Adams. 1st ed. 1st binding. dj. VG $75.00

STEINBECK, John. *Bombs Away.* 1942. Ills. Swope. 1st ed. dj. $20.00

STEINBECK, John. *Burning Bright.* 1950. Viking. 1st ed. dj. EX $40.00

STEINBECK, John. *Cannery Row.* 1945. New York. 1st ed. 208 pp. dj. EX $195.00

STEINBECK, John. *Cannery Row.* 1945. London. 1st Eng. ed. $30.00

STEINBECK, John. *Cup of Gold.* 1936. Covici-Friede. 1st ed. 2nd printing. dj. VG $40.00

STEINBECK, John. *East of Eden.* 1952. New York. Viking. 1st ed. 602 pp. $25.00

STEINBECK, John. *East of Eden.* 1955. Bantam. 1st ed. pb. wrappers. VG $4.00

STEINBECK, John. *Flight.* 1979. Tale Blazer. 1st ed. wrappers. VG $10.00

STEINBECK, John. *In Quest of America.* 1961. 1st ed. wrappers. VG $12.50

STEINBECK, John. *Life in Letters.* Ltd. ed. 1/1000. $50.00

STEINBECK, John. *Of Mice & Men.* 1947. World. 1st ed. dj. VG $17.50

STEINBECK, John. *Of Mice & Men.* 1937. Covici-Friede.1st ed. 2nd issue. VG $15.00

STEINBECK, John. *Pastures of Heaven.* New York. Modern Age. wrappers. G $15.00

STEINBECK, John. *Postitano.* 1959. 1st Eng. ed. wrappers. EX $90.00

STEINBECK, John. *Russian Journal.* 1948. Viking. 1st ed. dj. VG $35.00

STEINBECK, John. *Specches of Adlai Stevenson.* 1952. Random House. 1st ed. wrappers. VG $5.00

STEINBECK, John. *Sweet Thursday.* 1954. London. 1st ed. dj. VG $20.00

STEINBECK, John. *Sweet Thursday.* 1954. New York. 1st ed. 273 pp. $15.00

STEINBECK, John. *The Chrysanthemums.* 1979. Tale Blazer. 1st ed. wrappers. VG $10.00

STEINBECK, John. *The Grapes of Wrath.* 1939. London. 1st Eng. ed. dj. $185.00

STEINBECK, John. *The Grapes of Wrath.* 1940. Heritage. Ills. T.H. Benton. 1st ed. EX $200.00

STEINBECK, John. *The Grapes of Wrath.* 1939. New York. Viking. 1st ed. 1st issue. dj. $300.00

STEINBECK, John. *The Log from the Sea of Cortez.* 1951. Viking. 1st ed. dj. VG $12.50

STEINBECK, John. *The Log from the Sea of Cortez.* 1958. London. Heinemann. 1st Eng. ed. dj. $95.00

STEINBECK, John. *The Long Valley.* 1938. New York. 1st ed. dj. VG $75.00

STEINBECK, John. *The Moon is Down.* 1942. New York. 1st ed. dj. VG $35.00

STEINBECK, John. *The Moon is Down.* 1942. Viking. 2nd ed. VG $12.50

STEINBECK, John. *The Pastures of Heaven.* 1951. Bantam. 1st ed. wrappers. VG $12.50

STEINBECK, John. *The Pearl.* 1961. New York. Viking. ex-lib. 122 pp. $3.00

STEINBECK, John. *The Pearl.* 1947. Viking. Ills. 2nd ed. 122 pp. $10.00

STEINBECK, John. *The Pearl.* 1947. Bantam. 1st ed. wrappers. VG $12.50

STEINBECK, John. *The Red Pony.* 1965. Viking. Ills. Wesley Dennis. 1st ed. $10.00

STEINBECK, John. *The Red Pony.* 1945. Viking. Ills. Dennis. 1st ed. boxed. $25.00

STEINBECK, John. *The Short Novels of John Steinbeck.* 1953. New York. Viking. 407 pp. dj. $5.00

STEINBECK, John. *The Short Reign of Pippin IV.* 1957. New York. Viking. Ills. 1st ed. EX $40.00

STEINBECK, John. *The Short Reign of Pippin.* 1957. London. 1st ed. VG $40.00

STEINBECK, John. *The Wayward Bus.* 1947. New York. Viking. 312 pp. dj. VG $20.00

STEINBECK, John. *The Winter of Our Discontent.* 1961. Viking. 2nd ed. dj. $12.50

STEINBECK, John. *The Winter of Our Discontent.* 1961. New York. Viking. 1st ed. 311 pp. $17.50

STEINBECK, John. *The Winter of Our Discontent.* 1961. London. Heinemann. 1st ed. dj. VG $45.00

STEINBECK, John. *Their Blood Is Strong.* 1938. Lubin Society. VG $200.00

STEINBECK, John. *To a God Unknown.* 1933. New York. Ballou. dj. VG $450.00

STEINBECK, John. *Tortilla Flat.* 1947. New York. 1st ed. G $75.00

STEINBERG, Alfred. *Sam Johnson's Boy.* 1968. 1st ed. 871 pp. dj. $85.00

STEINBERG, Rafael. *The Cooking of Japan.* 1969. New York. Time Life. Ills. 208 pp. $10.00

STEINBERG, Saul. *The Passport.* 1954. Harper. 1st ed. dj. VG $10.00

STEINDLER, R.A. *Modern ABC's of Guns.* 1965. Harrisburg. Stackpole. Ills. 191 pp. dj. $7.50

STEINER, M.J. *Inside Pan-Arabia. An Incisive Analysis.* 1947. G $6.50

STEINER, Stan. *Diary & Paintings of Bonita Wa Wa Calachaw Nunez.* 1980. New York. Ills. 1st ed. 243 pp. $9.00

STEINER, Stan. *The Ranchers. A Book of Generations.* 1980. New York. 1st ed. dj. VG $10.00

STEINER. *A Point of View.* 1978. Wesleyan U. Press. 1st ed. $10.00

STELOFF, Frances. *Journal of Modern Literature.* 1975. Ills. 150 pp. index. wrappers. $20.00

STEMMONS. *Cemetery Record Compendium.* 1979. EX $30.00

STENDHAL. *The Red & the Black.* 1947. Heritage Press. boxed EX $7.50

STENHOUSE, T.B.H. *Rocky Mountain Saints.* 1873. New York. 1st ed. EX $75.00

STEPHENS, A. *The Reviewers Reviewed.* 1872. ex-lib. $22.50

STEPHENS, A. *The War Between the States.* 1868-70. ex-lib. 2 vol set. $32.50

STEPHENS, Ann S. *Malaeska: Indian Wife of the White Hunter.* 1860. New York. Ltd. 1st ed. EX $450.00

STEPHENS, C. Ralph. *Correspondence of Flannery O'Connor & B. Cheneys.* 1986. U. Press Miss. 1st ed. dj. VG $25.00

STEPHENS, C.A. *Stories of My Home Folks.* 1926. EX $15.00

STEPHENS, Hiram B. *Jacques Cartier & His Four Voyages.* 1890. Montreal. $75.00

STEPHENS, James. *Etched in Moonlight.* 1928. New York. Macmillan. reprint ed. sgn. $15.00

STEPHENS, James. *Hill of Vision.* 1912. Dublin. 1st ed. $25.00

STEPHENS, James. *In the Land of Youth.* 1924. New York. Macmillan. 1st Am. ed. $35.00

STEPHENS, James. *Irish Fairy Tales.* 1920. London. Ills. Rackham. 16 color pls. $200.00

STEPHENS, James. *Irish Fairy Tales.* 1924. London. Ills. Rackham. 318 pp. $65.00

STEPHENS, James. *Irish Fairy Tales.* 1920. New York. Ills. Rackham. 1st Am. ed. VG $75.00

STEPHENS, James. *The Crock of Gold.* 1926. New York. Ills. T. MacKenzie. 1st ed. $30.00

STEPHENS, James. *The Demi-Gods.* 1914. London. 1st ed. sgn. VG $40.00

STEPHENS, James. *The Insurrection in Dublin.* 1916. New York. 1st Am. ed. VG $20.00

STEPHENS, James. *Theme & Variations.* 1930. Macmillan. 1st ed. $12.50

STEPHENS, John L. *Incidents of Travel in Central America.* 1841. New York. G $95.00

STEPHENS. *Rifle Marksmanship.* 1941. Samworth. 217 pp. $6.50

STEPHENSON, George & Robert. *The Railway Revolution.* 1960. 356 pp. $3.85

STEPHENSON, J.B. *From Old Stencils to Silk Screening.* 1953. New York. dj. VG $20.00

STEPHENSON. *Pulp & Paper Manufacture.* 1950. McGraw Hill. 4 vol set. VG $47.50

STEPP, J.W. & Hill, I.W. *Mirror of War.* 1961. Ills. 378 pp. VG $10.00

STERLING, Claire. *The Masaryk Case.* 1969. NY. Harper. 366 pp. dj. VG $4.50

STERLING, Dorothy. *Captain of the Planter.* 1958. $6.50

STERLING, George. *The Caged Eagle.* 1916. San Francisco. 1st ed. VG $25.00

STERLING, George. *The House of Orchids.* 1911. San Francisco. 1st ed. sgn. VG $45.00

STERLING, Rod. *Patterns.* 1957. New York. Simon & Schuster. 1st ed. dj. $35.00

STERLING, Sara Hawks. *A Lady of King Arthur's Court.* 1907. Jacobs. Ills. Clara E. Peck. 1st ed. $40.00

STERLING. *Great French Paintings in the Hermitage.* Abrams. VG $45.00

STERN. *Young Ward's Diary.* 1935. New York. 1st ed. VG $25.00

STERN, Edward. *History of Free Franking of Mail in U.S.* 1936. New York. Ltd. ed. 1/100. sgn. $75.00

STERN, F.M. *The Citizen Army. Key to Defense in Atomic Age.* 1957. dj. VG $10.00

STERN, G.B. *Bouquet.* 1927. New York. Knopf. photos. 263 pp. VG $3.50

STERN, Geraldine. *Israel Woman.* 1974. 1st ed. sgn. dj. VG $10.00

STERN, Harold P. *Ukiyo-e Painting.* 1973. Ills. 319 pp. scarce. $85.00

STERN, Madeleine. *Imprints on His.* 1956. Indiana U. 1st ed. dj. $10.00

STERN, Philip Van Doren. *Prehistoric Europe Stone Age Man to Early Greeks.* 1969. Norton. Ills. 1st ed. 383 pp. dj. VG $10.00

STERN, Philip Van Doren. *Robert E. Lee. The Man & Soldier.* 1963. Ills. 256 pp. $12.50

STERN, Philip Van Doren. *The Annotated Uncle Tom's Cabin.* 1964. New York. dj. $15.00

STERN, Philip Van Doren. *The Confederate Navy.* 1962. Ills. 256 pp. $12.50

STERN, Philip Van Doren. *The Man Who Killed Lincoln.* 1939. G $10.00

STERN, Philip Van Doren. *The Moonlight Traveler.* 1943. New York. Doubleday. 1st ed. dj. EX $15.00

STERN. *Historical Imprint.* New York. 1st ed. dj. VG $15.00

STERNE, Laurence. *A Sentimental Journey Through France & Italy.* 1910. London. Ills. Ltd. ed. sgn. VG $175.00

STERNE, Laurence. *The Life & Opinions of Tristram Shady.* 1935. Heritage. boxed. EX $7.50

STERNE, Simon. *Constitutional History/Political Development U.S.* 1888. London. Putnam. revised ed. VG $15.00

STERNE. *The Passionate Eye/Life of William V. Valentier.* 1980. Wayne. $8.00

STERNER, Richard. *The Negro's Share.* 1943. New York. Harper. 433 pp. $5.00

STERRY, Iveagh H. & Garrigus. *They Found a Way: Connecticut's Restless People.* 1938. Stephen Daye Press. dj. VG $17.50

STETON, Ernest Thompson. *Rolf in the Woods.* 1911. Grosset & Dunlap. 437 pp. $4.50

STETTNER, L. *History of the Nude in American Photography.* 1966. Greenwich. 1st ed. wrappers. EX $15.00

STEVENS, Abel. *A Compendious History of American Methodism.* 1889. New York. Hunt & Eaton. 608 pp. pls. $15.00

STEVENS, Abel. *Centenary of American Methodism.* 1866. New York. G $10.00

STEVENS, Abel. *History of American Methodism.* 1867. New York. 1st ed. 11 pls. G $15.00

STEVENS, Charles Emery. *A History of Anthony Burns.* 1856. Boston. Jewett. 1st ed. 295 pp. $175.00

STEVENS, D.G. *1st 100 Years in American Baptist Public Society.* 1924. Philadelphia. Ills. VG $15.00

STEVENS, E. *This is Russia.* 1950. 200 pp. dj. $10.00

STEVENS. *Virginia House Tour.* 1964. dj. VG $30.00

STEVENS, Francis. *The Heads of Cerberus.* 1952. Reading, PA. Polaris Press. Ltd. ed. dj. $85.00

STEVENS, Frank. *Hawaiian Fungi.* 1925. Honolulu. 1st ed. stiff wrappers. $12.50

STEVENS, G.A. *Garden Flowers in Color.* 1936. New York. EX $18.00

STEVENS, George W. *The King & the Harper, Together with Other Poems.* 1901. Toledo. $12.50

STEVENS, Isaac I. *Campaigns of the Rio Grande & of Mexico.* 1851. New York. original printed wrappers. $300.00

STEVENS, J.L. *Riches & Marvels of Hawaii.* 1900. Philadelphia. Edgewood. 354 pp. 48 pls. $12.50

STEVENS, James. *Homer in the Sagebrush.* 1928. Knopf. VG $10.00

STEVENS, R. *Laggard.* 1953. London. Ills. 1st ed. dj. EX $12.50

STEVENS, R. *The Taming of Genghis.* 1975. Falconiformes. 127 pp. VG $15.00

STEVENS, W.B. *Victorious Mountaineer.* 1943. 1st ed. dj. VG $15.00

STEVENS, W.G. *Thirteen Months in the Rebel Army.* 1862. New York. $40.00

STEVENS, Walter B. *Centennial History of Missouri.* 1921. Chicago. 2 vol set. VG $50.00

STEVENS, William B. *History of the 50th Regiment M.V.M.* 1907. Ills. 1st ed. $55.00

STEVENS & MARKEY. *The Colonel's Lady.* 1948. Chicago. Ltd. ed. 1/300. VG $10.00

STEVENS & WESTCOTT. *A History of Sea Power.* 1947. maps. diagrams. G $10.00

STEVENS. *Clementina's Highwayman.* 1907. Grosset & Dunlap. Ills. $4.50

STEVENS. *From Capetown to Ladysmith.* 1900. New York. VG $10.00

STEVENSON, Allan. *Paper as Bibliographical Evidence.* 1962. London. inscr. wrappers. EX $25.00

STEVENSON, D.E. *Gerald & Elizabeth.* 1969. New York. 1st ed. dj. EX $10.00

STEVENSON, E. *Lafcadio Hearn.* 1961. $7.50

STEVENSON, J. *The Sama Veda.* 1842. London. 283 pp. G $45.00

STEVENSON, Philip. *The Gospel According to St. Luke's* 1931. New York. Longmans. 1st ed. dj. EX $45.00

STEVENSON, R. & Osborne, L. *The Wrecker.* 1892. London. $15.00

STEVENSON, R. Randolph. *Southern Side of Andersonville Prison.* 1876. VG $65.00

STEVENSON, Robert Lewis. *Across the Plains.* 1892. London. 1st ed. sgn. boxed. $125.00

STEVENSON, Robert Lewis. *Black Arrow.* 1942. Scribner. Ills. N.C. Wyeth. VG $15.00

STEVENSON, Robert Lewis. *St. Ives.* 1920. $5.00

STEVENSON, Robert Louis. *A Child's Garden of Verses.* 1940. Akron. Ills. Fern Bisel Peat. $35.00

STEVENSON, Robert Louis. *A Child's Garden of Verses.* 1934. Chicago. 64 pp. $3.50

STEVENSON, Robert Louis. *A Child's Garden of Verses.* 1929. New York. Ills. Jessie Wilcox Smith. VG $50.00

STEVENSON, Robert Louis. *A Child's Garden of Verses.* 1905. New York. Scribner. Ills. J.W. Smith. VG $22.50

STEVENSON, Robert Louis. *A Child's Garden of Verses.* 1926. New York. Sears & Co. Ills. Eva Noe. VG $17.50

STEVENSON, Robert Louis. *A Child's Garden of Verses.* 1930. Scribner. Ills. Jessie Wilcox Smith. VG $25.00

STEVENSON, Robert Louis. *A Child's Garden of Verses.* 1944. Ltd. Ed. Club. Ills. Roger Duvoisin. EX $25.00

STEVENSON, Robert Louis. *A Child's Garden of Verses.* 1929. New York. Platt & Munk. Ills. Eulalie. $25.00

STEVENSON, Robert Louis. *A Child's Garden of Verses.* 1932. New York. Platt & Munk. Ills. dj. EX $12.50

STEVENSON, Robert Louis. *A Child's Garden of Verses.* 1888. Scribner. 1st Am. ed. $15.00

STEVENSON, Robert Louis. *A Lodging for the Night.* 1923. Grolier Club. 1st ed. $20.00

STEVENSON, Robert Louis. *Ballads.* 1890. London. 1st Eng. ed. VG $35.00

STEVENSON, Robert Louis. *Catronia. A Sequel to Kidnapped.* 1893. London. 1st ed. VG $40.00

STEVENSON, Robert Louis. *Children's Garden of Verses.* 1961. New York. Platt & Munk. Ills. Eulalie. $15.00

STEVENSON, Robert Louis. *Complete Works of Robert Louis Stevenson.* 1903. Scribner. 26 vol set. tan cloth. $150.00

STEVENSON, Robert Louis. *David Balfour.* 1893. New York. 1st Am. ed. G $35.00

STEVENSON, Robert Louis. *Dr. Jekyll & Mr. Hyde.* 1886. Scribner. Ltd. ed. 1/1250. $350.00

STEVENSON, Robert Louis. *Edinburgh.* 1912. New York. Scribner. Ills. 208 pp. VG $35.00

STEVENSON, Robert Louis. *Island Night's Entertainment.* 1917. ex-lib. G $10.00

STEVENSON, Robert Louis. *Kidnapped.* 1930. London. Ills. Rowland Hilder. 1st ed. $30.00

STEVENSON, Robert Louis. *Kidnapped.* 1925. Philadelphia. Winston. Ills. Goodwin. VG $6.50

STEVENSON, Robert Louis. *Kidnapped.* Philadelphia. Ills. Eleanor Plaisted Abbott. $20.00

STEVENSON, Robert Louis. *Letters of Robert Louis Stevenson.* 1899. Scribner. 2 vol set. $30.00

STEVENSON, Robert Louis. *Letters to His Family & Friends.* 1899. London. 2 vol set. EX $30.00

STEVENSON, Robert Louis. *Moral Emblems.* 1921. Scribner. 1st ed. dj. $20.00

STEVENSON, Robert Louis. *More New Arabian Night. 2nd Series. The Dynamiter.* 1885. London. Longman Green. 207 pp. $75.00

STEVENSON, Robert Louis. *New Poems.* 1918. London. Chatto & Windus. $20.00

STEVENSON, Robert Louis. *Pan's Pipes.* 1910. Boston. Riverside. Ltd. ed. EX $50.00

STEVENSON, Robert Louis. *Poems.* 1913. London. Ltd. ed. 1/500. VG $45.00

STEVENSON, Robert Louis. *Silverado Squatters.* 1962. Grabhorn. VG $35.00

STEVENSON, Robert Louis. *The Merry Men.* 1887. London. 1st ed. VG $50.00

STEVENSON, Robert Louis. *The Wrecker.* 1906. New York. Ills. 553 pp. $5.00

STEVENSON, Robert Louis. *Treasure Island.* 1979. New York. Ills. Dulac. 1st Abaris ed. $25.00

STEVENSON, Robert Louis. *Treasure Island.* New York. World. no date. $3.00

STEVENSON, Robert Louis. *Treasure Island.* Garden City. no date. Ills. Dulac. $17.50

STEVENSON, Robert Louis. *Treasure Island.* 1917. New York. Ills. Wal Paget. 1st ed. VG $8.00

STEVENSON, Robert Louis. *Treasure Island.* Macmillan. Ills. Goble. 312 pp. dj. $30.00

STEVENSON, Robert Louis. *Treasure Island.* 1900. New York. Ills. Wal Paget. $20.00

STEVENSON, Robert Louis. *Treasure Island.* 1883. Cassell. 1st ed. green cloth. $450.00

STEVENSON, Robert Louis. *Treasure Island.* 1941. New York. Ltd. Ed. Club. Ills. Wilson. $60.00

STEVENSON, Robert Louis. *Underwoods.* London. 1st Eng. ed. VG $25.00

STEVENSON, Robert Louis. *Vailima Letters.* 1895. Chicago. 1st ed. 2 vol set. VG $50.00

STEVENSON, Robert Louis. *Weir of Hermiston.* 1896. London. 1st ed. VG $35.00

STEVENSON, Robert Louis. *Will o' the Mill.* 1901. New York. Roycroft. 53 pp. $22.50

STEVENSON, Robert. *Spanish Music in the Age of Columbus.* 1979. Westport, CT. Hyperion Press. EX $30.00

STEVENSON, W. *A Man Called Intrepid.* 1976. Ills. dj. EX $12.50

STEVENSON, W. *The Ghosts of Africa.* 1980. Harcourt. 1st ed. dj. VG $6.00

STEVENSON. *In the South Seas.* 1919. New York. 591 pp. $5.00

STEVERS & PENDLEBURY. *Sea Lanes. Man's Conquest of the Ocean.* 1935. Ills. maps. VG $10.00

STEWARD, J.W. *The Snakes of Europe.* 1971. Assoc. U. Pr. Ills. 1st Am. ed. 238 pp. dj. $10.00

STEWARD, Mary Norton. *Elmira, Girl Who Loved Poe.* 1966. 1st Am. ed. dj. EX $20.00

STEWART, A. *The Battle for Leyte Gulf.* 1979. London. Ills. maps. dj. EX $15.00

STEWART, Alexander. *Elements of Gaelic Grammar.* 1812. Edinburgh. 2nd ed. $45.00

STEWART, Basil. *On Collecting Japanese Colour Prints.* 1917. Ills. 124 pp. out of print. G $85.00

STEWART, Basil. *Subjects Portrayed in Japanese Colour Prints.* 1973. reprint. Ills. 382 pp. rare. $175.00

STEWART, Charles D. *Partners of Providence.* 1907. New York. Ills. C.J. Taylor. 1st ed. $12.50

STEWART, Donald Ogden. *Mr. & Mrs. Haddock in Paris, France.* 1926. Harper. Ills. Herb Roth. 1st ed. $12.50

STEWART, George R. *Earth Abides.* 1949. New York. 1st ed. sgn. VG $30.00

STEWART, George R. *Names on the Land.* 1945. New York. Random House. 1st printing. $16.00

STEWART, George R. *U.S. 40-Cross Section of the U.S. of America.* 1953. Boston. Houghton Mifflin. Ills. dj. $4.50

STEWART, George. *Names on the Land.* 1945. EX $6.00

STEWART, J. *Winds in the Woods, Story of John Muir.* 1975. Westminster. Ills. 126 pp. dj. EX $10.00

STEWART, J. & Hennessy, E.F. *Orchids of Africa.* 1981. Macmillan. Ills. 159 pp. dj. EX $45.00

STEWART, J.I.M. *Young Pattullo.* 1975. London. Gollancz. 1st ed. dj. $20.00

STEWART, J.T. *Indiana Co., PA; Her People, Past & Present.* 1913. Chicago. J.H. Bears Co. 2 vol set. G $48.00

STEWART, Jane L. *A Campfire Girls First Council Fire.* 1914. Saalfield. Campfire Girl Series, Vol. I. $4.50

STEWART, Jesse. *Taps for Private Tussie.* 1943. Book of Month Club. dj. $7.00

STEWART, M.M. *Amphibians of Malawi.* 1967. NY State U. Ills. 163 pp. dj. EX $15.00

STEWART, Mary. *This Wicked Day.* 1983. Morrow. proof copy. wrappers. VG $12.50

STEWART, Robert. *American Farmer's Horse Book.* 1867. Cincinnati. Ills. 600 pp. $35.00

STEWART. *Elements of the Philosophy of the Human Mind.* 1821. $35.00

STEWARTON. *Secret History of Court & Cabinet of St. Cloud.* 1895. London. Ills. Ltd. ed. 2 vol set. VG $100.00

STICK, David. *Graveyard of the Atlantic.* 1976. $12.50

STIDGER, William L. *Edwin Markham.* 1933. New York. Abingdon. sgn. $15.00

STIEGLITZ, Alfred. *America & Alfred Stieglitz.* 1934. 1st ed. EX $60.00

STIERI, Emanuele. *Aircraft Instruments.* 1943. New York. Ills. 312 pp. dj. $20.00

STIERLIN. *Art of the Maya.* 1981. Rizzoli. folio. $25.00

STILES, Henry Reed. *Bundling: Its Origins, Progress, & Decline.* Mt. Vernon, NY. Ills. Roth. 88 pp. $20.00

STILLMAN, Irwin & Baker. *Doctor's Quick Inches Off Diet.* 1969. Englewood Cliffs. 311 pp. $5.00

STILLSON, B. *Wings, Insects, Birds, Men.* 1954. dj. G $6.00

STILWELL, Joseph W. *The Stilwell Papers.* 1948. New York. 357 pp. dj. $10.00

STIMSON, E.J. *King Noanett.* 1896. Boston/NY. Wolf. Ills. map. G $17.50

STINE, Thomas Ostenson. *Scandinavians on Pacific, Puget Sound.* 1900. Seattle. Denny-Coryell. Ills. 1st ed. $85.00

STIRLING, John. *Fifty Years with the Rod.* 1929. VG $50.00

STIRLING, M.W. *Stone Monuments of Southern Mexico.* 1943. wrappers. VG $15.00

STIX, H. & Abbott, R.T. *The Shell.* 1978. Abrams. Ills. dj. EX $15.00

STOBART, Mrs. St. Clair. *Torchbearers of Spiritualism.* 1926. New York. 231 pp. dj. VG $27.50

STOBO, Robert. *Memoirs Major Robert Stobo of Virginia Regiment.* 1854. Pittsburgh. 1st Am. ed. 92 pp. $225.00

STOCKBRIDGE & PERRY. *Florida in the Making.* 1926. de Bower Pub. Ills. 351 pp. EX $10.00

STOCKBRIDGE. *So This Is Florida.* 1938. $7.50

STOCKHAM, Alice B. *Tokology. A Book for Every Woman.* 1884. Chicago. 301 pp. $17.50

STOCKING, C. & Totheroh, W.W. *The Business Man of Syria.* 1925. Chicago. 10th ed. index. $10.00

STOCKTON, Frank R. *Buccaneers & Pirates of Our Coasts.* 1926. Ills. G $6.00

STOCKTON, Frank R. *Buccaneers & Pirates of Our Coasts.* 1913. New York. Ills. VG $10.00

STOCKTON, Frank R. *Rudder Grange.* 1885. New York. Ills. A.B. Frost. $15.00

STOCKTON, Frank R. *Rudder Grange.* 1879. NY. Scribner. 1st ed. 1st issue. VG $45.00

STOCKTON, Frank R. *Story Teller's Pack.* 1897. New York. Ills Newell. 1st ed. VG $25.00

STOCKTON, Frank R. *Tales Out of School.* 1876. rebound. G $65.00

STOCKTON, Frank R. *The Bee-Man of Orn.* 1964. Winston. Ills. Sendak. 1st ed. VG $30.00

STOCKTON, Frank R. *The Christmas Wreck & Other Stories.* 1886. New York. Scribner. 1st ed. 242 pp. $10.00

STOCKTON, Frank R. *The Great Stone of Sardis.* 1898. New York. Harper. Ills. Newell. 1st ed. $40.00

STOCKTON, Frank R. *The Lady or the Tiger? & Other Stories.* 1899. New York. Scribner. 201 pp. $3.00

STOCKTON, Frank R. *The Late Mrs. Null.* 1886. New York. Scribner. 1st ed. $35.00

STODDARD, Amos. *Sketches, Historical, & Descriptive of Louisiana.* 1812. Philadelphia. 1st ed. 488 pp. $250.00

STODDARD, Anne. *Bingo Is My Name.* 1931. NY/London. Ills. Berta & Elmer Hader. $30.00

STODDARD, Henry L. *As I Knew Them. Presidents & Politics.* 1927. NY/London. Ills. 1st ed. 571 pp. index. $15.00

STODDARD, Henry L. *It Costs to Be President.* 1938. NY/London. 1st ed. 340 pp. index. $7.50

STODDARD, Henry L. *Presidential Sweepstakes.* 1948. New York. Putnam. exlib. 224 pp. VG $3.50

STODDARD, J.L. *Red Letter Days Abroad.* 1883. Boston. $15.00

STODDARD, Lothrop. *The Rising Tide of Color.* 1922. New York. Scribner. 320 pp. $3.50

STODDARD, William O. *The Lone Ranger at the Haunted Gulch.* 1941. New York. Grosset & Dunlap. 216 pp. $4.50

STODDARD, William O. *The Red Mustang.* 1918. New York. Harper. 246 pp. dj. $4.50

STODDARD. *Portfolio of Photographs of Famous Scenes.* Chicago. (ca.1895) 300 full pp. pls. $30.00

STODDARD. *The Works of Washington Irving with His Life.* 1881. Collier. $7.50

STOEVING. *The Art of Violin-Bowing.* London. (ca.1900) 171 pp. $20.00

STOFF, Joshua. *Dirigible.* 1985. New York. Ills. 106 pp. dj. EX $13.00

STOKER, Bram. *Dracula.* 1965. Ltd. Ed. Club. Ills. Hoffman. sgn. slipcase. $85.00

STOKER, Bram. *Dracula's Guest & Other Weird Stories.* London. Routledge. 11th impression. $20.00

STOKER, Bram. *Personal Reminiscences of Henry Irving.* 1906. New York. Ills. 1st ed. 2 vol set. VG $45.00

STOKER, Bram. *The Jewel of the Seven Stars.* 1904. New York. Harper. 1st Am. ed. VG $15.00

STOKES, D.W. *A Guide to the Behavior of Common Birds.* 1979. Little, Brown. Ills. Landsdowne. 1st ed. sgn. $15.00

STOKES. *How to Manage a Restaurant.* 1953. $10.00

STOKES. *Savannah.* 1951. 1st ed. dj. EX $15.00

STOKLEY, C.H. *African Camera Hunts.* 1948. London. Country Life. Ills. 1st ed. EX $35.00

STONE, A.A. & Gulvin, H.E. *Machines for Power Farming.* 1957. New York. Wiley & Sons. TB. G. $4.50

STONE, Amy Wentworth. *Going on Nine.* 1939. Boston. Ills. E. Wilkin. 1st ed. $20.00

STONE, Edward Durell. *Evolution of an Architect.* 1962. New York. Ills. 1st ed. dj. VG $45.00

STONE, Edward L. *A Book Lover's Bouquet.* 1931. New York. Rudge. Ltd. ed. 1/525. EX $35.00

STONE, Grace. *Bitter Tea of General Yen.* 1930. Indianapolis. Ills. B. MacFarlane. dj. VG $8.50

STONE, Herbert L. *The America's Cup Races.* 1930. Ills. new revised ed. VG $20.00

STONE, Horatio. *Freedom.* 1864. 1st ed. inscr. 81 pp. scarce. $35.00

STONE, I.F. *The Hidden Story of the Korean War.* 1952. dj. G $12.50

STONE, Irving. *Clarence Darrow for the Defense.* 1941. New York. Doubleday. 570 pp. $5.00

STONE, Irving. *Immortal Wife.* 1945. New York. Doubleday. 456 pp. VG $4.50

STONE, Irving. *Immortal Wife.* 1944. New York. 1st ed. sgn. G $12.50

STONE, Irving. *Love is Eternal.* 1954. New York. Doubleday. 468 pp. $3.00

STONE, Irving. *Men to Match My Mountains: Opening of Far West.* 1956. 1st ed. dj. VG $10.00

STONE, Irving. *Sailor on Horseback.* 1947. 1st ed. sgn. dj. VG $15.00

STONE, Irving. *The President's Lady.* 1951. 278 pp. worn dj. book EX $2.00

STONE, Isabel. *The City of 100 Gates.* 1942. Boston. Humphries. 1st ed. dj. EX $17.50

STONE, Leslie. *Out of the Void.* 1967. 1st ed. dj. EX $7.50

STONE, Lydia. *Pink Donkey Brown.* 1933. Rand McNally. Ills. Mary Dwyer. 64 pp. VG $4.50

STONE, Robert. *A Flag for Sunrise.* 1981. 1st Am. ed. dj. VG $15.00

STONE, Robert. *A Flag for Sunrise.* 1981. Knopf. 1st ed. dj. VG $15.00

STONE, Robert. *A Hall of Mirrors.* 1967. Boston. Houghton Mifflin. 1st ed. VG $75.00

STONE, Robert. *Hall of Mirrors.* 1967. 1st Am. ed. dj. $110.00

STONE, Robert. *Dog Soldiers.* 1974. Houghton. 1st ed. dj. VG $45.00

STONE, William L. *Life & Times of Sa-Go-Ye-Wat-Ha, or Red Jacket.* 1970. Scholarly Press. VG $15.00

STONE, William L. *Life & Times of Sa-Go-Ye-Wat-Ha, or Red Jacket.* 1866. Albany. J. Munsell. Ltd. ed. 1/75 $250.00

STONE, William L. *Life & Times of Sa-Go-Ye-Wat-Ha, or Red Jacket.* 1866. Albany. Ills. Ltd. ed. 1/550. index. G $95.00

STONE, William S. *The Ship of Flame.* 1945. New York. Ills. Nicolas Mordvinoff. dj. $15.00

STONE, William. *Life of Joseph Brant. Thayendanegea.* 1838. New York. 1st ed. 2 vol set. VG $150.00

STONE, Witmer & Cram, William. *American Animals: Popular Guide to Mammals.* 1903. New York. Ills. A.R. Dugmore. G $30.00

STONE, Witmer. *Bird Studies at Old Cape May.* 1937. Philadelphia. Ltd. ed. 2 vol set. VG $110.00

STONE & BLANCHARD. *Cruising Guide to Chesapeake.* 1973. dj. VG $7.50

STONEHOUSE, John Harrison. *Green Leaves.* 1931. London. Ills. revised ed. sgn. $85.00

STONER, Carol. *Stocking Up.* 1973. Emmaus, PA. Rodale. Ills. 351 pp. dj. $8.50

STONESTREET, Elizabeth Wilson. *Ancestors-Descendants of Isaac & Elizabeth Wilson.* 1979. Viennna, WV. Ills. 110 pp. wrappers. $12.50

STONG, Phil. *Horses & Americana.* 1939. New York. Ltd. ed. 1/250. sgn. VG $45.00

STOOKESBERRY, Sina Ethel. *Given Gold.* 1913. Carrolton, OH. 78 pp. $12.50

STOPPARD, Tom. *The Fifteen Minute Hamlet.* 1976. London. 1st ed. sgn. $55.00

STOPPARD, Tom. *Travesties.* 1975. London. Faber. 1st ed. dj. VG $25.00

STORER, T.I. & Tevis, L.P. *California Grizzly.* 1978. NB U. Press. Ills. 335 pp. EX $25.00

STOREY, David. *The Sporting Life.* 1960. New York. 1st Am. ed. dj. VG $12.50

STOREY, S. *To Golden Land.* 1889. London. 1st ed. map. photos. VG $35.00

STOTT, Raymond. *Maughamania. A Bibliography of Works of Maugham.* 1950. Doubleday. 1st ed. dj. $12.50

STOUFFER, Samuel. *Communism, Conformity, & Civil Liberties.* 1955. New York. Doubleday. 278 pp. dj. $3.50

STOUT, G. *The Shorebirds of North America.* 1967. New York. Ills. R.V. Clem. folio. dj. $115.00

STOUT, N.R. *The Royal Navy in America, 1760-1775.* 1973. dj. VG $20.00

STOUT, Rex. *A Family Affair.* 1975. New York. Viking. 1st ed. dj. VG $25.00

STOUT, Rex. *Death of a Doxy.* 1966. New York. dj. EX $35.00

STOUT, Rex. *In the Best Families.* 1950. 1st ed. dj. EX $45.00

STOUT, Rex. *The Doorbell Rang.* 1965. New York. Viking. 1st ed. dj. VG $35.00

STOUT, Rex. *The Illustrious Dunderheads.* 1942. New York. Knopf. 1st ed. EX $25.00

STOUT, Rex. *The Red Box.* 1937. New York. Farrar. 1st ed. VG $60.00

STOUT, Rex. *The Silent Speaker.* 1946. New York. Viking. 1st ed. dj. EX $45.00

STOUT, Rex. *Three for the Chair.* 1957. London. 1st ed. dj. VG $85.00

STOUT, Ruth & Rich. *No Work Garden Book.* 1971. Rodale, PA. Ills. 1st ed. dj. VG $12.00

STOUT, Ruth. *How to Have a Green Thumb Without Aching Back.* 1955. New York. 164 pp. dj. G. $4.00

STOUT, W.W. *Bullets by the Billion.* 1946. Ills. G $7.50

STOUT & GREENFIELD, eds. *Rue Morgue.* 1946. 1st Am. ed. dj. VG $25.00

STOWE, Charles Edward. *The Life of Harriet Beecher Stowe.* 1889. Boston. Ills. 1st ed. $15.00

STOWE, Harriet Beecher. *A Key to Uncle Tom's Cabin.* 1853. Boston. 1st ed. VG $42.50

STOWE, Harriet Beecher. *Lady Byron Vindicated.* 1870. Boston. 1st ed. 482 pp. $15.00

STOWE, Harriet Beecher. *Men of Our Times.* 1868. Ills. 574 pp. $11.50

STOWE, Harriet Beecher. *Tale of Great Dismal Swamp.* 1956. Boston. Phillips. 2 vol set. VG $50.00

STOWE, Harriet Beecher. *The Minister's Wooing.* 1859. New York. 578 pp. $10.00

STOWE, Harriet Beecher. *Uncle Sam's Emancipation.* 1853. Philadelphia. Hazard. VG $65.00

STOWE, Harriet Beecher. *We & Our Neighbors.* 1875. VG $25.00

STOWE, Lyman E. *My Wife Nellie & I.* 1895. Detroit. 130 pp. wrappers. $12.50

STOWELL, M.F.H. & Eric, F. *Nursery Games in Prose & Verse.* London/NY. Ills. Christie & Silver. VG $50.00

STRABOLGI, Lord. *The Conquest of Italy.* 1944. London. Ills. G $12.50

STRACHEY, Lytton. *Elizabeth & Essex.* 1928. New York. 1st ed. sgn. boxed. $30.00

STRACHEY, Lytton. *Queen Victoria.* 1921. New York. Harcourt Brace. photos. $5.00

STRACHEY, Lytton. *The Really Interesting Question & Other Papers.* 1973. New York. 1st ed. dj. VG $15.00

STRAHAN. *Art Truimphs.* 1882. New York. Ills. folio. $35.00

STRAHAN. *Etudes in Modern French Art.* 1882. New York. $40.00

STRAHORN, Robert. *To the Rockies & Beyond.* 1878. Omaha. fld map. $250.00

STRAIGHT, M. *Make This the Last War. Future of United Nations.* 1943. G $5.00

STRAIT, Raymond & Robinson, T. *Lanza: His Tragic Life.* 1980. Englewood Cliffs. 1st ed. dj. $25.00

STRAND, Paul. *The Years 1915-1946. The Years 1950-1968.* 1971. Aperture. Ltd. ed. 1/100. sgn. slipcase. $70.00

STRANGE, Edward Fairbrother. *Japanese Illustration. A History of Arts.* 1904. Ills. 155 pp. G $95.00

STRANGE, Edward Fairbrother. *The Colour Prints of Hiroshige.* 1925. Cassel & Co. 52 pls. 205 pp. $155.00

STRANGE, Michael. *Miscellaneous Poems.* 1916. New York. 101 pp. $7.50

STRANGE, Michael. *Who Tells Me True.* 1940. Scribner. Ills. Vg $10.00

STRANGE, T.A. *French Interiors, Furniture, Decoration, Woodwork.* 1968. New York. dj. EX $25.00

STRASBERG. *At the Actors' Studio.* 1965. Viking. 1st ed. dj. $12.50

STRATEMEYER, Edward. *A Young American in the Japanese Navy.* 1905. Lee & Shepard. Ills. Shute. 281 pp. VG $6.50

STRATTON, Clarence. *Swords & Statues.* 1937. New York. Ills. Robert Lawson. 1st ed. $20.00

STRATTON, R.B. *Captivity of the Oatman Girls.* 1859. 2nd ed. $50.00

STRATTON, R.B. *Captivity of the Oatman Girls.* 1859. New York. Ills. 3rd ed. 290 pp. $40.00

STRATTON-PORTER, Gene. *A Daughter of the Land.* 1918. New York. Doubleday. 1st ed. 475 pp. $22.50

STRATTON-PORTER, Gene. *Birds of the Bible.* 1909. New York. Abingdon. Ills. 469 pp. G $185.00

STRATTON-PORTER, Gene. *Freckles.* 1904. Doubleday. dj. EX $25.00

STRATTON-PORTER, Gene. *Her Father's Daughter.* 1921. New York. 486 pp. dj. $3.50

STRATTON-PORTER, Gene. *Morning Face.* 1916. Doubleday. 1st ed. rebound. $85.00

STRATTON-PORTER, Gene. *Moths of the Limberlost.* 1912. Garden City. 1st ed. VG $75.00

STRATTON-PORTER, Gene. *Moths of the Limberlost.* 1916. Doubleday. Ills. EX $60.00

STRATTON-PORTER, Gene. *Song of Cardinal.* 1903. Indianapolis. 1st ed. $75.00

STRATTON-PORTER, Gene. *The Magic Garden.* 1927. Doubleday. 1st ed. VG $25.00

STRATTON-PORTER, Gene. *White Flag.* 1923. Doubleday. 1st ed. VG $15.00

STRAUB, Peter. *Floating Dragon.* 1982. Ills. Dillon. Ltd. ed. 1/500. sgns. boxed. $100.00

STRAUB, Peter. *Floating Dragon.* 1983. New York. Putnam. 1st ed. dj. VG $25.00

STRAUB, Peter. *Ghost Story.* 1984. Ltd. reprint ed. sgn. dj. EX $50.00

STRAUB, Peter. *Ghost Story.* 1979. New York. Coward. 1st ed. dj. EX $25.00

STRAUB, Peter. *Marriages.* 1973. New York. proof copy. scarce. EX $250.00

STRAUB, Peter. *Shadowland.* 1980. New York. 1st ed. sgn. dj. VG $25.00

STRAUSS, Richard. *Der Hosenkavalier.* 1982. Boston. Ltd. Deluxe ed. 1/1000. sgn. $40.00

STRAWSON, J. *The Battle for North Africa.* 1969. Ills. maps. G $8.00

STRECKER, Edward. *Alcohol, One Man's Meat.* 1947. Macmillan. 5th ed. 230 pp. dj. $52.50

STREET, Donald M., Jr. *The Ocean Sailing Yacht.* 1973. New York. Norton. 702 pp. dj. $75.00

STREET, G.C. *Family Memoirs of Lockman, Porter, Street.* 1883. Chicago. re bound. EX $37.50

STREET, G.S. *The London Assurance 1729-1920.* 1920. London. Ills. only ed. $25.00

STREET, James. *By Valor & Arms.* 1944. 1st ed. $10.00

STREET, James. *Mingo Dabney.* 1950. New York. Dial Press. 1st ed. dj. VG $30.00

STREET, James. *Oh, Promised Land.* 1940. $10.00

STREET, James. *Tap Roots.* 1942. New York. 1st ed. $10.00

STREET, James. *The Revolutionary War.* 1954. New York. 1st ed. $10.00

STREET, James. *Tomorrow We Reap.* 1949. 1st ed. $10.00

STREET, P. *Vanishing Animals, Preserving Natures Rarities.* 1963. Dutton. Ills. 1st ed. 232 pp. dj. EX $10.00

STREET, P. *Wildlife Preservation.* 1971. Regenery. Ills. 141 pp. dj. VG $6.00

STREETER, Daniel. *An Arctic Rodeo.* 1929. New York. G $20.00

STREETER, Edward. *Dere Mable, Love Letters of a Rookie.* 1918. New York. Ills. 1st ed. dj. VG $10.00

STREETER, Edward. *Mr. Hobbs' Vacation.* 1954. New York. 1st ed. dj. VG $10.00

STREETER, Edward. *That's Me All Over, Mable.* 1919. Stokes. Ills. Bill Breck. $3.50

STREETER, Floyd Benjamin. *The Complete & Authentic Life of Ben Thompson.* 1957. New York. Ills. dj. VG $10.00

STREIBER, W. *The Hunger.* 1981. Morrow. 2nd ed. dj. EX $7.50

STREIBER, W. *The Wolfen.* 1978. New York. Morrow. 1st ed. dj. EX $40.00

STREIT, Clarence K. *Union Now with Britain.* 1941. New York. Harper & Bros. 240 pp. dj. $3.00

STRETTON, Charles. *Sport & Sportsmen: Book of Recollections.* 1866. London. 319 pp. $18.50

STRIBLING, T.S. *Clues of the Caribbees.* 1929. New York. Doubleday. 1st ed. VG $40.00

STRICK, Marv. *Beatnik Ball.* 1961. Van Nuys. Pike Books. wrappers. EX $10.00

STRICKLAND, W.P. *Autobiography of Rev. James B. Finley.* 1853. Cincinnati/NY. Ills. 455 pp. $15.00

STRICKLER. *Toledo Museum of Art: American Paintings.* 1979. Pennsylvania State Press. $10.00

STRIKER, Fran. *The Lone Ranger & the Gold Robbery.* 1939. Grosset & Dunlap. 185 pp. $5.00

STRIKER, Fran. *The Lone Ranger & the Outlaw Stronghold.* 1939. Grosset & Dunlap. dj. VG $17.50

STRIKER, Fran. *The Lone Ranger & Tonto.* 1940. VG $7.00

STRIKER, Fran. *The Lone Ranger on Powderhorn Trail.* 1949. New York. Grosset & Dunlap. 207 pp. $4.50

STRINGER. *Heroes All.* 1919. Fawcett. VG $8.50

STROBER, Jerry & Tomczak, R. *Jerry Falwell: Aflame for God.* 1979. Nashville, TN. 188 pp. dj. EX $5.00

STROKER, Bram. *Dracula.* Grosset & Dunlap. dj. $20.00

STRONG, Leah A. *Joseph Hopkins Twichell.* 1966. Athens, GA. 1st ed. sgn. 182 pp. dj. VG $12.50

STRONG, Phil. *The Adventure of 'Horse' Barnsby.* 1956. Garden City. 1st ed. dj. EX $10.00

STRONG, William R. *Canadian River Hunt.* 1960. U. of OK Press. reprint. Ltd. 1st ed. 1/1050. $50.00

STROOTMAN, Ralph. *History of the 363rd Infantry.* 1947. Infantry Journal. 1st ed. $15.00

STROUSE, J. *Alice James, a Bibliography.* 1980. Boston. Houghton Mifflin. 1st ed. dj. $25.00

STRUHSAKER, T.T. *The Red Colobus Monkey.* 1975. Chicago. Ills. 311 pp. dj. EX $22.50

STRUNG. *Spinfishing.* 1973. 1st ed. dj. EX $10.00

STRYKER, R. & Seidenberg, M. *A Pittsburgh Album 1758-1958.* 1959. Pittsburgh. 3rd printing. 95 pp. wrappers. $8.50

STRYON, Arthur. *Cast Iron Man. John C. Calhoun & Amer. Democracy.* 1935. NY/Toronto. 1st ed. 426 pp. dj. $15.00

STUART, Charles. *Lives & Works of Civil & Military Engineers of Am.* 1871. 24 Ills. ex-lib. 343 pp. G $52.00

STUART, Girdon. *Boy Scouts of the Air on Baldcrest.* 1922. $4.00

STUART, Ian. *The Satan Bug.* 1962. New York. Scribner. 1st ed. dj. EX $15.00

STUART, James & Rovett, N. *The Antiquities of Athens, Measured & Deliniated.* 1825. London. 1 vol of set of 4. VG $85.00

STUART, Jesse. *Album of Destiny.* 1944. Dutton. 1st ed. dj. G $50.00

STUART, Jesse. *Autumn Lovesong.* 1971. Hallmark. 1st ed. $15.00

STUART, Jesse. *Beyond the Dark Hills.* 1938. 1st ed. $55.00

STUART, Jesse. *Foretaste of Glory.* 1946. Dutton. 1st ed. $45.00

STUART, Jesse. *Hie to the Hunters.* 1950. New York. McGraw Hill. dj. VG $40.00

STUART, Jesse. *Hold April.* 1962. New York. 1st ed. inscr. dj. $37.50

STUART, Jesse. *Honest Confession of a Literary Sin.* Ltd. ed. sgn. EX $40.00

STUART, Jesse. *Man with a Bull-Tongue Plow.* 1936. New York. 3rd printing. VG $100.00

STUART, Jesse. *Man with a Bull-Tongue Plow.* 1934. New York. Dutton. 1st ed. dj. EX $325.00

STUART, Jesse. *Mr. Gallion's School.* 1967. New York. 1st ed. inscr. sgn. dj. $40.00

STUART, Jesse. *My Land Has a Voice.* 1966. New York. McGraw Hill. 3rd printing. dj. $20.00

STUART, Jesse. *Taps for Private Tussie.* 1943. New York. Ills. T.H. Benton. 303 pp. VG $15.00

STUART, Jesse. *The Thread that Runs So True.* 1955. Scribners. $3.00

STUART, Jesse. *The World of Jesse Stuart.* 1975. New York. McGraw Hill. 1st ed. dj. VG $30.00

STUART, Jesse. *Trees of Heaven.* 1940. New York. 1st ed. dj. VG $45.00

STUART, Ray. *Immortals of the Screen.* 1965. Ills. 224 pp. $8.00

STUART, Ruth McEnery. *George Washington Jones.* 1903. Philadelphia. Ills. 147 pp. $7.50

STUART, Ruth McEnery. *Sonny.* 1897. New York. inscr. sgn. VG $17.50

STUART, Ruth McEnery. *The River's Children. An Idyl of the Mississippi.* 1904. New York. Century. 179 pp. 5 pls. $12.50

STUART, Ruth McEnery. *The Unlived Life of Little Mary Ellen.* 1910. Boston. 91 pp. $7.50

STUBBERG, Friederich. *The Back-woodsman; or, Life on the Indian Frontier.* 1866. Boston. Ills. 1st Am. ed. 302 pp. $475.00

STUERMER, Gordon & Nina. *Starbound.* 1977. $5.50

STUHLDREHER, Harry A. *Knute Rockne, Man Builder.* 1931. New York. Grosset & Dunlap. 335 pp. $5.00

STURGEON, Theodore. *A Way Home.* 1955. New York. 1st ed. ex-lib. dj. G $8.00

STURGEON, Theodore. *Alien Cargo.* 1984. 1st Am. ed. dj. EX $15.00

STURGEON, Theodore. *Godbody.* 1986. proof copy. $25.00

STURGEON, Theodore. *Godbody.* 1986. 1st ed. dj. EX $25.00

STURGEON, Theodore. *Godbody.* 1986. Ltd. 1st ed. 1/350. $40.00

STURGEON, Theodore. *The Dreaming Jewels.* 1950. New York. Greenberg. 1st ed. dj. VG $25.00

STURGEON, Theodore. *The Player on the Other Side.* 1963. 1st Am. ed. dj. EX $30.00

STURGEON, Theodore. *The Rare Breed.* 1966. Gold Medal. 1st ed. pb. EX $17.50

STURGEON, Theodore. *Without Sorcery.* 1947. 1st ed. dj. EX $75.00

STURGEON, Theodore. *Without Sorcery.* 1948. Prime Press. 1st ed. VG $15.00

STURGES, Lillian Baker. *The Runaway Toys.* Rand McNally. no date. Ills. 64 pp. VG $4.50

STURGIS, Russell. *Appreciation of Sculpture.* 1904. $22.00

STURGIS, Russell. *How to Judge Arch.* 1903. $20.00

STURGIS, Russell. *Study in Handicrafts & Art Design.* 1905. New York. Ills. $37.50

STURGIS, Russell. *The Interdependence of the Arts of Design.* 1905. McClurg. 1st ed. $15.00

STURGIS, William. *Fly-Tying.* 1940. dj. VG $15.00

STURMS, C.C. *Reflections.* London. (ca.1800) 2 vol set. $35.00

STUTLEY. *Last Frontier.* 1930. New York. 1st ed. dj. $32.00

STYLES, S. *Forbidden Frontiers.* 1970. London. 1st ed. dj. EX $10.00

STYRON, William. *Lie Down in Darkness.* 1951. Indianapolis. 1st ed. dj. EX $100.00

STYRON, William. *Set This House on Fire.* 1960. Random House. 1st ed. sgn. dj. EX $55.00

STYRON, William. *Sophie's Choice.* Ltd. ed. 1/500. sgn. dj. EX $75.00

STYRON, William. *Sophie's Choice.* 1979. Random House. 1st trade ed. dj. VG $25.00

STYRON, William. *Sophie's Choice.* 1979. Cape. 1st Eng. ed. dj. VG $30.00

STYRON, William. *The Confessions of Nat Turner.* 1967. New York. Random House. 1st ed. dj. EX $35.00

STYRON, William. *The Quiet Dust.* 1982. New York. Ltd. ed. 1/250. sgn. slipcase. $85.00

STYRON, William. *The Quiet Dust.* 1982. Random House. 1st trade ed. dj. VG $15.00

STYRON, William. *The Quiet Dust.* 1982. Random House. 1st trade ed. sgn. dj. VG $30.00

SUCHOW. *Iowa Interiors.* 1926. 1st ed. dj. EX $10.00

SUCKOW, Ruth. *The Folks.* 1934. New York. New York Literary Guild. dj. $12.50

SUCKSDORFF, A.B. *Tiger in Sight.* 1970. Delacorte. Ills. 1st Am. ed. 110 pp. dj. $12.50

SUDDETH, James. *Aircraft Engine Maintenance.* 1944. 2nd ed. 400 pp. $125.00

SUE, Eugene. *The Gold Sickle; or, Hena, Virgin of Isle of Sen.* 1904. New York. Labor News. $4.00

SUE, Eugene. *The Mysteries of Paris.* New York. Lovell. 472 pp. $3.50

SUE, Eugene. *The Wandering Jew.* London. 1st Eng. ed. $90.00

SUGIMOTO, Etsu. *Daughter of the Narikin.* 1932. Doubleday. 1st ed. dj. $10.00

SUGRE, Francis. *Popes in the Modern World.* 1961. New York. Crownwell. 274 pp. dj. EX $5.00

SULLES, Foster Rhea. *Labor in America. A History.* 1960. New York. 435 pp. $5.00

SULLIVAN, Alan. *A Little Way Ahead.* 1930. New York. Dutton. 1st ed. dj. EX $15.00

SULLIVAN, Arthur. *Arthur Sullivan, His Life, Letters, & Diaries.* 1950. Cassell. 1st new & revised ed. dj. $10.00

SULLIVAN, Faith. *Mrs. Deming & the Mythical Beast.* 1985. Macmillan. advance copy. wrappers. EX $25.00

SULLIVAN, Judge. *The Disappearance of Dr. Parkman.* 1971. Ills. dj. VG $7.50

SULLIVAN, Mark. *Our Times. The United States 1900-1925, Vol. IV.* 1932. New York. Scribner. 629 pp. EX $4.50

SULLIVAN, May Kellogg. *A Woman Who Went to Alaska.* 1902. Boston. 1st ed. VG $25.00

SULLIVAN, Robert. *The Ten'a Food Quest.* 1942. Catholic U. 1st ed. stiff wrappers. $10.00

SULLIVAN, Sir Edward. *The Book of Kells.* 1914. London. The Studio. 1st ed. Ills. VG $80.00

SULLIVAN. *Christmas with Ed Sullivan.* 1959. New York. dj. VG $7.50

SULLIVAN. *The Empire Builder. Novel of James J. Hill.* 1928. 1st ed. VG $15.00

SULZERGER, C.L. *The Test. DeGaulle & Algeria.* 1962. dj. VG $7.50

SULZERGER, C.L. *World War II.* 1972. Ills. G $7.50

SUMER. *The Dawn of Art.* 1961. New York. dj. $45.00

SUMMERS, Florence Elizabeth. *Dere Bill, Mable's Love Letters to Her Rookie.* 1919. Stokes. Ills. Natalie Stokes. $3.50

SUMMERS, G. *Owned by an Eagle.* 1976. London. Collins. Ills. 1st ed. dj. EX $10.00

SUMMERS, G. *The Lure of the Falcon.* 1972. Ills. 1st ed. 283 pp. dj. EX $4.00

SUMMERS, M. *Vampire.* 1929. New York. 1st ed. G $15.00

SUMMERS, Montague. *The Physical Phenomena of Mysticism.* 1950. New York. Ills. 263 pp. index. $25.00

SUMMERS, Montague. *Works of Thomas Otway.* Nonsuch Press. Ltd. ed. 1/1250. 3 vol set. VG $65.00

SUMNER, Charles. *Promises of Declaration of Independence.* 1865. Boston. original wrappers. VG $15.00

SUMNER, David. *Rocky Mountains.* 1975. photos. dj. EX $40.00

SUMNER, G. Lynn. *Lincoln & His Books.* 1934. New York. Ills. 1st ed. $7.00

SUMNER, William Graham. *Financier & Finances of American Revolution.* 1891. New York. 1st ed. 2 vol set. VG $75.00

SUNDER, John. *Bill Sublette Mountain Man.* 1959. U. of OK. 1st ed. dj. $12.50

SUNDERMAN, James F. *Early Air Pioneers, 1862-1935.* 1961. New York. Ills. 282 pp. dj. VG $12.50

SUNDHEIM, Karl. *The Romance of Exploration.* 1935. New York. Ills. $6.50

SUNDMAN, Per Olaf. *The Flight of the Eagle.* 1st Am. ed. dj. VG $7.50

SUPER, R.H. *Matthew Arnold on the Classical Tradition.* 1960. 1st ed. dj. $8.50

SURETTE, Dick. *Trout & Salmon Fly Index.* 1974. 1st ed. inscr. $20.00

SURIEU, R. *Sarave' Maz.* Geneve. French text. Ills. $45.00

SURTEES, Robert S. *Ask Mamma.* 1858. Bradbury Evans. Ills. John Leech. 1st ed. VG $75.00

SURTEES, Robert S. *Handley Cross; or, Mr. Jorrock's Hunt.* 1930. Viking. Ltd. ed. 1/1050. G $27.50

SURTEES, Robert S. *Handley Cross; or, Mr. Jorrock's Hunt.* 1854. London. 17 colored engravings. $30.00

SURTEES, Robert S. *The Sporting Novels.* London. Ills. John Leech. EX $195.00

SURTON, S.D. *From Mission Hospital to Concentration Camp.* (ca. 1940) dj. VG $10.00

SUSAN. *Under the Sign of Saturn.* 1980. Farrar. 1st ed. sgn. dj. EX $30.00

SUSANN, Jacqueline. *Valley of the Dolls.* 1966. New York. Random House. 442 pp. $3.50

SUTCLIFE, Rob. *Travels in Some Parts of North America 1804-1806.* 1815. New York. 2nd ed. VG $55.00

SUTHERLAND, J.C. *At Sea with Joseph Conrad.* 1922. London. Ills. 1st ed. VG $25.00

SUTHERLAND, S.K. *Venomous Creatures of Australia.* 1981. Oxford. Ills. 1st ed. 128 pp. dj. EX $27.50

SUTLEY. *Last Frontier.* 1930. New York. 1st ed. dj. $32.00

SUTPHEN, Van Tassel. *The Doomsman.* 1906. New York. Harper. 1st ed. VG $25.00

SUTTON, David. *Complete Book of Model Railroading.* 1964. Castle. dj. VG $27.50

SUTTON, Fred & Macdonald, A.B. *Hands Up! Stories of Six-Gun Fighters of Old West.* 1927. Indianapolis. Ills. 1st ed. VG $40.00

SUTTON, G.M. *At a Bend in a Mexican River.* 1972. Eriksson. Ills. 184 pp. dj. EX $25.00

SUTTON, G.M. *Bird Student, an Autobiography.* 1980. Texas U. Press. Ills. 1st ed. 216 pp. dj. EX $10.00

SUTTON, G.M. *Fifty Common Birds of OK & Southern Great Plains.* 1977. OK U. Press. Ills. 1st ed. 113 pp. dj. EX $20.00

SUTTON, G.M. *Iceland Summer, Adventures of a Bird Artist.* 1961. OK U. Press. Ills. 1st ed. 253 pp. dj. EX $25.00

SUTTON, G.M. *Oklahoma Birds.* 1967. Norman. Ills. 1st ed. 674 pp. VG $20.00

SUTTON, G.M. *Portraits of Mexican Birds, 50 Selected Paintings.* 1975. OK U. Press. Ills. 1st ed. folio. 106 pp. $17.50

SUTTON, J. *The Missile Lords.* 1963. dj. VG $5.00

SUTTON, John Davison. *History of Braxton County & Central West Virginia.* 1919. Sutton, WV. Ills. 458 pp. index. $75.00

SUTTON, Margaret. *The Black Cat's Clue.* 1952. Grosset & Dunlap. $3.50

SUYIN, Han. *The Enchantress.* 1985. Bantam. proof copy. wrappers. VG $20.00

SUYIN, Han. *Till Morning Comes.* 1982. Bantam. 1st ed. dj. VG $15.00

SVENSEN, Carl. *Manual of Aircraft Drafting.* 1943. New York. Nostrand. 5th ed. 272 pp. dj. EX $150.00

SVENVO, Italo. *As a Man Grows Older.* New Directions. 1st ed. dj. VG $20.00

SVININE, Paul. *Sketch of the Life of General Moreau.* 1814. New York. 107 pp. rebound. VG $25.00

SWADOS, Harvey. *Nights in the Gardens of Brooklyn.* 1961. Boston. Little, Brown. 1st ed. EX $20.00

SWADOS, Harvey. *Out Went the Candle.* 1955. New York. 1st Am. ed. dj. VG $30.00

SWAIN, Virginia. *The Hollow Skin.* 1938. New York, Farrar. 1st ed. dj. EX $40.00

SWAN, Mabel Munson. *The Athenaeum Gallery, 1827-1873.* 1940. Boston. Merrymount Press. 312 pp. VG $40.00

SWAN, Michael. *Henry James.* 1950. London. 1st ed. wrappers. EX $15.00

SWAN, Oliver G. *Deep Water Days.* 1929. $12.50

SWANBERG, W.A. *Citizen Hearst. Biography William Randolph Hearst.* 1961. Scribner. 555 pp. dj. G $9.00

SWANBERG, W.A. *Luce, His Empire.* 1972. 529 pp. dj. $37.50

SWANBOROUGH, G. *Civil Aircraft of the World.* 1980. Ills. EX $10.00

SWANBOROUGH, G. *Turbine Engined Airliners of the World.* 1962. London. Ills. G $7.50

SWANBOROUGH, Gordon & Bowers. *United States Naval Aircraft Since 1911.* 1968. New York. 518 pp. dj. VG $12.00

SWANN, Peter Charles. *Hokusai.* 1959. Faber & Faber. Ills. wrappers. $35.00

SWANN, T.B. *Queens Walk in Dust.* 1977. Heritage Press. Ills. Jones. Ltd. ed. sgn. EX $25.00

SWANSON, Neil. *Unconquered. A Novel of the Pontiac Conspiracy.* 1947. New York. Doubleday. 376 pp. $3.50

SWANTON, John R. *Indian Tribes of North America.* 1953. Washington. 726 pp. $17.50

SWARD, Keith. *The Legend of Henry Ford.* 1948. Toronto. Rinehart. dj. VG $9.00

SWARZTRAUBER, S.A. *The Three Mile Limit of Territorial Sea.* 1972. dj. VG $12.50

SWEDENBORG, Emanuel. *Doctrine of the New Jerusalem Concerning the Lord.* 1784. London. 1st ed. VG $55.00

SWEDENBORG, Emanuel. *Heaven & Hell.* 1876. Philadelphia. VG $20.00

SWEDENBORG, Emanuel. *The Apocalypse Revealed.* 1876. Philadelphia. 1202 pp. VG $20.00

SWEDENBORG, Emanuel. *Treatise Concerning Heaven & Hell.* 1778. London. 1st. Eng. ed. VG $110.00

SWEENEY, John L. *The Painter's Eye.* 1956. London. Hart Davis. 1st ed. dj. EX $42.50

SWEENEY, R.C.H. *Grappling with a Griffon.* 1969. Pantheon. Ills. 1st Am. ed. 224 pp. dj. $10.00

SWEENY, C. *Moment of Truth.* 1943. G $7.50

SWEENY, C. *Naturalist in Sudan.* 1974. Taplinger. Ills. 1st Am. ed. dj. EX $15.00

SWEET. *Anglo-Saxon Primer.* 1974. Oxford U. Press. 129 pp. VG $3.50

SWEETMAN, Bill & Watanabe, R. *Avro Lancaster.* 1982. New York. Crown. 1st ed. EX $15.00

SWEETMAN, Bill & Watanabe, R. *Mosquito.* 1981. New York. Crown. 1st Am. ed. EX $15.00

SWEETMAN, Bill & Watanabe, R. *Spitfire.* 1980. New York. Crown. 1st ed. EX $15.00

SWEETSER, Arthur. *Opportunities in Aviation.* 1920. Harper. 113 pp. EX $12.50

SWEETSER, Kate Dickinson. *Ten Boys from Dickens.* 1901. New York. Ills. George A. Williams. dj. $20.00

SWEETSER, Kate Dickinson. *Ten Boys from Dickens.* 1925. NY/London. Ills. George A. Williams. dj. $17.00

SWEETSER, M.F. *Niagara Falls.* 1893. Boston. Ills. photos. 13 tinted pls. $42.50

SWEETSER, W.D. *Arthur Machen.* 1964. Twayne. 1st ed. pb. EX $7.50

SWENSON, A.A. *Cultivating Carnivorus Plants.* 1977. Doubleday. Ills. 1st ed. dj. EX $10.00

SWENSON, G.W.P. *Pictorial History of the Rifle.* 1972. New York. Drake. Ills. 184 pp. dj. VG $12.50

SWHIDHER, Jacob A. *Robert Gordon Cousins.* 1938. Iowa City. 307 pp. $12.50

SWIDEN, O.J. *Survivor of Babi-Yar.* 1980. EX $10.00

SWIERENGA. *Pioneers/Profits: Land Speculation on IA Frontier.* 1968. 1st ed. dj. EX $20.00

SWIFT, Dr. *Verses on the Death of Dr. Swift.* 1739. 3rd ed. rebound. $125.00

SWIFT, Graham. *Learning to Swim.* 1982. New York. Poseidon. 1st ed. dj. EX $20.00

SWIFT, Graham. *Waterland.* 1983. New York. Poseidon. 1st ed. dj. VG $20.00

SWIFT, Jonathan. *A Tale of a Tub.* 1930. New York. Ills. Chappell. 1st ed. $20.00

SWIFT, Jonathan. *Gulliver's Travels.* 1940. Heritage Press. 343 pp. $15.00

SWIFT, Jonathan. *Gulliver's Travels.* 1936. Chicago. Ills. Milo Winter. G $35.00

SWIFT, Jonathan. *Gulliver's Travels.* 1947. Grosset & Dunlap. Ills. dj. EX $6.50

SWIFT, Jonathan. *Gulliver's Travels.* 1981. New York. reprint. 70 Ills. $10.00

SWIFT, Jonathan. *Gulliver's Travels.* 1726. 3rd printing. 2 vol set. $550.00

SWIFT, Zephaniah. *A System of the Laws of State of Connecticut.* 1795. Windham. Vol I of II. $75.00

SWIFT. *Roman Sources of Christian Art.* 1951. Columbia U. Press. dj. $20.00

SWIGGETT. *Rebel Raider Morgan.* 1934. $12.00

SWINBURNE, A.C. *Laus Veneris.* 1866. New York. 1st Am. ed. $25.00

SWINBURNE, A.C. *The Springtide of Life/Poems of Childhood.* 1915. London. Ills. Rackham, Heinemann. G $35.00

SWINBURNE, A.C. *Under the Microscope.* 1899. Mosher Pub. Ltd. ed. 1/450. dj. boxed. EX $75.00

SWINDELL, Larry. *Spencer Tracy.* 1969. New York. World. dj. VG $4.00

SWINFORD. *Alaska.* 1898. fld map. VG $20.00

SWINNERTON, Frank. *The Adventures of a Manuscript.* 1956. London. Ltd. 1st ed. sgn. VG $20.00

SWINNERTON, Frank. *The Bookman's London.* 1969. London. Ills. revised ed. dj. EX $15.00

SWINNERTON, Frank. *The Bookman's London.* 1952. New York. Doubleday. 1st ed. 161 pp. $5.00

SWINTON. *Swinton's Condensed U.S. History.* 1879. Ills. TB. maps. $6.00

SWISHER, Carl B. *Stephen J. Field, Craftsman of the Law.* 1930. Washington. 473 pp. $12.50

SWISHER, Jacob A. *Iowa in Times of War.* 1943. $10.00

SWISHER, James. *How I Know, or 16 Years' Eventful Experience.* 1881. Cincinnati. Ills. 384 pp. $120.00

SWORD, Wiley. *Shiloh Bloody April.* 1974. Morrow. 1st ed. dj. VG $25.00

SYERS. *Off the Beaten Trail.* 1963-65. Fort Worth. 3 vol set. SftCvr. $15.00

SYKES. *Principles & Practice of Brewing.* 1897. London. 1st ed. 511 pp. $18.00

SYMAN, Susan. *Edward Lear's Birds.* 1980. Morrow. Ills. 1st Am. ed. dj. EX $45.00

SYMONDS, John Addington. *Shelley.* 1878. London. 1st ed. VG $35.00

SYMONS, A. *The Collected Drawings of A. Beardsley.* 1967. Bounty. $15.00

SYMONS, A.J.A. *The Quest for Corvo.* 1934. New York. 1st Am. ed. dj. VG $22.50

SYMONS, Julian. *Blackheath Poisonings.* 1st Eng. ed. dj. $12.00

SYMONS, Julian. *Bland Beginning.* 1949. London. Gollancz. 1st ed. dj. VG $60.00

SYMONS, Julian. *Charles Dickens.* 1951. London. 1st ed. dj. EX $35.00

SYMONS, Julian. *Detling Murders.* 1st Eng. ed. dj. $12.00

SYMONS, Julian. *Man Who Lost His Wife.* 1st Eng. ed. $12.00

SYMONS, Julian. *The Detective Story in Britain.* 1962. London. Longmans. 1st ed. wrappers. $25.00

SYMONS, Julian. *The End of Solomon Grundy.* 1964. London. 1st ed. dj. VG $22.00

SYMONS, Julian. *The 31st of February.* 1950. London. Gollanz. 1st ed. dj. VG $27.00

SYMONS, Julian. *Three Pipe Problem.* 1st Eng. ed. dj. $18.00

SYNGE, J.M. *Riders to the Sea.* 1911. Boston. 1st ed. VG $60.00

SYPHERD, Wilbur Owen. *Jephthal & His Daughter.* 1948. U. of DE. Ills. presentation copy. sgn. $10.00

SYROECHKOVSKII, E.E. *Wild Reindeer of the Soviet Union.* 1984. New Delhi. Oxonian Press. 309 pp. dj. EX $42.50

SZARKOWSKI, J. *Mirrors & Windows.* 1980. New York. dj. EX $25.00

SZARKOWSKI, J. *New Japanese Photography.* 1974. VG $22.50

SZARKOWSKI, J. *Photographer's Eye.* 1966. dj. VG $25.00

SZARKOWSKI. *The Face of Minnesota.* 1958. $25.00

SZASZ, F.M. *The Divided Mind of Protestant America 1880-1930.* 1982. EX $12.50

SZATHEMARY. *The Chefs' Secret Cookbook.* 1972. Chicago. 288 pp. dj. VG $10.00

SZOSTAK & LEIGHTON. *In the Footsteps of John Paul II.* 1980. 2nd printing. $10.00

SZYK, Arthur. *Anderson's Fairy Tales Illustrated by Szyk.* New York. Grosset & Dunlap. VG $10.00

SZYK, Arthur. *The Book of Ruth.* 1947. New York. Ills. Szyk. $35.00

SZYK, Arthur. *The New Order.* 1941. Putnam. 1st ed. dj. EX $90.00

T

TABER, Edward M. *Stowe Notes, Letters & Verses.* 1913. Boston. Ills. $15.00

TABER, Gladys & Kistner, R. *Flower Arranging for the American Home.* 1947. Philadelphia. Ills. sgn. Kistner. 221 pp. $30.00

TABER, Gladys & Webster, B. *Stillmeadow & Sugarbridge.* Book Club Ed. 282 pp. $22.50

TABER, Gladys & Webster, B. *Stillmeadow & Sugarbridge.* 1953. Philadelphia. Lippincott. Ills. 1st ed. VG $30.00

TABER, Gladys. *Another Path.* 1963. Philadelphia. 2nd ed. dj. VG $15.00

TABER, Gladys. *Best of Stillmeadow: Treasury of Country Living.* 1976. New York. Lippincott. 348 pp. $22.50

TABER, Gladys. *Book of Stillmeadow.* 1948. 3rd printing. VG $7.50

TABER, Gladys. *Conversations with Amber.* 1978. Philadelphia. Lippincott. 176 pp. $22.50

TABER, Gladys. *Country Chronicle.* 1974. Philadelphia. Lippincott. Ills. 220 pp. $18.50

TABER, Gladys. *Especially Dogs.* 1968. New York. 1st ed. dj. EX $30.00

TABER, Gladys. *Especially Spaniels.* 1945. Philadelphia. Macrae-Smith. 253 pp. $17.50

TABER, Gladys. *Harvest of Yesterdays.* 1976. Philadelphia. Lippincott. 224 pp. $17.50

TABER, Gladys. *Lyonnesse.* 1929. Bozart. 1st ed. VG $12.50

TABER, Gladys. *My Own Cape Cod.* 1970. Philadelphia. 2nd ed. dj. EX $12.50

TABER, Gladys. *My Own Cookbook.* 1972. Philadelphia. Lippincott. Ills. 312 pp. $15.00

TABER, Gladys. *Nurse in Blue.* 1944. Philadelphia. Blakiston. $20.00

TABER, Gladys. *One Dozen & One.* 1966. Philadelphia. Lippincott. 239 pp. $28.00

TABER, Gladys. *Still Cove Journal.* 1981. New York. Harper. 223 pp. $18.50

TABER, Gladys. *Stillmeadow Album.* 1969. Philadelphia. Lippincott. Ills. VG $27.50

TABER, Gladys. *Stillmeadow Calender.* 1967. Philadelphia. Lippincott. 256 pp. $20.00

TABER, Gladys. *Stillmeadow Cookbook.* 1965. Philadelphia. Lippincott. 335 pp. $38.00

TABER, Gladys. *Stillmeadow Daybook.* 1955. Philadelphia. Lippincott. 287 pp. $20.00

TABER, Gladys. *Stillmeadow Road.* 1962. Philadelphia. Lippincott. 287 pp. VG $20.00

TABER, Gladys. *Stillmeadow Sampler.* 1959. Philadelphia. Lippincott. 282 pp. $18.50

TABER, Gladys. *Stillmeadow Seasons.* 1949. Philadelphia. Macrae-Smith. $17.50

TABER, Gladys. *The Book of Stillmeadow.* 1948. Philadelphia. Macrae-Smith. Ills. 273 pp. $35.00

TABORI, Paul. *The Pen in Exile.* 1956. Great Britain. 252 pp. $125.00

TACITUS. *Works of Tacitus.* 1854. London. 2 vol set. VG $20.00

TAFT, Robert. *Artists & Illustrators of the Old West.* 1953. Scribner. 1st ed. $25.00

TAFT, Robert. *Photography & American Scenery.* 1938. VG $45.00

TAFT. *History American Sculpture.* 1903. $30.00

TAFT. *History American Sculpture.* 1930. new ed. $35.00

TAGORE, Abanindro Nath. *Rubaiyat of Omar Khayyam.* Philadelphia. (ca.1920) Ills. VG $25.00

TAGORE, Rabindranath. *Gitanjali.* Boston. wrappers. $7.50

TAINE, H.A. *History of English Literature.* 1873. Edinburgh. Edmonston & Douglas. 3 vol set. $15.00

TAINE, H.A. *Voyage aux Pyrenees.* 1860. Paris. Ills. Dore. 1st ed. VG $35.00

TAINE, John. *Quayle's Invention.* 1927. New York. 1st ed. VG $20.00

TAINE, John. *The Cosmic Geoids.* 1950. Los Angeles. 2nd printing. 179 pp. dj. EX $12.50

TAINE, John. *The Iron Star.* 1930. New York. 1st ed. VG $25.00

TAIT, S.W. *The Wildcatters.* 1946. Princeton. dj. G $12.50

TAKAHASHI, Masayoshi. *Color Atlas of Cancer Cytology.* 1981. Tokyo/NY. 2nd ed. dj. boxed. EX $65.00

TAKAHASHI, Seiichiro. *Traditional Woodblock Prints of Japan.* 1973. Weatherhill. Ills. 175 pp. dj. EX $44.00

TAKASHIMA, S. *The Hanami.* 1897. Tokyo. Ills. K. Ogawa. 25 pls. VG $175.00

TALBOT, Bishop. *My People of the Plains.* 1906. Harper. $17.50

TALBOT, Hake. *The Hangman's Handyman.* New York. Simon & Schuster. 1st ed. dj. $20.00

TALBOT, P.A. *In the Shadow of the Bush.* 1912. London. Ills. 500 pp. EX $70.00

TALBOTT, Strobe. *Deadly Gambits.* 1984. Knopf. 3rd ed. 280 pp. dj. $27.50

TALCOTT, Parsons & Clark. *The Negro American.* 1966. Houghton Mifflin. 1st ed. $3.50

TALENT, Elizabeth. *In Constant Flight.* 1983. New York. Knopf. 1st ed. dj. EX $25.00

TALESE, Gay. *Honor Thy Father.* 1971. New York. World. 490 pp. $5.00

TALESE, Gay. *The Over Reaches.* 1964. Harper. 1st ed. dj. EX $15.00

TALFOURD, Thomas Noon. *Final Memorials of Charles Lamb.* 1848. London. Moxon. 1st ed. 2 vol set. VG $55.00

TALFOURD, Thomas Noon. *The Works of Charles Lamb.* 1858. New York. Harper. 1166 pp. 2 vol set. $8.00

TALLACK, William. *Friendly Sketches in America.* 1861. London. 1st ed. $100.00

TALLENT. *Black Hills; or, Last Hunting Grounds of Dakotahs.* 1899. 1st ed. $90.00

TALMAGE, T. DeWitt. *Life's Looking Glass.* 1899. Chicago. 544 pp. $10.00

TALMAGE, T. DeWitt. *The Masque Torn Off.* 1880. Perrysville. Cline & Caraway. $12.50

TAMAKI, T. *Nisikigoi.* 1974. Hiroshimi. Tamaki Yogyoen. 1st ed. dj. EX $20.00

TAMPION, J. *Dangerous Plants.* 1982. Universe. Ills. 176 pp. dj. EX $15.00

TANNENBAUM, Frank. *Crime & the Community.* 1938. Boston. Ginn. 487 pp. VG $3.50

TANNER, Fred W. *Practical Bacteriology.* 1933. New York. TB. 235 pp. $3.50

TANNER, H. *Guns of the World.* 1977. New York. Ills. $15.00

TANNER, H.S. *Central Traveller, or Tourist's Guide PA, NJ, etc.* 1844. New York. 2nd ed. 2 fld maps. VG $35.00

TANNHAUSER. *Wagner's Poem Translated by Rolleston.* 1911. Crowell Co. Ills. Pogany. 1st Am. ed. VG $95.00

TAPPLY. *The Sportsman's Notebook.* 1964. VG $6.50

TARACOUZIO, T.A. *War & Peace in Soviet Diplomacy.* 1940. New York. Macmillan. ex-lib. 354 pp. G $3.00

TARBELL, Ida. *In the Footsteps of the Lincolns.* 1924. 1st ed. VG $25.00

TARBELL, Ida. *The Life of Abraham Lincoln.* 1907. New York. Ills. 4 vol set. VG $45.00

TARBELL, Tarbell. *The Life of Abraham Lincoln.* 1924. Lincoln Hist. Soc. 2 vol set. $16.00

TARDIEU, Andre. *France & America.* 1927. New York. ex-lib. 312 pp. G $3.50

TARG, W. *Bibliophile in the Nursery.* 1957. New York. 1st ed. dj. EX $37.50

TARG, W. *Indecent Pleasures.* 1975. New York. Macmillan. 1st printing. dj. $12.50

TARKINGTON, Booth. *Alice Adams.* 1921. New York. Doubleday Page. 434 pp. $3.00

TARKINGTON, Booth. *Beasley's Christmas Party.* 1911. Harper. Ills. Ruth Sypherd Clements. $8.50

TARKINGTON, Booth. *Beasley's Christmas Party.* 1909. New York. Harper. Ills. VG $20.00

TARKINGTON, Booth. *Cherry & Beasley's Christmas Party.* 1925. New York. Harper. 268 pp. $3.50

TARKINGTON, Booth. *Claire Ambler.* 1928. Doubleday. 1st ed. 253 pp. $75.00

TARKINGTON, Booth. *In the Arena.* 1905. McClure. 1st ed. $12.50

TARKINGTON, Booth. *Kate Fennigate.* 1943. Doubleday Doran. 1st ed. $7.00

TARKINGTON, Booth. *Little Orvie.* 1943. 1st ed. $17.50

TARKINGTON, Booth. *Looking Forward & Others.* 1926. Doubleday. $13.50

TARKINGTON, Booth. *Mary's Neck.* 1932. New York. 318 pp. $7.50

TARKINGTON, Booth. *Penrod.* Grosset & Dunlap. dj. VG $5.00

TARKINGTON, Booth. *Penrod-Penrod & Sam-Penrod Jashber.* 1943. New York. 590 pp. $7.00

TARKINGTON, Booth. *The Conquest of Canaan.* 1905. New York. Ills. Hitchcock. 389 pp. $3.50

TARKINGTON, Booth. *The Gentleman from Indiana.* 1900. New York. Doubleday/McClure. 384 pp. $10.00

TARKINGTON, Booth. *The Heritage of Hatcher Ide.* 1941. New York. Doubleday. 310 pp. $7.50

TARKINGTON, Booth. *The Turmoil.* 1915. New York. 349 pp. $7.50

TARKINGTON, Booth. *The Two Vanrevels.* 1902. Ills. Henry Hutt. 1st ed. $12.50

TARKINGTON, Booth. *Works of Booth Tarkington.* 1918. Garden City. Ltd. ed. 1/565. sgn. VG $125.00

TARNACRE, Robert. *Beyond the Swamps.* 1929. London. Lane. 1st ed. VG $35.00

TARRANT, Margaret. *Christmas Garland.* 1942. Boston. 1st ed. 19 color pls. G $15.00

TARRASCH. *The Game of Chess.* 1935. London. dj. VG $10.00

TASHI, Y. *Mental Efficiency/Timidity & How to Overcome It.* 1916. 179 pp. $5.50

TASHJIAN. *Skyscraper Primitives, Dada & America Avant Garde.* 1975. Wesleyan U. Press. $10.00

TASSO, T. *Jerusalem Delivered.* 1901. New York. Ills. VG $15.00

TATE, Allen & Wills, Ridley. *The Golden Mean & Other Poems.* Palaemon. 1st ed. wrappers. EX $30.00

TATE, Allen. *Collected Essays.* 1959. Denver. Swallow. 1st ed. sgn. dj. $65.00

TATE, Allen. *Collected Poems: 1919-1976.* 1977. Farrar. 1st ed. dj. VG $25.00

TATE, Allen. *Collected Poems: 1922-1947.* 1948. Scribner. 1st ed. dj. VG $55.00

TATE, Allen. *Essays of Four Decades.* 1970. Oxford. 1st English ed. dj. EX $30.00

TATE, Allen. *Jefferson Davis: His Rise & Fall.* 1929. New York. 2nd printing. VG $20.00

TATE, Allen. *Jefferson Davis: His Rise & Fall.* 1929. Ills. 1st ed. 311 pp. index. $35.00

TATE, Allen. *Memories & Essays: Old & New.* 1976. Carcanet. 1st English ed. dj. VG $30.00

TATE, Allen. *On the Limits of Poetry.* 1948. Denver. Swallow. 1st ed. dj. VG $80.00

TATE, N. *Angling: a Poem.* 1741. London. VG $360.00

TATE. *Fathers.* 1960. New York. presentation copy. sgn. dj. EX $35.00

TATE. *The United States & the Hawaiian Kingdom.* 1965. 1st ed. dj. EX $15.00

TATHAM, David. *Lure of Striped Pig: Ills. of Am. Music 1820-1870.* 1973. Barre, MA. Ltd. ed. 1/1950. sgn. EX $60.00

TATTERSALL, W.M. *A Review of Mysidacea of U.S. National Museum.* 1951. Ills. 292 pp. VG $7.50

TAUBES, Frederic. *Better Frames for Your Pictures.* 1968. VG $5.00

TAUBMAN, Harold. *Making of the American Theatre.* 1965. 2nd printing. dj. VG $10.00

TAUSSIG, H.B. *Congenital Malformations of the Heart.* 1947. Ills. 1st ed. 3rd printing. VG $45.00

TAVERNER, Eric. *Trout Fishing from All Angles.* London. 250 Ills. VG $15.00

TAVERNER, P.A. *Birds of Eastern Canada.* 1922. Ills. 2nd ed. VG $27.50

TAVIS, Walter. *Mockingbird.* proof copy. VG $15.00

TAYLOR, A.J.P. *War by Time Table. How the First World War Began.* 1969. Ills. maps. dj. G $6.50

TAYLOR, A.S. *Poisons in Relation to Jurisprudence & Medicine.* 1848. Philadelphia. 1st Am. ed. VG $125.00

TAYLOR, Ann. *Reciprocal Duties of Parents & Children.* 1825. Boston. 1st Am. ed. $45.00

TAYLOR, B.F. *Short Ravelings from a Long Yarn.* 1936. California. 168 pp. $125.00

TAYLOR, B.F. *The World on Wheels & Other Sketches.* 1874. Chicago. S.C. Griggs & Co. $65.00

TAYLOR, Bayard. *Boys of Other Countries.* 1876. New York. 1st ed. VG $65.00

TAYLOR, Bayard. *Egypt & Iceland in 1874.* New York. 282 pp. VG $25.00

TAYLOR, Bayard. *Eldorado, or Adventures in the Path of Empire.* 1850. New York. 1st ed. 2 vol set. VG $225.00

TAYLOR, Bayard. *Eldorado or Adventures in the Path of Empire.* 1850. New York. Ills. 2nd ed. 2 vol set. EX $250.00

TAYLOR, Bayard. *Home Pastoral.* 1875. G $30.00

TAYLOR, Bayard. *The Lands of the Saracen.* 1st ed. VG $125.00

TAYLOR, D. *Zoo Vet, Adventures of a Wild Animal Doctor.* 1977. Lippincott. Ills. 1st Am. ed. 255 pp. dj. $7.50

TAYLOR, D. Crane. *John L. Stoddard.* 1935. London. 1st ed. VG $15.00

TAYLOR, David. *Sycamore Men.* 1st ed. inscr. dj. $10.00

TAYLOR, David. *The Oldest Manuscripts in New Zealand.* 1955. Oxford. 1st ed. dj. $20.00

TAYLOR, Deems. *A Pictorial History of the Movies.* 1950. New York. 1st revised ed. VG $9.00

TAYLOR, Deems. *Treasury of Gilbert & Sullivan.* 1941. New York. Simon & Schuster. 403 pp. EX $6.00

TAYLOR, E.L. *Ohio Indians & Other Writings.* 1909. Columbus. Heer. Ills. 347 pp. $35.00

TAYLOR, Elizabeth. *Hester Lilly & 12 Short Stories.* 1954. New York. 1st ed. dj. VG $12.50

TAYLOR, Elizabeth. *Mrs. Palfrey at the Claremont.* 1971. Chatto/Windus. 1st ed. dj. VG $15.00

TAYLOR, Emerson Gifford. *New England in France, 1917-1919.* 1920. Boston. Ills. 325 pp. maps. VG $45.00

TAYLOR, Emily. *Dear Charlotte's Boys & Other Stories.* London. Ills. Whimper. VG $20.00

TAYLOR, Francis H. *Fifty Centuries of Art.* 1954. New York. Harper. 1st ed. G $15.00

TAYLOR, Geoffry. *Absurd World of Charles Bragg.* 1983. New York. Abrams. Ills. dj. EX $25.00

TAYLOR, George & Neu, Irene. *The American Railroad Network 1861-1890.* 1956. Harvard. 1st ed. dj. $10.00

TAYLOR, I. *Origin of the Ayrans.* 1889. VG $10.00

TAYLOR, J. *African Rifles & Cartridges.* 1948. dj. VG $215.00

TAYLOR, J. *An African Zoo in the Family.* 1965. Emerson. Ills. 185 pp. dj. VG $12.50

TAYLOR, J. *Pondoro, Last of the Ivory Hunters.* 1955. New York. Simon & Schuster. 1st ed. dj. $25.00

TAYLOR, J. Bayard. *Views A-Foot.* 1847. New York. Wiley. VG $20.00

TAYLOR, J.A. *History of Dentistry.* 1922. Philadelphia. Ills. 238 pp. $12.50

TAYLOR, J.C. *Wildlife in India's Tiger Kingdom.* 1980. Carlton. Ills. 366 pp. dj. EX $12.50

TAYLOR, J.M. *Field Trial Record of Dogs in America 1874-1907.* 1907. Ills. 545 pp. VG $100.00

TAYLOR, Jane & Ann. *Little Ann & Other Poems.* 1883. Warne. Ills. Greenaway. 1st ed. VG $75.00

TAYLOR, John R. & Jackson, A. *The Hollywood Musical.* 1971. London. Ills. dj. VG $20.00

TAYLOR, John W. & Munson, K. *History of Aviation, Full Story of Flight.* 1975. New York. 1500 color Ills. 1st Am. ed. $22.50

TAYLOR, John. *The Witchcraft Delusion in Colonial Connecticut.* 1908. New York. Grafton. 172 pp. $17.50

TAYLOR, Joseph. *The General Character of the Dog.* 1807. Philadelphia. $115.00

TAYLOR, L.B. Jr. *That Others May Live.* 1967. New York. Ills. ex-lib. 160 pp. dj. VG $5.00

TAYLOR, Malcolm. *Knight of the Air.* 1938. Boston. Ills. Allen Pope. 1st ed. $15.00

TAYLOR, Marie. *The Mysterious Five.* 1930. Boston. Christopher Pub. 1st ed. dj. $12.50

TAYLOR, Mrs. H.J. *The Last Survivor.* 1932. San Francisco. Ills. 22 pp. $15.00

TAYLOR, Peter. *The Early Guest.* 1982. Palaemon Press.Ltd. ed. 1/140. sgn. wrappers. $50.00

TAYLOR, Phoebe Atwood. *Proof of the Pudding.* 1945. London. Collins. 1st Eng. ed. dj. VG $25.00

TAYLOR, Phoebe Atwood. *Punch with Care.* 1947. London. 1st Eng. ed. dj. VG $22.00

TAYLOR, Phoebe Atwood. *The Crimson Patch.* 1936. New York. Norton. 1st ed. EX $20.00

TAYLOR, Robert Lewis. *Adrift in a Boneyard.* 1947. New York. Doubleday. 1st ed. dj. VG $25.00

TAYLOR, Robert. *W.C. Fields: His Follies & Fortunes.* 1949. Garden City. Doubleday. Ills. 1st ed. $17.50

TAYLOR, T. *Sword & Swastika.* 1952. New York. Simon & Schuster. ex-lib. G $15.00

TAYLOR, Walter. *Four Years with General Lee.* 1878. Appleton. $25.00

TAYLOR, William & Holub, E. *Africa Illustrated.* 1895. New York. 88 pp. photos. VG $18.00

TAYLOR, William. *California Life.* 1858. New York. Ills. VG $50.00

TAYLOR. *Deems, of Men & Music.* 1937. 1st ed. $6.50

TAYLOR. *Pictorial History of Scotland.* 1859. London. Ills. 2 vol set. $90.00

TAYLOR. *Principles of Scientific Management.* 1911. 1st ed. EX $35.00

TAYLOR. *The Horse America Made.* 1944. Ills. $12.50

TAZIEFF, Haroun. *Caves of Adventure.* 1953. New York. Harper. photos. 222 pp. dj. VG $3.50

TEAGUE, Charles Collins. *Recollections of Citrus & Walnut Industry.* 1944. Richie Press. 1st ed. sgn. $17.50

TEAL, Mildred & John. *Portrait of an Island.* 1964. New York. Ills. 1st ed. 167 pp. $7.50

TEALE, Edwin Way. *Adventures in Nature.* 1974. Dodd Mead. Ills. Ferguson. 304 pp. dj. EX $7.50

TEALE, Edwin Way. *Autumn Across America.* 1956. Dodd Mead. Ills. 386 pp. dj. $8.50

TEALE, Edwin Way. *Circle of Seasons.* 1953. Dodd Mead. Ills. 306 pp. dj. VG $5.00

TEALE, Edwin Way. *Journey into Summer.* 1965. Dodd Mead. Ills. 366 pp. dj. VG $5.00

TEALE, Edwin Way. *North with the Spring.* 1953. Dodd Mead. Ills. 358 pp. dj. VG $5.00

TEALE, Edwin Way. *The Golden Throng, a Book About Bees.* 1945. Dodd Mead. Ills. 208 pp. VG $10.00

TEALE, Edwin Way. *Wandering Through Winter.* 1965. New York. Dodd Mead. 370 pp. VG $5.00

TEALL. *The Pleasures of Collecting.* 1920. New York. $6.00

TEASDALE, Sara. *Collected Poems.* 1937. Macmillan. 1st ed. dj. $15.00

TEASDALE, Sara. *Dark of the Moon.* 1926. Macmillan. 1st ed. dj. $12.50

TEASDALE, Sara. *Star Tonight.* 1930. New York. Ills. Lathrop. 1st ed. dj. VG $35.00

TEASDALE, Sara. *Strange Victory.* 1933. Macmillan. 1st ed. dj. $12.50

TEGNER, E. *Frithiof's Saga.* 1908. Rock Island. pls. VG $35.00

TEGNER, E. *Frithiof's Saga.* 1850. Kiobenhavn. Danish text. 303 pp. VG $32.50

TEICHMANN, Howard. *George S. Kauffman.* 1972. New York. Atheneum. 1st ed. 371 pp. $5.00

TEITARO, D. Suzuki. *An Introduction to Zen Buddhism.* 1960. London. Rider & Co. 2nd ed. dj. G $10.00

TELLER, Thomas. *Life & Adventures of Robinson Crusoe.* 1849. New Haven. Ills. wrappers. $25.00

TELLER, Walter. *Twelve Works of Naive Genius.* 1972. New York. Harcourt. Ills. 1st ed. $5.00

TEMPLEMAN, Eleanor L. *Arlington Heritage.* 1959. New York. Avenel. Ills. dj. VG $10.50

TEMPLIER, Pierre-Daniel. *Erik Satie.* 1969. Cambridge. Ills. dj. VG $15.00

TENGGREN, Gustaf. *The Good Dog Book.* 1924. Boston. Houghton Mifflin. Ills. VG $20.00

TENGGREN. *D'Aulnoy's Fairy Tales.* 1923. Philadelphia. McKay. 8 color pls. VG $25.00

TENGGREN. *Sing for Christmas.* 1943. New York. Ills. dj. VG $45.00

TENN, William. *Of Men & Monsters.* 1969. 1st Am. ed. dj. EX $110.00

TENNANT, Alan. *A Field Guide to Texas Snakes.* 1985. TX Monthly Pr. Ills. 1st ed. 260 pp. dj. EX $20.00

TENNANT, Emma. *Wild Nights.* 1980. New York. Harcourt. 1st ed. dj. VG $20.00

TENNENT, J. Emerson. *Belgium.* 1841. London. 2 vol set. VG $60.00

TENNEY, A. Webster. *Practical Activities for Future Farmer Chapters.* 1941. Danville, IL. Interstate. Ills. 318 pp. $5.00

TENNEY. *Mark Twain, a Reference Guide.* 1977. 1st ed. 443 pp. EX $45.00

TENNIEL. *Alice's Adventures in Wonderland.* 1871. Boston. 42 Ills. VG $32.00

TENNYSON, Alfred Lord. *Ballads & Other Poems.* 1880. London. 1st ed. G $25.00

TENNYSON, Alfred Lord. *Enoch Arden.* 1864. Boston. VG $32.50

TENNYSON, Alfred Lord. *Idylls of the King.* 1873. London. gilt leather binding. $65.00

TENNYSON, Alfred Lord. *Locksley Hall. 60 Years After.* 1886. London. 1st ed. EX $25.00

TENNYSON, Alfred Lord. *Maud.* 1855. 1st ed. G $35.00

TENNYSON, Alfred Lord. *Poems.* 1911. VG $17.50

TENNYSON, Alfred Lord. *The Last Tournament.* 1872. Ills. G $20.00

TENNYSON, Alfred Lord. *Unpublished Early Poems.* 1931. London. Ltd. 1st ed. 1/1500. VG $45.00

TENNYSON, Alfred Lord. *Works of Alfred Lord Tennyson.* 1904. Boston. Riverside. ex-lib. 7 vol set. $165.00

TENNYSON, J.R. *A Singleness of Purpose, Story of Ducks Unlimited.* 1977. Ducks Unlimited. 127 pp. dj. $15.00

TENNYSON, Lord; Hallam, ed. *The Works of Tennyson.* 1923. New York. Macmillan. $5.50

TERESE, Robert & Owen, C. *A Flock of Lambs.* 1970. sgns. dj. EX $10.00

TERHUNE, Albert Payson. *Caleb Conover, Railroader.* 1907. London/NY. Ills. 322 pp. G $10.00

TERHUNE, Albert Payson. *Gray Dawn.* 1927. NY/London. Ills. Paul Bransom. 1st ed. $15.00

TERHUNE, Albert Payson. *Real Tales of Real Dogs.* 1935. Saalfield. Ills. Thorne. 1st ed. VG $25.00

TERHUNE, Albert Payson. *The Tiger's Claw.* 1924. New York. Doran. 1st ed. $10.00

TERHUNE, Albert Payson. *Water!* 1928. New York. 318 pp. $10.00

TERHUNE, Albert Payson. *Wolf.* 1925. Grosset & Dunlap. dj. EX $7.50

TERKEL, Studs. *American Dreams: Lost & Found.* 1980. Pantheon. 1st ed. dj. VG $10.00

TERKEL, Studs. *Division Street.* 1967. New York. Pantheon. 1st ed. dj. VG $75.00

TERKEL, Studs. *Talking to Myself.* 1977. Pantheon. 1st ed. dj. EX $15.00

TERKEL, Studs. *The Good War.* 1984. Pantheon. 1st ed. dj. EX $20.00

TERRELL, J. *Pueblos, Gods, & Spaniards.* 1973. 1st ed. dj. EX $15.00

TERRELL, John & Donna M. *Indian Women of the Western Morning.* 1974. New York. 1st ed. 214 pp. dj. EX $10.00

TERRELL, John Upton. *Bunkhouse Papers.* 1971. New York. Ills. 1st ed. 251 pp. $10.00

TERROUX, Gilles. *Face-Off of the Century.* 1972. Canada. Ills. SftCvr. pb. $10.00

TESNOHLIDEK, Rudolf. *The Cunning Little Vixen.* 1985. Farrar. Ltd. 1st ed. sgn. slipcase. EX $150.00

TETENS, Alfred. *Among the Savages of the South Seas.* 1958. Stanford. 1st ed. dj. $15.00

TEVIS, Walter. *The Man Who Fell to Earth.* 1963. Gold Medal. pb. VG $12.50

TEY, Josephine. *Richard Bordeaux by Gordon Daviott.* London. 1st ed. $55.00

THACKARY, William. *The Irish Sketch Book.* NY. New World. 1st Am. ed. wrappers. rare. VG $525.00

THACKERAY, Anne Isabella. *Old Kensington.* 1873. Tauchnitz. 1st ed. 2 vol set. $50.00

THACKERAY, William M. *Round About the Christmas Tree.* 1914. Marchblanks Pr. Ltd. ed. 1/250. VG $17.50

THACKERAY, William M. *Thackeray's Works.* 1891. Boston. Ills. Ltd. ed. 30 vol set. VG $125.00

THACKERAY, William M. *The Adventures of Philip.* 1st ed. 1st issue. 3 vol set. $250.00

THACKERAY, William M. *The End of the Play.* 1915. Torch Press. Ltd. ed. 1/200. $20.00

THACKERAY, William M. *The History of Henry Esmond.* 1950. Literary Guild. Ills. Hallman. $6.50

THACKERAY, William M. *The Newcomes: Memoirs of Most Respectable Family.* 1854. London. Ills. 1st ed. 2 vol set. $165.00

THACKERAY, William M. *The Rose & the Ring.* 1855. New York. Harper. VG $20.00

THACKERAY, William M. *The Virginians.* 1858. London. Ills. 1st ed. 2 vol set. VG $35.00

THACKERAY, William M. *Vanity Fair.* 1900. Harper. Becky Sharp, ed. Ills. 676 pp. $9.50

THACKERAY, William M. *Vanity Fair.* 1848. London. 1st ed. 1st issue. VG $375.00

THACKERAY, William M. *Vanity Fair.* 1860. Harper. Ills. $15.00

THACKERAY, William M. *Works of William Makepeace Thackeray.* 1886-1889. London. 24 vol set. $45.00

THACKERAY, William M. *Works of William Makepeace Thackeray.* 1899. London. Ills. 13 vol set. VG $525.00

THAL, Herbert Van. *Belloc-Biographical Anthology.* 1970. New York. 1st ed. dj. $10.00

THANE, Elswyth. *Dawn's Early Light.* 1943. Duel Sloan. 9th ed. dj. VG $15.00

THANE, Elswyth. *Dawn's Early Light.* 1943. New York. 1st ed. dj. VG $20.00

THANE, Elswyth. *Mt. Vernon: Legacy.* 1967. 1st ed. dj. VG $22.50

THANE, Elswyth. *Potomac Squire.* 1963. New York. 1st ed. 432 pp. $6.50

THANE, Elswyth. *The Family Quarrel.* 1959. New York. Ills. 308 pp. dj. $7.50

THARIN, R.S. *Arbitrary Arrests in the South.* 1863. New York 1st ed. $32.50

THARP, Louise Hall. *Appletons of Beacon Hill.* 1973. $10.00

THARP, Louise Hall. *Saint Gaudens & the Gilded Era.* 1969. VG $7.00

THARP, Louise Hall. *The Baroness & the General.* 1962. Boston/Toronto. Ills. 1st ed. 458 pp. dj. $10.00

THARP, Louise Hall. *The Peabody Sisters of Salem.* 1950. Boston. 372 pp. $52.50

THATCHER, B.B. *Indian Biography.* 1832. New York. $40.00

THATCHER, James. *Military Journal During Am. Revolutionary War.* 1827. Boston. 2nd ed. 487 pp. $50.00

THAW, Harry K. *The Traitor.* 1926. Philadelphia. Ills. 271 pp. dj. $12.50

THAXTER, Celia. *Among the Isles of Shoals.* 1873. Boston. Ills. 1st ed. VG $30.00

THAYER, Emma. *Wild Flowers of the Pacific Coast.* 1887. New York. G $35.00

THAYER, Emma. *Wild Flowers of the Rocky Mountains.* 1887. New York. 2nd ed. 24 color pls. EX $75.00

THAYER, G. *Concealing Coloration in the Animal Kingdom.* 1909. New York. Ills. sgn. VG $85.00

THAYER, Henry & Co. *Descriptive Catalogue of Fluid & Solid Extracts.* 1872. Cambridgeport. $55.00

THAYER, M. *Jacqueline Bouvier Kennedy.* 1961. 1st ed. VG $10.00

THAYER, Theodore. *Nathanael Greene Strategist of Am. Revolution.* 1960. Twayne. 1st ed. dj. $10.00

THAYER, William M. *Marvels of New West.* 1891. Norwich, CT. Ills. 6 vols in 1. 715 pp. $25.00

THAYER, William M. *Marvels of the New West.* 1887. Norwich. 1st ed. 715 pp. VG $27.50

THAYER, William M. *Marvels of the New West.* 1890. 6 books in 1 vol. VG $22.50

THAYER, William M. *Poor-House to Pulpit; or, Triumphs of Dr. Kitto.* 1859. Boston. 349 pp. $12.50

THAYER, William Roscoe. *The Life of John Hay.* 1915. Boston. Ills. 5th impression. 2 vol set. $12.50

THAYER, William. *Sumpter to Roanoke.* 1864. 347 pp. VG $17.00

THEAKER, H.G. *Ingoldsby Legends.* 1911. London. Ills. 1st ed. VG $45.00

THEAKER. *Water Babies.* London. 16 color pls. VG $30.00

THEMERSON, Stefan. *The Adventures of Reddy Bottom.* 1954. Gaberbocchus. 1st ed. EX $7.50

THEMERSON, Stefan. *Woolf Woolf; or, Who Killed Richard Wagner?* 1951. Gaberbocchus. 1st ed. dj. EX $10.00

THEOBALD. *Arizona Territory Post Offices & Postmasters.* 1961. Phoenix. Ills. SftCvr. $20.00

THEROUX, Paul. *A Christmas Card.* 1978. 1st ed. dj. EX $30.00

THEROUX, Paul. *Fong & the Indians.* 1968. Boston. dj. VG $35.00

THEROUX, Paul. *Girls at Play.* 1969. Boston. Houghton Mifflin. 1st ed. VG $45.00

THEROUX, Paul. *Half Moon Street.* 1984. 1st ed. dj. EX $15.00

THEROUX, Paul. *Jungle Lovers.* 1971. Boston. Houghton Mifflin. 1st ed. EX $50.00

THEROUX, Paul. *London Snow.* Great Britain. Ltd. ed. 1/450. sgn. VG $40.00

THEROUX, Paul. *Sailing Through China.* 1983. Great Britain. 1st ed. sgn. VG $25.00

THEROUX, Paul. *Sailing Through China.* 1984. Boston. Houghton Mifflin. 1st ed. dj. $15.00

THEROUX, Paul. *Saint Jack.* 1973. Boston. Houghton Mifflin. 1st ed. dj. $25.00

THEROUX, Paul. *The Black House.* 1974. Boston. Houghton Mifflin. 1st ed. VG $25.00

THEROUX, Paul. *The Black House.* 1974. 1st English ed. dj. EX $45.00

THEROUX, Paul. *The Consul's File.* 1977. Boston. 1st Am. ed. dj. VG $15.00

THEROUX, Paul. *The Great Railway Bazaar.* 1975. Boston. 1st ed. 1st issue. dj. VG $35.00

THEROUX, Paul. *The Kingdom by the Sea.* 1983. Boston. Ltd. 1st ed. slipcase. EX $75.00

THEROUX, Paul. *The Kingdom by the Sea.* 1983. Boston. Houghton Mifflin. 1st ed. dj. $17.50

THEROUX, Paul. *The Last Laugh.* 1981. Simon & Schuster. dj. VG $15.00

THEROUX, Paul. *The London Embassy.* 1983. Boston. 1st ed. dj. EX $15.00

THEROUX, Paul. *The Mosquito Coast.* Ltd. ed. 1/350. sgn. VG $30.00

THEROUX, Paul. *The Mosquito Coast.* 1982. Boston. 1st ed. dj. EX $15.00

THEROUX, Paul. *The Old Patagonian Express.* 1979. 1st ed. sgn. dj. EX $50.00

THEROUX, Paul. *V.S. Naipaul.* 1972. 1st English ed. dj. EX $55.00

THEROUX, Paul. *Waldo.* 1967. 1st ed. VG $85.00

THEROUX, Paul. *World's End & Other Stories.* 1980. Boston. Ltd. 1st ed. slipcase. EX $75.00

THEROUX, Paul. *World's End & Other Stories.* 1980. Boston. 1st ed. dj. EX $15.00

THEROUX, Phyllis. *California & Other States of Grace.* 1979. Morrow. proof copy. wrappers. VG $15.00

THIRKELL, Angela & Lejeune, C. *Three Score & Ten.* 1961. London. Hamilton. 1st ed. dj. VG $20.00

THIRKELL, Angela. *Jutland Cottage.* 1953. New York. 1st ed. EX $12.50

THIRKELL, Angela. *The Grateful Sparrow & Other Tales.* 1935. London. Ills. Richter. 1st ed. dj. VG $65.00

THOBURN, Bishop J.M. *India & Malaysia.* 1893. Ills. 566 pp. $15.00

THOLLANDER, Earl. *Back Roads of New England.* 1974. New York. 2nd printing. maps. dj. VG $10.00

THOM, Adam. *Claims to Oregon Territory Considered.* 1844. London. 1st ed. 44 pp. EX $100.00

THOM, Douglas J. *The Hockey Bibliography.* 1978. Ontario. 152 pp. SftCvr. EX $10.00

THOM, W.T., Jr. *Petroleum & Coal, the Keys to the Future.* 1929. Princeton. Ills. 223 pp. $10.00

THOMAS, A. *Fine Books.* 1967. New York. Putnam. Ills. $17.50

THOMAS, A. *Great Books & Book Collectors.* 1975. New York. Putnam. dj. VG $35.00

THOMAS, Benjamin. *Lincoln's New Salem.* 1934. Springfield. Ills. 1st ed. VG $8.00

THOMAS, Bob. *King Cohn: The Life & Times of Harry Cohn.* 1967. London. Barrie & Rockcliff. 381 pp. VG $5.00

THOMAS, Chauncey. *The Crystal Button.* 1891. Boston. VG $35.00

THOMAS, Clarence C. *Township Plat Book of Mercer County, IL.* 1935. Aldeo, IL. 32 pp. pb. G $15.00

THOMAS, D.H. *Swallow.* 1984. Denny. 1st Canadian ed. dj. VG $17.50

THOMAS, D.H. *The Devil & the Floral Dance.* 1978. Robson. Ills. Astrop. 1st ed. VG $20.00

THOMAS, D.H. *The White Hotel.* 1981. Viking. 1st Am. ed. dj. VG $22.50

THOMAS, D.M. *Ararat.* 1983. New York. Viking. 1st ed. dj. EX $20.00

THOMAS, D.M. *The Bronze Horseman.* 1982. New York. Viking. 1st ed. dj. VG $25.00

THOMAS, D.M. *The Flute Player.* 1979. New York. Dutton. 1st ed. dj. EX $30.00

THOMAS, David Y. *Arkansas in War & Reconstruction, 1861-1874.* 1926. Little Rock. Ills. 1st ed. 446 pp. $150.00

THOMAS, Dylan & Davenport, J. *The Death of the King's Canary.* 1976. London. Hutchinson. 1st ed. dj. VG $30.00

THOMAS, Dylan & Davenport, J. *The Death of the King's Canary.* 1977. Viking. 1st Am. ed. dj. VG $15.00

THOMAS, Dylan. *A Child's Christmas in Wales.* 1954. New Directions.1st ed. dj. $125.00

THOMAS, Dylan. *A Child's Christmas in Wales.* 1955. Norfolk. New Directions. dj. EX $45.00

THOMAS, Dylan. *A Prospect of the Sea.* 1955. London. Dent. 1st ed. dj. VG $65.00

THOMAS, Dylan. *Adventures in the Skin Trade.* 1955. London. Putnam. 1st ed. 1st issue. EX $135.00

THOMAS, Dylan. *Adventures in the Skin Trade.* 1955. London. Putnam. 1st ed. dj. VG $75.00

THOMAS, Dylan. *Collected Poems 1934-1952.* 1952. London. Dent. Ltd. 1st ed. dj. VG $110.00

THOMAS, Dylan. *Deaths & Entrances.* 1946. London. 1st ed. dj. VG $175.00

THOMAS, Dylan. *Eighteen Poems.* 1934. 1st Eng. ed. dj. $950.00

THOMAS, Dylan. *Letters to Vernon Watkins.* 1957. Dent. 2nd ed. dj. $8.50

THOMAS, Dylan. *Letters to Vernon Watkins.* 1957. London. Dent & Faber. 1st ed. dj. $45.00

THOMAS, Dylan. *Me & My Bike.* 1964. London. Ills. Leonora Box. Ltd. ed. VG $130.00

THOMAS, Dylan. *New Poems.* 1943. Norfolk. 32 pp. mauve wrappers. VG $70.00

THOMAS, Dylan. *Portrait of the Artist as a Young Dog.* 1948. London. First Guild Books ed. VG $30.00

THOMAS, Dylan. *Quite Early One Morning.* 1954. London. Dent. 1st ed. 1st issue. dj. $115.00

THOMAS, Dylan. *Rebecca's Daughters.* 1965. London. Triton. 1st ed. dj. VG $35.00

THOMAS, Dylan. *Rebecca's Daughters.* 1965. Little, Brown. 1st ed. dj. VG $20.00

THOMAS, Dylan. *The Beach of Falesa.* 1964. London. 1st Eng. ed. $60.00

THOMAS, Dylan. *The Doctor & the Devils.* 1953. London. Dent. 1st ed. dj. VG $95.00

THOMAS, Dylan. *The Map of Love.* 1939. 1st Eng. ed. dj. VG $200.00

THOMAS, Dylan. *The Outing.* 1985. London. Dent. Ills. 1st ed. dj. EX $35.00

THOMAS, Dylan. *Twenty Years A-Growing.* 1964. London. Dent. 1st ed. dj. VG $35.00

THOMAS, Dylan. *Under Milk Wood.* 1958. London. Dent. wrappers. $75.00

THOMAS, Dylan. *Under Milk Wood.* 1969. Toucan Press. Ltd. 1st ed. 1/250. wrappers. $30.00

THOMAS, Edward. *The Heart of England.* 1906. Dutton. Ills. H.L. Richardson. 1st ed. $35.00

THOMAS, G.C. *The Practical Book of Outdoor Rose Growing.* 1916. Philadelphia. Ills. G $12.00

THOMAS, Gordon & Witts, M.M. *The Day the World Ended.* 1969. New York. Ills. 306 pp. dj. EX $20.00

THOMAS, Hardy. *Selected Poems.* 1921. London/Boston. Ltd. VG $70.00

THOMAS, Henry & Dana. *Living Biographies of Famous Novelists.* 1943. Book League. $3.00

THOMAS, Isaiah. *Infernal Conference or Dialogues of Devils.* 1808. 288 pp. VG $55.00

THOMAS, Isaiah. *The Diary 1805-1828.* 1909. Worcester. 1st ed. 2 vol set. EX $150.00

THOMAS, Jean. *Big Sandy.* 1940. New York. Ills. 302 pp. index. dj. $32.50

THOMAS, Joseph B. *Hounds & Hunting Through the Ages.* 1929. Derrydale. Ltd. ed. 1/250. EX $150.00

THOMAS, L. *Count Luckner, the Sea Devil.* 1929. Ills. sgn. $15.00

THOMAS, L. *Storming Heaven.* 1970. 1st ed. dj. EX $10.00

THOMAS, L. *The Medusa & the Snail.* 1979. Viking. 175 pp. dj. EX $5.00

THOMAS, Lately. *Between Two Empires: Story of CA's 1st Senator.* 1969. Boston. Houghton Mifflin. dj. VG $6.00

THOMAS, Lately. *Delmonico's, a Century of Splendor.* 1967. Boston. Ills 1st ed. dj. VG $20.00

THOMAS, Leslie. *Dangerous Davies.* 1976. London. Methuen. 1st ed. dj. $15.00

THOMAS, Lowell. *Out of This World.* 1950. New York. photos. 320 pp. VG $3.50

THOMAS, Lowell. *Rolling Stone, Life & Adventures of A. R. Dugmore.* 1933. Garden City. 311 pp. $10.00

THOMAS, Lowell. *Seven Wonders of the World.* 1956. Ills. 283 pp. dj. EX $2.00

THOMAS, Lowell. *So Long Until Tomorrow. Quaker Hill to Kathmandu.* 1977. New York. 317 pp. $10.00

THOMAS, Lowell. *Tall Stories.* 1945. New York. 186 pp. $10.00

THOMAS, Lowell. *The First World Flight.* 1925. New York. 2nd impression. EX $45.00

THOMAS, Lowell. *These Men Shall Never Die.* 1943. Philadelphia. Ills. 307 pp. $10.50

THOMAS, Lowell. *Will Rogers, Ambassador of Good Will.* 1935. Philadelphia. 288 pp. $10.00

THOMAS, Lowell. *With Lawrence in Arabia.* 1924. Garden City. 408 pp. $6.50

THOMAS, M. *Bibliography of John Dewey, 1882-1930.* 1939. VG $15.00

THOMAS, Michael M. *Hard Money.* 1985. Viking. proof copy. wrappers. VG $30.00

THOMAS, Milton H. *John Dewey. A Centennial Bibliography.* 1962. U. Chicago Pr. ex-lib. 370 pp. VG $7.50

THOMAS, Norman. *Appeal to the Nations.* 1947. New York. Holt. 1st printing. 175 pp. VG $8.00

THOMAS, Norman. *As I See It.* 1932. New York. Macmillan. G $10.00

THOMAS, Norman. *Socialism Re-Examined.* 1963. New York. Norton. 1st ed. 280 pp. G $7.00

THOMAS, Pascoe. *True & Impartial Journal of South-Seas Voyage.* 1745. London. 1st ed. $485.00

THOMAS, R. *Glory of America: Memoirs & Exploits of Officers.* 1834. New York. Ills. 1st ed. $65.00

THOMAS, Ross. *Briarpatch.* 1984. New York. Simon & Schuster. 1st ed. dj. $30.00

THOMAS, Ross. *Chinaman's Chance.* 1978. 1st ed. dj. EX $40.00

THOMAS, Ross. *Missionary Stew.* 1983. New York. Simon & Schuster. 1st ed. dj. $20.00

THOMAS, Ross. *The Eighth Dwarf.* 1979. Random House. 1st ed. sgn. dj. EX $40.00

THOMAS, Ross. *The Eighth Dwarf.* 1979. Simon & Schuster. 1st ed. dj. $15.00

THOMAS, Ross. *The Money Harvest.* 1975. 1st ed. dj. EX $40.00

THOMAS, Ross. *The Mordida Man.* 1981. 1st ed. dj. EX $25.00

THOMAS, Ross. *The Porkchoppers.* 1972. 1st ed. inscr. dj. EX $80.00

THOMAS, Ross. *Yellow Dog Contract.* 1977. 1st ed. sgn. dj. EX $65.00

THOMAS, T.J. & Gallagher, D. *Spotlight on Ohio's Black Crime.* 1930. Cleveland. Ills. 127 pp. wrappers. $25.00

THOMAS, Will. *The Seeking.* 1953. New York. ex-lib. 290 pp. $3.50

THOMAS. *American & British Pewter: History Survey.* 1976. Universe Bks. $5.00

THOMAS. *No Questions Asked.* 1976. London. 1st ed. dj. EX $35.00

THOMAS. *Stranger in the Earth.* 1948. New York. 1st printing. 371 pp. dj. VG $25.00

THOMAS. *The Grand Heures of Jean, Duke of Berry.* 1971. New York. color pls. folio. dj. EX $40.00

THOMPSON, A.L. *Problems of Bird Migration.* 1926. Houghton Mifflin. 350 pp. VG $17.50

THOMPSON, Benjamin F. *History of Long Island.* 1839. New York. 1st ed. VG $75.00

THOMPSON, Buddie. *As I Know Them. A Midget's Story of Show People.* 1936. Indianapolis. 164 pp. $17.50

THOMPSON, Charles. *Halfway Down the Stairs.* 1957. New York. Harper. 277 pp. $5.00

THOMPSON, Craig. *Since Spindletop.* 1951. photos. 110 pp. EX $6.50

THOMPSON, Daniel. *Green Mountain Boy at Monticello.* 1962. Brattleboro. 1st ed. dj. $8.50

THOMPSON, Dorothy. *Once on Christmas.* 1938. New York. Oxford Press. Ills. Lenski. $5.00

THOMPSON, Ed Porter. *History of the Orphan Brigade.* 1898. Louisville, KY. enlarged ed. 2 pls. 1104 pp. $450.00

THOMPSON, Ernest Seton. *The Biography of a Grizzly.* 1900. New York. Ills. 1st ed. $17.50

THOMPSON, Harold W. *Body, Boots & Britches.* 1940. Phila./NY. 2nd impression. map. 530 pp. $10.00

THOMPSON, Hunter S. *Fear & Loathing in Las Vegas.* 1972. London. Paladin. 1st Eng. ed. VG $25.00

THOMPSON, Hunter S. *Fear & Loathing: On the Campaign Trail '72.* 1973. San Francisco. 1st ed. dj. EX $35.00

THOMPSON, Hunter S. *Great Shark Hunt.* advance copy. dj. EX $50.00

THOMPSON, J. Eric S. *The Rise & Fall of the Maya Civilization.* 1964. Norman. Ills. 6th printing. 288 pp. $10.00

THOMPSON, J.P. *Home Worship & Use of Bible in the Home.* 1882. New York. Ills. maps. 916 pp. $7.50

THOMPSON, James. *Seasons.* 1793. Ills. Singleton/Stothard. EX $125.00

THOMPSON, Jim. *Nothing but a Man.* 1970. New York. Popular Lib. 1st ed. dj. $20.00

THOMPSON, Jim. *Now & on Earth.* 1985. Belen. Ltd. ed. 1/400. dj. EX $35.00

THOMPSON, Jim. *South of Heaven.* 1967. Greenwich. Gold Medal. wrappers. EX $20.00

THOMPSON, Kay. *Eloise at Christmastime.* 1958. New York. Ills. 1st ed. dj. VG $42.50

THOMPSON, Kay. *Eloise in Moscow.* 1959. New York. Ills. 1st ed. EX $55.00

THOMPSON, Kay. *Eloise.* 1955. Ills. 3rd ed. 65 pp. EX $20.00

THOMPSON, L. *Robert Frost: Years of Triumph.* 1970. 2nd ed. $12.00

THOMPSON, L.M. & Troeh, F.R. *Soils & Soil Fertility.* 1978. New York. McGraw Hill. 4th ed. TB. dj. $4.00

THOMPSON, M. *Birds from North Borneo.* 1966. KS U. Press. EX $4.00

THOMPSON, Maurice. *Witchery of Archery.* 1928. Pinehurst, NC. dj. VG $30.00

THOMPSON, Morton. *Not as a Stranger.* 1954. New York. Scribner. 696 pp. dj. $4.00

THOMPSON, Mrs. E.L. *75 Years of Sully County, SD History, 1883-1958.* 1958. Onida, SD. 393 pp. SftCvr. G $30.00

THOMPSON, R.W. *Wild Animal Man.* 1934. 1st ed. dj. EX $10.00

THOMPSON, Ruth Plumly. *Captain Salt in Oz.* 1936. Chicago. reprint. Ills. Neill. dj. $55.00

THOMPSON, Ruth Plumly. *Handy Mandy in Oz.* 1937. Chicago. 1st ed. VG $135.00

THOMPSON, Ruth Plumly. *Hungry Tiger of Oz.* 1926. Chicago. reprint. dj. EX $50.00

THOMPSON, Ruth Plumly. *Lost King in Oz.* 1925. Chicago. 1st ed. 1st issue. EX $135.00

THOMPSON, Ruth Plumly. *Ojo in Oz.* 1933. Chicago. Ills. Neill. 1st ed. 304 pp. G $45.00

THOMPSON, Ruth Plumly. *Speedy in Oz.* 1934. Chicago. reprint. Ills. Neill. dj. $55.00

THOMPSON, Ruth Plumly. *The Royal Book of Oz.* 1921. Chicago. reprint. Ills. Neill. EX $45.00

THOMPSON, Ruth Plumly. *Wishing Horse of Oz.* 1935. Chicago. Ills. Neill. 1st ed. 298 pp. G $65.00

THOMPSON, Ruth Plumly. *Yellow Knight of Oz.* 1930. 1st ed. G $35.00

THOMPSON, S. Millett. *Regimental History of the 13th New Hampshire.* 1888. Boston. $70.00

THOMPSON, Thomas. *Richie.* 1973. New York. dj. $10.00

THOMPSON, Vance. *Diplomatic Mysteries.* 1905. Philadelphia. Lippincott. VG $15.00

THOMPSON, Vance. *Life of Ethelbert Nevin/Letters & Wife's Memories.* 1913. Boston. Ills. inscr. G $25.00

THOMPSON, Virginia. *Postmortem on Malaya.* 1943. New York. Macmillan. ex-lib. 323 pp. $3.00

THOMPSON, W.F. *Image of War, Pictorial Report of the Civil War.* 1960. 1st ed. $15.00

THOMPSON, W.M. *Lawson History of America's Cup.* 1902. Boston. Hudson Library. Ltd. ed. $125.00

THOMPSON, Wallace. *Rainbow Countries of Central America.* 1926. New York. Dutton. Ills. VG $15.00

THOMPSON, William. *Wigwam Wonder Tales.* 1919. New York. Ills. C.M. Boog. 156 pp. dj. $15.00

THOMPSON, Zadock. *History of Vermont.* 1842. Ills. 1st ed. 200 pp. fld. map. index. VG $75.00

THOMPSON. *Adventure Boys & the River of Emeralds.* 1927. Cupples & Leon. Ills. dj. EX $8.50

THOMPSON. *Great Shark Hunt.* 1979. 1st Am. ed. dj. EX $35.00

THOMPSON. *Gunman's Spawn.* Graphic Giant. pb. $3.00

THOMPSON. *Hell's Angels.* 1967. 1st Am. ed. dj. EX $90.00

THOMPSON. *On Growth & Form.* 1961. Cambridge. 1st ed. dj. VG $17.50

THOMPSON. *Rawhide Rider.* Popular. pb. $3.00

THOMSON, Hugh. *Tom Brown's School Days.* Boston. 412 pp. VG $17.50

THOMSON, J.A. *The Biology of Birds.* 1923. Macmillan. Ills. 436 pp. VG $10.00

THOMSON, John Stuart. *A Day's Song.* 1900. 1st ed. $8.50

THOMSON. *Marry Wives of Windsor.* 1910. Stokes. 40 color pls. VG $110.00

THONHOFF. *San Antonio Stage Lines. 1847-1881.* 1971. U. of TX. 38 pp. SftCvr. $15.00

THOREAU, Henry David. *A Week on the Concord & Merrimak Rivers.* 1893. Houghton Mifflin. 531 pp. G $6.00

THOREAU, Henry David. *Excursions.* 1863. Ticknor & Fields. ex-lib. VG $100.00

THOREAU, Henry David. *Men of Concord.* 1936. Boston. Ills. Wyeth. 1st ed. dj. EX $125.00

THOREAU, Henry David. *The Maine Woods.* 1950. Bramhall. 340 pp. VG $5.00

THOREAU, Henry David. *Walden.* 1942. Black. 358 pp. EX $7.50

THOREAU, Henry David. *Walden.* 1886. London. 1st Eng. ed. VG $200.00

THOREAU, Henry David. *Works of Henry David Thoreau.* 1981. Avenel. Ills. 713 pp. dj. EX $12.50

THORNBROUGH, Emma Lou. *Indian in the Civil War Era 1850-1880.* 1965. Indianapolis. 758 pp. wrappers. $10.00

THORNBROUGH, Gayle. *Correspondence of Badollet & Gallatin 1804-1856.* 1963. Indianapolis. 372 pp. wrappers. $10.00

THORNBURY, Walter. *Two Centuries of Song.* 1867. London. Ills. VG $45.00

THORNDIKE, Russell. *The Devil in the Belfry.* 1932. New York. Dial Press. 1st ed. VG $15.00

THORNDYKE, Helen Louise. *Honey Bunch: Her First Visit to the City.* 1923. New York. Grosset & Dunlap. 182 pp. $5.00

THORNTON, Francis B. *Sea of Glory.* 1953. 243 pp. dj. $4.00

THORNTON, J. Quinn. *Oregon & California in 1848.* 1849. New York. ex-lib. rebound. 2 vol set. $200.00

THORNTON, John W. *The First Records of Anglo-American Colonization.* 1859. Boston. Ltd. ed. 1/250. EX $85.00

THORNTON, R. *Elements of Botany.* 1812. Ills. 2 vol set. G $95.00

THORON, Ward. *The Letters of Mrs. Henry Adams.* 1936. Boston. 1st ed. dj. $15.00

THORP, R.W. *Wild West Doc Carver.* 1957. London. dj. VG $10.00

THORP, Willard. *Southern Reader.* 1955. Knopf. 1st ed. dj. VG $15.00

THORPE, T.B. *The Big Bear of Arkansas.* 1841. Baltimore. 1st ed. $50.00

THRASHER, Frederic. *Okay for Sound/How the Screen Found Its Voice.* 1946. New York. Ills. 301 pp. VG $25.00

THRASHER, Halsey. *Hunter & Trapper.* 1868. Ills. 95 pp. VG $40.00

THRILLING, Diana. *Claremont Essays.* 1964. New York. 1st ed. dj. EX $12.50

THROCKMORTON, P. *Lost Ships: Adventure in Undersea Archaeology.* 1964. Boston. Atlantic Monthly. Ills. dj. G $12.50

THRONE, Mildred. *Cyrus Clay Carpenter & Iowa Politics 1854-1898.* 1974. Iowa City. Ills. 302 pp. $10.00

THROOP, Benjamin H. *A Half Century in Scranton.* 1895. Scranton. Ills. 355 pp. $35.00

THRUELSEN, R. & Arnold. *East Mediterranean Sweep.* 1944. New York. dj. $20.00

THURBER, James. *Alarms & Diversions.* 1957. Harper $7.00

THURBER, James. *Credos & Curios.* 1962. Harper. 180 pp. dj. $52.50

THURBER, James. *My World & Welcome to It.* 1942. New York. Harcourt. 1st ed. 310 pp. $20.00

THURBER, James. *Selected Letters of James Thurber.* 1981. Boston. Little, Brown. 1st ed. dj. $7.50

THURBER, James. *The Beast in Me & Other Animals.* 1948. Harcourt Brace. 1st ed. VG $12.00

THURBER, James. *The Last Flower.* 1939. Knopf. 1st ed. dj. VG $30.00

THURBER, James. *The Thirteen Clocks.* 1950. New York. Ills. Simont. 1st ed. VG $40.00

THURBER, James. *The Thurber Carnival.* 1945. New York. Harper. 369 pp. dj. $12.50

THURBER, James. *The Thurber Album.* 1952. New York. Simon & Schuster. 1st ed. $42.50

THURBER, James. *The White Deer.* 1946. London. Ills. Thurber. dj. VG $40.00

THURBER, James. *The White Deer.* 1945. Harcourt. Ills. Thurber & Freeman. dj. $10.00

THURBER, James. *The Wonderful O.* 1957. New York. Ills. 1st ed. 73 pp. dj. $15.00

THURBER, James. *Thurber Country.* 1953. New York. Simon & Schuster. 1st ed. dj. $15.00

THURBER, James. *Thurber's Dogs.* 1955. New York. Ills. 1st ed. 294 pp. $15.00

THURBER, James. *Years with Ross.* 1959. Boston. 1st ed. dj. G $15.00

THURSTON, D.J. *Great Horse Omnibus from Homer to Hemingway.* 1949. Ills. 1st ed. $17.50

THURSTON, E. Temple. *The Flower of Gloster.* 1912. Dodd Mead. Ills. Dakon. 1st ed. 214 pp. $35.00

THURSTON, Howard. *200 More Tricks You Can Do.* 1927. A.L. Burt. 187 pp. ex-lib. $3.50

THURSTON, Lorrin A. *Handbook on the Annexation of Hawaii.* 1898. St. Joseph. 1st ed. 83 pp. $100.00

THURSTON, Robert. *Robert Fulton. His Life & Its Results.* 1891. 1st ed. ex-lib. 194 pp. G $30.00

THWAITES, Reuben Gold. *Collections of State Hist. Soc. of WI, Vol. I.* 1903. Madison. Ltd. ed. 164 pp. index. $15.00

THWAITES, Reuben Gold. *Early Western Travels: 1748-1846.* 1904. Clark. Ills. 364 pp. dj. G $15.00

THWING, Walter Eliot. *History of the First Church in Roxbury 1630-1904.* 1908. Boston. $32.50

TIBBLES, Thomas H. *The Ponca Chiefs.* 1879. Boston. 1st ed. 146 pp. wrappers. $150.00

TICKNOR, George. *Life of William Hickling Prescott.* 1864. Boston. Ills. inscr. 491 pp. G $27.50

TICKNOR & FIELDS. *The Money King.* 1860. Boston. G $10.00

TIDWELL, James N. *A Treasury of American Folk Humor.* 1956. New York. Crown. 620 pp. dj. $5.00

TIDY, C.M. *Legal Medicine.* 1882. New York. $120.00

TIERNEY, K. *Darrow, a Biography.* 1979. Crowell. Ills. 1st ed. 490 pp. dj. VG $17.50

TIFFANY, John K. *History of Postage Stamps of United States.* 1887. St.Louis. Ills. 1st ed. 278 pp. $35.00

TIFFANY, L.H. *Algae, Grass of Many Waters.* 1938. Thomas. Ills. 171 pp. dj. VG $10.00

TILDEN, F. *The National Parks.* 1968. Knopf. Ills. 1st revised ed. 562 pp. $12.50

TILDEN, Freeman. *Following the Frontier with F.J. Haynes.* 1964. New York. 1st ed. dj. VG $22.50

TILLOTSON, M.R. & Taylor, F.J. *Grand Canyon Country.* 1935. Stanford U. Pr. VG $7.50

TILLOTSON, M.R. & Taylor, F.J. *Grand Canyon Country.* 1930. Stanford U. Pr. Ills. revised ed. VG $7.50

TILLYARD, H.J.W. *Byzantine Music & Hymnography.* 1923. Charing Cross. 72 pp. G $12.00

TILNEY. *Master of Destiny, Biography of the Brain.* 1930. G $10.00

TILNEY. *Principles. Photographs. Pictorialism.* 1930. 1st ed. 80 photos. dj. VG $35.00

TIMBS, John & Gunn, Alexander. *Abbeys, Castles & Ancient Halls of England.* London. no date. 3 vol set. $30.00

TIME LIFE BOOKS. *Life Goes to War.* 1977. 304 pp. SftCvr. EX $7.50

TIME LIFE BOOKS. *Life Guide to Paris.* 1962. New York. Time Life. Ills. 204 pp. $4.00

TIME LIFE BOOKS. *Life's Picture History of Western Man.* 1951. New York. Ills. 1st ed. folio. dj. EX $12.00

TIME LIFE BOOKS. *The Time Life International Cookbook.* 1977. New York. 463 pp. dj. EX $4.00

TIMMONS, Bascom N. *Garner of Texas. A Personal History.* 1948. New York. special Texas ed. $10.00

TINBERGEN, N. *The Study of Instinct.* 1951. Oxford. Clarendon Press. 1st ed. $60.00

TINDALE, N.B. & Lindsay, H.A. *Aboriginal Australians.* 1963. Melbourne. Ills. 139 pp. dj. VG $10.00

TINKER, Ben. *Mexican Wilderness & Wildlife.* 1978. TX. U. Press. Ills. 131 pp. dj. EX $15.00

TINKER, Edward Larque. *Corridos & Calaveras.* U. of TX. Ills. folio. dj. VG $17.50

TINKER, F.G., Jr. *Some Still Live.* 1938. Funk & Wagnalls. Ills. 313 pp. $4.50

TINKER. *Strife. The Seventies.* 1931. New York. 1st ed. VG $15.00

TINKLE, Lon. *An American Original. Life of J. Frank Dobie.* 1978. Boston. Ills. 2nd printing. 264 pp. $12.50

TINKLE, Lon. *An American Original. Life of J. Frank Dobie.* 1978. 1st ed. dj. EX $25.00

TINKLE, Lon. *Mr. De: Biography of Everette Lee De Goyer.* 1970. Boston. 1st ed. dj. VG $8.00

TINKLE & MAXWELL. *Cowboy Reader.* 1959. Longmans. dj. VG $15.00

TINSLEY, R. *The Sailfish.* 1964. EX $75.00

TINTORI & BARSOOK. *Giotto: Reruzzi Chapel.* 1963. Abrams. dj. VG $35.00

TINYANOVA, H. *Stradivari the Violin Maker.* 1938. 1st ed. dj. VG $8.00

TIPTREE, James. *The Starry Rift.* 1986. 1st Am. ed. dj. EX $15.00

TISSANDIER, Gaston. *Histoire de mes Ascensions.* 1887. Paris. Ills. G $20.00

TISSOT, J. James. *The Life of Our Savior Jesus Christ.* 1903. New York. Ills. folio. VG $85.00

TISSOT, Roger. *Mont Blac.* 1924. photos. VG $12.00

TITIEV, Mischa. *Aruacanian Culture in Transition.* 1951. U. of MI. 1st ed. stiff wrappers. $10.00

TITUS. *I Conquered.* 1916. Chicago. Ills. Russell. 1st ed. VG $20.00

TOBE, J.H. *Hunza, Adventures in the Land of Paradise.* 1960. Rodale. Ills. 1st ed. 646 pp. G $7.00

TOBE, John H. *Health Giving, Live Saving 'No Cookbook.'* 1973. Provoker Press. 7th printing. 816 pp. $7.50

TOBIN, Agnes. *Love's Crucifix.* 1902. Ills. G. Robertson. 10 pls. VG $22.50

TOBIN, F.L. *Notes on Progress & Poverty/Reply to Henry George.* 1887. Pittsburgh. 1st ed. 52 pp. wrappers. $35.00

TOBOLDT, Bill. *Fix Your Ford V8s & 6s, 1960-1946.* 1960. Chicago, IL. 248 pp. dj. $8.00

TOBOLDT, Bill. *Fix Your Plymouth.* 1957. Goodheart-Wilcox. $7.50

TODD, John. *Early Settlement & Growth of Western Iowa.* 1906. Des Moines. 87 pp. index. wrappers. VG $10.00

TODD, Robert Bently. *Clinical Lectures on Paralysis.* 1855. Philadelphia. 1st Am. ed. 521 pp. $210.00

TODD, S.E. *The Young Farmer's Manual.* 1860. New York. Ills. 459 pp. $12.50

TODD, W. *Directory of Printers & Others in Allied Trades.* 1972. London. dj. EX $20.00

TODD, William B. *Swinburne Manuscripts at Texas.* 1959. 1st ed. 12 pp. wrappers. EX $20.00

TODD. *A New Astronomy.* 1906. $20.00

TODD. *The American Wheat Culturist.* 1868. Taintor Bros. Ills. $6.50

TODES, Charlotte. *Labor & Lumber.* 1931. New York. International. dj. EX $25.00

TODHUNTER. *Difficult Calculus.* 1890. $12.50

TODHUNTER. *Plane Coord Geometry.* 1867. $12.50

TODHUNTER. *Solution Key to Difficult Calculus.* 1924. $12.50

TOKLAS, Alice B. *Alice B. Toklas Cookbook.* 1954. London. $20.00

TOKLAS, Alice B. *Alice B. Toklas Cookbook.* 1954. Harper. dj. VG $20.00

TOKLAS, Alice B. *Staying on Alone: Letters of Alice B. Toklas.* 1973. Liveright. proof copy. wrappers. $30.00

TOKLAS, Alice B. *What is Remembered.* 1963. New York. 1st ed. dj. EX $10.00

TOKLAS, Alice. *What is Remembered.* 1963. London. 1st ed. dj. EX $15.00

TOKURIKI, T. *The Ten Oxherding Pictures.* no date. Ills. Japanese-bound. rare. VG $130.00

TOKURIKI, T. *Woodblock Print Primer.* 1970. Japan Pub. Ills. 61 pp. 1st ed. $35.00

TOLAND, J. *Battle: Story of the Bulge.* 1959. New York. dj. VG $15.00

TOLAND, J. *Hitler. Pictorial Documentary of His Life.* 1978. Ills. 205 pp. wrappers. EX $8.50

TOLAND, J. *Ships in the Sky.* 1957. New York. Ills. 1st ed. 352 pp. dj. $15.00

TOLAND, J. *The Last 100 Days.* 1966. New York. Random House. Ills. 630 pp. EX $5.00

TOLIVER, R.F. *The Interrogator. Story of Hans Scharff.* 1978. Ills. dj. EX $15.00

TOLKIEN, J.R.R. *Book of Lost Tales. Part I.* 1984. Houghton Mifflin. 1st Am. ed. $15.00

TOLKIEN, J.R.R. *Finn & Hengest: Fragment & Episode.* 1983. Boston. 1st Am. ed. dj. VG $15.00

TOLKIEN, J.R.R. *Smith of Woolton Major.* 1967. Ills. Baynes. 1st Am. ed. dj. $40.00

TOLKIEN, J.R.R. *The Adventures of Bambadil.* 1962. London. Allen & Unwin. 1st ed. dj. EX $50.00

TOLKIEN, J.R.R. *The Hobbit.* 1977. New York. Abrams. Ills. 1st ed. dj. EX $50.00

TOLKIEN, J.R.R. *The Hobbit.* 1966. Houghton Mifflin. Ills. boxed. $50.00

TOLKIEN, J.R.R. *The Letters of J.R.R. Tolkien.* 1981. Houghton. 1st Am. ed. dj. VG $17.50

TOLKIEN, J.R.R. *The Lord of the Rings Trilogy.* 1954-1955. 1st Eng. ed. 3 vol set. $950.00

TOLKIEN, J.R.R. *The Lord of the Rings.* 1978. Ballantine Books. Ills. VG $4.50

TOLKIEN, J.R.R. *The Return of the King.* 1955. London. Allen & Unwin. 1st ed. dj. EX $200.00

TOLKIEN, J.R.R. *The Silmarillion.* 1977. Boston. 1st ed. VG $30.00

TOLKIEN, J.R.R. *The Silmarillion.* 1977. Allen & Unwin. 1st ed. dj. VG $35.00

TOLKIEN, J.R.R. *The Two Towers.* 1955. London. 2nd impression. dj. VG $35.00

TOLKIEN, J.R.R. *The Two Towers.* 1955. London. Allen & Unwin. 1st ed. dj. EX $40.00

TOLKIEN & GORDON. *Sir Gawain & the Green Knight.* 1925. London. Oxford. 1st ed. VG $120.00

TOLLER, Ernst. *Look Through the Bars.* 1937. New York. 1st ed. 310 pp. $12.50

TOLLEY. *Yangtze Patrol.* 1971. 1st ed. dj. EX $32.50

TOLMAN. *Principles of Statistical Mechanics.* 1959. $25.00

TOLSTOY, Leo. *Anna Karenina.* 1939. Random House. color pls. 2 vol set. $50.00

TOLSTOY, Leo. *Anna Karenina.* 1886. New York. Crowell. 1st Am. ed. $125.00

TOLSTOY, Leo. *Ivan Ilyitch.* 1887. New York. 1st Am. ed. VG $75.00

TOLSTOY, Leo. *The Cossacks.* 1888. New York. 1st Am. ed. $75.00

TOLSTOY, Leo. *The Invaders.* 1887. New York. Crowell. 1st Am. ed. $50.00

TOLSTOY, Leo. *War & Peace.* 1949. Garden City. Ills. Whitman. 741 pp. $12.50

TOLSTOY, Leo. *War & Peace.* 1887-1888. New York. 6 vol set. $60.00

TOMASEVIC. *Magic World of Ivan Generalic.* 1976. $33.00

TOMASI, Mari. *Deep Grow the Roots.* 1930. Philadelphia. sgn. VG $20.00

TOMBLESON. *Tombleson's Views of the Rhine.* 1834. 68 pls. $140.00

TOMKINS, Calvin. *Eric Hoffer, an American Odyssey.* 1969. London. Ills. George Knight. 68 pp. $4.00

TOMLINSON, H.M. *All Our Yesterdays.* 1930. London. Heinnemann. Ltd. ed. 539 pp. $52.50

TOMLINSON, H.M. *Gallions Reach.* 1927. G $7.50

TOMLINSON, H.M. *The Sea & the Jungle.* 1971. Imprint Soc. Ills. Palmer. Ltd. ed. sgn. $25.00

TOMLINSON, H.M. *The Sea & the Jungle.* 1930. Harper. Ills. 1st ed. 333 pp. VG $12.50

TOMLINSON, H.M. *Tide Marks.* 1924. Harper. Ills. 1st ed. VG $15.00

TOMLINSON, R.R. *Crafts of Children.* 1935. London. VG $24.00

TOMLINSON. *All Hands.* 1937. London. 1st ed. $12.00

TOMLINSON. *Scouting with Daniel Boone.* 1931. Grosset & Dunlap. Ills. VG $15.00

TOMPKINS, S.R. *Alaska Promyshlennik & Sourdough.* 1945. OK U. Press. Ills. 1st ed. 350 pp. VG $25.00

TOMPKINS, Warwick M. *Two Sailors.* 1939. $7.00

TOOKER, Elva. *Nathan Trotter: Philadelphia Merchant 1787-1853.* 1955. Cambridge. Harvard U. Pr. Ills. 1st ed. $30.00

TOOLEY, R.V. *Maps & Map Makers.* 1949. London. Ills. 1st ed. VG $25.00

TOOLEY, R.V. *Maps & Map Makers.* 1961. Bonanza. Ills. 140 pp. dj. EX $20.00

TOOLEY, R.V. *Some English Books with Coloured Plates.* 1935. London. Ingpen & Grant. 1st ed. $85.00

TOOLEY, R.V. & Bricker, Chas. *Landmarks of Map Making.* 1968. Amsterdam. 1st ed. fld maps. folio. dj. $150.00

TOOMBS, Samuel. *New Jersey Troops in the Gettysburg Campaign.* 1888. Orange. VG $55.00

TOPPING, E.S. *Chronicles of the Yellowstone.* 1883. St. Paul. 1st ed. $100.00

TOPPING, E.S. *Chronicles of the Yellowstone.* 1968. Haines. reprint. map. dj. EX $15.00

TORDAY. *Camp & Tramp in African Wilds.* 1913. photos. $25.00

TORGESON, Roy. *Chrysalis.* 1980. Garden City. 1st ed. dj. VG $10.00

TORNABENE, Lyn. *Long Live the King.* 1976. New York. Putnam. 429 pp. VG $6.00

TORRE, Marie. *Don't Quote Me.* 1965. Doubleday. 1st ed. 254 pp. dj. $52.50

TORREY, Bradford. *Footing it in Franconia.* 1901. Boston. 1st ed. index. EX $20.00

TORREY, J. & Gray, Asa. *A Flora of North America.* 1969. Hafner. reprint. 2 vol set. djs. VG $20.00

TORREY, Marjorie. *Penny.* 1944. dj. EX $7.50

TORRINGTON. *A Catalog of Etchings of Levon West.* 1930. New York. Ltd. ed. 1/810. VG $75.00

TOTH, Steve. *Lost Angels.* 1984. Coffee House Pr. 1st ed. sgn. $10.00

TOTHEROH, W.W. *Why Not? Lawyer Truman's Story.* 1894. Chicago. 303 pp. $7.50

TOTTEN, Ruth Patton. *The Rolling Kitchen.* 1960. Boston. Houghton Mifflin. 98 pp. $5.00

TOTTENHAM, K. *A Way with Animals.* 1962. Nelson. Ills. 110 pp. dj. EX $5.00

TOULOUSE-LAUTREC, Henry de. *The Art of Cuisine.* 1966. New York. Ills. Loutrec. $20.00

TOULOUSE-LAUTREC, Henry de. *Unpublished Correspondence of Toulouse-Lautrec.* 1969. London. Phaidon. trans. 1st ed. dj. VG $15.00

TOURGEE, Albion W. *Bricks Without Straw.* 1880. New York. 521 pp. $75.00

TOUSEY, Sanford. *Airplane Andy.* 1942. Doubleday Doran. 44 pp. EX $4.50

TOUSEY, Sanford. *The Northwest Mounted Police.* 1945. Rand McNally. Ills. author. 35 pp. $4.50

TOW, J.S. *The Real Chinese in America.* 1923. New York. Academy Press. ex-lib. 168 pp. $3.50

TOWBRIDGE, J.T. *The South: Tour of Battlefields & Ruined Cities.* 1866. Hart. 1st ed. VG $45.00

TOWER, Walter S. *The Story of Oil.* 1916. New York. 270 pp. $10.00

TOWN, Salem. *Fourth Reader: or, Reading & Speaking Exercising.* 1847. Buffalo, NY. 408 pp. TB. $3.50

TOWN, Thomas. *The Complete Military Tutor.* 1809. Philadelhia. $100.00

TOWNE, C.W. *Her Majesty Montana.* 1939. $13.00

TOWNE, Dak. *Old Prairie Days.* 1941. Otsego Union Press. sgn. dj. $25.00

TOWNER, Daniel. *Six Poems.* 1980. Bits. 1st ed. wrappers. EX $3.00

TOWNSEND, C. W. *Captain Cartwright & His Labrador Journal.* 1911. Boston. 1st ed. VG $75.00

TOWNSEND, C.W. *Beach Grass.* 1923. Boston. Ills. 1st ed. dj. EX $30.00

TOWNSEND, Francis E. *The Townsend National Recovery Plan.* 1941. sgn. $6.50

TOWNSEND, G.W. *Memorial Life of William McKinley.* 1901. 520 pp. $5.00

TOWNSEND, Gilbert. *Carpentry.* 1953. Ills. 491 pp. $4.00

TOWNSEND, John K. *Narrative & Journey Across Rocky Mountains.* 1839. 1st ed. rare. $400.00

TOWNSEND, Luther Tracy. *Regimental History of the 16th NH.* 1897. Washington. VG $65.00

TOWNSEND, P.W. *Administration of Gordian III.* Yale. 1st ed. pamphlet. wrappers. $45.00

TOWNSEND, Sue. *Adrian Mole Diaries.* Arkham House. 1st ed. VG $12.50

TOWNSHEND, Chauncy. *Facts in Mesmerism.* 1841. 1st Am. ed. $95.00

TOYNBEE, Arnold. *Cities of Destiny.* 1967. McGraw Hill. dj. EX $75.00

TOYNBEE, Arnold J. *Greek Historical Thought.* 1924. London. 1st ed. 256 pp. EX $20.00

TRACY, Louis. *An American Emperor.* 1897. New York. Putnam. 1st Am. ed. VG $20.00

TRACY, Louis. *Son of the Immortals.* 1909. New York. Ills. Christy. VG $7.50

TRACY, Marion. *The Peasant Cookbook.* 1955. Garden City. Ills. 224 pp. $4.00

TRACY, Marion. *The Picnic Book.* 1957. New York. 224 pp. $4.00

TRACY. *African Dances of the Witwatersrand Gold Mines.* 1952. Johannesburg. dj. $30.00

TRADER, Vic. *Trader Vic's Pacific Island Cookbook.* 1968. New York. Doubleday. 287 pp. photos. dj. $3.50

TRAFTON, G.H. *Methods of Attracting Birds.* 1910. Houghton Mifflin. 1st ed. dj. $5.00

TRAGER. *Echoes of Silence.* 1972. Scroll Press. Ltd. private ed. 1/1000. sgn. $100.00

TRAGER. *Photographs of Architecture.* 1978. Wesleyan. $30.00

TRAIN, Arthur & Wood, R. *The Moon Maker.* 1958. Hamburg. Ills. McSherry. Ltd. ed. dj. $25.00

TRAIN, Arthur. *Mr. Tutt's Casebook.* 1948. Scribner. dj. VG $15.00

TRAIN, Arthur. *Mr. Tutt's Casebook.* 1936. New York. 1st ed. VG $10.00

TRAIN, Arthur. *The Butler's Story.* 1912. 2nd ed. $32.50

TRAIN, Arthur. *The Man Who Rocked the Earth.* 1915. New York. Doubleday. 1st ed. VG $50.00

TRAIN, Arthur. *Tut, Tut! Mr. Tut.* 1923. 1st ed. VG $9.00

TRAPP, M. *Around the Year with the Trapp Family.* 1955. Ills. 1st ed. VG $15.00

TRATMAN. *Railway Track & Track Work.* 1897. Ills. 1st ed. 418 pp. $70.00

TRAVEN, B. *Cotton Pickers.* 1969. 1st Am. ed. dj. EX $15.00

TRAVEN, B. *General from the Jungle.* 1954. London. 1st ed. dj. VG $25.00

TRAVEN, B. *General from the Jungle.* 1972. 1st Am. ed. dj. EX $15.00

TRAVEN, B. *Government.* 1971. 1st Am. ed. dj. EX $15.00

TRAVEN, B. *The Carreta.* 1970. 1st Am. ed. dj. EX $15.00

TRAVEN, B. *The Death Ship.* 1934. London. 1st Eng. ed. VG $110.00

TRAVEN, B. *The Death Ship.* 1934. New York. 1st ed. VG $50.00

TRAVEN, B. *The Kidnapped Saint & Other Stories.* 1978. London. 1st Eng. ed. dj. EX $45.00

TRAVEN, B. *The Night Visitor & Other Stories.* 1967. London. 1st Eng. ed. dj. EX $50.00

TRAVER, Robert. *Anatomy of a Fisherman.* 1964. 1st ed. dj. EX $60.00

TRAVER, Robert. *Horstein's Boy.* 1962. New York. sgn. inscr. dj. VG $15.00

TRAVER, Robert. *People Versus Kirk.* 1981. New York. St. Martins. 1st ed. dj. VG $25.00

TRAVER, Robert. *Trout Madness.* 1960. 1st ed. VG $12.50

TRAVIS, Robert J. *Travis (Travers) Family & Its Allies.* 1954. Savannah. 194 pp. VG $25.00

TRAYLOR, S.W. *Out of the Southwest: Texas Boy.* 1936. VG $32.50

TREAT, Mary. *Injurious Insects of the Farm & Garden.* 1882. Orange Judd Co.Ills. VG $14.00

TREECE, Henry. *The Black Seasons.* 1945. London. 1st ed. dj. VG $15.00

TREECE, Henry. *The Eagle King.* 1964. New York. Random House. 1st ed. dj. EX $8.50

TREFETHEN, G.A. *Strawberry Bank & Marquise de Lafayette in 1824.* 1950. Portsmouth, NH.Ills. 36 pp. wrappers. $3.00

TREFETHEN, J.B. *An American Crusade for Wildlife.* 1975. Winchester. Ills. 409 pp. dj. EX $15.00

TREFETHEN, J.B. *The Wild Sheep in Modern North America.* 1975. Boone & Crockett Club. 302 pp. $12.50

TREGASKIS, Richard. *Guadalcanal Diary.* 1943. New York. Random House. Ills. 263 pp. dj $4.50

TREGO, Charles. *Geography of Pennsylvania.* 1843. map. VG $65.00

TREHOLM. *Footprints on the Frontier.* 1943. Ltd. ed. 1/1000. sgn. $85.00

TRELAWNY, Edward John. *Records of Shelley, Byron, & Trelawny.* 1887. New York. VG $25.00

TREMAIN, Rose. *The Colonel's Daughter.* 1984. Summit. 1st Am. ed. dj. VG $15.00

TREMAIN, Rose. *The Cupboard.* 1982. St. Martins. 1st Am. ed. dj. VG $15.00

TREMAYNE, Peter. *The Revenge of Dracula.* Ills. D. Green. Ltd. 1st Am. ed. 1/1250. sgn. $20.00

TREMAYNE, Peter. *The Revenge of Dracula.* 1978. Ills. 1st Am. ed. sgn. EX $30.00

TREMBLY, R. *Trails of an Alaska Game Warden.* 1985. Alaska. Ills. 176 pp. dj. EX $10.00

TRENCH, Charles C. *A History of Marksmanship.* 1972. Chicago. Follett. Ills. 319 pp. dj. $18.50

TRENHOLM, Virginia. *The Arapahoes, Our People.* 1970. 1st ed. dj. EX $15.00

TRENTER. *Berge im Schnee.* 1935. Berlin. Ills. VG $15.00

TRESSELL, Robert. *The Ragged Trousered Philanthropists.* 1978. London. Lawrence & Wishart. 633 pp. $8.00

TREVELYAN, George O. *Marginal Notes by Lord Macaulay.* 1907. London. Longmans. 1st ed. 64 pp. $25.00

TREVERT, Edward. *The ABC of Wireless Telegraphy.* 1906. Lynn, MA. Ills. 116 pp. $3.00

TREVES, Sir Frederic. *The Elephant Man & Other Reminiscences.* New York. 1st Am. ed. dj. VG $35.00

TREVIS, Walter. *The Hustler.* 1959. New York. 1st ed. $35.00

TREVOR, William. *Angels at the Ritz.* 1976. New York. Viking. 1st Am. ed. VG $35.00

TREVOR, William. *Beyond the Pale & Other Stories.* 1982. New York. Viking. 1st ed. dj. EX $20.00

TREVOR, William. *Fools of Fortune.* 1983. London. Bodley Head. 1st ed. dj. EX $22.50

TREVOR, William. *The Children of Dynmouth.* 1976. London. Bodley Head. 1st ed. VG $35.00

TREVOR-ROPER, H. *Hermit of Peking.* 1977. New York. Knopf. dj. G $15.00

TRILLING, Diana. *We Must March My Darlings.* 1977. New York. VG $12.50

TRINDER, W.H. *Dowsing.* 1955. London. Ills. 137 pp. dj. $17.50

TRIPLETT, Frank. *Life, Times, & Treacherous Death of Jesse James.* 1970. Promontory Pr. Ills. 344 pp. index. dj. VG $10.00

TRIPLETT, Frank. *Life, Times & Treacherous Death of Jesse James.* 1970. Chicago. Ltd. ed. 1/250. sgn. $75.00

TRIPP. *Electric Development as an Aid to Agriculture.* 1926. Knickerbocker Press. Ills. $4.50

TRISTRAM, W. Outram. *Coaching Days & Coaching Ways.* 1924. Macmillan. Ills. H. Thompson/H. Railton. $35.00

TROEBST, C.C. *The Art of Survival.* 1965. Doubleday. Ills. 312 pp. VG $6.00

TROGDON, K.C. *History of Stephens County, GA.* 1973. Toccoa, GA. 568 pp. $25.00

TROLLOPE, Anthony. *An Editor's Tales.* 1870. London. Strahan & Co. 1st ed. VG $200.00

TROLLOPE, Anthony. *Barachester Towers.* 1945. Doubleday. Ills. McKay. Ltd. ed. sgn. $20.00

TROLLOPE, Anthony. *Christmas Day at Kirby Cottage.* 1947. London. Ills. Hassall. 1st ed. dj. VG $50.00

TROLLOPE, Anthony. *Framley Parsonage.* 1861. Tauchnitz. 1st ed. 2 vol set. VG $65.00

TROLLOPE, Anthony. *Orley Farm.* 1862. London. Ills. Millais. 2 vol set. VG $95.00

TROLLOPE, Anthony. *The Duke's Children.* 1880. Tauchnitz. 1st ed. $75.00

TROLLOPE, Anthony. *The Warden.* 1859. Tauchnitz. 1st ed. VG $40.00

TROLLOPE, Frances. *Life & Adventures of Michael Armstrong.* 1840. London. Ills. Herview & others. VG $125.00

TROLLOPE, T. Adolphus. *Girlhood of Catherine de Medici.* 1856. London. 1st ed. VG $45.00

TROMP, S.W. *Psychical Physics.* 1949. Rotterdam. Elesevier. Ills. 1st ed. $95.00

TROTSKY, Leon. *Writings of Leon Trotsky.* 1970. New York. Pathfinder Press. 1st ed. VG $8.00

TROUTMAN. *El Greco.* 1963. Spring Books. Ills. $4.50

TROW, Charles. *The Old Shipmasters of Salem.* 1905. New York. 1st ed. $60.00

TROWBRIDGE, J.T. *The Desolate South: 1856-66.* 1956. 1st ed. dj. VG $20.00

TROYAT, H. *The Mountain.* 1953. dj. EX $10.00

TROYER, Howard William. *Ned Ward of Grubstreet.* 1946. Harvard Press. 1st ed. dj. VG $10.00

TRUAX, Carol. *Ladies' Home Journal Cookbook.* 1963. New York. Doubleday. 728 pp. dj. $15.00

TRUDEAU, Margaret. *Beyond Reason.* 1979. New York. Paddington Press. ex-lib. dj. $5.00

TRUDELLC. *Colonial Yorktown.* 1938. 1st ed. $15.00

TRUE, F. *A Revision of the American Moles.* 1896. Smithsonian. Ills. 111 pp. dj. $5.00

TRUE, Mosephine Morse. *The Busy Little Honeybee.* 1937. Rand McNally. 63 pp. VG $3.50

TRUETT, Randle B. *Trade & Travel Around Southern Appalachians, 1830.* 1935. Chapel Hill. Ills. 1st ed. sgn. $45.00

TRUMAN, Ben C. *The Field of Honor.* 1884. New York. EX $30.00

TRUMBALL, Hammond. *Memorial Hist. of Hartford County CT. 1633-1884.* 1886. Edward Osgood Pub. VG $35.00

TRUMBALL, Henry. *History of the Indian Wars.* 1854. Philadelphia. Ills. VG $60.00

TRUMBO, Dalton. *Night of the Aurochs.* 1979. Viking. 1st ed. dj. VG $15.00

TRUMBO, Dalton. *The Remarkable Andrew.* 1941. Lippincott. 1st ed. dj. VG $40.00

TRUMBULL, H. Clay. *The Knightly Soldier.* 1865. Boston. Nichols & Noyes. G $7.50

TRUMBULL, Hammond. *Blue Laws True & False.* 1876. Hartford. VG $8.00

TRUMBULL, Henry. *History of Discovery of America.* 1812. Norwich, CT. G $25.00

TRUSS, Seldon. *The Bride that Got Away.* 1967. London. 1st ed. dj. VG $15.00

TRUSS, Seldon. *The High Wall.* 1954. London. Hodder & Stoughton. 1st ed. VG $15.00

TRUSSELL, Jake. *Collected Poems of Jake Trussell.* 1957. 1st ed. wrappers. EX $20.00

TRUSTA, H. *Little Mary or Talks & Tales for Children.* 1853. Boston. Phillips Sampson. VG $17.50

TRYON, R.M. *The Ferns & Fern Allies of Wisconsin.* 1940. WI U. Press. Ills. 158 pp. VG $27.50

TRYON, Thomas. *Harvest Home.* 1974. 1st Am. ed. sgn. dj. EX $25.00

TRYON, Thomas. *Lady.* 1974. Knopf. dj. EX $2.00

TRYON, Thomas. *The Other.* 1971. 1st Am. ed. dj. EX $25.00

TRYON, W.S. *Parnassus Corner. Life of James T. Fields.* 1963. Boston. Ills. 1st printing. 445 pp. $10.00

TUBB, E.C. *Alien Dust.* 1957. New York. Abalon Books. 223 pp. dj. EX $15.00

TUBBS, Floyd R. *Stahlelm.* 1971. Ills. 104 pp. wrappers. EX $8.00

TUCCI, G. *Minor Buddist Texts.* 1978. Kyoto. 2 vols in 1. 600 pp. dj. $85.00

TUCCI, G. *Nepal, Discovery of Malla.* 1962. New York. 1st ed. dj. EX $25.00

TUCCI, G. *Tibet. Land of Snow.* 1967. New York. Ills. G $40.00

TUCHMAN, B. *March of Folly.* Arkham House. 1st ed. VG $37.50

TUCHMAN, Barbara W. *The Guns of August.* 1962. New York. Macmillan. Ills. 511 pp. dj. G $6.50

TUCK, Dorothy. *Crowell's Handbook of Faulkner.* 1964. Crowell. 1st ed. pb. wrappers. EX $7.50

TUCKER, Beverly. *The Partisan Leader.* 1861. New York. 392 pp. $40.00

TUCKER, G. *Dawn Like Thunder.* 1963. 1st ed. $20.00

TUCKER, George. *Progress of United States in Population & Wealth.* 1843. New York. 1st ed. 211 pp. $150.00

TUCKER, Irwin St. John. *A Minstrel Friar.* 1949. Chicago. 1st ed. sgn. dj. EX $35.00

TUCKER, J. *Kanchenjunga.* 1966. New York. 1st ed. dj. EX $15.00

TUCKER, Wilson. *The Science Fiction Subtreasury.* 1954. New York. Rinehart. 1st ed. dj. EX $22.50

TUCKERMAN, Fred. *Poems.* 1869. Boston. 235 pp. $150.00

TUDOR, T.L. *High Peak to Sherwood.* McCrae Smith. 1st ed. EX $10.00

TUDOR, Tasha. *A Book of Christmas.* 1979. New York. Collins. Ills. EX $12.50

TUDOR, Tasha. *Fairy Tales from Hans Christian Andersen.* 1945. New York. Ills. 273 pp. dj. VG $22.50

TUDOR, Tasha. *The Tasha Tudor Book of Fairy Tales.* 1961. New York. Platt & Munk. Ills. 1st ed. EX $15.00

TUDOR, Tasha. *Thistly B.* 1949. Oxford U. Press. Ills. 1st ed. $5.00

TUGWELL, Rexford G. *The Battle for Democracy.* 1935. New York. Columbia U. Press. 330 pp. dj. $7.00

TUNEY, K. *Tallulah.* 1973. Ills. $7.50

TUNIS. *Champions Choice.* 1940. New York. World. 215 pp. VG $3.50

TUNNICLIFFE, C.F. *A Sketchbook of Birds.* 1979. Holt Rinehart. Ills. 1st ed. 135 pp. EX $17.50

TUPPER, H. Allen. *Around the World with Eyes Wide Open.* 1898. New York. Christian Herald. photos. VG $6.00

TURBFILL, Mark. *The Living Frieze.* 1921. Evanston. Ltd. ed. inscr. EX $125.00

TURBOTT, E.G. *Buller's Birds of New Zealand.* 1967. Honolulu. folio. 48 color pls. dj. EX $75.00

TURGEON. *Tante Maries French Pastry.* 1954. dj. VG $6.00

TURING, H.D. *Trout Fishing.* 1935. London. Ills. 1st ed. VG $17.50

TURKI, Fawaz. *The Disinherited; Journal of Palestinian Exile.* 1974. New York. 188 pp. $10.00

TURNBULL, A. *Thomas Wolfe.* 1967. Ills. $7.50

TURNBULL, Agnes. *The Bishop's Mantle.* 1948. New York. Macmillan. 314 pp. $3.50

TURNBULL, Agnes. *The Golden Journey.* 1955. Riverside. 303 pp. $27.50

TURNBULL, C. *The Mbuti Pygmies, an Ethnographic Survey.* 1965. Ills. VG $7.50

TURNBULL, E.R. & Denslow, Ray. *A History of Royal Arch Masonry.* 1956. 1st ed. 1617 pp. 3 vol set. VG $30.00

TURNBULL, Laurence. *Advantages & Accidents of Artificial Anesthesia.* 1879. Philadelphia. 2nd revised & enlarged ed. $25.00

TURNER, D. *Vampire Bat, a Field Study in Behavior & Ecology.* 1975. John Hopkins. Ills. 145 pp. dj. EX $12.50

TURNER, E.S. *All Heaven in a Rage.* 1965. St. Martins. Ills. 1st Am. ed. 324 pp. dj. $12.50

TURNER, Frederick J. *Correspondence French Ministers to U.S., 1791-97.* 1904. Washington. 1st ed. 110 pp. $35.00

TURNER, Frederick J. *Rise of the New West: 1819-1829.* 1906. New York. Ills. VG $25.00

TURNER, J.E.C. *Man Eaters & Memories.* 1959. London. 2nd ed. $30.00

TURNER, John Frayn. *British Aircraft of WWII.* 1975. New York. Stein & Day. 1st Am. ed. EX $12.00

TURNER, L. *Contributions to the Natural History of Alaska.* 1886. 1st ed. 11 color pls. $80.00

TURNER, W.J. *Mozart: Man & His Works.* 1928. New York. Ills. VG $22.00

TURNER. *Decorative Plasterwork in Great Britain.* 1927. Weyhe. $30.00

TURNER. *Red Men Calling on the Great White Father.* 1951. U. of OK Press. 1st ed. 235 pp. 12 pls. map. $20.00

TURNEY, Ida Virginia. *Paul Bunyan Comes West.* 1928. Boston/NY. Ills. Helen Rhodes. 1st ed. $15.00

TUROFF, M. *How to Make Pottery & Other Ceramics.* 1949. 1st ed. dj. VG $8.00

TURRILL, Gardner S. *Tale of Yellowstone: Wagon Through Western WY.* 1901. Jefferson, IA. Ills. 1st ed. 128 pp. $400.00

TUSHNET, L. *Uses Adversity.* 1966. New York. Yoseloff. Ills. dj. EX $15.00

TUTT, Ephraim. *Yankee Lawyer. The Autobiography of Ephraim Tutt.* 1943. Scribner. 1st ed. dj. $20.00

TUTTLE, B.R. *The Standard Book of Fishing.* 1950. New York. Ills. 532 pp. $10.00

TUTTLE, C.R. *General History of the State of Michigan.* 1873. Ills. G $45.00

TUTTLE, W.C. *Valley of Twisted Trails.* 1931. Boston. 1st ed. dj. $7.50

TUTTLE. *Shotgun Gold.* Popular. pb. $3.00

TWAIN, Mark. *A Connecticut Yankee in King Arthur's Court.* 1889. New York. 1st ed. 2nd issue. EX $125.00

TWAIN, Mark. *A Tramp Abroad.* 1880. Hartford. $195.00

TWAIN, Mark. *A Tramp Abroad.* 1966. Ltd. Eds. Club. sgn. boxed. EX $40.00

TWAIN, Mark. *Gems of Modern Wit & Humor.* 1903. Ills. Burdette. VG $15.00

TWAIN, Mark. *King Leopold's Soliloquy.* 1905. Boston. 1st ed. 4th issue. VG $125.00

TWAIN, Mark. *Life on the Mississippi.* 1920. New York. Harper. 527 pp. $7.50

TWAIN, Mark. *Life on the Mississippi.* 1883. London. 1st ed. EX $300.00

TWAIN, Mark. *Man That Corrupted Hadleyburg & Other Stories.* 1900. London. 1st Eng. ed. VG $190.00

TWAIN, Mark. *Mark Twain & the Happy Island.* 1913. Chicago. VG $40.00

TWAIN, Mark. *Mark Twain's Autobiography & First Romance.* Sheldon & Co. 1st ed. 2nd issue. $125.00

TWAIN, Mark. *Mark Twain's Autobiography.* 1924. New York. 1st ed. 2 vol set. VG $37.50

TWAIN, Mark. *Mark Twain's Notebook.* 1935. Harper. 1st ed. dj. EX $25.00

TWAIN, Mark. *Mark Twain's West.* 1983. Lakeside Press. VG $10.00

TWAIN, Mark. *Personal Recollections of Joan of Arc.* 1926. New York. Harper. Ills. G.B. Cutts. $15.00

TWAIN, Mark. *Prince & the Pauper.* 1882. Boston. Franklin Press. 1st issue. $125.00

TWAIN, Mark. *Pudd'nhead Wilson & Those Extraordinary Twins.* 1894. Hartford. 1st Am. ed. VG $100.00

TWAIN, Mark. *Saint Joan of Arc.* 1919. New York. Ills. H. Pyle. 1st ed. VG $90.00

TWAIN, Mark. *Stories of Humor in Two Parts.* 1908. New York. VG $15.00

TWAIN, Mark. *The Adventures of Huckleberry Finn.* 1884. London. 1st ed. EX $600.00

TWAIN, Mark. *The Adventures of Huckleberry Finn.* 1948. New York. Grosset & Dunlap. 373 pp. $3.50

TWAIN, Mark. *The Adventures of Huckleberry Finn.* 1885. Webster. 1st ed. boxed. $175.00

TWAIN, Mark. *The Adventures of Tom Sawyer.* 1876. Hartford. 1st Am. ed. 2nd printing. VG $185.00

TWAIN, Mark. *The American Claimant.* 1892. New York. 1st ed. G $50.00

TWAIN, Mark. *The American Claimant.* 1892. London. 1st ed. G $25.00

TWAIN, Mark. *The American Claimant.* 1892. New York. 1st ed. 2 inscr. VG $70.00

TWAIN, Mark. *The Choice Humorous Works.* 1880. Ills. VG $30.00

TWAIN, Mark. *The Family of Mark Twain.* Harper. no date. 1462 pp. VG $7.50

TWAIN, Mark. *The Innocents Abroad.* 1871. Am. Pub. 234 Ills. $35.00

TWAIN, Mark. *The Man that Corrupted Hadleyburg.* 1906. New York. Harper. 367 pp. $5.00

TWAIN, Mark. *The Niagara Book.* 1893. Buffalo. Ills. Harry Fenn. 1st ed. G $50.00

TWAIN, Mark. *The Tragedy of Pudd'nhead.* 1894. Hartford. Wilson. Ills. 1st Am. ed. EX $250.00

TWAIN, Mark. *Tom Sawyer.* 1890. VG $40.00

TWEED, T.F. *Blind Mouths.* 1934. Barker. 1st ed. dj. $40.00

TWEEDIE, M. *The World of Dinosaurs.* 1977. Morrow. Ills. 143 pp. dj. EX $12.50

TWEEDSMUIR, L. *Hudson's Bay Trader.* 1951. Norton. Ills. 1st ed. 195 pp. EX $15.00

TWIN. *Following the Equator.* 1897. Am. Pub. 1st ed. EX $95.00

TWISS, T. *The Oregon Territory, Its History & Discovery.* 1846. New York. 1st Am. ed. 264 pp. $125.00

TWITCHELL, Ralph. *The Military Occupation of New Mexico, 1845-1851.* 1909. Denver. 1st ed. 394 pp. VG $75.00

TWOMBLY, Alexander S. *The Life of John Lord.* 1896. New York. 277 pp. $12.50

TWYMAN, M. *Directory of London Lithographic Printers 1800-50.* 1976. London. EX $15.00

TYBOUT, Ella Middleton. *Poketown People.* 1904. Philadelphia. Ills. Verveck & Moore. 356 pp. $25.00

TYE, J.R. *Periodicals of the Nineties.* 1974. Oxford. 1st ed. 36 pp. wrappers. $15.00

TYLER, A. *Morgans Passing.* 1980. New York. 1st ed. dj. EX $15.00

TYLER, Anne. *A Slipping Down Life.* 1983. Severn House. 1st English ed. dj. VG $15.00

TYLER, Anne. *A Slipping Down Life.* 1970. New York. Knopf. 1st ed. dj. EX $40.00

TYLER, Anne. *A Visit with Eudora Welty.* Chicago. Pressworks. Ltd. ed. wrappers. $100.00

TYLER, Anne. *Celestial Navigation.* 1974. New York. Knopf. 1st Am. ed. VG $55.00

TYLER, Anne. *Dinner at the Homesick Restaurant.* 1982. Knopf. 1st ed. dj. VG $30.00

TYLER, Anne. *Earthly Possessions.* 1977. Knopf. 1st ed. dj. VG $45.00

TYLER, Anne. *If Morning Ever Comes.* 1984. Severn House. 1st English ed. dj. VG $15.00

TYLER, Anne. *The Accidental Tourist.* 1985. New York. 1st ed. sgn. dj. EX $40.00

TYLER, Anne. *The Accidental Tourist.* 1985. proof copy. EX $50.00

TYLER, Robert Ogden. *Memoir of Brevet Maj. Gen. Robert Ogden Tyler.* 1878. Philadelphia. 20 pp. $17.50

TYLER, Royall. *The Chestnut Tree.* 1931. Vermont. Driftwin Press. Ltd. 1st ed. $40.00

TYLER, Sydney. *The Japan-Russian War.* 1905. Philadelphia. Ills. & maps. 554 pp. VG. $4.00

TYNAN, Kenneth. *Bull Fever.* 1955. 1st ed. dj. $6.50

TYRRELL, R. & E. *Hummingbirds, Their Life, & Behavior.* 1985. Crown. Ills. 256 pp. EX $32.50

TYSON, C.B. *The Poconos.* 1929. Innes. Ills. 193 pp. VG $25.00

TYSON, James. *Diary of a Physician in California.* 1955. Oakland. Ltd. 1st CA ed. 1/500. EX $65.00

TYSON, Phillip. *Geology & Industrial Resources of California.* 1851. Baltimore. ex-lib. maps. $100.00

TZU, Chuang. *The Complete Works of Chuang Tzu.* 1970. Columbia U. trans. Burton Watson. $5.00

U.S. GOVERNMENT. *Abstract of Infantry Tactics.* 1830. Boston. Ills. 138 pp. $35.00

U.S. GOVERNMENT. *Handbook of the Hospital Corps, U.S. Navy. 1939.* Washington. 1015 pp. G $6.50

U.S. NAVY TRAINING OFFICE. *How to Survive on Land & Sea.* 1951. Washington. Ills. 323 pp. $5.00

U.S. NAVY TRAINING OFFICE. *Ordinance Instructions for U.S. Navy.* 1866. Washington, D.C. 400 pp. $75.00

U.S. OLYMPIC ASSOC. *U.S. 1956 Olympic Book.* 1957. Ills. 463 pp. $15.00

UDALL, Stewart L. *The National Parks of America.* 1966. New York. 1st ed. 225 pp. dj. $10.00

UDE, Louis Eustache. *The French Cook.* 1978. New York. Arco. dj. VG $7.50

ULLAH. *History of the Afghans.* 1965. New York. dj. VG $7.50

ULLMAN, Allan. *Sorry, Wrong Number.* 1948. New York. Random House. 1st ed. dj. VG $17.50

ULLMAN, J.R. *And Not to Yield.* 1970. New York. Doubleday. 432 pp. dj. $4.00

ULLMAN, J.R. *The Age of Mountaineering.* 1954. 1st Am. ed. maps. dj. VG $15.00

ULLMAN & TENZING. *Man of Everest: Autobiography of Tenzing.* 1956. reprint. sgn. dated. EX $20.00

ULLMAN J.R. *The White Tower.* 1945. New York. Lippincott. 479 pp. $3.50

ULLMAN. *Straight Up.* 1968. New York. 1st ed. dj. VG $7.50

ULLMANN, Liv. *Changing.* 1977. New York. Knopf. 244 pp. dj. EX $4.50

ULLOA, Don Antonio de & Juan. *A Voyage to South America.* 1772. London. 7 fld pls. fld map. 2 vol set. $250.00

ULMAN, Albert. *Landmark History of New York.* 1903. Appleton. $10.00

ULMAN, J.R. *High Conquest.* 1941. Philadelphia. Ills. 3rd ed. 5 maps. VG $12.50

ULMAN, J.R. *Kingdom of Adventure, Everest.* 1947. Sloane. Ills. 411 pp. dj. VG $15.00

UNDERHILL, Charles. *Your Soldier Boy Samuel.* 1929. private print. Ltd. ed. 1/400. dj. VG $30.00

UNDERHILL, D.C. *Arithmetical Primer.* New York. (ca.1854) wrappers. $20.00

UNDERHILL, Harold. *Deep Water Sail.* 1963. Brown & Ferguson. 2nd ed. dj. $17.50

UNDERHILL, Harold. *Sail Training & Cadet Ships.* 1973. Brown & Ferguson. 2nd ed. $17.50

UNDERHILL, Ruth M. *First Penthouse Dwellers of America.* 1938. New York. Ills. 1st ed. $15.00

UNDERHILL, Ruth M. *Here Come the Navaho!* no date. U.S. Indian Service. 285 pp. $25.00

UNDERHILL, Ruth M. *Indians of Pacific Northwest.* 1945. Riverside. Sherman Inst. Press. 232 pp. $17.50

UNDERHILL, Ruth M. *The Navajos.* 1956. Norman, OK. review copy. dj. VG $22.50

UNDERHILL, Ruth M. *The Navajos.* 1967. U. of OK Press. Ills. dj. $32.50

UNDERHILL, Ruth M. *The Navajos.* 1958. Norman. Ills. 2nd printing. 299 pp. EX $18.50

UNDERWOOD, Bob A. *Lunker.* 1975. McGraw Hill. Ills. 273 pp. VG $4.50

UNDERWOOD, G. *Our Falklands War.* 1983. Cornwall. Ills. 144 pp. wrappers. EX $10.00

UNDERWOOD, L. *Deer Book.* 1980. dj. EX $20.00

UNDERWOOD, Michael. *Goddess of Death.* 1982. St. Martins. 1st ed. dj. VG $10.00

UNDRY, Janice May. *Angie.* 1971. New York. Harper. Ills. 1st ed. VG $12.50

UNDSET, Sigrid. *Christmas & Twelfth Night.* New York. 2nd ed. dj. VG $7.50

UNGER, F.W. *Roosevelt's African Trip.* 1909. Ills. maps. 440 pp. G $12.50

UNGER, F.W. *Roosevelt's African Trip.* 1908. Ills. VG $20.00

UNITED BRETHREN CHURCH. *Origin, Doctrine, Constitution, & Discipline.* 1877. Dayton, Ohio. 140 pp. $10.00

UNSWORTH. *Everest.* 1981. 1st ed. dj. EX $20.00

UNSWORTH. *Peaks, Passes, & Glaciers.* 1981. 1st ed. dj. EX $15.00

UNTERMEYER, Louis. *Book of Noble Thoughts.* 1946. New York. Am. Art Group. Ills. Kent. dj. $10.00

UNTERMEYER, Louis. *The Donkey of God.* 1932. New York. Ills. J. MacDonald. sgn. $20.00

UNWIN, Philip. *Book Publishing as a Career.* 1965. London. Hamilton. 1st ed. dj. VG $15.00

UNWIN, Philip. *The Publishing Unwins.* 1972. London. Heinemann. Ills. 1st ed. dj. $15.00

UP DE GRAFF, F.W. *Head Hunters of the Amazon.* 1923. Garden City. 337 pp. G $9.00

UPCHURCH, Michael. *Jamboree.* 1st Am. ed. dj. EX $10.00

UPDIKE, D.B. *Printing Types: History, Forms, & Use.* 1922. Harvard U. Pr. 1st ed. VG $90.00

UPDIKE, J. *Kentavr.* 1966. U.S.S.R. 1st ed. G $25.00

UPDIKE, John. *A Child's Calendar.* 1965. New York. 1st ed. $30.00

UPDIKE, John. *A Month of Sundays.* 1975. New York. Knopf. 1st ed. dj. VG $25.00

UPDIKE, John. *A Month of Sundays.* 1975. New York. Book Club 1st ed. dj. EX $5.00

UPDIKE, John. *Assorted Prose.* 1965. Knopf. 1st ed. dj. VG $25.00

UPDIKE, John. *Bech is Back.* 1982. New York. 1st ed. sgn. VG $25.00

UPDIKE, John. *Bech is Back.* 1982. Knopf. 1st trade ed. dj. VG $15.00

UPDIKE, John. *Bech is Back.* 1983. Deutsch. 1st English ed. dj. VG $15.00

UPDIKE, John. *Bech: a Book.* 1970. New York. Ltd. ed. sgn. dj. EX $50.00

UPDIKE, John. *Bech: a Book.* 1970. New York. Knopf. 1st ed. dj. VG $15.00

UPDIKE, John. *Bech: a Book.* 1970. Knopf. 1st trade ed. dj. VG $30.00

UPDIKE, John. *Bottom's Dream.* 1969. New York. 1st ed. $25.00

UPDIKE, John. *Buchanan Dying.* 1974. Knopf. 1st ed. dj. EX $35.00

UPDIKE, John. *Confessions of a Wild Bore.* 1984. Tauchinitz. Ltd. 1st ed. 1/250. EX $35.00

UPDIKE, John. *Emersonianism.* 1985. Ewert. 1st ed. 1/203. sgn. VG $75.00

UPDIKE, John. *Facing Nature.* 1985. review copy. VG $65.00

UPDIKE, John. *Facing Nature.* 1985. Knopf. 1st ed. dj. VG $15.00

UPDIKE, John. *Five Poems.* Ltd. ed. 1/135. sgn. $45.00

UPDIKE, John. *Hawthorne's Creed.* 1981. Targ. Ltd. ed. 1/250. sgn. EX $60.00

UPDIKE, John. *Hoping for a Hoopoe.* 1959. Gollancz. 1st English ed. dj. VG $55.00

UPDIKE, John. *Jester's Dozen.* 1984. Lord John. Ills. Ltd. ed. 1/150. sgn. EX $75.00

UPDIKE, John. *Marry Me.* 1976. New York. Knopf. 1st ed. dj. EX $25.00

UPDIKE, John. *Marry Me.* 1976. review copy. dj. EX $25.00

UPDIKE, John. *Marry Me.* London. 1st ed. dj. VG $25.00

UPDIKE, John. *Midpoint & Other Poems.* 1969. Deutsch. 1st Eng. ed. dj. VG $30.00

UPDIKE, John. *Midpoint.* 1969. New York. Ltd. ed. 1/350. sgn. boxed. $110.00

UPDIKE, John. *Modern Fiction Studios.* 1974. 1st ed. wrappers. EX $12.00

UPDIKE, John. *More Stately Mansions.* 1986. Nouveau. Ltd. ed. 1/300. sgn. VG $65.00

UPDIKE, John. *More Stately Mansions.* 1986. Nouveau. Deluxe Ltd. ed. 1/40. sgn. EX $175.00

UPDIKE, John. *Pens & Needles Literary Caricatures by D. Levine.* 1969. Gambit. Ltd. 1st ed. 1/300. sgns. $45.00

UPDIKE, John. *Pens & Needles.* 1969. Ltd. ed. sgn. dj. EX $45.00

UPDIKE, John. *Pens & Needles.* 1969. 1st ed. dj. VG $20.00

UPDIKE, John. *Pigeon Feathers.* 1962. Knopf. 1st ed. dj. VG $75.00

UPDIKE, John. *Problems & Other Stories.* 1979. New York. Knopf. 1st ed. dj. EX $25.00

UPDIKE, John. *Rabbit Redux.* 1971. New York. Knopf. 1st ed. dj. EX $30.00

UPDIKE, John. *Roger's Version.* 1986. Franklin Soc. 1st ed. sgn. full leather. EX $45.00

UPDIKE, John. *Talk from the Fifties.* 1979. Lord John Pr. Ltd. ed. 1/300. sgn. dj. EX $60.00

UPDIKE, John. *Telephone Poles.* 1964. Deutsch. 1st English ed. dj. VG $35.00

UPDIKE, John. *The Best American Short Story.* 1984. Boston. Houghton Mifflin. dj. VG $15.00

UPDIKE, John. *The Carpentered Hen.* Knopf. 1st ed. sgn. VG $25.00

UPDIKE, John. *The Carpentered Hen.* 1982. New York. Knopf. 1st ed. dj. EX $8.50

UPDIKE, John. *The Centaur.* 1963. New York. Knopf. 1st ed. 303 pp. dj. $20.00

UPDIKE, John. *The Chaste Planet.* 1980. Ltd. ed. 1/300. sgn. wrappers. $40.00

UPDIKE, John. *The Coup.* review copy. sgn. VG $25.00

UPDIKE, John. *The Coup.* Ltd. ed. 1/350. sgn. boxed. $110.00

UPDIKE, John. *The Coup.* 1978. Knopf. 1st trade ed. dj. VG $20.00

UPDIKE, John. *The Coup.* 1978. New York. Knopf. 1st ed. 299 pp. dj. $10.00

UPDIKE, John. *The Music School.* 1966. Knopf. 1st ed. 2nd issue. dj. EX $35.00

UPDIKE, John. *The Rabbit Is Rich.* 1981. 1st ed. sgn. VG $25.00

UPDIKE, John. *The Rabbit Is Rich.* 1981. Knopf. 1st trade ed. dj. EX $15.00

UPDIKE, John. *The Ring.* 1964. Knopf. 1st ed. ex-lib. VG $35.00

UPDIKE, John. *The Same Door. Short Stories.* 1959. New York. dj. EX $65.00

UPDIKE, John. *The Witches of Eastwick.* 1984. Knopf. 307 pp. dj. EX $3.50

UPDIKE. *Couples.* 1st ed. dj. VG $22.50

UPDIKE. *Olinger Stories.* New York. 1st ed. wrappers. EX $25.00

UPFIELD, Arthur N. *Bony & the White Shadow.* 1961. London. Heinemann. 1st ed. dj. VG $17.50

UPFIELD, Arthur W. *Madman's Bend.* 1963. 1st English ed. dj. EX $45.00

UPFIELD, Arthur W. *Murder Must Wait.* 1953. 1st ed. dj. VG $45.00

UPFIELD, Arthur W. *The Bushman Who Came Back.* 1957. 1st ed. dj. VG $50.00

UPFIELD, Arthur W. *The Lure of the Bush.* 1965. 1st ed. dj. EX $45.00

UPFIELD, Arthur. *Death of a Swagman.* 1946. London. 1st Eng. ed. dj. VG $55.00

UPFIELD, Arthur. *The Mystery of Swordfish Reef.* 1960. London. 1st Eng. ed. dj. VG $55.00

UPHAM, Caroline E. *Salem Witchcraft in Outline.* 1891. Salem. Ills. 1st ed. VG $100.00

UPHAM, Caroline E. *Salem Witchcraft.* 1867. VG $55.00

UPSON, William Hazlett. *Earthworms in Europe.* 1931. New York. Farrar. 1st ed. sgn. 300 pp. $15.00

UPTON, E. *The Military Policy of the United States.* 1907. fld map. G $20.00

UPTON, F.K. *Golliwoggs Auto-Go-Cart.* 1901. Longmans. Ills. $125.00

UPTON, Harriet Taylor. *Our Early Presidents, Their Wives & Children.* 1890. Boston. Ills. 395 pp. $20.00

UPTON, John. *Diary of William Smith.* 1965. Champlain Soc. Ltd. ed. 1/750. VG $45.00

UPTON, R. *A Bird in Hand, Celebrated Falconers of the Past.* 1980. London. Debretts Peerage. Ills. dj. EX $22.50

URE, Stellanie. *Hawk Lady.* 1980. Doubleday. 215 pp. dj. EX $4.00

URIS, Leon. *The Angry Hills.* 1955. Random House. 1st ed. dj. VG $25.00

URQUHART, D.H. *Cocoa.* 1956. Longmans. Ills. 230 pp. dj. VG $10.00

URSIN, M.J. *Guide to Fishes of the Temperate Atlantic Coast.* 1977. Dutton. Ills. 262 pp. dj. EX $10.00

USBORNE, Richard. *Dr. Sir Pelham Wodehouse Old Boy.* 1977. Ltd. 1st ed. 1/500. VG $20.00

USDA YEARBOOKS. *Climate & Man, 1941.* 1942. Washington. 1248 pp. VG $7.50

USDA YEARBOOKS. *Farmers in a Changing World.* 1940. Washington. 1215 pp. VG $9.00

USDA YEARBOOKS. *Gardening for Food & Fun, 1977.* 1977. Washington. 392 pp. $3.50

USDA YEARBOOKS. *Grass, 1948.* 1949. Washington. ex-lib. 892 pp. G $6.00

USDA YEARBOOKS. *Living on a Few Acres.* 1978. Washington. 432 pp. EX $6.50

USDA YEARBOOKS. *Power to Produce, 1960.* 1960. Washington. 480 pp. VG $7.50

USDA YEARBOOKS. *Report of the Commissioner of Patents 1904.* 1905. Washington. 715 pp. VG $7.50

USDA YEARBOOKS. *Report of the Commissioner of Patents 1916.* 1917. Washington. 783 pp. VG $7.00

USDA YEARBOOKS. *Report of the Commissioner of Patents 1937.* 1937. Washington. 1497 pp. VG $7.50

USDA YEARBOOKS. *Report of the Commissioner of Patents.* 1858. Washington. 551 pp. G $15.00

USHER, Arland. *The XXII Keys of the Tarot.* 1969. Dolmen Press. 54 pp. dj. EX $15.00

USTINOV, Peter. *Photo Finish.* 1962. London. 1st ed. dj. VG $20.00

UTERMEYER, Louis. *Merry Christmas.* 1967. Golden Press. Ills. Joan Berg. $7.50

UTTERLIN. *Neither Fear Nor Hope.* 1964. New York. 1st ed. dj. EX $21.50

VAGTS, A. *Landing Operations: Strategy & Tactics.* 1952. Stackpole. 831 pp. VG $15.00

VAIL, Amanda. *Love Me Little.* 1957. 1st ed. dj. VG $15.00

VAIL, Charles H. *Ancient Mysteries & Modern Masonry.* 1909. New York. Macoy Pub. 1st ed 214 pp. VG $20.00

VAIL, Philip. *The Great American Rascal. Life of Aaron Burr.* 1973. New York. 243 pp. dj. VG $10.00

VAIL, R.W.G. *Knickerbocker Birthday.* 1954. New York. sgn. dj. VG $15.00

VAKA, D. *Haremlik.* 1914. Boston. 275 pp. G $12.50

VALDEZ, R. *Lords of the Pinnacles, Wild Goats of World.* 1985. Ltd. ed. sgn. 212 pp. dj. EX $60.00

VALDEZ, R. *The Wild Sheep of the World.* 1982. Ills. 1st ed. dj. EX $40.00

VALE, Robert B. *Wings, Fur, & Shot.* 1936. Ills. G. Sutton. VG $22.50

VALENTINE, Lewis J. *Night Stick.* 1947. New York. Dial Press. 1st ed. 318 pp. EX $17.50

VALENTINO, Rudolph. *Day Dreams.* 1923. New York. 1st ed. VG $12.50

VALENTINO, Rudolph. *My Private Diary.* 1929. Occult Pub. Ills. 313 pp. G $6.50

VALENZUELA, Luisa. *Clara.* 1st ed. sgn. $17.50

VALENZUELA, Luisa. *Strange Things Happen Here.* 1st ed. review copy. sgn. dj. $17.50

VALENZUELA, Luisa. *The Lizard's Tail.* 1983. Farrar. Ills. 1st Am. ed. dj. EX $17.50

VALERY, Paul. *Collected Works. Vol. 4.* 1956. New York. dj. VG $20.00

VALIN, Jonathan. *Day of Wrath.* 1982. New York. Congdon & Lattes. 1st ed. dj. $15.00

VALIN, Jonathan. *Dead Letter.* 1981. New York. Dodd Mead. 1st ed. dj. EX $25.00

VALIN, Jonathan. *Final Notice.* 1980. New York. Dodd Mead. 1st ed. dj. EX $35.00

VALLANCE, R. *Dickens' London Engravings.* 1966. Cruikshank Folio Soc. EX $25.00

VALLANDIGHAM, James L. *Life of Clement L. Vallandigham.* 1872. Baltimore. 1st ed. 573 pp. rebound. VG $65.00

VALLENTIN, Antonina. *Leonardo da Vinci.* 1938. color pls. $9.00

VALTIN, Jan. *Out of the Night.* 1941. New York. Alliance Book. 749 pp. G $10.00

VAN ALLSBURG, Chris. *The Polar Express.* 1985. 1st ed. VG $25.00

VAN BUREN, Martin. *Capture of Mexican Brig Urrea.* 1838. Washington. 1st ed. 46 pp. $85.00

VAN BUREN, Martin. *Mexico-Texas-Canada.* 1938. Washington. 1st ed. 54 pp. $75.00

VAN CLEVE, Spike. *40 Years' Gatherins.* 1977. Kansas City. Ills. 1st ed. 2nd printing. EX $12.50

VAN DE WATER, F. *Reluctant Rebel.* 1948. New York. 442 pp. $3.50

VAN DE WATER, F. *Rudyard Kipling's Vermont Feud.* 1937. New York. Ills. 1st ed. inscr. VG $10.00

VAN DEMAN, R. & Yeatman, F. *Aunt Sammy's Radio Recipes Revised.* 1931. Washington. VG $10.00

VAN DER POST, Laurens. *The Dark Eye of Africa.* 1955. New York. Morrow. 224 pp. dj. $3.00

VAN DER POST, Laurens. *Venture to the Interior.* 1951. Morrow. Ills. 253 pp. dj. EX $12.50

VAN DER POST. *Lost World of the Kalahari.* 1958. 1st ed. dj. VG $12.50

VAN DERVEER, Helen R. *Little Sally Mandy.* 1935. New York. Platt & Munk. Ills. B. Willis. $17.50

VAN DINE, S.S. *Casino Murder Case.* 1934. New York. dj. EX $15.00

VAN DINE, S.S. *The Bishop Murder Case.* 1929. New York. 1st ed. dj. VG $25.00

VAN DINE, S.S. *The Canary Murder Case.* 1927. 1st ed. VG $15.00

VAN DINE, S.S. *The Greene Murder Case.* 1928. Scribner. 1st ed. dj. VG $25.00

VAN DINE, S.S. *The Greene Murder Case.* 1928. 3rd ed. VG $15.00

VAN DINE, S.S. *The Scarab Murder Case.* 1930. New York. 1st ed. dj. VG $60.00

VAN DOREN, Carl. *Benjamin Franklin.* 1938. New York. 2nd printing. VG $6.00

VAN DOREN, Carl. *Secret History of the American Revolution.* 1941. New York. Ltd. ed. 1/590. sgn. slipcase. $60.00

VAN DOREN, M. *Travels of William Bartram.* Dover. reprint. Ills. 414 pp. EX $12.50

VAN DOREN, Mark. *An Autobiography of America.* 1929. New York. 737 pp. VG $10.00

VAN DOREN, Mark. *The Autobiography of Mark Van Doren.* 1958. $7.50

VAN DYKE, Henry. *Fisherman's Luck.* 1899. 1st ed. VG $25.00

VAN DYKE, Henry. *Music & Other Poems.* 1904. Scribner. 116 pp. VG $5.50

VAN DYKE, Henry. *The Ruling Passion.* 1901. Scribner. Ills. Clark. 1st ed. VG $12.00

VAN DYKE, Henry. *The Story of the Other Wise Man.* 1899. VG $8.00

VAN DYKE, Henry. *The Story of the Other Wise Man.* 1901. New York. Harper. 70 pp. $2.50

VAN DYKE, John C. *American Painting & Its Tradition.* 1919. New York. Ills. 1st ed. EX $15.00

VAN DYKE, John C. *How to Judge a Picture.* 1889. New York. Eaton & Mains. 168 pp. VG $15.00

VAN DYKE. *The New New York.* 1909. New York. Ills. J. Pennell. $7.50

VAN DYNE, Edith. *Aunt Jane's Nieces on the Ranch.* 1913. Chicago. 276 pp. $3.50

VAN EURIE, J.H. *White Supremacy, Negro Subordination.* 1868. New York. Ills. 2nd ed. 339 pp. $45.00

VAN EVRIE, J.H. *Negroes & Negro 'Slavery.'* 1863. New York. 339 pp. G $25.00

VAN FRISCH, Karl. *Animal Architecture.* 1974. Harcourt Brace Jovanovich. EX $7.50

VAN GORDEN, J.H. *Country Tradition.* 1975. Ills. sgn. dj. VG $12.50

VAN GORDEN, J.H. *The Susquehanna Flows On.* 1966. Ills. 281 pp. dj. VG $4.00

VAN GULIK, Robert H. *Essay on History Sanskrit Studies China & Japan.* 1956. Nagpur. 1st ed. 60 pls. 240 pp. VG $175.00

VAN GULIK, Robert H. *Gibbon in China.* 1967. Leiden. Brill. 1st ed. w/record. EX $37.50

VAN GULIK, Robert H. *Hsi K'ang & His Poetical Essay on the Lute.* 1969. Sophia University. dj. EX $45.00

VAN GULIK, Robert H. *Judge Dee at Work.* 1972. New York. 1st Am. ed. dj. EX $20.00

VAN GULIK, Robert H. *Lacquer Screen.* 1969. New York. 1st Am. ed. dj. EX $25.00

VAN GULIK, Robert H. *Lore of the Chinese Lute.* 1940. Tokyo. Sophia University. wrappers. $67.50

VAN GULIK, Robert H. *Sexual Life in Ancient China.* 1961. Leiden. Brill. dj. EX $95.00

VAN GULIK. *Phantom.* 1966. 1st ed. dj. EX $35.00

VAN HAGEN, V.W. *South American Zoo.* 1946. Messner. Ills. Jaques. 182 pp. dj. VG $7.00

VAN LAUN, Henri. *History of French Literature II.* 1877. New York. Putman. ex-lib. 392 pp. $3.00

VAN LAWICK-GOODALL, H. & J. *Innocent Killers.* 1971. Houghton Mifflin. 1st Am. ed. $17.50

VAN LAWICK-GOODALL, J. *My Friends the Wild Chimpanzees.* 1967. Nat. Geog. Soc. Ills. 204 pp. EX $10.00

VAN LOON, H. *The Story of Mankind.* 1929. Liveright. $10.00

VAN LOON, H. *The Story of Mankind.* 1922. Ills. 7th printing. VG $10.00

VAN LOON, Hendrick W. *Adventures & Escapes of Gustavus Vasa.* New York. Ills. dj. $15.00

VAN LOON, Hendrick W. *Ancient Man.* 1920. Boni & Liveright. 1st ed. VG $15.00

VAN LOON, Hendrick W. *Observations on the Mystery of Print.* 1937. Book Mfgrs. Inst. 1st ed. sgn. $35.00

VAN LOON, Hendrick W. *The Arts-Written & Illustrated.* 1937. New York. Simon & Schuster. 1st ed. G $7.00

VAN LOON, Hendrick W. *The Golden Book of the Dutch Navigators.* 1938. Appleton. Ills. revised ed. dj. VG $17.50

VAN LOON, Hendrick W. *Van Loon's Lives.* 1942. Simon & Schuster. 1st ed. $4.50

VAN LOON, Hendrik W. *An Elephant Up a Tree.* 1933. Simon & Schuster. VG $16.50

VAN LOON, Hendrick W. *How to Look at Pictures.* 1938. Modern Age Bks. VG $8.00

VAN LOON, Hendrick W. *The Arts.* 1939. New York. Simon & Schuster. 677 pp. EX $7.50

VAN LOON, Hendrick W. *The Message of the Bells.* 1942. New York. 1st ed. VG $12.50

VAN PASSEN, Pierre. *Days of Our Years.* 1939. New York. 1st ed. inscr. sgn. VG $20.00

VAN PASSEN, Pierre. *The Time Is Now.* 1941. New York. Dial Press. 80 pp. EX $3.00

VAN PELT, J. *Architecture Toscane.* 1923. New York. dj. EX $25.00

VAN RAVENSWAY. *Arts & Architecture of German Settlements in MO.* 1977. U. of MO. $25.00

VAN RENSELLAER, J.K. *Prophetical Educational & Playing Cards.* 1912. Philadelphia. Ills. 1st ed. EX $50.00

VAN RIPER, Guernsey, Jr. *Lou Gehrig, Boy of the Sand Lots.* 1949. New York. Bobbs Merrill. 194 pp. $5.00

VAN RJNDT, Phillippe. *Samaritan.* 1983. Dial Press. proof copy. wrappers. VG $10.00

VAN SCHAICK, George. *The Girl at Big Loon Post.* 1917. $4.00

VAN SICKLE, V.A. *The Wrong Body.* 1937. New York. Knopf. 1st ed. dj. VG $15.00

VAN SINDEREN. *Country of the Mountains of the Moon.* 1951. 1st ed. EX $15.00

VAN SLYKE, Helen. *No Love Lost.* 1980. Lippincott. 1st ed. dj. VG $7.50

VAN SLYKE, Helen. *The Best Place to Be.* 1976. Doubleday. 1st ed. dj. VG $7.50

VAN STOCKUM, Hilda. *Kersti & Saint Nicholas.* 1940. New York. Viking. Ills. 1st ed. $25.00

VAN TRAMP, John C. *Prairie & Rocky Mountain Adventures.* Columbus, OH. Gilmore & Brush. $30.00

VAN TRAMP, John. *Prairie & Rocky Mountain Adventures.* 1860. Columbus. Miller. Ills. 640 pp. VG $55.00

VAN VALKENBURG, Samuel. *Europe.* 1935. New York. Wiley. VG $15.00

VAN VECHTEN, C. *Nigger Heaven.* 1926. 1st ed. VG $35.00

VAN VECHTEN, C. *Red.* 1925. New York. Ltd. 1st ed. sgn. $55.00

VAN VOGT, A.E. *Destination: Universe!* 1952. New York. 1st ed. dj. VG $20.00

VAN VOGT, A.E. *Empire of the Atom.* 1956. Chicago. Shasta. 1st ed. dj. VG $25.00

VAN VOGT, A.E. *Far-Out Worlds of A.E. Van Vogt.* 1973. London. 1st ed. dj. EX $15.00

VAN VOGT, A.E. *The House that Stood Still.* 1950. Greenberg. 1st ed. dj. VG $25.00

VAN VOGT, A.E. *The Mind Cage.* 1957. New York. 1st ed. dj. VG $15.00

VAN VOGT, A.E. *The Mixed Men.* 1952. New York. Gnome. 1st ed. dj. VG $25.00

VAN VOGT, A.E. *The Violent Man.* 1962. New York. Farrar. 1st ed. dj. EX $15.00

VAN VOGT, A.E. *The Voyage of the Space Beagle.* 1950. Simon & Schuster. 1st ed. dj. $15.00

VAN VOGT, A.E. *The Weapon Makers.* 1952. New York. 1st revised ed. dj. VG $12.50

VAN VOGT. *The Weapon Makers.* 1947. Providence. Hadley. 1st ed. VG $35.00

VAN WORMER, J. *The World of the Black Bear.* 1966. Lippincott. Ills. 163 pp. dj. VG $15.00

VAN WORMER, J. *The World of the Pronghorn.* 1968. Lippincott. Ills. 190 pp. dj. EX $10.00

VAN WYCK, Mason. *Zanzibar Intrigue.* 1963. New York. 1st ed. dj. EX $10.00

VANCE, Ethel. *Escape.* 1939. Boston. 1st ed. VG $15.00

VANCE, J. *Augmented Agent.* 1986. Ltd. ed. 1/200. sgn. EX $50.00

VANCE, J. *Cugel's Saga.* 1983. New York. Timescape. 1st ed. dj. EX $25.00

VANCE, J. *Future Tense.* 1964. 1st printing. pb. EX $12.50

VANCE, J. *Galactic Effecutator.* 1980. Ltd. ed. 1/200. sgn. EX $50.00

VANCE, J. *Gold & Iron.* 1982. Ltd. ed. 1/200. sgn. EX $40.00

VANCE, J. *Gray Prince.* 1974. Bobbs Merrill. 1st ed. dj. EX $15.00

VANCE, J. *Green Magic.* 1979. Underwood & Miller. 1st ed. EX $25.00

VANCE, J. *Green Magic.* 1979. Ltd. ed. 1/175. sgn. EX $60.00

VANCE, J. *Green Pearl.* Ltd. ed. 1/600. sgn. $70.00

VANCE, J. *Houses of Iszm.* 1983. Ltd. ed. 1/200. sgn. EX $40.00

VANCE, J. *Last Castle.* 1980. Ills. Austin. Ltd. ed. 1/200. sgns. EX $50.00

VANCE, J. *Masque Thaery.* 1976. New York. Berkley. 1st ed. dj. EX $17.50

VANCE, J. *Quest for the Future.* 1971. London. 1st ed. dj. EX $15.00

VANCE, J. *Showboat World.* 1983. Ills. Dameron. Ltd. ed. 1/200. sgn. EX $40.00

VANCE, J. *Son of Tree.* 1983. Ltd. ed. 1/200. sgn. EX $40.00

VANCE, J. *The Blue World.* 1966. 1st printing. EX $10.00

VANCE, J. *The Dying Earth.* 1950. 1st Am. ed. wrappers. EX $110.00

VANCE, J. *The Killing Machine.* 1967. London. 1st hardcover ed. dj. EX $15.00

VANCE, J. *Trullion.* 1973. 1st printing. pb. EX $8.50

VANCE, Marguerite. *Lees of Arlington. Story of Mary & Robert E. Lee.* 1949. New York. Ills. Nedda Walker. 160 pp. $5.00

VANCOUVER, George. *Voyage of Discovery to North Pacific Ocean.* 1801. London. 2nd ed. 6 vol set. VG $1,250.00

VANDEGRIFT, A.A. *Once a Marine.* 1964. New York. Ills. 1st ed. map. index. VG $25.00

VANDENBERG, Arthur H. *The Private Papers of Senator Vandenberg.* 1952. Boston. 599 pp. VG $7.50

VANDENBERGH. *On the Trail of the Pygmies.* 1921. 1st ed. dj. VG $20.00

VANDERBILT, Amy. *Amy Vanderbilt's Complete Book of Etiquette.* 1955. New York. Doubleday. 700 pp. VG $5.00

VANDERBILT, Cornelius. *The Living Past of America.* 1966. New York. Crown. Ills. 234 pp. $10.00

VANDERBILT, G.F. *Social History of Flatbush.* 1899. New York. Ills. fld map. VG $25.00

VANDERCOOK, Margaret. *The Campfire Girls Amid the Snow.* 1913. Winston. Ills. G $4.50

VANDERCOOK, Margaret. *The Campfire Girls in After Years.* 1915. Philadelphia. Winston. 249 pp. $2.00

VANDERCOOK, Margaret. *The Campfire Girls in the Outside World.* 1914. Winston. 262 pp. $2.50

VANDERPOEL, Ambrose Ely. *History of Chatham, New Jersey.* 1959. Chatham. photos. 433 pp. EX $10.00

VANDERVELDE, Emile. *Collectivism & Industrial Evolution.* 1901. Chicago. trans. Kerr. 1st ed. $30.00

VANDERVELDE, Emile. *Socialism Versus the State.* 1919. Chicago. Kerr. 1st ed. EX $15.00

VANDIVER. *Mighty Stonewall.* 1957. New York. 1st ed. dj. VG $30.00

VANN, William. *Texas Institute of Letters 1936-1966.* 1967. Austin. Ltd. ed. sgn. EX $35.00

VANOT, Theodore. *Adventures of an African Slaver.* 1928. New York. Ills. VG $15.00

VANSITTART, Robert. *The Singing Caravan.* 1923. Gregynog Pr. Ltd. ed. 1/250. VG $40.00

VARADAY, D. *Gara-Yaka's Domain.* 1966. London. Collins. Ills. 192 pp. dj. VG $10.00

VARESCHI. *Mountains in Flower.* 1940. New York. 1st ed. dj. VG $15.00

VARLEY, John. *Blue Champagne.* 1986. Dark Harvest. Ltd. ed. sgn. slipcase. EX $60.00

VARLEY, John. *Demon.* 1984. Putnam. 1st ed. dj. EX $50.00

VARMA, Devendra P. *The Gothic Flame, Being History of Gothic Novel.* 1966. dj. $8.50

VARNEY, G.L. *Reminiscences of Henry Clay Barnabee.* 1913. Boston. Ills. sgn. 461 pp. $15.00

VASARI, Giorgio. *Artists of the Renaissance.* 1978. London. Crown. trans. Bull. Ills. EX $15.00

VASARI, Giorgio. *Lives of Eminent Painters, Sculptors, Architects.* 1912-1914 Medici Soc. Ills. 10 vol set. $175.00

VASS, George. *The Chicago Black Hawks' Story.* 1970. Chicago. Ills. 215 pp. dj. VG $8.50

VASSAR, T.E. *Uncle John Vassar; or, the Fight of Faith.* 1879. New York. 258 pp. $10.00

VASSEUR, John. *Typhon's Beard.* 1927. New York. Doran. 1st ed. VG $20.00

VASSOS, John. *A New Edition of Gray's Elegy.* 1931. New York. Dutton. Ills. $20.00

VAUGHAN, Beatrice. *The Ladies' Aid Cookbook.* 1971. Battleboro, VT.Greene. 186 pp. $6.50

VAUGHAN, Graham. *Ethnic Awareness & Attitudes in New Zealand.* 1964. Wellington. 1st ed. stiff wrappers. $8.50

VAUGHAN, Roger. *The Grand Gesture.* 1975. $5.50

VAVRA, Robert. *Unicorns I Have Known.* 1983. 1st ed. dj. VG $35.00

VAZQUEZ, P.R. *National Museum of Anthropology.* 1968. Mexico. Abrams. Ills. folio. dj. VG $42.50

VEACH, Wm. T. & Brown, H. E. *A Bon Vivant's Cookbook.* 1965. Boston. 236 pp. $7.50

VECHTEN. *Selected Writings of G. Stein.* 1st ed. VG $10.00

VEDDER, Elihu. *Rubaiyat of Omar Khayyam.* 1894. Boston. Houghton Mifflin. 1st ed. VG $60.00

VELIKOVSKY, I. *Worlds in Collision.* 1950. 1st Eng. ed. dj. VG $7.00

VELPEAU, A. *An Elementary Treatise on Midwifery.* 1831. Philadelphia. 584 pp. $45.00

VENABLE, Clarke. *Fleetfin.* 1925. 1st ed. VG $35.00

VENABLE, W.H. *Dramas & Dramatic Scenes.* 1874. Cincinnati/NY. Ills. 336 pp. $10.00

VENEGAS, Miguel. *A Natural & Civil History of California.* 1759. London. 1st ed. 2 vol set. $1,150.00

VENK, Ernest & Billiet, W. *Automotive Fundamentals.* 1961. Chicago. TB. 520 pp. EX $4.50

VERGA, G. *Mastro-Don Gesualdo.* 1923. New York. Seltzer. 1st ed. dj. $25.00

VERGES, Robert. *Okumura Masanobu, Early Ukiyo-e Master.* 1983. Kondansha. Ills. 1st ed. folio. dj. EX $35.00

VERHAEREN, Emile. *Plays.* 1916. Boston. Chiswick Press. VG $12.50

VERILL, A.H. *Thirty Years in the Jungle.* 1929. London. Lane. Ills. 1st ed. 281 pp. VG $20.00

VERNAM, G.R. *Rawhide Years.* 1976. 1st ed. dj. EX $10.00

VERNE, Jules. *Around the World in Eighty Days.* New York. Random House. $5.00

VERNE, Jules. *Doctor Ox.* 1874. Boston. Osgood. trans. Geo. M. Towle. $40.00

VERNE, Jules. *Journey to the Center of the Earth.* 1966. Heritage Press.Ills. Edward Wilson. dj. EX $20.00

VERNE, Jules. *The Castle of the Carathians.* 1900. New York. 211 pp. $5.00

VERNE, Jules. *The Mysterious Island.* 1933. Scribner. Ills. Wyeth. VG $16.50

VERNE, Jules. *Twenty Thousand Leagues Under the Sea.* 1956. Ltd. Eds. Club. Ills. E.A. Wilson. sgn. boxed. $60.00

VERNE, Jules. *Twenty Thousand Leagues Under the Sea.* 1952. Scribner. Ills. W.J. Aylward. VG $12.50

VERNE, Jules. *Un Hwernage dans les Glaces.* Paris. Ills. Adrien Marie. VG $10.00

VERNE, Jules. *Une Ville Flottante.* Paris. G $22.50

VERNER, Elizabeth. *Mellow by Time: Charleston Notebook.* 1959. Columbia, SC. Ills. EX $20.00

VERNET, Horace. *Costumes et Modes d'Autrefois.* 1955. Paris. Ltd. ed. 24 color pls. boxed. $27.50

VERNET, Joseph. *Le Ports De France Pents.* 1812. Paris. 23 of 26 pls present. $35.00

VERNON, Arthur. *History & Romance of the Horse.* 1940. Hayon House. Ills. Donnelly. VG $14.50

VERNON, S. *Antique Fishing Reels.* 1985. sgn. dj. EX $20.00

VERRILL, A.H. *Strange Birds & Their Stories.* 1938. Page. Ills. 203 pp. dj. VG $10.00

VERSEY-FITZGERALD, B. *The Worlds of Ants, Bees, & Wasps.* 1969. Pelham. Ills. 1st ed. 117 pp. dj. VG $7.50

VERVE. *Moods. Movement in Art.* 1959. $39.00

VERVLIET. *Sixteenth Century Printing Types of Low Countries.* 1968. Amsterdam. dj. EX $50.00

VESEY, Arthur H. *The Clock & the Key.* 1905. New York. Appleton. 2nd ed. VG $10.00

VESTAL, Stanley. *Dodge City Queen of the Cowtowns.* 1955. London. 285 pp. dj. VG $20.00

VESTAL, Stanley. *Kit Carson.* 1928. Boston. $10.00

VESTAL, Stanley. *Old Santa Fe Trail.* 1939. Houghton Mifflin. 1st ed. dj. $27.50

VESTAL, Stanley. *Short Grass Country.* 1941. New York. 1st ed. 304 pp. EX $30.00

VESTER, Bertha Spafford. *Flowers of the Holy Land.* 1962. Doubleday. Ills. 1st ed. dj. $3.50

VETROMILE, Eugene. *Indian Good Book.* 1857. Bangor, NY. Ills. 450 pp. $250.00

VETTER, H. *Mutiny at Koje Island.* 1965. dj. VG $15.00

VICKERS, Roy. *Murder Will Out.* 1950. London. Faber. 1st ed. dj. EX $35.00

VICKERS, Roy. *Murdering Mr. Velfrage.* 1959. London. 1st ed. dj. VG $20.00

VICKERS, Roy. *The Sole Survivor & the Kynsard Affair.* 1952. London. 1st Eng. ed. dj. VG $30.00

VICKROY, T.R. *Fonetic Furst Redur, Printed in Alfabet & Speling.* 1878. Cincinnati/NY. Ills. 48 pp. $10.00

VICTOR, Orville. *Incidents & Anecdotes of the War.* 1862. 1st ed. 400 pp. $28.50

VICTOR. *Book of Opera.* 1938. Ills. 9th revised ed. VG $11.00

VICTOR. *Boy Scouts Canoe Trip.* 1914. Chatterson. Ills. Mencl. $3.50

VICTOR. *Boy Scouts in the Canadian Rockies.* 1911. Platt & Peck. Ills. Mencl. $3.50

VICTOR. *Boy Scouts on the Yukon.* 1912. Hurst & Co. Ills. Mencl. dj. EX $7.50

VIDAL, Gore. *Creation.* 1981. Ltd. ed. 1/500. slipcase. EX $40.00

VIDAL, Gore. *Creation.* 1981. Random House. 1st ed. dj. VG $15.00

VIDAL, Gore. *Julian.* 1964. 1st ed. VG $65.00

VIDAL, Gore. *Kalki.* 1978. Random House. 1st ed. dj. VG $12.50

VIDAL, Gore. *Myra Breckinridge.* 1968. 1st ed. dj. VG $20.00

VIDAL, Gore. *Myron.* 1974. Random House. 1st ed. dj. VG $15.00

VIDAL, Gore. *Reflections from a Sinking Ship.* 1969. Little, Brown. 1st ed. dj. VG $22.50

VIDAL, Gore. *The City/The Pillar.* 1948. presentation copy. sgn. VG $65.00

VIDAL, Gore. *The Judgement of Paris.* 1952. New York. 1st ed. VG $10.00

VIDAL, Gore. *Two Sisters.* 1970. Little, Brown. 1st ed. dj. VG $15.00

VIDAL, Gore. *Views from a Window. Conversations with Vidal.* 1980. Stuart. 1st ed. dj. VG $15.00

VIDAL, Gore. *Washington, D.C.* 1967. Book Club. dj. $5.00

VIELE. *The Last of the Knickerbockers.* 1901. Stone & Co. 1st ed. VG $5.00

VIERECK, George Sylvester. *The House of the Vampire.* 1907. 1st Am. ed. G $15.00

VIERGE, Daniel. *Pen & Ink Drawings.* 1931. folio. 60 pls. VG $100.00

VIERTEL. *White Hunter, Black Heart.* 1953. 1st ed. VG $8.50

VIGDORVA. *Diary of a School Teacher.* 1954. Moscow. Ills. 344 pp. $20.00

VIGNON, Paul. *Le Linceul Du Christ Etude Scientifique.* 1902. Paris. 1st ed. exlib. $25.00

VIGNON, Paul. *The Shroud of Christ.* 1970. New York. Ills. 170 pp. $5.00

VIIRLAID, Arvel. *Graves Without Crosses.* 1972. Toronto. presentation copy. sgn. dj. VG $10.00

VILAS, C.N. & N.R. *Florida Marine Shells.* 1945. Aberdeen. Ills. 150 pp. dj. G $7.50

VILLA, Jose Garcia. *I Have Come, I Am Here.* 1942. Viking Press. 2nd ed. dj. VG $5.00

VILLAGRA, Gaspar Perez de. *History of New Mexico.* 1933. Los Angeles. Quivira Soc. Ltd. 1st ed. $200.00

VILLAR, R. *Piracy Today/Robbery & Violence at Sea Since 1980.* 1985. London. maps. dj. EX $20.00

VILLARD, Henry. *Lincoln on the Eve of '61.* 1941. Knopf. 105 pp. dj. VG $4.50

VILLARD, Henry. *Past & Present of the Pike's Peak Gold Region.* 1932. $22.50

VILLARD, O.G. *Some Newspapers & Newspaper Men.* 1932. New York. Knopf. 345 pp. G $10.00

VILLET, B. & G. *Those Whom God Chooses.* 1966. New York. 1st ed. dj. EX $7.50

VILLIARD, P. *Raising Small Animals for Fun & Profit.* 1973. Winchester. Ills. 160 pp. dj. EX $12.50

VILLIERS, Alan. *Captain John Cook.* 1967. Scribner. Ills. 1st ed. sgn. G $12.00

VILLIERS, Alan. *Falmouth for Order.* 1929. Holt. $12.50

VILLIERS, Alan. *Men, Ships, & the Sea.* 1962. Nat. Geo. Society. Ills. dj. $20.00

VILLIERS, Alan. *Monsoon Seas, Story of the Indian Ocean.* 1952. McGraw Hill. Ills. 337 pp. VG $10.00

VILLIERS, Alan. *The Coral Sea.* 1949. Whittlessey. Ills. 310 pp. VG $5.00

VILLIERS, Alan. *The Guest of the Schooner Argus.* 1951. $6.50

VILLIERS, Alan. *The Way of a Ship.* 1953. New York. 1st ed. sgn. $20.00

VILLIERS, Alan. *Whaling in the Frozen South.* 1931. McBride. sgn. dj. VG $35.00

VINCENT, Frank. *Around & About South America.* 1895. New York. 5th ed. VG $20.00

VINCENT, John Martin. *State & Federal Government in Switzerland.* 1891. Baltimore. 1st ed. VG $20.00

VINCENT, Lee Bain. *Earthly Footsteps of the Man of Galilee.* 1894. New York. Thompson. map. photos. EX $100.00

VINGE, Joan D. *World's End.* BlueJay Books. advance copy. wrappers. EX $20.00

VINING, Edward P. *The Mystery of Hamlet.* 1881. Philadelphia. 1st ed. 95 pp. $12.00

VINMONT, Rolf, Benjamin. *Our Presidents at a Glance.* 1932. New York. Ills. S.J. Patrick. 79 pp. $5.50

VINOGRADOFF, Paul. *English Society in the Eleventh Century.* 1908. Oxford. 1st ed. dj. $20.00

VIORST, Judith. *A Visit from St. Nicolas to a Liberated Household.* 1977. New York. Simon & Schuster. 1st ed. dj. $10.00

VIRGIL. *The Aeneid.* 1944. Heritage Press. Ills. Petrina. boxed. EX $7.50

VISSCHER, William L. *Thrilling & Truthful History of the Pony Express.* 1946. Chicago. Ills. 98 pp. $10.00

VISSER. *Asiatic Art in Private Collections of Holland.* 1948. New York. Beechurst Press. $30.00

VOGEL, Zdenek. *Reptile Life.* London. Spring Books. Ills. 80 pp. VG $25.00

VOGT, E.Z. & Hyman, Ray. *Water Witching U.S.A.* 1959. Chicago. Ills. 248 pp. dj. $17.50

VOGT, H. *Burden of Guilt.* 1964. New York. Oxford U.P. Ills. $15.00

VOIGHT, William. *Public Grazing Lands: Use/Misuse by Industry/Govt.* 1976. Rutgers. 1st ed. dj. VG $12.50

VOISIN, Gaston. *French Cooking for All.* London. (ca.1920) VG $10.00

VOLTAIRE. *Candide.* 1929. Literary Guild. Ills. Kent. $12.50

VOLTAIRE. *Candide.* Bodley Head. Ills. Tealby. 1st ed. VG $60.00

VOLTAIRE. *Candide.* 1930. Ills. Rockwell Kent. VG $10.00

VOLTAIRE. *Zadig.* 1929. New York. Ltd. ed. 1/999. boxed. VG $15.00

VON BARCHWITZ-KRAUSER, O. *Six Years with William Taylor in South America.* 1885. Boston. 332 pp. $12.50

VON DER OSTEN, H.H. *Die Welt der Perser.* 1956. Stuttgart. 299 pp. 118 pls. index. $17.50

VON FORSTNER. *Journal of Submarine Commander.* 1917. Boston. trans. Codman. 1st ed. $20.00

VON HAGEN, V.W. *Highway of the Sun.* 1955. Ills. 1st ed. dj. EX $20.00

VON HAGEN, V.W. *South America Called Them.* 1945. Knopf. Ills. 311 pp. VG $17.50

VON HAGEN, V.W. *South America: Green World of the Naturalists.* 1951. London. dj. VG $20.00

VON HAGEN, V.W. *The Ancient Sun Kingdoms of the Americas.* 1961. Cleveland/NY. Ills. Beltran. 1st ed. dj. $15.00

VON HAGEN, V.W. *The Golden Man, Quest for El Dorado.* 1974. London Book Classic Assoc. VG $14.00

VON HOLST. *The Constitutional & Political History of the U.S.* 1877. 505 pp. $8.50

VON KAISENBERG, Moritz. *The Memoirs of Baroness Cecile De Courtot.* 1900. New York. VG $12.50

VON KARMAN, Theodor. *Daniel Guggenheim Airship Institute Publication.* 1933. Akron. 68 pp. wrappers. $10.00

VON LANG, J. *Martin Bormann: Man Who Manipulated Hitler.* 1979. New York. Random House. Ills. VG $12.50

WALDEN. *The Boy Scout Afloat.* 1918. Barse & Hopkins. Ills. Wrenn. $3.50

WALDMAN, Max. *Waldman on Theater.* 1971. Garden City. EX $22.50

WALDRON, Malcolm. *Snow Man. John Honby in the Barren Lands.* 1931. Houghton Mifflin. 1st ed. $15.00

WALDSTEIN & SHOOBRIDGE. *Herculaneum.* 1908. London. $45.00

WALES, William W. *Sketch of St. Anthony & Minneapolis Territory.* 1857. Minneapolis. Ills. 1st ed. wrappers. $175.00

WALFORD, Lionel A. *Marine Game Fishes of Pacific Coast-AL to Equator.* 1937. Berkeley. VG $95.00

WALKDEN, S.L. *Aeroplanes in Gusts.* 1913. London. Ills. 2nd ed. 280 pp. VG $32.50

WALKER, Alexander. *Beauty Illustrated by Analysis & Classification.* 1852. London. 372 pp. $45.00

WALKER, Alexander. *Intermarriage.* 1839. New York. 1st Am. ed. $35.00

WALKER, Alice. *Good Night Willie Lee, I'll See You in Morning.* 1979. New York. Dial Press. 1st ed. dj. EX $50.00

WALKER, Alice. *Horses Make a Landscape More Beautiful.* 1984. NY. Harcourt. proof copy. wrappers. EX $45.00

WALKER, Alice. *You Can't Keep a Good Woman Down.* 1981. New York. Harcourt. 1st ed. dj. EX $50.00

WALKER, Ernest. *A History of Music in England.* 1907. Oxford. 364 pp. G $15.00

WALKER, Francis *General Hancock.* 1894. 332 pp. $13.50

WALKER, Franklin. *Ambrose Bierce, Wickedest Man in San Francisco.* 1941. Colt Press. Ltd. 1st ed. 1/550. $95.00

WALKER, Franklin. *The Wickedest Man in San Francisco.* 1941. Colt Press. Ltd. ed. 1/500. VG $35.00

WALKER, H.H. *Busy North Carolina Women.* 1931. sgn. VG $10.00

WALKER, J.B. *America Fallen!* 1915. New York. Dodd Mead. 1st ed. EX $40.00

WALKER, J.B. *Modern Warplanes of the World.* 1942. Ills. 64 pp. pb. G $7.50

WALKER, John. *The Universal Gazetteer.* 1797. Dublin. 8 fld map. EX $165.00

WALKER, Judson Elliott. *Campaigns of General Custer in North-West.* 1966. New York. Ills. 135 pp. dj. VG $10.00

WALKER, L.C. *Ecology & Our Forests.* 1972. Barnes. Ills. 175 pp. dj. EX $6.00

WALKER, Margaret. *For My People.* 1942. Yale. 2nd ed. inscr. dj. VG $10.00

WALKER, Margaret. *How I Wrote Jubilee.* 1972. 1st ed. wrappers. VG $30.00

WALKER, Margaret. *October Journey.* 1973. 1st ed. wrappers. VG $20.00

WALKER, Norman. *Loona, a Strange Tail.* 1931. London. Longman. dj. EX $25.00

WALKER, R. *Still Water Angling.* 1955. Ills. G $10.00

WALKER, R. *The Best of Beardsley.* 1983. London. Chancellor Press. $20.00

WALKER, Robert J. *Letter of Mr. Walker of Mississippi.* 1844. Washington. 32 pp. wrappers. VG $75.00

WALKER, Ryan. *Adventures of Henry Dubb.* 1914. New York. 1st ed. wrappers. VG $100.00

WALKER, Stanley. *Home to Texas.* 1956. 1st ed. dj. VG $15.00

WALKER, Stanley. *Texas.* 1962. New York. 1st ed. dj. $20.00

WALKER, T. *Red Salmon, Brown Bear, Story of an Alaskan Lake.* 1971. World Pub. 1st printing. 226 pp. dj. EX $10.00

WALKER, T. *The High Path.* 1982. London. Routledge. 1st ed. dj. EX $20.00

WALKER, Winifred. *All the Plants of the Bible.* 1945. Harper. Ills. dj. EX $20.00

WALKER & WALKER. *History of Reformed Church of Bronxville.* 1951. dj. VG $15.00

WALKER-BABER. *Longest Rope. Johnson County Wyoming Cattle War.* 1953. Caxton. 3rd ed. VG $22.50

WALL, Bernhardt. *Following Abraham Lincoln 1809-1865.* 1943. New York. sgn. VG $15.00

WALL, Joseph Frazier. *Henry Watterson, Reconstructed Rebel.* 1956. New York. VG $4.50

WALL, R. *Airliners. History of Meteoric Rise of Airliner.* 1980. Ills. dj. EX $20.00

WALL. *Chronicles of New Brunswick, New Jersey 1667-1931.* 1931. New Brunswick. VG $35.00

WALLACE, Alfred R. *Darwinism.* 1889. London. Macmillan. 1st ed. 494 pp. $165.00

WALLACE, Alfred R. *Exposition of Theory of Natural Selection.* 1889. London. 1st ed. VG $75.00

WALLACE, Alfred R. *Island Life.* 1880. London. Macmillan. 1st ed. $185.00

WALLACE, Dillon. *Beyond the Mexican Sierras.* 1910. Chicago. McClurg. Ills. 1st ed. map. VG $16.00

WALLACE, Dillon. *Saddle & Camp in the Rockies.* 1911. Outing Pub. 1st ed. $12.50

WALLACE, Dillon. *The Lure of the Labrador Wild.* 1905. London. Hodder Stoughton. 339 pp. G $10.00

WALLACE, E. *Sanders of the River.* 1930. 1st ed. VG $10.00

WALLACE, E. *The Crimson Circle.* 1929. 1st ed. VG $10.00

WALLACE, Edgar. *The Other Man.* 1911. 1st ed. VG $85.00

WALLACE, Ernest & Hoebel, E. *The Comanches. Lords of the South Plains.* 1954. Norman. Ills. 2nd printing. 381 pp. $18.50

WALLACE, Ernest. *Ronald S. Mackenzie on the Texas Frontier.* 1964. Lubbock. Ills. 1st ed. 214 pp. dj. $25.00

WALLACE, Frederick. *In the Wake of the Windships.* 1927. Sully. 1st ed. $15.00

WALLACE, George S. *Cabell County Annals & Families.* 1935. Richmond. Ills. 589 pp. VG $45.00

WALLACE, George S. *Huntington Through Seventy-Five Years.* 1947. Huntington. Ills. 288 pp. index. $25.00

WALLACE, H.B. *Art Scenery & Other Papers.* 1857. Philadelphia. $15.00

WALLACE, Henry A. *New Frontiers.* 1934. Reynal & Hitchcock. wrappers. $40.00

WALLACE, I. *Birds of Prey of Britain & Europe.* 1983. Oxford U. Pr. Ills. 1st ed. 96 pp. dj. EX $17.50

WALLACE, Ian. *Pan Sagittarius.* 1973. New York. 1st ed. dj. EX $8.00

WALLACE, Irving. *The Fabulous Showman: Life & Times of P.T. Barnum.* 1959. New York. Knopf. 280 pp. dj. G $4.00

WALLACE, Irving. *The Pigeon Project.* 1979. Simon & Schuster. 1st ed. dj. $12.50

WALLACE, Irving. *The World.* 1972. 576 pp. dj. $5.00

WALLACE, Irving. *The Writing of One Novel.* 1968. New York. 1st ed. $7.50

WALLACE, James F. *A Guide Book to the U.S. Navy.* 1943. Whitman. Ills. Barry Bart. 62 pp. $3.50

WALLACE, James F. *The U.S. Navy. Guide to Its Ships & Equipment.* 1942. Ills. Barry Bart. G $7.50

WALLACE, Joseph. *Past & Present of Springfield & Sangamon County.* 1904. Clarke Pub. 2 vol set. rebound. VG $80.00

WALLACE, Lew. *Ben-Hur. A Tale of the Christ.* 1880. New York. Harper. 552 pp. $27.50

WALLACE, Lew. *Life of General Benjamin Harrison.* 1888. Philadelphia. Ills. 1st ed. 578 pp. rebound. $27.50

WALLACE, Lew. *The Prince of India.* 1893. New York. Harper. 2 vol set. $10.00

WALLACE, Lily H. *New American Cookbook.* 1943. New York. 931 pp. VG $4.00

WALLACE, Lily H. *New American Cookbook.* 1949. $8.00

WALLACE, Lily H. *The Rumford Complete Cookbook.* 1923. Providence. 241 pp. VG $4.00

WALLACE, Lily H. *The Rumford Complete Cookbook.* 1918. Providence. VG $10.00

WALLACE, R.B., Jr. *Dress Her in White & Gold. Biography of GA Tech.* 1963. dj. VG $10.00

WALLACE, Robert. *Light Year '84.* 1983. dj. VG $12.50

WALLACE, Robert. *Light Year '85.* 1984. Bits. 1st ed. dj. VG $12.50

WALLACE, Robert. *The Author.* 1983. Bits. Ltd. ed. 1/60. sgn. wrappers. $8.00

WALLACE, Robert. *The Author.* 1983. Bits. Ltd. ed. 1/34. sgn. wrappers. $20.00

WALLACE, Wm. *The History of Canaan, NH.* 1910. Concord, NH. Rumford. Ills. 748 pp. $45.00

WALLACE. *Fur Trail Adventure.* 1st ed. VG $25.00

WALLACE. *Land of Pueblos.* 1890. Ills. ex-lib. $15.00

WALLACE. *The Man.* 1964. 1st ed. dj. VG $10.00

WALLACH, Ira. *Hopalong Freud.* 1951. 1st ed. dj. VG $25.00

WALLANT, Edward Lewis. *The Tenants of Moonbloom.* 1963. New York. Harcourt. 1st ed. dj. EX $40.00

WALLECHINSKY & IRVING. *The People's Almanac Presents the Book of Lists.* 1977. New York. Morrow. photos. 519 pp. $4.00

WALLER, Edmund. *The Works of Waller in Verse & Prose.* 1758. London. Tonson. 272 pp. G $75.00

WALLERSTEIN, James. *The Demon's Mirror.* 1951. New York. Harbinger. 1st ed. dj. VG $17.50

WALLIS, C.L. *Stories on Stone; American Epitaphs.* 1954. New York. dj. EX $30.00

WALLIS, Ruth. *How Children Grow.* 1931. U. of IA. 1st ed. inscr. $12.50

WALLMO, O.C. *Mule & Black-Tailed Deer in North America.* 1981. NB. U. Press. Ills. 605 pp. dj. EX $27.50

WALLOP, Douglass. *Baseball, an Informal History.* 1969. New York. W.W. Norton Co. Ills. 263 pp. $4.00

WALLWORK, J. *Desert Soil Fauna.* 1982. Praeger. Ills. 296 pp. EX $17.50

WALN. *House of Exile.* 1933. 1st ed. $6.50

WALPOLE, Fred. *4 Years in Pacific in Majesty's Ship, Collinwood.* 1849. London. Ills. 1st ed. 2 vol set. $265.00

WALPOLE, H. *The Duchess of Portland's Museum.* 1936. Grolier Club. Ltd. ed. 1/450. EX $110.00

WALPOLE, Horace. *On Modern Gardening.* 1931. New York. Ltd. ed. 1/325. $60.00

WALPOLE, Hugh. *Farmer John.* 1926. New York. VG $5.00

WALPOLE, Hugh. *Hans Frost.* 1929. New York. 1st ed. 356 pp. $4.50

WALPOLE, Hugh. *The Cathedral.* 1922. New York. 459 pp. EX $3.50

WALPOLE, Hugh. *The Fortress.* 1932. London. Macmillan. Ltd. ed. sgn. EX $65.00

WALPOLE, Hugh. *The Inquisitor.* 1935. New York. Literary Guild. 485 pp. $3.50

WALPOLE, Hugh. *The Inquisitor.* 1935. London. Macmillan. Ltd ed. sgn. dj. VG $50.00

WALPOLE, Hugh. *Vanessa.* 1933. New York. Doubleday. 620 pp. $3.50

WALPOLE, Hugh. *Vanessa.* 1933. London. Macmillan. Ltd. 1st ed. dj. VG $45.00

WALSH, J. *Strange Harp, Strange Symphony.* 1967. New York. 1st ed. dj. EX $12.50

WALSH, J. *The Making of Buffalo Bill.* 1928. Bobbs Merrill. Ills. 1st ed. VG $18.50

WALSH, J.C. *Walsh Family History.* New York. Kelmscott Press. $10.00

WALSH, R. *Writings of Christopher Gadsden.* 1966. U. of SC. 1st ed. VG $15.00

WALSH, William B. *A Ship Called Hope.* 1964. New York. Dutton. ex-lib. 224 pp. $8.00

WALSHE, Walter H. *Practice Treatise on Diseases of Lungs & Heart.* 1851. Philadelphia. 1st ed. 512 pp. VG $125.00

WALSTEAD, M. *The Life of Admiral Dewey.* 1899. 468 pp. $16.50

WALSTEAD. *Illustrious Life of William McKinley.* 1901. 464 pp. $6.50

WALT, Lewis G. *Strange War, Strange Strategy: Report on Vietnam.* 2nd printing. sgn. dj. EX $20.00

WALTARI, Mika. *The Etruscan.* 1956. EX $3.00

WALTARI, Mika. *The Roman.* 1966. dj. EX $3.50

WALTER, E. *Manual for the Essence Industry.* 1916. New York. Wiley. Ltd. 1st ed. 427 pp. VG $40.00

WALTERS, F.P. *A History of the League of Nations.* 1952. Oxford. 1st ed. 2 vol set. dj. $30.00

WALTERS, Lorenzo. *Tombstone's Yesterday.* 1928. Acme. 1st ed. rare. $75.00

WALTON, Bryce. *Sons of the Ocean Depth.* 1952. Philadelphia. 1st ed. dj. EX $15.00

WALTON, Clyde C. *John Francis Snyder: Selected Writings.* 1962. Springfield. 329 pp. $12.50

WALTON, Evangeline. *Witch House.* 1945. Sauk City. 1st ed. 200 pp. dj. EX $25.00

WALTON, Evangeline. *Witch House.* 1945. Arkham House. 1st ed. inscr. sgn. dj. VG $50.00

WALTON, F.L. *Tomahawks to Textiles: Fabulous Story of Worth St.* 1953. New York. Ills. 1st ed. maps. dj. VG $20.00

WALTON, G. *Sentinel of the Plains: Leavenworth & Am. West.* 1973. 1st ed. dj. VG $15.00

WALTON, Izaak & Cotton, Chas. *Complete Angler.* 1887. London. Chatto & Windus. Ills. EX $60.00

WALTON, Izaak & Cotton, Chas. *Complete Angler.* 1891. London/NY. 2 vols in 1. $85.00

WALTON, Izaak & Cotton, Chas. *Complete Angler.* 1835. London. VG $50.00

WALTON, Izaak. *Complete Angler or Contemplative Man's Recreation.* New York. Ills. Rackham. 223 pp. $12.50

WALTON, Izaak. *Complete Angler.* 1939. Penguin ed. Ills. Hermes. wrappers. VG $20.00

WALTON, Izaak. *Complete Angler.* 1929. London. Nonesuch Press. Ills. Ltd. ed. $250.00

WALTON, Izaak. *Waltoniana.* 1878. London. Pickering. 1st ed. G $45.00

WALTON, Izaak. *Complete Angler.* 1948. Heritage Press. Ills. Gorsline. boxed. $7.50

WALTON, O.F. *Christie's Old Organ.* Altemus. no date. (ca.1900) $5.00

WALTON, Perry. *The Story of Textiles.* 1937. New York. Ills. VG $16.00

WALTON, Perry. *The Story of Textiles.* 1936. New York. Ills. dj. VG $17.50

WALTON, W. *The Evidence of Washington.* 1966. Harper & Row. Ills. photos. folio. dj. VG $30.00

WALTON. *The Virgin & the Swine.* 1936. 1st ed. dj. VG $70.00

WAMBAUGH, Joseph. *The Black Marble.* 1st ed. dj. EX $10.00

WAMBAUGH, Joseph. *The Choirboys.* 1973. New York. Delacorte Press. 306 pp. $10.00

WAMBAUGH, Joseph. *The Secrets of Harry Bright.* 1985. New York. Morrow. proof copy. wrappers. $30.00

WANDELL, Sam & Minnigerode, M. *Aaron Burr.* 1925. New York. 1st ed. 2 vol set. EX $20.00

WANDREI, Donald. *Strange Harvest.* 1965. Sauk City. Arkham House. Ltd. ed. dj. EX $65.00

WANDREI, Donald. *The Web of Easter Island.* 1948. Sauk City. Arkham House. dj. $75.00

WANELL, S. *The Naga King's Daughter.* 1964. New York. 1st ed. 247 pp. dj. VG $15.00

WANLESS, Alexander. *Sun on the Water.* 1950. London. Ills. 1st ed. dj. VG $17.50

WANLEY, Humfrey. *Diary of Humfrey Wanley.* 1966. London. 1st ed. 2 vol set. $35.00

WANSELL, Geoffrey. *Haunted Idol. Story of Real Cary Grant.* 1984. New York. Ills. 1st ed. 336 pp. dj. VG $9.50

WAR DEPT. *Reports of the Sec. of War: 1861-1869.* 1869. Washington. 1,000 pp. $45.00

WARBURG, James P. *Still Hell Bent.* 1936. New York. Doubleday Doran. 88 pp. dj. $3.00

WARBURTON, George. *The Conquest of Canada.* 1850. New York. 1st Am. ed. 2 vol set. G $50.00

WARD, Aileen. *John Keats. The Making of a Poet.* 1963. New York. Viking. 1st ed. 450 pp. $6.50

WARD, Andrew. *Souvenir History of General U.S. Grant & His Tomb.* 1907. New York. 22 pp. wrappers. VG $17.50

WARD, C. *The American Carnation.* 1903. $15.00

WARD, C. *The War of the Revolution.* 1952. New York. 989 pp. 2 vol set. $12.00

WARD, C. *Twisted Tales.* 1924. New York. Holt. 1st ed. VG $15.00

WARD, Edward. *Marriage Among the Yoruba.* 1937. Catholic U. 1st ed. stiff wrappers. $7.50

WARD, J.S.M. *Secret Sign Languages.* 1969. New York. Ills. 245 pp. index. dj. VG $45.00

WARD, James W. *The Song of Higher-Water.* 1868. NY/Cincinnati. private print. 30 pp. $12.50

WARD, Leslie. *Forty Years a Spy.* 1915. New York. Ills. 1st Am. ed. VG $30.00

WARD, Lynd & Hicks, Granville. *One of Us; Story of John Reed.* 1935. New York. 1st ed. dj. VG $75.00

WARD, Lynd. *Gaudenzia.* 1960. Chicago. Ills. 1st ed. dj. VG $17.50

WARD, Lynd. *God's Man. J. Cape.* 1929. New York. Smith. Ills. 2nd printing. G $50.00

WARD, Lynd. *God's Man: Novel in Woodcuts.* 1929. Cape. 2nd ed. VG $30.00

WARD, Lynd. *Mad Man's Drum.* 1930. Cape Smith. 1st ed. VG $30.00

WARD, Lynd. *Prelude to a Million Years.* 1933. New York. Ltd. ed. 1/920. sgn. $125.00

WARD, Mrs. Humphrey. *The History of David Grieve.* 1892. New York. Macmillan. 576 pp. $3.50

WARD, R. Gerard. *American Activities in Central Pacific 1790-1870.* 1966. Gregg Press. 1st ed. 8 vol set. $85.00

WARD, Robert Plumer. *De Vere.* 1827. London. 1st ed. 4 vol set. $80.00

WARD, Roland. *Records of Big Game.* 1903. London. 4th ed. $80.00

WARD, W.E.F. *The Royal Navy & the Slavers.* 1969. $10.00

WARD, W.H. *The Architecture of the Renaissance in France.* 1926. London. 2nd ed. 2 vol set. VG $45.00

WARD. *A Book of Hours.* 1937. Putnam. 1st ed. dj. VG $10.00

WARDE, B.L. *Bombed But Unbeaten.* 1941. New York. Ltd. ed. 1/850. 100 pp. VG $25.00

WARDE, B.L. *The Nature of the Book.* 1930. Birmingham. 1st ed. 31 pp. slipcase. VG $45.00

WARDE, Beatrice. *Crystal Goblet. 16 Essays on Typography.* 1956. $20.00

WARDE & HAAS. *Bruce Rogers, Designer of Books.* 1968. EX $32.00

WARDNER, J. *Jim Wardner of Wardner, Idaho.* 1900. New York. 154 pp. $15.00

WARE, Eugene. *The Indian War of 1864.* 1960. St. Martins. 1st ed. 483 pp. dj. $10.00

WARE, Wallace F. *The Unforgettables.* 1965. Mimram Books. 160 pp. dj. G $4.00

WARE. *Occupational Shaving Mugs.* 1949. 1st ed. VG $20.00

WARGA, Wayne. *Hardcover.* 1985. New York. Arbor House. 1st ed. dj. EX $25.00

WARHOL, Andy. *Index Book.* 1967. New York. wrappers. EX $100.00

WARHOL, Andy. *The Philosophy of Andy Warhol.* 1975. New York. inscr. dj. $45.00

WARING, George E., Jr. *Street Cleaning & Disposal of a City's Wastes.* 1897. New York. 320 pp. $5.50

WARING, Guy. *My Pioneer Past.* 1936. Boston. Ills. 256 pp. photos. VG $30.00

WARLIMONT, W. *Inside Hitler's Headquarters.* 1964. New York. 1st ed. $45.00

WARLOCK, Peter. *Songs of the Gardens.* Nonsuch Press. Ltd. ed. 1/875. dj. VG $30.00

WARLOCK, Peter. *The Complete Book of Magic.* London. dj. VG $7.50

WARMAN, Cy. *Frontier Stories.* 1898. New York. 1st ed. G $65.00

WARNER, Anne. *Seeing France with Uncle John.* 1906. New York. Century. Ills. May Preston. $37.50

WARNER, C.F. *Picturesque Franklin, Massachusetts.* 1891. Northampton. 200 photos. 123 pp. $25.00

WARNER, Charles D. *On Horseback in Virginia, North Carolina, & Tenn.* 1888. Boston. 1st ed. VG $15.00

WARNER, Charles D. *Saunterings.* 1972. Boston. 1st ed. EX $25.00

WARNER, Langdon. *The Craft of the Japanese Sculptor.* 1936. New York. 1st ed. 55 pp. 85 pls. G $12.00

WARNER, Langdon. *The Enduring Art of Japan.* 1952. Harvard. Ills. 113 pp. scarce. VG $30.00

WARNER, Marina *The Dragon Empress.* 1972. Macmillan. Ills. VG $20.00

WARNER, O. *Great Battle Fleets.* 1973. London. Ills. EX $20.00

WARNER, O. *Great Sea Battles.* 1968. Ills. dj. VG $20.00

WARNER, O. *Nelson & Age of Fighting Sail.* 1963. London. Ills. maps. VG $10.00

WARNER, Oliver. *With Wolfe to Quebec, Path to Glory.* 1972. Toronto. Ills. maps. 224 pp. $12.00

WARNER, Peggy & Dennis. *The Great Road: Japan's Highway to Twentieth Cent.* 1979. Australia. Ills. 147 pp. dj. scarce. EX $55.00

WARNER, Sylvia Townsend. *Kingdoms of Elfin.* 1977. Viking. 1st ed. dj. EX $15.00

WARNER, Sylvia Townsend. *Letters.* 1982. London. 1st ed. dj. VG $18.00

WARNER, Sylvia Townsend. *Lolly Willows.* 1926. New York. 6th printing. dj. VG $25.00

WARNER, Sylvia Townsend. *Scenes of Childhood.* 1982. New York. Viking. proof copy. VG $45.00

WARNER, Sylvia Townsend. *The Cat's Cradle Book.* 1960. London. Chatto & Windus. proof copy. $30.00

WARNER, Sylvia Townsend. *The Salutation.* 1932. London. Chatto & Windus. 1st ed. VG $85.00

WARNER, Sylvia Townsend. *The Salutation.* 1932. New York. 1st ed. dj. EX $25.00

WARNER, Sylvia Townsend. *Twelve Poems.* 1980. London. Chatto & Windus. 1st ed. dj. $30.00

WARNER, W. Lloyd. *Black Civilization/A Study of Australian Tribe.* 1958. New York. Harper. 618 pp. dj. EX $6.50

WARNER, William W. *Beautiful Swimmers.* 1976. $5.00

WARNER. *Cree Life: Art of Allen Sapp.* 1977. Vancouver. Douglas. Ltd. ed. $12.00

WARNER. *First Annual Edition Knives: Today's Knives.* 1981. 1st ed. 192 pp. wrappers. EX $25.00

WARNER. *The Boxcar Children.* 1977. Whitman. Ills. Kate Deal. EX $10.00

WARREN, B.H. *Birds of Pennsylvania.* 1888. Harrisburg. Ills. 59 pls. 49 lithos. $55.00

WARREN, F.K. *California Illustrated.* 1892. Boston. Ills. 142 pp. VG $17.50

WARREN, G.F. *Elements of Agriculture.* 1915. New York. Macmillan. ex-lib. 434 pp. VG $4.00

WARREN, George A. *The Banner Boy Scouts Snowbound.* 1916. Saalfield Pub. $3.50

WARREN, George Washington. *History of Bunker Hill Monument Association.* 1877. Boston. Ills. 1st ed. 426 pp. G $17.50

WARREN, Robert Penn. *A Place to Come To.* 1977. Random House. 1st ed. dj. EX $30.00

WARREN, Robert Penn. *All the King's Men.* 1953. Modern Library.1st ed. dj. VG $15.00

WARREN, Robert Penn. *All the King's Men.* 1946. New York. 1st ed. dj. $25.00

WARREN, Robert Penn. *All the King's Men.* 1948. London. 1st Eng. ed. dj. VG $75.00

WARREN, Robert Penn. *Audubon.* 1969. Random House. 1st ed. dj. VG $35.00

WARREN, Robert Penn. *Band of Angels.* 1955. Random House. 1st ed. dj. VG $45.00

WARREN, Robert Penn. *Chief Joseph of the Nez Perce.* 1983. New York. Random House. 1st ed. EX $25.00

WARREN, Robert Penn. *Democracy & Poetry.* 1975. Harvard U. Pr. 1st ed. dj. VG $35.00

WARREN, Robert Penn. *Eleven Poems on the Same Theme.* 1942. New Directions.1st ed. sgn. wrappers. EX $45.00

WARREN, Robert Penn. *Flood.* 1964. New York. Random House. 1st ed. dj. EX $20.00

WARREN, Robert Penn. *John Brown.* 1929. New York. Ills. 1st ed. 474 pp. $27.50

WARREN, Robert Penn. *John Greenleaf Whittier's Poetry.* 1971. U. MN Press. 1st ed. sgn. dj. VG $40.00

WARREN, Robert Penn. *Meet Me in the Green Glen.* 1971. New York. Random House. 1st ed. dj. EX $35.00

WARREN, Robert Penn. *New & Selected Poems: 1923-1985.* 1985. Random House. Ltd. 1st ed. sgn. slipcase. EX $75.00

WARREN, Robert Penn. *Night Rider.* 1939. Boston. Houghton Mifflin. 1st ed. sgn. $100.00

WARREN, Robert Penn. *Or Else. Poems 1968-74.* 1974. New York. Random House. sgn. dj. VG $27.50

WARREN, Robert Penn. *Snowfall.* 1984. Ltd. ed. $50.00

WARREN, Robert Penn. *The Cave.* 1959. Random House. 1st ed. sgn. inscr. dj. EX $55.00

WARREN, Robert Penn. *Wilderness. A Tale of the Civil War.* 1961. New York. 1st ed. dj. EX $45.00

WARREN, Robert. *World Enough & Time.* 1950. Random House. 1st ed. VG $20.00

WARREN, William W. *History of the Ojibway Nation.* 1957. Minneapolis. 527 pp. dj. $17.50

WARREN COMMISSION. *Report of Assassination of President Kennedy.* 1964. New York. McGraw Hill. 726 pp. $7.00

WARREN. *Promises Poems 1954-56.* 1956. 1st ed. dj. VG $30.00

WARREN. *The Banner Boy Scouts on a Tour.* 1912. World Syndicate. Ills. EX. $6.50

WASHBURN, F.L. *Injurious Insects & Useful Birds.* 1918. Philadelphia. Lippincott. ex-lib. 453 pp. VG $4.50

WASHBURN, R.M. *Calvin Coolidge, His First Biography.* 1923. Boston. 150 pp. $10.00

WASHBURN, Sherwood. *Social Life of Early Man.* 1961. 1st ed. stiff wrappers. $12.50

WASHBURNE, E.B. *Sketch of Edward Coles, 2nd Governor of Illinois.* 1882. Chicago. 1st ed. sgn. 253 pp. $30.00

WASHEM, Yad. *Studies on European Jewish Catastrophe/Resistance.*1957. Jerusalem. Ills. Vol 1. G $10.00

WASHINGTON, Booker T. *The Future of the American Negro.* 1899. Boston. 1st ed. ex-lib. $100.00

WASHINGTON, Booker T. *The Story of My Life & Work.* 1900. Nichols. 1st ed. VG $25.00

WASHINGTON, Booker T. *Working with the Hands.* 1904. New York. Ills. 1st ed. $17.50

WASSON, R. Gordon. *Maria Sabina & Her Mazatec Mushroom Velada.* 1975. New York. 4 cassettes. boxed. EX $85.00

WASSON, R.G. & HEIM, R. *Les Champignons Hallucinogenes du Mexique.* 1958. Paris. National Nat. Hist. Museum. EX $190.00

WASTELL, W.F. *The Barnet Book of Photography.* 1922. London. VG $15.00

WATANNA, O. *Heart of Hyacinth.* 1903. 1st ed. EX $15.00

WATERFIELD. *Faberge Imperial Eggs.* 1978. New York. 143 pp. $25.00

WATERHOUSE, Benjamin. *Botanist: Botanical Part of a Course of Lectures.* 1811. Boston. J.T. Buckingham. 1st ed. $200.00

WATERHOUSE, David. *Images of Eighteenth Century Japan.* 1975. Ontario. Sir Edmund Walker Collection. $55.00

WATERHOUSE, Sylvester. *Adaptation of St. Louis to Iron Manufacturers.* 1869. St. Louis. 1st ed. 31 pp. $45.00

WATERLOO, Stanley. *The Story of AB.* 1897. Chicago. Way & Williams. 1st ed. VG $75.00

WATERMAN, Joseph. *With Sword & Lancet/Life of General Hugh Mercer.* 1941. Richmond. 177 pp. dj. $25.00

WATERMAN. *Hunting Upland Birds.* 1972. Winchester Press. Ills. dj. $10.00

WATERS, B. *Modern Training, Handling, & Kennel Management.* 1889. Chicago. Ills. 1st ed. 373 pp. VG $17.50

WATERS, Captain John M. *Bloody Winter.* 1967. Princeton. Ills. 1st ed. 279 pp. dj. VG $15.00

WATERS, Frank. *Masked Gods. Navaho & Pueblo Ceremonialism.* 1959. U. of NM. 1st ed. dj. $22.50

WATERS, Frank. *Pike's Peak.* 1971. Sage Books. dj. $15.00

WATKINS, L.W. *Early New England Potters & Their Wares.* 1950. Harvard U. Pr. Ills. 291 pp. $50.00

WATKINS, T.H. *Gold & Silver in the West.* 1971. Palo Alto. Ills. $25.00

WATKINS, Vernon. *Fidelities.* 1963. London. Faber. 1st ed. dj. EX $30.00

WATKINS, Vernon. *The Breaking of the Wave.* 1979. Ipswich. Golgonooza Press. 1st ed. dj. $15.00

WATKINS, Waterman. *A History of Cass County Michigan.* 1882. pls. G $55.00

WATKINS-PITCHFORD, Denys. *The Little Grey Men.* 1951. New York. dj. EX $7.00

WATSON, A. & Whalley, P.E.S. *Dictionary of Butterflies & Moths.* 1983. Exeter. Ills. 296 pp. dj. EX $35.00

WATSON, Aldren A. *Hand Bookbinding.* 1963. dj. VG $5.00

WATSON, Alfred E.T. *Fur, Feather & Fin Series. The Trout.* 1898. Longman Green. VG $35.00

WATSON, Colin. *Blue Murder.* 1979. London. Methuen. 1st ed. dj. $30.00

WATSON, Colin. *Hopjoy Was Here.* 1962. London. Eyre & Spottiswoode. 1st ed. $30.00

WATSON, David K. *History of American Coinage.* 1899. VG $15.00

WATSON, E.L.G. *Wonders of Natural History.* 1947. London. Pleides. Ills. Gregg. 192 pp. $4.00

WATSON, Elkanah. *Tour in Holland in 1784.* 1790. Isaiah Thomas. 1st Am. ed. VG $140.00

WATSON, F.E. *Our Common Butterflies.* 1926. Ills. 21 pp. VG $14.00

WATSON, H.B. Marriott. *The Privateers.* 1907. Doubleday Page. 1st ed. $3.00

WATSON, Ian. *The Book of the Stars.* 1984. London. 1st ed. dj. VG $12.50

WATSON, J. *The Sexual Adventures of Sherlock Holmes.* 1971. New York. Olympia Press. 1st ed. pb. EX $20.00

WATSON, James D. *The Double Helix.* 1968. New York. photos. 226 pp. dj. EX $4.00

WATSON, Margery. *Ruffles & Danny.* 1913. Cleveland. World Syndicate Co. 184 pp. $2.50

WATSON, P. *Sea Shepherd, My Fight for Whales & Seals.* 1982. Norton. Ills. 1st ed. dj. EX $5.00

WATSON, R. Spence. *A Visit to Wazan: Sacred City of Morocco.* 1880. London. 1st ed. fld map. EX $45.00

WATSON, Virginia. *The Princess Pocahontas.* 1916. New York. Ills. Edwards. 306 pp. $10.00

WATSON, Virginia. *With Cortez the Conqueror.* 1917. Philadelphia. Ills. Schoonover. 1st ed. $40.00

WATSON, W. *Adventures of a Dispatch Rider.* 1916. New York. VG $10.00

WATSON, William. *The Poems.* 1905. London. 2 vol set. VG $25.00

WATSON. *Forty Illustrators & How They Work.* 1946. Watson-Guptill. 1st ed. VG $37.50

WATT, Tom. *How to Play Hockey.* 1971. Canada. Ills. 176 pp. dj. EX $5.00

WATTENMAKER. *Punis de Chavannes & Modern Tradition.* 1976. Toronto. revised ed. $10.00

WATTS, Nellie. *Around the World Cookbook.* 1936. Culinary Arts Press. Ills. VG $5.00

WATTS, Nellie. *The Cookie Book.* 1937. Culinary Arts Press. $3.00

WATTS, Ralph L. *The Vegetable Growing Business.* 1940. New York. Ills. G $10.00

WATTS, Talbot. *Japan & the Japanese.* 1852. New York. $30.00

WATTS. *Psalms of David.* 1719. fine leather binding. $650.00

WATTS-DUNTON, Theodore. *Old Familiar Faces.* 1916. London. 1st ed. VG $25.00

WAUGH, Alec. *Hot Countries.* 1930. Literary Guild. Ills. Lynd Ward. VG $12.00

WAUGH, Evelyn. *A Little Learning.* 1964. London. Chapman & Hall. 1st ed. dj. VG $45.00

WAUGH, Evelyn. *Black Mischief.* 1932. Chapman & Hall. 1st ed. $15.00

WAUGH, Evelyn. *Brideshead Revisited.* 1945. Boston. 351 pp. dj. VG $3.50

WAUGH, Evelyn. *Helena.* 1950. London. Chapman & Hall. 1st ed. dj. $45.00

WAUGH, Evelyn. *Ordeal of Gilbert Pinfold.* 1957. Boston. 1st Am. ed. dj. $12.00

WAUGH, Evelyn. *Scott-King's Modern Europe.* 1947. London. Chapman & Hall. 1st ed. dj. $45.00

WAUGH, Evelyn. *The Loved Ones.* 1948. Little, Brown. 1st Am. ed. dj. VG $20.00

WAUGH, Harry. *Diary of a Winetaster.* 1972. New York. New York Times. $4.50

WAUGH, Hillary. *30' Manhattan East.* 1968. New York. Doubleday. 1st ed. 273 pp. dj. $4.50

WAUGH, W.T. *James Wolfe, Man & Soldier.* 1928. Montreal. Ills. maps. 333 pp. $25.00

WAUGH & GREENBERG. *The Fantastic Stories of Cornell Woolrich.* 1981. Carbondale. Southern IL U. Pr. 1st ed. dj. $25.00

WAXMAN. *The History of Jewish Literature.* 1960. 6 vol set. G $25.00

WAY, Frederick. *She Takes the Horns.* 1953. Cincinnati. Young & Klein. sgn. VG $25.00

WAY, Frederick. *The Log of the Betsy Ann.* 1933. McBride. 1st ed. dj. $15.00

WAY, Frederick. *Way's Packet Directory, 1848-1983.* 1983. Ohio U. 1st ed. dj. $20.00

WAY, Thomas E. *Frontier Arizona.* 1960. Carlton Press. 1st ed. dj. VG $8.50

WAY. *Time & Its Reckoning.* 1951. $15.00

WAYLAND, J.W. *History of Rockingham Co. Virginia.* 1912. Dayton, VA. 1st ed. VG $60.00

WAYLEN, E. *Ecclesiastical Reminiscences of the U.S.* 1846. New York. 501 pp. VG $12.50

WAYMAN, N. *Life on the River.* 1971. New York. 1st ed. VG $15.00

WAYNE, Dorothy. *Dorothy Dixon & the Double Cousin.* 1933. Chicago. Goldsmith. 253 pp. $3.50

WAYNE, Dorothy. *Dorothy Dixon Wins Her Wings.* 1933. Chicago. Goldsmith. dj. $3.00

WAYNE. *Ramrod from Hell.* Popular. pb. $3.00

WEAGE. *The Little Lame Prince.* 1916. Whitman. 8 color pls. G $9.00

WEATHERLY, F.E. *Told in the Twilight.* Dutton. (ca.1885) Ills. Edwards. G $12.00

WEATHERLY, F.E. & Watt. *Out of Town.* (ca.1884) VG $40.00

WEATHERWAX, Clara. *Marching! Marching!* 1935. New York. Day. 1st ed. EX $15.00

WEAVER, J. *The Wolves of Yellowstone.* 1978. Nat. Park Service. Ills. photos. maps. $7.50

WEAVER, M.P. *The Aztecs, Maya & Their Predecessors.* 1981. New York. 2nd ed. photos. maps. EX $25.00

WEAVER, Sarah Sanborne. *The White Buck. Legend of the Border.* 1957. San Antonio. 229 pp. dj. $9.00

WEAVER, Thomas. *Hist. Sketch of the Police Service of Hartford.* 1901. Hartford. Ills. 168 pp. ads. $35.00

WEAVER, Warren. *The Scientists Speak.* 1947. New York. Boni Gaer. $37.50

WEBB, C.S. *Odyssey of an Animal Collector.* 1954. London. Ills. 1st ed. dj. 368 pp. dj. $7.50

WEBB, Frank. *Switzerland of the Swiss.* 1909. New York. VG $15.00

WEBB, James. *A Quest Anthology.* 1976. New York. Arno Press. VG $25.00

WEBB, Mary. *Gone to Earth.* 1948. London. dj. VG $8.50

WEBB, Sharon. *Earth Song.* 1983. Atheneum. review copy. dj. VG $15.00

WEBB, Thomas Smith. *Freemason's Monitor. Ills. of Masonry: 2 Parts.* Providence. Cushing & Webb. 345 pp. VG $125.00

WEBB, Thomas Smith. *Freemason's Monitor; or, Illustrations of Masonry.* 1808. Boston. 336 pp. G $165.00

WEBB, W. *Coastguard! Official History of H.M. Coastguard.* 1976. London. Ills. dj. G $17.50

WEBB, W.E. *Buffalo Land: Authentic Account of Discoveries.* 1874. Phila./NY. Ills. 503 pp. $35.00

WEBB, Walter P. *Texas Rangers, a Century of Frontier Defense.* 1965. TX. Press. Ills. 2nd ed. 584 pp. index. $20.00

WEBB, Walter P. *The Great Plains.* 1931. New York. 1st ed. 2nd issue. dj. VG $50.00

WEBB, Walter P. *The Texas Rangers.* 1935. Boston. Ills. 1st ed. EX $55.00

WEBB, Walter P. *The Great Plains.* 1931. Boston. Ills. 1st ed. 525 pp. $45.00

WEBBER, C.W. *Romance of Natural History.* 1852. VG $37.50

WEBBER, Harry E. *Twelve Months with the 8th Mass. Infantry.* 1908. Salem. ex-lib. $35.00

WEBBER, Lucille R. *Japanese Woodblock Prints: Reciprocal Influence.* 1979. Ills. 154 pp. dj. scarce. EX $45.00

WEBBER. *Old Hicks the Guide.* 1848. New York. 1st ed. $125.00

WEBSTER, Barbara. *The Green Year.* 1956. New York. Norton. Ills. 1st ed. 270 pp. $12.50

WEBSTER, Charlotte E. *Ceremony of Innocence.* 1949. New York. 1st ed. dj. EX $10.00

WEBSTER, Clarence. *Town Meeting Country.* 1945. Duell. 2nd printing. dj. $6.50

WEBSTER, D.K. *Myth & Maneater, Story of the Shark.* 1963. Norton. Ills. 1st Am. ed. 223 pp. dj. $10.00

WEBSTER, Daniel. *The Works of Daniel Webster.* 1851. Boston. 1st ed. 6 vol set. EX $335.00

WEBSTER, F. *Results in Taxidermy.* 1905. scarce. VG $75.00

WEBSTER, Frank V. *The High School Rivals.* 1911. 206 pp. $3.50

WEBSTER, George Sidney. *The Seamen's Friend: Sketch of the Society.* 1932. 1st ed. $8.50

WEBSTER, H.T. *The Best of H.T. Webster.* 1953. New York. Simon & Schuster. 255 pp. VG $6.50

WEBSTER, J. *Dear Enemy.* 1915. New York. 1st Am. ed. sgn. dj. VG $8.00

WEBSTER, Jean. *Daddy Long Legs.* 1912. New York. 1st ed. VG $20.00

WEBSTER, Margaret. *Shakespeare Without Tears.* 1942. New York. 319 pp. VG $4.50

WEBSTER, Mrs. A.L. *The Improved Housewife or Book of Receipts.* 1852. Boston. $15.00

WEBSTER, Noah. *Elements of Useful Knowledge.* 1807, 1808. New Haven. 3rd ed. 2 vol set. $45.00

WEBSTER, Noah. *Letters of Noah Webster.* 1953. Library Pub. 1st ed. dj. $12.50

WEBSTER, Vere. *Spingle Spider & the Rose Pearl.* 1946. London. Ills. Elsie Thomas. 1st ed. $10.00

WEBSTER, Warren, Jr. *The Life & Times of Warren Webster.* 1942. private print. Ltd. ed. $10.00

WEBSTER. *Ben Hardy's Flying Machines.* 1911. Cupples & Leon. Ills. G $4.50

WEBSTER. *Bob Chester's Grit.* 1911. Saalfield. Ills. dj. EX $6.50

WEBSTER. *The Young Treasure Hunter.* 1937. Saalfield. Ills. dj. EX $6.50

WEBSTER. Noah. *The American Spelling Book.* 1843. Wells River, VT. revised ed. $30.00

WECHSBERG, J. *Blue Trout & Black Truffles.* 1953. New York. 1st ed. dj. VG $20.00

WECHSBERG, J. *Blue Trout & Black Truffles.* 1954. New York. 2nd printing. VG $15.00

WECHSBERG, Joseph. *The Waltz Emperors.* 1973. New York. 1st ed. dj. EX $15.00

WEDEMEYER, Albert C. *Wedemeyer Reports!* New York. Holt. 497 pp. VG $10.00

WEED, Clarence M. *Butterflies Worth Knowing.* 1923. Garden City. Ills. 286 pp. EX $22.50

WEED, Thurlow. *Autobiography of Thurlow Weed.* 1883. Boston. Houghton Mifflin. 2 vol set. $27.50

WEEDEN, Howard. *Bandanna Ballads.* 1899. New York. 1st ed. VG $25.00

WEEDEN & WARD. *Fairground Art.* 1981. New York. Abbeville. dj. EX $35.00

WEEDHAM, James. *Elementary Lessons in Zoology.* 1896. Am. Book Co. 304 pp. VG $3.00

WEEGEE. *Naked City.* 1945. New York. 1st ed. VG $25.00

WEEKLEY, Robert. *The House in Ruins.* 1958. 1st ed. 248 pp. dj. $47.50

WEEKLY, W.M. *Twenty Years on Horseback Itinerating in WV.* 1907. Dayton. 135 pp. VG $18.50

WEEKS, John E. *Diseases of the Eyes.* 1910. New York. 1st ed. 8 vol set. $65.00

WEEKS, Sara. *Tales of a Common Pigeon.* 1960. Houghton Mifflin. 1st ed. $3.50

WEEMS, John Edward. *Men Without Countries. 3 Adventures of Southwest.* 1969. Boston. Ills. 1st ed. 272 pp. dj. $7.50

WEEMS, M.L. *God's Revenge Against Murder.* 1808. Philadelphia. 5th ed. $50.00

WEEMS, Mason L. *The Life of Washington.* 1974. Ltd. Ed. Club. Ills/sgn Quackenbush. Ltd. ed. $35.00

WEESNER, Theodore. *The True Detective.* 1986. New York. Summit. proof copy. EX $15.00

WEGMANN. *Design & Construction of Dams.* 1911. New York. Ills. 529 pp. VG $85.00

WEHDE, Albert. *Since Leaving Home; Story of Great Adventure.* 1923. photos. $4.00

WEHLE. *Wing & Shot.* 1964. 1st ed. dj. EX $15.00

WEIDENREICH, Franz. *Giant Early Man from Java & South China.* 1945. 1st ed. stiff wrappers. $15.00

WEIDLING. *Checkered Sunshine, History of Ft. Lauderdale.* 1966. dj. $17.50

WEIDLINGER, Peter & Hamilton. *Aluminum Modern Architecture.* 1956. Louisville, KY. Ills. 2 vol set. EX $25.00

WEIDMAN. *Sound of Bow Bells.* 1962. New York. 1st printing. dj. VG $7.50

WEIGALL, T.H. *Boom in Florida.* 1931. Lane. 1st ed. dj. VG $10.00

WEIGAND, John. *Montana's Ring-Necked Pheasant History & Ecology.* 1976. MT. Dept. Game & Fish. $10.00

WEIGHT WATCHERS. *Weight Watchers 365-Day Menu Cookbook.* 1981. New York. Weight Watcher Inst. 343 pp. $4.00

WEIGL & HAMMER. *The Imagination as Glory, Poetry of James Dickey.* 1984. U. of IL. dj. VG $15.00

WEIK, Jesse. *The Real Lincoln: a Portrait.* 1922. Boston. Ills. 1st ed. VG $20.00

WEINBAUM, Stanley. *The Black Flame.* 1948. Fantasy Press. 1st trade ed. dj. EX $30.00

WEINBAUM, Stanley. *The Dark Other.* 1950. Los Angeles. 1st ed. dj. EX $25.00

WEINBAUM. *Red Peri.* 1952. 1st Am. ed. dj. EX $30.00

WEINBERG, George. *The Pliant Animal.* 1981. St.Martins. 1st ed. dj. $3.00

WEINBERGER. *History of Dentistry.* 1948. 1st ed. 2 vol set. $95.00

WEINER, Alexander S. *Blood Groups & Blood Transfusions.* 1935. Springfield. 1st ed. 8 vol set. $40.00

WEINER, Ed. *Damon Runyon Story.* 1948. New York. 1st ed. 258 pp. $6.50

WEINER. *Raspail, Scientist & Reformer.* 1968. Ills. VG $9.00

WEINLAND, H.A. *Now the Harvest.* 1957. New York. Exposition Press. 96 pp. G $4.50

WEINSTOCK, Herbert. *Rossini: a Biography.* 1968. New York. Ills. 1st ed. dj. VG $25.00

WEINTRAUB, Stanley. *Private Shaw & Public Shaw.* 1963. New York. 302 pp. dj. $4.00

WEIR, Albert E. *The Piano. Its History, Makers, Players, & Music.* 1940. New York. 1st ed. 467 pp. dj. VG $10.00

WEIR, Hugh C. *The Young Wheat Scout.* 1915. Boston/Chicago. 1st ed. $8.00

WEIR, Wilbert W. *Productive Soils.* 1920. Philadelphia. Lippincott. ex-lib. 398 pp. VG $4.50

WEISBERG, G.P. *Japonisme: Japanese Influence on French Art.* 1975. Cleveland. Ills. wrappers. VG $15.00

WEISS. *Advanced Bass Fishing.* 1976. Dutton. Ills. 356 pp. $3.50

WEIT, Paul & Denslow, W.W. *The Pearl & the Pumpkin.* 1904. New York. Dillingham. Ills. EX $35.00

WEITENKAMPF, Frank. *The Illustrated Book.* 1938. Cambridge. Ills. 314 pp. dj. VG $40.00

WEIZSACKER, C.F. *The History of Nature.* 1949. Chicago. Ills. 191 pp. EX $4.00

WELCH, Ned. *Who's Who in Thoroughbred Racing.* 1946. Washington. Ills. 1st ed. 2 vol set. EX $35.00

WELCH, Nell True. *Sunset Flower Arrangement Book.* 1942. Ills. pb. $1.00

WELCH. *Calligraphy in the Arts of the Muslim World.* 1979. TX. U. Press/ Asia Society. $12.00

WELCH. *King Books of Kings.* 1976. VG $27.00

WELCOME, John. *Best Crime Stories.* 1964. London. Faber. 1st ed. dj. EX $20.00

WELD, H.H. *Benjamin Franklin.* 1849. Ills. $25.00

WELD, Isaac. *Travels Through the States of North America.* 1799. London. Ills. 1st ed. 464 pp. VG $500.00

WELD, Isaac. *Voyage Au Canada.* 1800. Paris. Ills. 1st ed. 3 vol set. $385.00

WELD, Ralph F. *Brooklyn Village, 1816-1834.* 1938. CO. U. Pr.dj. $15.00

WELDON, Fay. *Remember Me.* 1976. Random House. 1st Am. ed. dj. VG $15.00

WELK, Lawrence & McGeehan, B. *Ah-One, Ah-Two! Life with My Music Family.* 1974. Englewood Cliffs. 215 pp. dj. $4.00

WELL, Nathaniel W. *The Picturesque Antiquities of Spain.* 1846. London. Ills. EX $110.00

WELLARD, J. *The French Foreign Legion.* 1974. Ills. maps. dj. VG $12.50

WELLER, Earle. *Keats & Mary Tighe.* 1928. New York. 1st ed. sgn. dj. EX $22.50

WELLES, G. *Diary of Gideon Welles, Secretary of Navy.* 1911. Boston. 1st ed. 3 vol set. $65.00

WELLES, Gideon. *Commodore Charles Wilkes's Court Martial.* 1964. Washington. 1st ed. $100.00

WELLES, Sumner. *The Time for Decision.* 1944. New York. Harper. 431 pp. $6.50

WELLINGTON, Elizabeth L. *The Years of the Sword.* 1969. 1st Am. ed. 548 pp. dj. $37.50

WELLMAN, Francis. *Luck & Opportunity.* 1938. 2nd ed. dj. VG $5.50

WELLMAN, Manly Wade. *After Dark.* 1980. New York. Doubleday. dj. EX $12.50

WELLMAN, Manly Wade. *Sherlock Holmes' War of the World.* 1975. New York. Warner. pb. VG $12.50

WELLMAN, Manly Wade. *The Hanging Stones.* 1982. Garden City. review copy. dj. VG $12.50

WELLMAN, Manly Wade. *The Old Gods Waken.* 1974. New York. Doubleday. uncorrected proofs. $22.50

WELLMAN, Manly Wade. *Voice of the Mountain.* 1984. Garden City. 1st ed. dj. EX $8.00

WELLMAN, Manly Wade. *Worse Things Waiting.* 1973. Chapel Hill. 1st ed. dj. VG $12.50

WELLMAN, P. *Thirty Year's Struggle for the Western Plains.* 1934. New York. 1st ed. photos. $35.00

WELLMAN, P. *Walls of Jericho.* 1947. 1st ed. $6.50

WELLMAN, Paul. *Death on the Prairie.* 1934. New York. sgn. 298 pp. $17.50

WELLMAN, Paul. *Glory, God & Gold: a Narrative History.* 1954. New York. Ills. 402 pp. map. index. dj. $10.00

WELLMAN, Paul. *Magnificent Destiny.* 1962. New York. Doubleday. 444 pp. dj. $3.50

WELLMAN, Paul. *The Commancheros. The Texas Rangers.* 1952. Garden City. 1st ed. 286 pp. dj. VG $20.00

WELLMAN, Paul. *The House Divides: Age of Jackson & Lincoln.* 1966. Mainstream. 1st ed. dj. VG $15.00

WELLMAN, Paul. *The Trampling Herd; Story of Cattle Range.* 1939. New York. Ills. F. Miller. 1st ed. dj. $40.00

WELLMAN. *Dynasty Western Outlaws.* Ills. Bjorklund. 1st ed. dj. $30.00

WELLS, A.W. *South Africa. A Planned Tour.* 1939. Philadelphia. Photos. Maps. VG $25.00

WELLS, Anna Maria. *The Floweret. A Gift of Love.* Boston. (ca.1847) Ills. wrappers. $25.00

WELLS, Basil. *Doorways to Space.* 1951. Los Angeles. 1st ed. dj. VG $20.00

WELLS, Carolyn. *Mother Goose's Menagerie.* 1901. Boston. Ills. Peter Newell. 1st ed. $75.00

WELLS, Carolyn. *The Lover's Baedeker & Guide to Arcady.* 1912. Stokes. Ills. Blashfield. 1st ed. VG $30.00

WELLS, Carolyn. *The Pete & Polly Stories.* 1902. Chicago. Ills. Fanny Cory. 228 pp. $12.50

WELLS, Carolyn. *The Rest of My Life.* 1937. Philadelphia. Ills. 295 pp. dj. VG $10.00

WELLS, Carveth. *Kapoot, Narrative of Search of Noah's Ark.* 1933. New York. photos. EX $15.00

WELLS, Carveth. *Six Years in the Malay Jungle.* 1925. New York. Garden City. Star Series. $7.50

WELLS, E. & Peterson, H.C. *The '49ers.* 1949. Doubleday. 1st ed. dj. $15.00

WELLS, Evelyn. *Champagne Days of San Francisco.* 1939. Garden City. Ills. 1st ed. $14.50

WELLS, Gabriel. *Human Nature & World Disorder.* NY/London. 1st ed. wrappers. $7.50

WELLS, H.G. *Bealby, a Holiday.* 1915. Donahue. $3.50

WELLS, H.G. *Brothers.* 1938. 1st ed. VG $15.00

WELLS, H.G. *Love & Mr. Lewisham.* 1924. New York. Scribners. 323 pp. EX $4.00

WELLS, H.G. *Men Like Gods.* 1923. 1st Eng. ed. dj. VG $150.00

WELLS, H.G. *Mind at the End of Its Tether.* 1946. Didier. 1st ed. dj. $8.50

WELLS, H.G. *Mr. Blettsworthy on Rampole Island.* 1928. 1st ed. G $8.50

WELLS, H.G. *Salvaging of Civilization.* 1922. VG $15.00

WELLS, H.G. *Star Begotten.* 1937. New York. Viking. 1st ed. 217 pp. $10.00

WELLS, H.G. *The Adventures of Tommy.* 1935. New York. Ills. Wells. $25.00

WELLS, H.G. *The Croquet Player.* 1937. Viking. 1st Am. ed. dj. VG $35.00

WELLS, H.G. *The Holy Terror.* 1939. London. 1st ed. $15.00

WELLS, H.G. *The Outline of History.* 1920. New York. Garden City. 1171 pp. $5.50

WELLS, H.G. *The Outline of History.* 1922. 3 vol set. $35.00

WELLS, H.G. *The Time Machine.* 1931. Random House. 1st ed. boxed. $15.00

WELLS, H.G. *The War of the Worlds.* 1898. Harper. Ills. 1st ed. 291 pp. $50.00

WELLS, H.G. *When the Sleeper Wakes.* 1899. NY/London. 1st Am. ed. dj. $85.00

WELLS, H.P. *Fly Rods & Fly Tackle.* 1885. New York. 1st ed. VG $45.00

WELLS, Henry. *A Christmas Garland. Carols & Poems.* 1885. London. 1st ed. $15.00

WELLS, J. Soelberg. *A Treatise on the Diseases of the Eye.* 1873. Henry Lea. 2nd Am. ed. 836 pp. $45.00

WELLS, Rhea. *Ali the Camel.* 1931. Garden City. Doubleday Doran. Ills. 1st ed. $40.00

WELLS, Rolla. *Episodes of My Life.* 1933. St. Louis. Ills. 1st ed. 510 pp. $125.00

WELLS. *Cherry Ames, Flight Nurse.* 1945. Grosset & Dunlap. VG $4.50

WELLS. *Cherry Ames at Hilton Hospital.* 1959. Grosset & Dunlap. Ills. VG $3.50

WELLS. *Star-Begotten.* 1937. 1st Am. ed. dj. EX $40.00

WELLS. *The Invisible Man.* 1967. Heritage Press. dj. slipcase. EX $27.50

WELTY, E. *The Shore Bird.* 1964. 1st ed. VG $50.00

WELTY, Eudora. *A Curtain of Green.* 1941. New York. 1st ed. $35.00

WELTY, Eudora. *Bye-Bye Brevoort.* 1980. New Stage. Ltd. 1st ed. 1/400. sgn. VG $50.00

WELTY, Eudora. *Collected Stories of Eudora Welty.* 1981. Boyars. 1st Eng. ed. sgn. dj. VG $60.00

WELTY, Eudora. *Collected Stories of Eudora Welty.* 1980. New York. Harcourt. 1st trade ed. dj. EX $35.00

WELTY, Eudora. *Delta Wedding.* 1946. Harcourt. 1st ed. dj. VG $10.00

WELTY, Eudora. *Fairy Tale of the Natchez Trace.* 1975. MS Hist. Soc. Ltd. 1st ed. sgn. EX $65.00

WELTY, Eudora. *Losing Battles.* 1982. London. Virago Press. 1st Eng. ed. dj. $45.00

WELTY, Eudora. *Losing Battles.* 1970. New York. 1st ed. dj. VG $15.00

WELTY, Eudora. *Retreat.* 1981. Palaemon. Ltd. ed. 1/150. sgn. wrappers. $100.00

WELTY, Eudora. *The Art of Willa Cather.* 1980. Alderman Lib. Ltd. 1st ed. sgn. wrappers. VG $50.00

WELTY, Eudora. *The Bride of the Innisfallen.* 1955. Harcourt. 1st ed. 2nd issue. dj. EX $35.00

WELTY, Eudora. *The Eye of the Story.* 1978. Random House. 1st trade ed. dj. EX $12.50

WELTY, Eudora. *The Optimist's Daughter.* 1972. Random House. 1st ed. dj. EX $20.00

WELTY, Eudora. *The Ponder Heart.* 1954. New York. Harcourt. 1st ed. dj. EX $75.00

WELTY, Eudora. *The Robber Bridegroom.* 1942. Doubleday. 1st ed. VG $20.00

WELTY, Eudora. *The Wide Net.* 1943. Harcourt. 1st ed. VG $25.00

WELTY, Eudora. *Three Papers on Fiction.* 1962. Smith College. 1st ed. wrappers. EX $75.00

WELTY, J.C. *The Life of Birds.* 1963. Knopf. Ills. 546 pp. EX $7.00

WELZL, J. *Thirty Years in the Golden North.* 1932. Macmillan. Ills. 1st ed. 336 pp. G $10.00

WENDEL, Tim. *Going for the Gold.* 1980. Lawrence Hill. Ills. 131 pp. dj. EX $12.50

WENDELL, Berry. *Salad.* New York. 1st ed. wrappers. EX $5.00

WENDT, H. *The Sex Life of Birds.* 1965. Ills. 383 pp. VG $6.00

WENGENROTH, Stow. *Making a Lithograph.* 1936. London. Studio. dj. VG $45.00

WENIGER, D. *Cacti of Texas & Neighboring States.* 1984. TX. U. Press. Ills. 1st ed. dj. EX $25.00

WENNER, David N. *The Practical Handbook of Car Care & Repair.* 1971. New York. Fawcett Pub. Ills. 128 pp. EX $3.50

WENNER, Linda. *Little History of a Little Town.* 1976. Ills. 2nd ed. sgn. 108 pp. $22.00

WENTWORTH, Patricia. *The Fingerprint.* 1959. London. Hodder & Stoughton. 1st ed. VG $15.00

WEPPNER, M. *North Star & Southern Cross.* 1880. New York. 3rd ed. G $20.00

WERFEL, Franz. *The Forty Days of Musa Daugh.* 1935. New York. Viking. 824 pp. $4.50

WERFEL, Franz. *The Song of Bernadette.* 1943. New York. Viking. 575 pp. $3.50

WERLER, John. *Poisonous Snakes of Texas.* 1978. TX Park & Wildlife Dept. Ills. $6.00

WERNER, A. *Butterflies & Moths.* 1956. Random House. Ills. 175 pp. dj. EX $30.00

WERNER, Elsa J. *Golden Geography: Child's Introduction to World.* 1953. New York. Ills. 1st ed. fld map. G $15.00

WERSBA, Barbara. *Twenty-Six Starlings Will Fly Through Your Mind.* 1980. New York. Ills. Palladini. 1st ed. $15.00

WERSTEIN, Irving. *The Lost Battalion.* 1966. New York. 191 pp. dj. VG $4.00

WERSTEIN, Irving. *The Many Faces of World War I.* 1963. New York. ex-lib. 191 pp. EX $4.00

WERTENBAKER, Charles C. *Invasion!* 1944. New York. Ills. 1st ed. 168 pp. dj. $15.00

WERTENBAKER, T.J. *Father Knickerbocker Rebels-NYC During Revolution.* 1948. New York. Scribner. 308 pp. pls. $12.50

WERTHAM, Frederic. *Dark Legend.* 1941. Duell, Sloan & Pearce. 1st ed. $25.00

WERTHAM, Frederic. *Seduction of the Innocent.* 1954. 2nd ed. dj. VG $80.00

WESCHLER, Lawrence. *Solidarity.* 1981. New York. Simon & Schuster. 221 pp. dj. $4.50

WESCOTT, Glenway. *Twelve Fables of Aesop.* 1954. New York. Ltd. ed. 1/975. boxed. $125.00

WESCOTT. *The Life of John Fitch, Inventor of Steamboat.* 1857. 1st ed. ex-lib. rebound. $42.00

WESCOTT, W.W. *Numbers, Their Occult Power & Mystic Virtues.* 1911. New York. 3rd ed. 127 pp. dj. VG $30.00

WEST, James E. & Hillcourt, W. *Scout Field Book.* 1948. New York. B.S.A. 8th printing 1953. G $2.50

WEST, John. *A Journal of a Mission to the Indians.* 1827. London. L.B. Seeley. 1st ed. $185.00

WEST, Morris. *The World is Made of Glass.* 1983. Morrow. proof copy. wrappers. VG $10.00

WEST, Nathaniel. *A Cool Million.* 1934. New York. $45.00

WEST, Nathaniel. *Complete Works of Farrar.* 1957. 1st ed. dj. $20.00

WEST, Nathaniel. *Day of the Locust.* 1951. London. 1st Eng. ed. dj. VG $40.00

WEST, Nathaniel. *Day of the Locust.* 1951. London. Grey Walls. 1st Eng. ed. VG $65.00

WEST, Nigel. *A Thread of Deceit; Espionage Myths of WWII.* 1985. New York. Random House. 166 pp. $7.00

WEST, R.B. Jr. *Kingdom of the Saints.* 1957. Viking. Ills. 1st ed. dj. EX $7.00

WEST, Rebecca. *Black Lamb & Grey Falcon.* 1944. London. 2 vol set. $25.00

WEST, Rebecca. *Black Lamb & Grey Falcon.* 1941. Viking. 2 vol set. slipcase. VG $50.00

WEST, Rebecca. *Fountain Overflows.* 1956. 1st ed. dj. VG $10.00

WEST, Rebecca. *The Judge.* 1922. 1st ed. $6.50

WEST, Richard. *Mr. Lincoln's Navy.* 1958. Longmans. 2nd printing. dj. $8.50

WEST, Wallace. *Everlasting Exiles.* 1967. 1st ed. dj. EX $7.50

WEST, Wallace. *The Bird of Time.* 1959. Hicksville, NY. Gnome Pr. 1st ed. 256 pp. dj. $10.00

WEST. *Diseases of Children.* 1860. Philadelphia. $40.00

WEST. *Dot & Dash at the Seashore.* 1940. Cupples & Leon. Ills. VG $4.00

WEST. *Dot & Dash in the North Woods.* 1938. Cupples & Leon. Ills. G $3.50

WEST. *Ghost Gold.* Pocketbook. pb. $3.00

WEST. *Miss Lonelyhearts.* New York. 1st ed. VG $125.00

WEST. *Outlaw Brand.* Pyramid. pb. $3.00

WESTCOTT, Edward. *David Harum.* 1899. Appleton. 392 pp. $3.50

WESTCOTT, Edward. *David Harum.* 1900. Appleton. Ills. Clinedinst. Ltd. 1st ed. $22.50

WESTER, D. *Love Letters of Mark Twain.* 1949. New York. Harper. 1st ed. dj. EX $15.00

WESTERKOV, K. *Know Your New Zealand Birds.* 1967. Ills. 144 pp. dj. EX $12.50

WESTERMEIR. *Trailing the Cowboy, His Life & Lore.* 1955. Caxton. 1st ed. dj. EX $25.00

WESTING. *The Locomotives that Baldwin Built.* 1966. 1st ed. dj. EX $25.00

WESTLAKE, Donald E. *Levine.* 1984. New York. Mysterious Press. 1st ed. dj. $20.00

WESTLAKE, Donald E. *Pity Him Afterwards.* 1964. New York. Random House. 1st Am. ed. VG $30.00

WESTLAKE. *Enough.* 1977. 1st Am. ed. sgn. dj. VG $25.00

WESTLAKE. *Nobody's Perfect.* 1977. 1st Am. ed. sgn. dj. VG $25.00

WESTMORE, Claude. *Sweepers of the Sea.* 1900. Indianapolis. Bowen Merrill. 1st ed. VG $60.00

WESTMORE, Helen Cody. *Last of the Great Scouts.* 1918. New York. dj. VG $15.00

WESTMORE, Helen Cody. *Last of Great Scouts: Life of Col. Wm. F. Cody.* 1899. Duluth. 1st ed. 267 pp. $100.00

WESTON, C.W. & Edward. *California & the West.* 1940. New York. 1st ed. VG $95.00

WESTON, Charis. *California & the West.* 1940. New York. 1st ed. $85.00

WESTON, Christine. *The Dark Wood.* 1946. New York. Scribner. 303 pp. $3.50

WESTON, Edward. *Idols Behind Altars.* 1929. 2nd printing. VG $35.00

WESTON, Edward. *Seeing California with Edward Weston.* 1939. no place. $250.00

WESTON. *Cats of Wildcat Hill.* 1947. $200.00

WESTON. *Fit for a King.* 1949. $38.00

WESTVELD, R.H. & Peck, R.H. *Forestry in Farm Management.* 1941. New York. Wiley & Sons. TB. 340 pp. $3.50

WESTVELD, R.H. & Peck, R.H. *Forestry in Farm Management.* 1945. 2nd printing. 339 pp. $3.50

WETMORE, A. *Birds of North America.* 1965. Nat. Geog. Soc.Ills. 1st printing. 643 pp. VG $20.00

WETZEL, G. *H.P. Lovecraft: Memoirs-Critiques-Bibliographies.* 1955. N. Tonawanda. Ltd. 1st ed. 1/200. wrappers. $55.00

WETZEL, Jan. *30 Years in the Golden North.* 1st Am. ed. fld map. dj. VG $10.00

WEY, Francis. *Rome.* London. (ca.1880) Ills. folio. EX $100.00

WEYER, E.M. *Jungle Quest.* 1955. Ills. 1st ed. $7.50

WEYER, E.M. *Strangest Creatures on Earth.* 1953. Sheridan House. 255 pp. G $5.00

WEYER, E.M. *The Eskimos; Their Environment & Folkways.* 1969. Archon Books. 491 pp. maps. dj. $25.00

WEYL, Hermann. *Symmetry.* 1952. Princeton. dj. VG $8.00

WHALEN, Philip. *Scenes of Life at the Capital.* 1971. Bolinas. 1st ed. dj. EX $15.00

WHALEN, Steve. *It Takes a Man to Cry.* 1980. Elliott. 1st ed. dj. VG $10.00

WHALL, W.B. *Rovers of the Deep.* 1953. New York. McBride. Ills. photos. VG $3.50

WHARFIELD, H. *With Scouts & Cavalry at Fort Apache.* 1965. Tuscon. Ills. maps. 124 pp. $30.00

WHARTON, Edith. *Custom of the Country.* 1913. 1st ed. VG $30.00

WHARTON, Edith. *Italian Backgrounds.* 1905. Scribner. Ills. 1st ed. $25.00

WHARTON, Edith. *Old New York New York.* 1924. 4 vol set. $20.00

WHARTON, Edith. *Sanctuary.* 1903. New York. Ills. W.A. Clark. 1st ed. VG $35.00

WHARTON, Edith. *The Age of the Innocence.* 1978. Ltd. Ed. Club. Ills/sgn Smith. 1/2000. boxed. $35.00

WHARTON, Edith. *The Children.* 1928. Appleton. 1st ed. VG $10.00

WHARTON, Edith. *The Fruit of the Tree.* 1907. New York. Scribner. 1st ed. 633 pp. $4.50

WHARTON, Edith. *The Greater Inclination.* 1899. Merrymount Pr. VG $80.00

WHARTON, Edith. *The House of Mirth.* 1975. Ltd. Ed. Club. Ills/sgn Harmon. 1/2000. VG $35.00

WHARTON, Edith. *The House of Mirth.* 1905. New York. 1st ed. EX $65.00

WHARTON, Edith. *The Valley of Decision.* 1902. 2 vol set. VG $60.00

WHARTON, Francis. *Correspondence of American Revolution.* 1889. 6 vol set. VG $185.00

WHARTON, William. *Birdy.* 1979. New York. 1st ed. dj. VG $45.00

WHARTON, William. *Birdy.* 1979. Cape. 1st English ed. dj. VG $35.00

WHARTON, William. *Dad.* 1981. New York. Knopf. 1st ed. dj. EX $25.00

WHEAT, Marvin T. *Travels in Western Slope of Mexican Cordillera.* 1857. San Francisco. Whitton, Towne. rebound. $100.00

WHEAT. *Books of the California Gold Rush.* 1949. Grabhorn. Ltd. ed. 1/500. $110.00

WHEATLEY, Dennis. *Murder Off Miami.* 1936. London. VG $45.00

WHEATLEY, Dennis. *The Malinsay Massacre.* 1938. London. Hutchinson. wrappers. $50.00

WHEATLEY, Dennis. *The Man Who Killed the King.* 1965. New York. Putnam. 1st ed. dj. VG $30.00

WHEATLEY, Dennis. *The Prisoner in the Mask.* 1957. London. Hutchinson. dj. VG $40.00

WHEATLEY, Dennis. *Total War.* 1942. London. Hutchinson. 1st ed. sgn. $30.00

WHEATLEY, Henry B. *Dedication of Books to Patron & Friend.* 1887. New York. 1st Am. ed. 257 pp. $22.50

WHEATLEY, Henry B. *How to Form a Library.* 1886. New York. 2nd ed. 248 pp. $12.50

WHEATLEY, Henry B. *Pepys' Diary.* 1892. Bell & Sons. 9 vol set. VG $150.00

WHEATLEY, James H. *Patterns in Thackeray's Fiction.* 1969. 157 pp. dj. $5.00

WHEATON, H. *Prekaska's Wife, a Year in the Aleutians.* 1945. Dodd Mead. Ills. 251 pp. VG $10.00

WHEELER, Dorothy M. *English Nursery Rhymes.* 1921. London. Black. Ills. ex-lib. VG $20.00

WHEELER, Esther & Lasker, A. *The Complete Book of Flowers & Plants.* 1957. New York. Hearthside Pr. Ills. 190 pp. $5.00

WHEELER, Homer W. *The Frontier Trail.* 1923. Los Angeles. 1st ed. inscr. $85.00

WHEELER, J.T. *The Maryland Press 1777-1790.* 1938. Baltimore. VG $47.50

WHEELER, Lucinda. *A Brief Sketch of the Christian Experience.* 1892. Clark's Corner. private print. 95 pp. $20.00

WHEELER, Opal. *H.M.S. Pinafore.* 1946. New York. Ills. Fritz Kredel. VG $20.00

WHEELER, Opal. *Sing for Christmas.* 1943. New York. Ills. 2nd printing. dj. VG $18.00

WHEELER, R. *The Bloody Battle for Suribachi.* 1965. Ills. dj. G $15.00

WHEELER, Ruth S. *Jane, Stewardess of the Air Lines.* 1934. Chicago. Goldsmith. 246 pp. dj. $3.00

WHEELER, Ruth S. *Janet Hardy in Hollywood.* 1935. Chicago. Goldsmith. 250 pp. dj. $3.00

WHEELER, Ruth S. *Janet Hardy in Radiocity.* 1935. Goldsmith. G $3.50

WHEELER, S.S. *The Friendly Goudys; Story of Visit to Deepdene.* 1932. Boston. photos. $20.00

WHEELER. *Buffalo Days.* 1925. $12.00

WHEELOCK, I.G. *Nestlings of Forest & Marsh.* 1902. McClurg. Ills. 1st ed. G $6.00

WHEELOCK, John Hall. *Poems Old & New.* 1956. New York. Scribner. 1st ed. sgn. 203 pp. $15.00

WHEELWRIGHT, Willaim Bond. *Life & Times of Alvah Crocker.* 1923. Boston. Ills. ex-lib. 114 pp. $12.50

WHELEN, T. & Angier, B. *On Your Own in the Wilderness.* 1958. Galahad. Ills. 330 pp. dj. EX $10.00

WHELEN, Townsend. *The Hunting Rifle: Design, Selection, Ballistics.* 1940. Harrisburg. Stackpole. 463 pp. VG $25.00

WHELEN, Townsend. *Why Not Load Your Own.* 1957. Barnes. Ills. 237 pp. dj. $8.50

WHERRY, Joseph H. *Indian Masks & Myths of the West.* 1969. New York. Ills. 1st ed. 273 pp. $12.50

WHIDDEN, J.D. *Ocean Life in Old Sailing Ship Days.* 1908. 1st ed. VG $7.50

WHIDDEN, J.D. *Old Sailing Ship Days.* 1925. Ills. G $25.00

WHIGHAM, H.J. *Manchuria & Korea.* 1904. Scribner. Ills. 1st ed. 245 pp. VG $25.00

WHINFIELD, E.H. *The Quatrains of Omar Khayyam.* 1882. Trubner. 1st ed. G $12.50

WHIPPLE, A. *Tall Ships & Great Captains.* 1960. Ills. dj. VG $15.00

WHIPPLE, A. *Yankee Whalers in the South Seas.* 1954. New York. Doubleday. 304 pp. dj. EX $10.00

WHIPPLE, A. *Yankee Whalers in the South Seas.* 1943. dj. VG $16.00

WHIPPLE, Leon. *The Story of Civil Liberty in the United States.* 1927. New York. 1st ed. 330 pp. $5.00

WHIPPLE, Wayne. *The Heart of Lincoln.* 1915. Philadelphia. 1st ed. dj. EX $10.00

WHISTLER, Rex. *Designs for the Theatre by Rex Whistler.* 1947. London. Ills. 1st ed. 2 vol set. $45.00

WHISTON, William. *Elements of Euclid.* 1726. London. 3rd ed. 5 fld pls. VG $100.00

WHISTON. *The Works of Flavius Josephus.* New York. (ca.1860) Ills. $50.00

WHITAKER, Herman. *The Planter.* 1909. $4.00

WHITAKER, R. *Common Indian Snakes.* 1978. India. Macmillan. Ills. 154 pp. VG $12.50

WHITAKER, Urban G. *Politics & Powers.* 1964. New York. Harper. VG $4.00

WHITAKER. *Rameses to Rockefeller, Story of Architecture.* 1934. Ills. VG $17.50

WHITE, A. *The Violin: Construction, Dye, & Varnish.* 1892. Boston. 2 fld pls. wrappers. G $25.00

WHITE, Alma. *With God in the Yellowstone.* 1920. Zarephath, NJ. Ills. 138 pp. $12.50

WHITE, Annee H. *The Story of Serapina.* 1951. Viking. Ills. Palazzo. 1st ed. VG $10.00

WHITE, C.R. *By the Sea.* 1890. Portland. photos. 27 pls. $42.50

WHITE, Colin. *Edmund Dulac.* 1976. New York. Scribner. Ills. VG $22.00

WHITE, Constance. *The Flip Flop Show.* 1909. Donohue. Ills. $35.00

WHITE, E.A. *The Principles of Floriculture.* 1915. New York. TB. 467 pp. VG $4.50

WHITE, E.B. *Charlotte's Web.* 1952. Harper. 1st ed. dj. VG $35.00

WHITE, E.B. *Essays of E.B. White.* 1977. New York. Harper. 1st ed. dj. EX $30.00

WHITE, E.B. *Letters of E.B. White.* 1976. New York. Harper. Ills. 686 pp. $10.00

WHITE, E.B. *Poems & Sketches of E.B. White.* 1981. New York. Harper. 1st ed. dj. EX $20.00

WHITE, E.B. *Points of My Compass.* 1962. Harper. 1st ed. dj. VG $35.00

WHITE, E.B. *Stuart Little in the Schoolroom.* 1945. 1st ed. Ills. Garth Williams. VG $50.00

WHITE, E.B. *The Second Tree from the Corner.* 1954. Harper. 1st ed. dj. VG $40.00

WHITE, E.B. & WHITE, K. *A Subtreasury of American Humor.* 1941. New York. Coward McCann. 814 pp. $4.00

WHITE, E.L. *Lukundoo.* 1927. New York. Doubleday. 1st ed. VG $30.00

WHITE, Edward. *Gold.* 1913. New York. Ills. Fogarty. 1st ed. VG $8.50

WHITE, George A. *Take Us North, Matilda.* 1957. New York. sgn. 77 pp. $10.00

WHITE, George. *Historical Collections of Georgia.* 1854. New York. Pudney/Russell. Ills. 1st ed. $125.00

WHITE, Gilbert. *The Natural History & Antiquities of Selborne.* 1911. London. Ills. George Collins. 1st ed. $50.00

WHITE, Gilbert. *The Natural History & Antiquities of Selborne.* 1941. Ills. Clare Leighton. VG $20.00

WHITE, Gilbert. *The Natural History & Antiquities of Selborne.* 1960. London. Cresset. Ills. 296 pp. dj. EX $10.00

WHITE, H. *Robert E. Lee & the Southern Confederacy.* 1897. New York. 1st ed. VG $35.00

WHITE, H.T. *America at Last. American Journal of H.T. White.* 1965. Putnam. 1st ed. dj. $7.50

WHITE, Henry Kirke. *History of Union Pacific Railway.* 1895. Chicago. Ills. 1st ed. 129 pp. $100.00

WHITE, J.E. & Wanless, Mrs. M. *Breakfast, Dinner, & Supper in Five Parts.* 1884. Battle Creek. 1st ed. $90.00

WHITE, J.H., Jr. *The American Railroad Passenger Car.* 1978. Baltimore. Ills. dj. G $60.00

WHITE, J.J. *Cranberry Culture.* 1870. Ills. $35.00

WHITE, J.J. *Funabout Fords.* 1915. Chicago. 56 pp. $37.50

WHITE, Jerry. *Beauty Photography 2.* 1965. New York. wrappers. VG $7.50

WHITE, Jon Manchip. *Diego Velazquez Painter & Courtier.* 1966. Chicago. 1st ed. dj. VG $15.00

WHITE, Leslie Turner. *Sir Rogue.* 1954. New York. Crown. 310 pp. EX $3.50

WHITE, Newman Ivy. *Portrait of Shelley.* 1945. New York. Knopf. dj. EX $20.00

WHITE, Owen P. *Them Was the Days: From El Paso to Prohibition.* London. Ills. Santee. 1st Eng. ed. dj. $27.00

WHITE, Patrick. *A Nation on Trial.* 1965. New York. 177 pp. EX $8.00

WHITE, Patrick. *The Cockatoos.* 1974. London. proof copy. wrappers. VG $40.00

WHITE, Patrick. *The Tree of Man.* 1956. London. 1st Eng. ed. dj. $45.00

WHITE, Rev. Henry. *Indian Battles: Incidents in Hist. of New England.* 1859. New York. 427 pp. indexed. $30.00

WHITE, S.E. & Adams, S.H. *The Mystery.* 1907. New York. 1st ed. VG $20.00

WHITE, Stewart Edward. *Camp & Trail.* 1917. Ills. 236 pp. $11.50

WHITE, Stewart Edward. *Conjuror's House, a Romance of the Free Forest.* 1908. New York. Ills. 1st ed. 260 pp. $12.50

WHITE, Stewart Edward. *Dog Days/Autobiography of a Man & His Dog Friends.* 1933. Doubleday. Ills. Crawford. 285 pp. G $10.00

WHITE, Stewart Edward. *Folded Hills.* 1934. New York. 1st ed. 479 pp. dj. VG $30.00

WHITE, Stewart Edward. *Gold.* 1913. Doubleday Page. Ills. Thomas Fogarty. VG $12.00

WHITE, Stewart Edward. *The Forest.* 1903. New York. Ills. Fogarty. 1st ed. 276 pp. $10.00

WHITE, Stewart Edward. *The Leopard Woman.* 1916. Garden City. Ills. 1st ed. 313 pp. $10.00

WHITE, Stewart Edward. *The Long Rifle.* 1932. New York. Ills. 1st ed. 537 pp. $7.50

WHITE, Stewart Edward. *The Silent Places.* 1904. New York. Ills. Goodwin. 1st ed. 304 pp. $4.50

WHITE, Stewart Edward. *The Story of California.* 1932. New York. Doubleday. 369 pp. $8.00

WHITE, T. *War with Spain & History of Cuba.* 1898. 300 Ills. salesman's copy. G $12.50

WHITE, T.H. *America in Search of History.* 1977. 1st ed. dj. VG $10.00

WHITE, T.H. *America in Search of Itself.* 1977. 1st ed. dj. VG $10.00

WHITE, T.H. *Breach of Faith.* 1975. New York. 373 pp. $5.50

WHITE, T.H. *In Search of History, a Personal Adventure.* 1978. New York. Harper. 561 pp. dj. $6.00

WHITE, T.H. *Mistress Masham's Repose.* 1946. New York. Putnam. Ills. Eichenberg. dj. $35.00

WHITE, T.H. *The Book of Beasts.* 1954. New York. 1st ed. dj. VG $35.00

WHITE, T.H. *The Book of Merlyn.* 1977. U. of TX Press. Ills. dj. EX $3.50

WHITE, T.H. *The Elephant & the Kangaroo.* 1948. London. 1st Eng. ed. dj. VG $45.00

WHITE, T.H. *The Goshawk: History of Falconry.* 1951. Putnam. 1st ed. dj. VG $30.00

WHITE, T.H. *The Making of the President 1960.* 1961. New York. 400 pp. VG $5.50

WHITE, T.H. *The Making of the President 1964.* 1965. New York. 459 pp. $5.50

WHITE, T.H. *The Making of the President 1968.* 1969. New York. 459 pp. 373 pp. $5.50

WHITE, T.H. *The Mountain Road.* 1950. New York. Duell Sloan. 347 pp. dj. $4.00

WHITE, T.H. *The Once & Future King.* 1958. London. Collins. 1st complete ed. $75.00

WHITE, T.H. *The Scandalmonger.* 1952. 1st ed. dj. VG $15.00

WHITE, T.H. *The Sword in the Stone.* 1939. New York. Ills. Robert Lawson. 1st ed. $20.00

WHITE, T.H. *The View from the Fortieth Floor.* 1960. New York. Duell Sloan. 341 pp. dj. $4.00

WHITE, T.H. & Jacoby A. *Thunder Out of China.* 1946. New York. 331 pp. VG $4.50

WHITE, W.L. *Queens Die Proudly.* 1943. New York. 273 pp. EX $5.00

WHITE, W.L. *They Were Expendable.* 1942. New York. 209 pp. EX $5.00

WHITE, Wallace B. *Milan Township & Village 150 Years.* 1959. Milan. 64 pp. wrappers. $8.50

WHITE, Walter. *How Far the Promised Land?* 1955. Viking. 1st ed. dj. VG $10.00

WHITE, Willan Allen. *A Certain Rich Man.* 1910. 1st ed. $6.50

WHITE, William Allen. *A Puritan in Babylon.* 1938. 1st ed. VG $15.00

WHITE, William Allen. *Defense for America.* 1940. New York. Macmillan. 205 pp. dj. VG $5.50

WHITE, William Allen. *Martial Adventures of Henry & Me.* 1918. New York. 1st ed. $10.00

WHITE, William Allen. *The Autobiography of William Allen White.* 1946. New York. Macmillan. 667 pp. $6.00

WHITE, William. *Byline: Ernest Hemingway.* 1967. 1st ed. dj. EX $45.00

WHITE, William. *The Taft Story.* 1954. Harper. 288 pp. dj. VG $4.50

WHITE. *Agent B-7.* Houghton Mifflin. dj. VG $6.50

WHITE. *Git Along, Little Dogies/Songs-Songmakers of West.* 1975. 1st ed. + record. dj. VG $15.00

WHITE. *Successful Houses & How to Build Them.* 1918. Macmillan. Ills. 520 pp. $15.00

WHITEHEAD, Don. *Border Guard.* 1963. New York. McGraw Hill. 274 pp. $2.50

WHITEHEAD, Don. *The FBI Story.* 1956. 4th printing. 368 pp. $12.00

WHITEHEAD, Eric. *Cyclone Taylor.* 1977. Doubleday. Ills. 1st ed. 205 pp. dj. EX $6.00

WHITEHEAD, Eric. *The Patricks, Hockey's Royal Family.* 1980. Doubleday. Ills. 280 pp. dj. EX $12.50

WHITEHEAD, H.S. *Junbee & Other Uncanny Tales.* 1944. Arkham House. 1st ed. $60.00

WHITEHEAD, H.S. *West India Lights.* 1946. Sauk City. 1st ed. 367 pp. dj. VG $35.00

WHITEHEAD, James. *Joiner.* 1971. Knopf. 1st ed. sgn. inscr. dj. VG $30.00

WHITEHEAD, John. *This Solemn Mockery.* 1973. London. Arlington Books. Ills. 1st ed. $20.00

WHITEING, Richard. *The Yellow Van.* 1903. New York. 379 pp. $15.00

WHITEING. *The Land of Enchantment, Pikes Peak to Pacific.* 1910. EX $15.00

WHITEMAN, Paul & McBride, M. *Jazz.* 1926. New York. Sears. 1st ed. dj. EX $75.00

WHITFIELD, Stephen. *Scott Nearing: Apostle of Am. Radicalism.* 1974. New York. Columbia Pr. 1st ed. 269 pp. $20.00

WHITFIELD. *Through Five Republics on Horseback.* 1921. Hauser. Ills. G $4.50

WHITFORD, Francis Peter. *Japanese Prints & Western Painters.* 1977. Macmillan. Ills. 264 pp. dj. scarce. EX $50.00

WHITING, E.M. *Whaling Wives.* 1953. Boston. Houghton Mifflin. 293 pp. pls. $12.50

WHITING, J.R. *Tales & Techniques of Boating.* 1959. Ills. G $7.50

WHITING, John D. *Practical Illustration: Guide for Artists.* 1920. New York. Ills. Pyle/Cootes/others. VG $40.00

WHITLEY, G.P. *Animals of the World. Australia.* 1968. Hamlyn. Ills. 125 pp. dj. VG $9.00

WHITLOCK, Brand. *Uprooted.* 1926. New York. 1st ed. 333 pp. $12.50

WHITLOCK, H.P. *The Story of the Gems.* 1936. Lee Furman. 1st ed. 206 pp. VG $15.00

WHITMAN, A. *Portrait: Adlai E. Stevenson.* 1965. New York. $10.00

WHITMAN, Roger B. *First Aid for the Ailing House.* 1942. New York. Ills. 359 pp. $5.50

WHITMAN, S.E. *The Troopers.* 1962. New York. Ills. Eggenhoffer. 254 pp. $12.50

WHITMAN, Walt. *Complete Prose Works.* 1897. Philadelphia. McKay. 522 pp. $12.50

WHITMAN, Walt. *Leaves of Grass.* 1936. Heritage Press. Ills. Rockwell Kent. 527 pp. $10.00

WHITMAN, Walt. *Leaves of Grass.* Boston. 1st Boston ed. dj. VG $175.00

WHITMAN, Walt. *Leaves of Grass.* 1940. Doubleday. Ills. L. Daniel. boxed. VG $15.00

WHITMAN, Walt. *Leaves of Grass.* 1930. Grabhorn Press. Ills. Angelo. Ltd. ed. 1/400. $1,100.00

WHITMAN, Walt. *Leaves of Grass.* 1892. Philadelphia. McKay. VG $135.00

WHITMAN, Walt. *Leaves of Grass.* 1942. Ltd. Eds. Club. Ills. Weston. 2 vol set. djs. $300.00

WHITMAN, Walt. *November Boughs.* 1888. Philadelphia. 1st ed. $90.00

WHITMAN, Walt. *Specimen Days & Collect 1882.* Philadelphia. McLay. 1st ed. 2nd issue. G $80.00

WHITMAN, Walt. *Specimen Days in America.* 1887. London. Scott. 1st ed. VG $65.00

WHITMAN, Wilson. *God's Valley.* 1939. New York. Viking. photos. 320 pp. $5.50

WHITNEY, A. *Mother Goose for Grown Folks.* 1882. New York. VG $10.00

WHITNEY, C.M. *The Bermuda Garden.* 1955. 1st ed. 11 pls. dj. $40.00

WHITNEY, E. *American Peace Society: a Centennial History.* 1928. Washington. 1st ed. 360 pp. $25.00

WHITNEY, George D. *Know Your First Aid for Dogs.* Netherland. $4.50

WHITNEY, GRINNELL & WISTER. *Musk-Ox, Bison, Sheep, & Goat.* 1904. Macmillan. Ills. 1st ed. 284 pp. VG $45.00

WHITNEY, Helen Hay. *Sonnets & Songs.* 1905. Harper. inscr. 81 pp. VG $15.00

WHITNEY, J.D. *The Metallic Wealth of the U.S.* 1854. Philadelphia. inscr. 510 pp. $75.00

WHITNEY, Phyllis. *Sea Jade.* 1964. 1st ed. 277 pp. $37.50

WHITNEY, W. Dwight. *A Sanskrit Grammar.* 1891. Leipzig/Boston. 2nd ed. 551 pp. VG $25.00

WHITSON, John H. *The Young Ditch Rider.* 1899. Chicago. 96 pp. wrappers. $10.00

WHITTAKER, E.T. *A History of the Theories of Aether & Electricity.* 1910. London. 475 pp. $15.00

WHITTAKER, James. *We Thought We Heard the Angels Sing.* 1944. Dutton. 139 pp. $37.50

WHITTIER, Jason. *Greenleaf.* 1893. Crowell. 1st ed. VG $10.00

WHITTIER, John Greenleaf. *Child Life in Prose.* 1874. Boston. Ills. 1st ed. $35.00

WHITTIER, John Greenleaf. *In War Time.* 1864. Boston. Ticknor & Fields. 1st ed. VG $40.00

WHITTIER, John Greenleaf. *Mabel Martin.* 1976. Martin. Ills. Moran /Waud/Hallack. VG $15.00

WHITTIER, John Greenleaf. *Snow Bound. A Winter Idyl.* 1911. Portland. Ltd. 1st ed. 1/925. $25.00

WHITTIER, John Greenleaf. *The King's Missive.* 1881. Boston. 1st ed. G $20.00

WHITTIER, John Greenleaf. *The Pennsylvania Pilgrim & Other Poems.* 1872. Boston. 1st ed. 129 pp. $12.50

WHITTIER, John Greenleaf. *The Tent on the Beach & Other Poems.* 1867. Ticknor & Fields. VG $22.50

WHITTIER, John Greenleaf. *The Tent on the Beach & Other Poems.* 1899. Houghton Mifflin. 1st Am. ed. $25.00

WHITTIER, John Greenleaf. *The Vision of Echard.* 1878. Boston. 1st ed. VG $20.00

WHITTING, J.D. *Trail of Fire, Story of Civil War Ship 'Alabama.'* 1930. Ills. G $12.50

WHITTINGTON, Harry. *The Devil Wears Wings.* 1960. London. Abelard Schuman. 1st ed. dj. $10.00

WHITTLESEY, Charles. *Early History of Cleveland, Ohio.* 1867. Cleveland. 487 pp. $75.00

WHITTON, F.E. *Wolfe & North America.* 1929. Boston. Ills. maps. 322 pp. $25.00

WHYMPER, Edward. *Scrambles Amongst the Alps.* New York. (ca.1889) EX $25.00

WHYMPER, Edward. *Travels Amongst the Great Andes of the Equator.* 1892. New York. EX $45.00

WHYMPER, Henry Josiah. *The Religion of Free Masonry.* 1888. London. 1st ed. 260 pp. VG $52.50

WHYMPER, R. *Cocoa & Chocolate, Their Chemistry & Manufacture.* 1912. Philadelphia. 327 pp. 12 pls. index. $15.00

WHYTE, William Foote. *Street Corner Society.* 1955. Chicago Press. 366 pp. dj VG $4.50

WIBBERLEY, Leonard. *Encounter Near Venus.* 1967. Ills. 1st printing. dj. EX $14.00

WIBBERLEY, Leonard. *Homeward to Ithaca.* 1978. Morrow. 1st ed. dj. VG $10.00

WIBBERLEY, Leonard. *The Time of the Lamb.* 1961. New York. Ills. Kredel. 1st ed. $7.50

WICHMANN, Siegfried. *Japanese Influence on Western Art 19th-20th Cent.* 1980. Harmony Books. Ills. 1st ed. EX $270.00

WICKENDEN, J. *A Claim in the Hills.* 1957. Rinehart. Ills. 275 pp. dj. EX $10.00

WICKERSHAM, Jason. *Old Yukon Trails, Trails, & Trails.* 1938. Washington. Ills. 514 pp. map. dj. $22.50

WICKSON, E.J. *The California Fruits & How to Grow Them.* 1891. San Francisco. Ills. G $35.00

WICKSON. *Rural California.* 1923. Macmillan. 399 pp. maps. charts. dj. VG $15.00

WIDDEMER, Margaret. *Ballads & Lyrics.* 1925. New York. $35.00

WIDDEMER, Margaret. *Winona of Camp Karonya.* 1917. New York. A.L. Burt. 318 pp. dj. $3.50

WIDDIFIELD, Hannah. *Widdifield's New Cookbook.* 1856. Philadelphia. G $45.00

WIDEMAN, John Edgar. *Hurry Home.* 1970. New York. Harcourt. 1st ed. dj. EX $30.00

WIDEMAN, John Edgar. *The Lynchers.* 1973. New York. Harcourt. 1st ed. dj. EX $25.00

WIEDERSEIM, G.G. *Little Sunbeam's Book.* 1918. Hurst. Ills. SftCvr. $45.00

WIEGAND, Sister. *Sketch Me Berta Hummel.* 1951. Indianapolis. 1st ed. dj. VG $15.00

WIENER. *Cybernetics.* 1948. $10.00

WIESE, Kurt. *Buddy the Bear.* 1936. New York. Ills. 1st ed. EX $25.00

WIESEL, Elie. *A Beggar in Jerusalem.* New York. 1st trade ed. sgn. dj. VG $45.00

WIESEL, Elie. *Legends of Our Time.* 1968. New York. Holt. proof copy. EX $40.00

WIESEL, Elie. *Legends of Our Time.* 1968. Holt. 1st ed. dj. VG $25.00

WIESEL, Elie. *One Generation After.* 1970. Random House. 1st ed. dj. VG $20.00

WIESEL, Elie. *Somewhere a Master.* 1982. New York. 1st ed. dj. VG $10.00

WIESEL, Elie. *The Oath.* 1973. Random House. 1st ed. dj. EX $30.00

WIGGIN, E. *History of Aroostook.* 1922. VG $30.00

WIGGIN, Kate Douglas. *Mother Carey's Chickens.* 1911. Boston. Houghton Mifflin. 1st ed. G $15.00

WIGGIN, Kate Douglas. *Penelope's Irish Experiences.* 1901. Boston. Houghton Mifflin. 1st ed. G $18.00

WIGGIN, Kate Douglas. *Romance of a Christmas Card.* 1916. Ills. Hunt. 1st ed. dj. EX $25.00

WIGGIN, Kate Douglas. *The Bird's Christmas Carol.* 1941. Boston. Ills. Memorial ed. dj. $15.00

WIGGIN, Kate Douglas. *The Bird's Christmas Carol.* 1888. Boston. Ills. dj. $12.50

WIGGIN, Kate Douglas. *The Old Peabody Pew.* 1907. Boston/NY. Ills. Stephens. 1st ed. $30.00

WIGGIN & SMITH. *Arabian Nights.* 1944. NY/London. Scribner. Ills. M. Parrish. G $16.00

WIGHTMAN, W.P.D. *Science & Monism.* 1934. Allen. 1st ed. $15.00

WIGHTMAN & CATE. *Early Days of Coastal Georgia.* 1955. 1st ed. VG $15.00

WIGHTON, C. *Heydrich.* 1962. $24.50

WIGSTON, W.F.C. *Bacon Shakespeare & the Rosicrucians.* 1888. London. 1st ed. 284 pp. $15.00

WIHOITE, Mariel & Horton, E. *Bobra of Bali.* 1936. New York. dj. EX $12.50

WIKLES, Charles. *Western America, Including California & Oregon.* 1849. Philadelphia. maps. wrappers. $375.00

WILBARGER. *Indian Depredations in Texas.* 1935. Austin. $75.00

WILBER, E.L. & Schoenholtz, E. *Silver Wings.* 1948. New York. Ills. Milton Caniff. dj. $20.00

WILBUR, D. *Iran, Past, & Present.* 1948. Ills. 1st ed. $7.50

WILBUR, Earl Morse. *A History of Unitarianism.* 1977. Boston. 2 vol set. djs. VG $12.50

WILBUR, Richard. *Ceremony & Other Poems.* 1950. New York. Harcourt Brace. 1st ed. VG $25.00

WILCOX, Cornelis DeWitt. *French-English Military Technical Dictionary.* 1899. Washington. 493 pp. $25.00

WILCOX, D.J. *Body Jewelry.* 1973. New York. dj. EX $22.50

WILCOX, E.V. & Smith, C.B. *Farmer's Encyclopedia of Agriculture.* 1922. New York. Judd Pub. 619 pp. G $4.00

WILCOX, Ella Wheeler. *Beautiful Land of Nod.* 1892. Chicago. Ills. Mears. 141 pp. VG $12.50

WILCOX, Frank N. *Ohio Indian Trails.* 1933. Gates Press. 2nd ed. sgn. dj. $80.00

WILCOX, James. *North Gladiola.* 1985. Harper. 1st ed. dj. VG $15.00

WILCOX, L.A. *Mr. Pepys' Navy. History of British Navy.* 1966. Ills. dj. VG $15.00

WILD, John. *Power Skating.* 1971. Prentice Hall. Ills. 128 pp. SftCvr. VG $5.50

WILDASH, P. *Birds of South Vietnam.* 1968. Tuttle. Ills. 1st ed. 234 pp. dj. EX $20.00

WILDE, Oscar. *Best Known Works.* Wise. no date. $3.00

WILDE, Oscar. *De Profundis.* 1905. 1st ed. VG $75.00

WILDE, Oscar. *Decay of Lying.* 1902. New York. Ltd. ed. 1/1000. VG $32.50

WILDE, Oscar. *Echoes from Kottabos.* 1906. London. Tyrell & Sullivan. 1st ed. $75.00

WILDE, Oscar. *For Love of the King.* 1922. London. Ltd. 1st ed. 1/1000. $75.00

WILDE, Oscar. *Importance of Being Earnest.* 1928. Tauchnitz. wrappers. VG $15.00

WILDE, Oscar. *Intentions. The Decay of Lying.* New York. Dodd Mead. Ltd. ed. 1/600. $50.00

WILDE, Oscar. *Prose Poems.* 1905. Greenwich. Ltd. ed. 1/300. EX $25.00

WILDE, Oscar. *Salome.* World. Ills. Aubrey Beardsley. $52.50

WILDE, Oscar. *The Birthday of the Infanta.* 1929. Macmillan. Ills. Ltd. ed. sgn. slipcase. $60.00

WILDE, Oscar. *The Happy Prince & Other Stories.* New York. Brentano. Ills. Robinson. VG $30.00

WILDE, Oscar. *The Picture of Dorian Gray.* 1908. Paris. Ills. 1st ed. VG $85.00

WILDE, Oscar. *The Trials of Oscar Wilde.* 1948. London. Ills. Toulouse-Lautrec. dj. EX $70.00

WILDER, G. *Fruits of the Hawaiian Islands.* 1911. Ills. revised ed. inscr. sgn. $25.00

WILDER, I. *The Morphology of Amphibian Metamorphosis.* 1925. Smith College. Ills. 161 pp. EX $12.50

WILDER, Kate Elenor. *Pussy Letters. Nature Stories.* 1929. Donahue. Ills. 194 pp. VG $5.50

WILDER, L.I. *Little House in the Big Woods.* 1932. Harper. Ills. H. Sewell. 1st ed. VG $40.00

WILDER, Robert. *Fruit of the Poppy.* 1965. London. Allen. 1st ed. dj. EX $25.00

WILDER, Robert. *Wind from the Carolinas.* 1964. New York. Putnam. 567 pp. $3.00

WILDER, Thornton. *Heaven's My Destination.* 1935. Harper. 1st ed. VG $12.00

WILDER, Thornton. *Lucrece.* 1933. Boston. Houghton Mifflin. 1st ed. VG $12.50

WILDER, Thornton. *Our Century. A Play in Three Scenes.* 1947. New York. Ltd. 1st ed. 1/1000. $17.50

WILDER, Thornton. *The Angel that Troubled the Waters.* 1928. New York. Ltd. 1st ed. dj. VG $42.50

WILDER, Thornton. *The Bridge of San Luis Rey.* 1927. 1st ed. inscr. VG $25.00

WILDER, Thornton. *The Eighth Day.* 1967. Harper. 1st ed. $8.50

WILDER, Thornton. *The Ides of March.* 1948. Harper. Ltd. ed. 1/750. sgn. dj. VG $20.00

WILDER, Thornton. *The Woman of Andros.* 1930. New York. 1st ed. dj. VG $17.50

WILDER, Thornton. *Theophilus North.* 1973. Harper. 1st ed. dj. EX $15.00

WILDER. *Since You Went Away.* 1943. 1st ed. dj. VG $7.50

WILDES, Harry Emerson. *Anthony Wayne, Trouble Shooter of Am. Revolution.* 1941. New York. 1st ed. 514 pp. maps. VG $45.00

WILDMAN, Frederick S., Jr. *A Wine Tour of France.* 1972. New York. $8.50

WILDON, J.C. *Three-Wheeling Through Africa.* 1936. Bobbs Merrill. Ills. 351 pp. G $6.00

WILDSCHUT, Wm. & Ewers, John. *Crow Indian Beadwork.* 1959. New York. Mus. Am. Indians. wrappers. EX $12.50

WILDSMITH, Brian. *Squirrels.* 1975. Watts Pub. Ills. 1st Am. ed. VG $20.00

WILDSMITH, Brian. *What the Moon Saw.* 1978. Oxford. Ills. 1st ed. EX $15.00

WILE, Frederic W. *Emile Berliner, Maker of the Microphone.* 1926. 1st ed. 353 pp. VG $25.00

WILEY, B.I. *Life of Johnny Reb. Common Soldier of Confederacy.* 1943. Bobbs Merrill. Ills. 1st ed. 444 pp. $20.00

WILEY, Farida A. *Ernest Thompson Seton's American Selections.* 1954. New York. Ills. 413 pp. index. $10.00

WILEY, Farida. *John Burrough's America.* 1951. Devin Adair. Ills. Jaques. 304 pp. VG $6.00

WILEY, Harvey W. *An Autobiography.* 1930. 1st ed. 339 pp. VG $15.00

WILEY, S.T. *History of Preston County.* 1882. Kingwood, WV. Ills. 1st ed. 529 pp. VG $35.00

WILEY. *Embattled Confederates.* 1964. Ills. 1st ed. 290 pp. $13.50

WILHELM, Donald. *Theodore Roosevelt as an Undergraduate.* 1910. Boston. 118 pp. $15.00

WILHELM, Kate. *Huysman's Pets.* 1986. BlueJay. 1st ed. dj. EX $10.00

WILHELM, R. *The Chinese Fairy Book.* 1922. London. Ills. Geo. W. Hood. 1st ed. VG $55.00

WILKENS-FREEMAN, Mary E. *Collected Ghost Stories.* 1974. Sauk City. 1st ed. 189 pp. dj. EX $12.50

WILKES, Charles. *U.S. Exploring Expedition During the Years.* 1845. Philadelphia. Ills. 5 vol set. maps. G $165.00

WILKES, Glenn. *Basketball Coach's Complete Handbook.* 1962. Englewood Cliffs. 306 pp. dj. $5.00

WILKES. *Columbia River to the Sacramento.* 1958. Oakland. Ltd. 1st CA ed. 1/600. EX $60.00

WILKIE, Wendell L. *One World.* 1943. 6th printing. dj. VG $6.50

WILKINS, Ernest Hatch. *Toward Unity.* 1946. Oberlin, Ohio. presentation copy. 116 pp. $7.50

WILKINS, H. *Family Adviser, Accommodated to Diseases of America.* 1804. New York. revised ed. $75.00

WILKINS, Mary E. *The Portion of Labor.* 1901. New York. 1st ed. VG $17.50

WILKINS, Robert P. & Wynona H. *God Giveth the Increase.* 1959. Fargo. 208 pp. dj. $10.00

WILKINS, Updike. *Memoirs of the Rhode Island Bar.* 1842. Boston. 1st ed. 311 pp. $50.00

WILKINS. *Cleverdale Mystery of Machine & Its Wheels.* 1887. New York. 1st ed. $30.00

WILKINSON, Charles K. *Iranian Ceramics.* 1963. New York. Asian House. Ills. inscr. VG $35.00

WILKINSON, D. *Land of the Long Day.* 1956. London. Harrap. Ills. 261 pp. dj. EX $15.00

WILKINSON, F. *Antique Arms & Armour.* 1972. New York. Drake. Ills. 192 pp. $16.50

WILKINSON, F. *Antique Guns & Gun Collecting.* 1974. Hamlyn. Ills. 96 pp. dj. VG $10.50

WILKINSON, F. *British & American Flintlocks.* 1971. dj. EX $12.50

WILKINSON, F. *Collecting Military Antiques.* 1976. London. Ills. dj. EX $20.00

WILKINSON, F. *Guns.* 1971. Ills. dj. VG $7.50

WILKINSON-LATHAM, John. *British Cut & Thrust Weapons.* 1971. Tuttle. 1st ed. dj. VG $12.50

WILLARD, D. *Montana, the Geological Story.* 1935. Lancaster, PA. 1st ed. inscr. 372 pp. VG $25.00

WILLARD, Mrs. Eugene S. *Kin-Da-Shon's Wife.* 1892. Chicago. Ills. 281 pp. $15.00

WILLARD, T.A. *The City of the Sacred Well.* 1926. Ills. 293 pp. EX $17.50

WILLARD, T.A. *The Lost Empires of the Itzaes & Mayas.* 1933. Clark. Ills. sgn. 449 pp. index. $75.00

WILLCOCK, C. *Africa's Rift Valley.* 1975. Time Life. Ills. 184 pp. EX $10.00

WILLIAM, Prince of Sweden. *Wild African Animals I Have Known.* 1923. London. Lane. Ills. 315 pp. VG $45.00

WILLIAM H. WISE & CO. *The 100 Best True Stories of World War II.* 1945. New York. Ills. 896 pp. VG $4.50

WILLIAMS, A.B. *Hampton & His Red Shirts.* 1935. 1st ed. VG $25.00

WILLIAMS, Alan. *Holy of Holies.* 1980. New York. Wade. proof copy. wrappers. EX $30.00

WILLIAMS, Albert. *A Pioneer Pastorate.* 1879. San Francisco. 255 pp. VG $45.00

WILLIAMS, Albert. *Through the Russian Revolution.* 1921. New York. 1st ed. photos. 311 pp. VG $12.50

WILLIAMS, Ben Ames. *Leave Her to Heaven.* 1944. Boston. 429 pp. dj. $3.50

WILLIAMS, Ben Ames. *The Strange Woman.* 1941. Boston. 507 pp. $3.50

WILLIAMS, C. *Mirrored Landmarks of Cincinnati.* 1939. Rutger Press. Ills. 1st ed. sgn. 205 pp. VG $15.00

WILLIAMS, C. *Zermatt Saga.* 1964. London. 1st ed. dj. VG $17.50

WILLIAMS, Car. *Sidelights on Williams Family History.* 1940. 89 pp. pb. VG $10.00

WILLIAMS, Carlos. *I Wanted to Write a Poem.* 1958. Beacon. 1st ed. dj. $15.00

WILLIAMS, Charles. *Aground.* 1960. New York. Viking. 1st ed. dj. VG $15.00

WILLIAMS, Charles. *Terrors of a Blizzard by One Who Has Had Experience.* 1902. Oshkosh, WI. Castle Pierce Pr. 1st ed. $85.00

WILLIAMS, D.W. *History of Jackson County, Ohio.* 1900. Jackson, OH. 188 pp. G $42.50

WILLIAMS, E. *Niagara: Queen of Wonders.* 1916. Boston. 1st ed. photos. VG $15.00

WILLIAMS, E.D. *Remember Me to Tom.* 1963. 1st ed. dj. VG $30.00

WILLIAMS, Ellen. *Harriet Monroe & the Poetry Renaissance.* 1977. U. of IL Press. 1st ed. 312 pp. dj. EX $7.50

WILLIAMS, G. *Timid Timothy.* 1944. Ills. L. Weisgard. VG $8.50

WILLIAMS, Gardner. *The Diamond Mines of South Africa.* 1905. New York. Ltd. 2nd ed. 1/1000. sgn. $185.00

WILLIAMS, George A. *The Boy's Book of Pirates.* 1913. Ills. $12.00

WILLIAMS, H.L. & Ottalie, K. *How to Furnish Old American Houses.* 1949. New York. Bonanza Books. Ills. dj. VG $15.00

WILLIAMS, H.T. *Window Gardening.* 1872. Ills. 300 pp. $15.00

WILLIAMS, Henry Smith. *Practical Radio.* 1923. New York. 2nd ed. ex-lib. 413 pp. $15.00

WILLIAMS, J. *Cowboys Out Our Way.* 1951. New York. G $6.00

WILLIAMS, J. *Field Guide to the National Parks of East Africa.* 1968. Houghton Mifflin. 352 pp. dj. $15.00

WILLIAMS, J. *The Redeemed Captive.* 1833. New York. Benedict. Ills. 116 pp. $40.00

WILLIAMS, J. David. *America Illustrated.* 1883. Boston. Ills. 121 pp. $12.50

WILLIAMS, J.G. & Arlott, N. *Field Guide to the Birds of East Africa.* 1980. London. Collins. Ills. 415 pp. EX $20.00

WILLIAMS, J.H. *Elephant Bill in Burma.* 1950. New York. Ills. 1st Am. ed. dj. EX $22.50

WILLIAMS, J.H. *Elephant Bill.* 1950. Doubleday. Ills. 1st ed. 250 pp. G $7.50

WILLIAMS, J.R. *Cowboys Out Our Way.* 1951. New York. 1st ed. VG $55.00

WILLIAMS, James. *The Rise & Fall of the Model Republic.* 1863. London. 1st ed. 424 pp. $125.00

WILLIAMS, Jay. *Stage Left. Radical Theatre in America.* 1974. dj. EX $10.00

WILLIAMS, Joan. *The Wintering.* 1971. Harcourt. 1st ed. sgn. dj. VG $35.00

WILLIAMS, John A. *Mothersill & the Foxes.* 1975. Garden City. Doubleday. sgn. dj. EX $30.00

WILLIAMS, John A. *Sissie.* 1963. NY. Farrar. advance copy. wrappers. $50.00

WILLIAMS, John A. *The Man Who Cried I Am.* 1967. Boston. Little, Brown. dj. EX $30.00

WILLIAMS, John H. *The Mountain that Was God.* 1911. 2nd ed. VG $25.00

WILLIAMS, Jonathan. *Portrait Photographs.* 1979. Gnome Press. Ltd. ed. slipcase. $75.00

WILLIAMS, L. *Heroic Enthusiasts. Ethical Poem by Giordano Bruno.* 1889. Redway & Quaritch. 2 vol set. $20.00

WILLIAMS, Mrs. H. Dwight. *A Year in China.* 1864. New York. VG $30.00

WILLIAMS, Neil W. *The Electric Theft.* 1906. Boston. 1st ed. VG $40.00

WILLIAMS, Ralph. *The Honorable Peter White. Biographical Sketch.* 1905. Cleveland. 1st ed. $20.00

WILLIAMS, Rhys. *The Soviets.* 1937. 1st ed. $6.50

WILLIAMS, S. Wells. *Our Relations with the Chinese Empire.* 1877. San Francisco. 1st ed. $75.00

WILLIAMS, Samuel. *The Natural & Civil History of Vermont.* 1794. Walpole, NH. 1st ed. VG $250.00

WILLIAMS, Sherley Anne. *Dessa Rose.* 1986. Morrow. proof copy. wrappers. EX $25.00

WILLIAMS, Stanley T. *A Bibliography of Writings of Washington Irving.* 1936. New York. 200 pp. $15.00

WILLIAMS, T. & Calvert, J. *Fiji & the Fijians.* 1860. Ills. EX $40.00

WILLIAMS, T. Harry. *A History of the United States.* 1961. New York. Alfred A. Knopf. VG $4.00

WILLIAMS, T. Harry. *Lincoln & His Generals.* New York. Knopf. Ills. 363 pp. VG $10.00

WILLIAMS, T. Harry. *Lincoln & His Generals.* Book of Month Club. dj. VG $6.00

WILLIAMS, Tennessee. *A Streetcar Named Desire.* 1949. London. 1st ed. dj. VG $50.00

WILLIAMS, Tennessee. *Cat on a Hot Tin Roof.* 1955. New Directions. 1st ed. dj. EX $65.00

WILLIAMS, Tennessee. *Hard Candy.* 1959. New Directions. 1st ed. dj. G $25.00

WILLIAMS, Tennessee. *In the Winter of Cities.* 1956. New Directions. 1st ed. $15.00

WILLIAMS, Tennessee. *One Arm.* 1948. New Directions. 1st ed. VG $12.00

WILLIAMS, Tennessee. *Period of Adjustment.* 1960. New York. 1st ed. dj. EX $37.50

WILLIAMS, Tennessee. *Suddenly Last Summer.* 1958. New Directions. 1st ed. dj. VG $70.00

WILLIAMS, Tennessee. *Suddenly Last Summer.* 2nd ed. sgn. dj. EX $50.00

WILLIAMS, Tennessee. *Summer & Smoke.* 1948. New Directions. 2nd ed. sgn. dj. VG $40.00

WILLIAMS, Tennessee. *The Milk Train Doesn't Stop Here Anymore.* 1964. London. 1st Eng. ed. dj. $20.00

WILLIAMS, Tennessee. *The Night of the Iguana.* 1962. 1st ed. VG $95.00

WILLIAMS, Tennessee. *The Remarkable Rooming-House of Mme. Le Monde.* 1984. Albondocani. Ltd. 1st ed. 1/150. wrappers. $55.00

WILLIAMS, Tennessee. *The Rose Tattoo.* 1950. New Directions. 1st ed. dj. VG $30.00

WILLIAMS, Thomas A. *Eliphas Levi, Master of Occultism.* 1975. 174 pp. dj. VG $25.00

WILLIAMS, W.C. *Want to Write Poem.* New York. 1st ed. dj. EX $25.00

WILLIAMS, W.W. *History of the Fire Lands, Huron & Erie Counties.* 1879. Cleveland. Ills. $37.50

WILLIAMS, Walter. *State of Missouri.* 1904. VG $17.50

WILLIAMS, William Carlos. *A Voyage to Pagnay.* 1928. New York. 1st ed. VG $25.00

WILLIAMS, William Carlos. *John Marin.* 1956. U. CA Press. Ills. 1st ed. dj. VG $22.50

WILLIAMS, William Carlos. *Make Light of It.* 1950. Random House. 1st ed. dj. $25.00

WILLIAMS, William Carlos. *Paterson.* 1948. New Directions. Ltd. 1st ed. 1/1577. VG $50.00

WILLIAMS, William Carlos. *The Build-Up.* 1952. Random House. 1st ed. dj. $20.00

WILLIAMS, William Carlos. *The Farmer's Daughter.* 1961. New Directions. 1st ed. $8.50

WILLIAMS, William Carlos. *Yes, Mrs. Williams.* 1959. McDowell. 1st ed. dj. $15.00

WILLIAMS. *American Illustrated.* 1876. New York. Ills. 121 pp. $30.00

WILLIAMS. *Appleton's Railroad & Steamboat Companion.* 1848. New York. 313 pp. $275.00

WILLIAMS. *Biog. Revolution Heroes Gen. Barton & Capt. Olney.* 1839. Providence. 1st ed. $30.00

WILLIAMS. *Dawn of the Tennessee Valley & Tennessee History.* 1937. Watauga Press. VG $20.00

WILLIAMS. *Henry VIII & His Court.* 1971. Macmillan. Ills. 271 pp. dj. $8.50

WILLIAMS. *Narratives & Adventures of Travelers in Africa.* no date. Ills. Alta ed. 340 pp. $5.50

WILLIAMS. *The Picturesque West. Empire Beyond Mississippi.* 1891. New York. Ills. 525 pp. EX $25.00

WILLIAMSON, Andreano, & Daum. *The American Petroleum Industry 1899-1959.* 1963. Evanston, IL. Northwestern Pub. 928 pp. dj. $5.00

WILLIAMSON, C.N. & A.M. *Rosemary in Search of a Father.* 1906. New York. Ills. Hatherell. 1st ed. $6.50

WILLIAMSON, H.D. *The Year of the Kangaroo.* 1977. Scribner. Ills. 1st ed. 187 pp. dj. EX $7.00

WILLIAMSON, Harold F. *Winchester, Gun that Won the West.* 1961. New York. Barnes. 2nd print. Ills. dj. $20.00

WILLIAMSON, Harold F. & Daum. *American Petroleum Industry. Age of Illumination.* 1959. Evanston. Ills. 864 pp. index. dj. $12.50

WILLIAMSON, Hugh Ross. *The Conspirators & the Crown.* 1959. New York. Hawthorne. Ills. 222 pp. $5.00

WILLIAMSON, Hugh. *Observations on Climate in America.* 1811. New York. 1st ed. 199 pp. $200.00

WILLIAMSON, J. *Humanoid Touch.* 1980. Phantasia Pr. Ltd. ed. 1/500. sgn. boxed. EX $50.00

WILLIAMSON, J. & Gunn, J. *Star Bridge.* 1955. New York. Gnome. 1st ed. dj. VG $12.50

WILLIAMSON, Jack. *Manseed.* 1982. New York. review copy. dj. EX $15.00

WILLIAMSON, Jack. *Seetee Shock.* 1950. New York. Simon & Schuster. 1st ed. dj. $35.00

WILLIAMSON, Jack. *The Cometeers.* 1950. Fantasy Press. 1st ed. dj. VG $35.00

WILLIAMSON, Jack. *The Cometeers.* 1950. Reading. Fantasy. 1st trade ed. dj. $25.00

WILLIAMSON, Jack. *The Humanoids.* 1949. New York. Simon & Schuster. 1st ed. dj. $12.50

WILLIAMSON, Jack. *The Legion of Time.* 1952. Reading. Fantasy. 1st ed. dj. EX $20.00

WILLIAMSON, James. *The Clyde Passenger Steamer.* 1904. Glasgow. VG $35.00

WILLIAMSON, Thames. *The Woods Colt.* 1933. New York. Harcourt. 1st ed. dj. VG $45.00

WILLINGHAM, Calder. *The Gates of Hell.* 1951. 1st ed. 190 pp. $15.00

WILLIS, Anson. *Our Rulers & Our Rights.* 1869. Philadelphia. 504 pp. $12.50

WILLIS, George. *Little Boy Blues.* 1947. New York. Dutton. 1st ed. dj. VG $10.00

WILLIS, John Tracy. *The Life of James Cardinal Gibbons.* 1963. Milwaukee. Bruce Pub. 223 pp. dj. EX $5.00

WILLIS, N.P. *Outdoors at Idlewild.* 1855. New York. 2 pls. EX $60.00

WILLIS. *Hurry-Graphs.* 1851. New York. 2nd ed. VG $14.00

WILLISON, George F. *Behold Virginia: the Fifth Crown.* 1951. New York. 1st ed. dj. VG $10.00

WILLISON, George F. *Saints & Strangers. Story of Mayflower & Plymouth.* 1945. New York. 1st ed. 512 pp. dj. $10.00

WILLISON, George F. *Saints & Strangers. Story of Mayflower & Plymouth.* 1966. London. 306 pp. $9.00

WILLMOTT, H.P. *Pearl Harbor.* 1981. Ills. dj. EX $7.50

WILLOCK, John. *Voyages & Adventures of John Willcok, Mariner.* 1798. Philadelphia. 1st Am. ed. $150.00

WILLOCK. *The Dalmatian.* 1927. Derrydale. Ltd. ed. sgn. EX $500.00

WILLOUGHBY, Charles. *Indian Burial Place at Winthrop Massachusetts.* 1924. Peabody Museum. Ills. 37 pp. EX $12.50

WILLOUGHBY, Malcolm F. *Rum War at Sea.* 1964. Washington. Ills. 183 pp. EX $20.00

WILLS, Garry. *Kennedy Imprisonment: Mediation on Power.* 1982. $10.00

WILLS, M.M. & Irwin, H.S. *Roadside Flowers of Texas.* 1961. TX. U. Press. Ills. 295 pp. dj. EX $15.00

WILLSON, Beckles. *The Great Company.* 1899. Toronto. Ills. 541 pp. fld map. G $62.50

WILMER, R.H. *Bishop of Alabama. Reminiscences of a Grandfather.* 1887. New York. Whittaker. 281 pp. $15.00

WILMORE, S.B. *Swans of the World.* 1974. London. David & Charles. Ills. 229 pp. $9.00

WILNER, Barry. *Wayne Gretzky: Countdown to Immortality.* 1982. Leisure Press. Ills. 232 pp. EX $8.00

WILSON, A.D. & Warburton, D.W. *Field Crops.* 1912. St. Paul, MN. ex-lib. 514 pp. G $3.50

WILSON, Arthur. *The Inconsistent Lady.* 1814. Oxford. Ltd. ed. 1/150. folio. EX $42.50

WILSON, Asa B. *Thirteen Years a Lunatic. Poems & Essays.* 1907. Reno, NV. Ills. 171 pp. $10.00

WILSON, Benjamin Franklin III. *Parthenon of Pericles & Reproduction in America.* 1937. Nashville, TN. Ills. 140 pp. dj. $9.00

WILSON, C. *Empire in Green & Gold. Story of Am. Banana Trade.* 1947. Holt. VG $12.50

WILSON, C. *The Glass Cage.* 1966. Random House. 1st ed. dj. VG $30.00

WILSON, Charles. *A Teacher is a Person.* 1956. New York. Holt. 1st ed. 285 pp. dj. $37.50

WILSON, Charles. *Trees & Test Tubes.* 1943. New York. photos. 352 pp. EX $4.00

WILSON, Colin. *Eagle & Earwig.* 1965. London. Baker. 1st ed. dj. VG $25.00

WILSON, Colin. *Outsider.* 1956. Boston. 1st Am. ed. 288 pp. dj. $22.50

WILSON, Colin. *The Personality Surgeon.* London. 1st ed. sgn. $25.00

WILSON, Colin. *The Space Vampires.* 1976. New York. 1st ed. dj. EX $12.50

WILSON, D. *Evidences of Christianity.* 1829. Boston. G $25.00

WILSON, D. & Ayerst, P. *White Gold, Story of African Ivory.* 1976. Taplinger. Ills. 184 pp. dj. EX $10.00

WILSON, Daniel. *300 Years of Quincy: 1625-1925.* 1926. Quincy. Ills. pls. $22.50

WILSON, Donald Powell. *My Six Convicts.* 1951. New York. 369 pp. dj. VG $5.00

WILSON, Dorothy C. *Stranger & Traveler.* 1975. Boston. 1st ed. 360 pp. dj. $10.00

WILSON, Dorothy C. *The Big-Little World of Doc Pritham.* 1971. New York. McGraw Hill. 320 pp. dj. $5.00

WILSON, Dorothy C. *The Gifts.* 1957. 1st ed. inscr. sgn. dj. VG $20.00

WILSON, E. *A Pilgrimage of Anglers.* 1952. Hartford. Ills. Ltd. ed. 1/450. sgn. VG $145.00

WILSON, E.A. *Iron Men & Wooden Ships.* 1926. Doubleday Page. Ills. VG $25.00

WILSON, Edmund. *A Piece of My Mind.* 1956. Farrar. 1st ed. dj. VG $25.00

WILSON, Edmund. *Patriotic Gore.* 1962. New York. Oxford U. Press. 816 pp. dj. $12.50

WILSON, Edmund. *The Cold War & the Income Tax: a Protest.* 1964. Signet Books. 1st ed. $10.00

WILSON, Edmund. *The Forties*. 1983. New York. Farrar. proof copy. EX $30.00

WILSON, Edmund. *The Fruits of the M.L.A.* 1968. NY Review Book.1st ed. wrappers. $6.00

WILSON, Edmund. *The Little Blue Light*. 1950. New York. 2nd printing. dj. $10.00

WILSON, Ernest H. *China Mother of Gardens*. 1929. Boston. 1st ed. sgn. VG $95.00

WILSON, Eugene. *A North Woods Rendezvous*. 1953. Hartford. Ills. Ltd. ed. sgn. slipcase. $50.00

WILSON, F. Paul. *The Keep*. 1981. New York. 1st Am. ed. dj. EX $15.00

WILSON, F. Paul. *Tomb*. 1984. Whispers Press. Ltd. ed. 1/250. sgn. boxed. EX $60.00

WILSON, F.A.C. *W.B. Yeats & Tradition*. 1958. Macmillan. 1st ed. dj. $10.00

WILSON, Francis. *The Eugene Field I Knew*. 1898. Scribner. ex-lib. $50.00

WILSON, H. *Boss of Little Arcady*. 1905. Boston. Ills. O'Neill. VG $5.00

WILSON, H. *Boss of Little Arcady*. 1905. Ills. O'Neill. 1st ed. VG $10.00

WILSON, Harry. *Morton of the Movies*. 1924. Grosset & Dunlap. Ills. $4.50

WILSON, Harry. *Morton of the Movies*. 1922. Garden City. Doubleday. 1st ed. 335 pp. $17.50

WILSON, Herbert Earl. *The Lore & the Lure of Sequoia*. 1928. Los Angeles. Ills. 628 pp. index. scarce $35.00

WILSON, J.G. *Life & Letters of Fitz-Green Halleck*. 1869. Appleton. 1st ed. $20.00

WILSON, John M. *Farmer's Dictionary. Encyclopedia of Agriculture*. 1850. London/NY. Ills. 2 vol set. $115.00

WILSON, Kinnier S.A. *Neurology*. 1940. 1st ed. 2 vols. 1,838 pp. $205.00

WILSON, Margaret Barclay. *A Carnegie Anthology*. 1915. New York. Ills. index. $35.00

WILSON, Mona. *The Life of William Blake*. 1927. London. Nonesuch Press. Ltd. ed. VG $90.00

WILSON, R. *Colt: an American Legend*. 1980. dj. EX $37.50

WILSON, R.R. *Out of the West*. 1936. New York. Ltd. ed. 1/300. sgn. dj. EX $22.50

WILSON, Robert. *Aideen MacLennon: Story of a Rebel*. 1952. New York. Fellowship Pub. sgn. 253 pp. $37.50

WILSON, Robert. *History of British Expedition to Egypt*. 1803. Philadelphia. maps. charts. ex-lib. G $75.00

WILSON, Sandy. *The Boy Friend*. 1955. London. Ills. 1st ed. dj. VG $50.00

WILSON, Sloan. *A Sense of Values*. 1960. New York. Harper. 604 pp. dj. $3.50

WILSON, Sloan. *Janus Island*. 1967. Boston. 399 pp. $3.50

WILSON, Theodore. *First Summit. Roosevelt & Churchill at Placentia*. 1941. Houghton Mifflin. dj. VG $10.00

WILSON, V.A. *Coaching Era*. New York. (ca.1900) Ills. 259; pp. $10.00

WILSON, W.B. *Acts & Actors in Civil War*. 1892. Philadelphia. Ills. 114 pp. $30.00

WILSON, William S. *Birthplace*. 1982. North-Point. 1st ed. dj. VG $15.00

WILSON, Woodrow. *Address of the President*. 1917. New York. dj. $20.00

WILSON, Woodrow. *Elements of Historical & Practical Politics*. 1903. Boston. revised ed. 656 pp. $12.50

WILSON, Woodrow. *George Washington*. 1896. New York. Harper. Ills. 1st ed. VG $20.00

WILSON, Woodrow. *History of the American People*. 1902. New York. Ills. 5 vol set. EX $40.00

WILSON, Woodrow. *Inaugural Presidential Address*. 1913. private print. $195.00

WILSON, Woodrow. *When a Man Comes to Himself*. 1915. Harper. New York. $4.00

WILSON & PENNELL. *Wiggles, a Funny Little Dog*. 1936. Houghton Mifflin. Ills. Davis. $3.50

WILSON. *Ben K. Green. A Descriptive Bibliography*. 1977. 1st ed. dj. EX $25.00

WILSON. *Bright Eyes. Story of Susette La Flesche*. 1974. 1st ed. dj. EX $15.00

WILSON. *History of Reconstructive Measures 1856-68*. 1868. Hartford. 1st ed. $25.00

WILSON. *John Slidell & the Confederates in Paris*. 1932. Ills. 1st ed. 296 pp. $12.50

WILSON. *Mind Parasites*. 1967. Arkham House. dj. EX $40.00

WILSON. *The Golden Gate*. 1962. Morrow. dj. G $10.00

WILSON. *Uncollected Works of Abraham Lincoln*. 1947. Ltd. ed. 2 vol set. djs. EX $45.00

WILSON. *Viking Art*. 1980. U. of MN. $6.00

WILSON. *With the Flag to Pretoria, History of Boer War*. 1900. Ills. $22.00

WILSTACH. *Hudson River Landings*. 1933. Indianapolis. 1st ed. VG $7.50

WIMENON. *Havoc by Accident*. 1943. New York. Harcourt. 1st ed. dj. EX $15.00

WINCH, Frank. *Thrilling Lives of Buffalo Bill & Pawnee Bill*. 1911. New York. 29 pls. G $15.00

WINCH, Frank. *Thrilling Lives of Buffalo Bill Cody, & Lillie*. 1911. New York. Ills. 1st ed. 224 pp. $20.00

WINCHELL, Alexander. *Walks & Talks in the Geological Field*. 1886. New York. 329 pp. $10.00

WINCHELL, Constance M. *Guide to Reference Books*. 1951. Chicago. 645 pp. VG $10.00

WINCHESTER-WESTERN. *Ball Powder Loading Data*. Ltd. ed. 1/73. 44 pp. $2.00

WINDHAM, Donald. *Two People*. 1965. Coward McCann. 1st ed. dj. VG $20.00

WINDSOR. *The Mississippi Basin*. 1895. 1st ed. $60.00

WINDWAR, Frances. *Oscar Wilde & the Yellow 'Nineties.'* 1941. New York. Blue Ribbon Books. 381 pp. $6.00

WINFIELD, Arthur. *The Rover Boys in New York*. Grosset & Dunlap. G $8.50

WINFIELD, Arthur. *The Rover Boys in the Air*. 1912. 288 pp. $7.50

WINFIELD, Arthur. *The Rover Boys on the Great Lakes*. 1901. Grosset & Dunlap. VG $5.50

WING, Frank. *The Fotygraft Album*. 1915. Reilly & Britton. Ills. $9.50

WINGARD, E.A. *Echoes & Other Poems*. 1899. Newberry, SC. 111 pp. G $5.00

WINGATE, William. *Crystal*. 1983. St. Martins. review copy. dj. VG $17.50

WINGFIELD, Sheila. *Collected Poems, 1938-1981*. 1982. Hill. proof copy. wrappers. EX $25.00

WINKLEMAN. *John D. Rockefeller*. 1937. Winston. Ills. $7.50

WINKLER, J.K. *The First Billion. Stillmans & National City Bank*. 1934. New York. 2nd printing. 277 pp. VG $10.00

WINKLER, J.K. *William Randolph Hearst*. 1955. New York. Ills. 325 pp. dj. $20.00

WINKLEY, J.W. *John Brown the Hero*. 1905. Boston. photo. $10.00

WINKS, Robert W. *Detective Fiction. Collection of Critical Essays*. 1980. Prentice Hall. 1st ed. dj. VG $15.00

WINN, Mary Day. *Macadam Trail, Ten Thousand Miles by Motor Coach*. 1931. New York. Ills. ex-lib. 319 pp. $5.00

WINRAM. *Violin Playing & Adjustment*. 1908. London. 126 pp. $25.00

WINSHIP, Albert E. *Horace Mann, the Educator*. 1896. Boston. New England Pub. 101 pp. G $4.00

WINSHIP, George Parker. *The Cambridge Press 1638-1692*. 1946. $15.00

WINSHIP. *The Journey of Coronado*. 1904. New York. VG $12.50

WINSLOW, M. *Memoir of Mrs. Harriet L. Winslow.* 1840. New York. Am. Tract Soc. 480 pp. $15.00

WINSLOW, Margaret E. *Sketch of Life of Alonzo Crittenden.* 1885. New York. Packer Collegiate Inst. G $15.00

WINSLOW, Ola Elizabeth. *Harper's Literary Museum.* 1927. New York. 1st ed. dj. VG $15.00

WINSOR, Frederick. *Space Child's Mother Goose.* 1958. New York. Ills. Parry. 1st ed. dj. $22.50

WINSOR, Justin. *Aboriginal America.* 1889. Boston. Houghton Mifflin. 470 pp. VG $20.00

WINSOR, Justin. *Narrative & Critical History of America.* 1899. New York. 8 vol set. VG $90.00

WINSOR, Justin. *The Memorial History of Boston 1630-1880.* 1882. Boston. Ills. 4 vol set. VG $90.00

WINSOR, Kathleen. *Forever Amber.* 1945. Macmillan. 652 pp. $3.50

WINSOR, Kathleen. *Star Money.* 1950. New York. 1st ed. dj. VG $15.00

WINSTOCK, Lewis. *Songs & Music of the Redcoats.* 1970. Harrisburg, PA.1st Am. ed. dj. VG $18.00

WINSTON, J.G. & Millar, W.J. *The Engineer's Encyclopedia.* 1890. Philadelphia. Ills. G $125.00

WINTER, E. *Enamel Painting Technics.* 1970. New York. dj. EX $17.50

WINTER, Lumen & Degner, Glenn. *Minute Epics of Flight.* 1933. New York. Ills. 160 pp. VG $9.00

WINTER, Milo. *A Wonder Book.* Rand McNally. 8 color pls. EX $15.00

WINTER, Milo. *Adventures of Perrine.* Rand McNally. 5 color pls. VG $12.00

WINTER, Milo. *Ivanhoe.* Rand McNally. 8 color pls. VG $15.00

WINTER, Milo. *Night Before Christmas.* 1947. Chicago. 1st ed. folio. EX $10.00

WINTER, Milo. *Robinson Crusoe.* Rand McNally. 5 color pls. dj. VG $17.00

WINTER, Milo. *Swiss Family Robinson.* Rand McNally. 8 color pls. $15.00

WINTER, Milo. *The Aesop for Children.* 1942. Rand McNally. VG $20.00

WINTER, Milo. *The Arabian Nights Entertainments.* 1914. Chicago. VG $25.00

WINTER, Milo. *The Bow Tie Book.* 1942. Chicago. 1st ed. EX $12.50

WINTER, Milo. *The Three Musketeers.* Rand McNally. 8 color pls. EX $15.00

WINTER, Milo. *Treasure Island.* 1915. Rand McNally. 14 color pls. VG $18.00

WINTER, William. *The Jefferson, American Actor Series.* 1881. Boston. $12.00

WINTERICH, John T. *A Primer of Book Collecting.* 1926. Greeneberg. 2nd printing. G $8.50

WINTERICH, John T. *Collector's Choice.* 1928. New York. dj. EX $15.00

WINTERICH, John T. *Early American Books & Printing.* 1935. Boston. 1st ed. $35.00

WINTERICH, John T. *Squads Write! A Selection Prose, Verse & Cartoon.* 1931. NY/London. Ills. 335 pp. dj. $15.00

WINTERICH, John T. *The Romance of Great Books & Their Authors.* New York. Halcyon House. 374 pp. $17.50

WINTERS, Yvor. *Uncollected Essays & Reviews.* 1974. Allan Lane. 1st English ed. dj. VG $20.00

WINTHER, O. *A Friend of the Mormons.* 1937. Grabhorn Press. Ltd. ed. 1/500. VG $45.00

WINTHER, Sophus Keith. *Eugene O'Neill, Critical Study.* 1934. Random House. VG $30.00

WINTHROP, Theodore. *The Canoe & the Saddle.* 1863. Boston. 5th ed. $12.00

WINTHROP, Theodore. *The Canoe & the Saddle.* 1863. Boston. 1st ed. $60.00

WINTON, J. *The Death of the Scharnhorst.* 1983. Ills. dj. EX $20.00

WINWAR, F. *Puritan City, Story of Salem.* 1938. Ills. 1st ed. $7.50

WINWAR, Francis. *The Life of the Heart.* 1945. New York. Harper. 3rd ed. 312 pp. $7.50

WISE, David & Ross, Thomas B. *The Invisible Government.* 1964. New York. Random House. dj. $4.00

WISE, David & Ross, Thomas B. *The U-2 Affair.* 1962. New York. Random House. photos. 269 pp. $3.50

WISE, Jennings C. *The Red Man in the New World Drama.* 1931. Washington. Ills. 628 pp. index. scarce $35.00

WISE, John S. *The End of an Era.* 1901. Boston/NY. 474 pp. index. VG $12.50

WISE, Lt., USN. *Los Gringos: or, Inside View of Mexico & CA.* 1849. New York. Baker & Scribner. 453 pp. $30.00

WISE, S.F. *Canadian Airmen & the First World War. Vol. I.* 1980. Ills. dj. EX $37.50

WISE, Thomas J. *Pauline; Fragment of a Confession.* 1866. London. 1833 reprint. Ltd. ed. 1/400. $70.00

WISE. *Encyclopedia of Cookery.* 1952. dj. $9.00

WISE. *Wildlife the World Over.* 1947. Ills. EX $10.00

WISEMAN, D.J. *Cylinder Seals of Western Asia.* Batchworth Press. 1st ed. dj. $17.50

WISSLER. *Indians of the United States.* 1940. $12.00

WISTER, Frances Anne. *25 Years of Philadelphia Orchestra 1900-1925.* 1925. Philadelphia. Ills. G $10.00

WISTER, Owen. *Roosevelt; Story of a Friendship 1880-1919.* 1930. New York. Macmillan. 373 pp. VG $4.00

WISTER, Owen. *The Dragon of Wantley.* 1892. Philadelphia. Lippincott. VG $35.00

WISTER, Owen. *The Virginian.* 1909. Grosset & Dunlap. 504 pp. $5.50

WISTER, Owen. *Ulysses S. Grant.* 1907. Maynard & Co. ex-lib. G $4.50

WISTER. *A Journey in Search of Christmas.* Toronto. Ills. Remington. 1st ed. VG $37.50

WISTER. *Lady Baltimore.* 1906. 1st ed. VG $20.00

WISTRICH, R. *Who's Who in Nazi Germany.* 1982. New York. Bonanza Books. dj. EX $15.00

WITCOVER, Jules. *Marathon: Pursuit of the Presidency 1972-1976.* 1977. New York. Viking. 684 pp. EX $5.50

WITHERS, Alexander S. *Chronicles of Border Warfare.* 1895. Cincinnati. 7th impression, 1920. EX $55.00

WITHERS, Alexander S. *Chronicles of Border Warfare.* 1958. Parsons, WV. reprint. Ltd. ed. $30.00

WITHERS, Percy. *A Buried Life.* 1940. London. Cape. 1st ed. $35.00

WITSHIRE, W. *Folk Pottery of the Shenandoah Valley.* 1975. New York. dj. EX $22.50

WITSON, A.R. & Walster, H.L. *Soils & Soil Fertility.* 1912. St.Paul, MN. TB. 315 pp. G $3.50

WITTER, Dean. *The Meandering Fisherman.* 1960. San Francisco. private print. VG $17.50

WITTIG, Monique. *The Lesbian Body.* 1975. New York. Morrow. 1st ed. dj. EX $22.50

WITTKOWER. *Baroque Art: The Jesuit Contribution.* 1972. Fordam U. Press. $12.00

WITTLIN, T. *Modigliani, Prince of Montparnasse.* 1964. 1st ed. dj. $8.50

WODEHOUSE, P.G. *Barmy in Wonderland.* 1952. London. 1st ed. VG $20.00

WODEHOUSE, P.G. *Big Money.* 1931. New York. 1st Am. ed. dj. VG $37.50

WODEHOUSE, P.G. *Big Money.* 1931. London. 1st Eng. ed. VG $50.00

WODEHOUSE, P.G. *Bill the Conqueror.* 1924. London. Methuen. 1st ed. VG $90.00

WODEHOUSE, P.G. *Carry On, Jeeves.* 1925. London. 1st ed. VG $60.00

WODEHOUSE, P.G. *Carry on Jeeves.* 1935. London. 5th ed. VG $20.00

WODEHOUSE, P.G. *Clicking of Cuthbert.* 1922. London. 2nd ed. VG $25.00

WODEHOUSE, P.G. *Code of Woosters.* 1939. London. 2nd ed. dj. VG $27.00

WODEHOUSE, P.G. *Company for Henry.* 1967. London. Jenkins. 1st Eng. ed. dj. EX $40.00

WODEHOUSE, P.G. *Doctor Sally.* 1932. London. Methuen. 1st ed. VG $65.00

WODEHOUSE, P.G. *French Leave.* 1959. New York. Simon & Schuster. 1st ed. dj. $35.00

WODEHOUSE, P.G. *Frozen Assets.* 1964. London. 1st Eng. ed. VG $45.00

WODEHOUSE, P.G. *Full Moon.* 1947. London. Jenkins. 1st Eng. ed. dj. VG $60.00

WODEHOUSE, P.G. *Good Morning Bill.* 1928. London. 1st ed. $75.00

WODEHOUSE, P.G. *Hot Water.* London. 5th ed. VG $17.50

WODEHOUSE, P.G. *If I Were You.* 1931. London. 1st Eng. ed. VG $55.00

WODEHOUSE, P.G. *Indiscretions of Archie.* London. Popular ed. G $20.00

WODEHOUSE, P.G. *Jeeves Omnibus.* 1931. London. Jenkins. 1st ed. 1st issue. $50.00

WODEHOUSE, P.G. *Louder & Funnier.* 1933. London. Faber. new ed. VG $55.00

WODEHOUSE, P.G. *Love Among the Chickens.* 1924. London. $50.00

WODEHOUSE, P.G. *Meet Mr. Mulliner.* 1927. London. Jenkins. 1st ed. 1st issue. $35.00

WODEHOUSE, P.G. *Meet Mr. Mulliner.* New York. A.L. Burt. 308 pp. $10.00

WODEHOUSE, P.G. *Meet Mr. Mulliner.* 1928. Garden City. 1st Am. ed. 308 pp. $16.00

WODEHOUSE, P.G. *Money in the Bank.* 1946. London. 1st ed. 1st issue. $50.00

WODEHOUSE, P.G. *Mr. Mulliner Speaking.* 1929. London. Jenkins. 1st ed. 1st issue. $45.00

WODEHOUSE, P.G. *Over Seventy.* 1957. London. Jenkins. 1st ed. dj. VG $70.00

WODEHOUSE, P.G. *Performing Flea: Self-Portrait in Letters.* 1953. London. Jenkins. 1st ed. dj. VG $50.00

WODEHOUSE, P.G. *Picadilly Jim.* 1922. London. VG $35.00

WODEHOUSE, P.G. *Service with a Smile.* 1961. London. Jenkins. 1st Eng. ed. dj. VG $35.00

WODEHOUSE, P.G. *Tales of St. Austin's.* Souvenir Press. 1st ed. $13.50

WODEHOUSE, P.G. *The Adventures of Sally.* 1928. Tauchnitz. 1st ed. wrappers. VG $45.00

WODEHOUSE, P.G. *The Best of Wodehouse.* 1949. New York. Pocket Books. wrappers. $10.00

WODEHOUSE, P.G. *The Golf Omnibus.* 1977. London. dj. $50.00

WODEHOUSE, P.G. *The Golf Omnibus.* 1968. Simon & Schuster. dj. EX $25.00

WODEHOUSE, P.G. *The Ice in the Bedroom.* 1961. New York. 1st Am. ed. dj. VG $15.00

WODEHOUSE, P.G. *The Luck of the Bodkins.* 1936. Boston. Little, Brown. 1st ed. 298 pp. $25.00

WODEHOUSE, P.G. *The Mating Season.* 1949. London. Jenkins. 1st ed. 1st printing. $30.00

WODEHOUSE, P.G. *The Small Bachelor.* 1927. London. Methuen. 1st ed. VG $40.00

WODEHOUSE, P.G. *The Weekend Wodehouse.* 1939. 1st ed. dj. VG $25.00

WODEHOUSE, P.G. *The White Feather.* 1922. London. G $35.00

WODEHOUSE, P.G. *Uncle Dynamite.* 1948. London. 1st ed. 1st issue. $50.00

WODEHOUSE, P.G. *Uncle Dynamite.* 1st Am. ed. pb. EX $10.00

WODEHOUSE, P.G. *Uncle Fred in the Springtime.* 1939. London. Jenkins. 1st Eng. ed. VG $40.00

WODEHOUSE, P.G. *Very Good Jeeves.* 1930. London. Jenkins. 1st Eng. ed. VG $40.00

WODEHOUSE, P.G. *William Tell Told Again.* London. Ills. Philip Dadd. $120.00

WODEHOUSE, P.G. & Bolton, G. *Bring on the Girls!* 1953. New York. Ills. 1st ed. dj. VG $15.00

WODEHOUSE. *Few Quick Ones.* 1959. 1st ed. dj. EX $20.00

WOELLNER, Robert. *General Mechanical Drawing for Beginners.* 1932. $3.00

WOELMONT, Le Baron Arnold de. *Nelly Mac Edwards: Moeurs Americaines* 1885. Paris. 1st ed. 297 pp. wrappers. $75.00

WOIWODE, L. *Beyond the Bedroom Wall.* 1975. Farrar. 1st ed. dj. VG $12.50

WOIWODE, L. *What I'm Going to Do, I Think.* 1969. dj. EX $4.00

WOJTYLE, Karol. *Easter Vigil & Other Poems.* 1979. Random House. 82 pp. dj. $37.50

WOLDERING, Irmagard. *Egypt. The Art of the Pharaohs.* 1965. London. Ills. color pls. slipcase. VG $25.00

WOLF, Edwin & Fleming, John. *Rosenbach. A Biography.* Cleveland. (ca.1960) Ltd. ed. sgn. boxed. $175.00

WOLF, Edwin & Fleming, John. *Rosenbach. A Biography.* 1960. London. Weidenfeld & Nicolson. 1st ed. $60.00

WOLF, W. *Die Welt der Aegypter.* 1955. Stuttgart. 293 pp. 118 pls. index. $25.00

WOLFE, Alfred. *In Alaskan Waters.* 1942. $10.00

WOLFE, Bernard. *Limbo.* 1952. Random House. 1st ed. presentation copy. dj. $65.00

WOLFE, Douglas. *Signs of a Migrant Worrier.* 1965. Coyote's Journal. wrappers. VG $15.00

WOLFE, Gene. *Gene Wolfe's Book of Days.* 1981. Garden City. review copy. dj. VG $25.00

WOLFE, Gene. *The Castle of the Otter.* 1982. Willimantic. Ziesing Bros. Ltd. 1st ed. dj. $100.00

WOLFE, Gene. *The Citadel of the Autarch.* 1983. New York. review copy. dj. VG $20.00

WOLFE, Gene. *The Citadel of the Autarch.* 1983. New York. Timescape. 1st ed. dj. EX $25.00

WOLFE, Gene. *The Claw of the Conciliator.* 1981. New York. 1st ed. dj. VG $20.00

WOLFE, Gene. *The Devil in a Forest.* 1976. Chicago. Follett. 1st ed. dj. $35.00

WOLFE, Gene. *The Shadow of the Torturer.* 1980. New York. Simon & Schuster. 1st ed. dj. $75.00

WOLFE, Gene. *The Sword of the Lictor.* 1981. New York. Timescape. dj. $50.00

WOLFE, Gene. *Wolfe Archipelago.* 1983. Willimantic. Ltd. 1st ed. sgn. 1/200. dj. $75.00

WOLFE, Humbert. *News of the Devil.* 1926. London. Ltd. 1st ed. sgn. dj. VG $15.00

WOLFE, Linnie. *Son of the Wilderness: Life of John Muir.* 1945. Knopf. 1st ed. dj. VG $10.00

WOLFE, Reese. *Yankee Ships.* 1953. New York. 287 pp. $3.50

WOLFE, Thomas. *America.* 1942. Chicago. 1st ed. dj. $100.00

WOLFE, Thomas. *Carolina Folk Plays.* 1924. New York. 1st ed. dj. VG $70.00

WOLFE, Thomas. *Carolina Folk Plays.* 1924. New York. VG $22.50

WOLFE, Thomas. *From Death to Morning.* 1935. New York. 1st ed. dj. $75.00

WOLFE, Thomas. *From Death to Morning.* 1936. London. 1st Eng. ed. dj. VG $75.00

WOLFE, Thomas. *In Our Time.* 1980. New York. $10.00

WOLFE, Thomas. *Look Homeward Angel.* 1971. 1st Russian ed. $25.00

WOLFE, Thomas. *Mauve Gloves & Madmen, Clutter & Vine.* 1976. Farrar. 1st ed. dj. VG $15.00

WOLFE, Thomas. *Radical Chic & Mau-Mauing the Flak Catchers.* 1971. Bantam. EX $2.50

WOLFE, Thomas. *Radical Chic & Mau-Mauing the Flak Catchers.* 1970. New York. Farrar. 1st ed. 153 pp. $10.00

WOLFE, Thomas. *The Face of the Nation.* 1939. Literary Guild.VG $15.00

WOLFE, Thomas. *The Hills Beyond.* 1941. Harper. 1st ed. $17.50

WOLFE, Thomas. *The Hound of Darkness.* 1986. Thomas Wolf Soc. Ltd. ed. $60.00

WOLFE, Thomas. *The Purple Decades.* 1982. Farrar. 1st ed. dj. VG $17.50

WOLFE, Thomas. *The Thomas Wolfe Reader.* 1962. Scribner. Book Club Ed. 690 pp. $7.50

WOLFE, Thomas. *The Web & the Rock.* 1939. Scribner. 1st ed. $17.50

WOLFE, Thomas. *You Can't Go Home Again.* 1940. New York. Harper. 1st ed. 743 pp. $35.00

WOLFE. *The Right Stuff.* 1979. $5.00

WOLFE. *Wolfe Portraiture & Genealogy.* 1959. Glasgow. Ills. Ltd 1st ed. 1/250. $45.00

WOLFE-AYLWARD, A.E. *The Pictorial Life of Wolfe.* 1927. Plymouth, Eng. Ills. 124 pp. $20.00

WOLFENSTEIN, M. & Leites, N. *Movies, a Psychological Study.* 1950. Free Press. $8.00

WOLFERT, Ira. *American Guerrilla in the Philippines.* 1945. New York. 301 pp. EX $5.00

WOLFF, H.D. *Rambling Recollections.* 1908. London. Macmillan. 2 vol set. G $30.00

WOLFF, Louis. *Electrocardiography: Fundamentals & Clinical Appl.*1950. Philadelphia. 1st ed. 187 pp. $45.00

WOLFF, W. *Island of Death.* 1973. Hacker. Ills. 228 pp. EX $12.50

WOLFSON, A. *Spinoza, Life of Reason.* 1932. New York. 347 pp. index. $15.00

WOLHUTER, H. *Memories of a Game Ranger.* 1984. Ills. 313 pp. dj. EX $25.00

WOLITZER, Hilma. *Hearts.* 1980. Farrar. 1st ed. dj. VG $12.50

WOLITZER, Hilma. *Hearts.* 1980. NY. Farrar. advance copy. wrappers. EX $15.00

WOLITZER, Hilma. *In the Palomar Arms.* 1983. NY. Farrar. advance copy. wrappers. EX $30.00

WOLLHEIM, Donald. *Mike Mars Flies the X-15.* 1961. Garden City. 1st ed. dj. EX $12.50

WOLLHEIM, Donald. *Terror in the Modern Vein.* 1955. Garden City. 1st ed. dj. VG $10.00

WOLLHEIM, Donald. *Terror in the Modern Vein.* 1955. New York. Hanover House. 1st ed. VG $20.00

WOLO. *Amanda.* 1941. 1st ed. sgn. VG $15.00

WOLOSHUK, Nicholas. *Edward Borein Drawings & Paintngs of Old West.* 1968. Flagstaff. Ltd. ed. 1/2000. sgn. $75.00

WOLSELEY, Viscount. *Story of a Soldier's Life.* 1903. New York. fld maps. 2 vol set. $65.00

WOLTERS, R.A. *Family Dog.* 1975. Dutton. Ills. 150 pp. dj. VG $6.00

WOLTERS, R.A. *Water Dog.* 1967. Dutton. Ills. 179 pp. dj. G $6.00

WOMAN'S HOME COMPANION. *Woman's Home Companion Cookbook.* 1944. New York. 950 pp. EX $7.00

WONG, Jade Snow. *Fifth Chinese Daughter.* 1950. Harper. Ills. Uhl. 1st ed. dj. VG $12.50

WONS, Tony. *Tony's Scrapbook.* 1940. $4.00

WOOD, Alan. *Study of J. Arthur Rank & British Films.* 1952. London. 1st ed. dj. VG $10.00

WOOD, Alexander Thomas. *Young Natural Philosopher 1773-1829.* 1954. Cambridge. 1st ed. dj. $10.00

WOOD, Alphonso. *New American Botanist & Florist.* 1889. $12.00

WOOD, Alphonso. *The American Botanist & Florist.* 1870. A.S. Barnes. 449 pp. G $5.50

WOOD, Charles R. *The Northern Pacific Main Street of the Northwest.*1968. dj. EX $6.00

WOOD, Clement. *Complete Rhyming Dictionary & Poet's Craft Book.* 1936. Garden City. 607 pp. $5.00

WOOD, Derek & Dempster, Derek. *Narrow Margin-Battle of Britain & Rise of Power.* New York. Ills. 1st Am. ed. 536 pp. $12.50

WOOD, Ernest. *An Englishman Defends Mother India.* 1929. Madras. Ills. EX $25.00

WOOD, F. *Turnpikes of New England.* 1919. Boston. 1st ed. photos. VG $40.00

WOOD, George. *The Dispensatory ot the U.S.A.* 1873. Philadelphia. 13th ed. G $30.00

WOOD, George. *The Gates Wide Open.* 1869. Boston. 354 pp. G $25.00

WOOD, Herbert Fairlie. *Famous Regiments, Kings Royal Rifle Corps.* 1967. London. Ills. 149 pp. dj. $15.00

WOOD, J.G. *Animate Creation.* 1898. New York. Ills. Prang. 6 vol set. VG $160.00

WOOD, J.G. *Common Objects of the Microscope.* London. (ca.1890) 12 color pls. $12.50

WOOD, J.G. *Uncivilized Races in All Countries of the World.* 1870. Hartford. 2 vol set. $24.00

WOOD, J.G. *Wood's Natural History.* 1882. Chicago. Ills. 229 pp. $52.50

WOOD, J.W. *Rose Petals.* 1926. Pasadena. pb. $12.00

WOOD, Kerry. *The Great Chief. Maskepeton: Warrior of the Crees.*1957. New York. Ills. John A. Hiam. 160 pp. $6.00

WOOD, Morrison. *Unusual Collection of Recipes with a Jug of Wine.* 1970. New York. Farrar. 379 pp. $7.50

WOOD, Mrs. Henry. *East Lynne.* 1862. Tauchnitz. 3 vol set. VG $65.00

WOOD, Mrs. Henry. *The Channings.* 1862. Tauchnitz. 1st ed. 2 vols in 1. VG $50.00

WOOD, Nancy. *When Buffalo Free the Mountains.* 1980. Doubleday. 1st ed. photos. $15.00

WOOD, R.E. *Life & Confessions of James Gilbert Jenkins.* 1864. Napa City, CA. 1st ed. 56 pp. wrappers. $225.00

WOOD, Robert. *Animal Analogues.* 1908. San Francisco. Ills. 28 pp. G $4.00

WOOD, Robert. *How to Tell the Birds from the Flowers.* 1907. San Francisco. Ills. 28 pp. G $4.00

WOOD, Roger. *Egypt in Color.* 1964. New York. $48.00

WOOD, W.B. & Edmonds. *Military History of the Civil War.* 1959. Jack Brussell. dj. $12.50

WOOD, William. *New England Prospect.* 1865. Boston. Ills. Ltd. ed. 131 pp. $75.00

WOOD, William. *Testaceologicus.* 1856. London. Willis & Sotheran. Ills. $235.00

WOOD & BACHE. *The Dispensatory of the United States.* 1839. Philadelphia. 4th ed. $30.00

WOOD. *The Pre-Raphaelites.* 1981. Viking. 1st ed. folio. dj. EX $55.00

WOOD. *The Seventh Regiment, a Record.* 1865. New York. VG $125.00

WOOD. *25 Years Painting in Arizona.* 1961. $28.00

WOODARD, Arthur. *Navajo Silversmithing.* 1938. Flagstaff. Ills. dj. VG $30.00

WOODBERRY, George E. *The Appreciation of Literature.* 1907. New York. 410 pp. VG $5.00

WOODBRIDGE, W.C. *School Atlas.* 1833. Hartford. Ills. $25.00

WOODBURN, James A. *Political Parties & Party Problems in the U.S.* 1924. New York. Putnam. ex-lib. 542 pp. VG $4.00

WOODBURY, A. *Maj. Gen. Ambrose E. Burnside & Ninth Army Corps.* 1867. Providence. 554 pp. VG $40.00

WOODBURY, George. *John Coffee's Legacy.* 1955. New York. 1st ed. dj. $10.00

WOODBURY, George. *John Coffee's Mills.* 1948. New York. Ills. 245 pp. dj. $10.00

WOODBURY, George. *The Story of a Stanley Steamer.* 1950. Norton. 1st ed. dj. $12.50

WOODFORD, A.F.A. *Kenning's Masonic Archaelogical Library.* 1878. London. 1st ed. 104 pp. VG $65.00

WOODFORD, M. *A Manual of Falconry.* 1966. London. Black. Ills. 194 pp. dj. VG $15.00

WOODGATE, W.B. *Rowing.* 1888. London. Badminton Library. Ills. maps. $22.50

WOODHAM-SMITH, Cecil. *Florence Nightingale, 1820-1910.* 1951. Ills. G $7.50

WOODHAM-SMITH, Cecil. *Queen Victoria.* 1972. New York. $15.00

WOODHOUSE, B. *Talking to Animals.* 1974. Stein Day. Ills. 208 pp. VG $6.00

WOODHOUSE. *Textbook of Naval Aeronautics.* 1917. New York. $50.00

WOODIN. *Home is the Desert.* 1964. 1st ed. dj. EX $15.00

WOODROFFE, Paul. *The Tempest.* 1908. Chapman & Hall. 20 color pls. EX $165.00

WOODRUFF, Hiram. *Trotting Horse of America, with Reminiscences.* 1869. New York. 1st ed. $25.00

WOODRUFF, Janette. *Indian Oasis.* 1939. Caldwell. Ills. 1st ed. $20.00

WOODS, D.R. *Successful Floriculture.* 1881. New Brighton. Ills. rubbed. G $40.00

WOODS, Henry. *God's Loaded Dice: Alaska 1897-1930.* 1948. Caxton. Ltd. 1st ed. 1/1000. sgn. $15.00

WOODS, John. *2 Years Residence on English Prairie of Illinois.* 1968. Chicago. Lakeside Classics. 242 pp. $15.00

WOODS, Junius. *The Negro in Chicago.* Chicago. wrappers. VG $25.00

WOODS, Margaret L. *Come Unto These Yellow Sands.* 1915. London/Toronto. Art Nouveau Ills. $75.00

WOODS, S. *Gunning for Upland Birds & Wildfowl.* 1976. dj. EX $12.50

WOODS, Sara. *Let's Choose Executors.* 1966. London. Collins. 1st ed. dj. VG $15.00

WOODS, Stuart. *Chiefs.* 1981. Norton. 1st ed. dj. VG $17.50

WOODS, Stuart. *Run Before the Wind.* 1983. Norton. proof copy. wrappers. VG $20.00

WOODSWORTH-ETTER, Mrs. M.B. *Signs & Wonders God Wrought in the Ministry.* 1916. Indianapolis. 584 pp. $10.00

WOODWARD, Alice. *Peter Pan & Racketty-Packetty House.* 1942. dj. G $7.50

WOODWARD, Kathleen. *Jipping Street, Childhood in a London Slum.* 1928. Harper. 1st ed. 150 pp. $75.00

WOODWARD, N.S. *Descendants of Richard Woodward, 1589-1982.* 1982. Baltimore. 280 pp. $15.00

WOODWARD, W.E. *Meet General Grant.* 1928. New York. 1st ed. 512 pp. $10.00

WOODWARD & CATES. *Encyclopedia of Chronology.* 1872. 1st ed. 1490 pp. $50.00

WOODWORTH, F.C. *A Budget of Willow Lane Stories.* 1854. New York. Scribner. 8 pls. $20.00

WOODWORTH, F.C. *The Diving Bell.* 1851. Boston. 8 pls. $25.00

WOODWORTH, F.C. *Uncle Reuben & His Budget of Stories.* 1856. New York. 7 pls. $25.00

WOODWORTH, Jim. *The Kodiak Bear Alaskan Adventure.* 1958. Stackpole. Ills. 1st ed. 204 pp. $40.00

WOOLF, Douglas. *Ya! & John-Juan.* 1971. New York. Harper. inscr. dj. EX $25.00

WOOLF, Virginia. *A Haunted House.* 1944. New York. Harcourt Brace. VG $5.00

WOOLF, Virginia. *A Writer's Diary.* 1954. Harcourt Brace. 1st ed. later issue. dj. EX $35.00

WOOLF, Virginia. *Diary of Virginia Woolf. Vol. III. 1925-1930.* 1980. New York. uncorrected proofs. wrappers. $40.00

WOOLF, Virginia. *Flush. A Biography.* 1933. New York. 1st ed. 185 pp. $15.00

WOOLF, Virginia. *Hours in a Library.* 1957. 1st ed. VG $25.00

WOOLF, Virginia. *Mrs. Dalloway.* 1925. Harcourt. 1st Am. ed. dj. VG $55.00

WOOLF, Virginia. *Orlando. A Biography.* 1928. Harcourt Brace. 1st ed. $40.00

WOOLF, Virginia. *The London Scene, Five Essays.* 1975. New York. Ltd. ed. 1/750. dj. EX $15.00

WOOLF, Virginia. *The Moment & Other Essays.* 1947. London. Hogarth. 1st ed. EX $45.00

WOOLF, Virginia. *The Second Common Reader.* 1932. New York. Harcourt. 295 pp. $7.50

WOOLF, Virginia. *The Waves.* 1931. Hogarth. 1st ed. dj. VG $90.00

WOOLF, Virginia. *The Years.* 1937. Harcourt. 9th ed. dj. G $5.00

WOOLF, Virginia. *The Years.* 1937. London. Hogarth. 1st ed. wrappers. $250.00

WOOLLCOTT, Alexander. *Woollcott's Second Reader.* 1937. New York. Viking. 1055 pp. VG $4.00

WOOLLCOTT. *Long, Long Ago.* 1943. 1st ed. $7.00

WOOLRICH, C. *A Young Man's Heart.* 1930. New York. Mason. 1st ed. VG $25.00

WOOLRICH, Cornell. *Angels of Darkness.* 1978. New York. Ltd ed. sgn. dj. slipcase. EX $90.00

WOOLRICH, Cornell. *Hotel Room.* 1958. New York. Random House. 1st ed. dj. EX $65.00

WOOLRICH, Cornell. *Nightwebs.* 1971. New York. Harper. 1st ed. dj. EX $25.00

WOOLRYCH, Humphry W. *Life of Judge Jeffreys.* 1827. London. rebound. $158.00

WOOSTER, A.S. *Quiltmaking.* 1972. New York. dj. EX $10.00

WOOTTEN, Bayard & Stoney, S. *Charleston, Azaleas, & Old Bricks.* 1937. Boston. Riverside Press. Ltd. ed. sgn. $100.00

WORCESTER, Donald. *Forked Tongues & Broken Treaties.* 1975. Caxton. dj. EX $12.00

WORCESTER. *Hunting the Lawless.* 1955. 1st ed. sgn. EX $20.00

WORCHESTER, G.R.G. *Junks & Sampans of Upper Yangtze.* 1940. Shanghai. Ills. pls. scarce. EX $300.00

WORDEN, Alfred. *Hello Earth: Greetings from Endeavor.* 1974. Los Angeles. Nash Pub. 1st ed. inscr. dj. $100.00

WORDEN, GREENE & RAMSAY. *The Monitor & the Merrimac.* 1912. Ills. G $15.00

WORDSWORTH, C. *A Church History to the Council of Nicaea.* 1881. New York. 481 pp. VG $75.00

WORDSWORTH, W. *Ode on the Intimations of Immortality.* Essex House. Ltd. ed. $125.00

WORELL, Eric. *Australian Snakes, Crocodiles, Tortoises, Lizards.* 1966. Sydney. Robertson. Ills. 64 pp. G $15.00

WORK, Paul. *The Tomato.* 1945. New York. Ills. G $10.00

WORTH, C.B. *A Naturalist in Trinidad.* 1967. Lippincott. Ills. 1st ed. 291 pp. dj. EX $25.00

WORTH, C.B. *Mosquito Safari, a Naturalist in Southern Africa.* 1971. Ills. 1st ed. dj. EX $20.00

WORTH, Patience & Curran, Mrs. *The Pot Upon the Wheel.* 1921. St. Louis. inscr. sgns. VG $35.00

WORTLEY, Lady E.S. *Travels in the United States.* 1851. New York. scarce $37.50

WORTLEY, R.S. *Letters from a Flying Officer.* 1982. Gloucester. Ills. 207 pp. wrappers. EX $6.00

WORTMAN, E. *Almost Too Late.* 1981. Random House. Ills. 1st ed. 211 pp. dj. EX $10.00

WORTMAN, H.R. *When Ships Were Ships & Not Tin Pots.* 1930. Ills. Francis Shields. G $10.00

WORTS, George. *Peter the Brazen.* 1919. Philadelphia. Lippincott. 1st ed. EX $40.00

WOUK, Herman. *Marjorie Morningstar.* 1955. Doubleday. 1st ed. dj. VG $30.00

WOUK, Herman. *The Winds of War.* 1971. Boston. Little, Brown. 1st ed. dj. VG $25.00

WOUK, Herman. *This is My God.* 1959. Doubleday. 1st ed. dj. VG $20.00

WOUK, Herman. *War & Remembrance.* 1978. Boston. Little, Brown. 1st ed. dj. EX $30.00

WOUK, Herman. *Youngblood Hawk.* 1962. Garden City. Doubleday. 1st ed. dj. EX $40.00

WPA ART PROGRAM. *1440 Early American Portrait Artists 1633-1860.* 1940. 306 pp. $48.00

WPA WRITER'S PROGRAM. *American Wild Life Illustrated.* 1940. New York. Ills. A. Baylitts. 749 pp. VG $13.50

WPA WRITER'S PROGRAM. *Arizona: State Guide.* 1940. Hastings House. Ills. 1st ed. VG $8.50

WPA WRITER'S PROGRAM. *California: Guide to the Golden State.* 1947. New York. Ills. 713 pp. fld map. $17.50

WPA WRITER'S PROGRAM. *Guide to Pennsylvania.* 1940. Oxford. 1st ed. 660 pp. dj. VG $25.00

WPA WRITER'S PROGRAM. *Houston, a History & Guide.* 1942. 1st ed. VG $40.00

WPA WRITER'S PROGRAM. *Michigan: Guide to the Wolverine State.* 1941. Oxford Press. Ills. ex-lib. 682 pp. VG $6.50

WPA WRITER'S PROGRAM. *Nevada: Guide to the Silver State.* 1957. Binfords & Mort. Ills. EX $10.00

WPA WRITER'S PROGRAM. *Oregon: End of the Trail.* 1940. Ills. 1st ed. dj. VG $20.00

WPA WRITER'S PROGRAM. *The Oregon Trail, Missouri River to Pacific Ocean.* 1939. New York. Ills. 1st ed. 244 pp. fld map. $22.50

WRAXALL. *The Backwoodsman.* 1866. Boston. $50.00

WREN, P.C. *Mysterious Way.* 1930. New York. 1st ed. dj. $125.00

WREN, Percival Christopher. *Beau Geste.* 1926. New York. 418 pp. $3.00

WRIGHT, A.M.R. *Old Ironsides.* 1926. Grosset & Dunlap. G $3.50

WRIGHT, Arthur. *Studies in Chinese Thought.* 1953. Am. Anthro. Assoc. 1st ed. $12.50

WRIGHT, Austen Tappan. *Islandia.* 1958. New York. VG $12.00

WRIGHT, Austin Tappan. *Islandia.* 1942. Farrar. 1st ed. $15.00

WRIGHT, B.S. *Ghost of North America, Story of Eastern Panther.* 1959. Vantage. Ills. 1st ed. 140 pp. dj. VG $15.00

WRIGHT, Basil. *The Long View.* 1974. Knopf. 1st Am. ed. VG $20.00

WRIGHT, Blanche Fisher. *The Real Mother Goose.* 1967. Ills. 128 pp. $4.50

WRIGHT, Caroll. *Industrial Evaluation of the United States.* 1902. New York. $8.00

WRIGHT, Dare. *Look at a Colt.* 1969. Ills. VG $10.00

WRIGHT, Dudley. *England's Masonic Pioneers.* 1925. London. Kenning & Son. 1st ed. 138 pp. $15.00

WRIGHT, Frank Lloyd. *An American Architecture.* 1955. New York. Horizon. 1st ed. dj. $45.00

WRIGHT, Frank Lloyd. *Frank Lloyd Wright, an Autobiography.* 1943. 1st Am. ed. VG $50.00

WRIGHT, Frank Lloyd. *The Japanese Print, an Interpretation.* 1967. New York. Horizon. reprint ed. boxed. $90.00

WRIGHT, Frank Lloyd. *The Living City.* 1958. 1st ed. dj. $65.00

WRIGHT, Frank Lloyd. *The Natural House.* 1954. New York. Horizon. 1st ed. dj. VG $55.00

WRIGHT, G. Frederick. *Story of My Life & Work.* 1916. Oberlin, OH. 459 pp. $15.00

WRIGHT, Harold Bell. *A Son of His Father.* 1925. New York. Appleton. VG $15.00

WRIGHT, Harold Bell. *Helen of the Old House.* 1921. New York. 372 pp. $5.00

WRIGHT, Harold Bell. *Ma Cinderella.* 1932. Harper. 1st ed. VG $60.00

WRIGHT, Harold Bell. *That Printer of Udell's.* 1911. New York. 346 pp. $3.50

WRIGHT, Harold Bell. *The Calling of Dan Mathews.* 1909. New York. 364 pp. $3.50

WRIGHT, Harold Bell. *The Eyes of the World.* 1914. New York. Ills. T.G. Cootes. 464 pp. $5.00

WRIGHT, Harold Bell. *The Eyes of the World.* 1914. Chicago. Book Supply. Ills. 1st ed. $4.50

WRIGHT, Harold Bell. *The Mine with the Iron Door.* 1923. Appleton. 1st ed. $12.00

WRIGHT, Harold Bell. *The Re-Creation of Brian Kent.* 1919. Book Supply. Ills. J. Allen St.John. $6.00

WRIGHT, Harold Bell. *The Shepherd of the Hills.* 1907. A.L. Burt. Ills. F. Graham Cootes. $8.00

WRIGHT, Harold Bell. *Their Yesterdays.* 1912. Chicago. Ills. Cootes. 1st ed. 311 pp. $5.00

WRIGHT, Harold Bell. *When a Man's a Man.* 1916. Book Supply. Ills. $6.00

WRIGHT, Helen S. *Great White North: Story of Polar Exploration.* 1910. New York. Ills. 1st ed. VG $12.00

WRIGHT, Jack. *The Scout Patrol Boys in the Frozen South.* 1933. New York. World. 110 pp. $3.00

WRIGHT, James Abell. *Parade of the Animals or Capers of Cattail Camp.* 1934. Ills. 1st ed. VG $27.50

WRIGHT, James. *Saint Judas.* 1959. Middletown. 1st ed. dj. VG $45.00

WRIGHT, Louis & Macleod, J. *The First Americans in North Africa.* 1945. Princeton. 1st ed. $12.50

WRIGHT, M.D. *Most Portable Position.* 1972. Ills. dj. EX $15.00

WRIGHT, Mabel O. *Four Footed Americans.* 1898. Macmillan. Ills. G $6.50

WRIGHT, Mabel Osgood. *My New York.* 1930. New York. Macmillan. Ills. 2nd ed. $10.00

WRIGHT, Marcus. *Official & Illustrated War Record.* 1898. Washington. $50.00

WRIGHT, Milton. *Inventions, Patents, & Trademarks.* 1933. New York. McGraw Hill. VG $15.00

WRIGHT, Mrs. Frank Lloyd. *Roots of Life.* 1963. New York. Horizon. 1st ed. dj. VG $27.50

WRIGHT, Richard B. *Final Things.* 1980. Dutton. 1st ed. dj. VG $10.00

WRIGHT, Richard B. *In the Middle of a Life.* 1973. Farrar. 1st ed. dj. VG $20.00

WRIGHT, Richard B. *The Weekend Man.* 1971. Farrar. 1st Am. ed. dj. VG $25.00

WRIGHT, Richard. *Black Boy.* 1945. New York. Harper. 228 pp. dj. $5.50

WRIGHT, Richard. *Pagan Spain.* 1957. New York. Harper. 1st ed. dj. $45.00

WRIGHT, Richard. *12 Million Black Voices.* 1941. Viking. Ills. 1st ed. dj. VG $45.00

WRIGHT, Richardson. *Another Gardener's Bed Book.* 1933. Lippincott. 1st ed. $5.00

WRIGHT, Richardson. *Flower Prints & Their Makers.* 1948. New York. Ills. $75.00

WRIGHT, Richardson. *Gardener's Day Book.* 1938. Lippincott. dj. VG $5.00

WRIGHT, Richardson. *Hawkers & Walkers in Early America.* 1927. Philadelphia. Ills. 1st ed. VG $10.00

WRIGHT, Richardson. *Truly Rural.* 1935. Lippincott. 5 color Ills. dj. VG $5.00

WRIGHT, S. Fowler. *The Hanging of Constance Hillier.* 1932. New York. Macmillan. 1st ed. dj. VG $10.00

WRIGHT, S. Fowler. *The Throne of Saturn.* 1949. Sauk City. Arkham House. VG $50.00

WRIGHT, T. *The Big Nail, Story of the Cook-Peary Feud.* 1970. Day. Ills. 368 pp. dj. EX $22.50

WRIGHT, T.M. *Strange Seed.* 1978. Everest House. 1st ed. dj. EX $7.50

WRIGHT, Thomas. *Caricature History of the Georges I, II, & III.* 1868. London. Ills. 689 pp. $25.00

WRIGHT, Thomas. *History of Caricature & Grotesque in Art.* 1865. London. Ills. EX $30.00

WRIGHT, Thomas. *History of Scotland from the Earliest Period.* Glasgow. Ills. 3 vol set. rebound. VG $145.00

WRIGHT, W.A. *The Complete Works of Shakespeare.* 1936. New York. 40 Ills. VG $10.00

WRIGHT, W.H. *The Grizzly Bear, Narrative of Hunter-Naturalist.* 1977. NB U. Press. reprint. Ills. 274 pp. EX $20.00

WRIGHT, William. *Heiress.* 1978. Washington. 1st ed. dj. VG $25.00

WRIGHT & JAGER. *Ethiopia Illuminated.* 1961. Paris. 32 color pls. folio. $65.00

WRIGHT. *Kachinas: A Hopi Artist's Documentary.* 1978. Northland. $25.00

WRIGHTSON, J. *Sheep Breeds & Management.* 1913. $10.00

WRONG, G.M. *A Canadian Manor & Its Seigneurs.* 1908. Toronto. Ills. 1st ed. VG $18.00

WULFF, Lee. *Lee Wulff's Handbook of Fresh-Water Fishing.* 1939. New York. Ills. VG $20.00

WULFF, Lee. *Silver Wedding.* 1948. London. $7.50

WULSIN, Frederick. *The Prehistoric Archaeology of N.W. Africa.* 1941. Peabody Museum. 1st ed. stiff wrappers. $12.50

WUORIO, Eva-Lis. *The Woman with the Portugese Basket.* 1964. 1st ed. ex-lib. $5.00

WURZER, Karl. *100 Styles of French Cooking.* 1981. New York. 1st printing. dj. VG $7.50

WYATT, Wyatt. *Catching Fire.* 1977. Random House. 1st Am. ed. dj. VG $30.00

WYATT & HORTON-SMITH. *Passing of Great Fleet. History of British Navy.* 1909. London. scarce. G $50.00

WYCOFF, Marjorie. *Christmas Carols.* 1946. New York. Ills. dj. VG $10.00

WYDEN, Peter & Barbara. *How the Doctors Diet.* 1968. New York. Trident. 258 pp. dj. $5.00

WYETH, Andrew. *Brandywine.* 1941. 1st ed. dj. EX $40.00

WYETH, Andrew. *Wyeth at Kuerners.* 1976. 1st ed. dj. boxed. EX $60.00

WYETH, John. *The Devil Forrest.* 1959. Harper. Ills. 1st ed. 614 pp. dj. VG $45.00

WYETH, N.C. *Men of Concord.* 1936. Boston. Houghton Mifflin. 1st ed. dj. $60.00

WYETH, N.C. *Mysterious Island.* 1951. New York. Scribner. Ills. Verne. VG $25.00

WYETH, N.C. *The Black Arrow.* 1916. New York. Ills. EX $60.00

WYETH, N.C. *The Bounty Trilogy.* 1951. Little, Brown. 8 pls. EX $15.00

WYETH, N.C. *The Boy's King Arthur.* 1952. Scribner. 14 color pls. EX $20.00

WYETH, N.C. *The Odyssey.* 1929. Houghton Mifflin. 16 pls. EX $95.00

WYETH, N.C. *The Scottish Chiefs.* 1937. Scribner. $25.00

WYETH, N.C. *The Scottish Chiefs.* 1934. Scribner. 9 color pls. VG $30.00

WYETH, N.C. *The White Company.* 1922. New York. Cosmopolitan. Ills. EX $60.00

WYETH, N.C. *The Yearling.* 1939. New York. Pulitzer ed. VG $22.50

WYETH, N.C. *The Yearling.* 1940. New York. 14 color pls. VG $15.00

WYETH, N.C. *Treasure Island.* 1947. Scribner. 9 color pls. VG $17.00

WYETH, W.C. *Westward Ho!* 1947. New York. Scribner. Ills. dj. VG $40.00

WYETH. *Pike County Ballads.* 1912. Houghton Mifflin. 12 pls. EX $35.00

WYETH. *The Long Roll.* 1911. Houghton Mifflin. 1st ed. VG $15.00

WYKES, A. *Snake Man, Story of C.J.P. Ionides.* 1960. London. Hamilton. Ills. 221 pp. EX $25.00

WYKES. *Complete Illustrated Guide to Gambling.* 1964. Doubleday. EX $20.00

WYLIE, Elinor. *The Orphan Angel.* 1926. New York. Knopf. Ltd. ed. sgn. boxed. EX $175.00

WYLIE, Max. *Clear Channels: T.V. & the American People.* 1955. 1st ed. dj. VG $10.00

WYLIE, Philip. *The Disappearance.* 1951. New York. Rinehart. advance copy. dj. VG $35.00

WYLIE, Philip. *The End of the Dream.* 1972. Garden City. 1st ed. dj. VG $10.00

WYLIE, W.W. *Yellowstone National Park; Great Am. Wonderland.* 1882. Kansas City. Ills. ex-lib. 99 pp. EX $35.00

WYLIE. *Generation of Vipers.* 1942. Rinehart. $5.50

WYLLIE, I. *The Cuckoo.* 1981. Universe. Ills. 176 pp. dj. EX $15.00

WYLLIE, R.E. *Orders, Decorations, & Insignia.* 1921. New York. Ills. ex-lib. 269 pp. index. $17.50

WYMAN, W.D. *Wild Horse of the West.* 1946. Caxton. dj. EX $15.00

WYMER, Norman. *English Town Crafts.* 1949. London. Ills. 1st ed. dj. VG $17.50

WYNDHAM, John. *Consider Her Ways.* 1961. London. Joseph. 1st ed. dj. VG $50.00

WYNDHAM, John. *The Day of the Triffids.* 1951. Garden City. 1st ed. dj. EX $30.00

WYNDHAM, John. *The Day of the Triffids.* 1951. London. 1st Eng. ed. dj. EX $125.00

WYNDHAM, John. *The Kraken Wakes.* 1953. London. 1st ed. dj. VG $45.00

WYNDHAM, John. *Web.* 1979. London. Joseph. 1st ed. dj. VG $15.00

WYNN, Marcia Rittenhouse. *Story Early Randsbury/Mojave Desert Mining Camp.* 1949. Carson City. Ills. Samelson. 1st ed. VG $15.00

WYSNER, Glora M. *The Kabyle People.* 1945. private print. sgn. 223 pp. VG $12.50

WYSOR, W.G. *The Southern States Story. First 35 Years.* 1959. Ills. 231 pp. wrappers. $6.00

WYSS, Johann R. *The Swiss Family Robinson.* Grosset & Dunlap. no date. VG $5.50

WYTHE, Major George. *Inter-Allied Games, Paris 22nd June to 6th July.* Paris. (ca.1920) Ills. 510 pp. $22.50

Y

YABLONSKY. *George Raft.* 1974. dj. VG $7.50

YAGGY & HAINES. *Museum of Antiquity.* 1881. Western Pub. House. Ills. EX $35.00

YAKHONTOFF, Victor A. *Russia & the Soviet Union in the Far East.* 1931. New York. Coward McCann. 454 pp. $5.00

YALLOP. *In God's Name.* 1984. 1st ed. dj. VG $15.00

YAMADA, Chisaburoh. *Dialogue in Art, Japan & the West.* 1976. Kodansha. Ills. 1st ed. 334 pp. EX $95.00

YANEKIAN, Adrienne. *The Telephone Pioneers of America 1911-1961.* 1961. New York. Ills. 367 pp. $10.00

YANTIS, N.S. *Genealogical Books in Print. Vol. I.* 1975. Springfield. 311 pp. wrappers. $5.00

YANTIS, N.S. *Genealogical Books in Print. Vol. II.* 1975. Springfield. 410 pp. wrappers. $7.50

YANTIS, N.S. *Genealogical Books in Print. Vol. III.* 1981. Springfield. 1000 pp. wrappers. $10.00

YARBRO, Chelsea. *False Dawn.* 1978. New York. Doubleday. 1st ed. dj. EX $12.50

YARD, Robert S. *The National Parks Portfolio.* 1921. Nat. Park Ser. Ills. 266 pp. G $5.00

YARDLEY, Herbert O. *The American Black Chamber.* 1931. Indianapolis. Ills. 375 pp. VG $15.00

YARDLEY, Herbert O. *The Chinese Black Chamber.* 1983. Boston. dj. EX $7.50

YARDLEY, Jonathan. *Ring, a Biography of Ring Lardner.* 1977. Random House. New York. 1st ed. 415 pp. $5.00

YAROSLAVA. *Tusya & the Pot of Gold.* 1971. Atheneum. 1st ed. VG $4.00

YASHIRODA, Kan. *Bonsai, Japanese Miniature Trees.* 1966. London. dj. $20.00

YATES, Elizabeth. *Piskey Folk, Cornish Legends of Enys Tregarthen.* 1940. Day Pub. Ills. 1st ed. VG $20.00

YATES, Frances A. *The Art of Memory.* 1966. Chicago. 1st ed. 400 pp. EX $12.50

YATES, Helen. *Bali, Enchanted Isle.* 1934. London. 188 pp. VG $8.00

YATES, R.F. & M.W. *Early American Crafts & Hobbies.* 1954. dj. EX $7.50

YATES, Raymond. *How to Restore China, Bric-A-Brac, & Sm. Antiques.* 1953. dj. VG $5.00

YATES, Richard. *Liars in Love.* Delacorte. proof copy. wrappers. EX $35.00

YATES, Richard. *Revolutionary Road.* 1961. Boston. Little, Brown. 1st ed. dj. EX $75.00

YATES, Richard. *Young Hearts Crying.* 1984. New York. Delacorte. 1st ed. dj. EX $15.00

YAVA. *Big Falling Snow.* 1978. 1st ed. dj. EX $15.00

YAVNO, Max. *The Los Angeles Book.* 1950. VG $25.00

YAVNO, Max. *The San Francisco Book.* 1948. dj. VG $32.50

YBARRA, T.R. *Young Man of Caracas.* 1914. New York. Washburn. 324 pp. $37.50

YEAGER, B. *B. Yeager's ABC of Figure Photography.* 1964. New York. wrappers. EX $7.50

YEARLY MEETING OF FRIENDS. *A Gateway to Good Will.* 1924. Philadelphia. 79 pp. wrappers. $5.00

YEATS, Jack B. *A Little Book of Bookplates.* 1979. County Doublin. Ills. 1st ed. 1/350. VG $40.00

YEATS, Jack B. *Collected Plays of Jack B. Yeats.* 1971. New York. $15.00

YEATS, Jack B. *Sligo.* 1930. London. 1st ed. dj. VG $120.00

YEATS, William Butler. *Irish Folk Tales.* 1973. Ltd. Ed. Club. Ills/sgn R. Friers. boxed. VG $35.00

YEATS, William Butler. *A Full Moon in March.* 1935. London. Macmillan. 1st ed. dj. VG $125.00

YEATS, William Butler. *Dramatis Personae.* 1936. New York. 1st Am. ed. dj. VG $22.50

YEATS, William Butler. *Fairy & Folk Tales of Irish Peasantry.* 1888. London. 1st ed. $200.00

YEATS, William Butler. *Four Plays for Dancers.* Macmillan. Ills. Dulac. 138 pp. $30.00

YEATS, William Butler. *Reveries over Childhood & Youth.* 1917. reprint. EX $37.50

YEATS, William Butler. *Sophocles' King Oedipus.* 1928. New York. 1st Am. ed. VG $17.50

YEATS, William Butler. *The Collected Plays of Yeats.* 1953. New York. Macmillan. 446 pp. $5.00

YEATS, William Butler. *The Green Helmet & Other Poems.* 1912. New York. Macmillan. VG $50.00

YEATS, William Butler. *The Green Helmet & Other Poems.* 1910. Cuala Press. Ltd. ed. 1/400. VG $150.00

YEATS, William Butler. *The Secret Rose.* 1897. Dodd Mead. Ills. 1st Eng. ed. VG $30.00

YEATS, William Butler. *The Senate Speeches of W.B. Yeats.* 1960. IN. U. 1st ed. dj. $10.00

YEATS, William Butler. *The Shadowy Waters.* 1900. London. 1st ed. sgn. G $45.00

YEATS, William Butler. *The Variorum Edition of Poems.* 1957. New York. sgn. slipcase. EX $275.00

YEATS, William Butler. *Wheels & Butterflies.* 1934. London. Ltd. 1st ed. 1/3000. VG $25.00

YEATS, William Butler. *Yeats' Letters to Katharine Tynan.* 1953. Macmillan. 1st ed. dj. $12.50

YEAZELL, R.B. *Death & Letters.* 1981. Berkeley. 1st ed. EX $15.00

YEE, Chiang. *The Silent Traveler in Dublin.* 1954. London. 12 color pls. dj. VG $12.50

YEE, Chiang. *The Silent Traveler in London.* 1939. London. dj. EX $15.00

YEE, Chiang. *The Silent Traveler in Oxford.* 1945. London. 2nd ed. 13 color pls. dj. VG $17.50

YEE, Chiang. *The Silent Traveler in San Francisco.* 1964. Norton. 1st ed. VG $17.50

YEE, Chiang. *The Silent Traveler in the Yorkshire Dales.* 1948. 1st Am. ed. 8 color pls. dj. $20.00

YEPSEN, R.B. *Organic Plant Protection.* 1977. Rodale. Ills. 688 pp. dj. EX $15.00

YERBY, Frank. *A Woman Called Fancy.* 1951. New York. Dial Press. 309 pp. VG $3.00

YERBY, Frank. *Fairoaks.* 1957. New York. Dial Press. 1st ed. dj. VG $25.00

YERBY, Frank. *Floodtide.* 1950. New York. Dial Press. 342 pp. VG $3.00

YERBY, Frank. *Gillian.* 1960. Dial Press. 1st ed. dj. VG $25.00

YERBY, Frank. *Pride's Castle.* 1949. New York. Dial Press. 312 pp. $3.00

YERBY, Frank. *The Devil's Laughter.* 1953. New York. Dial Press. 318 pp. dj. $3.50

YERBY, Frank. *The Golden Hawk.* 1948. New York. Dial Press. 312 pp. dj. $3.50

YERBY, Frank. *The Old God's Laugh.* 1964. New York. Dial Press. 1st ed. dj. VG $25.00

YERBY, Frank. *The Saracen Blade.* 1952. New York. Dial Press. $3.00

YERBY, Frank. *The Vixens.* 1947. New York. Dial Press. 347 pp. $3.00

YERKES, Robert. *The Dancing Mouse, a Study in Animal Behavior.* 1907. Macmillan. 1st ed. $35.00

YERKIES, Robert. *Chimpanzees. A Laboratory Colony.* 1943. Yale. 1st ed. dj. $25.00

YERKIES, Robert. *The Great Apes.* 1929. Yale. 1st ed. VG $45.00

YEVTUSHENKO, Yevgeny. *Yevtushenko Poems.* 1966. Dutton. trans. 1st Am. ed. dj. VG $20.00

YIP, Wai-Lim. *Ezra Pound's Cathay.* 1969. Princeton. dj. $10.00

YLLA. *Animals in India.* Macmillan. (ca.1950) Ills. 131 pp. EX $15.00

YMCA *Service with Fighting Men.* 1922. New York. Assoc. Press. Ills. 1300 pp. $12.00

YOE, S. *The Burman, His Life & Notions.* 1910. London. 609 pp. index. $22.50

YOLEN, Jane. *The Dream Weaver.* 1979. Collins. Ills. Hague. 1st ed. dj. VG $20.00

YONGE, Charlotte M. *Young Folk's History of Germany.* 1878. Boston. Ills. 1st ed. $15.00

YONGE, Charlotte. *The Little Duke.* 1927. New York. Ills. Marguerite De Angeli. VG $30.00

YONGE, Charlotte. *The Little Duke.* 1932. Saalfield. Ills. Lawson. dj. G $4.50

YOORS, Jan. *The Gypsies.* 1967. New York. 1st ed. pb. VG $5.00

YORKE, M. *Eric Gill, Man of Flesh & Spirit.* 1982. New York. dj. EX $22.50

YORKE. *The Seduction.* 1960. 1st ed. dj. VG $7.50

YOSHIDA, Kogoru. *Tanrokubon, Rare Books of Seventeenth Cent. Japan.* 1984. Kodansha. Ills. 228 pp. scarce. EX $65.00

YOSHIDA, Toshi & Yuki, Rei. *Japanese Print Making: Handbook of Techniques.* 1966. Tuttle. Ills. out of print. EX $225.00

YOSHIDA, Toshi. *Varieties of Japanese Print with 20 Hand Examples.* 1967. Tokyo. rare. $375.00

YOSHIKAWA, I. *Major Themes in Japanese Art.* 1976. 1st Eng. ed. Ills. 168 pp. EX $40.00

YOST, Fielding. *Football for Player & Spectator.* 1905. Ann Arbor. 1st ed. dj. G $75.00

YOST, Karl & Renner, Frederic. *Bibliography Published Works of Charles Russell.* 1971. U. of NB Press. 1st ed. dj. VG $40.00

YOUMANS, Edward L. *The Handbook of Household Science.* 1858. New York. 470 pp. $17.50

YOUMANS, Eleanor. *Skitter Cat & Major.* 1927. Indianapolis. Ills. Ruth Bennett. $15.00

YOUND, A.W. *History of Wayne Co. Indiana.* 1872. Cincinnati. Ills. VG $80.00

YOUNG, Ann Eliza. *Wife No. 19: Life in Bondage.* 1875. Hartford, CT. Ills. 1st ed. 605 pp. $70.00

YOUNG, Art. *Art Young, His Life & Times.* 1939. 1st ed. dj. VG $22.50

YOUNG, Arthur. *Troy & Her Legend.* 1948. U. of Pittsburgh. 1st ed. dj. $3.50

YOUNG, Bob & Jan. *Empire Builder Sam Brannan.* 1967. New York. dj. $37.50

YOUNG, Chic. *Blondie & Dagwood in Footlight Folly.* 1947. Dell. 1st ed. pb. VG $22.50

YOUNG, Collier. *The Todd Dossier.* 1969. Delacorte. 1st ed. 187 pp. $27.50

YOUNG, Desmond. *Rommel the Desert Fox.* 1950. New York. Harper. Ills. 264 pp. $5.00

YOUNG, Edgerton R. *By Canoe & Dog Train.* 1891. $22.00

YOUNG, Edward. *Night Thoughts on Life, Death, & Immortality.* 1816. Philadelphia. G $25.00

YOUNG, Egerton R. *My Dogs in the Northland.* 1902. New York. Ills. 1st ed. 285 pp. $17.50

YOUNG, Gordon R. *Savages.* 1921. New York. Doubleday. 1st ed. VG $25.00

YOUNG, James C. *Marse Robert: Knight of the Confederacy.* 1929. New York. VG $15.00

YOUNG, John D. *Young & the Colorado Gold Rush.* 1969. Chicago. $8.50

YOUNG, John H. *Our Deportment; or, Manners, Conduct & Dress.* 1882. Detroit, MI. 424 pp. $3.50

YOUNG, John L. *Books from the Manuscript to the Bookseller.* 1929. London. Pitman. Ills. 1st ed. dj. VG $25.00

YOUNG, John P. *Journalism in California.* 1915. San Francisco. $20.00

YOUNG, John Sacret. *The Weather Tomorrow.* 1981. New York. Random House. 1st ed. dj. VG $40.00

YOUNG, Ken. *The Bed Post.* 1962. London. 1st ed. VG $8.50

YOUNG, Kimball. *Isn't One Wife Enough?* 1954. Holt. Ills. 1st ed. 476 pp. index. $22.50

YOUNG, L.H. *Remarkable Events in the World's History.* no date. VG $14.00

YOUNG, Marguerite. *Angel in the Forest.* London. Peter Owen. 331 pp. dj. G $5.00

YOUNG, Marguerite. *Miss MacIntosh, My Darling.* 1965. New York. 1st ed. dj. VG $20.00

YOUNG, Paul H. *Making & Using the Dry Fly.* 1934. $80.00

YOUNG, Robert. *The Navajo Yearbook.* 1961. Windowrock. Ills. 609 pp. wrappers. VG $12.50

YOUNG, Robert. *The Worlds of Robert F. Young.* 1965. New York. Simon & Schuster. dj. EX $30.00

YOUNG, Roland. *Not for Children: Pictures & Verse.* 1930. New York. Doubleday. 1st ed. VG $15.00

YOUNG, Rosa. *The Story of Rosa Young as Told by Herself.* 1930. St. Louis. Ills. 2nd ed. 148 pp. $15.00

YOUNG, S. Hall. *Adventures in Alaska.* 1919. Revell. Ills. 181 pp. VG $25.00

YOUNG, S. Hall. *Alaska Days with John Muir.* 1915. New York. 226 pp. dj. VG $25.00

YOUNG, S.P. & Goldman, E.A. *The Wolves of North America.* 1944. Ills. 1st ed. 636 pp. VG $45.00

YOUNG, S.P. & Jackson, H.H.T. *The Clever Coyote.* 1978. NB U. Press. Ills. 411 pp. EX $10.00

YOUNG, Scott. *If You Can't Beat 'Em in the Alley.* 1981. Toronto. Ills. 290 pp. dj. EX $12.50

YOUNG, Staley P. & Goldman, E. *The Puma, Mysterious American Cat.* 1946. Washington. Ills. 1st ed. 358 pp. $27.50

YOUNG, Stanley. *The Wolf in North American History.* 1946. Caxton. 1st ed. dj. $12.50

YOUNG, Stark. *Theatre Practice.* 1926. Ills. 208 pp. $10.00

YOUNG, Thomas Daniel. *Conversations with Malcolm Cowley.* 1986. U. Miss. Press. 1st ed. dj. VG $20.00

YOUNG, Vernon. *Cinema Borealis, Ingmar Bergman & Swedish Ethos.* 1971. New York. Ills. 1st ed. dj. EX $10.00

YOUNG, William. *Shark Shark, Thirty Year Odyssey of Shark Hunter.* 1934. New York. Ills. 287 pp. sgn. $20.00

YOUNG & QUINN. *Foundation For Living; Story of C.S. Mott & Flint.* 1963. New York. 1st ed. sgn Mott. dj. VG $8.00

YOUNG FOLKS LIBRARY. *Famous Battles by Land & Sea.* 1902. Boston. Ills. 390 pp. $5.50

YOUNG. *Columbus & New World of His Discovery.* 1891. 1st English ed. 2 vol set. $25.00

YOUNG. *Guns of the Arrowhead.* Popular. pb. $3.00

YOUNG. *Two Gun Man.* Popular. pb. $3.00

YOUNGER. *Australia & the Australians.* 1970. Adelaide. dj. VG $10.00

YOUNGHUSBAND. *Light of Experience.* 1927. New York. 1st ed. VG $20.00

YOUNGSON. *The Making of Classical Edinburgh, 1750-1840.* 1966. Edinburgh U. Press. $12.00

YOUNT, John. *Hardcastle.* 1980. Marek. 1st ed. dj. VG $15.00

YOUNT, John. *The Trapper's Last Shot.* 1973. Random House. 1st ed. dj. VG $30.00

YOUNT, John. *Wolf at the Door.* 1967. Random House. review copy. dj. VG $50.00

YOUSSOUPOFF, Prince Felix. *Rasputin.* 1927. Dial Press. Ills. 246 pp. VG $30.00

YRIARTE, C. *Florence.* 1881. Paris. Ills. folio. $45.00

ZABEL, M.D. *In the Cage*. 1958. London. Hart Davies. dj. EX $20.00

ZABEL, M.D. *The Art of Travel*. 1958. New York. Doubleday. 1st ed. dj. EX $25.00

ZABRISKIE, George. *The Bon Vivant Companion*. 1948. Grady Press. Ltd. ed. 1/1200. VG $22.50

ZACHAROFF, L. *The Voice of Fighting Russia*. 1942. Ills. VG $20.00

ZAGAT, Arthur Leo. *Seven Out of Time*. 1949. Fantasy Press. Ills. Hannes Bok. 1st Am. ed. $20.00

ZAHL, Paul. *Coro Coro, the World of the Scarlet Ibis*. 1954. Bobbs Merrill. 1st ed. dj. $7.50

ZAHL, Paul. *To the Lost World*. 1939. New York. Ills. 1st ed. 268 pp. $10.00

ZARCHIN, M.M. *Jews in the Province of Posen*. 1939. Philadelphia. 115 pp. $17.50

ZECKENDORF. *Zeckendorf*. 1970. Holt. 1st ed. dj. VG $35.00

ZEIGLER, D.L. *The Okanogan Mule Deer*. 1978. Washington. Ills. 106 pp. $7.00

ZEITLIN, Ida. *Skazki, Tales & Legends of Old Russia*. 1926. Doran. Ills. 24 pls. 335 pp. $60.00

ZELAZNY, Dick & Roger. *Deus Irae*. 1976. 1st ed. dj. EX $25.00

ZELAZNY, Roger. *The Hand of Oberon*. 1976. Garden City. Doubleday. 1st ed. dj. EX $40.00

ZELAZNY. *Eye of Cat*. 1982. Ltd ed. 1/333. sgn. EX $65.00

ZELAZNY. *For Breath I Tarry*. 1980. Ills. Fabian. Ltd. ed. 1/200. sgn. EX $100.00

ZELAZNY. *Madwand*. 1981. Phantasia. Ltd. ed. 1/750. sgn. boxed. EX $60.00

ZELAZNY. *To Spin is Miracle Cat*. 1981. Ltd. ed. 1/200. sgn. boxed. EX $50.00

ZELAZNY. *Trumps of Doom*. 1985. Ltd. ed. 1/500. sgn. boxed. $40.00

ZEMPEL & VERKLER. *First Editions: Guide to Identification*. 1985. Peoria. Spoon River Press. dj. $20.00

ZERN, Ed. *To Hell with Fishing*. 1945. New York. Ills. H.T. Webster. 1st ed. VG $10.00

ZERVOS. *Les Oevvres de Greco en Espagne*. 1939. Paris. Cahiers D'Art. $30.00

ZETTERHOLM, Tore. *China: Dream of Man?* 1977. Ills. 237 pp. dj. EX $4.00

ZEVI, Bruno. *Architecture as Space*. 1957. New York. Horizon. 1st ed. dj. $15.00

ZEWEN, Wilson, & Drege. *The Great Wall*. 1981. Ills. 191 pp. dj. EX $10.00

ZHUKOV, Georgi K. *Marshal Zhukov's Greatest Battles*. 1969. 1st ed. 304 pp. dj. $50.00

ZIEGFELD, A.H. *Deutschland-das Gewissen Europas*. 1942. Berlin. Ills. 100 pp. wrappers. $25.00

ZIELEZINSKI, George. *24 Zeichnungen*. 1948. Munich. 24 black/white lithos. sgn. $40.00

ZIEMER, G. *Education of Death*. 1943. New York. 6th ed. G $17.50

ZIEMKE, Earl F. *German Northern Theater of Operations, 1940-1945*. 1959. Washington. Ills. 342 pp. 10 fld maps. G $37.50

ZIEMKE, Earl F. *Stalingrad to Berlin. German Defeat in the East*. 1968. Ills. G $27.50

ZIFF, Paul. *J.M. Hanson*. 1962. Ithaca, NY. Cornell U. Press. 1st ed. pls. $10.00

ZIFF, William B. *The Gentlemen Talk of Peace*. 1944. New York. Macmillan. 530 pp. dj. $3.50

ZIGROSSER, Carl. *Prints*. 1962. New York. Ills. 269 pp. dj. VG $35.00

ZILCZER. *Noble Buyer John Quinn: Patron of the Avant Garde*. 1978. Smithsonian Institute Press. $10.00

ZIMMER, H. *Myth & Symbols in Indian Art & Civilization*. 1946. Pantheon. Ills. 248 pp. dj. EX $10.00

ZIMMER, Norma. *Norma*. 1976. Wheaton, IL. photos. 368 pp. dj. $5.00

ZIMMERMAN & KAUFMAN. *Photographing Sports*. 1975. 1st printing. folio. wrappers. $10.00

ZIMMERMANN, Karl R. *A Decade of Delaware & Hudson*. 1978. $4.00

ZINCHE, E.B. *Egypt of the Pharoahs & the Kedive*. 1873. London. 2nd ed. map. $17.50

ZINMAN. *Saturday Afternoon at the Bijou*. 1973. Castle Books. Ills. 511 pp. EX $4.50

ZINSSER, H. *Rats, Lice, & History*. 1935. Blue Ribbon. 301 pp. VG $6.00

ZIPPIN. *Uses of Infinity*. 1962. $10.00

ZISLIN. *L'Album Zizlin. Dessins de Guerre*. 1916. Paris. 64 pls. wrappers. $22.50

ZOLA, Emile. *Best Known Works*. 1941. Book League of Am. $3.00

ZOLA, Emile. *Nana*. 1931. New York. 517 pp. VG $3.00

ZOLLNER, Johann C.F. *Transcendental Physics*. 1880. London. 1st ed. $125.00

ZOLOTOW, Charlotte. *Mr. Rabbit & the Lovely Present*. 1968. New York. Scolastic Books. Ills. 1st ed. $8.00

ZOLOTOW, Maurice. *It Takes All Kinds*. 1952. New York. 1st ed. dj. VG $8.50

ZORACH, William. *Zorach Explains Sculpture*. 1947. Ills. dj. VG $20.00

ZORBAUGH, Harvey Warren. *The Gold Coast & Slum, Sociological Study*. 1957. Chicago. Ills. 9th impression. 287 pp. $12.50

ZOUCH, Thomas. *Memoirs of Life & Writings of Sir Philip Sidney*. 1809. New York. 2nd ed. $35.00

ZSCHOKKE, Heinrich. *History of Switzerland for the Swiss People*. 1858. New York. map. VG $25.00

ZUBRZYCKI, Jerzy. *Settlers of the Latrobe Valley*. 1964. Canberra. 1st ed. VG $10.00

ZUCKERMAN, S. *Functional Affinities of Man, Monkeys, & Apes*. 1933. 1st ed. $15.00

ZUCKERMAN, S. *Nuclear Illusion & Reality*. 1982. New York. Viking. 154 pp. dj. $3.50

ZUCKERMAN, S. *The Social Life of Monkeys & Apes*. 1932. 1st ed. $15.00

ZUMBO, Jim. *Ice Fishing East & West*. 1978. McKay. Ills. Johnson. 182 pp. dj. $5.50

ZUMWALT, E.R., Jr. *On Watch. A Candid Memoir*. 1976. 568 pp. wrappers. G $7.50

ZWEIG, S. *Conqueror of the Seas, Story of Magellan*. 1938. Literary Guild. Ills. 1st ed. 335 pp. dj. VG $10.00

ZWEIG. *Mary, Queen of Scotland & the Isles*. 1935. Viking. Ills. $6.50

ZWEMER, S.M. *Arabia: Cradle of Islam*. 1900. Revell. Ills. 1st ed. EX $95.00

ZWILGMEYER. *Johnny Blossom*. 1948. Boston. 1st ed. dj. VG $25.00

Bookbuyers

In this section of the book we have listed buyers of books and related material. When you correspond with these dealers, be sure to enclose a self-addressed stamped envelope if you want a reply. Do not send lists of books for appraisal. If you wish to sell your books, quote the price you want or send a list and ask if there are any on the list they might be interested in and the price they would be willing to pay. If you want the list back, be sure to send a S.A.S.E. large enough for the listing to be returned. When you list your books, do so by author, full title, publisher and place, date, edition, and condition, noting any defects on cover or contents.

Adventure
D. Williams
P.O. Box 1185
St. Paul, MN 55101

Bunker Books
P.O. Box 1638
Spring Valley, CA 92077

Alaska
Martin's Books
Northward Bldg. Suite 115
3rd & Lacy Street
Fairbanks, AK 99701

Americana
Argosy Book Store
116 East 59 Street
New York, NY 10022

Fuller & Saunders, Books
3238 P Street NW
Washington, DC 20007

Gordon Totty
Scarce Paper Americana
576 Massachusetts Avenue W
Lunenburg, MA 01462

John L. Heflin
Civil War Books
5708 Brentwood Trace
Brentwood, TN 37027

Lawrence Golder
Rare Books
P.O. Box 144
Collinsville, CT 06022

Martin's Books
Northward Bldg. Suite 115
3rd & Lacy Street
Fairbanks, AK 99701

Melvin Marcher
Bookseller
6204 N. Vermont
Oklahoma City, OK 73112

Sykes & Flanders
Antiquarian Booksellers
P.O. Box 86
Weare, NH 03281

American Dancers & Painters
Cesi Kellinger
735 Philadelphia Ave.
Chambersburg, PA 17202

Antarctica
Old Mill Books
P.O. Box 21561
Alexandria, VA 22320

Antiques & Collectibles
The Library
P.O. Box 37
Des Moines, IA 50301

San Fernando Book Co.
P.O. Box 447
San Fernando, CA 91341

Archery
Melvin Marcher
Bookseller
6204 N. Vermont
Oklahoma City, OK 73112

Architecture
D. Williams
P.O. Box 1185
St. Paul, MN 55101

Arctic Regions
Martin's Books
Northward Bldg. Suite 115
3rd & Lacy Street
Fairbanks, AK 99701

Art Nouveau & Art Deco
Rachel A. Goodkind
c/o 45C Heritage Hills
Somers, NY 10589

Asia
Old Mill Books
P.O. Box 21561
Alexandria, VA 22320

Australia
Old Mill Books
P.O. Box 21561
Alexandria, VA 22320

Autographs
Argosy Book Store
116 East 59 Street
New York, NY 10022

Autographed Books
Signed by famous people.
Tomas Plasko, Books
57-15 246 Crescent
Douglaston, NY 11362

Aviation
Antheil Booksellers
2177 Isabelle Court
North Bellmore, NY 11710

BOOK
Box 547, Streetville
Mississauga, Ontario
Canada L5M 2C1

Baseball
Before 1970, hardcover only.
Ken Domonkos
Star Route 515 Box 119
Vernon, NJ 07462

Bibliographies
First Folio
3006 North Sheffield
Chicago, IL 60657

Limestone Hills Book Shop
P.O. BOX 1125
Glen Rose, TX 76043

Pre-1940 scientific biographies.
New Wireless Pioneers
James & Felicia Kreuzer
6270 Clinton Street
Elma, NY 14059

Biochemical Warfare
Vathek Books
250 Slocum Way
Fort Lee, NJ 07024

Books
Out-of-print books.
Martin's Books
Northward Bldg. Suite 115
3rd & Lacy Street
Fairbanks, AK 99701

Books about books, general out-of-print.
First Folio
3006 North Sheffield
Chicago, IL 60657

Miniature books.
Jo Ann Reisler, LTD.
360 Glyndon St., N.E.
Vienna, VA 22180

Books about books.
Limestone Hills Book Shop
P.O. Box 1125
Glen Rose, TX 76043

Proofs of science fiction, fantasy & horror.
Barry R. Levin Science Fiction & Fantasy
Literature, A.B.A.A.
2265 Westwood Blvd. #669
Los Angeles, CA 90064

Thornton Burgess
First editions & related ephemera.
S. Kruskall
Box 418
Dover, MA 02114

Cape Cod
E. May
Sea Watch Booklook
P.O. Box 251
East Orleans, MA 02643

Children's Books
Carol Myers
Box 7537
Boulder, CO 80306

E. May
Sea Watch Booklook
P.O. Box 251
East Orleans, MA 02643

First Folio
3006 North Sheffield
Chicago, IL 60657

Valerie Bonatis
1666 Bryan Avenue
Winter Park, FL 32789

Jo Ann Reisler, LTD.
360 Glyndon St., N.E.
Vienna, VA 22180

Civil War
North or South, new or old.
Donald S. Mull
1760 Girard Drive
Louisville, KY 40222

E. May
Sea Watch Booklook
P.O. Box 251
East Orleans, MA 02643

J.A. Baumhofer-Books
Box 65493
St. Paul, MN 55165

Fuller & Saunders, Books
3238 P Street NW
Washington, DC 20007

Melvin Marcher
Bookseller
6204 N. Vermont
Oklahoma City, OK 73112

Related ephemera including newspapers, magazines, documents, letters, stereoviews, photographs, covers, etc.
Gordon Totty
Scarce Paper Americana
576 Massachusetts Avenue
Lunenburg, MA 01462

Books, documents, letters, photos, envelopes, diaries, North & South, Confederate Money, slavery items, etc.
John L. Heflin, Jr.
Civil War Books
5708 Brentwood Trace
Brentwood, TN 37027

John K. King
Used and Rare Books
P.O. Box 363 A
Detroit, MI 48232

Comic Books
Pre-1965.
Calvin Slobodian
859-4th Avenue
Rivers, Manitoba
Canada ROK 1XO

Cookbooks
Natural food and vegetarian.
Rachel A. Goodkind
c/o 45C Heritage Hills
Somers, NY 10589

Before 1850.
Thomas Plasko, Books
57-15 246 Crescent
Douglaston, NY 11362

County Plat Books
Madigan's Books
846 Tenth
Charleston, IL 61920

Crime and Criminology
Patterson Smith, A.B.A.A.
23 Prospect Terrace
Montclair, NJ 07042

Decorative Arts
The Library
P.O. Box 37
Des Moines, IA 50301

Detective Fiction
Limestone Hills Book Shop
P.O. Box 1125
Glen Rose, TX 76043

Sykes & Flanders
Antiquarian Booksellers
P.O. Box 86
Weare, NH 03281

Detroit History
John K. King
Used and Rare Books
P.O. Box 363 A
Detroit, MI 48232

Elbert Hubbard
Richard Blancher
209 Plymouth Colony
Alps Rd.
Branford, CT 06405

Electricity
Pre-1900.
New Wireless Pioneers
James & Felicia Kreuzer
6270 Clinton Street
Elma, NY 14059

Engineering
Including technology and related history.
D. Williams
P.O. Box 1185
St. Paul, MN 55101

Farming
Whitlock Farm Booksellers
20 Sperry Road
Bethany, CT 06525

First Editions
Carol Myers
Box 7537
Boulder, CO 80306

Argosy Book Store
116 East 59 Street
New York, NY 10002

Rare.
Barry R. Levin Science Fiction & Fantasy
Literature, A.B.A.A.
2265 Westwood Blvd. #669
Los Angeles, CA 90064

19th & 20th century.
Sykes & Flanders
Antiquarian Booksellers
P.O. Box 86
Weare, NH 03281

Fishing
Melvin Marcher
Bookseller
6204 N. Vermont
Oklahoma City, OK 73112

Mainly trout and fly fishing.
R.F. Selgas
P.O. Box 227-B
Hershey, PA 17033

Florida Material
Douglas G. Hendriksen
P.O. Box 21153
Kennedy Space Center, FL 32815

Furniture
D. Williams
P.O. Box 1185
St. Paul, MN 55101

Fur Trade
Sykes & Flanders
Antiquarian Booksellers
P.O. Box 86
Weare, NH 03281

Gambling

Patterson Smith, A.B.A.A.
23 Prospect Terrace
Montclair, NJ 07042

Genealogy

Any items of genealogical interest as directories, county plat books, family or county histories, etc.
Madigan's Books
846 Tenth
Charleston, IL 61920

Monroe County Library System
3700 South Custer Road
Monroe, MI 48161

George Custer

Books, prints, magazines, maps, photos, etc. on the General and Battle of Little Big Horn.
Monroe County Library System
3700 South Custer Road
Monroe, MI 48161

Donald S. Mull
1706 Girard Drive
Louisville, KY 40222

Golf & Golfiana

George Owen
P.O. Box 29633
Dallas, TX 75229

Zane Grey

Any letters, signed books, ephemera, or associated items.
J.A. Baumhofer-Books
Box 65493
St. Paul, MN 55165

All books by and about Grey.
George Owen
P.O. Box 29633
Dallas, TX 75229

Guns & Weapons

Firearms, hunting and sport.
Melvin Marcher
Bookseller
6204 N. Vermont
Oklahoma City, OK 73112

Henry Ford

John K. King
Used and Rare Books
Box 363 A
Detroit, MI 48232

Histories

Pe Gee Antiques
R.R. #1 Box 172 C
Louisville, NE 68037

County and family histories or anything of interest to a genealogist.
Madigan's Books
846 Tenth
Charleston, IL 61920

Ice Skating

George Owen
P.O. Box 29633
Dallas, TX 75229

Illustrated Books

First Folio
3006 North Sheffield
Chicago, IL 60657

Sykes & Flanders
Antiquarian Booksellers
P.O. Box 86
Weare, NH 03281

On all subjects.
The Antiquarian Bookstore
1070 Lafayette Rd.
Portsmouth, NH 03801

Original illustrative art, early paper dolls and paper toys.
Jo Ann Reisler, LTD.
360 Glyndon St., N.E.
Vienna, VA 22180

Jewelry

Books and pamphlets printed in English before 1870; anything about people or religion.
Thomas Plasko, Books
57-15 246 Crescent
Douglaston, NY 11362

Karma

Bonita Summers
P.O. Box 96
Pacific, MO 63069

Kentucky Material

Especially non-fiction.
Donald S. Mull
1706 Girard Drive
Louisville, KY 40222

Kayaking

Rachel A. Goodkind
c/o 45C Heritage Hills
Somers, NY 10589

Literature

American and English.
Limestone Hills Book Shop
P.O. Box 1125
Glen Rose, TX 76043

Magazines

Pe Gee Antiques
R.R. # 1 Box 172C
Louisville, NE 68037

Old magazines in bulk.
The Antiquarian Bookstore
1070 Lafayette Road
Portsmouth, NH 03801

Sports.
ATC Books
321 East Superior Street
Duluth, MN 55802

Saturday Evening Post and other magazines with Rockwell covers.
Gordon Totty
Scarce Paper Americana
576 Massachusetts Avenue W
Lunenburg, MA 01462

Magic

Jack Curtis
P.O. Box 758
Stevens Point, WI 54481

Manuscripts

Barry R. Levin Science Fiction & Fantasy
Literature, A.B.A.A.
2265 Westwood Blvd. #669
Los Angeles, CA 90064

Part printed or full manuscript receipts, indentures, bills, statements, letters, etc.
Gordon Totty
Scarce Paper Americana
576 Massachusetts Avenue W
Lunenburg, MA 01462

Maps and Atlases

Samuel Lowe, Jr. Antiques Inc.
80 Charles Street
Boston, MA 02114

Pe Gee Antiques
R.R. #1 Box 172C
Louisville, NE 68037

Maps and antique prints.
Argosy Book Store
116 East 59 Street
New York, NY 10022

Pre-1865 maps and atlases of the North American continent.
Gordon Totty
Scarce Paper Americana
576 Massachusetts Avenue W
Lunenburg, MA 01462

Marine

Nonfiction.
Samuel Lowe, Jr. Antiques Inc.
80 Charles Street
Boston, MA 02114

Maritime

Antheil Booksellers
2177 Isabelle Court
North Bellmore, NY 11710

Masonry

Anything about history, morals or dogma.
Jack Bailes Books
P.O. Box 150
Eureka Springs, AR 72632

Mechanical Music

Books, all type literature, player pianos, rolls, music boxes, player organs, nickelodeons, etc.
William H. Edgerton
241 Long Neck Point Rd.
Darien, CT 06820

Vi & Si's Antiques
8970 Main Street
Clarence, NY 14031

Medical Books
History of medicine.
Argosy Book Store
116 East 59 Street
New York, NY 10022

*Current, rare, out-of-print and related
books.*
Richard Foster
Rittenhouse Book Store
1706 Rittenhouse Square
Philadelphia, PA 19103

Michigania
Michigan history and genealogy.
Monroe County Library System
3700 South Custer Road
Monroe, MI 48161

John K. King
Used and Rare Books
Box 363 A
Detroit, MI 48232

Military
Antheil Booksellers
2177 Isabelle Court
North Bellmore, NY 11710

ATC Books
321 East Superior St.
Duluth, MN 55802

Valerie Bonatis
1666 Bryan Avenue
Winter Park, FL 32789

Miscellaneous
Valerie Bonatis
1666 Bryan Avenue
Winter Park, FL 32789

General out-of-print.
First Folio
3006 North Sheffield
Chicago, IL 60657

Money and Banking
San Fernando Book Co.
P.O. Box 447
San Fernando, CA 91341

Musical Instruments
*Stringed instruments, their making and
makers.*
Rachel A. Goodkind
c/o 45C Heritage Hills
Somers, NY 10589

Mysteries
Paperback and hardcover.
Bunker Books
P.O. Box 1638
Spring Valley, CA 92077

D. Williams
P.O. Box 1185
St. Paul, MN 55101

National Geographic
*Issues 1888-1930 and all other publications
including books, maps, supplements,
rarities, etc.*
Edwin C. Buxbaum
P.O. Box 465
Wilmington, DE 19899

Natural History
All aspects.
Melvin Marcher
Bookseller
6204 N. Vermont
Oklahoma City, OK 73112

Whitlock Farm Booksellers
20 Sperry Road
Bethany, CT 06525

Naval
Antheil Booksellers
2177 Isabelle Ct.
North Bellmore, NY 11710

E. May
Sea Watch Booklook
P.O. Box 251
East Orleans, MA 02643

New England
Especially local history.
Whitlock Farm Booksellers
20 Sperry Road
Bethany, CT 06525

New Hampshire
Sykes & Flanders
Antiquarian Booksellers
P.O. Box 86
Weare, NH 03281

Newspapers
*Pre-1900 American & British, bound or
quantity; also illustrated as Harpers Week-
ly, Leslies, London News, etc.*
Gordon Totty
Scarce Paper Americana
576 Massachusetts Avenue W
Lunenburg, MA 01462

Novels
Valerie Bonatis
1666 Bryan Avenue
Winter Park, FL 32789

Numismatic Books
*Money and banking, silver and gold,
treasure hunting, etc.*
San Fernando Book Co.
P.O. Box 447
San Fernando, CA 91341

Jack Curtis
P.O. Box 758
Stevens Point, WI 54481

Oz Books and Oziana
First Folio
3006 North Sheffield
Chicago, IL 60657

George Owen
P.O. Box 29633
Dallas, TX 75229

Paperback Books
1930-1970
Bunker Books
P.O. Box 1638
Spring Valley, CA 92077

Polar Exploration
Pre-1930
Vathek Books
250 Slocum Way
Fort Lee, NJ 07024

Polo and Polo Horses
George Owen
P.O. Box 29633
Dallas, TX 75229

Gene Stratton-Porter
*Any letters, signed books, ephemera or
associated items*
J.A. Baumhofer-Books
Box 65493
St. Paul, MN 55165

Prints
Argosy Book Store
116 East 59 St.
New York, NY 10022

Samuel Lowe, Jr. Antiques Inc.
80 Charles Street
Boston, MA 02114

Radio, Telegraph
*Wireless and radio ephemera before 1925
and telegraph ephemera before 1900.*
New Wireless Pioneers
Jones & Felicia Kreuzer
6270 Clinton Street
Elma, NY 14059

Rare and Unusual
Argosy Book Store
116 East 59 Street
New York, NY 10022

Joseph J. Felcone Inc.
Rare Books
P.O. Box 366
Princeton, NJ 08540

Carol Myers
Box 7537
Boulder, CO 80306

Lawrence Golder
Rare Books
P.O. Box 144
Collinsville, CT 06022

Rare and out-of-print medical books.
Richard Foster
Rittenhouse Book Store
1706 Rittenhouse Square
Philadelphia, PA 19103

Curious books of all sorts.
Whitlock Farm Booksellers
20 Sperry Road
Bethany, CT 06525

Reincarnation
Survival of bodily death. Karma.
Bonita Summers
P.O. Box 96
Pacific, MO 63069

Reference
Americana, Civil War, military, wars, California, gold mining, travel, Twain, gazetters, etc.
Gorton Totty
Scarce Paper Americana
576 Massachusetts Avenue W
Lunenburg, MA 01462

Rome and Persia
Third century A.D.
Vathek Books
250 Slocum Way
Fort Lee, NJ 07024

Roycroft Printing Shop
Pre-1916 publications demonstrating hand-work, first editions, fine bindings, etc; also, ephemera.
Richard Blancher
209 Plymouth Colony
Alps Rd.
Branford, CT 06405

Science
Hoffman Research Services
P.O. Box 342
Rillton, PA 15678

Scientific Bibliographies.
New Wireless Pioneers
James & Felicia Kreuzer
6270 Clinton Street
Elma, NY 14059

Science Fiction
Bunker Books
P.O. Box 1638
Spring Valley, CA 92077

D. Williams
P.O. Box 1185
St. Paul, MN 55101

Proofs of science fiction, fantasy and horror.
Barry R. Levin Science Fiction & Fantasy
Literature, A.B.A.A.
2265 Westwood Blvd. #669
Los Angeles, CA 90064

Seminole Indians
Douglas G. Hendriksen
P.O. Box 21153
Kennedy Space Center, FL 32815

Silver and Gold
San Fernando Book Co.
P.O. Box 447
San Fernando, CA 91341

Ships and the Sea
BOOK
Box 547, Streetville
Mississauga, Ontario
Canada L5M 2C1

Hudson River shipwrecks and non-fiction ghost ships.
Vathek Books
250 Slocum Way
Fort Lee, NJ 07024

Spanish American War
Douglas G. Hendriksen
P.O. Box 21153
Kennedy Space Center, FL 32815

Sporting Books
ATC Books
321 East Superior Street
Duluth, MN 55802

Martin's Books
Northward Bldg. Suite 115
3rd & Lacy Street
Fairbanks, AK 99701

Sugar
Especially sugar cane or beet, one book or a collection.
Jack Bailes Books
P.O. Box 150
Eureka, Springs, AR 72632

Television
Pre-1940.
New Wireless Pioneers
James & Felicia Kreuzer
6270 Clinton Street
Elma, NY 14059

Travel & Travel Guides
Sykes & Flanders
Antiquarian Booksellers
P.O. Box 86
Weare, NH 03281

The Library
P.O. Box 37
Des Moines, IA 50301

Treasure Hunting
Numismatics, silver and gold.
San Fernando Book Co.
P.O. Box 447
San Fernando, CA 91341

TV Guides
1953-1973.
Bunker Books
P.O. Box 1638
Spring Valley, CA 92077

Texana
George Owen
P.O. Box 29633
Dallas, TX 75229

Washington, DC
History and area.
Fuller & Saunders, Books
3238 P. Street NW
Washington, DC 20007

Western Americana
Bunker Books
P.O. Box 1638
Spring Valley, CA 92077

George Owen
P.O. Box 29633
Dallas, TX 75229

Melvin Marcher
Bookseller
6204 N. Vermont
Oklahoma City, OK 73112

Carol Myers
Box 7537
Boulder, CO 80306

Northwest Americana.
Martin's Books
Northward Bldg. Suite 115
3rd & Lacy Street
Fairbanks, AK 99701

White Mountains
Sykes & Flanders
Antiquarian Booksellers
P.O. Box 86
Weare, NH 03281

P.G. Wodehouse
All books by and about Wodehouse.
George Owen
P.O. Box 29633
Dallas, TX 75229

Limestone Hills Book Shop
P.O. Box 1125
Glen Rose, TX 76043

Woodworking
D. Williams
P.O. Box 1185
St. Paul, MN 55101

World War I and II
E. May
Sea Watch Booklook
P.O. Box 251
East Orleans, MA 02643

H.B. Wright
Jack Bailes Books
P.O. Box 150
Eureka Springs, AR 72632

Schroeder's Antiques Price Guide

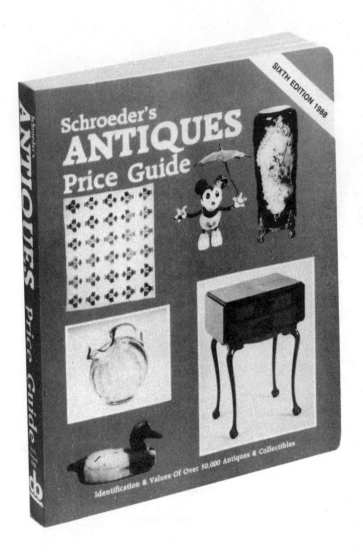

Schroeder's Antiques Price Guide has climbed its way to the top in a field already supplied with several well-established publications! The word is out, *Schroeder's Price Guide* is the best buy at any price. Over 500 categories are covered, with more than 50,000 listings. But it's not volume alone that makes Schroeder's the unique guide it is recognized to be. From ABC Plates to Zsolnay, if it merits the interest of today's collector, you'll find it in Schroeder's. Each subject is represented with histories and background information. In addition, hundreds of sharp original photos are used each year to illustrate not only the rare and the unusual, but the everyday "fun-type" collectibles as well -- not postage stamp pictures, but large close-up shots that show important details clearly.

Each edition is completely re-typeset from all new sources. We have not and will not simply change prices in each new edition. All new copy and all new illustrations make Schroeder's THE price guide on antiques and collectibles.

The writing and researching team behind this giant is proportionately large. It is backed by a staff of more than seventy of Collector Books' finest authors, as well as a board of advisors made up of well-known antique authorities and the country's top dealers, all specialists in their fields. Accuracy is their primary aim. Prices are gathered over the entire year previous to publication, from ads and personal contacts. Then each category is thoroughly checked to spot inconsistencies, listings that may not be entirely reflective of actual market dealings, and lines too vague to be of merit.

Only the best of the lot remains for publication. You'll find *Schroeder's Antiques Price Guide* the one to buy for factual information and quality.

No dealer, collector or investor can afford not to own this book. It is available from your favorite bookseller or antiques dealer at the low price of $11.95. If you are unable to find this price guide in your area, it's available from Collector Books, P. O. Box 3009, Paducah, KY 42001 at $11.95 plus $1.00 for postage and handling.

8½ x 11, 608 Pages $11.95